Dog & Pony Shows

Dog & Pony Shows

*How to Make Winning Presentations
when the Stakes Are High*

John Quick

McGraw-Hill, Inc.
New York St. Louis San Francisco Auckland Bogotá
Caracas Lisbon London Madrid Mexico Milan
Montreal New Delhi Paris San Juan São Paulo
Singapore Sydney Tokyo Toronto

Library of Congress Cataloging-in-Publication Data

Quick, John, date.
    Dog & pony shows : how to make winning presentations when the
stakes are high / John Quick.
        p.   cm.
    Includes index.
    ISBN 0-07-051078-4 (hc)   — ISBN 0-07-051077-6 (pbk)
    1. Public speaking. 2. Business presentations. 3. Visual
communication. 4. Business writing. I. Title. II. Title: Dog and
pony shows.
    PN4192.B87Q53 1992
    808.5'1—dc20   91-28427
                                                CIP

1 2 3 4 5 6 7 8 9 0 MAL/MAL 9 8 7 6 5 4 3 2

The sponsoring editor for this book was James H. Bessent, Jr., the
editing supervisor was David E. Fogarty, and the production
supervisor was Pamela A. Pelton. It was composed in Palatino by
McGraw-Hill's Professional Book Group composition unit.

Printed and bound by Malloy Lithographing, Inc.

For my wife, Maralyn

Contents

Preface

The presentation of ideas and solutions is becoming increasingly more prevalent and important. Here are just a few examples of what I'm talking about, situations in which professionals and nonprofessionals alike are making "homemade" presentations to explain ideas, close sales, advance causes, and—in general—persuade others.

- *Corporations.* Presentations to secure new business, form strategic partnerships, raise capital, introduce new products and services, recruit new employees, and inform and educate existing employees.

- *Small Businesses.* Presentations to banks, clients, prospects, prospective suppliers, and employees.

- *Science.* Lectures, presentations in support of foundation and federal grants.

- *Law.* Depositions and courtroom presentations, testimony of expert witnesses.

- *Engineering.* New-business "pitches," preliminary reports, final reports, presentation of technical papers at symposia and professional societies and associations.

- *Trade Associations.* Membership presentations, annual meetings.

- *Colleges and Universities.* Lecture materials, presentations in support of proposals for grants.

- *Elementary and Secondary Schools.* Aids to classroom teaching, proposals for increased resources.

- *Nonprofit Organizations and Special-Interest Groups.* Public information and membership presentations to citizens and government organizations.

- *Individuals.* This is the most important market of all. People need to learn how to create better opportunities for themselves—in securing new or better jobs and gaining increases in wages or salaries.

This book has been designed to help people get what they want: top-management people who must win large contracts; marketing and sales professionals who must develop more customers or clients; anybody who wants to gain approval, sponsorship, or funding for a good idea; individuals who must provide a solid justification for a raise or an important promotion; and special-interest groups who are trying to bring about change.

In short, the book will serve as a resource for anybody who wants to persuade anybody else as a means of getting *results*.

John Quick

Introduction: How to Use This Workbook

Dog & Pony Shows are about selling—selling products and services. That is their main purpose. And that is the purpose of this book.

Basic Organization

Every chapter of this workbook begins with a brief summary of its contents and ends with some strongly worded dos and don'ts in the Dog & Pony Checkpoints. Throughout *Dog & Pony Shows* are checklists that you can use to make sure you've covered all the important points when planning and delivering your presentation.

Contents of This Chapter

- Who makes important high-level presentations?
- What is the purpose of an important presentation?
- What are the 10 components of success?
  1. Verify the need for your solution.
  2. Analyze your audience.
  3. Differentiate yourself from your competition.
  4. Define quality, establish your price, and ask.
  5. Plan, schedule, and pick the right place to present.
  6. Develop the story about your solution.
  7. Gain your audience's commitment to attend.
  8. Convert your story into a show.

9. Make a persuasive presentation.

10. Follow up to assure your win.

- A score card to measure achievement.

- Dog & Pony Checkpoints.

Who Makes Important High-Level Presentations?

Basically, anybody does, but particularly people with a desire to convey a strong message in order to create change. In terms of size, there are three categories of people who produce winning presentations:

1. Large teams, often numbering six people or more

2. Smaller teams, usually consisting of two or three people

3. Individuals

People make presentations for a variety of reasons—most having to do with selling products and services, launching new ideas, or trying to get a better job in their organizations.

All presenters have the same objective: *to win.* And all depend upon the same basic rules for success.

But how *do* you win? And what *are* the rules? First we must agree on a definition of the *purpose* of a presentation.

What Is the Purpose of an Important Presentation?

The purpose of a major presentation is *to sell a solution,* specifically, *your solution!*

Your winning solution may involve products, services, or ideas, but it must *do* something. Your solution must solve a problem, answer a need, resolve an issue, create an opportunity, or do something worthwhile. It must have merit. It must be attractive. It must be compelling. It must work and show the promise of success. It must be timely. It must be *good.*

Success depends upon several factors, which can be broken down into 10 steps.

What Are the 10 Components of Success?

The 10 components of success, examined in detail in the chapters that follow, are outlined here and serve as a preview of the chapters.

1. *Verify the need for your solution.* As emphasized in Chap. 1, you must make sure that what you're going to present is *real,* that it's necessary, and that it can be applied. It must truly meet the needs of the people you've identified to talk to. It must be shown that it fits their specifications and is congruent with their situation and their or-

ganization. In order to succeed at this vital first step, you need to evaluate the following subjects:

- Your audience's vision of the future

- The symptoms, problems, and needs of your audience

- Possible objections your audience might raise

- Common gripes of senior people who have to sit through presentations

- Ways to substantiate the fact that your solution "fits" and is congruent with the audience's situation and organization

2. *Analyze your audience.* You must know as much as possible about the people you're talking to, the attitudes they have at present, and the attitudes and awareness that must be modified or created. Also, even though your solution may be perfectly valid and useful, there may be a number of obstacles to surmount or avoid. The people you're trying to convince may have misconceptions and prejudices about you or your solution that you will have to overcome. They may be behaving in nonrational ways that you will have to counter, possibly by employing their own brand of logic. Following are the key elements to interpret and understand:

- The type of audience you intend to present to

- The present or prevailing attitude of the audience

- The attitude you need to build

- The awareness you want to create

- Anthropological and philosophical viewpoints to understand

- The forces and attitudes that influence the audience's decision-making abilities

3. *Differentiate yourself from your competition.* As you will see in Chap. 3, everybody has direct or indirect competition. You must evaluate all competitive forces in order to position yourself and your ideas to win. Among the most noteworthy of "famous last words" are: "I don't *have* any competition!" (A simple example of indirect competition is as follows: Miniature golf courses compete with other miniature golf courses in the same market or region, but as well, in the broader context, they are also competing against other businesses that contend for the entertainment dollars of consumers—businesses such as movie theaters, amusement parks, racetracks, and ball games. Another example of competition, on a more personal basis, involves individuals within an organization. An individual in an organization may have a good idea, but it must be financed somehow, possibly by diverting money from another source. The individual is then, of course, competing against the other source either indirectly or—more likely—directly.) Here are the details covered in this chapter:

- Direct and indirect competitors

- Strengths and weaknesses of major competitors

- Ways to differentiate yourself from competitors
- Questions to ask about you and your company
- Ways to compete
- Relevant corporate or personal goals
- True benefits of your solution
- Key features of your solution
- Fundamental strategy for success

4. *Define quality, establish your price, and ask.* You must propose your own definition of—and level of—quality. Having established your own concept of quality, you can then determine price. Remember, there isn't necessarily a connection between cost and price. (For example, the same sandwich in a hotel's coffee shop, its restaurant, and its room service menu will have three different prices.) Above all, you must be comfortable in *asking* for what you want.

Here are the key elements of Chap. 4:

- The meaning of *good*
- A way to measure quality and performance
- Important values and beliefs
- The power of a promise
- Doing "better"
- Arriving at a price
- The society and the system
- A note about winning
- How to ask

5. *Plan, schedule, and pick the right place to present.* You mustn't leave the time and place to chance. Some times of the day (and days of the week) are much better than others. And you must *absolutely* control the environment in which you make your presentation. Here are some of the ideas that Chap. 5 covers in depth:

- Establishing a plan and a schedule
- Determining the best time to make your pitch
- Why the right room is so important

6. *Develop the story about your solution.* You must develop, and refine, the content and purpose of your presentation into a story for your audience. It is the story that explains why your solution is valuable, useful, or applicable to the people you're talking to, and how it will provide an advantage to them. You must produce a well-organized chronicle that is interesting and that provides any necessary proofs your audience may require. Here are some of the highlights of this chapter:

- Decide what you want your audience to *do*
- 10 questions to ask before you start writing
- An easy way to write a first draft
- How to design a winning presentation
- Key questions to review
- Ideas about tone and style

7. *Gain your audience's commitment to attend.* You must then develop a compelling "preview" of your story so that the people you select to see it and hear it will be enticed to attend your presentation. Invitations must then be made with sufficient advance notice. Calendars must be checked and times verified. Also, "preshow" material must be produced and distributed to your audience in advance of your presentation. Confirmations must be made two days before the event. Here are the ideas in this chapter:

- How to develop an inviting "preview"
- How to stimulate people to attend your presentation
- Ideas about invitations
- Distribution of a preshow summary
- Confirmations

8. *Convert your story into a* show. Make your presentation visually interesting and dynamic. Introduce drama and excitement. Develop a sense of pace and movement. Stimulate interaction by creating opportunities for your audience to think and to participate. You will find the following information very useful:

- Why the introduction is vital
- What to borrow from the theater
- The role of the director
- The role of the presenter
- Other correlations to the theater

9. *Make a persuasive presentation.* You must deliver your story and convince your audience. You must simultaneously sell yourself *and* your solution. You must gain your audience members' trust, and you must secure their commitment to do what you want them to do. You must show how you will implement your solution and make it work—and persuade them to proceed against your schedule for action. Your personality and your solution are inexorably linked. They are buying both you and *it*—your story. There is no way to make a successful presentation without adequate rehearsal. Here are some other vital areas to review:

- What to know about visual aids
- Technology—the old and the new

- Advantages and disadvantages of various media and why some are safer and more convenient than others.

- Sure-fire techniques

- Visuals that invite participation

- How to hit pay dirt (and the care and feeding of modern-day prospectors)

- Prove that an investment in your solution will yield positive dividends

10. *Follow up to preserve and protect your win.* Any advantage won in a perfect presentation could be lost if you don't follow up and consolidate your gains. This is most frequently expressed in a signed contract or other agreement to proceed with a plan. Some of the aspects to consider in this chapter include the following:

- How to gain verbal commitment

- How to secure a rough-draft written commitment

- Follow-up notes and letters

- Follow-on activities

A Scorecard to Measure Achievement

Figure I-1 is an outline of the scores you need to accumulate in preparing for, and making, a successful presentation. Be aware, though, that even if you score 100, *fully 60 percent of your success is often based on factors other than the presentation itself.*

There are several very strong messages that emerge from the tally in Fig. I-1, and they are explained as follows:

1. *Preliminary work to educate the audience.* You've got to do the groundwork in preparing your listeners to hear your solution and to be disposed to act on it. You can't catch them cold. You've got to prepare your way with thought-provoking, enticing previews of

THE VALUE OF YOUR EFFORTS	
1. Preliminary work to educate the audience	10
2. The right setting for the presentation	10
3. Your own self-confidence, leadership, and likability	20
4. Participation of the audience	20
5. Content—explanation of the solution	10
6. Quality of the solution and a strong cost-benefit story	20
7. Supporting visual materials	10
	Total score 100

Figure I-1.

information (and, when it is really called for, downright propaganda).

2. *The right setting for the presentation.* You must choose a setting in which the audience is comfortable, where you are in command, and where you and your audience will not be distracted or disturbed. An interruption is the worst thing that can happen to a presentation.

3. *Your own self-confidence, leadership, and likability.* Nobody knows for sure how many sales are made because the buyer liked and trusted the seller, frequently overlooking or ignoring the fact that the seller's solution was inferior to a competitor's. It is no secret that a large proportion of the sales made each year are personality-based rather than performance-based choices and are a function of the audience's reaction to the presence of real or apparent *leadership*.

4. *Participation of the audience.* Audience members will not make a decision without discussion, and they must participate easily and fully in discussion. At the beginning of every presentation, audiences should be told that questions will be handled at the end unless there is an urgent need to interrupt.

5. *Content—Explanation of the solution.* How your solution is described is of (relatively) minor significance. If it's truly a good idea, the quality will shine through.

6. *Quality of the solution and a strong cost-benefit story.* The *meaning* of your solution is more important than the explanation—since it tells precisely how it will help your audience in a cost-beneficial manner. This advantage must be conveyed at all costs.

7. *Supporting visual materials.* There have been plenty of successful presentations in which no visuals were used at all. So this may be of consequence only when the visuals are well chosen, selectively used, and vital to the story.

The KISS of Death

There are two overworked and incorrect little sayings or maxims to avoid.

The first is KISS (Keep it simple, stupid!). This is both self-deprecating and irrelevant. Some presentations have to be detailed or complicated because of the nature of the subject matter. This doesn't mean that they can't be interesting, clear, and understandable. They can, and *must*, be, but it requires creativity and imagination, not a dogged insistence on simplicity.

The other insipid and moth-eaten piece of advice is "Tell 'em what you're going to tell 'em; tell 'em; and then tell 'em what you told them." To actually *do* this would denigrate and insult your audience. There is *no* form of effective storytelling that works this way: not books, articles, newspaper stories, plays, movies, television news, proposals, commercials, or advertising, and most certainly not presentations. Ignore this idea altogether.

✔ Remember that every presentation has a solution. A solution must do two things: (1) it's got to work, and (2) it has to fit.

✔ Develop a solid understanding of your audience. Ask questions and remember that firsthand experience is better than second-hand and thirdhand research results.

✔ Keep in mind that people act (and react) nonrationally just about as often as they behave rationally.

✔ Capitalize on the weaknesses of competitors. Help them *lose.*

✔ Learn how to clearly differentiate yourself from competitors.

✔ Be clear about your responsibility to ask for what you want.

✔ Choose the right place and the best time to present.

✔ Learn how various aspects of theater apply to presentations.

✔ Remember that a winning presentation must gain a commitment from the audience.

✔ Don't forget the role of personality in presentations. People don't buy from people they don't like or can't trust.

✔ Don't be afraid to baby the people you're trying to convince. They may need to be cajoled into attending the presentation, believing you when they get there, and then agreeing to do what you want. This process depends more on patience than it does on logic.

Verify the Need for Your Solution

1

You must be absolutely sure that what you're going to present to your audience is *real*, that it's necessary, and that it can be applied. It must truly meet the needs of the people you've identified to talk to. It must be shown that it fits their specifications and is congruent with their situation and their organization. In order to succeed at this vital first step, you must learn to evaluate the following subjects:

Contents of This Chapter

- Your audience's vision of the future
- The symptoms, problems, and needs of your audience
- Possible objections your audience might raise
- Cutting through the biases and objections
- The view from the top
- Common gripes of senior people who have to sit through presentations
- Ways to substantiate the fact that your solution "fits" and is congruent with the audience's situation and organization
- A key to winning—Let the other guy lose!
- Dog & Pony checkpoints

An understanding and application of the first subjects in this chapter could represent the *greatest contributions to your success* in any presentation you ever make.

Begin with the dreams of your audience. Every organization (and most individuals) has a vision of what the future might hold.

Vision of the future—why should it matter to you?

Every organization has some idea, no matter how vague, of what it wants to do or be in the future. These intentions usually fall into one of two broad categories: *great dreams* and *other possibilities*. It is important to discover the intentions or directions of the people you're presenting to so that you can link your solution to their desires. Stated another way: If presented properly, your solution can be shown as *the bridge between the present and the future*—one of the important ways that your audience can secure its dream.

Where do you discover information about the future plans of your audience? If your audience's organization is a public company, you can find information in annual and quarterly reports, in 10-Qs and 10-Ks (quarterly and annual financial reports that must be filed with the Securities and Exchange Commission), and in brochures. Even a private company produces sales materials that will provide clues, and it's also important to do a literature search of newspapers, magazines, and trade publications for stories about the company, its officers, its products, and its plans for acquisition, expansion, retrenchment, or reorganization.

You can use the list of items in Fig. 1-1 to isolate what your targeted audience wants to accomplish in the future—its great dreams. Use a separate checklist for each vision analysis you undertake.

In addition to the great dreams, there are several other major objectives that occupy the thoughts of your audience. If any of these apply, list them at the bottom of Fig. 1-1. Or you can provide your own objectives.

To repeat, by understanding the dreams and intentions of your audience, you can more easily and intelligently tailor your presentation to support those ends or directions. You will help to make the vision of the audience more comprehensive, concrete, and achievable.

There are a great many companies that are content with the dubious strategy expressed in the statement: "Let's keep doing what we've always *been* doing." This typically contributes to a continuing decline.

You must always try to tie into whatever strategy a company is currently *talking* about doing—whether it's aggressively pursuing that strategy or not.

Possible Symptoms, Problems, and Needs of Your Audience

In most companies you can *absolutely count on* the existence of some of the negative circumstances seen in Fig. 1-2. I will stake my job on it. And if you find one prevailing negative condition, you will always find several corollary ones because of certain interconnections that are always present.

There are two basic kinds of management shortcomings: the external and the internal, and it's sometimes difficult to tell which is worse. One thing is true, however: Any time you can offer a non-

YOUR AUDIENCE'S VISION OF THE FUTURE

From the following list, check the "great dream(s)" that most closely match those of the organization for which you are planning your next presentation. Use a separate check sheet for each new presentation situation.

1. "Become the biggest and the best in the marketplace." .... ❏

2. "Grow the business and give it to our children or key employees so they will have a secure future." .... ❏

3. "Grow the business so that all of us will have more money, more time off, and more fun." .... ❏

4. "Take the business public, sell out, make a lot of money, and then do something else." .... ❏

5. "Sell the business immediately so that we can do something else." .... ❏

6. "Expand by teaming up with somebody and entering into a profitable joint-venture deal." .... ❏

7. "Expand by buying out our most successful competitors." .... ❏

8. "Focus our efforts. Prune back to the most profitable products, or highest-volume products, in order to concentrate our marketing efforts." .... ❏

9. "Diversify into new products or new businesses in order to meet the needs of the changing marketplace. If we keep doing what we're doing now, we'll go belly up." .... ❏

10. "Keep things as they are in order to keep doing pretty much what we're doing now. Little growth; continued profitability." .... ❏

11. "Hesitate. Establish a one-year moratorium on new capital equipment and new expenses, but don't prohibit the normal expenses." .... ❏

12. "License abroad. Capitalize on the use of our domestic technology, patent, know-how, brand franchise, and the like." .... ❏

13. "Export our products to foreign markets." .... ❏

14. "Develop an overseas business in the same industry but in a market with different characteristics." .... ❏

15. "Develop an overseas manufacturing capability for products to be sold in this country." .... ❏

Other Possibilities

_____

_____

_____

_____

Figure 1-1.

POSSIBLE SYMPTOMS, PROBLEMS, AND NEEDS OF YOUR AUDIENCE

There is every likelihood that the audience you've targeted or the situation you are addressing involves one or more of the negative elements included in this list. Therefore, your presentation should seek to eliminate any negative elements. For each audience and each corresponding presentation situation, check the items that apply. At the right, jot down a summary explanation.

Sales
- ❑ Weak or unsteady sales: _____
- ❑ Eroding market share: _____
- ❑ Little or no growth: _____
- ❑ Resistance to pricing: _____
- ❑ Sales cycle too long and costly: _____
- ❑ Untrustworthy forecasts: _____
- ❑ No strategy for sensible pricing: _____
- ❑ Poor competitive information: _____

Financial Performance
- ❑ Poor stock performance: _____
- ❑ Depressed price-earnings ratio: _____
- ❑ More external financing needed: _____
- ❑ Earnings not stabilized: _____
- ❑ Slow accounts receivable collection: _____

Product Development
- ❑ New-product problems: _____
- ❑ Lack of innovation: _____
- ❑ Little or no test marketing: _____
- ❑ No new technology: _____
- ❑ Poor application of old technology: _____
- ❑ Too little input from customers concerning new-product ideas: _____

Manufacturing and Distribution
- ❑ Poor quality control: _____
- ❑ Scrap rate too high: _____
- ❑ Production bottlenecks: _____
- ❑ Transportation troubles: _____
- ❑ Late-delivery problems: _____

Figure 1-2.

POSSIBLE SYMPTOMS, PROBLEMS, AND NEEDS OF YOUR AUDIENCE (CONT.)

Management Performance
- ❏ Little or no planning: _____
- ❏ Organization more reactive than proactive: _____
- ❏ Too many brushfires: _____
- ❏ Targets constantly changing: _____
- ❏ Regular dependence on ad hoc, piecemeal planning: _____
- ❏ No ongoing plans and schedules: _____
- ❏ Unproductive meetings: _____
- ❏ Same problems "solved" all the time: _____
- ❏ Poor resource allocation: _____
- ❏ Absence of leadership: _____

People Problems
- ❏ Labor problems: _____
- ❏ Turnover too high: _____
- ❏ No up-to-date job descriptions: _____
- ❏ No standards of performance: _____
- ❏ No clear expectations about performance: _____
- ❏ Problems finding, and keeping, good people: _____
- ❏ Too much paperwork: _____
- ❏ Too much duplication of effort: _____

External Relations
- ❏ Poor customer service and support: _____
- ❏ Trouble with environmentalists: _____
- ❏ Bad press: _____
- ❏ Takeover threats or rumors: _____
- ❏ Regulatory difficulties: _____

Other Possibilities
- ❏ _____
- ❏ _____
- ❏ _____
- ❏ _____
- ❏ _____

Figure 1-2   (*Continued*)

threatening solution to any of the difficult symptoms, you will come off a winner.

Have several people on your team review the material in Fig. 1-2, analyze it, and try to find any important additions to it.

It is imperative that you discover whatever you can about your audience's situation and tie your solution to one or more of your audience's obvious problems, shortcomings, or challenges.

There can be no major credibility gap in your presentation if you properly address an issue that is not only very real to your audience but also urgently in need of a solution.

Possible Objections the Audience Might Raise to Your Solutions

If an audience member raises an objection to what you're proposing, you must—*without hesitation*—make a carefully controlled and professional response. The only way to keep from becoming rattled and defensive is to have anticipated the objections that your particular audience is likely to bring up. This is an integral part of verifying the need for your proposed solution. You need to think about all possibilities well ahead of time and devise positive strategies to handle them.

Figure 1-3 lists a number of frequently heard objections. This is by no means a comprehensive or complete listing, so make it a point to review all the objections you've heard with respect to your particular organization, its products and services, and its policies and plans for the future.

The objections usually are silly. Or at least they may sound silly to you. But just remember that some illogical arguments or positions taken by businesspeople become official statements, indeed corporate *policy*. So be very skillful and patient in your efforts to help people over a bias they may have cherished for a long time.

Cutting through the Biases and Objections

Most people who sell products and services for a living agree with the following process for dealing with objections.

1. *Remain composed.* Learn to remain calm and confident in the face of any sort of objection or outburst. It is imperative that you neither lose your temper nor laugh out loud.

2. *Listen carefully.* When an objection is raised, do not attempt to interrupt the person who is voicing the concern. Also, don't start arguing. On the contrary, stay very calm and listen carefully to what's being said.

3. *Confirm.* After listening and—perhaps—gaining clarification of the objection, confirm that you understand it.

4. *Lay the groundwork.* Prepare the audience or the individual for the answer. This may consist of remarks such as: "This subject comes up frequently, and it's almost always due to a misunderstanding. Let me clarify it (simplify it) for you." Or "I can un-

POSSIBLE OBJECTIONS THE AUDIENCE MIGHT RAISE TO YOUR SOLUTION

As you plan any major presentation, try to anticipate the kinds of objections that could arise. The following checklist will help you sort out the objections you can expect to encounter. If you don't, fine, but it's better to be prepared in advance for tough questions.

Regarding Success
It won't work. ❏
It can't be made to work in time. ❏
It's too abstract. ❏
It's too much work right now. ❏
The benefits aren't clear enough. ❏
It would create a nightmare. ❏

Regarding Sufficiency
There isn't enough room. ❏
There aren't enough people. ❏
We're too busy right now. ❏
It needs to be analyzed more. ❏
It won't be efficient. ❏
It won't be thorough enough. ❏
It won't be complete enough. ❏
There won't be enough of it. ❏

Regarding Cost
It isn't in the budget. ❏
There isn't money *in* the budget. ❏
It costs too much. ❏
It won't be cost-effective. ❏

Regarding Scope or Scale
It's too complicated. ❏
It's too simple. ❏
It's too big. ❏
It's not big enough. ❏
The market's too little. ❏
There are too many competitors. ❏

Regarding Risk
It won't be safe. ❏
It's far too risky. ❏

The public isn't ready. ❏
I'm too scared to risk it. ❏

Regarding Timing
We don't have the time. ❏
This isn't the *right* time. ❏
It would *take* too much time. ❏
It doesn't *fit* right now. ❏

Regarding the Past
We already tried it and it failed. ❏
It's been done before. ❏
It's too late. ❏
Somebody else failed before. ❏

Regarding the Future
It's never been done before. ❏
It isn't in the plan. ❏
It's too soon. ❏
They're not ready. ❏

Regarding What Others Might Think
They probably won't like it. ❏
The committee won't approve it. ❏
Customers won't like it. ❏
(Top) management won't like it. ❏
Legal won't like it. ❏
The feds won't like it. ❏
Environmentalists will hate it. ❏

Regarding an Unspecified Barrier
You can't get there from here. ❏
It will cause trouble. ❏
I've got a funny feeling about this. ❏
It can't be approved. ❏

Other possible objections: _____

_____

_____

_____

Figure 1-3.

derstand why this might seem like a problem to you, but let me quickly show you how it isn't."

5. *Answer the objection.* Deal with it as directly and forthrightly as possible. Be clear in your answer.

6. *As you answer, stress an offsetting benefit.* Where possible, substitute one valuable feature or benefit for the one perceived as weak.

In Fig. 1-4 you'll find a checklist that will help you chart your progress in dealing with objections in a systematic way.

The following information will help you gain further insights into people's prejudices and how to counter them.

The View from the Top

If somebody tells you that most business presentations made in this country are crummy, lame, boring, and pointless, don't believe them. Most presentations are worse than that. That's right. Most are tedious and amateurish and hardly worth the time of the audience.

Am I making this up? No, I'm not. I got it from senior decision makers who have to *attend* presentations—people from such fields as banking, engineering, R&D, manufacturing, and consulting.

The following is what they had to say. It includes the top 10 gripes and the top 8 things they want from a presentation produced by people who should know what they're talking about and who ought to care about the audience they're trying to inform and persuade.

The top 10 gripes of people who have to attend important presentations

	Annoyance Rating
1. "Speakers didn't know our needs."	x x x x x x x x x x x x x x x x x x x x x
2. "Too long; too many details."	x x x x x x x x x x x x x x x x x
3. "No natural conclusion or decision step."	x x x x x x x x x x x x x x x x
4. "Needlessly technical."	x x x x x x x x x
5. "Speakers not properly prepared."	x x x x x x x x
6. "Cluttered visuals; often *unnecessary* visuals."	x x x x x
7. "Speakers got sidetracked."	x x x
8. "Too much about *them*; not enough about *us*."	x x x
9. "No clear continuity. Muddy organization."	x x
10. "Boring, not convincing."	x x

OBJECTION-HANDLING CHECKLIST

Use the following chart to analyze your objection-handling skills. After each presenting situation, check the Yes column for the items you performed correctly and the Needs Improvement column if you feel it could have gone better. After you have completed several of these, you will begin to see patterns of strengths and weaknesses and deal with them more systematically.

	Yes	Needs Improvement
1. Did I remain composed?		
a. Did I remain calm and confident in the face of objections?	_____	_____
b. Did I keep my temper under control?	_____	_____
c. Did I maintain a serious, professional demeanor?	_____	_____
2. Did I listen carefully?		
a. Did I avoid interrupting when an objection was raised?	_____	
b. Did I avoid argument?	_____	_____
c. Did I keep calm and hear the objection in full?	_____	_____
3. Did I acknowledge and confirm what I heard?		
a. Did I repeat what I heard back to the person objecting?	_____	_____
b. Did I seek clarification of any confusing points?	_____	_____
4. Did I lay the groundwork for my response?		
a. Did I assure the person that this has come up before?	_____	_____
b. Did I attempt to clarify any misunderstanding?	_____	_____
c. Did I address the perceived problem?	_____	_____
5. Did I answer the objection?		
a. Did I deal with the situation directly and forthrightly?	_____	_____
b. Was my response clear and unequivocal?	_____	_____
6. Did I emphasize benefits when handling the objection?		
a. Did I stress a benefit that would offset the perceived weakness?	_____	_____
b. Did I substitute value where lack of value was a problem?	_____	_____

Figure 1-4.

**ADDRESSING THE TOP 10 COMPLAINTS OF PEOPLE
WHO HAVE TO ATTEND IMPORTANT PRESENTATIONS**

1. What are the main needs of this audience? How do I let the audience members know I am aware of their needs? _____

_____

_____

_____

2. What do they need to know in order to make their decision? What unnecessary details can be cut from the presentation? How can I save them time? _____

_____

_____

_____

3. What am I asking them to do? What decision(s) should result from this presentation? How do I communicate the decision step to them? _____

_____

_____

_____

4. What information here might be considered overly technical? Have I avoided unnecessary jargon? Have I defined all technical terms that absolutely must be used? _____

_____

_____

_____

5. Have I prepared properly? What business and issues are involved here? What can I do to make this presentation more logical, to make it go more smoothly, to avoid confusion? _____

_____

_____

_____

6. How can the visuals be simplified? What can be done to keep the visuals relevant and clear? _____

_____

_____

_____

Figure 1-5.

7. Have I outlined the presentation so that I will not become sidetracked? What issues or questions might lead to getting sidetracked? What measures can be taken to keep the presentation moving toward the objective? _____

_____

_____

_____

8. How do I keep the presentation focused on the needs of the audience members? What are their problems and concerns? What do they absolutely have to know about me and my business? _____

_____

_____

_____

9. What can be done to improve the continuity of this presentation? What measures will ensure that it is perceived as clear and well organized? _____

_____

_____

_____

10. How can I keep the presentation lively? How can I maximize the credibility of the presentation?_____

_____

_____

_____

Figure 1-5 (*Continued*)

WORKSHEET FOR TAILORING YOUR PRESENTATION TO AUDIENCE NEEDS

1. What is this audience's current situation? How do the audience members operate? What do they need? How can I help? _____

   _____

   _____

   _____

2. What concrete recommendations can I make that will make the situation better? _____

   _____

   _____

   _____

3. What extraneous material in my presentation can be eliminated? _____

   _____

   _____

   _____

4. What things can be done to make the presentation more economical of time without forfeiting clarity?

   _____

   _____

   _____

5. Precisely how can available technology be applied to the benefit of this audience?

   _____

   _____

   _____

6. How better might the material be arranged in order to enhance communication?

   _____

   _____

   _____

7. Does the presentation include follow-up actions or implementation steps? What are they?

   _____

   _____

   _____

8. Have major points been adequately distinguished from minor ones? Have measures been taken to hold the presentation to the minimum needed for decision making, in terms of time and content? What are those measures? _____

   _____

Figure 1-6.

The top 8 things listeners say they want from a presentation

Importance Rating

1. "A better understanding of *our* current situation."   x x x x x.x x x x x x x x x x

2. "Practical solutions to real problems (and not a lot of emphasis on *theory*)."   x x x x x x x x x x x x x x

3. "Less background or introductory material."   x x x x x x x x x x x x x x

4. "A clear, concise presentation."   x x x x x x x x x x x

5. "What technology *does* for us, not what it *is*."   x x x x x x x x

6. "A well-organized presentation."   x x x x x x

7. "Clear-cut action steps to follow in case we *are* persuaded."   x x x x x x

8. "Less time devoted to minor points or details which are of little interest or importance."   x x x x

Remember that any presentation you develop must take into account the 10 most common audience complaints. You will be punished (and dismissed from the competition) for making any of the mistakes cited in the Top 10 Gripes list. The worksheet exercise in Fig. 1-5 will help you sidestep the complaints. You will be congratulated (and rewarded) by meeting your audience's needs and criteria mentioned in the Top 8 Things Listeners Say They Want list. The worksheet in Fig. 1-6 provides a framework for doing so.

A Key to Winning—Let the Other Guy Lose!

Obviously, you have to know your own industry, company, products, and services in order to succeed with winning presentations. Without that understanding, your solution will be empty. Likewise you need to know as many of the unique qualities and circumstances of your prospects and your competition as possible.

But an important fact is this: Your job is not so much to win, it is *to not lose!* Let your competitors keep doing what they're doing and look like they're stuck in a time warp when their substandard performance is compared with your superior one.

You don't have to do *everything* in this book to develop a competitive edge, but at least try to do as much as possible. And remember this very important fact about presentations (and management generally): People who *plan* always outperform those who do not.

✔ Understand, and cash in on, your audience's vision of the future.

✔ There are always problems and needs in an organization. Seek them out and develop solutions to correct them. For example, everybody would like to have more sales, higher profits, lower costs, less turnover of good people, easier ways to generate good leads, and better relationships with customers.

✔ Be prepared for every possible objection your audience could think of.

✔ Role-play and otherwise rehearse your (cool and confident) response to all possible objections.

✔ For every new presentation you work on, review The Top 10 Gripes of People Who Have to Attend Important Presentations. Ensure that you don't make any of these common mistakes.

✔ While you're at it, make sure you adequately address The Top 8 Things Listeners Say They Want from a Presentation.

✔ Do everything in your power to help your competitors *lose!*

✔ Plan!

2

Analyze Your Audience

You must learn as much as you can about the people you're talking to, the attitudes they have at present, and the attitudes and awareness that have to be modified or created. Also, even though your solution may be perfectly valid and useful, there may be a number of obstacles to surmount or avoid. The people you're trying to convince may have misconceptions and prejudices that you will have to overcome. They may be behaving in nonrational ways that you will have to counter, possibly by employing their own brand of logic. Following are the key elements to interpret and understand:

Contents of This Chapter

- Type of audience
- The present attitude of the audience
- The attitude you need to build
- The awareness you want to create
- The need to become a corporate anthropologist
- Some philosophical viewpoints to understand
- Factors that influence people's decisions (wanna versus gotta)
- Dog & Pony Checkpoints

Type of Audience

One of the first questions you need to be clear about when preparing a presentation is: "Whom am I talking to? Whom am I trying to persuade?" The checksheet shown in Fig. 2-1 represents four kinds of presentations with a breakdown of many of the audience types within each group. (There may be other categories that are important enough for you to stage a well-produced Dog & Pony Show—getting a raise, justifying a promotion, or otherwise gaining an advantage.)

A second reason for getting perspective on your audience is to see

TYPE OF AUDIENCE

As an aid in focusing your presentation, first check the major category that best describes your presentation situation: outside sale, deal, or pitch or report, or inside pitch or report. Then check off all applicable subcategories.

A. Outside Sale ❑
- Old customer .... ❑
- New customer .... ❑
- Old prospect .... ❑
- New prospect .... ❑
- "Bluebird" (unexpected sale) .... ❑
- Trade show .... ❑
- Government procurement group .... ❑
- Military procurement group .... ❑

B. Outside Deal ❑
- Private investor .... ❑
- Banker .... ❑
- Prospective buyer .... ❑
- Prospective joint venture partner or licensee .... ❑
- Supplier .... ❑
- Distributor, jobber, or broker .... ❑

C. Outside Pitch or Report ❑
- Thought or opinion leaders .... ❑
- The media .... ❑
- Local community .... ❑
- Union representatives .... ❑
- Legislators .... ❑
- Regulatory agencies .... ❑
- Trade association .... ❑
- Society or association conference .... ❑

D. Inside Pitch or Report ❑
- Shareholders .... ❑
- Stockholders .... ❑
- Board of directors .... ❑
- Corporate management .... ❑
- Sales force .... ❑
- Employees .... ❑

E. Other ❑
- _____ .... ❑
- _____ .... ❑
- _____ .... ❑
- _____ .... ❑
- _____ .... ❑

Figure 2-1.

if there is an opportunity for you to develop a secondary application for a particular presentation. After all, presentations are time-consuming and expensive to produce, so why not find other uses for the same effort? For example, a high-level presentation to an existing customer might be modified for use in a trade association meeting or for employee training and information.

The Present Attitude of the Audience

It's important also to figure out how the audience feels about you, your products and services, your ideas, or your company before you begin the preliminary stages of work on an important presentation. Don't *guess* about people's opinions and feelings,...ask these users and decision makers; have conversations with them.

Their attitudes can range from the top to the bottom of the spectrum shown in Fig. 2-2. Remember, the more positive the attitude of the audience, the more quickly you can proceed directly to your solution and its benefits. If the audience's attitude is neutral or negative, greater initial emphasis must be placed on your organization's qualifications, past history, other successful projects or products, quality of your employees, and so forth. In other words, this *general* foundation must be clarified and reinforced before you can successfully proceed to a *specific*.

Also, the more positive the audience is, the more *informal* your presentation can be. I speak later about the need to control the environment in which you're trying to persuade people. While this is tremendously important, it becomes somewhat less so if the audience is already on your side. That's why so much business is done in restaurants, in private clubs, and on golf courses. If an audience is neutral or downright negative, then you must do everything possible to appear knowledgeable, confident, and professional.

The Attitude You Need to Build

Attitudes are feelings or emotions about certain facts or conditions having to do with you, your organization, your performance, your ideas, and so forth. In most cases your objective is to reinforce the positive opinions or feelings in the first three categories in Fig. 2-3.

Note that at times certain *negative* attitudes are worth trying to stimulate. If you're in a business that's highly competitive—where there are really no new customers but merely a constant shuffling of market share among several competitors—then you generate interest in your products or services by exploiting a prospect's unhappiness with one of your rivals.

Remember that attitudes are usually nonrational or irrational, so don't try to apply too much logic to any given situation. People's feelings are usually influenced by the expression of other stronger feelings and emotions, and not necessarily facts. Hard facts, no matter how true or valid, may not be the ammunition to use in changing the minds of people who think their minds are made up.

THE PRESENT ATTITUDE OF THE AUDIENCE

It's important to figure out how the audience feels about you, your products and services, your ideas, or your company before you begin the preliminary stages of work on an important presentation. The attitudes of the audience members can range from the top to the bottom of this spectrum. For each presenting situation, get feedback from anyone who deals with you or your company. Then check the statement that most closely matches your situation. Determining your place on the attitude spectrum will help you know how far you need to go and what you need to say in your attempt at persuasion.

Positive

   A.   Very enthusiastic about you, your company, and its products .... ❑
   B.   Willing to experiment with new ideas and ready to begin .... ❑
   C.   Curious and willing to listen to what you have to say .... ❑
   D.   Open to change but in need of substantial proofs .... ❑
   E.   Unaware of — but open to— your products, people, or capabilities .... ❑

Neutral

   F.   Neutral and fearful of change and what it might bring .... ❑
   G.   Uncertain of what to do because of too many alternatives .... ❑
   H.   Confused about the facts and believing things that are untrue .... ❑
   I.   Ignorant of the facts about your products or services .... ❑
   J.   Lacking confidence in their ability to decide .... ❑

Negative

   K.   Dissatisfied with existing things and conditions .... ❑
   L.   Skeptical about your people, products, or services .... ❑
   M.   Distrustful of your company's reputation .... ❑
   N.   Apathetic about the need for your ideas or solutions .... ❑
   O.   Hostile or angry, for whatever reason or set of reasons .... ❑

Describe other possibilities: _____

_____

_____

_____

_____

Figure 2-2.

THE ATTITUDE YOU NEED TO BUILD

Consider the following possible categories: interpersonal, educational, emotional (in a strictly *positive* way), and emotional (in a way that's altogether *negative*). In planning your presentation, check off the most important attitudinal elements you want to try to instill.

Interpersonal

    A.   Confidence .... ❏
    B.   Trust .... ❏
    C.   Pride .... ❏
    D. Loyalty .... ❏

Educational

    E.   Certainty based upon proofs .... ❏
    F.   Awareness of company and industry .... ❏
    G. Knowledge of company's products and people .... ❏

Emotional (Positive)

    H. Satisfaction .... ❏
    I.   Feeling of security or safety .... ❏
    J.   Concern .... ❏
    K. Appreciation .... ❏
    L.   Longing .... ❏
    M. Possessiveness .... ❏

Emotional (Negative)

    N. Envy .... ❏
    O. Impatience .... ❏
    P.   Uncertainty .... ❏
    Q. Confusion .... ❏
    R.   Dissatisfaction .... ❏
    S.   Distrust .... ❏

Other possibilities: _____

_____

_____

_____

_____

_____

Figure 2-3.

In contrast to attitudes or opinions, awareness is much more a matter of information and reality. It is easily possible to affect awareness through various communications media, including advertising, promotion, and publicity—plus direct statements that you can make to a prospective audience ahead of time. Figure 2-4 shows a few examples of areas in which increased awareness can be cultivated.

Later I'll talk more explicitly about the factors that organizations and individuals use to *compete* and to *differentiate* themselves. The audience must be made to believe in the speaker and also in the strength or backbone of his or her argument—the fact that the solution being presented can be backed up with the requisite physical and intellectual capability. However, as I noted earlier, don't depend entirely upon logic in any given situation.

The Need to Become a Corporate Anthropologist

You can't make successful preparations unless you are aware of the extent to which your prospects (or, for that matter, you and your organization) may behave nonrationally. Not *irrationally,* mind you, but simply in ways that are not rational.

To understand this, it's helpful to understand something about cultural anthropology. Why? Because a lot of companies are like tribal villages in remote parts of the South Pacific—detached from the reality that you are familiar with.

Some companies—just like isolated societies—have their own languages, not to mention their own mores, conventions, mythology, history, and pecking orders. That's what's meant by the term *corporate culture.*

Here are some other similarities between companies and societies. See if any of these beliefs seem familiar to you from your own business experience.

- "Our society is best."

- "As a general rule, we distrust the ideas, tools, and technology of outside people."

- "History is the myth and legend that our tribal elders (senior people) agree upon; reality is what they choose reality to be."

- "We have our own language, with certain words having special meanings."

- "We also have special customs and ways of doing things, including a set of beliefs and unwritten laws including—of course—taboos."

- "Bad news is not tolerated. All forecasts must be optimistic."

- "Warriors (and salespeople) make false claims about their strength."

- "Off-islanders (customers) are usually wrong or confused. And it

THE AWARENESS YOU WANT TO CREATE

In what areas would increased awareness of you or your company make your presentation more likely to succeed? For each presentation you plan, use this list to check off the items that will best help create the kind of awareness you want.

Breadth of product line .... ❏	Management strength .... ❏
Business partnerships .... ❏	Marketing know-how .... ❏
Company name .... ❏	On-time delivery .... ❏
Competitive advantages .... ❏	Overall track record .... ❏
Concern for the environment .... ❏	Pioneering spirit, willingness to innovate .... ❏
Corporate goals .... ❏	Product/ brand identity .... ❏
Corporate business activities .... ❏	Product performance .... ❏
Corporate position on an issue .... ❏	Products .... ❏
Corporate social responsibility .... ❏	Quality .... ❏
Customer service .... ❏	Reputation .... ❏
Customer support .... ❏	R&D activities and capabilities .... ❏
Distribution system .... ❏	Record of growth .... ❏
Endorsements .... ❏	Role as an important employer .... ❏
Features .... ❏	Satisfied customers, references .... ❏
Hit rate; record of successes .... ❏	Services .... ❏
Industry leadership .... ❏	Testimonials .... ❏
Installed based .... ❏	Trademark or logotype .... ❏
Management methods .... ❏	Triumph over problems .... ❏
Management philosophy .... ❏	Technology, art, or craft .... ❏

Other possibilities: _____

_____

_____

_____

_____

_____

_____

Figure 2-4.

is easier to punish off-islanders (by raising prices) than it is to chastise islanders (by raising productivity)."

- "It is easier to chant in front of familiar idols (and hope for more sales) than it is to talk to off-islanders (to *get* more sales)."

- "Some old products gather much magic because of their age, and continue to be made whether anybody (such as a customer) wants them or not."

- "Some new products gather magic simply because of all the energy invested in them by the chief or tribal council members and will be produced whether anybody even knows about them or not."

- "Communications systems depend a lot on drums, smoke, and rumors."

Every company should write its own little book entitled *Island Fables* as a way to come to grips with reality and to illustrate the difference between what the company *says* it does and what it *really* does.

And you—as a presenter to village chiefs and elders—should by all means read that book or do some of your own research to write one.

Otherwise you will be driven to say things that may be perfectly true, but nevertheless *wrong!*

Some Philosophical Viewpoints to Understand

There is yet another level to investigate that will help you understand why people are able to deal with the same set of facts in altogether different ways. Part of it has to do with one's own mental outlook about information, future plans, and day-to-day work. It is important to understand the philosophical assumptions that drive certain people, and doubly important to avoid projecting our own assumptions on others.

My colleagues and I have developed something we call the "castle theory" to help understand some things about *points of view*—both yours and those of your audience. Here's why it's important.

Frequently a team of people (in your case, the team putting together a presentation or the team of people who will *attend* your presentation) can be in perfect agreement about the nature of the work to be done and also share a precise vocabulary of words to describe the work to be done.

Why, then, should there be any mix-ups? Why should team members occasionally look blankly at one another as if totally confused? It is because of divergent mental outlooks about information, future plans, and day-to-day work.

According to the theory, the castle has three characteristic parts to it (and three altogether different types of people residing there):

1. The tower

2. The courtyard

3. The dungeon

It is a top-to-bottom arrangement ranging from the clouds to the depths.

1. *The Tower.* This is the cheerful residence of Ms. Pollyanna and Mr. Goody Two-Shoes. It is a place of dreams, hopes, promising futures, rose-colored glasses, and certain marketing departments.

2. *The Courtyard.* The courtyard is at ground level, where practical people get results, have clear vision, and use common sense. These people can work out their differences in a logical manner.

3. *The Dungeon.* This is the dismal abode of Mr. and Mrs. It-Can't-Be-Done—a place of cynicism, suspicion, dissension, and negative attitudes. Nothing much good happens in the darkness of a dungeon.

Figure 2-5 depicts the castle hierarchy and categorizes an array of philosophical positions within each section of the castle. Figure 2-6 is an exercise that permits you to apply the castle theory for presentation planning or analysis.

The castle theory suggests that people in organizations have characteristic points of view that *they hold most of the time.* They are dependable in their optimism, practicality, or pessimism—at least given the three castle choices.

We also thought about some other categories that would define unusual behavior (if carried to an extreme), but they didn't fit in the above model. Maybe you should consider them, however, since they might turn up in a business situation.

- *Egoism.* A belief that self-interest is the motive for, and the valid end of, all conscious action.

- *Existentialism.* A philosophy based on the idea that no very good understanding or description can be had of human existence in either idealistic or scientific terms. It stresses the freedom and responsibility of individuals for themselves, even though the world may seem purposeless or chaotic.

- *Hedonism.* A belief that the principal good in life is the pursuit of one's own happiness and pleasure—the "go-for-it" attitude.

- *Intuitionism.* A belief that there are certain truths that we know only by intuition and that this forms the basis of knowledge.

- *Materialism.* The overriding belief that the most worthwhile things in life relate to material well-being and pleasure. It further holds that the reality of material supersedes spiritual feelings and intellectual ideas both in time and in logical importance.

- *Sensationalism.* A doctrine in which feeling is the sole criterion of what is good. If it feels good, it *is* good. It suggests that all our knowledge originates in sensation or sense perception (in contrast to rationalism).

THE CASTLE THEORY: Philosophical Viewpoints to Understand

The Tower

1. **Aestheticism —** Caring more about how things look than how or why they work.
2. **Altruism —** Having an overriding regard or concern for other people and their well-being, especially at the expense of bare-bone profitability.
3. **Escapism —** Diverting one's mind from reality with entertainment and daydreams. (Hoping that, when you get back, everything will be okay.)
4. **Idealism —** Placing lofty ideals ahead of practical considerations.
5. **Pacifism —** A belief in appeasement, smoothing things over and avoiding conflict.
6. **Perfectionism —** Believing that anything short of absolute perfection is unacceptable.
7. **Romanticism —** Seeing everything in dreamy, affectionate harmony.
8. **Utopianism —** Pursuing perfection; striving for ideal conditions, things, and people.

The Courtyard

9. **Eclecticism —** Taking a variety of useful beliefs and doctrines and putting them together in ways that work.
10. **Empiricism —** A belief in using observation and experience to verify knowledge. Placing more trust in firsthand observation than the extrapolation of secondhand and thirdhand research results.
11. **Pragmatism —** This is a refreshing point of view which suggests that truth can be tested by the practical consequences of believing in it.
12. **Rationalism —** Knowledge obtained by deductive means from a priori methods.
13. **Realism —** Not influenced by idealism, sentimentality, or speculation— just hard facts.
14. **Reductionism —** Reducing complicated information to its simplest terms in order to take action.

The Dungeon

15. **Defeatism —** The feeling (and practice) that "We're whipped no matter what we do!"
16. **Fatalism —** Believing that everything is preordained and that there's nothing anybody can do to change circumstances.
17. **Irrationalism —** Thinking that the universe is run by mysterious forces and that — therefore — it's okay to play wild hunches.
18. **Nihilism —** A conviction that most things merit total destruction, even though no alternative programs or systems are available.
19. **Skepticism —** Believing that there is no such thing as true knowledge because everything is uncertain. Reliable information can't be obtained.
20. **Stoicism —** An effort to not have any feelings about anything or anybody.

Other observations about philosophical points of view: _____

_____

_____

_____

_____

_____

Figure 2-5.

	A PHILOSOPHICAL PROFILE OF KEY PLAYERS IN YOUR PRESENTATION

This exercise can be used either before a presentation for planning what to say or after to analyze how you think the presentation was received. It can also be used both for the audience of the presentation and for the presenters themselves.

First, determine and write down in the space provided which part of the castle—tower, courtyard, or dungeon—each key player inhabits. Then choose from the list of philosophies accompanying each section (see Fig. 2.5), the set of assumptions that best seem to characterize that person's thinking. Finally, in the Remarks section, record how this information will shape your presentation and your future words and actions.

	Lives in	Major Philosophical Leaning	Remarks
Audience			
Member 1	_____	_____	_____
Member 2	_____	_____	_____
Member 3	_____	_____	_____
Member 4	_____	_____	_____
Member 5	_____	_____	_____
Member 6	_____	_____	_____
Presentation Team			
Member 1	_____	_____	_____
Member 2	_____	_____	_____
Member 3	_____	_____	_____
Member 4	_____	_____	_____
Member 5	_____	_____	_____
Member 6	_____	_____	_____

Figure 2-6.

- *Utilitarianism.* The concept that the useful is good. The way of deciding right conduct is to look at the usefulness of its consequences, e.g., the aim of action to promote the largest balance of pleasure over pain, or the greatest happiness for the greatest number. It's the-end-justifies-the-means argument.

You must be careful in projecting your own points of view and—most certainly—in understanding the viewpoints of the people you're presenting to.

Factors That Influence People's Decisions (*Wanna versus Gotta*)

Let's continue with some other nonrational influences on the way people think and—in particular—how they make choices. After all, the objective of a Dog & Pony Show is to influence the decision process. When it comes to decision making, people either (1) choose freely, based upon their own tastes or preferences, or (2) make a choice out of a sense of duty or moral obligation. It is the difference between *wanna* and *gotta*. The great thing about wanna is that you don't have to justify your choice. No explanations are necessary. Gotta, on the other hand, is tough. We inherit these attitudes directly from parents, other people in authority, and those we like or respect. Gotta puts us in the position of saying: "I'm doing this because I think I am expected to make this choice and I'll probably feel guilty if I don't."

Figure 2-7 contains 31 common factors that drive people to act in ways that may not make any sense.

Earlier, we spoke of the need to have well-rehearsed responses to objections. These responses should be standard to all presenters—consistent and as tightly reasoned as possible.

The same is true about the various wanna versus gotta explanations that might be expressed by audience members. You have to forecast these arguments and figure out sensible responses to them. Most of the gottas in Fig. 2-7 are false and are merely excuses to avoid or delay a decision.

Rehearse your responses in role-play situations so there is no confusion or hesitation in dealing with objections. Here's an example that sidesteps a number of the above "political" rationalizations.

> Most businesspeople agree that a good idea is one that meets all three of the following criteria: (1) it must demonstrate its capacity to either make money or save money; (2) it must promote the interests and intentions of the corporation and its shareholders; and (3) it must measurably contribute to customer satisfaction. The weight of this three-part test should be sufficient to suggest that personal or political objections be set aside.

AN EXERCISE FOR OVERCOMING COMMON OBJECTIONS TO YOUR PROPOSAL

It's a good idea to have ready answers to the most common excuses you'll encounter when presenting a new idea, product, service, or what have you. For each of the following response categories, write down your comeback. You might even consider talking these over with your colleagues, since different people will react to the excuses in different ways. Comparing notes will broaden the range of responses in your repertoire. And remember, even if you haven't encountered some of these, there is every likelihood that at some point in your career you will.

1. **Basic mistake:** "I'm stuck with the consequences of bad information or faulty advice, and there's nothing I can do about it. I'm too far in to get out." Or: "I know I've made a mistake, but I'm not going to admit it; I'm going to deny it."

2. **Circumstances:** "This is the only way I can choose because there are no alternatives. Things are the way they are, and I can't change them."

3. **Consistency:** "If we've always done it this way, then we'd better keep *doing* it this way. Don't confuse me with the facts."

4. **Duty:** "I am morally obliged (because of the tradition of the corps, the company, the flag, the nation) to choose thus."

5. **Ecology:** "My decision had better not hurt the environment, or I'll get complaints."

6. **Economics:** "Since things are getting better (or worse), I'd better choose this way."

7. **Expedient:** "This is the easy way out, and I'm going to take it. Now!"

8. **Experience:** "Practice suggests one thing, but a little voice is telling me something else."

9. **Family:** "Dad, mom, sis, and Uncle Jim all want me to choose this way."

10. **Geography:** "It's part of our culture to act the way we do."

11. **Habit:** "This is my own self-approved way of not looking at choices."

12. **Limited reason:** "I always look at (all of my favorite) alternatives."

13. **Luck:** "I'm glad (sad) to be at the right (wrong) place at the right (wrong) time."

14. **Military:** "I'll follow all orders that tell me when, how, and where to perform."

15. **Office politics:** "This is the politically 'smart' thing to do. I've got to cover my ass."

16. **Patriotism:** *"Gott mit uns* (God is with us) was on German Army belt buckles in World War I. It didn't help. " (Ambrose Bierce noted that God always seems to be on the side of the people with the biggest cannons.)

17. **Peer pressure:** "All my friends and colleagues are choosing this way."

Figure 2-7.

18.	**Personal bias:**	"I've always liked (hated) General Motors cars."
19.	**Prior agreement:**	"I signed up for four years, so I'll serve four years. That's the deal. I can't (won't) change it."
20.	**Point of view:**	"I am influenced by my coworkers' point of view, right or wrong."
21.	**Political system:**	"My choice will be consistent with the ideals of my peers."
22.	**Popularity:**	"Everybody (who is anybody) is doing it. It's the trendy thing to do."
23.	**Proximity:**	"Whoever is closest will have to make the decision (or be awarded the business)."
24.	**Religion:**	"If the Mormons here in Ogden don't drink Coke, I shouldn't either."
25.	**Research:**	"New evidence is accumulating that will affect my future choices. Maybe."
26.	**Revelation:**	"How can I argue with one who speaks directly to God?"
27.	**Secondhand bias:**	"L.A. is a terrible place. Plenty of people have told me so. I'm never going."
28.	**Stampeded:**	"They *made* me do it. It wasn't my idea."
29.	**Tradition:**	"My people (company, tribe, nation) have always chosen this way."
30.	**Technology:**	"I'd be a fool not to choose this new one."
31.	**Urgency:**	"I must decide quickly, or I will miss the chance." (False need for speed.)

Add any others you think might be appropriate. _____

_____

_____

_____

_____

_____

_____

Figure 2.7 *(Continued)*

- There are various types or kinds of audiences. You have to identify who they are as a guide to determining your content, continuity, pace, and tone.

- You must also diagnose the present attitude of the audience and learn where it is on a scale that starts at the top with wild enthusiasm and ends at the bottom with hostility and anger.

- If your audience is positive, you can make your presentation more informal. If your audience is neutral or negative, you must develop a much more structured and orderly approach.

- Once you know the prevailing attitude, you can select the new attitude that you would like to reinforce or build.

- Remember that people's attitudes and feelings are apt to be emotional and nonrational rather than logical. Be prepared to deal with this.

- You must be clear about the awareness you wish to create.

- Learn about the conventions and taboos of the "tribal leaders" in your audience. Avoid making obvious mistakes.

- Also understand how their "village" operates, especially with respect to decisions that have been made in the past and how those decisions were reached.

- Dreamers (ivory tower residents) are easy to flatter, but you mustn't get sucked into their impossible dreams.

- Remember that practical people will listen to the facts.

- Pessimists, defeatists, and skeptics are the hardest people to persuade and convince, so schedule three times as much effort to get around them. Typically, the best way is to convince their superiors, and then they will be dragged along by the decision of a higher-up.

3

Differentiate Yourself from Your Competition

Everybody has direct or indirect competition. You must evaluate all competitive forces in order to position yourself and your ideas to win. (Among the most noteworthy of "famous last words" are "I don't *have* any competition!") Then you must undertake the arduous job of showing how your solution is different from—and better than—the competition's.

Contents of This Chapter

- Important questions about your competition
- Questions to ask about you and your organization
- How to differentiate yourself from competitors
- Organizational goals
- Goals of individuals
- Key features of your solution
- Main benefits of your solution
- Ways to compete
- Strategy for success—navigating
- Dog & Pony checkpoints

As you compete against others, you must know whom you're up against and what they're likely to say. Marketing people must maintain up-to-date competitive information including price lists, catalogs, sales literature, annual reports, 10-Ks and 10-Qs, and articles in trade journals, scientific papers, and press releases.

Review the communications of your competitors and find the key themes they stress in all their sales messages—the major benefits of products, their key business values, and their goals for the future.

It is imperative—for at least two reasons—that you understand their positions and statements: (1) so that you don't embarrass yourself by accidentally using their exact words (colors, designs, slogans, etc.) and (2) so that you position yourself more favorably or attractively in the eyes of your audience.

Important Questions about Your Competition

As necessary for the development of your presentation, think about the correct answers to the questions contained in Fig. 3-1. Write your answers in the space provided.

Figure 3-2 shows a couple of forms that might be helpful in gaining a better understanding of your competitors. They are provided through the courtesy of Bob Wright, who operates a planning company in Boston.

Questions to Ask about You and Your Organization

The object of the exercise in Fig. 3-3 is to *write down* answers to the questions about your organization. There are two persuasive reasons for doing this.

First, it's a curious fact that when members of a management team are asked to answer these questions independently—in writing—*their answers almost never correspond*. The questions in Fig. 3-3 provide useful insights into why there is confusion and misunderstanding. It's simply a matter of people pulling in different directions and of having different viewpoints and expectations about what's going on now (and what can happen in the future). In preparing for a vital presentation, there must be no such difference of opinion or approach.

Second, a review of these questions will provide important clues about how to further differentiate yourself from strong competitors.

How to Differentiate Yourself from Competitors

This is just the beginning of your efforts to describe how you are different from—and therefore *better than*—your competition. There will be other valuable clues later in the book when we discuss such subjects as features, benefits, values, and how to compete. Don't worry about the fact that some of these categories may seem repetitive. Borrow any relevant material and reject the rest. Your task, after all, is to accumulate *your own list* of favorable facts that will help to position your organization and your solution well ahead of any competitor.

Use the Fig. 3-4 checksheet to focus the areas in which you either differ or would like to differ from your competitors.

Organizational Goals

Following is an entire category of differentiation—based not so much on what you have done in the past, but on what you propose to do

IMPORTANT QUESTIONS ABOUT YOUR COMPETITION

In developing your presentation, make sure you have the answers to the following list of questions. If you don't have the answers, there is a strong chance that your efforts will be misdirected or wasted.

1. First of all, what is the value of the industry you're in? What were the total annual sales (in dollars) last year? _____
_____
_____
_____

2. Is the value of the total industry growing or shrinking? _____
_____
_____
_____

3. What is *your* piece of the available pie? What is it worth? _____
_____
_____
_____

4. Who are the major competitors, and what is their share? _____
_____
_____
_____

5. Do shares change very often? How? _____
_____
_____
_____

6. Who sets the prices in your industry? _____
_____
_____
_____

7. What keeps people out of your industry? Is it money? Technology? Manufacturing? Distribution? Marketing and sales ability? _____
_____
_____
_____

Figure 3-1.

IMPORTANT QUESTIONS ABOUT YOUR COMPETITION (CONT.)

8. How quickly can you react to a competitor's action? How do you do it? _____
_____
_____
_____

9. What are the strengths of your major competitors? _____
_____
_____
_____

10. What are the weaknesses of your major competitors? _____
_____
_____
_____

11. How do they compete? What are the ways they compete? _____
_____
_____
_____

12. What are the strategic positions of your competitors? _____
_____
_____
_____

13. Are their product lines broadening or narrowing? _____
_____
_____
_____

14. How are your competitors regarded by their customers and prospects? _____
_____
_____
_____

15. What do your competitors think of you? _____
_____
_____
_____

Figure 3-1 (*Continued*)

16. What is your source of information about your competitors? _____

_____

_____

_____

17. Do you have a complete library of the sales materials used by your competitors, including brochures, catalogs, price lists, and so forth? If not, how soon can you develop such a library? _____

_____

_____

18. What are the future plans of your major competitors? _____

_____

_____

_____

19. What is your strategic position as compared with that of your major competitors? _____

_____

_____

_____

20. Where is each of your competitors' products in their life cycles? _____

_____

_____

_____

21. Can you create new customers, or must you take them from the competition? Explain. _____

_____

_____

_____

22. How can you differentiate yourself from the competition? _____

_____

_____

_____

Further observations: _____

_____

_____

_____

_____

Figure 3-1 (*Continued*)

GENERAL STATUS OF BUSINESS COMPETITORS

MEASURE	KEY COMPETITORS			OUR POSITION
	1	2	3	
Company sales				
Share of market				
Growth rate				
Geographic strength				
Competitive thrust				
Number of plants				
Square feet				
Total employees				
Total salespeople				
Accounts				
Installed units				
Key strength				
Key weakness Product importance				

STRATEGIC POSITIONS OF BUSINESS COMPETITORS

MEASURE	#1						#2						#3						OUR POSITION					
	D	S	F	T	W	N	D	S	F	T	W	N	D	S	F	T	W	N	D	S	F	T	W	N
Marketing																								
Engineering																								
Product design																								
Quality																								
Full line																								
Manufacturing cost																								
Pricing																								
Dealers																								
Distribution																								
Sales force																								
Promotion																								
Patents																								
Inventory																								
Other key measure																								

D-Dominant, controls the other competitors and has a wide choice of options. **S-Satisfactory,** able to take independent action without endangering long-term position. Can maintain position regardless of competitors' action. **F-Favorable,** has a strength which is exploitable in particular strategies. Has more than average opportunity to improve position. **T-Tenable,** sufficiently satisfactory performance to stay in business. Usually exists at the sufferance of the dominant player. Has less than average opportunity to improve position. **W-Weak,** currently unsatisfactory performance, but an opportunity exists for improvement. May have most of the characteristics of a better position, but obvious shortcomings. This is an inherently short-term condition and it must change. **N-Non-Viable,** currently unsatisfactory performance without opportunity for improvement. Must quit. (This material used by permission of Robert V. L. Wright, Boston.)

Figure 3-2.

COMPANY COMPETITIVE PROFILE: YOUR COMPANY

Company History

1. When was your organization founded, and what were the general business conditions at that time?

   _____

   _____

   _____

2. Why was it founded? _____

   _____

   _____

3. Did it have customers when it first started? If so, who were they? _____

   _____

   _____

4. How big is it now? ("Big" in terms of revenues, products, product lines, facilities, equipment, and so forth.) _____

   _____

   _____

5. Was it ever bigger than it is now? If so, explain when and why. _____

   _____

   _____

Purpose

6. In one paragraph, how would you write a statement of purpose for your organization? Describe its intentions and directions – where you think you're going and why. _____

   _____

   _____

Beliefs

7. What are the important values and beliefs of the company (expressed not just in words, but in the actions of the people in the organization)? _____

   _____

   _____

8. What is the working atmosphere of your company? _____

   _____

   _____

Figure 3-3.

9. What are some of the favorite myths of your organization (ideas that you keep talking about as real, but which are not)? _____

_____

_____

People

10. Who founded the company? What was the character of the founder? What were his or her intentions, values, and beliefs? _____

_____

_____

11. Can you draw a simple organization chart that shows the key people? _____

_____

_____

12. Which people are absolutely vital to your company? _____

_____

_____

13. What are your personnel turnover statistics? What are the chief causes of turnover? _____

_____

_____

14. What does it cost to go through the search, selection, indoctrination, and training of a new person?

_____

_____

_____

15. Are you understaffed? Overstaffed? Explain. _____

_____

_____

16. Divide annual sales revenues by the number of people in the organization. What is each person "worth" in terms of sales? Now go back and isolate the number of people in revenue-generating activities. Divide annual sales revenues by this smaller number. What does this say? _____

_____

_____

17. Is there a succession plan for the company? If so, describe it in brief. _____

_____

_____

Figure 3-3   *(Continued)*

COMPANY COMPETITIVE PROFILE: YOUR COMPANY (CONT.)

Products and Markets

18. What is your most important product, product line, or service? _____
_____
_____

19. Where are you doing business (i.e., locally, regionally, nationally, internationally)? Please explain. _____
_____
_____
_____

20. How many different businesses are you in? _____
_____
_____

21. What are your plans for introducing new products? _____
_____
_____

22. Are your product lines broadening or narrowing? Explain how and why. _____
_____
_____

23. Who are your major competitors? _____
_____
_____

24. Who sets prices in your industry? _____
_____
_____

Performance

25. How would you describe your performance over the last six years? _____
_____
_____

26. What is your present financial position? (If you are undercapitalized, what areas are most affected?) _____
_____
_____

Figure 3-3 (*Continued*)

COMPANY COMPETITIVE PROFILE: YOUR COMPANY (CONT.)

27. Do you have the necessary production and distribution capabilities to support your present sales objectives?

_____

_____

_____

28. At what percentage of total capacity are you presently operating? Please explain. _____

_____

_____

29. Do you perceive yourself to be "on schedule" with respect to the growth of your business? _____

_____

_____

_____

30. How would you increase your capacity to produce goods or provide services? Extra shifts? Overtime? New hires? New equipment or facilities? Outside vendors? Explain, and provide a simple cost-benefit analysis of each alternative. _____

_____

_____

31. Are you a leader or a follower in engineering and technological advances? What about new business developments generally? _____

_____

_____

32. What were the three smartest things your company did last year? What were the dumbest? _____

_____

_____

Planning

33. Do you have an operating budget? If so, describe it and indicate how long it has been in place. _____

_____

_____

34. Do you have a marketing plan (and budget)? If so, describe it and indicate how long it has been in place. ____

_____

_____

35. Do you have a long-range (or "strategic") plan? If so, describe it and indicate how long it has been in place.

_____

_____

_____

Figure 3-3 (*Continued*)

36. Do you have a cost-control system? If so, describe it and indicate how long it has been in place. _____
_____
_____

37. Describe your forecasting success. _____
_____
_____

The Present

38. What are the challenges facing your business today? _____
_____
_____

39. What do you see as your priorities at present? _____
_____
_____

40. What are your company's strengths? _____
_____
_____

41. What are your company's weaknesses? _____
_____
_____

The Future

42. Where are you going? (What should you do next?) _____
_____
_____

43. What happens if you keep doing exactly what you're doing now? _____
_____
_____

44. What social, political, economic, or market forces can influence the success or future growth of your business?
_____
_____

45. What specific proposed or pending federal or state legislation could affect the success or future growth of your business?
_____
_____

Figure 3.3 (*Continued*)

DIFFERENTIATING YOURSELF FROM COMPETITORS

Following are just a few of the areas in which an individual or company can excel. Choose the ones that represent points of differentiation for you or your company. When putting together your presentation, incorporate these points of distinction, in whatever combination you desire, to create an impression of uniqueness in the eyes of your client.

1. Track record at having solved serious customer problems .... ❏
2. On-time delivery (or sooner-than-expected-delivery) .... ❏
3. Accurate billing system; no time-consuming foul-ups for customers .... ❏
4. Superior customer service, generally .... ❏
5. Broader product line than nearby competitors .... ❏
6. National warehousing and distribution system .... ❏
7. Lower costs because of overseas production facilities .... ❏
8. More favorable guarantees or warranties .... ❏
9. Advantageous manufacturing capability .... ❏
10. More loyal or dependable work force .... ❏
11. Less turnover; better continuity of operations .... ❏
12. Higher standards and level of quality .... ❏
13. More responsive service people .... ❏
14. Better customer-complaint handling .... ❏
15. Superior design capabilities .... ❏
16. Dominant player in the industry; therefore the price-setter .... ❏
17. Preferable supplier because of better sales and service .... ❏
18. Leading product-development company .... ❏
19. Number one in customer satisfaction .... ❏
20. Outstanding engineering .... ❏
21. Cheaper than other competitors .... ❏
22. Bigger facilities .... ❏
23. Smarter management and planning .... ❏
24. Preeminent in the field .... ❏
25. A pronounced technological edge .... ❏
26. Greater savings .... ❏
27. Greater prominence, more name recognition .... ❏
28. Larger number of dealers and service centers .... ❏
29. Prettier; better designed .... ❏
30. Cleverer advertising .... ❏
31. Better environmental record .... ❏
32. More worthwhile features .... ❏
33. More favorable record of new-product introductions .... ❏
34. Better testing .... ❏
35. More installations .... ❏
36. Higher levels of quality control .... ❏
37. Better production planning and control .... ❏
38. Smarter inventory levels .... ❏
39. Better quality control .... ❏
40. Fewer legal hassles .... ❏
41. Higher levels of training .... ❏

Add your own: _____

_____

_____

Figure 3-4.

in the future. Goals are always a bit fuzzy, but they may provide something you can talk about in a convincing manner.

Goals are the ultimate, long-run, open-ended attributes that both organizations and individuals seek. Goals are frequently difficult—sometimes impossible—to measure. Figure 3-5 is a listing of some sample organizational goals that people think about in their ongoing efforts to be (or become) successful. If you know something about your audience's goals, you can try to connect with them in your presentation.

Goals of Individuals

Apart from organizational goals, there are also general goals, many of which are listed in Fig. 3-6, that people talk about having or of working toward in their lives. If you can link into any of the personal goals of people in your audience, then you stand a much greater chance of advancing your point of view. This, indirectly, is yet another way to compete for attention.

Key Features of Your Solution

The next checksheet, Fig. 3-7, is presented in this context to further amplify the differences between features and benefits. Features describe what a thing *is*. Benefits describe what a thing *means*, particularly to a user. Make additions to Fig. 3-7 regarding the distinctive features of your own particular solution.

Following is a sample summary of features that a company might make, not so much to tell a prospect or a client, but to position itself:

> Our products are well engineered and produced; our quality is high; we help clients create a competitive advantage; we're available and responsive; experienced; imaginative and creative; committed to customers; and we guarantee on-time delivery. We're also safe—a lot safer than competitors who don't know what they're doing. We're objective and can always advocate choices that are in the best interests of the audience rather than the presenter. Finally, we're economical in our own way, especially when people schedule enough time so that we can avoid rush or overtime charges.

Sound suspiciously like *your* company?

Main Benefits of Your Solution

Now let's review the idea of "benefits" selling for just a minute. Its major theme is that you must *not* go around crowing about all your important credentials if you don't have any meaning to the people you're trying to influence. All of your knowledge, reputation, experience, solutions, efficiency, and good ideas don't mean anything until they're applied to something your prospect or client wants or needs (or can be made to want or need).

ORGANIZATIONAL GOALS

For each presentation you do, check this list of organizational goals for the ones that are held by your prospective client. Make sure to tap into your client's organizational goals to whatever extent possible when planning and delivering the presentation. If your client's goal is not on the list, record it at the bottom of the page with a short explanation.

Achieve higher margins .... ❑

Advance _____ 's career .... ❑

Avoid costly risks or errors .... ❑

Be less crisis-oriented .... ❑

Become more innovative .... ❑

Break even .... ❑

Become profitable .... ❑

Control costs .... ❑

Contribute to our community .... ❑

Develop more qualified leads .... ❑

Develop new products .... ❑

Encourage more participation .... ❑

Establish better plans .... ❑

Establish new levels of quality .... ❑

Improve customer relations .... ❑

Improve customer service .... ❑

Improve internal training .... ❑

Improve morale .... ❑

Improve productivity .... ❑

Improve relationships with

_____ .... ❑

Increase market penetration .... ❑

Increase credibility .... ❑

Inspire initiative .... ❑

Make better forecasts .... ❑

Maximize revenues .... ❑

Minimize misunderstandings .... ❑

Protect competitive position .... ❑

Reduce red tape .... ❑

Finally resolve the _____

situation .... ❑

Seek new sources of revenue .... ❑

Steal share from competitors .... ❑

Survive .... ❑

Shorten the sales cycle .... ❑

Take the lead in a new idea .... ❑

Possible additions: _____

_____

_____

_____

_____

Figure 3-5.

GOALS OF INDIVIDUALS

To the extent possible, you should also try to link into the individual goals of the decision maker(s) in your audience. Casual conversation can often yield information on an individual's goals, apart from those of the organization. Choose from the following list any individual goals that you know are held by people you will be presenting to. Since some of these goals are contradictory, it is better to limit the number you choose to address, and to prioritize the ones you do choose.

Adventure ❏	Love ❏
Challenge ❏	Peace of mind, safety ❏
Comfort ❏	Playing it safe in order not to screw up ❏
Control of life (or self) ❏	Pleasure ❏
Enlightenment ❏	Possessions, property ❏
Equality ❏	Power, influence ❏
Fame ❏	Recognition, status ❏
Financial security ❏	Salvation ❏
Free time ❏	Self-confidence ❏
Friendship ❏	Self-esteem ❏
Fulfillment ❏	Sense of purpose ❏
Happiness ❏	Serenity, tranquillity ❏
Harmony ❏	Serving others ❏
Independence ❏	Strength ❏
Influence ❏	Survival ❏
Justice ❏	Wisdom, knowledge ❏
Keeping things as they are ❏	Work that has meaning ❏

Add others that may apply to specific audience members: _____

_____

_____

_____

_____

Figure 3-6.

KEY FEATURES OF YOUR SOLUTION

Features describe what a thing *is*. Benefits describe what a thing *means* or *does*, particularly to a user. This list can be used as a menu of generic features that describe a wide range of manufactured products, service products, ideas, and other kinds of "solutions." For each presentation, check the features of your solution that you will want to call the audience's attention to. Add any that are not on the list. And remember, it is best to concentrate on your two or three main features. Make additions to this list as necessary, regarding the distinctive features of your own particular solution.

Abrasion-resistant	❏	Handy	❏
Accurate	❏	Has many extras, options	❏
All-natural ingredients	❏	Heat-resistant	❏
Attractive, stylish, good-looking	❏	High tech	❏
Automatic	❏	Highest quality	❏
Available and responsive	❏	Imaginative and creative	❏
Battery-operated	❏	Latest fashions	❏
Broad selection	❏	Long-lasting	❏
Compact	❏	Long-range	❏
Committed to customers	❏	Made-to-order	❏
Compatible	❏	Many applications, same product	❏
Cordless	❏	Mildew-resistant	❏
Crashproof	❏	Needs no assembly	❏
Creates competitive advantage	❏	Nonskid, nonslip	❏
Deluxe	❏	On-time delivery	❏
Dependable operation	❏	Portable or mobile	❏
Dependable service	❏	Powerful	❏
Designed for outdoor use	❏	Range of colors	❏
Detachable components	❏	Remote controlled	❏
Doesn't break very often	❏	Resists shocks	❏
Economical	❏	Safe	❏
Experienced	❏	Scratch-resistant	❏
Factory-new or factory-perfect	❏	Solid (brass, steel, wood, etc.)	❏
Fast-acting	❏	Starts easily at all temperatures	❏
Fast response time	❏	State of the art, advanced	❏
Fireproof or fire-resistant	❏	Tough, sturdy, or rugged	❏
Folds up for storage	❏	Upgradable	❏
Fully adjustable	❏	Variable controls	❏
Genuine	❏	Waterproof	❏
Handmade or one of a kind	❏	Well engineered and produced	❏

DANGER: Since people care about benefits, avoid long lists of features. Just name your top three:

_____

_____

Figure 3-7.

Remember this well-known equation:

$$Needs + features = benefits$$

I first saw it in Xerox Corporation's popular *Professional Selling Skills*™ program. The equation means that:

1. You must learn about the real *needs* of your audience, and those needs may not always be fully amplified in a request for proposal (RFP) or a request for information (RFI), and it may not be clear in the minds of prospects.

2. When you have identified all of the audience members' needs, you can begin to adapt your *features* to them.

3. *Benefits* must then emerge from the marriage of their needs and your features.

It's best if the prospects or clients identify—and get excited about—the benefits inherent in what you've said. If this doesn't happen, you've got to jump in with the appropriate and persuasive information about obvious (and, in some cases, *not*-so-obvious) benefits.

Remember one thing: Objections are more effectively countered by reviewing benefits (or introducing new ones) than by restating features and getting bogged down in talking about yourself. People are more concerned about their own well-being and in gaining advantage than they are in listening to laundry lists of information that's of no interest to them.

Benefits (to *be* benefits) must always be capable of being expressed in *financially measurable terms*. (For example, it's not good enough to say: "We're good at reducing inventory investments." The positive way to say it is: "Under our direction, inventory investments can be reduced by $350,000 per quarter.")

Use Figs. 3-8 and 3-9 to check for benefits that will serve you and your prospects best—benefits that make money, save money, or improve productivity. There are two kinds:

A. The benefits in Fig. 3-8 can create *more* of something that is good or beneficial—in other words, build it up, encourage more of it, or promote it. An upward arrow (↑) identifies benefits such as these.

B. On the other hand, one can eliminate, minimize, or curtail those things, conditions, or activities that are not productive or harmonious, as indicated in Fig. 3-9. You can knock them down or discourage them. A downward arrow (↓) identifies benefits that head in this direction.

Please start with the "up" arrows and also measure the extent or degree to which you can guarantee a particular effect. Use a red pen to define the relative value of these benefits as they relate to your service or product. On this scale, 1 is the *least* powerful or effective and 10 is the *most*. What can you help to do? What contribution can you or your product really *make*?

MAIN BENEFITS OF YOUR SOLUTION—PART A (PUSH UP)

What contribution can you or your product really make?

Check the following for benefits that will best serve you and your audience — benefits that create an advantage because they make money, save money, improve productivity or quality, enhance customer satisfaction, and so forth. There are two ways to succeed. In category A, it is possible to create *more* of something that is good or beneficial — in other words, build it up, encourage more of it, or promote it. We indicate these benefits with an upward-pointing arrow. In category B, on the other hand, one can eliminate, minimize, or curtail those things, conditions, or activities that are not productive or harmonious. You can knock them down or discourage them. We indicate these benefits with a downward-pointing arrow.

Benefit	Least ⟶ Most
A-1 Aid decision making ↑.	1 2 3 4 5 6 7 8 9 10
A-2 Adapt to your specific needs ↑.	1 2 3 4 5 6 7 8 9 10
A-3 Advance _____'s career ↑.	1 2 3 4 5 6 7 8 9 10
A-4 Analyze complex situations ↑.	1 2 3 4 5 6 7 8 9 10
A-5 Arouse interest ↑.	1 2 3 4 5 6 7 8 9 10
A-6 Assure availability ↑.	1 2 3 4 5 6 7 8 9 10
A-7 Build a solid information base ↑.	1 2 3 4 5 6 7 8 9 10
A-8 Build confidence in people ↑.	1 2 3 4 5 6 7 8 9 10
A-9 Build enthusiasm generally ↑.	1 2 3 4 5 6 7 8 9 10
A-10 Clarify priorities ↑.	1 2 3 4 5 6 7 8 9 10
A-11 Conserve resources ↑.	1 2 3 4 5 6 7 8 9 10
A-12 Create a competitive edge ↑.	1 2 3 4 5 6 7 8 9 10
A-13 Create new demand ↑.	1 2 3 4 5 6 7 8 9 10
A-14 Create new products or processes ↑.	1 2 3 4 5 6 7 8 9 10
A-15 Develop better budgets ↑.	1 2 3 4 5 6 7 8 9 10
A-16 Develop better cost standards ↑.	1 2 3 4 5 6 7 8 9 10
A-17 Develop better customer relations ↑.	1 2 3 4 5 6 7 8 9 10
A-18 Develop better schedules ↑.	1 2 3 4 5 6 7 8 9 10
A-19 Develop new markets ↑.	1 2 3 4 5 6 7 8 9 10
A-20 Encourage creative thinking ↑.	1 2 3 4 5 6 7 8 9 10
A-21 Encourage proper follow-up ↑.	1 2 3 4 5 6 7 8 9 10
A-22 Enhance customer relations ↑.	1 2 3 4 5 6 7 8 9 10
A-23 Enhance image ↑.	1 2 3 4 5 6 7 8 9 10
A-24 Establish priorities for doing effective work ↑.	1 2 3 4 5 6 7 8 9 10
A-25 Estimate marketing and sales costs ↑.	1 2 3 4 5 6 7 8 9 10
A-26 Execute plans on time and in budget ↑.	1 2 3 4 5 6 7 8 9 10
A-27 Expand service ↑.	1 2 3 4 5 6 7 8 9 10
A-28 Find new uses for old technology ↑.	1 2 3 4 5 6 7 8 9 10
A-29 Gain power ↑.	1 2 3 4 5 6 7 8 9 10
A-30 Effectively gather information ↑.	1 2 3 4 5 6 7 8 9 10
A-31 Identify new customers ↑.	1 2 3 4 5 6 7 8 9 10
A-32 Improve communications ↑.	1 2 3 4 5 6 7 8 9 10
A-33 Improve forecasts ↑.	1 2 3 4 5 6 7 8 9 10

Figure 3-8.

MAIN BENEFITS OF YOUR SOLUTION—PART A (PUSH UP) (CONT.)

Benefit	Least $\rightarrow$ Most
A-34 Improve margins ↑.	1 2 3 4 5 6 7 8 9 10
A-35 Improve morale ↑.	1 2 3 4 5 6 7 8 9 10
A-36 Improve customer service ↑.	1 2 3 4 5 6 7 8 9 10
A-37 Improve on-the-job performance↑.	1 2 3 4 5 6 7 8 9 10
A-38 Improve efficiency or productivity ↑.	1 2 3 4 5 6 7 8 9 10
A-39 Improve financial performance ↑.	1 2 3 4 5 6 7 8 9 10
A-40 Improve our cash position ↑.	1 2 3 4 5 6 7 8 9 10
A-41 Improve our design capabilities ↑.	1 2 3 4 5 6 7 8 9 10
A-42 Improve quality ↑.	1 2 3 4 5 6 7 8 9 10
A-43 Improve reliability ↑.	1 2 3 4 5 6 7 8 9 10
A-44 Improve scheduling ↑.	1 2 3 4 5 6 7 8 9 10
A-45 Improve technology ↑.	1 2 3 4 5 6 7 8 9 10
A-46 Improve training ↑.	1 2 3 4 5 6 7 8 9 10
A-47 Increased market penetration ↑.	1 2 3 4 5 6 7 8 9 10
A-48 Increase profits ↑.	1 2 3 4 5 6 7 8 9 10
A-49 Increase return on investment ↑.	1 2 3 4 5 6 7 8 9 10
A-50 Improve safety ↑.	1 2 3 4 5 6 7 8 9 10
A-51 Increase sales or qualified leads ↑.	1 2 3 4 5 6 7 8 9 10
A-52 Increase satisfaction ↑.	1 2 3 4 5 6 7 8 9 10
A-53 Increase visibility ↑.	1 2 3 4 5 6 7 8 9 10
A-54 Invent new products (that customers *want*) ↑.	1 2 3 4 5 6 7 8 9 10
A-55 Maintain market share ↑.	1 2 3 4 5 6 7 8 9 10
A-56 Maximize performance ↑.	1 2 3 4 5 6 7 8 9 10
A-57 Preserve natural resources ↑.	1 2 3 4 5 6 7 8 9 10
A-58 Promote teamwork ↑.	1 2 3 4 5 6 7 8 9 10
A-59 Protect investments ↑.	1 2 3 4 5 6 7 8 9 10
A-60 Protect reputation ↑.	1 2 3 4 5 6 7 8 9 10
A-61 Provide long-term security for employees ↑.	1 2 3 4 5 6 7 8 9 10
A-62 Provide a final resolution to the situation ↑.	1 2 3 4 5 6 7 8 9 10
A-63 Provide satisfaction for people on the job ↑.	1 2 3 4 5 6 7 8 9 10
A-64 Speed up deliveries ↑.	1 2 3 4 5 6 7 8 9 10
A-65 Stabilize earnings ↑.	1 2 3 4 5 6 7 8 9 10
A-66 Steal market share ↑.	1 2 3 4 5 6 7 8 9 10
A-67 Stimulate new products ↑.	1 2 3 4 5 6 7 8 9 10
A-68 Streamline the organization ↑.	1 2 3 4 5 6 7 8 9 10
A-69 Understand competitive forces ↑.	1 2 3 4 5 6 7 8 9 10
A-70 Understand and control vulnerabilities ↑.	1 2 3 4 5 6 7 8 9 10
A-71 Win new customers ↑.	1 2 3 4 5 6 7 8 9 10
A-72 Win recognition for your accomplishments ↑.	1 2 3 4 5 6 7 8 9 10

Figure 3.8 *(Continued)*

And here are the B's — to hold down or minimize. What can you (your products, services, or ideas) do to help the following?

Benefit	Least $\longrightarrow$ Most
B-1 Avoid danger↓.	1 2 3 4 5 6 7 8 9 10
B-2 Avoid delays ↓.	1 2 3 4 5 6 7 8 9 10
B-3 Avoid or control overtime ↓.	1 2 3 4 5 6 7 8 9 10
B-4 Avoid or minimize unnecessary effort ↓.	1 2 3 4 5 6 7 8 9 10
B-5 Avoid production shortfalls↓.	1 2 3 4 5 6 7 8 9 10
B-6 Avoid regulatory surprises↓.	1 2 3 4 5 6 7 8 9 10
B-7 Avoid risk ↓.	1 2 3 4 5 6 7 8 9 10
B-8 Avoid shortages ↓.	1 2 3 4 5 6 7 8 9 10
B-9 Avoid shortfalls in production↓.	1 2 3 4 5 6 7 8 9 10
B-10 Avoid waste ↓.	1 2 3 4 5 6 7 8 9 10
B-11 Conserve important resources↓.	1 2 3 4 5 6 7 8 9 10
B-12 Control or reduce costs↓.	1 2 3 4 5 6 7 8 9 10
B-13 Control overtime ↓.	1 2 3 4 5 6 7 8 9 10
B-14 Cut costs ↓.	1 2 3 4 5 6 7 8 9 10
B-15 Determine products to discontinue ↓.	1 2 3 4 5 6 7 8 9 10
B-16 Eliminate or reduce production bottlenecks↓.	1 2 3 4 5 6 7 8 9 10
B-17 Eliminate duplication of effort↓.	1 2 3 4 5 6 7 8 9 10
B-18 Eliminate nuisances ↓.	1 2 3 4 5 6 7 8 9 10
B-19 Handle and minimize customer complaints↓.	1 2 3 4 5 6 7 8 9 10
B-20 Limit risk ↓.	1 2 3 4 5 6 7 8 9 10
B-21 Minimize duplication of effort↓.	1 2 3 4 5 6 7 8 9 10
B-22 Minimize errors ↓.	1 2 3 4 5 6 7 8 9 10
B-23 Minimize mistakes ↓.	1 2 3 4 5 6 7 8 9 10
B-24 Minimize late deliveries ↓.	1 2 3 4 5 6 7 8 9 10
B-25 Minimize paperwork at all levels↓.	1 2 3 4 5 6 7 8 9 10
B-26 Minimize wasted time↓.	1 2 3 4 5 6 7 8 9 10
B-27 Reduce canceled contracts↓.	1 2 3 4 5 6 7 8 9 10
B-28 Reduce faulty installations ↓.	1 2 3 4 5 6 7 8 9 10
B-29 Reduce inspection time and costs↓.	1 2 3 4 5 6 7 8 9 10
B-30 Reduce inventory investments↓.	1 2 3 4 5 6 7 8 9 10
B-31 Reduce maintenance costs ↓.	1 2 3 4 5 6 7 8 9 10
B-32 Reduce turnover ↓.	1 2 3 4 5 6 7 8 9 10
B-33 Reduce waste and scrap ↓.	1 2 3 4 5 6 7 8 9 10
B-34 Save work ↓.	1 2 3 4 5 6 7 8 9 10
B-35 Save valuable time ↓.	1 2 3 4 5 6 7 8 9 10
B-36 Shorten lead time to sales ↓.	1 2 3 4 5 6 7 8 9 10
B-37 Simplify policies and procedures↓.	1 2 3 4 5 6 7 8 9 10
B-38 Solve customer complaints ↓.	1 2 3 4 5 6 7 8 9 10
B-39 Solve problems ↓.	1 2 3 4 5 6 7 8 9 10

Figure 3-9.

Here are a few of the ways used by successful companies to develop—and retain—their customers. How do *you* compete? Have you ever formalized a statement about how you do it? Is what you *say* about how you compete really true? The abbreviated checksheet shown in Fig. 3-10 will help you refine or improve the way you do business. And remember to *add* to these possibilities wherever possible. As with all the other lists, this is only a general review and is not meant to be definitive.

1. *Accuracy.* This can relate to a product quality (Bulova Watch, for example) or an organizational quality. If your competition makes mistakes and you don't, then you have an advantage.

2. *Add-ons.* Examples of companies making their own add-ons to basic items of equipment include IBM and Pentax Camera. Others (such as computer software and peripheral manufacturers) provide products that work with equipment built by others.

3. *Agreeable and accommodating.* Having salespeople or sales representatives with this characteristic may represent an important way to compete. Avis Rent-A-Car Company comes to mind. Also Caterpillar Tractor's promise: "We provide spare parts anyplace in the world within 24 hours!"

4. *Appearance.* This is important, and it includes people, products, department store areas, vegetable displays in supermarkets, packaging, and everything else. *Styling* is an aspect of this, as exemplified in the Jaguar and Ferrari—and also in clothing fashion and architectural design.

5. *Associations and relationships.* Your associations and relationships can be better than your competition's. This could mean that you have suppliers, subcontractors, and consultants who can be counted on for dependable work, service, or advice. You may also have business and professional relationships that can be extremely valuable.

6. *Availability.* People in sales and service must be available when they are needed. Phones should be answered speedily and correctly. Advertised products must be in stock.

7. *Best people.* Having the best people is an effective means of competition. This means hiring and training the most competent, knowledgeable, and experienced people you can find.

8. *Commitment.* This is the concern for doing a good job on time and in budget, for providing the best customer service possible, and for sticking with a value (e.g., IBM's commitment to service or Sony's guarantee of quality).

9. *Communications.* Some goods and services are sold almost exclusively through programs of advertising, sales promotion, PR, publicity, trade show participation, and the like.

10. *Continuity.* Continuity is an important asset to companies that have been in business for a long time. Examples include West-

WAYS TO COMPETE

The sky's the limit when it comes to differentiating yourself from the competition. However, when the heat's on, it can be difficult to put your finger on specific areas of difference. Use this list to jump-start the differentiation process. If you think of factors not contained in the list, add them at the bottom of the form.

Accuracy .... ❑	Image .... ❑
Add-ons .... ❑	In business a long time .... ❑
Agreeable and accommodating .... ❑	Join ventures .... ❑
Appearance .... ❑	Knowledge, intelligence .... ❑
Associations and relationships .... ❑	Marketing know-how .... ❑
Availability .... ❑	Name or reputation .... ❑
Best people .... ❑	Objectivity, impartiality .... ❑
Commitment .... ❑	Only source of supply .... ❑
Communications .... ❑	Packaging .... ❑
Continuity .... ❑	Payment terms, financing .... ❑
Convenience .... ❑	Performance .... ❑
Coverage, distribution .... ❑	Price .... ❑
Craftsmanship, workmanship .... ❑	Prime location .... ❑
Delivery .... ❑	Product line .... ❑
Dependability .... ❑	Quality .... ❑
Discounts, deals .... ❑	Reliability .... ❑
Disposability, expendability .... ❑	Repairability .... ❑
Doesn't grow old .... ❑	Research .... ❑
Easy to order, to use .... ❑	Responds to a specific need .... ❑
Economy, no frills .... ❑	Saves time or labor .... ❑
Efficiency .... ❑	Security, safety .... ❑
Elegance .... ❑	Service .... ❑
Endorsements, testimonials .... ❑	Sex appeal .... ❑
Enthusiasm .... ❑	Specialization .... ❑
Experience .... ❑	Speed .... ❑
Facilities .... ❑	Status .... ❑
Features .... ❑	Tailor-made, unique .... ❑
First class, top of the line .... ❑	Terms .... ❑
Free samples, trials, or demonstrations .... ❑	Timeliness .... ❑
Giveaways .... ❑	Trade-in policy .... ❑
Guarantee .... ❑	Warranty .... ❑

What are the best ways for you to compete in order to sell *your* solution? _____

_____

Figure 3-10.

ern Union, Texaco, Bon Ami, Campbell's Soup, and Heinz products. Having been around a long time suggests dependability and quality.

11. *Convenience.* This is of great value to many customers or clients. People don't mind spending more money for things in a store that's open 24 hours a day. 7-11 and U-Tote-M are successful examples. There is also the convenience offered by bank card machines, Photo-Mat, and Midas Muffler and Brake Shops.

12. *Coverage, distribution.* Sometimes it's possible to control a market because you can deliver to it efficiently. The success of Federal Express is an excellent example. Book publishing and distribution is another.

13. *Craftsmanship, workmanship.* Craftsmanship or workmanship will sometimes provide a competitive edge by itself, all the way from inexpensive consumer items and craft products up to luxury automobiles. For example, it takes two people nearly a month to finish the leather upholstery and woodwork in a Rolls Royce.

14. *Delivery.* Delivery can provide a significant competitive edge if you can charge about the same price for a product as your competitor does but offer a delivery service—especially a free one. An example is Domino's Pizza's offer to deliver its product within 30 minutes.

15. *Dependability.* This is an advantage for those who have products and services that can be counted on without fail. Examples include Kodak's line of amateur and professional film products and Winchester Arms. The best example, of course, is Maytag—which has based a long-running series of TV commercials on this characteristic.

16. *Discounts, deals.* Discounts and deals are frequently offered to major customers as a reward for cash purchases or large orders or as part of a merchandising sale. Companies such as Buyers Club are able to discount their merchandise because they sell from warehouses.

17. *Disposability, expendability.* It's possible to compete successfully at the lower end of the quality line with expendable products such as watches, portable radios, and handheld calculators that are replaced rather than repaired, or with entirely disposable products such as Kleenex Tissues, Bic Razors, and Pampers diapers.

18. *Easy to order, easy to use.* Your product may be simpler to operate (or easier to get, start, use, repair, change, or update) than your competition's. Manufacturers of office copiers, dictating equipment, audio recorders, and home videocassette players are constantly looking for ways to make their systems more idiot-proof or easier to operate.

19. *Economy, no frills.* This sales approach has been taken by airlines, travel companies, car-rental companies, and discounters. Henry Ford followed this approach when he introduced automobiles to America with the Model T ("in any color you want, as long as it's black").

20. *Efficiency.* If your products (or your operations) are more efficient than those of your competition, then costs will be lower and profits higher. The original VW Beetle successfully competed on fuel economy, among other factors. Ad campaigns for flashlight batteries stress improved efficiency and longer shelf life.

21. *Elegance.* This is a way of competing at the highest end of any luxury market—where price is of no real concern to the purchaser. Examples include mansions, condominiums, yachts, women's gowns, and jewelry from such establishments as Cartier and Tiffany & Company.

22. *Endorsements, testimonials.* Endorsements and testimonials sharpen a competitive edge, especially if the product or service (or—as in the case of a presidential candidate—a person), has the approval and support of some important individual, institution, or business organization.

23. *Enthusiasm.* This may seem general and vague, but it's an ingredient that has been the key to the initial success of countless businesses—and the turnaround of many others. If businesspeople don't have enthusiasm, they can't expect growth or success.

24. *Experience.* This factor has value in every business or professional undertaking (and it takes on special personal significance when it comes to the selection of your own trusted plumber, stockbroker, surgeon, or mechanic).

25. *Facilities.* Some businesses capitalize on the fact that they have ample capacity in their central manufacturing facilities (or, conversely, in *de*centralized facilities to serve various geographical regions). Examples are Fiat (with car and truck manufacturing operations in South America) and Vick International (with manufacturing plants in each of the foreign countries it serves).

26. *Features.* This is the ability to say: "Our product has more features than our competition's." Excellent examples include automobiles loaded with extras and refrigerator-freezers complete with automatic ice makers and drink dispensers.

27. *First Class, top of the line.* There is always a limited, but profitable, market in this area. The latest example to come to my attention is the first-class section on Amtrak's Metroliner service between New York and Washington. Called Club Service, it provides better seating than in the regular section, a choice of four complimentary entrees, and service by an attendant.

28. *Free samples, trials, or demonstrations.* Demonstrations and trials are a standard part of selling cars, trucks, farm and construction equipment, boats, and airplanes. Also it's common for firms introducing a new detergent, shampoo, or other home product to send a generous sample through the mail.

29. *Giveaways.* This is a special variation of the above in which a customer is given something, usually in connection with an order. *Langiappe* (pronounced roughly "lon-yop") is a Cajun expression to describe this kind of gift—such as free lollipops—that a clerk might add to an order of groceries.

30. *Image.* Image is a highly valuable characteristic as it applies to people, facilities, products, and services. It may be literal, or simply imagined by satisfied customers. It is an ongoing concern of fine stores, hotels, restaurants, and major airlines.

31. *Joint ventures.* Sometimes a business fails to grow, usually because it has a shortage of cash to expand or because it can't develop new products or find new markets. One answer is to join with a more powerful player.

32. *Knowledge, intelligence.* Some business organizations operate on what they know at a given moment. Commodity traders, stockbrokers, and investment people are usually on the phone seeking the latest developments. It's how they compete.

33. *Marketing know-how.* Marketing know-how provides a competitive edge in an organization that can develop information about prospective customers and how to meet (or create) market needs. (And you don't have to be an IBM or a Xerox to successfully compete this way.)

34. *Name or reputation.* Imagine this kind of reputaion. At a place called Purdy's in London you may buy a shotgun if you are willing to (1) pay $7500 in advance, (2) sign an agreement that you'll pay *more* if the price goes up before delivery, and (3) wait two years or so to get your gun.

35. *Objectivity, impartiality.* Objectivity and impartiality become important competitive characteristics in certain kinds of service businesses, notably in various forms of consulting (e.g., Booz, Allen & Hamilton; Arthur D. Little; and the management advisory services groups in accounting firms).

36. *It doesn't grow old.* Some companies compete by having a timeless produce or service that doesn't become outdated over the years. Examples include such familiar consumer products as Hershey's Chocolate, Quaker Oats, and Ivory Soap (each of which has been around for more than 100 years and has satisfied generations of Americans).

37. *Only source of supply.* Having the only source of supply of a raw material, commodity, or product is an enviable way to compete. DeBeers ("A diamond is forever.") represents a monopoly in this area, controlling the price and availability of this gemstone worldwide.

38. *Packaging.* The attractiveness or sensibility of a company's packaging can sometimes make a great deal of difference. Chanel No. 5 and other expensive perfumes depend upon packaging and appearance for their appeal. Others use design and color.

39. *Payment terms, financing.* Obviously, your business will enjoy an advantageous position if your terms are easier or simpler than those of your competition. Bank cards and certain credit cards (Visa, etc.) try to compete in this way.

40. *Performance.* This is a key competitive factor. "How good is it? How well does it work?" are key questions in the minds of cus-

tomers. Mercedes Benz bases its advertising on this important characteristic (and uses this factor to justify the price of its automobiles).

41. *Price.* This is a principal way to compete in a business. A low-price approach will succeed only if an organization can do a better job than its competition in holding down costs without sacrificing quality. Price is also a way that a wealthy competitor can literally buy its way into a market.

42. *Prime location.* Prime location can be an important way to compete, especially for a business that depends on a great deal of customer walk-by or walk-through traffic. Best example: The post-card concession at the base of the Eiffel Tower in Paris.

43. *Product line.* If your product (or service) line is broader and offers more choice than your competition's, you may sometimes enjoy a competitive advantage. Other times, you may be better off with a narrower, but more profitable, product line.

44. *Quality.* An unswerving dedication to quality has marked the success of such firms as Sony, General Electric, DuPont, and Siemens. Lots of people talk about quality in annual reports and other communications. Quality is about *doing,* not talking.

45. *Reliability.* Reliability is different from dependability in that it describes an ability to continue to operate or perform once initiated.

46. *Repairability.* The Model A Ford of 50 years ago was an example of a product that could be maintained or repaired by the owner with a minimum of tools and experience. A contemporary example is the Land Rover, maintained by owners in Africa. It is also *versatile:* the grill is frequently removed from the front of the radiator and used as the other kind of grill (over a fire).

47. *Research.* The ability to conduct superior R&D efforts in a company provides a decided competitive advantage. Organizations that devote a substantial amount of money in this area include 3M, Proctor & Gamble, and Hewlett-Packard.

48. *Responds to a specific need.* The ability to respond to a specific need represents a useful way to compete. The need may be geographical, financial, cultural, etc.

49. *Saves time or labor.* Countless products and services compete on this basis: home appliances, office equipment, business services of all kinds, domestic services, computers, and many others (many of which misrepresent their real ability to save either time or effort).

50. *Security.* This is a way of competing by saying that your product or service will make people feel safer or more confident. Such products range all the way from Dial soap and Listerine to smoke detectors and life insurance.

51. *Service.* It is sometimes vital that when you sell and distribute a product, you also provide the necessary service and support to keep it operating the way it's supposed to. In another sense of the word, Sears has expanded its offerings to customers to include insurance and investment services.

52. *Sex appeal.* Men's and women's fashions, perfumes and colognes, jewelry, shoes, designer jeans, automobiles, and travel are just a few of the areas in which sex appeal is the name of the game. Dior, Clinique, Calvin Klein, Revlon, and Lord & Taylor are just a few examples.

53. *Specialization.* This is a way of competing by choosing one thing and doing it well. Familiar examples include Kentucky Fried Chicken, Hoover vacuum cleaners, H&R Block tax services, and Arm & Hammer baking soda.

54. *Speed.* There are a range of companies that compete on the basis of their prompt service. Jiffy Lube and Grease Monkey lube cars and change filters in 10 minutes, while you wait. One chain of optical houses will grind new lenses and fit your glasses in about an hour.

55. *Status.* There are any number of products designed to provide a feeling of status, exclusivity, or special treatment. It is the marketing thrust of top clothing designers, resort property developers, classic automobile dealers, and other extremely high-end businesses.

56. *Tailor-made, unique.* This is a way of competing by offering the customer a one-of-a-kind or customized version of a particular product or service. This attribute can be stressed at both the low and high ends: from cottage-industry products such as knitted goods and baskets, all the way up to custom-built homes and yachts.

57. *Terms.* It is possible that a company's terms of sale can be improved to make goods and services more appealing to prospective customers. Examples can be seen in TV advertising of consumer products such as furniture, cars and recreational vehicles, and major appliances.

58. *Timeliness.* Timeliness, as a way to compete, is usually linked to another business characteristic. For a high-end clothing retailer, for example, catching a trend and capitalizing on it is not merely desirable, but vital. Other examples include any service organization, since service and timeliness are very closely linked in the minds of customers.

59. *Trade-in policy.* A better, more liberal, trade-in policy than your competitor's will place you at an advantage. Singer and General Motors are examples of this successful way to compete.

60. *Warranty, guarantee.* This is a way to outpace competition by offering to do a better—and faster—job in the repair or replacement of a defective unit or part. Teradyne, a Boston manufacturer of electronic test equipment, offers a lifetime guarantee on some of its devices.

Note: Don't get bogged down in the similarities or differences among *goals, benefits, features,* and *ways to compete.* These lists are merely to help you remember key words and ideas that should be worked into your approach and your messages. They are among the ways you *differentiate.* Obviously, you have to be very selective about the words you choose. You can't present complicated laundry lists of all the things you do and believe. At best you should concentrate on the six or seven major ways in which you can successfully demonstrate the excellence of your solution.

Also keep in mind that some of these elements are *substitutable* for other ones. As you know from your own life, there has to be a time when enthusiasm, education, or energy is substitutable for experience since—when you first start work—you don't have any. Dependability is frequently substitutable for features (bells and whistles). And safety comes before price when necessary.

Strategy for Success—Navigating

Let's conclude this section about differentiation with some observations about planning and how necessary it is in developing not just *one* important Dog & Pony Show, but an ongoing series of them.

The analogy of *operating a ship* is a useful one. To properly navigate and steer a ship of any size requires a clear understanding of two important—but different—bodies of knowledge.

1. First of all, you must know exactly where you are at any given moment and what the ship's capabilities and resources are. In other words, you must have answers to the questions about how fast the ship will go, how far it will go, how much fuel it has, how seaworthy it is, how well the crew has been trained, and so forth.

2. As well, you must understand what confronts the ship in terms of forces that will work for it or against it as it sails from one point to another. In this case, you must know about prevailing winds, seasonal currents, weather conditions, possible hazards to navigation, and the situation in various ports (e.g., are dockworkers on strike, is a war imminent, could there be an embargo?).

Navigation is a match of two things: an understanding of the ship and an understanding of the world it's *in* (the environment). Exactly the same holds true in long-range planning for high-stakes presentations.

A long-range (strategic) approach in management permits an organization to better understand the *match* between what it represents (its internal resources, capabilities, goals, values, features, competences, and aspirations) and the external opportunities and risks it faces. It resembles navigation in the sense that one must carefully—and *continuously*—compare internal factors and resources against external ones, trying to see how the two can mesh as the organization (or the ship) tries to succeed in achieving its objectives—on time and within budget.

The key word in this description is *match*. Any time you try to match, or "fit," one thing or set of circumstances with another, you must understand them both very well. Businesses, especially new ones, must carefully assess their own internal capability to deliver goods and services and—more importantly—to know if (and where) *customers* exist in the external marketplace.

What holds true for an organization also holds true for you. You must make sure that you are creating solutions that match with what is needed. You must assure that your goals, values, skills, and beliefs are congruent with the needs of a possible marketplace that will give you the chance to work, live, and succeed. Just as in the operation of a business, *you* have internal resources that must be matched with the opportunities and risks of an external world.

It is our hope that the ideas in this book will help you compete more effectively and win more often.

Dog & Pony Checkpoints

- Admit that you have competition.
- Learn all you can about your competition. Don't take anything for granted.
- Even though you may not appear to have direct competition, determine who are the indirect competitors who are after your customers' or clients' dollars.
- Be acutely aware of the strengths of your direct and indirect competitors.
- Especially, capitalize on the weaknesses of your competitors.
- Review your own past history for clues to past achievements and success. Understand and capitalize on what you do best (and on what is the most profitable).
- Investigate the basic goals of your audience—find out what your audience wants and needs.
- Review your own goals—figure out what you really want.
- Describe the major benefits of your products or services so that prospects can see the real advantages.
- Learn how to talk about the key features of your products or services in ways that don't put people to sleep.
- Analyze, in great detail, all of your characteristic ways to compete.
- Write a statement about how you most effectively match your capabilities and potential with the needs of the marketplace.

4

Define Quality, Establish Your Price, and Ask

You must decide upon your own definition of—and *level* of—quality. Once you know what you mean by quality, you can then determine price. Remember, there's not necessarily a connection between cost and price. And, above all, you must be comfortable in *asking* for what you want.

Contents of This Chapter

- The meaning of *good*
- A grading system to measure quality and performance
- Values and beliefs of you and your organization
- The power of a promise
- Arriving at a price
- The society and the system
- A short soapbox speech about winning
- Asking
- Marketing and sales: two different things
- A final note on doing "better"
- Dog & Pony Checkpoints

The Meaning of Good

For some time now, people in the advertising business have talked about the idea of *performance-based pricing*. It holds that if the agency does a particularly good job for a client, the agency should be paid a performance bonus. One of the important measures of a "good" job is that the agency's advertising and promotion efforts pay off in terms of increased sales and profits for its client—not just pretty ad club awards that hang on a wall in the agency's or client's reception area.

I believe in performance bonuses for extraordinarily good work, and take this notion one step further. If my clients do an outstanding job, I believe *they* should be shown some consideration. What do I mean by that? I mean that if they go about the process of developing a presentation in a sensible way (without endless arguments and unnecessary little changes), they should be rewarded for it. After all, most people don't spend enough time in the development of their presentations and wind up trying to do everything on a *rush* basis. That's frustrating and costs too much.

So the essence of the deal is this: You do a good job, you get paid extra. Your clients do a good job, they get charged less.

Notice the word *good* keeps showing up in the conversation. What does *good* mean here? You can't have a definition of quality without agreeing on the meaning of it. There are several definitions for the word, which comes, itself, from Old English and Middle English and originally from the Sanskrit word *gahd*, "to hold fast."

In the context of presentations, *good* should have 10 important characteristics, and they must be present at all times in your presentations work with clients. Your products, direction, coaching, and advice must conform to the following criteria. *Good* means:

1. *Useful.* It has utility and value in every case.

2. *Beneficial.* This means *beyond* useful. It is also helpful.

3. *Sound.* It has integrity and won't fall apart or come undone.

4. *Ample.* There is *enough of it* to be effective.

5. *Wholesome.* It is healthy and safe and doesn't carry risk.

6. *Real.* It is tangible and permanent. Its effects can be seen and felt.

7. *True.* It is dependable, honest, accurate, and consistent.

8. *Reliable.* It works 100 percent of the time.

9. *Valuable.* It is extremely worthwhile and deserves appreciation.

10. *Agreeable.* It is pleasant and gratifying. Even fun.

These characteristics apply to good presentations. They apply to good visuals. And these 10 characteristics support the idea of *good* not only for presentations, but for however and wherever it is applied: to good friends, a good life, and good products of all kinds—even small and inexpensive ones.

Also, it turns out that the definition of *bad* (or, simply, *not good*) can be easily defined by flipping to the opposite terms of *good* as follows:

	Good		Bad
1.	Useful	1.	Useless, no utility or value
2.	Beneficial	2.	No benefits, not helpful
3.	Sound	3.	Weak, no integrity
4.	Ample	4.	Insufficient, ineffective
5.	Wholesome	5.	Unhealthy, unsafe, risky
6.	Real	6.	Bogus, intangible, impermanent
7.	True	7.	False, dishonest, undependable
8.	Reliable	8.	Can't be counted upon
9.	Valuable	9.	Worthless
10.	Agreeable	10.	Unpleasant and not gratifying

A Grading System to Measure Quality and Performance

You will not hesitate or falter in making choices about quality or sufficiency of your presentation if you use measuring systems that have no exact centers to "balance" on. You must be pushed or forced to one side or the other.

Consider for a moment an event that is familiar to everybody: parties. Everybody has been to *parties*. Some of the parties were good, and others were not. You generally gauge the success of a party by whether you had *fun* or not.

So—in the broadest sense—parties are either fun or dull.

To describe parties in this narrow either-or context does not permit much range. It can also tend to get you stuck in the middle if there is any question.

The worst thing that can happen in decision making is to get trapped in the middle and become powerless. When this happens, you can't go one way or the other.

What you need is a system that will tend to push you one way or the other—and also one that will give you the opportunity to expand the range of your qualitative measurements. You need to be able to *act*, without faltering and without getting bogged down.

Think of the middle as *dead center*. To be caught in the middle is poisonous. Remember this illustration.

You should use measuring systems that have no exact centers to balance on. The problem with a 5-point measuring system (1–2–3–4–5), in which 1 is good and 5 is bad, is that if you're at all uncertain, you might be tempted to pick 3 and sit on the fence right in the middle. When you "dead-center" yourself this way, you're taking the easy way out. This is wishy-washy and indecisive.

Effective measuring systems have *even numbers* of parts. Consider, for example, a system that consists of four parts: with two categories on the positive side and two on the negative side. In this 4-point system, A will be the best. F will be the least or the worst.

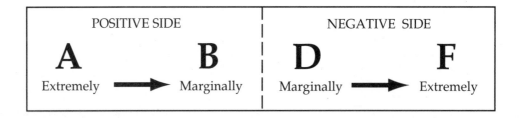

This is a way of showing a gradual deterioration of quality (or some other condition), from A all the way to F. At the extreme lower end of B, the condition becomes so marginal that it quickly turns into a negative factor. The scale then continues from D to F, getting worse as it goes.

Figure 4-1 shows another example. The scale shown in the figure is designed to take advantage of the familiar expression "going down-

COMFORT

A
Extremely
Comfortable

B
Generally
Comfortable

D
Marginally of Generally
Uncomfortable

F
Extremely
Uncomfortable

Figure 4-1 The typical slide down the comfort scale.

hill" to describe a condition or level of performance that gradually (or quickly) deteriorates over time. Such a scale can be used to describe a point on the range of comfort that we have experienced when shopping for a chair or a sofa. (It also, coincidentally, plots the continuum each of us experiences on a one-day 500-mile automobile trip. We start the day at position A, extremely comfortable, and progressively work through to F, extremely *uncomfortable*.

Here's a further discussion of the A–F "grades."

A—Maximum; superior quality; the most or the best

B—Average to above-average quality; quite sufficient

D—At least partially deficient or defective

F—Completely unacceptable; inferior or insufficient

This four-part range can be applied to some common conditions that affect all of us at one time or another. Figure 4-2 offers some familiar examples.

Values and Beliefs of You and Your Organization

Goals are where you're headed. Values and beliefs are the things you take along with you. They guide you in making decisions about what to do and how to act. Values and beliefs, however, become real only when they're acted upon. They must be more than verbal expressions of feelings, moods, or thoughts.

Finally, values and beliefs are interpreted differently, depending upon the personalities, interests, and intentions of others. For example, the values of an environmentalist would be interpreted according to the natural environment, and so there would be a specific meaning to the words *integrity* and *stability* as they were meant to

Colorful	(A) • • • (B) • • • (D) • • • (F)	Drab
Versatile	(A) • • • (B) • • • (D) • • • (F)	Limited
Reliable	(A) • • • (B) • • • (D) • • • (F)	Unreliable
Sufficient	(A) • • • (B) • • • (D) • • • (F)	Insufficient
Roomy	(A) • • • (B) • • • (D) • • • (F)	Cramped
Convenient	(A) • • • (B) • • • (D) • • • (F)	Inconvenient
Informed	(A) • • • (B) • • • (D) • • • (F)	Ignorant
Committed	(A) • • • (B) • • • (D) • • • (F)	Uncommitted
Creative	(A) • • • (B) • • • (D) • • • (F)	Unimaginative
Active	(A) • • • (B) • • • (D) • • • (F)	Lazy
Effective	(A) • • • (B) • • • (D) • • • (F)	Ineffective

Figure 4-2 Common areas of decline from desirable to undesirable.

pertain to the process of working to ensure that future generations will enjoy a wilderness area or a particular species.

Mathematicians view their field of study from the standpoint of the same words, *integrity* and *stability*, but have a different interpretation of them—a much different view of reality. The meanings of the two words differ once again when used by physicians, teachers, artists, architects, engineers, and others.

Some organizations *say* they have certain values—or they *talk as if* they believed certain things—but then behave otherwise. In a presentation, don't choose to talk about values that you don't really have.

Figure 4-3 lists a few examples of the kinds of things organizational leaders purport to value.

It is also a good idea to learn as much as possible about the values of the people you're presenting to, so that you can make the appropriate links between their beliefs and your own.

Now let's continue with another purely qualitative aspect of presenting important ideas—that of making promises based on the beliefs and values of both you and your organization.

The Power of a Promise

People have a *desire to believe* in clear-cut promises, sometimes despite what their own common sense tells them. They like—and frequently expect—promises, but be careful what you tell them. Promises might include such controversial statements as the ones detailed in Fig. 4-4.

As an example, a foreword to this workbook might include such promises and guarantees as:

> I promise that you will have some fun reading this workbook because parts of it are offbeat and nonacademic. I also promise to unravel a number of mysteries about why people act as they do, especially when they're part of an audience listening to you. Finally, I guarantee that if you actually *do* some of the things in this workbook, you will achieve faster results. You will succeed—chiefly by allowing your competition to fail by sticking relentlessly to their old, and now unacceptable, habits.

Price

Earlier in the chapter the discussion focused on quality, values, and essential goodness. Now the discussion turns to the issue of *price*.

I know a company president who says the following to customers:

> You may have any *two* of the following:
>
> 1. Quality
> 2. Delivery
> 3. Price
>
> Which two do you want?

VALUES AND BELIEFS OF YOU AND YOUR ORGANIZATION

This checklist can be used in either of two ways: to pinpoint the values and beliefs of your own organization for purposes of inclusion in your proposal presentation or to gauge the values and beliefs of the organization to which you are presenting. In either case, a clear focus on such guiding principles and a forthright declaration of them add power to any presentation.

A. Healthy atmosphere for discussion .... ❏
B. Achievement .... ❏
C. Advanced technology .... ❏
D. Advancement for women .... ❏
E. Organized system for suggestions and complaints .... ❏
F. Clear thinking and speaking .... ❏
G. Ethical behavior .... ❏
H. Harmony among people .... ❏
I. Helping people to grow .... ❏
J. Higher than average wages, benefits, and working conditions .... ❏
K. Honesty .... ❏
L. Integrating the needs of people with organizational objectives .... ❏
M. Integrity .... ❏
N. Job security .... ❏
O. Open communications .... ❏
P. Opportunities for minorities .... ❏
Q. Personal dignity .... ❏
R. Preservation of the environment .... ❏
S. Quality .... ❏
T. Reliability and dependability .... ❏
U. Stability .... ❏
V. Support of charities .... ❏
W. Physical health and safety of employees and customers .... ❏
X. Truth in advertising .... ❏
Y. Value of teamwork .... ❏
Z. Trust .... ❏
_____ .... ❏
_____ .... ❏
_____ .... ❏

Remember, values are to be *lived*, not merely talked about!

Figure 4-3.

PROMISES WITH POWER

Used judiciously, the generic promises contained here can help you get a favorable reception for your presentation. Although many of them are familiar from print and media advertising, they are all timeless, and tap into some of the common desires that people possess. For any given presentation, choose one or two that apply to your company or its products or services. Remember, though, don't promise it if you can't deliver.

A. Our product (service, or solution) will revolutionize the industry. .... ❑

B. Your knowledge (of a particular subject, industry, etc.) is now obsolete. .... ❑

C. Your old-fashioned equipment must be abandoned. .... ❑

D. Your investment will be fully recovered in three years. .... ❑

E. Our system is the fastest in the world. .... ❑

F. Without our help, you face financial disaster. .... ❑

G If you don't take action, you will only have a 50-50 chance of succeeding. .... ❑

H. You will have a 300 percent improvement in your odds. .... ❑

I. We'll answer our phone in no less than two rings. .... ❑

J. This product will last forever. .... ❑

K. Our system will change your life. .... ❑

L. All of your misconceptions will vanish. .... ❑

M. Mysteries will be revealed. .... ❑

N. Suddenly you will become an expert. .... ❑

O. Absolutely no preparation is required. .... ❑

P. You will be an instant winner. .... ❑

Q. This is the chance of a lifetime. .... ❑

R. There will never be an opportunity like this again. .... ❑

S. Satisfaction guaranteed. .... ❑

T. Satisfaction guaranteed or triple your money back. .... ❑

U. _____ .... ❑

V. _____ .... ❑

W. _____ .... ❑

X. _____ .... ❑

Y. _____ .... ❑

Z. _____ .... ❑

Figure 4-4.

I have found another way to deal with the prices that can be charged for services rendered. Most people think of "service" only in qualitative terms, but there are ways to express what it means (or what it *should* mean) in concrete terms.

When you need anything (such as a solution, a remedy, a tool, an idea, or a repair), you must find somebody (such as a colleague, a doctor, a hardware store clerk, a research librarian, or a mechanic) and open a conversation in order to initiate a process that will yield a desired result.

When you want to secure a service—or propose to *offer* a service—you must remember that the *process of the delivery* is frequently as important as the outcome you promise (and may, indeed, have a significant effect upon the price you propose to charge). The following steps must be taken, or tests met, in the order shown.

1. *Accessible.* You must be able to *reach* the person who can help. Somebody must pick up the phone—and in these days of recorded voices inviting you to push buttons for various options, this can be a substantial trick. And when you finally reach somebody, that person must be both knowledgeable and able to initiate some kind of positive action. People will frequently pay extra, in the form of a retainer, in order to secure services at their convenience (e.g., move to the head of the line).

2. *Capable.* Once you have successfully tapped the source, you must verify that the service provider is truly competent. You expect the best from the people you entrust with your health, your plumbing, your business and legal affairs, and your automobiles. You want the assurance that they have been well educated or trained and have extensive experience. The more persuasively these facts are presented, the more you are willing to pay.

3. *Available.* Merely *reaching* a capable specialist is meaningless if the person or team is unable, for whatever reason, to do what you wish. This is the point at which a great many negotiations break down. "Yes, I'm here. Yes, I'm capable and eminently qualified. And, yes, I'm available to do the sort of thing you wish. But I'm not available right this minute. As a matter of fact, I can't fit you in until the middle of next month." Availability is, therefore, frequently a matter of interpretation. Some stores and services (all the way from furnace repairers to hospital emergency rooms) advertise, and capitalize on, their 24-hour-a-day availability.

4. *Speed.* This is a crucial factor—the answer to exactly *when* you can get what you want. It is a part of the American way of doing things to expect fast results, and frequently people will pay a premium in order to get what they want when they want it. A number of businesses exist because they are able to charge double or triple for overnight—or virtually immediate—service.

5. *Terms.* Having successfully met the first four tests, the next logical step (*before* price) is a discussion of how easily the terms and conditions of delivery can be met. The payment *schedule* can often soften any shock associated with the price. And it is at this point that the client or customer must be reminded of the pre-

1.	Accessibility — Can you be reached?
2.	Capability — Can you truly do it?
3.	Availability — Are you able to deliver?
4.	Speed — Can you do it in time?
5.	Terms — Can you deliver it comfortably?
6.	Price — Can your "customer" perceive the value?

Figure 4-5 The six components of service.

mium charged in order to have successfully and agreeably met the first four criteria.

6. *Price.* This is the final step, and if the above elements have been skillfully illuminated, there is little or no resistance to the price or the fee.

So keep these ideas in mind when you offer to provide your solution. They are summarized in Fig. 4-5.

Also, remember the following words of John Ruskin. They were written more than 100 years ago:

> It is unwise to pay too much, but it's worse to pay too little. When you pay too much, you lose a little money, that is all. When you pay too little, you sometimes lose everything, because the thing you bought was incapable of doing what it was bought to do. The common law of business balance prohibits paying a little and getting a lot—it can't be done. If you deal with the lowest bidder, it is well to add something for the risk you run. And, if you do that, you will have enough for something better.

The Society and the System

Let me pursue the subject of business a bit further and touch upon *capitalism* and *winning,* and then move on to the subject of *how to ask for exactly what you want.*

America is an odd place to achieve success because it operates under two completely different sets of rules, neither of which is understood very well by the people (like you and me) who have to live and work here. We are not taught the rules very well, with the result that we can't negotiate very effectively for our own best interests and—more importantly—our share of the good life or however you describe *that which is important.*

Let me try to summarize a couple of things for you by saying that in the United States we have:

1. A democratic *society*

2. The capitalist *system*

They operate quite differently. If you don't have the rules clear in your mind, you can become schizophrenic and lose everything.

Democracy

Our democratic society is founded upon the Bill of Rights and the Declaration of Independence. These words speak of essential freedoms and fair treatment under the law. We are free to talk as we please, to travel at will, and to work wherever anybody will hire us. We are guaranteed the freedom of religious conscience and full political participation. Our personal beliefs are our business, and we don't have to answer to anybody about them, least of all the government.

Democracy is a system in which the people rule. The power vested in them is sometimes exercised by them directly, but more often it is exercised through representatives whom we vote into office in free elections. As you know, we elect people with varying points of view. We have conservatives who seek to preserve what has gone on before by way of certain institutions and traditions. They generally revere stability and prefer gradual development instead of abrupt change. Conservatives are almost invariably people who have something to conserve.

Liberals advocate progress, personal autonomy, the protection of civil liberties, and change that is far-reaching and progressive.

Radicals, of course, wish to see extreme changes in existing or predominating viewpoints, conditions, institutions, and so forth.

There is room for all these viewpoints in a democratic society.

The *system*, however, is quite different, as *it has nothing whatever to do with equality*.

Here are its highlights.

Capitalism

The capitalist system is an economic concept that holds that capital goods can be owned privately (or corporately); that investments are decided privately, not by the control of the state; and that a free market decides the production, distribution, and pricing of goods. The rules that apply in the free market (the free private enterprise system) are different from those that govern the society.

The capitalist system acknowledges that there will be winners and losers. Not everybody who goes into business succeeds at it. Nothing is automatic. Nothing is guaranteed. The people who try to start enterprises must understand the rules before they go in.

They could win. Or they could lose. But they can't stand around grumbling about their *fair share!* In business, there is no such thing as anybody's fair share. You get what you want by competing aggressively and successfully for it. *Competition* is at the very heart of the capitalist system.

Let's take a fast look at other concepts just to have a basis of comparison.

Socialism is a view that suggests that governments own and administer the means of production and the distribution of goods. In its purest form, it is a system of group living in which there is no property. Communism is a theory that doesn't believe in the ownership of private property, and holds that goods are owned by everybody and distributed to all as needed. It may also mean a system of government in which a single party controls the means of production and vows that it will create a classless society. History has shown, however, that the actions of these single-party advocates are always different from their words.

Attempts at socialist and communist forms of government invariably fall apart because social classes emerge and some people gain more wealth, power, privilege, and influence than others. Also, socialist and communist regimes profess high equality, which is almost never true. They are also low in freedom.

The lowest equality and the lowest freedom are found in fascist or totalitarian regimes. These systems exalt race or nation and depend upon a centralized government that controls all aspects of life and productive capacity in the country. It is marked by regimentation, fear, coercion, and forced suppression of any opposition.

Figure 4-6 shows a model developed by Robert Rokeach. As shown in the figure, both capitalism and democracy are characterized by a great deal of freedom. When it comes to equality, however, there is a great deal in democracy but very little in capitalism. Remember what we said earlier, capitalism is about *winners* and *losers*.

Capitalism is where we spend most of our time. The majority of wage and salary earners work for businesses. Businesses succeed by competing successfully against one another. As we said, they cannot go into the marketplace and *ask* for their *fair share* of customers. They'd be laughed at. There *is* no such thing.

A lot of social movements in this country have failed because the special-interest groups were trying to "win" by using the principles of the Constitution and the democratic society instead of the techniques of competition and the capitalist system. The rules are vastly different. To be the most successful, you have to learn how to apply the rules of the system.

Let's use an example: People insist on their constitutional right to speak any form of language they choose, to dress the way they want

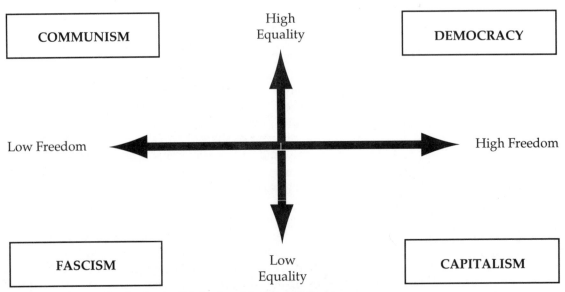

Figure 4-6   An equality-freedom model developed by Robert Rokeach.

to, and to look any way they please. Society says that's perfectly okay. But the society doesn't provide most of the jobs. The *system* does. And the system is far more rigorous in its requirements.

Businesses in the capitalist system prefer that people have a decent command of the English language and meet minimum standard of appropriate dress and neat appearance—especially among those workers who deal directly with customers. Common sense tells you that somebody who is sloppy looking or fat, and who can't speak grammatically correct English, isn't going to work in front of the public in sales or customer service operations.

People can squawk all they want to about it not being "fair," but social fairness doesn't have a thing to do with it. The realities of business, on the other hand, have *everything* to do with it.

Your share doesn't have to be equal to anybody else's. Fairness and equality are two different things. Everybody in this country ought to be equal under the law, but the shares are going to work out very differently. The people who dream the most, try the hardest, and prepare the best are going to get bigger shares than those who don't. That's the way it works. That's the reality of the system.

Let's proceed to another important concept that gets muddied up in the-society-versus-the-system struggle.

A Short Soapbox Speech about Winning

You've heard plenty of people use the expression "win-win." I'd like to encourage you to take it *out* of your vocabulary. Substitute the one-word version instead: "win!"

Nobody is sure where the *win-win* thing came from, but we have two theories:

One—it could have been started by a "motivation" expert who works with salespeople, especially the ones who have to sell hard-to-move merchandise such as life insurance, used automobiles, and $9.98 knife sets that last forever. The idea was to make buyers feel that they were winning when, in fact, they were getting stuck with something they didn't really like or need.

Or two—it was perfected by personnel departments that needed a technique to hypnotize workers into the belief that an annual salary increase of 1.75 percent was in the best interests of all concerned: "You see how it is, don't you? You win; we win; *everybody* wins!"

I just described how democracy is the province of fairness and equality—and how capitalism is linked with *competition*, and *not* with "fair share." Competition is at the very heart of the system, and the name of the game in free private enterprise is win-*lose*.

Neville Chamberlain flew back to England in 1938 from a win-win conference with Adolph Hitler. As an outcome, Hitler marched away with a big chunk of Europe and Chamberlain sauntered off with the illusion—however short-lived—that everything was going to be just swell.

And when it came to ending the war that followed, the Allies decided on the ultimate win-lose strategy: *unconditional surrender*. An end to appeasement.

And *appeasement* may not be a bad word to describe some of the misdirected application of *win-win* ideas in business. It can show up in sappy grins, insincere promises, and mediocre performances—small-time, and usually one-way, appeasement efforts in a process that prizes loyalty over creativity and tolerates a lot of do-nothings on the payroll. It camouflages defective ideas. It emphasizes the *appearance* of things going well.

Somebody ought to open a little win-lose college someplace where managers could go to learn—ahead of time—that there are certain unpleasant circumstances that must be faced in the business. Plants have to be shut down or relocated. Good people have to be let go. Certain projects have to be junked. Bullets have to be bitten. This doesn't fit at all with the win-win premise. People who fold businesses could have used more of the win-lose spirit on the part of everybody in their organizations.

Our country needs *innovation* as much as it needs technology. Great achievements can be made in controlling costs and finding how to do new things with proven, less-risky, old ideas. As the vice president of marketing at CMS Data, Robert Drucker, says: "We need to fully capitalize on *trailing-edge* technology."

This takes people who can take risks, not little players of internal politics. It takes fighters, not smilers. Boats need to be rocked. Weak participants need to lose.

Win-lose is the name of the game played daily in the offices of Coke and Pepsi. Neither is going to create any substantially new domestic market. Both realize that the market of people who drink colas is fairly stable. So any additional share must be taken from the hide of the other.

It may be unpleasant, but it's not *unfair,* not according to our system. Competing successfully in world markets doesn't have anything to do with our ability to take it; it has to do with our ability to dish it out. This means standing up straight and doing the right things: retiring certain products, junking favorite projects, reupholstering policies and procedures to meet modern needs, firing some folks who are just standing around, and learning to tolerate aggressive, impatient people who won't tolerate slow-moving bureaucracies.

Under capitalism, there is no such thing as *fair share*. Organizations (and individuals like you) are entitled to any share you can get and successfully hang onto. And there are completely ethical ways to go about it.

The simple message is this: *win*. And do everything you can to help your competitors *lose*.

The major part of winning has to do with asking for the business or asking for what you want. There has to be an agreement—a *close*—before there's a deal. Without deals, no business is conducted. Without business, there *is* no capitalism. And it's capital, after all, that defrays the operating costs of democracy and liberty.

Practically everybody growing up anywhere in this country was taught *not* to ask for anything. We grew up being told that it wasn't polite—that it would never be polite. It isn't gentlemanly to ask for things. It isn't ladylike.

As a matter of fact, we were even taught that it was impolite to accept things that were offered—like accepting cookies over at grandma's house.

"Here, Johnny, have a cookie,"

"Oh, no thanks, Grandma."

"But I want you to have one. And it's *okay* to have one."

So I'd have to get talked into it.

The biggest rule of capitalism (actually, the key to getting anything anywhere and under any circumstances) is this:

It Is Imperative that You Ask!

Otherwise nothing will get sold, produced, or delivered to anybody else. Also, if you—personally—don't ask for what you want, guess what? You won't get it.

If you hang around waiting for your fair share, all you're going to get is old. Correction, old and *poor*.

You must learn how to *ask*. You must learn how to ask *comfortably*. You must learn how to say such things as:

1. "Hey, I want you as a customer. *May I have your business?*"

2. "I deserve a big raise. Here's why. Can I *have* one?"

3. "I want a better job. May I *earn* one?"

It's that simple.

A lot of mythology has been built up about selling. Used-car salespeople and real estate salespeople have given selling a bad name. They are pushy and abrupt and don't mind selling things that customers don't need or want.

Selling is vital. Products and services must be sold by *somebody*. As noted at the beginning of this book, Dog & Pony Shows are about selling products and services. That is their chief purpose. They may seem like a branch of show business, but they are about *selling!*

And, by the way, don't use the word *marketing* when you mean *sales*.

Marketing and Sales: Two Different Things

At some point in the 1970s a certain number of weak people decided to use the word *marketing* instead of *sales*, because the word *marketing* sounded more gentile and sophisticated to them. This is a fundamental mistake. Here are the definitions to stick with:

Marketing, as an action, is simply *the process of finding out what customers want so that you can develop and produce it for them*.

Sales, as both an action *and* a management function, is *the process of persuading customers to buy something you've already developed and produced.*

Telemarketing should be called what it is: *telephone sales.* Nobody calls me to survey what I want! They call me to sell me what they have!

Be clear about the difference. And be clear—in case you're not already—that you must learn how to *ask* for the things you want.

Dog & Pony Shows are of all different sizes and kinds. They may take place in an elaborate conference room with lots of people or over lunch with just a couple of people. But such shows always include two parties: the asker and the asked. And it's the role of the asker to make it as easy and comfortable as possible for the asked to agree and say yes, freely and willingly—and without coercion.

Here's the next step.

Learn How to Ask for What You Want—Practice Asking!

Almost any time we broach this issue with people, they express the fear of seeming *obnoxious.* "They'll think I'm too pushy if I come right out and ask."

Don't worry about it. It isn't being pushy to simply ask for what you want. (It's important to understand the difference between being aggressive and being assertive. Here I'm simply talking about being assertive.)

Here is a simple example: You take a car in for service. You get an estimate, and then you either (A) express your wishes or (B) let the service station express its wishes.

It's okay for you to try to set a schedule that conforms to your needs rather than their convenience. It's neither pushy nor obnoxious to say:

"I'd like to pick up the car at noon tomorrow. Can you manage that?"

Or:

"Can you have the car ready by 10 in the morning? That way I can run over and pick it up on my break."

This approach is far superior to asking: "When can you have it ready?" Such a question can drop you to the bottom of the priority list as a person who will acquiesce to anything you're told.

Here are some other ways that you can gain control simply by asking.

In dealing with the phone company over an installation: "I can be available between 10 and 10:30 on Wednesday morning or between 4 and 4:30 Wednesday afternoon. Which is best for you?" (Otherwise the company will suggest that you hang around all day Wednesday.)

In a restaurant waiting for service: Flag down anybody and politely ask: "Excuse me, are you our waiter?"

Or, in a restaurant, unhappy with your meal: Flag down your

waiter and say: "This isn't to my taste. May I have something else? How about the haddock?"

In the furniture or appliance store: "I'll be available for awhile on Saturday. Would you please deliver it at 9 in the morning?"

Rehearse sentences like these out loud in front of a mirror. Look yourself straight in the eye and learn to say these things calmly and confidently:

"Excuse me,...can I have some assistance?"

"May I have your help?"

"If I write this up in contract form, will you sign it?"

"May I have your commitment for our team to begin work immediately?"

"Would you please deliver this to me this coming Monday at 6 in the evening?"

"May we have your business?"

"Would you like me to deliver the first 12 of these next week?"

"Would you please sign this contract for me?"

"We'd really like to do business with you. *May* we?"

"When can we start?"

"Could you help me with this, please?"

"If you'll sign this agreement today, we can start work on Monday. Will you please sign it?"

"With new customers we expect payment in advance. Do you have any problem with that?"

You must ask questions that require a yes-or-no answer. It's the only way you're going to get a yes.

On the off chance that somebody says no, immediately smile and calmly ask: "Why?"

A Final Note on Doing "Better"

The purpose of this workbook is to help people do a better job of making presentations. But care must be taken in how to go about helping people and how to encourage people to improve.

The theatrical director Charles Marowitz has some interesting things to say about *energy*. He says that in acting, as in sports, the value of increased energy is—or should be—that it sharpens skills. If it doesn't, it's just an increase of energy per se and doesn't accomplish anything worthwhile. It is nothing more than unharnessed physical effort and is bound to be counterproductive.

All work—in anybody's organization—is an amalgam of energy units, each of which requires the translation of energy into intention, attitude, and meaning. Calling for more energy, i.e., urging people to *try* harder, without deciding how this energy is to be used, is like building a supercharged sports car and neglecting to fit it with wheels or a steering wheel. To strain the analogy even further, one could complete the car and then not have a clue about how to drive it or where to *go* in it.

People's energy—especially *yours* in the context of presentations development—must be effectively translated into scope and meaning, direction and purpose—and should be used to generate light, not heat. It does no good to implore people to work or try harder—they must be shown ways to work *better*.

Dog & Pony Checkpoints

- Develop criteria for good and not good.

- Don't pay good money for stuff that's not good.

- Understand what you believe in—the standards from which you will not swerve.

- Understand the values and beliefs of the people you're presenting to.

- Develop a measuring system that won't allow you to get stuck in dead center.

- Discover the promises you can make (that people desperately want to hear).

- Spend your energy wisely. Trying harder isn't the answer. Trying better *is*.

- Remember that it's okay to charge people for quality.

- Keep in mind that it's okay to charge people for on-time (or *before-time*) delivery.

- Understand that there isn't necessarily a connection between cost and price.

- Learn how to do value pricing.

- Don't confuse the principles of equality and fairness (associated with democracy) with practices based upon aggressive competition (capitalism).

- Forget the childhood admonition that it's ungentlemanly or unladylike to ask for what you want. If you don't ask, you won't get squat. (No, I take that back...you *will* get squat!)

- Be mindful that sales is an okay word. Sales drives the international economy. Don't say *marketing* when you really mean *selling*.

- Learn the definition of *marketing*. People are always interested in having a hand in developing a solution that fits their exact needs.

5

Plan, Schedule, and Pick the Right Place to Present

You must take the time to develop a basic plan for your presentation. It doesn't need to be elaborate, but it must help remind you of the key elements. An example of a planning sheet is provided in this chapter. Also provided is a basic scheduling sheet and an explanation of the component parts of it. Finally, this chapter devotes attention to *when* to present and also *where*. You must realize that the time and place of a presentation must not be left to chance. Some times of the day (and days of the week) are much better than others. And you must *absolutely* control the environment in which you make your presentation. Here are some of the ideas that must be covered in depth:

Contents of this Chapter

- How to develop a presentation plan
- A schedule and a scheduling sheet
- Discussion of the schedule
- Tests of purposeful work
- The highlights of a schedule for an important presentation
- Determining the best time to make your pitch
- Why the right room is so important
- Case study: An actual example
- A few stage terms
- Dog & Pony checkpoints

Let's begin with the basic information that should appear on any planning sheet—that is to say, the key areas of subject matter that must at least be considered—whether they are selected for inclusion or not. The following material is presented as a form in Fig. 5-1.

Introductory material must include the following information:

- Presentation to: (identifying the organization)

- Date of the presentation

- Location of the presentation

- Type of audience

- Total time allocated

- Estimated length of formal presentation

- Director

- Budget

- The names, titles, and responsibilities of the audience members

- The names, titles, and responsibilities of the presenters

In the body of the form, these points must be addressed:

1. What you want the audience members to *do;* the action you'd like them to take

2. The audience's view of the future

3. Specific symptoms, problems, or needs of the audience that your solution can satisfy

4. Possible objections the audience might raise

5. Present attitude of the audience

6. The attitude you'd like to build

7. Awareness you'd like to create

8. Prominent philosophical views of audience members

9. Prevailing forces or attitudes that influence the audience's decisions

10. Direct or indirect competitors

11. Strengths and weaknesses of your competitors

12. How you will differentiate yourself from your major competitors

13. A review of your company's past performance

14. Ways you can compete

15. Relevant corporate, organizational, or personal goals

PRESENTATION PLANNING SHEET

Presentation to: _____   Date of presentation: _____

Location of presentation: _____   Type of audience: _____

Total time allocated: _____   Estimated length of formal presentation: _____

Director: _____   Budget: _____

Audience Members

Name	Title	Responsibility
_____	_____	_____
_____	_____	_____
_____	_____	_____
_____	_____	_____
_____	_____	_____
_____	_____	_____
_____	_____	_____
_____	_____	_____

Presenters

Name	Title	Responsibility
_____	_____	_____
_____	_____	_____
_____	_____	_____
_____	_____	_____
_____	_____	_____
_____	_____	_____
_____	_____	_____

Figure 5.1.

1. What you want the audience members to do; the action you'd like them to take: _____

_____

_____

2. The audience's view of the future: _____

_____

_____

_____

3. Specific symptoms, problems, or needs of the audience that your solution can satisfy: _____

_____

_____

_____

_____

_____

_____

_____

_____

4. Possible objections the audience might raise: _____

_____

_____

_____

_____

_____

_____

Figure 5.1 (*Continued*)

5. Present attitude of the audience: _____

_____

_____

6. The attitude you'd like to build: _____

_____

_____

7. Awareness you'd like to create: _____

_____

_____

8. Prominent philosophical views of audience members: _____

_____

_____

_____

9. Prevailing forces or attitudes that influence the audience's decisions: _____

_____

_____

10. Direct or indirect competitors: _____

_____

_____

_____

_____

_____

Figure 5.1 (*Continued*)

11. Strengths and weaknesses of your competitors: _____

_____

_____

_____

_____

_____

12. How you will differentiate yourself from your major competitors: _____

_____

_____

_____

_____

13. A review of your company's past performance: _____

_____

_____

_____

14. Ways you can compete: _____

_____

15. Relevant corporate, organizational, or personal goals: _____

_____

16. Your important values and beliefs:

_____

17. Key features of your solution: _____

_____

_____

Figure 5.1 *(Continued)*

18. True benefits of your solution: _____

_____

19. Your fundamental strategy for success: _____

_____

20. Promises you can make and keep: _____

_____

21. Your price and your pricing rationale: _____

_____

22. Description of your solution and its key elements: _____

_____

_____

_____

_____

_____

23. How your solution will help the audience achieve its goals and objectives: _____

_____

_____

_____

_____

24. How your solution "fits" and is congruent with the audience's present situation: _____

_____

_____

_____

Figure 5.1 (*Continued*)

25. Proof that an investment in your solution will yield positive dividends: _____

_____

_____

_____

_____

26. Requirements for visuals: _____

_____

_____

_____

_____

27. Brief highlights of "preview" material that will help to secure a meeting: _____

_____

_____

_____

_____

28. "Preshow summary" highlights: _____

_____

_____

_____

_____

_____

_____

_____

Figure 5.1 (*Continued*)

16. Your important values and beliefs

17. Key features of your solution

18. True benefits of your solution

19. Your fundamental strategy for success

20. Promises you can make and keep

21. Your price and your pricing rationale

22. Description of your solution and its key elements

23. How your solution will help the audience achieve its goals and objectives

24. How your solution "fits" and is congruent with the audience's present situation

25. Proof that an investment in your solution will yield positive dividends

26. Requirements for visuals

27. Brief highlights of "preview" material that will help to secure a meeting

28. "Preshow summary" highlights

A Schedule and a Scheduling Sheet

Figure 5-2 is a scheduling sheet that shows the optimum amount of time required to develop an effective presentation. It assumes a team effort and the involvement of several people, each of whom will handle a major component.

Insistence upon a scheduling sheet may seem unnecessarily academic or even downright impossible to you. But listen to the following accounts of executives about the major problems they used to have in developing high-level presentations (before the implementation of a more systematic approach):

> We used to find that presentations, even though we realized their importance, tended to disrupt our day-to-day business. Partly for this reason we procrastinated and did everything at the last minute—typically late at night and on weekends when we were the most tired, panicked, and under the gun. We should have developed a schedule and stuck to it.

> Preparations were usually frantic. We didn't allow enough time in the first place, and then we'd get into long-running arguments because of conflicting points of view about what to say and in what order. We'd compete with one another for air time. We needed a *system*.

> We didn't make the time to prepare very thoughtfully, so our presentations were frequently incomplete. Also, we'd cut and paste from a lot of other past sales pitches with the result that we'd forget important material that we should have covered. Even at that, our presentations were too long and would always run over the time limit.

	Week 1	Week 2	Week 3	Week 4
1. First meeting to define key elements	■			
2. Second meeting to discuss continuity	■			
3. Start of research and writing phase	■	■		
4. First draft of script		■		
5. First draft of preshow summary				
6. Group discussion of first drafts				
7. Travel arrangements				
8. Shipping arrangements				
9. Final draft of preshow summary			■	
10. Final draft of script				
11. First talk-through				
12. First draft of PC and chart visuals			■	
13. First walk-through, without visuals			■	
14. Blocking, without visuals				
15. Final draft of PC and chart visuals			■	
16. Production of visuals and summary			■	
17. Production of charts				
18. Delivery of preshow summary				■
19. First rehearsal with all final visuals				■
20. Name tents produced				
21. Rehearsal				■
22. Dress rehearsal				■
23. Final dress rehearsal				■
24. The presentation				■

SCHEDULE
Presentation To:
Date and Time:

Notes: Weekends are shown in gray on this standard four-week production and delivery schedule. The team should make every effort to keep projects on track and *not* have to work on Saturdays or Sundays. Space is provided on the last three lines for any special activities or requirements you may have. Be sure to add these extras on a master schedule (even if it's written on the back of an envelope) that shows who's doing what (according to which budget and timetable).

Figure 5-2.

Our habit, too often, was to show up unprepared and try to wing it. This didn't work very well, of course. But worse than that, we didn't have the concentration to be able to listen to our audience and understand what audience members were thinking and saying.

Our visuals were frequently weak because we'd make our suppliers and helpers do what they were told, not necessarily what was right. They knew how to do better work, but we wouldn't let them. We'd also jam them into a schedule that would make even substandard work difficult to deliver.

Nobody likes schedules; nobody. But we have found that, without them, we spend at least twice as much time to do a given amount of work, and as much as *triple* the budget to do things in an ad hoc, unplanned manner.

Discussion of the Schedule

Try not to laugh out loud at the idea of having a 4-*week* schedule to develop an important presentation. But do you know something? Organizations spend about as much *total* time doing things the wrong way as the approach discussed here suggests doing it the right way. And remember, the time is *elapsed* time, not total time—with an emphasis on quality. Also, this schedule is set up so that people can manage to do some of the work during regular hours instead of on their own time during evenings and weekends (when they're operating at reduced mental capacity). Please examine and evaluate the following schedule and the descriptions of its parts. Keep an open mind as you read about this approach. Modify it, as you wish, to accomplish the specific needs of your organization, your presentation, and the individuals contributing to it.

1. *First meeting to define key elements.* This meeting is broad-brush only. It's very short, maybe only 20 minutes, and it's used to select the right presenters (e.g., Maralyn will talk about marketing; Don will talk about R&D; Terry will ask for the business). You should only *estimate* content, since you won't know it with any precision until you've done the research and the thinking to arrive at the final form. Once you get more effective, fold the second meeting into this one and do both in 20 or 30 minutes.

2. *Second meeting to discuss continuity.* This is another short meeting, maybe 15 or 20 minutes, to guess at the probable organization of the presentation. But this isn't cast in concrete. You shouldn't develop an outline without further thought. (Forget all the advice about writing *outlines* before you begin work on a presentation or anything else—an article, a book, a film, and so forth. You can't know—ahead of time—what you don't know. So why guess? You can only develop an effective outline after you've done the majority of the writing, at which time you don't need one.)

3. *Start of research and writing phase.* This is where you can begin to get an idea of what's really going to happen. In doing research, you should take into account factors such as those listed below. (I'll

outline a basic system for collecting information that is actually *fun*. And I'll also show you a pathway that lets you gather information from a series of checklists that will help you to identify a lot of useful ideas about the following necessary components of your winning presentation.)

- Attitudes to build
- Audience attitudes
- Audience type
- Awareness to create
- Corporate goals

- Future visions
- Influencing factors
- Key features
- Major benefits
- People's attributes

- People's values
- Possible objections
- Symptoms and problems
- Ways to compete
- What is "good"

And this is only a partial list. I'll also present a method for collecting and then arranging information. The schedule calls for a 6-day period in which to accomplish this task. Obviously the entire 6 days aren't consumed in this effort, probably as little as 5 or 6 hours. But they will be highly *productive* hours.

4. *First draft of script.*   This is rough draft only and will be tuned up based upon the input of other presenters. A short meeting should be held to discuss one another's input, and is shown as item 6 on this schedule.

5. *First draft of preshow summary.*   What is a preshow summary? It is a brief piece designed as a tantalizing preview and delivered to audience members about a week ahead of the presentation. It includes biographical material about the presenters, and it highlights what you're up to (in a general way) and why you're going to appear. It's a very important technique in bringing an audience to your point of view.

6. *Group discussion of first drafts.*   Read the draft of other people *before* this short meeting and be prepared to comment with helpful and constructive remarks.

7. *Travel arrangements.*   Notice that travel arrangements are shown on the schedule as being made 2 weeks before the event. Do it sooner if you can. Also consider some contingency plans about how to get to a distant location in case of a blizzard that shuts down airports. Never, *never* take the last plane out of anywhere.

8. *Shipping arrangements.*   Shipping arrangements will be required only if you have mock-ups or prototypes that you want to show at the presentation.

9. *Final draft of preshow summary.*   This is shown as being completed by the beginning of the third week. This will then allow 5 working days for production before delivery (item 18 of the schedule), 1 week before the presentation.

10. *Final draft of script.*   This task should also be completed at the beginning of the third week, which then allows each team member another 10 working days to make adjustments, refinements, and necessary additions.

11. *First talk-through.*   The first talk-through is a 3-hour meeting in which team members go through their material for the first time.

This can be done while seated at a large worktable. It will provide insights into what components are too long or too short, and will also suggest suitable transitions from one segment to another.

12. *First draft of PC (personal computer) and chart visuals.* The day after the talk-through, it should be possible to develop the preliminary visuals to be used in the presentation. Work should begin approximately 10 working days before the presentation. Earlier would be even better.

13. *First walk-through, without visuals.* The purpose of this exercise is to begin to get an idea of where people are going to be positioned in the presentations area—where they will stand, walk, and interact with visuals and props.

14. *Placement of the presenters, without visuals.* On the same day, and possibly as a part of step 13, above, necessary movements and positions will be decided upon. (In theater, this is called *blocking.*)

15. *Final draft of PC and chart visuals.* After 5 days of effort, the visuals are ready for production, and some—no doubt—will already be in production.

16. *Production of PC visuals and summary.* At this point, both the visuals and the preshow summary must be solidly in the production cycle.

17. *Production of charts.* Any necessary charts can be easily produced if at least 4 working days are set aside for their completion.

18. *Delivery of preshow summary.* The summary should be delivered to the prospect at least 4 days before the presentation. Personalize one for each person who will attend.

19. *First rehearsal with all final visuals.* The first full rehearsals should begin at least 2 days before the event, and earlier if possible.

20. *Name tents produced.* By this point on the schedule—2 days before the event—the names of the audience members will be known for sure and production can begin on the name tents for them and for the people on the presentations team.

21. *Rehearsal.* Rehearsals continue 2 days before the presentation.

22. *Dress rehearsal.* A dress rehearsal takes place at the location the day before the presentation. No further adjustments are made to the presentation after this rehearsal.

23. *Final dress rehearsal.* This takes place in the afternoon or the evening before the presentation. This is only for polishing and for refining the timing.

Tests of Purposeful Work

Here are a few reminders about your approach in developing a presentation (or, for that matter, a plan of any kind). The tests of purposeful work are as follows. If you can't satisfy all these tests in what you're doing, then you are deluding yourself, and your proposed effort will probably fail. The checksheet in Fig. 5-3 will help you determine if your proposal is purposeful.

1. *Doable.* The work—your intention—must be clearly within the realm of possibility. Beyond that, it must be congruent with the aims and ambitions of both your organization and the one you're presenting to.

2. *Affordable.* The time, money, people, space, facilities, machines, materials, supplies, and other requirements must be available to pursue the work you propose.

3. *Somebody in charge.* A person—not a group—must be in control of *real* work to be done. He or she may ask for help from others, but the main point is that some stated individual must be vested with authority and responsibility.

4. *A timetable.* Real work must proceed on a schedule. It must have dates, deadlines, and milestones against which to measure progress. Vague approximations are not acceptable (e.g., sometime next quarter, within the next few weeks, one of these days).

5. *Capable of being negotiated with others.* Real work frequently impacts other people who are concerned with, affected by, or involved in the proposed effort. These people must be informed, and frequently they need to be motivated or persuaded to cooperate.

6. *Not in conflict.* Proposed work must not be in conflict with other solid efforts.

7. *Capable of being ranked.* Some objectives must be achievable simultaneously as well as individually. Otherwise they must be capable of being ranked in some logical way so that priorities can be established.

8. *Beneficial.* Benefits must accrue from purposeful work. There must be a payoff to you, to your organization, or to your organization's customers. Otherwise, why do it or even talk about it?

9. *Measurable.* Real work gets finished, not endlessly talked about in vague, nebulous terms. And the other good news is this: Purposeful work is always *financially measurable.*

Criterion 1 may seem stupid to a lot of people, who might say: "Of course, it's doable! Do you think I would have mentioned it if it weren't?" But it's our painful experience that senior people, especially, are fond of waving their hands and declaring something to be true or real when it simply isn't—and that the thing they're talking about has no possibility for birth, let alone success. A lot of people, both junior and senior, won't argue—they'll merely wander off and do what they were going to do anyway.

Determining the Best Time to Make Your Pitch

When *is* the best time to make your pitch? Here are some generalizations.

TESTS OF PURPOSEFUL WORK

1. Is it doable? _____

   _____

   a. Is this a realistic proposal?_____

   b. Does it fit with the aims and ambitions of your organization? _____

   c. Is it congruent with the aims and ambitions of your prospective client? _____

2. Is it affordable? _____

   a. Do you have the time? _____

   b. Do you have the money? _____

   c. Do you have the people? _____

   d. Do you have the space? _____

   e. Do you have the facilities? _____

   f. Do you have the machines and materials? _____

   g. Do you have the supplies? _____

   h. What other requirements are there? _____

3. Who's in charge? _____

4. What's the schedule? _____

   a. Relevant dates:_____

   _____

   _____

   _____

   b. Deadlines:_____

   _____

   _____

   _____

   c. Milestones:_____

   _____

   _____

Figure 5-3.

TESTS OF PURPOSEFUL WORK (CONT.)

5. Who else has a stake in the outcome of this project? _____
_____
_____

What is their interest? _____
_____

What power do they have to hamper or expedite progress? _____
_____

How do you influence them? _____
_____

6. Is this project in conflict with other efforts by your organization or the client organization? _____
If so, explain. _____
_____
_____

7. How can the work involved here be broken down and assigned priorities? _____
_____
_____
_____
_____

8. What's the payoff (the benefit)? _____
   a. To you: _____
   _____
   b. To the organization: _____
   _____
   c. To the client: _____
   _____

9. How do you measure results financially? _____
_____

How do you know when you're finished? _____
_____

Figure 5-3   (*Continued*)

Time of day

Avoid the early morning hours because certain audience members will not arrive on time. Likewise, avoid late afternoon time slots because of the possible need for some audience members to leave early.

It is my opinion that the best time for a presentation—especially one involving a number of audience members—is 10 in the morning. People have had time to arrive and review the material on their desks. They've also had their midmorning coffee and are reasonably alert.

If you schedule a presentation at this time, remember two things: (1) your audience will need a restroom break within about 45 minutes; and (2) you must promise that they will be able to have lunch at a reasonable time, preferably no later than 12:15.

Don't schedule a meeting right after lunch, because people are generally too sleepy to pay attention.

Day of the week

Don't schedule anything on a Monday (because it's too soon after the weekend) or on a Friday (because it's too close to the weekend). Also, busy people tend to have travel days at the beginning and ends of weeks.

Tuesdays and Wednesdays are the best days to present.

Week of the year

Common sense will tell you not to present in any week that has a major holiday in it. Particularly, don't schedule a presentation near Labor Day, near Thanksgiving, or between Christmas and New Year's Day.

Order of presentation

If you're competing against weaker competitors, try to go *last* with a very tight, shorter-than-expected presentation that answers all the audience members' questions without their ever having to ask them. If you're competing against stronger competitors, go *first* and set a high level and tone.

Why the Right Room Is So Important

People have done a lot of dumb things in the past with respect to the design of rooms and facilities for presentations. But they had very little precedent: boardrooms, classrooms, little theaters, screening rooms for films.

Nobody ever really sat down to think about the special needs of a true presentations room—which call for combining elements of stage lighting with the practical space limits (per person) of such a room, creating a place in which one should be very comfortable (in his or her seat in his or her "space") as a prerequisite to being comfortable with some new ideas or an important new proposal.

Let's talk about places to talk about business!

Frequently, the role of *the place* in which important presentations have been staged has made the difference between success and failure. And here, of course, I'm not talking about the obvious and specialized needs that scientists have for laboratories, that surgeons have for operating rooms, or that chefs have for kitchens. I'm talking about plain old *space,* an uncluttered room in which to spread things out.

I've spent a lot of time working with groups of adults who were either (1) trying to learn something new in a classroom or, more frequently, (2) convened someplace to develop a plan, make a decision, solve a problem, evaluate a new idea, or take action. I've worked in a variety of places under differing circumstances.

Some of the very worst facilities I've ever worked in include:

1. A wildly expensive but badly laid out conference room in Jakarta, Indonesia. It had one of those "Star Wars" podiums that couldn't be operated by any of the 40 graduate engineers present.

2. A resort in Houston staffed with well-meaning but untrained staff. Everything that could have gone wrong went wrong.

3. An elegant but windowless and dimly lighted miniature ballroom at the Amigo Hotel in Brussels. Since we couldn't see very well, we couldn't think very well, and we all wished we were outdoors, even in subzero weather.

4. An apparently unheatable conference facility in New Hampshire. Most of the right ingredients were present, including privacy, scenery, quiet, and a chance to pursue some ideas without interruptions or distractions. But the cold was too much to take, and so we abandoned the effort.

5. A hotel in London where most of the staff people were either unable or unwilling to speak any of the five languages known by the members of a market-planning team—English, French, German, Spanish, and Italian.

6. A ground-level conference room with too *many* windows at the Princess Hotel in Bermuda. The north side looked onto the swimming pool where there were lots of people in bathing suits. The east side looked seaward at a bunch of surf-sailers. And the south side looked onto the first tee of a golf course. There were altogether too many appealing distractions.

With only two exceptions, the conference and meeting rooms in every hotel, conference center, college, and management institute I've had anything to do with in three Asian and six European countries, twenty-three American states, and four Canadian provinces were substandard in one important way or another.

They were unacceptable because of one or more of the following:

- Inadequate or badly designed lighting

- Unsuitable seating arrangements

- Noise from adjacent rooms or kitchens or from the ventilation system

- Constant interruptions

- Badly designed rooms (would you believe an L-shaped room?)
- Uncomfortable chairs
- Inadequate resources (no markers, tape, paper, copier, etc.)
- Unhelpful help
- Poor food
- Inability to cool a hot room (or heat a cold one)
- Difficulty in getting to the facility in the first place

More about rooms

In a piece written for *The Boston Business Journal* a couple of years back, I described the following:

> There is an increasing need for a non-technological resource that few companies have bothered to invest in—an empty room. But not just *any* empty room.
>
> And I don't mean a conference room, which is usually formally outfitted and isn't empty at all, but filled with the ghosts of past executives, failed dreams, and frustrated efforts. No, I mean an empty room that is set aside for people *who need to concentrate on something— to do something without distractions.*
>
> Here are the specifications for such a room in which to work and think—especially about new-business presentations and other kinds of sales-related activities. It must be at least 16 by 20 feet. There should be windows along one of the long dimensions. There should be adjustable blinds on the windows, and the walls and ceilings should be off-white. And there should be plenty of incandescent (not fluorescent) lights in the ceiling.
>
> The three remaining walls should be covered with white boards to write on (in plenty of colors). The place should be furnished with a few comfortable chairs which swivel, tilt, and roll easily on the floor; two or three easily moved tables; and a couple of wastebaskets. It must have no distractions in it—no pictures, prints, clocks, or anything else. No shelves. There can be a phone jack in the room to make outgoing calls. No incoming calls should be accepted.
>
> Remember, that *this is not to be used as a meeting room.* It is to be used by individuals or small work groups for short periods of time to accomplish specific objectives. It is a room equipped to get messed up. The walls are for writing and to have pieces of paper taped to them. Tables and floors can be messy.
>
> It is not a room where unprepared speakers pontificate in front of bored audiences. It cannot have a lectern. It's a place to spread things out, to analyze as objectively as possible, to unify, to validate, to cross-check, to isolate, to confirm, to speculate, to wonder, and sometimes just look out the window. Seemingly unsystematic, it is a place to get out of ruts and see new possibilities.

There was feedback from this column. A number of people called who wanted to try it but had been told by their top management: "We don't have space for such a thing." Others tried some version of it for awhile but were then told: "I know we gave you the space, but now we need it for something more important." That's the story from the same top-management team that frequently goes to a retreat in the mountains or rents a nearby hotel suite in order to have somewhere to think without interruptions and to sort things out!

Turning our attention back to rooms for formal presentations, let's take a look at a couple of sample layouts of rooms that have been designed specifically for formal presentations involving a fairly large number of audience members.

Case Study: An Actual Example

In a high-level presentation for a large banking institution, the presentation group asked if it could take over one of the bank's biggest conference rooms for a couple of days before the event.

The bank consented. The facility was called the Lincoln Room—on the nineteenth floor of a 26-story building. The room itself was 50 feet long by 24 feet wide. It had 14 tables that were 5 feet by 2½ feet. Two people could sit at each one. The chairs were very comfortable and met the specifications of the presenters. It was also a very agreeable location because of large windows that could be left unrestricted for the view of the downtown area or could be closed off by drapes.

The room, the bank said, was usually set up in one of two configurations shown in Figs. 5-4 and 5-5.

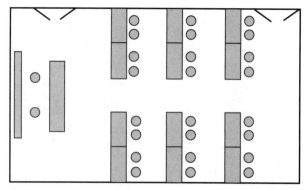

Figure 5-4 The classroom style of room arrangement—seating for up to 30.

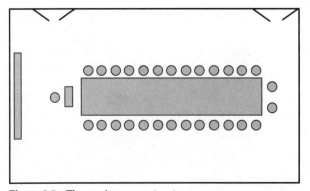

Figure 5-5 The conference style of room arrangement—seating for 28.

It is paramount that every person at a presentation be able to see every *other* person without straining. With classroom style (Fig. 5-4), this is impossible. In the conference style layout (Fig. 5-5), it would be necessary for people to lean forward. Therefore, neither of these configurations was acceptable.

The presentation team sought to find a new solution, shown in Fig. 5-6. The team created a 3-foot-square grid in order to develop a new floor plan in which there would be an equal number of the bank's participants (shown as gray circles in the figure) and presenters (shown as black circles). Each person can easily see everybody else in the U-shaped configuration.

As you can see from the diagram, visuals are generated with a Macintosh computer through a large-size video projector and onto a 12-foot screen. There is plenty of room for the presenters to stand either to the left of the screen (the less powerful position) or to the right of the screen (the strongest).

As the diagram shows, there is also ample room to "work the crowd" from the middle of the U-shaped area. Another way of ex-

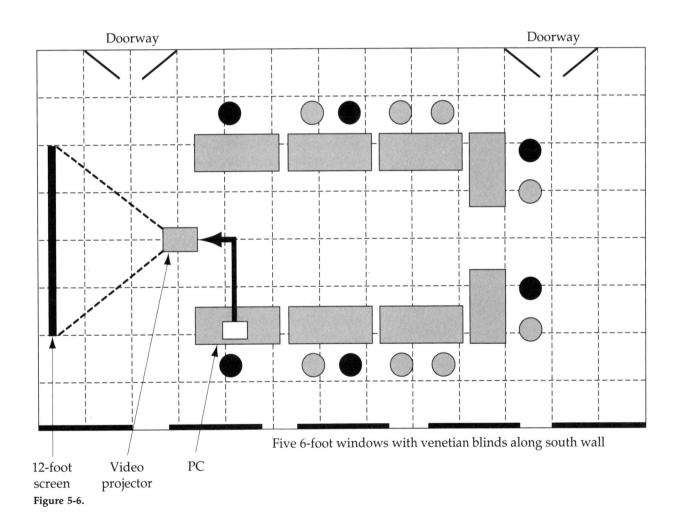

Five 6-foot windows with venetian blinds along south wall

12-foot screen   Video projector   PC

Figure 5-6.

pressing this is that the presenters can be considered as performers working in a theater-in-the-round setting.

Some stage rules apply that are worth talking about at this point, and then reinforced in Chap. 8.

A Few Stage Terms

Here are a few theatrical terms worth mentioning. They specifically pertain to theater stages, but you will do well to think of anyplace you present as a literal *stage*.

The term *downstage* always means the area of the stage closest to the audience. *Upstage* is the area *farthest* from the audience. In a theater-in-the-round setting, the audience surrounds the presenters, so the idea of downstage doesn't mean very much. The term *upstage,* however, has a meaning that you should understand, particularly when used in its verb form—to *upstage* somebody.

Suppose you and I are the only two performers on a regular stage. If so, we should be working on the same plane of the stage, with each of us the same distance from the audience.

While we appear to be looking at one another, we are actually positioned so that our bodies and our faces are "cheated" three-quarters to the audience so they can see us better. If you want to try to *upstage* me, all you have to do is move to the part of the set that is farthest from the audience, position yourself center stage and full face to the house, and deliver your line. I would then be obliged to turn *toward* you, thereby presenting my back to the audience. My character would be diminished, my position weakened, and the volume of my voice lessened because I would be projecting *away* from the audience instead of toward it.

This is the meaning of *upstaging,* and the only reason to mention it is so that you can avoid upstaging *yourself.* It happens all the time when people use visuals and then look at them while they talk, effectively presenting their *backs* to the audience.

You should either speak without looking at a visual or stand next to it and gesture toward it while still presenting yourself full front to the audience. Since most people are right-handed (and people read from left to right), the most powerful position for you to be in is to the right of the visual as seen from the audience.

Here are some other common terms that would be used in staging a play or an important presentation.

Blocking. The positioning of the presenters relative to the audience.

Crossing. Any movement of a presenter from one part of the "stage" area to another.

Business. Anything that you do with your hands, with or without a prop.

Walk-throughs. Rehearsals with scripts and without visuals.

Ensemble "acting." A group presentation where each person must work closely with everybody else: to introduce key players care-

PRESENTATIONS ROOM CHECKLIST

Use this list to ensure that all details of your presentation space have been taken care of.

1. Reservations .... ❏
2. Appropriate room size (usually, the larger the better) .... ❏
3. Room with windows, window coverings, and incandescent lights .... ❏
4. Maps showing people how to get to the location .... ❏
5. Transportation as required .... ❏
6. Comfortable seating .... ❏
7. Arrangement of the room (placement of tables and chairs) .... ❏
8. Appropriate equipment in good working order .... ❏
9. Trained equipment operator .... ❏
10. Room without distractions .... ❏
11. Name tents .... ❏
12. Location of fire escapes .... ❏
13. Location of rest rooms .... ❏
14. Electrical outlets and extension cords .... ❏
15. Easels and easel pads .... ❏
16. Markers .... ❏
17. Tape .... ❏
18. Adequate ventilation .... ❏
19. Special lighting requirements .... ❏
20. Arrangements for phone messages (no phone in room) .... ❏
21. Coffee, tea, juice, and rolls if a morning presentation .... ❏
22. Refreshments .... ❏
23. Meals, as required .... ❏
24. Hotel accommodations for out-of-town guests .... ❏
25. Person with whom to coordinate needs .... ❏
26. _____ .... ❏
27. _____ .... ❏

Figure 5-7.

fully and to keep them consistent and believable. The total picture seen by the audience must be harmonious. This includes the area in which everybody is working (hence the importance of the room), the positioning of everybody relative to one another, the lighting, and the other visual components of the presentation.

Figure 5-7 is a presentations room checklist.

Dog & Pony Checkpoints

- ✔ Always ask for the room you want. Specify exactly what you want.

- ✔ Be concerned about the type of room. Be aware of the layout of the room.

- ✔ Never meet in a windowless room. *Never!*

- ✔ Never—under any circumstances—seat decision makers in a classroom-style seating arrangement.

- ✔ Always put an important audience at tables placed in a U-shape or a semicircle, with you and your team controlling the open end.

- ✔ Never believe what a conference center employee tells you on the telephone. Always inspect an off-site location ahead of time.

- ✔ Always choose a presentations room that is a good deal larger than the "experts" say you need. *Spacious* is always better than *cramped.*

- ✔ Never—under any circumstances—make a presentation in a board room or conference room that is used for regular management meetings.

- ✔ Schedule your presentation for a Tuesday or a Wednesday.

- ✔ Meet in the morning (at 10 or 10:30 a.m.) rather than in the afternoon.

- ✔ If you're the best, present last. If you're less than the best, go first.

- ✔ You must be aware of the stage "picture" at every step of the show.

- ✔ You must create variety in room lighting.

- ✔ Never use lecterns. They are for the exclusive use of ministers, certain professors, and people who are frightened or uncertain.

- ✔ Don't use rear-screen projection systems.

- ✔ If possible, work in rooms that have incandescent lights, not fluorescent ones—especially cool white fluorescent lamps. (There are such things as "warm" white tubes, in case you didn't know.)

- ✔ Make people physically comfortable if you expect them to be intellectually or emotionally comfortable with your new ideas.

6

Develop the Story about Your Solution

You must develop—and refine—the content and purpose of your presentation. It is the story that explains why your solution is valuable, useful, or applicable to the people you're talking to, and how it will provide an advantage to them. You must produce a well-organized chronicle that is both interesting and provides any necessary proofs your audience may require. Here are some of the highlights of this chapter.

Contents of This Chapter

- Designing a winning presentation
- Deciding what you want your audience to do
- Understanding the steps that people must go through in order to take action
- Ten questions to ask before you start writing
- The easiest way in the world to write a first draft
- Common ways to organize your material
- Key questions to review
- Ideas about tone and style
- The impact of your solution on problems and circumstances
- Dog & Pony checkpoints

The very beginning

There are certain basic steps that need to be taken in designing a winning presentation. The audience has shown up at the appointed time and place. (Most people seem to think that Tuesday or Wednesday mornings are the best. Mondays are busy. Fridays are lazy. The favored time of day is 10 a.m. Decision makers will have arrived at work by then, and everybody will have had coffee or other refreshments.)

When you begin, you have the audience's undivided attention.

You will have communicated information ahead of time that explains what you're doing there—although you can't presume that everybody has *read* the information you sent them.

You must do several things simultaneously at the beginning.

1. Set a conversational, informal tone. This is really a theatrical ploy. The presenters only *look* relaxed and prepared to do something that is not stiff and formal. In fact, they are meticulously prepared. Do not use humor. Throw away your book of one-liners. High-stakes presentations aren't for laughs.

2. Gain control. Preserve control.

3. Begin building credibility.

4. Begin building confidence in the team of presenters.

5. Be amiable and likable. Start making friends with the audience.

6. Be professional. Gain respect for your professionalism. Begin the process of becoming partners with the key people in the audience.

Deciding What You Want Your Audience to Do

Cardinal rule: Don't start telling a story until you've figured out what you want your audience to do when you're finished. What do you *want?*

Every important presentation should have a *set* of objectives, not just one. Even though you may not achieve your primary purpose, you must win at something else and—at the very least—keep the discussion or the process moving forward to an eventual satisfactory conclusion.

It is vital that you and other team members remain focused on the content and the intention of the presentation. In the hours and minutes preceding an important show, there is a natural tendency to laugh and let off steam. This must be controlled, however; otherwise the presentation will get off to a very shaky and jittery start. Resist the temptation to joke around. Remain serious, and keep your concentration. Remember what you are there to accomplish. Figure 6-1 provides a menu that will help you pinpoint the thing or things you want your audience to do as a result of your presentation.

EXACTLY WHAT YOU WANT THE AUDIENCE TO DO

What will it take for you to feel like your presentation has been a success? Choose from the following menu of potential actions the ones you intend for your audience as a result of your efforts.

A.   Agree to pay for a proposal .... ❑

B.   Agree to share technology .... ❑

C.   Agree to sign a contract .... ❑

D.   Allocate resources .... ❑

E.   Create a detailed schedule .... ❑

F.   Develop a corporate or marketing plan .... ❑

G.   Enter into a joint-venture agreement .... ❑

H.   Enter into a partnership agreement .... ❑

I.   Justify a course of action .... ❑

J.   Make a recommendation .... ❑

K.   Prepare a contingency or succession plan .... ❑

L.   Prepare detailed work assignments .... ❑

M.   Provide equipment .... ❑

N.   Provide capital .... ❑

O.   Provide people .... ❑

P.   Sign a contract to begin work on an entire program .... ❑

Q.   Sign a contract to begin work on an initial project .... ❑

R.   Solve a problem .... ❑

S.   Win an important promotion .... ❑

Other possibilities: _____

_____

_____

_____

_____

Figure 6-1.

Here are some thoughts about how people make up their minds.

For some time now, I've been refining an idea that was originally developed some years ago by Russell Colley in a short book he wrote for the Association of National Advertisers, Inc., entitled *Defining Advertising Goals (for Measured Advertising Results)*. The usefulness of the idea has not diminished with time.

The concept describes how people go through successive stages in their thinking in order to take action. Here's where it starts.

No information

The lowest level of the communications spectrum is no understanding. At this level of unawareness are people who have never heard of you, your product or service, or your company. Any messages you may have directed to these people have not penetrated to the point where they recognize your name, a brand name, or your company name.

It's conceivable that people buy products or vote for candidates whose names are unknown to them. The chances are, however, that such a product makes few sales and such a candidate gets few votes.

Information

As a bare minimum, you must strive for a basic condition of awareness and information. In this state, not only are your prospects aware of you, your products or services, and your company—they may also know your company name or brand names, and they may recognize your packages, trademarks, and logos. They may also have a rough idea about what the product is and does. They are suddenly in possession of the facts—either because you provided them or because they got interested enough in the product, service, or idea to find the information for themselves.

There is also a direction associated with this process. It is upward.

Understanding

Facts, in themselves, are not enough. Understanding is the key. Unless people comprehend the information, they're not on the right track, and you'll never establish the correct relationship to begin the sale.

All too often the process stops right here. Audiences are given information without an opportunity to make sure they understand it completely and accurately. People write memos, reports, marketing plans, ads, and even books, seemingly with the idea that: "Here it is! I've written it all down! Now you can *do* it!"

But the world doesn't work that way. It is far better to take the time and effort necessary to help people understand what it means. It's surprising how often people misunderstand something that seems so clear and obvious to the writer or the speaker. There frequently needs to be discussion and feedback: questions and answers. Otherwise, you can't bring people to the next crucial step.

Conviction

This is the most important step of all. Only when people are convinced will they take *action,* especially the action you want them to take. This is the key element to keep in your thinking and planning

This ascending order of events takes place any time a new product or service is introduced. If a product or an idea is brand new, nobody has ever heard of it. Hence the need for advertising, promotion, and other programs of public information and awareness—maybe even a free sample or a hands-on demonstration. But it must be something convincing.

Action!

Action is the fifth and final step in the process and is taken at the point where a person says: "Aha! I now see how it works. It will do the job I need to get done. I'm convinced. I believe it. I'm ready to start. Where do I sign?"

You must take the necessary steps to move your prospects upward through the successive layers or states of mind as you provide information, ensure understanding of the features and advantages of what you're selling, and then stimulate the conviction (rational, nonrational, or emotional—it doesn't matter) that's necessary to take the action that leads to the desired sale or outcome.

Advertising and promotion are the chief forces providing information, understanding, conviction, and action. Other forces will vary, depending on whether you have a consumer, industrial, scientific, or some other specialized product or service.

These may include person-to-person selling, recommendations by users or retailers, publicity, and various other forms of mass communications such as displays, exhibits, videos, literature, and participation in regional or national trade shows.

Rarely does a single communication force a prospect through the entire cycle (although, as you know, mail-order-type advertising can move a reader through the entire spectrum from no information to a cash-in-advance sale in a few hundred words).

Usually, all the forces of marketing communication are brought together in a mix or blend to move the prospect step by step, even inch by inch, toward the ultimate goal of a satisfied customer.

> **Special note** Conviction is an extremely variable condition. Information (or the lack of it) is usually a one-way street: either you have it or you don't. Understanding is another condition that is mostly one way or the other: either you understand something or you don't (although you can have a general, hazy idea that may be sufficient to get you convinced enough to take action). Conviction, on the other hand, comes in a broad range of shades or intensities—all the way from (A) mildly convinced, e.g., "Okay, I'll go along with the decision because everybody else is"; through (B) "I'm really half and half on this one, but I guess I'll say yes"; to (C) fully committed, "I'm willing to stake my life on this decision!"

Pay attention to people's level of conviction. It frequently happens that a communications and sales job has been successful up to the point of a sale—to the moment of decision—only to fall apart because the deal was oversold. Don't keep selling after people have decided to buy. Stop. Be quiet. And sign the contract. Plenty of successful efforts have fallen apart because discussions continued and prospects literally talked themselves out of their decision to commit to a course of action.

General Karl von Clausewitz (1780–1831) had three things to say about strategy. They apply exactly to your need to inform, persuade, and convince your prospects and customers to take the action you want them to.

1. Pick the battlefield.

2. Know when you've won. (In other words, use only as much force—i.e., sales effort—as is needed to reach your objective. Then stop.)

3. Hang on to what you've gained.

Ten Questions to Ask Before You Start Writing

Let's begin with *the* most important questions you ought to ask before beginning work on a vital presentation.

1. *Do the audience members already know a great deal about the subject?* If they do, then you'll be spared a great deal of "teaching" or introductory material to get them up to speed.

2. *Does everybody in the audience know as much as everybody else?* If there is a serious discrepancy, then you'll have to adjust the balance of information and persuasion so that you educate the less knowledgeable while at the same time maintaining the interest and attention of the people who know considerably more.

3. *Are competitors talking to the audience about the same subject?* If they are, you need to give serious thought to *when* you compete. I firmly believe that if you are the strongest competitor, you should present *last*. If you're not so strong, try to be *first* to set the tone and quality of presentations for everybody who must follow.

4. *Is there a way to communicate with the members of the audience that's been successful in the past?* This is very interesting. It costs nothing to ask a prospective audience about presentations that have been successful at any time in the past; then try to emulate that approach. At the very least, you can find out what *hasn't* worked in the past and avoid similar mistakes.

5. *Are there ideas or themes that might antagonize them?* For example, there may be some old-fashioned management styles or opinions in a family-owned business that you'd be better off not criticizing in a preliminary meeting.

6. *Are there taboo words or subjects that you must be sure to avoid?* This brings up the subject of salty language. And the advice is

to not use coarse language in any circumstances—whether your listeners do or not. Maintain your professional bearing. And try to understand something about the history of the organizations you're talking to. For example, when speaking to Mitsubishi, it's okay to mention cars and TV sets, but try not to raise the question of who built a great many military aircraft in 1941. Some of which flew on Sundays. In early December. Near Hawaii.

7. *Are there concepts that might mislead or confuse them?* I heard a talk recently in which somebody summarized Journalism 101 in four words: "Oversimplify and then exaggerate." Don't do either. And don't confuse people with jargon or unnecessarily technical language.

8. *Are there things you can do ahead of time to influence the audience's thoughts or expectations about your team?* There are *always* things you can do. And they are well short of putting up a billboard in your prospective client's parking lot. Send notes and letters to audience members ahead of time. Send them reprints of articles in relevant trade publications. And—by all means— send them *a short summary* of what you're going to tell them when you meet for your presentation and include detailed biographical information on all the speakers. Get this information to them a few days before the presentation.

9. *Are there other connections between you and the audience that would be worth thinking about (church, political party, fraternity, club, sports, or other affiliations) and reminding them of?* It doesn't hurt a thing to find linkages, no matter how remote: having gone to the same summer camp, having gone to the same university at different years, having the same military veteran status, belonging to the same athletic club or golf club, whatever.

10. *Is there anything about the history or culture of the audience that would be worth exploiting or expanding as a theme running through the presentation?* By this is meant some well-known attribute or value that really *is* a part of the prospect's day-to-day business. For example, *service* is more than just a word at IBM. And *innovation* is a necessary aspect of life at 3-M. Any company that's been around for awhile knows that longevity is a salable virtue.

Figure 6-2 provides some blank space to help you organize your thoughts regarding this part of the presentation process.

The Easiest Way in the World to Write a First Draft

I'd like you to try an experiment that may help you produce a rough draft of a presentation (or anything else) with less hassle and in much less time than you're used to. There are four parts to the experiment:

TEN QUESTIONS TO ANSWER BEFORE YOU START WRITING

	Yes	No

1. Do the audience members already know a great deal about the subject? _____ _____

2. Does everybody in the audience know as much as everybody else? _____ _____

   If no, how do I deal with the discrepancy? _____

   _____

   _____

3. Are competitors talking to the audience about this same subject? _____ _____

   How do we compare in terms of strength?
   Should we present first, last, or in between? _____

   _____

   _____

4. Is there a way to communicate with the members of the audience that's been successful in the past? _____ _____

   If yes, what is it? Why did it work? _____

   _____

   _____

5. Are there ideas or themes that might antagonize them? _____ _____

   If yes, what are they? _____

   _____

   _____

6. Are there taboo words or subjects that you must be sure to avoid? _____ _____

   If yes, what are they? _____

   _____

   _____

   _____

Figure 6-2.

	Yes	No
7. Are there concepts that might mislead or confuse them?	_____	_____
a. Has the presentation been screened for such concepts?	_____	_____
b. Has it been screened for unnecessary jargon?	_____	_____
c. Has it been screened for technical language?	_____	_____
8. Are there things you can do ahead of time to influence the audience's thoughts or expectations about your team?	_____	_____

If yes, what are they? _____

_____

_____

_____

	Yes	No
9. Are there other connections between you and the audience that are worth thinking about (church, political party, fraternity, club, sports, or other affiliations) and reminding them of?	_____	_____

If yes, what are they? _____

_____

_____

_____

	Yes	No
10. Is there anything about the history or culture of the audience that would be worth exploiting or expanding as a theme running through the presentation?	_____	_____

If yes, elaborate on what it is and how it can be expanded upon. _____

_____

_____

_____

Figure 6.2 (*Continued*)

1. Don't try so hard

2. Goldilocks and the Three Bears revisited

3. One-sound words

4. Get a loved one out of a foreign prison

Here's how it works:

Don't try so hard

High school and college teachers probably told you that you can't write anything without first writing an *outline*. They were wrong. Writing an outline is, if you think about it, virtually *impossible*. How are you supposed to know *what you don't know yet* (since you haven't begun the process of observation, review, and analysis necessary to arrive at even a tentative position)? An effective outline can only be developed after you've finished *writing!* So don't bother.

Remember only this: The reasons for writing and speaking to others is to do some combination of the following:

- Give information on—or an appreciation of—a subject.

- Gain acceptance of a new point of view.

- Change basic attitudes.

- Provide detailed information.

- Teach a skill.

- Sell something.

- Stimulate in an entertaining way.

Do the easy stuff first   Here's how to start. Do easy stuff first. (And remember: No outline! The problem with an outline is that it forces you to consider the *order* of things before you even know the *importance* of things! That's out of the question.)

Here's an easy approach that's fun. Find either a shoe box or a big paper bag from the supermarket. Then cut 20 or 30 sheets of ordinary 8½ × 11-inch paper into quarters.

Start writing key ideas on the individual quarter pieces of paper, and put them in the box or bag. Write anything at all that might be relevant. Don't worry about order. And don't worry about completeness. Consult reference books or texts if you want to. Write down examples, analogies, and quotes. Look up facts and figures. Jot down ideas for visual aids. Keep doing this for 2 or 3 days.

Keep pencil and paper with you at all times, because you'll get your best ideas in bathrooms, on the street, or in aisle 8 of the supermarket. Don't worry about repeating yourself, and *don't look at the slips of paper.*

That's really the key to the success of this technique. Don't look at what you've done. Keep jotting down ideas. Continue to add slips of paper without worrying about the importance of what you're doing.

On the morning of day 3, clear off the largest table you can find (clear it *completely*), dump out the box or bag, and organize the slips of paper into three categories: (1) what you *must* cover, (2) what you *could* cover if you had the time, and (3) what you probably *won't or shouldn't* cover.

Keep in mind *what you want your listeners to remember when you're finished.* You'll be lucky if they remember two or three major points! There is plenty of evidence to show that people generally remember a greater percentage of something that's short than something that's long. If you try to cover too much ground, you will only confuse your audience.

Reorganize your notes   At this point you are ready to reorganize your notes into logical order and work out a structure that includes an introduction, the body, and a conclusion.

The introduction.   The introduction should be brief and to the point. It should present the theme and objective of your material in a way that arouses interest and curiosity right from the start. (In a presentation, opening remarks need to be planned and rehearsed with a lot of care, since it's your first impression that motivates your audience either to keep listening or to switch off. Above all, avoid beginning with an apology. It is seldom necessary or relevant, and it won't help you achieve your objective.) At the beginning of a presentation you may choose to (1) acquaint the audience with your qualifications or interests in dealing with a particular problem or opportunity, (2) arouse interest in the subject, (3) orient people to the problem, or (4) direct attention to some specific issue or issues. (Chapter 8 examines the introduction further, focusing on why the introduction is vital.)

The body.   In the body of your material, the main theme is developed in logical steps so that the most important points will be remembered. One step should quite naturally stem from the previous one, so that your audience is carried forward. Wherever you can, use illustrative examples related to the experience of the people you're writing or speaking to. And use visual aids to help people understand and remember what's important. In the body of the presentation you may decide to (1) describe the symptoms of the problem and the influence it seems to be having on people and events, (2) describe the problem, (3) explain the constraints on the solution, (4) summarize various possible solutions, and (5) recommend the best alternative or combination of alternatives.

The conclusion.   The type of conclusion you use will depend largely upon your objective, but at least give a brief recapitulation, in different words, of your main points—plus some indication of "Where we go from here." You might conclude by summarizing the main ideas, solutions, or opportunities that have emerged in your analysis. You must recommend and schedule *action*, even if it's only in the form of further discussion.

Since the quality of your conclusion may determine whether or not you achieve your overall objective, you need to devote a lot of thought to it. In a presentation you will be wise to memorize (and constantly rehearse *out loud*) your persuasive close.

Here's the second part of your writing experiment.

Goldilocks and the three bears revisited ————————

Do you have any idea how an engineer or scientist could prepare a checklist or breakdown of this familiar children's story?

It would look like this.

Forest	Cottage	Girl	Chairs
▪ Large	▪ Cute	▪ Blonde	▪ Hard
▪ Dark	▪ Small	▪ Lost	▪ Soft
▪ Scary	▪ Thatched	▪ Little	▪ Perfect

Porridge bowls	Beds	Bears
▪ Too hot	▪ Too hard	▪ Papa (gruff)
▪ Too cold	▪ Too soft	▪ Mama (sweet)
▪ Just right	▪ Just great	▪ Baby (cranky)

There isn't much you can do with this information as it stands. It's reasonably complete, but it's not a story yet.

Please take a ballpoint pen and write the following four words on the back of your hand (or—if you're self-conscious—somewhere else):

Content

Continuity

Pace

Tone

Content is the stuff above. Just the facts.

But if the facts aren't told in the correct *order,* they won't pay off. That's *continuity.*

Next is *pace.* You have to build up the story, and as you're telling it, you can adjust the speed to suit the needs of your listener. If the child gets bored, you can pick up the pace. If the child becomes completely entranced and engrossed, you can embellish the story and make it last longer.

Finally, the *tone* of voice you use in telling a story or making a presentation is very important. If you're too stern in your tone of voice with children, you can frighten them and make them cry. If you're too fatuous or pompous with a technical audience, you'll annoy them and they'll ignore you.

Leave these four words on the back of your hand (or wherever) for a couple of days and memorize them. It's the only memorization required in this whole book. You can handle four words, can't you? If all else fails, substitute four dirty words that start with C, C, P, and T; think of those, and then remember:

Content

Continuity

Pace

Tone

Now you're ready for the next step.

Try writing something using only one-sound words ――――――

One-sound words are words such as *yes, please, go, do, work,* and *now.* Technically speaking, a word like *stopped* has two syllables, but we call it a one-sound word because it comes out "stopt." We don't say "stop ped" in two parts.

Following is a one-sound-word version of a man and a woman meeting for the first time at the beach. It is only three sentences long.

1. She sits on the sand, and he walks up.

2. "Mind if I join you?" he asks.

3. "Yes, I mind, so take a hike," she says.

This makes for a very short story. Here is a longer version using the same theme. The scene, once again, is at the beach. In the next 28 lines there will be nothing but one-sound words.

1. A guy walks up to a girl on the beach.

2. "Hi," he says. "Mind if I sit with you?"

3. "Yes, I mind," she says. "Shove off."

4. "How come?" he asks. "You with a guy?"

5. "No, I'm not with a guy," she says. "But you can take a hike."

6. "You don't *like* guys? Is that it?"

7. "Yeah, I like guys. I just don't like *fat* guys."

8. "You think I'm plump?"

9. "I think you're *fat,* pal!"

10. "I'm real tall, though," he says.

11. "So what? You're still fat. So get lost."

12. "I'm a real nice guy."

13. "I don't care. Give me a break."

14. "I've got a real nice car, too."

15. "Oh, yeah?" she says.

16. "And a big house."

17. "You own a house?" she asks.

18. "Yes. It's mine."

19. "How *big* is it, this house of yours?"

20. "Real big," he says. "You know how come?"

21. "No. How come?"

22. "Cause I've got a lot of dough, that's why."

23. "You mean you're *rich?*"

24. "Yes."

25. "How rich?"

26. "Real rich," he says. "I've got scads of cash."

27. "Well, well, well," she says. "You know what? You have a real nice smile. Why don't you sit down for a sec?"

28. "Gee, thanks," he says. "I will."

Same story, but with a much better ending.

There's something interesting about one-sound words. Any dialogue written this way *cannot be misunderstood*. One-sound words place you in the here and now.

Almost everything can be explained and discussed in one-sound words. For example, some professions could be described by saying:

"I am an eye, ear, nose, and throat man."

"I fix pipes in your house."

"I dig in the ground for clues to the past."

"I fix cars."

"I watch stars and things in the sky."

"I help make sure that you are safe in the streets."

"I put out fires."

"I fly planes."

In the same way, some of the great discoveries and events of history can be simplified:

"I have seen the gulls; I think we can warp the wings." (Orville Wright and the development of control surfaces on airplanes.)

"They can now sleep through the worst part." (Invention of anesthesia.)

"If things are clean, you won't get sick so much." (Lister, antisepsis.)

"The thing that makes milk go sour will die if you boil the milk." (Pasteur.)

"Try this, and you will not be ill." (Jenner's smallpox vaccine, citrus fruit for scurvy, quinine for malaria.)

"I know we're right, so let's go for it!" (The Crusades, the Spanish Inquisition, both sides in the American Civil War.)

"We are smart and strong, and they are dumb and weak! So let's go for it!" (Genghis Khan, Alexander the Great, Adolph Hitler, Richard Nixon.)

"I may be short, but I'm in charge of the whole thing!" (Napoleon Bonaparte.)

"You seem like a nice kid; why not come up to my room?" (Casanova, Mae West.)

"I'll go for it one more time to show that I'm the champ." (Various prizefighters.)

This one-sound-words technique can also be applied to advertising. Some of the important selling propositions that businesses use can be summarized this way:

1. A child can use this.
2. It stays fresh a long time.
3. These are real cheap to run.
4. If it breaks down, we fix it. Fast.
5. You can have it *now,* and then pay it off when you can.
6. If we don't have it in stock, we'll go get it in our truck.
7. Trust our good name.
8. When you need things, we're here.
9. If you buy this (use this), you'll be safe.
10. We make the best ones of all.
11. This will make you look or feel nice.
12. This will make you smell great.
13. This one won't go out of date; you can add on to it.
14. If you want *speed,* this is the one for you!
15. Here's a deal with no *risk.*

I suggested this technique to a client of mine. The client's marketing people were spending a lot of time in meetings that weren't very productive. One-sound words helped them to be straight and clear. Figure 6-3 lists what they came up with.

Without one-sound words, organizations say things like:

> This group here assembled would be greatly obliged if you could entertain the possibility of modifying your behavior and follow guidelines that are consonant with our own, therefore performing to standards that have been established and maintained by us, or otherwise pursuing alternative possibilities for employment.

The short version of this is, of course: "Shape up or ship out."

Notice how easy it is to find one-sound equivalents for the words listed in Fig. 6-4.

To show how effective using one-sound words can be, read this example written by a senior financial analyst at one of my client locations—a person who had never been able to write (she said), and

---

THIS IS A GUIDE TO HOW WE'LL TALK WHEN WE MEET

We will tell the truth and be clear on these 12 points:

1. How does the team feel?
2. Are we on track?
3. We said we would do some things. Did we?
4. Were they done well? On time?
5. Did we make as much as we said we would?
6. Were the costs in line?
7. Did we ship when we said we would?
8. Did the stuff get there on time?
9. Did we break stuff on the way?
10. Can we fix the things we broke, or do we owe them new ones?
11. Where will the team go next?
12. What will the team do next? By what date?

Figure 6-3.

who expressed grave misgivings about ever writing anything with *spirit*. The following concerns an event that happened when she was in the third grade:

> I was 12 when the man crept in the house. It was in the dark of night. Rain poured down. Lights flashed, and loud sounds shook the sky. He came in through the front door, climbed the stairs, and stopped at my room. His hand turned the knob. In the next bolt of light I saw him as he stood at the door, the man in the dark pants and beige coat. He walked next to my bed and I screamed. My dad ran to my room. The man was gone. They thought I had a bad dream. But the wet prints on the rug let them know it was no dream. A man had crept in my room.

Okay, now you're ready for the last part.

Get a loved one out of a foreign prison

Here's an exercise to use after you've sorted through your slips of paper and given some thought to one-sound words. It's an easy way to write the first draft of anything—especially if it's loaded with information.

Imagine that somebody you really care about is being held prisoner by a country whose people need information in order to compete more effectively in world markets. They will consider releasing the loved one if you can write a letter that includes a lot of solid advice about how they can do better.

It has to be in letter form and personal—something they can easily understand (hence the importance of the one-sound-word exercise).

FINDING ONE-SOUND EQUIVALENTS

As an exercise, try coming up with one-sound equivalents for the following list of words:

1. Accomplish   _____

2. Utilization   _____

3. Compensation, remuneration   _____

4. Manufacture, fabricate   _____

5. Assistance   _____

6. Aggregate   _____

7. Primary   _____

8. Apprehension   _____

9. Substantiate   _____

10. Rigorous   _____

11. Termination   _____

12. Voluminous   _____

13. Visualize   _____

14. Variation   _____

15. Characterize   _____

16. Cognizant   _____

17. Determine   _____

18. Activate, instigate, initiate   _____

Figure 6-4.

A *letter*. Not a report. Not a chapter. Not a memo. Not an outline. Not an article for a magazine or a technical journal. Just a nice, clear letter containing your very best thinking. Don't worry about correct continuity and "proper" organization. Just start letting the ideas flow, and describe things that people really need to know in order to succeed.

Remember: The knowledge you impart must be meaty enough and complete enough—with enough provocative, imaginative, and solid ideas—to secure the loved one's release.

His or her freedom depends *only* on your writing an earnest letter, so what you write must be compelling, persuasive, and informative! Try it.

Leadership

This book is for people who already have some idea of how to speak, who are poised, and who are unafraid of audiences. One of the things that *must* be done in a high-level presentation is to project an additional characteristic that is in very short supply: *leadership*. You must project the quality of a person who can take full responsibility to get the job done.

A firm knowledge of your material provides the necessary confidence. You must also convey strength. You must convey professionalism. You must speak and act with authority. You must have a commanding presence. You must remain composed. The *only* way to do this is with adequate preparation and practice.

Under no circumstances can any members of the team display nervousness, uncertainty, or timidity. They must not laugh nervously. They mustn't get angry or rattled. They must never be defensive in their words or their attitude.

You must never preface a sentence with: "I *think*."

Common Ways to Organize Your Material

To help you convey the confidence of a real leader, you must be absolutely clear about the organization of your material. It must not be patched together with fragments from other presentations, proposals, technical papers, and articles. It must have a solid foundation and framework.

Figure 6-5 shows a number of basic ways to organize material. In a presentation with several speakers, more than one of the alternatives in Fig. 6-5 can be considered. It will add to the variety of the presentation to have more than one approach.

Let's examine some of the more common approaches from the list in more detail.

Analytical

The word *analyze* means to separate the whole into its constituent parts for careful scrutiny. For this reason, an analytical approach proves to be logical for many kinds of messages. For instance, when you write a résumé, you usually break it down into descriptive parts such as education, experience, personal data, and references.

Many business reports also separate a body of information into logical components. One example is a report or presentation about a company's performance which breaks the subject into the fundamental business functions of marketing and sales, R&D, engineering, production, distribution, finance, and human resources.

Cause and effect

This calls for a very straightforward exposition of the origin of a situation and the results or outcomes from it. Typical examples are reports of failures or accidents, engineering change orders, proposal debriefings, and other clear-cut examples in which there is a direct cause-effect relationship that can be established.

COMMON WAYS TO ORGANIZE A PRESENTATION

Following are a number of basic ways to organize material. For each presentation you plan, choose one or more of the methods from the list as an aid in structuring the presentation. In a presentation with several speakers, more than one of the alternatives might be selected to add variety to the presentation.

1. Advantages/ disadvantages	An objective look at pros and cons.	❏
2. Analytical	Break information into logical components.	❏
3. Applications	How to use a tool or technique.	❏
4. Benefits	Advantages of a solution or an approach.	❏
5. Cause and effect	"A" made "B" happen; here's how and why.	❏
6. Chronological	A sequence of acts or events.	❏
7. Comparative	How two or more things stack up.	❏
8. Deductive, inductive	General to specific or vice versa.	❏
9. Evaluations	This will work (not work) for these reasons.	❏
10. Fears and concerns	Things that are sneaking up to hurt us.	❏
11. General to specific	Example: Customer demand drives new products.	❏
12. Geographical	Example: Performance by regional offices.	❏
13. Highlights	The presentation of key ideas only.	❏
14. Historical	From the past to the present in easy steps.	❏
15. Innovations	Important developments of interest.	❏
16. Instructions	How to do something in simple, clear ways.	❏
17. Meeting criteria	Standards are set and then met.	❏
18. Price studies	Cost-benefit analyses in considerable depth.	❏
19. Plan or plans	A systematic look at how to do something.	❏
20. Problem or problems only	Clarifying a difficulty or difficulties.	❏
21. Problems and solutions	Here's the difficulty; here's what to do about it.	❏
22. Prospects for the future	Results of studies yield particular forecasts.	❏
23. Questions and answers	Obvious questions and not-so-obvious responses.	❏
24. Ranked	Urgent matters in their order of importance.	❏
25. Recommendations	Here is our choice and why we made it.	❏
26. Risks	Most options carry some risk of failure.	❏
27. Spatial	From top to bottom, side to side, and so forth.	❏
28. Specific to general	Example: A small new product drives a big market.	❏
29. Symptoms	Simple facts about how things appear to be.	❏

Figure 6-5.

Chronological

If a message features the order of events as the key dimension, then it uses the chronological approach.

Suppose you file an automobile accident claim with an insurance company. Sometimes during the process you will provide a narrative of events in the step-by-step sequence of their occurrence.

Chronological descriptions also tell how to perform production-line operations, how to assemble something, or how to write or tell the sequential story of a project or an event.

Comparative

The organization of a message often involves a comparative pattern. For example, a report could compare:

- Qualities of a decentralized versus a centralized organization plan

- Advantages and disadvantages of three proposed locations for a new plant site

- Views from both sides of a labor-management issue

- Alternative solutions to a problem or a business challenge

Deductive

The deductive or direct approach develops from the general to the specific or from the whole to the parts. It develops from the universe to the sample or from the conclusion or principle to the factual bits that fall under it.

The deductive approach works well for messages that include routine or pleasant information. For instance, a message of invitation usually begins with the invitation and then supplies the details.

Sales presentations can take advantage of this gradual building from acceptable general statements to a specific desired conclusion. Here's an example:

1. We have a national problem with crime.

2. Not only that, but crime is on the increase *locally*. Right here in this region.

3. As a matter of fact, your neighborhood could soon be a target for criminal activity.

4. Your house could be *next*.

5. With these facts in mind, let me explain what our company has produced to ensure the safety and security that your family deserves.

6. The new solid-state Universal Burglar & Fire Alarm system will meet your specific needs. (You owe it to your family to buy one today.)

Inductive

The inductive or indirect approach moves the message from the specific to the general, from the part to the whole. It moves from the sample to the universe and from the factual bits to a general conclusion or principle built from them.

The inductive approach is useful for delivering unpleasant messages. Used in those situations, induction establishes an indirect process that softens the blow of bad news. It also often appears in reports of research.

For example, if you were a bank officer and had to write a letter to refuse a request for credit, you would cite such factors as the applicant's poor credit record and insufficient income before actually making the refusal.

Historical

A variation of the chronological approach, this technique simply begins at the beginning (whenever you choose to start) and proceeds carefully and systematically to the present. In this reportorial style, it is unnecessary to inject opinion or analysis; it is simply a straightforward presentation of facts and events.

Problems and solutions

When using this approach, simply select the most important problems facing your client or prospect (or the client's organization, department, unit, etc.) and provide thoughtful answers to them. Limit the number of problems to just a few (six or seven), and—where necessary—provide alternative solutions.

Questions and answers

Use the same approach as you would for problems and solutions. Remember to keep the numbers of questions to a minimum; otherwise the reader or listener is likely to become confused or bored.

Ranked

You can arrange the components of a message in a ranked pattern. For example, when presenting alternatives, you might begin by listing the best choices first and the worst last (or—conversely—present the least desirable alternatives at the beginning, building toward the most desirable alternatives at the end).

Some other examples of ranked development include:

- Describing the qualities of good managerial style

- Ranking job factors in order of importance

- Asking questions in order of importance

- Arranging budget requests in order of importance

- Defining a list of priorities such as, for example, the requirements of new capital construction

Spatial

Some messages logically unfold through a spatial pattern. For example, if you write a report about your company's national operations, you could easily develop it by geographical areas.

Another spatial pattern covers the topic from top to bottom, from bottom to top, from right to left, from left to right, from inside to outside, from near to far, or from far to near. Topics natural to this kind of organizational approach include communications patterns for:

- Lateral flows

- Internal-to-external and external-to-internal processing

- Movements from a central office to decentralized offices or from decentralized offices back to a central one

Symptoms

This is another approach to reporting in which simple facts can be stated without any need for explanations, analyses, or expressions of opinions. In other words, present a cut-and-dried account of: "This is what appears to be happening." Or: "Based on what we can discover, this is what happened."

Key Questions to Review

Journalism 101 teaches freshmen to approach stories by asking questions about who, what, where, why, when, how many, how much, and how often.

The following questions are offered as a way to ensure that you haven't accidentally skipped anything of importance—a final test to make sure all the bases are covered. The questions were developed to help you examine facts and circumstances so that you can successfully solve problems, assess opportunities, verify objectives, understand conditions, foretell likely events, make decisions, and develop a better estimate of your competitive situation. A summary checklist is provided for your convenience in Fig. 6-6.

When preparing a specific presentation, evaluate the three most important questions on this list with respect to your particular presentation. Also try to come up with one or two others to add.

1. *Who are the key players on the prospect's team?* What are the names and relationships of the key players? Who is involved? Who has the clout or the authority?

2. *Who are the key players on your team?* Whom must you negotiate with for help, resources, or support? Who has the information? Who—on your own team—needs to be convinced of what?

3. *Who will not play a role?* It is sometimes just as important to know who will not play a part in the activity or the plan, and why they won't be a part of it. Needless to say, these people need to have the facts explained to them in order to allay fears and reduce uncertainty and confusion.

4. *Who is competing?* For what?

5. *Who cares?* Seriously—why does it matter? What difference does it make?

KEY QUESTIONS TO REVIEW

As a final review before writing up your presentation, quickly check the items on the following list to make sure you have covered all bases.

1. Who are the key players on their team? .... ❏
2. Who are the key players on your team? .... ❏
3. Who will *not* play a role? .... ❏
4. Who is competing? .... ❏
5. Who cares? Seriously — why does it matter? What difference does it make? .... ❏
6. What facts do you have? What assumptions are being made? .... ❏
7. What information do you need? And where do you have to go to get it? .... ❏
8. What existing rules, regulations, or procedures may apply? .... ❏
9. What's been done already? .... ❏
10. What is it: routine or nonroutine? .... ❏
11. What is it: concrete or abstract? .... ❏
12. What is the biggest challenge? .... ❏
13. What is the biggest obstacle? .... ❏
14. Where are you going, and when do you get there? .... ❏
15. *Where* is the problem? .... ❏
16. Where will it happen? .... ❏
17. Where can you go for help? .... ❏
18. Where are you now in the problem? The middle? The beginning? .... ❏
19. Why did it happen? Or why is it happening? .... ❏
20. Why are you doing what you're doing (or proposing what you're proposing)? .... ❏
21. Why are they in their present circumstances? .... ❏
22. When must something be done? What? In what order? By what date? .... ❏
23. How many? People? Units? Dollars? How many of *what*? .... ❏
24. How *much* is required now, or will be required in the future? .... ❏
25. How much is it going to cost? And what are the components of it? .... ❏
26. Can you look at it some new way? .... ❏
27. Can you analyze it easily? .... ❏
28. Is it right? Is it good (according to the earlier definition)? .... ❏
29. Is it timely? .... ❏
30. Is the payoff clear to you? .... ❏

Figure 6-6.

6. *What facts do you have?*   Or, in lieu of facts, what assumptions are being made?

7. *What information do you need?*   And where do you have to go to get it? Can you get it from books and reports? From talking to people? From a phone call to an expert?

8. *What existing rules, regulations, or procedures may apply?*

9. *What's been done already?*   Keep notes or records of what you've done already. Otherwise there's the possibility of forgetting important facts or having to redo work unnecessarily.

10. *Is a part of what you're struggling with routine or nonroutine?*   Has it ever happened before? Will it happen again? Don't be clever and inventive about activities that will happen routinely. Find a standard process or procedure for routine activities and then devote your best energies and efforts to *non*routine things.

11. *What is it: concrete or abstract?*   Is your perception of your situation clear, or is it hazy? Is what you're thinking about largely theoretical and complicated, or is it straightforward and simple to understand? Other questions you can ask are these: Is it subjective or objective? Qualitative or quantitative? Rational and logical or nonrational and illogical? Make pairs of lists if necessary.

12. *What is the biggest challenge?*

13. *What is the biggest obstacle?*

14. *Where are you going, and when do you get there?*

15. *Where is the problem?*   Notice that this doesn't ask: "What is the problem?" That is a different question. Example: If a problem is showing up in Detroit boilers, but not in the same boilers in other cities, then one might conclude that there's something specific about Detroit that is causing a difficulty.

16. *Where will it happen?*   Sometimes just knowing where will tell you a lot about what, why, when, and how many.

17. *Where can you go for help?*   Where can you find the answer? Where can you get the information you need? What's the fastest way? What's the closest place? Is there a cheap way out, or will you pay anything to get what you need?

18. *Where are you now in the problem?*   The middle? The beginning? Somewhere near the end? Can you make a map or chart of your situation, condition, or opportunity so as to show your precise location? Do you *know* where you—or they—are?

19. *Why did it happen?*   Or why is it happening? Why have things worked out the way they have so far? What were the key factors or causes?

20. *Why are you doing what you're doing?*   (Or proposing what you're proposing?)

21. *Why are they in their present circumstances?*

22. *When must something be done?* What must be done? In what order? By what date? How much time do you have to do what you have to do?

23. *How many?* People? Units? Dollars? How many of *what?*

24. *How much is required now, or will be required in the future?* One of the most frequently underforecasted elements is time. Most people fail to accurately account for the total number of hours, days, weeks, and months that an activity or a project will require.

25. *How much is it going to cost?* And what are the components of *it?* How many dollars for such elements as research, facilities, machines, quality control, advertising, procurement, training, storage, supplies, sales, inspection, people, legal expenses, lights, marketing, finance, planning, transportation, inventory, shipping, engineering—you name it.

26. *Can you look at it in some new way?* This thing you're thinking about—is it possible for you to turn it backward? What happens if you put the last thing first? Can it be turned upside down? Could you divide it in two and give half of it to somebody else? If you were suddenly two people, could you find two things to do simultaneously?

27. *Can you analyze it easily?* What is the most important thing about the subject? What is the least important thing? What is of medium importance? Where has most of your energy been going? There is frequently a substantial difference between what you think is truly important and where the bulk of your energy and concentration is focused.

28. *Is it right?* Is it good (*according to the earlier definition*)? Is it appropriate? Should you be doing it? Is it in your best long-term interests? Must you justify anything or rationalize anything in order to proceed? (To justify means to show that something is right or reasonable. To rationalize means to make things seem reasonable, or to present facts or reasons that are plausible, but—in the end—are untrue or unlikely. It's important to know when you're kidding others or yourself.)

29. *Is it timely?* You may be able to prove that the idea, the project, or the opportunity is worthwhile and appropriate, but is this really the time for it? And are you certain that you're *ready?*

30. *Is the payoff clear to you?* Is it substantial? Is it worth the effort? Is the payoff for you, for your organization, or for some greater cause? Is it altruism, capitalism, or exactly what?

Ideas about Tone and Style

Earlier in the chapter, you read about the value of one-sound words. They help cut through to the facts. Notice that commands like *Fire!* and *Stop!*—as well as most dirty words are very short and clear. That contributes to their forcefulness. Certainly, using one-sound words will help you write effectively.

In addition, these nine simple rules will help you in your writing:

1. Write the way you talk.

2. Be personal.

3. Use short words.

4. Use active verbs.

5. Use short sentences.

6. Identify benefits that accrue to the reader.

7. Write things down fast and in any order.

8. After you write, edit in a different color.

9. After you edit, wait awhile; then edit again.

Saul Bellow, American Nobel Prize winner in literature, summarized his approach as follows. (Actually, this is how my friend Herb Wolff *said* Saul Bellow summarized his approach. I hope Herb's right.)

1. First I write for ideas.

2. Then I go back and try to find better words.

3. Then I go back and work on the images the words are supposed to create.

Well-written work is crisp and to the point; it is clear. Good writing also uses only words that *count* and constructions which create vivid images in your mind. See what you think of the following.

A Getty ad in a magazine

One brisk June morning at the break of dawn, Bryan Allen attempted to become the first man to fly under his own power across the English Channel. After two years of intensive training, he was able to pedal with enough strength to keep the plane aloft. But against the Channel's unpredictable wind currents, sheer willpower would often be the only thing between him and disaster.

The flight took longer than expected. Yet even with cramps in both his legs and a severe case of exhaustion, he never gave in. And when he finally touched down on French soil, he had not only won his own personal victory, but he had paved the way for future experiments in manpowered flight.

Bryan Allen's accomplishment illustrates our belief that America gains most when individuals have great freedom to pursue goals without undue government interference. And although few of us would care to try what Bryan did, we nonetheless expect to pursue our own goals with equal freedom.

There are times, however, when neither you nor we can expect such freedom in our daily lives. Not when someone decides the government should protect us from it.

Something to think about from the people at Getty.

A story from the *New York Times* ───────────────────────────

BOMB PLOT CHARGED

After a police dog named Brandy sniffed out 13 sticks of dynamite hidden in a lunch box in a West Side garage, F.B.I. agents and New York City detectives last week arrested three Serbians, a priest, the operator of the garage and a machinist. They were charged with conspiring, along with two men in an Illinois Federal court complaint, to bomb the Yugoslav consulate in Chicago. Authorities said their evidence included recorded conversations about bomb attacks on Yugoslav diplomatic missions and residences. A defense lawyer described the three as staunch anti-Communists. By most accounts the arrests marked one of the first such actions in this country directed against Serbian opponents of Yugoslav's Communist government.

One sentence from Damon Runyon ───────────────────────────

It was on Judd Gray's forthright testimony that Damon Runyon wrote one of the all-time great news leads:

A plain little man in a plain gray suit sat on the witness stand this afternoon and talked his life away.

One paragraph from Anthony Carson ───────────────────────────

Once I worked as a clerk in an office and I grew thinner and my suits fell to bits and I watched the seagulls out of the window. The months passed and I knew I had taken the wrong road. "You're not paid to watch sea-gulls," said the manager. In my spare time I went to Victoria Station and bought cups of tea and watched the trains. The ceiling of the station shook with the thunder of wheels, and men with fur collars and attaché cases disappeared in clouds of steam. There was a faint imported smell of sea, a catch in the throat, a volley of shouts, and an explosion of children like fireworks. The Golden Arrow drew in. Out came the eternal over-wrapped exiles from operas and roulette, pampered ghosts from Anglo-French hotels, lovers, swindlers, actresses, impostors, believers, bores, and magicians. But all that mattered to me was the gold and blue of the places they had been to, the singing names, like Leman, Maggiore, Tropez, Cannes, Ischia, Ibiza.

Anthony Carson
Punch Magazine

An item from the J. Peterman Catalogue ───────────────────────────

THE RIGHT STUFF

The shops in Zurich, or on upper Madison Avenue or on Old Bond Street...the kind of shops where you have to ring a buzzer to get inside, have wallets these days made of ostrich, sea snake, lizard...and once in Hong Kong I actually saw wallets made from chicken feet...all costing so much that once you buy one you have nothing left over to put in them.

Accordingly, I now wish to draw your attention to something different; a wallet made out of a baseball mitt. This is not a joke.

Stop and think about that wonderful dark pocket of leather in the middle of a baseball glove, lovingly used and punished for half a lifetime. Is it wearing out? Is it ready to throw away? No, it's just quietly getting better.

This wallet is made out of *that* leather: baseball-glove leather. Center cut. Beautifully cut and sewn and made to last and made to darken; made to be with you for a long time.

Regular billfold size, 6 credit card pockets, 2 inside pockets, full-length compartment for bills, lined throughout.

Handsome, simple, hard to argue with.

Price: $56. We pay shipping. To order call toll free 800-231-7341.

Criteria for a good ad

Here are some ideas that were not established by the advertising industry. Instead, these criteria were dreamed up by businesspeople (financial analysts, actually—very dry, very literal) in a workshop called How to Write Stuff That People Wanna Read.

In our work together we analyzed lead sentences and paragraphs in newspapers and magazines (like the swell story about Brandy, which could be the outline of an entire movie), and we analyzed a lot of good ads.

Here are the criteria the analysts came up with:

1. It must be well organized.

2. It must have a logical flow.

3. It must be visually appealing (not cluttered with unnecessary design elements or words).

4. It must be interesting. It's got to attract, and hold, the attention of the reader or viewer.

5. It must present something desirable about the product—a benefit, something valuable or useful.

6. Material must be presented simply and clearly. There can be no ambiguity or uncertainty about how well the product works or how available it is.

7. There must be an action step or a way for the reader or viewer to connect with the product or the manufacturer (such as a number to call, a coupon to clip, or a place to visit).

I've thought a lot about these criteria. It occurs to me that they can be used to define a good memo, a good letter, a good report, or a good *presentation*.

The analysts did a great job. And so will you if you'll just give yourself a little extra time and a little extra thought.

The Impact of Your Solution on Problems and Circumstances

After you've written a draft of the presentation that tells the story of your solution, test its effectiveness by reviewing the extent to which it has solved a *problem* or altered *circumstances*.

In order for these ideas to matter, you must understand what they mean.

Solving a problem

One of the definitions of the word *problem* has to do with one's emotions—a problem as a source of irritation or perplexity, something mysterious and frustrating.

The primary definition, however, is this:

Problem—"A question raised for: (1) inquiry, (2) consideration, *or* (3) solution." (*Webster's Seventh New Collegiate Dictionary*)

This dictionary definition does two things. It allows no room or time for anger and frustration. And, most importantly, it provides a suggested pathway for problem *solving*.

Notice that at the beginning a question is raised. And having raised it, there are now three different things to do in a specific order.

You may, first of all, simply *inquire* into the question. (Your solution may only involve this first step. Plenty of research projects have been sold to merely inquire into the depth and nature of a problem). The process can stop at this point if you want it to. There may not be the need—or the possibility—to continue.

Should you choose to continue, you may proceed to the *consideration* step of the definition. You may consider either the question or the inquiries into it. This is the second step at which you can quit. (Your "solution" might merely be an evaluation of alternatives that have been uncovered in this important stage.)

Finally, with the first two steps clearly in mind and adequately covered, you may choose to try to *solve* the question or problem. Notice the critical word *or* in the above definition. Not all problems can be—or *need* to be—solved.

A simple illustration　In a management workshop a few years ago this process was challenged by somebody as being merely theoretical and of no real applicability. I invited him to think of a real problem, either business or personal, and he came up with the following:

"Here's the problem: it's real irritating. The washing machine at my beach house is broken, and I've got to replace it."

"In other words," I said, "you've elected to jump to the end of the process and select a *solution*, even without inquiry or consideration?"

"I'm not competent to inquire or consider. I'm not an appliance repairman."

I invited him to *inquire* anyway and ask a few fundamental questions.

Who *said* it was broken? *Answer:* The local washing machine distributor who both sells and repairs machines.

How is it broken? *Answer:* It doesn't work.

Do the hot and cold water run into the machine? *Answer:* Yes, they do. (Therefore, this is not a *hydraulic* problem.)

Does the motor work—does the machine still agitate and spin dry? *Answer:* Yes, it does. (Therefore, this is not a *mechanical* problem.)

Then what *is* the problem? *Answer:* The machine acts crazy; it's erratic; it doesn't do things in the right order. (Sounds like an electrical or an electronic problem if water runs and the motor operates.)

"Okay," I said. "Go to the next step and *consider* what you told us. Consider the facts."

"The valves seem to work, and the water runs. The motor isn't burned out. It's doing the job. And if the machine's crazy, it's because something's the matter with its 'brain.' I wonder if there's a circuit board in the control unit that's gotten corroded from the ocean air. The machine sits on the back porch, after all, and is pretty much exposed. I wonder if that's the answer?"

"What do you think?" I asked.

"It's certainly worth asking," he said. "Replacing a circuit board ought to be a helluva lot less expensive than a new washing machine. I'll ask. That's a very good idea."

His idea. Because he was forced to work through the logical steps.

Altering circumstances

Will the story about your solution change *circumstances?* Let's look into this for a minute.

Circumstances are defined as the facts, conditions, and events accompanying, conditioning, or determining others (i.e., other facts, conditions, and events). Don't get confused by this. The definition is rich with possibilities, as you will see in the simple illustration below.

Everything is linked to everything else. Every occurrence and every utterance has some impact, influence, or bearing—however small—upon something or someone.

One morning a while back, a large semi overturned on an east-west interstate (I-70) in the middle of Denver. It was a simple *event.* Trucks turn over all the time. But then an important *fact* came to light. The semi was carrying a load of U.S. Navy torpedoes. And nobody knew (1) the extent of damage to the cargo or (2) whether the torpedoes would explode if they were moved.

Also, the truck had overturned on the overpass above the north-south interstate (I-25). Because of the uncertainty of the situation, the authorities closed both major highways in both directions. This created a *condition* that quickly had an impact on thousands and thousands of commuters in and around Denver. Each person who was late for work had to face an altered set of personal facts, conditions, and events in his or her own life.

Events bear upon facts. Conditions create new facts and events. Things keep churning and changing. But it's usually for reasons that can be understood. A single *event* in the Middle East can trigger a new set of economic *facts* in international financial markets that will trickle down (or cascade) on each of us by way of new *conditions* that we face at the gas pump, airline ticket counter, and elsewhere.

When you make a presentation, you must be aware of the changes of *circumstances* that your solution will cause. One of your responsibilities is to demonstrate your willingness to take charge of the likely facts, conditions, and events associated with the implementation of your ideas.

Things happen

It is important to realize that things are going to happen, and circumstances will continue to change, whether you try to have any impact on them or not. The world keeps turning. Events take place. Conditions change. New facts will continue to be added to encyclopedias.

Even if we choose to hide in basement rooms, circumstances will continue to evolve.

Some businesses in recent decades have done the equivalent of hiding out and of deliberately not paying attention to what was going on outside their windows. They thought circumstances were stable, that products and services wouldn't change much, that the same mix of customers and competitors would prevail, and that government policies toward regulation and taxation were constant. Either they didn't *look* or they didn't pay any attention to what they saw.

Ross Webber, who teaches at the Wharton School of Management at the University of Pennsylvania, believes the environment faced by most managers today is a very turbulent one. He says [in his book, *Management* (Irwin, 1975)] that it is characterized by:

1. Continually changing products and services.

2. An ever-changing array of competitors, including market entries by big businesses.

3. Unpredictable governmental actions reflecting political interactions between the public and various advocacy groups (consumer protection, ecology, animal rights, and so forth).

4. Major technological innovations, including the introduction of innovations which render old ways of thinking and doing obsolete.

5. Rapid changes in the values and behavior of large numbers of people.

Your solutions—and the stories you develop to describe your solutions—must reflect your sensitivity to circumstances and how they must be creatively altered. You must demonstrate that you can accept ambiguity and cooperate with people with differing backgrounds and perspective (hence the understanding of people's goals, values, competences, and so forth).

The future can be changed. Circumstances can be adjusted to your advantage. The correct efforts taken in the present will benefit you in the near—and in the *distant*—future.

A part of this process and—possibly—the implementation of your solution may involve change. This may be difficult for some people, especially those in your audience. Here are some general observations by Ralph Besse appearing in George Steiner's book *Top Management Planning* (Macmillan, 1969). It will help you position your solution so as to create the least amount of dislocation. There is an accompanying worksheet in Fig. 6-7, the answers to which will help you build a change management element into your presentation.

CHANGE

1. Is more acceptable when those involved help create it than when it's imposed from the outside.

2. Is more tolerable when it doesn't affect security than when it does.

3. Is more liable to alteration when it results from application of

HOW TO MAKE PEOPLE MORE COMFORTABLE WITH CHANGE

As you plan your presentation, keep in mind the people who will have to execute your plan, work with your product or service, or in some other way implement your solution to their organization's problem. This means change for those people, and since their success impacts your success, it will behoove you to anticipate their needs. This checksheet will help.

For this presentation:

1. What measures can be taken to involve the people whose lives will be most affected? _____

   _____

   _____

   _____

2. What can be done to minimize the perception that the proposed solution will threaten their security, whether it's what they do or how they do it? _____

   _____

   _____

   _____

3. What prior experiences or practices of the organization in question can be used to increase the likelihood of acceptance of change? _____

   _____

   _____

   _____

4. What measures can be taken to increase the level of understanding of what is being proposed in this presentation? _____

   _____

   _____

   _____

5. How can leadership be led to plan for the change that is bound to accompany implementation of this proposal? How can the rank and file be convinced that any changes are indeed planned and not experimental? _____

   _____

   _____

   _____

Figure 6-7.

6. Are there other major changes or programs under way that could affect the success of this proposal? If so, what are they? Can the programs be merged or the timing altered so that they are more compatible or complementary? _____

_____

_____

_____

7. What is the balance of new versus veteran employees of the organization in question? What measures can be taken to address this "demographic" factor? _____

_____

_____

_____

8. What can be done to maximize the range of employees who will benefit from this solution? How can the benefits be successfully conveyed to them? _____

_____

_____

_____

9. To what extent is this organization already trained for major change or improvement? What has been added to the proposal presentation to address the issue of change readiness? _____

_____

_____

_____

Figure 6.7 (*Continued*)

previously established impersonal principles than when it is dictated by personal order.

4. Is more acceptable when it is understood than when it is not.

5. Is more unobjectionable if it is planned rather than experimental.

6. Is more successful when it is inaugurated after prior change has been assimilated than when it is inaugurated during the confusion of other major change.

7. Is much better received by people who are new on the job than by people who have been around for a long time and accustomed to the "old" ways.

8. Is more acceptable to people who share in the benefits of change than those who do not.

9. Is more acceptable if the organization has been trained to plan for improvement than it is if the organization is accustomed to static procedures.

Dog & Pony Checkpoints

✔ Prepare the audience with a preshow summary that explains what you're going to talk about and introduces the speakers.

✔ Don't use laser pointers. They're distracting.

✔ Present as a team, not as a solo performer.

✔ Don't use humor. There is nothing lighthearted about a major presentation—it's not a comedy workshop. Show your willingness to smile or laugh if the situation calls for it, but don't make any special efforts to be funny. It could be a tragic mistake.

✔ Don't use handouts during a presentation. They only serve to distract the audience from what you're trying to tell them. If you give something to people, they are bound to look at it, even though you've asked them not to. If they're busy *reading*, they're not watching and listening to you, and you will have completely derailed your own presentation.

✔ Work from an outline that is prepared on 3 × 5-inch cards, on a yellow pad, or in some other form. The speakers must, at all cost, appear to be under control and neither winging it nor working from too tight a script.

✔ Never use a podium.

✔ Never speak while you're sitting.

✔ Memorize the opening.

✔ Work from notes during the body of the presentation.

✔ Memorize the close.

✔ Don't think that people are going to take action based on the information you provide.

✔ Don't think that people are going to take action because you've gotten them to understand the information you've provided.

- Realize that people get convinced (or perhaps, more accurately, convince *themselves*) at different rates of speed—some faster, some slower.

- Understand the value of patience. Remember that you're trying to close deals that have long-term consequences, particularly to you.

- Keep in mind that it isn't the amount of work that goes into the development of a proposal or a presentation that's so important; it's the period of time over which the material is developed. The longer the period of elapsed time, the better the end product. It's not a matter of total hours that's so important, but the fact that there's been sufficient quality time to reflect.

- Define, in your own mind, what you want to accomplish in your presentation, and work systematically and rigorously toward that objective.

- Remember that the sooner you start preparing, the better off you'll be.

- Don't worry about writing an outline. Get your preliminary thoughts together in any order and any fashion that's comfortable for you. Those fragments will then suggest a sensible path—continuity.

- When conceptualizing about the content of a presentation (report, article, book, movie script, or whatever), be divergent not convergent.

- Use the fragments-in-a-bag (or box) approach.

- Remember that the most complicated ideas can be expressed in short words and sentences.

- Verify exactly how (where, why, when) your solution is going to solve a problem or answer a question.

- Investigate the ways or the extent to which your solution will affect circumstances.

- If your solution will introduce an uncomfortable level of change, suggest ways of minimizing its effects.

7

Gain Your Audience's Commitment to Attend

First, you have to present a story that is convincing enough in conversation with high-level people that you will be given the opportunity to schedule a detailed presentation. The schedule can then be set. Next, you must develop a compelling "preview" of your story so that other audience members who have been selected to see it and hear it will be enticed to attend your presentation. Invitations must then be made with sufficient advance notice. Calendars must be checked and times verified. Finally, "preshow" material must be produced and distributed to your audience in advance of your presentation. Confirmations must be made 24 hours before the event. Here is a brief look at important ideas in this chapter.

Contents of This Chapter

- Developing an inviting "preview" and stimulating the right people to attend your presentation
- Ideas about invitations
- Developing and distributing a "preshow summary"
- General guidelines for designing invitations and preshow summaries
- Confirmations
- Dog & Pony checkpoints

Developing an Inviting "Preview" and Stimulating the Right People to Attend Your Presentation

Here is the challenge. You have developed a desirable solution. (And remember, *a solution may be a product, a service, a process, a program, a system, an idea, or a company.*) Now you need to make a formal presentation about it in order to get it sold.

The strategy is to reveal your ideas in a condensed or abbreviated form that is so interesting and intriguing that when you talk about it, your prospective audience will be compelled to listen further to learn about your solution. Your audience will be happy to attend a presentation to hear the details and how the solution will be implemented.

Two things are required in the early stages: (1) the short form of your story and (2) a need to create a style, tone, or image for you and your solution. This is more a matter of *appearance* than substance. You've got to make it *look* good. It's got to feel right. You've got to impress your audience ahead of time and build trust. That's the first hook.

Here are the important steps.

1. *Conduct initial talks with important decision makers.* These may be face-to-face discussions or phone conversations. In this first critical step you must define your solution in such interesting terms that you create enough interest to justify a meeting and a formal presentation.

If the decision maker decides to involve other people in your presentation, you must find out who these people are. Chances are you won't be able to talk to them before the presentation, but you can at least send them written material ahead of time. The two things to send are an immediate invitation and a "preshow summary" a short time before the presentation.

2. *Send invitations.* Follow up with a written communication that reaffirms and reinforces your positive first step. Although this may be in the form of an invitation, it provides you with the opportunity to drive home a few of the outstanding benefits of your solution. Explain where the presentation is to be held, what's going to happen, and what you want your audience to do by way of preparation ahead of time. For the people that you have not met (and will not meet until the presentation), come up with a benefit that will be appealing to them on a *personal* basis. Suggest, somehow, that your solution will advance their career, make life easier, make more money for them, save them time or effort, whatever.

3. *Send a "preshow summary."* Just before the event send a *preshow summary* that provides some (but by no means all) of the details of your solution—how it works, how it can be applied, and why it's such a good idea. Include biographical information about (and pictures of) you and the other members of your presentation team. Make this summary personal. Make it easy for the audience members to relate to the presenters on a personal basis because of similar training and experiences in the past. Help the audience be disposed to *like* the presenters and their ideas.

Further exhibit your concern for their understanding and comfort by restating your invitation, including instructions on how to get to the presentation. One useful piece of advice is to provide transportation if it will make it more convenient for audience members to get to a location that you control.

Ideas about Invitations

You must convey the sense that you are calm, steady, thoughtful, distinguished, and professional and are under perfect control. If you get this feeling across, then you will create the illusion that your *solution* is of the same high quality.

> **Remember** The written invitation, or "preview," is merely to substantiate the reaction you got to your conversations. The communication is typically short—no more than one or two pages—and must not reveal so much information that the reader is no longer compelled to attend your presentation to hear the details about how you will implement your solution.
> The invitation must be clear about the following:

- Date of the presentation
- Time and duration of the presentation
- Location of the presentation and how to get there
- Brief outline of the agenda
- Those who will be in attendance (both audience and presenters)
- A phone number where you can be reached

Developing and Distributing a Preshow Summary

The preshow summary must be in the hands of the various audience members a few days before the presentation. It must be attractive, inviting, and easy to read. It must be designed to convey both information and also a note of friendliness and hospitality—a concern for the comfort of the audience, both intellectually and physically. The audience must be made to look forward to the presentation and not wonder whether it will be a big waste of time.

As mentioned earlier, the summary must include relevant parts of the story including the basic idea and how the solution will benefit the audience both directly and indirectly—also both generally and personally.

It must include biographical information and—if possible—pictures of the participants. It must outline their expertise, educational background, past job responsibilities, and competences in either explaining or implementing the solution to be presented.

General Guidelines for Designing Invitations and Preshow Summaries

In designing invitations and preshow summaries here are some things to keep in mind.

1. Make your story flow easily.

2. Stress benefits, not features.

3. Overcome skepticism.

4. Provide support for any promises or claims.

5. Keep it relevant.

6. Adopt a personal tone; use pronouns such as *you* and *we,* instead of an impersonal technical or legal approach.

7. If you can do so in ways that matter, compare yourself with competitors.

8. Compare your solution with alternatives (chiefly, your solution versus doing nothing).

9. Keep the design very simple and clean.

10. Be as visually interesting as possible—add easy-to-understand photos, drawings, and diagrams.

11. Use lots of headings and subheadings to break up the text.

12. Leave lots of white space at the top, bottom, and margins.

13. Use short paragraphs instead of dense, black areas of text.

14. Use quality paper—be concerned about its weight, texture, and finish.

15. Don't use colored papers.

16. Use a high-quality laser printer.

17. Print invitations and preshow summaries on standard-size 8½ × 11-inch stock. Do not fold. Mail them flat in oversize envelopes.

18. Don't use novelty typefaces.

19. Don't use type that is so small that it's hard to read.

20. Be extremely careful about a misuse of italics or reversed type (i.e., white letters on a black or colored background).

21. Do not "pad" the document with boilerplate from earlier proposals or presentation.

22. Likewise, don't bulk up the document with brochures or other printed promotional material that you happen to have around.

23. Use a binding system that allows material to lie flat.

24. Most important, keep the communication as short and easily readable as possible. Use the Fig. 7-1 checklist to narrow down issues that need attention for this all-important phase of your presentation.

GAINING YOUR AUDIENCE'S COMMITMENT TO ATTEND		

THE IMPORTANT STEPS	To Do	Done
1. Conduct initial talks with important decision makers.	_____	_____
2. Send invitations.	_____	_____

THE INVITATIONS AND THE PRESHOW SUMMARY	Yes	Needs Work
Does the invitation include the following?		
• Date of the presentation	_____	_____
• Time and duration of the presentation	_____	_____
• Location of the presentation and how to get there	_____	_____
• Brief outline of the agenda	_____	_____
• A note about who will be in attendance (both audience and presenters)	_____	_____
• A phone number where you can be reached	_____	_____

FOR BOTH THE INVITATION AND THE PRESHOW SUMMARY, HAVE YOU FOLLOWED THESE GUIDELINES?

1. Make your story flow easily.	_____	_____
2. Stress benefits, not features.	_____	_____
3. Overcome skepticism.	_____	_____
4. Provide support for any promises or claims.	_____	_____
5. Keep it relevant.	_____	_____
6. Adopt a personal tone; use pronouns such as *you* and *we*, instead of being impersonal.	_____	_____
7. If you can do so in ways that matter, compare yourself with competitors.	_____	_____
8. Compare your solution with alternatives (chiefly, your solution versus doing nothing).	_____	_____
9. Keep the design very simple and clean.	_____	_____
10. Be as visually interesting as possible — add easy-to-understand photos and drawings.	_____	_____
11. Use lots of headings and subheadings to break up the text.	_____	_____
12. Leave lots of white space at the top, bottom, and margins.	_____	_____
13. Use short paragraphs instead of dense, black areas of text.	_____	_____
14. Use quality paper—be concerned about its weight, texture, and finish.	_____	_____
15. Don't use colored papers.	_____	_____
16. Use a high-quality laser printer.	_____	_____
17. Print invitations and preshow summaries on standard-size $8 \frac{1}{2}$" x 11" stock. Do not fold. Mail them flat in oversize envelopes.	_____	_____
18. Don't use novelty typefaces or type that is so small that it's hard to read.	_____	_____
19. Don't use type that is so small that it's hard to read.	_____	_____
20. Be extremely careful about a misuse of italics or reversed type.	_____	_____
21. Do not "pad" the document with boilerplate from earlier proposals or presentations.	_____	_____
22. Likewise, don't bulk up the document with brochures or other printed material.	_____	_____
23. Use a binding system that allows material to lie flat when opened.	_____	_____
24. Most important, keep the communication as short and easily readable as possible.	_____	_____

Figure 7-1.

Confirmations

Confirm everyone's attendance 24 hours ahead of the presentation. If major decision makers will not be able to attend, cancel the meeting and reschedule it for a later date.

Do *not* agree to present to an audience of subordinates who do not have decision-making authority. It would serve only to introduce an intermediate step before higher-ups could make a decision, since you would probably have to make the presentation a second time. Too many things could go wrong in the process and the time interval.

Dog & Pony Checkpoints

✔ Polish an abbreviated version of the story of your solution so that you attract enough attention to schedule a presentation.

✔ Be rigorous and thorough in persuading audience members ahead of the event (especially the ones you were unable to talk to in preliminary conversations).

✔ Send carefully worded invitations.

✔ Provide a thoughtful and helpful preshow summary that includes what you want to happen as a result of the forthcoming presentation.

✔ Confirm the attendance of key audience members 24 hours ahead of the presentation (and be prepared to reschedule the presentation if they are, for any reason, unavailable).

8

Convert Your Story into a Show

This chapter has to do with the mechanics of making your presentation visually interesting and dynamic. You want to introduce drama and excitement, develop a sense of pace and movement, and stimulate interaction by creating opportunities for your audience to think and to participate. You will find the following information very useful:

Contents of This Chapter

- Why the introduction is vital
- Analogies to the theater
- Emotion and action
- Who's in charge
- The role of the director
- The responsibilities of the presenter
- Other correlations to the theater
- Dog & Pony checkpoints

Why the Introduction Is Vital

There are several key requirements of an effective introduction. Here are the rules to follow.

1. Be brief. Two minutes is more than enough for the introduction to a presentation involving several people.

2. Introduce one strong message.

3. Involve your listeners with issues that affect them.

4. Be clear—don't wander and get distracted.

5. Memorize your material and carefully rehearse your 2 minutes until it is absolutely tight and flawless. You mustn't appear confused about anything.

6. Set the *tone* and the *mood*. Be cordial and confidently professional. Try to emulate the calm of Winston Churchill or of John Kennedy in his TV addresses during the Cuban missile crisis.

7. Set the stage and establish control.

8. Raise excitement and anticipation for what's to come.

9. If possible, create an air of mystery or foreshadow possible action or a sense of "adventure" (at the frontiers of knowledge or technology—but be careful not to get too hokey).

10. Promise a break.

11. Promise to finish in much less time than the audience expects or than has been allotted. (This wins all kinds of free points. Everybody else takes too long.)

12. Promise a smooth presentation.

13. Promise satisfaction—with the approach, the technology, the people, and the ideas.

14. Be extremely polished in the first introduction and hand-off.

15. Use language that is clear and conversational. Do not use jargon or unnecessarily long words. It is crucial that you be clearly understood from the very beginning.

16. Call the audience's attention to a chart which (1) summarizes the reason for the meeting, (2) highlights some of the obvious concerns of the audience, or (3) presents vital questions that must be dealt with.

Here's an example of that last point.

I recently worked on a presentation with Charles H. "Rip" Harris, the founder of a company that develops software to manage documents. It was Rip's job to open a presentation to a large corporation, introduce several speakers, moderate the event, guide its flow and transitions, and play a role himself in an important segment of it.

In his opening, he pointed to two large charts that were easily readable by everybody in the room.

One, on the front wall, summarized the most important needs of the audience as gleaned from an RFI (Request for Information) that had been distributed ahead of time.

Addressing the audience, Rip began his presentation: "Let me begin our discussion this morning by confirming something. A number of concerns and requirements were stated in your Request for Information. Let's make sure we've identified the right ones."

He walked to the first chart in the front of the room (Fig. 8-1), pointed to it, and asked: "Is this accurate? Are these truly the objec-

> **OBJECTIVES YOU WANT TO ACHIEVE**
>
> 1. Contain costs.
> 2. Give our company a competitive edge.
> 3. Help our people work faster.
> 4. Help our people work with greater confidence.
> 5. Maintain flexibility.
> 6. Share information effectively among our offices.
> 7. Look at, find, and manage large amounts of paper.
> 8. Effectively combine visual, textual, graphical, image, and voice information.
> 9. Minimize resistance to change.
> 10. Achieve return on investment by improving productivity.

Figure 8-1.

tives you want, and *need,* to achieve? Is there anything that you would add to this list?"

He didn't expect a response and didn't get one, but audience members felt they had begun a real dialogue about their important needs.

Then he said: "I now call your attention to a second chart which shows the hardest questions we thought you could possibly ask."

He walked to the other end of the room and pointed to the chart shown in Fig. 8-2.

This kind of an opening makes it possible to do several things simultaneously:

- Convince your listeners that you're completely prepared.

- Show that you are addressing their real concerns.

- Exhibit a willingness to deal with sensitive or difficult issues.

> **QUESTIONS WE THOUGHT YOU MIGHT ASK**
>
> 1. How hard will it be to catch up to the technology of our *Fortune* 500 customers?
> 2. How will we really increase productivity?
> 3. How will your solution really affect our bottom line?
> 4. How will you tie our branch offices together?
> 5. How big a job will it be to retrain all of our people?
> 6. Who's going to install this?
> 7. How will you manage and deliver software?
> 8. Where and how do we get needed support?
> 9. How do we go about this? What's the timetable?
> 10. Can we really get more managers involved?

Figure 8-2.

- Establish levels of priority or importance in the show.

- Attract immediate interest.

- Build some excitement about *how* you'll address important issues.

The charts had two other important purposes.

The first purpose was to help the presenters keep on target—to assure them they weren't missing a step. As Rip and other presenters completed a subject or dealt with a question, they checked it off with a red marker.

The final purpose was to assure the audience that all the points had been successfully dealt with. Rip, who handled the close of the presentation as well as the opening, approached each chart, pointed to particular items, and disposed of them as having been sufficiently covered in the presentation.

Following is another approach at an introduction.

Example: asking for a loan

Here's a make-believe scenario in which we ask a bank for $4 million to develop a "presentations center."

We always start with a "housekeeping" opener, which is preliminary to the main introduction. It works this way:

> Good morning. Before we start, I'd like to clear up a few "housekeeping" issues. For those of you who are unfamiliar with this building, the fire escapes are at either end of the hall. In the unlikely event of an emergency, Maralyn Moore will lead the group to the fire escape to the right of the doorway to this room. And I will bring up the rear. The rest rooms are down the hall to the left. There are telephones in the lobby. We will be having a short break—only 8 minutes—in exactly 35 minutes from now.

These brief remarks are designed to express a knowledge of the surroundings, real concern for the needs of the audience, and a willingness to assume leadership in the event of a problem. I would then continue as follows:

> I hope everyone had a chance to review the biographical and summary material we sent over earlier in the week. If you haven't, let me summarize it.
>
> For some time we have talked about starting a separate company to help senior people design and produce winning presentations to high-level decision makers. Since we don't have a fully equipped "center" to do this—including properly designed conference rooms, and the most modern computers, cameras, processors, and video equipment, we are teaming up with another company to go after the financing to create one. You'll meet two people from that organization in a moment.
>
> Let me call your attention to this message.

I would then hang up a chart summarizing the purpose of the meeting (Fig. 8-3). It would remain on the wall during the entire presentation.

We would also have a "hard questions" chart, as illustrated by Fig. 8-4, the purpose of which is to cover all the major questions, *whether*

```
┌─────────────────────────────────┐
│            PURPOSE:             │
├─────────────────────────────────┤
│                                 │
│     WE ARE HERE TODAY TO        │
│     SECURE A $4 MILLION         │
│      LOAN TO DEVELOP A          │
│    NATIONAL CENTER TO           │
│   PRODUCE HIGH-LEVEL            │
│  PRESENTATIONS FOR U.S.         │
│     BUSINESS CLIENTS            │
│                                 │
└─────────────────────────────────┘
```

Figure 8-3.

```
┌───────────────────────────────────────────┐
│                        "HARD" QUESTIONS    │
├───────────────────────────────────────────┤
│    1. Is this a solid business idea?       │
│    2. What customers do you have now?      │
│    3. Is there a real need for such services? │
│    4. Have you the background and experience to do it? │
│    5. How will you promote this business?  │
│    6. Where will new customers come from?  │
│    7. What are your revenue projections?   │
│    8. How much capacity will you have to do it? │
│    9. What are your plans for growth in the future? │
│   10. Why will you be successful at it?    │
└───────────────────────────────────────────┘
```

Figure 8-4.

we chose to deal with them effectively or not. In other words, the hardest questions are already up, and the audience will have to ask different—probably easier—ones. These questions are outlined on the chart at the front of the room.

I would walk to this chart, point to the relevant components of it, and continue the narration as follows:

> To justify such a loan on the part of the bank, it will be necessary to discuss the elements needed to make such a project successful—the people, the equipment, the facilities, the technology, and the marketing know-how to make it happen.
>
> The various presenters will get the job done.
>
> We have the maturity and experience to operate such a business. We also have an understanding of the necessary *technology,* and not just the computer hardware and software capability, but the human relations and stagecraft necessary to develop successful "shows."
>
> Maralyn will begin with a very brief *marketing plan* and introduce the results of our market research.
>
> Bill Mach will then say a few words about the *design of rooms* in which people can do more effective work. He will also present an outline of the *proposed new facilities.*
>
> I will talk about how *presentations are designed* and the nature of their component parts.
>
> Don Cohen, president of Cimarron International, and a partner in

the proposed new venture, will then look at the *changing technology* of audiovisual communications and brand-new standards that have emerged.

He will also present some startling visuals as he describes how *high-tech graphics* will play a role in all future presentations of any importance.

Jack Reddish will be next, and he will talk about the impact of theater and the entertainment industry upon modern presentations.

Terry Cohen will describe some rather revolutionary ideas about performance-based pricing and how we'll charge for our services in ways that will be more understandable to our clients.

We will then have an ample period of time at the end in which to deal with questions.

It is 10:05 a.m. now. Our formal presentation will be over by 10:30, at which time we'll have a break. That will leave us plenty of time for questions and answers.

Speaking of which—if you have an urgent question as we go along, don't hesitate to ask it. We'll either deal with it on the spot or indicate that the answer will be forthcoming later in the presentation. Let me now introduce Maralyn Moore to lead off our presentation. Maralyn, . . .

In case you're interested, Fig. 8-5 shows visually how this particular Dog & Pony Show was developed. A blank action chart is provided for you in Fig. 8-6. The checklist in Fig. 8-7 can be used as a self-evaluation device for improving your skill at opening the presentation.

A note about foreshadowing

Foreshadowing is a theatrical technique in which the audience is given clues that make sense about information that is revealed later.

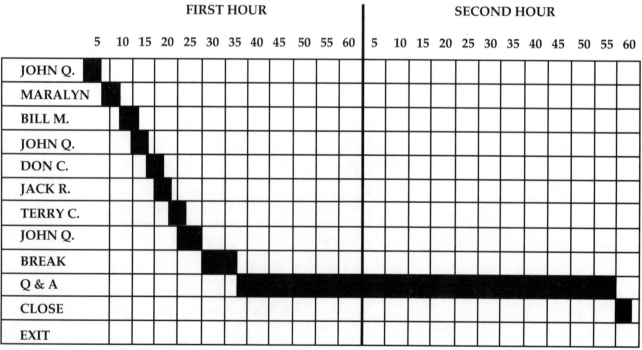

Figure 8-5.

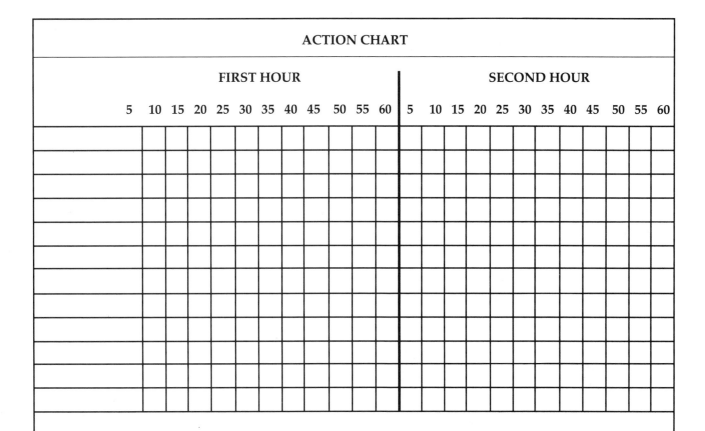

ACTION CHART

	FIRST HOUR												SECOND HOUR											
	5	10	15	20	25	30	35	40	45	50	55	60	5	10	15	20	25	30	35	40	45	50	55	60

The Action Chart can be used for more than just allocating time for a particular speaker. By using several colored pens you can indicate the precise point in time when you:

- Identify where various presenters begin and end.
- Change the room lighting for dramatic effect.
- Vary the tempo of the various presenters.
- Present visuals.
- Utilize props.
- Explain charts.
- Make a promise.
- Introduce conflict.
- Resolve a conflict or solve a problem.
- Introduce a feature or a benefit.
- Make a "trial" close.
- Begin and end major sections of the presentation.
- Commit to further action or activity.
- Indicate breaks.

Figure 8-6.

CHECKING THE VITALITY OF YOUR INTRODUCTION

The following checklist corresponds to the list on pages 153–154. For each presentation, the person in charge of the introduction should be sure to follow up with an evaluation of how well he or she executed the introduction. Although 16 items might seem like a lot to cover in 2 minutes, you'll find that with experience, it will become second nature.

	Yes	Needs Work
1. Did I hold it to 2 minutes or less?	_____	_____
2. Did I limit it to one or two major messages?	_____	_____
3. Did I touch on issues of relevance to the audience?	_____	_____
4. Was I clear, with no digressions?	_____	_____
5. Did I rehearse in advance?	_____	_____
6. Did I set a calm, confident tone?	_____	_____
7. Did I use the introduction to set the stage and establish control?	_____	_____
8. Did I create anticipation of what was to follow?	_____	_____
9. Was I able to create a sense of adventure?	_____	_____
10. Did I promise a break?	_____	_____
11. Did I promise to finish before the deadline?	_____	_____
12. Did I promise a smooth presentation?	_____	_____
13. Did I promise satisfaction with the solution?	_____	_____
14. Did I hand off effectively?	_____	_____
15. Did I keep it conversational and avoid jargon?	_____	_____
16. Did I create and use a supporting chart?	_____	_____

Figure 8-7.

You plant a seed without your audience being particularly conscious of it.

To demonstrate this, we have an easy task for you. Read the following paragraph. Can you identify the person being described?

> On a cold January day, a 43-year-old man was sworn in as chief executive of his country. By his side stood his predecessor, a famous general, who 15 years previously had commanded his country's armed forces in a war which resulted in the total defeat of the German nation. This young man was brought up in the Roman Catholic faith, and, after the ceremonies, spent 5 hours reviewing a parade in his honor and stayed up until 3 a.m. celebrating.

Who is this man?

We set you up for your answer because of a clue given in item 6 on page 154 at the beginning of this chapter. The name was planted there, and so it easily came to mind when you were asked the above question.

That's an example of foreshadowing. It's also a matter of deception and making you jump to a conclusion. The guy described above was Adolph Hitler.

Analogies to the Theater

Let's face it, when you make a truly important presentation to high-level decision makers, what you're doing might easily be defined as a branch of show business.

You're trying to be as expressive and persuasive as you can be. You are portraying leadership and expressing absolute conviction. Your presentation can be dramatic; it can be emotionally charged.

A stodgy interpretation of business communications might suggest that all you need to do is solemnly present the facts and that's all that's necessary for businesspeople to make a decision. But *persuasion* doesn't work that way. There is an emotional element that needs to be taken into account.

So let's approach the presentation from the standpoint of *theater* and see what it gets us.

How do individuals and playwrights get their messages across when they really want to? What are the emotions that are dealt with? What are the human conditions?

First of all, from your own experience, you know that *seduction* is an approach. Advertising attempts it all the time in efforts to make an idea or a person so attractive that it creates desire on the part of the viewer or listener.

As most everybody knows, there's an acronym called *AIDA* used by some salespeople. The letters are supposed to remind you of the need to do the following: Gain *attention*. Arouse *interest*. Create *desire*. Stimulate *action*. That's clever and easy to repeat, but how do you really do it? How do you gain attention in the first place?

At a cocktail party you do it by walking up to another person and introducing yourself. That's easy. The challenge is then to say something that's interesting enough to get a conversation going.

An important presentation has the *attention* component of the acronym pretty well covered. You have prearranged a meeting with a certain group of people. They have agreed to attend at a specified date, time, and place. They will sit where you ask them to sit, and they will be prepared—at least at the beginning of your presentation—to pay attention. It's then up to you to *keep* their attention and begin the process that will lead them to take the action you want them to take.

In short, then, business presentations stand to benefit by borrowing from the world of theater. Some rules to follow when doing so are shown in Fig. 8-8.

Emotion and Action

Every important presentation has the aim of *stimulating action that will be profitable or beneficial to the presenters.* (And, likewise, seem profitable and beneficial to the *audience!*)

The attention-getting step begins immediately.

But what's the appeal?

Here are a few of the "hooks" that writers and playwrights use to get people sufficiently intrigued at the beginning of a story to want to stay involved.

Mystery	Pity	Sorrow
Joy	Love	Humor
Intrigue	Conflict	Action
Adventure	Amazement	Confusion
Redemption	Punishment	Surprise
Danger	Honesty	Pride

These are key elements at the emotional core of stories. Usually there is more than one, and it's the emotional variety that keeps us interested. Let's examine a few of the common ones in more detail.

Conflict. Every story has some element of conflict. There has to be something in the plot for the hero or heroine to deal with: circumstances to overcome, problems to solve, or crises to face. A presentation frequently deals with a challenge to be met or a difficulty that needs to be handled. There may also be a considerable element of conflict in getting a solution adopted and installed.

Mystery. Everybody loves a mystery because everybody is eager to develop the clues to solve it or to watch with interest as somebody else solves it. There is a real element of mystery in high technology, particularly to people who are not technically trained. You must be careful, however, that you don't introduce mysteries you can't solve. This would only cause confusion.

Danger. Everyone is fascinated with dangerous situations, especially ones that are close geographically or are immediate in terms of time, risk, or money to be made or lost. There is great value in

WHAT TO BORROW FROM THE THEATER

Here are a few one-sentence rules that relate to theatrical production, all of which are of value when considered in the context of an important presentation, and which will be developed in greater detail in subsequent sections.

1. Remember that "costumes" are important. Don't dress like a buffoon.
2. Project the same excitement as an actor would in a performance. It *is* a performance.
3. Learn about stage "business."
4. But don't use stage business while other people are presenting.
5. Use props, but use only the props that work the best for you. Don't use distracting ones (such as, laser pointers.)
6. Don't move about when somebody else is talking.
7. Listen to fellow presenters with rapt attention—as if you'd never before heard what they were saying.
8. Learn how to loosen up (physically and mentally) before a performance.
9. Don't upstage anybody.
10. Don't upstage yourself.
11. It's okay to break the invisible wall between you and your audience; you're trying to establish a bond; develop a feeling of "tribe."
12. Establish "characters" convincingly and well.
13. Keep your "character" consistent.
14. Gain control and *preserve* control.
15. Elect somebody to be the director. Give him or her full power to make decisions that stick.
16. Don't be (or appear to be) disingenuous or phony.
17. Minimize distractions.
18. Stick to the script.
19. Stick to the plan.
20. Rehearse.
21. Use theaterlike movements on the stage.
22. Utilize dramatic lighting effects.
23. Use dramatic voice inflections (soft and loud intonations).
24. Use broad gestures. *You*, after all, are the most important visual aid of all.
25. Never sit while speaking to an important audience.
26. "Play" to your audience exactly as actors do in theater-in-the-round.
27. Use dramatic "hooks" to engage the audience's attention.

Figure 8-8.

being able to legitimately portray yourself as "the rescuer" and being able to save your audience from a desperate situation.

Adventure. Audience members are always eager to play a role in an adventure, especially if they can do it without risk or unnecessary expense.

Pride. This is a sure-fire hook, particularly when you can tie into something about which your listeners can take extreme interest—such as their own past accomplishments, choices, and successes.

Let's push forward to another direct parallel between business presentations and the theater. It has to do with who's in charge.

Who's in Charge?

Imagine being an investor in a Broadway show and having the producer call you up and say: "In order to save some dough, we're not going to hire a director for the show. We've found actors and actresses who've been in a lot of plays, so they should be able to figure out what to do. They can even *vote* on what to do and when to do it. It'll be very democratic, and everything's going to work out just great!"

That would be preposterous and completely unworkable. Actors can't direct themselves. (Even engineers and scientists have project managers and program directors.)

For the same practical reasons, an important presentation must have a director. Somebody has to be in charge—otherwise things fall apart. (America has had enough of things falling apart for lack of direction. Competition is becoming increasingly stiffer as time goes by. Everybody will have to work a lot harder and smarter to merely survive, let alone grow.)

This is an easy prediction: nobody can any longer afford to "wing" important presentations, patch things together, or struggle through last-minute preparations for important meetings with prospects, investors, and shareholders.

A brand-new profession will emerge, no doubt, from the ranks of people who have been through the mill—full-time, or at least part-time, Business Presentation Directors.

Let's look at both aspects of performance and presentation production:

1. What the director must do and be

2. What the presenters must do and be

The Role of the Director

The director must be an arbitrator, critic, and advisor, and must deal with power and influence in a calm, reflective, and rational way. This person must also be able to put the *audience's* interests ahead of those of the *presenters.*

Most importantly, the director must be invested with more power than anybody else connected with the presentation. He or she must have the authority to take charge, to say yes and no, to have the final say, and to both direct the presentation and provide advice about where the presentation is going.

The director of a presentation must be accomplished in myriad areas.

The challenge of big shots

The bigger the presentation to be done, the greater the involvement of CEOs, executive VPs, division heads, and other big shots. Since most of these people succeeded because they were smart or successful, they frequently think they know everything. But they frequently do *not*, especially when it comes to communicating ideas. As a matter of fact, technically proficient people are often the worst presenters of all. They know the most but manage to say the least.

Anyway, because of their power, the big shots can make all kinds of decisions that stick. They can decide on visuals that are too complicated to be seen (let alone be understood), and they can decide not to rehearse at all. After all, since they know everything, they can "wing it."

The challenge for the director, in this circumstance, is to use patience and leadership to help them do a better job. It is a difficult, but worthwhile, effort.

Most success comes from *showing* them a better way (not in merely talking about better ways since they frequently feel they don't have time to listen).

But you can persuade them to *watch*. And there are plenty of exciting new approaches to *see on screens* to draw them in. But it goes a lot further than just seeing.

Experts on human memory suggest that people remember about 10 percent of what they hear and 20 percent of what they see. The latter number doubles to 40 percent if they're allowed to *take part in a discussion* of the subject in question, and it more than doubles again (to 90 percent) when they're allowed to physically *do* something. So, while *telling* is important, allowing the audience to *do* something—to act—is even more so. Hence the value of a director's objectivity.

We talked about what a director must do. Figure 8-9 gives the important characteristics that a new business presentation director must *have*.

Finally, consider a couple of quotes about directors in the theater/film industry:

Tyrone Guthrie, the noted playwright and director, says:

> The director is partly an artist presiding over a group of other artists, excitable, unruly, childlike, and intermittently "inspired." He is also the foreman of a factory, the abbot of a monastery, and the superintendent of an analytic laboratory. It will do no harm if, in addition to other weapons, he arms himself with the patience of a good nurse, together with the voice and vocabulary of an old-time drill sergeant!

Frank Whiting, in his book *An Introduction to the Theater*, describes the director in these words:

WHAT'S YOUR "DIRECTOR QUOTIENT"

	Yes	No

1. Can you simultaneously handle technical content (form and meaning) and the artistic skills necessary to convey this content persuasively and convincingly?

2. Can you elicit ever-higher levels of performance?

3. Can you develop the themes and threads that hold the presentation together?

4. Can you create different roles or characters for the presenters on the team?

5. Can you establish logical relationships among presenters?

6. Can you achieve logical balance and a harmonious continuity?

7. Can you train and coach presenters?

8. Can you translate or interpret the content of the presentation (and not let speakers merely say what they wish)?

9. Can you simplify material?

10. Can you develop a methodical approach that guides the flow of energy from one presenter to the next or among the members of the group?

11. Can you provide visual and vocal variety and richness; i.e., vary the tempo, volume, lighting, and visuals?

12. Can you build tension and conflict, release it, and build it again?

13. Can you convey advice about positive changes in a way that's doable and acceptable to the presenter?

Those are the things a director must *do*. In addition, there are important characteristics that a new-business presentation director must *have*:

14. Do you have solid business management experience?

15. Do you have the maturity to deal with other senior people?

16. Do you have physical and emotional strength and capacity?

17. Are you responsible?

18. Do you have leadership capability?

19. Do you have enthusiasm?

20. Do you have tact?

21. Do you have intelligence?

22. Do you have the energy to work the long hours needed?

If you were able to say Yes to 16 or more of the above questions, you are probably director material. If you said Yes to 14 or more, you have potential, keep working. Below 14? Read on.

Figure 8-9.

The job of directing calls for the imagination and sensitivity of an artist, the skill and patience of a teacher, and the efficiency and organization of an executive....Theater...is a group art that demands teamwork. Even a mild amount of temperament or eccentricity—an amount that in a painter, an author, or even a farmer or minister, would go unnoticed, is a disaster in a director. Artistic and imaginative ability alone is not enough; ability as a teacher and executive is likewise fundamental.

The Responsibilities of the Presenter

The presenter must be able to do these things:

- Project his or her voice and personality.
- Move with agility and sureness.
- Develop tempo.
- Speak expressively.
- Concentrate.
- Project excitement and enthusiasm (this is, after all, a *performance*).
- Develop a sense of timing.
- Convey believability and credibility.
- Be literate and cogent.
- Stay focused.
- Know the cost of a stalemate or a delay in decision making.
- Be keenly aware of time limits.
- Redirect questions.
- Defuse objections.
- Develop skills as an "ensemble" player and work skillfully with others.
- Project both *self*-confidence and *subject* confidence.
- Pay attention to his or her fellow presenters.
- Pay careful attention to the mood and behavior of the audience.

Seeming Contradictions

An effective presenter is a performer, a salesperson, and a negotiator—all at once—and may have to have these seemingly contradictory skills and attributes and play these roles as necessary:

A	B
Scientist	Hunch player
Risk taker	Conservative
Detective	Inattentive bystander
Objective	Subjective about goals
Flexible, able to change as a result of new data	Inflexible on certain points
Decisive	Project indecisiveness as a ploy
Gutsy	Able to appear weak or vulnerable
Determined	Indifferent
Patient	Impatient
Attentive listener	Compelling, persuasive speaker
Creative enough to see the other person's point of view	Boring, stolid, and beyond influence
Specialist	Generalist
Tactician	Strategist

In short, the best presenters are—indeed—consummate *actors*.

Warm-up techniques for presenters

Most people aren't aware of the physiological requirements involved in having a conversation (while seated) and making a forceful presentation (while standing up). The transition is difficult to make without a lot of practice. You, as a presenter, must go from a condition of repose to one of being fully *on* in a matter of seconds!

So, before starting a presentation, go to a rest room or a deserted hallway and do the exercises outlined in Fig. 8-10 to get loosened up and *cranked up* for the presentation. But don't do it so strenuously that you get short of breath or start perspiring. If anybody asks what you're doing, tell them it's a religious ceremony.

About motivation

A person needs to be motivated to move from place to place on the "stage." This may arise from the story line, the character, or the director's need to make things appear more symmetrical or smooth.

Other Correlations to the Theater

Rehearsals

Hugh Morrison, a noted theatrical director, says that full-length plays should be rehearsed for 90 hours; musicals 125 hours. Is it asking too much that business presenters devote 16?

Costumes

My advice is clear and inflexible. There are *no* alternatives.

- *Suits.* If you're a man, you have only two or three choices to make about suits. You can choose which shade of gray or navy

---

PREPRESENTATION WARM-UP CHECKLIST

Here are a dozen loosening-up exercises to do before stepping into the breach. Every presenter should run through this checklist before going on.

- Wiggle your ears. _____
- Open (as far open as it will go) and close your mouth. _____
- Wiggle your jaw. _____
- Make big faces. _____
- Roll your head a few times. _____
- Stretch out your arms. _____
- Rotate your arms. _____
- Swing your arms. _____
- Shake each leg. _____
- Swing each leg. _____
- Stand on your tiptoes and rock up and down. _____
- Rotate your torso. _____

Figure 8-10.

blue you'd like and which conservative cut. And here's an idea: Bring a fresh suit on a hanger and change a few minutes before the presentation. Don't sit down and wrinkle it. (As for professional _women?_ They already know how to dress.)

- _Ties._ Silk rep ties are the norm. Fashion experts have declared that they're _out._ Fashion experts, however, are seldom required to appear in board rooms to make presentations involving millions (or billions) or dollars. So ignore them and stick with Brooks Brothers.

- _Shoes._ Black.

- _Shirts._ White. Cotton. Period.

If all this seems too conservative for you, just do this. Pay a visit to your nearest downtown business district. Arrive about the time people are going to work. Watch people going into three businesses: law firms, banks, and accounting firms. These are some of the men and women who attend important presentations. Dress like them. Period.

Props

A number of props can be used effectively. They include:

Pointers	Eyeglasses
Markers	Easel pads
Models	Exhibits
Photographs	Charts
Books	Pencils and pens

Actual pieces of equipment or components

Let the director work with you to develop ideas that look good in the context of the total stage picture. Otherwise, you will merely fiddle with the props and appear distracted. As mentioned earlier, laser pointers shouldn't be used for the simple reason that they are abused.

A caution about good presenters

As Charles Marowitz says: "Masters of illusion are frequently victims of delusion." They often think they're doing better than they're doing. Another of the director's roles is to remind the presenters of the limits of successfulness (have you done it *well*) and sufficiency (have you done *enough*).

Some Final Thoughts

1. Remember that when you set a conversational, informal tone, you are really developing a theatrical ploy. The presenters only *look* relaxed. They are carefully prepared to make a presentation that *seems* something other than stiff and formal.

2. Establish definitive characters such as the "Hero" or the "Colonel or General," the person who can make promises; the person who can lead everybody to victory. This person uses no visuals or props but depends upon sheer power of personality and stage "presence." Another character is "The Brain." This is the person who covers the technology and engineering aspects of the presentation and goes into levels of detail. This type includes Ph.D.s, who are *never* called "Doctor."

3. For the sake of variety, use more than one person in a presentation.

4. Learn to use your hands, especially to make broad gestures.

5. Learn to play to your audiences exactly as actors do in theater-in-the-round.

6. Never *sit* while speaking to an important audience.

7. Establish a friendly, but absolutely professional, tone and atmosphere in which there is not an adversarial relationship between your team of presenters and their team of presenters. Mix the group seated at the table to break down these perceptions.

8. Guard against being monotonous. There can be a natural *variety* in any material being presented. It can be achieved through (1) movement about the stage, (2) voice inflection (dramatic intonations,

both soft and loud), and (3) the lighting (which can be deliberately changed).

9. Do what you can to influence the *mood* of audiences. The director Charles Marowitz also had this to say about audiences: "The buzz of a theater audience before the curtain rises is a sure indication of how a performance will go. Absence of preperformance chatter almost always spells disaster. A good solid hum in the house is a harbinger of positive audience reaction."

You can only hope to affect the audience's mood in a Dog & Pony Show by the choice of the day and time you present, and through all the ways you tried to influence the audience ahead of time.

Encouraging a receptive mood is frequently an argument for having presentations off-site and away from the audience's facility so that you can set a tone of excitement, intrigue, mystery, or whatever. This is certainly the case of major shows for product introductions—which frequently involve actors, dancers, musicians, theatrical lights, and other Vegas show business elements.

10. Pay particular attention to the *denouement*. Most every play or movie has a brief segment at the very end of the production, after the climax or pivotal elements of action, in which the last pieces of the puzzle are put together. It is the final unraveling (as, for example, in a murder mystery in which the famous detective explains his or her successful approach), any necessary explanation or clarification of the story, or a smooth resolution (culminating in the ride into the sunset).

A business presentation should be engineered with exactly the same structure in mind. It should not merely have a conclusion, which—by the way—is normally very weak; it should have a dramatic climax and then a graceful and smooth denouement, a way to exit the presentation firmly and comfortably.

The final 5 minutes must be rehearsed very carefully. It is the point where conviction must be assured and where the audience is motivated to take exactly the action you suggest.

Dog & Pony Checkpoints

✔ Review the 16 rules about why the introduction is so important.

✔ Consider the use of charts that summarize:
1. What audience members want by way of a solution
2. The problems they (or you) think they have

✔ Develop an action chart that accurately shows time slots.

✔ Remember the analogies to the theater.

✔ Realize the importance of having a director, even though you may not use the title for the man or woman you put in charge. Either find or appoint one for the duration of the presentation preparations. It is essential that somebody be in charge of the overall effort—somebody with a final say about who will present, the order of presentation, and the subject matter to be covered.

- Don't take the role of the presenter lightly. If special training is required for senior people in an organization who must make formal presentations on a regular basis, then secure it from experts. Something to consider besides the usual public speaking courses is actual acting lessons.

- Develop unusual hooks to encourage attention (e.g., conflict, mystery, adventure). Audiences will happily play along with anything that you have carefully structured.

- Remember some warm-up techniques as a presenter. Your physical requirements change a great deal from being seated (and merely conversing) to standing (and projecting an image of leadership and knowledge).

- Be sure not to ignore the requirement for a theatrical denouement. It serves as a graceful transition from the formal part of your presentation to the informal part in which audience members can interact. It is in this vital interaction that your solution will be sold.

Make a Persuasive Presentation

You must *deliver* your story and convince your audience. You must simultaneously sell yourself *and* your solution. You must gain the trust of the audience members, and you must secure their commitment to do what you want them to do. You must show how you will implement your solution and make it work—and persuade them to proceed against your schedule for action. Your personality and your solution are inexorably linked. The audience is buying both you and *it*—your story. There is no way to make a successful presentation without adequate rehearsal. Here are some other vital areas to review:

Contents of This Chapter

- A brief word about computer-controlled graphics
- What to know about visual aids
- Technology—the old and the new
- Sure-fire techniques
- Visuals that invite participation
- A system for evaluating presentations
- Dog & Pony checkpoints

A Brief Word about Computer-Controlled Graphics

Please understand that the world has changed. Read the following paragraph for two reasons: (1) because the information in it is true, and (2) because if you ignore it, you'll look like a real amateur.

The *standard* visual medium that will be used from now on will be computer-controlled graphics that are either shown on a monitor or projected on a screen by a video projector. These graphics will include computer-generated visuals such as key words, graphs, charts, diagrams, still photos, and live or prerecorded video, and—most important of all—they will enable you to use very interesting animation techniques. Everything else is already obsolete, including overheads, 35 mm, and other alternatives.

Now forget about the present or the future for the time being. Let's look at what you should know about visual aids.

What to Know about Visual Aids

Let's start with some rules that must be applied *at all times:*

1. Never use visuals on an opening. Keep attention drawn to yourself.

2. Never use visuals on a close. Once again, you must keep the focus of attention on you—the *leader* who can make the solution come alive.

3. *Never use another overhead projector.* Let your competitors fumble with them and use their painfully complicated homemade visuals.

4. Unless speaking to an auditorium-sized audience, never use 35-mm slides.

5. Never use visuals as crutches or outlines.

6. Use visuals only to amplify a particular point or points for an audience. If a visual does not truly support or help to explain an idea, don't use it. Only spoken words should be used.

7. When you do use visuals, have somebody else be in charge of producing them. Speakers, understandably, have very little objectivity and are more focused on what they are going to *say* than on what the audience is properly supposed to hear and see.

8. Never advance your own visuals unless it is part of a demonstration that requires it.

9. Don't feel you *have* to use visuals. It may sound like a mere textbook theory, but the planning and preparation of visuals requires time, thought, and imagination. If you don't have these ingredients, you're better off by *not employing visuals at all.*

10. Don't allow yourself to be "upstaged" by your own visuals.

Problems

The following five points are sad but true! And the pathetic thing is that most people know perfectly well they're true but can't or won't do anything about them. Habits may die hard, but complete failure will kill you faster than anything. Here's the straight story:

- Most visuals are unnecessary in the first place.
- Most visuals are unreadable from anyplace in the room.
- Most visuals are unintelligible, even when they can be seen.
- Most visuals are badly designed and poorly produced.
- Most visuals are for the benefit of the speakers, not the audience.

The production of visual aids ———————————————

It's a simple fact that the *right* visuals can increase and reinforce understanding and learning. Not only can they add interest to a presentation by engaging more than one of the senses, but they also facilitate listening and remembering. They are especially useful when dealing with abstract concepts and unfamiliar subjects. However, and this is a very big *however: The planning and preparation of visuals requires time, thought, and imagination.*

It has become a habit with some people to design and produce visuals in a 24- to 48-hour time span. The activity should be extended over a 5- or 6-day period in order to properly develop ideas and refine concepts. Ideally, you should start 2 weeks ahead so that you've got a week to deal with roughs and a week to polish the finals.

Visuals should not be glued onto a presentation after the fact. Most presentations must be specially modified and simplified in order to make proper use of visuals. This is a good thing since many presentations are too complex and poorly organized, and the design process will improve them.

Only when you have a solid draft (after perhaps three or four attempts) should you begin to design visuals.

Go through your presentation sentence by sentence, idea by idea, and decide what truly needs to be visualized. This may include ideas, concepts, relationships, and processes.

Caution It is sometimes necessary to utilize an image that is very complicated. It is a fatal error, however, to present such a visual to an audience all at once. It must be built up item by item. An audience can readily absorb one idea at a time and will be quite ready to accept a complicated final picture.

For example, never present a statistical graph all filled in. First show the graph and explain the coordinates used. Then add the figures or computed points a few at a time.

Likewise, never present a complex industrial process as a completed visual. Show one piece of the equipment at a time (or a portion thereof) and keep adding pieces or portions. Different materials or values flowing through pipes or along circuits can be shown by different colored lines, added one at a time.

The chart in Fig. 9-1 provides a thorough run-down of dos and don'ts in planning, preparing, and using audiovisuals. Keep it as a handy reference for every presentation you do. The corollary Graphic Design Checklist shown in Fig. 9-2 covers in summary form

HOW TO USE VISUALS

PLANNING AND PREPARATION

Preparing visuals requires time, thought, and imagination in order to:

- Select the points to be visualized.
- Choose the right medium.
- Make the visuals
- Revise them as necessary.
- Translate ideas into suitable visual forms.
- Design the layouts and choose the colors.
- Evaluate their effectiveness.
- Use them effectively in a presentation.

VISUALS CAN BE USED TO:

1. Bring out a series of facts and the conclusion to which they lead.
2. Emphasize certain points.
3. Attract attention through unusual designs or colors.
4. Present complex (industrial, mathematical, chemical) processes.
5. Introduce new and unfamiliar concepts or objects.
6. Show relationships that exist among facts or objects.
7. Show in outline form the growth of a complex idea or the treatment of a subject so as to enable people to readily see which are the major and which are the subordinate points.

A METHOD TO FOLLOW

Use *pictures* wherever possible. Supplement them with words and numbers.

Use *words* (singly or in phrases) as a second choice.

Use the image area as a *graph* to present statistics and statistical processes, or mathematics.

Use the image area as a *form* to present accounting reports, statistical tabulations, and so forth.

Use unusual devices such as *lines, arrows,* and *multiple-layer images*.

Use color for coding and stressing *key facts*.

Use *complex images* only as appropriate and then build them up item by item. An audience can readily absorb one idea at a time and will be quite ready to accept a complicated final picture.

OTHER USES OF VISUALS

1. A visual can show the relationships existing between or among items or groups.
2. Important points or facts can be highlighted.
3. Sequences of events can be outlined over time.
4. Organizational relationships can be shown.
5. Cause-and-effect relationships can be defined.
6. Flowcharts explain how a process works.
7. Cutaways are used to understand how a thing is put together.
8. Diagrams or schematics make products or processes easier to understand.
9. Graphs with horizontal or vertical bars show relative values.
10. Rules can be explained.
11. Pie charts and divided bar graphs show the relationships of various parts or values.
12. A map can clarify geographical relationships.
13. Pictographs can be used to represent quantities through the use of symbols (such as a line of trucks or a stack of coins).

Figure 9-1.

GRAPHIC DESIGN CHECKLIST

RULES
1. Wherever possible, use graphics or pictures instead of words.
2. Use the simplest terms and relationships you can think of.
3. If a visual doesn't explain something better than words, it shouldn't be used.
4. A visual should never exceed 35 characters across, counting spaces. Anything much greater than this will not be readable from the back of the audience.
5. It should have a minimum number of lines, never more than eight.
6. Only highlights should be shown.
7. *Never* use a complete sentence, only key words and phrases.
8. Cover only one idea or key concept per visual, and don't dwell on it for more than a minute at most.
9. On graphs, never use more than three curves.
10. Use a minimum number of grid lines.
11. Omit subtitles and other extraneous words. *You're* there to pass along this information.
12. Eliminate supplementary notes.
13. Never use vertical printing.
14. For obvious reasons, a visual for a presentation should contain far less information than an illustration for a book or report. Under no circumstances should you use tables or exhibits from publications.

SIMPLE, BOLD, AND CLEAR

All visual aids, charts, graphs, models, diagrams, and so forth should aim to be:

Simple. Use only key elements or words. Never use a complete sentence. Keep lines and shapes understandable and to the point.

Bold. Visuals must be large enough to be easily seen by every member of the audience. One must be very careful in selecting colors, lettering style and size, and layout.

Clear. Is the visual aid easy to understand? Does it exactly reflect the message you're trying to get across? Is it logically arranged, well-spaced, and uncrowded? Do the main points stand out?

Figure 9-2.

the major rules and considerations to remember when producing graphics.

A special note about photographs ──────────────

Photos and videos are especially useful in telling stories. They can be used to show:

1. Products

2. The way to use (assemble) the products

3. Locations where the products are used

4. People using the products

5. People enjoying the benefits of the products

6. Plant locations

7. Key people in the organization

8. Laboratories and other operations

Summary ──────────────────────────────

The information just presented couldn't be simpler. Every presentation in America would be improved miraculously by adhering to only 30 percent of the advice.

But it's difficult to implement because of the reluctance of "experts" to accept outside help. It takes a great deal of patience to help presenters who are extremely knowledgeable in their fields to realize that their *information* is not being questioned, but that adjustments must be made not only in organization and continuity, but also in the pace and velocity with which the information should be conveyed.

Convince them that it's in the best interest of the *audience* to cooperate.

Familiarize yourself with the capabilities of computer-generated graphics, especially programs that allow animation features. It will become the standard. It is *presently* the standard against which everything else must be judged.

Technology—The Old and the New

Follies and "revolutions" ──────────────────

In my organization, we have always been outspoken in books, columns, speeches, and our own consulting activity. We were always among the first to denounce silly trends in the areas of presentations and audiovisual technology.

Before you explore the future, take a look at the past, especially at some of the great follies that have affected people's ability to win at presentations.

First there was an audiovisual revolution, then a multimedia revolution, and then a video revolution. None worked. Nothing really happened. Not in-house.

Equipment manufacturers did a terrific job of selling audiovisual equipment to just about everybody in the country. And the largest portion of this stuff is sitting in storerooms gathering dust because nobody knows how to use it. It was advertised to look so easy that anybody could use it. And it's true that just about anybody *can* turn the equipment on and off or lug it around. But very few people know how to *design* effective audiovisual material. Fewer still know how to produce the material once it's designed. And then there is the real minority—those who know how to use the material effectively once it's produced.

It's a job that requires a high level of imagination, creative ability, experience, and skill. It also takes unusual care and a considerable amount of time. So you've always got to be leery of the literature that explains how simple and easy everything is.

However, a few things *are* easy.

Some of the things that are easy

Chalkboards   These used to be called blackboards, but then they turned green, brown, and other colors. In whatever color, they are fairly cheap, big, and simple to use. They don't have cords to trip over, and there's no bulb to suddenly burn out at an important moment. You can place a lot of trust in your average chalkboard.

The chalkboard is not only a handy visual device; it is also a giant prop. It's a place to walk to—a destination—and it gives you something to do with your hands once you get there. You can walk up to some part of it, write something on it (or erase something from it), and walk away from it. This movement provides variety and a change of pace.

A chalkboard has a number of other advantages. You can easily make changes, there is plenty of room to write on, and you can create the impression that the information you write on it is very current—that the data are being revealed for the first time.

Another benefit, of course, is that you can display some of your audience's thoughts on it, thereby getting a lot more involvement and commitment on their part. People in an audience like to see their own ideas displayed.

The best chalkboard systems have several boards mounted on tracks so they can roll back and forth in front of each other (or slide up and down from above). Such systems enable you to prepare complex drawings or sets of figures ahead of time and move them into view when needed.

Whiteboards   To the disappointment of many people, some brands of whiteboards turned out to be *grunge*boards. They gradually discolored and became impossible to clean. The better brands aren't supposed to do that, being essentially fired enamel on steel. They have the additional advantage of accepting magnets. Everything said about the utility of chalkboards is likewise true for whiteboards.

Markers   As you know from your own painful experience, there are three distinctly different kinds of markers:

1. Easily erased markers for whiteboards

2. Solvent-based markers for charts and paper

3. Water-based markers for charts and paper

Whiteboard markers don't work very well on paper.

Solvent-based markers will both screw up a whiteboard and bleed through paper and screw up the painted wall or wallpaper behind it.

Water-based markers will *not* screw up a whiteboard (if accidentally applied) and will *not* bleed through paper onto a painted wall or wallpaper.

So can you guess what my recommendation is for markers to be used on charts and paper? One of the water-based brands I use is called Mr. Sketch and is manufactured by Sanford.

Carry a fresh set of markers with you wherever you go. I have yet to go to a hotel conference room or a major conference center that had appropriate markers. They always have plenty of dried-out markers and pale yellow or pink markers which can't be seen at a distance of more than 3 feet from the source.

Use water-based markers in the following standard colors: green, dark blue, black, red, orange, and brown.

Charts   There are two kinds of charts to use: the stiff kind made from illustration board (which are almost impossible to carry around, particularly on airplanes) and the flexible-paper kind that can be rolled up. The latter are called easel pads, and the individual pages can be flipped over the top like pages in a book.

Some fairly small flip charts are intended for conference rooms or office situations where they can be used on a tabletop with small audiences. Whatever their size, charts of this type are made up in advance, preferably by a professional who can do a good job.

I am a great believer in easel pads, in which the individual sheets can be torn off or flipped over the top of the pad. The pad is typically mounted on a tripod-type holder. (Most of these holders appear to have been designed by the diminutive artist, Henri de Toulouse-Lautrec, and are terrific if you are about 48 inches in height.)

If you intend to do much writing on an easel pad, tear the sheets off the pad and tape them on the wall as high as you can tape them.

Easel pads are cheap and easy to write on. You can produce lists of ideas and problems and tape them all over the walls of a room. Such a display of thoughts (easily added to or subtracted from) aids in problem solving. Important relationships between the information on the east wall and the data on the north can suddenly emerge.

The thing I like the most about both easel pads and whiteboards (or chalkboards) is the fact that the speaker generates the visual materials. This process keeps the speaker active, mobile, and animated, and lends a sense of immediacy and spontaneity to the information being presented.

All that is required of the presenter is legible handwriting—in letters that are large enough to be seen by the people in the back of the room. The lettering doesn't need to be artistic, just visible and understandable. Always print, and use capital letters.

Tape To affix easel pad sheets to the walls of rooms, you need *tape*.

There are two major classes of tapes: (1) those with enough strength to both hold up the sheets and also remove paint and wallpaper from the wall when you try to *remove* the sheets and (2) those with enough strength to hold up the sheets but that do *not* take paint and wallpaper off when removed.

I try to recommend the latter.

Go to a drafting supply store and buy some *drafting tape*. This is a safe way to hold up pieces of paper.

Never use transparent tape, duct tape, or any of the shiny-surfaced tapes used for sealing boxes or packages. The latter will do more than take off bits of paint or wallpaper; they can remove entire pieces of the wall, panels from doors, and panes from windows.

Always carry your own drafting tape with you. (It is my personal experience that *all* conference centers run out of tape the day before I get there.)

Relics: dinosaurs of an audiovisual past

Now let's take a walk through the museum of extinct species.

Opaque projectors Actually, the first one was about the size of a baby elephant and just about as easy to move around. In America, it was called an opaque projector (British people called it an "episcope"), and it was designed to project pages from books, reports, and other documents that people shouldn't have tried to use in a presentation anyway.

It was both a dumb idea and a very dim one (requiring a completely blacked-out room). It led to the *overhead* projector.

Overhead projectors As you know, overhead projectors use a transparency about 8 by 10 inches in size that lies flat when projected. A light source underneath the transparency shines upward through it. Part of the light is collected in a periscopelike device, the optics of which direct the image onto a screen or a wall. The rest of the light goes up to the ceiling in a nice, distracting puddle of white. Almost *nobody* does anything to prevent the distortion (keystoning) of the projected image.

In addition, overhead projectors are easily abused because the large format enables people to put enormous amounts of stuff on slides and then use them as crutches instead of honest aids to the audience. The cruelest trick of all is to produce material on a typewriter or a computer printer and then make a black-and-white transparency on a copy machine. Such a "visual" can't be seen by more than two people, and then only if they're seated within about 48 inches from the screen.

Rear-screen projection Speaking of screens, let me take a second to fire a salvo at one of the most expensive hoaxes ever played on American businesspeople, educators, and numerous others. It is the rear-screen projection system in which various kinds of projectors are placed behind a specially treated piece of glass and project reversed images onto it. The audience sees the right-reading image on the other side of the glass. There are only two small problems that will never be overcome. Number one, the image isn't as bright as a front-projection system (like the movie theater screens familiar to all of us). Number two, you have to sit straight on line with the projected image. If you're too far to the left or right (or too high or too low), you lose another 50 to 75 percent of the already attenuated brightness. This means that the very best picture can be seen by three or four people at the most. Dumb idea. The work of criminal minds.

"Star wars" lecterns   I've seen a lectern that was an electronic marvel—two rows of switches and controls, little bitty television monitors, gauges for sound levels, switches for projectors and dissolve units, dimmers for lights, automatic timers, and controls to make screens appear and disappear.

The lectern had only one small flaw. It didn't work. It *functioned* okay. The switches and gadgets performed as they were designed to. But taken as a whole, the lectern didn't work. Speakers couldn't focus even half of their attention on the audience while worrying about all the dials to watch and the controls to manage.

Engineers can get so caught up in their ability to create something that they forget why or for what purpose they're creating it. They lose track of such elements as applicability or reasonableness.

Multimedia   The "great multimedia" joke of the seventies was especially fun to write about. Tons of projection equipment, dissolve units, and programming computers were sold to industry, often to be put in their "electronic war rooms." This stuff now gathers dust or has long since been junked. Very few businesspeople used multiple-projector productions because said businesspeople were quite aware of the number of things that can (and usually do) go wrong with mechanical devices. Such devices require not only technical expertise but also considerable artistic ability. This technology is still used by people who produce expensive trade shows and special-events programming. But *they* do the elaborate creative and production work and the equipment maintenance, and they have qualified engineering people to run the shows. And they charge a fortune (which is usually worth it) to make things work out.

35-mm slides   Slides are almost as widely abused as overheads. It was the widespread use of 35-mm slides that gave rise to the idea that conference rooms shouldn't have any windows in them. That way the screen would be nice and bright. The room could be pitch black. And the speaker would become a disembodied voice and lose touch with his or her audience.

Why is 35-mm used at all? And why does it have those funny sprocket holes when other roll films (e.g., 2¼ by 2¼-inches) don't? Well, it's this way. The year 1889 was a big one for movies. A guy in England (William Friese-Greene) devised the first motion-picture camera to use sprocketed film (so that the film could be advanced at a steady rate in both cameras and projectors), and George Eastman invented flexible celluloid film and promoted motion-picture film for commercial use. Everybody agreed that 35-mm would be a swell format (that is to say, 35-mm from edge to edge including room for the sprockets).

At some point in the 1920s or 1930s some genius in the movie industry noticed that, in the course of film production, cinematographers ended up with short lengths of 35-mm film—perfectly good, but not long enough to record a scene. What do you do with it? Make an amateur camera that uses the same type of film, but instead of running it vertically through the camera, run it horizontally and get a bigger image area (36 × 24 mm) that can be processed as a slide and placed in a mount that is always 2 inches square.

As just noted, 35-mm cameras were originally developed for amateurs. Serious photographers usually use much larger formats because the negatives and prints (or transparencies) have a lot more detail. A great many advertising dollars have been spent in this country convincing people that they can take pictures. And, indeed, they can. (After all, modern 35-mm cameras are completely automated and are now almost to the stage of moving around town taking pictures on their own.) There are a lot of very competent picture takers in the population. A few of them even go on to become photographers.

But why is it that so few photographs (either prints or slides) are used in talks?

I'll explain why. The acquisition of a still photo or a slide is a fairly straightforward proposition—and involves consideration of what film to use, what lens, and what composition. The problem arises in the selection and organization of a *series* of pictures that are used to tell a *story*.

It is here that the project bogs down—not merely in pictures, but in words. It is a very complicated undertaking that requires more care than people are usually willing to take, or more imagination that most people *have*. The production of an audiovisual presentation requires more than the services of a photographer or a writer. It requires somebody who can think in terms of both verbal expressions and visual images.

Remember what I asked you to write on the back of your hand with respect to Goldilocks and the Three Bears? C_____t? C_____ −−y? P__e? And T__e? (See page 122.) Think about the extra dimension of applying visuals to the story against these four important criteria. There are very few people with this ability to be found in business communications. They are much more apt to be working in television or film production.

The 35-mm slide became particularly popular when it became possible to mechanically advance slides, as in a Kodak Carousel projector. Most of the time when projectors are used, they sit in the same room with the speaker. The projectors make a big racket because of their cooling fans.

Because of their convenience and ease of use, 35-mm projectors replaced lantern slide projectors.

Lantern slide projectors   You can tell by the very name that this is antique technology. The forerunners of these projectors were around before electricity (and literally used coal oil lanterns as a light source). They are big and heavy. They have a carriage that slides back and forth and will only accommodate two slides. To operate them, you slide the carriage to the left to project an image, put a new slide in the right, and slide it into place. It's a real pain in the neck and requires both a projection room and a projectionist. But do you know what my organization is going to use them for?

In our new facility we will employ front-screen projection in the main presentation area. In that room the screen area will cover most of an end wall, and we will use a portion of it for the video projection of animated visuals.

There will be times, however, when we'll want to use a slide of a product or a location. We'll have a 35-mm projector in the booth, and we'll start with it. It will project the image that most people are accustomed to although it will be clearer and crisper because there's a way to soup up a 35-mm projector to make it brighter. It will impress the viewers, and they'll "Ooh" and "Aah" a little bit. It will fill maybe 40 percent of the wall-sized screen.

Then the miracle will happen. We'll slowly dim the 35-mm projector and simultaneously bring up the power on one of our lantern slide projectors. The crystal-clear picture will fill the entire wall with about twice the brightness of the 35-mm.

The effect is fantastic! It's magical. And *why?* The image area of the lantern slide is the equivalent of about *eleven* 35-mm slides! The bulb is four times bigger. And the optical system has the quality of a photographic enlarger!

So we'll be glad to employ both the newest and the oldest technology in our facility. We'll be happy to take the *trouble.*

A summary of the advantages and disadvantages of the graphics choices, and some handling tips, is presented in Fig. 9-3.

A *System for* Evaluating *Presentations*

The form shown in Fig. 9-4 has been designed to provide an objective assessment of a presentation. Since it is difficult for you and your team to critique your own work, select colleagues from another part of your organization to attend a final rehearsal of your presentation and "grade" it according to the criteria provided on the following checklist.

Please note that this form uses a grading system that consists of A, B, D, and F, where A is outstanding, B is very good, D is below average, and F is entirely substandard and unacceptable. Everybody connected with an important presentation must be capable of A and B work. Merely "average" work will be demolished by well-organized competitors. Circle grades in red.

Most people, when asked to review a performance of any kind, have little besides their own subjective feelings to work with. Figure 9-4 is an alternative that tries to be more objective because it evaluates more aspects of a production.

Instead of thinking about presentations, however, let's talk for a moment about an experience that's common to everybody—watching movies. Consider several criteria that substantiate why you like or dislike certain movies. Before you start reading, have a movie in mind: one that either you were crazy about or you hated. Now

GRAPHIC CHOICES: A Summary Of Major Presentation Systems

Chalkboard:

ADVANTAGES: They are generally available and inexpensive. There is nothing to carry, and no advance preparation of visuals is needed.
Chalkboards are especially helpful for such matters as demonstrations of the construction of an item and use of mathematical and chemical equations where much erasing occurs.

DISADVANTAGES: They may encourage the speaker to talk to the board, not to the audience. A chalkboard can be seen from a limited distance and tends to be somewhat dusty and messy.

Dramatic, unusual effects are not possible.

HANDLING TIPS: Write for the audience, not for yourself. Print rather than write, and use all capitals for extra clarity. Keep the work neat and tidy; cut down to the essentials; don't crowd. Clean the board when the work is no longer relevant. Use colored chalk for emphasis.

White Boards—Enamel Boards

ADVANTAGES: They permit the wide use of color. They are less messy than chalkboards, and the markers write smoothly. The effect is bright, clean, and pleasant to look at.

DISADVANTAGES: If the surface of the board is not clean, the markers will not write evenly. If the wrong pens are used (which happens frequently), the indelible inks are difficult to remove without the proper solvents.

HANDLING TIPS: Same as for chalkboards. Since most white boards are made of enamel-covered steel, magnets can be used to hold visual materials to the board.

Flip Charts or Easel Pads

ADVANTAGES: These can be used in the same way as a chalkboard, or they can be previously prepared.

They are especially suitable for one-time briefings which do not justify much time and money in the preparation of more elaborate visuals.

They are good for telling a consecutive story in which a number of points need to be emphasized in outline form.

They are quick. They avoid mess and the time required to erase. If sheets are just flipped over and not torn off, material is available for recapitulation and review. Another technique is to remove each sheet as it is completed and use drafting tape to put it on the wall where it can be referred to as needed.

DISADVANTAGES: Pages have limited space. They can present a transportation problem if you have any great distance to travel. Dramatic effects are limited. Prepared drawings tend to curl unless they're stored flat.

HANDLING TIPS: Conceal the top of the chart with one or more blank sheets until you are ready to use it. That way the audience cannot read ahead. Roll sheets smoothly over the top so as to avoid a crinkle, which will become increasingly distracting as more sheets are turned over. Stand to one side when displaying and turning the chart.

If it is necessary to refer to special pages, mark them in some way, by, for example, folding the corners, using tape, or attaching paper clips. Keep extra pens on hand, as they tend to dry out with use. Drawings can be prepared "invisibly" in light yellow pencil.

Overhead Projectors

These machines come in a variety of weights and project large-size transparent images onto a screen under normal daylight conditions. They are most often abused when presenters try to photocopy typewritten pages or diagrams and other material from books. The material is inevitably too small for audience members to see, even if they're seated close to the screen.

ADVANTAGES: The speaker can always face the audience. The system permits the use of prepared visuals of varying levels of sophistication and the use of a roll of plastic for writing your own visuals in front of an audience. It permits elaborate effects: slides, flip-offs, and drop-downs. It permits the use of color and is quick and clean. It can be used without completely darkening the room, thus permitting note taking by the audience.

DISADVANTAGES: Some types of writing pens smudge easily or evaporate on the plastic. The equipment is not easily transported, and light from the projection lamp can be hard on the speaker's

Figure 9-3.

eyes. Also, the machine projects a keystone-shaped image unless the top of the screen can be tilted toward the audience.

There is no way to modify visuals in response to new situations and in answering questions, and it's not possible to quickly modify portions of hand-written visuals in answering questions.

HANDLING TIPS: Have the transparencies in exact sequence. Rehearse the use of special-effect visuals such as slide-offs, flip-offs, and flip-ons. For flip-offs, make sure that a tab is raised for you to take in your fingers. Fasten or mark guides on the projector so that visual frames can quickly be placed in exact positions.

Switch off the projector when not in use. Keep the focus of attention on yourself!

35-mm Slide Projectors

Slides represent one of the easiest amateur means of bringing real-life situations into a presentation. Less expensive to operate than film or video, and easier to edit and arrange, they have a great potential for adaption. The most common and dependable projector is the Kodak Carousel, which has circular trays that accommodate either 80 or 140 slides.

ADVANTAGES: The speaker can face the audience. A simple dissolve unit that controls two projectors creates a very professional looking presentation despite the relative simplicity of the slides themselves. Most people own 35-mm cameras or can borrow one for the purpose of developing a part of the presentations. Using 35-mm slides can be very colorful and interesting. Once the slides have been placed in proper order in the trays, they will stay in order. Also, 35-mm slides are easily transported from one place to another.

DISADVANTAGES: Changes cannot be made quickly (on the spot). If the room is darkened too much, the speaker tends to become a disembodied voice and loses touch with the audience.

Too many slides (especially of poor quality) can get very boring.

HANDLING TIPS: Set up the projector ahead of time and make sure that (1) it works, and (2) it's in focus. Make sure an extra projection bulb and a long extension cord are available. Use a black slide at the beginning and the end of the presentation. Never create a bare, dazzlingly white screen that blinds the audience. Make a duplicate set of slides for any presentation, just in case the originals are lost or misplaced.

Assign one of the participants to manage the room lights for you, so that you won't be crashing around in a darkened room. Also, if possible, have another person advance the slides for you if it will make the presentation go more smoothly.

Computer Graphics

Within the last few years, tremendous advances have been made in the area of presentation graphics for personal computers. At the present time there seems to be a considerable advantage in Apple Macintosh programs over DOS-based counterparts—especially when it comes to flexibility and capability.

ADVANTAGES: The speaker can face the audience. The system permits the use of several media in addition to the general appearance of a 35-mm word slide. It can utilize digitized still photography, live or prerecorded video inserts with voice and music, and animated visuals. It is the most sophisticated and advanced presentations medium.

DISADVANTAGES: For the best results, a budget must be set aside for outside professionals to design and produce presentations. When projected visuals are required for bigger audiences, a large-scale system must be rented or otherwise made available. For smaller audiences, large monitors must be rented.

HANDLING TIPS: Extensive rehearsals must be made with this medium so that the show proceeds very smoothly. It is imperative that an operator be available.

Figure 9-3 *(Continued)*

PRESENTATION EVALUATION FORM

A. OVERVIEW

1. In general, the producers of the presentation accomplished what they set out to do.. A B D F

2. The presentation seemed coherent and complete. .... A B D F

3. The presenters appeared to exercise absolute control from beginning to end. .... A B D F

4. The presenters clearly outlined the course of action that they wanted the audience to take. .... A B D F

5. It is my opinion the presentation will stimulate the audience to take the desired action. .... A B D F

Further general comments: _____

_____

_____

_____

B. PARTICIPATION

6. Immediately set the tone of professionalism and clarity of purpose, yet very open to discussion at any step. .... A B D F

7. Quickly established two-way communications. .... A B D F

8. Invited early participation. .... A B D F

9. Demonstrated that the presenters could integrate data from the audience into their presentation. .... A B D F

Further comments about participation: _____

_____

_____

_____

C. UNDERSTANDING OF THE AUDIENCE

10. Reflected an understanding of the audience's vision of the future. .... A B D F

11. Addressed specific symptoms, problems, or needs of the audience. .... A B D F

12. Foresaw possible objections the audience might raise. .... A B D F

13. Revealed the present attitude of the audience. .... A B D F

14. Conveyed the attitude the presenters wanted to build. .... A B D F

15. Imparted the awareness the presenters wanted to create. .... A B D F

Figure 9-4.

PRESENTATION EVALUATION FORM (CONT.)

16. Demonstrated an understanding of the prominent philosophical viewpoints of audience members. .... A B D F
17. Revealed a knowledge of the forces or attitudes that influence the audience's decision making. .... A B D F

Further comments about the presenters' understanding of the audience: ____________________

____

____

____

____

D. COMPETITION

18. Demonstrated an understanding of the competition's strengths and weaknesses. .... A B D F
19. Successfully differentiated themselves from the competition. .... A B D F
20. Described important ways to compete. .... A B D F
21. Discussed relevant corporate or personal goals. .... A B D F
22. Discussed important values and beliefs. .... A B D F

Further thoughts about competition: ____________________

____

____

____

____

E. THE SOLUTION

23. Successfully outlined the main elements of the solution. .... A B D F
24. Described the key features of the solution. .... A B D F
25. Accentuated the true benefits of the approach. .... A B D F
26. Described the highlights of a strategy for success. .... A B D F
27. Made certain promises that (it appears) can be kept. .... A B D F
28. Demonstrated that the solution was congruent with the audience's situation and organization. .... A B D F
29. Showed how the solution would help the audience members achieve their goals and objectives. .... A B D F

Figure 9-4. *(Continued)*

30. Provided proof that an investment in the solution would
    yield positive dividends. .... A B D F
31. Dealt easily and comfortably with the issue of price. .... A B D F

Further thoughts about the solution:_____

_____

_____

_____

_____

F. THE PRESENTATION

32. Presenters' knowledge of the subject. .... A B D F
33. Style and tone. .... A B D F
34. Clarity. .... A B D F
35. Duration—comfortable length of presentation. .... A B D F
36. Interest level. .... A B D F
37. Speed—pace. .... A B D F
38. Level of persuasion. .... A B D F
39. Worth the time. .... A B D F
40. Language (understandable? vague?). .... A B D F

Further comments about the presentation itself: _____

_____

_____

_____

_____

_____

_____

G. THE DESIGN OF THE STORY

41. Plot and structure. .... A B D F
42. Use of dramatic elements (e.g., desire, resistance, struggle, suspense,
    complications, crises). .... A B D F

Figure 9-4. *(Continued)*

43. Handling of the climax or concluding dramatic moment. .... A B D F

44. Denouement (the final unraveling, clarification, or resolution). .... A B D F

Further observations about the design of the story: _____

_____

_____

H. VISUALS

45. Clear and to the point. .... A B D F

46. Professionally designed and produced. .... A B D F

47. Truly useful in conveying information. .... A B D F

48. Easily seen by all members of the audience. .... A B D F

49. Smoothly utilized by presenters. .... A B D F

50. Helpful in making smooth transitions between parts. .... A B D F

Additional observations about the visuals: _____

_____

_____

_____

_____

_____

I. DIRECTION

51. Forceful directorial style. .... A B D F

52. Imaginative use of available resources. .... A B D F

53. Creative use of space. .... A B D F

54. Good "casting" and balance of presenters. .... A B D F

55. Good blocking and movement. .... A B D F

Further thoughts about the direction of the presentation: _____

_____

_____

Figure 9-4. (*Continued*)

J. THE PERFORMERS

56. Delivery. .... A B D F

57. Volume. .... A B D F

58. Tone of voice. .... A B D F

59. Diction—skill in phrasing. .... A B D F

60. Enthusiasm. .... A B D F

61. Posture. .... A B D F

62. General appearance. .... A B D F

63. Facial expression. .... A B D F

64. Eye contact. .... A B D F

65. Gestures. .... A B D F

66. Stage business, use of props and visuals. .... A B D F

Further thoughts about each performer: _____

_____

_____

_____

K. THE SETTING

67. General ambiance. .... A B D F

68. Temperature. .... A B D F

69. Seating. .... A B D F

70. Refreshments, food. .... A B D F

71. Freedom from distractions and interruptions. .... A B D F

Additional ideas about the setting: _____

_____

_____

CONCLUDING THOUGHTS

_____

_____

_____

_____

Figure 9-4. (*Continued*)

choose the answer that best describes your reaction to the movie you chose.

Your personal reaction to the film

A: I liked it from beginning to end. I felt satisfied and believe that nothing could have been done to improve it.

B: I liked it generally, but felt that there was room for improvement in a few places.

D: So-so and hardly worth the price of admission.

F: Boring, frustrating, and not worth watching. Totally unsatisfactory.

The basic idea behind the picture

A: Great or momentous.

B: Unusual, timely, or clever.

D: Little or no importance.

F: Not worthwhile; none worth mentioning.

The story

A: Interesting at all times.

B: Interesting most of the time.

D: Pretty ordinary and dull.

F: Trite, boring, or disgusting.

Social value of the picture

A: Made a contribution toward improving the social outlook of the audience. Makes the audience more tolerant of others. Shows the horror of war. Exposes injustice, snobbery, greed, jingoism. Is free from subtle propaganda for special interests. Avoids undue emphasis on sex, violence, and crime. Gives insight into real life.

B: Did not take fullest advantage of its opportunities to make a contribution.

D: Neutral, weak, harmless.

F: Destructive, insidious, without any value whatsoever.

Plot and structure

A: Flawless in development and continuity.

B: Generally well developed.

D: Some weaknesses and inconsistencies.

F: Incoherent, muddled, unintelligible.

Interest level

A: Dazzling, spellbinding, enthralling, spectacular.

B: Engaging, compelling, interesting, often riveting.

D: Many slow spots, monotonous.

F: Frustratingly slow paced, boring, endless.

Direction

A: Strikingly imaginative.

B: Generally okay, smooth, good.

D: Irregular, spotty.

F: Dull, weak, vapid.

Acting—the whole cast (speech and characterization included)

A: Sincere, convincing, intelligent by all members of the cast.

B: All acting was adequate; some was exceptional.

D: Poor acting by some.

F: The whole cast was below standard.

Acting—individuals

A: The character was well introduced and consistent throughout, extremely convincing and sincere.

B: The character was believable. Generally proficient acting job.

D: Inartistic, not credible, objectionable.

F: Fumbling, faltering, entirely unconvincing, offensive. Embarrassing to watch.

Photography and lighting

A: Distinguished, high artistic merit, helps interpret story.

B: Very good, highly effective for the most part.

D: Ordinary to substandard.

F: Extremely weak or poor.

Sets, costumes, makeup, props

A: Noteworthy for beauty and authenticity, well unified.

B: Appropriate and acceptable.

D: Inappropriate, inaccurate.

F: Crude, hackneyed, gaudy, ugly, overdone.

Dialogue, sound, and special effects

A: Natural, true to the situation, music (if any) well produced.

B: Satisfying, or good as comedy effects.

D: Distracting.

F: Unnatural, false.

Casting

A: Every actor was admirably suited to the character he or she was supposed to interpret.

B: Generally good, better than average.

D: Some of the characters were miscast.

F: Majority miscast.

Title of the picture

A: Appropriate and attention-getting.

B: Appropriate.

D: Misleading.

F: No connection with the picture whatever, sensational.

Dog & Pony Checkpoints

- ✔ Don't try multimedia at home, kids. Amateur-hour efforts are pitiful or comical.

- ✔ Try the world's oldest projector sometime. It's still the best.

- ✔ Don't use 35-mm. It was specially developed for lazy people.

- ✔ Don't use overhead visuals (and projectors). They are the pits.

- ✔ Be careful about buying whiteboards. Some turn quickly into smearboards.

- ✔ In markers, use standard, bold colors. Avoid light blue, yellow, and pink because they can't be seen very well. Lavender and purple? Well,...you be the judge.

- ✔ Keep in mind that rear-screen projection systems simply don't *work*. Don't believe anybody who tries to tell you otherwise!

- ✔ Remember that computer-based graphics are the way to go.

- ✔ Remember also that when it comes to visuals, amateurs must step aside for graphics professionals.

- ✔ Take advantage of easel pads and markers. There are still a lot of opportunities to use them.

- ✔ Learn to work with giant TV images. They are the wave of the future.

- ✔ Be aware that the future is here *right now!* (It arrived early.)

- ✔ And, finally, learn how to objectively critique a presentation.

10

Follow Up to Consolidate Your Gains

Any advantage won in a perfect presentation could be lost if you don't follow up and consolidate your gains. This is most frequently expressed in a signed contract or other agreement to proceed with a plan. Some of the aspects to consider in this chapter include the following:

Contents of This Chapter

- Don't celebrate—do some more work.
- Make sure you know the names of the audience members.
- Capture the essence of the postpresentation discussions.
- Write a follow-up report.
- Send thank-you letters to each audience member.
- Develop subsequent follow-up opportunities.

Don't Celebrate—Do Some More Work

To pull off a winning presentation is an exhilarating experience. You know that you have been successful when you leave the presentation with the agreement to begin efforts, when you've negotiated a price, when you've agreed upon a set of action steps to pursue.

But remember this important fact: Your euphoria is a very durable sensation and will last a long time—it's the outgrowth of a lot of planning and hard work. The audience doesn't *share* in this emotion, however, and you must remember that. The audience may have been enthusiastic, or even excited, but those feelings fade quickly and must be rekindled.

A great many past successes have evaporated and vanished because of insufficient follow-up. The audience—whether a group of people or an individual—needs to be reminded of the agreement and commitment and shown easy ways (or what *appears to be* easy ways) to proceed.

Step 1—Make Sure You Know the Names of Audience Members

This step must take place at the end of the presentation itself. You must make sure that you have the business cards of all those present so that you can write a thank-you letter to them for having attended. This is more than a mere courtesy. It is a vital part of conducting business.

Step 2—Capture the Essence of the Postpresentation Discussion

Instead of celebrating a big win with a party or a vacation, sit down *as soon as possible* and capture what was said while it's still fresh. Note especially the contributions made by the audience, and document those ideas in the audience's own words. Also make note of any negative comments so that you can assure the new client that these concerns will be attended to.

Step 3—Write a Follow-Up Report

Write a follow-up report of the meeting, and use as much detail as you possibly can. This document will be used to assure the audience members (now the "client") that you are paying close attention to their needs.

Step 4—Send Thank-You Letters to Each Audience Member

As soon as possible after the presentation, write a letter to every member of the audience. Thank the members for their attendance and attention. Make reference to any specific contributions that the particular individual made. Include a summary from the follow-up report mentioned in Step 3. (For some important members of the audience, include the *entire* follow-up report.) These letters should be in the hands of the audience within 1 or 2 working days after the presentation.

Step 5—Develop Subsequent Follow-Up Opportunities

Until work officially begins, find some reason—every 3 or 4 days—to be in touch with the decision makers. This effort is not being pushy. It's being attentive.

- Talk to them on the phone.
- Send them notes.
- Stay in close contact.

Dog & Pony Checkpoints

✔ Don't slack off just when things panned out for you.

✔ Don't worry about being a pest.

✔ Remember the possible *future* value of the relationship you're building, not just the immediate benefits.

11

Concluding Thoughts— On Becoming a Prospector and Hitting Pay Dirt

Let's continue now with a segment on how to hit pay dirt. Prospectors do that.

One of the first things prospectors learn is that they can't sit around on bar stools and lawn chairs. They have to go where the pay dirt is. It doesn't take an advanced degree, but it does take *going*.

This final chapter examines the following:

Contents of This Chapter

- How to hit pay dirt.
- Now, what is pay dirt?
- Personality types and prospecting.
- Dog & Pony checkpoints.

How to Hit Pay Dirt

Here are some tips to make the process successful:

1. As a prospector, make it easy for your competitors to lose. Encourage them to be as lazy and reckless as they've been in the past.

2. Make the effort. To try only *slightly* harder will yield a tremendous advantage. To work even harder than that will guarantee success.

3. If possible, leave the text and visuals to others. Based on the analogies to theater, it's a good idea to hire not only a director, but also a stage designer. Let professionals worry about what's being said (text) and what's being shown (visuals).

4. Identify the go-getters in the organization, and remove the obstacles to their success. They are the true prospectors and need to roam.

5. Understand what pay dirt actually is for you or your organization. You can't prospect for it if you can't recognize it.

6. Use the model (which follows) to become a modern-day prospector.

7. Free up the right people to go after new business.

8. Don't put obstacles in the way of the people to whom you expect to sell new business and make presentations.

9. *Ask* for what you want.

10. Take bureaucracy and politics out of the equation. Always ask the question: "Is what I'm doing in the best interests of my company, its profitability, and its customers?"

Now, What Is Pay Dirt?

It's a good new product or opportunity. It's a good new customer. Figure 11-1 shows some criteria.* You know it's good for your company when you can do any of the criteria listed in the figure—especially in the short term and with little capital investment.

Meeting the criteria requires that you be aggressive rather than conservative. It requires that you become a prospector and find pay dirt by *looking* for it.

Personality Types and Prospecting

Following are a couple of models that describe two common, but opposite, personality types frequently found in business.

The first is the rampaging, often radical, "one-man-band" sort of individual who demands constant action and can make decisions instantaneously. The second is the intelligent, conservative, and overly cautious person who requires increasing amounts of information and time to reach a decision of any kind.

The first personality type—the one-man band—describes prospectors, entrepreneurs, professional divers, and aggressive salespeople.

*Note: Based on what you've read in this book, which of the conditions or elements in Fig. 11-1 are goals? Purposeful work? Benefits? Ways to compete? Features? Things get pretty well mushed together unless you can make decisions on your own, especially with regard to presentations planning.

IDENTIFYING PAY DIRT OPPORTUNITIES

A situation only has to meet one of the following criteria to qualify as a pay dirt opportunity. When you think you've found a promising opportunity, run through this checklist and check off as many criteria as possible that apply to the situation. This is one case in which more is better. The more you identify, the more likely the opportunity is one you should pursue.

1. Meet an obvious customer need. _____
2. Solve a problem for customers. _____
3. Satisfy the quality needs of new and existing customers. _____
4. Establish an equitable price for the product or service. _____
5. Link directly to the company's capabilities and resources. _____
6. Tie directly to the company's long-term growth plans. _____
7. Contribute directly to short-and long-term financial targets. _____
8. Get better use of existing equipment and facilities. _____
9. Make better use of existing people. _____
10. Minimize training time or costs. _____
11. Improve new-product development possibilities. _____
12. Make it possible to develop new markets. _____
13. Make a contribution to fixed costs. _____
14. Produce positive cashflow. _____
15. Build confidence among employees. _____
16. Boost the image of the company and its offerings. _____
17. Tie into the existing distribution channels. _____
18. Tie into the same inventory system. _____
19. Utilize existing packaging technology. _____
20. Use the same sales force (distributors, brokers, etc.). _____
21. Create a private branding opportunity. _____
22. Stimulate co-op advertising opportunities. _____
23. Utilize existing financial systems, especially cost control. _____
24. Utilize existing service or support people. _____
25. Employ the same dealer network. _____
26. Where possible, extend or expand warranties. _____
27. Offer new trade discounts to exploit distributor networks. _____
28. Decrease raw materials costs and pass savings to customers. _____
29. Create profitable subcontracting possibilities. _____
30. Ease credit and financing restrictions. _____
31. Further expand the market for other, older products. _____
32. Satisfy profit objectives. _____
33. Contribute to business or market stability. _____
34. Outflank and weaken a major competitor. _____
35. Provide worthwhile experience for workers and managers. _____
36. Provide a framework for future growth. _____
37. Boost morale among all employees. _____
38. Crank up the sales force. _____

Figure 11-1.

The diving analogy is the easiest to follow. It starts with GO. And it works like this:

In order to *dive,* you must first climb a ladder or some stairs to a board or platform and then jump off. Diving is learned in midair, not from reading books, watching films, or interviewing people about diving. You must go *off the board.*

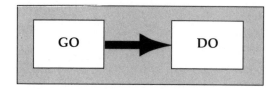

You are then in the DO phase of diving. You are in the air. You do the dive. Then you enter the water. At that point, you KNOW. You learned something by *doing* it—from the process. But first you had to GO.

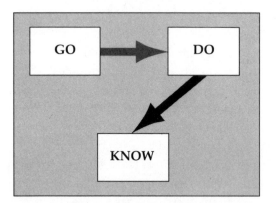

Only in this way can you gain immediate feedback about how well you did. Through this firsthand experience you come to KNOW how it felt. You get a sense of where your body was or should have been. But after the fact.

The model moves clockwise, so that the next time you GO, you proceed with increased skill and judgment. Maybe not much, but some. You have learned from firsthand experience. The loop is completed.

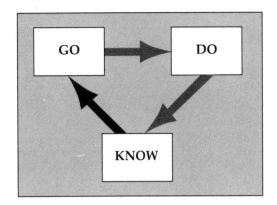

In most business situations, and in all *sales* situations, there is no substitute for *going and doing*. It's the only way. It is the key approach to business. It is the essence of making winning presentations—to GO out there and DO them. Conducting business is full of imponderables and surprises. The same things that worked last year and this year may not work *next* year. Businesspeople are constantly alert to the marketplace. They realize that their customers' needs are changing on almost a day-to-day basis. Nothing can be taken for granted. At least not for long.

All the frontiers were discovered and opened up by people who were prepared to *go*. They competed to see who could go the farthest (to the North and South Poles and to the moon), who could go the deepest (in submersibles in the Mariana Trench in the Pacific—nearly 36,000 feet in depth) and who could go the fastest (the various people who have set water, air, and land speed records).

The important thing to remember about this model is that learning *only* takes place when you GO and DO.

Now let's look at the second character type and a contrasting approach.

Professional people such as chemists, engineers, lawyers, doctors, architects, and physicists are trained according to a process that—out of necessity—*begins* with KNOW.

Since there is a large body of knowledge and historical information in the above professions, the process of learning begins with books and lectures. If you enter one of these disciplines, you can expect—at the beginning of your training—to sit through a lot of classes, write a great many papers, stare at miles of microfilm, and read plenty of books and periodicals.

The guiding principle at the beginning of training is to imitate professors (and follow procedures exactly as directed). It is only after a great deal of this activity that you are then permitted to DO anything at all, typically in a lab setting under careful supervision.

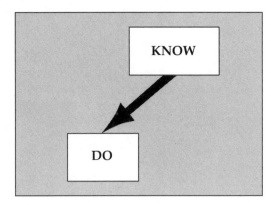

But the process calls for you to KNOW quite a bit before you DO even a little. After a certain amount of hands-on experience, you then go back to class to gain more book knowledge. Then you are permitted to DO again, but this time at a higher, more rigorous level. A loop is formed in which you are learning both from classes and from laboratory or fieldwork. The model now looks like this.

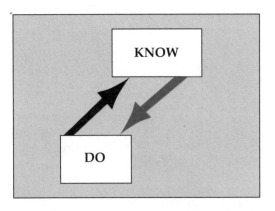

It is only at the completion of the course of study that you are permitted to DO an appreciable amount. Finally, at the very end of your training, you are certified by a board or special licensing authority and are permitted to GO forth on your own and practice your new profession. You are finally ready to start real work.

It is often obligatory that you continue to learn, through both classes and experience, but the process is more or less final upon graduation from the program and completion of an internship.

Let's compare the two approaches.

In the first (GO-DO-KNOW), people must be extremely self-reliant and self-directed.

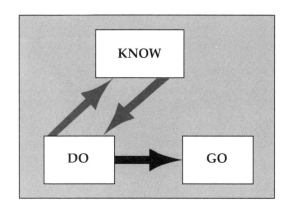

In the second, people are working within institutions and in groups. They enjoy the support of many other skilled people—plus facilities, specialized equipment, and sophisticated technology.

The risks of the second approach (if there are *any* for those who make it through the program) are all at the end, and they are minimal.

The risks of the first approach are all at the beginning, and they are substantial. Also, the risks are focused on the individual. There is little support and a great deal of uncertainty. The person never *knows* what's going to happen. And the winners are those who keep trying despite setbacks.

The ideal, of course, would be some combination of the two. The obstacle is that people accustomed to GO-DO-KNOW have little tolerance for or understanding of people who operate from KNOW-DO-GO. Some engineers and technical people desire absolute assurance that things are going to work out before they even start. Prospectors can seldom provide that assurance. People following the second approach think that people in the first are crazy. And—from their perspective—this is somewhat true.

When prospectors (or people like them) GO, they are self-authorized. It is an independent act, freely taken. They are not imitating anybody. The GO portion of the second approach, by contrast, is sanctioned by higher authority. That's why there isn't necessarily a connection between the two approaches. It would be convenient if the GO ending the second approach was the beginning GO of the first, but it's seldom the case.

This oversimplification is not meant to criticize the second approach—obviously it is essential to the development of professionals. It is unfortunate, however, that increased education sometimes leads to timidity and a disinclination to examine alternatives.

Academics often have trouble dealing with entrepreneurial behavior. For example, it's difficult for electrical engineers—for whom Ohm's law is Ohm's law, no matter where you go or what language you speak—to put on a sales hat and discover that there is nothing necessarily replicable about a sales call.

Another reason academics have so much trouble training entrepreneurs is that most professors are the personification of the second approach, the preservers and protectors of the idea that people must achieve perfection in *knowing* before they go forth and *try*.

Final message: Free up salespeople to *try*.

Go-getters depend on firsthand experience and observation more than on secondhand reports. They are persistent. They need to act as informally as possible. They shouldn't get bogged down in unnecessary ritual and paperwork. They should always be free to look for fresh alternatives.

Leave them alone. It's okay that you may not *know*. But it's imperative that you try—and that, in the course of trying, you remember the extent to which common sense and new technology can easily push you over the top.

Dog & Pony Checkpoints

- ✔ GO.
- ✔ Become a prospector.
- ✔ Don't forget your shovel.

Index

ABOUT THE AUTHOR

John Quick is a marketing, sales, and presentations expert who has helped clients—ranging from *Fortune* 500 companies to small startup enterprises—to win hundreds of millions of dollars in new business. His background in high-stakes presenting includes stints as an industrial motion picture writer and producer, corporate advertising manager, and creative director at the Interpublic Group of Companies in New York, the country's largest advertising agency conglomerate. After earning a doctorate in communications from Union Institute in Cincinnati, he spent 10 years as a consultant with the firm of Arthur D. Little, Inc., and also taught an ongoing planning program at Harvard's Center for Lifelong Learning. He is author of several other books, including the *Artists' and Illustrators' Encyclopedia* and *A Short Book on the Subject of Speaking*, both published by McGraw-Hill. Mr. Quick is president of The Quick Company in Denver, Colorado.

Alan Greenwood and his wife, Cleo, are the publishers of *Vintage Guitar* magazine, which they launched in 1986. *Vintage Guitar* is the largest monthly publication for guitar collectors, enthusiasts, and dealers. They also publish *Vintage Guitar®* Online at www.vintageguitar.com, and *The Official Vintage Guitar Magazine Price Guide*. His collection includes several vintage instruments from the '50s, '60s and '70s, as well as newer production and custom-made guitars and amps. He lives in Bismarck, North Dakota.

Gil Hembree began collecting guitars in 1966 as a college student working at Kitt's Music on G Street in Washington, DC. He graduated from American University in 1969 with a BSBA and two days after graduation he was hired by the General Motors Corporation. He held several assignments with GM including Financial Administrator of the Wichita Falls, Texas plant (where he obtained his MBA from Midwestern State University), and Supervisor of Corporate Audit in Detroit. In January of 2000, after a 30-year career, he retired from GM and he was immediately contracted by Vintage Guitar to co-author the Vintage Guitar Price Guide. Hembree maintains a small collection of '50s and '60s Fender and Gibson guitars and amps. He lives with his wife, Jane, in Austin, Texas.

The Official Vintage Guitar® Magazine Price Guide
By Alan Greenwood and Gil Hembree

Vintage Guitar Books
An imprint of Vintage Guitar Inc., PO Box 7301, Bismarck, ND 58507, (701) 255-1197, Fax (701) 255-0250, publishers of *Vintage Guitar®* magazine and Vintage Guitar® Online at www.vintageguitar.com. Vintage Guitar is a registered trademark of Vintage Guitar, Inc.

ISBN 1-884883-17-6

Cover and Back photos: 1968 Fender Telecaster (Pink Paisley and Blue Floral): Dave Rogers. 1965 Gibson Thunderbird: Steve Evans. 1957 Harmony Stratotone Newport H-42/1: Michael Wright.

Cover Design: Doug Yellow Bird/Vintage Guitar, Inc.

Printed in the United States of America

HAL•LEONARD®
CORPORATION
7777 W. BLUEMOUND RD. P.O. BOX 13819
MILWAUKEE, WISCONSIN 53213

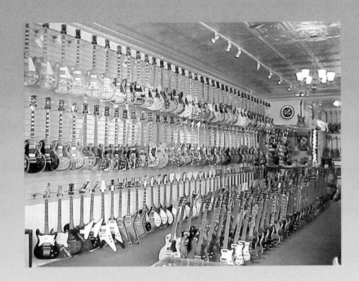

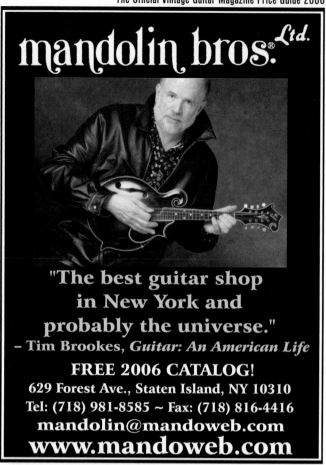

V

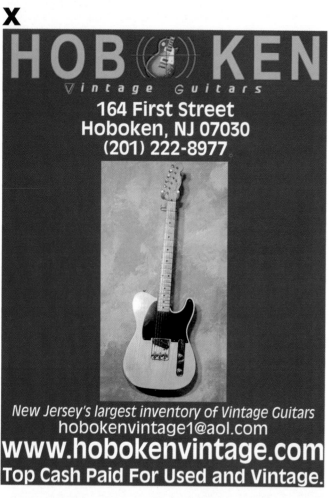
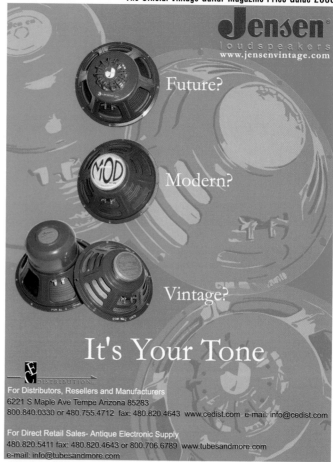

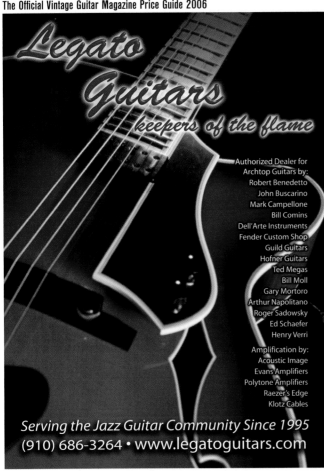
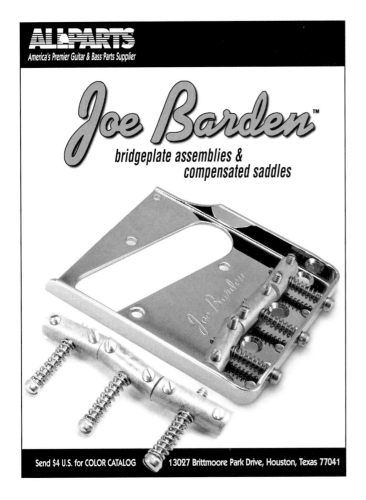

Table of Contents

1932 Gibson Mastertone Granada. Photo courtesy George Gruhn.

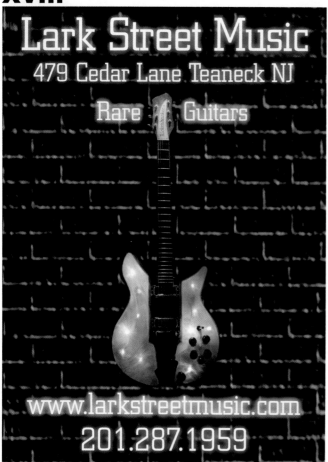

Using The Guide

Understanding the Values

The Official Vintage Guitar Price Guide conveys specific values for excellent-condition, all-original instruments. The Guide's definition of excellent condition allows for some wear, but the instrument should be well-maintained, with no significant blemishes, wear, repairs, or damage. An all-original instrument has the parts and finish it had when it left the factory. Replacement parts and refinishes can greatly affect value, as can the appropriate case (or cover) in excellent condition. In many instances, a "wrong" case will not greatly affect value, but with the top-dollar collectibles, it can.

Repairs affect value differently. Some repair is necessary to keep an instrument in playable condition, and the primary concern is the level of expertise displayed in the work. An amateurish repair will lower the value more than one that is obviously professional. A refinished guitar, regardless of the quality of the work, is generally worth 50% or less of the values shown in The Guide. A poorly executed neck repair or significant body repair can mean a 50% reduction in a guitar's value. A professional re-fret or minor, nearly invisible body repair will reduce a guitar's value by only 5%.

The values in the The Guide are for unfaded finishes. Slight color fade reduces the value by only 5%, but heavily faded examples can reduce the value by 25% to 50%.

We use a range of excellent-condition values, as there is seldom agreement on a single price point for vintage and used instruments. A tighter range suggests there is a general consensus, while a wide range means the market isn't in strict agreement. A mint-condition instrument can be worth more than the values listed here, and anything in less-than-excellent condition will have a reduced value.

Finding the Information

The table of contents shows the major sections. Each is organized in alphabetical order by brand, then by model. In a few instances, there are separate sections for a company's most popular models, especially when there is a large variety of similar instruments. Examples include Fender's Stratocasters, Telecasters, Precision and Jazz basses, and Gibson's Les Pauls. The outer top corner of each page uses a dictionary-type header that tells the models or brands on that page. This provides a quick way to navigate each section. The index at the back shows the page numbers for each type of instrument, by brand, and is a great place to start when looking for a specific model or brand.

The Guide has excellent brand histories and in most cases the guitar section has the most detailed information for each brand. When possible, The Guide lists each model's years of availability and any design changes that affect values.

More information on many of the brands covered in The Guide is available in the pages of Vintage Guitar magazine and on the "Brand Pages" section of our website, www.vintage-guitar.com.

The authors of The Guide always appreciate your help, so if you find any errors, or have additional information on certain brands or models, we'd like to hear from you. We are especially looking for info on any brand not yet listed. Whatever you may have to contribute, feel free to drop us a line at al@vguitar.com.

New Retail Pricing Information

The Guide continues to add information on individual luthiers and smaller shops. It's difficult to develop values on used instruments produced by these builders because much of their output is custom work, production is low, and/or they haven't been producing for a period of time sufficient to see their instruments enter the used/resale market. To give you an idea about their instruments, we've developed five grades of retail values for new instruments. These convey only the prices charged by the builder, and are not indicative of the quality of construction. The Guide applies this scale to all builders and manufacturers of new instruments.

The five retail-price grades are:
Budget - up to $250,
Intermediate - $251 to $1,000,
Professional - $1,001 to $3,000,
Premium - $3,001 to $10,000,
Presentation - more than $10,000.

The Guide uses the terms "production" and "custom" to differentiate between builders who do true custom work versus those who offer standard production models. "Production" means the company offers specific models, with no variations. "Custom" means they do only custom orders, and "production/custom" indicates they do both. Here's an example:

Greenwood Guitars

1977-present. Luthier Alan Greenwood builds his professional-grade, custom, solidbody guitars in Bismarck, North Dakota. He also builds basses.

This tells who the builder is, the type of instruments they build, where they build them, how long they've been operating under that brand, that they do only custom work, and that they ask between $1,000 and $3,000 for their guitars (professional-grade).

Again, we've applied the retail price grades and production and/or custom labels to most new-instrument manufacturers.

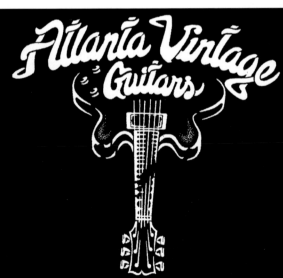

Introduction

The Vintage Market, 2006

If you own a couple of cool vintage guitars, congratulations! Not only have they provided great personal enjoyment, but they have also been great investments. Vintage guitars have been described as solid investments since 1978, but the news just keeps getting better

Again this year, we are providing financial information based on The 42 Index, which we developed to track the values of classic American instruments. The Index is comprised of excellent-condition instruments made in the 1960s or earlier. We chose 14 each from Fender, Gibson, and Martin, the companies accepted as the top manufacturers of that era. We omitted the highest-value collectibles of each brand, like the '58 Les Paul Standard, the pre-war D-45 and '50s custom-color Stratocasters, as those guitars can experience rapid increases in value and would skew our analysis of the overall market for that era.

The numbers in the following charts reference the guitars and basses in The 42 Index.

Chart 1 shows the accumulative appreciation percent of The 42 Index from 1991 to 2006. The increasing slope during the present decade indicates that vintage guitars are appreciating more quickly now than they were 10 years ago. You'll notice the appreciation is flat from 1999 to 2001.

There were "bears" who felt the vintage guitar market had peaked in '99 and the subsequent years would see declining values. Those bears suggested the supply of vintage guitars would begin to outstrip demand. There are many factors to consider when speculating, but a couple reasons given to support the bears' outlook were the high prices of '99, and a significant "Been there, done that!" mentality associated with a 35-year-old market.

Some forecasters, including the authors of *The Guide*, felt in '99 that the market would continue to appreciate at a healthy rate of about 3% per year. As you can see in our data, the market did much better from '02 to '06. One reason may be the collapse of the financial stock market in the early 2000s. Anecdotal evidence suggests that a lot of new money that left financial markets flowed to collectibles like guitars. This may well be true, but there are dozens of other reasons for the latest bull market in vintage guitars. It is very likely the market would have appreciated with or without the bust of the financial stock market. As proof, consider the vintage guitar market of

Guitar Dealer Participants

The information refined on these pages comes from several sources, including the input of many knowledgeable guitar dealers. Without the help of these individuals, it would be very hard for us to provide the information here and in each issue of *Vintage Guitar* magazine. We deeply appreciate the time and effort they provide.

Andy Eder
Andy's Guitars

Bob Page
Buffalo Brothers

Norm Moren
Cold Springs Electrical Works

Stan Werbin & S.J. "Frog" Forgey
Elderly Instruments

Dave Belzer & Drew Berlin
Guitar Center

Vallis Kolbeck
GuitarVille (Seattle)

Jim Singleton
Jim's Guitars

Dave Hinson
Killer Vintage

Timm Kummer
Kummer's Vintage Instruments

Buzzy Levine
Lark Street Music

Larry Wexer
Laurence Wexer, Ltd.

Stan Jay
Mandolin Brothers

Bob November
McKenzie River Music

Lowell Levinger
Players Vintage Instruments

Mike Reeder
Mike's Music

Eliot Michael
Rumble Seat Music

Bruce Barnes & Kenny Rardin
Solidbodyguitar.com

John DeSilva
Straight Shooter Guitars

Richard Friedman & David Davidson
We Buy Guitars

Nate Westgor
Willie's American Guitars

the mid '80s, when a bull stock market was developing. Plus, the vintage market did very well during the bull stock market of the late '90s.

Overall, vintage instruments have been sound investments over the past two decades, and Chart 2 shows that our "fantasy" investment of $150,000 (used to purchase the 42 guitars in 1991), has grown to $540,000 in 2006.

It's often said that a great guitar will *always* be a great guitar, and the 1958 Gibson ES-335 "dot-neck" in our fantasy 42 is a good example. *Guide* co-author Gil Hembree became familiar with this rare blond in 1966. Even at that time, guitar pros talked about the "rare blond 335," hoping to one day find one. Chart 3 shows the mid-point value (in our low-to-high value range for an all-original, excellent-condition instrument) from 1991 to 2006.

You'll notice the trend line for the '58 ES-335 in Chart 3 does not always go up. That's because the guitar truly defines rare and expert opinions concerning value can vary. One dealer might put a very high speculative value on the guitar, while a "put food on the table" dealer may have a difficult time selling if the price is too high.

Our advice concerning any vintage guitar purchase is to find the cleanest, most original one you can afford and deal with a reputable vintage guitar dealer that attests to the instrument's originality, and has a realistic return policy. You have to do your homework, as well. Be intimately familiar the model you're buying. For the '58 blond ES-335, be sure the guitar has the original (factory-installed) PAF humbucker pickups, pots, solder, natural finish, and tuners, shows no damage or changes, and has a fully functional truss rod and original frets (or notification of a re-fret with the size of wire used).

The Vintage Guitar Price Guide provides guidance pricing based on precedent values. Some guitars will be offered for

more than is indicated in *The Guide*. We do not take exception to that. Prices do rise when dealers break precedent and the new higher price is acceptable to several buyers.

The reverse can happen. Sometimes the market will rebuke excessive dealer speculation, and an overpriced guitar will remain unsold. In that case, the guitar will eventually be discounted, or as is more often the case, the dealer will wait for the market to catch up. This is called "putting a guitar back" until it can fetch the speculated price.

The *Guide* team is dedicated to setting accurate precedent value. A *Guide* value that's set too low may help a buyer because

THE 42 INDEX

FROM FENDER		
1952 blond Precision Bass	1964 Lake Placid Blue Jaguar	1964 sunburst Thunderbird II Bass
1952 blond Esquire	1964 sunburst Precision Bass	1965 EB-3 Bass
1953 blond Telecaster	1966 Candy Apple Red Stratocaster	1969 sunburst Citation
1956 sunburst Stratocaster	**FROM GIBSON**	**FROM MARTIN**
1958 sunburst Jazzmaster	1952 sunburst ES-5	1931 OM-28
1958 blond Telecaster	1952 Les Paul Model	1932 00-28 special order
1960 sunburst Stratocaster	1954 Les Paul Jr.	1935 D-18
1961 sunburst, stack knob, Jazz Bass	1958 sunburst EB-2 Bass	1944 scalloped-brace 000-28
1962 sunburst, 3-knob, Jazz Bass	1958 Les Paul Custom	1944 D-28
1963 sunburst Telecaster Custom	1958 natural ES-335	1950 D-28
1963 sunburst Esquire Custom	1958 Super 400CES	1958 000-18
	1959 Les Paul Jr.	1959 D-18
	1959 J-160E	1959 D-28E
	1961 sunburst ES-355	1962 D-28
	1961 Les Paul SG	1967 GT-75
		1968 000-18
		1969 N-20
		1969 D-45

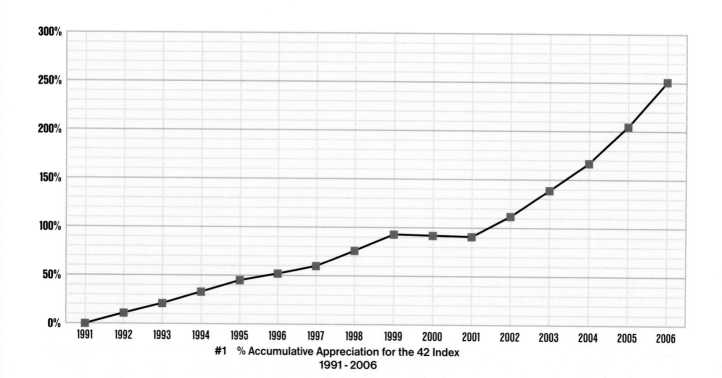

#1   % Accumulative Appreciation for the 42 Index
1991 - 2006

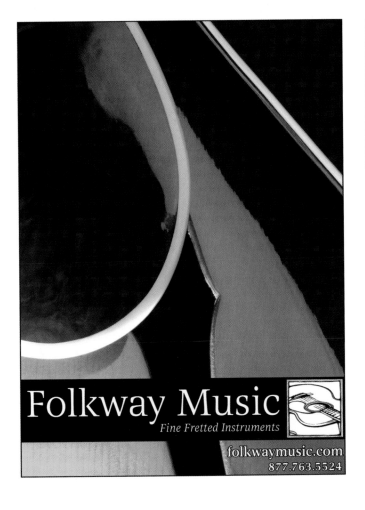

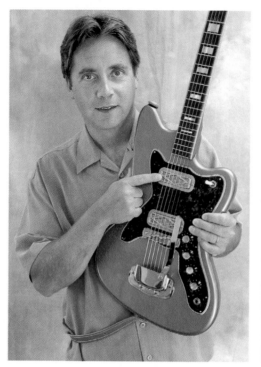

Authors Alan Greenwood and Gil Hembree.

the buyer will pay the *Guide* value to a seller, thinking the instrument is undervalued. But the same low *Guide* price may make it difficult to sell the guitar because a customer may object because the selling price is above the precedent price listed in the *Price Guide*. Conversely, if the *Price Guide* establishes a price that's too high, that makes it more difficult for a dealer to buy, but makes it easier for a dealer to sell at retail. The only win/win for everyone is to establish a correct precedent value in *The Guide*. When a correct price is set, the market takes care of the rest. That's what *The Guide* team strives for. It's our mission statement and our goal!

The Guide is a powerful tool because it's a precedent-value guide based on current selling prices. It sets a standard, and if a dealer rationalizes a different price than what is shown in *The Guide*, at least the public has a benchmark.

The 42 Index is specific to the guitars we track. If you develop your own index based on your collection, your data will look different. One caveat; old acoustic archtops and jazz guitars will not mimic the 42 Index trend line. Archtops and jazzers will show less appreciation, and in some cases will show declining values. Jazz guitars and acoustic archtops have been flat for several years. Old flat-tops? No problem, they're doing well. Mandolins – especially the collectible ones? Not a problem – they're in demand. Banjos? It's a party! Narrow-panel tweed amps? Doing great! You get the message – the vintage guitar market continues to be on fire!

More Information

The official website of *Vintage Guitar* magazine, vintage-

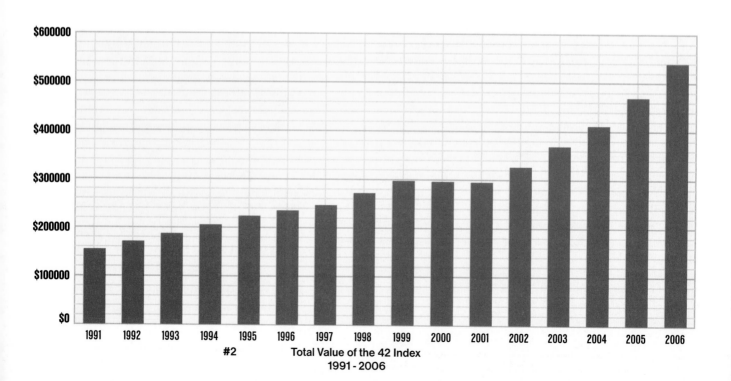

#2   Total Value of the 42 Index 1991 - 2006

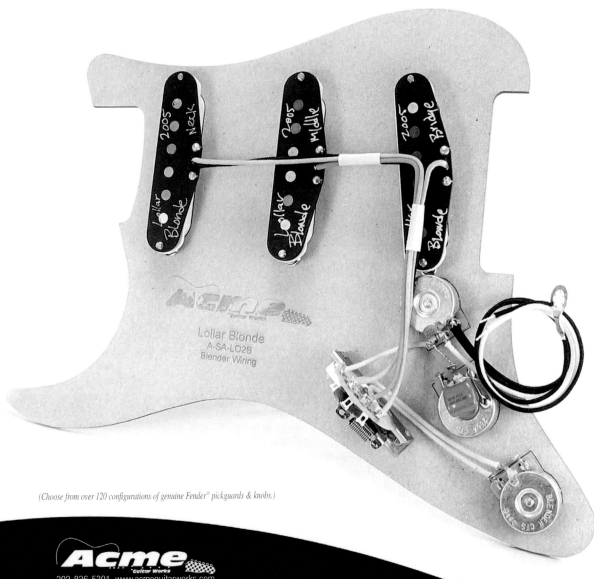

guitar.com, is updated five times a week from the magazine's inventory of articles. This expanding resource includes interviews with many of your favorite guitarists, reviews of new gear, and recordings and historic information on many of the brands and models covered in this book.

If a model is missing from *The Guide*, or if you'd like something clarified, please drop a line to gil@vguitar.com. If you're a builder and would like to be included, want to correct your info, or have information on your favorite brand, drop a line to al@vguitar.com.

Acknowledgments

Compiling *The Official Vintage Guitar Price Guide* is a massive undertaking that requires the talents of many people. We use many sources to determine the values, but the vintage instrument dealers who give their time and expertise to provide market information play an important role. Many of them provide info on brands and models, and they are acknowledged on page XXII.

Randy Klimpert provided the information and photos in the ukulele section. Many of the brand histories used in this edition are based on the work of Michael Wright, the longtime "Different Strummer" columnist for *VG*.

Several people at *VG* played an important role, as well. Doug Yellow Bird designs the cover and inside pages. Jeanine Shea assists with proofreading and, with James Jiskra, compiles the ads and dealer directory. Ward Meeker selects all the photos. Wanda Huether entered much of the data, and Jacob Strombeck and Bryan Engleson also helped with proofreading. We thank all of them for their usual fine work.

We always welcome suggestions, criticisms, and ideas to make future guides better. Contact us at Vintage Guitar, Inc., PO Box 7301, Bismarck, ND 58507, or by email at gil@vguitar.com or al@vguitar.com.

Thank you,

Alan Greenwood and Gil Hembree

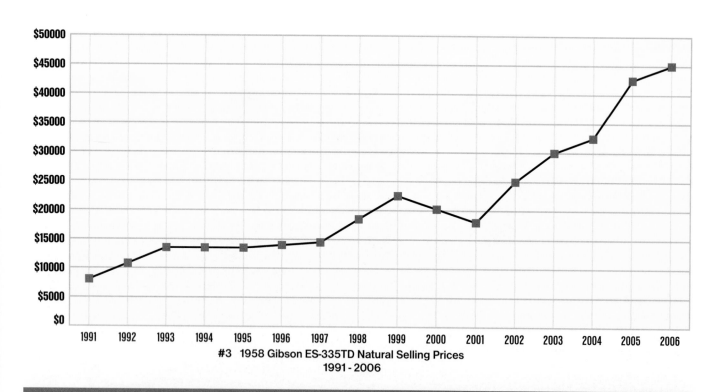

#3 1958 Gibson ES-335TD Natural Selling Prices
1991 - 2006

Builder Updates and Corrections

If you produce instruments for sale and would like to be included in the next *VG Price Guide*, send your infomation to al@vguitar.com. Include info on the types of instruments you build, model names and prices, yearly production, the year you started, where you are located and a short bio about yourself.

If you spot errors in the information about brands and models in this guide, or have information on a brand you'd like to see included, please contact us at the above email address. Your help is appreciated.

Guitars

Abyss NS ii archtop

*1963 Airline Super III
Res-O-Glas*

MODEL YEAR	FEATURES	EXC. COND. LOW	HIGH

A Fuller Sound

1998-present. Professional and premium grade, custom nylon and steel-string flat-tops built by Luthier Warren Fuller in Oakland, California.

Abel

1994-present. Custom aircraft-grade aluminum body, wood neck, guitars built by twins Jim and Jeff Abel in Evanston, Wyoming. They offered the Abel Axe from '94-'96 and 2000-'01, and still do custom orders. They also made the Rogue Aluminator in the late '90s.

Axe

1994-1996. Offset double-cut aluminum body with dozens of holes in the body, wood neck, various colors by annodizing the aluminum body. Abel Axe logo on the headstock.

1994-1996	Non-trem model	$800	$900
1994-1996	Trem model	$825	$925

Abilene

Budget and intermediate grade, production, acoustic and electric guitars imported by Samick.

Acoustic Guitars

2000-2002		$65	$150

Electric Guitars

Solidbody and hollowbody electrics, designs often based on classic American models.

2000-2002		$55	$110

Abyss

1997-present. Luthier Kevin Pederson builds his premium grade, production/custom, hollowbody and solidbody guitars in Forest City, Iowa.

Acoustic

Ca. 1965-ca. 1987, present. Mainly known for solidstate amps, the Acoustic Control Corp. of Los Angeles, California, did offer guitars and basses from around '69 to late '74. The brand was revived by Samick a few years ago on a line of amps.

Black Widow Guitar

1969-1970, 1972-1974. Both versions featured an unique black equal double-cut body with German carve, 2 pickups, a zero fret, and a protective spider design pad on back. The early version (called the AC500 Black Widow) had 22 frets, an ebonite 'board, and pickups with 1 row of adjustable polepieces. The later version was 24 frets, a rosewood 'board, and humbuckers with 2 rows of adjustable pole pieces (some '72s have the older style pickup). The jack and 4 control knobs were configured differently on the 2 versions, Acoustic outsourced the production of the guitars, possibly to Japan, but final 200 or so guitars produced by Semie Moseley. The AC700 Black Widow 12-string was also available for '69-'70.

1969-1970		$825	$925
1972-1974		$800	$900

Agile

1985-present. Budget grade, production, acoustic and electric guitars imported by Rondo Music of Union, New Jersey. They also offer mandolins.

Solidbody Electrics

2000s		$100	$175

Aims

Ca. 1974-ca. 1976. Aims instruments, distributed by Randall Instruments in the mid-'70s, were copies of classic American guitar and bass models. Randall also offered a line of Aims amps during the same time.

Airline

Ca. 1958-1968, 2004-present. Airline originally was a brand used by Montgomery Ward on acoustic, electric archtop and solidbody guitars and basses, amplifiers, steels, and possibly banjos and mandolins. Instruments manufactured by Kay, Harmony and Valco. In '04, the brand was revived on a line of imported intermediate grade, production, reissues from Eastwood guitars (see that listing for new info).

Acoustic Archtops (lower end)

1950s		$150	$300
1960s		$150	$300

Acoustic Archtops (higher end)

1950s		$325	$500
1960s		$325	$500

Acoustic Res-O-Glas Resonator

Res-o-glas, coverplate with M-shaped holes, asymmetrical peghead.

1964		$650	$850

Amp-In-Case Model

1960s. Double-cut, single pickup, short scale guitar with amplifier built into the case, Airline on grille.

1960s		$300	$350

Electric Hollowbodies

1950s	Kay Barney Kessel		
	Artist copy	$575	$750
1960s	ES-175 copy	$425	$600
1960s	Harmony H-54		
	Rocket II copy	$225	$450
1960s	Harmony H-75	$475	$650

Electric Res-O-Glas

Res-o-glas is a form of fiberglass. The bodies and sometimes the necks were made of this material.

1960s	JackWhite's		
	Red Jetson style	$1,100	$1,800
1960s	Other style, 1 & 2 pu	$650	$900

Electric Res-O-Glas Resonator

Res-o-glas is a form of fiberglass. These models have resonator cones in the body.

1960s		$650	$900

Electric Solidbodies (standard-lower end)

1960s		$200	$600

GUITARS

MODEL YEAR	FEATURES	EXC. COND. LOW	HIGH

Electric Solidbodies (deluxe-higher end)
Appointments may include multiple pickups, block inlays, additional logos, more binding.

1950s		$525	$900
1960s		$500	$575

Flat-Top (lower end, 13" body)

1960s		$75	$100

Alamo

1947-1982. Founded by Charles Eilenberg, Milton Fink, and Southern Music, San Antonio, Texas, and distributed by Bruno & Sons. Alamo started out making radios, phonographs, and instrument cases. In '49 they added amplifiers and lap steels. From '60 to '70, the company produced beginner-grade solidbody and hollow-core body electric Spanish guitars. The amps were all-tube until the '70s. Except for a few Valco-made examples, all instruments were built in San Antonio.

Electric Hollowbodies

1960s		$175	$325

Electric Solidbodies

1960s		$175	$325

Alamo Guitars

1999-present. The Alamo brand has been revived for a line of handcrafted, professional grade, production/custom, guitars by Alamo Music Products, which also offers Robin and Metropolitan brand guitars and Rio Grande pickups.

Tonemonger
1999-present. Ash or African Fakimba offset double cut solidbody, 3 single coils, tremolo.

1999-2004		$600	$900

Alan Carruth

1970-present. Professional and premium grade, production/custom, classical and archtop guitars built by luthier Alan Carruth in Newport, New Hampshire. He also builds violins, harps and dulcimers. He started out building dulcimers and added guitars in '74.

Albanus

Late 1950s-1973. Luthier Carl Albanus Johnson built around 100 high quality archtop guitars in Chicago, Illinois. He died in '73. He also built violins.

Alberico, Fabrizio

1998-present. Luthier Fabrizio Alberico builds his premium grade, custom, flat-top and classical guitars in Cheltenham, Ontario.

Alembic

1969-present. Premium and presentation grade, production/custom, guitars, baritones, and 12-strings built in Santa Rosa, California. They also build basses. Established in San Francisco by Ron and Susan Wickersham, Alembic started out as a studio working with the Grateful Dead and other

bands on a variety of sound gear. By '70 they were building custom basses, later adding guitars and cabinets. By '73, standardized models were being offered.

California Special
1988-present. Double-cut neck-thru solidbody, six-on-a-side tuners, various colors.

1990s		$1,600	$1,900

Orion
1990-present. Offset double-cut glued neck solidbody, various colors.

1990s		$1,500	$1,700

Series I
Early-1970s-present. Neck-thru, double-cut solidbody, bookmatched koa, black walnut core, 3 pickups, optional body styles available, natural.

1970s		$2,700	$2,900

Alhambra

1930s. The Alhambra brand was most likely used by a music studio (or distributor) on instruments made by others, including Regal-built resonator instruments.

Allen Guitars

1982-present. Premium grade, production resonators, steel-string flat-tops, and mandolins built by Luthier Randy Allen, Colfax, California.

Aloha

1935-1960s. Private branded by Aloha Publishing and Musical Instruments Company, Chicago, Illinois. Made by others. There was also the Aloha Manufacturing Company of Honolulu which made musical instruments from around 1911 to the late '20s.

Alray

1967. Electrics and acoustics built by the Holman-Woodell guitar factory in Neodesha, Kansas, who also marketed similar models under the Holman brand.

Alvarez

1965-present. Intermediate and professional grade, production, acoustic guitars imported by St. Louis Music. They also offer banjos and mandolins. Initially high-quality handmade Yairi guitars were exclusively distributed, followed by lower-priced Alvarez line. In '90 the Westone brand used on electric guitars and basses was replaced with the Alvarez name; these Alvarez electrics were offered until '02. Many Alvarez electric models designed by luthier Dana Sutcliffe; several models designed by Dan Armstrong.

Classic I, II, III
1994-1999. Designs based on classic solidbody American models.

1994-1999		$125	$175

1964 Alamo Fiesta I

Allen square-neck resophonic

Alvarez DY-91

*1969 Ampeg
Dan Armstrong lucite*

MODEL YEAR	FEATURES	EXC. COND. LOW	HIGH

Flat-Top (lower end)

1966-present. Beginner-grade instruments, solid or laminate tops, laminate back and sides, little or no extra appointments. Some are acoustic/electric.

1970s		$50	$75
1980s		$65	$100
1990s		$75	$125

Flat-Top (mid-level)

1966-present. Solid tops, laminated back and sides, lower appointments such as bound 'boards and headstocks, nickel hardware and pearl inlay.

1970s		$100	$200
1980s		$100	$200
1990s		$100	$200

Flat-Top (mid-to-high-end)

1966-present. Solid spruce tops, solid mahogany or rosewood backs, laminated mahogany or rosewood sides, may have scalloped bracing, mid-level appointments like abalone headstock inlay, soundhole rosettes and herringbone body binding.

1970s		$200	$325
1980s		$200	$325
1990s		$200	$325

Flat-Top (high end)

1966-present. Solid rosewood and/or mahogany backs and sides, solid spruce tops, may have dovetail neck joint, highest appointments like abalone inlay and real maple binding.

1980s		$450	$575
1990s		$475	$600

Fusion Series (with piezo and EQ)

1981-present. Single-cut, acoustic/electrics with EQ and transducer/piezo pickups. Earlier models had spruce tops with spruce or mahogany back and sides. More recent models have maple tops, backs and sides.

1980s		$275	$375
1990s		$275	$375

Alvarez Yairi

1966-present. Alvarez Yairi guitars are handcrafted and imported by St. Louis Music.

Flat-Top (higher-end)

Solid top of cedar or spruce, depending on model, higher-end appointments.

1970s		$550	$800
1980s		$550	$825
1990s		$675	$875
2000s		$700	$950

Flat-Top (mid-level)

Solid top of cedar or spruce, depending on model, mid-level appointments.

1970s		$275	$425
1980s		$300	$450
1990s		$325	$475

Flat-Top 9-String (DY-58)

Flat-top acoustic with 9 strings (doubles on the 3 high strings).

1989	Natural	$675	$800

MODEL YEAR	FEATURES	EXC. COND. LOW	HIGH

Fusion Series (with piezo and EQ)

1998-2002. Piezo bridge with volume and tone controls, higher-end appointments.

1990s		$650	$775

Alvarez, Juan

1952-present. Professional and premium grade, production/custom, classical and flamenco guitars made in Madrid, Spain, origianlly by luthier Juan Alvarez Gil and now by son Juan Miguel Alvarez.

American Acoustech

1993-2001. Production steel string flat-tops made by Tom Lockwood (former Guild plant manager) and Dave Stutzman (of Stutzman's Guitar Center) as ESVL Inc. in Rochester, New York.

American Archtop Guitars

1995-present. Premium and presentation grade, custom 6- and 7-string archtops by luthier Dale Unger, in Stroudsburg, Pennsylvania.

American Conservatory (Lyon & Healy)

Late-1800s-early-1900s. Guitars and mandolins built by Chicago's Lyon & Healy and sold mainly through various catalog retailers. Mid-level instruments above the quality of Lyon & Healy's Lakeside brand, and generally under thier Washburn brand.

Harp Guitar Style G2210

Early-1900s. Two 6-string necks with standard tuners, 1 neck fretless, rosewood back and sides, spruce top, fancy rope colored wood inlay around soundhole, sides and down the back center seam.

1917	Natural	$3,300	$3,700

American Showster

1986-present. Established by Bill Meeker and David Haines, Bayville, New Jersey. The Custom Series is made in the U.S.A., while the Standard Series (introduced in '97) is made in Czechoslovakia.

AS-57 Classic (original '57)

1987-present. Body styled like a '57 Chevy tail fin, basswood body, bolt-on neck, 1 humbucker or 3 single-coil pickups, various colors.

1987-1997		$2,100	$2,500

Ampeg

1949-present. Founded in '49 by Everett Hull as the Ampeg Bassamp Company in New York and has built amplifiers throughout its history. In '62 the company added instruments with the introduction of their Baby Bass and from '63 to '65, they carried a line of guitars and basses built by Burns of London and imported from England. In '66 the company introduced its own line of basses. In '67, Ampeg was acquired by Unimusic, Inc. From '69-'71 contracted with Dan Armstrong to produce lucite

MODEL		EXC. COND.	
YEAR	FEATURES	LOW	HIGH

"see-through" guitars and basses with replaceable slide-in pickup design. In '71 the company merged with Magnavox. Beginning around '72 until '75, Ampeg imported the Stud Series copy guitars from Japan. Ampeg shut down production in the spring of '80. MTI bought the company and started importing amps. In '86 St. Louis Music purchased the company. In '97 Ampeg introduced new and reissue American-made guitar and bass models. They discontinued the guitar line in 2001.

AMG1
1999-2001. Dan Amstrong guitar features, but with mahogany body with quilted maple top, 2 P-90-style or humbucker-style pickups.

1999-2001	Humbuckers, gold hardware	$925	$975
1999-2001	Kent Armstrong pickups	$425	$525
1999-2001	P-90s, standard hardware	$425	$525

Dan Armstrong Lucite Guitar
1969-1971. Clear plexiglas solidbody, with interchangable pickups, Dan Armstrong reports that around 9,000 guitars were produced, introduced in '69, but primary production was in '70-'71, reissued in '98.

1969-1971		$2,200	$2,900
1969-1971	Black smoke see-thru	$2,500	$3,500

Dan Armstrong Lucite Guitar Reissue
1998-2001. Produced by pickup designer Kent Armstrong (son of Dan Armstrong), offered in smoked (ADAG2) or clear (ADAG1).

1998-2001		$725	$825

Heavy Stud (GE-150/GEH-150)
1973-1975. Import from Japan, single-cut body, inexpensive materials, weight added for sustain.

1970s		$350	$400

Sonic Six (By Burns)
1964-1965. Solidbody, 2 pickups, tremolo, cherry finish, same as the Burns Nu-Sonic guitar.

1960s		$425	$525

Stud (GE-100/GET-100)
1973-1975. Import from Japan, double-cut, inexpensive materials, weight added for sustain, GET-100 included tremolo assembly.

1973-1975		$350	$400

Super Stud (GE-500)
1973-1975. Import from Japan, inexpensive materials, weight added for sustain, top-of-the-line in the Stud Series.

1970s		$375	$425

Thinline (By Burns)
1963-1964. Semi-hollowbody, 2 F-holes, 2 pickups, double-cut, tremolo, import by Burns of London, same as the Burns TR2 guitar.

1963-1964		$600	$700

Wild Dog (By Burns)
1963-1964. Solidbody, 3 pickups, shorter scale, tremolo, sunburst finish, import by Burns of London, same as the Burns Split Sound.

1963-1964		$600	$700

MODEL		EXC. COND.	
YEAR	FEATURES	LOW	HIGH

Wild Dog De Luxe (By Burns)
1963-1964. Solidbody, 3 pickups, bound neck, tremolo, sunburst finish, import by Burns of London, same as the Burns Split Sonic guitar.

1963-1964		$625	$725

Andersen Stringed Instruments
1978-present. Luthier Steve Andersen builds premium and presentation grade, production/custom flat-tops and archtops in Seattle, Washington. He also builds mandolins.

Andreas
1995-present. Luthier Andreas Pichler builds his aluminium-necked, solidbody guitars and basses in Dollach, Austria.

Angelica
Ca. 1967-1972. Entry-level guitars imported from Japan.
Electric Solidbodies
1970s		$125	$175

Angus
1976-present. Professional and premium grade, custom-made steel and nylon string flat-tops built by Mark Angus in Laguna Beach, California.

Antares
1980s-1990s. Korean-made budget electric and acoustic guitars imported by Vega Music International of Brea, California.
Double Neck 6/4
1990s. Cherry finish.
1990s		$400	$450
Solidbodies
1980s. Various models.
1980s		$125	$175

Antique Acoustics
1970s-present. Luthier Rudolph Blazer builds production/custom flat-tops, 12 strings, and archtops in Tubingen, Germany.

Antonio Lorca
Intermediate and professional grade, production, classical guitars made in Valencia, Spain.

Apollo
Ca. 1967-1972. Entry-level guitars imported by St. Louis Music. They also offered effects.
Electric
1967-1972. Japanese imports.
1967-1972	Advanced model, 4 pickups	$150	$250
1967-1972	Standard model, less features	$100	$150

1963 Ampeg Wild Dog Deluxe

Antique Acoustics Blazer SJ

GUITARS

Applegate flat-top

Aria Pro II Urchin Deluxe

MODEL YEAR	FEATURES	EXC. COND. LOW	HIGH

Applause

1976-present. Budget and intermediate grade, production, acoustic and acoustic/electric guitars. They also offer basses, mandolins and ukes. Kaman Music's entry-level Ovation-styled brand. The instruments were made in the U.S. until around '82, when production was moved to Korea. On the U.S.-made guitars, the back of the neck was molded Urelite, with a cast aluminum neck combining an I-beam neck reinforcement, fingerboard, and frets in one unit. The Korean models have traditional wood necks.

AA Models (acoustic)
Laminate top, plastic or composition body. Specs and features can vary on AA Models.

1976-1981	U.S.-made	$90	$140
1980s	Import	$80	$100

AE Models (acoustic/electric)
Laminate top, plastic or composition body. Specs and features can vary on AE Models.

1976-1981	U.S.-made	$175	$225
1980s	Import	$150	$175
1990s	Import	$150	$185

Applegate

2001-present. Premium grade, production/custom, acoustic and classical guitars built by luthier Brian Applegate in Minneapolis, Minnesota.

Arbor

1983-present. Budget and intermediate grade, production, classical, acoustic, and solid and semi-hollow body electric guitars imported by Musicorp (MBT).

Acoustic
1990s		$50	$150

Electric
1980s		$150	$225
1990s		$100	$150

Arch Kraft

1933-1934. Full-size acoustic archtop and flat-top guitars. Budget brand produced by the Kay Musical Instrument Company and sold through various distributors.

Acoustic (Archtop or Flat-top)
1930s		$250	$300

Aria Diamond

1960s. Brand name used by Aria in the '60s.

Electric
1960s. Various models and appointments in the '60s.

1960s		$300	$500

Aria/Aria Pro II

1960-present. Budget and intermediate grade, production, electric, acoustic, acoustic/electric, and classical guitars. They also make basses, mandolins, and banjos. Aria was established in Japan in '53 and started production of instruments in '60 using the Arai, Aria, Aria Diamond, and Diamond brands. The brand was renamed Aria Pro II in '75. Aria Pro II was used mainly on electric guitars, with Aria used on others. Over the years, they have produced acoustics, banjos, mandolins, electrics, basses, amplifiers, and effects. Around '87 production of cheaper models moved to Korea, reserving Japanese manufacturing for more expensive models. Around '95 some models were made in U.S., though most contemporary guitars sold in U.S. are Korean. In '01, the Pro II part of the name was dropped altogether.

Early Arias don't have serial numbers or pot codes. Serial numbers began to be used in the mid '70s. At least for Aria guitars made by Matsumoku, the serial number contains the year of manufacture in the first one or two digits (Y##### or YY####). Thus, a guitar from 1979 might begin with 79####. One from 1981 might begin with 1#####. The scheme becomes less sure after 1987. Some Korean-made guitars use a serial number with year and week indicated in the first four digits (YYWW####). Thus 9628#### would be from the 28th week of 1996. However, this is not the case on all guitars, and some have serial numbers which are not date-coded.

Models have been consolidated by sector unless specifically noted.

Acoustic Solid Wood Top
1960s-present. Steel string models, various appointments, generally mid-level imports.

1980s		$125	$250

Acoustic Veneer Wood Top
1960s-present. Steel string models, various appointments, generally entry-level imports.

1980s		$100	$200

Classical Solid Wood Top
1960s-present. Various models, various appointments, generally mid-level imports.

1980s		$125	$250

Classical Veneer Wood Top
1960s-present. Various models, various appointments, generally entry-level imports.

1980s		$75	$175

Fullerton Series
1995-2000. Various models with different appointments and configurations based on the classic offset double-cut solidbody.

1995-2000		$200	$275

Herb Ellis (PE-175/FA-DLX)
1978-1987 (Model PE-175) and 1988-1993 (Model FA-DLX). Archtop hollowbody, ebony 'board, 2 humbuckers.

1977-1987		$375	$600

Solidbody
1960s-present. Various models, various appointments, generally mid-level imports.

1960-1990		$225	$350

Titan Artist TA Series
1967-present. Double cut, semi-hollow bodies, 2 pickups, various models.

1980s		$225	$350

Armstrong, Rob

1971-present. Custom steel- and nylon-string flat-tops, 12 strings, and parlor guitars made in

MODEL YEAR	FEATURES	EXC. COND. LOW	HIGH

Coventry, England by luthier Rob Armstrong. He also builds mandolins and basses.

Arpeggio Korina

1995-present. Professional, premium and presentation grade, production/custom, korina wood solidbody guitars built by luthier Ron Kayfield in Pennsylvania.

58 Korina Reproduction V

1995		$825	$900

Art & Lutherie

Budget and intermediate grade, production, steel- and nylon-string acoustic and acoustic/electric guitars. Founded by luthier Robert Godin, who also has the Norman, Godin, Seagull, and Patrick & Simon brands of instruments.

Flat-Top Models

Various models.

2000s		$140	$160

Artesano

Professional grade, production, classical guitars built in Valencia, Spain, and distributed by Juan Orozco. Orozco also made higher-end classical Orozco Models 8, 10 and 15.

Models 20 to 50

1980s. Classical solid tops.

1980s		$200	$275

Artinger Custom Guitars

1997-present. Luthier Matt Artinger builds his professional and premium grade, production/custom, hollow, semi-hollow, and chambered solidbody guitars in Emmaus, Pennsylvania. He also builds basses.

Asama

1970s-1980s. Some models of this Japanese line of solidbody guitars featured built-in effects. They also offered basses, effects, drum machines and other music products.

Ashborn

1848-1864. James Ashborn, of Wolcottville, Connecticut, operated one of the largest guitar making factories of the mid-1800s. Models were small parlor-sized instruments with ladder bracing and gut strings. Most of these guitars will need repair. Often of more interest as historical artifacts or museum pieces versus guitar collections.

Model 2

1848-1864. Flat-top, plain appointments, no position markers on the neck, identified by Model number.

1855	Fully repaired	$450	$600

Model 5

1848-1864. Flat-top, higher appointments.

1855	Fully repaired	$1,300	$1,500

Asher

1982-present. Luthier Bill Asher builds his professional grade, production/custom, solidbody

electric guitars in Venice, California. He also builds lap steels.

Astro

1963-1964. The Astro AS-51 was a 1 pickup kit guitar sold by Rickenbacker.

Asturias

Professional and premium grade, production, classical guitars built on Kyushu island, in Japan.

Atkin Guitars

1993-present. Luthier Alister Atkin builds his production/custom steel and nylon string flat-tops in Canterbury, England. He also builds mandolins.

Audiovox

Ca. 1935-ca. 1950. Paul Tutmarc's Audiovox Manufacturing, of Seattle, Washington, was a pioneer in electric lap steels, basses, guitars and amps.

Austin

1999-present. Budget and intermediate grade, production, acoustic, acoustic/electric, resonator, and electric guitars imported by St. Louis Music. They also offer basses, mandolins and banjos.

Acoustic Flat-Top

Various models.

2000s		$100	$125

Solidbody Electric

Various models.

2001		$100	$145

Austin Hatchet

Mid-1970s-mid-1980s. Trademark of distributor Targ and Dinner, Chicago, Illinois.

Hatchet

1981. Travel guitar.

1981		$150	$175

Solidbody Electric

1970s-1980s. Various classic designs.

1980s		$100	$150

Avalon

1920s. Instruments built by the Oscar Schmidt Co. and possibly others. Most likely a brand made for a distributor.

Avante

1997-present. Intermediate grade, production, imported shape cutaway acoustic baritone guitars designed by Joe Veillette and Michael Tobias and offered by MusicYo. Originally higher priced instruments offered by Alvarez, there was the baritone, a 6-string and a bass.

AV-2 Baritone

1997-present. Baritone guitar tuned B to B, solid spruce cutaway top, mahogany sides and back.

1990s		$300	$350

Art & Lutherie Cedar

1855 Ashborn Model 2

Babicz D'Esque

Avanti

1960s. Guitar brand imported from Europe.
Electric Solidbody
1960s. Solidbody, 3 single-coils, dot markers.

MODEL YEAR	FEATURES	EXC. COND. LOW	HIGH
1960s		$125	$200

Babicz

2004-present. Started by luthier Jeff Babicz and Jeff Carano, who worked together at Steinberger, the company offers intermediate, professional, and premium grade, production/custom, acoustic and acoustic/electric guitars made in Poughkeepsie, New York, and overseas.

Bacon & Day

Established in 1921 by David Day and Paul Bacon, primarily known for fine quality tenor and plectrum banjos in the '20s and '30s. Purchased by Gretsch ca. '40.
Belmont
1950s. Gretsch era, 2 DeArmond pickups, natural.

1950s		$1,250	$1,350

Ramona Archtop
1938-1940. Sunburst.

1938-1940		$600	$1,000

Senorita Guitar
1940. Sunburst, mahogany back and sides.

1940		$700	$1,200

Sultana I
1930s. Large 18 1/4" acoustic archtop, Sultana engraved on tailpiece, block markers, bound top and back, sunburst.

1938		$3,600	$4,000

Baker U.S.A.

1997-present. Professional and premium grade, production/custom, solidbody electric guitars. Established by master builder Gene Baker after working at the Custom Shops of Gibson and Fender, Baker produced solid- and hollowbody guitars in Santa Maria, California. They also built basses. Baker also produced the Mean Gene brand of guitars from '88-'90. In September '03, the company was liquidated and the Baker U.S.A. name was sold to Robert English and Ed Roman. Gene Baker is no longer involved with Baker U.S.A.
B1/B1 Chambered/B1 Hollow
1997-present. Double-cut mahogany body, maple top, with a wide variety of options including chambered and hollowbody construction, set-neck.

1997-2003		$2,200	$2,700

BJ/BJ Hollow
1997-2003. Double-cut mahogany body, P-90-type pickups, several options available, set-neck.

1997-2003		$1,800	$2,200

BNT
1997-2000. Mahogany solidbody, maple top, neck-thru body, with various finishes and options.

1997-2000		$2,000	$2,500

1967 Baldwin Baby Bison

Baldwin

1965-1970. Founded in 1862, in Cincinnati, when reed organ and violin teacher Dwight Hamilton Baldwin opened a music store that eventually became one of the largest piano retailers in the Midwest. By 1965, the Baldwin Piano and Organ company was ready to buy into the guitar market but was outbid by CBS for Fender. Baldwin did procure Burns of London in September '65, and sold the guitars in the U.S. under the Baldwin name. Baldwin purchased Gretsch in '67. English production of Baldwin guitars ends in '70, after which Baldwin concentrates on the Gretsch brand.

Baby Bison (Model 560 by mid-1966)
1966-1970. Double-cut solidbody, V headstock, 2 pickups, shorter scale, tremolo, black, red or white finishes.

MODEL YEAR	FEATURES	EXC. COND. LOW	HIGH
1965-1966		$600	$700
1966-1970	Model 560	$500	$600

Bison (Model 511 by mid-1966)
1965-1970. Double-cut solidbody, scroll headstock, 3 pickups, tremolo, black or white finishes.

1965-1966		$900	$1,100
1966-1970	Model 511	$800	$1,000

Double Six (Model 525 by mid-1966)
1965-1970. Offset double-cut solidbody, 12 strings, 3 pickups, green or red sunburst.

1965-1966		$1,200	$1,300
1966-1970	Model 525	$1,100	$1,200

G.B. 65
1965-1966. Baldwin's first acoustic/electric, single-cut D-style flat-top, dual bar pickups.

1965-1966		$600	$700

G.B. 66 De Luxe
1965-1967. Same as Standard with added density control on treble horn, golden sunburst.

1965-1967		$700	$800

G.B. 66 Standard
1965-1966. Thinline Electric archtop, dual Ultra-Sonic pickups, offset cutaways, red sunburst.

1965-1966		$650	$750

Jazz Split Sound/Split Sound (Model 503 mid-1966)
1965-1970. Offset double-cut solidbody, scroll headstock, 3 pickups, tremolo, red sunburst or solid colors.

1965-1966		$600	$700
1966-1970	Model 503	$550	$650

Marvin (Model 524 by mid-1966)
1965-1970. Offset double-cut solidbody, scroll headstock, 3 pickups, tremolo, white or brown finish.

1965-1966		$1,200	$1,300
1966-1970	Model 524	$1,000	$1,100

Model 706
1967-1970. Double-cut semi-hollowbody, scroll headstock, 2 pickups, 2 f-holes, no vibrato, red or golden sunburst.

1967-1970		$600	$700

Model 706 V
1967-1970. Model 706 with vibrato.

1967-1970			$750

MODEL YEAR	FEATURES	EXC. COND. LOW	HIGH

Model 712 R Electric XII
1967-1970. Model 712 with regular neck, red or gold sunburst.

1967-1970		$700	$800

Model 712 T Electric XII
1967-1970. Model 712 with thin neck, red or gold sunburst.

1967-1970		$650	$750

Model 801 CP Electric Classical
1968-1970. Grand concert-sized classical with transducer based pickup system, natural pumpkin finish.

1968-1970		$700	$800

Nu-Sonic
1965-1966. Solidbody electric student model, 6-on-a-side tuners, black or cherry finish.

1965-1966		$425	$525

Vibraslim (Model 548 by late-1966)
1965-1970. Double-cut semi-hollowbody, 2 pickups, tremolo, 2 f-holes, red or golden sunburst. Notable spec changes with Model 548 in '66.

1965-1966		$700	$800
1966-1970	Model 548	$600	$700

Virginian (Model 550 by mid-1966)
1965-1970. Single-cut flat-top with 2 pickups, 1 on each side of soundhole, scroll headstock, tremolo, natural.

1965-1966		$700	$800
1966-1970	Model 550	$650	$750

Baranik Guitars
1995-present. Premium grade, production/custom steel-string flat-tops made in Tempe, Arizona by luthier Mike Baranik.

Barclay
1960s. Thinline acoustic/electric archtops, solidbody electric guitars and basses imported from Japan. Generally shorter scale beginner guitars.

Electric Solidbody Guitars
1960s. Various models and colors.

1960s		$150	$225

Barcus-Berry
1964-present. Founded by John Berry and Les Barcus introducing the first piezo crystal transducer. Martin guitar/Barcus-Berry products were offered in the mid-'80s. They also offered a line of amps from around '76 to ca. '80.

2500 Model Series
Mid-1980s. Various acoustic and acoustic/electric models.

1980s		$250	$350

Barrington
1988-1991. Imports offered by Barrington Guitar Werks, of Barrington, Illinois. Models included solidbody guitars and basses, archtop electrics, and acoustic flat-tops. Barrington Music Products is still in the music biz, offering LA saxophones and other products.

BGW-800 (acoustic/electric)
1988-1991. Acoustic/electric, flat-top single-cut with typical round soundhole, opaque white.

1988-1991		$450	$500

BRG-883 T (solidbody)
1988-ca 1991. Barrington's line of pointy headstock, double-cut solidbodies, black.

1988-1991		$125	$175

Bartell of California
1964-1969. Founded by Paul Barth (Magnatone) and Ted Peckles. Mosrite-inspired designs.

Electric 12
1967. Mosrite-style body.

1967		$1,150	$1,300

Bartolini
Early 1960s. European-made (likely Italian) guitars. Similar to Gemelli guitars, so most likely from same manufacturer.

Solidbody
1960s.

1960s		$375	$475

Bashkin Guitars
1998-present. Luthier Michael Bashkin builds his premium grade, custom, steel-string acoustics in Fort Collins, Colorado.

Baxendale & Baxendale
1975-present. Luthiers Scott Baxendale (father) and John Baxendale (son) build their professional and premium grade, custom, steel-string acoustic and solidbody electric guitars in Denver, Colorado. They were previously located in Tennessee and Texas.

Bay State
1865-ca.1910. Bay State was a trademark for Boston's John C. Haynes Co.

B.C. Rich
Ca. 1966/67-present. Budget, intermediate, and premium grade, production/custom, import and U.S.-made, electric and acoustic guitars. They also offer basses. Founded by Bernardo Chavez Rico in Los Angeles, California. As a boy he worked for his guitar-maker father Bernardo Mason Rico (Valencian Guitar Shop, Casa Rico, Bernardo's Guitar Shop), building first koa ukes and later, guitars, steel guitars and Martin 12-string conversions. He started using the B.C. Rich name ca. '66-'67 and made about 300 acoustics until '68, when first solidbody electric made using a Fender neck.

Rich's early models were based on Gibson and Fender designs. First production instruments were in '69 with 10 fancy Gibson EB-3 bass and 10 matching Les Paul copies, all carved out of single block of mahogany. Early guitars with Gibson humbuckers, then Guild humbuckers, and, from '74-'86, DiMarzio humbuckers. About 150 B.C. Rich Eagles were

1900 Bay State parlour guitar

Bashkin Placencia

1982 B.C. Rich Bich

B.C. Rich Eagle Supreme

imported from Japan in '76. Ca. '76 or '77 some bolt-neck guitars with parts made by Wayne Charvel were offered. Acoustic production ended in '82 (acoustics were again offered in '95).

For '83-'86 the B.C. Rich N.J. Series (N.J. Nagoya, Japan) was built by Masan Tarada. U.S. Production Series (U.S.-assembled Korean kits) in '84. From '86 on, the N.J. Series was made by Cort in Korea. Korean Rave and Platinum series begin around '86. In '87, Rich agrees to let Class Axe of New Jersey market the Korean Rave, Platinum and N.J. Series. Class Axe (with Neal Moser) introduces Virgin in '87 and in '88 Rave and Platinum names are licensed to Class Axe. In '89, Rico licensed the BC Rich name to Class Axe. Both imported and American-made BC Riches are offered during Class Axe management. In 2000, BC Rich became a division of Hanser Holdings.

During '90-'91, Rico begins making his upscale Mason Bernard guitars (approx. 225 made). In '94, Rico resumes making B.C. Rich guitars in California. He died in 1999.

First 340-360 U.S.-built guitars were numbered sequentially beginning in '72. Beginning in '74, serial numbers change to YYZZZ pattern (year plus consecutive production). As production increased in the late-'70s, the year number began getting ahead of itself. By '80 it was 2 years ahead; by '81 as much as four years ahead. No serial number codes on imports.

Assassin

1986-1998. Double-cut body, 2 humbuckers, maple thru-neck dot markers, various colors.

MODEL YEAR	FEATURES	EXC. COND. LOW	HIGH
1986-1989	1st Rico era	$750	$850
1989-1993	Class Axe era, neck-thru	$700	$800
1994-1998	2nd Rico era USA, neck-thru	$700	$800

B-28 Acoustic

Ca.1967-1982. Acoustic flat-top, hand-built, solid spruce top, rosewood back and sides, herringbone trim, pearl R headstock logo.

1970-1982		$400	$900

B-30 Acoustic

Ca.1967-1982. Acoustic flat-top.

1960s		$400	$900

B-38 Acoustic

Ca.1967-1982. Acoustic flat-top, cocobolo back and sides, herringbone trim.

1960s		$400	$900

B-41 Acoustic

1970s. Brazilian rosewood.

1970s		$1,400	$2,000

B-45 Acoustic

Hand-built, D-style rosewood body.

1970s		$1,900	$2,500

Bich (U.S.A. assembly)

1978-1998. Four-point sleek body, came in Standard top or Supreme with highly figured maple body and active EQ.

1978-1979	Supreme	$1,600	$1,900
1980-1989	Standard	$1,100	$1,200
1980-1989	Supreme	$1,400	$1,600

MODEL YEAR	FEATURES	EXC. COND. LOW	HIGH
1989-1993	Class Axe NJ era	$800	$900
1994-1998	2nd Rico era USA bolt-on	$800	$900
1994-1998	2nd Rico era USA neck-thru	$1,000	$1,200

Bich 10-String

1978-present. Doubles on 4 low strings.

1978-1982		$2,300	$3,000

Black Hole

1988. Bolt neck, rosewood 'board, integrated pickup design, Floyd Rose.

1988		$200	$300

Body Art Collection

2003-present. Imports with different exotic graphics on different models issued each month from January '03 to March '04, 25th Anniversary model still available.

2003	Boris Beast	$125	$175
2003	Space Face Ironbird	$125	$175
2003	Torchy ASM	$125	$175
2004	40 Lashes Mockingbird	$175	$225
2004	Umethar Jr. V	$145	$175

Bronze Series

2001-present. Made in China. Includes 2 models; Mockingbird and Warlock.

2000s		$75	$150

Doubleneck Models

1980s. Doublenecks were sporadically made and specs (and values) may vary.

1980s	Bich	$2,500	$3,500
1980s	Eagle	$3,000	$3,500
1980s	Iron Bird custom order	$2,000	$2,500
1980s	Mockingbird	$2,500	$3,000
1980s	Seagull custom order	$3,000	$3,500

Eagle (USA)

1977-1996, 2000-2004. Curved double-cut solidbody, neck-thru. Models included are the Standard, Deluxe, Special and Supreme which is a highly figured, higher end model.

1977-1979	Standard	$1,200	$1,500
1977-1979	Supreme	$1,700	$2,500
1977-1982	Special	$950	$1,300
1980-1982	Standard, 3-on-a-side tuners	$1,100	$1,400
1980-1982	Supreme	$1,500	$2,100
2000-2004	Supreme	$1,700	$2,000

Elvira

2001. Elvira (the witch) photo on black Warlock body, came with Casecore coffin case.

2000s		$375	$400

Exclusive EM1

1996-2004. Offset double-cut, bound top, 2 humbuckers.

2000s		$200	$250

Gunslinger

1987-1999. Inverted headstock, 1 (Gunslinger I) or 2 (Gunslinger II) humbuckers, recessed cutout behind Floyd Rose allows player to pull notes up 2 full steps.

1987-1989	Standard finish	$500	$700

MODEL YEAR	FEATURES	EXC. COND. LOW	HIGH
1987-1989	Various graphic designs	$750	$850
1989-1993	Class Axe New Jersey era	$500	$600
1994-1999	2nd Rico era, bolt-on	$500	$600
1994-1999	2nd Rico era, neck-thru	$500	$600

Ironbird
1983-2004. Pointy body and headstock.

1983-1984		$650	$850

Kerry King Wartribe1 Warlock
2004-present. Tribal Fire finish, 2 pickups.

2004		$210	$235

Mockingbird
1976-present. Includes Standard and Supreme (fancier features) models, bolt or neck-thru.

1976-1978	Earlier short horn	$1,900	$2,300
1976-1978	Supreme, short horn	$2,200	$2,700
1979-1983	Later long horn	$2,000	$2,400
1979-1983	Supreme	$2,200	$2,700
1984-1989	Last of 1st Rico era	$1,600	$2,400
1994-1999	2nd Rico era, bolt-on	$1,300	$1,700
1994-1999	2nd Rico era, Supreme	$1,600	$2,000

Mockingbird Ice Acrylic
2004-present. See-thru acrylic body.

2004		$275	$325

Nighthawk
1978-ca.1982. Eagle-shaped body with bolt neck.

1978-1982		$500	$675

NJ Series
1983-1986. Earlier models made in Japan. Made in Korea '86 forward. All NJ models fall within the same price range.. Models include; Assassin, Beast, Bich, Ironbird, Mockingbird, Outlaw, ST III, Virgin, Warlock.

1983-1986		$325	$475
1987-1989		$250	$450
1990-1999		$250	$450

Phoenix
1977-ca.1982. Mockingbird-shaped with bolt neck.

1977-1982		$550	$700

Platinum Series
1986-present. Imported versions including Assassin, Beast, Bich, Ironbird, ST, Warlock.

1986-1989		$250	$375
1990-1999		$250	$375

Rave Series
1986-ca. 1990. Korean-made down-market versions of popular models.

1980s		$180	$200

Seagull/Seagull II/Seagull Jr.
1972-1977. Solidbody, neck-thru, 2 humbuckers, Seagull ('72-'75) is single-cut, II and Jr. ('75-'77) double-cut.

1972-1975	Initial design	$1,000	$1,600
1972-1975	Supreme	$1,300	$1,700
1975-1977	II & Jr.	$1,000	$1,500

Stealth I Series
1983-1989. Includes Standard (maple body, diamond inlays) and Series II (mahogany body, dot inlays), 2 pickups.

1983-1989	Series II	$900	$1,200
1983-1989	Standard	$900	$1,200

ST-III (U.S.A.-made)
1987-1998. Double-cut solidbody, hum/single/single or 2 humbucker pickups, Kahler tremolo.

1987-1989	Bolt-on	$500	$600
1987-1989	Neck-thru	$600	$700
1989-1993	Class Axe era	$500	$600
1994-1998	New Rico era, neck-thru & bolt-on	$500	$600

The Mag
2000. U.S. Handcrafted Series Mockingbird Acoustic Supreme, solid spruce top, quilt maple back and sides, pickup with preamp and EQ optional, dark sunburst.

2000		$850	$950

Warlock (USA)
1981-present. Four-point sleek body style with widow headstock.

1981-1989	Standard	$1,100	$1,300
1981-1989	Supreme	$1,400	$1,800
1994-1999	2nd Rico era, bolt-on	$900	$1,000
1994-1999	2nd Rico era, neck-thru	$1,000	$1,400

Warlock Ice Acrylic
2004-present. See-thru acrylic body.

2004		$250	$350

Wave
1983. U.S.-made, very limited production based upon the Wave bass.

1983		$1,500	$2,000

Bear Creek Guitars
1995-present. Luthier Bill Hardin worked for OMI Dobro and Santa Cruz Guitar before introducing his own line of professional and premium grade, custom-made Wessenborn-style guitars, made in Kula, Hawaii. He also builds ukes.

Beardsell Guitars
1996-present. Production/custom flat-tops, classical and electric solidbody guitars built by luthier Allan Beardsell in Toronto, Ontario.

Behringer
1989-present. The German professional audio products company added budget, production, solidbody guitars in '03, sold in amp/guitar packages. They also offer effects and amps.

Beltona
1990-present. Production/custom metal body resonator guitars made in New Zealand by Steve Evans and Bill Johnson. Beltona was originally located in England. They also build ukes.

1979 B.C. Rich Mockingbird Deluxe

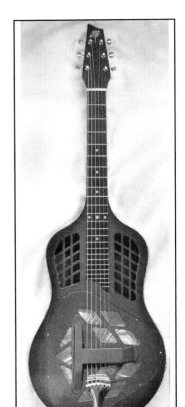

Beltona Pacifika Tricone

GUITARS

GUITARS

Benedetto Bravo

1985 Bently Series 10 graphite

MODEL YEAR	FEATURES	EXC. COND. LOW	HIGH

Beltone
1930s-1940s. Lower-end models.
Resonator Copy
1930s-1940s. Resonator copy but without a real resonator, rather just an aluminum plate on a wooden top, body mahogany plywood.

1938		$300	$400

Benedetto
1968-present. Archtop guitars, violins and a few solidbodies hand-crafted by Robert Benedetto in East Stroudsburg, Pennsylvania. He is especially known for refining the 7-string guitar. As of '99, Benedetto only makes special order instruments. He licensed the names of his standard models to Guild, which now makes them in their Custom Shop in Nashville, Tennessee. (Refer to Benedetto FMIC for post-'99 instruments.)
Benny
1990s. Electric semi-hollow, 14 1/2" body, cutaway, chambered Sitka spruce top, natural.

1990s		$4,000	$6,500

Benny Deluxe
1990s. Electric semi-hollow, chambered spruce top, abalone inlays, deluxe version of the Benny, sunburst.

1990s		$5,000	$7,500

Cremona
1988-1991. Acoustic/electric archtop, single-cut, 17" body, natural.

1988-1991		$18,000	$22,000

Fratello
1988-1999. Acoustic archtop, single-cut, 17" body, blond or sunburst.

1980s		$10,000	$13,000
1990s		$10,000	$13,000

La Venezia
1990s. Acoustic archtop, single-cut, 17" body, sunburst.

1990s		$12,000	$16,000

Limelite Custom
1990s. Single-cut, neck pickup, select aged wood, blond.

1990s		$20,000	$24,000

Manhattan
1989-1999. Archtop with 16" body, neck pickup, blond.

1989-1999		$11,000	$14,000

Manhattan Custom
1990s. Carved 17" body, blond.

1990s		$13,000	$16,000

Benedetto (FMIC)
1999-present. Premium and presentation, production/custom, acoustic and electric archtops. In '99, Bob Benedetto entered into an agreement with Fender (FMIC) to have the FMIC Guild Custom Shop, Nashville, Tennessee, build Benedetto guitars under his guidance and supervision. The guitars are now built in Fender's Corona, California, facility.

Artist/Artist Award
2000-2003. Full body, rounded cutaway, single neck pickup, natural or sunburst.

2000-2003		$4,500	$5,000

Fratello
2000-present. Single-cut archtop, block inlays, mini-humbucker.

2000-2003		$9,000	$10,500

Manhattan
2000-present. 17" single-cut archtop (3" deep), suspended mini-humbucking pickup.

2000-2003		$9,500	$11,000

Bently
ca.1985-1998. Student and intermediate grade copy style acoustic and electric guitars imported by St. Louis Music Supply. Includes the Series 10 electrics and the Songwriter acoustics (which have a double reversed B crown logo on the headstock). St. Louis Music replaced the Bently line with the Austin brand.
Series 10 (Electric)
1980s. Electric solidbody guitars, various colors.

1980s		$50	$100

Songwriter Series (Acoustic)
1980s. Acoustic guitars, spruce top, mahogany, natural finish.

1980s		$40	$90

Bernie Rico Jr. Guitars
Professional and premium grade, production/custom, solidbody electrics built by luther Bernie Rico, Jr., the son of BC Rich founder, in Hesperia, California. He also makes basses.

Bertoncini Stringed Instruments
1995-present. Luthier Dave Bertoncini builds his premium grade, custom, flat-top guitars in Olympia, Washington. He has also built solidbody electrics, archtops, mandolins and banjos.

Beyond The Trees
1976-present. Luthier Fred Carlson offers a variety of innovative designs for his professional and presentation grade, production/custom 6- and 12-string flat-tops in Santa Cruz, California. He also produces the Sympitar (a 6-string with added sympathetic strings) and the Dreadnautilus (an unique shaped headless acoustic).

Bigsby
1946-present. Pedal steel guitars, hollow-chambered electric Spanish guitars, electric mandolins, doublenecks, replacement necks on acoustic guitars, hand vibratos, all handmade by Paul Arthur Bigsby, machinist and motorcycle enthusiast (designer of '30s Crocker motorcycles), in Downey, California. Initially built for special orders.
Bigsby was a pioneer in developing pedal steels. He designed a hand vibrato for Merle Travis. In '48, his neck-through hollow electrics (with Merle Travis)

MODEL YEAR	FEATURES	EXC. COND. LOW	HIGH

influenced Leo Fender, and Bigsby employed young Semie Moseley. In '56, he designed the Magnatone Mark series guitars and 1 Hawaiian lap steel.

He built less than 50 Spanish guitars, 6 mandolins, 125 to 150 pedal steels and 12 or so neck replacements. SN was stamped on the end of fingerboard: MMD-DYY. In '65, the company was sold to Gibson president Ted McCarty who moved the tremolo/vibrato work to Kalamazoo. Bigsby died in '68. Fred Gretsch purchased the Bigsby company from Ted McCarty in '99. A solidbody guitar and a pedal steel based upon the original Paul Bigsby designs were introduced January, 2002. Early Bigsby guitars command high value on the collectible market.

Solidbody Guitars
Late-1940s-early-1950s. Solidbody, natural.

1948-1952	$20,000	$24,000

Bil Mitchell Guitars
1979-present. Luthier Bil Mitchell builds his professional and premium grade, production/custom, flat-top and archtop guitars originally in Wall, New Jersey, and since '02 in Riegelsville, Pennsylvania.

Bischoff Guitars
1975-present. Professional and premium-grade, custom-made flat-tops built by luthier Gordy Bischoff in Eau Claire, Wisconsin.

Bishline Guitars
1985-present. Luthier Robert Bishline builds custom-made flat-tops and resonators in Tulsa, Oklahoma. He also builds mandolins and banjos.

Black Jack
1960s. Violin-body hollowbody electric guitars and basses, possibly others. Imported from Japan by unidentified distributor. Manufacturers unknown, but some may be Arai.

Blackshear, Tom
1958-present. Premium and presentation grade, production, classical and flamenco guitars made by luthier Tom Blackshear in San Antonio, Texas.

Blade
1987-present. Intermediate and professional grade, production, solidbody guitars from luthier Gary Levinson and his Levinson Music Products Ltd. located in Switzerland. He also builds basses.

California Custom
1994-present. California Standard with maple top and high-end appointments.

1994-1999	$600	$1,000

California Deluxe/Deluxe
1994-1995. Standard with mahogany body and maple top.

1994-1995	$425	$700

California Hybrid
1998-1999. Standard with piezo bridge pickup.

1998-1999	$400	$650

California Standard
1994-present. Offset double-cut, swamp ash body, bolt neck, 5-way switch.

1994-1999	$275	$450

R 3
1988-1993. Offset double-cut maple solidbody, bolt maple neck, 3 single-coils or single/single/humbucker.

1988-1993	$300	$500

R 4
1988-1993. R 3 with ash body and see-thru color finishes.

1988-1992	$350	$600

Texas Series
2003-present. Includes Standard (3 single-coils) and Deluxe (gold hardware, single/single/hum pickups).

2003-2005 Deluxe	$500	$600
2003-2005 Standard	$450	$550

Blanchard Guitars
1994-present. Luthier Mark Blanchard builds premium grade, custom steel-string and classical guitars originally in Mammoth Lakes, California, and since May '03, in northwest Montana.

Blue Star
1984-present. Luthier Bruce Herron builds his production/custom guitars in Fennville, Michigan. He also builds mandolins, lap steels, dulcimers and ukes.

Travelmaster
1990s. Various colors.

1990s	$150	$250

Bluebird
1920s-1930s. Private brand with Bluebird painted on headstock, built by the Oscar Schmidt Co. and possibly others. Most likely made for distributor.

13" Flat-Top
1930s.

1930s	$100	$150

Blueridge
Early 1980s-present. Intermediate and professional grade, production, solid-top acoustic guitars distributed by Saga. In '00, the product line was redesigned with the input of luthier Greg Rich (Rich and Taylor guitars).

BR-263
2000-present. 000 size flat-top, solid spruce top, Brazilian rosewood back and sides.

2000-2003	$1,300	$1,500

Bluesouth
1991-present. Custom electric guitars built by luthier Ronnie Knight in Muscle Shoals, Alabama. He also built basses.

Boaz Elkayam Guitars
1985-present. Presentation grade, custom steel, nylon, and flamenco guitars made by luthier Boaz Elkayam in Chatsworth, California.

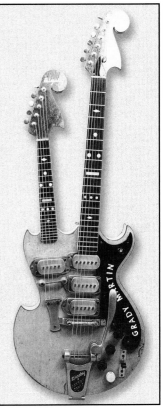

1952 Bigsby Grady Martin Doubleneck

Blueridge BR140

GUITARS

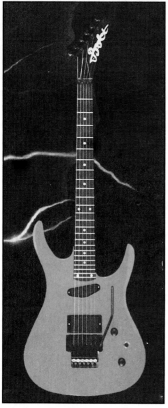

Bolt Viper 100

Bourgeois D-150

MODEL		EXC. COND.	
YEAR	FEATURES	LOW	HIGH

Bohmann

1878-ca. 1926. Acoustic flat-top guitars, harp guitars, mandolins, banjos, violins made in Chicago Illinois, by Joseph Bohmann (born 1848, in Czechoslovakia). Bohmann's American Musical Industry founded 1878. Guitar body widths are 12", 13", 14", 15". He had 13 grades of guitars by 1900 (Standard, Concert, Grand Concert sizes). Early American use of plywood. Some painted wood finishes. Special amber-oil varnishes. Tuner bushings. Early ovalled fingerboards. Patented tuner plates and bridge design. Steel engraved label inside. Probably succeeded by son Joseph Frederick Bohmann.

Ca. 1896 12" body faux rosewood, 13", 14" and 15" body faux rosewood birch, 12", 13", 14" and 15" body sunburst maple, 12", 13", 14" and 15" body rosewood. By 1900 Styles 0, 1, 2 and 3 Standard, Concert and Grand Concert maple, Styles 1, 2, 3, 4, 5, 6, 7, 8, 9, 10, 11 and 12 in Standard, Concert, and Grand Concert rosewood.

14 3/4" Flat-Top

Solid spruce top, veneered Brazilian rosewood back and sides, wood marquetry around top and soundhole, natural. Each Bohmann should be valued on a case-by-case basis.

1900		$1,000	$1,300

Bolin

1978-present. Professional and premium grade, production/custom, solidbody guitars built by luthier John Bolin in Boise, Idaho. Bolin is well-known for his custom work. His Cobra guitars are promoted and distributed by Sanderson Sales and Marketing as part of the Icons of America Series.

NS

1996-present. Slot-headstock, bolt-on neck, single-cut solidbody, Seymour Duncan passive pickups or EMG active, from '96 to the fall of 2001 custom-built serial numbers to 0050 then from the fall of '01 to the present production model build starting with SN 0051.

1996-2001	Custom-built	$2,000	$3,000
2001-2003	Standard		
	production	$1,400	$1,800

Bolt

1988-1991. Founded by luthier Wayne Bolt and Jim Dala Pallu in Schnecksville, Pennsylvania, Bolt's first work was CNC machined OEM necks and bodies made for Kramer and BC Rich. In '90, they started building solidbody Bolt guitars, many with airbrushed graphics. Only about 100 to 125 were built, around 40 with graphics.

Bond

1984-1985. Andrew Bond made around 1,400 Electraglide guitars in Scotland. Logo says 'Bond Guitars, London.'

ElectraGlide

1984-1985. Black carbon graphite 1-piece body and neck, double-cut, 3 single-coils (2 humbuckers were

MODEL		EXC. COND.	
YEAR	FEATURES	LOW	HIGH

also supposedly available), digital LED controls that required a separate transformer.

1984-1985		$900	$1,200

Bourgeois

1993-1999, 2000-present. Luthier Dana Bourgeois builds his professional and premium grade, production/custom, acoustic and archtop guitars in Lewiston, Maine. Bourgeois co-founded Schoenberg guitars and built Schoenberg models from '86-'90. Bourgeois' 20th Anniversary model was issued in '97. Bourgeois Guitars, per se, went of business at the end of '99. Patrick Theimer created Pantheon Guitars, which included 7 luthiers (including Bourgeois) working in an old 1840s textile mill in Lewiston, Maine and Bourgeois models continue to be made as part of the Pantheon organization.

Country Boy

1990s-present. Pre-war D-style model designed for Ricky Skaggs with Sitka spruce top, select mahogany back and sides, Bourgeois script logo headstock inlay, individually labeled with a Ricky Skaggs label, natural.

1990s		$1,600	$2,000

Country Boy Deluxe

2000-present. Country Boy with Adirondack spruce top.

2000s		$1,800	$2,100

D - 20th Anniversary

1997. 20 made, bearclaw spruce top, rosewood back and sides, mother-of-pearl 'board, ornate abalone floral pattern inlay, abalone rosette and border, natural.

1997		$3,100	$3,300

JOM

1990s-present. Jumbo Orchestra Model flat-top, 15 5/8". Model includes one with cedar top, mahogany back and sides, and one with spruce top, Brazilian rosewood back and sides.

1990s	Brazilian rosewood	$2,900	$3,700
1990s	Mahogany	$1,100	$1,400

JR-A

1990s. Artisan Series, 15 5/8", spruce top, rosewood back and sides.

1990s		$700	$1,000

Martin Simpson

1997-2003. Grand auditorium with unusual cutaway that removes one-half of the upper treble bout, Englemann spruce top, Indian rosewood back and sides, natural.

1997-2003		$2,400	$2,500

OM Soloist

1990s-present. Full-sized, soft cutaway flat-top, Adirondack spruce top, figured Brick Red Brazilian rosewood back and sides, natural.

1990s		$4,800	$5,000

Slope D

1993-present. D-size, 16", spruce top, mahogany back and sides.

1993-2000		$1,700	$1,900

MODEL YEAR	FEATURES	EXC. COND. LOW	HIGH

Bown Guitars

1981-present. Luthier Ralph Bown builds custom steel-string, nylon-string, baritone, and harp guitars in Walmgate, England.

Bozo

1964-present. Bozo (pronounced Bo-zho) Padunovac learned instrument building in his Yugoslavian homeland and arrived in the United States in '59. In '64 he opened his own shop and has built a variety of high-end, handmade, acoustic instruments, many being one-of-a-kind. He has built around 570 guitars over the years. There were several thousand Japanese-made (K. Yairi shop) Bell Western models bearing his name made from '79-'80; most of these were sold in Europe. He currently builds premium and presentation grade, production/custom guitars in Lindenhurst, Illinois.

Acoustic 12-String
1970-1980s. Indian rosewood.

1970-1980s		$1,500	$2,500

Cutaway 12-String
1977-1998. Often old world Balkan ornamentation, generally Sitka spruce top, Indian rosewood back and sides, widow-style headstock, ornamentation can vary (standard or elaborate).

1977	Standard	$1,500	$2,000
1993	Elaborate	$4,000	$5,000
1998	Elaborate custom	$5,000	$6,000

Bradford

Mid-1960s. Brand name used by the W.T. Grant Company, one of the old Five & Ten style retail stores similar to F.W. Woolworth and Kresge. Many of these instruments were made in Japan by Guyatone.

Acoustic Flat-Top
1960s. Various colors.

1960s		$75	$150

Electric Solidbody
1960s. Various colors.

1960s		$100	$175

Brawley Basses

Headquartered in Temecula, California, and designed by Keith Brawley, offering solidbody guitars made in Korea. They also made basses.

Breedlove

1990-present. Founded by Larry Breedlove and Steve Henderson. Intermediate, professional, premium, and presentation grade, production/custom, steel and nylon string flat-tops built in Tumalo, Oregon and imported. They also build mandolins. Several available custom options may add to the values listed here.

AD20/SM (Atlas Series)
2004-present. Imported solid spruce top, solid mahogany back and sides, pinless bridge.

2004		$250	$300

C1 (C10)
1990-2004. Shallow concert-sized flat-top, non-cut, solid spruce top, mahogany back and sides, natural.

1990s		$1,500	$1,700

C2 (C22)
1990-present. Highly figured walnut body with sitka spruce top, large sloping cutaway.

1990s		$1,800	$2,000

C5/Northwest
1995-present. Grand concert with large soft cutaway, sitka spruce top, figured myrtlewood body.

2000-2004		$2,200	$2,300

C15/R
1990-2004. Concert-size C1 with soft rounded cutaway, and optional cedar top and rosewood back and sides, gold tuners.

1990s		$1,800	$2,000

C-20
1990s-present. Concert series, mahgoany back and sides, sitka spruce top.

2000s		$1,800	$2,000

C25 Custom
1990s-present. Custom koa body, sitka spruce top.

2000-2004		$2,400	$2,600

CM
1990s-present. Unusual double-cut style, walnut body and top.

1990s		$3,700	$3,900

D20
2002-present. Sitka spruce top, mahogany body, non cut.

2002-2004		$1,900	$2,000

D25/R
2002-present. Cutaway, sitka spruce top, Indian rosewood back and sides.

2002-2004		$2,100	$2,200

Ed Gerhard
1997-present. Shallow jumbo, soft cut, Indian rosewood body.

2000s	Custom	$2,300	$2,500
2000s	Signature	$2,150	$2,250

J Series (Jumbo)
1990s-present. Spruce top, myrtlewood body.

2000s	J25	$2,500	$2,600

Myrtlewood Limited 01
Ca.1990s-2003. Acoustic/electric, D-size, solid spruce top, solid myrtlewood back and sides.

1990s		$1,650	$1,750

N25E
2000-present. Acoustic/electric version of N25.

2002		$1,700	$1,800

N25R
2000-present. Classical, Western red cedar top, solid Indian rosewood back and sides.

2000s		$1,800	$2,000

RD20 X/R
1999. Indian rosewood back and sides, sitka spruce top, winged bridge, abalone soundhole rosette.

1999		$1,650	$1,800

Bozo 40th Anniversary

Breedlove AD-25

1990s Brian Moore MC/1

MODEL YEAR	FEATURES	EXC. COND. LOW	HIGH
SC20			
	1990-present. Limited edition, various woods.		
1990-2000s		$1,600	$2,000
SC20-Z Custom			
	Mid-size with deep body, flat-top, Zircote back and sides, sitka spruce top.		
1999		$1,800	$2,000
SC25			
	1990-present. Limited edition, various woods.		
1990-2000		$1,700	$2,100
SJ20-12 W			
	1990s-present. 12-string, walnut (W) back and sides.		
2000s		$1,650	$1,800

Brentwood

1970s. Student models built by Kay for store or jobber.

K-100

1970s. 13" student flat-top, K-100 label inside back, K logo on 'guard.

1970s		$25	$50

Brian Moore

1992-present. Founded by Patrick Cummings, Brian Moore and Kevin Kalagher in Brewster, New York; they introduced their first guitars in '94. Initially expensive custom shop guitars with carbon-resin bodies with highly figured wood tops; later went to all wood bodies cut on CNC machines. The intermediate and professional grade, production, iGuitar/i2000series was introduced in 2000 and made in Korea, but set up in the U.S. Currently the premium grade, production/custom, Custom Shop Series guitars are handcrafted in La Grange, New York. They also build basses and electric mandolins.

C-45

1999-2001. Solidbody, mahogany body, bolt neck, 2 P-90-type pickups, natural satin.

1990s		$850	$1,050

C-55/C-55P

1997-2004. Solidbody, burl maple body, bolt neck, currently produced as a limited edition. C-55P indicates Piezo option.

1990s		$850	$1,050

C-90/C-90P

1996-present. Solidbody, figured maple top, mahogany body, bolt neck, hum-single-hum pickups, red sunburst. C-90P has Piezo option.

1990s		$1,300	$1,500

DC-1/DC-1P

1997-present. Quilted maple top, 2 humbuckers, single-cut, gold hardware. DC-1P has Piezo option.

1997-1998		$1,700	$2,000

i1

2000-present. Double-cut solidbody, maple top, mahogany body.

2000-2003		$475	$525

Briggs Avatar

MODEL YEAR	FEATURES	EXC. COND. LOW	HIGH
iGuitar 2.13			
	2000-present. The iGuitar series are Korean-made and are the same as the i2000 Series models, but feature a 13 pin RMC system for access to digital guitar processors.		
2000-2003		$700	$1,200
iGuitar 2P			
	2000-present. Single-cut solidbody, magnetic and piezo blend, maple top, Kalamta mahogany body and neck.		
2000-2003		$600	$700
iGuitar 8.13/81.13			
	2000-present. Mahogany body, figured maple top, 2 humbuckers, 13-pin adapter.		
2000-2003		$575	$775
MC1			
	1994-present. High-end model, quilted maple top, various pickup options including piezo and midi, gold hardware, currently produced as a limited edition- Should be evaluated on a case-by-case basis.		
1990s		$2,000	$3,000

Brian Stone Classical Guitars

Luthier Brian Stone builds his classical guitars in Corvallis, Oregon.

Briggs

1999-present. Luthier Jack Briggs builds his professional and premium grade, production/custom, chambered and solidbody guitars in Raleigh, North Carolina.

Broman

1930s. The Broman brand was most likely used by a music studio (or distributor) on instruments made by others, including Regal-built resonator instruments.

Brook Guitars

1993-present. Simon Smidmore and Andy Petherick build their production/custom Brook steel-string, nylon-strings, and archtops in Dartmoor, England.

Bruné, R. E.

1966-present. Luthier Richard Bruné builds his premium and presentation grade, custom, classical and flamenco guitars in Evanston, Illinois. He also offers his professional and premium grade Model 20 and Model 30, which are handmade in a leading guitar workshop in Japan. Bruné's "Guitars with Guts" column appears quarterly in *Vintage Guitar* magazine.

Bruno and Sons

1834-present. Established in 1834 by Charles Bruno, primarily as a distributor, Bruno and Sons marketed a variety of brands, including their own; currently part of Kaman.

Harp Guitar

1924		$2,000	$3,000

MODEL YEAR	FEATURES	EXC. COND. LOW	HIGH

Hollowbody Electrics
1960s-1970s. Various imported models.

1960s		$150	$250

Parlor Guitar
1880-1920. Various woods used on back and sides.

1880-1920	Birch	$300	$450
1880-1920	Brazilian rosewood	$800	$1,050
1880-1920	Mahogany	$400	$650

Bunker

1961-present. Founded by guitarist Dave Bunker, who started building custom guitars and basses while performing in Las Vegas in the '60s. Bunker began building guitars with his father and developed a number of innovations. Around '92 Bunker began PBC Guitar Technology in Allentown, Pennsylvania, building American-made instruments for Ibanez. PBC closed in '97 and Bunker moved back to Washington State to start Bunker Guitar Technology and resumed production of several Bunker models. In early 2002, Bunker Guitars became part of Maple Valley Tone Woods of Port Angeles, Washington. Currently Bunker offers intermediate, professional, and premium grade, production/custom, guitars and basses built in Port Angeles. Most early Bunker guitars were pretty much custom-made in low quantities.

Electric Solidbody or Archtop Guitars

1990s		$800	$900

Burns

1960-1970, 1974-1983, 1992-present. Intermediate and professional grade, production, electric guitars built in England and Korea. They also build basses. Jim Burns began building guitars in the late-'50s and established Burns London Ltd in '60. Baldwin Organ (see Baldwin listing) purchased the company in '65 and offered the instruments until '70. Burns tried the guitar biusiness a couple more times in the '70s and '80s. The Burns name was revived in '91 by Barry Gibson as Burns London, with Jim Burns' involvement, offering reproductions of some of the classic Burns models of the '60s. Jim Burns passed away in August '98.

Baby Bison
1965. Double-cut solidbody, scroll headstock, 2 pickups, shorter scale, tremolo.

1965		$700	$800

Bison
1964-1965. Double-cut solidbody, 3 pickups, tremolo, black or white, scroll-headstock, replaced flat headstock Black Bison. Has been reissued with both types of headstocks.

1964-1965		$1,100	$1,300
2000s	Reissue	$400	$475

Brian May Signature - Red Special
2002-present. Replica of May's original 'Red Special' but with added whammy-bar, red finish.

2000s		$600	$650

Cobra
2004-present. Double-cut solid, 2 pickups.

2000s		$150	$200

Double Six
1964-1965. Solidbody 12-string, double-cut, 3 pickups, greenburst. Has been reissued.

1964-1965		$1,400	$1,500

Flyte
1974-1977. Fighter jet-shaped solidbody, pointed headstock, 2 humbucking pickups, silver, has been reissued.

1974-1977		$700	$875

GB 66 Deluxe
1965. Like 66 Standard, but with bar pickups and add Density control.

1965		$800	$900

GB 66 Deluxe Standard
1965. Offset double-cut, f-holes, 2 Ultra-Sonic pickups.

1965		$750	$850

Jazz
1962-1965. Offset double-cut solid, shorter scale, 2 pickups.

1962-1965		$550	$650

Jazz Split Sound
1962-1965. Offset double-cut solid, 3 pickups, tremolo, red sunburst.

1962-1965		$700	$800

Marquee
2000-present. Offset double-cut solid, 3 pickups, scroll headstock

2000		$225	$275

Marvin
1964-1965. Offset double-cut solidbody, scroll headstock, 3 pickups, tremolo, white.

1964-1965		$1,400	$1,500

Nu-Sonic
1964-1965. Solidbody, 2 pickups, tremolo, white or cherry, has been reissued.

1964-1965		$500	$600

Sonic
1960-1964. Double shallow cut solid, 2 pickups, cherry.

1962-1964		$350	$450

Split Sonic
1962-1964. Solidbody, 3 pickups, bound neck, tremolo, red sunburst.

1962-1964		$725	$825

Steer
2000-present.

2000s		$250	$300

TR-2
1963-1964. Semi-hollw, 2 pickups, red sunburst.

1963-1964		$800	$900

Vibraslim
1964-1965. Double-cut, f-holes, 2 pickups, red sunburst.

1964-1965		$800	$900

Virginian
1964-1965. Burns of London model, later offered as Baldwin Virginian in '65.

1964-1965		$800	$900

Burns Flyte

Burns Vitasonic

GUITARS

Buscarino Virtuoso

Carvin CT-6M

MODEL YEAR	FEATURES	EXC. COND. LOW	HIGH

Vista Sonic
1962-1964. Offset double-cut solid, 3 pickups, red sunburst.

| 1962-1964 | | $650 | $750 |

Burnside
1987-1988. Budget solidbody guitars imported by Guild.

Solidbody Electric / Blade
1987-1988. Kramer-style solidbody, fat pointy head-stock, red-orange sunburst.

| 1987-1988 | | $300 | $400 |

Burns-Weill
1959. Jim Burns and Henry Weill teamed up to produce three solidbody electric and three solid-body bass models under this English brand.

Burton Guitars
1980-present. Custom classical guitars built by luthier Cynthia Burton in Portland, Oregon.

Buscarino Guitars
1981-present. Luthier John Buscarino builds his premium and presentation grade, custom archtops and steel-string and nylon-string flat-tops in Franklin, North Carolina.

Solidbody Electric - Custom-Built
1980-1990s.

| 1980-1990s | | $1,300 | $1,500 |

Byers, Gregory
1984-present. Premium grade, custom classical and Flamenco guitars built by luthier Gregory Byers in Willits, California.

C. Fox
1997-2002. Luthier Charles Fox built his premium grade, production/custom flat-tops in Healdsburg, California. In '02 he closed C. Fox Guitars and move to Portland, Oregon to build Charles Fox Guitars.

CA (Composite Acoustics)
1999-present. Professional grade, production, carbon fiber composite guitars built in Lafayette, Louisiana.

Callaham
1989-present. Professional, production/custom, solidbody electric guitars built by luthier Bill Callaham in Winchester, Virginia. They also make tube amp heads.

Camelli (Italy)
1960s. Line of solidbody electrics from Italy.

Solidbody Electric

| 1960s | | $375 | $475 |

Campellone
1978-present. Luthier Mark Campellone builds his premium grade, custom archtops in Smithfield, Rhode Island. He also made electrics and basses in the '70s and '80s, switching to archtops around '90.

Deluxe
1990-present. 17", middle of the company product line, archtop, blond or sunburst.

| 1990-1995 | | $5,400 | $6,200 |

Special
1994-present. 16" to 18" archtop, carved spruce top, carved flamed maple back, flamed maple sides, blond or sunburst.

| 1994-1999 | | $6,200 | $7,000 |

Canvas
2004-present. Budget and intermediate grade, production, solid and semi-hollow body guitars imported from China by American Sejung Corp. They also offer basses.

Carbonaro
1974-present. Luthier Robert Carbonaro builds his premium grade, production/custom, archtop and flat-top guitars in Santa Fe, New Mexico.

Carl Fischer
1920s. Most likely a brand made for a distributor. Instruments built by the Oscar Schmidt Co. and possibly others.

Carlos
ca.1976-late 1980s. Imported copies of classic American acoustics distributed by Coast Wholesale Music.

Model 240
1970s. Dreadnought with mahogany (laminate?) back and sides, spruce top, natural.

| 1978 | | $175 | $300 |

Model 275
1970s. Dreadnought with rosewood (laminate?) sides and three-piece back, spruce top, natural.

| 1978 | | $200 | $350 |

Carvin
1946-present. Intermediate and professional grade, production/custom, acoustic and electric guitars. They also offer basses and amps. Founded in Los Angeles by Hawaiian guitarist and recording artist Lowell C. Kiesel as the L.C. Kiesel Co. making pickups for guitars. Bakelite Kiesel-brand electric Hawaiian lap steels are introduced in early-'47. Small tube amps introduced ca. '47. By late-'49, the Carvin brand is introduced, combining parts of names of sons Carson and Gavin. Carvin acoustic and electric Spanish archtops are introduced in '54. Instruments are sold by mail-order only. The company relocated to Covina, California in '49 and to Escondido, California in '68. Two retail stores opened in Hollywood and Santa Ana, California

MODEL YEAR	FEATURES	EXC. COND. LOW	HIGH

in '91.

Approx. 2,000-4,000 guitars made prior to '70 with no serial number. First serial number appeared in '70, stamped on end of fingerboard, beginning with #5000. All are consecutive. Later SN on neck plates. Approximate SN ranges include:

1970:	First serial number #5000 to 10019 ('79).
'80-'83:	10768 to 15919.
'84-'87:	13666 to 25332.
'88-'90:	22731 to 25683.
'91-'94:	25359 to 42547.
'95-'99:	45879 to 81427.
'00-present:	56162 to ~95000.

Acoustic/Electric AC/AE Series
1990s		$400	$700

Soldibody B/C/D Series (Mid-level)
1990s		$350	$700

Solidbody Carved-Top (Higher-End)
2000s.
2000s		$1,000	$1,200

Solidbody DN/DB Series (Doubleneck)
1990s		$700	$1,500

Casa Montalvo

1987-present. Intermediate and professional grade, production/custom flamenco and classical guitars made in Mexico for George Katechis of Berkeley Musical Instrument Exchange.

Casio

1987-1988. Digital guitars imported from Japan, plastic body, synthesizer features.

DG10
1987. Self-contained digital guitar.
1987		$75	$125

DG20
Midi-capable digital guitar.
1987		$150	$250

PG-380
1987. Guitar synth, double-cut, over 80 built-in sounds, midi controller capable.
1987		$400	$650

Chandler

1984-present. Intermediate and professional grade, production/custom, solidbody electric guitars built by luthiers Paul and Adrian Chandler in Chico, California. They also build basses, laptops and pickups. Chandler started making pickguards and accessories in the '70s, adding electric guitars, basses, and effects in '84.

555 Model
1992-present. Sharp double-cut, three mini-humbucker pickups, retro slotted headstock.
1992	TV Yellow	$550	$650

Austin Special
1991-1999. Resembles futuristic Danelectro, lipstick pickups, available in 5-string version.
1991		$550	$650

Austin Special Baritone
1994-1999. Nicknamed Elvis, gold metalflake finish, mother-of-toilet-seat binding, tremolo, baritone.
1994		$550	$650

Metro
1995-2000. Double-cut slab body, P-90 in neck position and humbucker in the bridge position.
1994-2000		$550	$650

Telepathic
1994-2000. Classic single-cut style, 3 models; Basic, Standard, Deluxe.
1990s	Basic	$450	$500
1990s	Deluxe 1122 Model	$600	$700
1990s	Standard	$550	$650

Chapin

Professional and premium grade, production/custom, semi-hollow, solidbody, and acoustic electric guitars built by luthiers Bill Chapin and Fred Campbell in San Jose, California.

Chapman

1970-present. Made by Emmett Chapman, the Stick features 10 strings and is played by tapping both hands. The Grand Stick features 12 strings.

Stick
10 or 12 strings, touch-tap hybrid electric instrument.
1970-1999	10-string	$1,000	$1,400
1970-1999	12-string	$1,400	$1,600
2000-2003	10-string	$1,200	$1,400

Charles Fox Guitars

1968-present. Luthier Charles Fox builds his premium and presentation grade, custom, steel and nylon string guitars in Portland, Oregon. He also produced GRD acoustic and electric guitars for '78-'82 and C. Fox acoustic guitars for '97-'02. He also operates The American School of Lutherie in Portland.

Charles Shifflett Acoustic Guitars

1990-present. Premium grade, custom, classical, flamenco, resonator, and harp guitars built by luthier Charles Shifflett in High River, Alberta. He also builds basses and banjos.

Charvel

1979 (1980)-present. Intermediate and professional grade, production, solidbody electric guitars. Founded by Wayne Charvel as Charvel Manufacturing in '76, making guitar parts in Asuza, California. Moved to San Dimas in '78. Also in '78 Grover Jackson bought out Charvel. In '79 or early '80 Charvel branded guitars are introduced. U.S.-made to '85, a combination of imports and U.S.-made post-'85. Charvel also manufactured the Jackson brand. The earliest San Dimas Charvels were custom-built with wild graphics, locking trems, high-output pickups, and pointy headstocks.

Chandler Lectra-Slide

Charles Fox steel-string

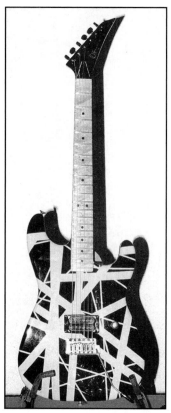

1983 Charvel Model 1

1987 Charvel Model 3

MODEL YEAR	FEATURES	EXC. COND. LOW	HIGH

Charvel licensed its trademark to IMC (Hondo) in '85. IMC bought Charvel in '86 and moved the factory to Ontario, California. On October 25, 2002, Fender Musical Instruments Corp. (FMIC) took ownership of Jackson/Charvel Manufacturing Inc.

Electric guitar manufacturing info:
1986-1989 Japanese-made Models 1 through 8
1989-1991 Japanese-made 550 XL, 650 XL/ Custom, 750 XL (XL=neck-thru)
1989-1992 Japanese-made Models 275, 375, 475, 575
1990-1991 Korean-made Charvette models
1992-1994 Korean-made Models 325, 425

Early Charvel serial numbers (provided by former Jackson/Charvel associate Tim Wilson): The first 500 to 750 guitars had no serial number, just marked "Made In U.S.A." on their neckplates. Five digit serial numbers were then used until November '81 when 4-digit number adopted, starting with #1001.
1981: 1001-1095
1982: 1096-1724
1983: 1725-2938
1984: 2939-4261
1985: 4262-5303
1986: 5304-5491

275 Deluxe Dinky
1989-1991. Made in Japan, offset double-cut solidbody, 1 single-coil and one humbucker ('89), 3 stacked humbuckers ('90-'91), tremolo.

1989	1 single, 1 humbucker	$300	$425
1990-1991	Stacked humbuckers	$300	$425

325SL
1992-1994. Dot inlays.

1992-1994		$300	$425

325SLX
1992-1994. Surfcaster-like thinline acoustic/electric, dual cutaways, F-hole, on-board chorus, shark inlays, made in Korea.

1992-1994		$300	$425

375 Deluxe
1989-1992. Maple or rosewood 'board, dot inlays, single-single-humbucker.

1989-1992		$300	$425

475
1989-1992. Humbucker-single-single configuration, bolt-on neck, dot markers.

1990s		$300	$425

475 Deluxe / Special
1989-1992. Introduced as Special, discontinued as Deluxe, bound rosewood 'board, shark fin markers, 2 oval stacked humbuckers and single bridge humbucker, various colors and finishes.

1989-1992		$325	$425

525
1990s. Acoustic-electric, single-cut.

1990s		$325	$425

625-C12
1990-2000s. Acoustic-electric cutaway 12-string.

1990-2000s		$250	$300

625F/625ACEL
1990-2000s. Acoustic-electric cutaway.

1990-2000s		$300	$350

Avenger
1990-1991. Randy Rhoads-style batwing-shaped solidbody, 3 stacked humbuckers, tremolo, made in Japan.

1990-1991		$300	$375

Charvette
1989-1992. Charvette Series made in Korea, super-strat-style, model number series 100 through 300.

1990-1991		$150	$200

Custom Shop
Late-1970-early-1980s. Custom order and built guitars, prior to factory production. Models may vary and each model should be valued individually.

1978-1983	Flying V	$1,500	$1,700
1978-1983	Van Halen	$600	$850

EVH Art Series/EVH-Guitars
Mid-2004. EVH guitars with hand stripe-work done by Edward Van Halen, classic early Charvel-Strat body with FMIC licensed Fender/Charvel headstock design, autographed by Ed, and sold in an on-line auction. These were the inspiration for the later Limited Edition EVH.

2004	Black w/yellow stripes	$10,000	$12,000
2004	Red w/black & white stripes	$10,000	$12,000
2004	White w/black stripes	$9,000	$11,000

Fusion Deluxe
1989-1991. Double-cut solidbody, tremolo, 1 humbucker and 1 single-coil pickup, made in Japan.

1988		$275	$400

Fusion Standard/AS FX 1
1993-1996. Double-cut solidbody, tremolo, 1 regular and 2 mini humbuckers, made in Japan, also named AS FX1.

1988		$225	$350

Model 1/1A/1C
1986-1989. Offset double-cut solidbody, bolt-on maple neck, dot inlays, 1 humbucker, tremolo, made in Japan. Model 1A has 3 single-coils. Model 1C has 1 humbucker and 2 single-coils.

1986-1988		$225	$275

Model 2
1986-1989. As Model 1, but with rosewood 'board.

1980s		$225	$325

Model 3/3A/3DR/3L
1986-1989. As Model 2, but with 1 humbucker, 2 single coils. Model 3A has 2 humbuckers. Model 3DR has 1 humbucker and 1 single-coil.

1986-1988		$325	$425

Model 4/4A
1986-1989. As Model 2, but with 1 regular humbucker and 2 stacked humbuckers mounted in the body (no pickguard), and with active electronics, shark-fin inlays. Model 4A has 2 regular humbuckers and dot markers.

1986-1988		$300	$425

MODEL YEAR	FEATURES	EXC. COND. LOW	HIGH

Model 5/5A
1986-1989. As Model 4A, but is neck-thru construction, with JE1000TG active elctronics. Model 5A is single humbucker and single knob version of Model 5, limited production, made in Japan.

1987		$300	$425

Model 6
1986-1989. As Model 4, but with shark's tooth 'board inlays, standard or various custom finishes.

1986-1989		$475	$625

Model 7
1988-1989. Single-cut solidbody, bound top, reversed headstock, 2 single-coils, made in Japan.

1988-1989		$475	$625

Model 88 LTD
1988. Double-cut solidbody, 1 slanted humbucker, shark fin inlay, 1000 built, made in Japan.

1988		$550	$700

San Dimas Bolt-On (U.S.-made)
1981-1986, 1995-1997. U.S.-made with San Dimas neck plate, bolt neck, rounded headstock early production, pointy headstock late production, reissued in mid-'90s. Serial numbers start with 100, and end with 5491 in early-'86.

Serial numbers as follows: 1981 1001-1095, 1982 1096-1724, 1983 1725-2938, 1984 2939-4261, 1985 4262-5303, 1986 5304-5491.

1981-1982	Soft headstock	$2,000	$3,500
1982-1986	Pointy headstock	$1,300	$1,600
1995-1997	Soft headstock	$650	$750

ST Custom
1990-1992. Offset double-cut ash solidbody, 2 single-coils and 1 humbucker, rosewood 'board, tremolo, made in Japan.

1990s		$325	$375

ST Deluxe
1990-1992. Same as ST Custom but with maple 'board.

1990s		$300	$350

Standard
2002-present. Typical offset double-cut Charvel body, 2 Seymour Duncan humbucker pickups, various opaque colors.

2002-2004		$225	$300

Star
1980. 4-point, kinda Explorer shape solid.

1980		$600	$800

Surfcaster
1991-1994. Offset double-cut, f-hole, various pickup options, bound body, tremolo, made in Japan.

1991-1993	1 single-coil, 1 humbucker	$700	$900
1991-1993	2 single-coils	$700	$900
1991-1993	3 single-coils	$800	$1,000
1991-1993	Optional custom color & features	$800	$1,200

Surfcaster 12
1991-1995. 12-string version of Surfcaster, no tremolo, made in Japan.

1991-1995		$700	$900

Surfcaster Double Neck
1992. Very limited production, 6/12 double neck, Charvel logo on both necks, black.

1992		$1,200	$2,000

Surfcaster HT (Model SC 1)
1992-1996. Made in Japan. Hard Tail (HT) non-tremolo version of Surfcaster, has single-coil and bridge humbucker.

1992-1996	Custom color & features	$650	$1,000
1992-1996	Standard colors & features	$550	$650

Chiquita
1979-present. Intermediate grade, production guitars made by Erlewine Guitars in Austin, Texas (see that listing). There was also a mini amp available.

Travel Guitar
1979-present. Developed by Mark Erlewine and ZZ Top's Billy Gibbons, 27" overall length solidbody.

1980s	Blond, natural or yellow	$225	$350
1980s	Red	$275	$325

Chrysalis Guitars
1998-present. Luthier Tim White builds his premium grade, production/custom Chrysalis Guitar System, which includes interchangeable components that can be quickly assembled into a full-size electric/acoustic guitar, in New Boston, New Hampshire. A variety of instruments may be created, including 6- and 12-string electrics and acoustics, electric and acoustic mandocello and acoustic basses.

Cipher
1960s. Solidbody electric guitars and basses imported from Japan by Inter-Mark. Generally strange-shaped bodies.

Electric Solidbody
Student-level import.

1960s		$150	$200

Citron
1995-present. Luthier Harvey Citron builds his professional and premium grade, production/custom solidbody guitars in Woodstock, New York. He also builds basses. In '75, Citron and Joe Veillette founded Veillette-Citron, which was known for handcrafted, neck-thru guitars and basses. That company closed in '83.

Custom-Made Electrics
2000s. A variety of solidbody and thin hollowbody mid- to high-end electrics.

2000s		$1,700	$2,700

Clifford
Clifford was a brand manufactured by Kansas City, Missouri instrument wholesalers J.W. Jenkins & Sons. First introduced in 1895, the brand also offered mandolins.

Charvel Surfcaster

Chrysalis

Collings OM2-H

Comins Chester Avenue

MODEL YEAR	FEATURES	EXC. COND. LOW	HIGH

Coleman Guitars

1976-1983. Custom made presentation grade instruments made in Homosassa, Florida, by luthier Harry Coleman. No headstock logo, Coleman logo on inside center strip.

Flat-Top

1976-1983		$5,000	$15,000

Collings

1986-present. Professional, premium, and presentation grade, production/custom, flat-top and archtop guitars built in Austin, Texas. They also build mandolins. Bill Collings started with guitar repair and began custom building guitars around '73. In '80, he relocated his shop from Houston to Austin and started Collings Guitars in '86.

00-41 (Brazilian rosewood)

2001. Premium Brazilian rosewood back and sides, Adirondack spruce top, abalone top purfling.

2001		$7,200	$7,500

000-1 (Mahogany)

1990s. Mahogany body, spruce top.

1990s		$2,450	$2,550

000-2H

1994-present. 15" 000-size, Indian rosewood back and sides, spruce top, slotted headstock, 12-fret neck, dot markers. AAA Koa back and sides in '96.

1994-1995	Indian rosewood	$2,000	$3,000
1996	AAA Koa	$3,000	$4,000

C-10 (Mahogany)

1994-present. 000-size, spruce top, mahogany back and sides, natural.

1995		$2,300	$2,700

C-10 Deluxe

1994-present. Indian rosewood or flamed maple back and sides, natural.

1994-2002	Flamed maple	$2,600	$3,000
1994-2002	Indian rosewood	$2,600	$3,000

C-100 (Mahogany)

1986-1995. Quadruple 0-size, spruce top, mahogany back and sides, natural, replaced by CJ Jumbo.

1986-1995		$2,300	$2,600

CJ Jumbo (Indian rosewood)

1995-present. Quadruple 0-size, spruce top, Indian rosewood back and sides, natural.

1995-2001		$2,900	$3,100

D-1 Gruhn

1989. Short run for Gruhn Guitars, Nashville, signed by Bill Collins, Indian rosewood back and sides, sitka spruce top.

1989		$2,000	$3,000

D-1/D-1SB/D-1A Custom

1994-present. D-style, 15 5/8", spruce top, mahogany back and sides, natural. D-1SB includes sunburst option. D-1A Custom includes upgrades to Adirondack spruce top and higher appointments, natural.

1995	D-1	$2,150	$2,250
1999-2002	D-1A Custom	$2,900	$3,300
2001	D-1SB	$2,300	$2,800

MODEL YEAR	FEATURES	EXC. COND. LOW	HIGH

D-2 (Indian rosewood)

1986-1995. D-1 with Indian rosewood back and sides, natural.

1986-1995		$2,700	$3,000

D-2H (Indian rosewood)

1986-present. Dreadnought, same as D-2 with herringbone purfling around top edge.

1986-2001		$2,700	$3,100

D-2H/D-2HBZ (Brazilian rosewood)

1994-2001. Grade AA Brazilian rosewood, spruce top.

1994-2001		$4,500	$5,500

D-3

1990-2000s. Similar to D-2H but with abalone purfling/rosette.

1990s	Brazilian rosewood	$5,500	$6,000
2000s	Indian rosewood	$2,700	$3,200

OM-1/OM-1A

1994-present. Grand concert, sitka spruce top, mahogany back and sides, natural. OM-1A includes Adirondack spruce upgrade.

1990s	OM-1	$2,300	$2,600
1990s	OM-1A	$2,400	$2,700

OM-2H (Indian rosewood)

1990-2000s.

1990-2000s.		$2,300	$2,800

OM-2HAV (Brazilian rosewood)

1998. Adirondack spruce top, Brazilian rosewood back and sides, ivoroid-bound body.

1998		$4,500	$5,500

OM-3 (Brazilian rosewood)

1998. Brazilian rosewood back and sides, Adirondack spruce top, fancy rosette.

1998		$5,500	$6,000

OM-3 (Indian rosewood)

2002.

2002		$2,400	$2,900

OM-3HC (Indian rosewood)

1986. Single rounded cutaway, 15", spruce top, Indian rosewood back and sides, herringbone purfling.

1986		$2,500	$3,000

OM-42B (Brazilian rosewood)

2000. Brazilian rosewood back and sides, Adirondack spruce top, fancy rosette and binding.

2000		$7,200	$7,500

SJ

Spruce top, quilted maple back and sides or Indian rosewood (earlier option).

1990s	Indian rosewood	$2,900	$3,300
2003	Maple	$2,900	$3,100

SJ-41 (Brazilian rosewood)

1996. Cedar top, Brazilian rosewood back and sides.

1996		$7,300	$7,500

Comins

1992-present. Premium grade, custom archtops built by luthier Bill Comins in Willow Grove, Pennsylvania. He also offers a combo amp built in collaboration with George Alessandro.

MODEL YEAR	FEATURES	EXC. COND. LOW	HIGH

Chester Avenue
1994-present. Electric archtop, solid spruce top and back, 17" or 18" cutaway, options can vary.

| 1994-1999 | 17" | $6,000 | $6,500 |
| 1994-1999 | 18" | $6,500 | $7,000 |

Classic
1995-present. Classic archtop jazz model, 17" cutaway, pickguard mounted neck pickup, block markers.

| 1995-1999 | | $5,000 | $6,000 |

Parlor
1995-present. 14" archtop with viola styling, violin golden brown.

| 1995-1999 | | $3,300 | $3,500 |

Renaissance
1996-present. 17" archtop cutaway, carved European spruce top, solid curly maple back and sides, unique removable sound baffles, blond.

| 1996-1999 | | $6,000 | $6,500 |

Concertone
Ca. 1914-1930s. Concertone was a brand made by Chicago's Slingerland and distributed by Montgomery Ward. The brand was also used on other instruments such as ukuleles.

Conklin
1984-present. Intermediate, professional and premium grade, production/custom, 6-, 7-, 8-, and 12-string solid and hollowbody electrics, by luthier Bill Conklin. He also builds basses. Originally located in Lebanon, Missouri, in '88 the company moved to Springfield, Missouri. Conklin instruments are made in the U.S. and overseas.

Conn Guitars
Ca.1968-ca.1978. Student to mid-quality classical and acoustic guitars, some with bolt-on necks. Imported from Japan by band instrument manufacturer and distributor Conn/Continental Music Company, Elkhart, IN.

Acoustic
1970s-1980s. Various models.

| 1970s | | $100 | $175 |
| 1980s | | $100 | $175 |

Classical
1980s. Various student-level modlels.

| 1970s | | $100 | $150 |

Solidbody Electric
1970s. Various models.

| 1970s. | | $150 | $200 |

Connor, Stephan
1995-present. Luthier Stephan Connor builds his premium grade, custom nylon-string guitars in Waltham, Massachusetts.

Conrad Guitars
Ca. 1968-1978. Mid- to better-quality copies of glued-neck Martin and Gibson acoustics and bolt-neck Gibson and Fender solidbodies. Also mandolins and banjos. Imported from Japan by David Wexler and Company, Chicago, Illinois.

Acoustic 12-String
1970s. D-style.

| 1970s | | $150 | $200 |

Acoustical Slimline 12-String 40100
1970s. Two DeArmond-style pickups, rosewood 'board, 12 strings, dot markers, sunburst.

| 1970s | | $200 | $300 |

Acoustical Slimline 40080/40085
1970s. Two or three DeArmond-style pickups, rosewood 'board, block markers, sunburst.

| 1970s | | $200 | $300 |

Bison (40035/40030/40065/40005)
1970s. One to four pickups, rosewood 'board with dot markers, six-on-side headstock.

| 1970s | | $175 | $250 |

Bumper (40223)
1970s. Armstrong Lucite copy, import.

| 1974 | | $225 | $325 |

De Luxe Folk Guitar
1970s. Resonator acoustic, mahogany back, sides and neck, Japanese import.

| 1974 | | $200 | $300 |

Electric Solidbody
1970s. Student-level.

| 1970s | | $200 | $400 |

Master Size 40178
1972-1977. Electric archtop, two pickups.

| 1970s | | $200 | $400 |

Violin-Shaped 12-String Electric 40176
1970s. Scroll headstock, 2 pickups, 500/1 control panel, bass side dot markers, sunburst.

| 1970s | | $200 | $300 |

Violin-Shaped Electric 40175
1970s. Scroll headstock, 2 pickups, 500/1 control panel, bass side dot markers, vibrato, sunburst.

| 1970s | | $200 | $300 |

White Styrene 1280 (solidbody)
1970s. Solid maple body covered with white styrene, 2 pickups, tremolo, bass side dot markers, white.

| 1970s | | $200 | $300 |

Contessa
1960s. Acoustic, semi-hollow archtop, solidbody and bass guitars made in Germany. They also made banjos.

Electric Solidbody
1967. Various models.

| 1967 | | $375 | $475 |

Contreras
See listing for Manuel Contreras and Manuel Contreras II.

Coral
Refer to Danelectro section.

Conklin F-Hole 8

1974 Conrad doubleneck

GUITARS

Corey James CJ Double

Cort Larry Coryell

MODEL YEAR	FEATURES	EXC. COND. LOW	HIGH

Córdoba

Line of classical guitars handmade in Portugal and imported by Guitar Salon International.

Classical

2000s	Gipsy King	$900	$1,000
2000s	Higher-end	$500	$600
2000s	Mid-level	$300	$400
2000s	Student-level	$225	$275

Cordova

1960s. Classical nylon string guitars imported by David Wexler of Chicago.

Grand Concert Model WC-026

1960s. Highest model offered by Cordova, 1-piece rosewood back, laminated rosewood sides, spruce top, natural.

1963		$200	$300

Corey James Custom Guitars

2005-present. Luthier Corey James Moilanen builds his professional and premium grade, production/custom solidbody guitars in Davisburg, Michigan. He also builds basses.

Coriani, Paolo

1984-present. Production/custom nylon-string guitars and hurdy-gurdys built by luthier Paolo Coriani in Modeila, Italy.

Cort

1973-present. North Brook, Illinois-based Cort offers budget, intermediate and professional grade, production/custom, acoustic and solidbody, semi-hollow, hollow body electric guitars built in Korea. They also offer basses.

Cort was the second significant Korean private-label (Hondo brand was the first) to come out of Korea. Jack Westheimer, based upon the success of Tommy Moore and Hondo, entered into an agreement with Korea's Cort to do Cort-brand, private-label, and Epiphone-brand guitars.

Doubleneck

Cherry, 6/12 necks, Asian import.

1970s		$350	$550

Electric

1973-present. A variety of models were offered, often copy guitars. These guitars were heavily distributed in the 1980s. New Cort models sell from $85 and should be evaluated on a model-by-model basis. The 2000s included a Matt 'Guitar' Murphy signature model and a Jim Triggs electric archtop.

1973-1989		$250	$350
1990-1999		$150	$300
2000s	Jim Triggs Archtop	$400	$450
2000s	Matt Murphy Signature	$350	$450

MODEL YEAR	FEATURES	EXC. COND. LOW	HIGH

Crafter

2000-present. Line of intermediate and professional grade, production, acoustic and acoustic/electric guitars from Hohner. They also offer mandolins and a bass.

Acoustic Flat-Top

2000s. Various production models.

2000s		$125	$300

Crafter USA

1986-present. Crafter offers budget and intermediate grade, production, classical, acoustic, acoustic/electric, and electric guitars made in Korea. They also build basses and amps. From '72 to '86 they made Sungeum classical guitars.

Crafters of Tennessee

See listing under Tennessee.

Cranium

1996-present. Professional grade, production/custom, hollow, semi-hollow, and solidbody electrics built by luthier Wayne O'Connor in Peterborough, Ontario.

Crescent Moon

1999-present. Professional grade, production/custom, solidbody guitars and basses built by luthier Craig Muller in Baltimore, Maryland.

Crestwood

1970s. Copies of the popular classical guitars, flat-tops, electric solidbodies and basses of the era, imported by La Playa Distributing Company of Detroit.

Electric

1970s. Various models include the 2043, 2045, 2047, 2020, 2073, 2078, 2082, and 2084.

1970s		$250	$350

Cromwell

1935-1939. Budget model brand built by Gibson and distributed by mail-order businesses like Grossman, Continental, and Richter & Phillips.

Acoustic Archtops

1935-1936. Archtop acoustic, F-holes, pressed mahogany back and sides, carved and bound top, bound back, 'guard and 'board, no truss rod.

1935-1939		$600	$800

Crown

1960s. Violin-shaped hollowbody electrics, solidbody electric guitars and basses, possibly others. Imported from Japan.

Acoustic Flat-Top

1960s. 6-string and 12-string.

1960s		$75	$150

MODEL YEAR	FEATURES	EXC. COND. LOW	HIGH

Electric Archtops
Double pointed cutaways, 2 humbucking pickups, laminated top, full-depth body.

1960s		$350	$450

Electric Solidbody/Semi-hollow
1960s. Student-level Japanese import.

1960s	Pointy violin-shaped body	$250	$275
1960s	Standard body styles	$125	$175

Crucianelli
Early 1960s. Italian guitars imported into the U.S. by Bennett Brothers of New York and Chicago around '63 to '64. Accordion builder Crucianelli also made Imperial, Elite, PANaramic, and Elli-Sound brand guitars.

Cumpiano
1974-present. Professional and premium grade, custom steel-string and nylon-string guitars, and acoustic basses built by luthier William Cumpiano in Northampton, Massachusetts.

Custom
1980s. Line of solidbody guitars and basses introduced in the early '80s by Charles Lawing and Chris Lovell, owners of Strings & Things in Memphis, Tennessee.

Custom Kraft
Late-1960s. A house brand of St. Louis Music Supply, instruments built by Valco, Chicago. They also offered basses.

Sound Saturator
1960s. 12-string.

1960s		$275	$400

Super Zapp
1960s.

1960s		$275	$400

D'Leco Guitars
1991-present. Luthier James W. Dale builds his premium grade, production/custom archtops in Oklahoma City, Oklahoma.

D'Agostino
1976-early 1990s. Acoustic and electric solidbody guitars and basses imported by PMS Music, founded in New York City by former Maestro executive Pat D'Agostino, his brother Steven D'Agostino, and Mike Confortti. First dreadnought acoustic guitars imported from Japan in '76. First solidbodies manufactured by the EKO custom shop beginning in '77. In '82 solidbody production moved to Japan. Beginning in '84, D'Agostinos were made in Korea. Overall, about 60% of guitars were Japanese, 40% Korean.

Acoustic Flat-Top
1976-1990. Early production in Japan, by mid-'80s, most production in Korea.

1970s		$175	$275

Electric Semi-Hollowbody
1981-early 1990s. Early production in Japan, later versions from Korea.

1980s		$275	$325

Electric Solidbody
1977-early 1990s. Early models made in Italy, later versions from Japan and Korea.

1970s		$275	$325

Daily Guitars
1976-present. Luthier David Daily builds his premium grade, production/custom classical guitars in Sparks, Nevada.

Daion
1978-1985. Mid- to higher-quality copies imported from Japan. Original designs introduced in the '80s.

Electric Guitars
1978-1985. Various solid and semi-hollow body guitars.

1978-1985		$400	$800

Daisy Rock
2001-present. Budget and intermediate grade, production, full-scale and 3/4 scale, solidbody, semi-hollow, acoustic, and acoustic/electric guitars. Founded by Tish Ciravolo as a Division of Schecter Guitars, the Daisy line is focused on female customers. Initial offerings included daisy and heart-shaped electric guitars and basses.

Electric or Acoustic
2001-present. Various models and features.

2001-2004		$150	$190

D'Ambrosio
2001-present. Luthier Otto D'Ambrosio builds his premium grade, custom/production, acoustic and electric archtop guitars in Providence, Rhode Island.

Dan Armstrong
Dan Armstrong started playing jazz in Cleveland in the late-'50s. He moved to New York and also started doing repairs, eventually opening his own store on 48th Street in '65. By the late-'60s he was designing his Lucite guitars for Ampeg (see Ampeg for those listings). He moved to England in '71, where he developed his line of colored stomp boxes. He returned to the States in '75. Armstrong died in '04.

Wood Body Guitar
1973-1975. Sliding pickup, wood body, brown.

1973-1975		$1,400	$1,600

Danelectro
1946-1969, 1996-present. Founded in Red Bank, New Jersey, by Nathan I. (Nate or Nat) Daniel, an electronics enthusiast with amplifier experience. In 1933, Daniel built amps for Thor's Bargain Basement in New York. In '34 he was recruited by Epiph-

1982 D'Agostino Bench Mark

Daisy Rock Heartbreaker

Danelectro Convertible

Danelectro Doubleneck 6/4

one's Herb Sunshine to build earliest Electar amps and pickup-making equipment. From '35 to '42, he operated Daniel Electric Laboratories in Manhattan, supplying Epiphone. He started Danelectro in '46 and made his first amps for Montgomery Ward in '47. Over the years, Danelectro made amplifiers, solidbody, semi-hollow and hollowbody electric guitars and basses, electric sitar, and the Bellzouki under the Danelectro, Silvertone, Coral, and Dane, brands. In '48, began supplying Silvertone amps for Sears (various coverings), with his own brand (brown leatherette) distributed by Targ and Dinner as Danelectro and S.S. Maxwell. He developed an electronic vibrato in '48 on his Vibravox series amps. In '50 he developed a microphone with volume and tone controls and outboard Echo Box reverb unit. In the fall of '54, Danelectro replaced Harmony as provider of Silvertone solidbody guitars for Sears. Also in '54, the first Danelectro brand guitars appeared with tweed covering, bell headstock, and pickups under the pickguard. The Coke-bottle headstock debuts as Silvertone Lightning Bolt in '54, and was used on Danelectros for '56 to '66. The company moved to Red Bank, New Jersey in '57, and in '58 relocated to Neptune, New Jersey. In '59, Harmony and Kay guitars replace all but 3 Danelectros in Sears catalog. In '66, MCA buys the company (Daniel remains with company), but by mid '69, MCA halts production and closes the doors. Some leftover stock is sold to Dan Armstrong, who had a shop in New York at the time. Armstrong assembled several hundred Danelectro guitars as Dan Armstrong Modified with his own pickup design.

Rights to name acquired by Anthony Marc in late-'80s, who assembled a number of thinline hollowbody guitars, many with Longhorn shape, using Japanese-made bodies and original Danelectro necks and hardware. In '96, the Evets Corporation, of San Clemente, California, introduced a line of effects bearing the Danelectro brand. Amps and guitars, many of which were reissues of the earlier instruments, soon followed. In early 2003, Evets discontinued offering guitar and amps, but revived the guitar line in '05.

MCA-Danelectro made guitars were called the Dane Series. Dane A model numbers start with an A (e.g. A2V), Dane B models start with a B (e.g. B3V), Dane C (e.g. C2N), and Dane D (e.g. D2N). The least expensive series was the A, going up to the most expensive D. All Dane Series instruments came with 1, 2, or 3 pickups and hand-vibrato options. The Dane Series were made from '67 to '69. MCA did carry over the Convertible, Guitarlin 4123, Long Horn Bass-4 and Bass-6 and Doubleneck 3923. MCA also offered the Bellzouki Double Pickup 7021. Each Dane Series includes an electric 12-string.

MODEL YEAR	FEATURES	EXC. COND. LOW	HIGH

Bellzouki
1961-1969. 12-string electric, teardrop-shaped body, single pickup, sunburst. Vincent Bell model has modified teardrop shape with 2 body points on both treble and bass bouts and 2 pickups.

1960s	Single pickups	$700	$1,000
1960s	Vincent Bell, 2 p/u	$900	$1,200

Convertible
1959-1969, 1999-2000. Acoustic/electric, double-cut, guitar was sold with or without the removable single pickup.

1950s	Pickup installed	$550	$750
1960s	Acoustic, no pickup	$400	$500
1960s	Pickup installed	$500	$700

Coral Firefly
1967-1969. Double-cut body, f-holes, 2 pickups, sold with or without vibrato.

1967		$450	$550

Coral Hornet 2
1967-1969. Solid body, 2 pickups, with or without vibrato.

1967		$550	$750

Coral Sitar
1967-1969. Six-string guitar with 13 drone strings and 3 pickups (2 under the 6 strings, 1 under the drones), kind of a USA-shaped body.

1967		$2,500	$3,000

Dane A Series
1967-1969. 1 and 2 pickup models, solid wood slab body, hard lacquer finish with 4 color options.

1967-1969		$350	$400

Dane B Series
1967-1969. 1 and 3 pickup models, semi-solid Durabody.

1967-1969		$400	$450

Dane C Series
1967-1969. 2 and 3 pickup models, semi-solid Durabody with 2-tone Gator finish.

1967-1969		$400	$450

Dane D Series
1967-1969. 2 and 3 pickup models, solid wood sculptured thinline body, 'floating adjustable pickguard-fingerguide', master volume with 4 switches.

1967-1969		$450	$500

Deluxe Double Pickup (6028)
Double-cut, 2 pointer knobs, 2 pickups, standard-size pickguard, master control knob, white (6026), dark walnut (6027), honey walnut (6028).

1960s		$700	$800

Deluxe Triple Pickup (6037)
Double-cut, 3 pointer knobs, 3 pickups, standard-size pickguard, master control knob, white (6036), dark walnut (6037), honey walnut (6038).

1960s		$1,000	$1,100

Doubleneck (3923)
1959-1969. A Shorthorn double-cut, bass and 6-string necks, 1 pickup on each neck, Coke bottle headstocks, white sunburst.

1960s		$1,500	$1,800

Electric Sitar

1967-1969. Traditional looking, oval-bodied sitar, no drone strings as on the Coral Sitar of the same period.

1967	$1,000	$1,200

Guitarlin (4123)

1963-1969. The Longhorn guitar, with 2 huge cutaways, 32-fret neck, and 2 pickups.

1960s	$1,400	$1,700

Hand Vibrato Double Pickup (4021)

1960s. Two pickups, double-cut, batwing headstock, simple design vibrato, black.

1960s	$400	$600

Hand Vibrato Single Pickup (4011)

1960s. One pickup, double-cut, batwing headstock, simple design vibrato, black.

1960s	$600	$700

Model C

1955-ca.1958. Single-cut, 1 pickup.

1956	$400	$500

Pro 1

1963-ca.1964. Odd-shaped double-cut electric with squared off corners, 1 pickup.

1963	$500	$600

Standard Double Pickup

1959-1967. A Shorthorn double-cut, 2 pickups, 2 stacked, concentric volume/tone controls, seal-shaped 'guard, Coke-bottle headstock, black version of this guitar is often referred to as the Jimmy Page model because he occasionally used one.

1950s	Black	$1,100	$1,200
1960s		$700	$900

Standard Single Pickup

1958-1967. A Shorthorn double-cut, 1 pickup, 2 regular control knobs, seal-shaped pickguard, Coke bottle headstock.

1960s	$500	$600

U-1

1956-ca.1960. Single-cut, 1 pickup, Coke bottle headstock.

1950s	Custom color	$900	$1,000
1950s	Standard color	$500	$600

U-1 '56 Reissue

1998-1999. Single-cut semi-hollow, masonite top and bottom, bolt-on neck, reissue of '56 U-1, with single 'lipstick tube' pickup, various colors.

1998-1999	$125	$175

U-2

1956-1959. Single-cut, 2 pickups, stacked concentric volume/tone controls, Coke bottle headstock.

1950s	Standard color	$700	$950

U-2 '56 Reissue

1998-2003. 2 pickup U-1.

1998-2003	$175	$225

U-3 '56 Reissue

1999-2003. Single-cut reissue of '56 U-3 with 3 'lipstick tube' pickups, various colors.

1999-2003	$200	$275

D'Angelico

John D'Angelico built his own line of archtop guitars, mandolins and violins from 1932 until his death in 1964. His instruments are some of the most sought-after by collectors.

D'Angelico (L-5 Snakehead)

1932-1935. D'Angelico's L-5-style with snakehead headstock, his first model, sunburst.

1932-1935	$11,500	$16,000

Excel/Exel (Cutaway)

1947-1964. Cutaway, 17" width, 1- and 3-ply bound F-hole, Larry Wexer noted from '50-'57, D'Angelico guitars suffer from severe binding problems and many have replaced bindings. Replaced bindings make the guitar non-original and these repaired guitars have lower values.

1947-1949	Natural, non-original binding	$19,000	$24,000
1947-1949	Natural, original binding	$35,000	$40,000
1947-1949	Sunburst, non-original binding	$14,000	$19,000
1947-1949	Sunburst, original binding	$33,000	$36,000
1950-1959	Natural, non-original binding	$19,000	$24,000
1950-1959	Natural, original binding	$33,000	$43,000
1950-1959	Sunburst, non-original binding	$14,000	$19,000
1950-1959	Sunburst, original binding	$33,000	$38,000
1960-1964	Natural	$33,000	$43,000
1960-1964	Sunburst	$33,000	$38,000

Excel/Exel (Non-cutaway)

1936-1949. Non-cut, 17" width, 1- and 3-ply bound F-hole, natural finishes were typically not offered in the '30s, non-cut Excels were generally not offered after '49 in deference to the Excel cutaway.

1936-1939	Sunburst, straight F-hole	$17,000	$24,000
1938-1939	Sunburst, standard F-hole	$17,000	$19,000
1940-1949	Natural	$17,000	$20,000
1940-1949	Sunburst, standard F-hole	$15,000	$19,000

New Yorker (Cutaway)

1947-1964. Cutaway, 18" width, 5-ply-bound F-hole, New Yorker non-cut orders were overshadowed by the cut model orders starting in '47, all prices noted are for original bindings, non-original (replaced) bindings will reduce the value by 33%-50%.

1947-1949	Natural, 4 made	$57,000	$71,000
1947-1949	Sunburst	$43,000	$57,000
1950-1959	Natural	$66,000	$71,000
1950-1959	Sunburst	$43,000	$57,000
1960-1964	Natural	$57,000	$71,000
1960-1964	Sunburst	$47,500	$57,000

1957 Danelectro U-1

1960 D'Angelico New Yorker

GUITARS

D'Angelico New Yorker NYL-2

D'Aquisto custom oval-hole

MODEL YEAR	FEATURES	EXC. COND. LOW	HIGH

New Yorker (Non-cutaway)

1936-1949. Non-cut, 18" width, 5-ply-bound F-hole, New Yorker non-cut orders were overshadowed by the cut model orders starting in '47, all prices noted are for original bindings, non-original (replaced) bindings will reduce the value by 33%-50%.

1936-1939	Sunburst	$19,000	$26,000
1940-1949	Natural	$24,000	$30,000
1940-1949	Sunburst	$19,000	$29,000

New Yorker Special

1947-1964. Also called Excel New Yorker or Excel Cutaway New YorkerCutaway, 17" width, New Yorker styling, prices are for original bindings, non-original (replaced) bindings reduce values by 33%-50%, not to be confused with D'Angelico Special (A and B style).

1947-1949	Natural	$33,000	$43,000
1947-1949	Sunburst	$33,000	$36,000
1950-1959	Natural	$33,000	$43,000
1950-1959	Sunburst	$33,000	$38,000
1960-1964	Natural	$33,000	$43,000
1960-1964	Sunburst	$33,000	$38,000

Special

1947-1964. Generally Style A and B-type instruments made for musicians on a budget, plain specs with little ornamentation, not to be confused with New Yorker Special.

1947-1964	Natural	$14,000	$17,000
1947-1964	Sunburst	$11,000	$14,000

Style A

1936-1945. Archtop, 17" width, unbound F-holes, block 'board inlays, multi-pointed headstock, nickel-plated metal parts.

1936-1939	Sunburst	$11,000	$12,500
1940-1945	Sunburst	$10,500	$11,500

Style A-1

1936-1945. Unbound F-holes, 17" width, arched headstock, nickel-plated metal parts.

1936-1939	Sunburst	$11,000	$12,500
1940-1945	Sunburst	$10,500	$11,500

Style B

1933-1948. Archtop 17" wide, unbound F-holes, block 'board inlays, gold-plated parts.

1936-1939	Sunburst	$12,000	$14,000
1940-1948	Sunburst	$11,000	$13,000

Style B Special

1933-1948. D'Angelico described variations from standard features with a 'Special' designation, Vintage dealers may also describe these instruments as 'Special'.

1936-1939	Sunburst	$13,000	$16,000
1940-1948	Sunburst	$13,000	$16,000

D'Angelico (Vestax)

1988-present. Premium and presentation grade, production/custom, archtop, flat-top, and solidbody guitars built by luthier Hidesato Shino and Vestax near Tokyo, Japan. Distributed in the U.S. by D'Angelico Guitars of America, in Westfield, New Jersey.

New Yorker NYL-2

17" single-cut archtop, spruce top, figured maple back and sides.

2000s	Natural	$1,900	$2,100

D'Angelico II

Mid-1990s. Archtops built in the U.S. and distributed by Archtop Enterprises of Merrick, New York.

Jazz Classic

1990s. Electric archtop, cutaway, carved spruce top, figured maple back and sides, single neck pickup, transparent cherry.

1990s		$3,900	$4,000

Daniel Friederich

1955-present. Luthier Daniel Friederich builds his custom/production, classical guitars in Paris, France.

D'Aquisto

1965-1995. James D'Aquisto apprenticed under D'Angelico until the latter's death, at age 59, in '64. He started making his own brand instruments in '65 and built archtop and flat top acoustic guitars, solidbody and hollowbody electric guitars. He also designed guitars for Hagstrom and Fender. He died in '95, at age 59.

Avant Garde

1987-1994. 18" wide, non-traditional futuristic model, approximately 5 or 6 instruments were reportedly made, because of low production this pricing is for guidance only.

1990	Blond	$80,000	$125,000

Centura/Centura Deluxe

1994 only. 17" wide, non-traditional art deco futuristic archtop, approximately 10 made, the last guitars made by this luthier, due to the low production this pricing is for guidance only.

1994	Blond	$80,000	$100,000

Excel (Cutaway)

1965-1992. Archtop, 17" width, with modern thin-logo started in '81.

1965-1968	Blond	$53,000	$55,000
1965-1968	Sunburst	$45,000	$53,000
1968-1979	Blond	$43,000	$46,000
1968-1979	Sunburst	$35,000	$39,000
1980-1989	Blond	$53,000	$55,000
1980-1989	Sunburst	$40,000	$41,000
1990-1992	Blond	$53,000	$55,000
1990-1992	Sunburst	$40,000	$41,000

Excel (Flat-Top)

1980s. Flat-top, 16", flamed maple back and sides, Sitka spruce top, about 15 made, narrow Excel-style headstock, oval soundhole, D'Aquisto script logo on headstock.

1980s		$15,000	$19,000

Hollow Electric

Early model with bar pickup, D'Aquisto headstock, '70s model with humbuckers.

1965	Sunburst	$10,500	$12,000
1972	Sunburst	$10,500	$12,000

MODEL YEAR	FEATURES	EXC. COND. LOW	HIGH
Jim Hall			
Hollow-body electric, carved spruce top, 1 pickup.			
1965	Laminate top	$10,500	$12,000
1978	Solid top	$10,500	$12,000
New Yorker Classic (Solidbody)			
1980s. Only 2 were reported to be made, therefore this pricing is for guidance only.			
1980s		$17,000	$18,500
New Yorker Deluxe (Cutaway)			
1965-1992. Most are 18" wide.			
1965-1967	Blond	$55,000	$63,000
1965-1967	Sunburst	$50,000	$63,000
1968-1979	Blond	$45,000	$49,000
1968-1979	Sunburst	$45,000	$49,000
1980-1989	Blond	$47,000	$49,000
1980-1989	Sunburst	$47,000	$49,000
1990-1992	Blond	$53,000	$55,000
1990-1992	Sunburst	$53,000	$55,000
New Yorker Special (7-String)			
1980s. Limited production 7-string, single-cut.			
1980s	Sunburst	$47,000	$49,000
New Yorker Special (Cutaway)			
1966-1992. Most are 17" wide.			
1966-1967	Blond	$55,000	$63,000
1966-1967	Sunburst	$50,000	$63,000
1970-1979	Blond	$45,000	$49,000
1970-1979	Sunburst	$45,000	$49,000
1980-1989	Blond	$47,000	$49,000
1980-1989	Sunburst	$47,000	$49,000
1990-1992	Blond	$53,000	$55,000
1990-1992	Sunburst	$53,000	$55,000
Solo/Solo Deluxe			
1992-1993. 18" wide, non-traditional non-cut art deco model, only 2 reported made, because of low production this pricing is for guidance only.			
1992-1993	Blond	$80,000	$100,000

D'Aquisto (Aria)

May 2002-present. Premium grade, production, D'Aquisto designs licensed to Aria of Japan by D'Aquisto Strings, Inc., Deer Park, New York.

Centura Electric

2002-present. Chambered solidbody, blond.

2002		$2,600	$2,300

Dauphin

1970s-present. Classical and flamenco guitars built in Spain..

Classical

Solid spruce top, rosewood back and sides.

1990s		$525	$600

Dave Maize Acoustic Guitars

1991-present. Luthier Dave Maize builds his professional and premium grade, production/custom, flat-tops in Cave Junction, Oregon. He also builds basses.

David Rubio

1960s-2000. Luthier David Spink built his guitars, lutes, violins, violas, cellos and harpsichords first in New York, and after '67, in England. While playing in Spain, he acquired his the nickname Rubio, after his red beard. He died in '00.

David Thomas McNaught

1989-present. Professional, premium, and presentation grade, custom, solidbody guitars built by luthier David Thomas McNaught and finished by Dave Mansel in Locust, North Carolina. In '97, they added the production/custom DTM line of guitars.

Solidbody High-End

2000s. High-end solidbody with indepth inlay (rhino, moonscape), heavily figured wood, various styles.

2000s		$4,000	$6,000

Vintage Double-Cut

Classic/modern offset double-cut, figured maple top, twin exposed humbuckers.

2002		$3,300	$3,500

Vintage Standard

2003		$3,300	$3,500

Davis, J. Thomas

1975-present. Premium and presentation grade, custom, steel-string flat-tops, 12-strings, classicals, archtops, Irish citterns and flat-top Irish bouzoukis made by luthier J. Thomas Davis in Columbus, Ohio.

Davoli

See Wandre listing.

de Jonge, Sergei

1972-present. Premium grade, production/custom classical and steel-string guitars built by luthier Sergei de Jonge originally in Oshawa, Ontario, and since '04 in Chelsea, Quebec.

De Paule Stringed Instruments

1969-1980, 1993-present. Custom steel-string, nylon-string, archtop, resonator, and Hawaiian guitars built by luthier C. Andrew De Paule in Eugene, Oregon.

Dean

1976-present. Intermediate, professional and premium grade, production/custom, solidbody, hollowbody, acoustic, acoustic/electric, and resonator guitars made in the U.S., Korea, the Czech Republic and China. They also offer basses, banjos, mandolins, and amps. Founded in Evanston, .. Illinois, by Dean Zelinsky. Original models were upscale versions of Gibson designs with glued necks, fancy tops, DiMarzio pickups and distinctive winged headstocks (V, Z and ML), with production beginning in '77. In '80 the factory was relocated to Chicago. Dean's American manufacturing ends in '86 when all production shifts to Korea. In '91 Zelinsky sold the company to Tropical Music in Miami, Florida. For '93-'94 there was again limited U.S. (California)

David Thomas McNaught G-5

1983 Dean Bel Air

Dean Baby ML

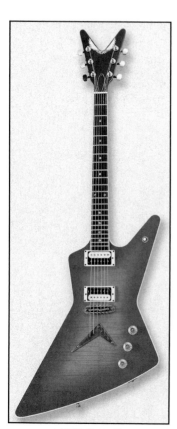

1978 Dean Z

production of the E'Lite, Cadillac and ML models under the supervision of Zelinsky and Cory Wadley. Korean versions were also produced. In '95, Elliott Rubinson's Armadillo Enterprises, of Clearwater, Florida, bought the Dean brand. In '97 and '98, Dean offered higher-end USA Custom Shop models. In '98, they reintroduced acoustics. In 2000, Zelinsky once again became involved in the company.

Baby ML
1982-1986. Downsized version of ML model.

MODEL YEAR	FEATURES	EXC. COND. LOW	HIGH
1980s	Import	$375	$425
1980s	U.S.-made	$575	$725

Baby V
1982-1986. Downsized version of the V model.

1980s	Import	$350	$400
1980s	U.S.-made	$500	$650

Baby Z
1982-1986. Downsized version of Z model.

1980s	Import	$350	$400
1980s	U.S.-made	$550	$700

Bel Aire
1983-1984. Solidbody, possibly the first production guitar with humbucker/single/single pickup layout, U.S.-made, an import model was introduced in '87

1980s	Import	$300	$350
1983-1984	U.S.-made	$500	$650

Budweiser Guitar
Ca.1987. Shaped like Bud logo.

1987		$500	$550

Cadillac (USA)
1979-1985. Single long treble horn on slab body.

1979-1982		$1,000	$1,100

Cadillac Deluxe (USA)
1993-1994, 1996-1997. Made in U.S., single longhorn shape, various colors.

1993-1994		$1,200	$1,300
1996-1997		$1,200	$1,300

Cadillac Reissue (Import)
1992-1994. Single longhorn shape, 2 humbuckers, various colors.

1994		$400	$450

Cadillac Standard
1996-1997. Slab body version.

1996		$1,000	$1,000

Eighty-Eight
1987-1990. Offset double-cut solidbody, import.

1987		$175	$275

E'Lite
1978-1985, 1994-1996. Single-horn shape.

1980s		$800	$950

E'Lite Deluxe
Single-horn shape.

1980s		$1,100	$1,300

Golden E'Lite
Single pointy treble cutaway, fork headstock, gold hardware, ebony 'board, sunburst.

1980		$1,100	$1,300

Hollywood Z (Import)
1985-1986. Bolt-neck Japanese copy of Baby Z, Explorer shape.

1985		$175	$200

Jammer (Import)
1987-1989. Offset double-cut body, bolt-on neck, dot markers, six-on-a-side tuners, various colors offered.

MODEL YEAR	FEATURES	EXC. COND. LOW	HIGH
1987-1989		$175	$225

Mach I (Import)
1985-1986. Limited run from Korea, Mach V with six-on-a-side tunes, various colors.

1985-1986		$175	$225

Mach V (Import)
1985-1986. Pointed solidbody, 2 humbucking pickups, maple neck, ebony 'board, locking trem, various colors, limited run from Korea.

1985-1986		$175	$225

Mach VII (USA)
1985-1986. Mach I styling, made in America, offered in unusual finishes.

1985-1986		$900	$1,000

ML (Import)
1983-1990. Korean-made.

1983-1990		$425	$475

ML (ML Standard/US-made)
1977-1986. There is a flame model and a standard model.

1977-1982		$1,500	$1,600

V (V Flame)
Flamed maple version of V Standard.

1977-1981	Unbound	$1,300	$1,400

V (V Standard)
1977-1986. V-shaped body, standard and flame model offered.

1977-1986	Bound	$1,300	$1,400

Z (Z Standard)
1977-1986. Solid body, long treble cutaway, 2 humbuckers.

1977-1983	U.S.-made, bound	$1,400	$1,500
1983-1986	Japanese import	$400	$450

Z Autograph (Import)
1985-1987. The first Dean import from Korea offset double-cut, bolt-on neck, dot markers, offered in several standard colors.

1985-1987		$250	$350

Z Coupe/Z Deluxe (USA Custom Shop)
1997-1998. Mahogany body offered in several standard colors, Z Deluxe with Floyd Rose tremolo.

1997-1998		$900	$1,150

Z Korina (USA Custom Shop)
1997-1998. Z Coupe with korina body, various standard colors.

1997-1998		$950	$1,200

Z LTD (USA Custom Shop)
1997-1998. Z Coupe with bound neck and headstock, offered in several standard colors.

1997-1998		$950	$1,150

Dean Markley

The string and pickup manufacturer offered a limited line of guitars and basses for a time in the '80s. They were introduced in '84.

MODEL YEAR	FEATURES	EXC. COND. LOW	HIGH

Electric Solidbodies

1980s. Includes the Concert, Vintage, and Custom Vintage models.

1980s		$300	$350

DeArmond Guitars

1999-2004. Solid, semi-hollow and hollow body guitars based on Guild models and imported from Korea by Fender. They also offered basses.

Electric

Late-1990s. Various import models, some with USA electronic components.

1999	Starfire	$425	$550
1999	X-155 hollowbody	$425	$550

Dearstone

1993-present. Luthier Ray Dearstone builds his professional and premium grade, custom, archtop and acoustic/electric guitars in Blountville, Tennessee. He also builds mandolin family instruments and violins.

DeCava Guitars

1983-present. Professional and premium grade, production/custom, archtop and classical guitars built by luthier Jim DeCava in Stratford, Connecticut. He also builds ukes, banjos, and mandolins.

Decca

Mid-1960s. Acoustic, solid and hollow body guitars made in Japan by Teisco and imported by Decca Records, Decca headstock logo, student-level instruments. They also offered amps and a bass.

Acoustic Flat-Top

1960s. Decca label on the inside back.

1960s		$100	$175

DeGennaro

2003-present. Premium grade, custom/production, acoustic, archtop, semi-hollow and solidbody guitars built by luthier William Degennaro in Grand Rapids, Michigan. He also builds basses and mandolins.

Del Pilar Guitars

1956-1986. Luthier William Del Pilar made his classical guitars in Brooklyn, New York.

Classical (Mahogany)

1980s. Mahogany back and sides, spruce top, red and green rosette.

1980s		$1,400	$1,500

Classical (Rosewood)

1950s. Brazilian rosewood back and sides, cedar top, quilt rosette, 9-ply top binding.

1950s		$3,500	$4,000

Del Vecchio

1902-present. Casa Del Vecchio builds a variety of Spanish instruments including acoustic and resonator guitars in São Paulo, Brazil.

Dell'Arte

1997-present. Production/custom Maccaferri-style guitars from John Kinnard and Alain Cola. In '96, luthier John Kinnard opened a small shop called Finegold Guitars and Mandolins. In '98 he met Alain Cola, a long time jazz guitarist who was selling Mexican-made copies of Selmer/Maccaferri guitars under the Dell'Arte brand. Cola wanted better workmanship for his guitars, and in October '98, Finegold and Dell'Arte merged. As of May '99 all production is in California.

Anouman Custom

1990s		$1,800	$2,000

Delta Guitars

2005-present. Acoustic, acoustic/electric, and solidbody electric guitars from Musician's Wholesale America, Nashville, Tennessee.

Dennis Hill Guitars

1991-present. Premium and presentation grade, production/custom, classical and flamenco guitars built by luthier Dennis Hill in Panama City, Florida. He has also built dulcimers, mandolins, and violins.

Desmond Guitars

1991-present. Luthier Robert B. Desmond builds his premium grade, production/custom classical guitars in Orlando, Florida.

DeTemple

1995-present. Premium grade, production/custom, solidbody electric guitars built by luthier Michael DeTemple in Sherman Oaks, California. He also builds basses.

DeVoe Guitars

1975-present. Luthier Lester DeVoe builds his premium grade, production/custom flamenco and classical guitars in Nipomo, California.

Diamond

Ca. 1963-1964. Line of sparkle finish solidbody guitars made in Italy for the Diamond Accordion company.

Ranger

Ca. 1963-1964. Rangers came with 1, 2, 3, or 4 pickups, sparkle finish.

1960s	4 pickups	$500	$675

Dick, Edward Victor

1975-present. Luthier Edward Dick currently builds his premium grade, custom, classical guitars in Denver, Colorado (he lived in Peterborough and Ottawa, Ontario until '95). He also operates the Colorado School of Luthrie.

Dickerson

1937-1947. Founded by the Dickerson brothers in '37, primarily for electric lap steels and small

Dell'Arte Anouman Custom

DeVoe archtop

DiPinto Galaxie 4

MODEL		EXC. COND.	
YEAR	FEATURES	LOW	HIGH

amps. Instruments were also private branded for Cleveland's Oahu company, and for the Gourley brand. By '47, the company changed ownership and was renamed Magna Electronics (Magnatone).

Dillion

2000-present. Dillion, of Cary, North Carolina, offers intermediate grade, production, acoustic, acoustic/electric, hollow-body and solidbody guitars made in Korea and Vietnam. They also have basses and mandolins.

Electric Solidbodies

2000-present. Includes various models.

2000-2004		$200	$400

Dillon

1975-present. Professional and premium grade, custom, flat-tops built by luthier John Dillon originally in Taos, New Mexico ('75-'81), then in Bloomsburg, Pennsylvania ('81-'01), and since 2001 back in Taos. He also builds basses.

DiPinto

1995-present. Intermediate and professional grade, production retro-vibe guitars from luthier Chris DiPinto of Philadelphia, Pennsylvania. He also builds basses. Until late '99, all instruments built in the U.S., since then all built in Korea.

Ditson

1916-1930. Ditson guitars were made by Martin and sold by the Oliver Ditson Company of Boston. The majority of production was from '16 to '22 with over 500 units sold in '21.

Concert Models

1916-1922. Similar in size to Martin size 0. Models include Style 1, Style 2 and Style 3.

1916-1922	Style 1	$1,900	$2,100
1916-1922	Style 2	$2,400	$2,600
1916-1922	Style 3	$2,900	$3,100

Standard Models

1916-1922. Small body similar to Martin size 3, plain styling. Models include Style 1, Style 2 and Style 3.

1916-1922	Style 1	$1,500	$2,000
1916-1922	Style 2	$2,000	$2,300
1916-1922	Style 3	$2,800	$3,000

Style 111 Dreadnought

Dreadnought-sized exceeding the Martin 000 size, initially intended to be a 6-string bass guitar, fan bracing on the top generally requires extensive restoration.

1916-1922		$4,000	$4,200

Dobro

1929-1942, ca. 1954-present. Currently, professional and premium grade, production, wood and metal body resophonic guitars offered by Gibson.

Founded 1929 in Los Angeles by John Dopyera, Rudy Dopyera, Ed Dopyera and Vic Smith (Dobro stands for "Dopyera Brothers"). Made instruments sold under the Dobro, Regal, Norwood Chimes,

1937 Dobro Model 27 (squareneck)

Angelus, Rex, Broman, Montgomery Ward, Penetro, Bruno, Alhambra, More Harmony, Orpheum, and Magn-o-tone brands.

Dobro instruments have a single cone facing outward with a spider bridge structure and competed with National products. Generally, model names are numbers referring to list price and therefore materials and workmanship (e.g., a No. 65 cost $65). Because of this, the same model number may apply to various different instruments. However, model numbers are never identified on instruments!

In '30, the company name was changed to Dobro Corporation, Ltd. In '32, Louis Dopyera buys Ted Kleinmeyer's share of National. Louis, Rudy and Ed now hold controlling interest in National, but in '32 John Dopyera left Dobro to pursue idea of metal resophonic violin. In December of '34 Ed Dopyera joins National's board of directors (he's also still on Dobro board), and by March of '35 Dobro and National have merged to become the National Dobro Corporation. Dobro moves into National's larger factory but continues to maintain separate production, sales and distribution until relocation to Chicago is complete. Beginning in early-'36 National Dobro starts relocating its offices to Chicago. L.A. production of Dobros continues until '37, after which some guitars continue to be assembled from parts until '39, when the L.A. operations were closed down. All resonator production ended in '42. Victor Smith, Al Frost and Louis Dopyera buy the company and change the name to the Valco Manufacturing Company. The Dobro name does not appear when production resumes after World War II.

In mid-'50s - some sources say as early as '54 - Rudy and Ed Dopyera began assembling wood-bodied Dobros from old parts using the name DB Original. In about '59, some 12-fret DB Originals were made for Standel, carrying both DB Original and Standel logos. In around '61, production was moved to Gardena, California, and Louis Dopyera and Valco transferred the Dobro name to Rudy and Ed, who produce the so-called Gardena Dobros. At this time, the modern Dobro logo appeared with a lyre that looks like 2 back-to-back '6s'. Dobro Original debuts ca. '62. In late-'64 the Dobro name was licensed to Ed's son Emil (Ed, Jr.) Dopyera. Ed, Jr. designs a more rounded Dobro (very similar to later Mosrites) and has falling out with Rudy over it.

In '66 Semi Moseley acquires the rights to the Dobro brand, building some in Gardena, and later moving to Bakersfield, California. Moseley introduced Ed, Jr's design plus a thinline double-cutaway Dobro. Moseley Dobros use either Dobro or National cones. In '67 Ed, Sr., Rudy and Gabriella Lazar start the Original Music Instrument Company (OMI) and produce Hound Dog brand Dobros. In '68 Moseley goes bankrupt and in '70 OMI obtains the rights to the Dobro brand and begins production of OMI Dobros. In '75 Gabriella's son and daughter, Ron Lazar and Dee Garland, take over OMI. Rudy Dupyera makes and sells Safari brand resonator mandolins. Ed, Sr. dies in '77 and

MODEL YEAR	FEATURES	EXC. COND. LOW	HIGH

Rudy in '78. In '84 OMI was sold to Chester and Betty Lizak. Both wood and metal-bodied Dobros produced in Huntington Beach, California. Chester Lizak died in '92. Gibson purchased Dobro in '93 and now makes Dobros in Nashville, Tennessee.

Dobros generally feature a serial number which, combined with historical information, provides a clue to dating. For prewar L.A. guitars, see approximation chart below adapted from Gruhn and Carter's Gruhn's Guide to Vintage Guitars (Miller Freeman, 1991). No information exists on DB Originals.

Gardena Dobros had D prefix plus 3 digits beginning with 100 and going into the 500s (reportedly under 500 made). No information is available on Moseley Dobros.

OMI Dobros from '70-'79 have either D prefix for wood bodies or B prefix for metal bodies, plus 3 or 4 numbers for ranking, space, then a single digit for year (D XXXX Y or B XXX Y; e.g., D 172 8 would be wood body #172 from '78). For '80-'87 OMI Dobros, start with first number of year (decade) plus 3 or 4 ranking numbers, space, then year and either D for wood or B for metal bodies (8 XXXX YD or 8 XXX YB; e.g., 8 2006 5B would be metal body #2008 from '85). From '88-'92, at least, a letter and number indicate guitar style, plus 3 or 4 digits for ranking, letter for neck style, 2 digits for year, and letter for body style (AX XXXX NYYD or AX XXX NYYB).

L.A. Guitars (approx. number ranges, not actual production totals)

1929-30	900-2999
1930-31	3000-3999
1931-32	BXXX (Cyclops models only)
1932-33	5000-5599
1934-36	5700-7699

Angelus
1933-1937. Wood body, round or square neck, 2-tone walnut finish, continues as Model 19 in Regal-made guitars.

1930s	Round neck	$1,300	$2,000
1930s	Square neck	$1,500	$2,500

Artist M-16
1934-1935. German silver alloy body, engraved.

1934-1935	H Square neck	$4,000	$4,500
1934-1935	M Round neck	$3,000	$3,500

Cyclops 45
1932-1933. Bound walnut body, 1 screen hole.

1932-1933	Round neck	$2,000	$3,000
1932-1933	Square neck	$2,500	$3,500

D-40 Texarkana
1965-1967. Mosrite-era (identified by C or D prefix), traditional Dobro style cone and coverplate, dot inlays, Dobro logo on headstock, sunburst wood body. Red and blue finishes available.

1965-1967	Sunburst, square neck	$1,200	$1,500

D-40E Texarkana
1965-1967. D-40 electric with single pickup and 2 knobs.

1965-1967		$1,400	$1,600

MODEL YEAR	FEATURES	EXC. COND. LOW	HIGH

DM-33 California Girl/DM-33H
1996-2004. Chrome-plated bell brass body, biscuit bridge, spider resonator, rosewood 'board. Girl or Hawaiian-scene (H) engraving.

2000s		$1,400	$1,800

Dobro/Regal 46/47
1935-1938 Dobro/Regal 46, renamed 47 1939-1942. Made by Regal of Chicago, aluminum body, round neck, 14 frets, slotted peghead, silver finish. Degraded finish was a common problem with the Dobro/Regal 47.

1935-1938	Model 46	$1,200	$1,600
1939-1942	Model 47, degraded finish	$600	$800
1939-1942	Model 47, original finish	$1,300	$1,700

Dobro/Regal 62/65
1935-1938 Dobro/Regal 62, continued as Dobro/Regal 65 for 1939-1942. Nickel-plated brass body, Spanish dancer etching, round or square neck. Note: Dobro/Regal 65 should not be confused with Dobro Model 65 which discontinued earlier.

1935-1938	Model 62, round neck	$3,200	$3,800
1935-1938	Model 62, square neck	$2,200	$2,800
1939-1942	Model 65, round neck	$3,200	$3,800
1939-1942	Model 65, square neck	$2,200	$2,800

Dobro/Regal Tenor 27-1/2
1930. Tenor version of Model 27.

1930		$800	$900

Dobrolektic
1990s-2000s. Resonator guitar with single-coil neck pickup, single-cut.

1990-2000s		$1,000	$1,150

DS-33/Steel 33
1995-2000. Steel body with light amber sunburst finish, resonator with coverplate, biscuit bridge.

1995-2000		$1,200	$1,300

DW-90C
2000s. Single sharp cutaway, wood body, metal resonator, F-hole upper bass bout.

2000s		$1,400	$1,500

Hula Blues
1980s-1990s. Dark brown wood body (earlier models have much lighter finish), painted Hawaiian scenes, round neck.

1991		$900	$1,100

Josh Graves
1996-present. Single bound ample body, spider cone, nickel plated.

1990s		$2,500	$2,600

Leader 14M/14H
1934-1935. Nickel plated brass body, segmented f-holes.

1934-1935	H Square neck	$2,500	$3,000
1934-1935	M Round neck	$2,000	$2,500

1930s Dobro Model 45

Dobro Josh Graves signature model

Dobro Model 19

1967 Domino Baron

MODEL YEAR	FEATURES	LOW	HIGH
Model 27 (OMI)			
1980s		$1,100	$1,300
Model 27 Cyclops			
1932-1933.			
1932-1933	Round neck	$1,000	$1,500
1932-1933	Square neck	$1,500	$2,000
Model 27 Deluxe			
1990s.			
1990s		$1,500	$1,700
Model 27/27G			
1933-1937. Regal-made, wooden body.			
1933-1937	Round neck	$1,500	$2,000
1933-1937	Square neck	$2,000	$2,500
Model 33 (Duolian)			
1972. Only made in '72, becomes Model 90 in '73.			
1972		$1,100	$1,500
1971-1974		$1,500	$1,600
Model 33 H			
1973-1997 (OMI & Gibson). Same as 33 D, but with etched Hawaiian scenes, available as round or square neck.			
1980s	Round neck	$1,600	$1,700
1980s	Square neck	$0	$0
Model 36			
1932-1937. Wood body with resonator, round or square neck.			
1932-1937	Round neck	$1,200	$1,700
1932-1937	Square neck	$2,000	$2,500
Model 36 S			
1970-1980s. Chrome-plated brass body, square neck, slotted headstock, dot markers, engraved rose floral art.			
1970-1980s		$1,500	$1,600
Model 37			
1933-1937. Regal-made wood body, mahogany, bound body and 'board, round or square 12-fret neck.			
1933-1937	Round neck	$1,100	$1,500
1933-1937	Square neck	$1,400	$2,000
Model 37 Tenor			
1933-1937 (Regal). Tenor version of No. 37.			
1930s		$800	$900
Model 55/56 Standard			
1929-1931 Model 55 Standard, renamed 56 Standard 1932-1934. Unbound wood body, metal resonator, bound neck, sunburst.			
1929-1931	Model 55	$2,000	$2,500
1932-1934	Model 56	$2,000	$2,500
Model 60			
1933-1936. Similar to Model 66/66B.			
1933-1936		$2,300	$2,800
Model 60 Cyclops			
1932-1933.			
1932-1933		$2,500	$3,000
Model 60/60 D (OMI)/60 DS			
1970-1993. Wood body (laminated maple) with Dobro resonator cone, model 60 until '73 when renamed 60 D, and various 60 model features offered, post-'93 was Gibson-owned production.			
1970s	Model 60	$1,100	$1,300
1980s	Model 60 D / 60 DS	$950	$1,300

MODEL YEAR	FEATURES	LOW	HIGH
Model 65/66/66 B			
1920s-1930s. Wood body with sandblasted ornamental design top and back, metal resonator, sunburst. Model 66 B has bound top.			
1929-1931	Model 65	$2,900	$3,300
1932-1933	Model 66	$2,900	$3,300
1932-1933	Model 66 B	$3,000	$3,400
Model 66 Cyclops			
1978		$1,100	$1,300
Model 90 (Duolian) (OMI)			
1972-1993. Chrome-plated, F-holes, etched Hawaiian scene.			
1972-1993		$1,100	$1,500
Model 90 (Woodbody)/WB90 G / WB90 S			
2000s. Maple body with upper bout F-holes or sound holes, round neck, metal resonator with spider bridge, sunburst.			
2002		$1,200	$1,500
Model 125 De Luxe			
1929-1934. Black walnut body, round or square neck, Dobro De Luxe engraved, triple-bound top, back and 'board, nickel-plated hardware, natural.			
1929-1934	Round neck	$3,500	$4,000
1929-1934	Square neck	$4,500	$5,500
Professional 15M/15H			
1934-1935. Engraved nickel body, round (M) or square (H) neck, solid peghead.			
1934-1935	H square neck	$3,000	$3,500
1934-1935	M round neck	$2,500	$3,000

Dodge

1996-present. Luthier Rick Dodge builds his intermediate and professional grade, production, solidbody guitars with changeable electronic modules in Tallahassee, Florida. He also builds basses.

Domino

Ca. 1967-1968. Solidbody and hollowbody electric guitars and basses imported from Japan by Maurice Lipsky Music Co. of New York, New York, previously responsible for marketing the Orpheum brand. Models are primarily near-copies of EKO, Vox, and Fender designs, plus some originals. Models were made by Arai or Kawai. Earlier models may have been imported, but this is not yet documented.

Electric

1967-1968. Various models include the Baron, Californian, Californian Rebel, Dawson, and the Spartan.

1967		$375	$475

Dommenget

1978-1985, 1988-present. Luthier Boris Dommenget (pronounced dommen-jay) builds his premium grade, custom/production, solidbody, flat-top, and archtop guitars in Balje, Germany. From '78 to '85 he was located in Wiesbaden, and from '88-'01 in Hamburg. He and wife Fiona also make pickups.

MODEL YEAR	FEATURES	EXC. COND. LOW	HIGH

Don Musser Guitars

1976-present. Custom, classical and flat-top guitars built by luthier Don Musser in Cotopaxi, Colorado.

Doolin Guitars

1997-present. Luthier Mike Doolin builds his premium grade, production/custom acoutics featuring his unique double-cut in Portland, Oregon.

Dorado

Ca. 1972-1973. Six- and 12-string acoustic guitars, solidbody electrics and basses. Brand used briefly by Baldwin/Gretsch on line of Japanese imports.

Acoustic Flat-Top/Acoustic Dobro

1972-1973. Includes folk D, jumbo Western, and grand concert styles (with laminated (?) rosewood back and sides), and Dobro-style.

1970s	Lower-range models	$75	$150
1970s	Mid-range models	$125	$200
1970s	Higher-range models	$175	$250

Solidbody Electric

1972-1973. Includes Model 5985, a double-cuty with 2 P-90-style pickups.

1970s		$125	$225

D'Pergo Custom Guitars

2002-present. Professional, premium, and presentation grade, production/custom, solidbody guitars built in Windham, New Hampshire. Every component of the guitars is built by D'Pergo.

Dragge Guitars

1982-present. Luthier Peter Dragge builds his custom, steel-string and nylon-string guitars in Ojai, California.

Dragonfly Guitars

1994-present. Professional grade, production/custom, sloped cutaway flat-tops, semi-hollow body electrics, and dulcitars built by luthier Dan Richter in Roberts Creek, British Columbia.

Drive

2000s. Student imports. Drive logo placed inside a rectangular border on the headstock.

DTM

1997-present. See David Thomas McNaught listing.

Dunwell Guitars

1996-present. Professional and premium grade, custom, flat-tops built by luthier Alan Dunwell in Nederland, Colorado.

Dupont

Luthier Maurice Dupont builds his classical, archtop, Weissenborn-style and Selmer-style guitars in Cognac, France.

Earthwood

1972-1985. Acoustic designs by Ernie Ball with input from George Fullerton. One of the first to offer acoustic basses.

Eastman

1992-present. Professional and premium grade, production, archtop and flat-top guitars mainly built in China, with some from Germany and Romania. Beijing, China-based Eastman Strings started out building violins and cellos. They added guitars in '02 and mandolins in '04.

Eastwood

1997-present. Mike Robinson's company imports budget and intermediate grade, production, solid and semi-hollowbody guitars, many styled after 1960s models. They also offer basses.

Airline J.B. Hutto Copy

2004. Supro/Airline copy, 6 knobs and switch on bass side of body, 1 knob near input jack on lower treble bout, 3 pickups, blue or white.

2004		$450	$550

Airline Jack White Copy

2004. Supro/Airline copy of Jack White's guitar, 4 knobs and toggle switch on treble side of body, block markers, 3 pickups, red or sunburst.

2004		$425	$475

Eaton, William

1976-present. Luthier William Eaton builds custom specialty instruments such as vihuelas, harp guitars, and lyres in Phoenix, Arizona. He is also the Director of the Robetto-Venn School of Luthiery.

Ed Claxton Guitars

1972-present. Premium grade, custom flat-tops made by luthier Ed Claxton, first in Austin, Texas, and currently in Santa Cruz, California.

Eduardo Duran Ferrer

1987-present. Luthier Eduardo Duran Ferrer builds his premium grade, classical guitars in Granada, Spain.

Egmond

1960-1972. Entry-level import from Holland. Prices include original guitar case, and an example without the case is worth considerably less.

Electric

1960s. Solid or semi-hollow bodies.

1960s		$350	$450

Ehlers

1985-present. Luthier Rob Ehlers builds his premium grade, production/custom, flat-top acoustic guitars in Oregon.

Dunwell parlor guitar

Eastwood Airline

1982 EKO CO-2 Cobra

EKO 500/3V

MODEL YEAR	FEATURES	EXC. COND. LOW	HIGH
15 CRC	*Cutaway, Western red cedar top, Indian rosewood back and sides.*		
1996		$2,800	$3,000
15 SRC	*Cutaway, European spruce top, Indian rosewood back and sides.*		
1998		$2,900	$3,100
16 BTM	*European spruce top, mahogany back and sides, Troubadour peghead, black lacquer finish.*		
1998		$2,900	$3,100
16 SK Concert	*16" lower bout, relatively small upper bout, small waist, European spruce top, flamed koa back and sides, diamond markers, natural.*		
1993		$2,400	$2,600
16 SM	*European spruce top, mahogany back and sides.*		
1999		$2,400	$2,500
16 SSC	*Cutaway, European spruce top, English sycamore back and sides.*		
1996		$3,000	$3,200
25 C	*Limited Edition Anniversary Model, European spruce top, Indian rosewood back and sides, abalone top border.*		
2001		$3,900	$4,100

Eichelbaum Guitars

1994-present. Luthier David Eichelbaum builds his premium grade, custom, flat-tops in Santa Barbara, California.

EKO

1959-1985, 2000-present. Originally acoustic, acoustic/electric, electric thinline and full-size archtop hollowbody, solidbody electric guitars and basses built by Oliviero Pigini and Company in Recanati, Italy, and imported by LoDuca Brothers, Milwaukee, Radio and Television Equipment Company in Santa Ana, California and others. First acoustic guitars followed by sparkle plastic-covered electrics by '62. Sparkle finishes are gone ca. '66. Pigini dies ca. '67. LoDuca Bros. phases out in early-'70s. By '75 EKO offers some copy guitars and they purchased a custom shop to make other brands by '78.

Since about 2000, budget and intermediate grade, production, classical, acoustic, acoustic/electric, solidbody, solidbody, and hollowbody EKO guitars are again available and made in Asia. They also make basses and amps. They we soon have the Italian-made Vintage Series available.

Barracuda/Barracuda 12-String

1966-ca.1978. Double-cut semi-hollow, 2 pickups, 6-string or 12-string.

1966-1978	6- and 12-string	$425	$475

MODEL YEAR	FEATURES	EXC. COND. LOW	HIGH
Cobra I/II/III/XII	*1966-1978. Double-cut solidbody, 2 knobs. Cobra I has 1 pickup, II 2 pickups and III 3 pickups. 12-string Cobra XII offered '67-'69, has 2 pickups.*		
1966-1978	Cobra I	$300	$350
1966-1978	Cobra II	$350	$400
1966-1978	Cobra III	$350	$400
1967-1969	Cobra XII	$375	$500
Condor	*1966-ca.1969. Double-cut solidbody with 3 or 4 pickups.*		
1966-1969		$450	$550
Dragon	*1967-ca.1969. Single-cut archtop, 2 F-holes, 3 pickups, tremolo.*		
1967-1969		$450	$550
Flat-Top Acoustic	*1960s. Various student-level flat-top acoustic models.*		
1960s		$175	$225
Florentine	*1964-ca.1969. Double-cut archtop, 2 pickups.*		
1964-1969		$500	$550
Kadett/Kadett XII	*1967-ca.1978. Double-cut solidbody with point on lower bass side of body, 3 pickups, tremolo. 12-string Kadett XII offered '68-'69.*		
1967-1978	Kadett	$450	$500
1968-1969	Kadett XII	$450	$500
Lancer	*1967-ca.1969. Double-cut solidbody, 2 pickups.*		
1967-1969		$275	$350
Lark I/II	*1970. Thin hollow cutaway, sunburst. Lark I has 1 pickup and Lark II 2.*		
1970	Lark I	$400	$450
1970	Lark II	$400	$450
Model 500/1 / 500/1V	*1961-1964. Plastic covered solid body, 1 pickup. 500/1 no vibrato, 1V with vibrato.*		
1961-1964	500/1	$350	$450
1961-1964	500/1V	$400	$500
Model 500/2 / 500/3V	*1961-1964. Plastic covered solid body, plastic sparkle finish. 500/2 no vibrato, 2 pickups. 3V with vibrato, 3 pickups.*		
1961-1964	500/2	$550	$650
1961-1964	500/3V	$600	$700
Model 500/4 / 500/4V	*1961-1964. Plastic covered solid body, 4 pickups. 500/4 no vibrato, 4V with vibrato.*		
1961-1964	500/4	$650	$750
1961-1964	500/4V	$700	$800
Model 540 (Classical)	*1960s. Nylon-string classical guitar.*		
1960s		$175	$225

MODEL YEAR	FEATURES	EXC. COND. LOW	HIGH

Model 700/3V
1961-1964. Map-shape/tulip-shape body, 3 pickups, vibrato, woodgrain plastic finish.

1961-1964		$1,000	$1,100

Model 700/4V
1961-1967. Map-shape/tulip-shape body, 4 pickups, multiple switches, vibrato.

1960s	Standard finish	$1,100	$1,200
1961-1967	Red, blue, silver sparkle	$1,300	$1,400

Ranger 6/12
1967-ca.1982. D-style flat-top acoustic, large 3-point 'guard, dot inlays, EKO Ranger label. Ranger 12 is 12-string.

1967-1982	Ranger 12	$325	$400
1967-1982	Ranger 6	$250	$350

Rocket VI/XII (Rokes)
1967-ca.1969. Rocket-shape design, solidbody, 6-string, says Rokes on the headstock, Rokes were a popular English band that endorsed EKO guitars, marketed as the Rocket VI in the U.S.; and as the Rokes in Europe, often called the Rok. Rocket XII is 12-string.

1967-1969	Rocket VI	$600	$850
1967-1969	Rocket XII	$650	$850

El Degas
Early-1970s. Japanese-made copies of classic America electrics and acoustics, imported by Buegeleisen & Jacobson of New York, New York.

Solidbodies
Early-1970s. Copies of classic American models.

1970s		$160	$180

Electar
See Epiphone listing.

Electra
1971-1984. Imported from Japan by St. Louis Music. Most instruments made by Matsumoku in Matsumoto, Japan. The Electra line replaced SLM's Japanese-made Apollo and U.S.-made Custom Kraft lines. First guitar, simply called The Electra, was a copy of the Ampeg Dan Armstrong lucite guitar and issued in '71, followed quickly by a variety of bolt-neck copies of other brands. In '75 the Tree-of-Life guitars debut with a leaf pattern carved into the top, and the Electra line expanded to 25 models. Open-book headstocks changed to wave or fan shape by '78. By around '81 ties with Matsumoku further solidified and decision eventually made to merge SLM's Electra brand with Matsumoku's Westone brand. Some Korean production begins in early-'80s. In the fall of '83, the Electra Brand becomes Electra Phoenix. By beginning of '84, the brand becomes Electra-Westone and by the end of '84 just Westone. Matsumoku-made guitars have serial number in which first 1 or 2 digits represent the year of manufacture. Thus a guitar with a serial number beginning in 0 or 80 would be from 1980.

Custom
1970s. Double-cut solidbody with 2 pickups, standard SG features, Custom logo on truss rod, cherry finish.

1970s		$350	$450

Elvin Bishop
1976-ca.1980. Double-cut semi-hollow with tree-of-life inlay.

1977		$625	$700

Flying Wedge
1970s. V body, six-on-a-side tuners.

1970s		$350	$450

MPC Outlaw
1976-1983. Has separate modules that plug in for different effects.

1976-1983		$325	$525

Omega
1970s. Single-cut, solid body, block inlays, Omega logo on truss rod, black finish with rosewood neck, or natural with figured top and maple neck.

1970s		$300	$500

Phoenix
1980-1984. Classic offset double-cut solidbody, Phoenix logo on headstock.

1980-1984		$250	$325

Rock
1971-1973. Single-cut, solid body, becomes the Super Rock in '73.

1971-1973		$300	$400

SLM
1970s. Single-cut, solid body, block markers, SLM logo on truss rod, black.

1970s		$250	$350

Super Rock
1973-ca.1978. Les Paul copy, renamed from Rock ('71-'73).

1973-1978		$300	$400

X145 60th Anniversary
1982. Classic offset double-cut only made one year, Anniversary plate on back of headstock, single/single/hum pickups.

1982		$250	$325

1981 Electra Outlaw

Electro
1964-1975. The Electro line was manufactured by Electro String Instruments and distributed by Radio-Tel. The Electro logo appeared on the headstock rather than Rickenbacker. Refer to the Rickenbacker section for models.

Elite
1960s. Guitars made in Italy by the Crucianelli accordion company, which made several other brands.

Elk
Late-1960s. Japanese-made by Elk Gakki Co., Ltd. Many were copies of American designs. They also offered amps and effects.

1978 Electra X350

Elliot classical

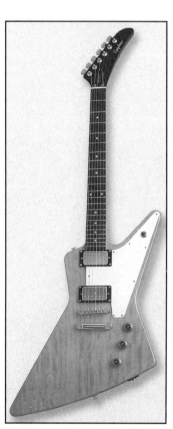

Epiphone 1958 Korina Explorer

MODEL YEAR	FEATURES	EXC. COND. LOW	HIGH

Elliott Guitars
1966-present. Premium and presentation grade, custom, nylon-string classical and steel-string guitars built by luthier Jeffrey Elliott in Portland, Oregon.

Elli-Sound
1960s. Guitars made in Italy by the Crucianelli accordion company, which made several other brands.

Emperador
1966-1992. Imported from Japan by Westheimer Musical Instruments. Early models appear to be made by either Teisco or Kawai; later models were made by Cort.

Acoustic Archtop

1960s		$100	$200

Electric Solidbody

1960s		$100	$225

English Electronics
1960s. Lansing, Michigan, company named after owner, some private branded guitars and amps by Valco (Chicago), many models with large English Electronics vertical logo on headstock.

Tonemaster

1965. National Val-Pro 84 with neck pickup and bridge mounted pickup, black.

1965		$650	$750

Epiphone
Ca. 1873-present. Budget, intermediate and professional grade, production, solidbody, archtop, acoustic, acoustic/electric, resonator, and classical guitars made in the U.S. and overseas. They also offer basses, amps, mandolins and banjos. Founded in Smyrna, Turkey, by Anastasios Stathopoulos and early instruments had his label. He emigrated to the U.S. in 1903 and changed the name to Stathoupoulo. Anastasios died in '15 and his son, Epaminondas ("Epi") took over. The name changed to House of Stathopoulo in '17 and the company incorporated in '23. In '24 the line of Epiphone Recording banjos debut and in '28 the company name was changed to the Epiphone Banjo Company. In '43 Epi Stathopoulo died and sons Orphie and Frixo took over. Labor trouble shut down the NYC factory in '51 and the company cut a deal with Conn/Continental and relocated to Philadelphia in '52. Frixo died in '57 and Gibson bought the company. Kalamazoo-made Gibson Epiphones debut in '58. In '69 American production ceased and Japanese imports began. Some Taiwanese guitars imported from '79-'81. Limited U.S. production resumed in '82 but sourcing shifted to Korea in '83. In '85 Norlin sold Gibson to Henry Juszkiewicz, Dave Barryman and Gary Zebrowski. In '92 Jim Rosenberg became president of the new Epiphone division.

MODEL YEAR	FEATURES	EXC. COND. LOW	HIGH

1958 Goth Explorer

2002-present. Flat black finish.

2002-2003		$375	$500

1958 Korina Explorer

1998-present. Explorer with typical appointments, korina body. This guitar was produced with a variety of specs, ranging from maple tops to spruce tops, different inlay markers were also used, different pickup combinations have been seen, natural or sunburst finish.

1998-2000		$400	$600

1958 Korina Flying V

1998-present. Typical Flying V configuration, korina body.

1998-2000		$400	$600

1963 Firebird VII/Firebird VII

2000-present. Three mini-humbuckers, gold hardware, Maestro-style vibrato, block markers, Firebird Red, reverse body. 1963 added after first year.

2000-2003		$475	$550

AJ-500R (Flat-Top)

2004-present. Masterbuild Series, sloped shoulder D-style, natural satin finish, solid spruce top, solid rosewood back and sides, pearl script logo.

2004		$400	$425

B.B. King Lucille

1997-present. Laminated double-cut maple body, 2 humbuckers, Lucille on headstock.

2000s		$500	$575

Barcelone (Classical)

1963-1968. Highest model of Epiphone '60s classical guitars.

1963-1965		$750	$900
1966-1968		$700	$850

Bard 12-String

1962-1969. Flat-top, mahogany back and sides, natural or sunburst.

1962-1964		$1,800	$2,200
1965-1969		$1,400	$1,800

Biscuit

1997-2000, 2002-present. Wood-body resonator with biscuit bridge, round neck.

1997-2000		$300	$350

Blackstone

1931-1950. Acoustic archtop, f-holes, sunburst.

1933-1934	Masterbuilt	$1,300	$1,600
1935-1937		$1,100	$1,400
1938-1939		$1,000	$1,300
1940-1941		$900	$1,200
1948-1949		$800	$1,200

Broadway (Acoustic)

1931-1958. Non-cut acoustic archtop.

1931-1938	Sunburst, walnut body	$2,700	$3,600
1939-1942	Sunburst, maple body	$2,700	$3,600
1946-1949	Natural	$2,700	$3,300
1946-1949	Sunburst	$2,600	$3,000
1950-1958	Sunburst	$2,700	$2,900

MODEL YEAR	FEATURES	EXC. COND. LOW	HIGH

Broadway (Electric)
1958-1969. Gibson-made electric archtop, single-cut, 2 New York pickups (mini-humbucking pickups by '61), Frequensator tailpiece, block inlays, sunburst or natural finish with cherry optional in '67 only.

1958-1964	Natural	$3,500	$4,000
1958-1964	Sunburst	$3,200	$3,400
1965-1969	Sunburst	$3,100	$3,300
1966-1968	Natural	$3,000	$3,500
1967	Cherry option	$3,200	$3,400

Broadway Regent (Acoustic Cutaway)
1950-1958. Single-cut acoustic archtop, sunburst.

1950-1958		$2,800	$3,200

Broadway Tenor
1937-1953. Acoustic archtop, sunburst.

1939		$1,000	$1,300
1950		$800	$1,100

Byron
1949-ca.1955. Acoustic archtop, mahogany back and sides, sunburst.

1949-1955		$375	$675

Caiola Custom
1963-1970. Introduced as Caiola, renamed Caiola Custom in '66, electric thinbody archtop, 2 mini-humbuckers, multi-bound top and back, block inlays, walnut or sunburst finish (walnut only by '68).

1963-1964		$3,200	$4,200
1965-1966		$3,000	$4,000
1967-1968		$2,800	$3,900
1969-1970		$2,800	$3,800

Caiola Standard
1966-1970. Electric thinbody archtop, 2 P-90s, single-bound top and back, dot inlays, sunburst or cherry.

1966		$2,600	$3,600
1967-1968		$2,500	$3,500
1969-1970		$2,400	$3,400

Casino (1 Pickup)
1961-1969. Thinline hollowbody, double-cut, 1 P-90 pickup.

1961-1963	Sunburst	$2,000	$2,400
1964-1966	Sunburst	$2,000	$2,600
1967-1968	Cherry	$1,700	$2,200
1967-1968	Sunburst	$2,000	$2,500
1969-1970	Cherry	$1,600	$2,000
1969-1970	Sunburst	$1,900	$2,300

Casino (2 Pickups)
1961-1970. Two pickup (P-90) version. '61-'63 known as Keith Richards model, '64-'65 known as Beatles model.

1961-1963	Royal Tan, black covers	$3,300	$3,500
1961-1963	Sunburst, black covers	$3,400	$3,600
1963-1966	Sunburst, chrome covers	$4,000	$5,000
1967-1968	Cherry option	$3,000	$4,000
1967-1968	Sunburst	$4,000	$5,000
1969-1970	Cherry option	$2,800	$3,100
1969-1970	Sunburst	$3,200	$3,800

Casino J.L. USA 1965
2003. 1,965 made.

2003		$1,900	$1,975

Casino Reissue
1995-present. Sunburst.

1995-1999		$500	$700
2000-2005		$450	$500

Century
1939-1970. Thinline archtop, non-cut, 1 pickup, trapeze tailpiece, walnut finish, sunburst finish available in '58, Royal Burgundy available '61 and only sunburst finish available by '68.

1949	Large rectangular pickup	$1,200	$1,400
1950	New York pickup	$1,400	$1,700
1951-1957	Sunburst	$1,350	$1,650
1958-1964	Sunburst, P-90 pickup	$1,300	$1,600
1965-1970	Sunburst or cherry	$1,200	$1,500

Classic (Classical)
1963-1970. Includes the Madrid, Entrada, Seville, Classic, Espana, and Barcelone models.

1963-1965		$500	$650
1966-1970		$450	$600

Collegiate
2004-present. Les Paul-style body, 1 pickup, various college graphic decals on body.

2004		$175	$225

Coronet (Electric Archtop)
1939-1949. Electric archtop, laminated mahogany body, 1 pickup, trapeze tailpiece, sunburst, name continued as an electric solidbody in '58.

1939-1949		$1,200	$1,400

Coronet (Solidbody)
1958-1969. Solidbody electric, 1 New York pickup ('58-'59), 1 P-90 ('59-'69), cherry or black finish, Silver Fox finish available by '63, reintroduced as Coronet USA '91-'94, Korean-made '95-'98.

1958		$1,900	$2,100
1959		$1,800	$2,000
1960		$1,800	$2,000
1961		$1,700	$1,900
1962		$1,600	$1,800
1963	Cherry or Silver Fox	$1,500	$1,700
1963	Green Stain (faded Pacific Blue)	$1,500	$1,700
1964	Cherry or Silver Fox	$1,400	$1,600
1964	Green Stain (faded Pacific Blue)	$1,400	$1,600
1965	Cherry or Silver Fox	$1,300	$1,500
1965	Green Stain (faded Pacific Blue)	$1,300	$1,500
1966-1969	Cherry	$1,200	$1,400

Coronet (Import)
1970s. Import electric, sunburst.

1970s		$275	$375

1965 Epiphone Casino

1962 Epiphone Coronet

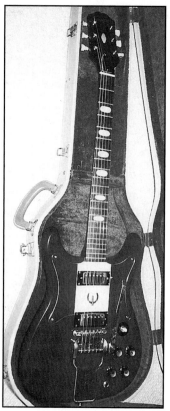

Epiphone Crestwood

Epiphone Elitist Broadway

MODEL YEAR	FEATURES	EXC. COND. LOW	HIGH
Crestwood Custom			

1958-1970. Solidbody, 2 New York pickups ('58-'60), 2 mini-humbuckers ('61-'70), symmetrical body ('58-'62), asymmetrical ('63-'70), slab body with no Gibson equivalent model.

MODEL YEAR	FEATURES	EXC. COND. LOW	HIGH
1958-1960	Cherry, New York pickups	$3,200	$3,900
1959	Sunburst	$2,700	$3,200
1961-1964	Cherry, mini-humbuckers	$2,900	$3,600
1961-1964	White, mini-humbuckers	$3,100	$3,800
1964-1966	Pacific Blue	$3,100	$3,800
1965-1966	Cherry	$2,500	$3,200
1965-1966	White	$2,700	$3,400
1967-1968	Cherry	$2,400	$3,100
1967-1968	White	$2,500	$3,200
1969-1970	Cherry or white	$2,400	$3,100
Crestwood Custom (Japan)			
1970s		$350	$400
Crestwood Deluxe			

1963-1969. Solidbody with 3 mini-humbuckers, block inlay, cherry or white finish.

1963-1964	Cherry	$3,500	$4,200
1963-1964	White	$3,600	$4,300
1965-1966	Cherry	$3,300	$4,000
1965-1966	White	$3,500	$4,200
1967-1968	Cherry	$3,100	$3,800
1967-1968	White	$3,200	$3,900
1969	Cherry or White	$2,900	$3,600
De Luxe			

1931-1957. Non-cut acoustic archtop, maple back and sides, trapeze tailpiece ('31-'37), frequensator tailpiece ('37-'57), gold-plated hardware, sunburst or natural finish.

1931-1934	Sunburst	$4,700	$5,600
1935-1939	Sunburst	$4,600	$5,500
1939	Natural, 1st year option	$5,600	$6,000
1940-1944	Natural	$5,400	$5,800
1940-1944	Sunburst	$4,400	$5,300
1945-1949	Natural	$4,700	$5,100
1945-1949	Sunburst	$3,700	$4,600
1950-1957	Natural	$3,300	$4,700
1950-1957	Sunburst	$2,800	$4,200
De Luxe Cutaway/Deluxe Cutaway			

1953-1970. Renamed from De Luxe Regent, cataloged Deluxe Cutaway by Gibson in '58, special order by '64 with limited production because acoustic archtops were pretty much replaced by electric archtops.

1953-1957	Epiphone NY-made	$3,500	$5,500
1958-1965	Gibson Kalamazoo, rounded cutaway	$3,500	$5,500
1965-1970	Special order only	$3,500	$6,000
De Luxe Electric (Archtop)			

1954-1957. Single-cut electric archtop, 2 pickups, called the Zephyr De Luxe Regent from '48-'54. Produced with a variety of specs, maple or spruce tops, different inlays and pickup combinations.

1954-1957	Natural	$3,700	$4,500
1954-1957	Sunburst	$3,500	$4,300

MODEL YEAR	FEATURES	EXC. COND. LOW	HIGH
De Luxe Regent (Acoustic Archtop)			

1948-1952. Acoustic cutaway archtop, high-end appointments, rounded cutaway, natural finish, renamed De Luxe Cutaway in '53.

1948-1952		$4,000	$6,000
Del Ray			

1995-2000. Offset double-cut body, 2 blade humbuckers, dot markers, tune-o-matic, flamed maple top.

1995-2000		$300	$375
Devon			

1949-1957. Acoustic archtop, non-cut, mahogany back and sides, sunburst finish, optional natural finish by '54.

1950-1953	Sunburst	$1,550	$1,700
1954-1957	Natural	$1,750	$2,000
1954-1957	Sunburst	$1,450	$1,600
Dot (ES-335 Dot)/Dot Archtop			

2000-present. Dot-neck ES-335.

2000-2003		$300	$325
Dot Studio			

2004-present. Simplified Dot, 2 control knobs, black hardware.

2004		$175	$225
Dwight			

1963, 1967. Coronet labeled as Dwight for dealer, 75 made in '63 and 36 in '67, cherry.

1963		$1,500	$1,700
1964		$1,400	$1,600
1965		$1,300	$1,500
1966-1967		$1,200	$1,400
EA/ET Series (Japan)			

1970-1979. Production of the Epiphone brand was moved to Japan in '70. Models included the EA (electric thinline) and ET (electric solidbody).

1970-1975	ET-270	$275	$325
1970s	EA-250	$350	$400
1975-1979	ET-290	$350	$400
El Diablo			

1990s. Offset double-cut acoustic/electric, on-board piezo and 3-band EQ, composite back and sides, spruce top, cherry sunburst.

1990s		$300	$350
El Dorado FT 90			

1963-1970. Dreadnought flat-top acoustic, mahogany back and sides, multi-bound front and back, natural.

1963-1964		$2,200	$2,600
1965-1970		$1,500	$2,300
Electar Model M			

1935-1939. Epiphone's initial entry into the new electric guitar market of the mid-'30s, 14 3/4" laminate maple archtop, horseshoe pickup, trap door on back for electronics, Electar logo on headstock, oblong pickup replaces horseshoe in late-'37.

1935-1936	2 control knobs	$1,150	$1,400
1937-1939	3 control knobs	$1,150	$1,400
Elitest Series			

2003-present. Made in Japan, higher-grade series, using finer woods and inlays and U.S.-made Gibson pickups.

2003-2004	1963 ES-335 Dot	$900	$950
2003-2004	1965 Casino	$900	$950

The *Vintage Guitar Price Guide* shows low to high values for items in all-original excellent condition, and, where applicable, with original case or cover.

MODEL YEAR	FEATURES	EXC. COND. LOW	HIGH
2003-2004	Les Paul Custom	$775	$825
2003-2004	Les Paul Standard	$700	$750

Emperor (Acoustic Archtop)

1935-1957. Acoustic archtop, non-cut, maple back and sides, multi-bound body, gold-plated hardware, sunburst, optional natural finish by '39.

1936-1938	Sunburst	$5,500	$6,500
1939-1949	Natural	$6,000	$7,000
1939-1949	Sunburst	$5,500	$6,500
1950-1954	Natural	$4,200	$6,200
1950-1954	Sunburst	$4,000	$6,000

Emperor (Thinline Electric)

1958-1969. Single-cut, thinline archtop, 3 New York pickups in '58-'60, 3 mini-humbuckers '61 on, multi-bound, gold-plated hardware, sunburst or natural finish until '65 when only sunburst was made.

1958-1960	Natural	$9,700	$11,500
1958-1960	Sunburst	$9,200	$11,000
1961-1962	Natural	$9,200	$11,000
1961-1962	Sunburst	$8,700	$10,500
1963-1968	Special order only	$8,700	$10,500

Emperor Cutaway (formerly Emperor Regent)

1953-1970 (Gibson-made 1958 on). Renamed from Emperor Regent, acoustic archtop, single-cut, maple back and sides, multi-bound body, gold-plated hardware, sunburst or natural finish.

1953-1958	Natural	$7,500	$9,000
1953-1958	Sunburst	$6,500	$8,000

Emperor Electric

1953-1957. Archtop, single-cut, 3 pickups, multi-bound body, sunburst, called the Zephyr Emperor Regent in '50-'53.

1953-1957		$4,700	$6,500

Emperor Regent

1948-1953. Acoustic archtop with rounded cutaway, renamed Emperor Cutaway in '53.

1948-1953	Natural	$7,500	$9,000
1948-1953	Sunburst	$6,500	$8,000

Emperor/Emperor II/Joe Pass Emperor II

1982-present. Single-cut archtop jazz guitar, 2 humbuckers, blocks, gold hardware. II added to name in '93, became Joe Pass Emperor II in '95, although his name was on the guitar as early as '91.

1990s		$450	$550
2000s		$400	$450

Entrada (Classical)

1963-1968. Classical, natural.

1963-1965		$400	$550
1966-1968		$350	$500

Espana (Classical)

1962-1968. Classical, maple back and sides, U.S.-made, natural, imported in '69 from Japan.

1962-1965		$500	$600
1966-1968		$450	$550

Exellente

1963-1969, 1994-1995. Flat-top, rosewood back and sides. Name revived on Gibson Montana insturment in '90s.

1963-1965		$4,500	$6,000
1966-1969		$3,500	$5,000

Firebird

1995-2000. Two mini-humbuckers, Firebird Red, dot markers.

1995-2000		$350	$400

Firebird 300

1986-1988. Korean import, Firebird Red.

1986-1988		$250	$325

Firebird 500

1986-1988. Korean import, Firebird Red.

1986-1988		$275	$350

Flying V/'58 Flying V

1989-1998. '67 specs, alder body, natural.

1989-1998		$400	$600

Folkster FT 95

1966-1969. 14" small body, mahogany back and sides, natural, double white 'guards.

1966-1969	Natural	$600	$900

FT 30

1941-1949. Acoustic flat-top, brown stain, mahogany back and sides, reintroduced as Gibson-made FT 30 Caballero in '58.

1941-1949		$900	$1,100

FT 30 Caballero

1958-1970. Reintroduced from Epiphone-made FT 30, Gibson-made acoustic flat-top, natural, all mahogany body, dot inlay, tenor available '63-'68.

1959-1961		$800	$1,000
1962		$700	$800
1963-1964		$600	$800
1965-1970		$550	$750

FT 45

1941-1948. Acoustic flat-top, walnut back and sides, cherry neck, rosewood 'board, natural top, reintroduced as Gibson-made FT 45 Cortez in '58.

1941-1948		$1,200	$1,400

FT 45 Cortez

1958-1969. Reintroduced from Epiphone-made FT 45, Gibson-made acoustic flat-top, mahogany back and sides, sunburst or natural top (sunburst only in '59-'62).

1958-1961	Sunburst	$1,000	$1,300
1962	Sunburst	$850	$1,000
1963-1965	Sunburst or natural	$750	$1,000
1966-1969	Sunburst or natural	$700	$950

FT 79

1941-1958. Acoustic 16" flat-top, square shoulder D-style, walnut back and sides until '49 and laminated maple back and sides '49 on, natural, renamed FT 79 Texan by Gibson in '58.

1941-1949	Walnut back & sides	$3,100	$3,300
1949-1958	Laminated pressed maple body	$2,600	$2,900

FT 79 Texan

1958-1970, 1993-1995. Renamed from Epiphone FT 79, Gibson-made acoustic flat-top, mahogany back and sides, sunburst or natural top, Gibson Montana made 170 in '93-'95.

1958-1961		$3,000	$3,500
1962-1964		$2,300	$3,300
1965-1966		$2,000	$3,000

1961 Epiphone Emperor

Epiphone Firebird

Epiphone FT-110

*Epiphone Noel Gallagher
Super Nova Union Jack*

MODEL YEAR	FEATURES	EXC. COND. LOW	HIGH
1967-1968		$1,500	$2,500
1969-1970		$1,500	$2,000

FT 110
1941-1958. Acoustic flat-top, natural, renamed the FT 110 Frontier by Gibson in '58.

1941-1949	Square shoulder	$3,000	$3,500
1949-1954	Round shoulder	$2,700	$3,000
1954-1958	Mahogany neck	$2,700	$3,000

FT 110 Frontier
1958-1970, 1994. Renamed from FT 110, acoustic flat-top, natural or sunburst, Gibson Montana made 30 in '94.

1958-1962		$2,700	$3,000
1962-1964		$2,700	$3,000
1965-1966		$2,500	$2,700
1967-1970		$1,700	$2,500

FT Series (Flat-Tops Japan)
1970s. In '70 Epiphone moved production to Japan. Various models were made, nearly all with bolt necks and small rectangular blue labels on the inside back.

1970s	FT 120	$75	$125
1970s	FT 130	$100	$150
1970s	FT 132	$125	$200
1970s	FT 133	$125	$200
1970s	FT 135	$200	$275
1970s	FT 140	$125	$175
1970s	FT 145	$200	$250
1970s	FT 146	$200	$275
1970s	FT 150	$300	$325
1970s	FT 155	$325	$375
1970s	FT 160 12-String	$200	$275
1970s	FT 160N	$200	$275
1970s	FT 165 12-String	$325	$350
1970s	FT 200 Monticello	$250	$300
1970s	FT 350	$325	$350
1970s	FT 550	$350	$400
1970s	FT 565 12-String	$350	$400
1970s	FT 570SB SuperJumbo	$350	$400

G 310
1989-present. SG-style model with large 'guard and gig bag.

1989-1999		$200	$275

G 400 Deluxe
1999-present. SG-style model with flamed maple top, 2 exposed humbuckers.

1996		$375	$425

G 400 Tony Iommi
2003-present. SG-style model with cross 'board inlay markers, black finish.

2003-2004		$450	$500

Genesis
1979-1980. Double-cut solidbody, 2 humbuckers with coil-taps, carved top, red or black, available as Custom, Deluxe, and Standard models, Taiwan import.

1979-1980		$450	$500

Granada (Cutaway)
1965-1970. Single-cut thinline archtop, 1 F-hole, 1 pickup, sunburst.

1965-1966		$850	$1,100
1967-1970		$800	$1,000

Granada (Non-cutaway Thinbody)
1962-1969. Non-cut thinline archtop, 1 F-hole, 1 pickup, trapeze tailpiece, sunburst finish.

1962-1966		$825	$925
1967-1969		$575	$825

Howard Roberts Custom
1965-1970. Single-cut archtop, bound front and back, 1 pickup, walnut finish (natural offered '66 only).

1965-1967		$2,900	$3,700
1968-1970		$2,300	$3,400

Howard Roberts III
1987-1991. Two pickups, various colors.

1987-1991		$575	$650

Howard Roberts Standard
1964-1970. Single-cut acoustic archtop, bound front and back, cherry or sunburst finish, listed in catalog as acoustic but built as electric.

1964-1965		$2,700	$3,500
1966-1967		$2,600	$3,400
1968-1970		$2,100	$3,200

Les Paul Custom
1989-present. Various colors.

1989-2000s		$400	$450

Les Paul Deluxe
1998-2000. Typical mini-humbucker pickups.

1998-2000		$400	$450

Les Paul LP-100
1993-present. Affordable single-cut Les Paul, bolt-on neck.

1990s		$150	$175

Les Paul Special
1994-2000. Double-cut, bolt neck.

1994-2000		$200	$250

Les Paul Special II
1996-present. Economical Les Paul, 2 pickups, single-cut, various colors.

1990s		$325	$350

Les Paul Standard
1989-present. Solid mahogany body, carved maple top, 2 humbuckers.

1989-2000s		$375	$475

Les Paul Standard Baritone
2004-present. 27-3/4" long-scale baritone model.

2004		$325	$350

Les Paul Studio
1995-present. Epiphone's version of Gibson LP Studio.

1990s		$225	$250

Les Paul XII
1998-2000. 12-string solidbody, trapeze tailpiece, flamed maple sunburst, standard configuration.

1998-2000		$450	$550

Madrid (Classical)
1962-1969. Classical, natural.

1962-1969		$350	$475

Navarre
1931-1940. Flat-top, mahogany back and sides, bound top and back, dot inlay, brown finish.

1936	Hawaiian, Masterbilt label	$1,450	$1,600

MODEL YEAR	FEATURES	EXC. COND. LOW	HIGH

Nighthawk Standard
1995-2000. Epiphone's version of the Gibson Nighthawk, single-cut, bolt neck, figured top.

1995-2000		$300	$375

Noel Gallagher Union Jack/Super Nova
1997-present. Limited edition, higher-end ES-335. Union Jack with British flag finish (introduced '99) or Supernova in solid blue.

2000s		$500	$575

Olympic (3/4 Scale Solidbody)
1960-1963. 22" scale, sunburst.

1960-1963		$700	$750

Olympic (Acoustic Archtop)
1931-1949. Mahogany back and sides.

1930s		$550	$800
1940s		$550	$800

Olympic Double (Solidbody)
1960-1969. Slab body, the same as the mid-'60s Coronet, Wilshire and Crestwood Series, single-cut '60-'62, asymmetrical-cut '63-'70, 2 Melody Maker single-coils, vibrato optional in '64 and standard by '65.

1960-1962	Sunburst, single-cut	$900	$1,200
1963-1965	Sunburst, double-cut	$850	$1,050
1966-1969	Cherry or sunburst	$750	$900

Olympic Single (Solidbody)
1960-1970. Slab body, the same as the mid-'60s Coronet, Wilshire and Crestwood Series, single-cut '60-'62, asymmetrical double-cut '63-'70, 2 Melody maker single-coil pickups, vibrato optional in '64 and standard by '65.

1960-1962	Sunburst, single-cut	$700	$1,100
1963-1965	Sunburst, double-cut	$600	$950
1966-1967	Cherry or sunburst	$600	$900
1968-1970	Cherry or sunburst	$575	$800

Olympic Special (Solidbody)
1962-1970. Short neck with neck body joint at the 16th fret (instead of the 22nd), single Melody Maker-style single-coil bridge pickup, small headstock, double-cut slab body, dot markers, Maestro or Epiphone vibrato optional '64-'65, slab body contour changes in '65 from symmetrical to asymmetrical with slightly longer bass horn, sunburst.

1964-1965		$700	$850
1966-1967		$650	$800
1968-1970		$600	$750

PR-200 (EA-20)
1992-2000. Imported D-style, spruce top with satin finish, mahogany back and sides, natural.

1992-2000		$150	$225

PR-350
1984-2000. Acoustic flat-top, mahogany D-style body, also available with a pickup.

1984-2000		$175	$250

PR-350 CE
1989-2000. Acoustic flat-top, cutaway, mahogany D-style body, also available with a pickup.

1989-2000		$250	$325

PR-600 ACS/ASB/N
1980-1985. Import 000-size flat-top, glued bridge, dot markers, sunburst.

1980-1985		$275	$400

PR-755S
1980-1985. Flat-top, single-cut, solid spruce top, laminate rosewood body, set mahogany neck, block markers, gold hardware, natural.

1981-1985		$275	$325

Pro 1
1989-1996. Solidbody, double-cut, 1 single-coil and 1 humbucking pickup, bolt-on neck, various colors.

1989-1996		$325	$400

Pro 2
1995-1998. Higher-end Pro I with Steinberger DB bridge, set-neck, 2 humbuckers, various colors.

1995-1998		$350	$400

Professional
1962-1967. Double-cut, thinline archtop, 1 pickup, mahogany finish.

1962-1967	With matching Professional Amp	$1,800	$2,300

Recording A
1928-1931.

1928-1931		$1,400	$1,600

Recording B
1928-1931. Asymmetrical body, cutaway bouts, flat-top, arched back, laminated maple back.

1928-1931		$2,000	$2,300

Recording C
1928-1931.

1928-1931		$2,400	$2,800

Recording D
1928-1931.

1928-1931		$3,000	$3,300

Recording E
1928-1931.

1928-1931		$4,100	$4,500

Riviera
1962-1970, 1993-1994. Double-cut thinline archtop, 2 mini-humbuckers, Royal Tan standard finish changing to sunburst in '65, cherry optional by '66-'70, additional 250 were made in Nashville in '93-'94, a Riviera import was available in '82 and for '94-present.

1962-1964	Tan or custom cherry	$3,000	$3,500
1965-1966	Sunburst or cherry	$2,700	$3,400
1966-1967	Burgundy Mist	$2,800	$3,500
1967-1968	Sunburst or cherry	$2,300	$3,300
1967-1968	Walnut	$2,200	$3,200
1969	Sunburst or cherry	$2,100	$3,000

Riviera 12-String
1965-1970. Double-cut, 12 strings, thinline archtop, 2 mini-humbuckers, sunburst or cherry.

1965-1966		$2,200	$2,700
1967-1968		$1,800	$2,300

1965 Epiphone Olympic

1966 Epiphone Riviera

Epiphone Sheraton II

Epiphone Wilshire

MODEL YEAR	FEATURES	EXC. COND. LOW	HIGH
Riviera 12-String Reissue (Korea)			
1997-present. Korean-made reissue, natural.			
1997		$425	$650
Riviera Reissue (Korea)			
1994-present. Korean-made contemporary reissue, natural.			
1997		$375	$450
Riviera Reissue (USA)			
1993. Part of Nashville USA Collection, limited run.			
1993		$1,600	$1,700
S-900			
1986-1989. Neck-thru-body, locking Bender tremolo system, 2 pickups with individual switching and a coil-tap control.			
1986-1989		$325	$400
Serenader 12-String FT 85			
1963-1969. 12 strings, mahogany back and sides, dot inlay, natural.			
1963-1964		$900	$1,300
1965-1966		$800	$1,100
1967-1969		$700	$900
Seville EC-100 (Classical)			
1938-1941, 1961-1969 (Gibson-made). Classical guitar, mahogany back and sides, natural, the '61-'63 version also available with a pickup.			
1961-1965		$400	$500
1966-1969		$350	$500
SG Special			
2000-present. SG body, dot markers, 2 open-coil humbuckers.			
2000s		$70	$90
Sheraton			
1958-1970, 1993-1994. Double-cut thinline archtop, 2 New York pickups '58-'60, 2 mini-humbuckers '61 on, frequensator tailpiece, multi-bound, gold-plated hardware, sunburst or natural finish with cherry optional by '65, an additional 250 American-made Sheratons were built			
1958-1959	Natural, New York pickups	$9,000	$10,000
1960	Natural, New York pickups	$8,000	$9,000
1961-1963	Natural, mini-humbuckers	$7,500	$8,000
1961-1963	Sunburst, mini-humbuckers	$7,000	$7,500
1964-1965	Natural	$6,800	$7,300
1964-1965	Sunburst	$6,000	$7,000
1965	Cherry	$6,200	$7,200
1966	Sunburst or cherry	$5,800	$6,700
1967	Sunburst or cherry	$5,000	$6,500
1968	Sunburst or cherry	$4,800	$6,000
1969	Sunburst	$4,300	$5,500
1993-1994	Model reintroduced	$575	$675
Sheraton (Japan)			
1978-1983. Early reissue, not to be confused with Sheraton II issued in late-'90s, natural or sunburst.			
1978-1983		$400	$450

MODEL YEAR	FEATURES	EXC. COND. LOW	HIGH
Sheraton II (Reissue)			
1997-present. Contemporary reissue, natural or sunburst.			
1997-1999		$400	$450
2000-2005		$350	$400
Sorrento (1 pickup)			
1960-1970. Single-cut thinline archtop, 1 pickup in neck position, tune-o-matic bridge, nickel-plated hardware, sunburst, natural or Royal Olive finish, (cherry or sunburst by '68).			
1960-1965		$1,600	$1,900
1966-1968		$1,500	$1,800
1969-1970		$1,450	$1,700
Sorrento (2 pickups)			
1960-1970. Single-cut thinline archtop, 2 pickups, tune-o-matic bridge, nickel-plated hardware, sunburst, natural or Royal Olive finish, (cherry or sunburst by '68).			
1960-1965		$1,900	$2,400
1966-1968		$1,700	$2,300
1969-1970		$1,500	$2,200
Sorrento (Reissue)			
1997-2000.			
1997-2000		$375	$450
Spartan			
1934-1949. Acoustic archtop, multi-bound, trapeze tailpiece, sunburst.			
1930s		$750	$1,100
1940s		$650	$900
Spider/The Spider			
1997-2000. Woold-body resonator and spider bridge, square neck.			
1997-2000		$300	$350
Spirit			
1979-1983. American-made electric solidbody, double-cut, carved top with 2 humbuckers, various colors.			
1979-1983		$600	$750
Trailer Park Troubadour Airscreamer			
2003-present. Airstream trailer-style body, identifying logo on headstock.			
2003-2004		$350	$400
Triumph			
1931-1957. 15 1/4" '31-'33, 16 3/8" '33-'36, 17 3/8" '36-'57, walnut back and sides until '33, laminated maple back and sides '33, solid maple back and sides '34, natural or sunburst.			
1931-1932	Sunburst, laminated walnut body	$1,100	$1,700
1933	Sunburst, laminated maple body	$1,100	$1,700
1934-1935	Sunburst, solid maple body	$1,500	$1,800
1936-1940	Sunburst 17 3/8" body	$1,800	$2,400
1941-1949	Natural	$1,800	$2,400
1941-1949	Sunburst	$1,700	$2,200
1950-1957	Natural	$1,700	$2,200
1950-1957	Sunburst	$1,500	$1,800

MODEL YEAR	FEATURES	EXC. COND. LOW	HIGH

Triumph Regent (Cutaway)

1948-1969. Acoustic archtop, single-cut, F-holes, renamed Triumph Cutaway in '53, then Gibson listed this model as just the Triumph from '58-'69.

1948-1958	Natural	$2,400	$3,000
1948-1958	Sunburst	$2,300	$2,800
1959-1965	Sunburst	$2,200	$2,700
1966-1968	Sunburst	$2,200	$2,600

Troubadour FT 98

1963-1969. 16" square shoulders, D-style, maple back and sides, gold-plated hardware, classical width 'board.

1963-1969		$1,500	$1,900

USA Map Guitar

1982-1983. Solidbody electric, mahogany body shaped like U.S. map, 2 pickups, American-made promotional model, natural.

1982-1983		$1,750	$2,025

Vee-Wee (Mini Flying V)

2003. Mini Flying V student guitar, Flying V shape with single bridge pickup, gig bag, solid opaque finish.

2003		$100	$125

Wildkat

2001-present. Thinline, single-cut, hollow-body, 2 P-90s, Bigsby tailpiece.

2001-2003		$400	$500

Wilshire

1959-1970. Double-cut solidbody, 2 pickups, tune-o-matic bridge, cherry.

1959	Symmetrical body	$3,000	$3,700
1960-1962	Thinner-style body, P-90s	$2,900	$3,600
1962	Mini-humbuckers	$2,700	$3,400
1963-1964	Asymmetrical body	$2,600	$3,300
1965-1966		$2,200	$2,900
1967-1968		$2,100	$2,800
1969-1970		$2,000	$2,700

Wilshire 12-String

1966-1968. Solidbody, 2 pickups, cherry.

1966		$2,300	$2,800
1967-1968		$1,900	$2,400

Wilshire II

1984-1985. Solidbody, maple body, neck and 'board, 2 humbuckers, 3-way switch, coil-tap, 1 tone and 1 volume control, various colors.

1984		$225	$300

Windsor

1959-1962. Archtop, 1 or 2 pickups, single-cut thinline, sunburst or natural finish.

1959-1960	New York pickup	$1,600	$1,900
1961-1962	Mini-humbucker	$1,600	$1,900

X-1000

1986-1989. Electric solidbody, Korean-made, various colors.

1986-1989		$225	$300

Zakk Wylde Les Paul Custom

2003-present. Bull's-eye graphic, block markers, split diamond headstock inlay.

2003-2004		$550	$625

Zenith

1931-1969. Acoustic archtop, bound front and back, F-holes, sunburst.

1931-1933		$950	$1,100
1934-1935	Larger 14 3/4" body	$950	$1,100
1936-1949	Still larger 16 3/8" body	$950	$1,100
1950-1958		$850	$1,000
1959-1961		$600	$950
1963-1964		$550	$900

Zephyr De Luxe (Non-cutaway)

1941-1954. Non-cut electric archtop, 1 or 2 pickups, multi-bound front and back, gold-plated hardware, natural or sunburst.

1941-1942	Natural	$2,700	$3,300
1945-1949	Natural	$2,700	$3,400
1950-1954	Natural	$2,200	$2,700
1950-1954	Sunburst	$2,000	$2,500

Zephyr De Luxe Regent (Cutaway)

1948-1954. Single-cut electric archtop, 1 or 2 pickups until '50, then only 2, gold-plated hardware, sunburst or natural finish. Renamed Deluxe Electric in '54.

1948-1949	Natural	$3,700	$4,500
1948-1949	Sunburst	$3,500	$4,300
1950-1954	Natural	$3,000	$3,800
1950-1954	Sunburst	$2,800	$3,600

Zephyr Electric (Cutaway)

1958-1964. Gibson-made version, thinline archtop, single-cut, 2 pickups, natural or sunburst.

1958-1959	Natural	$2,200	$2,700
1958-1959	Sunburst	$2,000	$2,500
1960-1964	Natural	$2,000	$2,400
1960-1964	Sunburst	$1,800	$2,200

Zephyr Emperor Regent

1950-1954. Archtop, single rounded cutaway, multi-bound body, 3 pickups, sunburst or natural finish, renamed Emperor Electric in '54.

1950-1954	Natural	$4,500	$5,200
1950-1954	Sunburst	$4,300	$5,000

Zephyr Regent

1950-1958. Single-cut electric archtop, 1 pickup, natural or sunburst, called Zephyr Electric for '54-'58.

1950	Sunburst	$1,500	$2,600
1951	Sunburst	$1,400	$2,500
1953	Sunburst or natural	$1,200	$2,400
1954	Sunburst or natural	$1,100	$2,200
1955	Sunburst or natural	$1,000	$2,100
1957	Sunburst or natural	$900	$2,100

Zephyr/Zephyr Electric

1939-1957. Non-cut electric archtop, 1 pickup, bound front and back, blond or sunburst (first offered '53), renamed Zephyr Electric '54. Name continued '58-'64 on thinline cutaway, 2 pickup model.

1939-1940	Blond, 16 3/8", metal handrest pickup	$1,500	$2,000
1941-1943	Blond, no metal handrest	$1,500	$2,000
1944-1946	Blond, top mounted pickup	$1,400	$2,000

Epiphone USA Map Guitar

*Epiphone Zephyr
De Luxe Regent*

ESP Horizon Custom

MODEL YEAR	FEATURES	EXC. COND. LOW	HIGH
1947-1948	17 3/8", metal covered pickup	$1,300	$1,800
1949-1952	Blond, New York pickup	$1,200	$1,800
1953-1957	Blond, New York pickup	$1,200	$1,600
1953-1957	Sunburst, New York pickup	$1,200	$1,500

Erlewine

1979-present. Professional and premium grade, production/custom guitars built by luthier Mark Erlewine in Austin, Texas. Erlewine also produces the Chiquita brand travel guitar.

ESP

1983-present. Intermediate, professional, and premium grade, production/custom, Japanese-made solidbody guitars and basses. Hisatake Shibuya founded Electronic Sound Products (ESP), a chain of retail stores, in '75. They began to produce replacement parts for electric guitars in '83 and in '85 started to make custom-made guitars. In '87 a factory was opened in Tokyo. In '86 ESP opened a sales office in New York, selling custom guitars and production models. In the '90s, ESP opened a California-based custom shop and in '96, they introduced the Korean-made LTD brand. Hisatake Shibuya also operated 48th Street Custom Guitars during the '90s but he closed that shop in 2003.

20th Anniversary
1995. Solidbody, double-cut, ESP95 inlaid at 12th fret, gold.

1995		$1,050	$1,200

Eclipse Custom/Custom T (Import)
1986-1988. Single-cut mahogany solidbody, earliest model with bolt-on dot marker neck, 2nd version with neck-thru design and block markers, the Custom T adds double locking tremolo.

1986-1987	Bolt, dots	$500	$550
1987-1988	Neck-through, Custom T	$500	$650
1987-1988	Neck-thru, blocks	$600	$650

Eclipse Deluxe
1986-1988. Single-cut solidbody, 1 single-coil and 1 humbucker pickup, vibrato, black.

1986-1988		$400	$525

Horizon
1986, 1996-2001. Double-cut neck-thru, bound ebony 'board, 1 single-coil and 1 humbucker, buffer preamp, various colors, reintroduced '96-'01with bolt neck, curved rounded point headstock.

1986		$400	$450
1996-2001		$275	$325

Horizon Classic (USA)
1993-1995. U.S.-made, carved mahogany body, set-neck, dot markers, various colors, optional mahogany body with figured maple top also offered.

1993-1995	Figured maple top	$1,200	$1,300
1993-1995	Standard mahogany body	$1,300	$1,500

ESP H100 ASB

Horizon Custom (USA)
1998-present. U.S. Custom Shop-made, mahogany body, figured maple top, bolt-on neck, mostly translucent finish in various colors.

1990s		$1,200	$1,300

Horizon Deluxe (Import)
1989-1992. Horizon Custom with bolt-on neck, various colors.

1989		$600	$700

Hybrid I (Import)
1986 only. Offset double-cut body, bolt-on maple neck, dot markers, six-on-a-side tuners, standard vibrato, various colors.

1986		$300	$400

Hybrid II (Import)
Offset double-cut, rosewood board on maple bolt-on neck, lipstick neck pickup, humbucker bridge pickup, Hybrid II logo on headstock.

1980s		$350	$450

LTD EC-1000
2002-present. Deluxe appointments including abalone inlays and figured-top, 2 humbuckers, Korean-made.

2000s		$700	$800

LTD EC-300
2002-2003. Single-cut solidbody, 2 humbuckers, Korean-made.

2000-2003		$350	$450

LTD H-100
1998-present. Offset double-cut solidbody, 2 humbuckers, made in Korea.

2000s		$175	$200

LTD Viper
2000-present. Double-cut SG style solidbody, 2 humbuckers.

2000s		$350	$450

Maverick/Maverick Deluxe
1989-1992. Offset double-cut, bolt-on maple or rosewood cap neck, dot markers, double locking vibrola, six-on-a-side tuners, various colors.

1989		$300	$400

Metal I
1986 only. Offset double-cut, bolt-on maple neck with rosewood cap, dot markers, various colors.

1986		$275	$375

Metal II
1986 only. Single horn V-style body, bolt on maple neck with rosewood cap, dot markers, various colors.

1986		$275	$375

Metal III
1986 only. Reverse offset body, bolt-on maple neck with maple cap, dot markers, gold hardware, various colors.

1986		$300	$400

M-I Custom
1987-1994. Offset double-cut thru-neck body, offset block markers, various colors.

1987-1994		$700	$800

MODEL YEAR	FEATURES	EXC. COND. LOW	HIGH

M-I Deluxe
1987-1989. Double-cut solidbody, rosewood 'board, 2 single-coils and 1 humbucker, various colors.

1987-1989		$600	$700

M-II
1989-1994, 1996-2000. Double-cut solidbody, reverse headstock, bolt-on maple or rosewood cap neck, dot markers, various colors.

1989-1994		$750	$850

M-II Custom
1990-1994. Double-cut solidbody, reverse headstock, neck-thru maple neck, rosewood cap, dot markers, various colors.

1990-1994		$950	$1,000

M-II Deluxe
1990-1994. Double-cut solidbody, reverse headstock, Custom with bolt-on neck, various colors.

1990-1994		$850	$950

Mirage Custom
1986-1990. Double-cut neck-thru solidbody, 2-octave ebony 'board, block markers, 1 humbucker and 2 single-coil pickups, locking trem, various colors.

1980s		$550	$650

Mirage Standard
1986 only. Single pickup version of Mirage Custom, various colors.

1986		$300	$400

Phoenix
1987 only. Offset, narrow waist, through-neck mahogany body, two pickups, black hardware, dot markers, various colors.

1987		$500	$600

Phoenix Contemporary
Late-1990s. Three pickups.

1998		$825	$875

S-454 / S-456
1986-1987. Offset double-cut, bolt-on maple or rosewood cap neck, dot markers, various colors.

1986-1987		$300	$500

S-500
1991-1993. Double-cut figured ash body, bolt-on neck, six-on-a-side tuners, various colors.

1991-1993		$500	$675

Traditional
1989-1990. Double-cut, 3 pickups, tremolo, various colors.

1989-1990		$550	$600

Vintage/Vintage Plus S
1995-1998. Offset double-cut, bolt maple or rosewood cap neck, dot markers, Floyd Rose or standard vibrato, various colors.

1995-1998		$650	$875

Espana

Early-1960s-early-1970s. Distributed by catalog wholesalers. Built in Sweden.

MODEL YEAR	FEATURES	EXC. COND. LOW	HIGH

Classical
Early-1960s-early-1970s. Guitars with white spruce fan-braced tops with either walnut, mahogany, or rosewood back and sides.

1970s		$100	$175

EL-36
1969-early-1970s. Thin hollow double-cut, 2 pickups, natural.

1970s		$125	$175

Jumbo Folk
1969-early-1970s. Natural.

1970s		$100	$175

Essex (SX)

1985-present. Budget grade, production, electric and acoustic guitars imported by Rondo Music of Union, New Jersey. They also offer basses.

Solidbody Electric
1980s-1990s. Copies of classic designs like the Les Paul and Telecaster.

1980s		$90	$110

Euphonon

1934-1944. This Larson-made brand was intended to compete with the competition's new larger body, 14-fret, solid peghead (unslotted) models. Standard and dreadnought models were offered. Three models were offered ranging from the small 13¾" student model, to the top end 15" and 16" models. Ornamentation and features are as important as rosewood vs. mahogany. Euphonons with truss rods were marketed as Prairie State models.

Standard 13"-15"
1934-1944. Fancy binding.

1934-1944		$8,000	$10,000

Standard 16"
1934-1944. D-style with various features.

1934-1944	D-46 appointments	$20,000	$30,000
1934-1944	Fancy binding	$10,000	$17,000
1934-1944	Pearl trim	$15,000	$25,000

Everett Guitars

1977-present. Luthier Kent Everett builds his premium grade, production/custom, steel-string and classical guitars in Atlanta, Georgia. From '01 to '03, his Laurel Series guitars were built in conjunction with Terada in Japan and set up in Atlanta. He has also built archtops, semi-hollow and solidbody electrics, Dobro-styles, and mandolins.

Evergreen Mountain

1971-present. Professional grade, custom, flat-top and tenor guitars built by luthier Jerry Nolte in Cove, Oregon. He also builds basses and mandolins and built over 100 dulcimers in the '70s.

Everly Guitars

1982-2001. Luthier Robert Steinegger built these premium grade, production/custom flat-tops in Portland, Oregon (also see Steinegger Guitars).

1986 ESP Traditional

Evergreen Mountain tenor guitar

GUITARS

Fender '51 NoCaster Relic

Fender Avalon

MODEL		EXC. COND.	
YEAR	FEATURES	LOW	HIGH

Falk

Custom archtop guitars built by luthier Dave Falk in Independence, Missouri.

Farnell

1989-present. Luthier Al Farnell builds his professional grade, production, solidbody guitars in Ontario, California. He also offers his intermediate grade, production, C Series which is imported from China. He also builds basses.

Favilla

1890-1973. Founded by the Favilla family in New York, the company began to import guitars in 1970, but folded in '73. American-made models have the Favilla family crest on the headstock. Import models used a script logo on the headstock.

Acoustic Classical

1960s-1973. Various nylon-string classical models.

1970-1973	Import	$200	$250

Acoustic Flat-Top

1960s-1973. Various flat-top models, 000- to D-styles, mahogany to spruce.

1960s-1969	U.S.-made, crest logo	$550	$750
1970-1973	Import, script logo	$350	$450

Fender

1946 (1945)-present. Budget, intermediate, professional and premium grade, production/custom, electric, acoustic, acoustic/electric, classical, and resonator guitars built in the U.S. and overseas. They also build amps, basses, mandolins, bouzoukis, banjos, violins, and PA gear.

Ca. 1939 Leo Fender opened a radio and record store called Fender Radio Service, where he met Clayton Orr 'Doc' Kauffman, and in '45 they started KF Company to build lap steels and amps. In '46 Kauffman left and Fender started the Fender Electric Instrument Company. By '50 Fender's products were distributed by F.C. Hall's Radio & Television Electronics Company (Radio-Tel, later owners of Rickenbacker). In '53 Radio-Tel is replaced by the Fender Sales Company which was run by Don Randall. In January '65 CBS purchased the company for $13 million and renamed it Fender Musical Instruments Corporation. Leo Fender was kept on as consultant until '70. Fender went on to design guitars for Music Man and G&L. Bill Schultz and Dan Smith were hired from Yamaha in '81. In '82 Fender Japan is established to produce licensed Fender copies for sale in Japan. Also in '82, the Fender Squier brand debuts on Japanese-made instruments for the European market and by '83 they were imported into U.S. In '85, the company was purchased by an investor group headed by Schultz but the purchase does not include the Fullerton factory. While a new factory was being established at Corona, California, all Fender Contemporary Stratocasters and Telecasters were made either by Fender Japan or in Seoul, Korea.

U.S. production resumes in '86 with American Standard Stratocaster. The Fender Custom Shop, run by Michael Stevens and John Page, opens in '87. The Mexican Fender factory is established in '90. In '95, Fender purchased the Guild guitar company. On January 3, '02, Fender Musical Instruments Corporation (FMIC) announced the sale of holdings in the company. FMIC recapitalized a minority portion of the common stock. The recapitalization partners included Roland Corporation U.S. (Los Angeles) and Weston Presidio, a private equity firm (San Francisco). As of January 1, '03, Fred Gretsch Enterprises, Ltd granted Fender the exclusive rights to develop, produce, market and distribute Gretsch guitars worldwide where FMIC is responsible for all aspects of the Gretsch product lines and brand-names, including development of new products. Fred Gretsch consulted during the changeover and will also consult on product development and quality control. Around the same time, Fender also acquired the Jackson/Charvel Guitar Company. In October, '04, Fender acquired Tacoma Guitars. FMIC brands also include Guild, Squire, DeArmond, Benedetto, Rodriguez, Tacoma, Sunn, SWR amps, Brand X amps and Floyd Rose.

Dating older Fender guitars is an imprecise art form at best. While serial numbers were used, they were frequently not in sequence, although a lower number will frequently be older than a substantially higher number. Often necks were dated, but only with the date the neck was finished, not when the guitar was assembled. Generally, dating requires triangulating between serial numbers, neck dates, pot dates, construction details and model histories.

From '50 through roughly '65, guitars had more-or-less sequential numbers in either 4 or 5 digits, though some higher numbers may have an initial 0 or - prefix. These can range from 0001 to 99XXX.

From '63 into '65, some instruments had serial numbers beginning with an L prefix plus 5 digits (LXXXXX). Beginning in '65 with the CBS take-over into '76, 6-digit serial numbers were stamped on F neckplates roughly sequentially from 10XXXX to 71XXXX. In '76 the serial number was shifted to the headstock decal. From '76-'77, the serial number began with a bold-face 76 or S6 plus 5 digits (76XXXXX).

From '77 on, serial numbers consisted of a 2-place prefix plus 5 digits (sometimes 6 beginning in '91): '77 (S7, S8), '78 (S7, S8, S9), '79 (S9, E0), '80-'81 (S9, E0, E1), '82 (E1, E2, E3), '84-'85 (E4), '85-'86 (no U.S. production), '87 (E4), '88 (E4, E8), '89 (E8, E9), '90 (E9, N9, N0), '91 (N0), '92 (N2).

Serial numbers on guitars made by Fender Japan consist of either a 2-place prefix plus 5 digits or a single prefix letter plus 6 digits: '82-'84 (JV), '83-'84 (SQ), '84-'87 (E), '85-'86+ (A, B, C), '86-'87 (F), '87-'88+ (G), '88-'89 (H), '89-'90 (I, J), '90-'91 (K), '91-'92 (L), '92-'93 (M).

Factors affecting Fender values: The CBS takeover is synonymous with a decline in quality - whether true or not is still debated, but the perception persists among musicians and collectors,

MODEL YEAR	FEATURES	EXC. COND. LOW	HIGH

and Pre-CBS Fenders are more valuable. Fender experienced some quality problems in the late-'60s. Small headstock is enlarged in '65 and the '70s introduced the 3-bolt neck and other design changes that weren't that popular with guitarists. With high value and relative scarcity of Pre-CBS Fenders, even CBS-era instruments are now sought by collectors. Custom color instruments, especially Strats from the '50s and early-'60s, can be valued much more than the standard sunburst finishes. In '75 Fender dropped the optional custom colors and started issuing the guitars in a variety of standard colors.

The various Telecaster, Stratocaster and Squier models are grouped under those general headings.

50th Anniversary Spanish Guitar Set Custom Shop
1996. 50 sets made, Tele Prototype reproduction with similar era copy of woodie amp.

Year	Features	Low	High
1996		$6,500	$9,000

'50s Relic/'51 No Caster Custom Shop
1996-present. Called the '50s Relic Nocaster for '96-'99, and '51 Nocaster in NOS, Relic, or Closet Classic versions at present, with the Relic Series being the highest offering.

Year	Features	Low	High
1999-2004	Closet Classic	$1,300	$1,500
1999-2004	Relic No Caster	$1,800	$1,900

Avalon
1984-1995. Acoustic, 6-on-a-side tuners, mahogany neck, back and sides (nato after '93), spruce top, various colors.

Year	Features	Low	High
1984-1992		$300	$400

Broadcaster
Mid-1950-early-1951. For a short time in early-'51, before being renamed the Telecaster, models had no Broadcaster decal; these are called No-casters by collectors.

Year	Features	Low	High
1950	Blond	$30,000	$40,000
1951	Clipped decal, "No Caster"	$30,000	$35,000

Broadcaster Leo Fender Custom Shop
1999 only. Leo Fender script logo signature replaces Fender logo on headstock, Custom Shop Certificate signed by Phyllis Fender, Fred Gretsch, and William Schultz, includes glass display case and poodle guitar case.

Year	Features	Low	High
1999		$6,000	$7,000

Bronco
1967-1980. Slab solidbody, 1 pickup, tremolo, red.

Year	Features	Low	High
1967-1969		$700	$800
1970-1980		$600	$700

Bullet
1981-1983. Solidbody, came in 2- and 3-pickup versions (single-coil and humbucker), and single- and double-cut models, various colors. Becomes Squire Bullet in '85.

Year	Features	Low	High
1981-1983	2 pickups	$275	$325
1981-1983	3 pickups	$325	$375

CG (Classical Guitar) Series
2000s. Various classical electric and/or acoustic models, an oval label on the inside back clearly indicates the model number. CG-35CE has solid cedar top and rosewood body.

Year	Features	Low	High
2000s	CG-35CE	$250	$350

Concert
1963-1970. Acoustic flat-top slightly shorter than King/Kingman, spruce body, mahogany back and sides (optional Brazilian or Indian rosewood, zebrawood or vermillion), natural, sunburst optional by '68.

Year	Features	Low	High
1963-1965	Natural	$700	$950
1966-1968	Natural or sunburst	$600	$850
1979-1970	Natural or sunburst	$600	$750

Concord
1987-1992. D-style flat-top, 6-on-a-side headstock, natural.

Year	Features	Low	High
1987-1992		$175	$275

Coronado I
1966-1970. Thinline semi-hollowbody, double-cut, tremolo, 1 pickup, single-bound, dot inlay.

Year	Features	Low	High
1966-1967	Blue custom color	$1,100	$1,400
1966-1967	Cherry Red	$750	$1,000
1966-1967	Orange custom color	$1,100	$1,400
1966-1967	Sunburst	$750	$1,000
1966-1967	White (unfaded)	$1,000	$1,300
1968-1970	Sunburst	$650	$900

Coronado II
1966-1969 (Antigua finish offered until '70). Thinline semi-hollowbody, double-cut, tremolo optional, 2 pickups, single-bound, block inlay, available in standard finishes but special issues offered in Antigua and 6 different Wildwood finishes (labeled on the pickguard as Wildwood I through Wildwood VI to designate different colors). Wildwood finishes were achieved by injecting dye into growing trees.

Year	Features	Low	High
1966-1967	Blue custom color	$1,400	$1,600
1966-1967	Cherry Red	$1,000	$1,200
1966-1967	Olympic White custom color	$1,300	$1,500
1966-1967	Orange custom color	$1,400	$1,600
1966-1967	Silver custom color	$1,400	$1,600
1966-1967	Sunburst	$1,000	$1,200
1966-1967	Wildwood (unfaded)	$1,400	$1,600
1967-1969	Antigua	$1,400	$1,600
1967-1969	Cherry Red	$900	$1,200
1967-1969	Orange custom color	$1,300	$1,600
1967-1969	Sunburst	$900	$1,200
1967-1969	Wildwood	$1,300	$1,600
1970	Antigua	$1,200	$1,400
1970-1973	Cherry Red	$700	$900
1970-1973	Sunburst	$700	$900

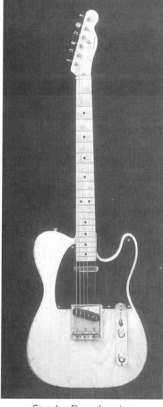

Fender Broadcaster

Fender Coronado II

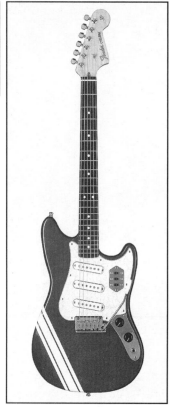

Fender Cyclone

1970s Fender Electric XII

MODEL YEAR	FEATURES	EXC. COND. LOW	HIGH

Coronado XII

1966-1969 (Antigua finish offered until '70). Thinline semi-hollowbody, double-cut, 12 strings, 2 pickups, block inlay, standard, Antigua and Wildwood finishes available.

Year	Features	Low	High
1966-1967	Cherry Red	$1,000	$1,200
1966-1967	Orange custom color	$1,400	$1,600
1966-1967	Sunburst	$1,000	$1,200
1966-1967	Wildwood Green	$1,400	$1,600
1968-1969	Antigua	$1,400	$1,600
1968-1969	Cherry Red	$900	$1,200
1968-1969	Orange custom color	$1,300	$1,600
1968-1969	Sunburst	$900	$1,200
1968-1969	Wildwood	$1,300	$1,600

Custom

1969-1971. Six-string solidbody that used up parts from discontinued Electric XII, asymmetrical-cut, long headstock, 2 split pickups, sunburst. Also marketed as the Maverick.

1969-1971		$1,400	$1,600

Cyclone

1998-present. Mexican import, solidbody, contoured offset waist, poplar body, various colors.

1998-2004		$350	$375

D'Aquisto Elite

1984, 1989-1994, 1994-present. Part of Fender's Master Series, archtop, single-cut, glued neck, 1 pickup, gold-plated hardware, made in Japan until '94, in '94 the Fender Custom Shop issued a version that retailed at $6,000, various colors.

1984	Japan made	$1,900	$2,200
1989-1994	Japan made	$1,900	$2,200

D'Aquisto Standard

1984 (Serial numbers could range from 1983-1985). Part of Fender's Master Series, archtop, single-cut, glued neck, 2 pickups, made in Japan, various colors.

1984		$1,800	$2,000

D'Aquisto Ultra

1994-2000. Custom Shop, made under the supervision of James D'Aquisto, flamed maple back and sides, spruce top, ebony tailpiece, bridge and 'guard, all hand carved.

1994-2000		$7,000	$8,500

Duo-Sonic

1957-1969. Solidbody, 3/4-size, single pickup, sand/natural ('57-'63) and 2 pickups, blue, red or white after, short- and long-scale necks, short-scale necks listed here (see Duo-Sonic II for long-scale), reissued Mexican-made in '94.

1957-1959	Maple neck	$1,200	$1,400
1960-1963	Rosewood 'board	$1,100	$1,300
1964-1965		$1,000	$1,200
1966-1969		$900	$1,100

Duo-Sonic II

1965-1969. Solidbody, 2 pickups, blue, red or white, long-scale neck, though the long-scale neck Duo-Sonic was not known as the Duo-Sonic II until '65, we have lumped all long-scales under the II for the purposes of this Guide.

1965-1969		$1,100	$1,400

MODEL YEAR	FEATURES	EXC. COND. LOW	HIGH

Duo-Sonic Reissue

1994-1997. Made in Mexico, black, red or white.

1994-1997		$200	$225

Electric XII

1965-1969. Solidbody, 12 strings, long headstock, 2 split pickups. Custom colors can fade or become darker; for example Lake Placid Blue changes to green. The price ranges below are for instruments that are relatively unfaded. Many older guitars have some color fade and minor fade is factored into these values. Each custom color should be evaluated on a case-by-case basis. Custom color Fenders can be forged and bogus finishes have been a problem. As the value of custom color Fenders has increased, so has the problem of bogus non-original finishes. The prices in the Guide are for factory original finishes in excellent condition. The prices noted do not take into account market factors such as fake instruments, which can have the effect of lowering a guitar's market value unless the guitar's provenance can be validated.

Year	Features	Low	High
1965-1966	Black	$2,300	$3,000
1965-1966	Blue Ice	$3,200	$4,200
1965-1966	Burgundy Mist	$3,400	$4,600
1965-1966	Candy Apple Red	$2,600	$3,600
1965-1966	Charcoal Frost	$3,200	$4,200
1965-1966	Dakota Red	$2,700	$3,900
1965-1966	Daphne Blue	$3,200	$4,200
1965-1966	Fiesta Red	$2,700	$3,900
1965-1966	Firemist Gold	$3,200	$4,200
1965-1966	Firemist Silver	$3,200	$4,200
1965-1966	Foam Green	$3,800	$4,800
1965-1966	Inca Silver	$3,200	$4,200
1965-1966	Lake Placid Blue	$2,600	$3,600
1965-1966	Ocean Turquoise	$3,200	$4,200
1965-1966	Olympic White	$2,600	$3,600
1965-1966	Sonic Blue	$3,200	$4,200
1965-1966	Sunburst, dots	$2,000	$2,300
1965-1966	Teal Green	$3,200	$4,200
1966	Sunburst (late '66), block	$1,900	$2,100
1967	Custom colors	$2,300	$4,000
1967	Sunburst, block	$1,900	$2,100
1968	Custom colors	$2,100	$3,800
1968	Sunburst	$1,700	$1,900
1969	Custom colors	$2,000	$3,600
1969	Sunburst	$1,600	$1,800

Esprit Elite

1983-1985. Part of the Master Series, made in Japan, double-cut, semi-hollow, carved maple top, 2 humbuckers, bound rosewood 'board, snowflake inlays, sunburst.

1983-1984		$1,100	$1,400

Esprit Standard

1983-1985. Part of the Master Series, made in Japan, double-cut, semi-hollow, carved maple top, 2 humbuckers, bound rosewood 'board, dot inlays, sunburst.

1983-1985		$1,000	$1,200

MODEL YEAR	FEATURES	EXC. COND. LOW	HIGH

Esprit Ultra

1984. Part of the Master Series, made in Japan, double-cut, semi-hollow, carved spruce top, 2 humbuckers, bound rosewood 'board, split-block inlays, sunburst, gold hardware.

1984		$1,200	$1,500

Esquire

1950-1970. Ash body, single-cut, 1 pickup, maple neck, black 'guard '50-'54, white 'guard '54 on.

1951	Blond, black 'guard	$15,000	$20,000
1952-1954	Blond, black 'guard	$14,000	$19,000
1954-1955	Blond, white 'guard	$10,500	$15,000
1956	Blond	$10,000	$14,000
1957	Blond	$10,000	$13,000
1958	Blond, backloader	$10,000	$12,000
1958	Blond, frontloader	$9,000	$11,000
1959	Blond, maple 'board	$7,000	$10,000
1959	Blond, slab 'board	$6,500	$9,000
1960	Blond	$6,500	$9,000
1960	Sunburst	$8,500	$10,500
1961	Blond	$6,200	$8,000
1961	Sunburst	$8,400	$12,000
1962	Blond, curved 'board	$6,000	$7,000
1962	Blond, slab 'board	$6,500	$7,500
1963	Blond	$5,400	$7,000
1963	Candy Apple Red	$7,000	$9,300
1963	Lake Placid Blue	$7,000	$9,300
1963	Olympic White	$6,000	$7,500
1964	Blond	$5,200	$7,000
1964	Burgundy Mist	$9,000	$12,200
1965	Blond	$4,800	$6,500
1965	Lake Placid Blue	$6,300	$8,600
1966	Blond	$4,200	$6,000
1966	Olympic White	$4,500	$6,500
1967	Blond	$3,500	$4,200
1967	Blue Ice	$5,700	$7,000
1967	Lake Placid Blue	$4,600	$5,500
1967	Olympic White	$3,700	$4,500
1968	Blond	$3,500	$4,200
1968	Sunburst	$4,100	$4,900
1969	Blond	$3,200	$3,800
1969	Sunburst	$3,000	$4,500
1970	Blond	$3,000	$3,600

Esquire Custom

1959-1970. Same as Esquire, but with bound alder sunburst body and rosewood 'board.

1959		$16,000	$23,000
1960		$15,000	$21,000
1961-1962		$12,000	$18,000
1963-1964		$9,000	$14,000
1965-1966		$7,000	$10,000
1967-1968		$6,000	$7,000
1969-1970		$5,000	$6,500

MODEL YEAR	FEATURES	EXC. COND. LOW	HIGH

Esquire Custom GT/Celtic/Scorpion

2003. Single-cut solidbody, 1 humbucker, 1 knob (volume), set-neck, solid colors.

2003		$250	$350

Esquire Custom Shop

Various colors.

1990s		$1,700	$2,200

Flame Elite

1984-1988. Part of the Master Series, made in Japan, neck-thru, offset double-cut, solidbody, 2 humbuckers, rosewood 'board, snowflake inlays.

1984-1988		$1,100	$1,400

Flame Standard

1984-1988. Part of the Master Series, made in Japan, neck-thru, offset double-cut, solidbody, 2 humbuckers, rosewood 'board, dot inlays.

1984-1988		$1,000	$1,200

Flame Ultra

1984-1988. Part of the Master Series, made in Japan, neck-thru, double-cut, solidbody, 2 humbuckers, rosewood 'board, split block inlays (some with snowflakes), gold hardware.

1984-1988		$1,200	$1,500

F-Series Dreadnought Flat-Top

1969-1981. The F-Series were Japanese-made flat-top acoustics, included were Concert- and Dreadnought-size instruments with features running from plain to bound necks and headstocks and fancy inlays, there was also a line of F-Series classical, nylon-string guitars. A label on the inside indicates model number. FC-20 is a classical with Brazilian rosewood. There was also an Asian (probably Korean) import Standard Series for '82-'90 where the models start with a F.

1969-1981	High-end solid top	$150	$250
1969-1981	Low-end laminated	$100	$150
1972-1981	FC-20 Classical	$250	$400

Gemini Series

1983-1990. Korean-made flat-tops, label on inside indicates model. I is classical nylon-string, II, III and IV are dreadnought steel-strings, there is also a 12-string and an IIE acoustic/electric.

1983-1987	Gemini II	$150	$175
1983-1988	Gemini I	$125	$150
1987-1990	Gemini III/IV	$175	$225

Harmony-Made Series

Early-1970s-mid-1970s. Harmony-made with white stencil Fender logo, mahogany, natural or sunburst.

1970s		$75	$150

Jag-Stang

1996-1999. Japanese-made, designed by Curt Cobain, body similar to Jaguar, tremolo, 1 pickup, oversize Strat peghead, Fiesta Red or Sonic Blue.

1996	1st issue, 50th Anniv. Label	$475	$575
1997-1999		$425	$525

Jaguar

1962-1975. Reintroduced as Jaguar '62 in '95-'99. Custom colors can fade and often the faded color has very little similarity to the original color. The values below are for an instrument that is relatively unfaded. Each custom color should be evaluated on a case-by-

1956 Fender Esquire

Fender Flame Ultra

1962 Fender Jaguar

1965 Fender Jaguar

case basis. Custom color Fenders can be forged and bogus finishes have been a problem. As the value of custom color Fenders has increased, so has the problem of bogus non-original finishes. The prices in the Guide are for factory original finishes in excellent condition.

MODEL YEAR	FEATURES	EXC. COND. LOW	HIGH
1962	Black	$3,000	$3,700
1962	Blond	$3,000	$3,700
1962	Burgundy Mist	$3,900	$4,800
1962	Dakota Red	$3,900	$4,800
1962	Daphne Blue	$3,700	$4,500
1962	Fiesta Red	$3,900	$4,800
1962	Foam Green	$4,300	$5,200
1962	Inca Silver	$3,700	$4,500
1962	Lake Pacid Blue	$3,300	$4,100
1962	Olympic White	$3,300	$4,100
1962	Shell Pink	$4,300	$5,200
1962	Sherwood Green	$3,900	$4,800
1962	Shoreline Gold	$3,900	$4,800
1962	Sonic Blue	$3,700	$4,500
1962	Sunburst	$2,300	$2,800
1962	Surf Green	$4,300	$5,200
1963-1964	Black	$2,900	$3,200
1963-1964	Blond	$2,900	$3,200
1963-1964	Burgundy Mist	$3,800	$4,500
1963-1964	Candy Apple Red	$3,200	$3,500
1963-1964	Fiesta Red	$3,800	$4,200
1963-1964	Lake Placid Blue	$3,200	$3,500
1963-1964	Olympic White	$3,200	$3,500
1963-1964	Shoreline Gold	$3,800	$4,200
1963-1964	Sonic Blue	$3,500	$4,100
1963-1964	Sunburst	$2,200	$2,400
1965	Black	$2,700	$3,000
1965	Blue Ice	$3,600	$4,000
1965	Burgundy Mist	$4,000	$4,400
1965	Candy Apple Red	$3,000	$3,400
1965	Fiesta Red	$3,500	$3,800
1965	Firemist Gold	$3,600	$4,000
1965	Firemist Silver	$3,600	$4,000
1965	Lake Placid Blue	$3,000	$3,400
1965	Ocean Turquoise	$3,600	$4,000
1965	Olympic White	$3,000	$3,400
1965	Sonic Blue	$3,600	$4,000
1965	Sunburst	$2,000	$2,200
1965	Teal Green	$3,600	$4,000
1966	Black	$2,600	$2,900
1966	Blond	$2,600	$2,900
1966	Blue Ice	$3,400	$3,800
1966	Candy Apple Red	$2,900	$3,200
1966	Fiesta Red	$3,200	$3,600
1966	Firemist Gold	$3,400	$3,800
1966	Firemist Silver	$3,400	$3,800
1966	Lake Placid Blue	$2,900	$3,200
1966	Olympic White	$2,800	$3,200
1966	Sonic Blue	$3,500	$3,800
1966	Sunburst, block markers	$1,600	$2,000
1966	Sunburst, dot markers (early '66)	$1,900	$2,100
1967	Custom colors	$2,500	$3,700
1967	Sunburst	$1,600	$2,000
1968-1970	Custom colors	$2,400	$3,600

MODEL YEAR	FEATURES	EXC. COND. LOW	HIGH
1968-1970	Sunburst	$1,500	$1,900
1971-1975	Custom colors	$2,300	$3,300
1971-1975	Sunburst	$1,300	$1,600

Jaguar '62

1994-present. Reintroduction of Jaguar, Japanese-made until '99, then U.S.-made, basswood body, rosewood 'board, various colors.

MODEL YEAR	FEATURES	EXC. COND. LOW	HIGH
1994-1999	Import	$550	$600
1999-2003	U.S.A.-made	$1,000	$1,150

Jazzmaster

1958-1980. Contoured body, 2 pickups, rosewood 'board, clay dot inlay, reintroduced as Japanese-made Jazzmaster '62 in '96. Custom color Fenders can be forged and bogus finishes have been a problem. As the value of custom color Fenders has increased, so has the problem of bogus non-original finishes. The prices in the Guide are for factory original finishes in excellent condition.

MODEL YEAR	FEATURES	EXC. COND. LOW	HIGH
1958	Sunburst	$4,200	$5,700
1958	Sunburst, rare maple 'board	$6,000	$6,500
1959	Custom colors, includes rare	$6,000	$10,000
1959	Sunburst	$4,000	$5,500
1960	Black	$4,500	$6,500
1960	Blond	$4,500	$6,500
1960	Burgundy Mist	$6,000	$8,500
1960	Dakota Red	$6,000	$8,500
1960	Daphne Blue	$5,500	$8,000
1960	Fiesta Red	$6,000	$8,500
1960	Foam Green	$6,500	$9,300
1960	Inca Silver	$5,500	$8,000
1960	Lake Placid Blue	$5,000	$7,300
1960	Olympic White	$5,000	$7,300
1960	Shell Pink	$6,500	$9,300
1960	Sherwood Green	$6,000	$8,500
1960	Shoreline Gold	$6,000	$8,500
1960	Sonic Blue	$5,500	$8,000
1960	Sunburst	$3,500	$5,000
1960	Surf Green	$6,500	$9,300
1961	Black	$4,400	$6,300
1961	Blond	$4,400	$6,300
1961	Burgundy Mist	$5,700	$8,000
1961	Dakota Red	$5,700	$8,000
1961	Daphne Blue	$5,200	$7,500
1961	Fiesta Red	$5,700	$8,000
1961	Foam Green	$6,100	$8,500
1961	Inca Silver	$5,200	$7,500
1961	Lake Placid Blue	$4,800	$7,000
1961	Olympic White	$4,800	$7,000
1961	Shell Pink	$6,100	$8,500
1961	Sherwood Green	$5,700	$8,000
1961	Shoreline Gold	$5,700	$8,000
1961	Sonic Blue	$5,200	$7,500
1961	Sunburst	$3,300	$4,700
1961	Surf Green	$6,100	$8,500
1962	Black	$4,000	$6,000
1962	Blond	$4,000	$6,000
1962	Burgundy Mist	$5,200	$7,800
1962	Dakota Red	$5,200	$7,800
1962	Daphne Blue	$4,800	$7,200

MODEL YEAR	FEATURES	EXC. COND. LOW	HIGH
1962	Fiesta Red	$5,200	$7,800
1962	Foam Green	$5,600	$8,400
1962	Inca Silver	$4,800	$7,200
1962	Lake Placid Blue	$4,400	$6,600
1962	Olympic White	$4,400	$6,600
1962	Shell Pink	$5,600	$8,400
1962	Sherwood Green	$5,200	$7,800
1962	Shoreline Gold	$5,200	$7,800
1962	Sonic Blue	$4,800	$7,200
1962	Sunburst	$3,000	$4,500
1962	Surf Green	$5,600	$8,400
1963-1964	Black	$3,500	$4,800
1963-1964	Blond	$3,500	$4,800
1963-1964	Burgundy Mist	$4,500	$6,200
1963-1964	Candy Apple Red	$3,800	$5,200
1963-1964	Dakota Red	$4,500	$6,200
1963-1964	Daphne Blue	$4,100	$5,700
1963-1964	Fiesta Red	$4,500	$6,200
1963-1964	Foam Green	$4,800	$6,700
1963-1964	Inca Silver	$4,200	$5,700
1963-1964	Lake Placid Blue	$3,800	$5,200
1963-1964	Olympic White	$3,800	$5,200
1963-1964	Sherwood Green	$4,500	$6,200
1963-1964	Shoreline Gold	$4,500	$6,200
1963-1964	Sonic Blue	$4,200	$5,700
1963-1964	Sunburst	$2,600	$3,600
1963-1964	Surf Green	$4,800	$6,700
1965	Black	$3,300	$4,200
1965	Blond	$3,300	$4,200
1965	Blue Ice	$4,200	$5,600
1965	Burgundy Mist	$4,600	$6,200
1965	Candy Apple Red	$3,500	$4,800
1965	Charcoal Frost	$4,200	$5,600
1965	Dakota Red	$4,000	$5,400
1965	Daphne Blue	$4,200	$5,600
1965	Fiesta Red	$4,000	$5,400
1965	Firemist Gold	$4,200	$5,600
1965	Firemist Silver	$4,200	$5,600
1965	Foam Green	$4,800	$6,500
1965	Lake Placid Blue	$3,500	$4,800
1965	Ocean Turquoise	$4,200	$5,600
1965	Olympic White	$3,500	$4,800
1965	Sonic Blue	$4,200	$5,600
1965	Sunburst	$2,300	$3,100
1966	Less common custom colors	$4,000	$5,800
1966	More common custom colors	$3,200	$4,000
1966	Sunburst, blocks (late '66)	$2,000	$2,800
1966	Sunburst, dots (early '66)	$2,100	$2,900
1967	Less common custom colors	$3,600	$5,400
1967	More common custom colors	$2,800	$3,600
1967	Sunburst	$1,900	$2,700
1968-1970	Less common custom colors	$3,400	$4,500
1968-1970	More common custom colors	$2,500	$3,400

MODEL YEAR	FEATURES	EXC. COND. LOW	HIGH
1968-1970	Sunburst	$1,800	$2,500
1971-1975	Custom colors	$2,200	$3,400
1971-1975	Sunburst	$1,400	$1,800
1976-1982	Custom colors	$1,800	$2,800
1976-1982	Sunburst	$1,300	$1,700

Jazzmaster '62
1994-present. Japanese-made reintroduction of Jazzmaster, basswood body, rosewood 'board, U.S.-made from '99, various colors.

1994-1999	Import	$575	$625
1999-2003	US	$950	$1,100

Jazzmaster The Ventures Limited Edition
1996. Japanese-made, ash body, 2 pickups, block inlay, transparent purple/black.

1996		$900	$1,100

Katana
1985-1986. Import, wedge-shaped body, bridge pickup, black.

1985-1986		$350	$400

King
1963-1965. Full-size 15 5/8" wide acoustic, natural. Renamed Kingman in '65.

1963-1965		$850	$1,000

Kingman
1965-1971. Full-size 15 5/8" wide acoustic, slightly smaller by '70, offered in 3 Wildwood colors, referred to as the Wildwood acoustic which is a Kingman with dyed wood.

1965-1968		$850	$1,000
1969-1971		$850	$950

Lead I
1979-1982. Double-cut solidbody with 1 humbucker, maple or rosewood 'board, black or brown.

1979-1982	Maple 'board	$325	$425

Lead II
1979-1982. Lead with 2 pickups, black or brown.

1979-1982	Maple 'board	$325	$425

Lead III
1982. Lead with 2 split-coil humbuckers, 2 3-way switches, various colors.

1982		$450	$700

LTD
1969-1975. Archtop electric, single-cut, gold-plated hardware, carved top and back, 1 pickup, multi-bound, bolt-on neck, sunburst.

1969-1975		$3,500	$5,000

Malibu
1965-1971, 1983-1992. Flat top, spruce top, mahogany back and sides, black, mahogany or sunburst. Name used on Asian import model in '80s.

1965-1971		$525	$600

Marauder
1965 only. The Marauder has 3 pickups, and some have slanted frets, only 8 were made, thus it is very rare. 1st generation has hidden pickups, 2nd has exposed.

1965	1st generation	$7,000	$14,000
1965	2nd generation	$5,000	$10,000

1959 Fender Jazzmaster

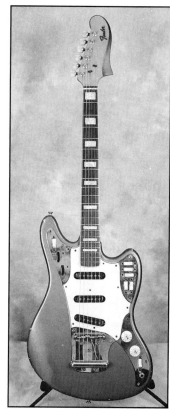

Fender Marauder

1964 Fender Musicmaster

Fender Squier '51

MODEL YEAR	FEATURES	EXC. COND. LOW	HIGH

Montego I/II
1968-1975. Electric archtop, single-cut, bolt-on neck, 1 pickup (I) or 2 pickups (II), chrome-plated hardware, sunburst.

1968-1975	I	$2,000	$2,500
1968-1975	II	$2,300	$2,700

Musiclander
1969-1972. Also called Swinger and Arrow, solidbody, 1 pickup, arrow-shaped headstock, no model name on peghead, red, white, and blue.

1969-1972		$1,300	$1,600

Musicmaster
1956-1980. Solidbody, 1 pickup, short-scale (3/4) neck, blond. Restyled in '64 like Mustang with red, white and blue available. Regular-scale necks were optional and are called Musicmaster II from '64 to '69, after '69 II is dropped and Musicmaster continues with regular-scale neck.

1956-1959	Blond	$900	$1,000
1960-1964	Blond	$700	$950
1964-1969	Red, white, blue	$600	$800
1970-1980	Red, white, blue	$500	$700

Musicmaster II
1964-1969. Solidbody, 1 pickup, long regular-scale neck version of Musicmaster, red, white, or blue.

1964-1969		$650	$850

Mustang
1964-1982, 1997-1998. Solidbody, 2 pickups. Reissued as '69 Mustang in 1996 and name changed back to Mustang '97-'98. Dakota Red, Daphne Blue and Olympic White with Competition Red, Blue and Orange finishes added ca. '69-'72. Competition finishes featured a racing stripe on the front of the body.

1964-1965	Various colors	$1,200	$1,400
1966-1969	Various colors	$1,000	$1,200
1970-1979	Various colors	$850	$1,100
1980-1982	Various colors	$750	$1,000

Mustang '69 Reissue
1996-1999. Japanese-made reissue of Mustang, blue or white, name changed back to Mustang in '97-'98.

1996-1999		$500	$550

Newporter
1965-1971, 1983-1992. Acoustic flat-top, mahogany back and sides. Name used on Asian import model in '80s.

1965-1968	Spruce top	$425	$525
1968-1971	Mahogany top	$325	$425

Palomino
1968-1971. Acoustic flat-top, spruce top, mahogany back and sides, triple-bound, black or mahogany.

1968-1971		$525	$600

Performer
1985-1986. Imported Swinger-like body design, 2 slanted humbuckers.

1985-1986		$875	$1,000

Prodigy
1991-1995. Electric solidbody, double-cut, chrome-plated hardware, 2 single-coil and 1 humbucker pickups, blue or black.

1991-1995		$375	$425

Redondo
1969-1971, 1983-1990. Mid-size flat-top, 14 3/8" wide, replaces Newport spruce top model. Name used on Asian import model in '80s.

1969-1971		$425	$525

Robben Ford
1989-1994. Symmetrical double-cut, 2 pickups, glued-in neck, solidbody with tone chambers, multi-bound, gold-plated hardware, sunburst. After '94 made in Fender Custom Shop.

1989-1994		$1,100	$1,400

Shenandoah 12-String
1965-1971. Acoustic flat-top, spruce top, mahogany back and sides.

1965-1968	Antigua	$900	$1,200
1965-1968	Blond	$650	$800
1969-1971	Antigua	$800	$1,100
1969-1971	Blond	$550	$750

Showmaster FMT (Custom Shop)
2000-present. Strat-style with bound figured maple top (FMT), 2 single-coil pickups and a bridge position humbucker, maple neck, Custom Shop certificate.

2000s		$1,100	$1,300

Showmaster HH (Import)
2002-present. 2 humbuckers, various models.

2002-2004		$500	$525

Squier '51
2004-present. Korean-made, Strat-style body with a Tele-style neck, various colors.

2004		$75	$125

Squier Bullet
1985-1988. Fender Japan was established in '82, Squier production began in '83, production was shifted to Korea in '87.

1985-1988	Sunburst, humbuckers	$250	$325
1985-1988	White	$175	$275

Squier II Stratocaster
1989-1990. Import from India.

1989-1990		$100	$125

Squier Katana
1985-1986. Import, wedge-shaped body, bridge pickup, black.

1985-1986		$275	$350

Squier Stratocaster Standard
1982-present. Fender Japan was established in '82 with Squier production beginning in '83. Production was shifted to Korea in '87 and later allocated to China, India (Squier II '89-'90) and Mexico. This model is the low-cost Stratocaster Standard version of the Squier line.

1982-1989		$250	$350
1990-1999		$175	$275
2000-2004	Indonesia	$100	$125

Squier Stratocaster Standard (Affinity Series)
1997-present. Made in China.

1997-2004		$75	$125

Squier Stratocaster Standard (Double Fat Strat)
2000-present. Made in China, 2 humbucker pickups.

2000-2004		$125	$175

The *Vintage Guitar Price Guide* shows low to high values for items in all-original excellent condition, and, where applicable, with original case or cover.

MODEL		EXC. COND.	
YEAR	FEATURES	LOW	HIGH

Squier Stratocaster Standard (Floyd Rose)
1995-1996. Floyd Rose tailpiece, fotoflame finish, large Fender script logo.

1995-1996		$300	$350

Squier Telecaster
1983-present. Fender Japan was established in '82 with Squier production beginning in '83. Production was shifted to Korea in '87 and later allocated to China, India (Squier II '89-'90) and Mexico. This model is the low-cost version of the Telecaster for Squier.

1983-1984	Blond, 1st year		
	'70s-style logo	$250	$350
1985-1989	Black or blond	$200	$300

Squier Telecaster Affinity (China)
1998-present. Standard Telecaster styling, various colors.

1999		$75	$125

Starcaster
1974-1980. Double-cut, thinline semi-hollowbody, 2 humbuckers, various colors. Fender currently uses the Starcaster name on a line of budget guitars sold through Costco stores.

1974-1980		$2,200	$2,800

Stratacoustic
2003-present. Thinline acoustic/electric, single-cut, spruce top, new state-of-the-art fiberglass body, on-board electronics.

2003		$200	$225

Stratocaster
The following are all variations of the Stratocaster. The first five listings are for the main U.S.-made models and the '85 interim production Japanese model. All others are listed alphabetically after that in the following order (Custom Shop models are grouped together).

Stratocaster
Standard Stratocaster (includes "Smith Strat")
Standard Stratocaster (Japan)
American Standard Stratocaster
American Series Stratocaster
25th Anniversary Stratocaster
40th Anniversary Stratocaster
'50s Stratocaster (Import)
'54 Stratocaster FMT
'57 Stratocaster (USA)
'57 Vintage Stratocaster (Japan)
'60s Stratocaster (Japan)
'62 Stratocaster (Japan)
'62 Stratocaster (USA)
'68 Stratocaster (Japan)
'68 Stratocaster (USA)
'70s Stratocaster (Mexico)
'72 Stratocaster (Japan)
American Classic Stratocaster
American Deluxe Fat Stratocaster
American Deluxe Stratocaster
American Series Stratocaster HSS/HH
Big Apple Stratocaster
Bill Carson Stratocaster

Blue Flower Stratocaster
Bonnie Raitt Stratocaster
Bowling Ball/Marble Stratocaster
Buddy Guy Stratocaster
Buddy Guy Stratocaster (Mexico)
California Stratocaster
Collector's Edition Stratocaster ('62 Reissue)
Contemporary Stratocaster (Import)
Custom Shop 21st Century Limited Ed. Stratocaster
Custom Shop 35th Anniversary Stratocaster
Custom Shop 50th Anniversary Stratocaster
Custom Shop 50th Anniversary Stratocaster Relic
Custom Shop '54 Stratocaster
Custom Shop '54 Stratocaster FMT
Custom Shop '56 Stratocaster
Custom Shop '57 Special Stratocaster
Custom Shop '57 Stratocaster
Custom Shop '58 Stratocaster
Custom Shop '58 Stratocaster (Dakota Red)
Custom Shop '60 FMT Stratocaster
Custom Shop '60 Stratocaster
Custom Shop '60 Stratocaster (Short-Run)
Custom Shop '65 Stratocaster
Custom Shop '66 Stratocaster
Custom Shop '68 Stratocaster
Custom Shop '69 Stratocaster
Custom Shop Aluminum Stratocaster
Custom Shop American Classic Holoflake Strat
Custom Shop American Classic Stratocaster
Custom Shop Contemporary Stratocaster
Custom Shop Dick Dale Stratocaster
Custom Shop Eric Clapton Gold Leaf Stratocaster
Custom Shop Eric Clapton Stratocaster
Custom Shop Floyd Rose Classic Relic Stratocaster
Custom Shop Freddy Tavares Aloha Stratocaster
Custom Shop Gold Stratocaster
Custom Shop Hank Marvin Stratocaster
Custom Shop Hellecaster Stratocaster
Custom Shop Homer Haynes HLE Stratocaster
Custom Shop Hot Wheels Stratocaster
Custom Shop Ike Turner Tribute Stratocaster
Custom Shop Jimi Hendrix Monterey Pop Stratocaster
Custom Shop Kon Tike Stratocaster
Custom Shop Moto Limited Edition Stratocaster
Custom Shop Moto Set Stratocaster
Custom Shop Playboy 40th Anniversary Stratocaster
Custom Shop Relic '50s Stratocaster
Custom Shop Relic '60s Stratocaster
Custom Shop Robin Trower Signature Stratocaster
Custom Shop Set-Neck Stratocaster
Custom Shop Texas Special Stratocaster
Custom Shop Tree of Life Stratocaster

Fender Stratacoustic

1954 Fender Stratocaster

1956 Fender Stratocaster

1957 Fender Stratocaster

Custom Shop Turquoise Sparkle Stratocaster
Custom Shop Western Stratocaster
Deluxe Strat Plus
Deluxe Stratocaster
Elite Stratocaster
Eric Clapton Stratocaster
Floyd Rose Classic Stratocaster
Foto Flame Stratocaster
Gold Stratocaster
Gold Elite Stratocaster
Harley-Davidson 90th Anniversary Strato-
  caster
Highway 1 Stratocaster/HSS
HM Stratocaster (USA/Import)
HRR Stratocaster
Jeff Beck Stratocaster
Jimi Hendrix Tribute Stratocaster
Jimi Hendrix Voodoo Stratocaster
Jimmy Vaughan Tex-Mex Stratocaster
Lone Star Stratocaster
Paisley Stratocaster
Powerhouse/Powerhouse Deluxe Stratocaster
Richie Sambora Stratocaster
Roadhouse Stratocaster
Robert Cray Stratocaster
Roland Stratocaster (Mexico)
Short-Scale (7/8) Stratocaster
Splatter Stratocaster
Standard Stratocaster (Mexico)
Stevie Ray Vaughan Stratocaster
Strat Plus
Stratocaster Special (Mexico)
Stratocaster XII
Sub Sonic Stratocaster
Super/Deluxe Super Stratocaster
Tanqurey Tonic Stratocaster
The Strat
U.S. Ultra/Ultra Plus Stratocaster
Ventures Limited Edition Stratocaster
Walnut Stratocaster
Walnut Elite Stratocaster
Yngwie Malmsteen Stratocaster

Stratocaster

1954-1981. Two-tone sunburst until '58, 3-tone after. Custom color finishes were quite rare in the '50s and early-'60s and are much more valuable than the standard sunburst finish. By the '70s, color finishes were much more common and do not affect the value near as much. In '75 Fender dropped the optional custom colors and started issuing the guitars in a variety of standard colors (sunburst, blond, white, natural, walnut and black). Custom color Fenders can be forged and bogus finishes have been a problem. As the value of custom color Fenders has increased, so has the problem of bogus non-original finishes. The prices in the Guide are for factory original finishes in excellent condition. Many of the Fender custom colors have been included in the listings. One color, Shell Pink, is notable because many vintage authorities ask, "Does a Shell Pink Strat even exist?" An ultra-rare custom color should have strong documented provenance and be verifiable by at least one (preferable two or more) well-known vintage authorities.

Three-bolt neck '72-'81, otherwise 4-bolt. Unless noted,

all Stratocasters listed have the Fender tremolo system. Non-tremolo models (aka hardtails) typically sell for less. Many guitarists feel the tremolo block helps produce a fuller range of sound. On average, many more tremolo models were made. One year, '58, seems to be a year where a greater percentage of non-tremolo models were made. Tremolo vs. non-tremolo valuation should be taken on a brand-by-brand basis; for example, a pre-'65 Gibson ES-335 non-tremolo model is worth more than a tremolo equipped model.

See Standard Stratocaster for '82-'84 (following listing), and American Standard Stratocaster for '86-2000. Currently called the American Series Stratocaster.

MODEL YEAR	FEATURES	EXC. COND. LOW	HIGH
1954	Sunburst	$35,000	$40,000
1955	Sunburst	$28,000	$33,000
1956	Blond, nickel hardware	$30,000	$35,000
1956	Mary Kaye, gold hardware	$35,000	$44,000
1956	Sunburst	$27,000	$30,000
1956	Sunburst, non-trem	$20,000	$25,000
1957	Blond, nickel hardware	$30,000	$35,000
1957	Custom colors	$35,000	$42,000
1957	Mary Kaye, gold hardware	$35,000	$44,000
1957	Sunburst, bakelite knobs	$25,000	$28,000
1957	Sunburst, plastic knobs	$22,000	$25,000
1958	Black	$28,000	$31,000
1958	Blond, nickel hardware	$29,000	$34,000
1958	Fiesta Red	$34,000	$37,000
1958	Mary Kaye, gold hardware	$34,000	$43,000
1958	Sunburst 2-tone	$21,000	$23,000
1958	Sunburst 3-tone	$17,000	$20,000
1958	Sunburst, non-trem	$13,000	$16,000
1959	Blond, nickel hardware	$27,000	$33,000
1959	Custom colors	$28,000	$37,000
1959	Mary Kaye, gold hardware	$33,000	$42,000
1959	Sunburst, maple 'board	$16,000	$19,000
1959	Sunburst, non-trem, slab	$11,000	$14,000
1959	Sunburst, slab 'board	$14,000	$18,000
1960	Black	$22,000	$25,000
1960	Blond	$22,000	$25,000
1960	Burgundy Mist	$26,000	$32,000
1960	Dakota Red	$28,000	$32,000
1960	Daphne Blue	$25,000	$29,000
1960	Fiesta Red	$28,000	$32,000
1960	Foam Green	$30,000	$35,000
1960	Inca Silver	$25,000	$29,000

MODEL YEAR	FEATURES	EXC. COND. LOW	HIGH
1960	Lake Placid Blue	$23,000	$27,000
1960	Olympic White	$23,000	$27,000
1960	Shell Pink	$34,000	$38,000
1960	Sherwood Green	$27,000	$31,000
1960	Shoreline Gold	$27,000	$31,000
1960	Sonic Blue	$25,000	$29,000
1960	Sunburst	$15,000	$18,000
1960	Surf Green	$29,000	$33,000
1961	Black	$21,000	$23,000
1961	Blond	$21,000	$23,000
1961	Burgundy Mist	$25,000	$30,000
1961	Dakota Red	$25,000	$30,000
1961	Daphne Blue	$24,000	$28,000
1961	Fiesta Red	$25,000	$30,000
1961	Foam Green	$28,000	$32,000
1961	Inca Silver	$24,000	$28,000
1961	Lake Placid Blue	$22,000	$26,000
1961	Olympic White	$22,000	$26,000
1961	Shell Pink	$32,000	$37,000
1961	Sherwood Green	$25,000	$30,000
1961	Shoreline Gold	$25,000	$30,000
1961	Sonic Blue	$24,000	$28,000
1961	Sunburst	$14,000	$17,000
1961	Surf Green	$27,000	$32,000
1962	Black, curve	$17,000	$20,000
1962	Black, slab	$20,000	$22,000
1962	Blond, curve	$17,000	$20,000
1962	Blond, slab	$20,000	$22,000
1962	Burgundy Mist, curve	$21,000	$26,000
1962	Burgundy Mist, slab	$24,000	$29,000
1962	Candy Apple Red, curve	$18,000	$22,000
1962	Dakota Red, curve	$23,000	$26,000
1962	Dakota Red, slab	$24,000	$29,000
1962	Daphne Blue, curve	$20,000	$24,000
1962	Daphne Blue, slab	$23,000	$27,000
1962	Fiesta Red, curve	$23,000	$26,000
1962	Fiesta Red, slab	$24,000	$29,000
1962	Foam Green, curve	$23,000	$28,000
1962	Foam Green, slab	$27,000	$31,000
1962	Inca Silver, curve	$20,000	$24,000
1962	Inca Silver, slab	$23,000	$27,000
1962	Lake Placid Blue, curve	$18,000	$22,000
1962	Lake Placid Blue, slab	$21,000	$26,000
1962	Olympic White, curve	$18,000	$22,000
1962	Olympic White, slab	$21,000	$26,000
1962	Shell Pink, slab	$31,000	$36,000
1962	Sherwood Green, curve	$21,000	$26,000
1962	Sherwood Green, slab	$24,000	$29,000
1962	Shoreline Gold, curve	$21,000	$26,000

MODEL YEAR	FEATURES	EXC. COND. LOW	HIGH
1962	Shoreline Gold, slab	$24,000	$29,000
1962	Sonic Blue, curve	$20,000	$24,000
1962	Sonic Blue, slab	$23,000	$27,000
1962	Sunburst, curve	$11,000	$15,000
1962	Sunburst, slab	$13,000	$16,000
1962	Surf Green, curve	$24,000	$28,000
1962	Surf Green, slab	$26,000	$31,000
1963	Black	$17,000	$20,000
1963	Blond	$17,000	$20,000
1963	Burgundy Mist	$21,000	$26,000
1963	Candy Apple Red	$18,000	$22,000
1963	Dakota Red	$23,000	$27,000
1963	Daphne Blue	$20,000	$24,000
1963	Fiesta Red	$23,000	$27,000
1963	Foam Green	$23,000	$28,000
1963	Inca Silver	$20,000	$24,000
1963	Lake Placid Blue	$18,000	$22,000
1963	Olympic White	$18,000	$22,000
1963	Sherwood Green	$21,000	$26,000
1963	Shoreline Gold	$21,000	$26,000
1963	Sonic Blue	$20,000	$24,000
1963	Sunburst	$11,000	$15,000
1963	Surf Green	$24,000	$28,000
1964	Black	$14,000	$18,000
1964	Blond	$14,000	$18,000
1964	Burgundy Mist	$21,000	$25,000
1964	Candy Apple Red	$14,000	$21,000
1964	Dakota Red	$21,000	$25,000
1964	Daphne Blue	$18,000	$23,000
1964	Fiesta Red	$16,000	$25,000
1964	Foam Green	$22,000	$27,000
1964	Inca Silver	$19,000	$23,000
1964	Lake Placid Blue	$16,000	$21,000
1964	Olympic White	$14,000	$21,000
1964	Sherwood Green	$16,000	$25,000
1964	Shoreline Gold	$18,000	$25,000
1964	Sonic Blue	$15,000	$23,000
1964	Sunburst, early '64 logo	$11,000	$15,000
1964	Sunburst, late trans logo	$10,000	$13,000
1964	Surf Green	$20,000	$26,000
1965	Black	$12,000	$15,000
1965	Blond	$12,000	$15,000
1965	Blue Ice	$17,000	$20,000
1965	Burgundy Mist	$20,000	$22,000
1965	Candy Apple Red	$14,000	$17,000
1965	Charcoal Frost	$17,000	$20,000
1965	Dakota Red	$16,000	$19,000
1965	Fiesta Red	$16,000	$19,000
1965	Firemist Gold	$17,000	$20,000
1965	Firemist Silver	$17,000	$20,000
1965	Foam Green	$20,000	$23,000
1965	Inca Silver	$17,000	$20,000
1965	Lake Placid Blue	$14,000	$17,000
1965	Ocean Turquoise	$18,000	$20,000
1965	Olympic White	$14,000	$17,000
1965	Sonic Blue	$18,000	$20,000
1965	Sunburst, F-plate	$9,000	$11,000

1958 Fender Stratocaster Mary Kaye

1964 Fender Stratocaster

GUITARS

1965 Fender Stratocaster

*1973 Fender Stratocaster
(hardtail)*

MODEL YEAR	FEATURES	EXC. COND. LOW	HIGH
1965	Sunburst, green 'guard	$10,000	$12,000
1965	Sunburst, white 'guard	$9,500	$11,500
1965	Teal Green	$18,000	$20,000
1966	Black	$10,000	$13,000
1966	Blond	$10,000	$13,000
1966	Candy Apple Red	$12,000	$15,000
1966	Charcoal Frost	$14,000	$17,000
1966	Dakota Red	$14,000	$17,000
1966	Fiesta Red	$14,000	$17,000
1966	Firemist Gold	$15,000	$18,000
1966	Firemist Silver	$15,000	$18,000
1966	Foam Green	$18,000	$21,000
1966	Ice Blue	$14,000	$17,000
1966	Lake Placid Blue	$12,000	$15,000
1966	Ocean Turquoise	$15,000	$18,000
1966	Olympic White	$12,000	$15,000
1966	Sonic Blue	$14,000	$17,000
1966	Sunburst	$8,500	$10,500
1966	Teal Green	$15,000	$18,000
1967	Black	$10,000	$13,000
1967	Blond	$10,000	$13,000
1967	Candy Apple Red	$11,000	$14,000
1967	Charcoal Frost	$14,000	$17,000
1967	Dakota Red	$13,000	$16,000
1967	Fiesta Red	$13,000	$16,000
1967	Firemist Gold	$14,000	$17,000
1967	Firemist Silver	$14,000	$17,000
1967	Ice Blue	$14,000	$17,000
1967	Lake Placid Blue	$11,000	$14,000
1967	Ocean Turquoise	$14,000	$17,000
1967	Olympic White	$11,000	$14,000
1967	Sonic Blue	$14,000	$17,000
1967	Sunburst, maple cap	$8,500	$10,500
1967	Sunburst, rosewood cap	$7,000	$9,500
1967	Teal Green	$14,000	$17,000
1968	Black	$10,000	$13,000
1968	Blond	$10,000	$13,000
1968	Candy Apple Red, maple cap	$12,000	$15,000
1968	Candy Apple Red, rosewood cap	$11,000	$14,000
1968	Dakota Red, maple cap	$14,000	$17,000
1968	Dakota Red, rosewood cap	$13,000	$16,000
1968	Fiesta Red, maple cap	$14,000	$17,000
1968	Fiesta Red, rosewood cap	$13,000	$16,000
1968	Lake Placid Blue, maple cap	$12,000	$15,000
1968	Lake Placid Blue, rosewood cap	$11,000	$14,000
1968	Olympic White, maple cap	$12,000	$15,000
1968	Olympic White, rosewood cap	$11,000	$14,000

MODEL YEAR	FEATURES	EXC. COND. LOW	HIGH
1968	Sonic Blue, maple cap	$15,000	$18,000
1968	Sonic Blue, rosewood cap	$14,000	$17,000
1968	Sunburst, maple cap	$7,500	$9,000
1968	Sunburst, rosewood cap	$6,500	$8,000
1969	Black, maple	$10,000	$12,000
1969	Black, rosewood cap	$9,000	$11,000
1969	Blond, maple cap	$10,000	$12,000
1969	Blond, rosewood cap	$9,000	$11,000
1969	Candy Apple Red, maple cap	$10,000	$12,000
1969	Candy Apple Red, rosewood cap	$9,000	$11,000
1969	Firemist Gold, rosewood cap	$11,000	$13,000
1969	Firemist Silver, rosewood cap	$11,000	$13,000
1969	Lake Placid Blue, rosewood cap	$10,000	$11,000
1969	Ocean Turquoise, rosewood cap	$12,000	$14,000
1969	Olympic White, maple cap	$10,000	$13,000
1969	Sonic Blue, maple cap	$13,000	$15,000
1969	Sonic Blue, rosewood cap	$12,000	$14,000
1969	Sunburst, maple cap	$6,500	$7,500
1969	Sunburst, rosewood cap	$6,000	$7,000
1970	Black, maple cap	$9,000	$12,000
1970	Black, rosewood cap	$8,000	$11,000
1970	Blond, maple cap	$9,000	$12,000
1970	Blond, rosewood cap	$8,000	$11,000
1970	Candy Apple Red, maple cap	$9,000	$12,000
1970	Candy Apple Red, rosewood cap	$8,000	$11,000
1970	Firemist Gold, maple cap	$10,000	$14,000
1970	Firemist Gold, rosewood cap	$9,000	$13,000
1970	Firemist Silver, maple cap	$10,000	$14,000
1970	Firemist Silver, rosewood cap	$9,000	$13,000
1970	Lake Placid Blue, maple cap	$9,000	$12,000
1970	Lake Placid Blue, rosewood cap	$8,000	$11,000
1970	Ocean Turquoise, maple cap	$10,000	$15,000

The *Vintage Guitar Price Guide* shows low to high values for items in all-original excellent condition, and, where applicable, with original case or cover.

MODEL YEAR	FEATURES	EXC. COND. LOW	HIGH
1970	Ocean Turquoise, rosewood cap	$9,000	$14,000
1970	Olympic White, maple cap	$9,000	$13,000
1970	Olympic White, rosewood cap	$8,000	$11,000
1970	Sonic Blue, maple cap	$9,000	$15,000
1970	Sonic Blue, rosewood cap	$8,000	$14,000
1970	Sunburst, maple cap	$6,000	$7,000
1970	Sunburst, rosewood cap	$5,500	$6,500
1971	Black	$7,000	$10,000
1971	Blond	$7,000	$10,000
1971	Candy Apple Red	$7,000	$10,000
1971	Firemist Gold	$9,000	$12,000
1971	Firemist Silver	$9,000	$12,000
1971	Lake Placid Blue	$7,000	$10,000
1971	Ocean Turquoise	$9,000	$12,000
1971	Olympic White	$7,000	$10,000
1971	Sonic Blue	$9,000	$12,000
1971	Sunburst	$4,700	$6,200
1972	Natural	$2,700	$3,200
1972	Solid colors	$3,000	$5,000
1972	Sunburst	$2,500	$3,000
1973	Natural, non-trem	$2,100	$2,700
1973	Natural, trem	$2,200	$3,000
1973	Solid colors	$3,000	$5,000
1973	Sunburst, non-trem	$2,100	$2,700
1973	Sunburst, trem	$2,200	$3,000
1974	Natural	$2,200	$3,000
1974	Solid colors	$3,000	$5,000
1974	Sunburst	$2,200	$3,000
1974	Sunburst, non-trem	$2,100	$2,700
1975	Natural, white parts	$2,000	$2,200
1975	Solid colors	$2,000	$2,700
1975	Sunburst, black parts	$1,900	$2,100
1975	Sunburst, white parts	$2,000	$2,200
1976	Natural	$1,800	$2,100
1976	Solid colors	$1,900	$2,400
1976	Sunburst	$1,800	$2,100
1977	Natural	$1,700	$1,900
1977	Solid colors	$1,800	$2,300
1977	Sunburst	$1,700	$1,900
1978	Antigua	$1,700	$2,000
1978	Natural	$1,600	$1,900
1978	Solid colors	$1,700	$2,000
1978	Sunburst	$1,600	$1,900
1979	Antigua	$1,400	$1,700
1979	Natural	$1,000	$1,500
1979	Solid colors	$1,400	$1,900
1979	Sunburst, standard colors	$1,000	$1,600
1980	Sunburst, standard colors	$1,000	$1,500

MODEL YEAR	FEATURES	EXC. COND. LOW	HIGH
1981	International colors	$975	$1,600
1981	Sunburst, standard colors	$875	$1,200

Standard Stratocaster (includes "Smith Strat")

1981-1984. Replaces the Stratocaster. Renamed the American Standard Stratocaster for '86-'00 (see next listing). Renamed American Series Stratocaster in '00. From '81/'82 to mid-'83, 4 knobs same as regular Strat but with 4-bolt neck. In August '81, Dan Smith was hired by Bill Schultz and Fender produced an alder body, 4-bolt neck, 21-fret, small headstock Standard Stratocaster that has been nicknamed the Smith Strat (made from Dec. '81-'83). Mid-'83 to the end of '84 2 knobs and 'guard mounted input jack. Not to be confused with current Standard Stratocaster, which is made in Mexico.

1981	Smith Strat, 4-bolt, 3 knobs	$1,100	$1,300
1982	Smith Strat, rare colors	$1,500	$1,900
1982	Smith Strat, various colors	$1,200	$1,500
1983	Smith Strat, various colors	$1,200	$1,500
1983-1984	Sunburst, 2-knob	$650	$850
1983-1984	Various colors, 2-knob	$600	$750

Standard Stratocaster (Japan)

1985. Interim production in Japan while the new Fender reorganized, standard pickup configuration and tremolo system, 3 knobs with switch, traditional style input jack, traditional shaped headstock, natural maple color.

1985	Black or red, white 'guard	$400	$700

American Standard Stratocaster

1986-2000. Fender's new name for the American-made Strat when reintroducing it after CBS sold the company. The only American-made Strats made in 1985 were the '57 and '62 models. See Stratocaster and Standard Stratocaster for earlier models, renamed American Series

1986-1989	Various colors	$700	$875
1989	Mary Kaye Limited Edition	$875	$975
1990-1999	Various colors	$600	$700
1995	Limited Edition matching headstock	$900	$1,075

American Series Stratocaster

2000-present. Fender's updated standard production model, ash or alder body, rosewood 'board, dot markers, 3 staggered single-coil pickups, 5-way switch, hand polished fret edges.

2000-2004	Alder body	$525	$625
2000-2004	Ash body	$550	$675
2000-2004	Limited Edition colors	$600	$700
2000-2004	Limited Edition matching headstock	$850	$950
2000-2005	Ash body, hardtail	$525	$625

1981 Fender Stratocaster

Fender American Series Stratocaster

*1979 Fender Silver
Anniversary Stratocaster*

*Fender American Vintage
'62 Stratocaster*

MODEL YEAR	FEATURES	EXC. COND. LOW	HIGH

25th Anniversary Stratocaster
1979-1980. Has "Anniversary" on upper body horn, silver metallic or white pearlescent finish.

1979	White, 1st issue, flaking	$1,100	$1,200
1979	White, 1st issue, no flaking	$1,300	$1,500
1979-1980	Silver, faded to gold	$1,100	$1,200
1979-1980	Silver, unfaded	$1,300	$1,500

40th Anniversary Stratocaster
1994 only. American Standard model (not Custom Shop model), plain top, appearance similar to a '54 maple-neck Stratocaster, sunburst. Not to be confused with the Custom Shop 40th Anniversary Diamond Edition.

| 1994 | | $1,000 | $1,400 |

'50s Stratocaster (Import)
1992-present. Part of Collectables Series, made in Japan, V-neck with skunk stripe, 8-screw single ply 'guard, various colors.

| 1992-1999 | | $450 | $500 |

'54 Stratocaster FMT
1993-1998. Custom Classic reissue, Flame Maple Top, also comes in gold hardware edition.

| 1993-1998 | | $1,600 | $1,750 |
| 1993-1998 | Gold hardware option | $1,700 | $1,850 |

'57 Stratocaster (USA)
1982-present. U.S.A.-made at the Fullerton, California plant ('82-'85) and at the Corona, California plant ('85-present).

1982-1984	Various colors	$900	$1,100
1986-1989	Blond, ash body	$1,000	$1,250
1986-1989	Various colors	$900	$1,100
1990-1999	Blond, ash body	$1,000	$1,250
1990-1999	Various colors	$900	$1,000
2000-2005	Various colors	$800	$900

'57 Vintage Stratocaster (Japan)
1984-1985. Japanese-made, various colors.

| 1984-1985 | | $400 | $700 |

'60s Stratocaster (Japan)
1992-present. Part of Collectables Series, made in Japan, U-neck slab board, various colors, some with Foto Flame.

| 1992-1999 | Foto-flame | $400 | $700 |
| 1992-1999 | Various colors | $400 | $700 |

'62 Stratocaster (Japan)
1984-1985.

| 1984-1985 | Various colors. | $400 | $700 |

'62 Stratocaster (USA)
1982-present. Made at Fullerton plant ('82-'85) then at Corona plant ('86-present).

1982-1984	Various colors	$1,000	$1,200
1986-1989	Blond, ash body	$1,100	$1,300
1986-1989	Various colors	$1,000	$1,200
1990-1999	Blond, ash body	$1,100	$1,300
1990-1999	Various colors	$1,000	$1,200

'68 Stratocaster (Japan)
1997-1999. '68 specs including large headstock, part of Collectables Series, sunburst, natural, Olympic White.

| 1997-1999 | | $400 | $700 |

'68 Stratocaster (USA)
Late 1990s. With special reverse 'large' headstock (post-CBS style), black.

| 1997 | | $700 | $750 |

'70s Stratocaster (Mexico)
Late 1990s. Made in Mexico, large headstock, white pickups and knobs, rosewood 'board.

| 1999 | | $350 | $400 |

'72 Stratocaster (Japan)
1988-1993. Made in Japan, white.

| 1988-1993 | | $400 | $700 |

American Classic Stratocaster
1993-2000. Custom Shop version of American Standard, 3 pickups, tremolo, rosewood 'board, nickel or gold-plated hardware.

| 1993-2000 | See-thru blond ash body | $1,500 | $1,600 |
| 1993-2000 | Various colors and options | $1,400 | $1,600 |

American Deluxe Fat Stratocaster
1998-2003. Made in USA, Fender DH-1 bridge humbucker for fat sound, premium alder or ash body.

| 1998-2003 | Ash body, transparent finish | $900 | $1,000 |
| 1998-2003 | Various colors | $800 | $900 |

American Deluxe Stratocaster
1998-present. Made in USA, premium alder or ash body.

1998-1999	Ash body, transparent finish	$875	$1,000
1998-1999	Various colors	$775	$875
2000-2003	Various colors	$800	$900

American Series Stratocaster HSS/HH
2004-present. Made in U.S., HSS has humbucker/single/single pickups, HH has 2 humbuckers.

| 2004 | Alder body | $600 | $675 |
| 2004 | Ash body, transparent finish | $650 | $725 |

Big Apple Stratocaster
1997-2000. Two humbucking pickups, 5-way switch, rosewood 'board or maple neck, non-tremolo optional.

| 1997-2000 | Various colors | $700 | $750 |

Bill Carson Stratocaster
Ca. 1992. Based on the '57 Strat, birdseye maple neck, Cimarron Red finish, 1 left-handed and 100 right-handed guitars produced, serial numbers MT000-MT100, made in Fender Custom Shop, and initiated by The Music Trader (MT) in Florida.

| 1992 | | $1,900 | $2,000 |

Blue Flower Stratocaster
1988-1993. Made in Japan, 1972 Strat reissue with a reissue '68 Tele Blue Floral finish.

| 1988-1993 | | $650 | $750 |

Bonnie Raitt Stratocaster
1995-2000. Alder body, often in blueburst, Bonnie Raitt's signature on headstock.

| 1995-2000 | | $950 | $1,100 |

MODEL YEAR	FEATURES	EXC. COND. LOW	HIGH

Bowling Ball/Marble Stratocaster
Ca.1983-1984. Standard Strat with 1 tone and 1 volume control, jack on 'guard, called Bowling Ball Strat due to the swirling, colored finish.

1984		$2,000	$2,400

Buddy Guy Stratocaster
1995-present. Maple neck, 3 Gold Lace Sensor pickups, ash body, signature model, blond or sunburst.

1995		$950	$1,050

Buddy Guy Stratocaster (Mexico)
1996-2004. Maple neck, polka-dot finish.

1996-2004		$400	$475

California Stratocaster
1997-1999. Made in the U.S., painted in Mexico, 2 pickups, various colors.

1997-1999		$450	$525

Collector's Edition Stratocaster ('62 Reissue)
1997. Pearl inlaid '97 on 12th fret, rosewood 'board, alder body, gold hardware, tortoise 'guard, nitro finish, sunburst, 1997 made.

1997		$1,175	$1,375

Contemporary Stratocaster (Import)
1985-1987. Import model used while the new Fender reorganized, black headstock with silver-white logo, black or white 'guard, 2 humbucker pickups or single-coil and humbucker, 2 knobs and slider switch.

1985-1987	Gray metallic, black 'guard	$250	$325

Custom Shop 21st Century Limited Ed. Stratocaster
2000. One of first 100 to leave Fender in 2000, certificate with CEO William C. Schultz, 21st logo on headstock.

2000		$1,100	$1,250

Custom Shop 35th Anniversary Stratocaster
1989-1991. Custom Shop model, figured maple top, Lace Sensor pickups, Eric Clapton preamp circuit, sunburst.

1989-1991		$2,200	$2,800

Custom Shop 50th Anniversary Stratocaster
1995-1996. Flame maple top, 3 vintage-style pickups, gold hardware, gold 50th Anniversary coin on back of the headstock, sunburst, 2500 made.

1995-1996		$1,350	$1,500

Custom Shop 50th Anniversary Stratocaster Relic
1995-1996. Relic aged played-in feel, diamond headstock inlay, Shoreline Gold finish, 200 units planned.

1995-1996		$2,400	$2,700

Custom Shop '54 Stratocaster
1993-1998 (Custom Shop Classic reissue), 1997-present. Ash body, Custom '50s pickups, gold-plated hardware.

1993-1998	Various options	$1,500	$1,700

Custom Shop '54 Stratocaster FMT
1993-1998. Flame maple top version.

1993-1998		$1,600	$1,750
1993-1998	Gold hardware option	$1,700	$1,850

Custom Shop '56 Stratocaster
1999-present. Most detailed replica (and most expensive to date) of '56 Strat, including electronics and pickups, offered with rosewood or maple 'board, gold hardware is +$100.

1999-2004	Closet Classic, all colors	$1,700	$1,800
1999-2004	NOS, all colors	$1,600	$1,700
1999-2004	Relic, all colors	$1,900	$2,000

Custom Shop '57 Special Stratocaster
1992-1993. Flamed maple top, birdseye maple neck, run of 60 made, sunburst.

1992-1993		$1,700	$1,800

Custom Shop '57 Stratocaster
Mid-1990s. Custom Shop, replaced by the more authentic, higher-detailed '56 Custom Shop Stratocaster by '99, Custom Shop models can be distinguished by the original certificate that comes with the guitar.

1994-1996	Various colors	$1,200	$1,500

Custom Shop '58 Stratocaster
1996-present. Ash body, Fat '50s pickups, chrome or gold hardware (gold is +$100.), Custom Shop models can be distinguished by the original certificate that comes with the guitar.

1996-1999	Various colors	$1,400	$1,700

Custom Shop '58 Stratocaster (Dakota Red)
1996. Run of 30 made in Dakota Red with matching headstock, maple neck, Texas special pickups, gold hardware.

1996		$1,500	$1,700

Custom Shop '60 FMT Stratocaster
1997-1999. Flame maple top.

1997-1999		$1,600	$1,750

Custom Shop '60 Stratocaster
1999-present. Most detailed Replica (and most expensive to date) of '60 Strat, including electronics and pickups, gold hardware is +$100.

1999-2004	Closet Classic, all colors	$1,700	$1,800
1999-2004	NOS, all colors	$1,600	$1,700
1999-2004	Relic, all colors	$1,900	$2,000

Custom Shop '60 Stratocaster (Short-Run)
Short-run production during the 1990s, permanent product line 1999-present. Various colors.

1994		$1,500	$1,600

Custom Shop '65 Stratocaster
2003-present. '65 small-headstock specs, rosewood or maple cap 'board, transition logo, offered in NOS, Relic, or Closet Classic versions.

2003-2004	Closet Classic, all colors	$1,700	$1,800
2003-2004	NOS, all colors	$1,600	$1,700
2003-2004	Relic, all colors	$1,900	$2,000

Fender Custom Shop '56 Stratocaster NOS

Fender '60s Closet Classic Stratocaster

To get the most from this book, be sure to read "Using *The Guide*" in the introduction.

1994 Fender Custom Shop Aluminum Stratocaster

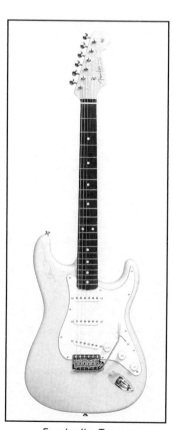

Fender Ike Turner Tribute Stratocaster

MODEL YEAR	FEATURES	EXC. COND. LOW	HIGH
Custom Shop '66 Stratocaster			
2004-present. Offered in NOS, Relic, or Closet Classic versions.			
2004	Closet Classic	$1,700	$1,800
2004	NOS	$1,600	$1,700
2004	Relic	$1,900	$2,000
Custom Shop '68 Stratocaster			
1990s. Jimi Hendrix-style, maple cap neck.			
1990s		$1,600	$1,800
Custom Shop '69 Stratocaster			
1997-present. Large headstock, U-shaped maple neck with rosewood or maple cap options, '69-style finish, gold hardware is +$100, since 2000, offered in NOS, Relic, or Closet Classic versions.			
2000-2004	Closet Classic	$1,700	$1,800
2000-2004	NOS	$1,600	$1,700
2000-2004	Relic	$1,900	$2,000
Custom Shop Aluminum Stratocaster			
1994-1995. Aluminum with anodized marble-variant finish.			
1994-1995		$1,475	$1,775
Custom Shop American Classic Holoflake Strat			
1992-1993. Splatter/sparkle finish, pearloid 'guard.			
1992-1999		$1,300	$1,400
Custom Shop American Classic Stratocaster			
1992-1999. Custom Shop version of American Standard, 3 pickups, tremolo, rosewood 'board, nickel or gold-plated hardware, various colors.			
1992-1999	Blond, transparent finish	$1,500	$1,600
1992-1999	Various colors	$1,400	$1,500
Custom Shop Contemporary Stratocaster			
1989-1998. U.S.-made, 7/8 scale body, hum/single/ single pickups, various colors.			
1989-1998		$1,100	$1,300
Custom Shop Dick Dale Stratocaster			
1994-present. Dick Dale signature model, alder body, reverse headstock, chartreuse sparkle finish.			
1990s		$1,500	$1,800
Custom Shop Eric Clapton Gold Leaf Stratocaster			
2004. Special build for Guitar Center, 50 made, 23k gold leaf finish/covering.			
2004		$7,000	$8,000
Custom Shop Eric Clapton Stratocaster			
2004. Re-creation of Clapton's personal guitar, standard non-active single-coil pickups, black or blue finish.			
2004		$1,700	$1,800
Custom Shop Floyd Rose Classic Relic Stratocaster			
1998-1999. Late '60s large headstock, 1 humbucker and 1 Strat pickups.			
1998-1999		$1,300	$1,700
Custom Shop Freddy Tavares Aloha Stratocaster			
1993-1994. Hollow aluminum body with hand engraved Hawaiian scenes, custom inlay on neck, 153 made.			
1993-1994		$4,100	$4,400

MODEL YEAR	FEATURES	EXC. COND. LOW	HIGH
Custom Shop Gold Stratocaster			
1989. 500 made, gold finish with gold anodized and white 'guards included.			
1989		$2,100	$2,200
Custom Shop Hank Marvin Stratocaster			
1995-1996. Feista red.			
1995-1996		$1,400	$1,600
Custom Shop Hellecaster Stratocaster			
1997. Gold sparkle 'guard, gold hardware, split single-coils, rosewood 'board.			
1997		$1,300	$1,600
Custom Shop Homer Haynes HLE Stratocaster			
1988-1989. 1959 Strat basics with gold finish, gold anodized guard, and gold hardware, limited edition of 500.			
1988-1989		$1,500	$1,800
Custom Shop Hot Wheels Stratocaster			
2003. Commissioned by Hot Wheels, 16 made, orange flames over blue background, large Hot Wheels logo.			
2003		$2,900	$3,500
Custom Shop Ike Turner Tribute Stratocaster			
2005. 100 made, replica of Ike Turner's Sonic Blue Strat.			
2005		$1,900	$2,000
Custom Shop Jimi Hendrix Monterey Pop Stratocaster			
1997-1998. Near replica of Monterey Pop Festival sacrifice guitar, red psychedelic-style finish.			
1997		$7,000	$8,000
Custom Shop Kon Tike Stratocaster			
2003. Limited run of 25, Tiki Green including Tike 3-color art work on headstock.			
2003		$1,300	$1,450
Custom Shop Moto Limited Edition Stratocaster			
1990s. Pearloid cover in various colors, includes Certificate of Authenticity, not to be confused with white pearloid Moto Strat which is part of a guitar and amp set (as listed below).			
1990s		$1,500	$1,600
Custom Shop Moto Set Stratocaster			
1995-1996. Custom Shop set including guitar, case, amp and amp stand, white pearloid finish.			
1995		$3,700	$4,100
Custom Shop Playboy 40th Anniversary Stratocaster			
1994. Nude Marilyn Monroe graphic on body.			
1994		$6,000	$6,500
Custom Shop Relic '50s Stratocaster			
1996-1999. Relatively faithful reproduction of '50s (ca. '57) era Strat with 'played-in' feel, gold hardware is +$100, see-thru Mary Kaye ash body is +$100, replaced by '56 Strat.			
1996-1999	Various colors	$1,300	$1,700
Custom Shop Relic '60s Stratocaster			
1996-1999. Relatively faithful reproduction of '60s era Strat with played-in feel, gold hardware is +$100, see-thru Mary Kaye ash body is +$100, replaced by '60 Relic.			
1996-1999	Various colors	$1,300	$1,700

*The **Vintage Guitar Price Guide** shows low to high values for items in all-original excellent condition, and, where applicable, with original case or cover.*

MODEL YEAR	FEATURES	EXC. COND. LOW	HIGH

Custom Shop Robin Trower Signature Stratocaster

2004. 100 made, large headstock (post '65-era styling), with '70s logo styling, post '71 3-bolt neck, bullet truss rod, white.

| 2004 | | $2,100 | $2,400 |

Custom Shop Set-Neck Stratocaster

1992-1999. Mahogany body and figured maple top, 4 pickups, glued-in neck, active electronics, by '96 ash body.

| 1992-1996 | | $1,100 | $1,300 |

Custom Shop Texas Special Stratocaster

1991-1992. 50 made, state of Texas map stamped on neck plate, Texas Special pickups, maple fretboard, sunburst.

| 1991-1992 | | $1,650 | $2,000 |

Custom Shop Tree of Life Stratocaster

1993. 29 made, tree of life fretboard inlay, 1-piece quilted maple body.

| 1993 | | $7,000 | $10,000 |

Custom Shop Turquoise Sparkle Stratocaster

2001. Limited run of 75 for Mars Music, turquoise sparkle finish.

| 2001 | | $1,100 | $1,200 |

Custom Shop Western Stratocaster

1995. Only 5 made, featured in Fender Custom Shop book from the 1990s.

| 1995 | | $9,000 | $12,000 |

Deluxe Strat Plus

1987-1998. Three Lace Sensor pickups, Floyd Rose, alder (poplar available earlier) body with ash veneer on front and back, various colors, also see Strat Plus.

| 1987-1998 | | $675 | $775 |

Deluxe Stratocaster

Late 1990s-2000s. USA-made, vintage noiseless single-coil Strat-style pickups, ash body, various colors.

| 1998-2002 | | $825 | $875 |

Eric Clapton Stratocaster

1988-present. U.S.-made, '57 reissue features, active electronics.

| 1988-1999 | | $950 | $1,000 |

Elite Stratocaster

1983-1984. The Elite Series feature active electronics and noise-cancelling pickups, push buttons instead of 3-way switch, Elite script logo on 4-bolt neck plate, various colors. Also see Gold Elite Stratocaster and Walnut Elite Stratocaster.

| 1983-1984 | | $850 | $1,100 |

Floyd Rose Classic Stratocaster

1992-1997. Two single-coils, bridge humbucker, Floyd Rose tremolo, various colors.

| 1992-1997 | | $725 | $825 |

Foto Flame Stratocaster

1994-1996, 2000. Japanese-made Collectables model, alder and basswood body with Foto Flame (simulated woodgrain) finish on top cap and back of neck.

| 1994-1996 | | $400 | $600 |
| 2000 | | $400 | $600 |

Gold Stratocaster

1981-1983. Gold metallic finish and gold-plated brass hardware, 4-bolt neck, revised small headstock, maple 'board, skunk stripe, tremolo.

| 1981-1983 | | $1,000 | $1,400 |

Gold Elite Stratocaster

1983-1984. The Elite series feature active electronics and noise-cancelling pickups, the Gold Elite has gold hardware and pearloid tuner buttons, also see Elite Stratocaster and Walnut Elite Stratocaster.

| 1983-1984 | | $1,000 | $1,250 |

Harley-Davidson 90th Anniversary Stratocaster

1993. Custom Shop, 109 total made, Harley-Davidson and Custom Shop V logo on headstock (Diamond Edition, 40 units), 9 units produced for the Harley-Davidson company without diamond logo, 60 units were not Diamond Edition, chrome-plated engraved metal body, engraved 'guard, Custom Shop Certificate important attribute.

| 1993 | | $9,000 | $12,000 |

Highway 1 Stratocaster/HSS

2003-present. U.S.-made, alder body, satin lacquer finish, HSS version has humbucker/single/single pickups.

| 2003-2004 | | $450 | $475 |

HM Stratocaster (USA/Import)

1988-1992 ('88 Japanese-made, '89-'90 U.S.- and Japanese-made, '91-'92 U.S.-made). Heavy Metal Strat, Floyd Rose, regular or pointy headstock, black hardware, 1 or 2 humbuckers, 1 single-coil and 1 humbucker, or 2 single-coils and 1 humbucker. Later models have choice of 2 humbuckers and 1 single-coil or 2 single-coils and 1 humbucker.

1988-1990	Bud Dry logo finish	$350	$425
1988-1990	Import	$200	$275
1989-1992	US	$300	$400

HRR Stratocaster

1990-1995. Japanese-made, hot-rodded vintage-style Strat, Floyd Rose tremolo system, 3 pickups, maple neck, Foto Flame, black, Olympic White or sunburst.

| 1990-1995 | | $350 | $500 |

Jeff Beck Stratocaster

1994-present. Alder body, Lace Sensor pickups, special designed tremolo, various colors but mostly Surf Green.

| 1990s | | $950 | $1,000 |

Jimi Hendrix Tribute Stratocaster

1997-2000. Left-handed guitar strung right-handed, maple cap neck, Olympic White finish.

| 1997-2000 | | $1,100 | $1,200 |

Jimi Hendrix Voodoo Stratocaster

1998-2002. Right-handed body with reverse peghead, maple neck, sunburst, Olympic White, or black.

| 1998-2002 | | $1,150 | $1,300 |

Fender Highway 1 Stratocaster Stratocaster

Fender Jeff Beck Stratocaster

*Fender Robert Cray
Stratocaster*

*Fender Stevie Ray Vaughan
Stratocaster*

MODEL YEAR	FEATURES	EXC. COND. LOW	HIGH

Jimmy Vaughan Tex-Mex Stratocaster
1997-present. Poplar body, maple 'board, Jimmy Vaughan signature on headstock, 3 Tex-Mex pickups, various colors.

1997-2004		$375	$450

Lone Star Stratocaster
1996-2000. Alder body, 1 humbucker and 2 single-coil pickups, rosewood 'board or maple neck, various colors.

1996-2000		$650	$675

Paisley Stratocaster
Ca.1988-1995. Japanese-made '72 Strat reissue with a reissue '68 Tele Pink Paisley finish.

1988-1995		$750	$1,050

Powerhouse/Powerhouse Deluxe Stratocaster
1997-present. Import Standard Strat configuration with pearloid 'guard, various colors.

1997-2003		$425	$475

Richie Sambora Stratocaster
1993-2002. Alder body, Floyd Rose tremolo, maple neck, sunburst. There was also a cheaper Richie Sambora Standard Stratocaster in blue or white.

1993-2002		$1,000	$1,175

Roadhouse Stratocaster
1997-2000. U.S.-made, poplar body, tortoise shell 'guard, maple 'board, 3 Texas Special pickups, various colors.

1997-2000		$550	$675

Robert Cray Stratocaster
1991-present. Custom Shop signature model, rosewood 'board, chunky neck, lighter weight, non-tremolo, alder body, gold-plated hardware, various colors. There is also a chrome hardware Robert Cray Standard Stratocaster model.

1991-1999		$1,000	$1,200

Roland Stratocaster (Mexico)
1998-present. Single synth pickup and 3 standard single-coil pickups, made in Mexico.

1998-2003		$425	$500

Short-Scale (7/8) Stratocaster
1989-1994. Similar to Standard Strat, but with 2 control knobs and switch, 24" scale vs. 25" scale, sometimes called a mini-Strat, Japanese import, various colors.

1989-1994		$525	$600

Splatter Stratocaster
2004. Made in Mexico, splatter paint job, various color combinations, with gig bag.

2004		$250	$300

Standard Stratocaster (Mexico)
1990-present. Fender Mexico started guitar production in '90. Not to be confused with the American-made Standard Stratocaster of '81-'84. High end of range includes a hard guitar case, while the low end of the range includes only a gig bag, various colors.

1990-1999		$250	$275
2000-2005		$260	$285

Stevie Ray Vaughan Stratocaster
1992-present. U.S.-made, alder body, sunburst, gold hardware, SRV 'guard, lefty tremolot, Brazilian rosewood 'board (pau ferro by '93).

1992-1999		$1,000	$1,100

Strat Plus
1987-1999. Three Lace Sensor pickups, alder (poplar available earlier) body, tremolo, rosewood 'board or maple neck, various colors. See Deluxe Strat Plus for ash veneer version.

1987-1999		$675	$775

Stratocaster Special (Mexico)
1993-1995. A humbucker and a single-coil pickup, 1 volume, 1 tone.

1993-1995		$275	$350

Stratocaster XII
1988-1995. Alder body, maple neck, 21-fret rosewood 'board, 3 vintage Strat pickups, Japanese-made, various colors.

1988-1995		$525	$625

Sub Sonic Stratocaster
2000-2001. Baritone model tuned B-E-A-D-G-B, single-single-hum pickup configuration, Strat-styling.

2000-2001		$700	$900

Super/Deluxe Super Stratocaster
1997-2003. Import made in Mexico, part of Deluxe Series, Standard Strat features with maple neck.

1997-2003		$260	$300

Tanqurey Tonic Stratocaster
1988. Made for ad campaign giveaway.

1988		$850	$1,050

The Strat
1980-1983. Alder body, 4-bolt neck, large STRAT on painted peghead, gold-plated brass hardware, various colors.

1980-1983	Rare colors	$1,200	$1,500
1980-1983	Various common colors	$900	$1,200

U.S. Ultra/Ultra Plus Stratocaster
1990-1997. Alder body with figured maple veneer on front and back, single Lace Sensor pickups in neck and middle, double Sensor at bridge, ebony 'board, sunburst.

1990-1997		$775	$875

Ventures Limited Edition Stratocaster
1996. Japanese-made tribute model, matches Jazzmaster equivalent, black.

1996		$875	$1,000

Walnut Stratocaster
1981-1983. American black walnut body and 1-piece neck and 'board.

1981-1983		$1,600	$2,200

Walnut Elite Stratocaster
1983-1984. The Elite Series features active electronics and noise-cancelling pickups, Walnut Elite has a walnut body and neck, gold-plated hardware and pearloid tuner buttons. Also see Elite Stratocaster and Gold Elite Stratocaster.

1983-1984		$1,900	$2,400

Yngwie Malmsteen Stratocaster
1988-present. U.S.-made, maple neck, scalloped 'board, 3 single-coil pickups, blue, red, white.

1988-2001		$950	$1,100

The *Vintage Guitar Price Guide* shows low to high values for items in all-original excellent condition, and, where applicable, with original case or cover.

MODEL YEAR	FEATURES	EXC. COND. LOW	HIGH

Telecaster

The following are all variations of the Telecaster. The first five listings are for the main U.S.-made models and the '85 interim production Japanese model. All others are listed alphabetically after that in the following order (Custom Shop models are grouped together).

Telecaster
Standard Telecaster
Standard Telecaster (Japan)
American Standard Telecaster
American Series Telecaster
'50s Telecaster (Import)
'52 Telecaster
'62 Custom Telecaster (Import)
'69 Blue Flower Telecaster
'69 Pink Paisley Telecaster
'69 Rosewood Telecaster
'69 Telecaster Thinline
'72 Custom Telecaster (Import)
'72 Telecaster Thinline
'90s Telecaster Thinline
Albert Collins Telecaster
Aluminum Telecaster
American Deluxe Telecaster
Black and Gold Telecaster
California Telecaster
California Fat Telecaster
Collector's Edition Telecaster
Contemporary Telecaster (Import)
Custom Shop 40th Anniversary Telecaster
Custom Shop 50th Anniversary Telecaster
Custom Shop '60s Telecaster Custom
Custom Shop '63 Closet Classic Telecaster
Custom Shop American Classic Holoflake Telecaster
Custom Shop American Classic Telecaster
Custom Shop Buck Owens Ltd Edition Telecaster
Custom Shop Danny Gatton Telecaster
Custom Shop Jerry Donahue Telecaster
Custom Shop John Jorgenson Telecaster
Custom Shop Jr. Telecaster
Custom Shop Sparkle Telecaster
Custom Shop Thinline Telecaster
Deluxe Nashville Telecaster (Mexico)
Deluxe Telecaster (USA)
Elite Telecaster
Foto Flame Telecaster
Highway 1 Telecaster/Texas Telecaster
HMT Telecaster
James Burton Telecaster
NHL Premier Edition Telecaster
Plus/Plus Deluxe Telecaster
Rosewood Telecaster
Set-Neck Telecaster
Standard Telecaster (Mexico)
Telecaster Custom
Telecaster Deluxe (Import)
Telecaster Thinline/Thinline II

MODEL YEAR	FEATURES	EXC. COND. LOW	HIGH

Telecaster

1951-1981. See Standard Telecaster (following listing) for '82-'84, and American Standard Telecaster for '88-2000. Currently called American Series Telecaster.

1951	Blond, black 'guard	$23,000	$28,000
1952	Blond, black 'guard	$22,000	$25,000
1953	Blond, black 'guard	$20,000	$24,000
1954	Blond, black 'guard	$19,000	$23,000
1954	Blond, white 'guard	$17,000	$19,000
1955	Blond, white 'guard	$15,500	$17,500
1956	Blond	$15,000	$17,000
1957	Blond	$14,500	$16,000
1957	Custom colors	$20,000	$30,000
1958	Black	$14,000	$16,000
1958	Blond, backloader	$13,000	$14,700
1958	Blond, top loader	$11,000	$12,500
1958	Fiesta Red	$17,000	$20,000
1958	Sunburst, backloader	$13,500	$15,700
1958	Sunburst, top loader	$11,500	$13,500
1959	Blond, maple	$10,500	$12,000
1959	Blond, slab	$9,000	$11,000
1959	Custom colors	$14,000	$20,000
1959	Sunburst, maple	$11,000	$12,500
1959	Sunburst, slab	$9,500	$11,500
1960	Blond	$8,800	$10,800
1960	Less common custom colors	$12,000	$20,000
1960	More common custom colors	$9,400	$12,000
1960	Sunburst	$10,200	$12,500
1961	Black	$10,900	$13,500
1961	Blond	$8,300	$10,300
1961	Burgundy Mist	$14,400	$17,900
1961	Dakota Red	$12,100	$15,000
1961	Daphne Blue	$12,700	$15,800
1961	Fiesta Red	$12,100	$15,000
1961	Foam Green	$15,600	$19,300
1961	Inca Silver	$12,700	$15,800
1961	Lake Placid Blue	$11,000	$13,700
1961	Olympic White	$8,900	$11,000
1961	Shell Pink	$0	$0
1961	Sherwood Green	$13,300	$16,500
1961	Shoreline Gold	$13,000	$16,100
1961	Sonic Blue	$13,700	$17,000
1961	Sunburst	$9,800	$12,100
1961	Surf Green	$15,600	$19,300
1962	Black	$10,500	$12,500
1962	Blond, curved	$7,500	$9,000
1962	Blond, slab	$8,000	$9,500
1962	Burgundy Mist, slab	$14,000	$16,500
1962	Dakota Red, slab	$11,600	$13,800

1958 Fender Telecaster

1959 Fender Telecaster

GUITARS

1965 Fender Telecaster

1966 Fender Telecaster
(Lake Placid Blue)

MODEL YEAR	FEATURES	EXC. COND. LOW	HIGH
1962	Daphne Blue, slab	$12,200	$14,500
1962	Fiesta Red, slab	$11,600	$13,800
1962	Foam Green, slab	$15,000	$17,800
1962	Inca Silver, slab	$13,200	$15,600
1962	Lake Placid Blue, curved	$9,600	$11,800
1962	Lake Placid Blue, slab	$10,600	$12,600
1962	Olympic White, slab	$8,500	$10,000
1962	Sherwood Green, slab	$12,800	$15,200
1962	Shoreline Gold, slab	$12,500	$14,800
1962	Sonic Blue, slab	$13,200	$15,600
1962	Sunburst, slab	$9,400	$11,200
1962	Surf Green, slab	$15,000	$17,800
1963	Black	$9,800	$11,000
1963	Blond	$7,500	$8,500
1963	Burgundy Mist	$13,000	$14,700
1963	Dakota Red	$11,000	$12,300
1963	Daphne Blue	$11,500	$13,000
1963	Fiesta Red	$11,000	$12,300
1963	Foam Green	$14,000	$16,000
1963	Inca Silver	$12,300	$14,000
1963	Lake Placid Blue	$10,000	$11,300
1963	Olympic White	$8,000	$9,000
1963	Sherwood Green	$12,000	$13,600
1963	Shoreline Gold	$11,700	$13,200
1963	Sonic Blue	$12,300	$14,000
1963	Sunburst	$8,800	$10,000
1963	Surf Green	$14,000	$16,000
1964	Black	$9,200	$10,700
1964	Blond	$7,000	$8,200
1964	Burgundy Mist	$12,100	$14,200
1964	Dakota Red	$10,100	$12,000
1964	Daphne Blue	$10,700	$12,500
1964	Fiesta Red	$10,100	$12,000
1964	Foam Green	$13,000	$15,300
1964	Inca Silver	$11,500	$13,500
1964	Lake Placid Blue	$9,300	$11,000
1964	Olympic White	$7,500	$8,800
1964	Sherwood Green	$11,200	$13,000
1964	Shoreline Gold	$11,000	$12,800
1964	Sonic Blue	$11,500	$13,500
1964	Sunburst	$8,200	$9,600
1964	Surf Green	$13,000	$15,300
1965	Black	$8,500	$9,800
1965	Blond	$6,500	$7,500
1965	Blue Ice	$10,700	$12,300
1965	Candy Apple Red	$8,600	$10,000
1965	Charcoal Frost	$10,700	$12,300
1965	Dakota Red	$9,500	$11,000
1965	Fiesta Red	$9,500	$11,000
1965	Firemist Gold	$10,700	$12,300
1965	Firemist Silver	$10,700	$12,300
1965	Lake Placid Blue	$8,600	$10,000
1965	Ocean Turquoise	$10,700	$12,300
1965	Olympic White	$6,900	$8,000
1965	Sonic Blue	$10,700	$12,300
1965	Sunburst	$7,600	$8,800

MODEL YEAR	FEATURES	EXC. COND. LOW	HIGH
1965	Teal Green	$10,700	$12,400
1966	Black	$7,200	$8,500
1966	Blond	$5,500	$6,500
1966	Blue Ice	$9,000	$10,700
1966	Candy Apple Red	$7,300	$8,600
1966	Charcoal Frost	$9,000	$10,700
1966	Dakota Red	$8,000	$9,500
1966	Fiesta Red	$8,000	$9,500
1966	Firemist Gold	$9,000	$10,700
1966	Firemist Silver	$9,000	$10,700
1966	Lake Placid Blue	$7,300	$8,600
1966	Ocean Turquoise	$9,000	$10,700
1966	Olympic White	$5,800	$6,900
1966	Sonic Blue	$9,000	$10,700
1966	Sunburst	$6,500	$7,600
1966	Teal Green	$9,000	$10,700
1967	Black	$5,700	$6,800
1967	Blond, Bigsby	$4,200	$4,600
1967	Blond, maple cap	$4,600	$5,200
1967	Blond, rosewood cap	$4,400	$4,800
1967	Blue Ice	$7,200	$8,500
1967	Candy Apple Red	$5,800	$6,900
1967	Charcoal Frost	$7,200	$8,500
1967	Dakota Red	$6,400	$7,500
1967	Fiesta Red	$6,400	$7,500
1967	Firemist Gold	$7,200	$8,500
1967	Firemist Silver	$7,200	$8,500
1967	Lake Placid Blue	$5,800	$6,900
1967	Ocean Turquoise	$7,200	$8,500
1967	Olympic White	$4,700	$5,500
1967	Sonic Blue	$7,200	$8,500
1967	Sunburst	$5,200	$6,100
1967	Teal Green	$7,200	$8,500
1968	Black	$5,700	$6,800
1968	Blond, Bigsby	$4,200	$4,600
1968	Blond, maple cap	$4,600	$5,200
1968	Blond, rosewood cap	$4,400	$4,800
1968	Blue Floral	$7,000	$11,000
1968	Blue Ice	$7,200	$8,500
1968	Candy Apple Red	$5,800	$6,900
1968	Charcoal Frost	$7,200	$8,500
1968	Dakota Red	$6,700	$7,500
1968	Fiesta Red	$6,400	$7,500
1968	Firemist Gold	$7,200	$8,500
1968	Firemist Silver	$7,200	$8,500
1968	Lake Placid Blue	$5,800	$6,900
1968	Ocean Turquoise	$7,200	$8,500
1968	Olympic White	$4,700	$5,500
1968	Pink Paisley	$8,000	$12,000
1968	Sonic Blue	$7,200	$8,500
1968	Sunburst	$5,200	$6,100
1968	Teal Green	$7,200	$8,500
1969	Blond, maple cap	$4,200	$4,800
1969	Blond, rosewood cap	$4,000	$4,400
1969	Blue Floral	$7,000	$11,000
1969	Less common custom colors	$6,000	$8,000

The *Vintage Guitar Price Guide* shows low to high values for items in all-original excellent condition, and, where applicable, with original case or cover.

MODEL YEAR	FEATURES	EXC. COND. LOW	HIGH
1969	More common custom colors	$4,300	$6,000
1969	Pink Paisley	$8,000	$12,000
1969	Sunburst	$4,500	$5,500
1970	Blond	$3,200	$4,200
1970	Blond, Bigsby	$3,000	$4,000
1970	Less common custom colors	$5,800	$7,300
1970	More common custom colors	$4,200	$5,800
1970	Sunburst	$3,800	$5,000
1971	Blond	$3,000	$3,600
1971	Less common custom colors	$4,700	$6,200
1971	More common custom colors	$4,000	$4,700
1971	Sunburst	$3,500	$4,200
1972	Blond	$2,400	$3,000
1972	Less common custom colors	$4,000	$5,200
1972	More common custom colors	$3,000	$4,000
1972	Natural	$2,600	$3,200
1972	Sunburst	$2,800	$3,500
1973	Blond	$2,100	$3,000
1973	Custom colors	$2,200	$5,000
1974	Blond	$2,100	$3,000
1974	Custom colors	$2,200	$5,000
1975	Blond	$1,900	$2,700
1975	Custom colors	$2,000	$2,700
1976	Blond	$1,800	$2,100
1976	Custom colors	$1,900	$2,400
1977	Blond	$1,700	$1,900
1977	Custom colors	$1,800	$2,300
1978	Antigua	$1,700	$2,000
1978	Blond	$1,600	$1,900
1978	Custom colors	$1,700	$2,000
1979	Antigua	$1,600	$1,900
1979	Blond	$1,000	$1,600
1979	Custom colors	$1,400	$1,900
1980	Blond	$1,000	$1,500
1980	Custom colors	$1,200	$1,500
1981	Custom colors	$875	$1,200
1981	International colors	$975	$1,600

Standard Telecaster

1982-1984. See Telecaster for '51-'81, and American Standard Telecaster (following listing) for '88-2000. Not to be confused with the current Standard Telecaster, which is made in Mexico.

1982-1984	Blond	$650	$1,100
1982-1984	Jewel or various colors	$700	$1,500

Standard Telecaster (Japan)

1985. Interim production in Japan while the new Fender reorganized.

1985		$400	$700

American Standard Telecaster

1988-2000. Name used when Fender reissued the standard American-made Tele after CBS sold the company. The only American-made Tele available for '86 and '87 was the '52 Telecaster. See Telecaster for '51-'81, and Standard Telecaster for '82-'84. All '94 models have a metal

40th Anniversary pin on the headstock, but should not be confused with the actual 40th Anniversary Telecaster model (see separate listing), all standard colors, renamed the American Series Telecaster in 2000.

1988-1989		$675	$825
1990-1999		$600	$700

American Series Telecaster

2000-present. Current name for the regular U.S.-made Telecaster. See Telecaster for '51-'81, Standard Telecaster for '82-'84, and American Standard for '88-'99.

2000-2004		$600	$650

'50s Telecaster (Import)

1992-1999. Import from Japan, basswood body, blond finish, black 'guard.

1992-1999		$400	$650

'52 Telecaster

1982-present. Ash body, maple neck or rosewood 'board.

1982-1999	Blond	$900	$1,050
1990-1999	Copper (limited number)	$900	$1,050

'62 Custom Telecaster (Import)

1985-1984, 1986-1999. Made in Japan, bound top and back, rosewood 'board, sunburst or red.

1982-1999		$400	$650

'69 Blue Flower Telecaster

Ca.1986-1994. Import, Blue Flower finish.

1986-1989		$650	$900
1990-1994		$500	$650

'69 Pink Paisley Telecaster

Ca.1986-1998. Import, Pink Paisley finish.

1986-1989		$650	$900
1990-1998		$500	$650

'69 Rosewood Telecaster

1986-1996. Japanese-made reissue, rosewood.

1986-1996		$1,700	$2,400

'69 Telecaster Thinline

1988-1998. Import, 2 Tele pickups, natural.

1988-1998		$400	$650

'72 Custom Telecaster (Import)

1986-1999. Import, black or red.

1986-1999		$550	$600

'72 Telecaster Thinline

1988-1998. Import, 2 humbuckers, natural.

1988-1998	Natural	$400	$650

'90s Telecaster Thinline

1997-present. Ash body, single f-hole, natural Foto-Flame or transparent crimson.

1997-1999		$900	$1,000

Albert Collins Telecaster

1990-present. U.S.-made Custom Shop signature model, bound swamp ash body, humbucker pickup in neck position.

1990-1999	Natural	$1,150	$1,300
1995	Silver sparkle	$1,250	$1,400

Aluminum Telecaster

1994-1995. Aluminum with anodized marble-variant finish.

1994-1995		$1,475	$1,775

American Deluxe Telecaster

1998-present. Premium ash or alder body with see-thru finishes.

1998-1999	Alder	$700	$850

1968 Fender Telecaster (Pink Paisley)

Fender '69 Telecaster Thinline

To get the most from this book, be sure to read "Using **The Guide**" in the introduction.

Fender James Burton Telecaster

Fender Highway 1 Texas Telecaster

MODEL YEAR	FEATURES	EXC. COND. LOW	HIGH
1998-1999	Ash	$825	$925
2000-2003	Alder	$775	$875
2000-2003	Ash	$850	$950

Black and Gold Telecaster
1981-1982. Black finish, gold-plated brass hardware.

1981-1982		$1,100	$1,250

California Telecaster
1997-1998. Alder body, maple 'board, sunburst, Tex-Mex Strat and Tele pickup configuration.

1997-1998		$450	$525

California Fat Telecaster
1997-1998. Alder body, maple 'board, Tex-Mex humbucker and Tele pickup configuration.

1997-1998		$450	$525

Collector's Edition Telecaster
1998. Mid-1955 specs including white 'guard, offered in sunburst with gold hardware (which was an option in '55), 1,998 made.

1998		$1,175	$1,375

Contemporary Telecaster (Import)
1985-1987. Japanese-made while the new Fender reorganized, 2 or 3 pickups, vibrato, black chrome hardware, rosewood 'board.

1985-1987		$250	$325

Custom Shop 40th Anniversary Telecaster
1988, 1999. Custom Shop limited edition run of 300, 2-piece flamed maple top, gold hardware ('88), flamed maple top over ash body, gold hardware ('99).

1988	1st run, high-end	$3,500	$4,000
1999	2nd run, plain top	$1,300	$1,600

Custom Shop 50th Anniversary Telecaster
1995-1996. Flame maple top, 2 vintage-style pickups, gold hardware, sunburst, gold 50th Anniversary coin on back of the headstock, 1250 made.

1995-1996		$1,250	$1,400

Custom Shop '60s Telecaster Custom
1997-1998. U.S. custom shop, bound alder body, black or custom colors.

1997-1998		$1,200	$1,600

Custom Shop '63 Closet Classic Telecaster
1999-present. Alder body (or blond on ash), original spec pickups, C-shaped neck, rosewood 'board.

1999-2004		$1,600	$1,900

Custom Shop American Classic Holoflake Telecaster
1996-1999. Splatter/sparkle finish, pearloid 'guard.

1996-1999		$1,300	$1,400

Custom Shop American Classic Telecaster
1996-1999. Handcrafted version of American Standard, thin lacquer-finished ash body, maple or rosewood 'board, various options and colors, earlier versions had gold hardware and custom-color options.

1996-1999		$1,300	$1,400

Custom Shop Buck Owens Ltd Edition Telecaster
1998-2002. Red, white and blue sparkle finish, gold hardware, gold 'guard, rosewood 'board, by Fender Japan.

1998-2002		$875	$975

Custom Shop Danny Gatton Telecaster
1990-present. Like '53 Telecaster, maple neck, 2 humbuckers.

1990s	Frost Gold	$1,700	$1,900

Custom Shop Jerry Donahue Telecaster
1992-2001. Designed by Donahue, Tele bridge pickup and Strat neck pickup, birdseye maple neck and top, basswood body, special passive circuitry, there was also a Japanese J.D. Telecaster.

1992-1999	Sunburst	$1,100	$1,200
1992-1999	Various colors, gold hardware	$1,400	$1,600

Custom Shop John Jorgenson Telecaster
1998-2000. Double-coil stacked pickups, sparkle or black finish, korina body.

1998-2000	Gold sparkle	$1,300	$1,900

Custom Shop Jr. Telecaster
1994, 1997-present. Transparent blond ash body, 2 P-90-style pickups, set neck, 11 tone chambers, 100 made in '94, reintroduced in '97.

1994		$1,500	$1,700

Custom Shop Sparkle Telecaster
1993-1995. Poplar body, white 'guard, sparkle finish: champagne, gold, silver.

1993-1995		$1,300	$1,400

Custom Shop Thinline Telecaster
1990s. Gold sparkle.

1990s		$1,400	$1,600

Deluxe Nashville Telecaster (Mexico)
1998-present. Made in Mexico, Tex-Mex Strat and Tele pickup configuration, various colors.

1998-2003		$500	$600

Deluxe Telecaster (USA)
1972-1981. Two humbucker pickups, various colors.

1972-1974		$2,000	$2,500
1975-1978		$1,600	$2,000
1978-1979	Antigua	$1,700	$2,200
1979-1981		$1,000	$1,600

Elite Telecaster
1983-1985. Two active humbucker pickups, Les Paul-style 3-way switch, 2 volume knobs, 1 presence and filter controls, chrome hardware, various colors.

1983-1985		$800	$1,000

Foto Flame Telecaster
1994-1996. Import, sunburst or transparent.

1994-1996		$400	$600

Highway 1 Telecaster/Texas Telecaster
2003-present. U.S.-made, alder body, satin lacquer finish, Texas version (introduced in '04) has ash body and Hot Vintage pickups.

2003-2004		$450	$475

HMT Telecaster
1990-1993. Japanese-made Metal-Rock Tele, available with or without Floyd Rose tremolo, 1 Fender Lace Sensor pickup and 1 DiMarzio bridge humbucker pickup, black.

1990-1993		$200	$275

James Burton Telecaster
1990-present. Ash body, 3 Fender Lace pickups, available in black with Gold Paisley, black with Candy Red Paisley, Pearl White, and Frost Red.

1990-1999	Black and gold paisley, gold hardware	$850	$1,000

MODEL YEAR	FEATURES	EXC. COND. LOW	HIGH
1990-1999	Frost Red, black hardware	$550	$750
1990-1999	Pearl white, gold hardware	$550	$750
1990-2000	Black and red paisley, black hardware	$850	$1,000

NHL Premier Edition Telecaster

1999-2000. Limited edition of 100 guitars with NHL hockey art logo on the top.

1999-2000	Chicago Blackhawks	$1,200	$1,400
1999-2000	Philly Flyers	$1,200	$1,400

Plus/Plus Deluxe Telecaster

1990-1997. Strat 3-pickup combination, American Standard tremolo system, various colors.

1990-1997		$675	$775

Rosewood Telecaster

1969-1972. Rosewood body and neck.

1969-1972		$4,500	$6,000

Set-Neck Telecaster

1990-1996. Glued-in neck, Custom Shop, 2 humbucking pickups, Set-Neck CA (Country Artist) has 1 humbucker and 1 Tele pickup, various colors.

1990-1996		$1,100	$1,300

Standard Telecaster (Mexico)

1990-present. Guitar production at the Mexico facility started in '91. High end of range includes a hard guitar case, while the low end of the range includes only a gig bag, various colors.

1990-1999		$250	$275
2000-2004		$260	$285

Telecaster Custom

1959-1972. Body bound top and back, rosewood 'board, 2 Tele pickups, see Telecaster Custom (2nd Edition) for the 1 Tele/1 humbucker version.

1959	Sunburst, maple	$21,000	$27,000
1960	Custom colors	$22,000	$45,000
1960	Sunburst	$20,000	$25,000
1961	Less common custom colors	$25,000	$37,000
1961	More common custom colors	$19,000	$25,000
1961	Sunburst	$18,000	$20,000
1962	Less common custom colors	$26,000	$33,000
1962	More common custom colors	$17,000	$26,000
1962	Sunburst	$16,000	$18,000
1963	Less common custom colors	$23,000	$30,000
1963	More common custom colors	$15,000	$23,000
1963	Sunburst	$14,000	$16,000
1964	Less common custom colors	$20,000	$26,000
1964	More common custom colors	$13,000	$20,000
1964	Sunburst	$12,000	$14,000
1965	Less common custom colors	$17,000	$22,000

MODEL YEAR	FEATURES	EXC. COND. LOW	HIGH
1965	More common custom colors	$11,000	$17,000
1965	Sunburst	$10,000	$12,000
1966	Less common custom colors	$15,000	$18,000
1966	More common custom colors	$10,000	$15,000
1966	Sunburst	$9,000	$10,000
1967	Less common custom colors	$15,000	$17,000
1967	More common custom colors	$9,000	$15,000
1967	Sunburst	$8,000	$9,000
1968	Less common custom colors	$15,000	$17,000
1968	More common custom colors	$9,000	$15,000
1968	Sunburst, maple cap	$9,000	$9,500
1968	Sunburst, rosewood cap	$8,000	$9,000
1968	White	$8,000	$9,300
1969	Custom colors	$8,000	$13,000
1969	Sunburst	$7,000	$8,000
1970	Custom colors	$7,200	$12,000
1970	Sunburst	$6,200	$7,200
1971	Custom colors, 4-bolt	$6,100	$10,000
1971	Sunburst, 3-bolt	$2,600	$3,100
1971	Sunburst, 4-bolt	$4,700	$6,100
1972	Custom colors, 3-bolt	$3,000	$5,000
1972	Sunburst, 3-bolt	$2,400	$3,000

Telecaster Custom II

1972-1981. One humbucking and 1 Tele pickup, standard colors, see above for 2 Tele pickup version. Also called Custom Telecaster.

1972-1974		$2,100	$2,500
1975-1978		$1,600	$2,100
1979-1981		$1,400	$1,600

Telecaster Deluxe (Import)

1995-1998. Import, 1 Tele-style bridge pickup and 2 Strat-style pickups, rosewood 'board, Foto Flame '95-'97 and non-Foto Flame '97-'98.

1995-1998		$425	$475

Telecaster Thinline/Thinline II

1968-1980. Semi-hollowbody, 1 F-hole, 2 Tele pickups, ash or mahogany body, in late-'71, the tilt neck was added and the 2 Tele pickups were switched to 2 humbuckers.

1968	Less common custom colors	$6,100	$7,300
1968	More common custom colors	$4,000	$6,100
1968	Natural ash	$3,800	$4,200
1968	Natural mahogany	$4,800	$5,000
1968	Sunburst	$3,800	$4,200
1969	Less common custom colors	$5,500	$6,600
1969	More common custom colors	$3,800	$5,500
1969	Natural ash	$3,600	$3,800

1965 Fender Telecaster Custom

1971 Telecaster Thinline

GUITARS

1974 Telecaster Thinline

Fender Toronado

MODEL YEAR	FEATURES	EXC. COND. LOW	HIGH
1969	Natural mahogany	$4,600	$4,800
1969	Sunburst	$3,600	$3,800
1970	Less common custom colors	$5,300	$6,400
1970	More common custom colors	$3,700	$5,300
1970	Natural ash	$3,500	$3,700
1970	Natural mahogany	$4,500	$4,700
1970	Sunburst	$3,500	$3,700
1971	Less common custom colors	$4,000	$6,400
1971	More common custom colors	$2,700	$4,000
1971	Natural ash, 3-bolt neck	$2,500	$3,100
1971	Natural ash, 4-bolt neck	$3,500	$3,700
1971	Natural mahogany, 3-bolt neck	$3,000	$3,500
1971	Sunburst, 3-bolt neck	$2,500	$3,100
1972-1974	Less common custom colors	$3,300	$5,200
1972-1974	Mahogany, humbuckers	$2,500	$3,200
1972-1974	More common custom colors	$2,300	$3,500
1972-1974	Natural ash, humbuckers	$2,200	$3,000
1972-1974	Sunburst, humbuckers	$2,200	$3,000
1975-1978	Blond, custom option	$2,300	$3,100
1975-1978	Natural ash, humbuckers	$1,700	$2,200
1975-1978	Sunburst, humbuckers	$1,700	$2,200

Toronado/Toronado Deluxe

1999-present. Contoured offset-waist body with 2 Atomic Humbucker pickups, offered in black, Arctic White, Candy Apple Red, and brown sunburst.

1999-2001	Atomic humbuckers	$350	$400
1999-2001	DE-9000 P-90s	$350	$400

Villager 12-String

1965-1969. Acoustic flat top, spruce top, mahogany back and sides, 12 strings, natural.

1965-1969		$575	$750

Violin - Electric

1958-1976. Sunburst is the standard finish.

1958-1960	Natural, with bow	$1,500	$1,700
1960-1969	Natural, with bow	$1,400	$1,600
1970-1976	Natural, with bow	$1,200	$1,400

Wildwood

1963-1971. Acoustic flat top with Wildwood dyed top.

1966-1971	Various (faded)	$900	$1,000
1966-1971	Various (unfaded)	$1,100	$1,500

Fernandes

1969-present. Established in Tokyo. Early efforts were classical guitars, but they now offer a variety of guitars and basses.

MODEL YEAR	FEATURES	EXC. COND. LOW	HIGH

AFR-120

1988-1998. Bolt-on neck, locking tremolo, graphic finishes, natural.

1988		$350	$450

APG-100

1989-1996. Carved and bound maple top, mahogany back, maple neck, rosewood 'board, various pickup configurations, sunburst.

1991-1996		$550	$600

Dragonfly Pro Sustainer

2000s. Offset double cut, single/single/humbucker, dot markers, figured top.

2000s		$275	$300

Dragonfly/Dragonfly X

2000s. Offset double cut, single/single/humbucker, dot markers.

2000s		$125	$165

FR-552

Introduced in 1987. One-piece maple neck, 24-fret 'board, deep cutaway, Fernandes Floyd Rose locking tremolo, black.

1980s		$250	$300

FV-105RRR Randy Rhoads

1990s. Limited production Randy Rhoads, bold white polka dots on solid background.

1990s		$1,800	$2,000

LE-1

Introduced in 1987. Double-cut alder body, maple or rosewood 'board, various colors.

1980s		$250	$300

LE-2 G

1991-1998. LE-2 with gold hardware, sunburst.

1990s		$350	$400

LE-2/LE-2X

1991-1998. Double-cut, hum/single/single pickups, Floyd-style vibrato (LE-2X double-locking).

1990s		$250	$300

Nomad Travel/Nomad Deluxe

2000s. Unusual body style, extra large banana headstock, built-in effects, low-power amplifier, and speaker. Deluxe models have added features.

2000s	Deluxe	$250	$300
2000s	Hot Rod Deluxe	$250	$300
2000s	Standard	$150	$175
2000s	USA Deluxe	$260	$310

Revival

Late-1990s. Single-cut solidbody.

1990s		$250	$300

Sustainer/Sustainer Elite

2000s. Sustainer electronic. Sustainer is single-cut, Elite is offset double-cut.

2000s	Elite	$400	$500
2000s	Sustainer	$400	$500

TE-3

1993-1998. Natural.

1990s		$450	$550

TE-59/60

Introduced in 1987. Single-cut alder body, natural.

1980s		$250	$300

MODEL YEAR	FEATURES	EXC. COND. LOW	HIGH

Vertigo Deluxe/Vertigo Elite

1990s-2000s. Solid body, split trapazoid markers, dual mini-humbuckers, mahogany body.

1990-2000s Deluxe		$425	$575
1990-2000s Elite		$425	$575

Fina

Production classical and steel-string guitars built at the Kwo Hsiao Music Wooden Factory in Huiyang City, Guang Dong, mainland China. They also build acoustic basses.

Fine Resophonic

1988-present. Professional and premium grade, production/custom, wood and metal-bodied resophonic guitars (including reso-electrics) built by luthiers Mike Lewis and Pierre Avocat in Vitry Sur Seine, France. They also build ukes and mandolins.

First Act

1995-present. Budget and professional grade, production/custom, acoustic, solid and semi-hollow body guitars built in China and in their Custom Shop in Boston. They also make basses, violins, and other instruments.

Flaxwood

2004-present. Professional grade, production/custom, solid and semi-hollow body guitars built in Finland, with bodies of natural fiber composites.

Fleishman Instruments

1974-present. Premium and presentation grade, custom flat-tops made by luthier Harry Fleishman in Sebastopol, California. He also offers basses and electric uprights. Fleishman is the director of Luthiers School International.

Fletcher Brock Stringed Instruments

1992-present. Custom flat-tops and archtops made by luthier Fletcher Brock originally in Ketchum, Idaho, and currently in Seattle, Washington. He also builds mandolin family instruments.

Flowers Guitars

Premium grade, custom, archtop guitars built by luthier Gary Flowers in Baltimore, Maryland.

Floyd Rose

2004-present. Floyd Rose, inventor of the revolutionary Floyd Rose Locking Tremolo, introduced a guitar line at Winter NAMM, January 2004. Innovations accompany the new models, including the SpeedLoader headstock nut and automatic electronic tuner that eliminates the need for tuning keys. The Redmond Series includes 6 models simply named Model 1 through Model 5, plus the Model K (made of Karina limba).

Fontanilla Guitars

1987-present. Luthier Allan Fontanilla builds his premium grade, production/custom, classical guitars in San Francisco, California.

Fouilleul

1978-present. Production/custom, classical guitars made by luthier Jean-Marie Fouilleul in Cuguen, France.

Frame Works

1995-present. Professional grade, production/custom, steel- and nylon-string guitars built by luthier Frank Krocker in Burghausen, Germany. The instruments feature a neck mounted on a guitar-shaped frame. Krocker has also built traditional archtops, flat-tops, and classicals.

Framus

1946-1977, 1996-present. Professional and premium grade, production/custom, guitars made in Markneukirchen, Germany. They also build basses and amps. Frankische Musikindustrie (Framus) founded in Erlangen, Germany by Fred Wilfer, relocated to Bubenreuth in '54, and to Pretzfeld in '67. Begun as an acoustic instrument manufacturer, Framus added electrics in the mid-'50s. Earliest electrics were mostly acoustics with pickups attached. Electric designs begin in early-'60s. Unique feature was a laminated maple neck with many thin plies. By around '64-'65 upscale models featured the organtone, often called a spigot, a spring-loaded volume control that allowed you to simulate a Leslie speaker effect. Better models often had mutes and lots of switches.

In the '60s, Framus instruments were imported into the U.S. by Philadelphia Music Company. Resurgence of interest in ca. '74 with the Jan Akkermann hollowbody followed by original mid-'70s design called the Nashville, the product of an alliance with some American financing. The brand was revived in '96 by Hans Peter Wilfer, the president of Warwick, with production in Warwick's factory in Germany. Distributed in the U.S. by Dana B. Goods.

Atilla Zoller AZ-10

Early-1960s-late-1970s. Single-cut archtop, 2 pickups, neck glued-in until the '70s, bolt-on after, sunburst. Model 5/65 (rounded cutaway) and Model 5/67 (sharp cutaway).

1960s	Model 5/65	$650	$850
1960s	Model 5/67	$700	$900

Big 18 Doubleneck

Late 1960s. Model 5/200 is a solidbody and Model 5/220 is acoustic.

1960s	Model 5/200	$650	$850
1960s	Model 5/220	$675	$875

Caravelle 5/117

Ca.1965-1977. Double-cut archtop, tremolo, 2 pickups, cherry or sunburst.

1960s		$600	$800

First Act Delia

Floyd Rose Redmond

Framus Television

Froggy Bottom Model K

MODEL YEAR	FEATURES	EXC. COND. LOW	HIGH

Jan Akkerman
1974-1977. Single-cut semi-hollowbody, 2 pickups, gold hardware.

1974-1977		$300	$500

Missouri 5/60 (E Framus Missouri)
Ca.1960-1977. Non-cut acoustic archtop until '65, single-cut archtop with 2 pickups after, natural or sunburst.

1960s		$500	$600

New Sound Series
1960s. Gibson ES-335 copy. Model 5/116 I has 2 pickups and Model 5/116 II has 3.

1960s	Model 5/115/54	$650	$850
1960s	Model 5/116/52	$600	$800

Sorella Series
Ca.1955-1977. Model 5/59 is single-cut acoustic archtop, Model 5/59/50 is electric 1-pickup, Model 5/59/52 is electric 2-pickup.

1959-1965	Model 5/59	$250	$450
1959-1966	Model 5/59/50	$300	$500
1959-1967	Model 5/59/52	$350	$550

Sorento
Ca.1965-1970. Oversized semi-hollowbody, single-cut, 2 pickups, organ effect, F-holes.

1960s	Model 5/112/52	$400	$600

Strato de Luxe Series
Ca.1964-1972. 1, 2, or 3 pickups, some models have gold hardware. Model 5/068 is 12-string, 2 pickups, tremolo.

1960s	Model 5/068	$550	$750
1960s	Model 5/168/52, 2 pus	$550	$750
1960s	Model 5/168/52, 3 pus	$600	$800

Strato Super
1960s. Economy version of Strato de Luxe.

1960s	Model 5/155/52	$350	$550

Studio Series
1960s. Model 5/51 is acoustic archtop, cutaway and Model 5/51E is electric, 1 pickup.

1960s	Model 5/51	$150	$400
1960s	Model 5/51E	$200	$450

Television Series
1960s. Offset double-cut, thinline hollowbody, cherry or sunburst. Model 5/118/52 has 2 pickups and Model 5/118/54 3 pickups.

1960s	Model 5/118/52	$550	$750
1960s	Model 5/118/54	$650	$850

Texan Series
1960s. Sunburst or natural, 6- or 12-string.

1960s	Natural, 12-string	$375	$550
1960s	Natural, 6-string	$325	$500
1960s	Sunburst, 12-string	$350	$525
1960s	Sunburst, 6-string	$300	$475

Fresher
1973-1985. The Japanese-made Fresher brand was introduced in '73. The guitars were mainly copies of popular brands and were not imported into the U.S., but they do show up at guitar shows.

Solidbody Electric
1970s. Import from Japan.

1970s		$275	$375

Froggy Bottom Guitars
1970-present. Luthier Michael Millard builds his premium and presentation grade, production/custom flat-tops in Newfane, Vermont (until '84 production was in Richmond, New Hampshire).

Fukuoka Musical Instruments
1993-present. Custom steel- and nylon-string flat-tops and archtops built in Japan.

Futurama
Late 1950s-mid to late 1960s. Futurama was a brand name used by Selmer in the United Kingdom. Early instruments made in Czechoslovakia, models for '63-'64 made by Sweden's Hagstrom company. Some later '60s instruments may have been made in Japan. Hobbyists will recognize the brand name as Beatle George Harrison's first electric.

Futurama/Futurama II
1960s. Offset double-cut, 2- or 3-pickup versions available, large Futurama logo on headstock with reverse upper-case F.

1960s		$350	$500

Fylde Guitars
1973-present. Luthier Roger Bucknall builds his professional and premium grade, production/custom acoustic guitars in Penrith, Cumbria, United Kingdom. He also builds basses, mandolins, mandolas, bouzoukis, and citterns.

G & L
1980-present. Intermediate and professional grade, production/custom, solidbody and semi-hollowbody electric guitars made in the U.S. and overseas. They also make basses. Founded by Leo Fender and George Fullerton following the severance of ties between Fender's CLF Research and Music Man. Company sold to John MacLaren and BBE Sound, when Leo Fender died in '91. In '98 they added their Custom Creations Department. In '03 G & L introduced the Korean-made G & L Tribute Series.

ASAT
1986-1998. Called the Broadcaster in '85. Two or 3 single-coil or 2 single-coil/1 humbucker pickup configurations until early-'90s, 2 single-coils after.

1986		$675	$800
1987	Leo Fender sig. on headstock	$725	$850
1988-1991	Leo Fender sig. on body	$825	$950
1992-1998		$575	$700

ASAT III
1988-1991, 1996-1998. Single-cut, 3 single-coil pickups.

1988-1991	1st version, Leo era, 150 made	$900	$1,050
1996-1998	Post Leo era	$675	$800

MODEL YEAR	FEATURES	EXC. COND. LOW	HIGH

ASAT 20th Anniversary
2000. Limited Edition of 50, ash body, tinted birdseye maple neck, 2-tone sunburst.

2000		$1,250	$1,500

ASAT '50
1999. Limited edition of 10.

1999		$950	$1,250

ASAT Classic
1990-present. Two single-coil pickups, individually adjustable bridge saddles, neck-tilt adjustment and tapered string posts.

1990-1991	Signature on neck	$825	$1,050
1992-1997	3-bolt neck	$725	$950
1997-2003	4-bolt neck	$675	$900

ASAT Classic B-Bender
1997. 12 made with factory-original B-Bender.

1997		$1,050	$1,200

ASAT Classic Blues Boy
2001-present. Humbucker neck pickup, single-coil at bridge.

2001-2003		$725	$900

ASAT Blues Boy Limited Edition
1999. Limited edition of 20.

1999		$950	$1,200

ASAT Classic Blues Boy Semi-Hollow
1997-present. Chambered Classic with f-holes.

1997-1999		$775	$950

ASAT Blues Boy Semi-Hollow Limited Edition
1999. Limited edition of 12, thin semi-hollow.

1999		$950	$1,400

ASAT Classic Commemorative
1991-1992. Leo Fender signature and birth/death dating.

1991	Australian lacewood, 6 made	$3,850	$6,000
1991-1992	Cherryburst, 350 made	$2,300	$2,600

ASAT Classic Custom
1996-1997, 2002-present.

1996-1997	1st version	$825	$950
2002-2003	2nd version, 4-bolt neck	$675	$750

ASAT Classic Custom Semi-Hollow
2002-present.

2002-2003		$725	$850

ASAT Classic Semi-Hollow
1997-present.

1997-2003		$675	$800

ASAT Classic Three
1998. Limited Edition of 100 units.

1998		$950	$1,400

ASAT Custom
1996. No pickguard, 25 to 30 made.

1996		$775	$900

ASAT Deluxe
1997-present. Two humbuckers, flamed maple top, bound body.

1997	3-bolt neck, less than 100 made	$950	$1,400
1997-2003	4-bolt neck	$950	$1,100

ASAT Deluxe Semi-Hollow
1997-present. Two humbuckers.

1997-2003		$1,050	$1,300

ASAT Junior Limited Edition
1998-2002. Single-cut semi-hollowbody, 2 single-coil pickups, short run of 250 units.

1998-2002		$875	$1,100

ASAT S-3
1998-2000. Three soap-bar single-coil pickups, limited production.

1998-2000		$675	$900

ASAT Semi-Hollow
1997-present. Semi-hollow version of ASAT Special.

1997-2003		$675	$800

ASAT Special
1992-present. Like ASAT, but with 2 larger P-90-type pickups, chrome hardware, various colors.

1992-1997	3-bolt neck	$575	$800
1997-1998	4-bolt neck	$575	$750

ASAT Special Deluxe
2001-present. No 'guard version of the Special with figured maple top.

2001-2003		$775	$850

ASAT Z-2 Limited Edition
1999. Limited edition of 10 instruments, semi-hollow construction, natural ash, tortoise bound, engraved neckplate.

1999		$900	$1,050

ASAT Z-3
1998-present. Three offset-style Z-3 high output pickups, sunburst.

1998-2003		$675	$800

ASAT Z-3 Semi-Hollow
1998-present. Semi-hollowbody-style, 3 offset-style Z-3 high output pickups.

1998-2003		$775	$900

Broadcaster
1985-1986. Solidbody, 2 single-coils with adjustable polepieces act in humbucking mode with selector switch in the center position, black parts and finish, name changed to ASAT in early-'86.

1985-1986	Signed by Leo, ebony board	$1,725	$2,100
1985-1986	Signed by Leo, maple board	$1,725	$2,200

Cavalier
1983-1986. Offset double-cut, 2 humbuckers, 700 made, sunburst.

1983-1986		$675	$1,000

Climax
1992-1996. Offset double-cut, bolt maple neck, six-on-a-side tuners, double locking vibrato, blue.

1992-1996		$725	$850

G&L ASAT 3

G&L ASAT Z-3 Semi-Hollow

G&L Comanche

G&L Legacy

MODEL YEAR	FEATURES	EXC. COND. LOW	HIGH
Climax Plus			
1992-1996. Two humbuckers replace single-coils of the Climax, plus 1 single-coil.			
1992-1996		$725	$850
Climax XL			
1992-1996. Two humbuckers only.			
1992-1996		$720	$850
Comanche V			
1988-1991. Solidbody, 3 Z-shaped single-coil humbuckers, maple neck in choice of 3 radii, rosewood 'board, vibrato, fine tuners, Leo Fender's signature on the body, sunburst.			
1988-1991		$825	$950
Comanche VI			
1990-1991. Leo Fender's signature on the body, 6 mini-toggles.			
1990-1991		$950	$1,300
Comanche (Reintroduced)			
1998-present. Reissue with either swamp ash or alder body, bolt-on maple neck, 3 Z-coil pickups, standard or premium finish options.			
1998-2003	Premium finish, flame top	$875	$1,000
1998-2003	Standard finish	$725	$850
Commemorative			
1992-1997. About 350 made, Leo Fender signature on upper bass bout.			
1993	Sunburst	$1,925	$2,400
F-100 (Model I and II)			
1980-1986. Offset double-cut solidbody, 2 humbuckers, natural. Came in a I and II model - only difference is the radius of the 'board.			
1980-1986		$675	$900
F-100 E (Model I and II)			
1980-1982. Offset double-cut solidbody, 2 humbuckers, active electronics, pre-amp, natural. Came in a I and II model - only difference is the radius of the 'board.			
1980-1982		$675	$900
G-200			
1981-1982. Mahogany solidbody, maple neck, ebony 'board, 2 humbucking pickups, coil-split switches, natural or sunburst, 209 made.			
1981-1982		$950	$1,300
GBL-LE (Guitars by Leo Limited Edition)			
1999. Limited edition of 25, semi-hollowbody, 3 pickups.			
1999		$950	$1,300
George Fullerton Signature			
1995-present. Double-cut solidbody, sunburst.			
1995-1997	3-bolt neck	$775	$1,000
1997-2003	4-bolt neck	$675	$800
HG-1			
1982-1983. Offset double-cut, 1 humbucker, dot inlays.			
1982-1983		$1,825	$2,100
HG-2			
1982-1984. Two-humbucker HG, body changes to classic offset double-cut in '84.			
1982-1983		$950	$1,500
1984		$950	$1,500

MODEL YEAR	FEATURES	EXC. COND. LOW	HIGH
Interceptor			
1983-1991. To '86 an X-shaped solidbody (about 70 made), either 3 single-coils, 2 humbuckers, or 1 humbucker and 2 single-coils, '87-'89 was an offset double-cut solidbody (about 12 made).			
1983-1985	1st X-body	$1,150	$1,400
1985-1986	2nd X-body	$1,450	$1,700
1988-1991	Double-cut	$675	$900
Invader			
1984-1991, 1998-present. Double-cut solidbody, 2 single-coil and 1 humbucker pickups.			
1984-1991	1st version	$475	$700
1998-2003	2nd version	$775	$900
Invader Plus			
1998-present. Two humbuckers and single blade pickup in the middle position.			
1998-2003		$775	$900
Invader XL			
1998-present. Two humbuckers.			
1998-2003		$725	$850
John Jorgenson Signature Model ASAT			
1995. About 190 made, Silver Metalflake finish.			
1995		$975	$1,250
Legacy			
1992-present. Classic double-cut configuration, various colors.			
1992-1994	3-bolt neck, Duncan SSLs	$625	$800
1995-1997	3-bolt neck, Alnicos	$575	$750
1997-2003	4-bolt neck, Alnicos	$525	$700
Legacy Deluxe			
2001-present. No 'guard, figured maple top.			
2001-2003		$675	$850
Legacy HB			
2001-present. One humbucker pickup at bridge position plus 2 single-coil pickups.			
2001-2003		$575	$750
Legacy 2HB			
2001-present. Two humbucker pickups.			
2001-2003		$525	$700
Legacy Special			
1993-present. Legacy with 3 humbuckers, various colors.			
1992-1997	3-bolt neck	$575	$700
1998-2003	4-bolt neck	$525	$600
Nighthawk			
1983. Offset double-cut solidbody, 3 single-coil pickups, 269 made, sunburst, name changed to Skyhawk in '84.			
1983		$625	$950
Rampage			
1984-1991. Offset double-cut solidbody, hard rock maple neck, ebony 'board, 1 bridge-position humbucker pickup, sunburst.			
1984-1991		$575	$800
Rampage (Reissue)			
2000. Limited Edition of 70 units, supplied with gig bag and not hard case, ivory finish.			
2000		$475	$700

MODEL YEAR	FEATURES	EXC. COND. LOW	HIGH

S-500

1982-present. Double-cut mahogany or ash solidbody, maple neck, ebony or maple 'board, 3 single-coil pickups, vibrato.

1982-1987	No mini-toggle	$750	$950
1988-1991	Mini-toggle, Leo's sig. on body	$775	$1,000
1992-1997	3-bolt neck	$625	$800
1997-2003	4-bolt neck	$575	$700

S-500 Deluxe

2001-present. Deluxe Series features, including no 'guard and flamed maple top, natural.

2001-2003		$775	$900

SC-1

1982-1983. Offset double-cut solidbody, 1 single-coil pickup, tremolo, sunburst, 250 made.

1982-1983		$575	$800

SC-2

1982-1983. Offset double-cut solidbody, 2 MFD soapbar pickups, about 600 made.

1982-1983	Shallow cutaways	$475	$700
1983	Deeper, pointed cutaways	$475	$600

SC-3

1982-1991. Offset double-cut solidbody, 3 single-coil pickups, tremolo.

1982-1983	Shallow cutaways	$525	$750
1984-1987	Deeper cutaways, no 'guard	$475	$700
1988-1991	Deeper cutaways, 'guard	$475	$600

Skyhawk

1984-1991. Renamed from Nighthawk, offset double-cut, 3 single-coils, signature on headstock '84-'87, then on body '88-'91.

1984-1987		$625	$750
1988-1991		$725	$850

Superhawk

1984-1987. Offset double-cut, maple neck, ebony 'board, G&L or Kahler tremolos, 2 humbuckers, signature on headstock.

1984-1987		$525	$750

Will Ray Signature Model

2002-present. Will Ray signature on headstock, 3 Z-coil pickups, Hipshot B-Bender.

2002-2003		$925	$1,000

G.L. Stiles

1960-1994. Built by Gilbert Lee Stiles (b. October 2, 1914, Independence, West Virginia; d. 1994) primarily in the Miami, Florida area. First solidbody, including pickups and all hardware, built by hand in his garage. Stiles favored scrolls, fancy carving and walnut fingerboards. His later instruments were considerably more fancy and refined. He moved to Hialeah, Florida by '63 and began making acoustic guitars and other instruments. His acoustics featured double stressed (bent) backs for increased tension. He later taught for the Augusta Heritage Program and Davis and Elkins College in Elkins, West Virginia. Only his solidbodies had consecu-

tive serial numbers. Stiles made approximately 1000 solidbodies and 500 acoustics.

Gabriel's Guitar Workshop

1979-present. Production/custom steel- and nylon-stringed guitars built by luthier Gabriel Ochoteco in Germany until '84 and in Brisbane, Australia since.

Gagnon

1998-present. Luthier Bill Gagnon builds his premium and presentation grade, production/custom, archtop guitars in Beaverton, Oregon.

Galanti

Ca.1962-ca.1967. Electric guitars offered by the longtime Italian accordion maker. They may have also offered acoustics.

Electric

1962-1967. Solidbody or hollowbody.

1962-1967		$400	$600

Galiano

New Yorkers Antonio Cerrito and Raphael Ciani offered guitars under the Galiano brand during the early part of the last century. They used the brand both on guitars built by them and others, including The Oscar Schmidt Company.

Gallagher

1965-present. Professional and premium grade, production/custom, flat-top guitars built in Wartrace, Tennessee. J. W. Gallagher started building Shelby brand guitars in the Slingerland Drum factory in Shelbyville, Tennessee in '63. In '65 he and his son Don made the first Gallagher guitar, the G-50. Doc Watson began using Gallagher guitars in '68. In '76, Don assumed operation of the business when J. W. semi-retired. J. W. died in '79.

71 Special

1970-present. Rosewood back and sides, spruce top, herringbone trim, bound ebony 'board, natural.

1970s		$1,600	$1,900

A-70 Ragtime Special

1978-present. Smaller auditorium/00 size, spruce top, mahogany back and sides, G logo, natural.

1980s		$1,600	$1,800

Custom 12-String

Introduced in 1965. Mahogany, 12-fret neck, natural.

1965		$1,000	$1,350

Doc Watson 12-String

1995-2000. Natural.

1995-2000		$1,500	$1,700

Doc Watson Model

1974-present. Spruce top, mahogany back and sides, scalloped bracing, ebony 'board, herringbone trim, natural.

1974-1979		$1,700	$2,000
1980-1989		$1,600	$1,800
1990-1999		$1,500	$1,700

G&L S-500 Deluxe

Gallagher Doc Watson

Ganz Gula

Garrison G-25

MODEL YEAR	FEATURES	EXC. COND. LOW	HIGH

Doc Watson Model (Cutaway)
1975-present. Spruce top, mahogany back and sides, scalloped bracing, ebony 'board, herringbone trim, natural.

| 1980s | | $1,700 | $2,000 |

G-45
1970-present. Mahogany back and sides, spruce top, ebony 'board, natural.

| 1980s | | $1,000 | $1,100 |

G-50
1980s-present. Mahogany back and sides, spruce top, ebony 'board, natural.

| 1980s | | $1,100 | $1,300 |

G-65
1980s-present. Rosewood back and sides, spruce top, ebony 'board, natural.

| 1980s | | $1,300 | $1,500 |

G-70
1978-present. Rosewood back and sides, herringbone purfling on top and soundhole, mother-of-pearl diamond 'board inlays, bound headstock, natural.

| 1980s | | $1,400 | $1,600 |

Gallagher, Kevin
1996. Kevin Gallagher, luthier, changed name brand to Omega to avoid confusion with J.W. Gallagher. See Omega listing.

Galloup Guitars
1994-present. Luthier Bryan Galloup builds his professional and premium grade, production/custom flat-tops in Big Rapids, Michigan. He also operates the Galloup School of Lutherie and The Guitar Hospital repair and restoration business.

Gamble & O'Toole
1978-present. Premium grade, custom classical and steel string guitars built by luthier Arnie Gamble in Sacramento, California, with design input and inlay work from his wife Erin O'Toole.

Ganz Guitars
1995-present. Luthier Steve Ganz builds his professional grade, production/custom classical guitars in Bellingham, Washington.

Garcia
Made by luthier Federico Garcia in Spain until late-1960s or very early-'70s when production moved to Japan.

Classical
1960s-1970s. Mid-level, '60s model is solid spruce top with solid mahogany, rosewood or walnut back and sides, '70s model is Spanish pine top with walnut back and sides.

1960s	Mahogany	$225	$275
1960s	Rosewood	$400	$450
1960s	Walnut	$375	$425
1970s	Spanish pine/walnut	$175	$225

MODEL YEAR	FEATURES	EXC. COND. LOW	HIGH

Garrison
2000-present. Intermediate and professional grade, production, acoustic and acoustic/electric guitars designed by luthier Chris Griffiths using his Active Bracing System (a single integrated glass-fiber bracing system inside a solid wood body). He started Griffiths Guitar Works in 1993 in St. John's, Newfoundland, and introduced Garrison guitars in 2000.

G Series
2000-present.

| 2000-2004 | | $300 | $550 |

Gemelli
Early 1960s. European-made (likely Italian) guitars. Similar to Bartolini guitars, so most likely from same manufacturer.

Giannini
1900-present. Classical, acoustic, and acoustic/electric guitars built in Salto, SP, Brazil near Sao Paolo. They also build violas, cavaquinhos and mandolins. Founded by guitar-builder Tranquillo Giannini, an Italian who traveled to Brazil in 1890 and discovered the exotic woods of Brazil. The company was producing 30,000 instruments a year by '30. They began exporting their acoustic instruments to the U.S. in '63. They added electric guitars in '60, but these weren't imported as much, if at all. Gianninis from this era used much Brazilian Rosewood.

Classical
Early-1970s. Nylon string import, small body.

| 1970s | | $125 | $250 |

CraViola
1970s. Kidney bean-shaped rosewood body, acoustic, natural, line included a classical, a steel string, and a 12-string.

| 1972-1974 | | $225 | $350 |

CraViola 12-String
Early-1970s. Kidney bean-shaped body, 12 strings.

| 1972-1974 | | $250 | $350 |

Gibson
1880s (1902)-present. Intermediate, professional, and premium grade, production/custom, acoustic and electric guitars made in the U.S. They also build basses, mandolins, amps, and banjos under the Gibson name. Gibson also offers instruments under the Epiphone, Kramer, Steinberger, Dobro, Tobias, Valley Arts, Slingerland (drums), Baldwin (pianos), Trace Elliot, Electar (amps), Maestro, Gibson Labs, Oberheim, and Echoplex brands.

Founded in Kalamazoo, Michigan by Orville Gibson, a musician and luthier who developed instruments with tops, sides and backs carved out of solid pieces of wood. Early instruments included mandolins, archtop guitars and harp guitars. By 1896 Gibson had opened a shop. In 1902 Gibson was bought out by a group of investors who incor-

MODEL YEAR	FEATURES	EXC. COND. LOW	HIGH

porated the business as Gibson Mandolin-Guitar Manufacturing Company, Limited. The company was purchased by Chicago Musical Instrument Company (CMI) in '44. In '57 CMI also purchased the Epiphone guitar company, transferring production from Philadelphia to the Gibson plant in Kalamazoo. Gibson was purchased by Norlin in late-'69 and a new factory was opened in Nashville, Tennessee in '74. The Kalamazoo factory ceased production in '84. In '85, Gibson was sold to a group headed by Henry Juskewiscz. Gibson purchased the Flatiron Company in '87 and built a new factory in '89, moving acoustic instrument production to Bozeman, Montana.

The various models of Firebirds, Flying Vs, Les Pauls, SGs, and Super 400s are grouped together under those general headings. Custom Shop and Historic instruments are listed with their respective main model (for example, the '39 Super 400 Historical Collection model is listed with the Super 400s).

335 S Custom

1980-1981. Solidbody, 335-shaped, mahogany body, unbound rosewood 'board, 2 exposed Dirty Finger humbuckers, coil-tap, TP-6 tailpiece.

1980-1981	Sunburst	$750	$900

335 S Deluxe

1980-1982. Same as 335 S Custom but with bound ebony 'board, brass nut.

1980-1982	Cherry	$750	$900
1980-1982	Silverburst	$850	$1,100
1980-1982	Sunburst	$750	$900

335 S Standard

1980-1981. Solidbody, 335-shaped, maple body and neck, 2 exposed split-coil humbuckers, stop tailpiece, no coil-tap, unbound 'board.

1980-1981	Sunburst	$700	$800

'63 Corvette Sting Ray (Custom shop)

1996-1997. SG-style body carved to simulate split rear window on '63 Corvette, Sting Ray inlay, 150 instruments built, offered in black, white, silver or red.

1996-1997	Black	$3,000	$4,500

Advance Jumbo Reissue/AJ Special Edition

1990-1999, 2001-present. Issued as a standard production model, but soon available only as a special order for most of the '90s; currently offered as standard production. Renamed 1936 Advanced Jumbo for '97-'98. There were also some limited-edition AJs offered during the '90s.

1990s	Reissue	$1,800	$2,000
1990s	Special Edition, flamed maple	$2,000	$3,000
2000s	Reintroduced	$1,900	$2,000
2000s	Special Edition, Indian rosewood	$2,000	$3,000

Advanced Jumbo

1936-1940. Dreadnought, 16" wide, round shoulders, Brazilian rosewood back and sides, sunburst, reintroduced '90-'97.

1936-1937		$40,000	$45,000
1938-1939		$38,000	$45,000
1940		$35,000	$42,000

B.B. King Custom

1980-1988. Lucille on peghead, 2 pickups, multi-bound, gold-plated parts, Vari-tone, cherry or ebony, renamed B.B. King Lucille in '88.

1980-1988		$1,500	$1,700

B.B. King Lucille

1988-present. Introduced as B.B. King Custom, renamed B.B. King Lucille. Lucille on peghead, 2 pickups, multi-bound, gold-plated parts, Vari-tone, cherry or ebony.

1988-1999		$1,500	$1,700

B.B. King Standard

1980-1985. Like B.B. King Custom, but with stereo electronics and chrome-plated parts, cherry or ebony.

1980-1985		$1,350	$1,500

B-15

1967-1971. Mahogany, spruce top, student model, natural finish.

1967-1971		$500	$700

B-25

1962-1977. Flat-top, mahogany, bound body, cherry sunburst (natural finish is the B-25 N).

1962-1964		$1,100	$1,500
1965-1966		$875	$1,200
1967-1969		$800	$1,100
1970-1977		$675	$900

B-25 3/4

1962-1968. Short-scale version, flat-top, mahogany body, cherry sunburst (natural finish is the B-25 3/4 N).

1962-1964		$750	$1,100
1965-1966		$650	$850
1967-1968		$575	$800

B-25 N

1962-1977. Flat-top, mahogany, bound body, natural (cherry sunburst finish is the B-25).

1962-1964		$1,150	$1,550
1965-1966		$900	$1,225
1967-1969		$825	$1,125
1970-1977		$700	$950

B-25 N 3/4

1966-1968. Short-scale version, flat-top, mahogany body, natural (cherry sunburst finish is the B-25 3/4).

1966-1968		$675	$825

B-25-12

1962-1970. Flat-top 12-string version, mahogany, bound body, cherry sunburst (natural finish is the B-25-12 N).

1962-1964		$900	$1,300
1965-1966		$800	$1,100
1967-1968		$650	$800
1969-1970		$500	$750

B-25-12 N

1962-1977. Flat-top 12-string version, mahogany, bound body, natural (cherry sunburst is the B-25-12).

1962-1964		$1,000	$1,400
1965-1966		$900	$1,200
1967-1969		$750	$900
1970-1977		$600	$850

1981 Gibson 335S Deluxe

1965 Gibson B-25-12 N

1959 Gibson Byrdland

1957 Gibson C-2

MODEL YEAR	FEATURES	EXC. COND. LOW	HIGH
B-45-12			

1961-1979. Flat-top 12-string, mahogany, round shoulders for '61, square after, sunburst (natural finish is the B-45-12 N).

MODEL YEAR	FEATURES	LOW	HIGH
1961-1962	Round shoulders	$2,000	$2,400
1962-1964	Square shoulders	$1,800	$2,200
1965-1969	Non-pin bridge introduced	$1,400	$1,800
1970-1979	Pin bridge reintroduced	$1,000	$1,300

B-45-12 Limited Edition

1991-1992. Limited edition reissue with rosewood back and sides, natural.

1991-1992		$1,200	$1,350

B-45-12 N

1962-1979. Flat-top 12-string, mahogany, natural (cherry sunburst finish is the B-45-12).

1962-1964	Square shoulders	$1,850	$2,250
1965-1969	Non-pin bridge introduced	$1,450	$1,850
1970-1979	Pin bridge reintroduced	$1,050	$1,350

Barney Kessel Custom

1961-1973. Double-cut archtop, 2 humbuckers, gold hardware, cherry sunburst.

1961-1964		$3,300	$4,000
1965-1966		$3,200	$3,800
1967-1969		$3,000	$3,300
1970-1973		$2,700	$3,200

Barney Kessel Regular

1961-1974. Double-cut archtop, 2 humbuckers, nickel hardware, cherry sunburst.

1961-1964		$3,000	$3,200
1965-1966		$2,800	$3,000
1967-1969		$2,600	$3,000
1970-1973		$2,300	$2,800

Blue Ridge

1968-1979, 1989-1990. Flat-top, dreadnought, laminated rosewood back and sides, natural finish.

1968-1969		$1,000	$1,200
1970-1979		$950	$1,100

Blue Ridge 12

1970-1978. Flat-top, 12 strings, laminated rosewood back and sides, natural finish.

1970-1978		$600	$850

Blueshawk

1996-present. Small Les Paul single-cut-type body with f-holes, 2 single-coil hum cancelling Blues 90 pickups, 6-way Varitone rotary dial.

1996-2002		$500	$650

Byrdland

1955-1992. Thinline archtop, single-cut (rounded until late-'60, pointed '60-late-'69, rounded after '69, rounded or pointed '98-present), 2 pickups, now part of the Historic Collection.

1956-1957	Natural, P-90s	$9,000	$9,500
1956-1957	Sunburst, P-90s	$7,000	$7,500
1958-1959	Natural, PAFs	$11,000	$12,000
1958-1959	Sunburst, PAFs	$9,000	$10,000
1960-1962	Natural, PAFs	$10,000	$11,000
1960-1962	Sunburst, PAFs	$8,000	$9,000

MODEL YEAR	FEATURES	EXC. COND. LOW	HIGH
1963-1964	Natural, pat #	$7,000	$7,700
1963-1964	Sunburst, pat #	$6,500	$7,200
1965-1969	Natural	$5,000	$6,000
1965-1969	Sunburst	$4,000	$5,500
1970-1979	Various colors	$3,000	$4,000
1980-1992	Various colors	$3,500	$4,500

Byrdland Historic Collection

Various colors.

1993-2002	Natural	$4,000	$4,500
1993-2002	Sunburst	$3,500	$4,000
1993-2002	Wine Red	$3,000	$3,500

C-0 Classical

1962-1971. Spruce top, mahogany back and sides, bound top, natural.

1962-1971		$350	$475

C-1 Classical

1957-1971. Spruce top, mahogany back and sides, bound body, natural.

1957-1971		$400	$550

C-1 E Classical Electric

1960-1967. C-1 with ceramic bridge pickup, catalog notes special matched amplifier that filters out fingering noises.

1960-1967		$500	$650

C-1 S Petite Classical

1961-1966. Petite 13 1/4" body, natural spruce top, mahogany back and sides.

1961-1966		$450	$500

C-2 Classical

1960-1971. Maple back and sides, bound body, natural.

1960-1971		$500	$600

C-4 Classical

1962-1968. Maple back and sides, natural.

1962-1968		$750	$900

C-5 Classical

1957-1960. Rosewood back and sides, previously named GS-5 Classical in '54-'56.

1957-1960		$850	$1,000

C-6 Classical

1958-1971. Rosewood back and sides, gold hardware, natural.

1958-1971		$1,000	$1,500

C-8 Classical

1962-1969. Rosewood back and sides, natural.

1962-1969		$1,300	$2,500

CF-100

1950-1958. Flat-top, pointed cutaway, mahogany back and sides, bound body, sunburst finish.

1950-1958		$2,300	$2,500

CF-100 E

1951-1958. CF-100 with a single-coil pickup.

1950-1958		$2,500	$3,400

Challenger I

1983-1985. Single-cut Les Paul-shaped solidbody, 1 humbucker pickup, bolt-on maple neck with rosewood 'board and dot markers, silver finish standard.

1983-1985		$400	$450

Challenger II

1983-1985. Single-cut Les Paul-shaped solidbody, 2 humbucker pickups, bolt-on maple neck with rosewood 'board and dot markers, various colors.

1983-1985		$425	$475

MODEL YEAR	FEATURES	EXC. COND. LOW	HIGH

Chet Atkins CE
1981-1995. CE stands for Classical Electric, single-cut, multi-bound body, rosewood 'board with standard width nut, gold hardware, various colors. In '95, the Atkins CE and CEC were consolidated into 1 model, the Chet Atkins CE/CEC, with an ebony 'board with a standard (CE) and classical (CEC) nut.

| 1981-1995 | | $850 | $1,000 |

Chet Atkins CEC
1981-1995. Same as CE but with ebony 'board and 2" classical width nut, black or natural. In '95, the Atkins CE and CEC were consolidated into 1 model, the Chet Atkins CE/CEC, with an ebony 'board with a standard (CE) and classical (CEC) nut.

| 1981-1995 | | $1,000 | $1,300 |

Chet Atkins Country Gentleman
1987-present. Thinline archtop, single rounded cutaway, 2 humbuckers, multi-bound, gold hardware, Bigsby. Currently part of Gibson's Custom line.

| 1987-1995 | | $1,500 | $2,200 |

Chet Atkins SST
1987-present. Steel string acoustic/electric solid-body, single-cut, bridge transducer pickup, active bass and treble controls, gold hardware.

| 1986-2001 | | $950 | $1,200 |

Chet Atkins SST-12
1990-1994. 12-string model similar to 6-string, mahogany/spruce body, preamp circuit controls single transducer pickup, natural or ebony finish.

| 1990-1994 | | $1,400 | $1,700 |

Chet Atkins Tennessean
1990-present. Single rounded cutaway archtop, 2 humbuckers, f-holes, bound body. Currently part of Gibson's Custom line.

| 1990-2000 | | $1,400 | $1,500 |

Chicago 35
1994-1995. Flat-top dreadnought, round shoulders, mahogany back and sides, prewar script logo.

| 1994-1995 | Natural, factory electronics | $900 | $1,050 |

Citation
1969-1971. 17" full-depth body, single-cut archtop, 1 or 2 floating pickups, fancy inlay, natural or sunburst. Only 8 shipped for '69-'71, reissued the first time '79-'83 and as part of the Historic Collection in '93.

| 1969-1971 | | $10,000 | $15,000 |

Citation (1st Reissue)
1979-1983. Reissue of '69-'71 model, reintroduced in '93 as part of Gibson's Historic Collection.

| 1979-1983 | | $10,000 | $15,000 |

Citation (2nd Reissue)
1993-present. Limited production via Gibson's Historic Collection, natural or sunburst.

| 1994-1999 | Natural | $10,000 | $14,000 |
| 1994-1999 | Sunburst | $10,000 | $14,000 |

CL-20/CL-20+
1997-1998. Flat-top, laminated back and sides, 4-ply binding with tortoiseshell appointments, abalone diamond inlays.

| 1997-1998 | | $1,400 | $1,600 |

CL-30 Deluxe
1997-1998. J-50 style dreadnought, solid spruce top, Bubinga back and sides. Discontinued after '98.

| 1997-1998 | | $775 | $975 |

Corvus I
1982-1984. Odd-shaped solidbody with offset V-type cut, bolt maple neck, rosewood 'board, 1 humbucker, standard finish was silver gloss, but others available at an additional cost.

| 1982-1984 | | $350 | $400 |

Corvus II
1982-1984. Same as Corvus I, but with 2 humbuckers, 2 volume controls, 1 master tone control.

| 1982-1984 | | $400 | $500 |

Corvus III
1982-1984. Same as Corvus I, but with 3 single-coil pickups, master volume and tone control, 5-way switch.

| 1982-1984 | | $550 | $650 |

Crest Gold
1969-1971. Double-cut thinline archtop, Brazilian rosewood body, 2 mini-humbuckers, bound top and headstock, bound f-holes, gold-plated parts.

| 1969-1971 | | $3,000 | $3,500 |

Crest Silver
1969-1972. Silver-plated parts version of Crest.

| 1969-1972 | | $2,500 | $3,000 |

Dove
1962-1996, 1999-2003. Flat-top acoustic, maple back and sides, square shoulders.

1962-1964	Sunburst	$4,500	$5,000
1963-1964	Natural	$5,000	$5,500
1965	Natural	$4,500	$5,000
1965	Sunburst	$4,200	$4,600
1966	Natural	$4,100	$4,500
1966	Sunburst	$3,800	$4,200
1967	Natural	$3,500	$4,000
1967	Sunburst	$3,300	$3,600
1968	Natural	$3,100	$3,400
1968	Sunburst	$2,800	$3,100
1969-1970	Natural	$2,500	$2,750
1969-1970	Sunburst	$2,400	$2,650
1971-1984	Natural	$2,200	$2,400
1971-1984	Sunburst	$2,100	$2,300
1984-1989	Sunburst, black, natural	$1,600	$1,750
1990-1996	Natural	$1,300	$1,550
1990-1996	Sunburst	$1,300	$1,550

'60s Dove
1997-1999. Spruce top, maple back and sides, Dove appointments.

| 1997-1999 | | $1,600 | $1,750 |

Dove Commemorative
1994-1996. Heritage or Antique Cherry finish.

| 1994 | | $1,600 | $2,000 |

Doves In Flight
1996-present. Gibson Custom model, maple back and sides, doves in flight inlays.

| 1996-2002 | | $2,800 | $3,000 |

1986 Gibson Corvus

Gibson Dove

1956 Gibson ES-5

1957 Gibson ES-5 Switchmaster

MODEL YEAR	FEATURES	EXC. COND. LOW	HIGH

EAS Deluxe
1992-1994. Single-cut flat-top acoustic/electric, solid flamed maple top, 3-band EQ.

| 1993 | Vintage Cherry Sunburst | $850 | $950 |

EBS(F)-1250 Double Bass
1962-1970. Double-cut SG-type solidbody, double-neck with bass and 6-string, originally introduced as the EBSF-1250 because of a built-in fuzztone, which was later deleted, only 22 made.

1962-1964		$8,000	$10,000
1965-1966		$6,000	$8,000
1967-1969		$5,000	$7,000
1970		$4,000	$6,000

EC-10 Standard
1997-1998. Jumbo single-cut, on-board electronics, solid spruce top, maple back and sides.

| 1997-1998 | | $650 | $700 |

EC-20 Starburst
1997-1998. Jumbo single-cut, on-board electronics, solid spruce top, maple back and sides, renamed J-180 EC in '99.

| 1997-1998 | | $1,150 | $1,250 |

EC-30 Blues King Electro (BKE)
1997-1998. Jumbo single-cut, on-board electronics, solid spruce top, figured maple back and sides, renamed J-185 EC in '99.

| 1997-1998 | | $1,500 | $1,600 |

EDS-1275 Double 12
1958-1968, 1977-1990. Double-cut doubleneck with one 12- and one 6-string, thinline hollowbody until late-'62, SG-style solidbody '62 on.

1958-1959	Black or cherry	$16,000	$20,000
1958-1959	Sunburst	$13,000	$15,000
1958-1959	White	$17,000	$21,000
1960-1962	Black or cherry	$15,000	$19,000
1960-1962	Sunburst	$12,000	$14,000
1960-1962	White	$16,000	$20,000
1968	Black or cherry	$6,000	$8,000
1968	Jimmy Page exact specs	$8,000	$12,000
1968	White	$7,000	$9,000
1977-1979	Sunburst, walnut, or white	$2,800	$3,200
1980-1991	Sunburst, walnut, or white	$2,400	$2,600
1995-2000	Various colors	$2,000	$2,200

EDS-1275 Double 12 (Historic Collection)
1991-1994. Historic Collection reissue.

| 1991-1994 | White | $2,000 | $2,200 |

EDS-1275 Double 12 Centennial
1994. Guitar of the Month (May), gold medallion on back of headstock, gold hardware.

| 1994 | Cherry | $2,000 | $2,200 |

EMS-1235 Double Mandolin
1958-1968. Double-cut, doubleneck with 1 regular 6-string and 1 short 6-string (the mandolin neck), thinline hollowbody until late-1962, SG-style solidbody '62-'68, black, sunburst or white, total of 61 shipped.

| 1958-1961 | | $11,000 | $16,000 |
| 1962-1964 | | $5,500 | $8,000 |

MODEL YEAR	FEATURES	EXC. COND. LOW	HIGH
1965-1968		$3,500	$5,500

ES-5
1949-1955. Single-cut archtop, 3 P-90 pickups, renamed ES-5 Switchmaster in '55.

| 1949-1955 | Natural | $7,500 | $8,500 |
| 1949-1955 | Sunburst | $6,500 | $7,500 |

ES-5 Switchmaster
1956-1962. Renamed from ES-5, single-cut (rounded until late-'60, pointed after) archtop, 3 P-90s until end of '57, humbuckers after, switchmaster control. The PAF pickups in this model are worth as much as the rest of the guitar. We have listed a non-original '58 with replaced pickups to demonstrate how value is reduced when the original PAFs are removed.

1956-1957	Natural, P-90s	$7,500	$8,500
1956-1957	Sunburst, P-90s	$6,500	$7,500
1957-1960	Natural, humbuckers	$11,000	$14,000
1957-1960	Sunburst, humbuckers	$10,000	$12,000
1957-1960	Sunburst, non-original pickups	$5,000	$6,000
1960-1962	Pointed Florentine cutaway	$10,000	$12,000

ES-5/ES-5 Switchmaster Custom Shop Historic
1995-2002.

| 1995-2002 | ES-5, P-90s, sunburst | $3,000 | $3,200 |
| 1995-2002 | Switchmaster, humbuckers, Wine Red | $3,100 | $3,300 |

ES-100
1938-1941. Archtop, 1 pickup, bound body, sunburst, renamed ES-125 in '41.

| 1938-1941 | | $1,000 | $1,300 |

ES-120 T
1962-1970. Archtop, thinline, 1 f-hole, bound body, 1 pickup, sunburst.

| 1962-1966 | | $900 | $1,000 |
| 1967-1970 | | $600 | $800 |

ES-125
1941-1943, 1946-1970. Archtop, non-cut, 1 pickup, sunburst, renamed from ES-100.

1941-1943	Blade pickup	$1,300	$1,400
1946-1950	1st non-adj., P-90s	$1,300	$1,500
1951-1964	Adj. P-90s with poles	$1,200	$1,400
1965-1970		$1,000	$1,300

ES-125 C
1966-1970. Wide body archtop, single pointed cutaway, 1 pickup, sunburst.

| 1966-1970 | | $1,000 | $1,300 |

ES-125 CD
1966-1970. Wide body archtop, single-cut, 2 pickups, sunburst.

| 1966-1970 | | $1,500 | $1,700 |

ES-125 D
1957. Limited production (not mentioned in catalog), 2 pickup version of thick body ES-125, sunburst.

| 1957 | | $1,400 | $1,700 |

*The **Vintage Guitar Price Guide** shows low to high values for items in all-original excellent condition, and, where applicable, with original case or cover.*

MODEL YEAR	FEATURES	EXC. COND. LOW	HIGH

ES-125 T
1956-1969. Archtop thinline, non-cut, 1 pickup, bound body, sunburst.

1956-1964		$1,300	$1,600
1965-1969		$1,200	$1,500

ES-125 T 3/4
1957-1970. Archtop thinline, short-scale, non-cut, 1 pickup, sunburst.

1957-1964		$800	$900
1965-1970		$600	$700

ES-125 TC
1960-1970. Archtop thinline, single pointed cutaway, bound body, 1 P-90 pickup, sunburst.

1960-1964		$1,550	$1,650
1965-1970		$1,450	$1,600

ES-125 TD
1957-1963. Archtop thinline, non-cut, 2 pickups, sunburst.

1957-1963		$1,300	$1,500

ES-125 TDC or ES-125 TCD
1960-1971. Archtop thinline, single pointed cutaway, 2 P-90 pickups, sunburst.

1960-1964		$1,600	$2,100
1965-1966		$1,400	$2,000
1966-1971		$1,200	$1,800

ES-130
1954-1956. Archtop, non-cut, 1 pickup, bound body, sunburst, renamed ES-135 in '56.

1954-1956		$1,200	$1,500

ES-135
1956-1958. Renamed from ES-130, non-cut archtop, 1 pickup, sunburst, name reused on a thin body in the '90s.

1956-1958		$1,200	$1,500

ES-135 (Thinline)
1991-2002. Single-cut archtop, laminated maple body, 2 humbuckers or 2 P-90s, chrome or gold hardware, sunburst.

1991-2002	Stoptail	$1,050	$1,150
1991-2002	Trapeze	$875	$1,000

ES-140 (3/4)
1950-1956. Archtop, single-cut, 1 pickup, bound body, short-scale.

1950-1956	Natural option	$1,700	$2,300
1950-1956	Sunburst	$1,500	$1,800

ES-140 3/4 T
1957-1968. Archtop thinline, single-cut, bound body, 1 pickup, short-scale, sunburst.

1957-1968		$1,500	$1,800

ES-150
1936-1942, 1946-1956. Historically important archtop, non-cut, bound body, Charlie Christian bar pickup from '36-'39, various metal covered pickups starting in '40, sunburst.

1936-1939	Charlie Christian pickup	$4,200	$5,000
1940-1942	Metal covered pickup	$3,200	$4,000
1946-1956	P-90 pickup	$1,600	$2,000

ES-150 DC
1969-1975. Archtop, double rounded cutaway, 2 humbuckers, multi-bound.

1969-1975	Cherry or walnut	$2,000	$2,200
1969-1975	Natural	$2,200	$2,500

ES-165 Herb Ellis Model
1991-present. Single pointed cut hollowbody, 1 humbucker, gold hardware.

1991-1995		$1,500	$1,700

ES-175
1949-1971. Archtop, single pointed cutaway, 1 pickup (P-90 from '49-early-'57, humbucker early-'57-'71), multi-bound.

1949-1951	Natural	$4,000	$4,500
1949-1951	Sunburst	$3,500	$4,000
1952-1956	Natural, P-90	$3,500	$4,000
1952-1956	Sunburst, P-90	$3,000	$3,500
1957-1959	Natural, humbucker	$6,000	$7,000
1957-1959	Sunburst, humbucker	$5,500	$6,000
1960	Sunburst	$5,200	$5,800
1961	Sunburst	$5,000	$5,600
1962	Sunburst	$4,700	$5,200
1963	Sunburst	$4,500	$4,800
1964	Sunburst	$4,000	$4,400
1965	Sunburst	$3,500	$4,200
1966	Natural	$3,200	$4,000
1966	Sunburst	$3,100	$3,800
1967-1969	Various colors	$3,000	$3,600
1970-1971	Various colors	$2,200	$3,000

ES-175 CC
1978-1979. 1 Charlie Christian pickup, sunburst or walnut.

1978-1979		$2,500	$3,000

ES-175 D
1951-present. Archtop, single-cut, 2 pickups (P-90s from '53-early-'57, humbuckers early-'57 on). Humbucker pickups were converted from PAF-stickers to Pat. No.-stickers in '62. Different models were converted at different times. An ES-175 model, made during the transitional time, with PAFs, will fetch more. In some of the electric-archtop models, the transition period may have been later than '62. Cataloged as the ES-175 Reissue in the '90s, Currently as the ES-175 under Gibson Custom.

1952-1956	Natural	$5,500	$6,500
1952-1956	Sunburst	$4,500	$5,500
1957-1959	Natural, humbuckers	$7,500	$8,500
1957-1959	Sunburst, humbuckers	$7,000	$7,500
1960	Natural	$6,500	$7,500
1960	Sunburst	$6,000	$7,000
1961	Natural	$6,400	$7,400
1961	Sunburst	$5,900	$6,900
1962	Natural	$5,500	$6,500
1962	Sunburst	$5,000	$6,000
1963	Natural	$5,000	$6,000
1963	Sunburst	$4,500	$5,500
1964	Natural	$4,500	$5,500

1962 Gibson ES-125TDC

1958 Gibson ES-175

GUITARS

Gibson ES-225 TDN

1959 Gibson ES-330 TD

MODEL YEAR	FEATURES	EXC. COND. LOW	HIGH
1964	Sunburst	$4,000	$5,000
1965	Natural	$4,000	$5,000
1965	Sunburst	$3,500	$4,500
1966	Natural	$3,800	$4,800
1966	Sunburst	$3,600	$4,200
1967-1969	Various colors	$3,000	$3,500
1970-1972	Various colors	$2,500	$3,000
1973-1979	Various colors	$2,000	$2,500
1980-1989	Various colors	$1,600	$2,300
1990-1999	Various colors	$1,600	$2,100
2000-2003	Various colors	$1,600	$2,100

ES-175 T

1976-1980. Archtop thinline, single pointed cutaway, 2 humbuckers, various colors.

1976-1980		$2,200	$2,600

ES-225 T

1955-1959. Thinline, single pointed cutaway, 1 P-90 pickup, bound body and neck.

1955-1959	Natural	$1,700	$2,200
1955-1959	Sunburst	$1,500	$1,900

ES-225 TD

1956-1959. Thinline, single-cut, 2 P-90s, bound body and neck.

1956-1959	Natural	$2,000	$3,000
1956-1959	Sunburst	$1,700	$2,200

ES-250

1939-1940. Archtop, carved top, special Christian pickup, multi-bound, high-end appointments.

1939-1940	Natural,	$18,000	$21,000
1939-1940	Sunburst	$8,000	$10,000

ES-295

1952-1958. Single pointed cutaway archtop, 2 pickups (P-90s from '52-late-'58, humbuckers after), gold finish, gold-plated hardware.

1952-1957	P-90s	$5,500	$7,500
1957-1958	Humbuckers	$15,000	$17,000

ES-295 Reissue

1990-1993. Gold finish, 2 P-90 pickups, Bigsby.

1990-1993		$2,400	$2,500

ES-295 '52 Historic Collection

1993-2000. Higher end reissue, Antique Gold finish, 2 P-90 pickups, Bigsby.

1994-1995		$2,500	$2,600

ES-300

1940-1942, 1945-1953. Archtop, non-cut, f-holes, had 4 pickup configurations during its run, sunburst or natural.

1940-1942	Natural, 1 pickup	$3,500	$4,000
1940-1942	Sunburst, 1 pickup	$2,500	$3,500
1945-1948	Sunburst, 1 pickup	$2,000	$2,500
1949-1953	Sunburst, 2 pickups	$2,500	$3,000

ES-320 TD

1971-1974. Thinline archtop, double-cut, 2 single-coil pickups, bound body, cherry, natural, or walnut.

1971-1974		$1,000	$1,100

ES-325 TD

1972-1978. Thinline archtop, double-cut, 2 mini-humbuckers, 1 f-hole, bound body, cherry or walnut.

1972-1978		$1,100	$1,300

ES-330 T

1959-1963. Double rounded cutaway, thinline, 1 pickup, bound body and neck, in the '60s came with either an original semi-hard case (better than chip board) or a hardshell case. Prices quoted are for hardshell case; approximately $100 should be deducted for the semi-hard

1959-1961	Natural	$3,500	$5,000
1959-1961	Sunburst	$2,300	$2,800
1962-1963	Cherry or sunburst	$2,100	$2,500

ES-330 TD

1959-1972. Double rounded cutaway, thinline, 2 pickups, bound body and neck, in the '60s came with either an original semi-hard case (better than chip board) or a hardshell case. Prices noted for the hardshell case; approximately $100 should be deducted for the semi-hard case.

1959-1960	Natural	$4,500	$6,000
1959-1960	Sunburst	$3,000	$3,500
1961	Cherry or sunburst	$3,000	$3,500
1962-1964	Cherry or sunburst	$2,600	$3,300
1965-1969	Various colors	$2,200	$2,600
1969-1972	Various colors, long neck	$2,000	$2,500

ES-335 TD

1958-1981. The original design ES-335 has dot 'board inlays and a stop tailpiece. Block inlays replaced dots in mid-'62, in late-'64 the stop tailpiece was replaced with a trapeze tailpiece. Replaced by the ES-335 DOT in '81.

1958	Natural, unbound neck	$40,000	$50,000
1958	Natural, unbound neck, Bigsby	$31,000	$39,000
1958	Sunburst, bound neck	$26,000	$30,000
1958	Sunburst, bound neck, Bigsby	$20,000	$25,000
1958	Sunburst, unbound neck	$27,000	$31,000
1958	Sunburst, unbound neck, Bigsby	$21,000	$27,000
1959	Natural, bound neck	$40,000	$50,000
1959	Natural, bound neck, Bigsby	$31,000	$39,000
1959	Sunburst	$26,000	$30,000
1959	Sunburst, factory Bigsby	$20,000	$23,000
1960	Cherry, factory Bigsby	$15,000	$17,000
1960	Cherry, factory stop tail	$20,000	$22,000
1960	Natural, factory Bigsby	$27,000	$35,000
1960	Natural, factory stop tail	$35,000	$45,000
1960	Sunburst, factory Bigsby	$15,000	$17,000

MODEL YEAR	FEATURES	EXC. COND. LOW	HIGH
1960	Sunburst, factory stop tail	$20,000	$22,000
1961	Cherry, factory Bigsby	$14,000	$15,000
1961	Cherry, factory stop tail	$18,000	$20,000
1961	Sunburst, factory Bigsby	$15,000	$16,000
1961	Sunburst, factory stop tail	$19,000	$21,000
1962	Cherry, blocks, PAFs	$13,000	$15,000
1962	Cherry, blocks, pat. #	$10,000	$12,000
1962	Cherry, dots, PAFs	$14,000	$16,000
1962	Cherry, dots, pat. #	$11,000	$13,000
1962	Sunburst, blocks, PAFs	$14,000	$16,000
1962	Sunburst, blocks, pat. #	$11,000	$13,000
1962	Sunburst, dots, PAFs	$15,000	$17,000
1962	Sunburst, dots, pat. #	$12,000	$14,000
1963-1964	Cherry	$9,000	$11,000
1963-1964	Cherry, factory Bigsby	$7,800	$9,300
1963-1964	Cherry, with Maestro	$7,800	$9,300
1963-1964	Sunburst	$10,000	$12,000
1963-1964	Sunburst, factory Bigsby	$7,800	$9,300
1965	Cherry or sunburst, trapeze or tremolo	$4,700	$5,500
1966-1968	Burgundy Metallic (unfaded)	$4,700	$6,000
1966-1968	Cherry or sunburst, trapeze or tremolo	$3,700	$4,500
1966-1968	Pelham Blue (unfaded)	$6,000	$8,000
1969	Cherry or sunburst, trapeze or tremolo	$3,000	$3,500
1970	Cherry or sunburst, trapeze or tremolo	$2,500	$3,300
1971-1976	Cherry or sunburst, trapeze or tremolo	$2,300	$2,600
1977-1979	Various colors, coil tap	$1,800	$2,300
1980-1981	Various colors	$1,500	$1,700

ES-335 Dot
1981-1990. Reissue of 1960 ES-335 and replaces ES-335 TD. Name changed to ES-335 Reissue. Various color options including highly figured wood.

1982-1990		$1,800	$2,500

ES-335 Reissue/1959 Dot Reissue
1991-present. Replaced the ES-335 DOT, dot inlays, various color options including highly figured wood. Renamed the 1959 ES-335 Dot Reissue in '98. A block

---

inlay version, called the 1963 ES-335 Block Reissue also became available in '98.

1991-1999		$1,700	$2,400
2000-2005		$1,700	$2,000

ES-335-12
1965-1971. 12-string version of the 335.

1965-1966	Cherry or sunburst	$2,500	$3,000
1967-1969	Various colors	$2,000	$2,500

ES-335 '59 Historic Collection
Historical Series based upon 1959 ES-335 dot neck, figured maple top, nickel hardware, replica Orange label, cherry.

1998		$2,200	$2,500

ES-335 '63 Historic Collection
Historical Series based upon 1962 ES-335 with small block markers, maple top, nickel hardware, replica Orange label, cherry.

2000-2001		$2,200	$2,500

ES-335 Artist
1981. Off-set dot markers, large headstock logo, metal truss rod plate, gold hardware, 3 control knobs with unusual toggles and input specification.

1981		$2,100	$2,300

ES-335 Centennial
1994. Centennial edition, gold medallion in headstock, diamond inlay in tailpiece, cherry.

1994		$3,500	$4,000

ES-335 TD CRR
1979. Country Rock Regular, 2 stereo pickups, coil-tap, sunburst.

1979		$1,900	$2,400

ES-335 Custom Shop
1980s-1990s. Gibson Custom Shop logo on the back of the headstock, various color options including highly figured wood.

1980s		$2,200	$3,000
1990s		$2,200	$3,000

ES-335 Dot CMT
1983-1985. Custom Shop ES-335 Dot with curly maple top and back, full-length center block, gold hardware, various colors.

1983-1985		$2,200	$3,000

ES-335 Jimmy Wallace Reissue
1980	Blond	$2,500	$3,300

ES-335 Pro
1979-1981. Two humbucking pickups with exposed coils, bound 'board, cherry or sunburst.

1979-1981		$1,400	$1,550

ES-335 Showcase Edition
1988. Guitar of the Month series, limited production, transparent white/beige finish, black gothic-style hardware, EMG pickups.

1988		$1,700	$1,800

ES-335 Studio
1986-1991. No f-holes, 2 Dirty Finger humbuckers, bound body, cherry or ebony.

1986-1991		$1,200	$1,550

ES-336
1996-2002. Custom Shop smaller sized ES-335 with smaller headstock, dot markers.

1996-2002		$1,500	$1,600

1960 Gibson ES-335

1960s Gibson ES-335-12

1960 Gibson ES-345TD
(Cherry Red)

Gibson ES-355

MODEL YEAR	FEATURES	EXC. COND. LOW	HIGH

ES-340 TD
1968-1973. The 335 with a laminated maple neck, master volume and mixer controls, various colors.

1968-1969		$2,500	$2,900
1970-1973		$2,100	$2,700

ES-345 TD
1959-1983. The 335 with Vari-tone, stereo, 2 humbuckers, gold hardware, double parallelogram inlays, stop tailpiece '59-'64 and '82-'83, trapeze tailpiece '65-'82.

1959	Cherry, Bigsby	$12,750	$14,250
1959	Cherry, stud tail	$17,000	$19,000
1959	Natural, Bigsby	$22,000	$27,000
1959	Natural, stud tail	$32,000	$37,000
1959	Sunburst, Bigsby	$12,750	$14,250
1959	Sunburst, stud tail	$17,000	$19,000
1960	Cherry, Bigsby	$12,000	$13,500
1960	Cherry, stud tail	$16,000	$18,000
1960	Natural, Bigsby	$17,000	$22,000
1960	Natural, stud tail	$27,000	$32,000
1960	Sunburst, Bigsby	$12,000	$13,500
1960	Sunburst, stud tail	$16,000	$18,000
1961	Cherry, Bigsby	$12,000	$13,500
1961	Cherry, stud tail	$16,000	$18,000
1961	Sunburst, Bigsby	$12,000	$13,500
1961	Sunburst, stud tail	$16,000	$18,000
1962-1964	Bigsby	$6,750	$7,500
1962-1964	Stud tail	$9,000	$10,000
1965-1967	Various colors	$3,700	$4,500
1968	Various colors	$3,000	$3,700
1969	Various colors	$2,600	$3,400
1970	Various colors	$2,400	$2,600
1971-1976	Various colors	$2,300	$2,500
1977-1983	Various colors	$1,500	$2,300

ES-345 Reissue
2002-present. ES-345 features with 6-position Varitone selector, gold hardware, stop tailpiece, various colors.

2002-2005		$2,000	$2,200

ES-347 TD/ES-347 S
1978-1993. 335-style with gold hardware, tune-o-matic bridge, 2 Spotlight double-coil pickups, coil-tap, bound body and neck, S added to name in '87.

1978-1986		$1,800	$2,000
1987-1993		$1,800	$2,000

ES-350
1947-1956. Originally the ES-350 Premier, full body archtop, single-cut, 1 P-90 pickup until end of '48, 2 afterwards.

1947-1956	Natural	$5,500	$6,000
1947-1956	Sunburst	$4,500	$5,500

ES-350 T
1955-1963. McCarty era, called the ES-350 TD in early-'60s, thinline archtop, single-cut (round '55-'60 and '77-'81, pointed '61-'63), 2 P-90 pickups '55-'56, humbuckers after, gold hardware.

1956	Natural, P-90s	$5,000	$5,500
1956	Sunburst, P-90s	$4,000	$5,000
1957-1959	Natural, humbuckers	$7,000	$8,000
1957-1959	Sunburst, humbuckers	$6,500	$7,000
1960-1963	Natural	$6,000	$6,500
1960-1963	Sunburst	$5,500	$5,800

ES-350 T (2nd Issue)
1977-1981. Norlin era, second issue of ES-350 T.

1977-1981	Natural	$2,500	$3,000
1977-1981	Sunburst	$2,300	$2,800

ES-350 T Limited Edition Reissue
1990s. Special medallion on back of headstock.

1990s		$3,200	$3,300

ES-355 Centennial
1994. Custom Shop Guitar of the Month in June '94, high-end custom appointments, gold-plated hardware, sunburst.

1994		$3,500	$4,000

ES-355 TD
1958-1970. A 335-style with large block inlays, multi-bound body and headstock, 2 humbuckers, the 355 model was standard with a Bigsby, sideways or Maestro vibrato, non-vibrato models were an option. The prices shown assume a vibrato tailpiece, a factory stop tailpiece was considered an advantage and will fetch more. Early examples have factory Bigsby vibratos, early '60s have sideways vibratos, and late '60s have Maestro vibratos, cherry finish was the standard finish.

1958-1962	Cherry, PAFs, stop tail	$18,750	$20,000
1958-1962	Cherry, PAFs, vibrato	$15,000	$16,000
1963-1964	Cherry, pat. #, vibrato	$7,800	$8,700
1965	Burgundy Metallic (unfaded)	$5,700	$6,500
1965	Cherry or sunburst	$4,700	$5,500
1966	Burgundy Metallic (unfaded)	$4,700	$5,500
1966	Cherry or sunburst	$3,700	$4,500
1967	Burgundy Metallic (unfaded)	$4,700	$5,500
1967	Cherry or sunburst	$3,700	$4,500
1968-1969	Various colors	$3,000	$4,500

ES-355 TDSV
1959-1982. Stereo version of ES-355 with Vari-tone switch, a mono version was available but few were made, the 355 model was standard with a Bigsby, sideways or Maestro vibrato, non-vibrato models were an option. The prices shown assume a vibrato tailpiece. A factory stop tailpiece was considered an advantage and will fetch more, early examples have factory Bigsby vibratos, early-'60s have sideways vibratos and late-'60s have Maestro vibratos, cherry finish was standard, walnut became available in '69.

1959-1960	Bigsby	$13,000	$16,000
1961-1962	Sideways, late PAFs	$11,000	$13,000
1963-1964	Maestro, pat. #	$7,000	$8,500
1965		$5,200	$6,200
1966		$4,400	$5,200

MODEL YEAR	FEATURES	EXC. COND. LOW	HIGH
1967-1969	Maestro '67-'68, Bigsby '69	$4,000	$5,000
1970-1979	Bigsby	$2,500	$3,500

ES-369

1982. A 335-style with 2 exposed humbucker pick-ups, coil-tap, sunburst.

1982		$1,400	$1,700

ES-775

1990-1993. Single-cut hollowbody, 2 humbuckers, gold hardware, ebony, natural or sunburst.

1990-1993		$2,400	$2,800

ES-Artist

1979-1985. Double-cut thinline, semi-hollowbody, no f-holes, 2 humbuckers, active electronics, gold hardware, ebony, fireburst or sunburst.

1979-1985		$1,800	$2,500

EST-150

1937-1940. Tenor version of ES-150, renamed ETG-150 in '40, sunburst.

1937-1940		$2,800	$3,000

ETG-150

1940-1942, 1947-1971. Renamed from EST-150, tenor version of ES-150, 1 pickup, sunburst.

1947-1971		$1,300	$1,400

Everly Brothers

1962-1972. Jumbo flat-top, huge double 'guard, star inlays, natural is optional in '63 and becomes the standard color in '68, reintroduced as the J-180 Everly Brothers in '86.

1962-1964	Black	$8,000	$9,000
1963	Natural option	$8,000	$9,000
1965-1967	Black	$6,000	$6,500
1968-1969	Natural replaces black	$3,500	$3,800
1970-1972	Natural	$3,300	$3,500

Explorer

1958-1959, 1963. Some '58s shipped in '63, korina body, 2 humbuckers. The Explorer market is a very specialized and very small market, with few genuine examples available and a limited number of high-end buyers. The slightest change to the original specifica-tions can mean a significant drop in value. The nar-row price ranges noted are for all original examples that have the original guitar case.

1958-1959		$135,000	$160,000
1963		$110,000	$135,000

Explorer (Mahogany body)

1976-1982. Mahogany body, 2 humbucking pick-ups.

1976-1982		$1,500	$1,700

Explorer (Alder body)

1983-1989. Alder body, 2 humbuckers, maple neck, ebony 'board, dot inlays, triangle knob pattern, re-ferred to as Explorer 83 in '83.

1983-1989	Custom colors limited run	$1,000	$1,300
1983-1989	Standard finishes	$800	$900

Explorer (Limited Edition Korina)

1976. Limited edition korina body replaces standard mahogany body, natural.

1976		$2,700	$3,500

Explorer Heritage

1983. Reissue of '58 Explorer, korina body, gold hardware, inked serial number, limited edition.

1983	Black	$2,500	$3,000
1983	Natural	$3,000	$3,500
1983	White	$2,500	$3,000

Explorer Korina

1982-1984. Korina body and neck, 2 humbucking pickups, gold hardware, standard 8-digit serial (versus the inked serial number on the Heritage Explorer of the same era).

1982-1984		$2,500	$3,000

Explorer '76/X-plorer

1990-present. Mahogany body and neck, rosewood 'board, dot inlays, 2 humbucking pickups, name changed to X-plorer in 2002.

1990-1999	Standard finish	$800	$900
1998	Sunburst or natural limited run	$900	$1,200
2000-2005	Various colors	$700	$800

Explorer 90 Double

1989-1990. Mahogany body and neck, 1 single-coil and 1 humbucker, strings-thru-body.

1989-1990		$550	$700

Explorer Centennial

1994 only. Les Paul Gold finish, 100 year banner inlay at 12th fret, diamonds in headstock and gold-plated knobs, Gibson coin in rear of headstock, only 100 made.

1994		$3,200	$3,800

Explorer CMT/The Explorer

1981-1984. Maple body, exposed-coil pickups, TP-6 tailpiece.

1981-1984		$900	$1,100

Explorer Gothic

1998-2003. Gothic Series with black finish and hardware.

1998-2003		$600	$900

Explorer II (E/2)

1979-1983. Five-piece maple and walnut laminate body sculptured like V II, ebony 'board with dot inlays, 2 humbucking pickups, gold-plated hardware, natural finish.

1979-1983	Figured maple top option	$1,500	$1,700

Explorer III

1984-1985. Alder body, 3 P-90 pickups, 2 control knobs.

1984-1985	Chrome hardware	$700	$900
1984-1985	Chrome hardware, locking trem	$600	$800
1985	Black hardware, Kahler	$600	$800

F-25 Folksinger

1963-1971. 14-1/2" flat-top, mahogany body, most have double white 'guard, natural.

1963-1964		$1,200	$1,400
1965-1969		$1,000	$1,200
1970-1971		$800	$1,000

1967 Gibson Everly Brothers

1959 Gibson Explorer

1964 Gibson Firebird I

1964 Gibson Firebird VII

MODEL YEAR	FEATURES	EXC. COND. LOW	HIGH
Firebird I			

1963-1969. Reverse body and 1 humbucking pickup '63-mid-'65, non-reversed body and 2 P-90 pickups mid-'65-'69.

MODEL YEAR	FEATURES	EXC. COND. LOW	HIGH
1963	Sunburst, reverse	$5,000	$6,500
1964	Cardinal Red, reverse	$6,000	$7,000
1964	Sunburst, reverse	$4,000	$6,000
1965	Cardinal Red, reverse	$5,500	$6,500
1965	Golden Mist, non-reverse	$3,500	$4,500
1965	Sunburst, non-reverse	$2,500	$3,500
1965	Sunburst, reverse	$3,500	$5,000
1966-1969	Sunburst, non-reverse	$2,000	$3,000

Firebird I Custom Shop

1991-1992. Limited run from Custom Shop, reverse body, 1 pickup, gold-plated, sunburst.

1991		$1,500	$1,600

Firebird 76

1976-1978. Reverse body, gold hardware, 2 pickups.

1976	Bicentennial White	$2,500	$3,000
1977-1978		$1,500	$2,500

Firebird I/ Firebird 76

1980-1982. Reintroduced Firebird 76 but renamed Firebird I.

1980-1982		$2,000	$2,500

Firebird I 1963 Reissue Historic Collection

1999-present. Neck-thru, reverse body, Firebird logo on 'guard.

1999	Sunburst	$1,600	$1,700
2002	Blue Swirl limited edition	$1,800	$2,200

Firebird II/Firebird 2

1981-1982. Maple body with figured maple top, 2 full size active humbuckers, TP-6 tailpiece.

1981-1982		$1,500	$2,000

Firebird III

1963-1969. Reverse body and 2 humbucking pickups '63-mid-'65, non-reversed body and 3 P-90 pickups mid-'65-'69.

1963	Cardinal Red	$7,500	$9,000
1963	Golden Mist	$7,500	$8,500
1963	Polaris White	$7,000	$8,000
1963	Sunburst	$5,500	$7,000
1964	Cardinal Red, reverse	$7,500	$9,000
1964	Polaris White, reverse	$7,000	$8,500
1964	Sunburst, reverse	$5,000	$6,500
1965	Frost Blue, reverse	$7,500	$9,000
1965	Inverness Green, non-reverse	$5,000	$7,000
1965	Sunburst, non-reverse	$3,000	$3,500
1965	Sunburst, reverse	$4,000	$5,500

MODEL YEAR	FEATURES	EXC. COND. LOW	HIGH
1966	Sunburst, non-reverse	$2,500	$3,500
1967	Frost Blue	$3,500	$5,000
1967-1969	Pelham Blue	$3,500	$5,000
1967-1969	Sunburst	$2,500	$3,500

Firebird V

1963-1969, 1994-present. Two humbucking pickups, reverse body '63-mid-'65, non-reversed body mid-'65-'69.

1963	Pelham Blue	$9,000	$11,000
1963	Sunburst	$6,500	$9,000
1964	Cardinal Red, reverse	$7,500	$10,000
1964	Sunburst, reverse	$6,000	$7,000
1965	Cardinal Red, reverse	$7,800	$9,000
1965	Sunburst, non-reverse	$3,500	$4,500
1965	Sunburst, reverse	$4,500	$6,000
1966	Sunburst, non-reverse	$3,000	$4,000
1967-1969	Sunburst	$3,000	$4,000

Firebird V Celebrity Series

1990-1993. Reverse body, gold hardware, 2 humbuckers, various colors.

1990-1993		$1,200	$1,500

Firebird V Guitar Trader Reissue

1982. Guitar Trader commissioned Firebird reissue, only 15 made.

1982	Sunburst	$1,700	$2,200
1982	White	$2,200	$2,700

Firebird V Medallion

1972-1973. Reverse body, 2 humbuckers, Limited Edition medallion mounted on body.

1972-1973		$4,000	$4,500

Firebird V Reissue/Firebird Reissue

1990-present. Based on Firebird V specs, reverse body, several colors available with Cardinal Red optional in '91.

1990-1999	Various colors	$1,300	$1,500

Firebird V-12

1966-1967. Non-reverse Firebird V-style body with standard six-on-a-side headstock and split diamond headstock inlay (like ES-335-12 inlay), dot markers, special twin humbucking pickups (like mini-humbuckers).

1966-1967	Custom colors	$5,000	$6,500
1966-1967	Sunburst	$4,000	$4,500

Firebird VII

1963-1969. Three humbucking pickups, reverse body '63-mid-'65, non-reversed body mid-'65-'69, sunburst standard.

1963		$10,500	$15,000
1964		$10,000	$14,000
1965	Reverse	$9,000	$10,000
1966	Non-reverse	$5,000	$7,000
1967		$4,500	$6,500
1968		$4,500	$6,500
1968	Custom colors	$6,500	$8,500

The Vintage Guitar Price Guide shows low to high values for items in all-original excellent condition, and, where applicable, with original case or cover.

MODEL YEAR	FEATURES	EXC. COND. LOW	HIGH

Firebird VII (Historic/Custom Shop)
1997-present. Standard color is Vintage Sunburst, other colors available.

1997-2004	Custom colors	$2,800	$3,500
1997-2004	Sunburst	$2,500	$3,000

Firebird VII Centennial
1994 only. Headstock medallion, sunburst.

1994		$3,000	$4,000

Firebird VII Reissue (production model)

2003-2005		$1,300	$1,400

FJ-N Jumbo Folk Singer
1963-1967. Square shoulders, jumbo flat-top, natural finish with deep red on back and sides.

1963-1964		$1,500	$1,700
1965-1967		$1,200	$1,500

Flamenco 2
1963-1967. Natural spruce top, 14 3/4", cypress back and sides, slotted headstock, zero fret.

1963-1967		$550	$750

Flying V
1958-1959, 1962-1963. Only 81 shipped in '58 and 17 in '59, guitars made from leftover parts and sold in '62-'63, natural korina body, string-thru-body design. As with any ultra high-end instrument, each instrument should be evaluated on a case-by-case basis. The Flying V market is a very specialized market, with few untouched examples available, and a limited number of high-end buyers. The price ranges noted are for all-original, excellent condition guitars with the original Flying V case. The slightest change to the original specifications can mean a significant drop in value.

1958-1959		$90,000	$115,000

Flying V (Mahogany)
1966-1969, 1975-1980. Mahogany body, around 200 were shipped for '66-'70. Gibson greatly increased production of Flying Vs in '75. See separate listing for the '71 Medallion V version.

1966-1967	Cherry or sunburst	$13,000	$15,000
1969-1971	Cherry or sunburst	$10,000	$13,000
1975	Various colors	$3,000	$3,500
1976	Various colors	$2,500	$3,000
1979	Silverburst	$3,000	$3,500
1979	Various colors	$2,500	$3,000
1980	Various colors	$2,300	$2,500

Flying V (Mahogany string-through-body)
1981-1982. Mahogany body, string-thru-body design, only 100 made, most in white, some red or black possible.

1981-1982	Black, red or white	$1,700	$2,000

Flying V Heritage
1981-1982. Limited edition based on '58 specs, korina body, 4 colors available.

1981-1982	Natural	$2,500	$3,500
1981-1982	Various colors	$2,500	$3,200

Flying V (Korina)
1983. Name changed from Flying V Heritage, korina body, various colors.

1983		$2,500	$3,500

Flying V '90 Double
1989-1990. Mahogany body, stud tailpiece, 1 single-coil and 1 double-coil humbucker, Floyd Rose tremolo, ebony, silver or white.

1989-1990		$600	$800

Flying V '98
1998. Mahogany body, '58 style controls, gold or chrome hardware.

1998		$800	$950

Flying V CMT/The V
1981-1985. Maple body with a curly maple top, 2 pickups, stud tailpiece, natural or sunburst.

1981-1985		$850	$1,150

Flying V Custom (Limited Edition)
2002. Appointments similar to Les Paul Custom, including black finish, only 40 made.

2002		$3,400	$3,800

Flying V Gothic/'98 Gothic
1998-2003. Satin black finish, black hardware, moon and star markers.

1998-2000		$700	$950

Flying V Historic Collection
1991-present. Based on '58 Flying V, gold hardware, natural korina.

1991-1999		$4,500	$6,000

Flying V I/V '83/Flying V (no pickguard)
1981-1988. Introduced as Flying V I, then renamed Flying V '83 in 1983, called Flying V from '84 on. Alder body, 2 exposed humbuckers, maple neck, ebony 'board, dot inlays, black rings, no 'guard, ebony or ivory finish, designed for lower-end market.

1981-1988		$500	$800

Flying V II
1979-1982. Five-piece maple and walnut laminate sculptured body, ebony 'board with dot inlays, 2 V-shaped pickups (2 Dirty Fingers humbuckers towards end of run), gold-plated hardware, natural.

1979-1982		$1,300	$1,600

Flying V Medallion
1971. Mahogany body, stud tailpiece, numbered Limited Edition medallion on bass side of V, 350 made in '71 (3 more were shipped in '73-'74).

1971-1974		$5,500	$6,500

Flying V Primavera
1994. Primavera (light yellow/white mahogany) body, gold-plated hardware.

1994	Natural yellow/white	$1,450	$1,550
1994	Various special colors	$1,300	$1,400

Flying V Reissue/'67 Flying V/V Factor X
1990-present. Called Flying V Reissue first year, then '67 Flying V until '03, then V Factor X, mahogany body, X dropped in '05.

1990-1999	Various colors	$900	$1,100
1993	Cardinal Red (custom)	$1,200	$1,500

Hendrix Hall of Fame Flying V
Late-1991-1993. Limited Edition (400 made), numbered, black.

1991-1993		$1,750	$1,900

1958 Gibson Flying V

1979 Gibson Flying V (mahogany)

1970s Gibson Heritage

1974 Gibson Howard Roberts

MODEL YEAR	FEATURES	EXC. COND. LOW	HIGH
Lonnie Mack Flying V			
1993-1994. Mahogany body with Lonnie Mack-style Bigsby vibrato, cherry.			
1993-1994		$2,600	$2,900
Futura			
1982-1984. Deep cutout solidbody, 2 humbucker pickups, gold hardware, black, white or purple.			
1982-1984		$600	$750
GB-1			
1922-1923. Guitar-banjo, 6-string neck, walnut, renamed GB-5 in '23.			
1922-1923		$1,500	$2,000
GB-3			
1923-1931. Style 4 appointments, maple.			
1923-1937		$2,000	$2,500
GB-4			
1923-1931. Style 4 appointments, 14" rim.			
1923-1931		$2,500	$3,000
Gospel			
1973-1979. Flat-top, square shoulders, laminated maple back and sides, arched back, Dove of Peace headstock inlay, natural.			
1973-1979		$800	$950
Gospel Reissue			
1992-1997. Flat-top, cutaway with laminated mahogany back and sides and arched back, natural or sunburst.			
1992-1997		$850	$1,000
GS-1 Classical			
1950-1956. Mahogany back and sides.			
1950-1956		$400	$550
GS-2 Classical			
1950-1956. Maple back and sides.			
1950-1956		$500	$600
GS-5 Classical			
1954-1956. Rosewood back and sides, renamed C-5 Classical in '57.			
1954-1956		$800	$950
GS-35 Classical/Gut String 35			
1939-1942. Spruce top, mahogany back and sides, only 39 made.			
1939-1942		$1,900	$2,900
GS-85 Classical/Gut String 85			
1939-1942. Rosewood back and sides.			
1939-1942		$4,200	$6,000
GY (Army-Navy)			
1918-1921. Slightly arched top and back, low-end budget model.			
1918	Sheraton Brown	$800	$1,100
Harley Davidson Limited Edition			
1994-1995. Body 16" wide, flat-top, Harley Davidson in script and logo, 1500 sold through Harley dealers.			
1994-1995	Black	$2,250	$3,000
Heritage			
1964-1982. Flat-top dreadnought, square shoulders, rosewood back and sides (Brazilian until '67, Indian '68 on), bound top and back, natural finish.			
1964-1968	Brazilian rosewood	$2,400	$2,600
1968-1982	Indian rosewood	$1,100	$1,400
Heritage-12			
1968-1970. Flat-top dreadnought, 12 strings, Indian rosewood back and sides, bound top and back, natural finish.			
1968-1970		$900	$1,300
HG-00 (Hawaiian)			
1932-1942, 1991-present. Hawaiian version of L-00, 14 3/4" flat-top, mahogany back and sides, bound top, natural.			
1937-1942		$2,000	$2,500
HG-20 (Hawaiian)			
1929-1933. Hawaiian, 14 1/2" dreadnought-shaped, maple back and sides, round soundhole and 4 f-holes.			
1929-1933		$2,400	$2,500
HG-22 (Hawaiian)			
1929-1932. Dreadnought, 14", Hawaiian, round soundhole and 4 f-holes, white paint logo, very small number produced.			
1929-1932		$2,500	$2,800
HG-24 (Hawaiian)			
1929-1932. 16" Hawaiian, rosewood back and sides, round soundhole plus 4 f-holes, small number produced.			
1929-1932		$4,000	$4,500
HG-Century (Hawaiian)			
1937-1938. Hawaiian, 14 3/4" L-C Century of Progress.			
1937-1938		$2,400	$2,700
Howard Roberts Artist			
1976-1980. Full body single-cut archtop, soundhole, 1 humbucking pickup, gold hardware, ebony 'board, various colors.			
1976-1980		$2,100	$2,400
Howard Roberts Artist Double Pickup			
1979-1980. Two pickup version of HR Artist.			
1979-1980		$2,300	$2,600
Howard Roberts Custom			
1974-1981. Full body single-cut archtop, soundhole, 1 humbucking pickup, chrome hardware, rosewood 'board, various colors.			
1974-1981		$1,900	$2,200
Howard Roberts Fusion			
1979-1988. Single-cut, semi-hollowbody, 2 humbucking pickups, chrome hardware, ebony 'board, TP-6 tailpiece, various colors, renamed Howard Roberts Fusion IIL in '88.			
1979-1988		$1,500	$1,700
Howard Roberts Fusion III			
1991-present. Renamed from Howard Roberts Fusion IIL, same specs except for finger-style tailpiece and gold hardware, ebony or sunburst.			
1991-1999		$1,500	$1,700
Hummingbird			
1960-present. Flat-top acoustic, square shoulders, mahogany back and sides, bound body and neck.			
1960	Cherry Sunburst, 156 shipped	$3,800	$4,500
1961-1962	Cherry Sunburst, 1000 shipped	$3,600	$4,200

MODEL YEAR	FEATURES	EXC. COND. LOW	HIGH
1962-1963	Cherry Sunburst, maple option	$3,600	$4,200
1963-1964	Cherry Sunburst, 2700 shipped	$3,100	$3,700
1965-1966	Cherry Sunburst or natural	$2,600	$3,300
1967-1968	Screwed 'guard	$2,300	$3,000
1969-1970	Natural or sunburst	$1,800	$2,500
1971-1980	Double X, block markers	$1,600	$2,000
1981-1983	Non-volute neck	$1,500	$1,900
1984	Double para. Markers	$1,200	$1,400
1985-1988	Single X	$1,300	$1,500
1989-1999	25 1/2" scale	$1,400	$1,600
2000-2004		$1,500	$1,700

J-25

1983-1985. Flat-top, laminated spruce top, synthetic semi-round back, ebony 'board, natural or sunburst.

1983-1985		$375	$450

J-30

1985-1993. Dreadnought-size flat-top acoustic, mahogany back and sides, sunburst, renamed J-30 Montana in '94.

1985-1993		$900	$1,000

J-30 Montana

1994-1997. Renamed from J-30, dreadnought-size flat-top acoustic, mahogany back and sides, sunburst.

1994-1997		$1,100	$1,250

J-40

1971-1982. Dreadnought flat-top, mahogany back and sides, economy satin finish.

1971-1982	Natural satin finish	$700	$800

J-45

1942-1982, 1984-1993, 1999-present. Dreadnought flat-top, mahogany back and sides, round shoulders until '68 and '84 on, square shoulders '69-'82, sunburst finish (see J-50 for natural version) then natural finish also available in '90s, renamed J-45 Western in '94, renamed Early J-45 in '97 then renamed J-45 in '99. The prices noted are for all-original crack free instruments. A single professionally repaired minor crack that is nearly invisible will reduce the value only slightly. Two or more, or unsightly repaired cracks will devalue an otherwise excellent original acoustic instrument. Repaired cracks should be evaluated on a case-by-case basis.

1942	Sunburst, banner logo	$4,500	$5,000
1943	Sunburst, banner logo	$4,400	$4,800
1944	Sunburst, banner logo	$4,300	$4,700
1945	Sunburst, banner logo	$4,300	$4,600
1946	Sunburst, banner logo	$4,000	$4,500
1947	Sunburst	$3,600	$4,400
1948	Sunburst	$3,500	$4,300
1949	Sunburst	$3,300	$4,200
1950-1953	Sunburst	$3,000	$4,100

MODEL YEAR	FEATURES	EXC. COND. LOW	HIGH
1954-1955	Sunburst	$3,000	$4,000
1956-1957	Sunburst	$3,000	$4,000
1958-1959	Sunburst	$2,500	$3,500
1960-1962	Sunburst	$2,400	$3,000
1963	Sunburst	$2,300	$2,700
1964	Sunburst	$2,200	$2,600
1965	Sunburst	$2,000	$2,500
1966	Sunburst	$2,000	$2,200
1967	Sunburst	$2,000	$2,100
1968	Black, round shoulders	$2,000	$2,100
1968	Sunburst, round shoulders	$2,000	$2,100
1969	Sunburst, round shoulders	$2,000	$2,100
1969	Sunburst, square shoulders	$1,500	$1,700
1970	Sunburst, square shoulders	$1,400	$1,600
1971	Sunburst	$1,200	$1,500
1972	Sunburst	$1,200	$1,400
1973	Sunburst	$1,000	$1,300
1974	Sunburst	$900	$1,200
1975-1981	Sunburst	$850	$950
1984-1993	Various colors	$850	$1,000

Early J-45

1997-1998. J-45 model name for '97 and '98.

1997-1998		$1,150	$1,500

J-45 Buddy Holly Limited Edition

1995. 250 made.

1995		$1,550	$1,700

J-45 Celebrity

1985. Acoustic introduced for Gibson's 90th anniversary, spruce top, rosewood back and sides, ebony 'board, binding on body and 'board, only 90 made.

1985		$1,700	$1,800

J-45 Rosewood

2000s. Rosewood body, spruce top.

2000s		$1,500	$1,600

J-45 Western

1994-1997. Previously called J-45, name changed to Early J-45 in '97.

1994-1997		$1,000	$1,100

J-50

1942, 1945-1981, 1990-1995, 1998-present. Dreadnought flat-top, mahogany back and sides, round shoulders until '68, square shoulders after, natural finish (see J-45 for sunburst version).

1945		$4,300	$4,600
1946		$4,000	$4,500
1947		$3,600	$4,400
1948		$3,500	$4,300
1949		$3,300	$4,200
1950-1953		$3,000	$4,100
1954-1955		$3,000	$4,000
1956-1957		$3,000	$4,000
1958-1959		$2,500	$3,500
1960-1962		$2,400	$3,000
1963		$2,300	$2,700
1964		$2,200	$2,600
1965		$2,000	$2,500

Gibson Hummingbird

'40s Gibson J-45

1973 Gibson J-50 Deluxe

1956 Gibson J-160E

MODEL YEAR	FEATURES	EXC. COND. LOW	HIGH
1966		$2,000	$2,200
1967		$2,000	$2,100
1968	Round shoulders	$2,000	$2,100
1969	Round shoulders	$2,000	$2,100
1969	Square shoulders	$1,500	$1,700
1970	Square shoulders	$1,400	$1,600
1971		$1,200	$1,500
1972		$1,200	$1,400
1973		$1,000	$1,300
1974		$900	$1,200
1975-1981		$850	$950
1990-1995		$850	$1,000
1998-2001		$1,050	$1,350

J-55 (Jumbo 55) Limited Edition

1994 only. 16" flat-top, spruce top, mahogany back and sides, 100 made, sunburst.

1994		$1,550	$1,700

J-55 (Reintroduced)

1973-1982. Flat-top, laminated mahogany back and sides, arched back, square shoulders, sunburst. See Jumbo 55 listing for '39-'43 version.

1973-1982		$850	$1,000

J-60

1992-1999. Solid spruce top dreadnought, square shoulders, Indian rosewood back and sides, multiple bindings, natural or sunburst.

1992-1999		$900	$1,100

J-60 Curly Maple

1993 and 1996. Curly maple back and sides, limited edition from Montana shop, natural.

1993		$2,100	$2,500

J-100

1970-1974, 1985-1997, 2003-present. Flat-top jumbo, multi-bound top and back, black 'guard, dot inlays, mahogany back and sides, '80s version has maple back and sides, dot inlays and tortoise shell 'guard, current model has maple back and sides, no 'guard, and J-200 style block 'board inlays.

1972-1974	Mahogany	$1,500	$1,700
1985-1989	Maple	$1,300	$1,500
1990-1997		$1,200	$1,300

J-100 Xtra

1991-1997, 1999-2003. Jumbo flat-top, mahogany back and sides, moustache bridge, dot inlays, various colors, J-100 Xtra Cutaway also available, reintroduced in '99 with maple back and sides and single-bound body.

1991-1997		$1,150	$1,300

J-160E

1954-1979. Flat-top jumbo acoustic, 1 bridge P-90 pickup, tone and volume controls on front, sunburst finish, reintroduced as J-160 in '90.

1954-1961		$3,400	$3,900
1962	Beatles' vintage June '62	$4,000	$5,000
1963		$3,500	$4,000
1964	Lennon's 2nd model	$4,000	$4,500
1965		$3,200	$3,600
1966		$3,100	$3,500
1967		$2,800	$3,200
1968		$2,500	$2,800

MODEL YEAR	FEATURES	EXC. COND. LOW	HIGH
1969		$1,900	$2,500
1970		$1,500	$1,900
1971-1979		$1,300	$1,600

J-160E Reissue

1991-1997. Reintroduced J-160E with solid spruce top, solid mahogany back and sides.

1991-1997		$1,550	$1,800

J-180/Everly Brothers/The Everly Brothers

1986-present. Reissue of the '62-'72 Everly Brothers model, renamed The Everly Brothers ('92-'94), then The Everly ('94-'96), then back to J-180, black.

1986-1991		$1,100	$1,300
1992-1994	Everly Brothers	$1,100	$1,300
1994-1999	The Everly	$1,300	$1,500

J-185

1951-1959. Flat-top jumbo, figured maple back and sides, bound body and neck.

1951-1956	Natural	$8,500	$9,000
1951-1956	Sunburst	$8,000	$8,500
1957-1959	Natural	$7,500	$8,500
1957-1959	Sunburst	$7,000	$8,000

J-185 Reissue

1990-1995, 1999-present. Flat-top jumbo, figured maple back and sides, bound body and neck, natural or sunburst, limited run of 100 between '91-'92.

1990-1995		$1,650	$2,000

J-185 EC

1999-present. Acoustic/electric, rounded cutaway, sunburst.

1999-2002		$1,550	$1,900

J-200/SJ-200

1947-1996. Labeled SJ-200 until ca.'54. Super Jumbo flat-top, maple back and sides, see SJ-200 for '38-'42 rosewood back and sides model, called J-200 Artist for a time in the mid-'70s, renamed '50s Super Jumbo 200 in '97 and again renamed SJ-200 Reissue in '99, standard finish is sunburst.

1947-1949	Natural option	$13,000	$16,000
1947-1949	Sunburst	$12,000	$14,000
1950-1954	Natural option	$10,000	$13,000
1950-1954	Sunburst	$9,000	$11,000
1955-1959	Natural option	$9,500	$10,500
1955-1959	Sunburst	$8,500	$10,000
1960	Natural	$9,000	$10,000
1960	Sunburst	$7,500	$9,000
1961-1963	Natural option	$7,000	$9,000
1961-1963	Sunburst	$6,000	$7,500
1964	Natural	$5,500	$7,000
1964	Sunburst	$4,500	$6,500
1965	Natural or sunburst	$4,000	$5,500
1966-1967	Natural or sunburst	$3,500	$4,000
1969	Natural or sunburst	$2,700	$3,000
1970-1972	Natural or sunburst	$2,500	$2,700
1973	Natural or sunburst	$2,300	$2,500
1974-1992	Natural or sunburst	$2,200	$2,400
1985-1989	Natural or sunburst	$2,000	$2,300
1990-1996	Natural or sunburst	$1,900	$2,100
1996-1999	Natural or sunburst	$1,900	$2,100
2000s	Super J-200, natural	$2,100	$2,300

MODEL YEAR	FEATURES	EXC. COND. LOW	HIGH

J-200 Celebrity
1985-1987. Acoustic introduced for Gibson's 90th anniversary, spruce top, rosewood back, sides and 'board, binding on body and 'board, sunburst, only 90 made.

1985-1987		$2,600	$3,000

J-200 Koa
1994. Figured Hawaiian Koa back and sides, spruce top, natural.

1994		$2,600	$2,700

J-250 R
1972-1973, 1976-1978. A J-200 with rosewood back and sides, sunburst, only 20 shipped from Gibson.

1972-1973		$2,300	$2,700
1976-1978		$1,800	$2,300

J-2000/J-2000 Custom/J-2000 R
1991-1993. Cutaway acoustic, rosewood back and sides (a few had Brazilian rosewood or maple bodies), ebony 'board and bridge, Sitka spruce top, multiple bindings, sunburst or natural, 28 made. Name changed to J-2000 Custom in '93 when it became available only on a custom-order basis.

1986	J-2000 R, rosewood	$2,400	$2,600
1986	J-2000, maple	$2,400	$2,600
1992	Rosewood	$2,300	$2,500
1993-1996	J-2000 Custom	$2,300	$2,500
1999	J-2000 Custom Cutaway	$3,000	$3,400

JG-0
1970-1972. Economy square shouldered jumbo, follows Jubilee model in '70.

1970-1972		$750	$825

JG-12
1970. Economy square shouldered jumbo 12-string, follows Jubilee-12 model in '70.

1970		$600	$725

Johnny A Signature Series
Ca.2004-present. Thinline semi-hollow, sharp double-cut, flamed maple top, humbucking pickups, Johnny A truss rod cover, gold plated hardware, Bigsby vibrato (part of his signature style), sunburst, includes certificate of authenticity.

2004		$2,300	$2,400

Johnny Smith
1961-1989. Single-cut archtop, 1 humbucking pickup, gold hardware, multiple binding front and back, natural or sunburst.

1961-1962		$8,000	$9,000
1963-1964		$7,000	$8,000
1965-1967		$6,500	$7,000
1968-1969		$5,500	$6,500
1970-1989		$5,000	$5,500

Johnny Smith Double
1963-1989. Single-cut archtop, 2 humbucking pickups, gold hardware, multiple binding front and back, natural or sunburst.

1963-1964		$7,500	$8,500
1965-1967		$7,000	$7,500
1968-1969		$6,000	$7,000
1970-1989		$5,500	$6,000

Jubilee
1969-1970. Flat-top, laminated mahogany back and sides, single bound body, natural with black back and sides.

1969-1970		$750	$825

Jubilee Deluxe
1970-1971. Flat-top, laminated rosewood back and sides, multi-bound body, natural finish.

1970-1971		$900	$975

Jubilee-12
1969-1970. Flat-top, 12 strings, laminated mahogany back and sides, multi-bound, natural.

1969-1970		$675	$875

Jumbo
1934-1936. Gibson's first Jumbo flat-top, mahogany back and sides, round shoulders, bound top and back, sunburst, becomes the 16" Jumbo 35 in late-'36.

1934		$15,000	$20,000
1935		$14,000	$19,000
1936		$14,000	$18,000

Jumbo 35/J-35
1936-1942. Jumbo flat-top, mahogany back and sides, silkscreen logo, sunburst, reintroduced as J-35, square-shouldered dreadnought, in '83.

1936		$9,000	$13,000
1937		$8,500	$12,000
1938		$8,000	$10,000
1939		$7,500	$9,500
1940-1942		$7,000	$9,000

Jumbo 55/J-55
1939-1943. Flat-top dreadnought, round shoulders, mahogany back and sides, pearl inlaid logo, sunburst, reintroduced in '73 as J-55.

1939-1943		$15,000	$16,000

Jumbo Centennial Special
1994. Reissue of 1934 Jumbo, natural, 100 made.

1994		$2,200	$2,400

Junior Pro
1987-1989. Single-cut, mahogany body, KB-X tremolo system 1 humbucker pickup, black chrome hardware, various colors.

1987-1989		$375	$450

Kalamazoo Award Model
1978-1981. Single-cut archtop, bound f-holes, multi-bound top and back, 1 mini-humbucker, gold-plated hardware, woodgrain 'guard with bird and branch abalone inlay, highly figured natural or sunburst.

1978-1981	Natural	$13,000	$16,000
1978-1981	Sunburst	$12,000	$15,000

L-0
1926-1933, 1937-1942. Acoustic flat-top, maple back and sides '26-'27, mahogany after.

1926-1933	Amber Brown	$1,800	$2,500
1937-1942	Various colors	$1,800	$2,500

L-00
1932-1946. Acoustic flat-top, mahogany back and sides, bound top to '36 and bound top and back '37 on.

1932-1939	Black or sunburst	$2,100	$3,000
1940-1946	Natural or sunburst	$2,100	$3,000

1961 Gibson Johnny Smith

Gibson Johnny A. signature

GUITARS

1929 Gibson L-1

1915 Gibson L-4

MODEL YEAR	FEATURES	EXC. COND. LOW	HIGH
L-00/Blues King			
1991-1997. Mahogany back and sides, spruce top, ebony or sunburst.			
1991-1997		$1,100	$1,300
L-1 (Archtop)			
1902-1925. Acoustic archtop, single-bound top, back and soundhole, name continued on flat-top model in '26.			
1902-1907	Standard 12.5" body	$1,150	$1,300
1908-1925	Standard 13.5" body	$1,250	$1,400
L-1 (Flat-Top)			
1926-1937. Acoustic flat-top, maple back and sides '26-'27, mahogany after.			
1926-1927	13 1/2" maple body, 12 frets	$2,200	$3,150
1928-1930	13 1/2" mahogany body, 12 frets	$2,200	$3,150
1931	14 3/4" mahogany body	$2,200	$3,150
1932-1937	14 frets	$2,200	$3,150
L-2 (Archtop)			
1902-1926. Round soundhole archtop, pearl inlay on peghead, 1902-'07 available in 3 body sizes: 12.5" to 16", '24-'26 13.5" body width.			
1902-1907	Standard 12.5" body	$1,350	$1,500
1924-1926	Standard 13.5" body	$1,450	$1,600
L-2 (Flat-Top)			
1929-1935. Acoustic flat-top, rosewood back and sides except for mahogany in '31, triple-bound top and back, limited edition model in '94.			
1929-1930	Natural, 14 3/4" body, 13 frets	$3,300	$4,000
1931	Argentine Gray, 13 frets	$2,300	$3,300
1932-1933	Natural, 13 frets	$2,300	$3,300
1934-1935	Natural, 14 frets	$2,300	$3,300
L-3 (Archtop)			
1902-1933. Acoustic archtop, available in 3 sizes: 12 1/2", 13 1/2", 16".			
1902-1907	Standard 12.5" body	$1,550	$1,700
1908-1926	Standard 13.5" body	$1,650	$1,800
1927-1929	Oval soundhole	$1,850	$2,100
L-4			
1912-1956. Acoustic archtop, 16" wide.			
1912-1927	Oval soundhole	$2,000	$2,500
1928-1934	Round soundhole	$2,000	$2,500
1935-1945	F-holes	$2,000	$2,500
1946-1956	Crown peghead inlay, triple bound	$1,800	$2,200
L-4 A			
2000s. 15 3/4" lower bout, mid-size jumbo style with rounded cutaway, factory electronics with preamp.			
2000s		$1,100	$1,200
L-4 C/L-4 CN			
1949-1971. Single-cut acoustic archtop.			
1949-1959	Natural	$3,000	$3,500
1949-1959	Sunburst	$2,800	$3,000
1960-1965	Natural	$2,900	$3,400
1960-1965	Sunburst	$2,700	$2,900
1966-1969	Sunburst	$2,500	$3,000
1969-1971	Sunburst	$2,400	$2,600

MODEL YEAR	FEATURES	EXC. COND. LOW	HIGH
L-4 CES			
1958, 1969, 1986-present. Single pointed cutaway archtop, 2 humbuckers, gold parts, natural or sunburst, now part of Gibson's Custom Collection.			
1986-2003		$2,200	$2,400
L-4 Special Tenor/Plectrum			
Late-1920. Limited edition 4-string flat-top.			
1929		$2,200	$2,500
L-5			
1922-1958. Acoustic archtop, non-cut, multiple bindings, Lloyd Loar label until '24, 17" body by '35, Master Model label until '27, sunburst with natural option later.			
1922-1924	Lloyd Loar label	$55,000	$60,000
1924	Lloyd Loar signed (Mar-Dec)	$60,000	$65,000
1925-1927	Master Model label	$25,000	$30,000
1928	Last dot markers	$15,000	$25,000
1929	Early 1929	$10,000	$13,000
1929-1930	Block markers	$10,000	$12,000
1931-1932	Kaufman vibrola	$12,000	$14,000
1931-1932	Standard trapeze	$9,000	$10,500
1933-1934	16" body	$8,000	$9,500
1935-1940	17" body	$5,500	$7,500
1939-1940	Natural option	$6,500	$8,500
1946-1949	Natural option	$6,500	$8,000
1946-1949	Sunburst	$5,000	$6,000
1950-1958	Natural	$5,000	$7,000
1950-1958	Sunburst	$5,000	$6,000
L-5 Premier/L-5 P			
1939-1947. Introduced as L-5 Premier (L-5 P) and renamed L-5 C in '48, single rounded cutaway acoustic archtop.			
1939-1940	Natural option	$18,000	$20,000
1939-1940	Sunburst	$16,000	$18,000
L-5 C			
1948-1982. Renamed from L-5 Premier (L-5 P), single rounded cutaway acoustic archtop, sunburst.			
1948		$13,000	$15,000
1949		$12,000	$15,000
1950-1959		$12,000	$13,000
1960-1962		$9,000	$11,000
1964-1965		$8,000	$10,000
1966-1967		$7,500	$9,000
1968		$7,000	$8,500
1969		$6,000	$7,500
1970-1972		$5,000	$7,000
1973-1975		$4,500	$5,500
1976-1982		$4,000	$5,000
L-5 CES			
1951-present. Electric version of L-5 C, single round cutaway (pointed mid-'60-'69), archtop, 2 pickups (P-90s '51-'53, Alnico Vs '54-mid-'57, humbuckers after), now part of Gibson's Historic Collection.			
1951-1957	Natural, single coils	$14,000	$17,000
1951-1957	Sunburst, single coils	$12,000	$14,000
1958-1960	Natural, humbuckers	$25,000	$30,000

The *Vintage Guitar Price Guide* shows low to high values for items in all-original excellent condition, and, where applicable, with original case or cover.

MODEL YEAR	FEATURES	EXC. COND. LOW	HIGH
1958-1960	Sunburst, humbuckers	$18,000	$21,000
1961-1962	Natural, PAFs	$18,000	$21,000
1961-1962	Sunburst, PAFs	$15,000	$18,000
1963-1964	Natural, pat. #	$12,000	$14,000
1963-1964	Sunburst, pat. #	$9,000	$11,500
1965-1969	Natural	$7,000	$9,000
1965-1969	Sunburst	$6,000	$8,000
1970-1972	Various colors	$5,500	$6,500
1973-1984	Kalamazoo made	$5,500	$6,200
1985-1992	Nashville made	$5,500	$6,000

L-5 CES Custom Shop Historic Collection

1990s. Historic Collection Series, sunburst.

1990s	100th Anniversary, black	$6,400	$6,600
1990s	Sunburst	$5,500	$6,300

L-5 CT (George Gobel)

1959-1961. Single-cut, thinline archtop acoustic, some were built with pickups, cherry, currently available in Gibson's Historic Collection.

1959-1961		$14,000	$19,000

L-5 CT Reissue

1998-present. Natural.

1998		$4,500	$5,000

L-5 S

1972-1985, 2004-present. Single-cut solidbody, multi-bound body and neck, gold hardware, 2 pickups (low impedence '72-'74, humbuckers '75 on), offered in natural, cherry sunburst or vintage sunburst, 1 humbucker version reissued in 2004 from Gibson's Custom, Art & Historic division.

1972-1974	Natural, gold hardware, low impedence pickups	$3,000	$3,500
1972-1974	Sunburst, low impedence pickups	$2,500	$3,300
1975-1980	Natural, gold hardware, humbuckers	$3,500	$4,500
1975-1980	Sunburst, humbuckers	$3,000	$4,000

L-5 Studio

1996-2000. Normal L-5 dual pickup features, marble-style 'guard, translucent finish..

1996-2000		$2,300	$2,700

L-5 Wes Montgomery Custom Shop

1993-present. Various colors.

1993-1999		$4,400	$4,600

L-6 S

1973-1975. Single-cut solidbody, 2 humbucking pickups, stop tailpiece, cherry or natural, renamed L-6 S Custom in '75.

1973-1975		$650	$850

L-6 S Custom

1975-1980. Renamed from the L-6 S, single-cut solidbody, 2 humbucking pickups, stop tailpiece, cherry or natural.

1975-1980		$650	$850

L-6 S Deluxe

1975-1981. Single-cut solidbody, 2 humbucking pickups, strings-thru-body design, cherry or natural.

1975-1981		$650	$850

L-7

1932-1956. Acoustic archtop, bound body and neck, fleur-de-lis peghead inlay, 16" body '32-'34, 17" body X-braced top late-'34.

1932-1934	16" body	$2,800	$3,200
1935-1939	17" body, X-braced	$2,800	$3,300
1940-1950	Natural or sunburst	$2,700	$3,100
1951-1956	Natural or sunburst	$2,500	$3,000

L-7 C

1948-1972. Single-cut acoustic archtop, triple-bound top, sunburst or natural finish. Gibson revived the L-7 C name for a new acoustic archtop in 2002.

1948-1949	Natural	$4,500	$4,900
1948-1949	Sunburst	$3,800	$4,300
1950-1951	Natural	$4,300	$4,700
1950-1951	Sunburst	$3,600	$4,100
1952-1964	Natural	$3,500	$3,800
1952-1964	Sunburst	$3,100	$3,600
1965-1967	Sunburst	$3,000	$3,200
1968-1971	Sunburst	$2,900	$3,000

L-10

1929-1939. Acoustic archtop, single-bound body and 'board.

1929-1933	Black, 16" body	$2,500	$3,000
1934-1939	Black or sunburst, 17" body, X-braced	$3,000	$3,300

L-12

1930-1955. Acoustic archtop, single-bound body, 'guard, neck and headstock, gold-plated hardware, sunburst.

1930-1934	16" body	$3,200	$3,400
1935-1938	17" body, X-braced	$3,200	$3,400
1939-1941	Parallel top braced	$3,200	$3,400
1946-1955	Post-war	$3,000	$3,200

L-12 Premier/L-12 P

1947-1950. L-12 with rounded cutaway, sunburst.

1947-1950		$4,500	$4,700

L-30

1935-1943. Acoustic archtop, single-bound body, black or sunburst.

1935-1943		$1,100	$1,400

L-37

1937-1941. 14-3/4" acoustic archtop, flat back, single-bound body and 'guard, sunburst.

1937-1941		$1,100	$1,400

L-48

1946-1971. 16" acoustic archtop, single-bound body, sunburst.

1946-1965		$950	$1,100
1966-1971		$650	$800

L-50

1932-1971. 14 3/4" wide acoustic archtop, flat or arched back, round soundhole or f-holes, pearl logo pre-war, decal logo post-war, sunburst.

1932-1933	14 3/4" body, round hole	$1,400	$1,600
1934	Longer body, f-holes	$1,400	$1,600

Gibson L-5 CT reissue

Gibson L-50

To get the most from this book, be sure to read "Using *The Guide*" in the introduction.

Gibson Le Grande

Gibson Les Paul Indian

MODEL YEAR	FEATURES	EXC. COND. LOW	HIGH
1935-1943	16" body, f-holes	$1,400	$1,600
1946-1965	Decal logo, trapezoid inlay	$1,200	$1,400
1966-1971		$1,000	$1,200

L-75

1932-1939. 14 3/4" archtop with round soundhole and flat back, size increased to 16" with arched back in '35, small button tuners, dot markers, lower-end style trapeze tailpiece, pearl script logo, sunburst.

1932-1934	14 3/4" body	$1,900	$2,200
1935-1939	16" body	$2,400	$2,700

L-130

2000s. 14 7/8" lower bout, small jumbo, solid spruce top, solid bubinga back and sides, factory electronics with preamp.

2000s		$1,100	$1,200

L-C Century

1933-1941. Curly maple back and sides, bound body, white pearloid 'board and peghead (all years) and headstock (until '38), sunburst.

1933-1941		$3,700	$4,000

L-C Reissue

1994. Pearloid headstock and 'board.

1994		$2,300	$2,500

LC-1 Cascade

2002-present. Released November '02, LC-Series acoustic/electric, advanced L-00-style, solid quilted maple back and sides.

2002-2003		$900	$1,300

LC-3 Caldera

2003-present. 14 3/4" flat-top, soft cutaway, solid cedar top, solid flamed Koa back and sides, fancy appointments.

2003		$1,900	$2,000

Le Grande

1993-present. Electric archtop, 17", formerly called Johnny Smith.

1993-2003		$5,500	$7,000

Les Paul

Following are models that bear the Les Paul name, beginning with the original Les Paul Model. All others are listed alphabetically as follows:

Les Paul Model
'52 Les Paul Goldtop
'54 Les Paul Goldtop
'56 Les Paul Goldtop
'57 Les Paul Goldtop
'57 Les Paul Jr. Historic Collection
'58 Les Paul Flametop
'59 Les Paul Flametop Historic Collection
'60 Corvette (Custom Shop)
'60 Les Paul Flametop
'60 Les Paul Jr. Historic Collection
Les Paul (All Maple)
Les Paul 25/50 Anniversary
Les Paul 25th Silver Anniversary (Guitar Center)
Les Paul 30th Anniversary
Les Paul 40th Anniversary (from 1952)
Les Paul 40th Anniversary (from 1959)
Les Paul 55

Les Paul Ace Frehley Signature
Les Paul Artisan
Les Paul Artist/Les Paul Active
Les Paul Bird's-Eye Standard
Les Paul Centennial
Les Paul Classic
Les Paul Classic Plus
Les Paul Classic Premium Plus
Les Paul Custom
Les Paul Custom 20th Anniversary
Les Paul Custom 35th Anniversary
Les Paul Custom '54
Les Paul Custom Historic '54
Les Paul Custom Historic '57 Black Beauty/2-pickup
Les Paul Custom Historic '57 Black Beauty/3-pickup
Les Paul Custom Historic '68
Les Paul Custom Lite
Les Paul Custom Lite (Show Case Ed.)
Les Paul Custom Plus
Les Paul Custom SG 30th Anniversary
Les Paul DC Pro
Les Paul DC Standard
Les Paul DC Standard Plus
Les Paul DC Studio
Les Paul Deluxe
Les Paul Deluxe Hall of Fame
Les Paul Deluxe Limited Edition
Les Paul Dickey Betts Goldtop
Les Paul Dickey Betts Red Top
Les Paul Elegant (Custom Shop)
Les Paul Gary Moore Model
Les Paul Guitar Trader Reissue
Les Paul Heritage 80
Les Paul Heritage 80 Award
Les Paul Heritage 80 Elite
Les Paul Indian Motorcycle
Les Paul Jim Beam (Custom Shop)
Les Paul Jimmy Page Signature
Jimmy Page Signature Custom Shop
Les Paul Jimmy Wallace Reissue
Les Paul Joe Perry Signature
Les Paul Jr.
Les Paul Jr. 3/4
Les Paul Jr. Double Cutaway
Les Paul Jumbo
Les Paul KM (Kalamazoo Model)
Les Paul Leo's Reissue
Les Paul Limited Edition (3-tone)
Les Paul Old Hickory
Les Paul Pee Wee
Les Paul Personal
Les Paul Pro-Deluxe
Les Paul Professional
Les Paul Recording
Les Paul Reissue Flametop
Les Paul Reissue Goldtop
Les Paul Signature
Les Paul SmartWood Standard
Les Paul SmartWood Studio
Les Paul Special
Les Paul Special (Reissue)

The *Vintage Guitar Price Guide* shows low to high values for items in all-original excellent condition, and, where applicable, with original case or cover.

MODEL YEAR	FEATURES	EXC. COND. LOW	HIGH
Les Paul Special 3/4			
Les Paul Special Centennial			
Les Paul Special Custom Shop			
Les Paul Special Double Cutaway			
Les Paul Spotlight Special			
Les Paul Standard (Sunburst)			
Les Paul Standard (SG body)			
Les Paul Standard (reintroduced)			
Les Paul Standard '58			
Les Paul Standard '82			
Les Paul Standard Lite			
Les Paul Standard Plus			
Les Paul Standard Sparkle			
Les Paul Strings and Things Standard			
Les Paul Studio			
Les Paul Studio Baritone			
Les Paul Studio Custom			
Les Paul Studio Gem			
Les Paul Studio Gothic			
Les Paul Studio Lite			
Les Paul Studio Plus			
Les Paul Studio Swamp Ash/Swamp Ash Studio			
Les Paul Supreme			
Les Paul Supreme Figured			
Les Paul Tie Dye Custom Shop			
Les Paul TV			
Les Paul TV 3/4			
Les Paul Ultima			
Les Paul Voodoo/Voodoo Les Paul			
Les Paul XR-I/XR-II/XR-III			
Les Paul Zack Wylde Signature			
The Les Paul			
The Paul			
The Paul Firebrand Deluxe			
The Paul II			

Les Paul Model

1952-1958. The Goldtop, 2 P-90 pickups until mid-'57, humbuckers after, trapeze tailpiece until late-'53, stud tailpiece/bridge '53-mid-'55, Tune-o-matic bridge '55-'58, renamed Les Paul Standard in '58.

1952	1st made, unbound neck	$15,000	$17,000
1952	5/8" knobs	$10,000	$11,000
1952	5/8" knobs, all gold option, trapeze	$10,000	$11,000
1953	1/2" knobs, early-'53 trapeze	$9,500	$10,500
1953	1/2" knobs, late-'53 wrap-around	$15,000	$16,500
1953	1/2" knobs, mid-'53 wrap-around	$13,000	$14,000
1955-1957	All gold option, P-90s	$26,000	$28,000
1955-1957	Tune-o-matic, all mahogany body	$22,000	$24,000
1955-1957	Tune-o-matic, P-90s	$25,000	$27,000
1957-1958	All mahogany, stud tail, humbuckers	$50,000	$53,000

MODEL YEAR	FEATURES	EXC. COND. LOW	HIGH
1957-1958	Bigsby, humbuckers	$40,000	$43,000
1957-1958	Stud tail, humbuckers	$55,000	$60,000

'52 Les Paul Goldtop

1990s-present. By '98 The Gibson Historic Collection offered guitars reissued with incredible accuracy. Goldtop finish, two P-90s, '52-style trapeze tailpiece/bridge.

1997		$1,700	$1,900

'54 Les Paul Goldtop

1990s-present. Goldtop finish, 2 P-90s, '53-'54 stud tailpiece/bridge.

1997		$1,700	$1,900

'56 Les Paul Goldtop

1991-present. Renamed from Les Paul Reissue Goldtop. Goldtop finish, 2 P-90 pickups, now part of Gibson's Historic Collection.

1991-2002		$1,700	$1,900

'57 Les Paul Goldtop

1993-present. Goldtop finish, 2 humbuckers, now part of Gibson's Historic Collection.

1993-1999		$1,700	$1,990

'57 Les Paul Jr. Historic Collection

1998-present. High quality Historic reissue of '57 slab body, double-cut Les Paul Jr.

1990s	TV Yellow	$1,400	$1,800

'58 Les Paul Flametop

Part of Gibson's Historic Collection, sunburst.

2001		$2,800	$3,000

'59 Les Paul Flametop Historic Collection

1991-present. Renamed from Les Paul Reissue Flametop, flame maple top, 2 humbuckers, thick '59-style neck, sunburst finish, part of Gibson's Historic Collection. By '98 Gibson guaranteed only AAA Premium grade maple tops would be used.

1991-2004		$3,000	$3,500

'60 Corvette (Custom Shop)

1995-1997. Custom Shop Les Paul, Chevrolet Corvette styling from '60, distinctive styling, offered in 6 colors.

1995-1997		$4,000	$5,500

'60 Les Paul Flametop

1991-1999. Renamed from Les Paul Reissue Flametop, flame maple top, 2 humbuckers, thinner neck, sunburst finish, part of Gibson's Historic Collection.

1991-1999		$3,000	$3,500

'60 Les Paul Jr. Historic Collection

Introduced in 1992. High quality Historic reissue of '60 slab body, double-cut Les Paul Jr., cherry.

1992-2003		$1,400	$1,800

Les Paul (All Maple)

1984. Limited run, all maple body, Super 400-style inlay, gold hardware.

1984		$3,000	$3,400

Les Paul 25/50 Anniversary

1978-1979. Regular model with 25/50 inlay on headstock, sunburst.

1978-1979	Moderate flame	$2,700	$3,000
1978-1979	Premium flame	$3,300	$4,500

1952 Gibson Les Paul Model

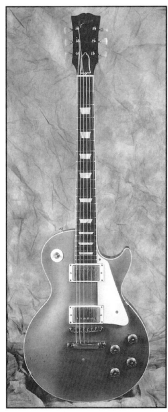

1957 Gibson Les Paul Model

GUITARS

1977 Gibson Les Paul Artisan

1956 Gibson Les Paul Custom

MODEL YEAR	FEATURES	EXC. COND. LOW	HIGH

Les Paul 25th Silver Anniversary (Guitar Center)

1978. Special order of 50 Les Paul Customs with metallic silver top, back, sides and neck, commissioned by Guitar Center of California, most have 25th Anniversary etched in tailpiece.

1978		$2,300	$2,500

Les Paul 30th Anniversary

1982-1984. Features of a 1958 Les Paul Goldtop, 2 humbuckers, 30th Anniversary inlay on 19th fret.

1982-1984		$2,400	$2,600

Les Paul 40th Anniversary (from 1952)

1991-1992. Black finish, 2 soapbar P-100 pickups, gold hardware, stop tailpiece, 40th Anniversary inlay at 12th fret.

1991-1992		$1,800	$1,900

Les Paul 40th Anniversary (from 1959)

1999. Reissue Historic, highly figured.

1999		$3,300	$3,800

Les Paul 55

1974, 1976-1981. Single-cut Special reissue, 2 pickups.

1974	Sunburst	$750	$900
1976-1981	Sunburst or Wine Red	$750	$900

Les Paul Ace Frehley Signature

1997-2001. Ace's signature inlay at 15th fret, 3 humbuckers, sunburst.

1997-2001		$2,700	$3,000

Les Paul Artisan

1976-1982. Carved maple top, 2 or 3 humbuckers, gold hardware, hearts and flowers inlays on 'board and headstock, ebony, sunburst or walnut.

1976-1982		$2,000	$2,400

Les Paul Artist/L.P. Artist/Les Paul Active

1979-1982. Two humbuckers (3 optional), active electronics, gold hardware, 3 mini-switches, multibound.

1979	Sunburst	$1,350	$1,500
1980-1982	Ebony or sunburst	$1,350	$1,500

Les Paul Bird's-Eye Standard

Birdseye top, gold hardware, 2 humbucking pickups.

1999	Transparent amber	$1,900	$2,100

Les Paul Centennial ('56 LP Standard Goldtop)

1994. Part of the Guitar of the Month program commemorating Gibson's 100th year, limited edition of 100, Goldtop Les Paul mahogany body with '56-style configuration, gold hardware, gold truss rod plate, gold medallion, engraved light-gold 'guard.

1994		$4,500	$6,000

Les Paul Centennial ('59 LP Special)

1994. Part of the Guitar of the Month program commemorating Gibson's 100th year, limited edition, slab body Les Paul Special-style configuration, 100 made, gold hardware, P-90 pickups, gold medallion, commemorative engraving in 'guard, cherry.

1994		$3,000	$4,000

MODEL YEAR	FEATURES	EXC. COND. LOW	HIGH

Les Paul Classic

1990-1998, 2001-present. Early models have 1960 on pickguard, 2 exposed humbucker pickups, Les Paul Model on peghead until '93, Les Paul Classic afterwards.

1990-1998	All gold neck and body	$1,600	$1,700
1990-1998	Various colors, plain top	$1,300	$1,500
2001-2005	Various colors	$1,300	$1,500

Les Paul Classic Plus

1991-1996, 1999-2000. Les Paul Classic with fancier maple top, 2 exposed humbucker pickups.

1991-1996	Price depends on top figure	$1,700	$2,100

Les Paul Classic Premium Plus

1993-1996, 2000-2002. Les Paul Classic with AAA-grade flame maple top, 2 exposed humbucker pickups.

1993-1996	Price depends on top figure	$2,100	$2,700

Les Paul Custom

1953-1963 (renamed SG Custom late-1963), 1968-present. Les Paul body shape except for SG body '61-'63, 2 pickups (3 humbuckers mid-'57-'63 and '68-'70, 3 pickups were optional various years after).

1954-1957	Single coils	$12,500	$14,000
1954-1957	Single coils with factory Bigsby	$11,000	$12,000
1957-1960	Humbuckers	$20,000	$22,000
1957-1960	Humbuckers with factory Bigsby	$16,000	$18,000
1961-1963	Black, SG body	$9,000	$12,000
1961-1963	White, SG body	$8,000	$9,000
1968-1969	Black, 1-piece body	$8,000	$8,500
1968-1969	Black, 3-piece body	$6,000	$6,500
1970-1972	Volute, 2 pickups	$2,200	$2,400
1970-1972	Volute, 3 pickups	$2,400	$2,700
1973-1974	Volute, 2 pickups	$2,100	$2,300
1973-1974	Volute, 3 pickups	$2,300	$2,500
1975-1976	Volute, 2 pickups, chrome hardware	$1,700	$2,000
1975-1976	Volute, 2 pickups, gold hardware	$1,800	$2,100
1977-1978	Volute, 2 pickups	$1,650	$1,800
1977-1978	Volute, 3 pickups	$2,000	$2,200
1979-1982	2 pickups	$1,650	$1,800
1979-1982	Silverburst, volute, 2 pickups	$2,500	$3,000
1983-1985	2 pickups	$1,550	$1,700
1983-1985	3 pickups	$1,700	$1,900
1986-1989	Various colors	$1,550	$1,700
1990-1999	Limited Edition color series	$1,750	$1,900
1990-1999	Various colors	$1,550	$1,700
2000-2002	Various colors	$1,600	$1,900

Les Paul Custom 20th Anniversary

1974. Regular 2-pickup Custom, with 20th Anniversary inlay at 15th fret, black or white.

1974		$2,000	$2,200

The Official Vintage Guitar Magazine Price Guide 2006 **Gibson** LP Custom 35th Ann. — **Gibson** LP Guitar Trader **97**

GUITARS

MODEL YEAR	FEATURES	EXC. COND. LOW	HIGH

Les Paul Custom 35th Anniversary
1989. Gold hardware, 3 pickups, carved, solid mahogany body and neck, 35th Anniversary inlay on headstock, black.

| 1989 | | $2,100 | $2,400 |

Les Paul Custom '54
1972-1973. Reissue of 1954 Custom, black finish, Alnico V and P-90 pickups.

| 1972-1973 | Black | $3,200 | $3,600 |

Les Paul Custom Historic '54
1990s Historic Collection, 1954 appointments and pickup configuration, black, gold hardware.

| 1997-2000 | | $1,900 | $2,200 |

Les Paul Custom Historic '57 Black Beauty/2-pickup
1991-present. Black finish, gold hardware, 2 humbucker pickups, part of Gibson's Historic Collection.

| 1991-1999 | | $1,700 | $2,000 |

Les Paul Custom Historic '57 Black Beauty/3-pickup
1991-present. Black finish, gold hardware, 3 humbucker pickups, part of Gibson's Historic Collection.

| 1991-1999 | | $1,800 | $2,100 |

Les Paul Custom Historic '68
Historic Collection, ebony block marked fretboard, gold hardware, flamed maple top available, 2 pickups.

| 2000-2001 | | $2,000 | $2,300 |

Les Paul Custom Lite
1987-1990. Full-thickness carved maple top, ebony 'board, pearl block position markers, gold hardware, PAF pickups, bound neck, headstock and body, black.

| 1987-1990 | | $1,400 | $1,800 |

Les Paul Custom Lite (Show Case Ed.)
1988. Showcase Edition, only 200 made, gold top.

| 1988 | | $2,000 | $2,100 |

Les Paul Custom Plus
1991-1998. Regular Custom with figured maple top, sunburst finish or colors.

| 1991-1998 | | $1,700 | $2,200 |

Les Paul Custom SG 30th Anniversary
1991. 30th Anniversary limited edition of SG-style Les Paul Custom introduced in '61, Opaque TV Yellow finish including back of neck, typical split-diamond headstock inlay, block markers, tune-o-matic, gold hardware, 30th Anniversary logo.

| 1991 | | $1,900 | $2,000 |

Les Paul DC Pro
1997-1998. Custom Shop, body like a '59 Les Paul Junior, carved highly figured maple top, various options.

| 1997-1998 | | $1,700 | $1,900 |

Les Paul DC Standard
1998-1999, 2001-present. Offset double-cut, highly flamed maple top, mahogany set-neck, translucent lacquer finishes in various colors, typical Les Paul Model stencil logo on headstock and 'Standard' notation on truss rod cover, reintroduced as Standard Lite in '99 but without Les Paul designation on headstock or truss rod cover.

| 1998-1999 | | $1,100 | $1,300 |

MODEL YEAR	FEATURES	EXC. COND. LOW	HIGH

Les Paul DC Standard Plus
2001-present. Reintroduction of LP DC Standard, flamed top, gold hardware, cherry.

| 2001-2004 | | $1,050 | $1,150 |

Les Paul DC Studio
1997-1999. DC Series double-cut like late '50s models, carved maple top, 2 humbucker pickups, various colors.

| 1997-1999 | | $675 | $725 |

Les Paul Deluxe
1969-1985. In 1969, the Goldtop Les Paul Standard was renamed the Deluxe. Two mini-humbuckers (regular humbuckers optional in mid-'70s). Mid-'70s sparkle tops, made at the request of the Sam Ash chain, are worth more than standard finishes. The market slightly favors the Goldtop finish, but practically speaking condition is more important than finish, such that all finishes fetch about the same amount (with the exception of the sparkle finish). Initially, the Deluxe was offered only as a Goldtop and the first year models are more highly prized than the others. Cherry sunburst was offered in '71, cherry in '71-'75, walnut in '71-'72, brown sunburst in '72-'79, natural in '75, red sparkle in '75 only, blue sparkle in '75-'77, wine red/see-thru red offered '75-'85. In '99, the Deluxe was reissued for its 30th anniversary.

1969	Goldtop	$3,400	$3,800
1970	Goldtop	$2,500	$2,800
1971-1975	Various colors	$2,000	$2,300
1975	Red sparkle, fewer made	$4,000	$4,500
1975-1977	Blue sparkle, more made	$3,100	$3,500
1976-1979	Various colors	$1,900	$2,100
1980-1985	Various colors	$1,725	$1,900

Les Paul Deluxe Hall of Fame
1991. All gold finish.

| 1991 | | $1,725 | $1,900 |

Les Paul Deluxe Limited Edition
1999-2002. Limited edition reissue with Les Paul Standard features and Deluxe mini-humbuckers, black.

| 1999-2002 | | $1,300 | $1,500 |

Les Paul Dickey Betts Goldtop
2001-2003. Aged gold top.

| 2001-2003 | | $5,200 | $5,700 |

Les Paul Dickey Betts Red Top
2003. Transparent red, gold hardware.

| 2003 | | $2,600 | $2,900 |

Les Paul Elegant (Custom Shop)
1996-present. Custom Shop highly flamed maple top, abalone Custom Shop headstock inlay.

| 1996-1999 | | $2,400 | $2,700 |

Les Paul Gary Moore Model
2000-2002. Signature Series model, Gary Moore script logo on truss rod cover, flamed maple top.

| 2000-2002 | | $1,850 | $2,050 |

Les Paul Guitar Trader Reissue
1982-1983. Special order flametop Les Paul by the Guitar Trader Company, Redbank, New Jersey. Approximately 47 were built, the first 15 guitars ordered

Gibson Les Paul DC Classic

Gibson Les Paul Deluxe

GUITARS

Gibson Les Paul Heritage 80

1956 Gibson Les Paul Junior

MODEL YEAR	FEATURES	EXC. COND. LOW	HIGH

received original PAFs, all were double black bobbins (except 1 Zebra and 1 double white), 3 of the guitars were made in the '60-style. The PAF equipped models were based on order date and not build date. The serial number series started with 9 1001 and a second serial number was put in the control cavity based upon the standard Gibson serial number system, which allowed for exact build date identification. Gibson's pickup designer in the early-'80s was Tim Shaw and the pickups used for the last 32 guitars have been nicknamed "Shaw PAFs." After Gibson's short run for Guitar Trader, 10 non-Gibson replica or bootleg Les Pauls were made. These GT bootleg guitars have a poorly done Gibson logo and other telltale issues.

1982-1983	Actual PAFs installed	$7,800	$8,500
1982-1983	Shaw PAFs	$5,100	$5,500
1983	"Bootleg" Les Paul	$1,500	$2,500

Les Paul Heritage 80
1980-1982. Copy of '59 Les Paul Standard, curly maple top, mahogany body, rosewood 'board, sunburst.

1980-1982	Sunburst	$2,500	$2,700

Les Paul Heritage 80 Award
1982. Ebony 'board, 1-piece mahogany neck, gold-plated hardware, sunburst.

1982		$3,200	$3,500

Les Paul Heritage 80 Elite
1980-1982. Copy of '59 Les Paul Standard, quilted maple top, mahogany body and neck, ebony 'board, chrome hardware, sunburst.

1980-1982		$2,900	$3,200

Les Paul Indian Motorcycle
2002. 100 made, has Indian script logo on fretboard and chrome cast war bonnet on the body, crimson red and cream white.

2002		$3,500	$4,000

Les Paul Jim Beam (Custom Shop)
2000. Jim Beam logo art on top of guitar, award-ribbon-style B Bean logo on headstock, white background with logo, JBLP serial number series.

2000		$1,550	$1,650

Les Paul Jimmy Page Signature
1995-1999. Jimmy Page signature on 'guard, mid-grade figured top, push-pull knobs for phasing and coil-tapping, Grover tuners, gold-plated hardware. This is not the '04 Custom Shop Jimmy Page Signature Series Les Paul (see separate listing).

1995	Highly figured, 1st year	$4,000	$4,300
1995	Low to moderate figure, 1st year	$3,600	$4,000
1996-1999	Highly figured	$3,700	$4,100
1996-1999	Low to moderate figure	$3,500	$3,900

Jimmy Page Signature Les Paul Custom Shop
2004. Introduced at the January '04 NAMM Show, 175 planned production, the first 25 were personally inspected, played-in, and autographed by Jimmy Page. Initial retail price for first 25 was $25,000, the

MODEL YEAR	FEATURES	EXC. COND. LOW	HIGH

remaining 150 instruments had an initial retail price of $16,400. Cosmetically aged by Tom Murphy to resemble Page's No. 1 Les Paul in color fade, weight, top flame, slab cut attribution on the edges, neck size and profile.

2004	1st 25 made	$22,000	$25,000
2004	Factory order 26-150	$14,000	$16,000

Les Paul Jimmy Wallace Reissue
1978-1997. Les Paul Standard '59 reissue with Jimmy Wallace on truss rod cover, special order by dealer Jimmy Wallace, figured maple top, sunburst.

1978-1983	Kalamazoo-made	$4,400	$4,900
1983-1989	Nashville-made	$3,500	$3,900
1990-1997		$3,500	$3,900

Les Paul Joe Perry Signature
1997-2001. Unbound slab body with push-pull knobs and Joe Perry signature below bridge, Bone-Yard logo model with typical Les Ppaul Standard bound body, configuration and appointments.

1997-2001	Bone-Yard option with logo	$2,400	$2,600
1997-2001	Unbound standard model	$1,800	$2,000

Les Paul Jr.
1954-1963, 1986-1992. One P-90 pickup, single-cut solidbody '54-mid-'58, double-cut '58-early-'61, SG body '61-'63, renamed SG Jr. in '63, reintroduced as single-cut for '86-'92, reissued as the 1957 Les Paul Jr. Single Cutaway in '98.

1954	Sunburst, single-cut	$3,800	$4,500
1955-1958	Sunburst, single-cut	$3,700	$4,400
1959-1961	Cherry, double-cut	$3,400	$4,100
1961-1963	Cherry, SG body	$2,400	$2,600

Les Paul Jr. 3/4
1956-1961. One P-90 pickup, short-scale, single-cut solidbody '54-mid-'58, double-cut '58-early-'61.

1956-1958	Sunburst, single-cut	$2,450	$2,700
1958-1961	Cherry, double-cut	$2,300	$2,500

Les Paul Jr. Double Cutaway
1986-1992, 1995-1996. Copy of '50s double-cut Jr., cherry or sunburst, reissued as the 1957 Les Paul Jr. Double Cutaway in '98.

1986-1992		$825	$950

Les Paul Jumbo
1969-1970. Single rounded cutaway, flat-top dreadnought acoustic/electric, 1 pickup, rosewood back and sides, natural.

1969-1970		$2,500	$2,800

Les Paul KM (Kalamazoo Model)
1979. Regular Les Paul Standard with 2 exposed humbuckers, KM on headstock, sunburst, approximately 1500 were made in the Kalamazoo plant.

1979		$1,500	$2,500

Les Paul Leo's Reissue
1980-1985. Special order from Gibson's Nashville facility for Leo's Music, Oakland, California. Identified by serial number with L at the beginning, flamed maple top. About 800 guitars were made, with about 400 being exported to Japan. Kalamazoo-made Leo's have a 2nd serial number in the control cavity, Nash-

MODEL YEAR	FEATURES	EXC. COND. LOW	HIGH

ville-made Leo's do not have a 2nd serial number.

| 1980-1983 | Kalamazoo-made | $4,000 | $4,500 |
| 1983-1985 | Nashville-made | $3,800 | $4,300 |

Les Paul Limited Edition (3-tone)

1997. Limited Edition stamped on the back of the headstock, Les Paul Standard configuration with cloud inlay markers, 2-piece 3-tone sunburst finish over non-figured maple top.

| 1997 | | $1,900 | $2,200 |

Les Paul Old Hickory

1998 only. Limited run of 200, tulip poplar body from The Hermitage, Custom-style trim.

| 1998 | | $2,500 | $4,000 |

Les Paul Pee Wee

1999. 3/4" sized Les Paul Jr. style guitar, included battery-powered amp.

| 1999 | | $425 | $475 |

Les Paul Personal

1969-1972. Two angled, low impedence pickups, phase switch, gold parts, walnut finish.

| 1970 | | $950 | $1,200 |

Les Paul Pro-Deluxe

1978-1982. Two P-90 pickups, chrome-plated hardware, Pro engraved on truss rod cover, various colors.

| 1978-1982 | | $1,250 | $1,600 |

Les Paul Professional

1969-1971, 1977-1979. Single-cut, 2 angled, low impedence pickups, carved top, walnut finish.

| 1969-1971 | | $975 | $1,200 |

Les Paul Recording

1971-1980. Two angled, low impedence pickups, high/low impedence selector switch, various colors.

| 1971-1980 | | $975 | $1,200 |

Les Paul Reissue Flametop

1983-1990. Flame maple top, 2 humbuckers, thicker '59-style neck, sunburst finish, renamed '59 Les Paul Flametop in '91.

| 1983-1990 | Highly figured | $2,800 | $3,300 |

Les Paul Reissue Goldtop

1983-1991. Goldtop finish, 2 P-100 pickups, renamed '56 Les Paul Goldtop in '91.

| 1983-1989 | | $1,400 | $1,700 |
| 1990-1991 | | $1,500 | $1,900 |

Les Paul Signature

1973-1978. Thin semi-hollowbody, double-cut, 2 low impedence pickups, f-holes, various colors.

| 1973-1978 | | $1,750 | $2,000 |

Les Paul SmartWood Standard

1996-2002. Smartwood Series, figured maple top, mahogany body, Smartwood on truss rod cover.

| 1996-2002 | Antique natural | $950 | $1,200 |

Les Paul SmartWood Studio

2002-present. Released December '02 as part of Les Paul Exotics guitar series, Muiracatiara (Muir) top and mahogany back, Preciosa (Prec) 'board, initial production will use Muir wood until replaced by another exotic wood, full-depth body style, Studio model appointments including pearl-style dot markers.

| 2002-2003 | | $750 | $900 |

Les Paul Special

1955-1959. Slab solidbody, 2 pickups (P-90s in '50s, P-100 stacked humbuckers on later version), single-cut until end of '58, double in '59, the '89 reissue is a single-cut, renamed SG Special in late-'59.

| 1955-1959 | TV Yellow | $6,000 | $8,000 |
| 1959 | Cherry (mid- to late-'59) | $5,000 | $6,500 |

Les Paul Special (Reissue)

1989-1998. Briefly introduced as Les Paul Junior II but name changed to Special in the first year, single-cut, 2 P-100 stacked humbucking pickups, tune-o-matic bridge, TV Yellow, in '90 there was a run of 300 with LE serial number, renamed Special SL in '98.

| 1989-1998 | | $800 | $950 |

Les Paul Special 3/4

1959. Slab solidbody, 2 P-90 pickups, double-cut, short-scale, cherry finish, renamed SG Special 3/4 in late-'59.

| 1959 | | $3,700 | $4,500 |

Les Paul Special Centennial

1994 only. 100 made, double-cut, cherry, 100 year banner at the 12th fret, diamonds in headstock and in gold-plated knobs, gold-plated Gibson coin in back of headstock.

| 1994 | | $3,000 | $3,500 |

Les Paul Special Custom Shop

1999-present. 1960 Special, offered in single- or double-cut version.

| 1999 | | $1,000 | $1,200 |

Les Paul Special Double Cutaway

1976-1979, 1993-1998. Double-cut, 2 pickups (P-90s in '70s, P-100 stacked humbuckers in later version), various colors.

| 1976-1979 | | $1,200 | $1,500 |
| 1993-1998 | | $1,100 | $1,200 |

Les Paul Spotlight Special

1983-1984. Curly maple and walnut top, 2 humbuckers, gold hardware, multi-bound top, Custom Shop Edition logo, natural or sunburst.

| 1983-1984 | | $1,900 | $2,200 |

Les Paul Standard (Sunburst)

1958-1960, special order 1972-1975. Les Paul Sunbursts from '58-'60 should be individually valued based on originality, color and the amount and type of figure in the maple top, changed tuners or a Bigsby removal will drop the value. The noted price ranges are guidance valuations. Each '58-'60 Les Paul Standard should be evaluated on a case-by-case basis. As is always the case, the low and high range are for an all original, excellent condition, undamaged guitar. About 70% of the '58-'60 Les Paul Standards have relatively plain maple tops. Approximately 15% came with the Bigsby tailpiece. The majority of '58-'60 Les Paul Standards have moderate or extreme color fade. Wider fret wire was introduced in early-'59. White bobbins were introduced in early- to mid-'59. Double ring Kluson Deluxe tuners were introduced in late-'60. It has been suggested that all '58-'60 models have 2-piece centerseam tops. This implies that 1-piece tops, 3-piece tops and off-centerseam tops do not exist.

Sunburst language includes terms such as: arching

Gibson Les Paul Recording

Gibson Les Paul Smartwood Studio

*1960 Gibson
Les Paul Standard*

*1962 Gibson Les Paul Standard
(SG body)*

MODEL YEAR	FEATURES	EXC. COND. LOW	HIGH

medullary grain, swirling medullary grain, ribbon-curl, chevrons, Honey-Amber, receding red aniline, pinstripe, bookmatched, double-white bobbins, zebra bobbins, black bobbins, fiddleback maple, sunburst finish, Honeyburst, lemon drop, quarter sawn, blistered figure, width of gradation, flat sawn, Teaburst, Bigsby-shadow, rift sawn, heel size, aged clear lacquer, 3-dimensional figure, intense fine flame, tag-shadow, red pore filler, Eastern maple fleck, medium-thick flame, shrunk tuners, wave and flame, flitch-matched, elbow discoloration, ambered top coat, natural gradation, grain orientation, script oxidation, asymmetrical figure Tangerineburst, Greenburst, and birdseye. The bobbins used for the pickup winding were either black or white. The market has determined that white bobbin PAFs are the most highly regarded. Generally speaking, in '58 bobbins were black, in '59 the bobbin component transitioned to white and some guitars have 1 white and 1 black bobbin (aka zebra). In '60, there were zebras and double blacks returned.

Rather than listing separate line items for fade and wood, the Guide lists discounts and premiums as follows. The price ranges shown below are for instruments with excellent color, excellent wood, with the original guitar case. The following discounts and premiums should be considered.

An instrument with a plain top should be discounted about 50%.

An instrument with an average top should be discounted about 30%.

An instrument with moderate or total fade should be discounted about 10%.

An instrument with a factory Bigsby should be discounted about 10%-15%.

Original jumbo frets are preferred over original small frets and are worth +10%.

An instrument with a non-original Les Paul case is worth $2,500 less.

1958	Highly flamed, strong color	$190,000	$210,000
1959	Highly flamed, strong color	$225,000	$250,000
1960	Highly flamed, strong color	$190,000	$210,000

Les Paul Standard (SG body)

1961-1963 (SG body those years). Renamed SG Standard in late-'63.

1961-1962	Cherry, side vibrola, PAFs	$10,000	$12,000
1962	Ebony block, SG body, PAFs	$12,000	$14,000
1962	Ebony block, SG body, pat. #	$8,000	$11,000
1963	Cherry	$7,000	$10,000

Les Paul Standard (reintroduced then renamed)

1968-1969. Comes back as a goldtop with P-90s for '68-'69 (renamed Les Paul Deluxe, '69), available as special order Deluxe '72-'76.

1968	P-90s, small headstock	$7,500	$9,000
1968-1969	P-90s, large headstock	$5,200	$6,000

Les Paul Standard (reintroduced)

1976-present. Available as special order Deluxe '72-'76, reintroduced with 2 humbuckers '76-present.

1972-1974	Special order goldtop, P-90s	$2,800	$3,200
1972-1974	Special order sunburst, P-90s	$2,800	$3,200
1974-1975	Special order sunburst, humbuckers	$2,800	$3,200
1976	Sunburst, 4-piece pancake body	$1,800	$1,950
1976	Wine Red or natural	$1,650	$1,800
1977	Sunburst	$1,650	$1,800
1978	Natural	$1,650	$1,800
1978	Sunburst	$1,650	$1,800
1979	Brown Sunburst	$1,650	$1,800
61979	Cherry Sunburst	$1,600	$1,800
51979	Goldtop	$1,750	$1,900
61979	Natural	$1,650	$1,800
1979	Wine Red	$1,650	$1,800
1980	Black	$1,650	$1,800
1980	Natural	$1,650	$1,800
1980	Sunburst	$1,650	$1,800
1980	Sunburst, mild flame	$1,750	$2,000
1980	Wine Red	$1,650	$1,800
1981	Sunburst	$1,650	$1,800
1981	Wine Red	$1,650	$1,800
1982	Black	$1,650	$1,800
1982	Brown Sunburst	$1,650	$1,800
1982	Candy Apple Red, gold hardware, LD	$1,750	$1,900
1982	Cherry Sunburst	$1,650	$1,800
1982	Goldtop	$1,750	$1,900
1982	Natural	$1,750	$1,900
1982	Wine Red	$1,650	$1,800
1983	Black	$1,550	$1,700
1983	Natural	$1,550	$1,700
1983	Sunburst	$1,550	$1,700
1984	Sunburst	$1,550	$1,700
1985	Black	$1,550	$1,700
1985	Wine Red	$1,550	$1,700
1986	Sunburst	$1,450	$1,700
1987	Various colors	$1,450	$1,700
1988	Various colors	$1,450	$1,700
1989	Various colors	$1,300	$1,600
1990-1999	Limited Edition colors	$1,600	$2,000
1990-1999	Various colors	$1,450	$1,650
2000-2002	Various colors	$1,550	$1,600

Les Paul Standard '58

1971-1975. Goldtop, called the '58, but set up like a '54 Goldtop with 2 soapbar pickups and stop tailpiece.

1971-1975		$3,500	$4,500

MODEL YEAR	FEATURES	EXC. COND. LOW	HIGH

Les Paul Standard '82
1982. Standard 82 on truss rod cover, made in Kalamazoo, Made in USA stamp on back of the headstock, generally quilted maple tops.

1982		$2,500	$4,000

Les Paul Standard Lite
1999-2001. A member of DC body-style, renamed from DC Standard in '99, reintroduced as Les Paul Standard DC Plus in 2001, various translucent finishes, available in 2004 under this name also.

1999-2001		$850	$1,000

Les Paul Standard Plus
2000s. Cherry sunburst standard with mid-level flame.

2000s		$1,600	$1,700

Les Paul Standard Sparkle
2001. Sparkle holoflake top, reflective back, Standard logo on truss rod.

2001		$2,000	$2,500

Les Paul Strings and Things Standard
1975-1978. Special order flamed maple top Les Paul Standard model, built for Chris Lovell, owner of Strings and Things, a Gibson dealer in Memphis, approximately 28 were built, authentication of a Strings and Things Les Paul is difficult due to no diffinitive attributes, valuation should be on a case-by-case basis, sunburst.

1975-1978	2-piece top	$4,000	$5,000
1975-1978	3-piece top	$2,500	$3,000

Les Paul Studio
1983-present. Alder body, 2 humbuckers, various colors.

1983-1999		$800	$900
2000-2004		$800	$875

Les Paul Studio Baritone
2004-present. 28" baritone scale.

2004		$875	$975

Les Paul Studio Custom
1984-1985. Alder body, 2 humbucking pickups, multibound top, gold-plated hardware, various colors.

1984-1985		$850	$1,000

Les Paul Studio Gem
1996-1998. Limited edition with Les Paul Studio features, but using P-90 pickups instead of humbucker pickups, plus trapezoid markers and gold hardware.

1996-1998		$850	$950

Les Paul Studio Gothic
2000s. Gothic Black.

2000-2001		$675	$750

Les Paul Studio Lite
1987-1998. Carved maple top, mahogany back and neck, 2 humbucker pickups, various colors.

1987-1998		$800	$925

Les Paul Studio Plus
2002-present. Two-piece AA flamed unbound top, gold hardware, Desert Burst or see-thru black.

2002-2005		$975	$1,075

Les Paul Studio Swamp Ash/Swamp Ash Studio
2004. Studio model with swamp ash body.

2004		$700	$775

Les Paul Supreme
2004. Same as Supreme Figured (listed below), various opaque finishes and less figured wood.

2004		$1,900	$2,100

Les Paul Supreme Figured
2004. Highly figured AAAA maple top and back, custom binding, deluxe split style pearl inlay markers, chambered mahogany body, globe logo on headstock, various colors.

2004		$2,200	$2,300

Les Paul Tie Dye Custom Shop
2002. Limited series of one-off colorful finishes, Custom Shop logo.

2002		$3,550	$3,700

Les Paul TV
1954-1959. Les Paul Jr. with limed mahogany (TV Yellow) finish, single-cut until mid-'58, double-cut after, renamed SG TV in late-'59.

1955-1958	Single-cut	$6,000	$8,000
1958-1959	Double-cut	$5,000	$6,500

Les Paul TV 3/4
1954-1957. Limed mahogany (TV Yellow) Les Paul Jr. 3/4, short-scale, single-cut.

1954-1957		$3,100	$3,700

Les Paul Ultima
1996-present. Custom Shop model, flame or quilted sunburst top, fancy abalone and mother-of-pearl tree of life, harp, or flame fingerboard inlay, multi abalone bound body.

1996-1999		$5,200	$6,000

Les Paul Voodoo/Voodoo Les Paul
2004. Single-cut, swamp ash body, 2 exposed humbuckers, black satin finish.

2004		$900	$975

Les Paul XR-I/XR-II/XR-III
1981-1983. No frills model with Dirty Finger pickups, dot markers, Les Paul stencil logo on headstock, goldburst, silverburst and cherryburst finishes.

1981-1983	XR-I, silverburst	$550	$850
1981-1983	XR-II	$550	$850
1981-1983	XR-III	$550	$850

Les Paul Zack Wylde Signature
2003-present. Custom shop, black and antique-white bullseye graphic finish.

2003-2005	Black/white bullseye	$2,500	$2,800
2003-2005	Green Camo bullseye option	$2,500	$2,800

The Les Paul
1976-1980. Figured maple top, 2 humbuckers, gold hardware, rosewood binding, 'guard, 'board, knobs, cover plates, etc., natural or rosewood finishing, natural only by '79.

1976-1980	Natural or rosewood	$11,000	$13,000

The Paul
1978-1982. Walnut body, 2 exposed humbuckers.

1978-1982		$650	$750

Gibson Les Paul Supreme

1950s Gibson Les Paul TV

GUITARS

1970 Gibson Melody Maker

Gibson Melody Maker ³/₄

MODEL YEAR	FEATURES	EXC. COND. LOW	HIGH
The Paul Firebrand Deluxe			

1980-1982. Single-cut mahogany solidbody, rough natural finish, Gibson branded in headstock, 2 exposed humbuckers.

MODEL YEAR	FEATURES	LOW	HIGH
1980-1982	Pelham Blue	$625	$700
1980-1982	Rough natural	$550	$600
The Paul II			

1996-1998. Mahogany body, 2 humbucking pickups, rosewood dot neck, renamed The Paul SL in '98.

1996-1998		$500	$550
LG-0			

1958-1974. Flat-top acoustic, mahogany, bound body, rosewood bridge '58-'61 and '68-'74, plastic bridge '62-'67, natural.

1958-1961	Rosewood bridge	$800	$1,100
1962-1964	Plastic bridge	$600	$800
1965-1967	Plastic bridge	$550	$750
1968-1969	Rosewood bridge	$500	$750
1970-1974		$400	$700
LG-1			

1943-1968. Flat-top acoustic, spruce top, mahogany back and sides, bound body, rosewood bridge '43-'61, plastic bridge after, examples seen to '74, sunburst.

1943		$1,800	$2,000
1944		$1,700	$1,900
1945		$1,600	$1,800
1946		$1,500	$1,700
1947-1949		$1,300	$1,500
1950-1961		$1,000	$1,300
1962-1965		$750	$1,000
1966-1968		$700	$950
LG-2			

1942-1962. Flat-top acoustic, spruce top, mahogany back and sides (some with maple '43-'46), banner headstock '42-'46, bound body, X-bracing, sunburst finish, replaced by B-25 in '62.

1942		$2,400	$2,800
1943		$2,300	$2,700
1944		$2,200	$2,600
1945		$2,000	$2,500
1946		$1,900	$2,400
1947-1949		$1,800	$2,300
1950-1961		$1,600	$2,100
1962	Ajustable bridge	$1,250	$1,800
LG-2 3/4			

1949-1962. Short-scale version of LG-2 flat-top, wood bridge, sunburst.

1949-1962		$1,100	$2,200
LG-2 H			

1945-1955. Flat-top, Hawaiian, natural or sunburst.

1945-1955		$1,300	$1,800
LG-3			

1942-1964. Flat-top acoustic, spruce top, mahogany back and sides, bound body, natural finish, replaced by B-25 N.

1942		$2,600	$3,000
1943		$2,500	$2,900
1944		$2,400	$2,800
1945		$2,200	$2,700

MODEL YEAR	FEATURES	EXC. COND. LOW	HIGH
1946		$2,100	$2,600
1947-1949		$1,900	$2,400
1950-1962	Wood bridge	$1,700	$2,200
1962-1964	Plastic bridge	$1,250	$1,900
LG-12 (12-string)			

1967-1973. 14-1/8" wide, mahogany back and sides, bound top, natural.

1967-1969	Adjustable saddle	$650	$850
1970-1974	Set saddle	$550	$750
Mach II			

1990-1991. Renamed from U-2, offset double-cut, 2 single coils and 1 humbucking pickup.

1990-1991		$600	$750
Map Guitar			

1983, 1985. Body cutout like lower 48, 2 humbuckers, limited run promotion, '83 version in natural mahogany or red, white and blue, '85 version red, white and blue stars and stripes on a white background.

1983	Natural	$1,900	$2,100
1983	Red, white and blue	$2,100	$2,400
Marauder			

1975-1980. Single-cut solidbody, pointed headstock, 2 pickups, bolt-on neck, various colors.

1975-1980		$550	$650
Melody Maker			

1959-1971. Slab solidbody, 1 pickup, single-cut until '61, double '61-'66, SG body '66-'71, reintroduced as single-cut in '86-'93.

1959	Sunburst, single-cut	$850	$1,300
1960	Sunburst, single-cut	$800	$1,150
1961	Sunburst, single-cut	$750	$1,050
1962	Cherry, double-cut	$700	$1,000
1962	Sunburst, double-cut	$700	$1,000
1963	Cherry, double-cut	$650	$950
1964	Cherry, double-cut	$650	$900
1964	Sunburst, double-cut	$650	$900
1965-1966	Cherry, double cut	$600	$850
1966	Blue or red, SG body	$750	$1,100
1967-1969	Blue or red, SG body	$700	$1,050
1968-1970	Walnut, SG body	$700	$1,050
Melody Maker 3/4			

1959-1970. Short-scale version.

1959-1965	Melody Maker body	$550	$950
1966-1970	SG body	$650	$1,050
Melody Maker D			

1960-1970. Two pickup version of Melody Maker, reintroduced as Melody Maker Double in '77.

1960	Sunburst, single-cut	$1,000	$1,250
1961	Sunburst, single-cut	$950	$1,200
1962	Sunburst, double-cut	$900	$1,150
1963	Cherry, double-cut	$850	$1,050
1964	Cherry, double-cut	$800	$950
1965-1966	Cherry, double-cut	$850	$900
1966	Blue or red, SG body	$1,050	$1,150
1967-1969	Blue, red or white SG body	$1,000	$1,200
1968-1970	Walnut, SG body	$1,000	$1,200
Melody Maker Double			

1977-1983. Reintroduction of Melody Maker D, double-cut solidbody, 2 pickups, cherry or sunburst.

1977-1983		$625	$700

MODEL YEAR	FEATURES	EXC. COND. LOW	HIGH

Melody Maker III
1965-1971. SG-style double-cut solidbody, 3 pickups, various colors.

1967-1969		$1,200	$1,400
1970-1971		$1,000	$1,300

Melody Maker 12
1967-1971. SG-style solidbody, 12 strings, 2 pickups, red, white or Pelham Blue.

1967-1971		$1,100	$1,200

MK-35
1975-1978. Mark Series flat-top acoustic, mahogany back and sides, black-bound body, natural or sunburst.

1975-1978		$650	$850

MK-53
1975-1978. Mark Series flat-top acoustic, maple back and sides, multi-bound body, natural or sunburst.

1975-1978		$750	$900

MK-72
1975-1978. Mark Series flat-top acoustic, rosewood back and sides, black-bound body, natural or sunburst.

1975-1978		$850	$1,000

MK-81
1975-1978. Mark Series flat-top acoustic, rosewood back and sides, multi-bound body, gold tuners, high-end appointments, natural or sunburst.

1975-1978		$900	$1,100

Moderne Heritage
1981-1983. Limited edition, korina body, 2 humbucking pickups, gold hardware.

1981-1983	Black or white	$2,500	$3,500
1981-1983	Natural	$2,500	$3,200

Nick Lucas
1928-1938. Flat-top acoustic, multi-bound body and neck, sunburst, reintroduced in '91 and '99.

1928	Mahogany, 12-fret, 13 1/3"	$6,000	$7,000
1928	Rosewood, 12-fret, 13 1/2"	$7,000	$8,000
1929-1933	Rosewood, 13-fret, 14 3/4"	$8,000	$9,000
1934-1938	Maple, 14-fret, 14 3/4"	$7,000	$8,000

Nick Lucas Reissue
1991-1992, 1999-2004. Limited edition flat-top acoustic, sunburst.

1991-1992		$1,600	$1,750
1999-2004		$1,900	$2,100

Nighthawk Custom
1993-1998. Flame maple top, ebony 'board, gold hardware, fireburst, single/double/mini pickups.

1993-1998		$1,000	$1,100

Nighthawk Special
1993-1998. Single-cut solidbody, figured maple top, double-coil and mini-pickup or with additional single-coil options, dot marker inlay, cherry, ebony or sunburst.

1993-1998		$550	$600

Nighthawk Standard
1993-1998. Single-cut solidbody, figured maple top, 2 or 3 pickups, double-parallelogram inlay, amber, fireburst or sunburst.

1993-1998		$850	$900

Nouveau NV6T-M
1986-1987. A line of Gibson flat-tops with imported parts assembled and finished in the U.S., acoustic dreadnought, bound maple body, natural.

1986-1987		$400	$450

Q-100
1985-1986. Offset double-cut solidbody, Kahler trem, 6-on-a-side tuners, 1 humbucker, black hardware.

1985-1986		$300	$325

Q-200/Q2000
1985-1986. Like Q-100, but with 1 single-coil and 1 humbucker, black or chrome hardware.

1985-1986		$325	$375

Q-300/Q3000
1985-1986. Like Q-100, but with 3 single-coils, black or chrome hardware.

1985-1986		$400	$450

RD Artist
1978-1982. Double-cut solidbody, 2 humbuckers, TP-6 tailpiece, active electronics, ebony 'board, block inlays, gold-plated parts, various colors, called just RD (no Artist) in '81 and '82.

1978-1982		$1,100	$1,400

RD Custom
1977-1979. Double-cut solidbody, 2 humbuckers, stop tailpiece, active electronics, dot inlays, maple 'board, chrome parts, natural or walnut.

1977-1979		$1,050	$1,350

RD Standard
1977-1979. Double-cut solidbody, 2 humbuckers, stop tailpiece, rosewood 'board, dot inlays, chrome parts, natural, sunburst or walnut.

1977-1979		$1,000	$1,300

Roy Smeck Radio Grande Hawaiian
1934-1939. Dreadnought acoustic flat-top, rosewood back and sides, bound body and neck, natural.

1934-1939		$8,000	$12,000

Roy Smeck Stage Deluxe Hawaiian
1934-1942. Dreadnought acoustic flat-top, mahogany back and sides, bound body, natural.

1934-1942		$6,000	$8,000

S-1
1976-1980. Single-cut solidbody, pointed headstock, 3 single-coil pickups, similar to the Marauder, various colors.

1976-1980		$700	$825

SG
Following are models, listed alphabetically, bearing the SG designation:

SG '61 Reissue
1993-present. Double-cut SG body, 2 humbuckers, cherry, see SG Reissue for '86-'87, and SG '62 Reissue for '88-'91.

1993-2002		$900	$1,400

1977 Gibson RD Custom

1976 Gibson S-1

1963 Gibson SG Custom

*Gibson SG Pete
Townshend Signature*

MODEL YEAR	FEATURES	EXC. COND. LOW	HIGH

SG '62 Reissue Showcase Edition
1988. Guitar of the Month, bright blue opaque finish, 200 made.

1988		$1,100	$1,300

SG '62 Reissue/SG Reissue
1986-1991. Called SG Reissue '86-'87, SG '62 Reissue '88-'91, and SG '61 Reissue '93-present, cherry.

1986-1987	SG Reissue	$900	$1,200
1988-1991	'62 Reissue	$900	$1,200

SG 90 Double
1988-1990. SG body, updated electronics, graphite reinforced neck, 2 pickups, cherry, turquoise or white.

1988-1990		$550	$650

SG 90 Single
1988-1990. SG body, updated electronics, graphite reinforced neck, 1 humbucker pickup, cherry, turquoise or white.

1988-1990		$500	$600

SG Corvette Sting Ray L.E. (Custom Shop)
1996 only. SG-style body, Sting Ray inlay, 150 instruments built, offered in black, red or silver.

1996		$2,000	$2,300

SG Custom
1963-1980. Renamed from Les Paul Custom, 3 humbuckers, vibrato, made with Les Paul Custom plate from '61-'63 (see Les Paul Custom), white finish until '68, walnut and others after.

1963	White, pat. #	$6,800	$9,900
1964	White	$5,800	$9,400
1965	White	$5,200	$8,300
1966	White	$4,700	$7,700
1967	White	$3,700	$5,000
1968	White	$3,200	$5,000
1969	Walnut	$2,700	$3,900
1969	White	$3,200	$4,400
1970-1973	Walnut	$2,100	$3,000
1970-1973	White option	$3,000	$3,700
1974-1976	Various colors	$2,100	$3,000
1977-1980	Various colors	$1,900	$2,700

SG Custom '67 Reissue/Les Paul SG '67 Custom
1991-1993. The SG Custom '67 Reissue has a wine red finish, the Les Paul SG '67 Custom ('92-'93) has a wine red or white finish.

1991-1993		$1,750	$1,800

SG Deluxe
1971-1972, 1981-1985, 1998-present. The '70s models were offered in natural, cherry or walnut finishes, reintroduced in '98 with 3 Firebird mini-humbucker-style pickups in black, Ice Blue or red finishes.

1971-1972	Cherry	$1,375	$1,675
1971-1972	Natural or walnut	$1,155	$1,450
1981-1985	Various colors	$750	$825
1998-1999	Various colors	$850	$925

SG Exclusive
1979. SG with humbuckers, coil-tap and rotary control knob, block inlay, pearl logo (not decal), black/ebony finish.

1979		$900	$950

MODEL YEAR	FEATURES	EXC. COND. LOW	HIGH

SG Firebrand
1980-1982. Double-cut mahogany solidbody, rough natural finish, Gibson branded in headstock, 2 exposed humbuckers, Firebrand logo on The SG (Standard) model.

1980-1982		$650	$750

SG I
1972-1977. Double-cut, mahogany body, 1 mini-humbucker pickup (some with SG Jr. P-90), cherry or walnut.

1972-1977		$700	$900

SG II
1972-1976. 2 mini-humbuckers (some in '75 had regular humbuckers), cherry or walnut.

1972-1976		$750	$950

SG III
1972-1974. The sunburst version of the II, some shipped as late as '79.

1972-1974		$750	$950

SG Jr.
1963-1971, 1991-1994. One pickup, solidbody.

1963	Alpine White	$2,500	$3,000
1963	Cherry	$1,900	$2,300
1964	Cherry	$1,700	$2,100
1964	White	$2,400	$2,800
1965	Cherry	$1,600	$1,900
1965	White	$2,200	$2,600
1966	Cherry	$1,600	$1,750
1966	White	$2,200	$2,500
1967	Cherry	$1,500	$1,600
1967	White	$1,800	$2,200
1968	Cherry	$1,250	$1,550
1968	White	$1,600	$2,000
1969	Cherry	$1,150	$1,450
1970	Cherry	$1,050	$1,260
1971	Cherry or walnut	$950	$1,150
1991-1994	Various colors	$750	$950

SG Les Paul Custom
1987-1992. Three pickups, called the SG '90 Les Paul Custom towards the end of its run.

1987-1989	Antique Ivory	$1,575	$1,900
1990-1992	White	$1,350	$1,700

SG Les Paul Custom 30th Anniversary
1991. SG body, 3 humbuckers, gold hardware, TV Yellow finish, 30th Anniversary on peghead.

1991		$1,575	$2,100

SG Pete Townshend Signature (Historic/ Custom Shop)
2000-2003. SG Special with '70 specs, large 'guard, 2 cases, cherry red.

2000-2003		$2,150	$2,400

SG Pro
1971-1973. Two P-90 pickups, tune-o-matic bridge, vibrato, cherry, mahogany or walnut.

1971-1973	Cherry	$1,250	$1,450
1971-1973	Mahogany or walnut	$1,050	$1,250

SG Special
1959-1978, 1986-1996, 2000-2001. Rounded double-cut for '59-'60, switched to SG body early-'61, 2 P-90s '59-'71, 2 mini-humbuckers '72-'78, 2 regular size

humbuckers on current version, reintroduced variation to the SG line in '86-'99, then reintroduced again in 2000.

MODEL YEAR	FEATURES	EXC. COND. LOW	HIGH
1959	Cherry, slab, high neck pickup	$4,700	$5,800
1960	Cherry, slab, lower neck pickup	$5,250	$6,000
1961	Cherry, SG body	$3,300	$4,200
1962	Cherry	$3,000	$3,500
1962	White	$3,700	$4,200
1963	Cherry	$2,700	$3,200
1963	White	$3,500	$4,000
1964	Cherry	$2,600	$3,100
1964	White	$3,300	$3,900
1965	Cherry	$2,200	$2,500
1965	White	$2,800	$3,100
1966	Cherry, large 'guard	$2,000	$2,300
1966	Cherry, small 'guard	$2,100	$2,400
1966	White, large 'guard	$2,400	$2,750
1966	White, small 'guard	$2,600	$3,000
1967	Cherry	$1,900	$2,200
1967	White	$2,200	$2,500
1968-1971	Cherry	$1,600	$1,875
1972-1975	Cherry or walnut	$1,250	$1,475
1976-1978	Cherry or walnut	$1,050	$1,250
1986-1996	Various colors	$675	$775
2000-2004	Various colors	$625	$675

SG Special Faded/Faded SG Special
2003. Aged worn cherry finish.

2003		$400	$550

SG Standard
1963-1981. Les Paul Standard changes to SG body, 2 humbuckers, some very early models have optional factory Bigsby.

1963	Cherry	$6,000	$7,700
1964	Cherry	$5,250	$7,200
1965	Cherry	$5,250	$6,600
1965	Pelham Blue (faded)	$5,500	$7,700
1965	Pelham Blue (unfaded)	$7,400	$11,000
1966	Cherry	$4,200	$5,500
1967	Burgundy Metallic	$4,700	$6,600
1967	Cherry	$2,600	$3,900
1967	White	$3,700	$5,500
1968	Cherry	$2,600	$3,800
1969	Cherry, engraved lyre	$2,100	$3,300
1970	Cherry, engraved lyre	$2,000	$2,600
1970	Cherry, non-lyre tailpiece	$1,600	$2,100
1971	Cherry	$1,400	$1,900
1972-1975	New specs and colors	$1,350	$1,675
1976-1981	New color line-up	$1,125	$1,350
1983-1999	Various colors	$875	$950

SG Standard Korina
1993-1994. Korina version of SG Standard, limited run, natural.

1993-1994		$1,700	$2,100

SG Supreme
2004-present. '57 humbuckers, flamed maple top, split-diamond markers, various colors.

2004		$1,250	$1,350

SG Tommy Iommi Signature (Historic/Custom Shop)
2001-2003. Signature humbuckers without poles, cross inlays, ebony or wine red.

2001-2003		$1,850	$2,200

SG TV
1959-1968. Les Paul TV changed to SG body, double rounded cutaway solidbody for '59-'60, SG body '61-'68, 1 pickup, limed mahogany (TV yellow) finish.

1959-1961	TV Yellow, slab body	$5,000	$6,500
1961-1963	White, SG body	$2,500	$3,500

SG Voodoo/Voodoo SG
2004-2005. Black satin finish.

2004-2005		$750	$850

SG-100
1971-1972. Double-cut solidbody, 1 pickup, cherry or walnut.

1971-1972	Melody Maker pickup	$600	$750
1971-1972	P-90 pickup option	$750	$900

SG-200
1971-1972. Two pickup version of SG-100 in black, cherry or walnut finish, replaced by SG II.

1971-1972	Melody Maker pickups	$700	$800

SG-250
1971-1972. Two-pickup version of SG-100 in cherry sunburst, replaced by SG III.

1971-1972	Melody Maker pickups	$700	$800

SG-X (All American)
1995-1999. Renamed the SG-X in '98, previously part of the all American series, SG body with single bridge humbucker, various colors.

1995-1999		$550	$600

The SG
1979-1980. Normal SG specs, solid walnut body and neck, ebony 'board, 2 exposed-coil humbuckers, model name logo on truss rod, Firebrand logo added in '80, refer to SG Firebrand listing.

1979-1980		$700	$750

The SG (Standard)
1983-1987. Normal SG specs, exposed humbucker pickups, model name logo on truss rod, walnut neck and walnut body, natural and other colors.

1983-1987		$700	$750

1965 Gibson SG Standard

1983 Gibson The SG

*1983 Gibson
Sonex 180 Deluxe*

Gibson Style U

MODEL YEAR	FEATURES	EXC. COND. LOW	HIGH
SJ (Southern Jumbo)			

1942-1969,1991-1996. Flat-top, sunburst standard, natural optional starting in '54 (natural finish version called Country-Western starting in '56), round shoulders (changed to square in '62), catalog name changed to SJ Deluxe in '70, refer to that listing.

MODEL YEAR	FEATURES	LOW	HIGH
1942-1944		$5,000	$5,500
1947-1948		$4,000	$4,900
1949-1950		$3,500	$4,400
1951-1955		$3,500	$4,200
1954-1956	Natural option, round shoulder	$3,700	$4,500
1954-1956	Sunburst, round shoulder	$3,500	$4,000
1956-1961	Round shoulder	$3,000	$3,600
1962-1964	Square shoulder	$2,700	$3,000
1965-1966		$2,600	$2,800
1967-1968		$2,500	$2,700
1969-1974	Below belly bridge	$1,700	$2,200

SJ Deluxe (Southern Jumbo)

1970-1978. SJ name changed to SJ Deluxe in catalog, along with a series of engineering changes.

1970-1971	Non-adj. saddle	$1,500	$1,700
1972-1973	Unbound 'board	$1,000	$1,500
1974-1978	4-ply to binding	$850	$1,000

SJ-100 1939 Centennial

1994. Acoustic flat-top, limited edition, sunburst

1994		$1,600	$1,800

SJ-200 Ray Whitley/J-200 Custom Club

1994-1995. Based on Ray Whitley's late-1930s J-200, including engraved inlays and initials on the truss rod cover, only 37 made, one of the limited edition models the Montana division released to celebrate Gibson's 100th anniversary.

1994-1995		$7,200	$9,000

SJN (Country-Western)

1956-1969. Flat-top, natural finish version of SJ, round shoulders '56-'62, square shoulders after that, called the SJN in '60 and '61, the SJN Country Western after that, catalog name changed to SJN Deluxe in '70, refer to that listing.

1956-1961	Round shoulders	$3,600	$4,400
1962-1964	Square shoulders	$3,200	$3,800
1965-1966	Square shoulders	$2,900	$3,200
1967-1968	Square shoulders	$2,700	$2,900
1969	Below belly bridge	$1,900	$2,400

SJN Deluxe (Country-Western Jumbo)

1970-1978. SJN name changed to SJN Deluxe in catalog, along with a series of engineering changes.

1970-1971	Non-adj. saddle	$1,700	$1,900
1972-1973	Unbound 'board	$1,200	$1,700
1974-1978	4-ply to binding	$950	$1,200

Sonex-180 Custom

1980-1982. Two Super humbuckers, coil-tap, maple neck, ebony 'board, single-cut, body of Multi-Phonic synthetic material, various colors.

1980-1982		$500	$550

MODEL YEAR	FEATURES	EXC. COND. LOW	HIGH
Sonex-180 Deluxe			

1980-1984. Hardwood neck, rosewood 'board, single-cut, body of Multi-Phonic synthetic material, 2 pickups, no coil-tap, various colors.

1980-1984		$425	$475

Spirit I

1982-1988. Double rounded cutaway, 1 pickup, chrome hardware, various colors.

1982-1988		$400	$450

Spirit II XPL

1985-1987. Double-cut solidbody, Kahler tremolo, 2 pickups, various colors.

1985-1987		$450	$550

SR-71

1987-1989. Floyd Rose tremolo, 1 humbucker, 2 single-coil pickups, various colors, Wayne Charvel designed.

1987-1989		$450	$550

Star

1992. Star logo on headstock, star position markers, single sharp cutaway flat-top, sunburst.

1992		$1,500	$1,650

Style O

1902-1925. Acoustic archtop, oval soundhole, bound top, neck and headstock, various colors.

1910-1925		$4,500	$4,800

Style U Harp Guitar

1902-1939. Acoustic 6-string, with 10 or 12 sub-bass strings, maple back and sides, bound soundhole, black.

1915-1919		$5,600	$6,400

Super 300 (Non-Cutaway)

1948-1955. Acoustic archtop, non-cut, bound body, neck and headstock, sunburst.

1948-1955		$3,500	$4,500

Super 300 C (Cutaway)

1954-1958. Acoustic archtop, rounded cutaway, bound body, neck and headstock, sunburst with natural option.

1954-1957	Sunburst	$5,500	$6,500

Super 400

1934-1941, 1947-1955. Acoustic archtop, non-cut, multi-bound, f-holes, sunburst (see Super 400 N for natural version).

1934	Super L-5 Deluxe (intro. Model)	$30,000	$40,000
1934-1935		$11,000	$13,000
1936-1940		$9,500	$10,500
1941-1947		$8,000	$9,000
1948-1955		$8,000	$8,500

Super 400 N

1940, 1948-1955. Natural finish version of Super 400, non-cut, acoustic archtop.

1940		$10,000	$14,000
1948-1955		$9,000	$10,000

Super 400 P (Premier)

1939-1941. Acoustic archtop, single rounded cutaway, '39 model 'board rests on top, sunburst finish.

1939		$25,000	$27,000
1940-1941		$23,000	$25,000

The *Vintage Guitar Price Guide* shows low to high values for items in all-original excellent condition, and, where applicable, with original case or cover.

GUITARS

Super 400 C

1948-1982. Introduced as Super 400 Premier, acoustic archtop, single-cut, sunburst finish (natural is called Super 400 CN).

MODEL YEAR FEATURES	EXC. COND. LOW	HIGH
1948-1951	$12,000	$15,000
1952-1957	$12,000	$14,000
1958-1959	$11,000	$13,000
1960-1963	$10,000	$12,000
1964-1965	$9,000	$11,000
1966-1969	$6,500	$10,000
1970-1974	$5,500	$8,000
1975-1982	$4,500	$7,000

Super 400 PN (Premium Natural)

1939-1940. Rounded cutaway, '39 'board rests on top, natural finish.

1939	$40,000	$45,000
1940	$35,000	$40,000

Super 400 CN

1950-1987. Natural finish version of Super 400 C.

1950-1957	$14,000	$16,000
1958-1959	$13,000	$15,000
1960-1964	$12,000	$14,000
1965-1969	$11,000	$12,500

Super 400 CES

1951-present. Electric version of Super 400 C, archtop, single-cut (round '51-'60 and '69-present, pointed '60-'69), 2 pickups (P-90s '51-'54, Alnico Vs '54-'57, humbuckers '57 on), sunburst (natural version called Super 400 CESN), now part of Gibson's Historic Collection.

1951-1953	P-90s	$13,000	$18,000
1954-1956	Alnico Vs	$14,000	$20,000
1957-1959	PAFs	$17,000	$22,000
1960-1962	PAFs	$16,000	$17,000
1963-1964	Pat. #	$13,000	$15,000
1965-1966		$8,000	$12,000
1967-1969		$7,500	$10,000
1970-1974		$7,000	$9,500
1975-1979		$6,500	$7,500
1980-1987		$6,000	$6,500

Super 400 CESN

1952-present. Natural version of Super 400 CES, now part of Gibson's Historic Collection.

1952		$19,000	$25,000
1953-1956	Single coils	$18,000	$22,000
1957-1960	PAFs	$31,000	$35,000
1961	Sharp cut introduced	$29,000	$32,000
1962	PAFs	$25,000	$29,000
1963-1964	Pat. #	$18,000	$20,000
1965-1966		$11,500	$14,500
1967-1969		$11,000	$12,500
1970-1982		$6,500	$10,000

'39 Super 400 Historical Collection

1993-2000. Reissue of non-cut '39 version. Part of Gibson's Historic Collection.

1993-1995	Sunburst	$5,500	$6,500
1993-1995	Wine Red Burgundy	$5,500	$6,500

Super Jumbo 100

1939-1943. Jumbo flat-top, mahogany back and sides, bound body and neck, sunburst, reintroduced as J-100 with different specs in '84.

1939-1943	$18,000	$23,000

Super Jumbo/Super Jumbo 200

1938-1947. Initially called Super Jumbo in '38 and named Super Jumbo 200 in '39. name then changed to J-200 (see that listing) by '47 (with maple back and sides) and SJ-200 by the '50s. Named for super large jumbo 16 7/8" flat-top body, double braced with rosewood back and sides, sunburst finish.

1938-1939	$45,000	$55,000
1940-1942	$45,000	$55,000

Super V CES

1978-1993. Archtop, L-5 with a Super 400 neck, natural or sunburst.

1978-1993	$5,200	$5,700

Tal Farlow

1962-1971, 1993-present. Full body, single-cut archtop, 2 humbucking pickups, triple-bound top, reintroduced '93, now part of Gibson's Historic Collection.

1962-1964	Viceroy Brown	$7,000	$9,000
1965-1966	Viceroy Brown	$6,500	$8,500
1967-1969	Viceroy Brown	$6,000	$7,250
1970-1971	Viceroy Brown	$4,500	$5,800
1993-1999	Cherry or Viceroy Brown	$2,700	$2,900
1993-1999	Natural, figured wood	$3,000	$3,200

TG-0 (L-0 based)

1927-1933. Acoustic tenor based on L-0, mahogany body, light amber.

1927-1933	$1,000	$1,200

TG-0 (LG-0 based)

1960-1974. Acoustic tenor based on LG-0, mahogany body, natural.

1960-1964	$550	$750
1965-1969	$450	$650
1970-1974	$350	$550

TG-00 (L-00 based)

1932-1943. Tenor flat-top based on L-00.

1932-1943	$1,100	$1,300

TG-1/L-1 Tenor/L-4 Tenor (and Plectrum)

1927-1937. Acoustic flat-top, tenor or plectrum guitar based on L-1, mahogany back and sides, bound body, sunburst.

1927-1933	$2,200	$2,500
1934-1937	$1,700	$2,200

TG-7

1934-1940. Tenor based on the L-7, sunburst.

1934-1940	$1,700	$2,200

TG-25/TG-25 N

1962-1970. Acoustic flat-top, tenor guitar based on B-25, mahogany back and sides, natural or sunburst.

1962-1964	$675	$800
1965-1969	$575	$700
1970	$475	$600

1959 Gibson Super 400 CES

Gibson Tal Farlow

1967 Gibson Trini Lopez

MODEL YEAR	FEATURES	EXC. COND. LOW	HIGH

TG-50
1934-1958. Acoustic archtop, tenor guitar based on L-50, mahogany back and sides, sunburst.

1934-1940		$1,100	$1,400
1947-1949		$1,000	$1,300
1950-1958		$900	$1,200

Trini Lopez Deluxe
1964-1970. Double pointed cutaway, thinline archtop, 2 humbuckers, triple-bound, sunburst.

1964-1970		$2,500	$2,800

Trini Lopez Standard
1964-1970. Double rounded cutaway, thinline archtop, 2 humbuckers, tune-o-matic bridge, trapeze tailpiece, single-bound, cherry, sparkling burgundy and Pelham Blue finishes.

1964-1970	Cherry	$1,800	$2,300
1964-1970	Sparkling Burgundy custom	$2,000	$2,600

U-2
1987-1989. Double-cut, 1 humbucker and 2 single-coil pickups, ebony or red, renamed Mach II in '90-'91.

1987-1991		$675	$750

U-2 Showcase Edition
1988. November 1988 Guitar of the Month series, 250 made.

1988		$775	$900

US-1/US-3
1986-1991. Double-cut maple top with mahogany back, 3 humbucker pickups (US-1), or 3 P-90s (US-3), standard production and Custom Shop.

1986-1991	US-3, P-90s	$525	$650

Victory MV II (MV 2)
1981-1984. Asymetrical double-cut with long horn, 3-way slider, maple body and neck, rosewood 'board, 2 pickups.

1981-1984		$700	$1,100

Victory MV X (MV 10)
1981-1984. 3 humbuckers, 5-way switch, various colors.

1981-1984		$1,000	$1,300

XPL Custom
1985-1986. Explorer-like shape, exposed humbuckers, locking tremolo, bound maple top, sunburst or white.

1985-1986		$575	$650

Giffin

1977-1988, 1997-present. Professional and premium grade, production/custom, hollow-, semi-hollow-, and solidbody guitars built by luthier Roger Giffin in West San Fernando Valley, California. For '77-'88, Giffin's shop was in London. From '88 to '93, he worked for the Gibson Custom Shop in California as a Master Luthier. In '97, Giffin set up shop in Sweden for a year, moving back to California in the Spring of '98. He also built small numbers of instruments during '67-'76 and '94-'96 (when he had a repair business).

Gigliotti Special

MODEL YEAR	FEATURES	EXC. COND. LOW	HIGH

Micro Series
1997. Double-cut with long, sharp bass horn, bolt-on neck, quilted maple top over ash body, relatively small and light body, single and humbucker pickups.

1997		$650	$800

Model T
2000s. Double-cut solidbody, 1 bridge position P-90.

2000s		$550	$650

Gigliotti

2000-present. Premium grade, production/custom, electric guitars with a metal plate top and tone chambers and designed by Patrick Gigliotti in Tacoma, Washington.

GS
2004-present. Offset double-cut solidbody, 3 pickups, custom made to order.

2004		$1,800	$1,900

Gila Eban Guitars

1979-present. Premium grade, custom, classical guitars built by luthier Gila Eban in Riverside, Connecticut.

Gilbert Guitars

1965-present. Custom classical guitars by luthiers John Gilbert and William Gilbert in Paso Robles, California. Son William has handled all production since 1991.

Girl Brand Guitars

1996-present. Premium-grade, production/custom, guitars built by luthier Chris Larsen in Tucson, Arizona.

Crossroadsgirl
2004. Single-cut, semi-hollow, 2 single-coils, various artistic custom option finishes and appointments.

2004		$1,500	$2,000

Gitane

2003-present. Classic Selmer-Maccaferri style jazz guitars made in China for Saga.

Gittler

1974-ca.1985. Minimalistic electric guitar designed by Allan Gittler, consisting basically of a thin rod with frets welded to it. A total of 560 were built, with Gittler making the first 60 in the U.S. from '74 to the early '80s. The remainder were made around '85 in Israel by the Astron corporation under a licensing agreement. Three Gittler basses were also built. Gittler emigrated to Israel in the early '80s and changed his name to Avraham Bar Rashi. He died in 2002. An U.S.-made Gittler is the only musical instrument in the Museum of Modern Art in New York.

Metal Skeleton Gittler
1971-1999.

1971-1982		$2,700	$3,500
1982-1999		$1,600	$2,000

The *Vintage Guitar Price Guide* shows low to high values for items in all-original excellent condition, and, where applicable, with original case or cover.

MODEL YEAR	FEATURES	EXC. COND. LOW	HIGH

Godin

1987-present. Intermediate and professional grade, production, solidbody electrics and nylon and steel string acoustic/electrics from luthier Robert Godin. They also build basses and mandolins. Necks and bodies are made in La Patrie, Quebec with final assembly in Berlin, New Hampshire. Godin is also involved in the Seagull, Norman, Art & Lutherie, and Patrick & Simon brand of guitars.

Acousticaster 6

1987-present. Thin line single-cut chambered maple body, acoustic/electric, maple neck, 6-on-a-side tuners, spruce top.

1987-1999		$525	$575
2000-2003		$575	$650

Acousticaster 6 Deluxe

1994-present. Acousticaster 6 with mahogany body.

1994-1999		$575	$675

Artisan ST I/ST I

1992-1998. Offset double-cut solidbody, birdseye maple top, 3 pickups.

1992-1998		$600	$700

Flat Five X

2002-present. Single-cut, semi-hollow with f-holes, 3-way pickup system (magnetic to transducer).

2002-2003		$700	$1,000

G-1000

1993-1996. Double-cut with long bass horn, gold hardware, single-single-humbucker configuration, sunburst.

1993-1996		$250	$425

Glissentar A11

2000-2004. Electric/acoustic nylon 11-string, solid cedar top, chambered maple body, fretless, natural.

2000-2004		$425	$500

Jeff Cook Signature

1994-1995. Quilted maple top, light maple back, 2 twin rail and 1 humbucker pickups.

1994-1995		$525	$600

LG/LGT

1995-present. Single-cut carved slab mahogany body, 2 Tetrad Combo pickups ('95-'97) or 2 Duncan SP-90 pickups ('98-present), various colors, satin lacquer finish. LGT with tremolo.

1997-2001		$325	$425

LGX/LGXT

1996-present. Single-cut maple-top carved solidbody, 2 Duncan humbuckers, various quality tops offered. LGXT with tremolo.

1997-2000	AA top	$700	$900
1997-2000	AAA top	$1,000	$1,200
1997-2000	Standard top	$600	$800

Montreal

2004-present. Chambered body carved from solid mahogany, f-holes, 2 humbuckers, saddle transducer, stereo mixing output.

2004		$800	$900

Multiac Series

1994-present. Single-cut, thinline electric with solid spruce top, RMC Sensor System electronics, available in either nylon string or steel string versions, built-in EQ, program up/down buttons.

1994-1999	Duet Nylon, classical	$525	$675
1994-1999	Steel string	$525	$725
2000-2003	ACS (nylon) SA	$700	$900
2000-2003	Jazz SA	$750	$1,000
2000-2003	Steel string	$550	$750

Radiator

1999-present. Single-cut, dual pickup, pearloid top, dot markers.

1999-2002		$225	$300

Solidac - Two Voice

2000-present Single-cut, 2-voice technology for electric or acoustic sound.

2000-2003		$350	$500

TC Signature

1980s-1999. Single-cut, quilted maple top, 2 Tetrad Combo pickups.

1990s		$600	$700

Golden Hawaiian

1920s-1930s. Private branded lap guitar most likely made by one of the many Chicago makers for a small retailer, publisher, cataloger, or teaching studio.

Guitars

1920s	Sunburst	$275	$475
1930s	Sunburst	$275	$475

Goodall

1972-present. Premium grade, custom flat-tops and nylon-strings, built by luthier James Goodall originally in California and, since '92, in Kailua-Kona, Hawaii.

Acoustic

1980s. Full-size, various models.

1980s		$2,000	$3,000

Gordon-Smith

1979-present. Intermediate and professional grade, production/custom, semi-hollow and solidbody guitars built by luthier John Smith in Partington, England.

Graduate 60

2000s. Single-cut solidbody, exotic woods may be used, dot markers, 2 humbuckers.

2000s		$800	$850

Gould Musical Instruments

Wholesale-importer owned by the Gould family since 1964, Rochester, Minnesota. Student-level imports.

Acoustic

1980s. D-size, laminated (WRM41) or solid wood top (WRM41ST).

1980s	WRM41	$75	$125
1980s	WRM41ST	$100	$150

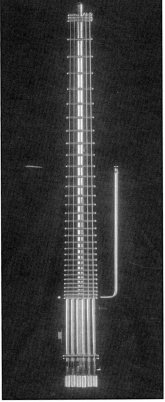

Gittler

Godin Detour

GUITARS

60s Goya Rangemaster

1974 Grammer S-20

MODEL YEAR	FEATURES	EXC. COND. LOW	HIGH

Electric

1980s. Various models include Nighthawk, Snowbird, Warlock and Starfire.

1980s	Nighthawk	$75	$150
1980s	Snowbird	$65	$140
1980s	Starfire	$50	$125
1980s	Warlock	$75	$155

Gower

1955-1960s. Built in Nashville by Jay Gower, later joined by his son Randy. Gower is also associated with Billy Grammer and Grammer guitars.

G-55-2 Flat-Top

1960s. Square shoulder-style flat-top, triple abalone rosette, abalone fretboard trim, small block markers, natural.

1960s		$1,250	$1,500

G-65 Flat-Top

1960s. Square shoulder-style flat-top, lower belly bridge with pearl dots on bridge, dot markers, sunburst.

1960s		$800	$1,200

Solidbody Electric

1960s. Mosrite influenced odd-shaped body, 2 single-coils, bolt neck, Bigsby bridge.

1960s		$500	$800

Goya

1955-present. Brand initially used by Hershman Musical Instrument Company of New York City, New York, in mid-'50s for acoustic guitars made in Sweden by Levin, particularly known for its classicals. From '58 to '61 they imported Hagstrom-made electrics labeled as Goya. By '63 the company had become the Goya Musical Instrument Corporation, marketing primarily Goya acoustics. Goya was purchased by Avnet, Inc., prior to '66, when Avnet purchased Guild Guitars. In '69, Goya was purchased by Kustom which offered the instruments until '71. Probably some '70s guitars were made in Japan. The brand name was purchased by C.F. Martin in the mid-'70s, with Japanese-made acoustic guitars, solidbody electric guitars and basses, banjos and mandolins imported in around '78 and continuing through the '80s. The brand is currently used on Korean-made acoustic and acoustic/electric guitars, banjos and mandolins.

Classical

1955-1980s. Various models low- to high-end. Kustom ownership (imports) in the '70s and Martin ownership (Asia imports) in the '80s.

1955-1959		$300	$800
1960s		$200	$800
1970s		$100	$300
1980s		$100	$300

Folk

1960-1980s. Various models low- to high-end. Kustom ownership (imports) in the '70s and Martin ownership (Asia imports) in the '80s.

1960s		$250	$800
1970s		$100	$300
1980s		$100	$300

MODEL YEAR	FEATURES	EXC. COND. LOW	HIGH

Model 80/Model 90

1959-1962. Single-cut body, replaceable modular pickup assembly, sparkle top.

1959-1962		$700	$1,800

Panther S-3

1960s. Double-cut solidbody, 3 pickups, Panther S-3 Goya logo, volume and tone knobs with 6 upper bass bout switches, bolt-on neck.

1960s		$500	$700

Rangemaster

1967-1969. Double-cut with 2 offset double-coil pickups and lots of buttons, made by EKO, sunburst.

1967-1969		$500	$700

Graf, Oskar

1970-present. Luthier Oskar Graf builds his premium grade, production/custom flat-top, classical, and flamenco guitars in Clarendon, Ontario. He also builds basses and lutes.

Grammer

1965-1970. Founded by Bill Grammer then sold to Ampeg.

G-10

1965-1970. Solid Brazilian rosewood back and sides, solid spruce top, large crown-shaped bridge, pearl dot markers, natural.

1965-1970		$1,300	$1,700

G-20

1965-1970. Natural.

1965-1970		$1,300	$1,700

G-30

1965-1970. Natural.

1965-1970		$1,300	$1,700

G-58

1965-1970. Top-of-the-line Grammer, Brazilian rosewood back and sides, Adirondack spruce top.

1965-1970		$2,100	$2,400

S-30

1965-1970. Solid spruce top, solid ribbon mahogany back and sides.

1965-1970		$1,100	$1,300

Granada

1970s-1980s. Japanes-made acoustic, electric solid, semi-hollow and hollowbody guitars, many copies of classic American models. They also offered basses.

Solidbodies

Various copy models.

1970s		$200	$300

Granata Guitars

1989-present. Luthier Peter Granata builds his professional grade, custom, flat-top and resonator guitars in Oak Ridge, New Jersey.

Graveel

Production/custom, solidbody guitars built by luthier Dean Graveel in Indianapolis, Indiana.

MODEL YEAR	FEATURES	EXC. COND. LOW	HIGH

GRD

1978-1982. High-end acoustic and electric guitars produced in Charles Fox's Guitar Research & Design Center in Vermont. GRD introduced the original thin-line acoustic-electric guitar to the world at the '78 Winter NAMM show.

Greco

1960s-present. Brand name used in Japan by Fuji Gen Gakki, maker of many Hoshino/Ibanez guitars; thus often Greco guitars are similar to Ibanez. During the '70s the company sold many high-quality copies of American designs, though by '75 they offered many weird-shaped original designs, including the Iceman and carved people shapes. By the late-'70s they were offering neck-through-body guitars. Currently owned by Kanda Shokai and offering solidbody, hollowbody and acoustic guitars.

Electric Archtop

1960s		$250	$575

Electric Solidbody

1960s		$250	$575

Electric Violin-Shape

1960s. Beatles violin-shape copy.

1960s		$250	$575

Folk 12-String

1960s		$225	$300

Green, Aaron

1990-present. Premium and presentation grade, custom, classical and flamenco guitars built by luthier Aaron Green in Waltham, Massachusetts.

Greene & Campbell

2002-present. Luthier Dean Campbell builds his intermediate and professional grade, production/custom, solidbody guitars in Westwood, Massachusetts. Founding partner Jeffrey Greene left the company in '04; Greene earlier built guitars under his own name.

Greene, Jeffrey

2000-2002. Professional grade, production/custom, electric solidbody guitars built by luthier Jeffrey Greene in West Kingston, Rhode Island. He went to work with Dean Campbell building the Greene & Campbell line of guitars.

Greenfield Guitars

1997-present. Premium grade, production/custom, flat-top, classical, and electric archtop guitars built by luthier Michael Greenfield in Montreal, Quebec.

Gretsch

1883-present. Currently Gretsch offers intermediate, professional, and premium grade, production, acoustic, solidbody, hollowbody, double neck, resonator and Hawaiian guitars. They also offer basses, amps and lap steels. Previous brands included Gretsch, Rex, 20th Century, Recording King (for Montgomery Ward), Dorado (Japanese imports).

Founded by Friedrich Gretsch in Brooklyn, New York, making drums, banjos, tambourines, and toy instruments which were sold to large distributors including C. Bruno and Wurlitzer. Upon early death of Friedrich, son Fred Gretsch, Sr. took over business at age 15. By the turn of the century the company was also making mandolins. In the '20s, they were distributing Rex and 20th Century brands, some made by Gretsch, some by others such as Kay. Charles "Duke" Kramer joined Gretsch in '35. In '40 Gretsch purchased Bacon & Day banjos. Fred Gretsch, Sr. retired in '42 and was replaced by sons Fred, Jr. and Bill. Fred departs for Navy and Bill runs company until his death in '48, when Fred resumes control. After the war the decision was made to promote the Gretsch brand rather than selling to distributors, though some jobbing continues. Kramer becomes Chicago branch manager in '48.

In '67 Baldwin of Cincinnati buys Gretsch. During '70-'72 the factory relocates from Brooklyn to Booneville, Arkansas and company headquarters moves to Cincinnati. A '72 factory fire drastically reduces production for next two years. In '78 Baldwin buys Kustom amps and sells Gretsch to Kustom's Charlie Roy, and headquarters are moved to Chanute, Kansas. Duke Kramer retires in '80. Guitar production ends '80-'81. Ca. '83 ownership reverts back to Baldwin and Kramer was asked to arrange the sale of the company. In '84 Fred Gretsch III was contacted and in '85 Gretsch guitars came back to the Gretsch family and Fred Gretsch Enterprises, Ltd (FGE). Initial Gretsch Enterprise models were imports made by Japan's Terada Company. In '95, some U.S.-made models were introduced.

As of January 1, 2003, Fred Gretsch Enterprises, Ltd granted Fender Musical Instruments Corporation the exclusive rights to develop, produce, market and distribute Gretsch guitars worldwide where FMIC is responsible for all aspects of the Gretsch stringed instrument product lines and brands, including development of new products. Fred Gretsch consulted during the changeover and on product development and quality control.

12-String Electric Archtop (6075/6076)

1967-1972. 16" double-cut, 2 Super Tron pickups, 17" body option available, sunburst (6075) or natural (6076).

1967	Natural	$1,800	$2,100
1967	Sunburst	$1,700	$2,000

12-String Flat-Top (6020)

1969-1972. 15 1/5" body, mahogany back and sides, spruce top, slotted headstock, dot markers.

1969-1972		$500	$850

Green Concert Classical0

Greenfield Philmore

1966 Gretsch Anniversary

Gretsch Burl Ives

MODEL YEAR	FEATURES	EXC. COND. LOW	HIGH

Anniversary (6124/6125)

1958-1971, 1993-1999. Single-cut hollowbody archtop, 1 pickup (Filtron '58-'60, Hi-Lo Tron '61 on), bound body, named for Gretsch's 75th anniversary. 6124 is 2-tone green with 2-tone tan an option, 6125 sunburst. Model numbers revied in '90s.

1958-1959	Green 2-tone	$1,800	$2,000
1958-1959	Sunburst	$1,600	$1,900
1960-1961	Green 2-tone	$1,800	$2,000
1960-1961	Sunburst	$1,600	$1,900
1962-1964	2-tone green or tan	$1,400	$1,800
1962-1964	Sunburst	$1,300	$1,700
1963	Tan 2-tone	$1,700	$2,100
1965-1966	Various colors	$1,300	$1,600
1967-1969	Various colors	$1,200	$1,400
1970-1971	Various colors	$1,000	$1,200

Anniversary (G6117/G6118)

1993-present. 2 pickup like Double Anniversary, 6118 in 2-tone green with (T) or without Bigsby, 6117 is sunburst.

2002-2004	Green 2-tone	$1,100	$1,200

Astro-Jet (6126)

1965-1967. Solidbody electric, double-cut, 2 pickups, vibrato, 4/2 tuner arrangement, red top with black back and sides.

1965-1967		$1,300	$1,600

Atkins Axe (7685/7686)

1976-1980. Solidbody electric, single pointed cutaway, 2 pickups, ebony stain (7685) or red rosewood stain (7686), called the Super Axe with added onboard effects.

1976-1980		$1,200	$1,400

Atkins Super Axe (7680/7681)

1976-1981. Single pointed cutaway solidbody with built-in phaser and sustain, five knobs, three switches, Red Rosewood (7680) or Ebony (7681) stains.

1976-1981		$1,700	$2,100

Belle (6122)

1982.

1982		$1,100	$1,200

Bikini (6023/6024/6025)

1961-1962. Solidbody electric, separate 6-string and bass neck-body units that slide into 1 of 3 body butterflies - 1 for the 6-string only (6023), 1 for bass only (6024), 1 for double neck (6 and bass - 6025). Components could be purchased separately.

1961-1962	6023/6024, single neck	$700	$900
1961-1962	6025, double neck	$1,550	$1,800

Black Falcon G6136BK (Limited Edition 1955)

1993-1999, 2003-present. Black version of White Falcon G6136 with G tailpiece. Had the 1955 or Limited Edition 1955 designation in the '90s.

1993-1999		$2,100	$2,600

Black Falcon G7593BK (Limited Edition 1955)

1993-1999, 2003-present. G63136BK with Bigsby. Had the Limited Edition 1955 designation in the early '90s.

1993-1999		$2,100	$2,600

Black Falcon G7594BK

1994-1999. Black version of G7594 White Falcon, double-cut, 2" thick body, Bigsby.

1994-1999		$2,000	$2,500

Black Hawk (6100/6101)

1967-1972. Hollowbody archtop, double-cut, 2 pickups, G tailpiece or Bigsby vibrato, bound body and neck, sunburst (6100) or black (6101).

1967-1969	6100, sunburst	$1,900	$2,300
1967-1969	6101, black	$1,700	$2,100
1970-1972	6100, sunburst	$1,800	$2,200
1970-1972	6101, black	$1,600	$2,000

Bo Diddley (6138)

2000-present. Reproduction of rectangle-shaped, semi-hollow guitar originally made for Diddley by Gretsch, Firebird Red.

2000		$1,450	$1,600

Brian Setzer Signature (G6120-SSL)

1994-present. Hollowbody electric, double-cut, 2 Alnico PAF Filtertron pickups, based on the classic Gretsch 6120, formerly called the Brian Setzer Nashville.

1994-1999	Western Orange	$1,800	$2,000

Broadkaster (Hollowbody)

1975-1980. Double-cut archtop, hollowbody, 2 pickups, natural or sunburst.

1975-1977	7603, Bigsby, natural	$1,100	$1,200
1975-1977	7604, Bigsby, sunburst	$1,000	$1,200
1975-1977	7607, G tailpiece, natural	$1,000	$1,100
1975-1977	7608, G tailpiece, sunburst	$900	$1,100
1977-1980	7609, red	$900	$1,100

Broadkaster (Solidbody)

1975-1979. Double-cut, maple body, 2 pickups, bolt-on neck, natural (7600) or sunburst (7601).

1975-1979		$600	$800

BST 1000 Beast

1979-1980. Single-cut solidbody, bolt-on neck, mahogany body, available with 1 pickup in walnut stain (8210) or red stain (8216) or 2 pickups in walnut (7617, 8215, 8217) or red stain (8211).

1979-1980		$450	$550

BST 2000 Beast

1979. Symmetrical double-cut solidbody of mahogany, 2 humbucking pickups, bolt-on neck, walnut stain (7620 or 8220) or red stain (8221).

1979		$500	$600

BST 5000 Beast

1979-1980. Asymmetrical double-cut solidbody, neck-thru, walnut and maple construction, 2 humbucker pickups, stud tailpiece, natural walnut/maple (8250).

1979-1980		$550	$650

Burl Ives (6004)

1949-1955. Flat-top acoustic, mahogany back and sides, bound body, natural top (6004).

1949-1955		$500	$600

MODEL YEAR	FEATURES	EXC. COND. LOW	HIGH

Chet Atkins Country Gentleman (6122/7670)

1957-1981. Hollowbody, single-cut to late-'62 and double after, 2 pickups, painted f-holes until '72, real after, mahogany finish (6122). Model number changes to 7670 in '71.

1957-1960		$5,800	$6,400
1961		$5,700	$6,300
1962		$5,000	$5,700
1962-1963		$3,400	$4,000
1964		$3,060	$3,400
1965		$2,970	$3,300
1966		$2,880	$3,200
1967-1970		$2,790	$3,100
1971-1981	#7670	$1,800	$2,400

Chet Atkins Hollowbody (6120)

1954-1964. Archtop electric, single-cut to '61, double after, 2 pickups, vibrato, f-holes (real to '61 and fake after), G brand on top '54-'56, orange finish (6120). Renamed Chet Atkins Nashville in '64.

1954-1956		$7,300	$8,100
1957-1959		$6,400	$7,100
1960		$5,800	$6,400
1961		$5,500	$6,000
1961-1964		$3,000	$3,300

Chet Atkins Junior

1970. Archtop, single-cut, 1 pickup, vibrato, open f-holes, double-bound body, orange stain.

1970		$1,125	$1,250

Chet Atkins Nashville (6120/7660)

1964-1980. Replaced Chet Atkins Hollowbody (6120), electric archtop, double-cut, 2 pickups, amber red (orange). Renumbered 7660 in '71, reissued in '90 as the Nashville 6120.

1964		$3,000	$3,300
1965-1968		$2,700	$3,000
1969-1970		$2,610	$2,900
1971	#7660	$2,100	$2,600
1972	#7660	$1,800	$2,300
1973-1977	#7660	$1,700	$2,200
1978-1980	#7660	$1,400	$1,900

Chet Atkins Solidbody (6121)

1955-1963. Solidbody electric, single-cut, maple or knotty pine top, 2 pickups, Bigsby vibrato, G brand until '57, multi-bound top, brown mahogany, orange finish (6121).

1955-1956		$6,400	$7,100
1957	G brand	$6,300	$7,100
1957	No G brand	$6,000	$6,300
1958-1959		$5,800	$6,300
1960		$5,600	$6,100
1961-1963		$5,100	$5,600

Chet Atkins Tennessean (6119/7655)

1958-1980. Archtop electric, single-cut, 1 pickup until '61 and 2 after, vibrato. Renumbered as the 7655 in '71.

1958		$3,000	$3,000
1959		$2,900	$3,200
1960-1961	1 pickup	$2,800	$3,100
1961-1964	2 pickups	$2,600	$2,900
1965		$2,400	$2,700

1966-1967		$2,300	$2,550
1968-1970		$2,100	$2,200
1971-1972	#7655	$1,700	$2,200
1973-1980	#7655	$1,500	$2,100

Clipper (6185/6186/6187/7555)

1958-1975. Archtop electric, single-cut, sunburst, 1 pickup (6186) until '72 and 2 pickups (6185) from '72-'75, also available in 1 pickup natural (6187) from '59-'61.

1958-1961	#6186	$1,000	$1,200
1959-1961	#6187	$1,100	$1,300
1962-1967	#6186	$900	$1,100
1968-1971	#6186	$800	$950
1972-1975	#7555	$1,000	$1,200

Committee (7628)

1977-1980. Neck-thru electric solidbody, double-cut, walnut and maple body, 2 pickups, 4 knobs, natural.

1977-1980		$650	$750

Constellation

1955-1960. Renamed from Synchromatic 6030 and 6031, archtop acoustic, single-cut, G tailpiece, humped block inlay.

1955-1956		$2,000	$2,500
1957-1958		$1,900	$2,400
1959-1960		$1,700	$2,200

Convertible (6199)

1955-1958. Archtop electric, single-cut, 1 pickup, multi-bound body, G tailpiece, renamed Sal Salvadore in '58.

1955-1958		$2,200	$3,000

Corsair

1955-1960. Renamed from Synchromatic 100, archtop acoustic, bound body and headstock, G tailpiece, available in sunburst (6014), natural (6015) or burgundy (6016).

1955-1959		$700	$1,000
1960-1965		$650	$950

Corvette (Hollowbody)

1955-1959. Renamed from Electromatic Spanish, archtop electric, 1 pickup, f-holes, bound body, Electromatic on headstock, non-cut, sunburst (6182), natural or Jaguar Tan (6184), and ivory with rounded cutaway (6187).

1955-1959	6182, sunburst	$1,200	$1,500
1955-1959	6184, Jaguar Tan	$1,700	$1,900
1955-1959	6184, natural	$1,700	$1,900
1957-1959	6187, ivory	$1,700	$1,900

Corvette (Solidbody)

1961-1972, 1976-1978. Double-cut slab solidbody. Mahogany 6132 and cherry 6134 1 pickup for '61-'68. 2 pickup mahogany 6135 and cherry 7623 available by '63-'72 and '76-'78. From late-'61 through '63 a Twist option was offered featuring a red candy stripe 'guard. Platinum gray 6133 available for '61-'63 and the Gold Duke and Silver Duke sparkle finishes were offered in '66.

1961-1962	Mahogany, cherry	$700	$900
1961-1963	Platinum gray	$1,100	$1,500
1961-1963	Twist 'guard	$1,300	$1,700
1963-1965	Custom color	$900	$1,200

Gretsch Chet Atkins 6120

1963 Gretsch Corvette

1966 Gretsch Country Club

*1959 Gretsch
Double Anniversary*

MODEL YEAR	FEATURES	EXC. COND. LOW	HIGH
1963-1965	Mahogany, cherry, 1 pickup	$600	$800
1963-1965	Mahogany, cherry, 2 pickups	$800	$1,100
1966	Gold Duke	$1,100	$1,500
1966	Silver Duke	$1,100	$1,500
1966-1968	Mahogany, cherry, 1 pickup	$500	$700
1966-1968	Mahogany, cherry, 2 pickups	$700	$1,000
1969-1972	Mahogany, cherry, 2 pickups	$600	$900
1976-1978	7623, 2 pickups	$500	$650

Country Club

1954-1981. Renamed from Electro II Cutaway, archtop electric, single-cut, 2 pickups (Filter Trons after '57), G tailpiece, multi-bound, various colors.

1954-1956	Cadillac Green or natural	$3,300	$4,300
1954-1956	Sunburst	$2,300	$3,300
1957-1958	Cadillac Green or natural	$3,800	$4,800
1957-1958	Sunburst	$2,800	$3,800
1959	Cadillac Green or natural	$3,800	$4,500
1959	Sunburst	$2,700	$3,500
1960	Cadillac Green	$3,600	$4,400
1960	Sunburst	$2,700	$3,500
1961	Natural	$3,300	$4,000
1961	Sunburst	$2,600	$3,300
1962	Cadillac Green or natural	$3,300	$4,000
1962-1963	Sunburst	$2,500	$3,200
1964	Cadillac Green	$3,100	$4,000
1964	Sunburst	$2,500	$2,800
1965-1967	Sunburst or walnut	$2,300	$2,500
1970-1972	Various colors	$2,100	$2,300
1973-1981	Various colors	$1,900	$2,100

Country Club 1955 (G6196-1955)(FGE)

1995-1999. U.S.-made reissue of Country Club, single-cut, 2 DeArmond pickups, hand-rubbed lacquer finish.

1995-1999		$2,700	$2,900

Country Roc (7620)

1974-1978. Single-cut solidbody, 2 pickups, belt buckle tailpiece, western scene fretboard inlays, G brand, tooled leather side trim.

1974-1978		$1,800	$2,200

Deluxe Chet (7680/7681)

1972-1974. Electric archtop with rounded cutaway, Autumn Red (7680) or brown walnut (7681) finishes.

1972-1974		$2,300	$2,750

Deluxe Flat-Top (7535)

1972-1978 16" redwood top, mahogany back and sides.

1972-1978		$1,700	$2,000

Double Anniversary Mono (6117/6118)

1958-1976. Archtop electric, single-cut, 2 pickups, stereo optional until '63, sunburst (6117) or green 2-tone (6118). Reissued in '93 as the Anniversary 6117 and 6118.

1958-1960	Green 2-tone	$2,500	$2,900

MODEL YEAR	FEATURES	EXC. COND. LOW	HIGH
1958-1960	Sunburst	$2,300	$2,700
1960-1961	Green 2-tone	$2,200	$2,600
1960-1961	Sunburst	$2,100	$2,500
1962-1964	Green 2-tone	$2,000	$2,400
1962-1964	Sunburst	$1,900	$2,300
1963	Tan 2-tone	$2,400	$2,800
1965-1966	Various colors	$1,500	$2,100
1967-1969	Various colors	$1,400	$2,000
1970-1974	Various colors	$1,300	$1,700
1975-1976	Various colors	$1,200	$1,600

Double Anniversary Stereo (6111/6112)

1961-1963. One stereo channel/signal per pickup, sunburst (6111) or green (6112).

1961-1963	Green	$2,500	$2,900
1961-1963	Sunburst	$2,300	$2,700

Duo-Jet (6128)

1953-1971. Solidbody electric, single-cut until '61, double after, 2 pickups. black (6128) with a few special ordered in green, sparkle finishes were offered '63-'66, reissued in '90.

1953-1956	Black	$4,700	$5,100
1956-1957	Cadillac Green	$7,000	$8,000
1957	Black	$4,400	$4,900
1958-1960	Black	$4,000	$4,600
1961-1964	Black	$3,300	$4,200
1963-1966	Sparkle-gold, champagne, burgundy or tangerine	$3,500	$4,500
1964-1966	Silver sparkle	$3,500	$4,500
1965-1967	Black	$2,400	$3,300
1968-1971	Black	$2,000	$2,400

Duo-Jet Reissue (G6128)

1990-present. Reissue of the '50s solidbody, black, optional Bigsby (G6128T).

1990-2002		$1,100	$1,300

Duo-Jet Tenor

1959-1960. Electric tenor, 4 strings, block inlays, black.

1959-1960		$2,000	$2,400

Eldorado (6038/6039)

1959-1968. The smaller 17" version, named Fleetwood from '55 to '58, sunburst (6038) or natural (6039).

1960-1963	Natural	$1,900	$2,300
1960-1963	Sunburst	$1,700	$2,100
1964-1965	Natural	$1,700	$2,100
1964-1965	Sunburst	$1,500	$1,900
1966-1968	Natural	$1,600	$2,000
1966-1968	Sunburst	$1,500	$1,800

Eldorado (6040/6041)

1955-1970, 1991-1997. This is the larger 18" version, renamed from Synchromatic 400, archtop acoustic, single-cut, triple-bound fretboard and peghead, sunburst (6040) or natural (6041). Reintroduced in '91, made by Heritage in Kalamazoo, as the G410 Synchromatic

Eldorado in sunburst or natural (G410M).

1955-1959	Natural	$2,700	$3,100
1955-1959	Sunburst	$2,500	$2,800
1960-1963	Natural	$2,300	$2,700

MODEL YEAR	FEATURES	EXC. COND. LOW	HIGH
1960-1963	Sunburst	$2,100	$2,400
1964-1965	Natural	$2,000	$2,400
1964-1965	Sunburst	$1,800	$2,200
1966-1967	Natural	$1,900	$2,300
1966-1967	Sunburst	$1,700	$2,100
1968-1969	Sunburst	$1,600	$2,000
1991-1997	Natural	$1,800	$2,200
1991-1997	Sunburst	$1,500	$1,900

Electro Classic (6006/6495)
1969-1973. Classical flat-top with piezo pickup.

1969-1970	#6006	$700	$1,000
1971-1973	#6495	$600	$1,000

Electro II Cutaway (6192/6193)
1951-1954. Archtop electric, single-cut, Melita bridge by '53, 2 pickups, f-holes, sunburst (6192) or natural (6193). Renamed Country Club in '54.

1951-1954	Natural	$3,300	$4,200
1951-1954	Sunburst	$2,300	$3,200

Electromatic Spanish (6185/6185N)
1940-1955. Hollowbody, 17" wide, 1 pickup, sunburst (6185) or natural (6185N). Renamed Corvette (hollowbody) in '55.

1940-1949	Sunburst	$1,200	$1,500
1950-1955	Natural	$1,700	$1,900
1950-1955	Sunburst	$1,200	$1,500

Fleetwood (6038/6039)
1955-1958. Named Synchromatic prior to '55, sunburst (6038) or natural (6039). Renamed Eldorado in '59, available by custom order.

1955-1968		$2,500	$2,800

Folk/Folk Singing (6003/7505/7506)
1963-1975. Lower-model of Gretsch flat-tops, 14 1/4", mahogany back and sides. Renamed from Jimmie Rodgers model, renamed Folk Singing in '63.

1963-1965		$600	$900
1966-1969		$500	$800
1970-1975		$400	$700

Golden Classic (Hauser Model/Model 6000)
1961-1969. Grand Concert body size, nylon-string classical, 14 1/4" spruce top, mahogany back and sides, multiple inlaid sound hole purfling, inlaid headstock.

1961-1969		$500	$800

Grand Concert (6003)
1955-1959. Lower-model of Gretsch flat-tops, 14 1/4", mahogany back and sides. Renamed from Model 6003 and renamed Jimmie Rodgers in '59.

1955-1959		$450	$700

Jet Firebird (6131)
1955-1971, 1990-present. Solidbody electric, single-cut until '61, double '61-'71, 2 pickups, black body with red top, reissued in '90.

1955-1956		$4,400	$4,800
1957		$4,100	$4,600
1958-1960		$3,700	$4,300
1961-1964		$3,000	$3,700
1965-1967		$2,000	$3,000
1968-1971	Super Trons	$1,900	$2,000

Jet FirebirdReissue (G6131/G6131T)
1991-1999, 2003-present. Based on '58 specs, single-cut, red top, black neck and back, 2 FilterTrons, thumbprint markers, Bigsby available (T).

2003-2004		$1,200	$1,500

Jimmie Rodgers (6003)
1959-1962. 14" flat-top with round hold, mahogany back and sides, renamed from Grand Concert and renamed Folk Singing in '63.

1959-1962		$450	$700

Jumbo Synchromatic (125F)
1947-1955. 17" flat-top, triangular soundhole, bound top and back, metal bridge anchor plate, adjustable wood bridge, natural top with sunburst back and sides or optional translucent white-blond top and sides.

1947-1955	Natural	$1,600	$2,100
1947-1955	White-blond	$1,700	$2,200

Model 25 (Acoustic)
1933-1939. 16" archtop, no binding on top or back, dot markers, sunburst.

1933-1939		$650	$800

Model 30 (Acoustic)
1939-1949. 16" archtop, top binding, dot markers, sunburst.

1939-1949		$700	$900

Model 35 (Acoustic)
1933-1949. 16" archtop, single-bound top and back, dot markers, sunburst.

1933-1949		$800	$1,000

Model 50/50R (Acoustic)
1936-1939. Acoustic archtop, F-holes. Model 50R has round soundhole.

1936-1939	Model 50	$900	$1,200

Model 65 (Acoustic)
1933-1939. Archtop acoustic, bound body, amber.

1933-1939		$1,000	$1,300

Model 6003
1951-1955. 14 1/4", mahogany back and sides, renamed Grand Concert in '55.

1951-1954		$500	$700

Model TW300T (Traveling Wilburys)
1988-1990. Promotional guitar, solidbody electric, single-cut, 1 and 2 pickups, 6 variations, graphics.

1988-1990		$275	$325

Monkees
1966-1969. Hollowbody electric, double-cut, 2 pickups, Monkees logo on 'guard, bound top, f-holes and neck, vibrato, red.

1966-1969		$1,600	$1,900

New Yorker
Ca.1949-1970. Archtop acoustic, f-holes, sunburst.

1949-1951		$650	$800
1952-1954		$600	$750
1955-1959		$550	$700
1960-1965		$500	$650
1966-1970		$450	$600

Ozark/Ozark Soft String (6005)
1965-1968. 16" classical, rosewood back and sides.

1965-1968		$700	$1,200

Gretsch Jet Firebird Reissue

Gretsch Monkees

1954 Gretsch Roundup (6130)

1954 Gretsch Silver Jet

MODEL YEAR	FEATURES	EXC. COND. LOW	HIGH

Princess (6106)
1963. Corvette-type solidbody double-cut, 1 pickup, vibrato, gold parts, colors available were white/grape, blue/white, pink/white, or white/gold, often sold with the Princess amp.

1963		$1,750	$2,200

Rally (6104/6105)
1967-1969. Archtop, double-cut, 2 pickups, vibrato, racing strip on truss rod cover and pickguard, green or yellow.

1967-1969		$1,600	$1,800

Rambler (6115)
1957-1961. Small body electric archtop, single-cut, 1 pickup, G tailpiece, bound body and headstock.

1957-1961		$1,200	$1,400

Rancher
1954-1980. Flat-top acoustic, triangle soundhole, Western theme inlay, G brand until '61 and '75 and after, golden red (orange), reissued in '90.

1954-1955	G brand	$4,000	$5,000
1956-1957	G brand	$4,000	$5,000
1958-1961	G brand	$3,500	$4,500
1962-1964	No G brand	$3,000	$4,000
1965-1966	No G brand	$2,500	$3,500
1967-1969	No G brand	$2,000	$3,000
1970-1974	No G brand	$1,600	$2,500
1975-1980	G brand	$1,600	$2,500

Roc I/Roc II (7635/7621)
1974-1976. Electric solidbody, mahogany, single-cut, Duo-Jet-style body, 1 pickup (7635) or 2 pickups (7621), bound body and neck.

1974-1976	Roc I	$700	$900
1974-1977	Roc II	$800	$1,000

Roc Jet
1969-1980. Electric solidbody, single-cut, 2 pickups, adjustamatic bridge, black, cherry, pumpkin or walnut.

1970-1972		$1,100	$1,500
1973-1976		$1,000	$1,400
1977-1980		$900	$1,300

Round-Up (6130)
1954-1960. Electric solidbody, single-cut, 2 pickups, G brand, belt buckle tailpiece, maple, pine, knotty pine or orange. Reissued in '90.

1954-1956	Knotty pine (2 knots)	$12,000	$15,000
1954-1956	Knotty pine (4 knots)	$15,000	$20,000
1954-1956	Maple	$9,000	$12,000
1954-1956	Pine	$9,000	$12,000
1957-1960	Orange	$8,000	$11,000

Round-Up Reissue (G6121)
1990-1995, 2003-present. Based on the '50s model, Western Orange, G brand.

1990-1995		$1,250	$1,350

Sal Fabraio (6117)
1964-1968. Double-cut thin electric archtop, distinctive cats-eye f-holes, 2 pickups, sunburst, ordered for resale by guitar teacher Sal Fabraio.

1964-1968		$2,000	$2,400

Sal Salvador (6199)
1958-1968. Electric archtop, single-cut, 1 pickup, triple-bound neck and headstock, sunburst.

1958-1959		$2,200	$3,500
1960-1962		$2,100	$3,200
1963-1964		$2,000	$2,600
1965-1966		$1,800	$2,500
1967-1968		$1,700	$2,300

Sho Bro (Hawaiian/Spanish)
1969-1978. Flat-top acoustic, multi-bound, resonator, lucite fretboard, Hawaiian version non-cut, square neck and Spanish version non- or single-cut, round neck.

1969-1978	Hawaiian	$700	$750
1969-1978	Spanish	$700	$950

Silver Classic (Hauser Model/Model 6001)
1961-1969. Grand Concert body size, nylon-string classical. Similar to Golden Classic but with less fancy appointments.

1961-1969		$350	$550

Silver Falcon G6136SL (1955)
1993-1999, 2003-present. Silver version of White Falcon G6136 with G tailpiece. Had the 1955 designation in the '90s.

1995-1999		$2,100	$2,600

Silver Falcon G7594SL
1995-1999. Silver version of G7594 White Falcon, double-cut, 2" thick body, Bigsby.

1995-1999		$2,000	$2,500

Silver Jet (6129)
1954-1963. Solidbody electric, single-cut until '61, double '61-'63, 2 pickups, Duo-Jet with silver sparkle top, reissued in '90. Optional sparkle colors were offered but were not given their own model numbers; refer to Duo-Jet listing for optional colors.

1954-1956	Silver	$5,500	$7,000
1957	Silver	$5,000	$6,500
1958-1960	Silver	$4,500	$5,500
1961-1963	Silver, double-cut	$4,000	$5,000

Silver Jet 1957 Reissue (G6129-1957)
1990-present. Reissue of single-cut '50s Silver Jet, silver sparkle.

1990-1993		$1,225	$1,300
1994-1996		$1,325	$1,400
1997-1999		$1,425	$1,500

Southern Belle (7176)
1983. Electric archtop, walnut, Country Gentleman parts from the late-'70s assembled in Mexico and marketed as Southern Belle, based upon Belle (6122).

1983		$1,100	$1,200

Sparkle Jet
1994-present. Electric solidbody, single-cut, 2 pickups, Duo-Jet with sparkle finish.

1995-1999		$1,100	$1,300

Streamliner Double Cutaway (6102/6103)
1968-1973. Reintroduced from single-cut model, electric archtop, double-cut, 2 pickups, G tailpiece, cherry or sunburst.

1968-1969		$1,500	$1,900
1970-1973		$1,400	$1,800

The *Vintage Guitar Price Guide* shows low to high values for items in all-original excellent condition, and, where applicable, with original case or cover.

MODEL YEAR	FEATURES	EXC. COND. LOW	HIGH

Streamliner Single Cutaway (6189/6190/6191)

1955-1959. Electric archtop, single-cut, maple top, G tailpiece, 1 pickup, multi-bound, Bamboo Yellow (6189), sunburst (6190), or natural (6191), name reintroduced as a double-cut in '68.

1955-1959		$2,100	$2,500

Sun Valley (6010/7515/7514)

1959-1977. Flat-top acoustic, laminated Brazilian rosewood back and sides, multi-bound top, natural or sunburst.

1959-1964		$800	$1,300
1965-1969		$700	$1,200
1970-1977		$600	$1,000

Super Chet (7690/7690-B/7691/7691-B)

1972-1980. Electric archtop, single rounded cutaway, 2 pickups, gold hardware, mini control knobs along edge of 'guard, Autumn Red or walnut.

1972-1976		$2,600	$3,200
1977-1980		$2,100	$2,700

Supreme (7545)

1972-1978. Flat-top 16", spruce top, mahogany or rosewood body options, gold hardware.

1972-1978	Mahogany	$1,300	$1,600
1972-1979	Rosewood	$1,700	$2,000

Synchromatic (6030/6031)

1951-1954. 17" acoustic archtop, becomes Constellation in '55.

1951-1955		$1,700	$2,000

Synchromatic (6038/6039)

1951-1955. 17" acoustic archtop, single-cut, G tailpiece, multi-bound, sunburst (6038) or natural (6039), renamed Fleetwood in '55.

1951-1955	Sunburst	$1,900	$2,200

Synchromatic 75

1939-1949. Acoustic archtop, f-holes, multi-bound, large floral peghead inlay.

1939-1949		$1,200	$1,500

Synchromatic 100

1939-1955. Renamed from No. 100F, acoustic archtop, double-bound body, amber, sunburst or natural, renamed Corsair in '55.

1939-1949	Natural	$1,400	$1,700
1939-1949	Sunburst	$1,200	$1,500
1950-1955	Sunburst	$1,000	$1,300

Synchromatic 160 (6028/6029)

1939-1943, 1947-1951. Acoustic archtop, catseye soundholes, maple back and sides, triple-bound, natural or sunburst.

1939-1943	Sunburst	$1,300	$1,700
1947-1951	Sunburst	$1,200	$1,400
1948-1951	Natural	$1,400	$1,700

Synchromatic 200

1939-1949. Acoustic archtop, cats-eye soundholes, maple back and sides, multi-bound, gold-plated hardware, amber or natural.

1939-1949		$1,800	$2,100

Synchromatic 300

1939-1955. Acoustic archtop, cats-eye soundholes until '51 and f-holes after, multi-bound, natural or sunburst.

1939-1949	Natural	$2,500	$3,000

MODEL YEAR	FEATURES	EXC. COND. LOW	HIGH
1939-1949	Sunburst	$2,200	$2,700
1950-1955	Natural	$2,200	$2,700
1950-1955	Sunburst	$2,000	$2,500

Synchromatic 400

1940-1955. Acoustic archtop, cats-eye soundholes until '51 and f-holes after, multi-bound, gold hardware, natural or sunburst.

1940-1949	Natural	$6,000	$6,500
1940-1949	Sunburst	$5,500	$6,000
1950-1955	Natural	$5,500	$6,000
1950-1955	Sunburst	$5,000	$5,500

Synchromatic Limited (G450/G450M)

1997. Acoustic archtop, hand carved spruce (G450) or maple (G450M) top, floating pickup, sunburst, only 50 were to be made.

1997	Maple	$1,300	$1,500
1997	Spruce	$1,200	$1,400

Synchromatic Sierra

1949-1955. Renamed from Synchromatic X75F (see below), acoustic flat-top, maple back and sides, triangular soundhole, sunburst.

1949-1955		$1,200	$1,500

Synchromatic X75F

1947-1949. Acoustic flat-top, maple back and sides, triangular soundhole, sunburst, renamed Synchromatic Sierra in '49.

1947-1949		$1,200	$1,500

TK 300 (7624/7625)

1977-1981. Double-cut maple solidbody, 1 humbucker, bolt-on neck, six-on-a-side tuners, hockey stick headstock, Autumn Red or natural.

1977-1981		$575	$700

Town and Country (6021)

1954-1959. Renamed from Jumbo Synchromatic 125 F, flat-top acoustic, maple back and sides, triangular soundhole, multi-bound.

1954-1959		$1,900	$2,100

Van Eps 7-String (6079/6080)

1968-1978. Electric archtop, single-cut, 2 pickups, 7 strings, sunburst or walnut.

1968-1978		$2,500	$3,100

Viking (6187/6188/6189)

1964-1975. Electric archtop, double-cut, 2 pickups, vibrato, sunburst (6187), natural (6188) or Cadillac Green (6189).

1964-1967	Cadillac Green	$2,500	$3,000
1964-1967	Natural	$2,500	$3,000
1964-1967	Sunburst	$2,000	$2,700
1968-1970	Cadillac Green	$2,100	$2,300
1968-1970	Natural	$2,200	$2,500
1968-1970	Sunburst	$2,300	$2,700
1971-1972	Various colors	$2,100	$2,300
1973-1975	Various colors	$1,900	$2,100

Wayfarer Jumbo (6008)

1969-1971. Flat-top acoustic dreadnought, non-cut, maple back and sides, multi-bound.

1969-1971		$500	$900

1973 Gretsch Super Chet

*1940s Gretsch
Synchromatic 400*

Gretsch White Falcon 6136T

Grosh Custom T Carve

MODEL YEAR	FEATURES	EXC. COND. LOW	HIGH

White Falcon Mono (6136/7595)
1955-1981. Includes the single-cut 6136 of '55-'61, the double-cut 6136 of '62-'70, and the double-cut 7594 of '71-'81.

1955	Single-cut 6136	$25,000	$30,000
1956		$24,000	$29,000
1957		$23,000	$28,000
1958		$22,000	$25,000
1959-1961		$21,000	$24,000
1962-1963	Double-cut 6136	$10,000	$12,000
1964		$9,000	$11,000
1965		$7,500	$10,000
1966		$7,000	$9,000
1967-1969		$6,200	$8,200
1970		$5,000	$6,000
1971-1972	Model 7594	$4,500	$5,700
1973-1979		$4,000	$5,600
1980-1981		$3,500	$5,300

White Falcon Stereo (6137/7595)
1958-1981. Features Project-O-Sonic Stereo, includes Includes the single-cut 6137 of '58-'61, the double-cut 6137 of '62-'70, and the double-cut 7595 of '71-'81.

1958	Early stereo specs	$25,000	$30,000
1959-1961	Single-cut 6137	$24,000	$28,000
1962-1963	Double-cut 6137	$11,000	$14,000
1964		$10,000	$13,000
1965		$8,000	$12,000
1966		$8,000	$10,400
1967-1969		$7,100	$9,400
1970		$5,800	$6,900
1971-1972	Model 7595	$5,200	$6,600
1973-1979		$4,600	$6,400
1980-1981		$4,000	$6,100

White Falcon G6136-1955 Custom USA
1995-1999. U.S.-made, single-cut, DynaSonic pickups, gold sparkle appointments, rhinestone embedded knobs, white. In '04, Current U.S. model called G6136CST is released. The import White Falcon has sometimes been listed with the 1955 designation and is not included here.

1995-1999		$4,200	$5,700

White Falcon G7593/G7593 I
1993-present. G6136 with added Bigsby. Currently sold as G7593 White Falcon I.

1991-1999		$2,100	$2,600

White Falcon I/G6136
1991-present. Single-cut, white, 2.75" thick body, Cadillac G tailpiece. Called the White Falcon I for '91-'92 (not to be confused with current White Falcon I G7593). See Black and Silver Falcons under those listings.

1991-1999		$2,100	$2,600

White Falcon II/G7594
1991-present. Double-cut, white, 2" thick body, Bigsby. Called the White Falcon II for '91-'92, the G7594 for '93-ca. '02, and White Falcon II G7594 since.

1991-1999		$2,000	$2,500

MODEL YEAR	FEATURES	EXC. COND. LOW	HIGH

White Penguin (6134)
1955-1964. Electric solidbody, single-cut until '62, double '62-'64, 2 pickups (DeArmond until '58 then Filter Tron), fewer than 100 made, white, gold sparkle bound, gold-plated parts. More than any other model, there seems a higher concern regarding forgery.

1956-1958		$80,000	$100,000
1959-1960		$70,000	$90,000
1961-1962		$70,000	$80,000
1962-1964		$65,000	$80,000

White Penguin G6134
1996-present. White, single-cut, metalflake binding, gold hardware, jeweled knobs, Cadillac G tailpiece.

1996-1999		$2,900	$3,300

Greven
1969, 1975-present. Luthier John Greven builds his premium grade, production/custom, acoustic guitars in Portland, Oregon.

Griffin String Instruments
1976-present. Luthier Kim Griffin builds his professional and premium grade, production/custom, parlor, steel-string, and classical guitars in Greenwich, New York.

Grimes Guitars
1974-present. Premium and presentation grade, custom, flat-tops, nylon-strings, archtops, semi-hollow electrics made by luthier Steve Grimes originally in Port Townsend, Washington, and since '82 in Kula, Hawaii.

Groove Tools
2002-2004. Korean-made, production, intermediate grade, 7-string guitars that were offered by Conklin Guitars of Springfield, Missouri.

Solidbody Electrics
2002-2004.

2002-2004		$225	$325

Grosh, Don
1993-present. Professional and premium grade, production/custom, solid and semi-hollow body guitars built by luthier Don Grosh in Santa Clarita, California. He also builds basses. Grosh worked in production for Valley Arts from '84-'92. Guitars generally with bolt necks until '03 when set-necks were added to the line.

Classical Electric
1990s. Single-cut solidbody with nylon strings and piezo-style hidden pickup, highly figured top.

1990s		$1,200	$1,700

Custom S Bent Top
Offset double-cut, figured maple carved top, 2 pickups.

2003		$1,400	$1,900

Custom T Carve Top
Single-cut, figured maple carved top, 2 pickups.

2003		$1,400	$1,900

MODEL YEAR FEATURES	EXC. COND. LOW	HIGH
Retro Classic		
1993-present. Offset double-cut, 3 pickups.		
2001	$1,400	$1,800
Retro Vintage T		
1993-present. Single-cut, black 'guard.		
2001	$1,400	$1,800

Gruen Acoustic Guitars

1999-present. Luthier Paul Gruen builds his professional grade, custom steel-string guitars in Chapel Hill, North Carolina. His speciality is his E.Q. model, which features 5 soundholes, 4 of which can be plugged with wooden stoppers to give different tonal balances.

Gruggett

Mid 1960s-present. In the 1960s, luthier Bill Gruggett worked with Mosrite and Hallmark guitars as well as building electric guitars under his own name in Bakersfield, California. He still makes his Stradette model for Hallmark guitars.

Guernsey Resophonic Guitars

1989-present. Production/custom, resonator guitars built by luthier Ivan Guernsey in Marysville, Indiana.

Guild

1952-present. Professional and premium grade, production/custom, acoustic, acoustic/electric, hollowbody and semi-hollowbody guitars. Founded in New York City by jazz guitarist Alfred Dronge, employing many ex-Epiphone workers. The company was purchased by Avnet, Inc., in '66 and the Westerly, Rhode Island factory was opened in '68. Hoboken factory closed in '71 and headquarters moved to Elizabeth, New Jersey. Company was Guild Musical Instrument Corporation in '86 but was in bankruptcy in '88. Purchased by Faas Corporation, New Berlin, Wisconsin, which became the U.S. Musical Corporation. The brand was purchased by Fender Musical Instrument Corporation in '95. The Guild Custom Shop opened in Nashville in '97. The Guild Custom Shop remains in Nashville, while all other Guild U.S. production has been moved to Corona, , California.

A-50
1994-1996. Original A-50 models can be found under the Cordoba A-50 listing, the new model drops the Cordoba name, size 000 flat top, spruce top, Indian rosewood body.

	EXC. COND. LOW	HIGH
1994-1996	$900	$1,000

Aragon F-30
1954-1986. Acoustic flat-top, spruce top, laminated maple arched back (mahogany back and sides by '59), reintroduced as just F-30 in '98.

1954-1959	$950	$1,200
1960-1969	$850	$1,100
1970-1986	$700	$800

Aragon F-30 NT
1959-1985. Natural finish version of F-30.

	EXC. COND. LOW	HIGH
1959-1969	$1,000	$1,300
1970-1985	$750	$850

Aragon F-30 R
1973-1995. Rosewood back and sides version of F-30, sunburst.

1973-1979	$850	$950

Aristocrat M-75
1955-1963, 1967-1968. Electric archtop, single-cut, 2 pickups, blond or sunburst, name changed to Bluesbird M-75 in '68.

1955-1959	$2,600	$3,000
1960-1963	$2,400	$2,900
1967-1968	$1,200	$1,500

Aristocrat M-75 Tenor
Mid-late 1950s. Tenor version of 6-string Aristocrat electric, dual soapbar pickups, 4 knobs.

1950s	$2,400	$2,600

Artist Award
1961-1999. Renamed from Johnny Smith Award, single-cut electric archtop, floating DeArmond pickup (changed to humbucker in '80), multi-bound, gold hardware, sunburst or natural.

1961-1969	$4,100	$4,600
1970-1979	$4,000	$4,500
1980-1989	$3,600	$4,100
1990-1999	$3,300	$3,800

Artist F-312 12-String
1963-1973. Flat-top, rosewood back and sides, spruce top, no board inlay (but some in '72 may have dots).

1964-1968	Brazilian rosewood	$1,800	$2,000
1969-1973	Indian rosewood	$1,200	$1,400

Bluegrass D-25/D-25 M
1968-1999. Flat-top, mahogany top until '76, spruce after, mahogany back and sides, various colors, called Bluegrass D-25 M in late-'70s and '80s, listed as D-25 in '90s.

1968-1979	$800	$900
1980-1989	$750	$825
1990-1999	$700	$775

Bluegrass D-25-12
1987-1992, 1996-1999. 12-string version of D-25.

1987-1992	$700	$800
1996-1999	$675	$800

Bluegrass D-35
1966-1988. Acoustic flat-top, spruce top and mahogany back and sides, rosewood 'board and bridge, natural.

1966-1969	$850	$1,000
1970-1979	$800	$950
1980-1988	$775	$875

Bluegrass F-47
1963-1976. 16" narrow-waist style, mahogany sides and back, acoustic flat-top, spruce top, mahogany back and sides, bound rosewood 'board and bridge, natural.

1963-1969	$1,300	$1,500
1970-1976	$1,200	$1,400

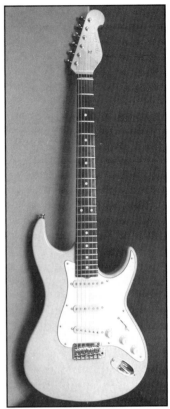

Grosh Retro Classic

1970s Guild Bluesbird

Guild Brian May BHM-1

1970s Guild Bluesbird

MODEL YEAR	FEATURES	EXC. COND. LOW	HIGH
Bluegrass Jubilee D-40			
1963-1992. Acoustic flat-top, spruce top, mahogany back and sides, rosewood 'board and bridge, natural.			
1963-1969		$1,000	$1,200
1970-1979		$950	$1,150
1980-1992		$900	$1,100
Bluegrass Jubilee D-40 C			
1975-1991. Acoustic flat-top, single Florentine cutaway, mahogany back and sides, rosewood 'board and bridge, natural.			
1975-1979		$900	$1,050
1980-1991		$875	$1,000
Bluegrass Jubilee D-44			
1965-1972. Acoustic flat-top, spruce top, pearwood back and sides, ebony 'board, rosewood bridge.			
1965-1969		$1,000	$1,200
1970-1972		$950	$1,050
Bluegrass Jubilee D-44 M			
1971-present. Acoustic flat top, spruce top, maple back & sides, ebony fingerboard, rosewood bridge.			
1971-1979		$900	$1,200
1980-1985		$850	$1,050
Bluegrass Special D-50			
1963-1993. Acoustic flat-top, spruce top, rosewood back and sides, ebony fretboard, multi-bound.			
1963-1968	Brazilian rosewood	$2,500	$3,000
1969-1979		$1,900	$2,100
1980-1993		$1,500	$1,900
Blues 90			
Ca. 1997-present. Single-cut with 2 P-90 style pickups.			
1997-1998		$925	$1,025
Bluesbird M-75 (Hollowbody)			
1968-1970. Reintroduced from Aristocrat M-75, thinbody electric archtop of maple, spruce or mahogany, single-cut, 2 pickups, reintroduced as a solidbody in '70.			
1968-1970		$1,200	$1,500
Bluesbird M-75 (Solidbody)			
1970-1978. Solidbody version of hollowbody Bluesbird M-75, mahogany body, rounded cutaway, 2 pickups.			
1970-1978		$1,200	$1,500
Bluesbird (Reintroduced)			
1998-2004. AAA flamed top.			
1998-2001		$1,150	$1,250
2002-2004		$1,150	$1,250
Brian May BHM-1			
1984-1987. Electric solidbody, double-cut, vibrato, 3 pickups, bound top and back, red or green, Brian May Pro, Special and Standard introduced in '94.			
1984-1987		$2,200	$2,600
Brian May Pro			
1994-1995. Electric solidbody, double-cut, vibrato, 3 pickups, bound top and back, various colors.			
1994-1995		$1,700	$2,100

MODEL YEAR	FEATURES	EXC. COND. LOW	HIGH
CA-100 Capri			
1956-1973. Acoustic archtop version of CE-100, sharp Florentine cutaway, solid spruce top, laminated maple back and sides, rosewood 'board and bridge, nickel-plated metal parts, natural or sunburst.			
1956-1959		$1,100	$1,400
1960-1969		$1,100	$1,400
1970-1973		$1,000	$1,300
Capri CE-100			
1956-1985. Electric archtop, single Florentine cutaway, 1 pickup (2 pickups by '83), maple body, Waverly tailpiece, sunburst, in '59-'82 CE-100 D listed with 2 pickups.			
1956-1959		$1,100	$1,400
1960-1969		$1,100	$1,400
1970-1979		$1,000	$1,300
1980-1985		$1,000	$1,200
Capri CE-100 D			
1956-1982. Electric archtop, single Florentine cutaway, 2 pickups, maple body, sunburst, Waverly tailpiece (D dropped, became the Capri CE-100 in '83).			
1956-1959		$1,500	$1,700
1960-1969		$1,400	$1,700
1970-1979		$1,300	$1,600
1980-1982		$1,200	$1,500
Citron X-92			
1984. Electric solidbody, detachable body section, 3 pickups.			
1984		$300	$350
Cordoba A-50			
1961-1972. Acoustic archtop, lowest-end in the Guild archtop line, named Granda A-50 prior to '61.			
1961-1972		$575	$625
Cordoba T-50 Slim			
1961-1973. Thinbody version of Cordoba X-50.			
1961-1973		$850	$1,000
Cordoba X-50			
1961-1970. Electric archtop non-cut, laminated maple body, rosewood 'board, 1 pickup, nickel-plated parts.			
1961-1970		$850	$1,000
Custom F-412 12-String			
1968-1986. Special order only from '68-'74, then regular production, 17" wide body 12-string version of F-50 flat-top, spruce top, maple back and sides, arched back, 2-tone block inlays, gold hardware, natural finish.			
1968-1974		$1,550	$1,800
1975-1979		$1,350	$1,600
1980-1986		$1,250	$1,500
Custom F-512 12-String			
1968-1986. 1968-1986, 1990. Rosewood back and sides version of F-412.			
1968-1969		$1,600	$1,900
1970-1979		$1,400	$1,700
1980-1986		$1,300	$1,600
Custom F-612 12-String			
1972-1973. Acoustic 12-string, similar to Custom F-512, but with 18" body, fancy mother-of-pearl inlays, and black/white marquee body, neck and headstock binding..			
1972-1973		$1,800	$2,100

MODEL YEAR	FEATURES	EXC. COND. LOW	HIGH

Custom Shop 45th Anniversary
1997. Built in Guild's Nashville Custom Shop, all solid wood, spruce top, maple back and sides, with high-end appointments.

1997	Natural, Gold hardware	$2,200	$2,500

D-4 Series
1991-2002. Dreadnought flat-top, mahogany sides, dot markers.

1991-2002	6-String	$525	$575
1992-1999	12-String	$700	$725

D-6 (D-6 E/D-6 HG/D-6 HE)
1992-1995. Flat-top, 15 3/4", mahogany back and sides, natural satin non-gloss finish, options available.

1992-1995		$650	$725

D-15 Mahogany Rush
1983-1988. Dreadnought flat-top, mahogany body and neck, rosewood 'board, dot inlays, stain finish.

1983-1988		$625	$725

D-16 Mahogany Rush
1984-1986. Like D-15, but with gloss finish.

1984-1986		$675	$800

D-17 Mahogany Rush
1984-1988. Like D-15, but with gloss finish and bound body.

1984-1988		$725	$850

D-25
2003. Solid mahogany body. Refer to Bluegrass D-25 for earlier models.

2003		$450	$550

D-30
1987-1999. Acoustic flat top, spruce-top, laminated maple back and solid maple sides, rosewood 'board, multi-bound, various colors.

1987-1989		$900	$1,000
1990-1999		$800	$950

D-40
1999-2003. Solid spruce top, mahogany back and sides, rosewood' board. See earlier models under Bluegrass Jubilee D-40.

1999		$900	$975

D-46
1980-1985. Dreadnought acoustic, ash back, sides and neck, spruce top, ebony 'board, ivoroid body binding.

1980-1985		$950	$1,100

D-60
1987-1990, 1998-2000. Renamed from D-66, rosewood back and sides, 15 3/4", scalloped bracing, multibound top, slotted diamond inlay, G shield logo.

1987-1990		$1,550	$1,650
1998-1999		$1,425	$1,600

D-64
1984-1986. Maple back and side, multi-bound body, notched diamond inlays, limited production.

1984-1986		$1,300	$1,550

D-66
1984-1987. Amber, rosewood back and sides, 15 3/4", scalloped bracing, renamed D-60 in '87.

1984-1987		$1,550	$1,650

D-70
1981-1985. Dreadnought acoustic, spruce top, Indian rosewood back and sides, multi-bound, ebony 'board with mother-of-pearl inlays.

1981-1985		$1,950	$2,150

D-212 12-String
1981-1983. 12-string version of D-25, laminated mahogany back and sides, natural, sunburst or black, renamed D-25-12 in '87, reintroduced as D-212 '96-present.

1981-1983	Sunburst	$850	$1,050

D-412 12-String
1990-1997. Dreadnought, 12 strings, mahogany sides and arched back, satin finished, natural.

1990-1997		$850	$1,100

DCE True American
1993-2000. Cutaway flat-top acoustic/electric, 1 with mahogany back and sides, 5 with rosewood.

1993-2000	DCE1	$650	$750
1994-2000	DCE5	$675	$775

Del Rio M-30
1959-1964. Flat-top, 15", all mahogany body, satin non-gloss finish.

1959-1964		$700	$950

Detonator
1987-1988. Electric solidbody, double-cut, 3 pickups, bolt-on neck, Guild/Mueller tremolo system, black hardware.

1987-1988		$250	$450

Duane Eddy Deluxe DE-500
1962-1974, 1984-1987. Electric archtop, single rounded cutaway, 2 pickups (early years and '80s version have DeArmonds), Bigsby, master volume, spruce top with maple back and sides, available in blond (BL) or sunburst (SB).

1962	Natural	$5,500	$6,500
1962	Sunburst	$4,500	$5,500
1963	Natural	$5,400	$6,400
1963	Sunburst	$4,400	$5,400
1964	Natural	$5,300	$6,300
1964	Sunburst	$4,300	$5,300
1965	Natural	$4,800	$5,800
1965	Sunburst	$3,800	$5,000
1966	Natural	$4,300	$5,300
1966	Sunburst	$3,500	$4,700
1967-1969	Various colors	$3,300	$4,500
1970-1974	Various colors	$3,100	$4,000
1984-1987	Natural or sunburst	$3,000	$3,500

Duane Eddy Standard DE-400
1963-1974. Electric archtop, single rounded cutaway, 2 pickups, vibrato, natural or sunburst, less appointments than DE-500 Deluxe.

1963	Natural	$4,100	$4,700
1963	Sunburst	$3,900	$4,200
1964	Natural	$3,800	$4,300
1964	Sunburst	$3,400	$3,800
1965	Natural	$3,400	$4,000
1965	Sunburst	$3,000	$3,400

1997 Guild D-55

Guild Duane Eddy Deluxe DE-500

GUITARS

Guild JF-30

*Guild George Barnes
AcoustiLectric*

MODEL YEAR	FEATURES	EXC. COND. LOW	HIGH
1966	Natural	$3,100	$3,700
1966	Sunburst	$2,800	$3,200
1967-1969	Various colors	$2,500	$2,700
1970-1974	Various colors	$2,300	$2,500

DV Series

1963-1974. 1992-1999. Acoustic flat-top, spruce top, solid mahogany or rosewood back and sides, ebony or rosewood 'board and bridge, mahogany neck, satin or gloss finish.

1993-1999	DV-52, rosewood, satin	$925	$1,050
1996-1999	DV-6, mahogany, satin	$725	$825

Economy M-20

1958-1965, 1969-1973. Mahogany body, acoustic flat-top, natural or sunburst satin finish.

1958-1965		$700	$900
1969-1973		$500	$700

F-4 CEHG

2000s. Single-cut flat-top, on-board electronics, sunburst.

2001		$850	$900

F-5 CE

1992-2001. Acoustic/electric, single cutaway, rosewood back and sides, dot inlays, chrome tuners.

1992-2001		$975	$1,100

F-30 R-LS

1990s. Custom Shop model, other F-30 models are listed under Aragon F-30 listing, rosewood sides and back, bearclaw spruce top, limited production.

1990s		$1,200	$1,300

F-45 CE

1983-1992. Acoustic/electric, single pointed cutaway, active EQ, preamp, spruce top, mahogany back and sides, rosewood 'board, natural finish.

1983-1992		$900	$1,000

F-47 RCE Grand Auditorium

1999-2003. Cutaway acoustic/electric, solid spruce top, solid maple back and sides, block inlays.

1999-2003		$1,300	$1,350

F-65 CE

1992-2001. Acoustic/electric, single cutaway, rosewood back and sides, block inlay, gold tuners.

1992-2001		$1,350	$1,400

F-212 12-String

1964-1982. Acoustic flat-top jumbo, 12 strings, spruce top, mahogany back and sides.

1964-1969		$1,000	$1,200
1970-1979		$875	$1,050
1980-1982		$800	$975

F-412

2002-present. Solid spruce top, solid maple back and sides, block inlays, 12-string. See Custom F-412 for earlier models.

2005		$950	$1,100

Freshman M-65

1958-1973. Electric archtop, single-cut, mahogany back and sides, 1 single-coil pickup, sunburst or natural top.

1958-1959		$1,000	$1,225
1960-1969		$950	$1,125
1970-1973		$900	$1,025

Freshman M-65 3/4

1958-1973. Short-scale version of M-65, electric archtop, single rounded cutaway, 1 pickup.

1958-1959	Natural or sunburst	$900	$1,125
1960-1969	Cherry, natural or sunburst	$850	$1,025
1970-1973	Cherry or sunburst	$825	$925

FS-46 CE

1983-1986. Flat-top acoustic/electric, pointed cutaway, black, natural or sunburst.

1983-1986		$625	$725

G-5P

1988-ca.1989. Handmade in Spain, cedar top, gold-plated hardware.

1988-1989		$575	$625

G-37

1973-1986. Acoustic flat-top, spruce top, laminated maple back and sides, rosewood 'board and bridge, sunburst or natural top.

1973-1986		$900	$1,000

G-41

1974-1978. Acoustic flat-top, spruce top, mahogany back and sides, rosewood 'board and bridge, 20 frets.

1975-1978		$850	$1,000

G-75

1975-1977. Acoustic flat-top, 3/4-size version of D-50, spruce top, rosewood back and sides, mahogany neck, ebony 'board and bridge.

1975-1977		$850	$1,200

G-212 12-String

1974-1983. Acoustic flat-top 12-string version of D-40, spruce top, mahogany back and sides, natural or sunburst.

1974-1983		$875	$1,050

G-212 XL 12-String

1974-1983. Acoustic flat-top, 12 strings, 17" version of G-212.

1974-1983		$875	$1,050

G-312 12-String

1974-1987. Acoustic flat-top 12-string version of the D-50, spruce top, rosewood back and sides.

1974-1987		$1,000	$1,150

George Barnes AcoustiLectric

1962-1972. Electric archtop, single-cut, solid spruce top, curly maple back and sides, multi-bound, 2 humbuckers, gold-plated hardware, sunburst or natural finish.

1962-1972		$3,000	$3,400

GF-30

1987-1991. Acoustic flat-top, maple back, sides and neck, multi-bound.

1987-1991		$875	$950

MODEL YEAR	FEATURES	EXC. COND. LOW	HIGH

GF-50
1987-1991. Acoustic flat-top, rosewood back and sides, mahogany neck, multi-bound.

1987-1991		$925	$1,100

Granda A-50 (Acoustic Archtop)
1956-1960. Lowest-end acoustic archtop in the Guild line, renamed Cordoba A-50 in '61.

1956-1960		$600	$650

Granda X-50
1954-1961. Electric archtop, non-cut, laminated all maple body, rosewood 'board and bridge, nickel-plated metal parts, 1 pickup, sunburst. Renamed Cordoba X-50 in '61.

1955-1959		$900	$1,050
1960-1961		$850	$1,000

GV Series
1994. Flat-top, rosewood back and sides, various enhancements.

1993-1995	GV-52, jumbo, rosewood	$875	$925
1993-1995	GV-70, abalone soundhole ring	$925	$975
1993-1995	GV-72, herringbone, extra trim	$975	$1,025

Jet Star S-50
1963-1970. Electric solidbody, double-cut, mahogany or alder body, 1 pickup, vibrato optional by '65, asymmetrical headstock until '65, reintroduced as S-50 in '72-'78 with body redesign.

1963-1965	3-on-side tuners, single-coil	$800	$1,200
1966-1970	6-in-line tuners, single-coil	$600	$1,000
1972-1973	Single-coil	$500	$700
1974-1978	Humbucker	$550	$750

JF-30
1987-2004. Jumbo 6-string acoustic, spruce top, laminated maple back, solid maple sides, multi-bound.

1987-1999		$925	$1,000
2000-2003		$950	$1,025

JF-30 E

1994-2004		$950	$1,050

JF-30-12
1987-2004. 12-string version of the JF-30.

1987-1999		$950	$1,050

JF-50 R
1987-1988. Jumbo 6-string acoustic, rosewood back and sides, multi-bound.

1987-1988		$1,000	$1,500

JF-55
1989-2000. Jumbo flat-top, spruce top, rosewood body.

1989-2000		$1,300	$1,600

JF-55-12
1991-2000. 12-string JF-55.

1991-2000		$1,450	$1,600

JF-65 R
1987. Renamed from Navarre F-50 R, Jumbo flat-top acoustic, spruce top, rosewood back and sides, multi-bound, gold tuners, reintroduced as JF-55 in '89.

1987		$1,000	$1,300

JF-65-12
1987-2001. Jumbo flat-top 12-string, spruce top, laminated maple back and solid maple sides, multi-bound, gold tuners, natural or sunburst.

1987-2001		$1,150	$1,500

JF-65R-12
1987. Rosewood body version of JF-65-12.

1987		$1,300	$1,600

Liberator Elite
1988. Limited Edition, top-of-the-line, set-neck, offset double-cut solidbody, 2-piece figured maple top, mahogany body, rising-sun inlays, 3 active Bartolini pickups, 2 knobs and 4 toggles, last of the Guild solidbodies.

1988		$900	$1,050

M-80 CS
1975-1984. Solidbody, double-cut, 2 pickups, has M-80 on truss rod cover, called just M-80 from '80-'84.

1975-1984		$675	$700

Manhattan X-170 (Mini-Manhattan X-170)
1985-2002. Called Mini-Manhattan X-170 in '85-'86, electric archtop hollowbody, single rounded cutaway, maple body, f-holes, 2 humbuckers, block inlays, gold hardware, natural or sunburst.

1985-1989		$1,300	$1,400
1990-2002		$1,350	$1,450

Manhattan X-175 (Sunburst)
1954-1985. Electric archtop, single rounded cutaway, laminated spruce top, laminated maple back and sides, 2 pickups, chrome hardware, sunburst.

1954-1959		$2,050	$2,300
1960-1969		$1,950	$2,200
1970-1985		$1,650	$1,900

Manhattan X-175 B (Natural)
1954-1976. Natural finish X-175.

1954-1959		$2,200	$2,600
1960-1969		$2,100	$2,400
1970-1976		$1,800	$2,200

Mark I
1961-1972. Classical, Honduras mahogany body, rosewood 'board, slotted headstock.

1961-1969		$300	$500
1970-1973		$275	$400

Mark II
1961-1987. Like Mark I, but with spruce top and body binding.

1961-1969		$425	$550
1970-1979		$400	$525
1980-1987		$375	$500

Mark III
1961-1987. Like Mark II, but with Peruvian mahogany back and sides and floral soundhole design.

1961-1969		$650	$750
1970-1979		$600	$700
1980-1987		$500	$600

Mark IV
1961-1985. Like Mark III, but with flamed pearwood back and sides (rosewood offered in '61, maple in '62).

1961-1969	Pearwood	$850	$950
1970-1979	Pearwood	$750	$850
1980-1985	Pearwood	$700	$800

1964 Guild Jet Star S-50

1955 Guild Manhattan X-175

To get the most from this book, be sure to read "Using *The Guide*" in the introduction.

Guild Mark V

Guild Starfire II

MODEL YEAR	FEATURES	EXC. COND. LOW	HIGH

Mark V
1961-1987. Like Mark III, but with rosewood back and sides (maple available for '61-'64.

1961-1968	Brazilian rosewood	$1,500	$2,500
1969-1979	Indian rosewood	$1,100	$1,200
1980-1987	Indian rosewood	$1,000	$1,100

Mark VI
1962-1973. Rosewood back and sides, spruce top, wood binding.

| 1962-1968 | Brazilian rosewood | $1,800 | $2,900 |
| 1969-1973 | Indian rosewood | $1,400 | $1,500 |

Mark VII Custom
1968-1973. Special order only, spruce top, premium rosewood back and sides, inlaid rosewood bridge, engraved gold tuners.

| 1962-1968 | Brazilian rosewood | $1,900 | $3,000 |
| 1969-1973 | Indian rosewood | $1,500 | $1,600 |

Navarre F-48
1972-1975. 17", mahogany, block markers.

| 1972-1975 | | $1,100 | $1,200 |

Navarre F-50/F-50
1954-1986, 1994-1995, 2002-present. Acoustic flat-top, spruce top, curly maple back and sides, rosewood 'board and bridge, 17" rounded lower bout, laminated arched maple back, renamed JF-65 M in '87. Reissued in '94 and in '02.

1954-1956		$2,600	$3,200
1957-1962	Pearl block markers added	$2,400	$2,600
1963-1969	Ebony 'board added	$2,200	$2,400
1970-1975		$1,900	$2,400
1976-1979		$1,800	$2,400
1980-1986		$1,700	$2,200
1994-1995		$1,300	$1,400

Navarre F-50 R/F-50 R
1965-1987, 2002-present. Rosewood back and side version of F-50, renamed JF-65 R in '87. Reissued in '02.

1965-1968	Brazilian rosewood	$3,000	$4,000
1969-1975	Indian rosewood	$2,100	$2,600
1976-1979		$2,000	$2,500
1980-1987		$1,900	$2,300

Nightbird
1985-1987. Electric solidbody, single sharp cutaway, tone chambers, 2 pickups, multi-bound, black or gold hardware, renamed Nightbird II in '87.

| 1985-1987 | | $1,400 | $1,550 |

Nightbird I
1987-1988. Like Nightbird but with chrome hardware, less binding and appointments, 2 pickups, coil-tap, phaser switch.

| 1987-1988 | | $1,200 | $1,400 |

Nightbird II
1987-1992. Renamed from Nightbird, electric solidbody, single sharp cut, tone chambers, 2 pickups, multi-bound, black hardware, renamed Nightbird X-2000 in '92.

| 1987-1992 | | $1,400 | $1,550 |

Nightbird X-2000
1992-1996. Renamed from Nightbird II.

| 1992-1996 | | $1,300 | $1,400 |

Polara S-100
1963-1970. Electric solidbody, double-cut, mahogany or alder body, rosewood 'board, 2 single coil pickups, built-in stand until '70, asymmetrical headstock, in '70 Polara dropped from title (see S-100), renamed back to Polara S-100 in '97.

| 1963-1970 | | $1,000 | $1,200 |

Roy Buchanan T-200
1986. Single-cut solidbody, 2 pickups, pointed six-on-a-side headstock, poplar body, bolt-on neck, gold and brass hardware.

| 1986 | | $575 | $650 |

S-60/S-60 D
1976-1981. Double-cut solidbody, 1 pickup, all mahogany body, rosewood 'board. Renamed S-60 D in '77 with 2 DiMarzio pickups.

| 1976 | S-60 | $400 | $500 |
| 1977-1981 | S-60 D | $425 | $500 |

S-65 D
1980-1981. Electric solidbody, double-cut, 3 DiMarzio pickups, rosewood 'board.

| 1980-1981 | | $425 | $500 |

S-90
1972-1977. Double-cut SG-like body, 2 humbuckers, dot inlay, chrome hardware.

| 1972-1977 | | $625 | $725 |

S-100
1970-1978, 1994-1996. S-100 Standard is double-cut solidbody, 2 humbuckers, block inlays. Deluxe of '72-'75 had added Bigsby. Standard Carved of '74-'77 has acorns and oakleaves carved in the top.

1970-1978	Standard	$900	$1,100
1972-1975	Deluxe	$900	$1,100
1974-1977	Standard Carved	$925	$1,125

S-100 Reissue
1994-1997. Renamed Polara in '97.

| 1994-1997 | | $700 | $800 |

S-261
Ca.1985. Double-cut, maple body, black Kahler tremolo, 1 humbucker and 2 single-coil pickups, rosewood 'board.

| 1985 | | $400 | $550 |

S-275
1982-1983. Offset double-cut body, 2 humbuckers, bound figured maple top, sunburst or natural.

| 1982-1983 | | $450 | $700 |

S-280 Flyer
1983-1984. Double-cut poplar body, 2 humbuckers or 3 single-coils, maple or rosewood neck, dot markers.

| 1983-1984 | | $450 | $700 |

S-281 Flyer
1983-1988. Double-cut poplar body S-280 with locking vibrato, optional pickups available.

| 1983-1988 | | $400 | $650 |

S-300 Series
1976-1983. Double-cut mahogany solidbody with larger bass horn and rounded bottom, 2 humbuckers. S-300 A has ash body, D has exposed DiMarzio humbuckers.

| 1976-1983 | S-300 | $700 | $1,100 |

MODEL YEAR	FEATURES	EXC. COND. LOW	HIGH
1977-1982	S-300 D	$600	$950
1977-1983	S-300 A	$650	$1,000

Savoy A-150 (Natural)
1958-1973. Natural finish, acoustic archtop version of X-150, available with floating pickup.

1958-1961		$1,375	$1,650

Savoy A-150 (Sunburst)
1958-1973. Sunburst, acoustic archtop version of X-150, available with floating pickup.

1958-1961		$1,300	$1,600

Savoy X-150
1954-1965, 1998-present. Electric archtop, single rounded cutaway, spruce top, maple back and sides, rosewood 'board and bridge, 1 single-coil pickup, sunburst, blond or sparkling gold finish, reintroduced in '98.

1954	Sunburst	$1,500	$2,000
1955-1959	Sunburst	$1,500	$1,900
1960-1961	Sunburst	$1,400	$1,850

Slim Jim T-100
1958-1973. Electric archtop thinline, single-cut, laminated all-maple body, rosewood 'board and bridge, Waverly tailpiece, 1 pickup, natural or sunburst.

1958-1960		$900	$1,150
1961-1969		$850	$1,100
1970-1973		$750	$900

Slim Jim T-100 D
1958-1973. Semi-hollowbody electric, single Florentine cutaway, thinline, 2-pickup version of the T-100, natural or sunburst.

1958-1959		$1,000	$1,250
1960-1969		$950	$1,200
1970-1973		$850	$1,100

Songbird S-4
1987-1991. Designed by George Gruhn, flat-top, mahogany back, spruce top, single pointed cutaway, pickup with preamp, multi-bound top, black, natural or white.

1987-1991		$750	$900

Standard F-112 12-String
1968-1982. Acoustic flat-top, spruce top, mahogany back, sides and neck.

1968-1969		$975	$1,150
1970-1979		$875	$1,050
1980-1982		$875	$1,050

Standard F-212 XL 12-String
1966-1986. Acoustic flat-top, 12 strings, spruce top, mahogany back and sides, ebony fingerboard.

1966-1969		$1,025	$1,225
1970-1979		$925	$1,125
1980-1986		$825	$1,025

Starfire I
1960-1964. Electric archtop, single-cut thinline, laminated maple or mahogany body, bound body and neck, 1 pickup.

1960-1961	Starfire Red	$900	$1,100
1962-1964		$800	$1,000

Starfire II
1960-1976, 1997-2001. Electric archtop, single-cut thinline, laminated maple or mahogany body, bound body and rosewood neck, 2 pickups, reissued '97-present.

1960-1961	Sunburst	$1,200	$1,400
1962	Emerald Green	$1,400	$2,800
1962-1966	Special color options	$1,200	$2,800
1962-1966	Sunburst, Starfire Red	$1,100	$1,300
1967-1969	Sunburst, Starfire Red	$1,000	$1,200
1970-1975	Sunburst, Starfire Red	$950	$1,050
1997-1999	Reissue model	$950	$1,100

Starfire III
1960-1974, 1997-present. Electric archtop, single-cut thinline, laminated maple or mahogany body, bound body and rosewood neck, 2 pickups, Guild or Bigsby vibrato, Starfire Red, reissued '97.

1960-1961	.	$1,300	$1,500
1962	Emerald Green	$0	$0
1962-1966		$1,200	$1,400
1967-1969		$1,100	$1,300
1970-1973		$900	$1,000
1997-2003	Reissue model	$1,000	$1,200

Starfire IV
1963-1987, 1991-present. Thinline, double-cut semi-hollowbody, laminated maple or mahogany body, F-holes, 2 humbuckers, rosewood 'board, cherry or sunburst, reissued in '91.

1963-1966		$1,800	$2,000
1967-1969		$1,700	$1,900
1970-1975		$1,600	$1,800
1976-1979		$1,400	$1,600
1980-1987		$1,200	$1,400
1991-2001	Reissue model	$1,100	$1,200

Starfire IV Special (Custom Shop)
2001-2002. Nashville Custom Shop.

2001-2002		$1,900	$2,100

Starfire V
1963-1973, 1999-2002. Same as Starfire IV but with block markers, Bigsby and master volume, natural or sunburst finish, reissued in '99.

1963-1966		$2,000	$2,300
1967-1969		$1,800	$2,200
1970-1973		$1,700	$2,100

Starfire VI
1964-1979. Same as Starfire IV but with higher appointments such as ebony 'board, pearl inlays, Guild/Bigsby vibrato, natural or sunburst.

1964-1966		$3,000	$3,500
1967-1969		$2,900	$3,300
1970-1975	Sunburst or blond	$2,800	$3,200
1976-1979		$2,700	$3,000

Guild Standard F-212XL

Guild Starfire IV

Guild Stratford X-375

Guild Thunderbird S-200

MODEL YEAR	FEATURES	EXC. COND. LOW	HIGH

Starfire XII

1966-1973. Electric archtop, 12-string, double-cut, maple or mahogany body, set-in neck, 2 humbuckers, harp tailpiece.

1966-1967		$1,700	$2,000
1968-1969		$1,600	$1,900
1970-1973		$1,500	$1,800

Stratford A-350

1956-1973. Acoustic archtop, single rounded cutaway, solid spruce top with solid curly maple back and sides, rosewood 'board and bridge (changed to ebony by '60), sunburst.

1956-1959		$2,400	$2,700
1960-1965		$2,300	$2,600
1966-1969		$2,200	$2,500
1970-1973		$2,100	$2,400

Stratford A-350B

1956-1973. A-350 in blond/natural finish option.

1956-1959		$2,600	$2,900
1960-1965		$2,500	$2,800
1966-1969		$2,400	$2,700
1970-1973		$2,300	$2,600

Stratford X-350

1954-1965. Electric archtop, single rounded cutaway, laminated spruce top with laminated maple back and sides, rosewood 'board, 6 push-button pickup selectors, sunburst finish (natural finish is X-375).

| 1953-1959 | | $2,900 | $3,300 |
| 1960-1965 | | $3,200 | $3,600 |

Stratford X-375/X-350 B

1954-1965. Natural finish version of X-350, renamed X-350 B in '58.

| 1953-1959 | X-375 | $2,800 | $3,400 |
| 1960-1965 | X-350 B | $2,700 | $3,100 |

Stuart A-500

1956-1969. Acoustic archtop single-cut, 17" body, A-500 sunburst, available with Guild logo, floating DeArmond pickup.

1956-1959		$2,500	$2,800
1960-1965		$2,400	$2,700
1966-1969		$2,300	$2,600

Stuart A-550/A-500 B

1956-1969. Natural blond finish version of Stuart A-500, renamed A-500 B in '60.

1956-1959		$2,700	$3,000
1960-1965		$2,600	$2,900
1966-1969		$2,500	$2,800

Stuart X-500

1953-1995. Electric archtop, single-cut, laminated spruce top, laminated curly maple back and sides, 2 pickups, sunburst.

1953-1959		$3,000	$3,400
1960-1964		$2,800	$3,200
1965-1969		$2,600	$3,000
1970-1979		$2,400	$2,800
1980-1995		$2,200	$2,600

MODEL YEAR	FEATURES	EXC. COND. LOW	HIGH

Stuart X-550/X-500 B

1953-1995. Natural blond finish Stuart X-500, renamed X-500 B in '60.

1953-1959		$3,200	$3,700
1960-1964		$3,000	$3,500
1965-1969		$2,800	$3,300
1970-1979		$2,600	$3,100
1980-1995		$2,400	$2,900

Studio 301/ST301

1968-1970. Thinline, semi-hollow archtop Starfire-style but with sharp horns, I pickup, dot inlays, cherry or sunburst.

| 1968-1969 | Single-coil | $1,200 | $1,300 |
| 1970 | Humbucker | $1,300 | $1,400 |

Studio 302/ST302

1968-1970. Like Studio 301, but with 2 pickups.

| 1968-1969 | Single-coils | $1,400 | $1,500 |
| 1970 | Humbucker | $1,500 | $1,600 |

Studio 303/ST303

1968-1970. Like Studio 301, but with 2 pickups and Guild/Bigsby.

| 1968-1969 | Single-coils | $1,400 | $1,500 |
| 1970 | Humbucker | $1,500 | $1,600 |

Studio 402/ST402

1969-1970. Inch thicker body than other Studios, 2 pickups, block inlays.

| 1969-1970 | Humbuckers | $1,600 | $1,700 |
| 1969-1970 | Single-coils | $1,500 | $1,600 |

T-250

1986-1988. Single-cut body and pickup configuration with banana-style headstock.

| 1986-1988 | | $575 | $650 |

Thunderbird S-200

1963-1968. Electric solidbody, offset double-cut, built-in rear guitar stand, AdjustoMatic bridge and vibrato tailpiece, 2 humbucker pickups until changed to single-coils in '66.

| 1963-1965 | Humbuckers | $4,000 | $5,000 |
| 1966-1968 | Single-coils | $3,000 | $3,500 |

Troubador F-20

1956-1987. Acoustic flat-top, spruce top with maple back and sides (mahogany '59 and after), rosewood 'board and bridge, natural or sunburst.

1956-1959		$750	$850
1960-1969		$700	$800
1970-1979		$650	$750
1980-1987		$600	$700

TV Model D-55/D-65/D-55

1968-1987, 1990-present (special order only for 1968-1973). Dreadnought acoustic, spruce top, rosewood back and sides, scalloped bracing, gold-plated tuners, renamed D-65 in '87. Reintroduced as D-55 in '90.

1968-1969		$2,000	$2,400
1970-1975		$1,900	$2,100
1976-1979		$1,700	$1,900
1980-1987		$1,600	$2,000
1990-1999		$1,500	$1,600
2000-2003		$1,500	$1,600

The *Vintage Guitar Price Guide* shows low to high values for items in all-original excellent condition, and, where applicable, with original case or cover.

MODEL		EXC. COND.	
YEAR	FEATURES	LOW	HIGH

Valencia F-40
1954-1963. Acoustic flat-top, rounded lower bout, spruce top, maple back and sides, rosewood 'board and bridge, sunburst finish. Renamed F-47 in '63.

| 1954-1956 | | $1,800 | $2,000 |
| 1957-1962 | | $1,500 | $1,700 |

X-79 Skyhawk
1981-1986. Four-point solidbody, 2 pickups, coil-tap or phase switch, various colors.

| 1981-1986 | | $650 | $700 |

X-80 Skylark/Swan
1982-1986. Solidbody with 2 deep cutaways, banana-style 6-on-a-side headstock, renamed Swan in '85.

| 1983-1986 | | $600 | $800 |

X-88 Flying Star Motley Crue
1984-1986. Pointy 4-point star body, rocketship meets spearhead headstock on bolt neck, 1 pickup, optional vibrato.

| 1984-1986 | | $575 | $625 |

X-100/X-110
1953-1954. Guild was founded in 1952, so this is a very early model, 17" non-cut, single-coil soapbar neck pickup, X-100 sunburst finish, X-110 natural blond finish.

| 1953-1954 | X-100 | $1,200 | $1,400 |
| 1953-1954 | X-110 | $1,400 | $1,600 |

X-160 Savoy
1989-1993. No Bigsby, black or sunburst.

| 1989-1993 | | $1,100 | $1,300 |

X-161/X-160B Savoy
1989-1993. X-160 Savoy with Bigsby, black or sunburst.

| 1989-1993 | | $1,300 | $1,400 |

X-200/X-220
1953-1954. Electric archtop, spruce top, laminated maple body, rosewood 'board, non-cut, 2 pickups. X-200 is sunburst and X-220 blond.

| 1953-1954 | X-200 | $1,500 | $2,000 |
| 1953-1954 | X-220 | $1,700 | $2,200 |

X-300/X-330
1953-1954. No model name, non-cut, 2 pickups, X-300 is sunburst and X-330 blond. Becomes Savoy X-150 in '54.

| 1953-1954 | X-300 | $1,500 | $2,000 |
| 1953-1954 | X-330 | $1,700 | $2,200 |

X-400/X-440
1953-1954. Electric archtop, single-cut, spruce top, laminated maple body, rosewood 'board, 2 pickups, X-400 in sunburst and X-440 in blond. Becomes Manhattan X-175 in '54.

| 1953-1954 | X-400 | $2,050 | $2,300 |
| 1953-1954 | X-440 | $2,300 | $2,600 |

X-600/X-660
1953. No model name, single-cut, 3 pickups, X-600 in sunburst and X-660 in blond. Becomes Statford X-350 in '54.

| 1953 | X-600 | $2,900 | $3,300 |
| 1953 | X-660 | $3,200 | $3,600 |

X-700
1994-present. Rounded cutaway, 17", solid spruce top, laminated maple back and sides, gold hardware, natural or sunburst.

| 1994-2000 | | $1,700 | $2,200 |

Guillermo Roberto Guitars
2000-present. Professional grade, solidbody electric bajo quintos made in San Fernando, California.

Gurian
1965-1981. Luthier Michael Gurian started making classical guitars on a special order basis, in New York City. In '69, he started building steel-string guitars as well. 1971 brought a move to Hinsdale, Vermont, and with it increased production.

JM
1970s. Mahogany, jumbo body with relatively wide waist (versus D-style or SJ-style), herringbone/rope trim.

| 1970s | | $1,550 | $1,750 |

JR3
Rosewood back and sides.

| 1970s | | $1,900 | $2,000 |

S-2-M
Mahogany, acoustic.

| 1970s | | $1,100 | $1,300 |

S-3-M
Mahogany.

| 1970s | | $1,100 | $1,300 |

S-3-R
Indian rosewood.

| 1970s | | $1,400 | $1,700 |

Guyatone
1933-present. Made in Tokyo by Matsuki Seisaku-jo, founded by Hawaiian guitarists Mitsuo Matsuki and Atsuo Kaneko (later of Teisco). Guya brand Rickenbacker lap copies in '30s. After a hiatus for the war ('40-'48), Seisakujo resumes production of laps and amps as Matsuki Denki Onkyo Kenkyujo. In '51 the Guyatone brand is first used on guitars, and in '52 they changed the company name to Tokyo Sound Company. Guyatones are among the earliest U.S. imports, branded as Marco Polo, Winston, Kingston and Kent. Other brand names included LaFayette and Bradford. Production and exports slowed after '68.

Electric Hollowbody Archtops
Various models.

| 1950s | | $350 | $450 |
| 1960s | | $350 | $450 |

Electric Solidbody
Various models.

| 1950s | | $350 | $450 |
| 1960s | | $350 | $450 |

Guild X-700 Stuart

Guild X-88D Flying Star

Hagstrom HL-550

Hallmark Sweptwing Vintage

Hagenlocher, Henner

1996-present. Luthier Henner Hagenlocher builds his premium grade, custom, nylon-string guitars in Granada, Spain.

Hagstrom

1958-1983, 2004-present. Intermediate, professional, and premium grade, production/custom, solidbody, semi-hollowbody and acoustic guitars made in the U.S. and imported. Founded by Albin Hagström of Älvdalen, Sweden, who began importing accordions in 1921 and incorporated in '25. The name of the company was changed to A.B. Hagström, Inc. in '38, and an American sales office was established in '40. Electric guitar and bass production began in '58 with plastic-covered hollowbody De Luxe and Standard models. The guitars were imported into the U.S. by Hershman Music of New York as Goya 90 and 80 from '58-'61. Bass versions were imported in '61. Following a year in the U.S., Albin's son Karl-Erik Hagström took over the company as exclusive distributor of Fender in Scandinavia; he changed the U.S. importer to Merson Musical Instruments of New York (later Unicord in '65), and redesigned the line. The company closed its doors in '83. In 2004 American Music & Sound started manufacturing and distributing the Hagstrom brand under license from A.B. Albin Hagstrom.

Corvette

1963-1967. Offset double-cut solidbody, 3 single-coil pickups, multiple push-button switches, spring vibrato, called the Condor on U.S. imports.

1965	Red	$950	$1,150

D'Aquisto Jimmy

1969, 1976-1979. Designed by James D'Aquisto, electric archtop, f-holes, 2 pickups, sunburst, natural, cherry or white. The '69 had dot inlays, the later version had blocks. From '77 to '79, another version with an oval soundhole (no f-holes) was also available.

1976-1979	$900	$1,100

H-12 Electric/Viking XII

1965-1967. Double-cut, 2 pickups, 12 strings.

1965-1967	$600	$700

H-22 Folk

1965-1967. Flat-top acoustic.

1965-1967	$500	$550

Impala

1963-1967. Two-pickup version of the Corvette, sunburst.

1965	$800	$950

Model I

1965-1971. Small double-cut solidbody, 2 single-coils, early models have plastic top.

1965-1971	Rare finish	$650	$800
1965-1971	Standard finish	$400	$500

Model II/F-200 Futura/H II

1965-1972, 1975-1976. Offset double-cut slab body with beveled edge, 2 pickups, called F-200 Futura in U.S., Model II elsewhere, '75-'76 called H II. F-200 reissued in 2004.

1965-1972	$400	$500

Model III/F-300 Futura/H III

1965-1972, 1977. Offset double-cut slab body with beveled edge, 3 pickups, called F-300 Futura in U.S., Model III elsewhere, '77 called H III.

1965-1972	$500	$550
1977	$500	$550

Swede

1970-1982, 2004-present. Bolt-on neck, single-cut solidbody, black, cherry or natural, '04 version is set-neck.

1979-1982	$800	$850

Super Swede

1979-1983, 2004-present. Glued-in neck upgrade of Swede, '04 version is maple top upgrade of Swede.

1979-1983	$850	$1,000

Viking

1965-1968, 1972-1979, 2004-present. Double-cut thinline, 2 f-holes, also advertised as the V-1.

1965-1968	$600	$700
1972-1979	$600	$700

Hallmark

1965-1967, 2004-present. Imported and U.S.-made, intermediate and premium grade, production/custom, guitars from luthiers Bob Shade and Bill Gruggett, and located in Greenbelt, Maryland. They also make basses. The brand was originally founded by Joe Hall in Arvin, California, in '65. Hall had worked for Semie Moseley (Mosrite) and had also designed guitars for Standel in the mid-'60s. Bill Gruggett, who also built his own line of guitars, was the company's production manager. Joe Hall estimates that less than 1000 original Hallmark guitars were built. The brand was revived by Shade in '04.

Sweptwing

1965-1967. Pointed body, sorta like a backwards Flying V.

1965-1967	$450	$600

Hamer

1974-present. Intermediate, professional and premium grade, production/custom, electric guitars made in the U.S. and overseas. Hamer also makes basses and the Slammer line of instruments. Founded in Arlington Heights, Illinois, by Paul Hamer and Jol Dantzig. Prototype guitars built in early-'70s were on Gibson lines, with first production guitar, the Standard (Explorer shape), introduced in '75. Hamer was puchased by Kaman Corporation (Ovation) in '88. The Illinois factory was closed and the operations were moved to the Ovation factory in Connecticut in '97.

Artist/Archtop Artist/Artist Custom

1995-present. Similar to Sunburst Archtop with semi-solid, f-hole design, named Archtop Artist, then renamed Artist (with stop tailpiece)/Artist Custom in '97.

1995-2003	Sunburst	$1,000	$1,200

MODEL YEAR	FEATURES	EXC. COND. LOW	HIGH

Blitz

1982-1984 (1st version), 1984-1990 (2nd version). Explorer-style body, 2 humbuckers, three-on-a-side peghead, dot inlays, choice of tremolo or fixed bridge, second version same except has angled six-on-a-side peghead and Floyd Rose tremolo.

| 1982-1984 | 3-on-a-side peghead | $500 | $900 |
| 1984-1990 | 6-on-a-side peghead | $500 | $750 |

Californian

1987-1997. Solidbody double cut, bolt neck, 1 humbucker and 1 single-coil, Floyd Rose tremolo.

| 1987-1989 | | $500 | $900 |
| 1990-1997 | | $500 | $750 |

Californian Custom

1987-1997. Downsized contoured body, offset double-cut, neck-thru-body, optional figured maple body, Duncan Trembucker and Trem-single pickups.

| 1987-1989 | | $500 | $900 |
| 1990-1997 | | $500 | $750 |

Californian Elite

1987-1997. Downsized contoured body, offset double-cut, optional figured maple body, bolt-on neck, Duncan Trembucker and Trem-single pickups.

| 1987-1989 | | $675 | $875 |
| 1990-1997 | | $650 | $850 |

Centaura

1989-1995. Contoured body of alder or swamp ash, offset double-cut, bolt-on neck, 1 humbucker and 2 single-coil pickups, Floyd Rose tremolo, sunburst.

| 1989-1995 | | $500 | $700 |

Chaparral

1985-1987 (1st version), 1987-1994 (2nd version). Contoured body, offset double-cut, glued maple neck, angled peghead, 1 humbucker and 2 single-coils, tremolo, second version has bolt neck with a modified peghead.

| 1985-1987 | Set-neck | $450 | $750 |
| 1987-1994 | Bolt-on neck | $400 | $600 |

Daytona

1993-1997. Contoured body, offset double-cut, bolt maple neck, dot inlay, 3 single-coils, Wilkinson VSV tremolo.

| 1993-1997 | | $550 | $600 |

Diablo

1992-1997. Contoured alder body, offset double-cut, bolt maple neck, rosewood 'board, dot inlays, reversed peghead '92-'94, 2 pickups, tremolo.

| 1992-1997 | | $500 | $550 |

Duo-Tone

1993-present. Acoustic/electric semi-hollowbody, double-cut, bound top, glued-in neck, rosewood 'board, 2 humbuckers, EQ.

| 1993-1999 | | $350 | $500 |

Eclipse

1994-2003. Asymmetrical double-cut slab mahogany body, glued neck, three-on-a-side peghead, rosewood 'board, dot inlays, 2 Duncan Mini-Humbuckers, cherry.

| 1994-2003 | | $600 | $750 |

FB I

1986-1987. Reverse Firebird-style body, glued-in neck, reverse headstock, 1 pickup, rosewood 'board with dot inlays, also available in non-reverse body.

| 1986-1987 | | $400 | $500 |

FB II

1986-1987. Reverse Firebird-style, glued-in neck, ebony 'board with boomerang inlays, angled headstock, 2 humbuckers, Floyd Rose tremolo, also available as a 12-string.

| 1986-1987 | | $500 | $550 |

Korina Standard

1995-1996. Limited run, Korina Explorer-type body, glued-in neck, angled peghead, 2 humbuckers.

| 1995-1996 | | $1,000 | $1,200 |

Maestro

1990. Offset double-cut, 7 strings, tremolo, bolt-on maple neck, 3 Seymour Duncan rail pickups.

| 1990 | | $700 | $800 |

Miller Music Guitar

1985-1986. Miller (Beer) Music graphic art (white letters on red background), shaped like Miller bottle label. There was a matching bass. Trapezoid-shaped Miller Genuine Draft guitars and basses were offered in '87

| 1985-1986 | | $1,100 | $1,350 |

Mirage

1994-1998. Double-cut carved figured koa wood top, transparent flamed top, initially with 3 single-coil pickups, dual humbucker option in '95.

| 1994-1998 | | $1,050 | $1,200 |

Monaco Elite

2003-present. Single-cut solidbody, 2 humbuckers, three-in-a-line control knobs, tune-o-matic-style bridge, mother-of-pearl inlaid 'victory' position markers, carved flamed maple cap over mahogany body, flamed maple sunburst.

| 2003 | | $1,200 | $1,400 |

Phantom A5

1982-1884, 1985-1986 (2nd version). Contoured offset double-cut, glued neck, 3-on-a-side peghead, 1 triple-coil and 1 single-coil pickup, second version same but with 6ix-on-a-side peghead and Kahler tremolo.

| 1982-1984 | | $500 | $650 |

Phantom GT

1984-1986. Contoured body, offset double-cut, glued-in fixed neck, six-on-a-side peghead, 1 humbucker, single volume control.

| 1984-1986 | | $400 | $550 |

Prototype

1981-1985. Contoured mahogany body, double-cut with 1 splitable triple-coil pickup, fixed bridge, three-on-a-side peghead, Prototype II has extra pickup and tremolo.

| 1981-1985 | | $700 | $800 |

Scarab I

1984-1986. Multiple cutaway body, six-on-a-side peghead, 1 humbucker, tremolo, rosewood or ebony 'board, dot inlays.

| 1984-1986 | | $450 | $600 |

Hamer Duo-Tone

Hamer Monaco III

GUITARS

Hamer Standard Flametop

Harmony Buck Owens

Scarab II
1984-1986. Two humbucker version of the Scarab.

1984-1986	$475	$650

Scepter
1986-1990. Explorer-type body, ebony 'board with boomerang inlays, angled six-on-a-side peghead, Floyd Rose tremolo.

1986-1990	$400	$550

Special
1980-1983 (1st version), 1984-1985 (Floyd Rose version), 1992-1997 (2nd version). Double-cut solidbody, flame maple top, glued neck, 3-on-a-side peghead, 2 humbuckers, Rose version has mahogany body with ebony 'board, the second version is all mahogany and has tune-o- matic bridge, stop tailpiece and Duncan P-90s, cherry red.

1980-1983	1st version	$600	$800
1984-1985	With Floyd Rose	$550	$750
1992-1997	2nd version	$500	$700

Special FM
1993-1997. Special with flamed maple top and 2 humbuckers, renamed the Special Custom in '97.

1993-1999	$850	$950

Standard
1974-1985, 1995-1999. Explorer-shaped body, maple top, bound or unbound body, glued neck, angled headstock, either unbound neck with dot inlays or bound neck with crown inlays, 2 humbuckers. Reissued in '95 with same specs but unbound mahogany body after '97. Higher dollar Standard Custom still available.

1974-1975	Pre-production, about 20 made	$2,000	$4,000
1975-1977	Production, about 50 made, PAFs	$2,000	$3,000
1977-1979	Dimarzio PAF-copies	$1,500	$2,500
1980-1985		$1,500	$2,300
1995-1999		$1,200	$1,500

Stellar 1
1999-2000. Korean import, double-cut, 2 humbuckers.

1999-2000	$150	$160

Steve Stevens I
1984-1992. Introduced as Prototype SS, changed to Steve Stevens I in '86, contoured double-cut, six-on-a-side headstock, dot or crown inlays, 1 humbucker and 2 single-coil pickups.

1984-1992	$700	$750

Steve Stevens II
1986-1987. One humbucker and 1 single-coil version.

1986-1987	$650	$700

Studio
1993-present. Double-cut, flamed maple top on mahogany body, dual humbucker pickups, cherry or natural.

1993-1999	$750	$850

Sunburst
1977-1983, 1990-1992. Double-cut bound solidbody, flamed maple top, glue-in neck, bound neck and crown inlays optional, 3-on-a-side headstock, 2 humbuckers.

1977-1979	$1,200	$1,700

1980-1983	Arlington Heights built	$1,000	$1,500
1990-1992		$900	$1,250

Sunburst Archtop
1991-present. Sunburst model with figured maple carved top, 2 humbuckers, offered under various names:

Standard - unbound neck and dot inlays, tune-o-matic and stop tailpiece '91-'93.

Custom - a Standard with bound neck and crown inlays '91-'93.

Archtop - bound neck with crown inlays '94-'97.

Studio Custom - bound neck with crown inlays '97-present.

Studio - unbound body, by '95 stud wrap-around tailpiece '93-present.

Archtop GT - Gold top with P-90 soapbar-style pickups '93-'97.

1991-1997	$900	$1,250

T-51
1993-1997. Classic single-cut southern ash body, 2 single-coils.

1993-1997	$700	$750

T-62
1991-1995. Classic offset double-cut solidbody, tremolo, pau ferro 'board, Lubritrak nut, locking tuners, 3-band active EQ, various colors.

1991-1995	$700	$750

TLE
1986-1992. Single-cut mahogany body, maple top, glued neck, 6-on-a-side headstock, rosewood 'board, dot inlays, 3 pickups.

1986-1992	$700	$800

TLE Custom
1986-1992. Bound, single-cut solidbody with maple top, glued-in neck, angled headstock, ebony 'board with boomerang inlays, 3 pickups.

1986-1992	$700	$800

Harmony

1892-1976, late 1970s-present. Huge, Chicago-based manufacturer of fretted instruments, mainly budget models under the Harmony name or for many other American brands and mass marketers. Harmony was at one time the largest guitar builder in the world. In its glory days, Harmony made over one-half of the guitars built in the U.S., with '65 being their peak year. But by the early-'70s, the crash of the '60s guitar boom and increasing foreign competition brought an end to the company.

The Harmony brand appeared on Asian-built instruments starting in the late '70s to the '90s with sales mainly is mass-retail stores. In 2000, the Harmony brand was distributed by MBT International. In '02, former MBT International marketing director Alison Gillette announced the launch of Harmony Classic Reissue Guitars and Basses.

Many Harmony guitars have a factory order number on the inside back of the guitar which often contains the serial number. Most older Harmony acoustics and hollowbodies have a date ink-stamped

MODEL YEAR	FEATURES	EXC. COND. LOW	HIGH

inside the body. DeArmond made most of the electronic assemblies used on older Harmony electrics, and they often have a date stamped on the underside.

Archtone H1215
1950s. Lower-end archtop, sunburst.

1950-1960s		$100	$150

Blond H62
1950s-1960s. Thin body, dual pickup archtop, curly maple back and sides, spruce top, blond.

1950s		$550	$800
1960s		$450	$700

Brilliant Cutaway H1310
1962-1965. 16 1/2" body (Grand Auditorium), acoustic archtop cutaway, block markers, sunburst.

1962-1965		$500	$550

Broadway H954
1930s-1971. 15-3/4" body, acoustic archtop, dot markers, sunburst.

1960s		$300	$350

Buck Owens
Acoustic flat-top, red, white and blue.

1969		$600	$800

Cremona
1930s-1952. Full-size archtop line, Harmony and Cremona logo on headstock, natural. Cutaways became available in '53.

1940s		$125	$250

Espanada H63/H64
1950s-1960s. Thick body, single-cut, jazz-style double pickups, black finish with white appointments.

1950s		$550	$800
1960s		$450	$700

Grand Concert H165
1960s. Flat-top, all mahogany body.

1960s		$225	$250

H72/H72V Double Cutaway Hollowbody
1966-1971. Two pickups, multiple bindings, cherry red, H72V has Bigsby.

1966-1971		$300	$450

H73 Double Cutaway Hollowbody
Double cutaway, 2 pickups.

1960s		$300	$450

H75 Double Cutaway Hollowbody
1960-1970. Three pickups, multi-bound body, 3-part f-holes, block inlays, bolt neck, brown sunburst.

1960-1970		$550	$700

H76 Double Cutaway Hollowbody
Late-1960s. Three pickups, Bigsby vibrato tailpiece, sunburst.

1960s		$550	$700

H77 Double Cutaway Hollowbody
1964-1970. Same as H75, but in cherry sunburst.

1964-1970		$550	$700

H78 Double Cutaway Hollowbody
Late-1960s. Three pickups, Bigsby vibrato tailpiece, cherry.

1960s		$550	$700

H79 Double Cutaway Hollowbody 12-String
1966-1970. Unique slotted headstock, cherry finish.

1966-1970		$650	$800

Hollywood H37/H39/H41
Auditorium-sized 15 3/4" non-cut electric archtop, H37 has a single pickup and bronze finish, H39 has a single pickup and brown mahogany shaded finish, H41 has dual pickups and brown finish.

1960s		$250	$350

Master H945
1965-1966. 15" (Auditorium) acoustic archtop, block markers, music note painted logo on headstock, sunburst.

1965-1966		$225	$300

Meteor H70/H71
1958-1966. Single rounded cutaway 2" thin body, 2 pickups, 3-part F-holes, block inlays, bolt neck, H70 sunburst, H71 natural (ended '65), lefty offered '65-'66, reintroduced as H661 and H671 (without Meteor name) in '72-'74.

1960s	H70	$350	$600
1960s	H71	$375	$650

Monterey H950/H952/H1325/H1456/H1457/H6450
1930s-1974. Line of Auditorium and Grand Auditorium acoustic archtop models.

1950s	H952 Colorama	$350	$400
1960s		$250	$300
1970s	H6450	$200	$250

Patrician F63
Archtop.

1940s		$275	$350

Rebel H81
1968-1971. Single pickup version of Rebel, brown sunburst.

1968-1971		$200	$275

Rebel H82/H82G
Listed as a new model in 1971. Thin body, hollow tone chamber, double-cut, 2 pickups, H82 sunburst, H82G greenburst avacado shading (renumbered as H682 and H683 in '72).

1970s	H82	$275	$325
1970s	H82G	$325	$350

Rocket H53/H54/H56/H59
1959-1973. Single-cut, F-holes, dot inlays, 2-tone brown sunburst ('59-'62) or red sunburst ('63 on), came with 1 pickup (Rocket I H53 '59-'71), 2 pickups (Rocket II H54 has 2 pickups, Rocket VII H56 has 2 pickups and vibrato, Rocket III H59 has 3 pickups. Rockets were single-cut, brown sunburst in the early-'60s and double-cut red sunburst in the early-'70s.

1959-1973	1 pickup	$250	$350
1959-1973	2 pickups	$250	$450
1959-1973	3 pickups	$550	$650

Silhouette De Luxe Double H19
1964-1967. Double-cut solidbody, deluxe pickups, block markers, advanced vibrato, sunburst.

1965-1969		$375	$425

Harmony H-82G Rebel

Harmony Rocket

GUITARS

1957 Harmony Stratotone Newport

Heiden Dreadnought

MODEL YEAR	FEATURES	EXC. COND. LOW	HIGH

Silhouette H14/H15/H17

1964-1967. Double-cut solidbody, H14 single pickup, H15 dual pickup, H17 dual with vibrato (offered until '66).

1965-1967	H14	$175	$225
1965-1967	H15	$225	$325
1965-1966	H17	$250	$350

Singing Cowboys H1057

Western chuck-wagon scene stencil top, Singing Cowboys stenciled on either side of upper bouts, brown background versus earlier Supertone version that had black background.

1950s		$200	$300

Sovereign Jumbo H1260

1960s-1970s. Jumbo shape, 16" wide body, natural.

1960s		$500	$550
1970s		$425	$500

Sovereign Jumbo Deluxe H1266

1960s-1970s. Jumbo nearly D-style, 16" wide body with out-size 'guard, natural.

1960s		$550	$600
1970s		$475	$550

Sovereign Western Special Jumbo H1203

1960s-1970s. 15" wide body, 000-style.

1960s		$550	$600

Stratotone Deluxe Jupiter H49

1958-1968. Single-cut, tone chamber construction, 2 pickups, bound spruce top, curly maple back and 6 control knobs.

1958-1959		$350	$450

Stratotone Mars Electric H45/H46

1958-1968. Single-cut, tone chamber construction, H45 with 1 pickup and sunburst finish, H46 with 2 pickups.

1958-1959		$225	$350

Stratotone Mercury Electric H47/H48

1958-1968. Single-cut, tone chamber construction, H47 with 1 pickup, block inlay and curly maple sunburst top, H48 is the same with a blond top.

1958-1959		$300	$400

TG1201 Tenor

Spruce top, two-on-a-side tuners, Sovereign model tenor, natural

1950s		$225	$300

Harptone

1893-ca. 1975. The Harptone Manufacturing Corporation was located in Newark, New Jersey. They made musical instrument cases and accessories and got into instrument production from 1934 to '42, making guitars, banjos, mandolins, and tiples. In '66 they got back into guitar production, making the Standel line from '67 to '69. Harptone offered flat-tops and archtops under their own brand until the mid-'70s when the name was sold to the Diamond S company, which owned Micro-Frets.

E-6N

D-style body, spruce top and mahogany back and sides, unique Harptone headstock, natural.

1970s		$900	$950

MODEL YEAR	FEATURES	EXC. COND. LOW	HIGH

Harwood

Harwood was a brand introduced in 1885 by Kansas City, Missouri instrument wholesalers J.W. Jenkins & Sons. May have been built by Jenkins at first, but was later contracted out to Harmony.

Hascal Haile

Late 1960s-1986. Luthier Hascal Haile started building acoustic, classical and solidbody guitars in Tompkinsville, Kentucky, after retiring from furniture making. He died in '86.

Hayes Guitars

1993-present. Professional and premium grade, production/custom, steel and nylon string guitars made by luthier Louis Hayes in Paonia, Colorado.

Hayman

1970-1973. Solid and semi-hollow body guitars developed by Jim Burns and Bob Pearson for Ivor Arbiter of the Dallas Arbiter Company and built by Shergold in England.

Haynes

1865-early 1900s. The John C. Haynes Co. of Boston, also made the Bay State brand.

Parlor Guitar

1900s-1920s. Small 12 1/2" parlor guitar with typical narrow bouts, spruce top, Brazilian rosewood back and sides, multicolored wood marquetry trim, natural.

1910		$850	$1,000

Heartfield

1989-1994. Founded as a joint venture between Fender Musical Instrument Corporation (U.S.A.) and Fender Japan (partnership between Fender and distributors Kanda Skokai and Yamano Music) to build and market more advanced designs (built by Fuji Gen-Gakki). First RR and EX guitar series and DR Bass series debut in '90. Talon and Elan guitar series and Prophecy bass series introduced in '91. The brand was dead by '94.

Elan

1989-1994. Carved-style bound double-cut body, flamed top, 2 humbuckers, offset headstock.

1989-1994		$450	$550

EX

1990-1994. 3 single-coils, Floyd Rose tremolo.

1990-1994		$250	$350

Talon

1989-1994. Offset double-cut, wedge-triangle headstock, dot markers, hum/single/hum pickups.

1989-1994		$250	$350

Heiden Stringed Instruments

1974-present. Luthier Michael Heiden builds his premium grade, production/custom, flat-top guitars in Chilliwack, British Columbia. He also builds mandolins.

MODEL YEAR	FEATURES	EXC. COND. LOW	HIGH

Heit Deluxe

Ca. 1967-1970. Imported from Japan by unidentified New York distributor. Many were made by Teisco, the most famous being the Teisco V-2 Mosrite copy.

Acoustic Archtop
1967-1970. Various models.

1967-1970		$125	$200

Electric Solidbody
1967-1970. Various models.

1967-1970		$125	$200

Hemken, Michael

1993-present. Luthier Michael Hemken builds his premium grade, custom, archtops in St. Helena, California.

Heritage

1985-present. Professional, premium, and presentation grade, production/custom, hollow, semi-hollow, and solidbody guitars built in Kalamazoo, Michigan. They have also made banjos, mandolins, flat-tops, and basses in the past. Founded by Jim Deurloo, Marvin Lamb, J.P. Moats, Bill Paige and Mike Korpak, all former Gibson employees who did not go to Nashville when Norlin closed the original Gibson factory in '84.

Eagle
1986-present. Single rounded cutaway semi-hollowbody, mahogany body and neck, 1 jazz pickup, f-holes, sunburst or natural.

1986-1999		$1,400	$1,700
2000-2003		$1,500	$1,900

Eagle Custom
Eagle with custom inlays.

2001		$2,000	$2,400

Gary Moore Model
1989-1991. Single-cut solidbody, 2 pickups, chrome hardware, sunburst.

1989-1991		$1,900	$2,300

Golden Eagle
1985-present. Single-cut hollowbody, back inlaid with mother-of-pearl eagle and registration number, multi-bound ebony 'board with mother-of-pearl cloud inlays, bound f-holes, gold-plated parts, ebony bridge inlaid with mother-of-pearl, mother-of-pearl truss rod cover engraved with owner's name, 1 Heritage jazz pickup, multi-bound curly maple 'guard.

1985-1999		$2,200	$2,600
2000-2003		$2,400	$2,800

H-140 CM
1985-present. Single pointed cutaway solidbody, bound curly maple top, 2 humbuckers, chrome parts.

1985-1994	Curly maple top	$725	$800
1985-1994	Goldtop	$725	$800

H-147
1990-1991. Single-cut solidbody, 2 humbuckers, mahogany body, mother-of-pearl block inlays, black with black or gold hardware.

1990-1991		$625	$675

H-150 C/H-150 CM
1985-present. Single rounded cutaway solidbody, curly maple top, 2 pickups, chrome parts, cherry sunburst.

1985-1999		$825	$875
2000-2003		$925	$975

H-157 Ultra
Single-cut solidbody, large block markers, highly figured maple top.

1993-1994		$1,250	$1,350

H-204 DD
1986-1989. Single-cut solidbody of mahogany, curly maple top, 1-piece mahogany neck, 22-fret rosewood 'board.

1986-1989		$500	$600

H-207 DD
1986-1989. Double-cut solidbody of mahogany, curly maple top, 1-piece mahogany neck, 22-fret rosewood 'board.

1986-1989		$500	$600

H-357
1989-1994. Asymmetrical solidbody, neck-thru.

1989-1994		$2,000	$2,100

H-535
1987-present. Double-cut semi-hollowbody archtop, rosewood 'board, 2 humbucker pickups.

1987-1999		$1,000	$1,100
1987-1999	Flamed maple top	$1,100	$1,200
2000-2003		$1,200	$1,300

H-550
1990-present. Single-cut hollow body, laminated maple top and back, multiple bound top, white bound 'guard, f-holes, 2 humbuckers.

1990-2000		$1,800	$2,100

H-555
1989-present. Like 535, but with maple neck, ebony 'board, pearl and abalone inlays, gold hardware.

1989-2003		$1,300	$1,500

H-575
1987-present. Single sharp cut hollow body, solid maple top and back, cream bound top and back, wood 'guard, f-holes, 2 humbuckers.

1987-1999		$1,400	$1,500

H-576
1990-present. Single rounded cut hollow body, laminated maple top and back, multiple bound top, single bound back and f-holes and wood 'guard, 2 humbuckers.

1990-1999		$1,200	$1,400

HFT-445
1987-2000. Flat-top acoustic, mahogany back and sides, spruce top, maple neck, rosewood 'board.

1987-2000		$600	$700

Johnny Smith
1989-2001. Custom hand-carved 17" hollowbody, single-cut, f-holes, 1 pickup.

1989-1999	Optional colors	$3,000	$3,300
1989-1999	Sunburst	$2,700	$3,000

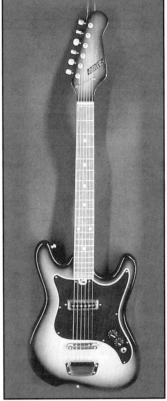

Heit Deluxe

Heritage Johnny Smith

Hoffman Concert 12

1967 Höfner Committee

MODEL YEAR	FEATURES	EXC. COND. LOW	HIGH

Millennium 2000

2000-present. Single-cut semi-solidbody, multiple bound curly maple top, single-bound curly maple back, F-holes, 2 humbuckers.

| 2000 | | $1,000 | $1,200 |

Millennium SAE

2000-present. Single-cut semi-solidbody, laminated arch top, single cream bound top and back, f-holes, 2 humbuckers.

| 2000-2003 | | $1,000 | $1,200 |

Parsons Street

1989-1992. Offset double-cut, curly maple top on mahogany body, single/single/hum pickups, pearl block markers, sunburst or natural.

| 1989-1992 | | $700 | $800 |

Roy Clark

1992-present. Thinline, single-cut semi-hollow archtop, gold hardware, 2 humbuckers, block markers, cherry sunburst.

| 1992-2002 | | $1,700 | $1,900 |

SAE Custom

1992-2000. Single-cut maple semi-hollow body, f-holes, 2 humbuckers and 1 bridge pickup.

| 1992-2000 | | $1,000 | $1,100 |

Super Eagle

1988-present. 18" body, single-cut electric archtop.

| 1989-1999 | Optional colors | $2,700 | $3,000 |
| 1989-1999 | Sunburst | $2,500 | $2,700 |

Sweet 16

1987-present. Single-cut maple semi-hollowbody, spruce top, 2 pickups, pearl inlays.

| 1987-2000 | Optional colors | $2,400 | $2,800 |
| 1987-2000 | Sunburst | $2,100 | $2,600 |

Hermann Hauser

Born in 1882, Hauser started out building zithers and at age 23 added classical guitars and lutes, most built in his shop in Munich, Germany. He died in 1952. His son and grandson, Hermann II and III, continued the tradition.

Hermann Hauser II

Born in 1911 and the son of Hermann Hauser I, he built between 500 and 600 classical guitars in Germany during his career. He died in 1988.

Hermann Hauser III

1988-present. Hermann III started build guitars in '74, and took over the family business upon the death of his father in '88. He continues to build classical guitars in Munich, Germany.

Hill Guitar Company

1972-1980, 1990-present. Luthier Kenny Hill builds his professional and premium grade production/custom, classical and flamenco guitars in Felton, California and Michoacan, Mexico.

Hirade Classical

1968-present. Professional grade, production, solid top, classical guitars built in Japan by Taka-

mine. The late Mass Hirade was the founder of the Takamine workshop. He learned his craft from master luthier Masare Kohno. Hirade represents Takamine's finest craftsmanship and material.

H-5

Solid cedar top, laminate rosewood body.

| 1980s | | $900 | $1,100 |

H-8

1989-1996. Solid spruce top, solid rosewood body.

| 1989-1996 | | $1,200 | $1,400 |

HD-5C

Solid cedar top, rosewood laminate body, cutaway, pickup and preamp.

| 1980s | | $1,000 | $1,200 |

Hoffman Guitars

1971-present. Premium grade, custom flat-tops and harp guitars built by luthier Charles Hoffman in Minneapolis, Minnesota.

Höfner

1887-present. Budget, intermediate, and professional grade, production, archtop, acoustic, and classical guitars built in Germany and the Far East. They also produce basses and bowed-instruments. Founded by Karl Hofner in Schonbach, Germany. The company was already producing guitars when sons Josef and Walter joined the company in 1919 and '21 and expanded the market worldwide. They moved the company to Bavaria in '50 and to Hagenau in '97.

Beatle Electric Model 459TZ

1966-1967. Violin-shaped 500/1 body, block-stripe position markers, transistor-powered flip-fuzz and treble boost, sunburst.

| 1966-1967 | | $1,600 | $1,700 |

Beatle Electric Model 459VTZ

1966-1967. Violin-shaped 500/1 body, same as Model 459TZ except with vibrato tailpiece, sunburst.

| 1966-1967 | | $1,600 | $1,700 |

Beatle Electric Model G459TZ Super

1966-1967. Violin-shaped 500/1 body, deluxe version of Model 459TZ, including flamed maple sides, narrow grain spruce top, gold hardware, elaborate inlays and binding, natural blond.

| 1966-1967 | | $1,800 | $1,900 |

Beatle Electric Model G459VTZ Super

1966-1967. Violin-shaped 500/1 body, same as G459TZ Super but with vibrato tailpiece, narrow grain spruce top, gold hardware, natural blond.

| 1966-1967 | | $1,800 | $1,900 |

Club Model 126

1954-1970. Mid-sized single-cut Guild Bluesbird or Les Paul-style body, dot markers, flamed maple back and sides, spruce top, sunburst. Listed with Hofner Professional Electric Series.

| 1954-1970 | | $600 | $700 |

Committee Model 4680 Thin Electric

1961-1968. Thinline archtop single-cut Byrdland-style body, dual pickups, split-arrowhead markers, no vibrato, sunburst.

| 1961-1968 | | $1,300 | $1,400 |

MODEL YEAR	FEATURES	EXC. COND. LOW	HIGH

Deluxe Model 176
1964-1983. Double-cut, 3 pickups, polyester varnished sunburst finish, vibrola tailpiece, similar to Model 175 polyester varnished red and gold version.

1964-1983		$600	$700

Galaxy Model 175
1963-1966. Double-cut, 3 pickups, red and gold vinyl covering, fancy red-patch 'guard, vibrola, similar to Model 176 polyester varnished sunburst version.

1963-1966	Red and gold vinyl	$1,300	$1,500
1963-1966	Sunburst	$1,200	$1,400

Golden Hofner
1959-1963. Single-cut archtop, blond, 2 pickups, F-holes.

1959-1963		$1,200	$1,300

Jazzica Custom
2000-present. Full body, single soft cutaway, acoustic/electric archtop, carved German spruce top, sunburst.

2000-2004		$1,600	$1,700

Model 172 II (R) (S) (I)
1962-1963. Double-cut body, polyester varnished wood (S) or scruff-proof red (R) or white (I) vinyl, 2 pickups, vibrato.

1962-1963		$450	$500

Model 173 II (S) (I)
1962-1963. Double-cut body, polyester varnished wood (S) or scuffproof vinyl (I), 3 pickups, vibrato.

1962-1963	Gold foil vinyl	$450	$500
1962-1963	White vinyl	$450	$500

Model 180 Shorty Standard
1982. Small-bodied, single-cut, solidbody, 1 pickup, travel guitar, the Shorty Super had a built-in amp and speaker.

1982		$300	$400

Model 470SE2 Electric Archtop
1961-1993. Large single rounded cutaway electric archtop on Hofner's higher-end they call "superbly flamed maple (back and sides), carved top of best spruce," 2 pickups, 3 control knobs, gold hardware, pearl inlay, natural finish only.

1969-1977		$1,200	$1,300

Model 471SE2 Electric Archtop
1969-1977. Large single pointed cutaway electric archtop, flamed maple back and sides, spruce top, black celluloid binding, ebony 'board, pearl inlays, sunburst version of the 470SE2.

1969-1977		$1,200	$1,300

Model 490 Acoustic
Late 1960s. 16" body, 12-string, spruce top, maple back and sides, dot markers, natural.

1960s		$350	$400

Model 490E Acoustic Electric
Late 1960s. Flat-top 12-string with on-board pickup and 2 control knobs.

1960s		$400	$450

Model 491 Flat-Top
1960s-1970s. J-45-slope shoulder body style, spruce top, mahogany back and sides, shaded sunburst.

1970s		$400	$450

Model 492 Acoustic
Late 1960s. 16" body, 12-string, spruce top, mahogany back and sides, dot markers.

1960s		$500	$550

Model 492E Acoustic Electric
Late 1960s. Flat-top 12-string with on-board pickup and 2 control knobs.

1960s		$550	$600

Model 496 Jumbo Flat-Top
1960s. J-185-style body with selected spruce top and highly flamed maple back and sides, gold-plated hardware, ornamented vine pattern 'guard, sunburst.

1960s		$950	$1,100

Model 514-H Classical Concert
1960s. Concert model, lower-end of the Hofner classical line, natural.

1960s		$250	$300

Model 4575VTZ/Verythin (Professional Extra Thin)
1960s. Extra-thinline acoustic, double-cut with shallow rounded horns, 2 or 3 pickups, vibrato arm, treble boost and flip-fuzz, straight-line markers. The Verythin Standard was reintroduced in '01.

1960s	2 pickups	$800	$850
1960s	3 pickups	$900	$950

Model 4578TZ President
1959-1970. Double-cut archtop..

1959-1965		$800	$1,000
1966-1970		$700	$900

Model 4600/V2 (Professional Extra Thin)
1968-1970. Thinline acoustic, double-cut, 2 pickups, vibrato arm, dot markers, sunburst.

1960s		$600	$800

Verythin Standard
2000-present. Update of the 1960s Verythin line.

2000-2004	Reissue Verythin	$800	$950

Hohner
1857-present. Budget and intermediate grade, production, acoustic and electric guitars. They also have basses, ukes and mandolins. Matthias Hohner, a clockmaker in Trossingen, Germany, founded Hohner in 1857, making harmonicas. Hohner has been offering guitars and basses at least since the early '70s. HSS was founded in 1986 as a distributor of guitars and other musical products. By 2000, Hohner was also offering the Crafter brands of guitars.

Alpha Standard
Designed by Klaus Scholler, solidbody, stereo outputs, Flytune tremolo.

1987		$225	$300

G 2T/G 3T Series
1980s-1990s. Steinberger-style body, 6-string, neck-thru, locking tremolo.

1980-1990s		$200	$300

Jacaranda Rosewood Dreadnought
Flat-top acoustic.

1978		$250	$350

Höfner Deluxe 176

Hohner G3T Headless

Hohner ST Custom

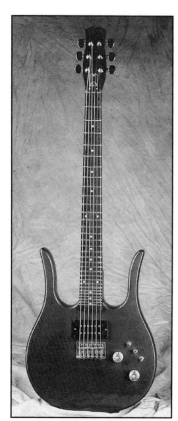

1978 Hondo II Longhorn

MODEL YEAR	FEATURES	EXC. COND. LOW	HIGH

Jack
1987-1990s. Mate for Jack Bass. Headless, tone circuit, tremolo, 2 single-coils and 1 humbucker.

1987-1992		$200	$300

L 59/L 75 Series
Late-1970s-1980s. Classic single-cut solidbody, 2 humbuckers, glued neck, sunburst, 59 has upgrade maple body with maple veneer top.

1970s		$250	$300

Miller Beer Guitar
Solidbody, shaped like Miller beer logo.

1985		$350	$400

Professional
1980s. Single-cut solidbody, maple neck, extra large 'guard, natural.

1980s		$250	$300

Professional Series - TE Custom
1980s-1990s. Single-cut solidbody, bolt neck.

1980-1990s		$1,000	$1,400

Professional Series - TE Prinz
Late 1980s-early 1990s. Based on Prince's No. 1 guitar, 2 single-coils, bolt neck, Professional The Prinz headstock logo, natural.

1989-1990		$1,000	$1,400

SE 35
1989-mid-1990s. ES-335-style, 22 frets, graphite nut, 2 humbucker pickups, natural.

1989		$350	$450

SG Lion
1980s-1990s. Offset double-cut, pointy headstock, glued neck.

1980-1990s		$200	$300

ST Series
1986-1990s. Includes the bolt neck ST 57, ST Special, ST Special S, Viper I, Viper II (snakeskin finish option), ST Victory, ST Metal S, and the ST Custom.

1986-1992		$150	$275

Standard Series - EX Artist
1970s-1980s. Solidbody, 2 humbuckers, gold hardware, neck-thru, solid maple body, rosewood 'board, tremolo.

1970-1980s		$200	$300

Standard Series - RR Custom
1970s-1980s. Randy Rhoads V body, 2 humbuckers, chrome hardware, glued neck, mahogany body, rosewood 'board, tremolo.

1970-1980s		$200	$300

Standard Series - SR Heavy
1970s-1980s. Hybrid body, 2 humbuckers, neck-thru, solid maple body, rosewood 'board, tremolo.

1970-1980s		$200	$300

Holiday
Student-level, private-branded similar to Stella but may have solid tops.

Hollenbeck Guitars
1970-present. Luthier Bill Hollenbeck builds his premium grade, production/custom, hollow and semi-hollow body acoustics and electric guitars in Lincoln, Illinois.

MODEL YEAR	FEATURES	EXC. COND. LOW	HIGH

Holman
1966-1968. Built by the Holman-Woodell guitar factory in Neodesha, Kansas. The factory was started to build guitars for Wurlitzer, but that fell through by '67.

Hondo
1969-1987, 1991-present. Budget grade, production, imported acoustic, classical and electric guitars. They also offer basses and mandolins. Originally imported by International Music Corporation (IMC) of Fort Worth, Texas, founded by Jerry Freed and Tommy Moore and named after a small town near San Antonio, Texas. Early pioneers of Korean guitarmaking, primarily targeted at beginner market. Introduced their first electrics in '72. Changed brand to Hondo II in '74. Some better Hondos made in Japan '74-'82/'83. In '85 IMC purchases major interest in Jackson/Charvel, and the Hondo line was supplanted by Charvels. 1987 was the last catalog before hiatus. In '88 IMC was sold and Freed began Jerry Freed International and in '91 he revived the Hondo name. Acquired by MBT International in '95.

Acoustic Flat-Top
1969-1987, 1991-present.

1970s		$125	$250

Electric Hollowbody
1969-1987, 1991-present.

1980s		$225	$400

Electric Solidbody
1969-1987, 1991-present.

1969-1987		$225	$400
1991-1999		$125	$300
2000s		$60	$75

H 752 Fame
1990s. Single-cut solidbody, black single-ply 'guard, maple neck, blond.

1990s		$175	$225

H 756 BTS Fame
1990s. Double-cut solidbody, white 'guard, maple body, rosewood or maple 'board, natural or sunburst.

1990s		$175	$225

Longhorn 6/12 Doubleneck Copy
1970s-1980s. Copy of Danelectro Longhorn 6/12 Doubleneck guitar, Dano coke bottle-style headstock, white sunburst.

1980s		$650	$800

Longhorn Copy
Ca. 1978-1980s. Copy of Danelectro Long Horn guitar, Dano Coke bottle-style headstock, brown-copper.

1970s		$325	$450

M 16 Rambo-Machine Gun
1970s-1980s. Machine gun body-style, matching machine gun-shaped guitar case, black or red.

1970-1980s		$450	$600

MODEL YEAR	FEATURES	EXC. COND. LOW	HIGH

Hopf

1906-present. Intermediate, professional, premium, and presentation grade, production/custom, classical guitars made in Germany. They also make basses, mandolins and flutes.

The Hopf family of Germany has a tradition of instrument building going back to 1669, but the modern company was founded in 1906. Hopf started making electric guitars in the mid-'50s. Some Hopf models were made by others for the company. By the late-'70s, Hopf had discontinued making electrics, concentrating on classicals.

Explorer Standard
1960s. Double-cut semi-hollow, sharp horns, center block, 2 mini-humbuckers.

1960s		$450	$500

Saturn Archtop
1960s. Offset cutaway, archtop-style soundholes, 2 pickups, white.

1960s		$550	$700

Super Deluxe Archtop
1960s. Archtop, 16 3/4", catseye soundholes, carved spruce top, flamed maple back and sides, sunburst.

1960s		$650	$800

Horabe

Classical and Espana models made in Japan.

Model 25 Classical
Solid top.

1960s		$450	$600

Model 40 Classical
Solid cedar top, rosewood back and sides.

1960s		$650	$800

Model 60 Classical
1980s. German spruce top, solid Indian rosewood rims.

1980s		$850	$1,200

Hoyer

1874-present. Intermediate grade, production, flat-top, classical, electric, and resonator guitars. They also build basses. Founded by Franz Hoyer, building classical guitars and other instruments. His son, Arnold, added archtops in the late-1940s, and solidbodies in the '60s. In '67, Arnold's son, Walter, took over, leaving the company in '77. The company changed hands a few times over the following years. Walter started building guitars again in '84 under the W.A. Hoyer brand, which is not associated with Hoyer.

Junior
Early-1960s. Solidbody with unusual sharp horn cutaway, single neck pickup, bolt-on neck, dot markers, Arnold Hoyer logo on headstock, shaded sunburst.

1960s		$475	$525

Soloist Electric
Single-cut archtop, 2 pickups, teardrop F-holes, sunburst.

1960-1962		$500	$550

Humming Bird

1947-ca.1968. Japanese manufacturer. By 1968 making pointy Mosrite inspirations. Probably not imported into the U.S.

Electric Solidbody

1950s		$125	$300

Humphrey, Thomas

1970-present. Premium and presentation grade, custom, nylon-string guitars built by luthier Thomas Humphrey in Gardiner, New York. In 1996 Humphrey began collaborating with Martin Guitars, resulting in the Martin C-TSH and C-1R. Often the inside back label will indicate the year of manufacturer.

Classical
1976-1984. Brazilian or Indian rosewood back and sides, spruce top, traditionally-based designs evolved over time with Millenium becoming a benchmark design in 1985, values can increase with new designs. Valuations depend on each specific instrument and year and type of construction, price ranges are guidance only; each instrument should be evaluated on a case-by-case basis.

1976-1984		$6,000	$7,500

Millenium (Classical)
1985-present. Professional performance-grade high-end classical guitar with innovative taper body design and elevated 'board, tops are generally spruce (versus cedar) with rosewood back and sides.

1995-1996		$9,000	$13,000

Huss and Dalton Guitar Company

1995-present. Luthiers Jeff Huss and Mark Dalton build their professional and premium grade flat-tops and banjos in Staunton, Virginia.

CM Custom
15 1/4" lower bout, soft cutaway, sitka spruce top, mahogany back and sides.

2000s		$2,500	$2,700

OM
15 1/8" lower bout, sitka spruce top, Indian rosewood back and sides, fancy inlay markers.

2000s		$2,100	$2,300

Ibanez

1932-present. Budget, intermediate, and professional grade, production/custom, acoustic and electric guitars. They also make basses, amps, mandolins, and effects.

Founded in Nagoya, Japan, by Matsujiro Hoshino as book and stationary supply, started retailing musical instruments in 1909. He began importing instruments in '21. His son Yoshitaro became president in '27 and began exporting. Manufacturing of Ibanez instruments began in '32. The company's factories were destroyed during World War II, but the business was revived in '50. Junpei Hoshino, grandson of founder, became president in '60; a new factory opened called Tama Seisakusho (Tama

Thomas Humphrey La Catalina

Huss and Dalton TD-R

*Ibanez AR-1200
Doubleneck Arist*

1977 Ibanez Artist Professional

MODEL YEAR	FEATURES	EXC. COND. LOW	HIGH

Industries). Brand names by '64 included Ibanez, Star, King's Stone, Jamboree and Goldentone, supplied by 85 factories serving global markets. Sold acoustic guitars to Harry Rosenblum of Elger Guitars ('59-ca.'65) in Ardmore, Pennsylvania, in early-'60s. Around '62 Hoshino purchased 50% interest in Elger Guitars, and ca. '65 changed the name to Ibanez.

Jeff Hasselberger headed the American guitar side beginning '73-'74, and the company headquarters were moved to Cornwells Heights, Pennsylvania in '74. By '75 the instruments are being distributed by Chesbro Music Company in Idaho Falls, Idaho, and Harry Rosenblum sells his interest to Hoshino shortly thereafter. Ca. '81, the Elger Company becomes Hoshino U.S.A. An U.S. Custom Shop was opened in '88.

Most glued-neck guitars from '70s are fairly rare.

Dating: copy guitars begin ca. '71. Serial numbers begin '75 with letter (A-L for month) followed by 6 digits, the first 2 indicating year, last 4 sequential (MYYXXXX). By '88 the month letter drops off. Dating code stops early-'90s; by '94 letter preface either F for Fuji or C for Cort (Korean)

470S/S470
1992-present. Offset double-cut mahogany solidbody, single-single-hum pickups until about '95 (470 S), hum-single-hum (S470) afterwards.
1992-2004 $400 $450

540S/Pro 540S/Saber 540S
1987-1994. Offset double-cut solidbody, maple neck, rosewood 'board, dots, single-single-hum pickups, called the Pro 540 in '87, the Saber 540S in '88, there was also a double humbucker model (541S-HH).
1987-1994 $550 $600

540SFM/S540FM
1991-1998. Solidbody, flame maple top, maple neck, rosewood 'board, single-single-hum pickups until '94 (540SFM), hum-single-hum (S540FM) afterwards.
1991-1998 $650 $800

540SLTD/S540LTD
1989-1998. Offset double-cut mahogany solidbody, maple neck, bound rosewood 'board, sharktooth inlays, hum-single-hum pickups, model changed to S540LTD in '94.
1989-1998 $650 $800

AE40
1994. Acoustic/electric, single-cut, flame maple.
1994 $325 $375

AH10 (Allan Holdsworth)
1985-1987. Offset double-cut solidbody, bolt neck, bridge humbucker, dots, various colors.
1985-1987 $350 $450

AM50 Stagemaster
1983-1984. Small double cut semi-hollow body, 2 humbuckers, no pickguard.
1983-1984 $600 $750

MODEL YEAR	FEATURES	EXC. COND. LOW	HIGH

AM70
1985-1987. Small double-cut semi-hollow body, f-holes, 2 humbuckers.
1985-1987 $625 $800

AM75/AM75T
1985-1987. Small double cut semi hollow body, vibrato, 2 humbuckers.
1985-1987 $700 $800

AM100 Stagemaster
1983-1984, 1989-1990. Small double cut semi-hollow body, 2 humbuckers. Model name used again, without "Stagemaster" in '89-'90.
1983-1984 $650 $850

Artcore Electric Hollowbody (China)
2002-present. Artcore semi-acoustics have mahogany necks, rosewood 'boards, 24 3/4" scale with 22 frets, 2 Artcore medium output pickups, f-holes with binding.
2002-2004 $130 $200

Artcore United Electric Hollowbody (China/Japan)
2002-present. Body made in China and assembled in Japan, 2 Artcore medium output pickups, f-holes with binding.
2002-2004 $450 $500

Artist 2640/AR1200 Doubleneck
1977-1984. Double cut solidbody, set 6/12 necks, 4 humbuckers, gold hardware. Called 2640 until '79 when changed to AR1200.
1977-1984 $1,100 $1,300

Artist AR100
1979-1984. Set neck double cut maple top solidbody, 2 humbuckers.
1979-1984 $550 $650

Artist AS100/AS100
1979-1982, 1989-1990. Double cut set neck semi-hollow body, sunburst, dots, replaced Artist 2629. Artist dropped from name when it becomes hollow body archtop in '82.
1979-1981 Semi-hollow body $900 $1,200

Artist AS200/AS200
1979-1991. Double cut flame maple semi-hollow body, block markers, gold hardware, 2 humbuckers, replaced Artist 2630. Artist dropped from name when model becomes hollowbody archtop in '82.
1979-1981 Semi-hollow body $1,200 $1,300

Artist Model 2612
1974-1975. Rounded double-cut solidbody, black finish, birch top, gold hardware, bound rosewood 'board, 2 humbuckers, fleur-de-lis inlay.
1974-1975 $800 $850

Artist Model 2613
1974-1975. Natural version of 2612.
1974-1975 $800 $850

Artist Model 2617
1976-1980. Pointed double-cut natural ash solidbody, set-neck, German carved top, spilt block inlays, bound ebony 'board, 2 humbuckers, later would evolve into the Professional model.
1976-1980 $1,000 $1,100

MODEL YEAR	FEATURES	EXC. COND. LOW	HIGH

Artist Model 2618
1976-1979. Like 2617, but with maple and mahogany body and dot markers. Becomes AR200 in '79.

| 1976-1979 | | $800 | $850 |

Artist Model 2619
1976-1979. Like 2618, but with split block markers. Becomes AR300 in '79.

| 1976-1979 | | $800 | $850 |

Artist Model 2630 Artist Deluxe
1976-1979. Double cut semi-hollow body, sunburst, name changed to AS200 in '79.

| 1976-1979 | | $900 | $1,100 |

AS50 Artstar
1998-1999. Laminated maple body, bound rosewood 'board, dot inlays, 2 humbuckers.

| 1998-1999 | | $700 | $850 |

AS80 Artstar
1994-2002. Double cut semi-hollow body, dot markers, chrome hardware.

| 1994-2002 | | $400 | $500 |

AW300
1996-1998. Grand concert size flat-top, solid spruce top, mahogany body, bound rosewood 'board.

| 1996-1998 | | $250 | $300 |

AX125
2001-present. Double-cut solidbody, 2 humbuckers, bolt neck.

| 2001-2004 | | $125 | $175 |

Blazer Series
1980-1982, 1997-1998. Offset double-cut, 10 similar models in the '80s with different body woods and electronic configurations. Series name returns on 3 models in late '90s.

| 1980-1982 | Various models | $225 | $325 |

Bob Weir Model 2681
1975-1980. Double-cut solidbody of carved solid ash, maple neck, ebony 'board with tree-of-life inlay, gold-plated Super 70 pickups, only 3 to 6 of these were ever produced.

| 1975-1980 | | $1,800 | $2,100 |

Bob Weir Standard Model 2680
1976-1980. Double-cut solidbody of carved solid ash, maple neck, ebony 'board, dot markers, gold-plated Super 70 pickups, production model.

| 1976-1980 | | $900 | $1,100 |

Concert CN200 Custom
1978-1979. Carved maple top, mahogany body, 7 layer black/white binding, bolt-on neck, gold hardware, block inlays, 2 Super 80 pickups.

| 1978-1979 | | $350 | $450 |

Concert CN250
1978-1979. Like CN200 but with vine inlay.

| 1978-1979 | | $400 | $500 |

Concord 673
1974-1978. D-style flat-top, laminated spruce top, laminated maple and jacaranda body, maple 'board, natural finish, gold tuners. Just the 637 for '74-'75, Concord added to name in '76.

| 1974-1978 | | $400 | $550 |

Destroyer II DT400/DT500
1980-1984. Basswood body, set-neck, 2 pickups, cherry sunburst. Model changed to DT500 in '82.

| 1980-1984 | | $550 | $650 |

Destroyer II DT555 Phil Collen
1983-1987. Bound basswood solidbody, 3 humbuckers, vibrato, black.

| 1983-1987 | | $750 | $850 |

Destroyer II DTX120
2000-present. 4-point maple/basswood body, 2 humbuckers.

| 2000-2004 | | $250 | $350 |

EG80 Star
1957-1961. Single cut set neck solidbody, 1 oval pickup, large 'guard.

| 1957-1961 | | $200 | $350 |

EX Series
1988-1993. Double cut solidbodies with long thin horns, various models, all models may not be included.

1991-1993	EX370	$200	$300
1992-1993	EX1700	$200	$300
1992-1993	EX3700FM maple top	$250	$350

FA-100
1978-1982. Hollowbody, single-cut, 2 pickups, f-holes, block inlays.

| 1978-1982 | | $800 | $1,100 |

FG-360S
1973-1974. Single-cut solidbody, bolt neck, trapezoid markers, maple top, sunburst.

| 1973-1974 | | $400 | $500 |

GAX70
1998-present. Symmetrical double-cut, 2 humbuckers, set neck, dot markers.

| 1998-2000 | | $150 | $225 |

GAX75
2001-present. GAX70 with Downshifter bridge.

| 2001 | | $150 | $225 |

George Benson GB10
1977-present. Single-cut, laminated spruce top, flame maple back and sides, 2 humbuckers, 3-piece set-in maple neck, ebony 'board.

1977-1979	Blond	$1,700	$2,000
1977-1979	Sunburst	$1,600	$1,800
1980-1989	Blond	$1,600	$1,800
1980-1989	Sunburst	$1,500	$1,700
1990-1999	Blond	$1,500	$1,700
1990-1999	Sunburst	$1,400	$1,600

George Benson GB20
1978-1982. Larger than GB10, laminated spruce top, flame maple back and sides.

| 1978-1982 | | $1,500 | $1,700 |

George Benson GB100 Deluxe
1993-1996. GB-10 with flamed maple top, pearl binding, sunburst finish 'guard, pearl vine inlay tailpiece, gold hardware.

| 1993-1996 | | $2,500 | $2,800 |

1975 Ibanez Artist 2616

Ibanez George Benson GB10

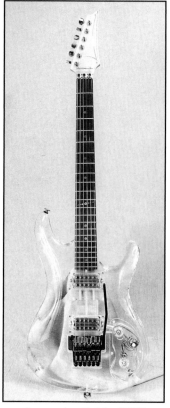

Ibanez Joe Satriani Y2K

Ibanez JEM 777

MODEL YEAR	FEATURES	EXC. COND. LOW	HIGH

Iceman 2663/2663 TC/2663 SL
1975-1978. The original Iceman Series models, called the Flash I, II and III respectively, I has 2 humbuckers, II (TC) and III (SL) have 1 triple-coil pickup.

1975-1978		$600	$800

Iceman IC200
1978-1980. Continuation of 2 humbucker Iceman 2663, 555 made.

1978-1980		$700	$850

Iceman IC250
1978-1979. Flame maple top, 64 made.

1978-1979		$900	$1,200

Iceman IC300
1995-2003. Reintroduced line, made in Korea, standard model without tremolo.

1994-2003		$425	$500

Iceman IC300 (Korina)
1978-1979. Korina finished ash body, engraved twin Super 80 pickups, 137 made.

1978-1979		$700	$850

Iceman IC350
1995-1996. Reintroduced Korean version with tremolo, black.

1995		$425	$500

Iceman IC400
1978-1979, 1981-1982. Mahogany body, maple top, set neck, 2 pickups, parallelogram inlays in first version, blocks in second.

1978-1982		$800	$1,000

Iceman IC-400 CS
1981 only. 28 made.

1981		$900	$1,000

Iceman IC500
1994. Limited production primarily for Japanese domestic market.

1994		$850	$950

Iceman PS10 Paul Stanley
1978-1981. Limited edition Paul Stanley model, abalone trim, Stanley's name engraved at 21st fret, reissued in '95 with upgraded model names.

1978-1981	Korina finish	$1,700	$2,200
1978-1981	Sunburst or black	$1,500	$2,000

Iceman PS10 II Paul Stanley
1995-1996. Reissue of original PS-10

1995-1996		$1,500	$1,600

IMG-2010 Guitar Controller MIDI
1985-1987. Similar to Roland GR-707, slim triangle-wedge body with treble horn.

1985-1987		$400	$500

JEM 10th Anniversary
1996. Limited Edition signature Steve Vai model, bolt neck, vine metal 'guard, vine neck inlays and headstock art.

1996		$1,600	$2,000

JEM 90th Anniversary
1997. Limited Edition signature Steve Vai model, textured silver finish, chrome 'guard.

1997		$1,600	$2,000

MODEL YEAR	FEATURES	EXC. COND. LOW	HIGH

JEM 77 Series
1988-1999, 2003-present. Basswood body, monkey grip handle, 3 pickups, 'board with tree of life or pyramids inlay, finishes include floral pattern or multicolor swirl. Current version has dot inlays and solid finish.

1980s	Floral	$1,400	$1,700
1980s	Multicolor	$1,400	$1,700

JEM 555
1994-2000. Basswood, dots and vine inlay, 3 pick-ups.

1994-2000		$600	$700

JEM 777 Series
1987-1996. Basswood body, monkey grip 3 pickups, pyramids or vine inlay.

1987	LG Loch Ness Green, limited edition	$1,500	$2,000
1988-1989	SK Shocking Pink, pyramids	$600	$1,000
1988-1996	DY Desert Sun Yellow, pyramids	$700	$1,000
1989-1993	VBK black, vines	$800	$1,200
1989-1993	VDY yellow, vines	$800	$1,200

JEM Y2KDNA (limited edition)
2000. Red Swirl marble finish using Steve Vai's blood in the paint.

2000		$3,600	$4,000

Joe Pass Model JP20
1981-1990. Full body, single-cut, 1 pickup, abalone and pearl split block inlay, JP inlay on headstock.

1981-1990	Sunburst	$1,700	$1,900

Joe Satriani JS100
1994-present. Offset double cut basswood body, 2 humbuckers, vibrato, red, black or white.

1994-2002		$325	$375

Joe Satriani Y2K
2000. Clear see-thru plexi-style body.

2000		$1,850	$2,200

JPM100 John Petrucci/JPM100P3
1996-1999. Offset double-cut solidbody, 2 pickups, available in multi-color art finish.

1996-1999		$1,600	$2,000

Lee Ritenour LR10
1981-1987. Flame maple body, bound set neck, Quick Change tailpiece, 2 pickups, dark red sunburst, foam-filled body to limit feedback.

1981-1987		$900	$1,200

M340
1978-1979. Flat-top, spruce top, flamed maple back and sides, maple 'board.

1978-1979		$400	$450

Maxxas
1987-1988. Solidbody (MX2) or with internal sound chambers (MX3, '88 only), 2 pickups, all-access neck joint system.

1987-1988	MX2	$800	$850

Model 600 Series
1974-1978. Copy era acoustic flat-tops with model numbers in the 600 Series, basically copies of classic American square shoulder dreadnoughts. Includes

MODEL		EXC. COND.	
YEAR	FEATURES	LOW	HIGH

the 683, 684, 693,and the six-on-a-side 647; there were 12-string copies as well.

1974-1978		$450	$700

Model 700 Series

1974-1977. Upgraded flat-top models such as the Brazilian Scent 750, with more original design content than 600 Series.

| 1974-1977 | | $450 | $700 |

Model 1453

1971-1973. Copy of classic single-cut hollowbody, replaced by Model 2355 in '73.

| 1971-1973 | | $800 | $1,100 |

Model 1912

1971-1973. Double-cut semi-hollow body, sunburst finish.

| 1971-1973 | | $1,000 | $1,100 |

Model 2020

1970. Initial offering of the copy era, offset double-cut, 2 unusual rectangular pickups, block markers, raised nailed-on headstock logo, sunburst.

| 1970 | | $500 | $650 |

Model 2336 Les Jr.

1974-1976. Copy of classic slab solidbody, TV Lime.

| 1974-1976 | | $450 | $550 |

Model 2340 Deluxe '59er

1974-1977. Copy of classic single-cut solidbody, flametop, Hi-Power humbuckers.

| 1974-1977 | | $550 | $650 |

Model 2341 Les Custom

1974-1977. Copy of classic single-cut solidbody.

| 1974-1977 | | $600 | $700 |

Model 2342 Les Moonlight/Sunlight Special

1974-1977. Copy of classic slab solidbody, black (Moonlight) or ivory (Sunlight).

| 1974-1977 | | $450 | $550 |

Model 2343 FM Jr.

1974-1976.

| 1974-1976 | | $400 | $450 |

Model 2344

1974-1976. Copy of classic Double-cut solidbody.

| 1974-1976 | | $350 | $400 |

Model 2345

1974-1976. Copy of classic sharp double-cut solidbody, set neck, walnut or white, vibrato, 3 pickups.

| 1974-1976 | | $500 | $600 |

Model 2346

1974. Copy of classic sharp double-cut solidbody, vibrato, set neck, 2 pickups.

| 1974 | | $500 | $600 |

Model 2347

1974-1976. Copy of classic sharp double-cut solidbody, set-neck, 1 pickup.

| 1974-1976 | | $400 | $450 |

Model 2348 Firebrand

1974-1977. Copy of classic reverse solidbody, mahogany body, bolt neck, 2 pickups.

| 1974-1977 | | $600 | $650 |

Model 2350 Les

1971-1977. Copy of classic single-cut solidbody, bolt neck, black, gold hardware, goldtop version (2350G Les) also available. A cherry sunburst finish (2350 Les Custom) was offered by '74.

| 1971-1977 | | $550 | $650 |

Model 2351

1974-1977. Copy of classic single-cut solidbody, gold top, 2 pickups.

| 1974-1977 | | $500 | $600 |

Model 2351DX

1974-1977. Copy of classic single-cut solidbody, gold top, 2 mini-humbuckers.

| 1974-1977 | | $500 | $550 |

Model 2352 Telly

1974-1978. Copy of early classic single-cut solidbody, 1 bridge pickup, white finish.

| 1974-1978 | | $500 | $600 |

Model 2352CT

1974-1978. Copy of classic single-cut solidbody, single-coil bridge and humbucker neck pickup.

| 1974-1978 | | $500 | $600 |

Model 2352DX Telly

1974-1978. Copy of classic single-cut solidbody, 2 humbuckers.

| 1974-1978 | | $500 | $600 |

Model 2354

1974-1977. Copy of classic sharp double-cut solidbody, 2 humbuckers, vibrato.

| 1974-1977 | | $500 | $600 |

Model 2354S

1972-1977. Stop tailpiece version of 2354.

| 1972-1977 | | $500 | $600 |

Model 2355/2355M

1973-1977. Copy of classic single-cut hollowbody, sunburst or natural maple (M).

| 1973-1977 | | $1,300 | $1,400 |

Model 2356

1973-1975. Copy of classic double pointed cutaway hollowbody, bowtie markers, sunburst. There was another Model 2356 in '74, a copy of a different hollowbody.

| 1973-1975 | | $800 | $1,100 |

Model 2363R

1973-1974. Cherry finish copy of classic varitone double-cut semi-hollow body.

| 1973-1974 | | $1,000 | $1,100 |

Model 2364 Ibanex

1971-1973. Dan Armstrong see-thru Lucite copy, 2 mounted humbuckers.

| 1971-1973 | | $600 | $700 |

Model 2368 Telly

1974-1978. Copy of classic single-cut thinline, chambered f-hole body, single coil pickup, mahogany body.

| 1974-1978 | | $500 | $600 |

Model 2368F

1973-1978. 2368 with 1 humbucker and 1 single coil.

| 1973-1978 | | $550 | $650 |

1970 Ibanez Model 2020

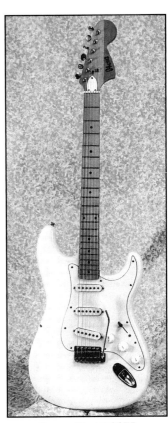

Ibanez Model 2375

Ibanez Model 2384

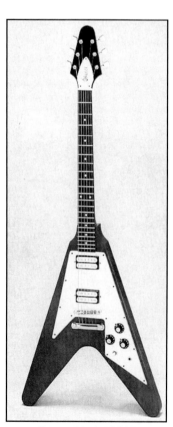

*Ibanez Model 2387
Rocket Roll*

MODEL YEAR	FEATURES	EXC. COND. LOW	HIGH

Model 2370
1972-1977. Sunburst version of Model 2363R.

1972-1977		$1,000	$1,100

Model 2372 Les Pro/2372DX Les Pro
1972-1977. Copy of classic single-cut solidbody, bolt neck, low impedance pickups, DX with gold hardware available for '73-'74.

1972-1977		$550	$650

Model 2374 Crest
1974-1976. Copy of classic double-cut semi-hollow body, walnut finish.

1974-1976		$900	$1,000

Model 2375 Strato
1971-1978. Copy of classic offset double-cut solidbody, 3 single-coils, sunburst.

1971-1978		$400	$600

Model 2375ASH Strato
1974-1978. 2375 with ash body.

1974-1978		$550	$650

Model 2375WH/N/BK Strato
1974-1978. 2375 in white (WH), natural (N), and black (BK) finishes.

1974-1978		$400	$600

Model 2377
1974-1975. Copy of classic double sharp-cut solidbody, short production run, dot markers.

1974-1975		$400	$450

Model 2380
1973-1977. Copy of classic double-cut solidbody with low impedence pickups, small block markers.

1973-1977		$550	$650

Model 2383
1974-1976. Copy of classic double sharp cut solidbody, white or walnut, 3 humbuckers, gold hardware.

1974-1976	Walnut	$600	$700
1974-1976	White	$650	$750

Model 2384 Telly
1974-1976. Copy of classic single-cut, f-holes, 2 humbuckers, ash body.

1974-1976		$500	$600

Model 2387 Rocket Roll/Rocket Roll Sr.
1975-1977. Copy of classic v-shpaed solidbody, set-neck, dot markers, gold-covered pickups.

1975-1977		$1,100	$1,400

Model 2390
1974-1976. Copy of classic double-cut semi-hollow body, maple 'board, walnut finish.

1974-1976		$900	$1,000

Model 2395
1974-1976. Natural finished 2390.

1974-1976		$900	$1,000

Model 2397
1974-1976. Double-cut semi-hollow body, low impedance electronics, trapezoid markers, goldtop.

1974-1976		$900	$1,000

Model 2399DX Jazz Solid
1974-1976. Single-cut solidbody, sunburst, set-neck, gold hardware.

1974-1976		$600	$800

Model 2401 Signature
1974-1976. Double-cut semi-hollow archtop, gold top, bolt neck.

1974-1976		$900	$1,000

Model 2402/2402DX Double Axe
1974-1977. Double sharp cut solidbody 6/12 doubleneck, cherry or walnut, DX model has gold hardware and white finish.

1974-1977		$900	$1,200

Model 2404 Double Axe
1974-1977. Double sharp cut solidbody guitar/bass doubleneck copy, walnut, white available '75 only.

1974-1977		$1,000	$1,400

Model 2405 Custom Agent
1974-1977. Single-cut solidbody, set neck, scroll headstock, pearl body inlay, 2 humbuckers.

1974-1977		$1,400	$1,600

Model 2406 Double Axe
1974-1977. Double sharp cut solidbody doubleneck, two 6-strings, cherry or wlanut.

1974-1977		$1,000	$1,400

Model 2407 Strato Jazz
1974-1976. Offset double-cut solidbody double-neck.

1974-1976		$800	$1,200

Model 2451
1974-1977. Single-cut solidbody, maple 'board, black or natural, set neck.

1974-1977		$500	$600

Model 2453 Howie Roberts
1974-1977. Single-cut archtop, round soundhole, maple body, set neck, rosewood 'board, block markers, 1 pickup, gold hardware, burgundy or sunburst.

1974-1977		$1,000	$1,200

Model 2454
1974-1977. Copy of classic double-cut semi-hollow body, set-neck, small block markers, cherry finish over ash.

1974-1977		$900	$1,000

Model 2455
1974-1977. Copy of classic single-cut archtop, 2 pickups, natural.

1974-1977		$1,200	$1,800

Model 2459 Destroyer
1975-1977. Korina finished mahogany body.

1975-1977		$750	$1,000

Model 2460
1975-1977. Copy of classic single-cut archtop, natural.

1975-1977		$1,000	$1,600

Model 2461
1975-1977. Copy of classic single-cut archtop, laminated spruce top, curly maple body, set-neck, ebony 'board, pearl blocks, 2 pickups, gold hardware, sunburst or natural.

1976-1979		$1,600	$1,800

Model 2464
1975-1977. Copy of classic single-cut thinline arcthop, natural.

1975-1977		$1,300	$1,600

MODEL YEAR	FEATURES	EXC. COND. LOW	HIGH

Model 2469 Futura
1976-1977. Korina finished furturistic model copy.

1976-1977		$1,100	$1,400

Musician MC Series
1978-1982. Solidbodies, various models.

1978-1982	Bolt neck	$550	$600
1978-1982	Neck-thru body	$700	$800
1978-1982	Set neck	$650	$750

Performer PF100 Standard
1978-1979. Single cut solidbody, plain birch top, mahogany body, bolt neck, dot inlays, 2 humbuckers.

1978-1979		$350	$450

Performer PF200 Custom
1978-1979. Maple top PF100.

1978-1979		$350	$500

Performer PF300
1978-1980. Single cut solidbody, maple top, mahogany body, set neck, 2 humbuckers, Tri-Sound.

1978-1980		$500	$600

Performer PF400
1978-1979. Single cut solidbody, flame maple top, alder body, set neck, block inlays, 2 humbuckers, Tri-Sound.

1978-1979		$500	$650

PF Performance Series Acoustics
1987-present. Line of mostly dreadnought size flat-tops, various models.

1987-1998	PF-10	$200	$300
1987-1998	PF1012 12-string	$350	$400

PM20 Pat Metheny
1997-1999. Double-cut semi-hollow body, f-holes, 1 pickup, rosewood 'board.

1997-1999		$1,000	$1,100

Pro Line PL1770/PLZ1770
1985-1987. Alder solidbody, ebony 'board, hum/single/single pickups, locking trem, Z added in '87.

1985-1987		$350	$450

Pro Line PL2550/PLZ2550
1985-1987. Alder solidbody, neck-thru body, hum/single/single pickups, locking trem, Z added in '87.

1986-1987		$450	$550

Pro Line PR1660
1985. Randy Rhoads-style body, 2 humbuckers.

1985		$300	$350

RG220
1994-1999. Offset double-cut solidbody, 2 humbuckers.

1998-1999		$250	$300

RG270
1994-2002. Offset double-cut solidbody, 2 humbuckers.

1994-2001		$250	$300

RG320
1998-2000. Offset double-cut solidbody, 2 humbuckers.

1998-2000		$250	$300

RG350DX
1998-2001. Offset double-cut solidbody, hum/single/hum pickups.

1998-2001		$250	$300

RG470
1993-2002. Double long pointy cut basswood solidbody, hum/single/hum pickups, dot markers.

1993-2000		$300	$400

RG520QS
1997-2002. Offset double-cut mahogany solidbody, quilt top, 2 humbuckers, dot markers.

1998-2001		$450	$600

RG550/RG550 DX
1987-1993, 1997-2002. Pointy headstock, long thin horn double-cut solidbody, hum/single/hum pickups. Roadstar Deluxe series until '91, than RG series.

1987-1993		$575	$675

RG560
1988-1992. Offset double cut, single/single/hum pickups, Roadstar Deluxe series until '91, than RG series.

1988-1992		$450	$500

RG570
1989-1992, 1996-2002. Offset double cut, hum/single/hum pickups, Roadstar Deluxe series until '91, than RG series.

1989-1992		$450	$500

RG760
1989-1992. Offset double cut, shark tooth inlays, single/single/hum pickups mounted in body. Roadstar Deluxe series until '91, than RG series.

1989-1992		$375	$450

RG770
1990-1993. Hum/single/hum version of RG760. Roadstar Deluxe series until '91, than RG series.

1990-1993		$425	$475

RG1200
1992. Offset double-cut, hum/single/hum pickups, flame maple top.

1992		$500	$550

RG7620/RG7621
1997-2000. 7-string models in the RG Series, 7621, available '98 only, had fixed bridge.

1997-2000		$550	$600

RGT42
2002-2004. Offset double cut, 2 humbuckers, dot markers.

2002-2004		$375	$450

Roadstar Deluxe Series
1986-1991. Offset double cut basswood (or maple top) solidbodies, various models, higher appointments than original series, but still says Roadstar II on headstock.

1986	RG530 (2 hum, maple)	$400	$500
1986-1887	RG440 (h\s\s)	$450	$600
1986-1987	RG410 (1 hum)	$350	$450
1986-1987	RG420 (2 hum)	$400	$500
1986-1987	RG430 (3 SC)	$450	$600

Roadstar II/Roadstar Standard
1983-1988. Various offset double-cut solidbodies, Roadstar II for '83-'85, Roadstar Standard '86-'88. Says Roadstar II on headstock for all years.

1986-1987	RG120/135/140	$250	$275

Ibanez PF 1055

1984 Ibanez Roadstar

Ibanez UV777

Imperial Tonmaster Elite

MODEL YEAR	FEATURES	EXC. COND. LOW	HIGH
1987	RG240 (more features)	$275	$300
1987	RG250 (flame maple)	$300	$325

Roadster
1979-1983. Offset double-cut, maple 'board, bolt neck, replaced by Roadstar series in '83.

1979-1983		$300	$350

Rocket Roll II RR550
1982-1984. Flying V body, six-on-side headstock, pearloid blocks, cherry sunburst, maple top, set neck.

1982-1984		$400	$500

RT Series
1992-1993. Offset double-cut, bolt neck, rosewood 'board, dot markers, hum/single/hum pickups. 150 has lower pickup quality, 650 has flamed top.

1992-1993	RT150	$250	$300
1992-1993	RT650	$450	$500

RX20/GRX20
1994-present. Offset double cut maple solidbody, 2 humbuckers, maple 'board, became the agathis or alder body, rosewood 'board GRX in '98.

1994-1998		$225	$250

Studio ST50 Jr.
1979-1981. Set-neck, small offset sharp double-cut mahogany solidbody, 2 exposed pickups.

1979-1981		$450	$550

Studio ST300
1978-1980. Maple/ash body, active tone system, tri-sound switch, natural, gold hardware, 2 humbuckers.

1978-1980		$500	$600

Talman TC420
1995-1997. Offset double cut, bolt neck, 2 humbuckers, dot markers.

1995-1997		$400	$450

Talman TC620
1994-1997. 2 stacked P-90 style pickups, BP version was black with pearloid 'guard.

1995-1996		$300	$400

Talman TC630
1995-1997. 3 lipstick pickups, dot markers.

1995-1997		$450	$550

Universe UV7/7P/77
1990-1997. Basswood 7-strings, hum/single/hum pickups. The '90-'93 white 7P and multi-colored 77 have pyramid inlays, the black '90-'97 7 has dots.

1990-1993	7P	$1,000	$1,100
1990-1997	7 and 77	$1,200	$1,300

Universe UV777GR
1991-1993. Basswood 7-string, pyramid inlays, maple 'board, hum/single/hum pickups.

1991-1993		$1,600	$2,100

USRG-10 (U.S.A.)
1994-1995. RG style guitars built in the U.S. by PBC Guitar Technology.

1994-1995		$750	$850

V300
1978-1991. Vintage Series acoustic dreadnought, spruce top, mahogany back and sides, sunburst or various colors.

1978-1991		$300	$475

Ibanez, Salvador

1875-1920. Salvador Ibanez was a Spanish luthier who operated a small guitar-building workshop. In the early 1900s he founded Spain's largest guitar factory. In 1929 Japan's Hoshino family began importing Salvador Ibanez guitars. Demand for the Salvador Ibanez guitars became so great that the Hoshino family began building their own guitars, which ultimately became known as the Ibanez brand. Guitars from 1875-1920 were mostly classical style and often can be identified by a label on the inside back which stipulates Salvador Ibanez.

Ignacio Rozas

1987-present. Luthier Ignacio M. Rozas builds his classical and flamenco guitars in Madrid, Spain. He also offers factory-made guitars built to his specifications.

Imperial

Ca.1963-ca.1970. Imported by the Imperial Accordion Company of Chicago, Illinois. Early guitars made in Italy by accordion builder Crucianelli. By ca. '66 switched to Japanese guitars.

Electric Solidbody
1963-1968. Italian-made until '66, then Japanese-made, includes the Tonemaster line.

1963-1968		$150	$250

Infeld

2003-present. Solidbody guitars and basses offered by string-maker Thomastik-Infeld of Vienna.

Infinox

1980s. Infinox by JTG, of Nashville, offered a line of 'the classic shapes of yesterday and the hi tech chic of today'. Classic shapes included copies of many classic American solidbody designs with the block letter Infinox by JTG logo on headstock, special metallic 'grafteq' paint finish, space-age faux graphite-feel neck, Gotoh tuning machines, Gotoh locking nut tremolo with fine tuners, all models with 1 or 2 humbucker pickups.

Interdonati

1930s. Guitars built by luthier Philip Interdonati, of Staten Island, New York, originally professional grade, luthier's label is on the inside back.

Size 000 Flat-Top

1930s		$3,500	$7,500

Italia

1999-present. Intermediate grade, production, solid, semi-solid, and hollow body guitars designed by Trevor Wilkinson and made in Korea. They also build basses.

J Burda Guitars

Flat-top guitars built by luthier Jan Burda in Berrien Springs, Michigan.

MODEL YEAR	FEATURES	EXC. COND. LOW	HIGH

J. Frog Guitars

1978-present. Professional and premium grade, production/custom, solidbody guitars made in Las Vegas, Nevada, by Ed Roman.

J.B. Player

1980s-present. Budget and intermediate grade, production, imported acoustic, acoustic/electric, and solidbody guitars. They also offer basses, banjos and mandolins. Founded in United States. Moved production of guitars to Korea but maintained a U.S. Custom Shop. MBT International/Musicorp took over manufacture and distribution in '89.

J.R. Zeidler Guitars

1977-present. Luthier John Zeidler builds his premium and presentation grade, custom, flat-top, 12-string, and archtop guitars in Wallingford, Pennsylvania. He also builds mandolins.

Auditorium Cutaway

Introduced in 1982. Sitka or Adirondack spruce top, Indian rosewood sides, gold hardware.

1990s		$4,500	$5,500

Concert

1990s. Spruce top, Indian rosewood back and sides, the name does not denote the size, which approximates 00 Grand Concert.

1992		$5,500	$6,000

J.T. Hargreaves Basses And Guitars

1995-present. Luthier Jay Hargreaves builds his premium grade, production/custom, classical and steel string guitars in Seattle, Washington. He also builds basses.

Jack Daniel's

2004-present. Acoustic and electric guitar models, some with custom Jack Daniel's artwork on the body and headstock, built by Peavey for the Jack Daniel's Distillery. There is also an amp model.

Jackson

1980-present. Currently Jackson offers intermediate, professional, and premium grade, production, electric guitars. They also offer basses. In '78 Grover Jackson bought out Charvel Guitars and moved it to San Dimas. Jackson made custom-built bolt-on Charvels. In '82 the pointy, tilt-back Jackson headstock became standard. The Jackson logo was born in '80 and used on a guitar designed as Randy Rhoad's first flying V. Jacksons were neck-through construction.

The Charvel trademark was licensed to IMC in '85. IMC moved the Jackson factory to Ontario, California in '86. Grover Jackson stayed with Jackson/Charvel until '89 (see Charvel). On October 25, 2002, Fender Musical Instruments Corp (FMIC) took ownership of Jackson/Charvel Manufacturing Inc.

DR3

1996-2001. Dinky Reverse, double-cut solidbody, reverse headstock, triangle markers, dual humbuckers, locking vibrato, various colors, made in Japan, flamed maple top available.

1996-1999		$375	$425

DR5

1996 only. Offset double-cut solidbody, 2 Kent Armstrong humbuckers, rosewood 'board, dot markers.

1996		$375	$425

JSX94

1994-1995. Offset double-cut solidbody, single/single/hum, rosewood 'board, dot markers.

1994-1995		$275	$375

KE2 USA Kelly

1998-present. Alder solidbody, flame maple top, neck-thru.

1998-2003		$1,100	$1,200

Kelly Custom

1984-early 1990s. Neck-thru solidbody, Kahler tremolo, 2 humbuckers, ebony 'board with shark's tooth inlays, bound neck and headstock.

1984-1993	Bolt-on	$550	$800

Kelly Pro

1994-1995. Pointy-cut solidbody, neck-thru, 2 humbuckers, bound ebony 'board, sharkfin inlays.

1994-1995		$550	$800

Kelly Standard

1993-1995. Pointy cutaway solidbody, bolt neck, 2 humbuckers, dot markers.

1993-1995	Bolt-on	$450	$725

Kelly XL

1994-1995. Pointy cutaway solidbody, bolt neck, 2 humbuckers, bound rosewood 'board, sharkfin inlays.

1994-1995		$550	$800

King V Pro

1993-1995. Soft V-shaped neck-thru solidbody, sharkfin markers, 2 humbuckers.

1993-1995		$500	$700

King V STD

1993-1995. Bolt neck version of King V.

1993-1995		$275	$325

Phil Collen

1989-1991, 1993-1995. Offset double-cut maple neck-thru solidbody, six-on-a-side tuners, 1 volume, bound ebony 'board, U.S.-made, early version has poplar body, 1 humbucker; later version with basswood body, 1 single-coil and 1 humbucker.

1993-1995		$950	$1,150

Phil Collen PC1 (U.S.A.)

1996-present. Quilt maple top, bolt-on maple neck, maple board, koa body '96-'00, mahogany body '01-present, 1 humbucker and 1 single coil '96-'97, humbucker, stacked humbucker, and single coil '98-present.

1996-2000		$1,050	$1,250

Phil Collen PC3 (Import)

1996-2001. Downscale version of Collen model, poplar body, bolt neck, humbucker\single\single.

1996-2000		$450	$525

Jack Daniel's USA Custom

Jackson Phil Collen

Jackson Randy Rhoads

1970s Jacobacci doubleneck

MODEL YEAR	FEATURES	EXC. COND. LOW	HIGH

PS2
1994-2000. Offset double-cut solidbody, single/single/hum, rosewood 'board, dot markers.

| 1994-2000 | | $165 | $185 |

PS3
1994-2000. Rhoads wedge-style body, 2 humbuckers, rosewood 'board, dot markers.

| 1994-2000 | | $165 | $185 |

Randy Rhoads (U.S.A.)
1983-present. V-shaped neck-thru solidbody, 2 humbuckers, originally made at San Dimas plant, serial numbers RR 0001 to RR 1929, production moved to the Ontario plant by '87, serial numbers RR 1930 to present in sequential order.

1983	Early serial #, no trem	$2,000	$2,500
1983-1986	Kahler trem	$1,100	$1,500
1983-1986	Rose trem or string-thru	$1,500	$2,000
1987-1989	Early Ontario-built	$1,100	$1,400
1990-1999	Ontario-built	$1,000	$1,300
2000-2002		$900	$1,000
2002	FMIC, RR5	$700	$800

Randy Rhoads Custom Shop
1999. U.S.-made Custom Shop, special features.

| 1999 | | $1,000 | $1,100 |

Randy Rhoads Custom Shop RR1T
2002 only. U.S.-made Custom Shop, only 50 made, Randy Rhoads body.

| 2002 | | $1,350 | $1,550 |

Randy Rhoads Limited Edition
1992 only. Shark fin-style maple neck-thru body, gold hardware, white with black pinstriping, block inlays, six-on-a-side tuners, U.S.-made, only 200 built.

| 1992 | | $1,300 | $1,400 |

Randy Rhoads Performer/RR Performer
2000s. Randy Rhoades body style, Performer logo on headstock.

| 2000s | | $300 | $325 |

Randy Rhoads (Import)
1990s. Bolt-on import version.

| 1990s | | $325 | $350 |

San Dimas Custom-Built
1980-1982. Various custom-built solidbody models, values vary depending on each individual instrument.

| 1980-1982 | | $2,000 | $3,500 |

Soloist
1984-1990. Double-cut, neck-thru, string-thru solidbody, 2 humbuckers, bound rosewood 'board, U.S.-made, replaced by the Soloist USA in '90.

| 1984-1986 | San Dimas-built | $1,100 | $1,500 |
| 1986-1990 | Ontario-built | $975 | $1,025 |

Soloist Custom
1993-1995. Double-cut, neck-thru solidbody, 1 humbucker and 2 single-coils, bound ebony 'board, shark's tooth inlays, U.S.-made.

| 1993-1995 | | $875 | $950 |

MODEL YEAR	FEATURES	EXC. COND. LOW	HIGH

Soloist Student J1 (U.S.A.)
1984-1999. Double-cut neck-thru solidbody, Seymour Duncan single-single-hum pickups, rosewood 'board, dot inlays, no binding.

| 1984-1986 | San Dimas-built | $600 | $800 |
| 1986-1999 | Ontario-built | $725 | $850 |

Soloist USA
1990-1995. Replaces Soloist, sharkfin markers, single-single-hum.

| 1990-1995 | | $975 | $1,025 |

Warrior Pro (Import)
1990-1992. Japanese version.

| 1990-1992 | | $225 | $300 |

Warrior USA
1990-1992. Four point neck-thru solidbody, 1 humbucker and 1 single-coil, triangle markers, active electronics, U.S.-made, the Warrior Pro was Japanese version.

| 1990s | Red | $1,100 | $1,500 |

Jackson-Guldan/Jay G Guitars
1920s-1960s. The Jackson-Guldan Violin Company, of Columbus, Ohio, mainly built inexpensive violins, violas, cellos, etc. but also offered acoustic guitars in the 1950s and early '60s, some of which were distributed by Wards. Their sales flyers from that era state "Made in America by Jackson-Guldan Craftsman." Very similar to small (13"-14") Stella economy flat-tops. Jay G name with quarter-note logo is sometimes on the headstock. They also offered lap steels and small tube amps early on.

Jacobacci
1930s-1994. Founded in France by Italian Vincent Jacobacci and originally building basso-guitars, banjos, and mandolins. Sons Roger and Andre joined the company and encouraged pop to add lapsteels and electric and regular acoustic guitars around '52. The guitars are sometimes labeled as Jaco and, from ca. '54 to ca. '66, as Jaco Major. In '58 the company introduced aluminum neck models, and in '59 their first solidbodies. In the '60s they also made instruments branded Royal, Texas, Ohio, Star and made instruments for Major Conn and other companies. By the mid '60s, they were producing mainly jazz style guitars.

James R. Baker Guitars
1996-present. Luthier James R. Baker builds his premium grade, custom, archtops in Shoreham, New York.

James Tyler
Early 1980s-present. Luthier James Tyler builds his professional and premium grade, custom/production, solidbody guitars in Van Nuys, California, and also has a model built in Japan. He also builds basses.

MODEL		EXC. COND.	
YEAR	FEATURES	LOW	HIGH

Janofsky Guitars

1978-present. Production classical and flamenco guitars built by luthier Stephen Janofsky in Amherst, Massachusetts.

Jaros

1995-present. Professional and premium grade, production/custom, solidbody and acoustic/electric guitars originally built by father and son luthiers Harry and Jim Jaros in Rochester, Pennsylvania. In '01 Ed Roman in Las Vegas, bought the brand. He sold it in '04 to Dave Weiler in Nashville.

Jasmine

1994-present. Budget and intermediate grade, production, steel and classical guitars offered by Takamine Jasmine or Jasmine by Takamine. Student level instruments.

Jay Turser

1997-present. Budget and intermediate grade, production, imported acoustic, acoustic/electric, electric and resonator guitars. They also offer basses and amps. Designed and developed by Tommy Rizzi for Music Industries Corp.

Jeff Traugott Guitars

1991-present. Premium and presentation grade, custom, flat-top, nylon-string, and acoustic/electric guitars built by luthier Jeff Traugott, in Santa Cruz, California.

Jeremy Locke Guitars

1985-present. Premium grade, production/custom, classical and flamenco guitars built by luthier Jeremy Locke in Coomera, South East Queensland, Australia.

Jeronimo Pena Fernandez

1967-present. Luthier Jeronimo Pena Fernandez started building classical guitars in Marmolejo, Spain, in the '50s. In '67, he went full-time and soon became well-known for his fine work. He is now retired, but still builds a few guitars a year.

Classical

Brazilian rosewood back and sides, cedar top, full-size classical guitar, higher-end luthier.

1960-1990s		$5,000	$8,000

Jerry Jones

1981-present. Intermediate grade, production, semi-hollow body electric guitars and sitars from luthier Jerry Jones, built in Nashville, Tennessee. They also build basses. Jones started building custom guitars in '81, and launched his Danelectro-inspired line in '87.

Electric Models

Various models include Baritone 6-string ('89-present); Electric Sitar ('90-present) with buzz-bar sitar bridge, individual pickup for sympathetic strings and custom color gator finish; Longhorn Guitarlin ('89-'00,

MODEL		EXC. COND.	
YEAR	FEATURES	LOW	HIGH

'05-present) with large cutaway Guitarlin-style body, 24 frets in '89 and 31 after; and the Neptune 12-string ('81-present) single-cut with 3 pickups.

1990s	Baritone 6-string	$500	$600
1990s	Electric Sitar	$550	$650
1990s	Longhorn Guitarlin	$550	$650
1990s	Neptune Electric 12-string	$600	$800

Jersey Girl

1991-present. Premium grade, production/custom, solidbody guitars made in Japan. They also build effects.

Jewel

1920s. Instruments built by the Oscar Schmidt Co. and possibly others. Most likely a brand made for a distributor.

Jim Redgate Guitars

1992-present. Luthier Jim Redgate builds his premium grade, custom, nylon-string classical guitars in Belair, Adelaide, South Australia.

John Le Voi Guitars

1970-present. Production/custom, gypsy jazz, flat-top, and archtop guitars built by luthier John Le Voi in Lincolnshire, United Kingdom. He also builds mandolin family instruments.

John Price Guitars

1984-present. Custom classical and flamenco guitars built by luthier John Price in Australia.

Johnson

Mid-1990s-present. Budget, intermediate and professional grade, production, acoustic, classical, acoustic/electric, resonator and solidbody guitars imported by Music Link, Brisbane, California. Johnson also offers basses, amps, mandolins, ukuleles and effects.

Jon Kammerer

1995-present. Luthier Jon Kammerer builds his professional grade, custom, acoustic and electric guitars in Keokuk, Iowa. He also builds the Sinister Custom Shop Bass for Sinister Guitars.

Jones

See TV Jones listing.

Jordan

1981-present. Professional and premium grade, custom, flat-top and archtop guitars built by luthier John Jordan in Concord, California. He also builds electric violins and cellos.

Jose Oribe

1962-present. Presentation grade, production, classical, flamenco, and steel-string acoustic guitars built by luthier Jose Oribe in Vista, California.

Jay Turser JT-136 Vine

Jerry Jones Electric Sitar

Kalamazoo KG--14

Jose Ramirez

1882-present. Professional, premium, and presentation grade, custom/production, classical guitars built by luthier José Ramirez IV in Madrid, Spain. The company was founded by his great-grandfather.

K & S

1992-1998. Hawaiian-style and classical guitars distributed by George Katechis and Marc Silber and handmade in Paracho, Mexico. A few 16" wide Leadbelly Model 12-strings were made in Oakland, California by luthier Stewart Port. K & S also offered mandolins, mandolas and ukes. In '98, Silber started marketing guitars under the Marc Silber Guitar Company brand and Katechis continued to offer instruments under the Casa Montalvo brand.

Kakos, Stephen

1972-present. Luthier Stephen Kakos builds his premium grade, production/custom, classical guitars in Mound, Minnesota.

Kalamazoo

1933-1942, 1965-1970. Budget brand built by Gibson. Made flat-tops, solidbodies, mandolins, lap steels, banjos and amps. Amps and solidbodies were built '65-'67.

KG-1/KG-1 A

1965-1969. Offset double-cut (initial issue) or SG-shape (second issue), 1 pickup, Model 1 A with spring vibrato, red, blue or white.

		LOW	HIGH
1965-1969		$150	$200

KG-2/KG-2 A

1965-1970. Offset double-cut (initial shape) or SG-shape, 2 pickups, Model 2 A with spring vibrato, red, blue or white.

		LOW	HIGH
1965-1970		$275	$375

KG-11

1933-1941. Flat-top, all mahogany, 14" with no 'guard, sunburst.

		LOW	HIGH
1933-1941		$500	$750

KG-14

1936-1940. Flat-top L-0-size, mahogany back and sides, with 'guard, sunburst.

		LOW	HIGH
1936-1940		$750	$1,000

KG-16

1939-1940. Gibson-made archtop, small body, f-hole.

		LOW	HIGH
1939-1940		$700	$800

KG-21

1936-1941. Early model 15" archtop (bent, not curved), dot markers, bound top, sunburst.

		LOW	HIGH
1936-1941		$700	$750

KG-31

1935-1940. Archtop L-50-size, 16" body, non-carved spruce top, mahogany back and sides.

		LOW	HIGH
1935-1940		$750	$825

Kathy Wingert flat-top

KG-32

1939-1942. Archtop, 16" body.

		LOW	HIGH
1939-1942		$800	$850

KTG-14 Tenor

1936-1940. Flat-top L-0-size tenor, mahogany back and sides, bound top, sunburst.

		LOW	HIGH
1936-1940		$225	$350

Kamico

Brand started in 1947. Flat-top acoustic guitars. Low-end budget brand made by Kay Musical Instrument Company and sold through various distributors.

Acoustic Flat-Tops

1940s. Made by Kay.

		LOW	HIGH
1940s		$175	$250

Kapa

Ca. 1962-1970. Begun by Dutch immigrant and music store owner Kope Veneman in Hyattsville, Maryland whose father had made Amka guitars in Holland. Kapa is from K for Kope, A for son Albert, P for daughter Patricia, and A for wife Adeline. Crown shield logo from Amka guitars. The brand included some Hofner and Italian imports in '60. Ca. '66 Kapa started offering thinner bodies. Some German Pix pickups ca. '66. Thinlines and Japanese bodies in '69. Kapa closed shop in '70 and the parts and equipment were sold to Micro-Frets and Mosrite. Later Veneman was involved with Bradley copy guitars imported from Japan. Approximately 120,000 Kapas were made.

Electric Guitars

1962-1970. Various models include Challenger with 3-way toggle from '62-'66/'67 and 2 on/off switches after; Cobra with 1 pickup; Continental and Continental 12-string; Minstrel and Minstrel 12-string with teardrop shape, 3 pickups; and the Wildcat, mini offset double-cut, 3

		LOW	HIGH
1962-1970	Various models	$300	$600

Kasha

1967-1997. Innovative classical guitars built by luthier Richard Schneider in collaboration with Dr. Michael Kasha. Schneider also consulted for Gibson and Gretsch. Schneider died in '97.

Kathy Wingert Guitars

1996-present. Luthier Kathy Wingert builds her premium grade, production/custom, flat-tops in Rancho Palos Verdes, California.

Kawai

1927-present. Kawai is a Japanese piano and guitar maker. They started offering guitars around '56 and they were imported into the U.S. carrying many different brand names, including Kimberly and Teisco. In '67 Kawai purchased Teisco. Odd-shaped guitars were offered from late-'60s through the mid-'70s. Few imports carrying the Kawai brand until the late-'70s; best known for high quality basses. By

MODEL YEAR	FEATURES	EXC. COND. LOW	HIGH

'90s they were making plexiglass replicas of Teisco Spectrum 5 and Kawai moon-shaped guitar. Kawai recently quit offering guitars and basses.

Acoustic Hollowbody Archtops
1956-1990s.

1960s		$225	$275

Electric Archtops
1956-1990s.

1960s	Various	$275	$400
1970s	Various	$225	$400

Kay

Ca. 1931 (1890)-present. Originally founded in Chicago, Illinois as Groehsl Company (or Groehsel) in 1890, making bowl-backed mandolins. Offered Groehsl, Stromberg, Kay Kraft, Kay, Arch Kraft brand names, plus made guitars for S.S.Maxwell, Old Kraftsman (Spiegel), Recording King (Wards), Supertone (Sears), Silvertone (Sears), National, Dobro, Custom Kraft (St.Louis Music), Hollywood (Shireson Bros.), Oahu and others.

In 1921 the name was changed to Stromberg-Voisinet Company. Henry Kay "Hank" Kuhrmeyer joined the company in '23 and was secretary by '25. By the mid-'20s the company was making many better Montgomery Ward guitars, banjos and mandolins, often with lots of pearloid. First production electric guitars and amps are introduced with big fanfare in '28; perhaps only 200 or so made. Last Stromberg instruments seen in '32. Kuhrmeyer becomes president and the Kay Kraft brand was introduced in '31, probably named for Kuhrmeyer's middle name, though S-V had used Kay brand on German Kreuzinger violins '28-'36. By '34, if not earlier, the company is changed to the Kay Musical Instrument Company. A new factory was built at 1640 West Walnut Street in '35. The Kay Kraft brand ends in '37 and the Kay brand is introduced in late-'36 or '37. Violin Style Guitars and upright acoustic basses debut in '38. In '40 the first guitars for Sears, carrying the new Silvertone brand, are offered. Kamico budget line introduced in '47 and Rex flat-tops and archtops sold through Gretsch in late-'40s. Kuhrmeyer retires in '55 dies a year later. New gigantic factory in Elk Grove Village, Illinois opens in '64. Seeburg purchased Kay in '66 and sold it to Valco in '67. Valco/Kay went out of business in '68 and its assets were auctioned in '69. The Kay name went to Sol Weindling and Barry Hornstein of W.M.I. (Teisco Del Rey) who began putting Kay name on Teisco guitars. By '73 most Teisco guitars are called Kay. Tony Blair, president of Indianapolis-based A.R. Musical Enterprises Inc. (founded in '73) purchased the Kay nameplate in '79 and currently distributes Kay in the U.S. See Guitar Stories Volume II, by Michael Wright, for a complete history of Kay with detailed model listings.

Barney Kessel Artist
1957-1960. Single-cut, 15 1/2" body, 1 (K6701) or 2 (K6700) pickups, Kelvinator headstock, sunburst or blond.

1957-1960		$1,200	$1,500

Barney Kessel Pro
1957-1960. 13" hollowbody, single-cut, Kelvinator headstock, ebony 'board with pearl inlays, white binding, 1 or 2 pickups, sunburst.

1957-1960		$1,500	$1,700

K20
1939-1942. 16" archtop, solid spruce top, maple back and sides, sunburst.

1939-1942		$225	$300

K22
1950s. Flat-top similar to Gibson J-100 17", spruce top, mahogany back and sides.

1955-1959		$375	$600

K26
1955-1959. Flat-top, block markers, natural.

1955-1959		$475	$700

K44
1947-1951. Non-cut archtop, solid spruce top, 17" curly maple veneered body, block markers, sunburst.

1947-1951		$375	$500

K45
1952-1954. Non-cut archtop, 17" body, engraved tortoiseshell-celluloid headstock, large block markers, natural.

1952-1954		$425	$550

K46
1947-1951. Non-cut archtop, solid spruce top, 17" curly maple-veneered body, double-eighth note headstock inlay, sunburst.

1947-1951		$450	$600

K48 Artist
1947-1951. Non-cut archtop, 17" solid spruce top with figured maple back and sides, split block inlays, sunburst or black.

1947-1951		$900	$1,200

K48/K21 Jazz Special
Late-1960s. Slim solidbody with 3 reflective pickups, garden spade headstock, fancy position Circle K headstock logo.

1968	White	$375	$500

K100 Vanguard
1961-1966. Offset double-cut slab solidbody, genuine maple veneered top and back over hardwood body, sunburst.

1961-1966		$135	$165

K102 Vanguard
1961-1966. Double pickup version of the K100, sunburst.

1961-1966		$140	$190

K161 Thin Twin "Jimmy Reed"
1952-1958. Cutaway semi-hollow, 2 pickups, birdseye maple, often called the Jimmy Reed, sunburst.

1952-1958		$500	$650

Kawai KS-700

1957 Kay Barney Kessel

1950s Kay Upbeat

Kay 573 Speed Demon

MODEL YEAR	FEATURES	EXC. COND. LOW	HIGH

K300 Double Cutaway Solid Electric
1962-1966. Two single-coils, block inlays, some with curly maple top and some with plain maple top, natural.

1962-1966		$500	$575

K535
1961-1965. Thinline double-cut, 2 pickups, vibrato, sunburst.

1961-1965		$400	$575

K571/K572/K573 Speed Demon
1961-1965. Thinline semi-acoustic/electric, single pointed cutaway, some with Bigsby vibrato, with 2 (K571), 2 (K572) or 3 (K573) pickups. There was also a Speed Demon solidbody.

1961-1965	K571	$300	$400
1961-1965	K572	$400	$500
1961-1965	K573	$450	$650

K592
1962-1966. Thinline semi-acoustic/electric, double Florentine cut, 2 or 3 pickups, Bigsby vibrato, pie-slice inlays, cherry.

1962-1966		$450	$600

K671/K672 Swingmaster
1961-1965. Single rounded cutaway semi-hollow-body, with 1 (K671) or 2 (K672) pickups.

1961-1965	K671	$600	$750
1961-1965	K672	$700	$850

K1160 Standard
1957-1964. Small 13" (standard) flat-top, laminated construction.

1957-1965		$50	$70

K1961/K1962/K1963
1960-1965. Part of Value Leader line, thinline single-cut, hollowbody, identified by single chrome-plated checkered, body-length guard on treble side, laminated maple body, maple neck, dot markers, sunburst, with 1 (K1961), 2 (K1962) or 3 (K1963) pickups.

1960-1965	K1961	$350	$450
1960-1965	K1962	$450	$500
1960-1965	K1963	$450	$600

K1982/K1983 Style Leader/Jimmy Reed
1960-1965. Part of the Style Leader mid-level Kay line. Sometimes dubbed Jimmy Reed of 1960s. Easily identified by the long brushed copper dual guardplates on either side of the strings. Brown or gleaming golden blond (natural) finish, laminated curly maple body, simple script Kay logo, with 2 (K1982) or 3 (K1983) pickups.

1960-1965	K1982	$450	$525
1960-1965	K1983	$450	$600

K3500 Student Concert
1966-1968. 14 1/2" flat-top, solid spruce top, laminated maple back and sides.

1966-1968		$70	$100

K5113 Plains Special
1968. Flat-top, solid spruce top, laminated mahogany back and sides.

1968		$140	$200

K5160 Auditorium
1957-1965. Flat-top 15" auditorium-size, laminated construction.

1957-1965		$90	$125

K6100 Country
1950s-1960s. Jumbo flat-top, spruce x-braced top, mahogany back and sides, natural.

1957-1962		$325	$400

K6116 Super Auditorium
1957-1965. Super Auditorium-size flat-top, laminated figured maple back and sides, solid spruce top.

1957-1965		$175	$250

K6120 Western
1960s. Jumbo flat-top, laminated maple body, pin-less bridge, sunburst.

1962		$150	$200

K6130 Calypso
1960-1965. 15 1/2" flat-top with narrow waist, slotted headstock, natural.

1960-1965		$225	$300

K6533/K6535 Value Leader
1961-1965. Value Leader was the budget line of Kay, full body archtop, sunburst, with 1 (K6533) or 2 (K6535) pickups.

1961-1965	K6533	$225	$300
1961-1965	K6535	$225	$300

K7000 Artist
1960-1965. Highest-end of Kay classical series, fan bracing, spruce top, maple back and sides.

1960-1965		$375	$450

K7010 Concerto
1960-1965. Entry level of Kay classical series.

1960-1965		$75	$150

K7010 Maestro
1960-1965. Middle level of Kay classical series.

1960-1965		$225	$275

K8110 Master
1957-1960. 17" master-size flat-top which was largest of the series, laminated construction.

1957-1960		$125	$175

K8127 Solo Special
1957-1965. Kay's professional grade flat-top, narrow waist jumbo, block markers.

1957-1965		$425	$550

K8995 Upbeat
1958-1960. Less expensive alternative to Barney Kessel Jazz Special, 2 pickups, sunburst.

1958-1960		$850	$1,050

Kay Kraft
Ca.1931-1937. First brand name of the Kay Musical Instrument Company as it began its transition from Stromberg-Voisinet Company to Kay (see Kay for more info).

Kay Kraft Recording King

1931-1937		$350	$550

Keller Custom Guitars
1994-present. Professional grade, production/custom, solidbody guitars built by luthier Randall Keller in Mandan, North Dakota.

MODEL YEAR	FEATURES	EXC. COND. LOW	HIGH

Keller Guitars

1975-present. Premium grade, production/custom, flat-tops made by luthier Michael L. Keller in Rochester, Minnesota.

Ken Franklin

2003-present. Luthier Ken Franklin builds his premium grade, production/custom, acoustic guitars in Ukiah, California.

Kendrick

1989-present. Premium grade, production/custom, solidbody guitars built in Texas. Founded by Gerald Weber in Pflugerville, Texas and currently located in Kempner, Texas. Mainly known for their handmade tube amps, Kendrick also offers speakers and effects.

Kent

1961-1969. Imported from Japan by Buegeleisen and Jacobson of New York, New York. Manufacturers unknown but many early guitars were made by Guyatone and Teisco.

Acoustic Flat-Tops
1962-1969.

1962-1969		$125	$150

Acoustic/Electric Guitars
1962-1969.

1962-1969		$175	$225

Electric 12-String
1960s. Thinline electric, double pointy cutaways, 12 strings, slanted dual pickup, sunburst.

1965-1969		$300	$450

Semi-Hollow Electric
1960s. Thinline electric, offset double pointy cutaways, slanted dual pickups, various colors.

1962-1969		$300	$450

Solidbody Electrics
1962-1969. Models include Polaris I, II and III, Lido, Copa and Videocaster.

1962-1969	Century Red	$150	$250

Kevin Ryan Guitars

1989-present. Premium grade, custom, flat-tops built by luthier Kevin Ryan in Westminster, California.

Kiesel

See Carvin.

Kimberly

Late-1960s-early-1970s. Private branded import made in the same Japanese factory as Teisco.

May Queen
1960s. Same as Teisco May Queen with Kimberly script logo on headstock and May Queen Teisco on the 'guard.

1960s		$450	$600

Kingsley

1960s. Early Japanese imports, Teisco-made.

Soldibody Electric
1960s. Four pickups with tremolo.

1960s		$350	$375

Kingston

Ca. 1958-1967. Imported from Japan by Jack Westheimer and Westheimer Importing Corporation of Chicago, Illinois. Early examples made by Guyatone and Teisco.

Electric
1958-1967. Imported from Japan. Various models include: B-1, soldibody with 1 pickup; B-2T/B-3T/B-4T, solidbodies with 2/3/4 pickups and tremolo; SA-27, thin hollowbody with 2 pickups and tremolo.

1958-1967		$150	$375

Kinscherff Guitars

1990-present. Luthier Jamie Kinscherff builds his premium grade, production/custom, flat-top guitars in Austin, Texas.

Klein Acoustic Guitars

1972-present. Luthiers Steve Klein and Steven Kauffman build their production/custom, premium and presentation grade flat-tops in Sonoma, California. They also build basses.

Klein Electric Guitars

1988-present. Steve Klein added electrics to his line in '88. In '95, he sold the electric part of his business to Lorenzo German, who continues to produce professional grade, production/custom, solidbody guitars in Linden, California. He also builds basses.

Klira

The company founded by Johannes Klira in 1887 in Schoenbach, Germany, mainly made violins, but added guitars in the 1950s. The guitars of the '50s and '60s were original designs, but by the '70s most models were similar to popular American models. The guitars of the '50s and '60s were aimed at the budget market, but workmanship improved with the '70s models.

Hollowbody Electrics
1960s		$225	$400

Solidbody Electrics
1960s		$175	$400

Knutsen

1890s-1920s. Luthier Chris J. Knutsen of Tacoma and Seattle, Washington, experimented with and perfected Hawaiian and harp guitar models. He moved to Los Angeles, California around 1916, where he also made steels and ukes.

Convertible
1909-1914. Flat-top model with adjustable neck angle that allowed for a convertible Hawaiian or Spanish setup.

1909-1914		$2,000	$2,500

1964 Kent No. 540

Kendrick Canary

GUITARS

Knutson Songbird

1977 Kramer 650G

MODEL YEAR	FEATURES	EXC. COND. LOW	HIGH

Harp Guitar
1900s. Normally 11 strings with fancy purfling and trim.

| 1900-1910 | | $6,500 | $7,000 |

Knutson Luthiery
1981-present. Professional and premium grade, custom, archtop and flat-top guitars built by luthier John Knutson in Forestville, California. He also builds basses and mandolins.

Kohno
1960-present. Luthier Masaru Kohno built his classical guitars in Tokyo, Japan. When he died in '98, production was taken over by his nephew, Masaki Sakurai.
Classical
Brazilian rosewood back and sides, spruce top.

| 1970s | | $2,800 | $3,200 |

Koll
1990-present. Professional and premium grade, custom/production, solidbody, chambered, and archtop guitars built by luthier Saul Koll, originally in Long Beach, California, and since '93, in Portland, Oregon. He also builds basses.

Kona
1920s. Acoustic Hawaiian guitars sold by C.S. Delano and others, and thought to be made by Herman Weissenborn. Weissenborn appointments in line with style number, with thicker body and solid neck construction.
Style 3
| 1920s | Koa | $3,100 | $3,600 |

Style 4
| 1920s | Brown koa | $3,800 | $4,500 |

Koontz
1970-late 1980s. Luthier Sam Koontz started building custom guitars in the late '50s. Starting in '66 Koontz, who was associated with Harptone guitars, built guitars for Standel. In '70, he opened his own shop in Linden, New Jersey, building a variety of custom guitars. Koontz died in the late '80s. His guitars varied greatly and should be valued on a case-by-case basis.

Kramer
1976-1990, 1995-present. Currently Kramer offers budget and intermediate grade, production, imported acoustic, acoustic/electric, semi-hollow and solidbody guitars. They also offer basses, amps and effects.

Founded by New York music retailer Dennis Berardi, ex-Travis Bean sales rep Gary Kramer and ex-Norlin executive Peter LaPlaca. Initial financing provided by real estate developer Henry Vaccaro. Parent company named BKL Corporation (Berardi, Kramer, LaPlaca), located in Neptune City, New Jersey. The first guitars were designed by Berardi

MODEL YEAR	FEATURES	EXC. COND. LOW	HIGH

and luthier Phil Petillo and featured aluminum necks with wooden inserts on back to give them a wooden feel. Guitar production commenced in late-'76.

Control passed to Guitar Center of Los Angeles for '79-'82, which recommended a switch to more economical wood necks. Aluminum necks were phased out during the early-'80s, and were last produced in '85. In '89, a new investment group was brought in with James Liati as president, hoping for access to Russian market, but the company went of business in late-'90. In '95 Henry Vaccaro and new partners revived the company and designed a number of new guitars in conjunction with Phil Petillo. However, in '97 the Kramer brand was sold to Gibson. In '98, Henry Vaccaro released his new line of aluminum-core neck, split headstock guitars under the Vacarro brand.

Non-U.S.-made models include the following lines: Aerostar, Ferrington, Focus, Hundred (post-'85 made with 3 digits in the 100-900), Showster, Striker, Thousand (post-'85 made with 4 digits in the 1000-9000), XL (except XL-5 made in '80s). **Serial numbers for import models include:**

Two alpha followed by 4 numbers: for example AA2341 with any assortment of letters and numbers.

One alpha followed by 5 numbers: for example B23412.

Five numbers: for example 23412.

Model number preceeding numbers: for example XL1-03205.

The notation "Kramer, Neptune, NJ" does indicate U.S.A.-made production.

Most post-'85 Kramers were ESP Japanese-made guitars. American Series were ESP Japanese components that were assembled in the U.S.

The vintage/used market makes value distinctions between U.S.-made and import models. **Headstock and logo shape can help identify U.S. versus imports as follows:**

Traditional or Classic headstock with capital K as Kramer: U.S.A. '81-'84.

Banana (soft edges) headstock with all caps KRAMER: U.S.A. American Series '84-'86.

Pointy (sharp cut) headstock with all caps KRAMER: U.S.A. American Series '86-'87.

Pointy (sharp cut) headstock with downsized letters Kramer plus American decal: U.S.A. American Series '87-'94.

Pointy (sharp cut) headstock with downsized letters Kramer but without American decal, is an import.

100-ST (Import)
1985-late-1980s. Offset double-cut, 1 slanted bridge humbucker, maple bolt-on neck, rosewood 'board, dot markers.

| 1985-1987 | | $225 | $300 |

250-G Aluminum Neck
1977-1979. Offset double-cut, tropical woods, aluminum neck, dot markers, 2 pickups.

| 1977-1979 | | $500 | $550 |

MODEL YEAR	FEATURES	EXC. COND. LOW	HIGH

300-HST (Import)
1988-1991. Offset double-cut body, pointy-style headstock with large Kramer logo.

1988-1991		$200	$300

450-G Aluminum Neck
1977-1979. Offset double-cut, tropical woods, aluminum neck, ebonol 'board, 20 Petillo frets + zero fret, 2 pickups, 3-way switch, stop tailpiece, natural koa.

1977-1979		$500	$550

650-G Artist Aluminum Neck
1977-1980. Aluminum neck, ebonol 'board, double-cut solidbody, 2 humbuckers.

1977-1980		$550	$700

Baretta
1984-1986. Offset double-cut, banana six-on-a-side headstock, 1 pickup, Floyd Rose tremolo, black hardware, U.S.A.-made.

1984-1986	Custom finish	$700	$850
1984-1986	Standard opaque finish	$650	$750

DMZ Custom Series
1978-1981. Solidbody double-cut with larger upper horn, bolt-on aluminum T-neck, slot headstock, stop tailpiece, models include various pickup numbers and styles.

1978-1981	DMZ-1000	$400	$450
1978-1981	DMZ-2000	$450	$500
1978-1981	DMZ-3000	$500	$550
1978-1981	DMZ-4000	$550	$600
1978-1981	DMZ-6000	$550	$600

Duke Custom/Standard
1981-1982. Headless aluminum neck, 22-fret neck, 1 pickup, Floyd Rose tremolo.

1981-1982		$450	$600

Duke Special
1982-1985. Headless aluminum neck, two pickups, tuners on body.

1982-1985		$450	$600

E.E. Pro I
1987-1988. Designed by Elliot Easton, offset double-cut, six-on-a-side headstock, Floyd Rose tremolo, 2 single-coils and 1 humbucker.

1987-1988		$375	$450

E.E. Pro II
1987-1988. Same as E.E. Pro I, but with fixed-bridge tailpiece, 3 pickups, 5-position switching and master volume.

1987-1988		$400	$475

Ferrington
1985-1990. Acoustic-electric, offered in single- and double-cut, bolt-on electric-style neck, transducers, made in Korea.

1985-1990		$350	$475

Focus Series (Import)
1984-1989.

1984-1989		$225	$400

Gene Simmons Axe
1980-1981. Axe-shaped guitar, aluminum neck, 1 humbucker, slot headstock, stop tailpiece, 25 were made.

1980-1981		$2,250	$3,500

Gorky Park (import)
1986-1989. Triangular balalaika, bolt-on maple neck, pointy droopy six-on-a-side headstock, 1 pickup, Floyd Rose tremolo, red with iron sickle graphics, tribute to Russian rock, reissued in late-'90s.

1986-1989		$500	$600

Nightswan
1987-1990. Offset double-cut, six-on-a-side headstock, 2 Duncan humbuckers, Floyd Rose tremolo, blue metallic.

1987-1990		$850	$950

Pacer Series

1982-1984	Pacer	$450	$600
1983-1986	Pacer Custom	$500	$650
1983-1986	Pacer Deluxe	$500	$650

ProAxe (U.S.A.-made)
1989-1990. Offset double-cut, sharp pointy headstock, dot markers, 2 or 3 pickups.

1989-1990		$350	$550

Striker Series (Import)
1984-1989. Korean imports, offset double-cut, single-single-double pickup layout, various colors, series included Striker 100, 200, 300, 400, 600 and 700 Bass.

1984-1989		$200	$325

Vanguard Series
1981-1986, 1999-present. U.S.-made or American Series (assembled in U.S.). V shape, 1 humbucker, aluminum (Special '81-'83) or wood (Custom '81-'83) neck. Added for '83-'84 were the Imperial (wood neck, 2 humbuckers) and the Headless (alum neck, 1 humbucker). For '85-'86, the body was modified to a Jackson Randy Rhoads style V body, with a banana headstock and 2 humbuckers. In '99 this last design was revived as an import.

1981-1986		$350	$475

Voyager
1980s. Kramer and Voyager Series logo on headstock.

1982-1983		$350	$475

XKG-10
1980s. Aluminum neck, V-shaped body.

1980		$400	$500

ZX Aerostar Series (Import)
1986-1989. Offset double-cut solidbodies, pointy six-on-a-side headstock. Models include the 1 humbucker ZX-10, 2 humbucker ZX-20, 3 single coil ZX-30, and hum/single/single ZX-30H.

1986-1989		$100	$200

Kramer-Harrison, William
1977-present. Luthier William Kramer-Harrison builds his premium grade, custom, classical and flat-top guitars in Kingston, New York.

Kubicki
1973-present. Kubicki is best known for their Factor basses, but did offer a few guitar models in the early '80s. See Bass section for more company info.

1979 Kramer DMZ-2000

Kramer Focus

1967 La Baye 2x4

Lace Twister

MODEL YEAR	FEATURES	EXC. COND. LOW	HIGH

Kustom

1968-present. Founded by Bud Ross in Chanute, Kansas, and best known for the tuck-and-roll amps, Kustom also offered guitars from '68 to '69. See Amp section for more company info.

Electric Hollowbody

1968-1969. Hollowed-out 2-part bodies; includes the K200A (humbucker, Bigsby), the K200B (single-coils, trapeze tailpiece), and the K200C (less fancy tuners), various colors.

1960s		$775	$875

Kyle, Doug

1990-present. Premium grade, custom, Selmer-style guitars made by luthier Doug Kyle in England.

L Benito

2001-present. Professional grade, steel and nylon string acoustics from luthier Lito Benito and built in Chile.

La Baye

1967. Designed by Dan Helland in Green Bay, Wisconsin and built by the Holman-Woodell factory in Neodesha, Kansas. Introduced at NAMM and folded when no orders came in. Only 45 prototypes made. A few may have been sold later as 21st Century.

2x4 6-String

1967. Narrow plank body, controls on top, 2 pickups, tremolo, 12-string version was also made.

1967		$1,200	$1,500

LA Guitar Factory

1997-present. Founded by Ari Lehtela and Luke Lukuer in Charlotte, North Carolina. Lehtela became the sole owner in 2000. From '97 to '03, LA offered production and custom models. Currently, Lehtela uses the LA Guitar Factory brand on his professional and premium grade, production, solid-body and tone chambered guitars and basses. He markets his premium grade, custom guitars - mainly jazz body carved tops - under Lehtela guitarCraft.

La Mancha

1996-present. Professional and premium grade, production/custom, classical guitars made in Mexico under the supervision of Kenny Hill and Gil Carnal and distributed by Jerry Roberts of Nashville.

Style F Classical

1996-present . Solid cedar top, solid rosewood back and sides.

1996-2002		$1,900	$2,100

La Patrie

Production, classical guitars. Founded by luthier Robert Godin, who also has the Norman, Godin, Seagull, and Patrick & Simon brands of instruments.

La Scala

Ca. 1920s-1930s. La Scala was another brand of the Oscar Schmidt Company of New Jersey, and was used on guitars, banjos, and mandolins. These were often the fanciest of the Schmidt instruments. Schmidt made the guitars and mandolins; the banjos were made by Rettberg & Lang.

Lace Music Products

1979-present. Intermediate and professional, production, electric guitars from Lace Music Products, a division of Actodyne General Inc. which was founded by Don Lace Sr., inventor of the Lace Sensor Pickup. In '96 Lace added amplifiers and in 2001 they added guitars. In '02, they also started offering the Rat Fink brand of guitars.

Lado

1973-present. Founded by Joe Kovacic, Lado builds professional and premium grade, production/custom, solidbody guitars in Lindsay, Ontario. Some model lines are branded J. K. Lado. They also build basses.

Lafayette

Ca. 1963-1967. Sold through Lafayette Electronics catalogs. Early Japanese-made guitars from pre-copy era, generally shorter scale beginner guitars. Many made by Guyatone, some possibly by Teisco.

Acoustic Thinline Archtop

1963-1967. Various models.

1963-1967		$150	$250

Lakeside (Lyon & Healy)

Late-1800s-early-1900s. Mainly catalog sales of guitars and mandolins from the Chicago maker. Marketed as a less expensive alternative to the Lyon & Healy Washburn product line.

Harp Guitar - Jumbo Style G3740

Early-1900s. Spruce top, rosewood finished birch back and sides, two 6-string necks with standard tuners, 1 neck is fretless without dot markers, rectangular bridge.

1917	Natural	$2,000	$3,000

Lakewood

1986-present. Luthier Martin Seeliger builds his professional and premium grade, production/custom, steel and nylon string guitars in Giessen, Germany. He also builds mandolins.

Langejans Guitars

1971-present. Premium grade, production/custom, flat-top, 12-string, and classical guitars built by luthier Delwyn Langejans in Holland, Michigan.

Larrivee

1968-present. Professional and premium grade, production/custom, acoustic, acoustic/electric, and classical guitars built in Vancouver, British

MODEL YEAR	FEATURES	EXC. COND. LOW	HIGH

Columbia. Founded by Jean Larrivee, who apprenticed under Edgar Monch in Toronto. He built classic guitars in his home from '68-'70 and built his first steel string guitar in '71. Moved company to Victoria, BC in '77 and to Vancouver in '82. In '83, he began building solidbody electric guitars until '89, when focus again returned to acoustics.

Up to 2004, Larrivee used the following model designations: 05 Mahogany Standard, 09 Rosewood Standard, 10 Deluxe, 19 Special, 50 & 60 Standard (unique inlay), 70 Deluxe, and 72 Presentation. The 2004 designations used are: 01 Parlor, 03 Standard, 05 Select Mahogany, 09 Rosewood Artist, 10 Rosewood Deluxe, 19 California Anniv. Special Edition Series, 50 Traditional Series, 60 Traditional Series, E = Electric, R = Rosewood.

00-10
2000s. 00-size 14" lower bout, spruce top, rosewood back and sides, gloss finish.
2000s $1,500 $1,600

C-10 Deluxe
Late-1980s-1990s. Sitka spruce top, Indian rosewood back and sides, sharp cutaway, fancy binding.
1980s $1,600 $2,000

C-72 Cutaway Presentation
Spruce top, Indian rosewood back and sides, sharp cutaway, ultra-fancy abalone and pearl hand-engraved headstock.
1990s Mermaid headstock $2,600 $3,000

C-72 Presentation
Spruce top, Indian rosewood back and sides, non-cut Style D, ultra-fancy abalone and pearl hand-engraved headstock.
1990s Jester headstock $2,100 $2,600

D-10 Deluxe
2000s. Spruce top, rosewood rims, abalone top and soundhole trim.
2000s $1,700 $2,000

D-70 Deluxe
1990s $1,600 $2,000

D-Style Classical
1970s. Rosewood body, unicorn inlays.
1970s $2,100 $2,300

J-05 12
2000s. Jumbo acoustic-electric 12-string, spruce top, mahogany back and sides.
2000s $1,200 $1,400

JV-05 Mahogany Standard
2000s $1,100 $1,200

L-0 Standard Series
1980s-1990s. Models include L-03 (satin finish), L-05 (mahogany) and L-09 (Indian rosewood).
1980s L-05 $800 $1,100
1983-1987 L-09 $1,000 $1,500
1990s L-03 $700 $800

L-72 Presentation Custom
Mid- to late-1990s. Spruce top, Indian rosewood rims, ornate vase and vine inlays.
1990s $3,100 $3,500

Parlor Walnut
Early 2000s. Spruce top, solid walnut back and sides.
2002 $425 $500

RS-4 CM Carved Top
1988-1989. Carved top solidbody, curly maple top, single-single-humbucker pickups, sunburst or translucent finishes.
1988-1989 $950 $1,200

Larson Brothers (Chicago)
Late 1890s-1944. Chicago's Carl and August Larson built guitars under a variety of names, (refer to Stetson, Maurer and Prairie State listings).

Laskin
1973-present. Luthier William "Grit" Laskin builds his premium and presentation grade, custom, steel-string, classical, and flamenco guitars in Toronto, Ontario. Many of his instruments feature extensive inlay work.

Leach Guitars
1980-present. Luthier Harvey Leach builds his professional and premium grade, custom, flat-tops, archtops, and solidbody electrics and travel guitars in Cedar Ridge, California. He also builds basses.

Lehmann Stringed Instruments
1971-present. Luthier Bernard Lehmann builds his professional and premium grade, production/custom, flat-top, archtop, classical and Gypsy guitars in Rochester, New York. He also builds lutes, vielles and rebecs.

Lehtela guitarCraft
2003-present. Premium grade, custom, guitars - mainly jazz body carved tops - built by luthier Ari Lehtela in Charlotte, North Carolina. He markets his non-custom production models under LA Guitar Factory.

Les Stansell Guitars
1980-present. Luthier Les Stansell builds his premium grade, custom, nylon-string guitars in Pistol River, Oregon.

Levin
1900-1973. Founded by Herman Carlson Levin and located in Gothenburg, Sweden, Levin was best known for their classical guitars, which they also built for other brands, most notably Goya from ca. 1955 to the mid '70s. They also built mandolins and ukes.

Linc Luthier
Professional and premium grade, custom/production, electric and acoustic guitars built by luther Linc Luthier in Upland, California. He also builds basses and double-necks.

Larrivee L-19

Larson Brothers Euphanon

Loprinzi CM-36

1912 Larson Bros./Dyer harp guitar

MODEL YEAR	FEATURES	EXC. COND. LOW	HIGH

Lindert

1986-present. Luthier Chuck Lindert makes his intermediate and professional grade, production/ custom, Art Deco-vibe electric guitars in Chelan, Washington.

Line 6

1996-present. Professional grade, production, imported solidbody and acoustic modeling guitars able to replicate the tones of a variety of instruments. Line 6 also builds effects and amps.

Lopez, Abel Garcia

1985-present. Luthier Abel Garcia Lopez builds his premium grade, custom, classical guitars in Mexico.

Loprinzi

1972-present. Professional and premium grade, production/custom, classical and steel-string guitars built in Clearwater, Florida. They also build ukes.

Founded by Augustino LoPrinzi and his brother Thomas in New Jersey. The guitar operations were taken over by AMF/Maark Corp. in '73. LoPrinzi left the company and again started producing his own Augustino Guitars, moving his operations to Florida in '78. AMF ceased production in '80, and a few years later, LoPrinzi got his trademarked name back.

Classical

Various models.

1970s	Mahogany	$500	$800
1970s	Rosewood	$1,000	$1,300

Lord

Mid-1960s. Acoustic and solidbody electric guitars imported by Halifax.

Acoustic

Various models.

1960s		$100	$200

Lotus

Late-1970-present. Budget grade acoustic and electric guitars imported originally by Midco International, of Effingham, Illinois, and most recently by Musicorp. They also make basses, banjos and mandolins.

Louis Panormo

Early to mid-1800s. Spanish guitars made in London, England by luthier Louis (Luis) Panormo. He was born in Paris in 1784, and died in 1862.

Lowden

1973-present. Luthier George Lowden builds his production/custom, acoustic guitars in Newtownards, Northern Ireland and supervises productions of others. From '80 to '85, he had some models made in Japan.

Flat-Tops

2000s. Standard models include D, F, O, and S sizes and models 10 thru 32.

2000s	12-string	$1,300	$1,800
2000s	Premium 6-string	$1,900	$2,200
2000s	Standard 6-string	$1,200	$1,600

LSR Headless Instruments

1988-present. Professional and premium grade, production/custom, solidbody headless guitars made in Las Vegas, Nevada by Ed Roman. They also make basses.

LTD

1995-present. Intermediate grade, production, Korean-made solidbody guitars offered by ESP. They also offer basses. See ESP for models.

Lucas Custom Instruments

1989-present. Premium and presentation grade, production/custom, flat-tops built by luthier Randy Lucas in Columbus, Indiana.

Lucas, A. J.

1990-present. Luthier A. J. Lucas builds his production/custom, classical and steel string guitars in Lincolnshire, England.

LOM-28

1999		$5,800	$6,200

Lyle

Ca. 1969-1980. Imported by distributor L.D. Heater of Portland, Oregon. Generally higher quality Japanese-made copies of American designs by unknown manufacturers, but some early ones, at least, were made by Arai and Company.

Acoustic

1969-1980. Various models.

1969-1980		$150	$200

Electric

1969-1980. Various copy models include double-cut semi-hollow A-790, and the sharp double-cut solidbodies S750 (1 pickup) and S-760 (2 pickups).

1970s	A-790	$225	$275
1970s	S-750	$150	$175
1970s	S-760	$175	$225

Lyon & Healy

In the 1930s, Lyon & Healy was an industry giant. It operated a chain of music stores, and manufactured harps (their only remaining product), pianos, Washburn guitars and a line of brass and wind instruments. See Washburn, American Conservatory, Lakeside, and College brands.

Lyra

1920s. Instruments built by the Oscar Schmidt Co. and possibly others. Most likely a brand made for a distributor.

MODEL		EXC. COND.	
YEAR	FEATURES	LOW	HIGH

Lyric

1996-present. Luthier John Southern builds his professional and premium grade, custom, semi-hollow and solidbody guitars in Tulsa, Oklahoma. He also builds basses.

M. Campellone Guitars

See listing under Campellone Guitars

Maccaferri

1923-1990. Built by luthier and classical guitarist Mario Maccaferri (b. May 20, 1900, Cento, Italy; d. 1993, New York) in Cento, Italy; Paris, France; New York, New York; and Mount Vernon, New York. Maccaferri was a student of Luigi Mozzani from '11 to '28. His first catalog was in '23, and included a cutaway guitar. He designed Selmer guitars in '31. Maccaferri invented the plastic clothespin during World War II and used that technology to produce plastic ukes starting in '49 and Dow Styron plastic guitars in '53. He made several experimental plastic electrics in the '60s and plastic violins in the late-'80s. See *Guitar Stories Volume II*, by Michael Wright, for a complete history of Maccaferri with detailed model listings.

Plastic (Dow Styron)

1950s. Plastic construction, models include Deluxe (archtop, crown logo), Islander (Islander logo), TV Pal (4-string cutaway) and Showtime (Showtime logo).

1950s	Deluxe	$175	$250
1950s	Islander	$175	$200
1950s	Showtime	$175	$200
1950s	TV Pal	$125	$150

Madeira

Late-1970s. Imports serviced and distributed exclusively by Guild Guitars.

Magnatone

Ca. 1937-1971. Founded as Dickerson Brothers in Los Angeles, California and known as Magna Electronics from '47, with Art Duhamell president. Brands include Dickerson, Oahu (not all), Gourley, Natural Music Guild, Magnatone. In '59 Magna and Estey merged and in '66 the company relocated to Pennsylvania. In '71, the brand was taken over by a toy company.

Cyclops

1930s. Dobro-made resonator guitar.

1930s		$650	$950

Tornado

1965-1966. Offset double-cut body, 3 DeArmond pickups, vibrato.

1965-1966		$600	$700

Typhoon

1965-1966. Double-cut solidbody, 3 DeArmond pickups, vibrato.

1965-1966		$475	$600

MODEL		EXC. COND.	
YEAR	FEATURES	LOW	HIGH

Zephyr

1965-1966. Double-cut with 2 DeArmond single-coil pickups, metallic finish, vibrato.

1965-1966		$450	$550

Magno-Tone

1930s. Brand most likely used by a music studio (or distributor) on instruments made by others, including Regal-built resonator instruments.

Mako

1985-1989. Line of budget to lower-intermediate solidbody guitars from Kaman (Ovation, Hamer). They also offered basses and amps.

Solidbodies

1985-1989	Various models	$175	$275

Manuel Contreras

1962-1994. Luthier Manuel Gonzalez Contreras worked with José Ramírez III, before opening his own shop in Madrid, Spain, in '62.

Guitarra de Estudio

1970s. Designed as a student model, but with solid cedar top and solid mahogany back and sides.

1970s		$500	$600

Manuel Contreras II

1986-present. Professional grade, production/custom, nylon-string guitars made in Madrid, Spain, by luthier Pablo Contreras, son of Manuel.

C5

2000s. Solid close-grained cedar top, Indian rosewood back and sides.

2000s		$700	$975

Manuel Rodriguez and Sons, S.L.

1905-present. Professional, premium, and presentation grade, custom flat-top and nylon-string guitars from Madrid, Spain.

Manuel Velázquez

1933-present. Luthier Manuel Velázquez has built his classical guitars in Puerto Rico, New York City, Virginia, and Florida.

Manzanita Guitars

1993-present. Custom, steel-string, Hawaiian, and resonator guitars built by luthiers Manfred Pietrzok and Moritz Sattler in Rosdorf, Germany.

Manzer Guitars

1976-present. Luthier Linda Manzer builds her premium and presentation grade, custom, steel-string, nylon-string, and archtop guitars in Toronto, Ontario.

Maccaferri G-40

Manuel Contreras II Double Top

Mark Lacey Orpheus

1935 Martin O-15

MODEL YEAR	FEATURES	EXC. COND. LOW	HIGH

Maple Lake

2003-present. Intermediate grade, production, flat-top and acoustic/electric imported guitars from luthier Abe Wechter. Wechter also builds guitars under his own name.

Mapson

1995-present. Luthier James L. Mapson builds his premium and presentation grade, production/custom, archtops in Santa Ana, California.

Marc Silber Guitar Company

1998-present. Intermediate and professional grade, production, flat-top, nylon-string, and Hawaiian guitars designed by Marc Silber and made in Mexico. These were offered under the K & S Guitars and/or Silber brands for 1992-'98. Silber also has ukuleles.

Marchione Guitars

1993-present. Premium and presentation grade, custom, archtops and solidbodies built by Stephen Marchione originally in New York City, but currently in Houston, Texas.

Marcia

1920s. Instruments built by the Oscar Schmidt Co. and possibly others. Most likely a brand made for a distributor.

Marco Polo

1960-ca. 1964. Imported from Japan by Harry Stewart and the Marco Polo Company of Santa Ana, California. One of the first American distributors to advertise inexpensive Japanese guitars. Manufacturers unknown, but some acoustics by Suzuki, some electrics by Guyatone.

Acoustic Hollowbody Guitars

1960-1964. Various models.

1960s		$100	$200

Mark Lacey Guitars

1974-present. Luthier Mark Lacey builds his premium and presentation archtops and flat-tops in Nashville, Tennessee.

Mark Wescott Guitars

1980-present. Premium grade, custom, flat-tops, built by luthier Mark Wescott in Marmora, New Jersey.

Marling

Ca. 1975. Budget line instruments marketed by EKO of Recanati, Italy; probably made by them, although possibly imported.

Acoustic Guitars

1975. Includes the steel-string S.110, and the dreadnoughts W.354 Western, and W.356 Western.

1975		$75	$100

Electric Guitars

1975. Includes the E.400 (semi-acoustic/electric), E.490 (solidbody), E.480 (single-cut-style), and the 460 (Manta-style).

1975		$75	$150

Martelle

1934. Private brand attributed to Gibson and some to Kay.

De Luxe

1934. Gibson 12-fret round shoulder Jumbo construction, mahogany back and sides, sunburst, Hawaiian or Spanish option.

1934		$8,500	$9,000

Martin

1833-present. Intermediate, professional, premium, and presentation grade, production/custom, acoustic, acoustic/electric, archtop and resonator guitars. Founded in New York City by Christian Frederick Martin, former employee of J. Staufer in Vienna, Austria. Moved to Nazareth, Pennsylvania in 1839. Early guitars were made in the European style, many made with partners John Coupa, Charles Bruno and Henry Schatz. Scalloped X-bracing was introduced in the late-1840s. The dreadnought was introduced in 1916 for the Oliver Ditson Company, Boston; and Martin introduced their own versions in 1931.

Martin model size and shape are indicated by the letter prefix (e.g., 0, 00, 000, D, etc.); materials and ornamentation are indicated by number, with the higher the number, the fancier the instrument (e.g., 18, 28, 35, etc.). Martin offered electric thinline guitars from '61-'68 and electric solidbodies from '78-'82. The Martin Shenandoah was made in Asia and assembled in U.S. Japanese Martin Sigma ('72-'73) and Korean Martin Stinger ('85 on) imported solidbodies. See Michael Wright's Guitar Stories Vol. II for more information on Martin's electric guitars.

0-15

1935, 1940-1943, 1948-1961. All mahogany, unbound rosewood 'board, slotted peghead and 12-fret neck until '34, solid peghead and 14-fret neck thereafter, natural mahogany.

1935	2 made, maple/birch	$2,300	$2,600
1940-1943		$1,800	$2,000
1948-1949		$1,600	$1,800
1950-1959		$1,400	$1,600
1960-1961		$1,000	$1,400

0-15 T

1960-1963. Tenor with Style 15 appointments, natural mahogany.

1960-1963		$900	$1,000

0-16

1961 only. Six made.

1961		$1,700	$1,800

MODEL YEAR	FEATURES	EXC. COND. LOW	HIGH

0-16 NY
1961-1995. Mahogany back and sides, 12 frets, slotted peghead, unbound extra-wide rosewood 'board, natural.

1961-1969		$1,000	$1,800
1970-1979		$850	$1,500
1980-1989		$850	$1,500
1990-1995		$850	$1,500

0-17
1906-1917, 1929-1948, 1966-1968. First version has mahogany back and sides, 3 black soundhole rings, rosewood bound back, unbound ebony 'board, 12 frets, slotted peghead. Second version ('29 and on) is all mahogany, 3 white-black-white soundhole rings, top bound until '30, thin black backstripe, 12 frets and slotted peghead until '34, solid peghead and 14 frets thereafter, natural mahogany.

1906-1917	Gut braces	$1,450	$1,700
1929-1934	Bar frets, 12 fret-style	$1,800	$2,100
1934-1939	T-frets, 14 fret-style	$2,000	$2,300
1940-1945		$1,800	$2,200
1946-1948		$1,700	$2,000
1966-1968	7 made	$1,000	$1,800

0-17 H
1930, 1935-1941. Hawaiian, mahogany back and sides, 12 frets clear of body, natural.

1930	60 made	$1,700	$1,800
1935-1941		$1,700	$1,800

0-17 T
1932-1960. Mahogany back and sides, tenor, natural.

1932-1949		$1,300	$1,600
1950-1960	Mahogany	$1,200	$1,500

0-18
1898-1996. Rosewood back and sides until 1917, mahogany back and sides after, Adirondack spruce top until 1946, slotted peghead and 12 frets until 1934, solid peghead and 14 frets after 1934, braced for steel strings in 1923, improved neck in late-1934, non-scalloped braces appear late-'44, natural.

1917-1922	Mahogany, gut braces	$2,500	$2,700
1923-1939	Steel braces	$3,100	$3,300
1940-1944	Scalloped braces	$2,800	$3,100
1945-1949		$2,300	$2,600
1950-1959		$2,200	$2,300
1960-1969		$1,000	$2,200
1970-1996		$900	$1,000

0-18 G
1960s. Special order classical nylon-string model, natural.

1961		$1,300	$2,200

0-18 K
1918-1935. Hawaiian, all koa wood, braced for steel strings in 1923, T-frets and steel T-bar neck in late-1934, natural.

1918-1922		$2,300	$2,600
1923-1927	Steel braces	$2,500	$2,700
1928-1935		$2,600	$2,800

0-18 T
1929-1995. Mahogany body, spruce top, tenor, natural.

1929-1939		$1,400	$1,900
1940-1959		$1,300	$1,800
1960-1964		$1,300	$1,500
1965-1969		$1,200	$1,400
1970-1979		$1,100	$1,200
1980-1989		$1,000	$1,100
1990-1995		$900	$1,000

0-21
1898-1948. Rosewood back and sides, Adirondack spruce top until 1946, 12 frets, braced for steel strings in 1923, T-frets and steel T-bar neck in late-1934, non-scalloped braces in late-1944, natural.

1898-1926	Gut braces	$2,800	$3,200
1927-1943	Steel braces	$3,000	$4,000
1944-1948	Non-scalloped	$2,400	$3,200

0-26
1850-1890. Rosewood back and sides, ivory-bound top, rope-style purfling.

1850-1890		$3,000	$3,500

0-27
1850-1898. Rosewood back and sides, ivory-bound top.

1850-1898		$3,500	$4,500

0-28
1870s-1931, 1937 (6 made), 1969 (1 made). Brazilian rosewood back and sides, braced for steel strings in 1923, herringbone binding until 1937, natural.

1870-1927		$4,400	$5,200
1928-1931		$5,500	$6,500

0-28 K
1917-1931, 1935. Hawaiian, all koa wood, braced for steel strings in '23, natural.

1917	Spruce top option	$4,500	$5,500
1917-1924	Figured koa	$4,500	$5,500
1925-1931	Steel braces	$5,000	$6,000

0-28 T
1930-1931. Tenor neck.

1930-1931		$3,000	$3,500

0-30
1899-1921. Brazilian rosewood back and sides, ivory-bound body, neck and headstock.

1899-1921		$4,500	$5,500

0-42
1870s-1942. Brazilian rosewood back and sides, 12 frets, natural.

1890-1926	Gut braces	$8,000	$12,000
1927-1930	Steel braces	$10,000	$15,000

0-45
1904-1939. Brazilian rosewood back and sides, natural, special order only for '31-'39.

1904-1928	Gut braces	$25,000	$30,000
1929-1930	Steel braces	$32,000	$38,000

00-16 C
1962-1977, 1980-1981. Classical, mahogany back and sides, 5-ply bound top, satin finish, 12 frets, slotted peghead, natural.

1962-1969		$1,100	$1,200
1970-1977		$900	$1,100

1936 Martin 0-17

1923 Martin 0-21

1957 Martin 00-18

Martin 00-18V

MODEL YEAR	FEATURES	EXC. COND. LOW	HIGH
1980-1981	2 made	$900	$1,100

00-17

1908-1917, 1930-1960, 1982-1988. Mahogany back and sides, 12 frets and slotted headstock until '34, solid headstock and 14 frets after '34, natural mahogany, reissued in 2002 with a high gloss finish.

1908-1917	Limited production	$1,900	$2,200
1930-1939		$2,400	$2,700
1940-1944		$2,300	$2,400
1945-1949		$2,000	$2,200
1950-1960		$1,700	$2,000
2002	Reissue model	$1,000	$1,100

00-17 H

1934-1935. Hawaiian set-up, mahogany body, no binding.

1934-1935		$2,000	$2,200

00-18

1898-1995. Rosewood back and sides until 1917, mahogany after, braced for steel strings in 1923, improved neck in late-1934, war-time design changes 1942-1946, non-scalloped braces in late-1944, Adirondack spruce top until 1946, natural.

1898-1917	Rosewood	$4,500	$5,000
1918-1922	Mahogany	$4,100	$4,400
1923-1939	Steel braces in '23	$5,200	$5,500
1934-1939	Sunburst option	$5,000	$6,000
1940-1941		$5,000	$5,200
1942-1943	Ebony rod	$4,500	$4,800
1944	Scalloped braces early '44	$4,200	$4,500
1944-1946	Non-scalloped	$3,300	$3,400
1946	Steel bar neck	$3,100	$3,300
1947-1949		$2,800	$3,100
1950-1952		$2,600	$2,800
1953-1959		$2,400	$2,600
1960-1962		$2,100	$2,400
1963-1965		$1,900	$2,100
1966	Tortoise guard early '66	$1,600	$2,100
1966	Black guard late '66	$1,500	$1,800
1967		$1,400	$1,700
1968		$1,300	$1,600
1969		$1,200	$1,400
1970-1979		$1,000	$1,200
1980-1989		$1,000	$1,200
1990-1995		$1,000	$1,200

00-18 C

1962-1995. Renamed from 00-18 G in '62, mahogany back and sides, classical, 12 frets, slotted headstock, natural.

1962-1969		$1,500	$1,600
1970-1979		$1,300	$1,400

00-18 E

1959-1964. Flat top Style 18, single neck pickup and 2 knobs, heavier bracing, natural.

1959-1964		$2,500	$2,600

00-18 G

1936-1962. Mahogany back and sides, classical, natural, renamed 00-18 C in '62.

1936-1939		$1,700	$2,500
1940-1949		$1,600	$2,300

MODEL YEAR	FEATURES	EXC. COND. LOW	HIGH
1950-1962		$1,500	$1,700

00-18 Gruhn Limited Edition

1995. Sitka spruce top, C-shaped neck profile, 25 made.

1995		$1,450	$1,600

00-18 H

1935-1941. Hawaiian, mahogany back amd sides, 12 frets clear of body, natural. The Price Guide is generally for all original instruments. The H conversion is an exception, because converting from H (Hawaiian-style) to 00-18 specs is considered by some to be a favorable improvement and something that adds value.

1935-1941		$3,600	$4,000
1935-1941	Converted to Spanish	$4,100	$5,500

00-18 SH Steve Howe

1999-2000. Limited edition run of 250.

1999-2000		$2,500	$2,600

00-21

1898-1996. Brazilian rosewood back and sides, changed to Indian rosewood in 1970, dark outer binding, unbound ebony 'board until 1947, rosewood from 1947, slotted diamond inlays until 1944, dot after, natural.

1898-1926	Gut braces	$6,400	$6,800
1927-1931	Steel braces in '27	$8,000	$8,500
1932-1939		$7,500	$8,000
1934-1939	Sunburst option	$7,000	$7,500
1940-1944	Scalloped braces	$6,000	$7,000
1944-1949	Non-scalloped	$4,000	$4,500
1950-1959		$3,600	$4,000
1960-1965		$3,400	$3,600
1966-1969	Brazilian rosewood, black guard	$3,200	$3,400
1970-1996	Indian rosewood	$1,600	$1,700

00-21 H

Special order limited production Hawaiian.

1914	1 made	$6,600	$7,000
1952	1 made	$6,600	$7,000
1955	1 made	$6,600	$7,000

00-21 NY

1961-1965. Brazilian rosewood back and sides, no inlay, natural.

1961-1965		$3,400	$3,600

00-28

1898-1941, 1958 (1 made), 1977 (1 made), 1984 (2 made). Brazilian rosewood back and sides, changed to Indian rosewood in 1977, herringbone purfling through 1941, white binding and unbound 'board after 1941, no inlays before 1901, diamond inlays from 1901-'41, dot after, natural.

1898-1924	Gut braces	$8,000	$12,000
1925-1931	Steel braces in '25	$10,000	$15,000
1932-1941	Special order	$10,000	$15,000
1958	Special order	$3,300	$3,600

GUITARS

MODEL YEAR	FEATURES	EXC. COND. LOW	HIGH

00-28 C

1966-1995. Renamed from 00-28 G, Brazilian rosewood back and sides, changed to Indian rosewood in '70, classical, 12 frets, natural.

1966-1969	Brazilian rosewood	$3,100	$4,000
1970-1979	Indian rosewood	$1,600	$1,800

00-28 G

1936-1962. Brazilian rosewood back and sides, classical, natural, reintroduced as 00-28 C in '66.

1936-1939	$5,600	$6,000
1940-1949	$5,100	$5,500
1951-1962	$4,100	$5,000

00-28 K Hawaiian

1919-1921, 1926-1933. Koa back and sides, Hawaiian set-up.

1919-1921	34 made	$6,600	$7,000
1926-1933	1 made per year	$7,100	$9,000

00-40 H

1928-1939. Hawaiian, Brazilian rosewood back and sides, 12 frets clear of body, natural. H models are sometimes converted to standard Spanish setup, in higher-end models this can make the instrument more valuable to some people.

1928-1939		$10,000	$13,000
1928-1939	Converted to Spanish	$13,000	$16,000

00-40 K

Few were made (only 6), figured koa, natural.

1918	1 made	$20,000	$22,000
1930	5 made	$20,000	$22,000

00-42

1898-1942, 1973 (one made), 1994-1996. Brazilian rosewood back and sides, Indian rosewood in 1973, pearl top borders, 12 frets, ivory bound peghead until 1918, ivoroid binding after 1918, natural.

1898-1926	Gut braces	$16,800	$20,000
1927-1942	Steel braces	$21,000	$25,000
1973	1 made	$2,500	$3,500
1994-1996		$2,000	$3,000

00-42 K

1919. Koa body, 1 made.

1919	$20,000	$25,000

00-44 Soloist/Olcott-Bickford Artist Model

1913-1939. Custom-made in small quantities, Brazilian rosewood, ivory or faux-ivory-bound ebony 'board.

1913-1939	$25,000	$45,000

00-45

1904-1938, 1970-1995. Brazilian rosewood back and sides, changed to Indian rosewood in '70, 12 frets and slotted headstock until '34 and from '70 on 14 frets, and solid headstock from '34-'70, natural.

1904-1927	Gut braces	$35,000	$45,000
1928-1938	Steel braces	$45,000	$55,000

00-45 K

1919. Koa body, 1 made.

1919	$35,000	$45,000

00-45 Stauffer Commemorative Limited Edition

1997. Stauffer six-on-a-side headstock, 45-style appointments, 00-size body, Sitka spruce top, Brazilian rosewood back and sides.

1997	$8,000	$10,000

000-1 R

1996-2002. Solid spruce top with laminated Indian rosewood sides.

1996-2002	$700	$900

000-15 Auditorium

1997-present. All solid wood mahogany body, dot markers, natural.

1997-1999	$625	$725

000-16

1989-1995. Acoustic, mahogany back and sides, diamonds and squares inlaid, name changed to 000-16 T Auditorium in '96, sunburst.

1989-1995	$1,000	$1,400

000-16 T

1996-1999. All solid wood mahogany back and sides, higher appointments than 000-15.

1996-1999	$850	$1,000

000-18

1911-present (none in 1932-1933). Rosewood back and sides until '17, mahogany back and sides from '17, longer scale in '24-'34, 12 frets clear of body until '33, changed to 14 frets in '34. Improved neck late-'34, war-time changes '41-'46, non-scalloped braces in late-'44, switched from Adirondack spruce to Sitka spruce top in '46 (though some Adirondack tops in '50s and '60s), natural. Now called the 000-18 Auditorium.

1924-1927	Gut/nylon braces, 12-fret	$5,000	$7,000
1928-1931	Steel braces, 12-fret	$7,000	$9,000
1934-1939	24.5" scale, 14-fret clear	$10,000	$12,500
1934-1939	Sunburst option	$12,000	$15,500
1940-1941	Natural	$8,500	$10,500
1942-1944	Scalloped braces	$7,500	$9,000
1942-1944	Sunburst option	$9,500	$11,500
1944-1946	Non-scalloped	$5,300	$6,500
1944-1946	Sunburst option	$6,000	$7,300
1947-1949	Natural	$5,200	$6,000
1947-1949	Sunburst option	$5,800	$6,700
1950-1952	Natural	$4,000	$4,500
1953-1959		$3,800	$4,100
1960-1962		$3,100	$3,500
1963-1965		$2,800	$3,000
1966	Black guard late '66	$2,400	$2,700
1966	Tortoise guard early '66	$2,600	$2,800
1967	Last of Maple bridgeplate	$2,200	$2,600
1968		$1,800	$2,100
1969		$1,500	$1,800
1970-1975		$1,300	$1,500
1976-1979		$1,200	$1,600
1980-1985		$1,100	$1,500
1986-1989		$1,000	$1,400
1990-1999		$1,000	$1,300

Martin 00-21GE

1937 Martin 000-18

1957 Martin 000-28

Martin 000-28 EC

MODEL YEAR	FEATURES	EXC. COND. LOW	HIGH
2000-2004		$1,000	$1,200

000-21
1902-1924 (22 made over that time), 1931(2), 1938-1959, 1965 (1), 1979 (12). Brazilian rosewood back and sides, changed to Indian rosewood in '70, natural.

1902-1937	Low production mostly gut	$12,000	$15,000
1938-1941	Pre-war specs	$15,000	$17,000
1942-1944	Ebony rod, scalloped braces	$11,000	$14,000
1944-1946	Non-scalloped	$8,300	$10,000
1947-1949	Herringbone, non-scalloped	$6,000	$6,500
1950-1959		$5,000	$6,000
1965	1 made	$4,000	$6,000
1979	12 made	$1,800	$2,000

000-28
1902-present. Brazilian rosewood back and sides, changed to Indian rosewood in '70, herringbone purfling through '41, white binding and unbound 'board after '41, no inlays before '01, slotted diamond inlays from '01-'44, dot after, 12 frets until '32, 14 frets '31 on (both 12 and 14 frets were made during '31-'32), natural.

1902-1927	Gut/nylon braces	$19,000	$29,000
1928-1931	Steel braces	$25,000	$35,000
1933		$30,000	$34,000
1934-1939		$25,000	$29,000
1940-1941		$22,000	$27,000
1942-1944	Scalloped braces	$20,000	$25,000
1944-1946	Herringbone, non-scalloped	$15,000	$20,000
1947-1949	Start of non-herringbone '47	$9,000	$11,000
1950-1952		$8,000	$9,500
1953-1958	Last of Kluson early '58	$6,500	$8,000
1958-1959	Grover tuners late '58	$6,000	$7,500
1960-1962		$5,000	$7,100
1963-1965		$5,000	$6,000
1966	Black guard late '66	$4,100	$5,300
1966	Tortoise guard early '66	$4,500	$5,500
1967	Last of maple bridgeplate	$4,000	$5,200
1968	Rosewood bridgeplate	$3,900	$5,000
1969	Last of Brazilian rosewood	$3,800	$4,400
1970-1979	Indian rosewood	$1,800	$2,000
1980-1989	Indian rosewood	$1,600	$2,000
1990-1999	Indian rosewood	$1,500	$1,700
2000-2004		$1,300	$1,500

000-28 C
1962-1969. Brazilian rosewood back and sides, classical, slotted peghead, natural.

1962-1969		$3,500	$4,500

000-28 EC Eric Clapton Signature
1996-present. Sitka spruce top, Indian rosewood back and sides, herringbone trim, natural.

1996-1999		$2,000	$2,200

000-28 ECB Eric Clapton Brazilian
2003. Limited edition, 2nd edition of EC Signature Series with Brazilian rosewood.

2003		$6,000	$6,500

000-28 G
1937-1955. Special order, very limited production.

1937-1940	3 made	$10,000	$18,000
1946-1949	10 made	$8,000	$10,000
1950-1955	4 made	$6,000	$8,000

000-28 Golden Era
1996 only. Sitka spruce top, rosewood back and sides, scalloped braces, herringbone trim, 12-fret model, natural.

1996		$2,900	$3,200

000-28 H
2000-2001. Herringbone top trim.

2000-2001		$1,650	$1,750

000-28 K
1921. Non-catalog special order model, only 2 known to exist, koa top, back and sides.

1921		$20,000	$28,000

000-41
1996. Custom shop style 000-41.

1996		$2,550	$2,700

000-42
1918, 1921-1922, 1925, 1930, 1934, 1938-1943. Brazilian rosewood back and sides, natural.

1918-1934	Special order	$35,000	$40,000
1938-1943		$40,000	$45,000

000-42 EC Eric Clapton
1995. Style 45 pearl-inlaid headplate, ivoroid bindings, Eric Clapton signature, 24.9" scale, flat top, sunburst top price is $8320 ('95 price), only 461 made.

1995		$7,200	$8,000

000-45
1906, 1911-1914, 1917-1919, 1922-1942, 1971-1993. Brazilian rosewood back and sides, changed to Indian rosewood in '70, 12-fret neck and slotted headstock until '34 (but 7 were made in '70 and 1 in '75), 14-fret neck and solid headstock after '34, natural.

1906-1919		$50,000	$65,000
1922-1927	Gut braces	$50,000	$65,000
1928-1929	Steel braces	$65,000	$80,000
1930-1933		$75,000	$90,000
1934-1936	14 frets, C.F.M. inlaid	$85,000	$100,000
1937-1939		$80,000	$95,000
1940-1942		$75,000	$90,000

000-45 JR Jimmie Rodgers Golden Era
1997. Adirondack spruce top, Brazilian rosewood back and sides, scalloped high X-braces, abalone trim, natural, 100 made.

1997		$9,500	$11,000

MODEL YEAR	FEATURES	EXC. COND. LOW	HIGH

000C Series
Late-1990s-2000s. French-style small soft cutaway (like vintage Selmer), models include; 000C-1E (mahogany body) and 000C-16RGTE (premium, rosewood body).

1990s	000C-1E	$1,000	$1,100
2000s	000C-16 RGTE	$1,000	$1,100

000C-16
1990-1995. Cutaway acoustic, mahogany back and sides, diamonds and squares inlay, name changed to 000-C16T Auditorium in '96.

1990-1995		$1,025	$1,150

0000-28 Series
1997-2000. Several models, jumbo-size 0000 cutaway body, models include; H (herringbone trim), Custom (Indian rosewood, sitka spruce top), H-AG (Arlo Guthrie 30th anniversary, Indian rosewood back and sides, only 30 made), H Custom Shop (herringbone).

1997-2000	0000-28 H	$1,900	$2,400
1998	0000-28 Custom	$2,800	$3,000
1999	0000-28 H-AG	$3,800	$4,200
2000	0000-28 H Custom Shop	$1,700	$1,900

1-17
1906-1917 (1st version), 1931-1934 (2nd version). First version has spruce top, mahogany back and sides, second version has all mahogany with flat natural finish.

1906-1917		$1,300	$1,500
1930-1934		$1,500	$1,700

1-18
1899-1927. Brazilian rosewood or mahogany back and sides.

1918-1927	Mahogany	$2,200	$2,500

1-21
1860-1926. Initially offered in size 1 in the 1860s, ornate soundhole rings.

1860-1899		$2,200	$3,000
1900-1926		$2,300	$3,000

1-26
1850-1890. Rosewood back and sides, ivory-bound top, rope-style purfling.

1850-1890		$2,800	$3,200

1-27
1880-1907.

1880-1907		$3,300	$4,300

1-28
1880-1923. Style 28 appointments including Brazilian rosewood back and sides.

1900-1923		$4,000	$5,000

1-42
1958-1919. Rosewood back and sides, ivory-bound top and 'board.

1858-1919		$5,000	$8,000

1-45
1904-1919. Only 6 made, slotted headstock and Style 45 appointments.

1904-1919		$18,000	$23,000

2-15
1939-1964. All mahogany body, dot markers.

1939	Special order	$1,200	$1,400

2-17
1910, 1922-1938. 1910 version has spruce top, mahogany back and sides. '22 on, all mahogany body, no body binding after '30.

1910	6 made	$1,400	$1,700
1922-1930		$1,400	$1,700

2-17 H
1927-1931. Hawaiian, all mahogany, 12 frets clear of body.

1927-1931		$1,400	$1,700

2-20
1855-1899. Rare style only offered in size 2.

1855-1899		$2,500	$3,000

2-24
1857-1898.

1857-1898		$2,700	$3,000

2-27
1857-1907. Brazilian rosewood back and sides, pearl ring, zigzag back stripe, ivory bound ebony 'board and peghead.

1857-1899		$3,500	$4,000
1900-1907		$3,500	$4,000

2-28 T
1929-1930. Tenor neck, Brazilian rosewood back and sides, herringbone top purfling.

1929-1930		$2,000	$2,500

2-30
1902-1921. Similar to 2-27.

1902-1921	7 made	$3,800	$4,200

2-34
1870-1898. Similar to 2-30.

1870-1898		$3,900	$4,300

2 1/2-17
1856-1897, 1909-1914. The first Style 17s were small size 2 1/2 and 3, these early models use Brazilian rosewood.

1890-1897		$1,400	$1,700
1909-1914		$1,400	$1,700

2 1/2-18
1865-1923. Parlor-size body with Style 18 appointments.

1865-1898		$2,000	$2,500
1901-1917	Brazilian rosewood	$2,000	$2,500
1918-1923	Mahogany	$2,000	$2,500

3-17
1856-1897, 1908 (one made). The first Style 17s were small size 2 1/2 and 3. The early models use Brazilian rosewood, spruce top, bound back, unbound ebony 'board.

1890-1897		$1,300	$1,700
1908	1 made	$1,300	$1,700

5-15 T
1949-1963. All mahogany, non-gloss finish, tenor neck.

1949-1963		$1,100	$1,500

5-17 T
1927-1949. All mahogany, tenor neck.

1927-1949		$1,200	$1,600

Martin 000-45 JR

Martin 0000-28

Martin D12-28

Martin DC-1E

5-18

1898-1989. Rosewood back and sides (changed to mahogany from 1917 on), 12 frets, slotted headstock.

YEAR	FEATURES	LOW	HIGH
1918-1922	Gut braces, mahogany	$1,600	$1,900
1923-1939	Steel braces in '23	$1,900	$2,200
1940-1944		$1,800	$2,200
1945-1949		$1,700	$2,000
1950-1959		$1,600	$1,900
1960-1969		$1,300	$1,500
1970-1989		$800	$1,200

5-21 T

1926-1928. Tenor guitar with 21-styling.

YEAR	FEATURES	LOW	HIGH
1926-1928		$2,200	$2,400

5-28

2001-2002. Special edition, 1/2-size parlor guitar size 15 with Terz tuning, Indian rosewood back and sides.

YEAR	FEATURES	LOW	HIGH
2001-2002		$1,800	$2,100

7-28

1980-1995, 1997-2002. 7/8-body-size of a D-model, Style 28 appointments.

YEAR	FEATURES	LOW	HIGH
1980-1995		$1,800	$2,100
1997-2002		$1,800	$2,100

Alternative X Midi

2001-present. Thin 00-size body, solid aluminum top, laminate back and sides, Stratabond aluminate neck, black micarta 'board, micro-dot markers. Roland GK Midi pickup with 13-pin output, additional Fishman Prefix Pro pickup and preamp system, requires Roland GA-20 (or substitute) Midi interface.

YEAR	FEATURES	LOW	HIGH
2001-2004		$825	$875

C-1

1931-1942. Acoustic archtop, mahogany back and sides, spruce top, round hole until '33, f-holes appear in '32, bound body, sunburst.

YEAR	FEATURES	LOW	HIGH
1931-1933	Round, 449 made	$2,000	$2,500
1932-1942	F-hole, 786 made	$2,000	$2,500

C-2

1931-1942. Acoustic archtop, Brazilian rosewood back and sides, carved spruce top, round hole until '33, f-holes appear in '32, zigzag back stripe, multi-bound body, slotted-diamond inlay, sunburst.

YEAR	FEATURES	LOW	HIGH
1931-1933	Round, 269 made	$3,000	$4,000
1932-1942	F-hole, 439 made	$3,000	$4,000

C-2 Conversion

1931-1942. The VG Price Guide lists original, excellent condition instruments. A C-2 Conversion is an exception. The C-2 archtop was generally less popular than a flat-top with similar appointments. C series archtops and H series Hawaiians converted to Spanish setup flat- tops have more appeal to some players and collectors. The C-2 Conversion requires removal of the arched top and installation of a high quality spruce top. Appointments may vary.

YEAR	FEATURES	LOW	HIGH
1931-1942	High-end appointments	$6,000	$12,000

C-3

1931-1934. Archtop, Brazilian rosewood back and sides, round soundhole until early '33, f-holes after.

YEAR	FEATURES	LOW	HIGH
1931-1933	Round, 53 made	$4,500	$6,000
1933-1934	F-hole, 58 made	$4,500	$6,000

C-TSH (Humphrey/Martin)

Late-1990s. Designed by high-end classical guitar luthier Thomas Humphrey for Martin, based on his Millenium model, arched Englemann spruce top, rosewood back and sides.

YEAR	FEATURES	LOW	HIGH
1998		$2,100	$2,200

Custom OM-45 Deluxe

1998-1999. Limited custom shop run of 14, Adirondack spruce and typical Style 45 appointments.

YEAR	FEATURES	LOW	HIGH
1998-1999		$13,500	$15,000

D-1

1992-present. Name first used for the prototype of the D-18, made in 1931, name revived for current model with mahogany body, A-frame bracing, available as an acoustic/electric.

YEAR	FEATURES	LOW	HIGH
1992-1999		$550	$700

D-3-18

1991. Sitka spruce top, 3-piece mahogany back, 80-piece limited edition.

YEAR	FEATURES	LOW	HIGH
1991		$1,800	$2,300

D12-18

1973-1995. Mahogany back and sides, 12 strings, 14 frets clear of body, solid headstock.

YEAR	FEATURES	LOW	HIGH
1973-1979		$1,300	$1,450
1980-1989		$1,200	$1,350
1990-1995		$1,100	$1,300

D12-20

1964-1991. Mahogany back and sides, 12 strings, 12 frets clear of body, slotted headstock.

YEAR	FEATURES	LOW	HIGH
1964-1969		$1,500	$1,800
1970-1979		$1,400	$1,500
1980-1991		$1,300	$1,400

D12-28

1970-present. Indian rosewood back and sides, 12 strings, 14 frets clear of body, solid headstock.

YEAR	FEATURES	LOW	HIGH
1970-1979		$1,500	$1,700
1980-1989		$1,500	$1,600
1990-1999		$1,400	$1,500

D12-35

1965-1995. Brazilian rosewood back and sides, changed to Indian rosewood in '70, 12 strings, 12 frets clear of body, slotted headstock.

YEAR	FEATURES	LOW	HIGH
1965-1969	Brazilian rosewood	$3,000	$3,500
1970-1979	Indian rosewood	$1,500	$1,700
1980-1989		$1,500	$1,600
1990-1995		$1,400	$1,500

D12-45

1970s. Special order instrument, not a standard catalog item, with D-45 appointments, Indian rosewood.

YEAR	FEATURES	LOW	HIGH
1970-1979		$5,000	$6,000

D-15

1997-present. All mahogany body.

YEAR	FEATURES	LOW	HIGH
1997-2002		$450	$550

D-16 A

1987-1990. North American ash back and sides, solid spruce top, scalloped bracing, rosewood 'board and bridge, solid mahogany neck.

YEAR	FEATURES	LOW	HIGH
1987-1990		$1,050	$1,200

MODEL YEAR	FEATURES	EXC. COND. LOW	HIGH

D-16 GT/D-16 RGT

1999-present. D-16 T specs, GT with glossy top and mahogany back and sides, RGT with satin top and rosewood back and sides.

1999-2003	Mahogany, gloss	$750	$800
1999-2003	Rosewood, satin	$800	$850

D-16 H

1991-1995. Full-size dreadnought, mahogany back and sides with satin finish, herringbone marquetry, vintage X-bracing, scalloped braces, optional acoustic pickup or active preamp system, replaced by D-16 T in '96.

1991-1995		$1,050	$1,200

D-16 M

1986, 1988-1990. Mahogany back and sides, non-gloss satin finish.

1988-1990		$825	$900

D-16 T

1995-2002. Solid spruce top, solid mahogany back and sides, scalloped braces, satin finish.

1995-2002		$875	$975

D-16 TR

1995-2002. Indian rosewood version of 16 T.

1995-2002		$1,250	$1,350

D-17

2000-2005. All solid mahogany back, sides and top, natural brown mahogany finish.

2000-2005		$875	$925

D-18

1932-present. Mahogany back and sides, spruce top, black back stripe, 12-fret neck, changed to 14 frets in '34.

1932-1933	12-fret neck	$25,000	$26,000
1934-1939	14-fret neck	$20,000	$23,000
1940-1941		$14,000	$17,000
1942-1944	Scalloped braces	$12,500	$14,000
1944-1946	Non-scalloped	$7,500	$9,000
1947-1949		$6,500	$7,500
1950-1952		$5,500	$6,500
1953-1959		$4,500	$5,500
1960-1962		$3,200	$4,500
1963-1965		$3,000	$3,500
1966	Black guard late '66	$2,600	$2,800
1966	Tortoise guard early '66	$2,800	$3,000
1967	Last of maple bridgeplate	$2,300	$2,600
1968	Rosewood bridgeplate	$1,800	$2,100
1969		$1,500	$1,800
1970-1979		$1,400	$1,500
1980-1989		$1,300	$1,400
1990-1999		$1,200	$1,300
2000-2003		$1,100	$1,200

D-18 Andy Griffith

2003. D-18 specs with bear claw spruce top, Andy's script signature on 18th fret.

2003		$2,000	$2,250

D-18 DC David Crosby

2002. David Crosby signature at 20th fret, Adirondack spruce top, quilted mahogany back and sides, 250 made.

2002		$1,950	$2,200

D-18 E

1958-1959. D-18 factory built with DeArmond pickups which required ladder bracing (reducing acoustic volume and quality).

1958-1959		$3,000	$3,500

D-18 GE Golden Era

1995. Part of the Golden Era Series, copy of '37 D-18, 272 made.

1995		$1,800	$2,250

D-18 LE

1986-1987. Limited Edition, quilted or flamed mahogany back and sides, scalloped braces, gold tuners with ebony buttons.

1986-1987		$1,750	$1,900

D-18 MB

1990. Limited Edition Guitar of the Month, flame maple binding, Engelmann spruce top signed by shop foremen, X-brace, total of 99 sold.

1990		$1,650	$1,800

D-18 S

1967-1993. Mahogany back and sides, 12-fret neck, slotted headstock, majority of production before '77, infrequent after that.

1967-1969		$2,000	$2,400
1970-1979		$1,500	$1,600
1980-1993		$1,500	$1,600

D-18 V (Vintage)

1992. Guitar of the Month, low-profile neck, scalloped braces, bound, total of 218 sold.

1992		$1,650	$1,800

D-18 VM/V

1996-present. 14-fret vintage series, mahogany body, M dropped from name in '99.

1996-1999		$1,350	$1,500

D-18 VMS

1996-2002. VM with 12-fret neck and slotted headstock.

1996-1999		$1,700	$1,800

D-19

1977-1988. Deluxe mahogany dreadnought, optional mahogany top, multi-bound but unbound rosewood 'board.

1977-1988		$1,250	$1,400

D-21

1955-1969. Brazilian rosewood back and sides, rosewood 'board, chrome tuners.

1955-1958	Klusons to early '58	$6,100	$6,800
1958-1959	Grover tuners late '58	$5,700	$6,300
1960-1962		$5,000	$5,500
1963-1965		$4,500	$5,000
1966-1967		$4,000	$4,500
1968-1969		$3,500	$4,000

Martin D-18

Martin D-18V

Martin D-25 K2

1966 Martin D-35

MODEL YEAR	FEATURES	EXC. COND. LOW	HIGH

D-25 K
1980-1989. Dreadnought-size with koa back and sides and spruce top.

| 1980-1989 | | $1,550 | $1,750 |

D-25 K2
1980-1989. Same as D-25K, but with koa top and black 'guard.

| 1980-1989 | | $1,650 | $1,850 |

D-28
1931-present. Brazilian rosewood back and sides (changed to Indian rosewood in '70), '36 was the last year for the 12-fret model, '44 was the last year for scalloped bracing, '47 was the last year herringbone trim was offered, natural. Ultra high-end D-28 Martin guitar (pre-'47) valuations are very sensitive to structural and cosmetic condition. Finish wear and body cracks for ultra high-end Martin flat tops should be evaluated on a case-by-case basis. Small variances within the 'excellent condition' category can lead to notable valuation differences.

1931-1932		$55,000	$70,000
1933		$55,000	$65,000
1934-1936	14-fret neck	$55,000	$60,000
1937-1939		$36,000	$55,000
1940-1941		$34,000	$36,000
1942-1944	Scalloped braces	$27,000	$34,000
1944-1946	Herringbone, non-scalloped	$18,000	$21,000
1947-1949	Non-herringbone starting '47	$9,000	$11,000
1950-1952		$7,700	$9,000
1953-1958	Klusons to early '58	$7,100	$7,700
1958-1959	Grover tuners late '58	$6,500	$7,100
1960-1962		$6,100	$6,500
1963-1965		$5,600	$6,100
1966	Black guard late '66	$5,000	$5,500
1966	Tortoise guard early '66	$5,100	$5,600
1967	Last of maple bridgeplate	$4,800	$5,400
1968	Rosewood bridgeplate	$4,400	$4,800
1969	Last of Brazilian rosewood	$4,000	$4,400
1970-1979	Indian rosewood	$1,800	$2,000
1980-1989		$1,800	$2,000
1990-1999		$1,800	$2,000
2000-2002		$1,500	$1,700

D-28 (1935 Special)
1993. Guitar of the Month, 1935 features, Indian rosewood back and sides, peghead with Brazilian rosewood veneer.

| 1993 | | $1,650 | $2,200 |

D-28 50th Anniversary
1983. Stamped inside 1833-1983 150th Anniversary, Indian rosewood back and sides.

| 1983 | | $1,600 | $1,800 |

D-28 CW/CWB Clarence White
2002-2004. CW has Indian rosewood back and sides, the CWB Brazilian, only 150 CWBs were to be built.

| 2002-2004 | CW | $2,200 | $2,400 |
| 2002-2004 | CWB | $4,400 | $4,800 |

D-28 DM Del McCourey Signature
2003. Limited edition of 115 instruments, natural.

| 2003 | | $2,500 | $2,600 |

D-28 E
1959-1964. Electric, Brazilian rosewood back and sides, 2 DeArmond pickups, natural.

| 1959-1964 | | $3,500 | $4,000 |

D-28 GE Golden Era
1999-2002. GE (Golden Era), Brazilian rosewood.

| 1999-2002 | | $5,500 | $5,900 |

D-28 LSH
1991. Guitar of the Month, Indian rosewood back and sides, herringbone trim, snowflake inlay, zigzag back stripe.

| 1991 | | $1,650 | $1,800 |

D-28 P
1988-1990. P stands for low-profile neck, Indian rosewood back and sides.

| 1988-1990 | | $1,250 | $1,500 |

D-28 S
1954-1993. Rosewood back and sides, 12-fret neck.

1954-1965		$5,400	$6,500
1966-1969	Brazilian rosewood	$5,000	$5,400
1970-1979	Indian rosewood	$2,100	$2,400
1980-1993		$2,100	$2,400

D-28 V
1983-1985. Brazilian rosewood back and sides, Limited Edition, herringbone trim, slotted diamond inlay.

| 1983-1985 | | $4,300 | $4,900 |

D-2832 Shenandoah
1984-1992. Dreadnought acoustic, Thinline pickup, spruce top, V-neck, laminated rosewood sides, 3-piece rosewood back.

| 1984-1992 | | $550 | $800 |

D-35
1965-present. Brazilian rosewood back and sides, changed to Indian rosewood in '70, 3-piece back, natural with sunburst option.

1965		$4,700	$4,800
1966		$4,500	$4,700
1967		$3,700	$4,500
1968		$3,400	$3,700
1969	Brazilian rosewood	$3,200	$3,400
1970-1979	Indian rosewood	$1,700	$1,900
1980-1989		$1,500	$1,700
1990-1999		$1,300	$1,600
2000-2003		$1,300	$1,900

D-35 Ernest Tubb
2003. Indian rosewood back and sides, special inlays, 90 built.

| 2003 | | $2,100 | $2,400 |

MODEL YEAR	FEATURES	EXC. COND. LOW	HIGH

D-35 S
1966-1993. Brazilian rosewood back and sides, changed to Indian rosewood in '70, 12-fret neck, slotted peghead.

1966-1969	Brazilian rosewood	$3,600	$4,300
1970-1979	Indian rosewood	$1,800	$2,000
1980-1989		$1,700	$1,900
1990-1993		$1,600	$1,800

D-3532 Shenandoah
1984-1993. Dreadnought acoustic, spruce top, V-neck, laminated rosewood sides, 3-piece rosewood back.

1984-1993		$550	$800

D-37 K
1980-1995. Dreadnought-size, koa back and sides, spruce top.

1980-1995		$2,100	$2,300

D-37 K2
1980-1995. Same as D-37 K, but has a koa top and black 'guard.

1980-1995		$2,100	$2,300

D-40
1997-2005. Rosewood back and sides, hexagon inlays.

1997-2005		$2,200	$2,300

D-41
1969-present. Brazilian rosewood back and sides for the first ones in '69 then Indian rosewood, bound body, scalloped braces, natural.

1969	Brazilian rosewood	$9,000	$14,000
1970-1979	Indian rosewood	$3,100	$3,600
1980-1989		$2,600	$3,300
1990-1999		$2,500	$3,300
1990-1999	Sunburst option	$2,800	$3,300
2000-2003		$2,300	$2,400

D-41 BLE
1990. Limited Edition Guitar of the Month, Brazilian rosewood back and sides, pearl top border except around 'board.

1989		$2,900	$3,700

D-42
1996-present. Dreadnought, Indian rosewood back and sides, spruce top, pearl rosette and inlays, snowflake 'board inlays, gold tuners, gloss finish.

1996-2002		$2,600	$3,000

D-42 K/D-42 K2
2000-present. K has koa back and sides, K2 has all koa body.

2000-2004		$2,200	$2,500

D-42 LE
1988 only. D-42-style, limited edition (75 sold), scalloped braces, low profile neck.

1988		$2,150	$2,500

D-42 V
1985. Vintage Series, 12 made, Brazilian rosewood, scalloped braces.

1985		$7,750	$9,000

D-45
1933-1942 (96 made), 1968-present. Brazilian rosewood back and sides, changed to Indian rosewood during '69. The pre-WW II D-45 is one of the holy grails. A pre-war D-45 should be evaluated on a case-by-case basis. The price ranges are for all-original guitars in excellent condition and are guidance pricing only. These ranges are for a crack-free guitar. Unfortunately, many older acoustics have a crack or two and this can make ultra-expensive acoustics more difficult to evaluate than ultra-expensive solidbody electrics. Technically, a repaired body crack makes a guitar non-original, but the vintage market generally considers a professionally repaired crack to be original. Crack width, length and depth can vary, therefore extra attention is suggested.

1936	Only 2 made	$230,000	$250,000
1937	Only 2 made	$210,000	$235,000
1938	Only 9 made	$200,000	$225,000
1939	Only 14 made	$185,000	$210,000
1940	Only 19 made	$175,000	$200,000
1941	Only 24 made	$175,000	$200,000
1942	Only 19 made	$160,000	$200,000
1968-1969	Brazilian rosewood	$30,000	$35,000
1970-1974	Indian rosewood, 105 made	$6,500	$7,500
1975-1979		$6,000	$7,000
1980-1989		$5,000	$6,000
1990-1999		$4,000	$5,000
2000-2002		$4,000	$5,000

D-45 (1939 Reissue)
High-grade spruce top, figured Brazilian rosewood back and sides, high X and scalloped braces, abalone trim, natural, gold tuners.

1992		$12,000	$13,500

D-45 200th Anniversary (C.F. Martin Sr. Deluxe)
1996 only. Commemorative model for C.F. Martin Sr.'s birth in 1796, Brazilian Deluxe Edition, natural.

1996		$13,000	$14,500

D-45 Custom
Various options and models, Brazilian rosewood back and sides.

1991-1992		$5,000	$15,000

D-45 Deluxe
1993 only. Guitar of the Month, Brazilian rosewood back and sides, figured spruce top, inlay in bridge and 'guard, tree-of-life inlay on 'board, pearl borders and back stripe, gold tuners with large gold buttons, total of 60 sold.

1993		$16,000	$17,000

D-45 Gene Autry
1994 only. Gene Autry inlay (2 options available), natural.

1994		$13,000	$17,000

D-45 S
1969-1993. Brazilian rosewood back and sides, 12-fret neck, S means slotted peghead, only 50 made.

1988-1993		$6,500	$8,000

D-45 Steven Stills Signature
2002. Limited edition of 91.

2002		$12,000	$14,000

1976 Martin D-35

1997 Martin D-45

Martin HD-28

1963 Martin F-65

MODEL YEAR	FEATURES	EXC. COND. LOW	HIGH

D-45 V
1983-1985. Brazilian rosewood back and sides, scalloped braces, snowflake inlay, natural, name revived in '99.

1983-1985		$12,000	$13,000

D-45 VR
1997-Present. Scalloped braces, high X-bracing, vintage aging toner, snowflake inlay, name changed to D-45 V in '99.

1997-2001		$4,900	$5,300

D-62
1989-1995. Dreadnought, flamed maple back and sides, spruce top, chrome-plated enclosed Schaller tuners.

1989-1995		$1,650	$2,000

D-62 LE
1986. Flamed maple back and sides, spruce top, snowflake inlays, natural, Guitar of the Month October '86.

1986		$1,850	$2,200

D-76
1975-1976. Limited Edition, Indian rosewood back and sides, 3-piece back, herringbone back stripe, pearl stars on 'board, eagle on peghead, only 200 made in '75 and 1,976 made in '76.

1976		$2,800	$3,000

DC-1 E/DC-1 M
1995-present. Cutaway design, all solid wood, mahogany back and sides, spruce top, transducer pickup.

1995-1999		$850	$950

DC-16 GTE Premium
2000s. D-style rounded cutaway, all solid wood, gloss finish top, satin finish mahogany back and sides.

2000s		$950	$1,000

DM
1990-present. Solid sitka spruce top, laminated mahogany back and sides, dot markers, natural satin.

1990-1999		$500	$600

DXM
1998-present. Wood composite mahogany laminate D body, solid wood neck, decal rosette, screened headstock logo, unique DX bracing.

1998-2001		$350	$400

D12XM
1999-2000. 12-string version of the DXM.

1999-2000		$325	$425

E-18
1979-1982. Offset double-cut, maple and rosewood laminate solidbody, 2 DiMarzio pickups, phase switch, natural.

1979-1982		$650	$800

EM-18
1979-1982. Offset double-cut, maple and rosewood laminate solidbody, 2 exposed-coil humbucking pickups, coil split switch.

1979-1982		$650	$800

MODEL YEAR	FEATURES	EXC. COND. LOW	HIGH

EMP-1
1998-1999. Employee series designed by Martin employee team, cutaway solid spruce top, ovangkol wood back and sides with rosewood middle insert (D-35-style insert), on-board pickup.

1998-1999		$1,850	$2,200

F-1
1940-1942. Mahogany back and sides, carved spruce top, multi-bound, f-holes, sunburst.

1940-1942	91 made	$1,950	$2,200

F-2
1940-1942. Rosewood back and sides, carved spruce top, multi-bound, f-holes.

1940-1942	46 made	$2,400	$3,000

F-7
1935-1942. Brazilian rosewood back and sides, f-holes, carved top, back arched by braces, multi-bound, sunburst top finish.

1935-1942		$6,200	$7,000

F-9
1935-1941. Highest-end archtop, Brazilian rosewood, Martin inlaid vertically on headstock, 7-ply top binding, 45-style back strip, sunburst.

1935-1941		$10,500	$14,000

F-50
1961-1965. Single-cut thinline archtop with laminated maple body, 1 pickup.

1961-1965		$1,100	$1,350

F-55
1961-1965. Single-cut thinline archtop with laminated maple body, 2 pickups.

1961-1965		$1,100	$1,450

F-65
1961-1965. Electric archtop, double-cut, f-holes, 2 pickups, square-cornered peghead, Bigsby, sunburst.

1961-1965		$1,400	$1,800

GT-70
1966-1968. Electric archtop, bound body, f-holes, single-cut, 2 pickups, tremolo, burgundy or black finish.

1966-1968		$1,200	$1,400

GT-75
1966-1968. Electric archtop, bound body, f-holes, double-cut, 2 pickups, tremolo, burgundy or black finish.

1966-1968		$1,500	$1,700

Hawaiian X
2002-2004. Hawaiian scene painted on top, similar to the Cowboy guitar model, limited edition of 500.

2002-2004		$800	$950

HD-28 Standard Series
1976-present. Indian rosewood back and sides, scalloped bracing, herringbone purfling.

1976-1979		$1,800	$2,100
1980-1989		$1,800	$2,100
1990-1999		$1,800	$2,100
2000-2002		$1,500	$1,800

HD-28 BLE
1990. Guitar of the Month, Brazilian rosewood back and sides, herringbone soundhole ring, low profile neck (LE), chrome tuners, aging toner finish.

1990		$4,100	$5,000

The *Vintage Guitar Price Guide* shows low to high values for items in all-original excellent condition, and, where applicable, with original case or cover.

MODEL		EXC. COND.	
YEAR	FEATURES	LOW	HIGH

HD-28 GM LSH
1994. Grand Marquis, Guitar of the Month, rosewood back and sides, large soundhole with double herringbone rings, snowflake inlay in bridge.

1994		$2,600	$3,000

HD-28 KM Keb Mo Signature Edition
2001. 252 made.

2001		$2,000	$2,300

HD-28 LE
1985. Guitar of the Month, rosewood back and sides, scalloped bracing, herringbone top purfling, diamonds and squares 'board inlay, V-neck.

1985		$2,600	$2,800

HD-28 MP
1990. Bolivian rosewood back and sides, scalloped braces, herringbone top purfling, zipper back stripe, low profile neck.

1990		$1,600	$1,800

HD-28 P
1987-1989. Rosewood back and sides, scalloped braces, herringbone, low profile neck (P), zigzag back stripe.

1987-1989		$1,600	$1,800

HD-28 V/VR
1996-present. 14-fret vintage series, rosewood body, R dropped from name in '99.

1999		$1,850	$1,950

HD-35
1978-present. Indian rosewood back and sides, herringbone top trim, zipper back stripe.

1978-1979		$1,750	$1,950
1980-1989		$1,750	$1,950
1990-1999		$1,750	$1,950

HD-40 MK Mark Knopfler Edition
2001-2001. Limited edition of 251 made, Mark Knopfler signature inlay 20th fret, herringbone trim, fancy marquetry soundhole rings.

2001-2002		$2,500	$2,700

HD-282 R
1994 only.

1994		$1,500	$1,700

HOM-35
1989. Herringbone Orchestra Model, Guitar of the Month, scalloped braces, 3-piece Brazilian rosewood back, bookmatched sides, 14-fret neck, only 60 built.

1989		$3,200	$4,600

HPD-41
1999-2001. Like D-41, but with herringbone rosette, binding.

1999-2001		$2,900	$3,100

J-1 Jumbo
1997-2002. Jumbo body with mahogany back and sides.

1997-2002		$825	$900

J12-16 GT
2000s. 16" jumbo 12-string, satin solid mahogany back and sides, gloss solid spruce top.

2001		$775	$825

J12-40
1985-1996. Called J12-40 M from '85-'90, rosewood back and sides, 12 strings, 16" jumbo size, 14-fret neck, solid peghead, gold tuners.

1996		$1,550	$1,800

J12-65
1985-1995. Called J12-65M for '84-'90, Jumbo style 65 12-string, spruce top, figured maple back and sides, gold tuning machines, scalloped bracing, ebony 'board, tortoiseshell-style binding, natural.

1985-1995		$1,550	$1,800

J-18/J-18M
1987-1996. J-size body with Style 18 appointments, natural, called J-18M for '87-'89.

1987-1996		$1,250	$1,350

J-40
1990-present. Called J-40 M from '85-'89, Jumbo, Indian rosewood back and sides, triple-bound 'board, hexagonal inlays.

1990-1999		$1,850	$2,200

J-40 M
1985-1989. Jumbo, Indian rosewood back and sides, triple-bound 'board, hexagonal inlays, name changed to J-40 in '90.

1985-1989		$1,850	$2,200

J-65/J-65 E/J-65 M
1985-1995. Jumbo acoustic featuring maple back and sides, gold-plated tuners, scalloped bracing, ebony 'board, tortoise shell-style binding.

1985-1995		$1,850	$2,200

M-21 Custom
December 1984. Guitar of the Month, low profile neck M-Series, Indian rosewood back and sides, special ornamentation.

1984		$1,850	$2,100

M-36
1978-1997. Indian rosewood back and sides, bound 'board, low profile neck, multi-bound, white-black-white back stripes.

1978-1997		$1,500	$1,600

M-38
1977-1996. Indian rosewood back and sides, multi-bound, low profile neck, gold-plated tuners, stained top.

1977-1996		$2,000	$2,200

MC-28
1981-1996. Rosewood back and sides, single-cut acoustic, oval soundhole, scalloped braces, natural.

1981-1996		$1,600	$1,700

MC-68
1985-1995. Auditorium-size acoustic, rounded cutaway, maple back and sides, gold tuners, scalloped bracing, ebony 'board, tortoiseshell-style binding, natural or sunburst.

1985-1995		$1,700	$2,200

MTV-1 Unplugged
1996. Body is 1/2 rosewood and 1/2 mahogany, scalloped bracing, MTV logo on headstock.

1996		$1,550	$1,650

1966 Martin GT-75

Martin J-40

Martin OM-42

1937 Martin R-18

MODEL YEAR	FEATURES	EXC. COND. LOW	HIGH

N-10

1968-1995. Classical, mahogany back and sides, fan bracing, wood marquetry soundhole ring, unbound rosewood 'board, 12-fret neck and slotted peghead from '70.

1968-1969	Short-scale	$1,350	$1,700
1970-1979	Long-scale	$1,250	$1,550
1980-1989	Long-scale	$1,200	$1,450
1990-1995	Long-scale	$1,100	$1,350

N-20

1968-1995. Classical, Brazilian rosewood back and sides (changed to Indian rosewood in '69), multibound, 12-fret neck, solid headstock (changed to slotted in '70), natural.

1968-1969	Brazilian rosewood, short-scale	$3,000	$3,500
1970-1979	Indian rosewood, long-scale	$1,500	$1,800
1980-1989	Long-scale	$1,400	$1,700
1990-1995	Long-scale	$1,350	$1,650

OM-18

1930-1934. Orchestra Model, mahogany back and sides, 14-fret neck, solid peghead, banjo tuners (changed to right-angle in '31).

1930-1933	Natural	$15,000	$18,000
1934	Sunburst option	$16,000	$19,000

OM-18 GE Golden Era 1930/Special Edition GE

2003-present. Mahogany back and sides, Brazilian rosewood purfling and binding.

2003-2004		$2,000	$2,300

OM-18 V

1999-present. Vintage features.

1999-2002		$1,550	$1,800

OM-18 VLJ/OMC-18 VLJ

2002. 133 made.

2002		$2,200	$3,000

OM-21 Standard Series

1992-1997. Triple 0-size, 15 1/8", spruce top, rosewood back and sides, natural.

1992-1997		$1,250	$1,350

OM-28

1929-1933. Orchestra Model, Brazilian rosewood back and sides, 14-fret neck, solid peghead, banjo tuners (changed to right-angle in '31), reintroduced with Indian rosewood in '90.

1929-1930	Small guard, banjo tuners	$35,000	$40,000
1931-1933	Large guard	$30,000	$35,000

OM-28 Reissue

1990-1996. Indian rosewood back and sides.

1990-1996		$1,850	$2,200

OM-28 PB Perry Bechtel

1993. Guitar of the Month, signed by Perry Bechtel's widow Ina, spruce top, Indian rosewood back and sides, zigzag back stripe, chrome tuners, V-neck, only 50 made.

1993		$4,900	$5,300

MODEL YEAR	FEATURES	EXC. COND. LOW	HIGH

OM-28 VR

1990-1996. Orchestra Model, reintroduced OM-28 with rosewood back and sides.

1990-1996		$1,850	$2,100

OM-42 PS Paul Simon

1997. Bookmatched sitka spruce top, Indian rosewood back and sides, 42- and 45-style features, low profile PS neck, 500 made.

1997		$3,900	$4,200

OM-42 Reissue

1999-present. Indian rosewood back and sides, Style 45 snowflake inlays, rounded neck profile.

1999-2002		$2,800	$3,200

OM-45 Deluxe/OM-45

1930-1933. OM-style, 45 level appointments with pearl inlay in 'guard and bridge, only 14 OM-45 Deluxe instruments made. Regular OM-45 with normal 45-style appointments. Condition is critically important on this or any ultra high-end instrument, minor flaws are critical to value.

1930	OM-45 Deluxe	$200,000	$225,000
1930-1933	OM-45	$100,000	$125,000

OM-45 Deluxe Reissue

1994.

1994		$4,000	$4,300

OMC-28

1990. Guitar of the Month with rounded cutaway, gold tuners, low profile neck, pearl Martin script logo in headstock, label signed by C.F. Martin IV.

1990		$1,750	$2,100

R-17

1934-1942. All mahogany, arched top and back, 3-segment f-holes (changed to 1-segment in '37), 12-fret neck, sunburst.

1934-1942	940 made	$1,000	$1,500

R-18

1933-1942. Spruce arched top (carved top by 1937), mahogany back and sides, 14-fret neck, bound top, sunburst.

1933-1942	1,928 made	$1,500	$2,500

SPD-16 R

2000s. Special edition D-style, solid spruce top, solid rosewood back and sides, gloss finish.

2002		$1,000	$1,200

SPD-16 TR/R

1997-2000. East Indian rosewood back and sides, abalone snowflake markers.

1997-2000		$1,000	$1,200

SPDC-16 TR/R

1997-2000. Cutaway version of SPD-16 R.

1997-2000		$1,250	$1,350

Stauffer

1830s-ca.1850s. One of C.F. Martin's earliest models, distinguished by the scrolled, six-on-a-side headstock, ornamentation varies from guitar to guitar.

1830s	Plain, no ivory	$3,500	$7,000
1830s	Very fancy, ivory board and bridge	$5,500	$12,000

MODEL		EXC. COND.	
YEAR	FEATURES	LOW	HIGH

T-17 Tiple
1926-1948. Ten-string instrument with double and triple strings, mahogany. In Argentina tiple means 'small guitar'.

1926-1948		$1,000	$1,400

T-28 Tiple
1922-1927. Tiple with style 28 appointments, natural.

1922-1927		$1,900	$2,400

Marvel
Ca. 1950s- ca. 1960s. Brand name used for budget instruments marketed by Peter Sorkin Company in New York, New York. Sorkin manufactured and distributed Premier guitars and amplifiers made by its Multivox subsidiary. Marvel instruments were primarily beginner-grade. Brand disappears by mid-'60s.

Electric Solidbody Guitars
1950s-mid-1960s. Various models.

1950s		$125	$225

Masaki Sakurai
See Kohno brand.

Mason
1936-1939. Henry L. Mason on headstock, wholesale distribution, similar to Gibson/Cromwell, pressed wood back and sides.

Student/Intermediate Student
1936-1939. Various flat-top and archtop student/budget models.

1936-1939		$350	$750

Mason Bernard
1990-1991. Founded by Bernie Rico (BC Rich founder). During this period BC Rich guitars were liscensed and controlled by Randy Waltuch and Class Axe. Most Mason models were designs similar to the BC Rich Assassin, according to Bernie Rico only the very best materials were used, large MB logo on headstock. Around 225 guitars were built bearing this brand.

MB-1/MB-2 Assassin

1990-1991		$550	$700

Maton
1946-present. Intermediate and professional grade, production/custom, acoustic, acoustic/electric, hollow body and solidbody guitars built in Box Hill, Victoria, Australia. Founded by Bill May and his brother Reg and still run by the family. Only available in USA since '82.

Mauel Guitars
1995-present. Luthier Hank Mauel builds his premium grade, custom, flat-tops in Auburn, California.

Maurer
1897-1944. Robert Maurer built instruments under his own name and the Champion brand in his Chicago-based woodworking shop. He sold the shop to the Larson Brothers in 1900, but the Maurer name was retained. The Larsons offered low-end and high quality Maurer models. They also branded instruments for various retailers.

13" Acoustic Flat-Top (Standard)
Early-1900s. Rosewood back and sides, spruce top, 12 3/4", made by Larson Brothers of Chicago.

1910		$2,000	$2,700

13" Higher-End Flat-Top (Brazilian)
Early-1900s. Spruce top, 13 5/8", Brazilian rosewood back and sides, high-end pearl appointments, slotted headstock.

1910	Natural	$3,500	$4,700

14" Flat-Top (Brazilian)
1920s-1930s. Mid-sized (about 14") with Brazilian rosewood back and sides, attractive appointments.

1920s	Abalone trim	$6,000	$8,000
1930s		$6,000	$8,000

14" Flat-Top (Mahogany)
1920s-1930s. Mid-sized (about 14") with mahogany back and sides, standard appointments.

1930s		$2,500	$3,700

15" High-end Flat-Top (Brazilian)
Early-1900s. Brazilian rosewood back and sides, tree of life inlay, 15", pearl-bound.

1920s		$9,000	$11,000

McAlister Guitars
1997-present. Premium grade, custom, flat-tops built by luthier Roy McAlister in Watsonville, California.

McCollum Guitars
1994-present. Luthier Lance McCollum builds his premium grade, custom, flat-top and harp guitars in Colfax, California.

McCurdy Guitars
1983-present. Premium grade, production/custom, archtops built by luthier Ric McCurdy originally in Santa Barbara, California and, since '91, New York, New York.

McGill Guitars
1976-present. Luthier Paul McGill builds his premium grade, production/custom, classical, resonator, and acoustic/electric guitars in Nashville, Tennessee.

MCI, Inc
1967-1988. MusiConics International (MCI), of Waco, Texas, introduced the world to the Guitorgan, invented by Bob Murrell. Later, they also offered effects and a steel guitar. In the '80s, a MIDI version was offered. MCI was also involved with the Daion line of guitars in the late '70s and early '80s.

McCollum flat-top

Maton MS500/12

McInturff Sportster

Megas Athena solidbody

MODEL YEAR	FEATURES	EXC. COND. LOW	HIGH

GuitOrgan B-35

1970s (ca. 1976-1978?). Duplicated the sounds of an organ and more. MCI bought double-cut semi-hollow body guitars from others and outfitted them with lots of switches and buttons. Each fret has 6 segments that correspond to an organ tone. There was also a B-300 and B-30 version, and the earlier M-300 and 340.

1970s		$1,300	$1,700

McInturff

1996-present. Professional and premium grade, production/custom, solidbody guitars built by luthier Terry C. McInturff originally in Holly Springs, North Carolina, and since '04, in Moncure, North Carolina. McInturff spent 17 years during guitar repair and custom work before starting his own guitar line.

Taurus Standard

Single-cut, carved flamed maple top on chambered mahogany body, dual humbucker pickups, gold hardware.

1996-2001	Sunburst	$1,800	$2,100

McPherson Guitars

1981-present. Premium grade, production, flat-tops built by luthier Mander McPherson in Sparta, Wisconsin.

Mean Gene

1988-1990. Heavy metal style solidbodies made by Gene Baker, who started Baker U.S.A. guitars in '97, and Eric Zoellner in Santa Maria, California. They built around 30 custom guitars.

Megas Guitars

1989-present. Luthier Ted Megas builds his premium grade, custom, archtop and solidbody guitars, originally in San Franciso, and currently in Portland, Oregon.

Melancon

Professional and premium grade, custom/production, solid and semi-hollow body guitars built by luthier Gerard Melancon in Thibodaux, Louisiana. They also build basses.

Mello, John F.

1973-present. Premium grade, production/custom, classical and ftat-top guitars built by luthier John Mello in Kensington, California.

Melophonic

1960s. Brand built by the Valco Company of Chicago.

Resonator Guitar

Valco-made.

1965		$600	$700

Melville Guitars

1988-present. Luthier Christopher Melville builds his premium grade, custom, flat-tops in Milton, Queensland, Australia.

Mercurio

Luthier Peter Mercuio builds his custom/production solidbody guitars, featuring his interchangeable PickupPak system to swap pickups, in Chanhassen, Minnesota.

Mermer Guitars

1983-present. Luthier Richard Mermer builds his premium grade, production/custom, steel-string, nylon-string, and Hawaiian guitars in Sebastian, Florida.

Merrill Brothers

1998-present. Premium grade, production/custom, steel-string and harp guitars built by luthiers Jim and Dave Merrill in Williamsburg, Virginia.

Mesrobian

1995-present. Luthier Carl Mesrobian builds his professional and premium grade, custom, archtop guitars in Salem, Massachusetts.

Messenger

1967-1968. Built by Musicraft, Inc., originally of 156 Montgomery Street, San Francisco, California. The distinguishing feature of the Messengers is a metal alloy neck which extended through the body to the tailblock, plus mono or stereo outputs. Sometime before March '68 the company relocated to Astoria, Oregon. Press touted "improved" magnesium neck, though it's not clear if this constituted a change from '67. Brand disappears after '68.

Electric Hollowbody Archtop

1967-1968. Symmetrical double-cut body shape, metal neck with rosewood 'boards, stereo.

1967-1968	Rojo Red	$2,000	$2,750

Metropolitan

1995-present. Professional and premium grade, production/custom, retro-styled solidbodies designed by David Wintz reminiscent of the '50s National Res-o-glas and wood body guitars. They feature full-scale set-neck construction and a wood body instead of Res-o-glas. Wintz also makes Robin and Alamo brand instruments.

Glendale Custom

1997-present. Single-cut, African fakimba body, set-neck, 2 pickups, various colors.

1997-2000		$1,450	$1,700

Glendale Custom Acoustic

1997-2004. Single-cut, African fakimba body, set-neck, 3 pickups including piezo.

1997-2004		$1,950	$2,300

Glendale Deluxe

1997-present. Single-cut, African fakimba body, set-neck, 2 pickups, dot markers.

1997-2000		$850	$1,100

Glendale Super Acoustic

1997-2004. Single-cut, flamed maple top, 3 pickups

MODEL YEAR	FEATURES	EXC. COND. LOW	HIGH

including piezo, gold hardware.

1997-2004 $2,950 $3,400

Tanglewood Custom

1996-present. Map-shape basswood body, German body carve front and back, 2 humbuckers, bound ebony 'board, butterfly inlays, various colors.

1996-1997 $1,450 $1,700

Tanglewood Custom Acoustic

1996-2004. Tanglewood Custom with added piezo bridge pickup, various colors.

1996-2004 $1,950 $2,300

Tanglewood Deluxe

1996-present. Similar to Custom, but with unbound rosewood 'board, dot inlays, German body carve on top only.

1996-2000 $850 $1,100

Westport Custom

1997-present. Single-cut, 3 pickups, art deco design, African fakimba body, set-neck, various colors.

1997-2000 $1,450 $1,700

Westport Custom Acoustic

1997-2004. Single-cut, 3 pickups, art deco design, African fakimba body, set-neck.

1997-2004 $1,950 $2,300

Westport Deluxe

1997-present. Single-cut, 2 humbuckers.

1997-2000 $850 $1,000

Westport Super Acoustic

1997-2004. Single-cut, 3 pickups with piezo, art deco design, Africa fakimba body, set-neck.

1997-2004 $3,100 $3,500

Miami

1920s. Instruments built by the Oscar Schmidt Co. and possibly others. Most likely a brand made for a distributor.

Michael Dunn Guitars

1968-present. Luthier Michael Dunn builds his production/custom Maccaferri-style guitars in New Westminster, British Columbia. He also offers a harp uke and a Weissenborn- or Knutsen-style Hawaiian guitar, and has built archtops.

Michael Kelly

1999-present. Intermediate and professional grade, production, acoustic, solidbody and archtop guitars imported by Mailbox Music of Clearwater, Florida. They also offer mandolins and basses.

Michael Lewis Instruments

1992-present. Luthier Michael Lewis builds his premium and presentation grade, custom, archtop guitars in Grass Valley, California. He also builds mandolins.

Michael Menkevich

1970-present. Luthier Michael Menkevich builds his professional and premium grade, production/custom, flamenco and classical guitars in Elkins Park, Pennsylvania

Segovia

Solid cedar top, solid Indian rosewood back and sides, Spanish cedar neck.

1990s $2,500 $2,600

Michael Silvey Custom Guitars

2003-present. Solidbody electric guitars built by Michael Silvey in North Canton, Ohio.

Michael Thames

1972-present. Luthier Michael Thames builds his premium grade, custom/production, classical guitars in Taos, New Mexico.

Classical

1990s. Solid cedar top, solid Indian rosewood back and sides, mahogany neck.

1990s $3,400 $3,600

Michael Tuttle

2003-present. Professional and premium grade, custom, solid and hollow body guitars built by luthier Michael Tuttle in Saugus, California. He also builds basses.

Microfrets

1967-1975, 2004-present. Professional grade, production, electric guitars built in Myersville, Maryland. They also build basses. Founded by Ralph S. Jones, Sr. in Frederick, Microfrets offered over 20 models of guitars that sported innovative designs and features, with pickups designed by Bill Lawrence. The brand was revived, again in Frederick, by Will Meadors and Paul Rose in '04.

Serial numbers run from about 1000 to about 3800. Not all instruments have serial numbers, particularly ones produced in '75. Serial numbers do not appear to be correlated to a model type, but are sequential by the general date of production.

Instruments can be identified by body styles as follows; Styles 1, 1.5, 2, and 3. An instrument may be described as a Model Name and Style Number (for example, Covington Style 1). Style 1 has a wavey-shaped pickguard with control knobs mounted below the guard and the 2-piece guitar body has a particle board side gasket. Style 1.5 has the same guard and knobs, but no side body gasket. Style 2 has an oblong pickguard with top mounted control knobs and a pancake style seam between the top and lower part of the body. Style 3 has a seamless 2-piece body and a Speedline neck.

Metropolitan Glendale Deluxe

Michael Lewis San Rafael

GUITARS

1972 Microfrets Calibra I

Mike Lull TX

MODEL YEAR	FEATURES	EXC. COND. LOW	HIGH

Baritone Signature
1971. Baritone version of Signature Guitar, sharply pointed double-cut, with or without f-holes, single- or double-dot inlays.

1971		$600	$700

Baritone Stage II
1971-ca. 1975. Double-cut, 2 pickups.

1971-1975		$600	$700

Calibra I
1969-1975. Double-cut, 2 pickups, f-hole.

1969-1975		$500	$600

Covington
1967-1969. Offset double-cut, 2 pickups, f-hole.

1967-1969		$800	$900

Golden Comet
1969-1971. Double-cut, 2 pickups, f-hole.

1969-1971		$600	$700

Golden Melody
1969-1971, 2004-present. Offset double-cut, 2 pickups, f-hole, M-shaped metal design behind tailpiece.

1969-1971		$800	$900

Huntington
1969-1975. Double-cut, 2 pickups.

1969-1975		$800	$900

Orbiter
1967-1969. Odd triple cutaway body, thumbwheel controls on bottom edge of 'guard.

1967-1969		$800	$900

Plainsman
1967-1969. Offset double-cut, 2 pickups, f-hole, thumbwheel controls on bottom edge of 'guard.

1967-1969		$900	$1,000

Signature
1967-1969. Double-cut, 2 pickups.

1967-1969		$600	$700

Spacetone
1969-1971, 2004-present. Double-cut semi-hollow body, 2 pickups.

1969-1971		$700	$800

Stage II
1969-1975. Offset double-cut, 2 pickups.

1969-1975		$600	$700

Swinger
1971-1975. Offset double-cut, 2 pickups.

1971-1975		$700	$800

Wanderer
1969. Double-cut, 2 pickups.

1969		$600	$700

Mike Lull Custom Guitars

1995-present. Professional and premium grade, production/custom, guitars built by luthier Mike Lull in Bellevue, Washington. He also builds basses.

Milburn Guitars

1990-present. Luthiers Orville and Robert Milburn build their premium grade, custom, classical guitars in Sweet Home, Oregon.

MODEL YEAR	FEATURES	EXC. COND. LOW	HIGH

Minarik

Luthier M.E. Minarik builds his professional and premium grade, custom/production, solid and chambered body guitars in Van Nuys, California.

Mirabella

1997-present. Professional and premium grade, custom archtops, flat-tops, hollowbody, and solidbody guitars built by luthier Cristian Mirabella in Babylon, New York. He also builds mandolins and ukes.

Mitre

1983-1985. Bolt neck, solidbody guitars made in Aldenville (or East Longmeadow), Massachusetts, featuring pointy body shapes, 2 humbuckers, active or passive electronics and with or without trems. They also offered a bass.

MJ Guitar Engineering

1993-present. Professional and premium grade, production/custom, hollow-body, chambered and solidbody guitars built by luthier Mark Johnson in Rohnert Park, California. He also builds basses.

Mobius Megatar

2000-present. Professional grade, production, hybrid guitars designed for two-handed tapping, built in Mount Shasta, California. Founded by Reg Thompson, Henri Dupont, and Traktor Topaz in '97, they released their first guitars in '00.

True Tapper
1999-present. Similar to Chapman Stick, 2 pickups.

2000-2004		$600	$800

Modulus

1978-present. Founded by Geoff Gould in the San Francisco area, currently built in Novato, California. Modulus currently offers professional grade, production/custom, solidbody electric guitars. They also build electric basses.

Genesis 2/2T
1996-present. Double-cut, long extended bass horn alder body, bolt-on carbon fiber/red cedar neck, hum-single-single pickups, locking vibrato (2T model).

1996-1999		$1,100	$1,300

Moll Custom Instruments

1996-present. Luthier Bill Moll builds his professional and premium grade, archtops in Springfield, Missouri. He has also built violins, violas and cellos.

Monrad, Eric

1993-present. Premium, custom, flamenco and classical guitars built by luthier Eric Monrad in Healdsburg, California.

MODEL YEAR	FEATURES	EXC. COND. LOW	HIGH

Montalvo
See listing under Casa Montalvo.

Montaya
Late-1980s. Montaya Hyosung 'America' Inc., Korean acoustic and electric import copies.

Monteleone
1976-present. Presentation grade, production/custom, archtop guitars built by Luthier John Monteleone in Islip, New York.

Eclipse
17" electric archtop, natural orange.

1991-1992		$14,000	$19,000
2003		$19,000	$24,000

OM-42
1970s. Styled like an old Martin OM, spruce top, Brazilian rosewood back.

1975		$11,000	$15,000

Radio City
18" acoustic archtop cutaway, art deco fretboard inlays, golden blond.

1996		$19,000	$23,000

Monty
1980-present. Luthier Brian Monty builds his professional and premium grade, production, archtop, semi-hollow, solidbody, and flatop guitars originally in Lennoxville, Quebec, and currently in Anne de Prescott, Ontario.

Moon (Japan)
1979-present. Professional and premium grade, production/custom, guitars made in Japan. They also build basses.

Moon (Scotland)
1979-present. Intermediate, professional and premium grade, production/custom, acoustic and electric guitars built by luthier Jimmy Moon in Glasgow, Scotland. They also build mandolin family instruments.

Moonstone
1972-present. Professional, premium, and presentation grade production/custom flat-top, solid and semi-hollow electric guitars, built by luthier Steve Helgeson in Eureka, California. He also builds basses. Higher unit sales in the early-'80s. Some models have an optional graphite composite neck built by Modulus.

Eclipse Standard
1979-1983. Figured wood body, offset double-cut, neck-thru, dot markers, standard maple neck, natural finish.

1979-1983		$1,600	$2,100

Explorer
1980-1983. Figured wood solidbody, neck-thru, standard maple neck, natural finish.

1980-1983		$1,600	$2,100

Flaming V
1980-1984. Figured wood body, V-shaped, neck-thru, standard maple neck, natural finish.

1980-1984		$1,600	$2,100

M-80
1980-1984. Figured wood double-cut semi-hollow body, standard maple or optional graphite neck, natural finish.

1980s	Optional graphite neck	$2,500	$3,500
1980s	Standard maple neck	$1,800	$2,200

Vulcan Deluxe
1979-1983. Figured maple carved-top body, offset double-cut, diamond markers, standard maple neck, natural finish.

1979-1983		$2,000	$2,500

Vulcan Standard
1979-1983. Mahogany carved-top body, offset double-cutaway, dot markers, standard maple neck, natural finish.

1979-1983		$1,900	$2,400

Morales
Ca.1967-1968. Made in Japan by Zen-On, not heavily imported into the U.S., if at all.

More Harmony
1930s. Private branded by Dobro for Dailey's More Harmony Music Studio. Private branding for catalog companies, teaching studios, publishers, and music stores was common for the Chicago makers. More Harmony silk-screen logo on the headstock.

More Harmony Dobro
1930s. 14" wood body with upper bout f-holes and metal resonator.

1930s	Sunburst	$600	$800

Morgaine Guitars
1994-present. Luthier Jorg Tandler builds his professional and premium grade, production/custom electrics in Germany.

Morgan Monroe
1999-present. Intermediate grade, production, acoustic, acoustic/electric and resonator guitars made in Korea and distributed by SHS International of Indianapolis, Indiana. They also offer mandolins, basses, banjos, and fiddles.

Morris
1970s-present. Intermediate, professional and premium grade, production, acoustic guitars imported by Moridaira of Japan. Morris guitars were first imported into the U.S. from the early '70s to around '90. They are again being imported into the U.S. starting in 2001.

Monteleone Eclipse

Moonstone Eagle

GUITARS

'60s Mosrite Celebrity

Mosrite Ventures

MODEL YEAR	FEATURES	EXC. COND. LOW	HIGH

000 Copy
1970s. Brazilian rosewood laminate body, import.

1970s		$350	$450

D-45 Copy
1970s. Brazilian laminate body.

1970s		$450	$550

Mortoro Guitars
1992-present. Luthier Gary Mortoro builds his premium grade, custom, archtop guitars in Miami, Florida.

Mosrite
The history of Mosrite has more ups and downs than just about any other guitar company. Founder Semie Moseley had several innovative designs and had his first success in 1954, at age 19, building doubleneck guitars for super picker Joe Maphis and protégé Larry Collins. Next came the Ventures, who launched the brand nationally by playing Mosrites and featuring them on album covers. At its '60s peak, the company was turning out around 1,000 guitars a month. The company ceased production in '69, and Moseley went back to playing gospel concerts and built a few custom instruments during the '70s.

In the early-'80s, Mosrite again set up shop in Jonas Ridge, North Carolina, but the plant burned down in November '83, taking about 300 guitars with it. In early-'92, Mosrite relocated to Booneville, Arkansas, producing a new line of Mosrites, of which 96% were exported to Japan, where the Ventures and Mosrite have always been popular.

Semie Moseley died, at age 57, on August 7, '92 and the business carried on until finally closing its doors in '93. The Mosrite line has again been revived, offering intermediate and premium grade, production, reissues.

Throughout much of the history of Mosrite, production numbers were small and model features often changed. As a result, exact production dates are difficult to determine.

Brass Rail
1970s. Double-cut solidbody, has a brass plate running the length of the 'board.

1970s		$850	$950

Celebrity 1
Late-1960s-1970s. Thick hollowbody, 2 pickups.

1970s	Sunburst	$900	$1,000

Celebrity 2 Standard
Late-1960s-1970s. Thin hollowbody, 2 pickups, in the '70s, it came in a Standard and a Deluxe version.

1970s		$900	$1,000

Celebrity 3
Late-1960s. Thin hollowbody, double-cut, 2 pickups, f-holes.

1960s		$900	$1,000

MODEL YEAR	FEATURES	EXC. COND. LOW	HIGH

Combo Mark 1
1966-1968. Bound body, 1 f-hole.

1966-1968		$1,600	$1,800

Custom-Built
1950s. Pre-production custom instruments hand-built by Semie Moseley, guidance pricing only, each instrument will vary.

1950s		$5,000	$10,000

D-40 Resonator Guitar
1960s.

1960s		$750	$900

D-100 Californian
1960s. Double-cut, resonator guitar with 2 pick-ups.

1967		$850	$1,200

Joe Maphis Mark 1
1960s. Semi-hollow double-cut, 2 single-coils, spruce top, walnut back, rosewood 'board.

1960s	Natural	$1,500	$1,800

Joe Maphis Mark XVIII
1960s. 6/12 doubleneck, double-cut, 2 pickups on each neck, Moseley tremolo on 6-string.

1960s		$3,500	$4,000

Mosrite 1988
1988-early-1990s. Has traditional Mosrite body styling, Mosrite pickups and bridge.

1988		$600	$900

Ventures Model
1963-1968. Double-cut solidbody, triple-bound body '63, no binding after, Vibramute for '63-'64, Moseley tailpiece '65-'68.

1963	Blue or red, bound	$6,000	$7,500
1963	Sunburst, bound	$5,500	$7,000
1964	Blue or red, Vibramute	$5,000	$7,000
1964	Sunburst, Vibramute	$5,000	$6,500
1965	Blue, red, sunburst, Moseley tailpiece	$4,000	$5,000
1965	Blue, red, sunburst, Vibramute	$5,000	$6,300
1966	Moseley tailpiece	$3,500	$4,000
1967	Moseley tailpiece	$3,000	$3,500
1968	Moseley tailpiece	$2,500	$3,000

Ventures (Jonas Ridge/Boonville)
1982-1993. Made in Jonas Ridge, NC or Booneville, AR, classic Ventures styling.

1982-1993		$1,800	$2,400

Ventures Mark V
1963-1968. Double-cut solidbody.

1960s		$1,900	$2,100

Ventures 12-String
1966-1968. Double-cut solidbody, 12 strings.

1967		$1,700	$1,800

Mossman
1965-present. Professional and premium grade, production/custom, flat-top guitars built in Sulphur Springs, Texas. They have also built acoustic basses. Founded by Stuart L. Mossman in Winfield, Kansas. In '75, fire destroyed one company build-

MODEL YEAR	FEATURES	EXC. COND. LOW	HIGH

ing, including the complete supply of Brazilian rosewood. They entered into an agreement with C.G. Conn Co. to distribute guitars by '77. 1200 Mossman guitars in a Conn warehouse in Nevada were ruined by being heated during the day and frozen during the night. A disagreement about who was responsible resulted in cash flow problems for Mossman. Production fell to a few guitars per month until the company was sold in '86 to Scott Baxendale. Baxendale sold the company to John Kinsey and Bob Casey in Sulphur Springs in '89.

Flint Hills
1970-mid-1980s. Flat-top acoustic, rosewood back and sides.

1970-1979		$1,400	$1,650

Great Plains
1970-mid-1980s. Flat-top, Indian rosewood, herringbone trim.

1970-1979		$1,400	$1,650

Southwind
1976-ca. 1986, mid-1990s-2002. Flat-top, abalone trim top.

1976-1979		$1,600	$1,850

Tennessee
1975-1979. D-style, spruce top, mahogany back and sides, rope marquetry purfling, rope binding.

1975-1979		$1,000	$1,200

Tennessee 12-String
1975-1979.

1975-1979		$1,000	$1,200

Winter Wheat
1976-1979, mid-1990s-present. Flat-top, abalone trim, natural finish.

1976-1979		$1,600	$1,850

Winter Wheat 12-String
1976-1979. 12-string version of Winter Wheat, natural.

1976-1979		$1,600	$1,850

Mozzani
Built in shops of Luigi Mozzani (b. March 9, 1869, Faenza, Italy; d. 1943) who opened lutherie schools in Bologna, Cento and Rovereto in 1890s. By 1926 No. 1 and 2 Original Mozzani Model Mandolin (flat back), No. 3 Mandola (flat back), No. 4 6-String Guitar, No. 5 7-, 8-, and 9-String Guitars, No. 6 Lyre-Guitar.

Acoustic Flat-Top

1920s		$300	$450

Murph
1965-1966. Mid-level electric semi-hollow and solidbody guitars built by Pat Murphy in San Fernado, California. Murph logo on headstock.

Electric Solidbody

1965-1966		$650	$850

Electric XII

1965-1966		$700	$900

Music Man
1972-present. Professional grade, production, solidbody guitars built in San Luis Obispo, California. They also build basses. Founded by ex-Fender executives Forrest White and Tom Walker in Orange County, California. Music Man originally produced guitar and bass amps based on early Fender ideas using many former Fender employees. They contracted with Leo Fender's CLF Research to design and produce a line of solidbody guitars and basses. Leo Fender began G & L Guitars with George Fullerton in '82. In '84, Music Man was purchased by Ernie Ball and production was moved to San Luis Obispo.

Axis
1996-present. Offset double-cut solidbody, figured maple top, basswood body, 2 humbucker pickups, Floyd Rose.

1996-2002		$1,000	$1,100

Edward Van Halen
1990-1995. Basswood solidbody, figured maple top, bolt-on maple neck, maple 'board, binding, 2 humbuckers, named changed to Axis.

1990-1995		$2,100	$2,200

Sabre I
1978-1982. Offset double-cut solidbody, maple neck, 2 pickups, Sabre I comes with a flat 'board with jumbo frets.

1978-1982		$650	$750

Sabre II
1978-1982. Same as Sabre I, but with an oval 7 1/2" radius 'board.

1978-1982		$650	$750

Silhouette
1986-present. Offset double-cut, contoured beveled solidbody, various pickup configurations.

1987-1995		$800	$900

Steve Morse Model
1987-present. Solidbody, 4 pickups, humbuckers in the neck and bridge positions, 2 single-coils in the middle, special pickup switching, 6-bolt neck mounting, maple neck.

1987-1995		$850	$950

Stingray I
1976-1982. Offset double-cut solidbody, flat 'board radius.

1976-1979		$700	$800
1980-1982		$700	$800

Stingray II
1976-1982. Offset double-cut solidbody, rounder 'board radius.

1976-1979		$800	$900
1980-1982		$800	$900

Musicvox
1996-present. Intermediate grade, production, Korean-made retro-vibe guitars and basses from Matt Eichen of Cherry Hill, New Jersey.

1976 Mossman Southwind

Music Man Van Halen

1985 Nady Lightning

1955 National Debonaire

MODEL YEAR	FEATURES	EXC. COND. LOW	HIGH

Nady

Wireless sound company Nady Systems offered guitars and basses with built-in wireless systems for 1985-'87. Made by Fernandes in Japan until '86, then by Cort in Korea.

Lightning/Lightning I

1985-1987. Double-cut, neck-thru, solidbody, 24 frets, built-in wireless, labeled as just Lightning until cheaper second version came out in '86.

1985	Fernandes	$650	$750
1986-1987	Cort	$600	$700

Lightning/Lightning II

1986-1987. Cheaper, bolt-neck version of the Lightning I.

1986-1987	Cort	$350	$550

Napolitano Guitars

1993-present. Luthier Arthur Napolitano builds his professional and premium grade, custom, archtop guitars in Allentown, New Jersey.

Nashville Guitar Company

1985-present. Professional and premium grade, custom, flat-top guitars built by luthier Marty Lanham in Nashville, Tennessee. He has also built banjos.

Custom Slide

Weissenborn Hawaiian copy with hollow neck, natural koa.

1997		$3,300	$3,500

National

Ca. 1927-present. Founded in Los Angeles, California as the National String Instrument Corporation by John Dopyera, George Beauchamp, Ted Kleinmeyer and Paul Barth. In '29 Dopyera left to start the Dobro Manufacturing Company with Rudy and Ed Dopyera and Vic Smith. The Dobro company competed with National until the companies reunited. Beauchamp and Barth then left National to found Ro-Pat-In with Adolph Rickenbacker and C.L. Farr (later becoming Electro String Instrument Corporation, then Rickenbacher). In '32 Dopyera returns to National and National and Dobro start their merger in late-'33, finalizing it by mid-'34. Throughout the '30s, National and Dobro maintained separate production, sales and distribution. National Dobro moved to Chicago, Illinois in '36. In Chicago, archtop and flat top bodies are built primarily by Regal and Kay; after '37 all National resonator guitar bodies made by Kay. L.A. production is maintained until around '37, although some assembly of Dobros continued in L.A. (primarily for export) until '39 when the L.A. offices are finally closed. By ca. '39 the Dobro brand disappears.

In '42, the company's resonator production ceased and Victor Smith, Al Frost and Louis Dopyera buy the company and change name to Valco Manufacturing Company. Post-war production resumes in '46. Valco is purchased by treasurer Robert Engelhardt in '64. In '67, Valco bought Kay, but in '68 the new Valco/Kay company went out of business. In the Summer of '69 the assets, including brandnames, were auctioned off and the National and Supro names were purchased by Chicago-area distributor/importer Strum 'N Drum (Noble, Norma brands). The National brand is used on copies in early- to mid-'70s, and the brand went into hiatus by the '80s.

In '88 National Resophonic Guitars is founded in San Luis Obispo, California, by Don Young, with production of National-style resonator guitars beginning in '89 (see following). In the '90s, the National brand also resurfaces on inexpensive Asian imports.

National Resonator guitars are categorized by materials and decoration (from plain to fancy): Duolian, Triolian, Style 0, Style 1, Style 2, Style 3, Style 4, Don #1, Style 97, Don #2, Don #3, Style 35.

National guitars all have serial numbers which provide clues to date of production. This is a complex issue. This list combines information included in George Gruhn and Walter Carter's Gruhn's Guide to Vintage Guitars, which was originally provided by Bob Brozman and Mike Newton, with new information provided by Mike Newton.

Pre Chicago numbers

A101-A450	1935-1936

Chicago numbers

A prefix (some may not have the prefix)	1936-mid-1997
B prefix	Mid-1937-1938
C prefix	Late-1938-1940
G prefix up to 200	Ea. 1941-ea. 1942
G suffix under 2000	Ea. 1941-ea. 1942
G suffix 2000-3000s (probably old parts)	1943-1945
G suffix 4000s (old parts)	Late 1945-mid-1947
V100-V7500	1947
V7500-V15000	1948
V15000-V25000	1949
V25000-V35000	1950
V35000-V38000	1951
X100-X7000	1951
X7000-X17000	1952
X17000-X30000	1953
X30000-X43000	1954
X43000-X57000	1955
X57000-X71000	1956
X71000-X85000	1957
X85000-X99000	1958
T100-T5000	1958
T5000-T25000	1959
T25000-T50000	1960
T50000-T75000	1961
T75000-T90000	1962
G100-G5000	1962
T90000-T99000	1963
G5000-G15000	1963
G15000-G40000	1964
1 prefix	1965-ea. 1968
2 prefix	Mid-1968

MODEL YEAR	FEATURES	EXC. COND. LOW	HIGH

Aragon De Luxe
1939-1942. Archtop with resonator (the only archtop resonator offered), spruce top and maple back and sides, light brown.

1939-1942		$6,000	$8,000

Bel-Aire
1953-1961. Single pointed cut archtop, 2 pickups until '57, 3 after, master tone knob and jack, bound body, sunburst.

1953-1961		$700	$900

Bluegrass 35
1963-1965. Acoustic, non-cut single-cone resonator, Res-O-Glas body in Arctic White.

1963-1965		$800	$900

Bobbie Thomas
Ca.1967-1968. Double-cut thinline hollowbody, bat-shaped F-holes, 2 pickups, Bobbie Thomas on 'guard, vibrato.

1967-1968		$300	$600

Bolero
1956-1957. Les Paul-shape, control knobs mounted on 'guard, single pickup, trapeze tailpiece, sunburst.

1956-1957		$550	$700

California
1949-1955. Electric hollowbody archtop, multi-bound, F-holes, trapeze tailpiece, 1 pickup, natural.

1949-1955		$650	$950

Club Combo
1952-1955, 1959-1961. Electric hollowbody archtop, 2 pickups, rounded cutaway.

1952-1955		$700	$1,000
1959-1961		$950	$1,100

Don Style 1
1934-1936. Plain body with engraved borders, pearl dot inlay, 14 frets, single-cone, silver (nickel-plated).

1934-1936		$5,500	$6,500

Don Style 2
1934-1936. Geometric Art Deco body engraving, 14 frets, single-cone, fancy square pearl inlays and pearloid headstock overlay, silver (nickel-plated).

1934-1936		$6,500	$10,000

Don Style 3
1934-1936. Same as Style 2 but more elaborate floral engravings, fancy pearl diamond inlays, 14 frets, single-cone, silver (nickel-plated), only a very few made.

1934-1936		$7,500	$11,000

Duolian
1930-1939. Acoustic steel body, frosted paint finish until '36, mahogany-grain paint finish '37-'39, round neck, square neck available in '33, 12-fret neck until '34 then 14-fret.

1930-1934	Round neck, 12 frets	$2,300	$2,800
1935-1939	Round neck, 14 frets	$2,200	$2,700

El Trovador
1933 only. Wood body, 12 frets.

1933		$1,300	$1,400

Electric Spanish
1935-1938. 15 1/2" archtop with Pat. Appl. For bridge pickup, National crest logo, fancy N-logo 'guard, black and white art deco, sunburst, becomes New Yorker Spanish '39-'58.

1935-1938		$1,200	$1,500

Estralita
1934-1942. Acoustic with single-cone resonator, f-holes, multi-bound, 14-fret, mahogany top and back, shaded brown.

1934-1942		$1,300	$1,400

Glenwood
1954-1958. Les Paul-shaped solidbody, wood body, not fiberglass, single-cut, multi-bound, 2 pickups, natural, renamed Glenwood Deluxe with Bigsby in '59.

1954-1958		$1,200	$1,300

Glenwood 95
1962-1964. Glenwood 98 without third bridge-mount pickup.

1962-1964	Vermillion Red/ Flame Red	$1,900	$2,300

Glenwood 98
1964-1965. USA map-shaped solidbody of molded Res-O-Glas, 2 regular and 1 bridge pickups, vibrato, pearl white finish.

1964-1965	Pearl White	$2,100	$2,500

Glenwood 99
1962-1965. USA map-shaped solidbody of molded Res-O-Glas, 2 regular and 1 bridge pickups, butterfly inlay.

1962-1963	Snow White	$2,500	$3,000
1964-1965	Sea Foam Green	$3,000	$3,500

Glenwood Deluxe
1959-1961. Renamed from Glenwood, Les Paul-shaped solidbody, wood body, not fiberglass, multi-bound, 2 pickups, factory Bigsby, vibrato, natural.

1959-1961		$1,500	$1,700

Model 1155
1948-1961. Flat top acoustic with Gibson body, mahogany back and sides, bolt-on neck.

1948-1961		$850	$1,000

N-600 Series
1968. Offset double-cut solidbody, 1, 2, and 3 pickup models, with and without vibrato.

1968		$450	$650

N-800 Series
1968. Double-cut semi-hollow body, various models with or without Bigsby.

1968	No Bigsby	$650	$750
1968	With Bigsby	$750	$850

Newport 82
1963-1965. Renamed from Val-Pro 82, USA map-shaped Res-O-Glas, 1 pickup, red finish.

1963-1965	Pepper Red	$1,300	$1,600

Newport 84
1963-1965. Renamed from Val-Pro 84, USA map-shaped Res-O-Glas, 1 regular and 1 bridge pickup, Sea Foam Green finish.

1963-1965	Sea Foam Green	$1,500	$1,800

National Bel-Aire

1933 National El Trovador

1930s National Style N

National Triolian

MODEL YEAR	FEATURES	EXC. COND. LOW	HIGH

Newport 88
1963-1965. Renamed from Val-Pro 88, USA map-shaped Res-O-Glas, 2 regular and 1 bridge pickup, black finish.

| 1963-1965 | Raven Black | $1,600 | $1,900 |

Pro Dual Pickup
1960s. Non-catalog Jetson-style res-o-glas type body, National logo, 2 pickups, red.

| 1960s | | $800 | $1,200 |

Reso-phonic
1956-1964. Pearloid-covered, single-cut semi-solid-body acoustic, single resonator, maroon or white, also a non-cut, square neck version was offered, which is included in these values.

| 1956-1964 | Round neck | $900 | $1,000 |
| 1956-1964 | Square neck | $800 | $900 |

Rosita
1933-1939. Plywood body by Harmony, plain metal resonator, plain appointments.

| 1933-1939 | | $800 | $1,000 |

Silvo (Electric Hawaiian)
1937-1941. Nickel-plated metal body flat-top, small upper bout, f-holes, square neck, multiple straight line body art over dark background, Roman numeral parallelogram markers, National badge headstock logo, Silvo name on coverplate.

| 1937-1941 | Silver | $2,500 | $3,500 |

Studio 66
1961-1964. Electric solidbody of Res-O-Glas, single-cut, 1 pickup, renamed Varsity 66 in '65.

| 1961-1962 | Sand Buff, bridge pickup | $1,100 | $1,400 |
| 1963-1964 | Jet Black, neck pickup | $1,050 | $1,350 |

Style 0
1930-1942. Acoustic single-cone brass body (early models had a steel body), Hawaiian scene etching, 12-fret neck '30-'34, 14-fret neck '35 on, round (all years) or square ('33 on) neck.

1930-1934	Round neck, 12-fret	$3,500	$4,000
1933-1942	Square neck	$2,500	$3,000
1935-1942	Round neck, 14-fret	$3,500	$4,000

Style 1 Tricone
1927-1943. German silver body tricone resonator, ebony 'board, mahogany square (Hawaiian) or round (Spanish) neck, plain body, 12-fret neck until '34, 14-fret after.

| 1927-1932 | Round neck | $4,500 | $6,000 |
| 1928-1932 | Square neck | $2,500 | $3,000 |

Style 1 Tricone Plectrum
1928-1935. 26" scale versus the 23" scale of the tenor.

| 1928-1935 | | $2,700 | $3,000 |

Style 1 Tricone Tenor
1928-1935. Tenor, 4 strings, 23" scale, square neck is Hawaiian, round neck is Spanish.

| 1928-1935 | | $2,500 | $3,000 |

MODEL YEAR	FEATURES	EXC. COND. LOW	HIGH

Style 2 Tricone
1927-1942. German silver body tricone resonator, wild rose engraving, square (Hawaiian) or round (Spanish) neck, 12-fret neck until '34, 14-fret after.

| 1930s | Round neck | $9,500 | $12,000 |
| 1930s | Square neck | $4,000 | $5,000 |

Style 2 Tricone Plectrum
1928-1935. 26" scale versus the 23" scale of the tenor.

| 1928-1935 | | $4,000 | $4,300 |

Style 2 Tricone Tenor
1928-1935. Tenor.

| 1928-1935 | | $3,800 | $4,300 |

Style 3 Tricone
1928-1941. German silver body tricone resonator, lily-of-the-valley engraving, square (Hawaiian) or round (Spanish) neck, 12-fret neck until '34, 14-fret after, reintroduced with a nickel-plated brass body in '94.

| 1930s | Round neck | $15,000 | $17,000 |
| 1930s | Square neck | $6,500 | $7,500 |

Style 3 Tricone Plectrum
1928-1935. 26" scale versus the 23" scale of the tenor.

| 1928-1935 | | $4,600 | $5,500 |

Style 3 Tricone Tenor
1928-1939.

| 1928-1939 | | $4,300 | $5,500 |

Style 4 Tricone
1928-1940. German silver body tricone resonator, chrysanthemum etching, 12-fret neck until '34, 14-fret after, reissued in '95 with same specs.

| 1930s | Round neck | $24,000 | $26,000 |
| 1930s | Square neck | $8,000 | $10,000 |

Style 35
1936-1942. Brass body tricone resonator, sand-blasted minstrel and trees scene, 12 frets, square (Hawaiian) or round (Spanish) neck.

| 1936-1942 | Round neck | $8,000 | $10,000 |
| 1936-1942 | Square neck | $4,000 | $5,000 |

Style 97
1936-1940. Nickel-plated brass body tricone resonator, sandblasted scene of female surfrider and palm trees, 12 frets, slotted peghead.

| 1930s | Round neck | $8,500 | $10,000 |
| 1930s | Square neck | $4,000 | $5,000 |

Style N
1930-1931. Nickel-plated brass body single-cone resonator, plain finish, 12 frets.

| 1930-1931 | | $4,000 | $5,000 |

Triolian
1928-1941. Single-cone resonator, wood body replaced by metal body in '29, 12-fret neck and slotted headstock '28-'34, changed to 14-fret neck in '35 and solid headstock in '36, round or square ('33 on) neck available.

| 1928-1936 | Various colors | $2,800 | $3,000 |
| 1937 | Fake rosewood grain finish | $2,300 | $2,700 |

MODEL YEAR	FEATURES	EXC. COND. LOW	HIGH

Triolian Tenor
1928-1936. Tenor, metal body.

1928-1936		$1,200	$1,700

Trojan
1934-1942. Single-cone resonator wood body, F-holes, bound top, 14-fret round neck.

1934-1942		$800	$1,000

Val-Pro 82
1962-1963. USA map-shaped Res-O-Glas, 1 pickup, Vermillion Red finish, renamed Newport 82 in '63.

1962-1963		$1,300	$1,600

Val-Pro 84
1962-1963. USA map-shaped Res-O-Glas, 1 regular and 1 bridge pickup, snow white finish, renamed Newport 84 in '63.

1962-1963		$1,600	$1,900

Val-Pro 88
1962-1963. USA map-shaped Res-O-Glas, 2 regular and 1 bridge pickup, black finish, renamed Newport 88 in '63.

1962-1963		$1,700	$2,000

Varsity 66
1964-1965. Renamed from Studio 66 in '64, molded Res-O-Glas, 1 pickup, 2 knobs, beige finish.

1964-1965		$1,100	$1,400

Westwood 72
1962-1964. USA map-shaped solid hardwood body (not fiberglas), 1 pickup, Cherry Red.

1962-1964		$700	$900

Westwood 75
1962-1964. USA map-shaped solid hardwood body (not fiberglas), 1 regular and 1 bridge pickup, cherry-to-black sunburst finish.

1962-1964		$800	$1,000

Westwood 77
1962-1965. USA map-shaped solid hardwood body (not fiberglas), 2 regular and 1 bridge pickup.

1962-1963	Blond-Ivory	$900	$1,100

National Reso-Phonic
1988-present. Professional and premium grade, production/custom, single cone, acoustic-electric, and tricone guitars (all with resonators), built in San Luis Obispo, California. They also build basses and ukes. McGregor Gaines and Don Young formed the National Reso-Phonic Guitar Company with the objective of building instruments based upon the original National designs.

Reso-Lectric
1990-present. Thin single-cut body with single-cone resonator, maple veneer top, lipstick neck pickup until '96 when changed to P-90 and added saddle transducer.

1993-1996		$800	$1,000
1997-2003		$1,200	$1,300

New Orleans Guitar Company
1992-present. Luthier Vincent Guidroz builds his premium grade, production/custom, solid and semi-hollow body guitars in New Orleans, Louisiana.

Nickerson Guitars
1983-present. Luthier Brad Nickerson builds his professional and premium grade, production/custom, archtop and flat-top guitars in Northampton, Massachusetts.

Nielsen
2004-present. Premium grade, custom/production, archtop guitars built by luthier Dale Nielsen in Duluth, Minnesota.

Nioma
1930s. Brand most likely used by a music studio (or distributor) on instruments made by others, including Regal-built resonator instruments.

Noble
Ca. 1950-ca. 1969. Instruments made by others and distributed by Don Noble and Company of Chicago. Plastic-covered guitars made by EKO debut in '62. Aluminum-necked Wandré guitars added to the line in early-'63. By ca. '65-'66 the brand is owned by Chicago-area importer and distributor Strum 'N Drum and used mainly on Japanese-made solidbodies. Strum 'N Drum bought the National brand name in '69 and imported Japanese copies of American designs under the National brand and Japanese original designs under Norma through the early '70s. The Noble brand disappears at least by the advent of the Japanese National brand, if not before.

Norma
Ca.1965-1970. Imported from Japan by Strum 'N Drum, Inc. of Chicago (see Noble brand info). Early examples were built by Tombo, most notably sparkle plastic covered guitars and basses.

Electric Solidbody
1965-1970s. Type of finish has affect on value. Various models include; EG-350 (student double-cut, 1 pickup), EG-403 (unique pointy cutaway, 2 pickups), EG-400 (double-cut, 2 pickups), EG-450 (double-cut, 2 split-coil pickups), EG-421 (double-cut, 4 pickups), EG-412-12 (double-cut, 12-string).

1965-1968	Blue, red, gold sparkle	$350	$550
1965-1970	Non-sparkle	$200	$350

Norman
1972-present. Intermediate grade, production, acoustic and acoustic/electric guitars built in LaPatrie, Quebec. Norman was the first guitar production venture luthier Robert Godin was involved with. He has since added the Seagull, Godin, and Patrick & Simon brands of instruments.

Northworthy Guitars
1987-present. Professional and premium grade, production/custom, flat-top and electric guitars built by luthier Alan Marshall in Ashbourne, Derbyshire, England. He also builds basses and mandolins.

National Val-Pro 82

1960s Norma Solidbody

Novax Expression Classic

1999 Olson SJ

MODEL YEAR	FEATURES	EXC. COND. LOW	HIGH

Norwood

1960s. Budget guitars imported most likely from Japan.

Electric Solidbodies

1960s. Offset double-cut body, 3 soapbar-style pickups, Norwood label on headstock.

1960s		$150	$200

Novax Guitars

1989-present. Luthier Ralph Novak builds his fanned-fret professional and premium grade, production/custom, solidbody and acoustic guitars in San Leandro, California. He also builds basses.

Nyberg Instruments

1993-present. Professional grade, custom, flat-top and Maccaferri-style guitars built by luthier Lawrence Nyberg in Hornby Island, British Columbia. He also builds mandolas, bouzoukis and citterns.

Oahu

1926-1985, present. The Oahu Publishing Company and Honolulu Conservatory, based in Cleveland, Ohio was active in the sheet music and student instrument business in the '30s. An instrument, set of instructional sheet music, and lessons were offered as a complete package. Lessons were often given to large groups of students. Instruments, lessons, and sheet music could also be purchased by mail order. The Oahu Publishing Co. advertised itself as The World's Largest Guitar Dealer. Most '30s Oahu guitars were made by Kay with smaller numbers from the Oscar Schmidt Company.

Guitar Models from the Mid-'30s include: 71K (jumbo square neck), 72K (jumbo roundneck), 68B (jumbo, vine body decoration), 68K (deluxe jumbo square neck), 69K (deluxe jumbo roundneck), 65K and 66K (mahogany, square neck), 64K and 67K (mahogany, roundneck), 65M (standard-size, checker binding, mahogany), 53K (roundneck, mahogany), 51 (black, Hawaiian scene, pearlette 'board), 51K (black, pond scene decoration), 52K (black, Hawaiian scene decoration), 50 and 50K (student guitar, brown). The brand has been revived on a line of tube amps.

Round Neck 14" Flat-Top

1930s. Spruce top, figured maple back and sides, thin logo.

1932		$1,000	$1,500

Style 50K Student Guitar

Student-size guitar, brown finish.

1935		$200	$275

Style 65M

Standard-size mahogany body, checker binding, natural brown.

1933		$275	$350

Style 68K De Luxe Jumbo

Hawaiian, 15.5" wide, square neck, Brazilian back and sides, spruce top, fancy pearl vine inlay, abalone trim on top and soundhole, rosewood pyramid bridge, fancy pearl headstock inlay, butterbean tuners, lad-

MODEL YEAR	FEATURES	EXC. COND. LOW	HIGH

der-braced, natural. High-end model made for Oahu by Kay.

1935		$4,000	$4,500

Odessa

1981-1990s. Budget guitars imported by Davitt & Hanser (BC Rich). Mainly acoustics in the '90s, but some electrics early on.

O'Hagan

1979-1983. Designed by clarinetist and importer Jerol O'Hagan in St. Louis Park, Minnesota. Primarily neck-thru construction, most with German-carved bodies. In '81 became Jemar Corporation and in '83 it was closed by the I.R.S., a victim of recession.

SN=YYM(M)NN (e.g., 80905, September '80, 5th guitar); or MYMNNN (e.g., A34006, April 1983, 6th guitar). Approximately 3000 total instruments were made with the majority being NightWatches (approx. 200 Twenty Twos, 100-150 Sharks, 100 Lasers; about 25 with birdseye maple bodies).

Electric

1979-1983. Models include; Laser (solidbody, double-cut, maple or walnut body, set-thru neck, 3 single-coil Schaller pickups), Shark (Explorer-looking solidbody) and Twenty Two (Flying V copy, 2 humbuckers).

1979-1983		$350	$500

Ohio

1959-ca. 1965. Line of electric solidbodies and basses made by France's Jacobacci company, which also built under its own brand. Sparkle finish, bolt-on aluminum necks, strings-thru-body design.

Old Kraftsman

Ca. 1930s-ca. 1960s. Brandname used by the Spiegel catalog company for instruments made by other American manufacturers, including Regal, Kay and even Gibson. The instruments were of mixed quality, but some better grade instruments were comparable to those offered by Wards.

Archtops

1930s-1960s. Various models.

1930s	17", Stauffer-style headstock	$500	$600
1950s		$350	$450
1960s		$300	$350

Thin Twin Jimmy Reed Model

1950s		$500	$650

Olson Guitars

1977-present. Luthier James A. Olson builds his presentation grade, custom, flat-tops in Circle Pines, Minnesota.

Omega

1996-present. Luthier Kevin Gallagher builds his premium grade, custom/production acoustic guitars in East Saylorsburg, Pennsylvania.

MODEL YEAR	FEATURES	EXC. COND. LOW	HIGH

Oncor Sound

1980-ca. 1981. This Salt Lake City-based company made both a guitar and a bass synthesizer.

Opus

1975-1976. Line of flattops made by Harmony. The original Harmony company closed soon after these were produced.

Orpheum

1897-1942, 1944-early 1970s, 2001-present. Intermediate grade, production, acoustic and resonator guitars. They also offer mandolins. Orpheum originally was a brand of Rettberg and Lange, who made instruments for other companies as well. William Rettberg and William Lange bought the facilities of New York banjo maker James H. Buckbee in 1897. Lange went out on his own in '21 to start the Paramount brand. He apparently continued using the Orpheum brand as well. He went out of business in '42. In '44 the brand was acquired by New York's Maurice Lipsky Music Co. who used it primarily on beginner to medium grade instruments, which were manufactured by Regal, Kay, and United Guitar (and maybe others). In the early '60s Lipsky applied the brand to Japanese and European imports. Lipsky dropped the name in the early '70s. The brand was revived in '01 by Tacoma Guitars.

Cutaway Thin Electric (Kay Thin Twin K-161)

Introduced 1952-1953 by Kay and also sold as the Orpheum Cutaway Thin Electric, 2 tube/bar pickups, 4 knobs, block markers, curly maple top and back, mahogany sides, natural.

1953		$500	$650

Orpheum Special (Regal-made)

1930s. Slot head, Dobro-style wood body, metal resonator, sunburst.

1930s		$800	$1,100

Ultra Deluxe Professional Cutaway Model 899

1950s. 17" cutaway, 2 pickups, 2 knobs, maple back and sides, top material varies, dot markers, finishes as follows: E-C copper, E-G gold, E-G-B gold-black sunburst, E-B blond curly maple, E-S golden orange sunburst.

1953	All finishes	$1,300	$1,900

Oscar Schmidt

1879-ca. 1939, 1979-present. Budget and intermediate grade, production, acoustic, acoustic/electric, and electric guitars distributed by U.S. Music Corp. (Washburn, Randall, etc.). They also offer mandolins, banjos, ukes and the famous Oscar Schmidt autoharp.

The original Oscar Schmidt Company, Jersey City, New Jersey, offered banjo mandolins, tenor banjos, guitar banjos, ukuleles, mandolins and guitars under their own brand and others (including Sovereign and Stella). By the early 1900s, the company had factories in the U.S. and Europe producing instruments. Oscar Schmidt was also an early contributor to innovative mandolin designs and the company participated in the '00-'30 mandolin boom. The company hit hard times during the Depression and was sold to Harmony by the end of the '30s. In '79, Washburn acquired the brand and it is now part of U.S. Music.

Stella Model No. 501D

1921	Decalcomania top	$175	$275

Otwin

1950s-1960s. A brand used on electric guitars made by the Musima company of East Germany. Musima also produced guitars under their own brand.

Outbound Instruments

1990-2002. Intermediate grade, production, travel-size acoustics from the Boulder, Colorado-based company.

Ovation

1966-present. Intermediate and professional grade, production, acoustic and acoustic/electric guitars built in the U.S. They also build basses and mandolins.

Ovation's parent company, helicopter manufacturer Kaman Corporation, was founded in 1945 by jazz guitarist and aeronautical engineer Charles Huron Kaman in Bloomfield, Connecticut. In the '60s, after losing a government contract, Kaman began looking to diversify. When offers to buy Martin and Harmony were rejected, Kaman decided to use their helicopter expertise (working with synthetic materials, spruce, high tolerances) and designed, with the help of employee and violin restorer John Ringso, the first fiberglass-backed (Lyracord) acoustic guitars in '65. Production began in '66 and the music factory moved to New Hartford, Connecticut, in '67. Early input was provided by fingerstyle jazz guitarist Charlie Byrd, who gave Kaman the idea for the name Ovation. C. William Kaman II became president of the company in '85. Kaman Music purchased Hamer Guitars in '88, and Trace Elliot amplifiers (U.K.) in '90.

Adamas 1587

1979-1998. Carbon top, walnut, single-cut, bowl back, binding, mini-soundholes.

1985	Black Sparkle	$1,600	$1,900

Adamas 1597

2000s. On-board electronics.

2000s	Black	$900	$1,000

Adamas 1687

1977-1998. Acoustic/electric, carbon top, non-cut, bowl back, mini-soundholes.

1990	Sunburst	$1,800	$1,900

Adamas II 1881 NB-2

1993-1998. Acoustic/electric, single-cut, shallow bowl.

1990s	Brown	$1,600	$1,900

Oscar Schmidt OE

Ovation Adamas 1687

Ovation Breadwinner

Ovation Deacon 12-string

MODEL YEAR	FEATURES	EXC. COND. LOW	HIGH

Anniversary Electric 1657

1978. Deep bowl, acoustic/electric, abalone inlays, gold-plated parts, carved bridge, for Ovation's 10th anniversary. They also offered an acoustic Anniversary.

| 1978 | | $550 | $800 |

Balladeer 1111

1968-1983, 1993-2000. Acoustic, non-cut with deep bowl, bound body, natural top, later called the Standard Balladeer.

| 1976-1983 | Natural | $300 | $400 |

Balladeer Artist 1121

1968-1990. Acoustic, non-cut with shallow bowl, bound body.

| 1972 | Natural | $325 | $450 |

Balladeer Classic 1122

1970s. Classical shallow-bowl version of Concert Classic, nylon strings, slotted headstock.

| 1970s | | $300 | $400 |

Balladeer Custom 1112

1976-1990. Acoustic, deep bowl, diamond inlays.

| 1976-1990 | Natural | $350 | $500 |

Balladeer Custom 12-String Electric 1655/1755

1982-1994. 12-string version of Balladeer Custom Electric.

| 1982-1994 | Sunburst | $350 | $500 |

Balladeer Custom Electric 1612/1712

1976-1990. Acoustic/electric version of Balladeer Custom, deep bowl.

| 1976-1990 | Natural | $350 | $450 |

Balladeer Standard 1761

1990s. Acoustic/electric, deep bowl, rounded cutaway.

| 1990s | | $550 | $600 |

Breadwinner 1251

1971-1983. Axe-like shaped single-cut solidbody, 2 pickups, textured finish, black, blue, tan or white.

| 1971-1983 | | $650 | $750 |

Celebrity CC-57

1990-1996. Laminated spruce top, shallow bowl, mahogany neck.

| 1990-1996 | Black | $200 | $300 |

Celebrity CK-057

2000s. Acoustic/electric rounded cutaway, shallow back.

| 2000s | | $400 | $450 |

Celebrity CS-257 (Import)

1992-present. Super shallow bowl back body, single-cut, Adamas soundholes, alternating dot and diamond markers, made in Korea.

| 1992-2003 | Black | $375 | $400 |

Classic 1613/1713

1971-1993. Acoustic/electric, non-cut, deep bowl, no inlay, slotted headstock, gold tuners.

| 1971-1993 | Natural | $400 | $500 |

Classic 1663/1763

1982-1998. Acoustic/electric, single-cut, deep bowl, cedar top, EQ, no inlay, slotted headstock, gold tuners.

| 1982-1998 | | $500 | $600 |

Classic 1863

1989-1998. Acoustic/electric, single-cut, shallow bowl, no inlay, cedar top, EQ, slotted headstock, gold tuners.

| 1989-1998 | | $500 | $600 |

Collectors Series

1982-present. Limited edition, different model featured each year and production limited to that year only, the year designation is marked at the 12th fret, various colors (each year different).

| 1982-2002 | | $700 | $1,000 |

Concert Classic 1116

1970s. Deep-bowl nylon string classical, slotted headstock.

| 1970s | | $350 | $450 |

Contemporary Folk Classic Electric 1616

1974-1990. Acoustic/electric, no inlay, slotted headstock, natural or sunburst.

| 1974-1990 | Natural | $300 | $450 |

Country Artist Classic Electric 1624-4

1970s-1980s. Nylon strings, slotted headstock, standard steel-string sized neck to simulate a folk guitar, on-board electronics with single control knob.

| 1970-1980s | | $350 | $600 |

Country Artist Classic Electric 6773

1990s. Classic electric, soft-cut, solid spruce top, slotted headstock, Ovation pickup system.

| 1990s | Natural | $850 | $1,000 |

Country Artist Electric 1624

Introduced in 1971. Acoustic/electric, non-cut, shallow bowl, slotted headstock, no inlay, chrome tuners.

| 1971-1975 | Natural | $550 | $625 |

Custom Legend 1117

1970s. Non-electrical 2nd generation Ovation, higher-end with abalone inlays and gold hardware, open V-bracing pattern. Model 1117-4, natural.

| 1970s | | $550 | $600 |

Custom Legend 1619

1970s. Acoustic/electric 2nd generation Ovation, electric version of model 1117, higher-end with abalone inlays and gold hardware, open V-bracing pattern. Model 1619-4, natural.

| 1970s | | $600 | $750 |

Custom Legend 1719

1970s. Acoustic/electric 2nd generation Ovation, deep bowl, AAA sitka spruce top, abalone inlay.

| 1970s | | $650 | $750 |

Custom Legend 1959

1980-present. Acoustic/electric, abalone top border, 'board binding, abalone floral inlay, gold tuners, natural or sunburst.

| 1980s | | $700 | $800 |

Custom Legend 1959-12

1980s. Acoustic/electric 12-string, deep bowl, AAA sitka spruce top, abalone inlay.

| 1980s | | $600 | $700 |

Deacon 1252

1973-1980. Axe-shaped solidbody electric, active electronics, diamond fret markers.

| 1973-1980 | Sunburst | $500 | $600 |

MODEL YEAR	FEATURES	EXC. COND. LOW	HIGH

Deacon 12-String 1253
1975. Axe-shaped solidbody, diamond inlay, 2 pickups. only a few made.

| 1975 | | $500 | $600 |

Elite 1718
1982-1997. Acoustic/electric, non-cut, deep bowl, solid spruce top, Adamas-type soundhole, volume and tone controls, stereo output.

| 1982-1997 Sunburst | | $650 | $700 |

Elite 1758
1990-1998. Acoustic/electric, non-cut, deep bowl.

| 1990-1998 | | $650 | $750 |

Elite 1768
1990-1998. Acoustic/electric, cutaway, deep bowl.

| 1990-1998 Natural | | $650 | $750 |

Elite 1868
1983-present. Acoustic/electric, cutaway, shallow bowl.

| 1983-2000 Sunburst | | $650 | $750 |

Elite Doubleneck
Six- and 12-string necks, can be ordered with a variety of custom options.

| 1989 | | $750 | $900 |

Folklore 1614
Introduced 1972. Acoustic/electric, 12-fret neck on full-size body, wide neck, on-board electronics.

| 1970s | | $500 | $700 |

Glen Campbell 12-String 1118 (K-1118)
1968-1982. Acoustic, 12 strings, shallow bowl version of Legend, gold tuners, diamond inlay.

| 1968-1982 | | $550 | $700 |

Glen Campbell Artist Balladeer 1127
1968-1990. Acoustic, shallow bowl, diamond inlay, gold tuners.

| 1968-1990 Natural | | $450 | $500 |

Hurricane 12-String K-1120
1968-1969. ES-335-style electric semi-hollowbody, double-cut, 12 strings, F-holes, 2 pickups.

| 1968-1969 | | $400 | $500 |

Josh White 1114
1967-1970, 1972-1983. Designed by and for folk and blues singer Josh White, has wide 12-fret to the body neck, dot markers, classical-style tuners.

| 1967-1970 | | $550 | $700 |
| 1972-1983 | | $450 | $600 |

Legend 1117
1972-1999. Deep bowl acoustic, 5-ply top binding, gold tuners, various colors (most natural).

| 1972-1999 | | $450 | $500 |

Legend 12-String 1866
1989-present. Acoustic/electric, cutaway, 12 strings, shallow bowl, 5-ply top binding.

| 1989-2000 Black | | $650 | $750 |

Legend 1717
1990-1998. Acoustic/electric, 5-ply top binding, various colors.

| 1990-1998 | | $650 | $750 |

Legend 1869
1994. Acoustic/electric, cutaway, super shallow bowl.

| 1994 Natural | | $650 | $750 |

Legend Cutaway 1667
1982-1996. Acoustic/electric, cutaway, deep bowl, abalone, gold tuners.

| 1982-1989 | | $650 | $750 |
| 1990-1996 | | $650 | $750 |

Legend Electric 1617
1972-1998. Acoustic/electric, deep bowl, abalone, gold tuners, various colors.

| 1972-1998 | | $500 | $600 |

Pacemaker 12-String 1115/1615
1968-1980s. Originally called the K-1115 12-string, Renamed Pacemaker in '72.

| 1968-1982 | | $650 | $750 |

Patriot Bicentennial
*1976. Limited run of 1776 guitars, Legend Custom model with drum and flag decal and "1776*1976" decal on lower bout.*

| 1976 | | $750 | $900 |

Pinnacle
1990-1992. Spruce or sycamore top, broad leaf pattern rosette, mahogany neck, piezo bridge pickup.

| 1990-1992 Sunburst | | $400 | $500 |

Pinnacle Shallow Cutaway
1990-1994. Pinnacle with shallow bowl body and single-cut.

| 1990-1994 Sunburst | | $450 | $550 |

Preacher 1281
1975-1982. Solidbody, mahogany body, double-cut, 2 pickups.

| 1975-1982 | | $500 | $600 |

Preacher 12-String 1285
1975-1983. Double-cut solidbody, 12 strings, 2 pickups.

| 1975-1983 | | $500 | $600 |

Preacher Deluxe 1282
1975-1982. Double-cut solidbody, 2 pickups with series/parallel pickup switch and mid-range control.

| 1975-1982 | | $550 | $650 |

Thunderhead 1460
1968-1972. Double-cut, 2 pickups, gold hardware, phase switch, master volume, separate tone controls, pickup balance/blend control, vibrato.

| 1968-1972 | | $450 | $550 |

Tornado 1260
1968-1973. Same as Thunderhead without phase switch, with chrome hardware.

| 1968-1973 | | $400 | $500 |

UK II 1291
1980-1982. Single-cut solidbody, 2 pickups, body made of Urelite on aluminum frame, bolt-on neck, gold hardware.

| 1980-1982 | | $650 | $800 |

Ultra GS
1985. Double-cut solidbody electrics, 1, 2, or 3 pickups.

| 1985 | | $175 | $275 |

Viper 1271
1975-1982. Single-cut, 2 single-coil pickups.

| 1975-1982 | | $400 | $500 |

Ovation Hurricane

Ovation K-1360

To get the most from this book, be sure to read "Using *The Guide*" in the introduction.

Ovation Viper III

*Pantheon Bourgeois
Vintage Dreadnought*

MODEL YEAR	FEATURES	EXC. COND. LOW	HIGH

Viper EA 68
1994-present. Thin acoustic/electric, single-cut mahogany body, spruce top over sound chamber with multiple upper bout soundholes.

1994-1999 Black		$500	$600

Viper III 1273
1975-1982. Single-cut, 3 single-coil pickups.

1975-1982		$500	$600

P. W. Crump Company
1975-present. Luthier Phil Crump builds his custom flat-top guitars in Arcata, California. He also builds mandolin-family instruments.

Pagan
Guitars made in Germany and imported into the U.S. by a guitar shop.

Palen
1998-present. Premium grade, production/custom, archtop guitars built by luthier Nelson Palen in Beloit, Kansas.

Palmer
Early 1970s-present. Budget and intermediate grade, production acoustic, acoustic/electric and classical guitars imported from Europe and Asia. They also have offered electrics.

PANaramic
1961-1963. Guitars made in Italy by the Crucianelli accordion company and imported by PANaramic accordion. They also offered amps made by Magnatone.

Pantheon Guitars
2000-present. Patrick Theimer created Pantheon which offers premium grade, production/custom, flat-tops built by seven luthiers (including Dana Bourgeois) working in an old 1840s textile mill in Lewiston, Maine.

Paramount
1930s-1942, Late 1940s. The William L. Lange Company began selling Paramount banjos, guitar banjos and mandolin banjos in the early 1920s, and added archtop guitars in '34. The guitars were made by Martin and possibly others. Lange went out of business by '42; Gretsch picked up the Paramount name and used it on acoustics and electrics for a time in the late '40s.

GB
1920s-1930s. Guitar banjo.

1920s		$1,500	$1,900

Style C
1930s. 16" acoustic archtop, maple back and sides.

1930s		$600	$700

Style L
1930s. Small body with resonator, limited production to about 36 instruments.

1930s		$2,500	$3,500

MODEL YEAR	FEATURES	EXC. COND. LOW	HIGH

Parker
1992-present. U.S.-made and imported intermediate, professional, and premium grade, production/custom, solidbody guitars featuring a thin skin of carbon and glass fibers bonded to a wooden guitar body. They also build basses. Located northwest of Boston, Parker was founded by Ken Parker and Larry Fishman (Fishman Transducers). Korg USA committed money to get the Fly Deluxe model into production. Production started July '93. Parker announced the opening of the Parker Custom Shop January 1, 2003 to produce custom special build instruments and non-core higher-end models that were no longer available as a standard product offering. In early '04, Parker was acquired by U.S. Music Corp.

Concert
1997 only. Solid sitka spruce top, only piezo system pickup, no magnetic pickups, transparent butterscotch.

1997		$1,350	$1,450

Fly
1993-1994. There are many Parker Fly models, the model simply called Fly is similar to the more common Fly Deluxe, except it does not have the Fishman piezo pickup system.

1993-1994		$1,000	$1,350

Fly Artist
1998-1999. Solid sitka spruce top, vibrato, Deluxe-style electronics, transparent blond finish.

1998-1999		$1,750	$1,850

Fly Classic
1996-1998, 2000-present. One-piece Honduras mahogany body, basswood neck, electronics same as Fly Deluxe.

1996-2002		$1,000	$1,500

Fly Deluxe
1993-present. Poplar body, basswood neck, 2 pickups, Fishman bridge transducer, '93-'96 models were offered with or without vibrato, then non-vibrato discontinued. The Deluxe normally came with a gig bag, but also offered with a hardshell case, which would add about $50 to the values listed.

1993-2003		$900	$1,400

Fly Maple Classic
2000. Classic with maple body (vs. mahogany), transparent butterscotch.

2000		$1,400	$1,500

Fly Supreme
1996-1999. One-piece flame maple body, electronics same as the Fly Deluxe, includes hard molded case.

1990s	Highly flamed butterscotch	$2,300	$2,500

NiteFly/NiteFly NFV1/NFV3/NFV5
1996-1999. Three single-coil pickup NiteFly, Fishman piezo system, bolt neck, maple body for '96-'98, ash for '99. Called the NiteFly in '96, NiteFly NFV1 ('97-'98), NiteFly NFV3 ('98), NiteFly NFV5 ('99).

1996-1999		$550	$700

MODEL YEAR FEATURES	EXC. COND. LOW	HIGH

NiteFly/NiteFly NFV2/NFV4/NFV6/SA

1996-present. Two single-coil and 1 humbucker pickup NiteFly, Fishman piezo system, bolt neck, maple body for '96-'98, ash for '99-present. Called the NiteFly in '96, NiteFly NFV2 ('97-'98), NiteFly NFV4 ('98), NiteFly NFV6 ('99), NiteFly SA ('00-present).

1996-2003	$550	$700

P Series

2000-2003. Various models include P-38 (ash body, bolt maple neck, rosewood 'board, vibrato, piezo bridge pickup and active Parker Alnico humbucker and 2 single-coils, gig bag); P-40 (as P-38, but with pickups mounted on body, no 'guard); P-44 (mahogany body, flamed maple top, piezo bridge pickup and 2 special Parker humbuckers).

2000-2003	$400	$500

Tulipwood Limited Edition

1998. Limited build of 35 guitars, standard Deluxe features with tulipwood body.

1998	$1,300	$1,500

Patrick Eggle Guitars

1991-present. Founded by Patrick Eggle and others in Birmingham, England, building solid and semi-solid body electric guitars. They also builds basses. In '95, Eggle left the company to build acoustics.

Patrick James Eggle

2001-present. Eggle cofounded the Patrick Eggle Guitar company in '91 building solidbodies. In '95, he left to do repairs and custom work. In '01 he opened a new workshop in Bedforshire, England, building professional and premium grade, production/custom, archtop and flatop guitars. He has since relocated to Hendersonville, North Carolina.

Paul Reed Smith

1985-present. Intermediate, professional and premium grade, production/custom, solid and semi-hollow body guitars made in the U.S. and imported. They also build basses. Paul Reed Smith built his first guitar in '75 as an independent study project in college and refined his design over the next 10 years building custom guitars. After building two prototypes and getting several orders from East Coast guitar dealers, Smith was able to secure the support necessary to start PRS in a factory on Virginia Avenue in Annapolis, Maryland. On '95, they moved to their current location on Kent Island in Stevensville. In 2001 PRS introduced the Korean-made SE Series.

10th Anniversary

1995. Only 200 made, offset double-cut, carved maple figured top, mahogany body, ebony 'board, mother-of-pearl inlays, abalone purfling, gold McCarty pickups, either 22-fret wide-fat or wide-thin mahogany neck, 10th Anniversary logo.

1995	$5,000	$6,000

MODEL YEAR FEATURES	EXC. COND. LOW	HIGH

513 Rosewood

Dec.2003-present. Brazilian rosewood neck, newly developed PRS pickup system with 13 sound settings, hum-single-hum pickups.

2003-2005	$3,200	$3,350

Artist/Artist I/Artist 24

1991-1994. Carved maple top, offset double-cut mahogany body, 24-fret neck, bird markers, less than 500 made. A different Custom 24 Artist package was subsequently offered in the 2000s.

1991-1994	$3,700	$4,700

Artist II/Artist 22

1993-1995. Curly maple top, mahogany body and neck, maple purfling on rosewood 'board, inlaid maple bound headstock, abalone birds, 22 frets, gold hardware, short run of less than 500 instruments.

1993-1995	$2,500	$3,500

Artist III

1996-1997. Continuation of the 22-fret neck with some changes in materials and specs, figured maple tops, short run of less than 500 instruments.

1996-1997	Black Cherry	$2,700	$3,700

Artist IV

1996. Continuation of the 22-fret neck with some upgrades in materials and specs, short run of less than 70 instruments.

1996	$3,500	$4,500

Artist Limited

1994-1995. Like the Artist II with 14-carat gold bird inlays, abalone purfling on neck, headstock and truss rod cover, Brazilian rosewood 'board, 165 made.

1994-1995	$3,500	$4,500

CE 22

1994-2000. Double-cut carved alder (1995) or mahogany (post 1995) body, bolt-on maple neck with rosewood 'board, dot inlays, 2 humbuckers, chrome hardware, translucent colors, options include vibrato and gold hardware and custom colors.

1994-1995	Alder, standard features	$1,200	$1,400
1994-1995	Alder, upgrade options	$1,300	$1,500
1996-1999	Mahogany, standard features	$1,000	$1,300
1996-1999	Mahogany, upgrade options	$1,100	$1,400
2000-2004	Upgrade options	$1,100	$1,400

CE 22 Maple Top

1994-present. CE 22 with figured maple top, upgrade options included gold hardware, custom colors or 10 top.

1994-1995	Standard features	$1,200	$1,600
1994-1995	Upgrade options	$1,300	$1,700
1996-1999	Standard features	$1,100	$1,500
1996-1999	Upgrade options	$1,200	$1,600
2000-2004	Upgrade options	$1,200	$1,600

Parker PM-10N

PRS CE 22 Maple Top

GUITARS

PRS Custom 24

*PRS Dave Navarro
signature model*

CE 24 (Classic Electric, CE)

1988-2000. Double-cut alder body, carved top, 24-fret bolt-on maple neck, 2 humbuckers, dot inlays, upgrade options included gold hardware, custom colors or 10 top.

MODEL YEAR	FEATURES	EXC. COND. LOW	HIGH
1988-1991	Standard features, rosewood board	$1,400	$2,000
1988-1991	Upgrade, rosewood board	$1,500	$2,200
1992-1995	Standard features	$1,200	$1,500
1992-1995	Upgrade options	$1,300	$1,600
1996-1999	Standard features	$1,100	$1,400
1996-1999	Upgrade options	$1,200	$1,500
2000-2004	Standard features	$1,100	$1,400
2000-2004	Upgrade options	$1,200	$1,500

CE 24 Maple Top (CE Maple Top)

1989-present. CE 24 with figured maple top, 24-fret 'board, upgrade options may include any or all the following: gold hardware, custom colors or 10 top.

MODEL YEAR	FEATURES	EXC. COND. LOW	HIGH
1988-1991	Standard features	$1,500	$2,100
1988-1991	Upgrade options	$1,600	$2,300
1992-1995	Standard features	$1,200	$1,600
1992-1995	Upgrade options	$1,300	$1,700
1996-1999	Standard features	$1,100	$1,500
1996-1999	Upgrade options	$1,200	$1,600
2000-2004	Standard features	$1,200	$1,500
2000-2004	Upgrade options	$1,300	$1,600

Custom (Custom 24/PRS Custom)

1985-present. Double-cut solidbody, curly maple top, mahogany back and neck, pearl and abalone moon inlays, 24 frets, 2 humbuckers, tremolo, options include quilted or 10 Top, bird inlays, and gold hardware.

MODEL YEAR	FEATURES	EXC. COND. LOW	HIGH
1985	Standard features	$4,000	$9,000
1985	Upgrade options	$5,000	$10,000
1986	Standard features	$3,700	$5,000
1986	Upgrade options	$4,300	$5,500
1987	Standard features	$3,200	$4,500
1987	Upgrade options	$3,500	$5,000
1988	Standard features	$2,600	$3,800
1988	Upgrade options	$2,700	$4,000
1989-1991	Standard features	$2,500	$3,100
1989-1991	Upgrade options, rosewood board	$2,600	$3,200
1992	Upgrade options	$2,200	$2,900
1993	Upgrade options	$2,200	$2,600
1994-1995	Upgrade options	$2,000	$2,400
1996-1999	Standard features	$1,500	$2,000
1996-1999	Upgrade options	$1,600	$2,100
2000-2004	Standard features	$1,650	$1,750
2000-2004	Upgrade options	$1,750	$1,850

Custom 22

1993-present. Custom 22 with flamed or quilted maple top on mahogany body, 22-fret set-neck, upgrade option is gold hardware, normally the quilt top is higher than flamed top.

MODEL YEAR	FEATURES	EXC. COND. LOW	HIGH
1993-1995	Standard features	$1,800	$2,200
1993-1995	Upgrade options	$2,000	$2,400
1996-1999	Standard features	$1,500	$2,000
1996-1999	Upgrade options	$1,600	$2,100
2000-2004	Standard features	$1,650	$1,750
2000-2004	Upgrade options	$1,750	$1,850

Custom 22 (Brazilian)

2003-2004. Limited run of 500 with Brazilian rosewood 'board, figured 10 top, pearl bird inlays.

MODEL YEAR	FEATURES	EXC. COND. LOW	HIGH
2003-2004		$2,200	$2,400

Custom 22/12

December 2003-present. 12-string version, flame or quilt maple top, hum/single/hum pickups.

MODEL YEAR	FEATURES	EXC. COND. LOW	HIGH
2003-2004		$1,950	$2,050

Custom 24 (Brazilian)

2003-2004. Limited run with Brazilian rosewood 'board, figured 10 top, pearl bird inlays.

MODEL YEAR	FEATURES	EXC. COND. LOW	HIGH
2003-2004		$2,200	$2,400

Custom 24 (Walnut)

1992. Seamless matched walnut over mahogany, 3 made.

MODEL YEAR	FEATURES	EXC. COND. LOW	HIGH
1992		$5,000	$5,500

Dave Navaro Signature

2005-present. Carved maple top, bird inlays, trem, white.

MODEL YEAR	FEATURES	EXC. COND. LOW	HIGH
2005		$1,950	$2,050

Dragon I

1992. 22 frets, PRS Dragon pickups, wide-fat neck, gold hardware, 'board inlay of a dragon made of 201 pieces of abalone, turquoise and mother-of-pearl, limited production of 50 guitars.

MODEL YEAR	FEATURES	EXC. COND. LOW	HIGH
1992		$16,000	$25,000

Dragon II

1993. 22 frets, PRS Dragon pickups, wide-fat neck, gold hardware, 'board inlay of a dragon made of 218 pieces of gold, coral, abalone, malachite, onyx and mother-of-pearl, limited production of 100 guitars.

MODEL YEAR	FEATURES	EXC. COND. LOW	HIGH
1993		$12,000	$20,000

Dragon III

1994. Carved maple top, mahogany back, 22 frets, PRS Dragon pickups, wide-fat neck, gold hardware, 'board inlay of a dragon made of 438 pieces of gold, red and green abalone, mother-of-pearl, mammoth ivory, and stone, limited production of 100 guitars.

MODEL YEAR	FEATURES	EXC. COND. LOW	HIGH
1994		$15,000	$20,000

Dragon 2000

1999-2000. Three-D dragon inlay in body versus neck inlay of previous models, limited production of 50 guitars.

MODEL YEAR	FEATURES	EXC. COND. LOW	HIGH
1999-2000		$10,000	$18,000

Dragon 2002

2002. Limited edition of 100 guitars, ultra-inlay work depicting dragon head on the guitar body.

MODEL YEAR	FEATURES	EXC. COND. LOW	HIGH
2002		$10,000	$17,000

EG II

1991-1995. Double-cut solidbody, bolt-on neck, 3 single-coils, single-single-hum, or hum-single-hum pickup options, opaque finish.

MODEL YEAR	FEATURES	EXC. COND. LOW	HIGH
1991-1995		$1,000	$1,300

EG II Maple Top

1991-1995. EG II with flamed maple top, chrome hardware.

MODEL YEAR	FEATURES	EXC. COND. LOW	HIGH
1993		$1,200	$1,500

EG 3

1990-1991. Double-cut solidbody, bolt-on 22-fret neck, 3 single-coil pickups.

MODEL YEAR	FEATURES	EXC. COND. LOW	HIGH
1990-1991	Flamed 10 top	$1,300	$1,500
1990-1991	Opaque finish	$1,000	$1,300

MODEL YEAR	FEATURES	EXC. COND. LOW	HIGH

EG 4

1990-1991. Similar to EG 3 with single-single-hum pickup configuration, opaque finish.

| 1990-1991 | | $1,000 | $1,300 |

Golden Eagle

1997-1998. Very limited production, eagle head and shoulders carved into lower bouts, varied high-end appointments.

| 1997-1998 | | $16,000 | $23,000 |

Limited Edition

1989-1991, 2000. Double-cut, semi-hollow mahogany body, figured cedar top, gold hardware, less than 300 made. In '00, single-cut, short run of 5 antique white and five black offered via Garrett Park Guitars.

| 2000 | White | $2,200 | $2,500 |

McCarty Model

1994-present. Mahogany body with figured maple top, upgrade options may include a 10 top, gold hardware, bird inlays.

1994-1995	Standard features	$1,700	$1,900
1994-1995	Upgrade options	$1,800	$2,000
1995-1999	Standard features	$1,600	$1,800
1995-1999	Upgrade options	$1,700	$1,900
2000-2003	Standard features	$1,675	$1,800
2000-2003	Upgrade options	$1,750	$1,850

McCarty Archtop (Spruce)

1998-2000. Deep mahogany body, archtop, spruce top, 22-fret set-neck.

| 1998-2000 | Chrome hardware | $1,950 | $2,250 |
| 1998-2000 | Gold hardware | $2,050 | $2,350 |

McCarty Archtop Artist

1998-2002. Highest grade figured maple top and highest appointments, gold hardware.

| 1998-2002 | | $4,700 | $5,300 |

McCarty Archtop II (Maple)

1998-2000. Deep mahogany body, archtop, figured maple top, 22-fret set-neck.

1998-2000	Flamed 10 top, chrome hardware	$2,400	$2,800
1998-2000	Flamed 10 top, gold hardware	$2,500	$3,000
1998-2000	Quilted 10 top	$2,500	$3,000

McCarty Hollowbody (Spruce)

2000-present. Similar to Hollowbody I with less appointments.

| 2000-2003 | Standard features | $1,900 | $2,200 |
| 2000-2003 | Upgrade options | $2,200 | $2,400 |

McCarty Hollowbody/Hollowbody I

1998-present. Medium deep mahogany hollowbody, spruce top, 22-fret set-neck, chrome hardware.

| 1998-1999 | Standard features | $1,950 | $2,250 |
| 1998-1999 | Upgrade options | $2,050 | $2,350 |

McCarty Hollowbody II (Maple)

1998-present. Medium deep mahogany hollowbody, figured maple top, 22-fret set-neck, chrome hardware.

| 1998-2004 | Upgrade options | $2,200 | $2,500 |

McCarty Soapbar/Soapbar Standard

1998-present. Solid mahogany body, P-90-style soapbar pickups, 22-fret set-neck, nickel-plated hardware, upgrade options may include gold hardware and bird inlays.

1998-1999	Standard features	$1,600	$1,775
1998-1999	Upgrade options	$1,700	$1,825
2000-2004	Standard features	$1,600	$1,775
2000-2004	Upgrade options	$1,700	$1,825

McCarty Soapbar (Maple)

1998-present. Soapbar with figured maple top option, nickel hardware.

| 1998-2003 | | $1,750 | $1,850 |

McCarty Standard

1994-present. McCarty Model with carved mahogany body but without maple top, nickel-plated hardware, upgrade options may include gold hardware and bird inlays.

1994-1995	Standard features	$1,600	$1,800
1994-1995	Upgrade options	$1,800	$2,000
1996-1999	Standard features	$1,500	$1,700
1996-1999	Upgrade options	$1,700	$1,900
2000-2004	Standard features	$1,500	$1,700
2000-2004	Upgrade options	$1,800	$1,900

Metal

1985-1986. Solid mahogany body with custom 2-color striped body finish and graphics, 24-fret set-neck, nickel hardware, 2 humbuckers.

| 1985-1986 | | $4,000 | $8,000 |

Modern Eagle

2004-present. Higher-end model based on Private Stock innovations, standard PRS double-cut, flying eagle markers, satin nitrocellulose finish, Brazilian rosewood neck.

| 2004 | | $4,000 | $4,500 |

Private Stock Program

April 1996-present. One-off custom instruments based around existing designs such as the McCarty Model. Values may be somewhat near production equivalents or they may be higher. The Private Stock option was reintroduced by 2003 and a '03 typical offering might retail at about $7,500, but a '03 Santana I Private Stock might retail at over $15,000, so each guitar should be evaluated on a case-by-case basis.

| 1996-2002 | Hollowbody, typical specs | $7,000 | $9,000 |
| 1996-2002 | Solidbody, typical specs | $6,000 | $9,000 |

PRS Guitar

1985-1986. Set-neck, solid mahogany body, 24-fret 'board, 2 humbuckers, chrome hardware, renamed Standard from '87-'98 then Standard 24 from '98.

| 1985 | Sunburst and optional colors | $4,000 | $12,000 |
| 1986 | Sunburst and optional colors | $4,000 | $8,000 |

Rosewood Ltd.

1996. Mahogany body with figured maple top, 1-piece rosewood neck with ultra-deluxe tree-of-life neck inlay, gold hardware.

| 1996 | | $10,000 | $12,000 |

PRS McCarty Soapbar

PRS Modern Eagle

PRS Santana SE

PRS SE EG

MODEL YEAR	FEATURES	EXC. COND. LOW	HIGH

Santana

1995-1998. Mahogany body, slightly wider lower bout than other models, figured maple top, 24-fret set-neck, symmetric Santana headstock, unique body purfling, chrome and nickel-plated hardware, limited production special order.

1995-1998		$6,000	$7,000

Santana II

1998-present. Three-way toggle replaces former dual mini-switches, special order.

1998-2004		$3,800	$4,000

Santana III

2001-present. Less ornate version of Santana II.

2001-2004		$2,200	$2,300

Santana SE

2001-present. Solid mahogany body, set mahogany neck, 2 humbuckers, thin diagonal line position markers.

2001-2004		$350	$400

SE EG

December 2003-present. 3 single-coils, SE logo on headstock, 2 knobs, set-neck.

2003-2004		$300	$350

SE Soapbar/Soapbar II

Dec.2003-present. Single-cut, soapbar pickups. Replaced by Soapbar II with classic PRS double-cut introduced in early-'05.

2003-2004	Single-cut	$300	$350
2005	Double-cut	$275	$325

Signature/PRS Signature

1987-1991. Solid mahogany body, figured maple top, set-neck, 24 frets, hand-signed signature on headstock, limited run of 1,000.

1987-1991		$5,200	$6,000

Single Cut

2000-2004. Single-cut mahogany body, maple top, 22-fret 'board, upgrade options may include either or all of the following: 10 top flamed maple, gold hardware, bird inlays.

2000-2004	Standard features	$1,800	$2,500
2000-2004	Upgrade options	$2,100	$2,700

Special

1987-1990, 1991-1993. Similar to Standard with upgrades, wide-thin neck, 2 HFS humbuckers. From '91-'93, a special option package was offered featuring a wide-thin neck and high output humbuckers.

1987-1990	Solid color finish	$2,500	$3,500
1991-1993	Special order only	$3,000	$3,500

Standard

1987-1998. Set-neck, solid mahogany body, 24-fret 'board, 2 humbuckers, chrome hardware. Originally called the PRS Guitar from '85-'86 (see that listing), renamed Standard 24 from '98.

1987-1989	Sunburst and optional colors	$2,000	$3,000
1990-1991	Last Brazilian board	$1,700	$1,900
1992-1995		$1,500	$1,800
1995-1998		$1,400	$1,700

Standard 22

1994-present. 22-fret Standard.

1994-1995		$1,400	$1,800
1995-1999		$1,300	$1,700
2000-2004		$1,300	$1,700

Standard 24

1998-present. Renamed from Standard, solid mahogany body, 24-fret set-neck.

1998-1999		$1,200	$1,600
2000-2004		$1,300	$1,700

Studio

1988-1991. Standard model variant, solid mahogany body, 24-fret set-neck, chrome and nickel hardware, single-single-hum pickups, special Studio package offered '91-'96.

1988-1991		$1,500	$1,800

Studio Maple Top

1990-1991. Mahogany solidbody, bird 'board inlays, 2 single-coil and 1 humbucking pickups, tremolo, transparent finish.

1990-1991		$1,800	$2,300

Swamp Ash Special

1996-present. Solid swamp ash body, 22-fret bolt-on maple neck, 3 pickups, upgrade options available.

1996-2004	Figured maple neck option	$1,300	$1,700

Tremonti SE (Import)

2002-2004. Single-cut, contoured mahogany body, 2 humbuckers, stop tailpiece.

2002-2004		$375	$475

Pawar

1999-present. Founded by Jay Pawar, Jeff Johnston and Kevin Johnston in Willoughby Hills, Ohio, Pawar builds professional and premium grade, production/custom, solidbody guitars that feature the Pawar Positive Tone System with over 20 single coil and humbucker tones.

Stage Turn of the Century

1999-present. Chambered swamp ash double-cut solidbody, figured maple top, bass-side scroll horn, set-neck.

2000		$1,200	$1,500

Peavey

1965-present. Headquartered in Meridan, Mississippi, Peavey builds budget, intermediate, professional, and premium grade, production/custom, acoustic and electric guitars. They also build basses, amps, PA gear, effects and drums. Hartley Peavey's first products were guitar amps. He added guitars to the mix in '78.

Axcelerator/AX

1994-1998. Offset double-cut swamp ash or poplar body, bolt-on maple neck, dot markers, AX with locking vibrato, various colors.

1994-1998		$275	$325

Cropper Classic

1995-2005. Single-cut solidbody, 1 humbucker and 1 single coil, figured maple top over thin mahogany body, transparent Onion Green.

1995-2005		$425	$500

MODEL YEAR	FEATURES	EXC. COND. LOW	HIGH

Defender

1994-1995. Double-cut, solid poplar body, 2 humbuckers and 1 single-coil pickup, locking Floyd Rose tremolo, metallic or pearl finish.

1994-1995		$150	$200

Destiny

1989-1992. Double-cut, mahogany body, maple top, neck-thru-bridge, maple neck, 3 integrated pickups, double locking tremolo.

1989-1992		$300	$400

Destiny Custom

1989-1992. Destiny with figured wood and higher-end appointments, various colors.

1989-1992		$400	$550

Detonator AX

1995-1998. Double-cut, maple neck, rosewood 'board, dot markers, hum/single/hum pickups, black.

1995-1998		$200	$275

EVH Wolfgang

1996-2004. Offset double-cut, arched top, bolt neck, stop tailpiece or Floyd Rose vibrato, quilted or flamed maple top upgrade option.

1996	Pat. Pending early production	$850	$1,100
1996-2004	Flamed maple	$850	$1,200
1996-2004	Standard top	$550	$850

EVH Wolfgang Special

1997-2004. Offset double-cut lower-end Wolfgang model, various opaque finishes, flamed top optional.

1997-2004	Flamed maple top	$600	$750
1997-2004	Standard finish	$500	$650

Falcon/Falcon Active/Falcon Custom

1987-1992. Double-cut, 3 pickups, passive or active electronics, Kahler locking vibrato.

1987-1992	Custom color	$250	$350
1987-1992	Standard color	$175	$275

Firenza

1994-1999. Offset double-cut, bolt-on neck, single-coil pickups.

1994-1999		$200	$275

Firenza AX

1994-1999. Upscale Firenza Impact with humbucking pickups.

1994-1999		$300	$375

Generation S-1/S-2

1988-1994. Single-cut, maple cap on mahogany body, bolt-on maple neck, six-on-a-side tuners, active single/hum pickups, S-2 with locking vibrato system.

1988-1994		$225	$275

Horizon/Horizon II

1983-1985. Extended pointy horns, angled lower bout, maple body, rear routing for electronics, 2 humbucking pickups. Horizon II has added blade pickup.

1983-1985		$150	$225

Hydra Doubleneck

1985-1989. Available as a custom order, 6/12-string necks each with 2 humbuckers, 3-way pickup select.

1985-1989		$400	$550

Impact 1/Impact 2

1985-1987. Offset double-cut, Impact 1 has higher-end synthetic 'board, Impact 2 with conventional rosewood 'board.

1985-1987		$200	$275

Mantis

1984-1989. Hybrid X-shaped solidbody, 1 humbucking pickup, tremolo, laminated maple neck.

1984-1989		$175	$225

Milestone/Milestone Custom

1983-1986. Import, offset double-cut.

1983-1986		$100	$200

Milestone 12-String

1985-1986. Offset double-cut, 12 strings.

1985-1986		$175	$275

Mystic

1983-1989. Double-cut, 2 pickups, stop tailpiece initially, later Power Bend vibrato, maple body and neck.

1983-1989		$150	$220

Nitro I/II/III

1986-1989. Offset double-cut, banana-style headstock, 1 humbucker (I), 2 humbuckers (II), or single/single/hum pickups (III).

1986-1989	Nitro I	$100	$175
1986-1989	Nitro II	$125	$200
1986-1989	Nitro III	$175	$250

Nitro I Active

1988-1990. Active electronics.

1988-1990		$225	$300

Odyssey

1990-1994. Single-cut, figured carved maple top on mahogany body, humbuckers.

1990-1994		$400	$550

Odyssey 25th Anniversary

1990. Single-cut body, limited production.

1990		$550	$700

Patriot

1983-1987. Double-cut, single bridge humbucker.

1983-1987		$125	$175

Patriot Plus

1983-1987. Double-cut, 2 humbucker pickups, bi-laminated maple neck.

1983-1987		$150	$200

Patriot Tremolo

1986-1990. Double-cut, single bridge humbucker, tremolo, replaced the standard Patriot.

1986-1990		$125	$200

Predator/Predator AX/Predator DX

1985-1988, 1990-2000. Double-cut poplar body, 2 pickups until '87, 3 after, vibrato.

1985-1988		$150	$200
1990-2000		$125	$200

Raptor I/Plus/Plus TK/Plus EXP

1997-present. Offset double-cut solidbody, 3 single-coils early, hum/single/single later.

1997-2002		$120	$130

Pawar Stage

Peavey Predator Plus

Peavey Razer

1988 Peavey Vandenberg

MODEL YEAR	FEATURES	EXC. COND. LOW	HIGH
Razer			
1983-1989. Double-cut with arrowhead point for lower bout, 2 pickups, 1 volume and 2 tone controls, stop tailpiece or vibrato.			
1983-1989		$275	$400
Reactor			
1993-1999. Classic single-cut style, 2 single-coils.			
1993-1999		$275	$325
T-15			
1981-1983. Offset double-cut, bolt-on neck, dual ferrite blade single-coil pickups, natural.			
1981-1983		$125	$200
T-15 Amp-In-Case			
1981-1983. Amplifier built into guitar case and T-15 guitar.			
1981-1983		$225	$300
T-25			
1979-1985. Synthetic polymer body, 2 pickups, cream 'guard, sunburst finish.			
1979-1985		$150	$225
T-25 Special			
1979-1985. Same as T-25, but with super high output pickups, phenolic 'board, black/white/black 'guard, ebony black finish.			
1979-1985		$150	$225
T-26			
1982-1986. Same as T-25, but with 3 single-coil pickups and 5-way switch.			
1982-1986		$175	$250
T-27			
1981-1983. Offset double-cut, bolt-on neck, dual ferrite blade single-coil pickups.			
1981-1983		$175	$250
T-30			
1982-1985. Short-scale, 3 single-coil pickups, 5-way select, by '83 amp-in-case available.			
1982-1985		$175	$250
T-60			
1978-1988. Contoured offset double-cut, ash body, six-in-line tuners, 2 humbuckers, thru-body strings, by '87 maple bodies, various finishes.			
1978-1988	Black	$250	$300
1978-1988	Natural	$200	$250
1978-1988	Red, sunburst, white	$250	$325
T-1000 LT			
1992-1994. Double-cut, 2 single-coils and humbucker with coil-tap.			
1992-1994		$200	$250
Tracer/Tracer II			
1987-1994. Offset scooped double-cut with extended pointy horns, poplar body, 1 pickup, Floyd Rose.			
1987-1994		$125	$200
Tracer Custom			
1989-1990. Tracer with 2 single/hum pickups and extras.			
1989-1990		$125	$200
Vandenberg Signature			
1988-1992. Double-cut, reverse headstock, bolt-on neck, locking vibrato, various colors.			
1988-1992		$425	$575
Vandenberg Quilt Top			
1989-1992. Vandenberg Custom with quilted maple top, 2 humbuckers, glued-in neck, quilted maple top, mahogany body and neck.			
1989-1992		$800	$1,200
Vortex I/Vortex II			
1986. Streamlined Mantis with 2 pickups, 3-way, Kahler locking vibrato. Vortex II has Randy Rhoads Sharkfin V.			
1986		$250	$325

Pedro de Miguel

1991-present. Luthiers Pedro Pérez and Miguel Rodriguez build their professional and premium grade, custom/production, classical guitars in Madrid, Spain. They also offer factory-made instruments built to their specifications.

Pegasus Guitars and Ukuleles

1977-present. Premium grade, custom steel-string guitars built by luthier Bob Gleason in Kurtistown, Hawaii, who also builds ukulele family instruments.

Penco

Ca. 1974-1978. Generally high quality Japanese-made copies of American acoustic, electric and bass guitars. Probably (though not certainly) imported into Philadelphia during the copy era. Includes dreadnoughts with laminated woods, bolt-neck solidbody electric guitars and basses, mandolins and banjos.

MODEL YEAR	FEATURES	EXC. COND. LOW	HIGH
Acoustic Flat-Top			
1974-1978. Various models.			
1974-1978		$150	$225
Electric Solidbody			
1974-1978. Various copies.			
1974-1978		$200	$275

Pensa (Pensa-Suhr)

1982-present. Premium grade, production/custom, solidbody guitars built in the U.S. They also build basses. Rudy Pensa, of Rudy's Music Stop, New York City, started building Pensa guitars in '82. In '85 he teamed up with John Suhr to build Pensa-Suhr instruments. Name changed back to Pensa in '96.

MODEL YEAR	FEATURES	EXC. COND. LOW	HIGH
Classic			
1992-Ca. 1998. Offest double-cut, 3 single-coils, gold hardware.			
1992-1998		$1,500	$1,700
MK 1 (Mark Knopfler)			
1985-present. Offset double-cut solidbody, carved flamed maple bound top, 2 single-coils and 1 humbucker, gold hardware, dot markers, bolt-on neck.			
1985-1992		$1,600	$1,800

MODEL		EXC. COND.	
YEAR	FEATURES	LOW	HIGH

Suhr Custom

1985-1989. Two-piece maple body, bolt-on maple neck with rosewood 'board, custom order basis with a variety of woods and options available.

| 1985-1989 | Flamed maple top | $1,600 | $1,800 |

Suhr Standard

1985-1991. Double-cut, single/single/hum pickup configuration, opaque solid finish normally, dot markers.

| 1985-1991 | | $1,400 | $1,600 |

Perlman Guitars

1976-present. Luthier Alan Pearlman builds his premium grade, custom, steel-string and classical guitars in San Francisco, California.

Perry Guitars

1982-present. Premium grade, production/custom, classical guitars built by luthier Daryl Perry in Winnipeg, Manitoba. He also builds lutes.

Petillo Masterpiece Guitars

1965-present. Luthiers Phillip J. and David Petillo build their intermediate, professional and premium grade, custom, steel-string, nylon-string, 12-string, resonator, archtop, and Hawaiian guitars in Ocean, New Jersey.

Petros Guitars

1992-present. Premium grade, production/custom, flat-top, 12-string, and nylon-string guitars built by luthier Bruce Petros in Kaukauna, Wisconsin.

Apple Creek

1992-1999.

| 1992-1999 | | $2,500 | $3,300 |

Phantom Guitar Works

1992-present. Intermediate grade, production/custom, classic Phantom, and Teardrop shaped solid and hollowbody guitars assembled in Clatskanie, Oregon. They also offer basses and the MandoGuitar. Phantom was established by Jack Charles, former lead guitarist of the band Quarterflash. Some earlier guitars were built overseas.

Pieper

2005-present. Premium grade, custom, solidbody guitars built by luthier Robert Pieper in New Haven, Connecticut. He also builds basses.

Pimentel and Sons

1951-present. Luthiers Lorenzo Pimentel and sons build their professional, premium and presentation grade, flat-top, jazz, cutaway electric, and classical guitars in Albuquerque, New Mexico.

Flamenco

1960s. Spruce top, cyprus back and sides.

| 1960s | | $1,000 | $1,300 |

W1 Classical

1970s. Cedar top, walnut back and sides.

| 1970s | | $900 | $950 |

MODEL		EXC. COND.	
YEAR	FEATURES	LOW	HIGH

Player

1984-1985. Player guitars featured interchangable pickup modules that mounted through the back of the guitar. They offered a double-cut solidbody with various options and the pickup modules were sold separately. The company was located in Scarsdale, New York.

MDS-1B

1984-1985. Offset double-cut, bolt neck, 1, 2 or 3 pickups, Player headstock logo.

1984-1985	1 pickup	$200	$250
1984-1985	2 pickups	$400	$450
1984-1985	3 pickups	$550	$650

Pleasant

Late 1940s-ca.1966. Solidbody electric guitars, obviously others, Japanese manufacturer, probably not imported into the U.S.

Electric Solidbodies

1940s-1966. Various models.

| 1950s | | $125 | $200 |

Prairie State

Late 1920s-ca. 1940. Larson Brothers brand, basically a derivative of Maurer & Company, but advertised as "a new method of guitar construction." The Prairie State equivalent models were slightly more expensive than the Maurer models (on average 5% to 10% more). Prairie State guitars were also promoted "reinforced with steel" and "the tube or support near the top withstands the strain of the strings, leaving the top or sound-board free and resilient." One or more steel tubes are noticable running from the neck block to the tail block, when looking through the round soundhole. These guitars were advertised as being suitable for playing steel (high nut and steel strings). Steel strings were the rage in the 1920s (re: Martin finally converting all guitar models to steel strings by 1928).

1932 Prairie State Catalog Models - description and prices:

Style 225 Concert	$65.00
Style 425 Auditorium	$70.00
Style 426 Style 425 Steel	$70.00
Style 427 Reinforced Neck	$75.00
Style 428 Style 427 Steel	$75.00
Style 235 Concert with trim	$80.00
Style 335 Grand Concert + trim	$83.00
Style 435 Auditorium with trim	$85.00
Style 340 Grand Concert fancy	$90.00
Style 350 Grand Concert fancy	$97.00
Style 440 Auditorium fancy trim	$93.00
Style 450 Auditorium fancy trim	$100.00

Small Higher-End Flat-Top

Spruce top, 13 5/8" scale, Brazilian rosewood back and sides, high-end pearl appointments, slotted headstock, natural.

| 1920s | | $5,000 | $7,000 |

Phantom Deluxe

Petros Prairie FS

1959 Premier Custom

Rahbek Classic

MODEL		EXC. COND.	
YEAR	FEATURES	LOW	HIGH

Mid-Size Mid to High End Flat-Top

15" spruce X-braced top, Brazilian rosewood back and sides, solid headstock, mid- to high-end appointments.

1920s		$7,000	$10,000

Premier

Ca.1938-ca.1975, 1990s-present. Budget and intermediate grade, production, import guitars. They also offer basses.

Brands originally offered by Premier include Premier, Multivox, Marvel, Belltone and Strad-O-Lin. Produced by Peter Sorkin Music Company in Manhattan, New York City, New York, who began in Philadelphia, relocating to NYC in '35. First radio-sized amplifiers and stick-on pickups for acoustic archtops were introduced by '38. After World War II, they set up the Multivox subsidiary to manufacture amplifiers ca. '46. First flat-top with pickup appeared in '46.

Most acoustic instruments made by United Guitar Corporation in Jersey City, New Jersey. Ca. '57 Multivox acquires Strad-O-Lin. Ca.'64-'65 their Custom line guitars are assembled with probably Italian bodies and hardware, Japanese electronics, possibly Egmond necks from Holland. By ca. '74-'75, there were a few Japanese-made guitars, then Premier brand goes into hiatus.

The rights to the Premier brand are held by Entertainment Music Marketing Corporation in New York. The Premier brand reappears on some Asian-made solidbody guitars and basses beginning in the '90s.

Bantam Custom

1950s-1960s. Model below Special, single-cut archtop, dot markers, early models with white potted pickups, then metal-covered pickups, and finally Japanese-made pickups (least valued).

1950-1960s		$550	$700

Bantam Deluxe

1950s-1960s. Single-cut archtop, fully bound, sparkle knobs, early models with white potted pickups, then metal-covered pickups, and finally Japanese-made pickups (least valued), block markers, single or double pickups (deduct $100 for single pickup instrument).

1950-1960s	Blond	$1,000	$1,300
1950-1960s	Sunburst	$900	$1,100

Bantam Special

1950s-1960s. Model below Deluxe, single-cut archtop, dot markers, early models with white potted pickups, then metal-covered pickups, and finally Japanese-made pickups (least valued), single or double pickup models offered (deduct $100 for single pickup instrument).

1950-1960s		$650	$800

Custom Solidbody

1958-1970. Notable solidbody bass scroll cutaway, various models with various components used, finally import components only.

1958-1970	1 pickup	$400	$500
1958-1970	2 pickups	$500	$600
1958-1970	3 pickups	$600	$700

MODEL		EXC. COND.	
YEAR	FEATURES	LOW	HIGH

Deluxe Archtop

1950s-1960s. Full body 17 1/4" archtop, square block markers, single-cut, early models with white potted pickups, later '60s models with metal pickups.

1950-1960s	Blond	$1,200	$1,600
1950-1960s	Sunburst	$1,200	$1,400

Semi-Pro 16" Archtop

1950s-early-1960s. Thinline electric 16" archtop with 2 1/4" deep body, acoustic or electric.

1950-1960s	Acoustic	$700	$750
1950-1960s	Electric	$800	$850

Semi-Pro Bantam Series

1960s. Thinline electric archtop with 2 3/4" deep body, offered in cutaway and non-cut models.

1960s		$300	$350

Special Archtop

1950s-1960s. Full body 17 1/4" archtop, less fancy than Deluxe, single-cut, early models with white potted pickups, '60s models with metal pickups.

1950-1960s		$850	$1,000

Studio Six Archtop

1950s-early-1960s. 16" wide archtop, single pickup, early pickups white potted, changed later to metal top.

1950-1960s		$550	$600

Prestige

Intermediate, professional, and premium grade, production/custom, acoustic, solidbody and hollowbody guitars from Vancouver, British Columbia. They also offer basses.

Queen Shoals Stringed Instruments

1972-present. Luthier Larry Cadle builds his production/custom, flat-top, 12-string, and nylon-string guitars in Clendenin, West Virginia.

Queguiner, Alain

1982-present. Custom flat-tops, 12 strings, and nylon strings built by luthier Alain Quiguiner in Paris, France.

R.C. Allen

1951-present. Luthier R. C. "Dick" Allen builds professional and premium grade, custom hollowbody and semi-hollowbody guitars in El Monte, California. He has also built solidbody guitars.

Rahan

1999-present. Professional grade, production/custom, solidbody guitars built by luthiers Mike Curd and Rick Cantu in Houston, Texas.

Rahbek Guitars

2000-present. Professional and premium grade, production/custom, solidbody electrics built by luthier Peter Rahbek in Copenhagen, Denmark.

MODEL YEAR	FEATURES	EXC. COND. LOW	HIGH

Raimundo

2000s. Classical guitars made in Spain.

Classical 130

2000s. Solid cedar top, solid rosewood sides.

2000s		$500	$600

RainSong

1991-present. Professional grade, production, all-graphite and graphite and wood acoustic guitars built in Woodinville, Washington. The guitars were developed after years of research by luthier engineer John Decker with help from luthier Lorenzo Pimentel, engineer Chris Halford, and sailboard builder George Clayton. The company was started in Maui, but has since moved to Woodinville.

Ramirez

1882-present. Founded by José Ramirez, the company is now in its fourth generation of family ownership in Madrid, Spain.

1A

1970s. Classical.

1970s		$4,000	$5,000

De Camera

1980s. Classical, cedar top, Brazilian rosewood back and sides.

1980s		$4,000	$5,000

Flamenco

European spruce top, cyprus back and sides.

1960-1969		$3,500	$4,500

R4 Classical

1995-1997. All solid wood, Western red cedar top, rosewood back and sides.

1995-1997		$1,500	$1,700

Randy Reynolds Guitars

1996-present. Luthier Randy Reynolds builds his premium grade, production/custom classical and flamenco guitars in Colorado Springs, Colorado.

Randy Wood Guitars

1968-present. Premium grade, custom/production, archtop, flat-top, and resonator guitars built by luthier Randy Woods in Bloomingdale, Georgia. He also builds mandolins and banjos.

Rarebird Guitars

1978-present. Luthier Bruce Clay builds his professional and premium grade, production/custom, acoustic, electric solidbody and hollowbody guitars and mini guitars, originally in Arvada, Colorado, but since '05 in Paonia, Colorado. He also builds basses.

Rat Fink

2002-present. Intermediate grade, production, guitars from Lace Music Products, the makers of the Lace Sensor pickup, featuring the artwork of Ed "Big Daddy" Roth. They also offer basses and amps.

MODEL YEAR	FEATURES	EXC. COND. LOW	HIGH

Recording King

1936-1941. Brand name used by Montgomery Ward for instruments made by various American manufacturers, including Kay, Gibson and Gretsch. Generally mid-grade instruments. M Series are Gibson-made archtops.

Carson Robison/Model K

1936-1939. Flat-top, 14 3/4", mahogany back and sides, renamed Model K in early-'38.

1936-1939		$900	$1,100

M-2

1936-1941. Gibson-made archtop with carved top and F-holes, maple back and sides.

1936-1941		$550	$700

M-3

1936-1941. Gibson-made archtop, F-holes, maple back and sides, carved top.

1936-1941		$850	$1,100

M-5

1936-1941. Gibson-made archtop with F-holes, maple back and sides, trapeze tailpiece, checkered top binding.

1936-1938	16" body	$1,100	$1,400
1939-1941	17" body	$1,400	$1,600

M-6

1938-1939. M-5 with upgraded gold hardware.

1938-1939		$1,500	$1,800

Ray Whitley

1939-1940. High-quality model made by Gibson, round shoulder flat-top, mahogany or Brazilian rosewood back and sides, 5-piece maple neck, Ray Whitley stencil script peghead logo, pearl crown inlay on peghead, fancy inlaid markers.

1939-1940	Rosewood	$17,000	$19,000

Regal

Ca. 1884-1966, 1987-present. Intermediate and professional grade, production, acoustic and wood and metal body resonator guitars. They also build basses.

Originally a mass manufacturer founded in Indianapolis, Indiana, the Regal brand was first used by Emil Wulschner & Son. In 1901 new owners changed the company name to The Regal Manufacturing Company. The company was moved to Chicago in '08 and renamed the Regal Musical Instrument Company. Regal made brands for distributors and mass merchandisers as well as marketing its own Regal brand. Regal purchased the Lyon & Healy factory in '28. Regal was licensed to co-manufacture Dobros in '32 and became the sole manufacturer of them in '37 (see Dobro for those instruments). Most Regal instruments were beginner-grade; however, some very fancy archtops were made during the '30s. The company was purchased by Harmony in '54 and absorbed. From '59 to '66, Harmony made acoustics under the Regal name for Fender. In '87 the Regal name was revived on a line of resonator instruments by Saga.

Rainsong WS1000

Rat Fink RF3

Renaissance Model T

Reverend Wolfman

MODEL YEAR / FEATURES	EXC. COND. LOW	HIGH

Concert Folk H6382
1960s. Regal by Harmony, solid spruce top, mahogany back and sides, dot markers, natural.

| 1960s | $250 | $325 |

Deluxe Dreadnought H6600
1960s. Regal by Harmony, solid spruce top, mahogany back and sides, bound top and back, rosewood 'board, dot markers, natural.

| 1960s | $250 | $375 |

Dreadnought 12-String H1269
1960s. Regal by Harmony, solid spruce top, 12-string version of Deluxe, natural.

| 1960s | $250 | $375 |

Model 27
1933-1942. Birch wood body, mahogany or maple, 2-tone walnut finish, single-bound top, round or square neck.

| 1933-1942 | $1,000 | $1,500 |

Model 45
1933-1937. Spruce top and mahogany back and sides, bound body, square neck.

| 1933-1937 | $1,500 | $2,500 |

Model 55 Standard
1933-1934. Regal's version of Dobro Model 55 which was discontinued in '33.

| 1933-1934 | $1,200 | $1,500 |

Model 75
1939-1940. Metal body, square neck.

| 1939-1940 | $2,000 | $3,000 |

RD45B
1990s-2000s. Standard style Dobro model with wood body, metal resonator, dual screen holes, gloss black finish.

| 1990-2000s | $225 | $250 |

Spirit Of '76
1976. Red-white-blue, flat-top.

| 1976 | $250 | $400 |

Reliance
1920s. Instruments built by the Oscar Schmidt Co. and possibly others. Most likely a brand made for a distributor.

Renaissance
1978-1980. Plexiglass solidbody electric guitars and basses. Founded in Malvern, Pennsylvania, by John Marshall (designer), Phil Goldberg and Daniel Lamb. Original partners gradually leave and John Dragonetti takes over by late-'79. The line is redesigned with passive electronics on guitars, exotic shapes, but when deal with Sunn amplifiers falls through, company closes. Brandname currently used on a line of guitars and basses made by Rick Turner in Santa Cruz, California.

Fewer than 300 of first series made, plus a few prototypes and several wooden versions; six or so prototypes of second series made. SN=M(M)YYXXXX: month, year, consecutive number.

Electric Plexiglas Solidbody
1978-1980. Models include the SPG ('78-'79, DiMarzio pickups, active electronics), T-200G ('80, Bich-style with 2 passive DiMarzio pickups), and the S-200G ('80, double-cut, 2 DiMarzio pickups, passive electronics).

| 1978-1980 | $500 | $700 |

Renaissance Guitars
1994-present. Professional grade, custom, semi-acoustic flat-top, nylon-string and solidbody guitars built by luthier Rick Turner in Santa Cruz, California. He also builds basses and ukuleles.

Model 1/Model One Lindsey Buckingham
1990s-present. Originally built for Buckingham in '79, with 1 humbucker or will added piezo, soft cutaway old-style body.

| 1996-2003 | $2,500 | $3,200 |

Model T
1996-present. Mahogany, fade-away single-cut, Kay Kraft-style body, bolt-on neck, horseshoe pickup.

| 1996-2003 | $850 | $1,000 |

RS-6
1997-present. Acoustic/electric, solid cedar top, semi-hollow rosewood body, no soundhole, bolt maple neck.

| 1997-2003 | $1,150 | $1,300 |

Reuter Guitars
1984-present. Professional and premium grade, custom, flat-top, 12-string, resonator, and Hawaiian guitars built by luthier John Reuter, the Director of Training at the Roberto-Venn School of Luthiery, in Tempe, Arizona.

Reverend
1996-present. Intermediate grade, production, guitars built in Warren, Michigan, by luthier Joe Naylor, who also founded Naylor Amps. They also build basses and amps. Reverend offered effects for 2000-'04.

Semi-Hollow Electric
1997-present. Offset double-cut semi-hollowbody, bolt maple neck, various pickup options. Models include Avenger, Commando, Hitman, Rocco, Slingshot and Spy. By 2004 the Workhorse Series included the Avenger TL, Commando, and Slingshot Custom, which were all factory-direct instruments.

| 1997-1999 | Various models and options | $550 | $675 |
| 2000s | Workhorse Series | $400 | $475 |

Rex
1930s-1940s. Generally beginner-grade guitars made by Harmony and Kay and sold through Fred Gretsch distributors.

Acoustic Flat-Top
1940s. Various models.

| 1940s | $275 | $350 |

MODEL		EXC. COND.	
YEAR	FEATURES	LOW	HIGH

Ribbecke Guitars

1972-present. Premium and presentation grade, custom thinline, flat-top, and archtop guitars built by luthier Tom Ribbecke in Healdsburg, California.

Rich and Taylor

1993-1996. Custom acoustic and electric guitars and banjos from luthiers Greg Rich and Mark Taylor (Crafters of Tennessee).

Richard Schneider

1960s-1997. Luthier Richard Schneider built his acoustic guitars in Washington state. Over the years, he collaborated with Dr. Michael A. Kasha on many guitar designs and innovations. Originally from Michigan, he also was involved in designing guitars for Gretsch and Gibson. He died in early '97.

Richter Mfg.

1930s. One of many Chicago makers of the era.
Small 13"
1930s. Typical small 13" lower bout body, slotted headstock, decalmania art over black finish, single dot markers.

1930s		$375	$450

Rick Turner

1979-1981, 1990-present. Rick Turner has a long career as a luthier, electronics designer and innovator. He also makes the Renaissance line of guitars in his shop in Santa Cruz, California.

Rickenbacker

1931-present. Professional and premium grade, production/custom, acoustic and electric guitars built in California. They also build basses. Founded in Los Angeles as Ro-Pat-In by ex-National executives George Beauchamp, Paul Barth and National's resonator cone supplier Adolph Rickenbacher. Rickenbacher was born in Basel, Switzerland in 1886, emigrated to the U.S. and moved to Los Angeles in 1918, opening a tool and die business in '20.

In the mid-'20s, Rickenbacher began providing resonator cones and other metal parts to George Beauchamp and Louis Dopyera of National String Instrument Corporation and became a shareholder in National. Beauchamp, Barth and Harry Watson came up with wooden "frying pan" electric Hawaiian lap steel for National in '31; National was not interested, so Beauchamp and Barth joined with Rickenbacher as Ro-Pat-In (probably for ElectRO-PATent-INstruments) to produce Electro guitars. Cast aluminum frying pans were introduced in '32. Some Spanish guitars (flat-top, F-holes) with Electro pickups were produced beginning in '32.

Ro-Pat-In changes their name to Electro String Instrument Corporation in '34, and brand becomes Rickenbacher Electro, soon changed to Rickenbacker, with a "k." Beauchamp retires in '40. There

was a production hiatus during World War II. In '53, Electro was purchased by Francis Cary Hall (born 1908), owner of Radio and Television Equipment Company (Radio-Tel) in Santa Ana, California (founded in '20s as Hall's Radio Service, which began distributing Fender instruments in '46). The factory was relocated to Santa Ana in '62 and the sales/distribution company's name is changed from Radio-Tel to Rickenbacker Inc. in '65.

1950s serial numbers have from 4 to 7 letters and numbers, with the number following the letter indicating the '50s year (e.g., NNL8NN would be from '58). From '61 to '86 serial numbers indicate month and year of production with initial letter A-Z for the year A=1961, Z=1986) followed by letter for the month A-M (A=January) plus numbers as before followed by a number 0-9 for the year (0=1987; 9=1996). Rickenbacker used the term Combo for solidbody models. To avoid confusion, we have listed all instruments by model number. For example, the Combo 400 is listed as Model 400/Combo 400.
Electro ES-16
1964-1971. Double-cut, set neck, solidbody, 3/4 size, 1 pickup. The Electro line was manufactured by Rickenbacker and distributed by Radio-Tel. The Electro logo appears on the headstock.

1964-1971		$800	$900

Electro ES-17
1964-1975. Cutaway, set neck, solidbody, 1 pickup.

1964-1969		$900	$1,000
1970-1975		$600	$800

Electro Spanish (Model B Spanish)
1935-1943. Small guitar with a lap steel appearance played Spanish-style, hollow bakelite body augmented with 5 chrome plates, called the Model B ca. '40.

1935-1936		$3,500	$4,500
1938-1939		$3,200	$4,200
1940-1943	Model B	$3,000	$4,000

Model 230 Hamburg
1983-1991. Offset double-cut, 2 pickups, dot inlay, rosewood 'board, chrome-plated hardware.

1983-1991		$675	$725

Model 250 El Dorado
1983. Deluxe version of Hamburg, gold hardware, white binding.

1983		$700	$800

Model 310
1958-1970, 1981-1985. Two-pickup version of Model 320.

1966	16 made	$2,000	$2,400

Model 315
1958-1974. Two-pickup version of Model 325.

1966	6 made	$2,300	$2,800

Model 320
1958-1992. Short-scale hollowbody, 3 pickups, f-holes optional in '61 and standard in '64 and optional again in '79.

1966	4 made	$7,000	$15,000
1968	1 made	$7,000	$10,000

Rick Turner Model One

Ribbecke 7-string

Rickenbacker 325

Rickenbacker 331 Light Show

MODEL YEAR	FEATURES	EXC. COND. LOW	HIGH

Model 325

1958-1975, 1985-1992. This was a low production model, with some years having no production. In the mid-'60s, the 325 was unofficially known as the John Lennon Model due to his guitar's high exposure on the Ed Sullivan Show and in the Saturday Evening Post.

MODEL YEAR	FEATURES	LOW	HIGH
1958-1960	29 made	$7,000	$15,000
1964-1965	Fireglo (24 Fireglo, 3 black)	$7,000	$12,000
1966	Fireglo or black, 40 made	$7,000	$10,000
1966	Mapleglo, 6 made	$7,000	$12,000
1968	10 made	$5,000	$8,000
1970-1979		$1,400	$1,800
1980-1992		$1,100	$1,700

Model 325 JL/325V59 John Lennon

1989-1993. John Lennon Limited Edition, 3 vintage Ric pickups, vintage vibrato, maple body; 3/4-size rosewood neck, a 12-string and a full-scale version are also available.

1989-1990		$1,800	$2,400

Model 325C58

2002. Designed as near-copy of the '58-made model that John Lennon saw in Germany.

2002		$1,450	$1,600

Model 330

1958-present. Thinline hollowbody, 2 pickups, slash soundhole, natural or sunburst.

1958-1959	56 made	$2,100	$3,000
1960-1965	190 made	$2,100	$2,700
1966	264 made	$2,000	$2,500
1984-1989		$825	$975
1990-1999		$825	$975
2000-2003		$825	$975

Model 330/12

1965-present. Thinline, 2 pickups, 12-string version of Model 300.

1964-1965		$2,100	$4,000
1966	392 made	$2,000	$3,000
1968-1969	14 made	$1,500	$2,200
1970s		$1,400	$2,000
1980s		$1,000	$1,300
1990s		$900	$1,050

Model 330S/12

1964 (1 made)-1965 (2 made).

1964-1965	3 made	$2,500	$4,000

Model 331 Light Show

1970-1975. Model 330 with translucent top with lights in body that lit up when played, needed external transformer. The first offering's design, noted as Type 1, had heat problems and a fully original one is difficult to find. The 2nd offering's design, noted as Type 2, was a more stable design and is more highly valued in the market.

1970-1971	Type 1 1st edition	$7,000	$8,000
1972-1975	Type 2 2nd edition	$8,500	$10,000

Model 335 Capri

1958-1960. Thinline, 2 pickups, vibrato. The Capri Model name is technically reserved for the '58 to mid-'60s vintage, these models had a 2" depth. Ca. mid-'60

MODEL YEAR	FEATURES	EXC. COND. LOW	HIGH

the body depth was reduced to 1 1/2". Rickenbacker dropped the Capri name in '60.

1958-1960	Autumnglo, 37 made	$3,500	$4,500
1958-1960	Fireglo, 13 made	$3,500	$4,500
1958-1960	Mapleglo, 28 made	$3,500	$4,500

Model 335

1961-1978. Thinline, 2 pickups, vibrato, Fireglo, called the 330VB from '85-'97.

1961-1965	90 made	$3,000	$4,000
1966	442 made	$2,100	$3,500

Model 336/12

1966-1974. Like 300-12, but with 6-12 converter comb.

1966	7 made	$3,000	$4,000

Model 340

1958-present. Thin semi-hollowbody, thru-body maple neck, 2 single-coil pickups, sharp point horns, very limited production '58-'65, with first notable volume of 45 units starting in '66.

1958	1 made	$3,100	$5,000
1962	1 made	$3,100	$5,000
1963	1 made	$3,100	$5,000
1964	2 made	$3,100	$5,000
1965	4 made	$3,100	$5,000
1966	43 made, 3 pickups	$2,600	$4,000
2000		$650	$800

Model 345 Capri

1958-1960. Thinline 330-345 series, version with 3 pickups and vibrato tailpiece. The Capri Model name is technically reserved for the '58 to mid-'60s vintage, these models had a 2" depth. Body depth was reduced to 1 1/2" ca. mid-'60 and Capri name was dropped.

1958-1960	97 made	$3,600	$5,500

Model 345

1961-1974. Thinline 330-345 series, version with 3 pickups and vibrato tailpiece, in the mid-'60s Jetglo Black was a very unusual color, caution advised.

1961-1962	23 made	$2,500	$4,000
1964-1966		$2,500	$4,000
1974	Dual humbuckers, slant frets	$1,000	$1,300

Model 350 Liverpool

1983-1997. Thinline, 3 pickups, vibrato, no soundhole.

1983-1997		$850	$1,000

Model 350V63 Liverpool

1994-present. Like 355 JL, but without signature.

1994-2003		$1,200	$1,400

Model 355 JL

1989-1993. John Lennon model, signature and drawing on 'guard.

1989-1993		$2,200	$2,600

Model 355/12 JL

1989-1993. 12-string 355 JL, limited production.

1989-1993		$2,600	$3,000

Model 360

1958-present. Deluxe thinline, 2 pickups, slash soundhole.

1958-1959	24 in '58, 96 in '59	$3,100	$3,300
1960-1963	60 in '60, 26 in '61	$3,000	$3,200

MODEL YEAR	FEATURES	EXC. COND. LOW	HIGH
1964	NS new style, 7 made	$2,900	$3,100
1965-1969		$2,800	$3,000
1970-1972		$1,900	$2,300
1973-1977		$1,500	$1,900
1978-1979		$1,400	$1,700
1980-1989		$1,100	$1,300
1990-1994		$1,050	$1,300
1995-1999		$950	$1,050
2000s		$900	$1,000

Model 360 WB

1991-1998. Two pickups, double bound body, vibrato optional.

1991-1998	Non-vibrato	$1,100	$1,300
1991-1998	Vibrato option	$1,100	$1,300

Model 360/12

1964-present. Deluxe thinline, 2 pickups, 12-string version of Model 360, Rick-O-Sound stereo.

1964	7 old style, 29 new style	$4,000	$15,000
1965	29 old style, 480 new style	$4,000	$15,000
1966	1164 made	$2,800	$3,800
1967-1969		$2,700	$3,500
1967-1969	Custom or rare color	$3,200	$4,000
1970-1979		$1,300	$1,800
1980-1999		$1,100	$1,300
2000-2003		$1,000	$1,200

Model 360/12V64

1985-2001. Deluxe thinline with '64 features, 2 pickups, 12 strings, slanted plate tailpiece.

1985-2001		$1,700	$2,100

Model 365

1958-1974. Deluxe thinline, 2 pickups, vibrato, called Model 360 VB from '84-'97.

1958-1959	Late	$2,400	$3,300
1960-1963		$2,100	$3,000
1966	Old style	$2,000	$3,000
1970-1974		$2,100	$2,500

Model 365 F

1960 and 1962. Thin full-body (F designation) with recorded production only in '60.

1960	10 made	$4,100	$5,000
1962	2 made	$4,100	$5,000

Model 366/12 Convertible

1966-1974. Two pickups, 12 strings, comb-like device that converts it to a 6-string, production only noted in '68, perhaps available on custom order basis.

1966	7 made	$3,500	$4,500
1968	125 made	$3,500	$4,500

Model 370

1958-1990, 1994-present. Deluxe thinline, 3 pickups. Could be considered to be a dealer special order item from '58-'67 with limited production ('58=0, '59=4, '60=0, '61=3, '62-'67=0), then started more regularly in '68).

1959	4 made	$3,500	$5,000
1961	3 made	$3,000	$4,000
1966	6 made, new style	$3,000	$4,000

MODEL YEAR	FEATURES	EXC. COND. LOW	HIGH
1968-1969	Larger scale production	$2,600	$3,500
1970s		$1,300	$2,000
1980-2000s		$1,300	$1,500

Model 370/12

1965-1990, 1994-present. Not regular production until '80, deluxe thinline, 3 pickups, 12 strings. Could be considered to be a dealer special order item in the '60s and '70s with limited production.

1966	5 made, special order	$3,500	$5,000
1985-1990		$1,100	$1,500
1994-2003		$1,100	$1,300

Model 370/12 Limited Edition (Roger McGuinn)

1988. Roger McGuinn model, 1000 made, higher-quality appointments.

1988		$3,500	$4,400

Model 375

1958-1974. Deluxe thinline, 3 pickups, vibrato.

1958-1959	16 made	$3,500	$4,400
1960-1964	42 made	$4,000	$4,200
1965-1970	Sporadic limited production	$2,500	$3,500

Model 381

1958-1963,1969-1974. Double-cut archtop, 2 pickups, slash soundhole, solid 'guard, reintroduced in '69 with double split-level 'guard.

1958-1963	Light sporadic production	$4,100	$5,000
1969-1974	Various colors, some rare	$2,100	$4,000

Model 381 JK

1988-1997. John Kay model, 2 humbucking pickups, active electronics, stereo and mono outputs.

1988-1997		$1,600	$2,500

Model 381V68

1987-1990. Renamed V69 in '91.

1987-1990		$1,750	$1,900

Model 381V69

1991-1998. Reissue of vintage 381, originally called 381V68.

1991-1998		$1,750	$1,900

Model 381/12V69

1987-present. Reissue of 381/12, deep double-cut body, sound body cavity, catseye soundhole, triangle inlays, bridge with 12 individual saddles. Finishes include Fireglo, Mapleglo and Jetglo.

1987-2003		$1,800	$2,000

Model 400/Combo 400

1956-1958. Double-cut tulip body, neck-thru, 1 pickup, gold anodized 'guard, 21 frets, replaced by Model 425 in '58. Available in black (216 made), blue turquoise (53), Cloverfield Green (53), Montezuma Brown (41), and 4 in other custom colors.

1956-1958	Black	$1,500	$2,500
1956-1958	Other colors	$2,000	$2,800

1967 Rickenbacker 365

Rickenbacker Combo 400

Rickenbacker Model 625

Robin Avalon Classic

MODEL YEAR	FEATURES	EXC. COND. LOW	HIGH

Model 420
1965-1983. Non-vibrato version of Model 425, single pickup.

1965-1968	42 in '65, 15 in '66, 13 in '68	$1,200	$1,500
1969-1983		$975	$1,200

Model 425
1958-1973. Double-cut solidbody, 1 pickup, sunburst.

1958-1959	1 in '58, 129 in '59	$1,500	$2,000
1960	139 made	$1,400	$1,700
1961-1966	615 made	$1,300	$1,600
1968	3 made	$1,100	$1,400
1969-1973		$1,000	$1,200

Model 450/Combo 450
1957-1984. Replaces Combo 450, 2 pickups (3 optional '62-'77), tulip body shape '57-'59, cresting wave body shape after.

1958-1959	180 made	$2,000	$2,500
1960	266 made	$1,500	$2,500
1961	148 made	$1,500	$2,400
1962	20 made	$1,500	$2,300
1963	44 made	$1,500	$2,200
1964	34 made	$1,500	$2,100
1965	126 made	$1,500	$1,900
1966	248 made	$1,500	$1,800
1970-1979		$1,400	$1,600
1980-1984		$900	$1,200

Model 450/12
1964-1985. Double-cut solidbody, 12-string version of Model 450, 2 pickups.

1964	12 made	$2,100	$2,500
1965	336 made	$1,800	$2,300
1966	1164 made	$1,800	$2,200
1967-1969		$1,700	$2,100
1970-1979		$1,400	$1,700
1980-1985		$1,100	$1,400

Model 456/12 Convertible
1968-1978. Double-cut solidbody, 2 pickups, comb-like device to convert it to 6-string.

1968-1969		$1,600	$2,000
1970-1978		$1,400	$1,600

Model 460
1961-1985. Double-cut solidbody, 2 pickups, neck-thru-body, deluxe trim.

1961-1965	Small consistent production	$1,800	$2,600
1966-1969		$1,700	$2,100
1970-1979		$1,300	$1,900
1980-1985		$1,100	$1,600

Model 480
1973-1984. Double-cut solidbody with long thin bass horn in 4001 bass series style, 2 pickups, cresting wave body and headstock, bolt-on neck.

1973-1979		$950	$1,050
1980-1984		$850	$950

Model 600/Combo 600
1954-1966. Modified double-cut.

1954-1957	Blond/white, 46 made	$2,000	$3,000

1956-1958	OT/Blue Turquoise, 16 made	$2,500	$3,500
1966		$1,200	$1,400

Model 610
1985-1991. Cresting-wave cutaway solidbody, 2 pickups, trapeze R-tailpiece, Jetglo.

1985-1991		$700	$775

Model 615
1962-1966, 1969-1977. Double-cut solidbody, 2 pickups, vibrato.

1962-1966	Very small consistent production	$2,000	$2,400
1969-1977		$1,900	$2,200

Model 620
1974-present. Double-cut solidbody, deluxe binding, 2 pickups, neck-thru-body.

1974-1979		$1,075	$1,175
1980-1989		$975	$1,075
1990-2000s		$800	$975

Model 620/12
1981-present. Double-cut solidbody, 2 pickups, 12 strings, standard trim.

1981-1989		$1,075	$1,275
1990-1999		$875	$1,150
2000-2005		$850	$1,125

Model 625
1962-1977. Double-cut solidbody, deluxe trim, 2 pickups, vibrato.

1962-1965		$3,000	$3,300
1966-1969		$2,500	$3,000
1970-1977		$2,100	$2,500

Model 650/Combo 650
1958. Standard color, 1 pickup.

1958		$1,500	$2,000

Model 650A Atlantis
1991-2004. Cresting wave solidbody, neck-thru, 2 pickups, chrome hardware, turquoise.

1991-2004		$625	$700

Model 650C Colorado
1993-present. Maple neck and body, neck-thru, 2 pickups..

1993-2004		$625	$700

Model 650D Dakota
1993-present. Tulip-shaped neck-thru solidbody, single pickup, chrome hardware, walnut oil-satin finish.

1993-1999		$625	$700

Model 650 E Excalibur/F Frisco
1991-2003. African Vermilion, gold hardware, gloss finish. Name changed to Frisco in '95.

1991-2003		$625	$700

Model 650S Sierra
1993-present. Tulip-shaped neck-thru solidbody, single pickup, gold hardware, walnut oil-satin finish.

1993-1999		$675	$750

Model 660/12 TP
1991-2000s. Tom Petty model, 12 strings, cresting wave body, 2 pickups, deluxe trim, limited run of 1000.

1991-2000s		$1,500	$1,700

MODEL YEAR	FEATURES	EXC. COND. LOW	HIGH

Model 800/Combo 800

1954-1966. Offset double-cut, 1 horseshoe pickup until late-'57, second bar type after, called the Model 800 in the '60s.

1954-1959	Blond/white, 89 made	$2,300	$3,300
1954-1959	Blue or green, 15 made	$2,800	$3,600
1966		$1,400	$1,700

Model 850/Combo 850

1957-1959. Extreme double-cut, 1 pickup until '58, 2 after, maple or turquoise, called Model 850 in the '60s.

1957-1959	Autumnglo, 2 made	$2,500	$3,500
1957-1959	Blue or green, 15 made	$2,000	$3,000
1957-1959	Mapleglo, 21 made	$2,000	$3,000
1957-1959	White, 1 made	$2,500	$3,500

Model 900

1957-1980. Double-cut tulip body shape, 3/4 size, 1 pickups. Body changes to cresting wave shape in '69.

1958-1966		$1,300	$1,600

Model 950/Combo 950

1957-1980. Like Model 900, but with 2 pickups, 21 frets. Body changes to cresting wave shape in '69.

1957-1964		$1,500	$1,900
1965-1980		$1,400	$1,700

Model 1000

1957-1970. Like Model 900, but with 18 frets. Body does not change to cresting wave shape.

1958-1966		$1,200	$1,500

RKS

2003-present. Professional and premium grade, production/custom, electric hollowbody and solidbody guitars designed by Ravi Sawhney and guitarist Dave Mason and built in Thousand Oaks, California. They also build basses.

Robert Cefalu

1998-present. Luthier Robert Cefalu builds his professional grade, production/custom, acoustic guitars in Buffalo, New York. The guitars have an RC on the headstock.

Robert Guitars

1981-present. Luthier Mikhail Robert builds his premium grade, production/custom, classical guitars in Summerland, British Columbia.

Robertson Guitars

1995-present. Luthier Jeff Robertson builds his premium grade, production/custom flat-top guitars in South New Berlin, New York.

Robin

1982-present. Professional and premium grade, production/custom, guitars from luthier David Wintz and built in Houston, Texas. Most guitars were Japanese-made until '87; American produc-

tion began in '88. Most Japanese Robins were pretty consistent in features, but the American ones were often custom-made, so many variations in models exist. They also make Metropolitan (since '96) and Alamo (since '00) brand guitars.

Artisan

1985-late 1980s. Double-cut bound mahogany solidbody, 2 humbuckers, bound rosewood 'board, flamed top, sunburst.

1985		$625	$700

Avalon Classic

1994-present. Single-cut, figured maple top, exposed humbuckers.

1994		$1,100	$1,400

Medley Special

1992-1995. Ash body, maple neck, rosewood 'board, 24 frets, various pickup options.

1992-1995		$425	$500

Medley Standard

1985-present. Offset double-cut swamp ash solidbody, bolt neck, originally with hum-single-single pickups, but now also available with 2 humbuckers.

1985-1992		$525	$600

Octave

1982-1990s. Tuned an octave above standard tuning, full body size with 15 1/2" short-scale bolt maple neck. Japanese-made production model until '87, U.S.-made custom shop after.

1990s	With original case	$550	$800

Raider I/Raider II/Raider III

1985-1991. Double-cut solidbody, 1 humbucker pickup (Raider I), 2 humbuckers (Raider II), or 3 single-coils (Raider III), maple neck, either maple or rosewood 'board, sunburst.

1985-1991	1 pickup	$375	$450
1985-1991	2 pickups	$425	$500
1985-1992	3 pickups	$450	$525

Ranger Custom

1982-1986, 1988-present. Swamp ash bound body, bolt-on maple neck, rosewood or maple 'board, 2 single coils and 1 humbucker, orange, made in Japan until '86, U.S.-made after.

1988-1999	U.S.-made	$575	$775

RDN-Doubleneck Octave/Six

1982-1985. Six-string standard neck with 3 pickups, 6-string octave neck with 1 pickup, double-cut solidbody.

1982-1985	With original case	$550	$750

Soloist

1982-1986. Mahogany double-cut solidbody, carved bound maple top, set neck, 2 humbuckers, only about 125 made.

1982-1986		$425	$550

Wrangler

1990s. Classic '50s single-cut slab body, 3 Rio Grande pickups, opaque finish.

1990s		$425	$750

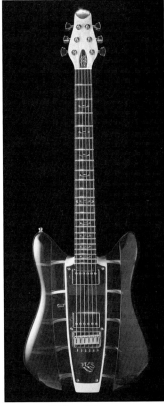

RKS solidbody

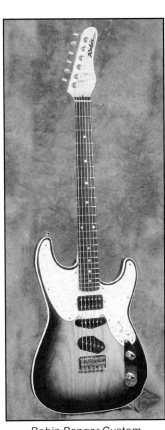

Robin Ranger Custom

Roman Pearlcaster

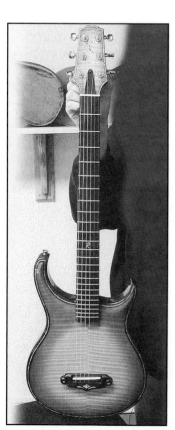

Rowan Cimarron

MODEL YEAR	FEATURES	EXC. COND. LOW	HIGH

Rogands

Late 1960s. Produced by France's Jacobacci company and named after brothers Roger and Andre. Short-lived brand; the brothers made instruments under several other brands as well.

Rogue

2001-present. Budget and intermediate grade, production, acoustic, resonator and sitar guitars. They also offer amps, mandolins, banjos, effects, ukes and basses.

Roland

Best known for keyboards, effects, and amps, Roland offered synthesizer-based guitars and basses from 1977 to '86.

GR-707 Synth Guitar

1983-1986. Slab-wedge asymmetrical body, bass bout to headstock support arm, 2 humbucker pickups, multi-controls.

1983-1986	Silver	$1,000	$1,250

GS-500 Synth Guitar/Module

1977-1986. Snyth functions in a single-cut solidbody guitar. The GS-300 was the same electronics in a classic offset double-cut body.

1977-1986	Sunburst	$750	$1,100

Roman & Lipman Guitars

1989-2000. Production/custom, solidbody guitars made in Danbury, Connecticut by Ed Roman. They also made basses.

Roman Abstract Guitars

1989-present. Professional grade, production/custom, solidbody guitars made in Las Vegas, Nevada by Ed Roman.

Roman Centurion Guitars

2001-present. Premium and presentation grade, custom guitars made in Las Vegas, Nevada by Ed Roman.

Roman Pearlcaster Guitars

1999-present. Professional and premium grade, production/custom, solidbody guitars made in Las Vegas, Nevada by Ed Roman.

Roman Quicksilver Guitars

1997-present. Professional and premium grade, production/custom, solid and hollow-body guitars made in Las Vegas, Nevada by Ed Roman.

Roman Vampire Guitars

2004-present. Professional and premium grade, production/custom, solidbody guitars made in Las Vegas, Nevada by Ed Roman.

Rono

1967-present. Luthier Ron Oates builds his professional and premium grade, production/custom, flat-top, jazz, Wiesenborn-style, and resonator guitars in Boulder, Colorado. He also builds basses and mandolins.

Rowan

1997-present. Professional and premium grade, production/custom, solidbody and acoustic/electric guitars built by luthier Michael Rowan in Garland, Texas.

Royal

ca. 1954-ca. 1965. Line of jazz style guitars made by France's Jacobacci company, which also built under its own brand.

Royden Guitars

1996-present. Professional grade, production/custom, flat-tops and solidbody electrics built by luthier Royden Moran in Peterborough, Ontario.

RS Guitarworks

1994-present. Professional grade, production/custom, solid and hollowbody guitars built by luthier Roy Bowen in Winchester, Kentucky.

Rubio, German Vasquez

1993-present. Luthier German Vasquez Rubio builds his professional and premium grade, production/custom classical and flamenco guitars in Los Angeles, California.

Ruck, Robert

1966-present. Premium grade, custom classical and flamenco guitars built by luthier Robert Ruck in Kalaheo, Hawaii.

Custom Classical

1966-present. Premium grade classical with solid spruce top and solid rosewood back and sides.

1990s		$7,000	$8,200

Running Dog Guitars

1994-present. Luthier Rick Davis builds his professional and premium grade, custom flat-tops in Richmond, Vermont.

Rustler

1993-ca. 1996. Solidbody electrics with hand-tooled leather bound and studded sides and a R branded into the top, built by luthier Charles Caponi in Mason City, Iowa.

RVC Guitars

1999-present. Professional and premium grade, production/custom, solidbody guitars made in Las Vegas, Nevada by Ed Roman.

RWK

1991-present. Luthier Bob Karger builds his intermediate grade, production/custom, solidbody electrics and travel guitars in Highland Park, Illinois.

MODEL YEAR	FEATURES	EXC. COND. LOW	HIGH

Ryder

1963. Made by Rickenbacker, the one guitar with this brand was the same as their solidbody Model 425.

S. B. Brown Guitars

1994-present. Custom flat-tops made by luthier Steve Brown in Fullerton, California.

S. B. MacDonald Custom Instruments

1988-present. Professional and premium grade, custom/production, flat-top, resonator, and solid-body guitars built by luthier Scott B. MacDonald in Huntington, New York.

S. Yairi

Ca. 1965-1980s. Steel string folk guitars and classical nylon string guitars by master Japanese luthier Sadao Yairi, imported by Philadelphia Music Company of Limerick, Pennsylvania. Early sales literature called the brand Syairi. Most steel string models have dreadnought bodies and nylon-string classical guitars are mostly standard grand concert size. All models are handmade. Steel string Jumbos and dreadnoughts have Syairi logo on the headstock, nylon-classical models have no logo. The Model 900 has a solid wood body, others assumed to have laminate

S.D. Curlee

1975-1982. Founded in Matteson, Illinois by music store owner Randy Curlee, after an unsuccessful attempt to recruit builder Dan Armstrong. S.D. Curlee guitars were made in Illinois, while S.D. Curlee International instruments were made by Matsumoku in Japan. The guitars featured mostly Watco oil finishes, often with exotic hardwoods, and unique neck-thru-bridge construction on American and Japanese instruments. These were the first production guitars to use a single-coil pickup at the bridge with a humbucker at the neck, and a square brass nut. DiMarzio pickups. Offered in a variety of shapes, later some copies. Approximately 12,000 American-made basses and 3,000 guitars were made, most of which were sold overseas. Two hundred were made in '75-'76; first production guitar numbered 518.

Electric Solidbody

1975-1982. Models include the '75-'81Standard I, II and III, '76-'81? International C-10 and C-11, '80-'81 Yanke, Liberty, Butcher, Curbeck, Summit, Special, and the '81-'82 Destroyer, Flying V.

1975-1982		$350	$550

S101

2002-present. Budget and intermediate grade, production, classical, acoustic, resonator, solid and semi-hollow body guitars imported from China by American Sejung Corp. They also offer basses, mandolins and banjos.

Sadowsky

1980-present. Professional and premium grade, production/custom, solidbody, archtop, and electric nylon-string guitars built by luthier Roger Sadowsky in Brooklyn, New York. He also builds basses. In '96, luthier Yoshi Kikuchi started building Sadowsky Tokyo instruments in Japan.

T Custom

1990-2000s		$1,800	$2,000

Vintage Style

Swamp ash body, Barden pickups, vintage-style gears, bridge, control plate and 'guard, sunburst.

1982-1987		$1,200	$1,600

Saga

Saga Musical Instruments, of San Francisco, California distributes a wide variety of instruments and brands, occasionally including their own line of solidbody guitars called the Saga Gladiator Series (1987-'88, '94-'95). In the 2000s, Saga also offered component kits ($90-$130) that allowed for complete assembly in white wood.

Sahlin Guitars

1975-present. Luthier Eric Sahlin builds his premium grade, custom, classical and flamenco guitars in Spokane, Washington.

Samick

1958-2001, 2002-present. Budget, intermediate and professional grade, production, imported acoustic and electric guitars. They also offer basses, mandolins, ukes and banjos. Samick also distributes Abilene and Silvertone brand instruments.

Samick started out producing pianos, adding guitars in '65 under other brands. In '88 Samick greatly increased their guitar production. The Samick line of 350 models was totally closed out in 2001. A totally new line of 250 models was introduced January 2002 at NAMM. All 2002 models have the new compact smaller headstock and highly styled S logo.

Sammo

1920s. Labels in these instruments state they were made by the Osborne Mfg. Co. with an address of Masonic Temple, Chicago, Illinois. High quality and often with a high degree of ornamentation. They also made ukes and mandolins.

Sand Guitars

1979-present. Luthier Kirk Sand opened the Guitar Shoppe in Laguna Beach, California in 1972 with James Matthews. By '79, he started producing his own line of premium grade, production/custom-made flat-tops.

Santa Cruz

1976-present. Professional, premium and presentation grade, production/custom, flat-top, 12-string, and archtop guitars from luthier Richard Hoover

1976 S.D. Curlee Standard

Jim Hall archtop

*Santa Cruz
Tony Rice Professional*

Schecter Jazz Elite

MODEL YEAR	FEATURES	EXC. COND. LOW	HIGH

in Santa Cruz, California. Founded by Hoover, Bruce Ross and William Davis. Hoover became sole owner in '89. Custom ordered instruments with special upgrades may have higher values than the ranges listed here.

Archtop
Early 1980s-present. Originally called the FJZ, but by mid-'90s, called the Archtop, offering 16", 17" and 18" cutaway acoustic/electric models, often special order. Spruce top, curly maple body, ebony 'board, floating pickup, f-holes, sunburst or natural. Many custom options

1980-1990s		$4,000	$7,000

D 12-Fret
1994-present. 15 1/2" scale, 12-fret neck, slotted headstock, round shoulders, spruce top, mahogany back and sides, notch diamond markers, herringbone trim and rosette, natural. Special order models will vary in value and could exceed the posted range.

1990s		$2,500	$3,000

D Koa
1980s-1990s. Style D with koa back and sides.

1990s		$2,400	$2,600

D PW
2001-present. Pre-war D-style.

2001-2002		$1,600	$1,800

F
1976-present. 15 7/8" scale with narrow waist, sitka spruce top, Indian rosewood back and sides, natural.

1990s		$2,400	$2,650

F46R
1980s. Brazilian rosewood, single-cut.

1980s		$4,000	$4,400

FS (Finger Style)
1988-present. Single-cut, cedar top, Indian rosewood back and sides, mahogany neck, modified X-bracing.

1988-2000s		$2,500	$3,000

H/H13
1976-present. Parlor size acoustic, offered in cutaway and non-cut versions, and options included koa, rosewood or maple, special inlays, slotted headstock, and shallow or deep bodies.

1980-1990s		$2,300	$2,800
2000s		$2,100	$2,200

OM (Orchestra Model)
1987-present. Orchestra model acoustic, sitka spruce top, Indian rosewood (Brazilian optional) back and sides, herringbone rosette, scalloped braces.

1987-1999	Brazilian rosewood	$4,100	$4,800
1987-1999	Indian rosewood	$1,600	$1,800

Tony Rice
1980s-present. Dreadnought-size, Indian rosewood body, sitka spruce top, solid peghead, zigzag back stripe, pickup optional.

1980-1990s		$2,300	$2,600
2000s		$2,000	$2,300

Tony Rice Professional
1980s-present. Brazilian rosewood back and sides, carved German spruce top, zigzag back stripe, solid peghead.

1980-1990s		$4,100	$4,800

Vintage Artist Custom
2000s. Martin D-42 style, mahogany body, Indian rosewood back and sides, sitka spruce top, zigzag back stripe, solid peghead, scalloped X-bracing, pickup optional.

2000s		$3,000	$3,200

VJ (Vintage Jumbo)
2000-present. 16" scale, round shouldered body, sitka spruce, figured mahogany back and sides, natural.

1990-2000s		$2,200	$2,500

Sawchyn Guitars
1972-present. Professional and premium grade, production/custom, flat-top and flamenco guitars and mandolins built by luthier Peter Sawchyn in Regina, Saskatchewan.

Schaefer
1997-present. Premium grade, production/custom electric archtops handcrafted by luthier Edward A. Schaefer, who was located in Fort Worth, Texas, until '03 and is currently in Duluth, Minnesota.

Schecter
1974-present. Intermediate, professional and premium grade, production/custom, acoustic and electric guitars. They also offer basses. Guitar component manufacturer founded in California by four partners (David Schecter's name sounded the best), later offering complete instruments. The company was bought out and moved to Dallas, Texas in the early '80s. By '88 the company was back in California and in '89 was purchased by Hisatake Shibuya. Schecter Custom Shop guitars are made in Burbank, California and their Diamond Series is made in South Korea.

A1/A7
1997-2000. Diamond series, offset double-cut, long pointed bass horn, arched mahogany body, bolt neck. A7 is 7-string.

1997-2000	Various models	$275	$400

Avenger
1997-2004. Diamond series, offset double-cut, long pointed bass horn, arched mahogany body, bolt neck, 2 humbuckers.

1997-2004	Custom color	$400	$500
1997-2004	Sunburst	$300	$400

Avenger 7
1997-2003. 7-string Avenger option.

1997-2003	Custom color	$550	$750

Genesis
1985-late 1980s. Offset double-cut, bolt neck, single-single-hum pickups, dot markers.

1980s		$250	$300

Jazz Elite
2004-present. Diamond series, thinline hollowbody, single-cut, 2 humbuckers.

2004-2005		$350	$375

MODEL YEAR	FEATURES	EXC. COND. LOW	HIGH

Omen 7
2001-present. Diamond series, offset double-cut, 2 humbuckers, bolt neck, 7-string.

2001-2004		$200	$275

Scheerhorn
1989-present. Professional and premium grade, custom, resonator and Hawaiian guitars built by luthier Tim Scheerhorn in Kentwood, Michigan.

Schoenberg
1986-present. Premium grade, production/custom, flat-tops offered by Eric Schoenberg of Tiburon, California. From '86-'94 guitars made to Schoenberg's specifications by Martin. From '86-'90 constructed by Schoenberg's luthier and from '90-'94 assembled by Martin but voiced and inlaid in the Schoenberg shop. Current models made to Schoenberg specs by various smaller shops.

Schon
1986-1991. Designed by guitarist Neal Schon, early production by Charvel/Jackson building about 200 in the San Dimas factory. The final 500 were built by Larrivee in Canada. Leo Knapp also built custom Schon guitars from '85-'87, and '90s custom-made Schon guitars were also available.

Standard (Canadian-made)
1987-1991. Made in Canada on headstock.

1987-1988	Single-cut	$325	$425
1989-1991	Reverse double-cut	$325	$425

Standard (U.S.A.-made)
1986 only. San Dimas/Jackson model, single-cut, pointy headstock shape, Made in U.S.A. on headstock.

1986		$1,500	$2,000

Schramm Guitars
1990-present. Premium grade, production/custom, classical and flamenco guitars built by luthier David Schramm in Clovis, California.

Schroder Guitars
1993-present. Luthier Timothy Schroeder builds his premium grade, production/custom, archtops in Northbrook, Illinois.

Schwartz Guitars
1992-present. Premium grade, custom, flat-top guitars built by luthier Sheldon Schwartz in Concord, Ontario.

ScoGo
2001-present. Professional and premium grade, production/custom, solidbody guitars built by luthier Scott Gordon in Parkesburg, Pennsylvania.

Scorpion Guitars
1998-present. Professional and premium grade, custom, solidbody guitars made in Las Vegas, Nevada by Ed Roman.

MODEL YEAR	FEATURES	EXC. COND. LOW	HIGH

Seagull
1982-present. Intermediate grade, production, acoustic and acoustic/electric guitars built in Canada. Seagull was founded by luthier Robert Godin, who also has the Norman, Godin, and Patrick & Simon brands of instruments.

Artist Mahogany Folk
1997-2003. Small body 14 3/4" lower bout, cedar top, mahogany back and sides, script Artist logo on headstock.

1997-2003		$400	$450

M6 Cedar GT
2003-present. Cedar top, mahogany back and sides.

2000s		$275	$300

S6+ Folk
1993-present. Wild cherry back and sides, cedar top,

1993-2003		$225	$275

Sebring
1980s-mid-1990s. Entry level Korean imports distributed by V.M.I. Industries.

Seiwa
Early 1980s. Entry-level to mid-level Japanese electric guitars and basses, logo may indicate Since 1956.

Sekova
Mid-1960s-mid-1970s. Entry level instruments imported by the U.S. Musical Merchandise Corporation of New York.

Selmer
1932-1952. France-based Selmer & Cie was primarily a maker of wind instruments when they asked Mario Maccaferri to design a line of guitars for them. The guitars, with an internal sound chamber for increased volume, were built in Mante La Ville. Both gut and steel string models were offered. Maccaferri left Selmer in '33, but guitar production continued, and the original models are gradually phased out. In '36, only the 14 fret oval model is built. Production is stopped for WWII and resumes in '46, finally stopping in '52. Less than 900 guitars are built in total.

Classique
1942. Solid Rosewood back and sides, no cutaway, solid spruce top, round soundhole, classical guitar size, possibly only 2 built.

1942		$5,000	$7,000

Concert
1932-1933. For gut strings, cutaway, laminated Indian rosewood back and sides, internal resonator, spruce top with D hole, wide walnut neck, ebony 'board, only a few dozen built.

1932-1933		$15,000	$20,000

Schon Standard

1968 Sekova Grecian

MODEL YEAR	FEATURES	EXC. COND. LOW	HIGH

Sheppard Minstral Grand Concert

Eddie Freeman Special

1933. For steel strings, 4 strings, laminated Indian rosewood back and sides, cutaway, no internal resonator, solid spruce top, D hole, black and white rosette inlays, walnut 12 fret neck, ebony 'board, 640mm scale, approx. 100 made.

1933		$5,000	$8,000

Espagnol

1932. For gut strings, laminated Indian rosewood back and sides, no cutaway, internal resonator, solid spruce top, round soundhole, wide walnut neck, ebony 'board, only a few made.

1932		$8,000	$10,000

Grand Modele 4 Cordes

1932-1933. For steel strings, 4 string model, laminated back and sides, cutaway, internal resonator, solid spruce top, D hole, walnut neck, ebony 'board, 12 fret, 640mm scale, 2 or 3 dozen made.

1932-1933		$8,000	$13,000

Harp Guitar

1933. For gut strings, solid mahogany body, extended horn holding 3 sub bass strings, 3 screw adjustable neck, wide walnut neck, ebony 'board, only about 12 built.

1933		$13,000	$15,000

Hawaienne

1932-1934. For steel strings, 6 or 7 strings, laminated back and sides, no cutaway, internal resonator, solid spruce top, D hole, wide walnut neck, ebony 'board, 2 or 3 dozen built.

1932-1934		$17,000	$25,000

Modele Jazz

1936-1942, 1946-1952. For steel strings, laminated Indian rosewood back and sides (some laminated or solid mahogany), cutaway, solid spruce top, small oval soundhole, walnut neck, ebony 'board (latest ones with rosewood necks), 14 fret to the body, 670mm scale. Production interrupted for WWII.

1936-1952		$22,000	$27,000

Modeles de Transition

1934-1936. Transition models appearing before 14 fret oval hole model, some in solid maple with solid headstock, some with round soundhole and cutaway, some 12 fret models with oval hole.

1934-1936		$15,000	$18,000

Orchestre

1932-1934. For steel strings, laminated back and sides, cutaway, internal resonator, solid spruce top, D hole, walnut neck, ebony 'board, about 100 made.

1932-1934		$25,000	$30,000

Tenor

1932-1933. For steel strings, 4 strings, laminated back and sides, internal resonator, solid spruce top, D hole, walnut neck, ebony 'board, 12 fret, 570mm scale, 2 or 3 dozen built.

1932-1933		$5,000	$8,000

Serge Guitars

1995-present. Luthier Serge Michaud builds his production/custom, classical, steel-string, resophonic and archtop guitars in Breakeyville, Quebec.

Sho-Bro resonator

Sexauer Guitars

1967-present. Premium and presentation grade, custom, steel-string, 12-string, nylon-string, and archtop guitars built by luthier Bruce Sexauer in Petaluma, California.

Shanti Guitars

1985-present. Premium and presentation grade, custom, steel-string, 12-string, nylon-string and archtop guitars built by luthier Michael Hornick in Avery, California.

Shelley D. Park Guitars

1991-present. Luthier Shelley D. Park builds her professional grade, custom, nylon- and steel-string guitars in Vancouver, British Columbia.

Shelton-Farretta

1967-present. Premium grade, production/custom, flamenco and classical guitars built by luthiers John Shelton and Susan Farretta origianlly in Portland, Oregon, and since '05 in Alsea, Oregon.

Sheppard Guitars

1993-present. Luthier Gerald Sheppard builds his premium grade, production/custom, steel-string guitars in Kingsport, Tennessee.

Shergold

1968-1992. Founded by Jack Golder and Norman Houlder, Shergold originally made guitars for other brands like Hayman and Barnes and Mullins. In '75, they started building guitars and basses under their own name. By '82, general guitar production was halted but custom orders were filled through '90. In '91, general production was again started but ended in '92 when Golder died.

Sherwood

c.1950s. Private brand made by Chicago manufacturerers such as Kay.

Shifflett

1990-present. Luthier Charles Shifflett builds his premium grade, production/custom, flat-top, classical, flamenco, resophonic, and harp guitars in High River, Alberta. He also builds basses and banjos.

Sho-Bro

1969-1978. Spanish and Hawaiian style resonator guitars made by Sho-Bud in Nashville, Tennessee and distributed by Gretsch. Designed Shot Jackson and Buddy Emmons.

Grand Slam

1978. Acoustic, spruce top, mahogany neck, jacaranda sides and back, and mother-of-pearl inlays, abalone soundhole purfling.

1970s		$425	$550

MODEL YEAR	FEATURES	EXC. COND. LOW	HIGH

Resonator

1972-1978. Flat-top style guitar with metal resonator with 2 small circular grilled soundholes.

| 1972-1978 | | $525 | $650 |

Siegmund Guitars & Amplifiers

1993-present. Luthier Chris Siegmund builds his professional, premium, and presentation grade, custom/production, archtop, solidbody, and resonator guitars in Los Angeles, California. He founded the company in Seattle, moving it to Austin, Texas for '95-'97. He also builds effects pedals and amps.

Sigma

1970-present. Budget and intermediate grade, production, import acoustic guitars distributed by C.F. Martin Company.

DR Series

1970-2003. Various dreadnought models.

1970-1996	DR-28H	$350	$450
1970-1996	DR-35H	$375	$475
1970-2003	DR-41	$400	$500

GCS-6

Grand concert semi-narrow waist body, laminated spruce top, mahogany back and sides, natural.

| 1994 | | $150 | $225 |

Signet

Ca. 1973. Acoustic flat-top guitars, imported from Japan by Ampeg/Selmer.

Silber

1992-1998. Solid wood, steel-string guitars designed by Marc Silber, made in Paracho, Mexico, and distributed by K & S Music. Silber continues to offer the same models under the Marc Silber Music brand.

Silvertone

1941-ca. 1970, present. Brand of Sears instruments which replaced their Supertone brand in '41. The Silvertone name was used on Sears phonographs, records and radios as early as the 'teens, and on occasional guitar models. When Sears divested itself of the Harmony guitar subsidiary in '40 it turned to other suppliers including Kay. In '40 Kay-made archtops and Hawaiian electric lap steels appeared in the catalog bearing the Silvertone brand, and after '41-'42, all guitars, regardless of manufacturer, were called Silvertone.

Sears offered Danelectro-made solidbodies in the fall of '54. Danelectro hollowbodies appeared in '56. By '65, the Silvertones were Teisco-made guitars from W.M.I., but never sold through the catalog. First imports shown in catalog were in '69. By '70, most guitars sold by Sears were imports and did not carry the Silvertone name. Currently, Samick offers a line of amps under the Silvertone name.

Amp-In-Case

The 1-pickup guitar, introduced in 1962, came with a smaller wattage amp without tremolo. The 2-pickup model, introduced in '63, came with a higher-watt amp with tremolo and better quality Jensen speaker. Gray tolex covered the guitar-amp case.

| 1960s | 1 pickup | $375 | $425 |
| 1960s | 2 pickups | $475 | $525 |

Belmont

1950s. Single-cut solidbody, double pickup, black.

| 1958 | | $350 | $400 |

Espanada

Bigsby, 2 pickups, black.

| 1960s | | $225 | $425 |

Estrelita

Semi-hollowbody archtop, 2 pickups, black, Harmony-made.

| 1960s | | $225 | $425 |

Gene Autry Melody Ranch

1941-1955. 13" Harmony-made acoustic, Gene Autry signature on belly, cowboy roundup stencil, same as earlier Supertone Gene Autry Roundup.

| 1941-1955 | | $250 | $450 |

Meteor

Single-cut, 1 pickup, sunburst.

| 1955 | | $225 | $350 |

Student-level 13" Flat-Top

Harmony-made, 13" lower bout.

| 1960s | | $50 | $75 |

Ultra Thin Professional

1960s. Harmony-made, thin hollow cutaway, 3 pickups, Bigsby tailpiece.

| 1960s | | $450 | $750 |

Simon & Patrick

1985-present. Intermediate and professional grade, production, acoustic and acoustic/electric guitars built in Canada. Founded by luthier Robert Godin and named after his sons. He also produces the Seagull, Godin, and Norman brands of instruments.

Skylark

1981. Solidbody guitars made in Japan and distributed by JC Penney. Two set-neck models and one bolt-neck model were offered. Most likely a one-time deal as brand quickly disappeared.

Slammer

1990-present. Budget and intermediate grade, production, guitars imported by Hamer. They also offer basses. Originally Slammers were upscale copies of Hamer models made in Korea. In '96, production of a more budget line was switched to Indonesia.

Slingerland

1930s-mid-1940s. The parent company was Slingerland Banjo and Drums, Chicago, Illinois. The company offered other stringed instruments into the '40s. They also marketed the May Bell

Siegmund Outcaster

'60s Silvertone semi-hollow-body

GUITARS

Smart J-2

Spector Arc 6

MODEL		EXC. COND.	
YEAR	FEATURES	LOW	HIGH

brand. The guitars were made by other companies. Slingerland Drums is now owned by Gibson.

Nitehawk
1930s. 16" archtop, Nitehawk logo on headstock, fancy position neck markers.

1930s		$550	$700

Songster Archtop/Flat-Top
1930s.

1930s	Archtop	$450	$650
1930s	Flat-Top	$900	$1,100

Smart Musical Instruments

1986-present. Luthier A. Lawrence Smart builds his professional and premium grade, custom, flat-top guitars in McCall, Idaho. He also builds mandolin-family instruments.

Smith, George

1959-present. Custom classical and flamenco guitars built by luthier George Smith in Portland, Oregon.

Smith, Lawrence K.

1989-present. Luthier Lawrence Smith builds his professional and premium grade, production/custom, flat-top, nylon-string, and archtop guitars in Thirrow, New South Wales, Australia.

Somervell

1979-present. Luthier Douglas P. Somervell builds his premium and presentation grade, production/custom, classical and flamenco guitars in Brasstown, North Carolina.

Somogyi, Ervin

1971-present. Luthier Ervin Somogyi builds his presentation grade, production/custom, flat-top, flamenco, and classical guitars in Oakland, California.

SonFather Guitars

1994-present. Luthier David A. Cassotta builds his production/custom, flat-top, 12-string, nylon-string and electric guitars in Rocklin, California.

Southwell Guitars

1983-present. Premium grade, custom, nylon-string guitars built by luthier Gary Southwell in Nottingham, England.

Sovereign

Ca. 1899-ca. 1938. Sovereign was originally a brand of The Oscar Schmidt Company of Jersey City, New Jersey, and used on guitars, banjos and mandolins starting in the very late 1800s. In the late '30s, Harmony purchased several trade names from the Schmidt Company, including Sovereign and Stella. Sovereign then ceased as a brand, but Harmony continued using it on a model line of Harmony guitars.

MODEL		EXC. COND.	
YEAR	FEATURES	LOW	HIGH

Specimen Products

1984-present. Luthier Ian Schneller builds his professional and premium grade, production/custom, aluminum and wood body guitars in Chicago, Illinois. He also builds basses, ukes, amps and speaker cabs.

Spector/Stuart Spector Design

1975-1990 (Spector), 1991-1998 (SSD), 1998-present (Spector SSD). Known mainly for basses, Spector offered U.S.-made guitars during '75-'90 and '96-'99, and imports for '87-'90 and '96-'99. Since 2003, they again offer U.S.-professional grade, production, solidbody guitars. See Bass Section for more company info.

St. George

Mid to late 1960s. Early Japanese brand imported possibly by Buegeleisen & Jacobson of New York, New York.

St. Moritz

1960s. Imported from Japan by unidentified distributor. Manufacturers unknown, but some appear to be either Teisco or Kawai. Generally shorter scale beginner guitars, some with interesting pickup configurations.

Stahl

1900-1941. William Stahl ran a publishing company in Milwaukee and sold instruments from a variety of builders under his own name. By at least 1906, some of his better instruments were coming from the Larson Brothers of Chicago. The guitars listed here were built by the Larsons and valuation is based on style number.

Style 4 Flat-Top
1930s. Mahogany body.

1930s		$2,500	$4,000

Style 5 Flat-Top
1930s. Mahogany body.

1930s		$2,500	$4,000

Style 6 Orchestra Special Flat-Top
1930s. Rosewood body.

1929-1930		$4,500	$7,500

Style 7 Special Solo Flat-Top
1930s. 13 1/2" scale, choice rosewood body, white spruce top, fancy appointments.

1930s		$5,000	$8,000

Style 8 Special Solo Flat-Top
1930s. Choicest rosewood body, finest white spruce top, fancy appointments.

1930s		$6,000	$9,000

Style 9 Artist Special Flat-Top
1930s. Choicest rosewood body, finest white spruce top, fancy appointments.

1930s		$7,000	$10,000

MODEL		EXC. COND.	
YEAR	FEATURES	LOW	HIGH

MODEL		EXC. COND.	
YEAR	FEATURES	LOW	HIGH

Stambaugh

1995-present. Luthier Chris Stambaugh builds his professional grade, custom/production, solid-body guitars in Stratham, New Hampshire. He also builds basses.

Standel

1952-1974, 1997-present. Amp builder Bob Crooks offered instruments under his Standel brand 3 different times during the '60s. In '61 Semie Moseley, later of Mosrite fame, made 2 guitar models and 1 bass for Standel, in limited numbers. Also in '61, Standel began distributing Sierra steels and Dobro resonators, sometimes under the Standel name. In '65 and '66 Standel offered a guitar and a bass made by Joe Hall, who also made the Hallmark guitars. In '66 Standel connected with Sam Koontz, who designed and produced the most numerous Standel models (but still in relatively small numbers) in Newark, New Jersey. These models hit the market in '67 and were handled by Harptone, which was associated with Koontz. By '70 Standel was out of the guitar biz. See Amp section for more company info.

Custom Solidbody 201/201X

1967-1968. Solidbody, 2 pickups, vibrola, 2 pointed cutaways, headstock similar to that on Fender XII, 201X has no vibrato, sunburst, black, pearl white and metallic red.

1967-1968		$800	$1,000

Custom Deluxe Solidbody 101/101X

1967-1968. Custom with better electronics, 101X has no vibrato, sunburst, black, pearl white and metallic red.

1967-1968		$1,000	$1,300

Custom Thin Body 202/202X

1967-1968. Thin body, headstock similar to that on Fender XII, 202X has no vibrato, offered in sunburst and 5 solid color options.

1967-1968		$900	$1,100

Custom Deluxe Thin Body 102/102X

1967-1968. Custom with better electronics, 102X has no vibrato, offered in sunburst and 5 solid color options.

1967-1968		$1,100	$1,500

Starfield

1992-1993. Solidbody guitars from Hoshino (Ibanez) made in the U.S. and Japan. U.S. guitars are identified as American models; Japanese ones as SJ models. Hoshino also used the Starfield name on a line of Japanese guitars in the late '70s. These Starfields had nothing to do with the '90s versions and were not sold in the U.S.

Starforce

Ca. 1989. Import copies from Starforce Music/ Starforce USA.

Stauffer

1800s. Old World violin and guitar maker, Georg Stauffer. Valid attributions include "signed or labeled by the maker" indicating the guitar was actually made by Stauffer, as opposed to "attributed to Stauffer or one of his contemporaries."

Guitar

1830	Fancy model,		
	pearl trim	$11,000	$12,000

Stefan Sobell Musical Instruments

1982-present. Premium grade, production/custom, flat-top, 12-string, and archtop guitars built by luthier Stefan Sobell in Hetham, Northumberland, England. He also builds mandolins, citterns and bouzoukis.

Steinberger

1979-present. Currently Steinberger offers budget, intermediate, and professional grade, production, electric guitars. They also offer basses. Founded by Ned Steinberger, who started designing NS Models for Stuart Spector in '76. In '79, he designed the L-2 headless bass. In '80, the Steinberger Sound Corp. was founded. Steinberger Sound was purchased by the Gibson Guitar Corp. in '87, and in '92, Steinberger relocated to Nashville, Tennessee.

Headless model codes for '85-'93 are:
First letter is X for bass or G for guitar.
Second letter is for body shape: M is regular offset double-cut guitar body; L is rectangle body; P is mini V shaped body.
Number is pickup designation: 2 = 2 humbuckers, 3 = 3 single coils, 4 = single/single/humbucker.
Last letter is type of tremolo: S = S-Trem tremolo; T = Trans-Trem which cost more on original retail.

Steinegger

1976-present. Premium grade, custom steel-string flat-top guitars built by luthier Robert Steinegger in Portland, Oregon.

Stella

Ca. 1899-1974, present. Stella was a brand of the Oscar Schmidt Company which started using the brand on low-mid to mid-level instruments in the very late 1800s. Oscar Schmidt produced all types of stringed instruments and was very successful in the 1920s. Company salesmen reached many rural areas and Stella instruments were available in general stores, furniture stores, and dry goods stores, ending up in the hands of musicians such as Leadbelly and Charlie Patton. Harmony acquired the Stella brand in '39 and built thousands of instruments with that name in the '50s and '60s. Harmony dissolved in '74. The Stella brand has been reintroduced by MBT International.

1968 Standel 510

Stefan Sobell Model 1

GUITARS

Stella/Harmony

1952 Stromberg Master 400

MODEL YEAR	FEATURES	EXC. COND. LOW	HIGH

00 Style
Early-1900s. Oak body flat-top.

1908		$750	$1,000

Harp Guitar
Early-1900s.

1915		$2,000	$2,500

Singing Cowboy
Late-1990s. Copy of Supertone (black background)/ Silvertone/Harmony Singing Cowboy, import with laminated wood construction and ladder bracing.

2000	Stencil over black	$50	$75

Stetson
1910s-1925. Stetson was a house brand of William John Dyer's St. Paul, Minnesota, music store. The guitars were built by Chicago's Larson Brothers. He also carried Dyer brand instruments made by Knutsen.

Small Higher-End Flat-Top

1910s		$3,200	$4,000

Stevenson
1999-present. Professional grade, production/ custom, solidbody electric guitars built by luthier Ted Stevenson in Lachine, Quebec. He also builds basses and amps.

Strad-O-Lin
Ca.1920s-ca.1960s. The Strad-O-Lin company was operated by the Hominic brothers in New York, primarily making mandolins for wholesalers. Around '57 Multivox/Premier bought the company and also used the name on guitars, making both electrics and acoustics. Premier also marketed student level guitars under the U.S. Strad brand.

Stromberg
1906-1955, 2001-present. Intermediate and professional grade, production, archtop guitars imported by Larry Davis.

Founded in Boston by master luthier Charles Stromberg, a Swedish immigrant, building banjos and drums. Son Harry joined the company in 1907and stayed until '27. Son Elmer started in 1910 at age 15. The shop was well known for tenor banjos, but when the banjo's popularity declined, they began building archtop orchestra model guitars. The shop moved to Hanover Street in Boston in '27 and began producing custom order archtop guitars, in particular the 16" G-series and the Deluxe. As styles changed the G-series was increased to 17 3/8" and the 19" Master 400 model was introduced in '37. Stromberg designs radically changed around '40, most likely when Elmer took over guitar production. Both Charles and Elmer died within a few months of each other in '55.

Larry Davis of WD Music Products revived the Stromberg name and introduced a series of moderately priced jazz guitars in June, 2001. The models are crafted by a small Korean shop with component parts supplied by WD.

MODEL YEAR	FEATURES	EXC. COND. LOW	HIGH

Deluxe
1927-1955. Non-cut, 16" body to '34, 17 3/8" body after '35, also sometimes labeled Delux.

1927-1930		$9,000	$10,000
1931-1939		$11,000	$12,000
1940-1955		$11,000	$12,000

G-1
1927-1955. Non-cut, 16" body to '35, 17 3/8" body after '35, sunburst.

1927-1935	16" body	$9,000	$10,000
1936-1955	17 3/8" body	$9,000	$10,000

G-3
Early 1930s. Archtop, 16 3/8", 3 segment F-holes, ladder bracing, gold hardware, engraved tailpiece, 8-ply 'guard, 5-ply body binding, laminate maple back, fancy engraved headstock with Stromberg name, less total refinement than higher-end Stromberg models.

1927-1935		$10,000	$11,000

Master 300
1937-1955. 19" non-cut.

1937-1955	Natural	$35,000	$40,000
1937-1955	Sunburst	$30,000	$35,000

Master 400
1937-1955. 19" top-of-the-line non-cut, the most common of Stromberg's models.

1937-1955	Natural	$40,000	$50,000
1937-1955	Sunburst	$35,000	$45,000

Master 400 Cutaway
1949. Only 7 cutaway Strombergs are known to exist.

1949	Natural	$75,000	$85,000

Stromberg-Voisinet
1921-ca.1932. Marketed Stromberg (not to be confused with Charles Stromberg of Boston) and Kay Kraft brands, plus guitars of other distributors and retailers. Stromberg was the successor to the Groehsl Company (or Groehsel) founded in Chicago, Illinois in 1890; and the predecessor .... to the Kay Musical Instrument Company. In 1921, the name was changed to Stromberg-Voisinet Company. Henry Kay "Hank" Kuhrmeyer joined the company in '23 and was secretary by '25. By the mid-'20s, the company was making many better Montgomery Ward guitars, banjos and mandolins, often with lots of pearloid.

Joseph Zorzi, Philip Gabriel and John Abbott left Lyon & Healy for S-V in '26 or '27, developing 2-point Venetian shape, which was offered in '27. The first production of electric guitars and amps was introduced with big fanfare in '28; perhaps only 200 or so made. The last Stromberg acoustic instruments were seen in '32. The Kay Kraft brand was introduced by Kuhrmeyer in '31 as the company made its transition to Kay (see Kay). See Guitar Stories Volume II, by Michael Wright, for a complete history of Stromberg-Voisinet/Kay with detailed model listings.

MODEL YEAR	FEATURES	EXC. COND. LOW	HIGH

Archtop Deluxe
1920s-1930s. Venetian cutaways, oval soundhole, decalomania art on top, trapeze tailpiece, light sunburst. Later offered under the Kay-Kraft brand.

1930s		$450	$650

Archtop Standard
1920s-1930s. Venetian cutaways, oval soundhole, no decalomania art, plain top, trapeze tailpiece, light sunburst. Later offered under the Kay-Kraft brand.

1930s		$400	$600

Stuart Custom Guitars
2004-present. Professional and premium grade, production/custom, solid and semi-hollow body guitars built by luthier Fred Stuart in Riverside, California. Stuart was a Senior Master Builder at Fender. He also builds pickups.

Suhr Guitars
1997-present. Luthier John Suhr builds his professional and premium grade, production/custom, solidbody electrics in Lake Elsinore, California. He also builds basses. He previously built Pensa-Suhr guitars with Rudy Pensa in New York.

Superior Guitars
1987-present. Intermediate grade, production/custom Hawaiian, flamenco and classical guitars made in Mexico for George Katechis Montalvo of Berkeley Musical Instrument Exchange. They also offer mandolin-family instruments.

Supersound
1958. England's Jim Burns first production brand, about 20 short scale, single-cut solidbodies were produced bearing this name.

Supertone
1914-1941. Brand used by Sears, Roebuck and Company for instruments made by various American manufacturers, including especially its own subsidiary Harmony (which it purchased in 1916). When Sears divested itself of Harmony in '40, instruments began making a transition to the Silvertone brand. By '41 the Supertone name was gone.

Acoustic Flat-Top (13" Wide, Non-Stencil)

1930s		$150	$250

Acoustic Flat-Top (High-End Appointments)

1920s	Pearl trim 00-42 likeness	$1,300	$2,200
1920s	Pearl trim, Lindbergh model	$1,300	$1,800

Gene Autry Roundup
1932-1939. Harmony made acoustic, Gene Autry signature on belly, cowboy roundup stencil, 13" body until '35, then 14".

1932-1939		$250	$400

Lone Ranger
1936-1941. Black with red and silver Lone Ranger and Tonto stencil, silver-painted fretboard, 13 1/2" wide. "Hi-Yo Silver" added in '37, changed to "Hi-Ho Silver" in '38.

1936-1941		$200	$325

Singing Cowboys
1938-1943. Stencil of guitar strumming cowboys around chuck wagon and campfire, branded Silvertone after '41.

1938-1943		$250	$325

Supertone Wedge
1930s. Triangle-shaped wedge body, laminate construction, blue-silver Supertone label inside sound chamber, art decals on body.

1930s		$225	$300

Supro
1935-1968. Budget brand of National Dobro Company. Some Supro models also sold under the Airline brand for Montgomery Ward. In '42 Victor Smith, Al Frost and Louis Dopyera bought National and changed the name to Valco Manufacturing Company. Valco Manufacturing Company name changed to Valco Guitars, Inc., in '62. Company treasurer Robert Engelhardt bought Valco in '64. In '67 Valco bought Kay and in '68 Valco/Kay went out of business. In the summer of '69, Valco/Kay brands and assets were sold at auction and the Supro and National names purchased by Chicago-area importer and distributor Strum N' Drum (Norma, Noble). TIn the early-'80s, ownership of the Supro name was transferred to Archer's Music, Fresno, California. Some Supros assembled from new-old-stock parts.

Belmont
1955-1964. For '55-'60, 12" wide, single-cut, 1 neck pickup, 2 knobs treble side in 'guard, reverse-stairs tailpiece, No-Mar plastic maroon-colored covering. For '60, size increased to 13 1/2" wide. For '62-'64, Res-o-glas fiberglas was used for the body, a slight cutaway on bass side, 1 bridge pickup, 2 knobs on opposite sides. Polar White.

1955-1962	Black or white No-Mar	$700	$950
1961-1964	Polar White Res-o-glas	$1,050	$1,350

Bermuda
1962 only. Slab body (not beveled), double pickups, dot markers, cherry glass-fiber finish.

1962		$950	$1,250

Collegian Spanish
1939-1942. Metal body, 12 frets. Moved to National line in '42.

1939-1942		$1,100	$1,300

Coronado/Coronado II
1961-1967. Listed as II in '62 15 1/2" scale, single-cut Gibson thinline-style, 2 pickups with 4 knobs and slider, natural blond spruce top. Changed to slight cutaway on bass side in '62 when renamed II.

1961-1962	Blond, natural spruce top	$1,100	$1,350
1963-1967	Black fiberglass	$1,300	$1,800

Suhr Standard

1965 Supro S-555

1958 Supro Dual-Tone

Tacoma RM6C

MODEL YEAR	FEATURES	EXC. COND. LOW	HIGH

Dual-Tone
1954-1966. The Dual Tone had several body style changes, all instruments had dual pickups. '54, 11 1/4" body, No Mar Arctic White plastic body ('54-'62). '55, 12" body. '58, 13" body. '60, 13 1/2" body. '62, Res-o-glas Ermine White body, light cutaway on bass side.

| 1954-1961 | Arctic White No-Mar | $900 | $1,200 |
| 1962-1964 | Ermine White Res-o-glas | $1,000 | $1,300 |

Folk Star/Vagabond
1964-1967. Molded Res-o-glas body, single-cone resonator, dot inlays, Fire Engine Red. Name changed to Vagabond in '66.

| 1964-1967 | | $700 | $900 |

Kingston
1962-1963. Double-cut slab body, bridge pickup, glass-fiber sand finish, similar to same vintage Ozark.

| 1962-1963 | | $450 | $550 |

Martinique
1962-1967. Single-cut, 13 1/2" wide, 2 standard and 1 bridge pickups, 6 knobs on bass side, 1 knob and slider on treble side, block markers, cataloged as "Supro's finest electric," Val-Trol script on 'guard, Bigsby vibrato tailpiece, blue or Ermine White Polyester Glas.

| 1962-1967 | | $1,900 | $2,300 |

Ozark
1952-1954, 1958-1967. Non-cut, 1 pickup, dot inlay, white pearloid body, name reintroduced in '58 as a continuation of model Sixty with single-cut, Dobro tailpiece.

1952-1954	White pearloid	$450	$550
1958-1961	Red	$450	$550
1962-1967	Jet Black or Fire Bronze	$450	$550

Ranchero
1948-1960. Full body electric archtop, neck pickup, dot markers, bound body, sunburst.

| 1948-1960 | | $550 | $650 |

Sahara
1960-1964. 13 1/2" body-style similar to Dual-Tone, single pickup, 2 knobs, Sand-Buff or Wedgewood Blue.

| 1960-1964 | | $800 | $900 |

Silverwood/Val-Trol
1960-1962. Single-cut, 13 1/2" wide, 2 standard and 1 bridge pickups, 6 knobs on bass side, 1 knob and slider on treble side, block markers, cataloged as "Supro's finest electric", natural blond, Val-Trol script on 'guard, renamed Martinique in '62.

| 1960-1962 | | $1,350 | $1,800 |

Sixty
1955-1958. Single-cut, single pickup, white No-Mar, becomes Ozark in '58.

| 1955-1958 | | $450 | $550 |

Special 12
1958-1960. Single-cut, replaces Supro Sixty, neck pickup 'guard mounted.

| 1958-1960 | | $450 | $550 |

MODEL YEAR	FEATURES	EXC. COND. LOW	HIGH

Strum 'N' Drum Solidbody
1970s. Student-level import, 1 pickup, large Supro logo on headstock.

| 1970s | | $250 | $350 |

Super
1958-1964. 12" wide single-cut body style like mid-'50s models, single bridge pickup, short-scale, ivory.

| 1958-1964 | | $450 | $500 |

Super Seven
1965-1967. Offset double-cut solidbody, short scale, middle pickup, Calypso Blue.

| 1965-1967 | | $350 | $400 |

Suprosonic 30
1963-1967. Introduced as Suprosonic, renamed Suprosonic 30 in '64, double-cut, single neck pickup, vibrato tailpiece, more of a student model, Holly Red.

| 1963-1967 | | $500 | $600 |

Tremo-Lectric
1965. Fiberglas hollowbody, 2 pickups, unique built-in electric tremolo (not mechanical), Wedgewood Blue finish, multiple controls associated with electric tremolo.

| 1965 | | $1,200 | $1,800 |

White Holiday/Holiday
1963-1967. Introduced as Holiday, renamed White Holiday in '64, fiberglas double-cut, vibrato tailpiece, single bridge pickup, Dawn White.

| 1963-1967 | | $800 | $900 |

Suzuki Takeharu
See listing for Takeharu.

SX
See listing for Essex.

T. H. Davis
1976-present. Professional and premium grade, custom, steel string and classical guitars built by luthier Ted Davis in Loudon, Tennessee. He also builds mandolins.

Tacoma
1995-present. Intermediate, professional, and premium grade, production, acoustic guitars produced in Tacoma, Washington. They also build acoustic basses and mandolins. In October, '04, Fender acquired Tacoma.

C-1C/C-1CE Chief
1997-present. Cutaway flat-top with upper bass bout soundhole, solid cedar top, mahogany back and sides, rosewood 'board. Sides laminated until 2000, solid after, CE is acoustic/electric.

| 1997-2000 | | $375 | $400 |
| 1997-2000 | Fishman electronics | $575 | $625 |

CB-10E4 Thunderchief
2000-present. 17 3/4 flat-top, solid spruce top, solid mahogany back, laminated mahogany sides, rounded cutaway, bolt-on neck, natural satin finish, factory Fishman Prefix Plus pickup system (E4), dot markers.

| 2000-2002 | | $700 | $750 |

MODEL YEAR	FEATURES	EXC. COND. LOW	HIGH

DM Series
1997-present. Dreadnought, solid spruce top, mahogany back and sides, satin finish, natural. Models include DM-8, -9, -10 and -14.

1997-2003	DM-9, DM-10	$325	$475

DR Series
1997-present. Dreadnought, solid sitka spruce top, solid rosewood back and sides, natural. Models include DR-20 (non-cut, herringbone trim, abalone rosette), DR-8C (cutaway), and DR-38.

1997-2004	DR-20	$650	$750
2000s	DR-38	$1,000	$1,100
2000s	DR-8C	$600	$700

JK-50CE4 Jumbo Koa
1997-2003. Jumbo cutaway, 17" lower bout, sitka spruce top, figured koa back and sides.

1997-2003		$1,100	$1,300

JR-14C Jumbo Rosewood
Late-1990s. Jumbo cutaway, 16 5/8" lower bout, gloss spruce top, satin rosewood body.

1998		$950	$1,050

P-1/P-2 Papoose
1995-present. Travel-size mini-flat-top, all solid wood, mahogany back and sides (P-1) or solid rosewood (P-2), cedar top, natural satin finish.

1995-1999	P-1	$350	$400
1995-2002	P-2	$400	$500

PK-30 Parlor
1997-2003. Smaller 14 3/4" body, solid spruce top, figured koa back and sides, natural gloss finish.

1997-2003		$1,050	$1,150

PM-15
1997-1998. Solid spruce top, solid mahogany back and sides.

1997-1998		$500	$600

PM-20
1997-2003. Solid spruce top, solid mahogany back and sides, gloss finish.

1997-2003		$650	$700

Takamine
1962-present. Intermediate and professional grade, production, steel- and nylon-string, acoustic and acoustic/electric guitars. They also make basses. Takamine is named after a mountain near its factory in Sakashita, Japan. Mass Hirade joined Takamine in '68 and revamped the brand's designs and improved quality. In '75, Takamine began exporting to other countries, including U.S. distribution by Kaman Music (Ovation). In '78, Takamine introduced acoustic/electric guitars. They offered solidbody electrics and some archtops for '83-'84.

Acoustic Electrics (laminate construction)
All laminate (plywood) construction, non-cut, standard features, pickup and preamp.

1980s		$250	$400
1990s		$250	$400

Acoustic Electric Cutaways (laminate)
All laminate (plywood) construction, cutaway, standard features, pickup and preamp.

1980s		$250	$400
1990s		$250	$400

Acoustic Electrics (solid top)
Solid wood top, sides and back can vary, cutaway, standard features, preamp and pickup.

1980s		$450	$900
1990s		$450	$900

Classical Guitars (solid top)
Solid wood (often cedar) top, classical, sides and back can vary.

1980s		$450	$600
1990s		$450	$600

Collectors (limited edition)
Each year a different limited edition collector's guitar is issued. '97 - solid top, koa body, cutaway, natural finish, preamp and pickup. '98 - solid top, rosewood body, cutaway, natural finish, preamp and pickup. '99 - solid top, rosewood body, cutaway, natural finish, preamp and pickup. '00 - solid top, rosewood body, cutaway, natural finish, preamp and pickup. '01 - solid top, rosewood body, cutaway, natural finish, preamp and pickup.

1990s		$950	$1,100

Takeharu (by Suzuki)
Mid-1970s. Classical guitars offered by Suzuki as part of their internationally known teaching method (e.g. Violin Suzuki method), various sized instruments designed to eliminate the confusion of size that has been a problem for classroom guitar programs.

Taku Sakashta Guitars
1994-present. Premium and presentation grade, production/custom, archtop, flat-top, 12-sting, and nylon-string guitars, built by luthier Taku Sakashta in Sebastopol, California.

Tama
Ca. 1959-1967, 1974-1979. Hoshino's (Ibanez) brand of higher-end acoutic flat-tops made in Japan. Many of the brand's features would be transferred to Ibanez's Artwood acoustics.

Taylor
1974-present. Intermediate, professional, premium, and presentation grade, production/custom, steel- and nylon-string, acoustic and acoustic/electric guitars built in El Cajon, California. Founded by Bob Taylor, Steve Schemmer and Kurt Listug in Lemon Grove, California, the company was originally named the Westland Music Company, but was soon changed to Taylor (Bob designed the guitars and it fit on the logo). Taylor and Listug bought out Schemmer in '83.

Bob Taylor was the first commercially successful guitar maker to harness CAD/CAM CNC technology for acoustic guitars. The CNC technology

Tacoma Papoose P1

Taylor XXX-KE

Taylor Baby

Taylor 310ce

allowed Taylor to build a less expensive guitar model without resorting to offshore manufacturing. Taylor's CNC-based intermediate priced all wood acoustic was the Model 410. Soon other builders followed Bob Taylor's lead.

Baby
1996-present. Solid spruce top, 3/4 dreadnought, mahogany laminated back and sides until '99, sapele laminate after.

MODEL YEAR / FEATURES	LOW	HIGH
1996-2003	$200	$250

Baby Mahogany (M)
1998-present. Solid mahogany top version of Baby, mahogany laminated back and sides until '99, sapele laminate after.

1998-2003	$250	$325

Baby Rosewood
2000-2003. Laminated Indian rosewood back and sides version, solid sitka spruce top

2000-2003	$275	$375

Big Baby
2000-present. 15/16"-size dreadnought, solid sitka spruce top, sapele-mahogany laminated back and sides, satin finish, gig bag.

2000s	$300	$450

Dan Crary Signature Model
1986-2000. Dreadnought, Venetian cutaway, thin spruce top, Indian rosewood back and sides, Crary signature on headstock.

1986-2000	$1,300	$1,500

LKSM6/12 Leo Kottke
1997-present. Jumbo 17" body, 6- or 12-string, rounded cutaway, sitka spruce top, mahogany back and sides, gloss finish, Leo Kottke signature.

1997-2003 12-string	$1,800	$1,900
1997-2003 6-string	$1,600	$1,700

Model 310 Dreadnought
1998-present. D-style solid spruce top, sapele-mahogany back and sides.

1998-2003	$800	$900

Model 310ce Dreadnought
1998-present. D-style Venetian cutaway, solid spruce top, sapele-mahogany back and sides, on-board electronics.

1998-2003	$900	$1,000

Model 312ce Grand Concert
1998-present. Grand Concert Venetian cutaway, solid spruce top, sapele-mahogany back and sides, on-board electronics.

1998-2003	$800	$900

Model 314 Grand Auditorium
1998-present. Mid-size Grand Auditorium-style, solid spruce top, sapele-mahogany back and sides.

1998-2003	$800	$900

Model 314ce Grand Auditorium
1998-present. Grand Auditorium Venetian cutaway, solid spruce top, sapele-mahogany back and sides, on-board electronics.

1998-2003	$1,100	$1,200

Model 314cek Grand Auditorium
2000. Limited edition of this model with flamed koa body.

MODEL YEAR / FEATURES	LOW	HIGH
2000	$1,000	$1,200

Model 315ce Jumbo
1998-present. Jumbo-style Venetian cutaway, solid spruce top, sapele-mahogany back and sides, on-board electronics.

1998-2003	$1,000	$1,100

Model 355 Jumbo 12-String
1998-present. Jumbo 12-string, solid spruce top, sapele-mahogany back and sides.

1998-2003	$900	$1,000

Model 355ce Jumbo 12-String
1998-present. Jumbo 12-string cutaway, solid spruce top, sapele-mahogany back and sides, on-board electrics.

1998-2003	$950	$1,050

Model 410 Dreadnought
1991-present. D-style, solid spruce top, mahogany back and sides until '98, African ovangkol back and sides after '98.

1991-2003	$900	$1,000

Model 410ce Dreadnought
1991-present. Cutaway, solid spruce top, mahogany back and sides until '98, African ovangkol back and sides after '98, satin finish.

1991-2003	$1,000	$1,200

Model 412 Grand Concert
1991-1998. Solid spruce top, mahogany back and sides until '98, African ovangkol back and sides after '98.

1991-1998	$800	$900

Model 412ce Grand Concert
1998-present. Cutaway electric version replaced the 412 in '98.

1998-2003	$1,000	$1,100

Model 414 Grand Auditorium
1998-present. Solid sitka spruce top, ovangkol back and sides, pearl dot inlays, natural.

1998-2003	$1,000	$1,100

Model 414ce Grand Auditorium
1998-present. Cutaway version, solid sitka spruce top, ovangkol back and sides, pearl dot inlays, natural.

1998-2003	$1,100	$1,200

Model 415 Jumbo
1998-present. Solid sitka spruce top, ovangkol back and sides, pearl dot inlays.

1998-2003	$900	$1,000

Model 420
1990-1997. D-style, sitka spruce top, maple back and sides, natural.

1990-1997	$900	$1,000

Model 450 12-String
1996-1997. Dreadnought 12-string, satin finish.

1996-1997	$900	$1,000

Model 455 12-String
2001-present. Solid Sitka spruce top, ovangkol back and sides, dot markers.

2001-2003	$1,000	$1,100

MODEL YEAR	FEATURES	EXC. COND. LOW	HIGH

Model 455ce 12-String
2001-present. Cutaway electric version, solid sitka spruce top, ovangkol back and sides, dot markers, on-board electronics.

2001-2003		$1,100	$1,200

Model 510 Dreadnought
1978-present. All solid wood, spruce top, mahogany back and sides.

1978-1979		$1,250	$1,400
1980-2003		$1,150	$1,300

Model 510 Dreadnought Limited
2002. Limited edition.

2002		$1,300	$1,400

Model 510ce Dreadnought
1978-present. Cutaway version of Model 510.

1978-1979		$1,350	$1,550
1980-1989		$1,300	$1,450
1990-2003		$1,300	$1,400

Model 512 Grand Concert
1978-2000. Solid Engelmann spruce top, solid American mahogany back and sides, dot markers.

1978-2000		$1,200	$1,300

Model 512ce Grand Concert
1978-present. Solid Engelmann spruce top, solid American mahogany back and sides, dot markers.

1978-2000s		$1,600	$1,800

Model 514c Grand Auditorium
1990-1998. Venetian cutaway, solid spruce or solid red cedar top, mahogany back and sides, no electronics, natural.

1990-1998		$1,600	$1,800

Model 514ce Grand Auditorium
1998-present. Venetian cutaway, solid red cedar top, mahogany back and sides, on-board electronics.

1998-2002		$1,650	$1,850

Model 555 Jumbo 12-String
1978-present. Solid sitka spruce top, solid mahogany back and sides, higher-end appointments.

1994-2003		$1,600	$1,700

Model 555ce Jumbo 12-String
1994-present. Cutaway, solid sitka spruce top, solid mahogany back and sides, higher-end appointments, on-board electronics.

1994-2003		$1,800	$1,900

Model 610 Dreadnought
1978-1998. Solid spruce top, solid maple back and sides, generally with amber stained finishes.

1978-1998		$1,300	$1,400

Model 610ce Dreadnought
1998-present. Solid spruce top, solid maple back and sides, generally with opaque finishes, on-board electronics.

1998-2003		$1,400	$1,500

Model 612 Grand Concert
1984-1998. Solid spruce top, solid maple back and sides, generally with amber stained finishes.

1984-1998		$1,500	$1,700

Model 612ce Grand Concert
1998-present. Solid spruce top, solid maple back and sides, generally with opaque finish, on-board electronics.

1998-2003		$1,500	$1,800

Model 614 Grand Auditorium
1978-1998. Solid spruce top, solid maple back and sides, generally with amber stained finishes.

1978-1998		$1,600	$1,800

Model 614ce Grand Auditorium
1998-present. Solid spruce top, solid maple back and sides, generally with opaque finish, on-board electronics.

1998-2004		$1,600	$1,900

Model 615
1981-1998. Jumbo, spruce top, flamed maple back and sides, non-cut.

1981-1998		$1,700	$1,850

Model 655 Jumbo
1978-present. Solid spruce top, solid maple back and sides, generally with Amber stained finishes.

1978-1998		$1,600	$1,700

Model 655 Jumbo 12-String
1978-1991, 1996-present. Solid spruce top, solid maple back and sides, generally with amber stained finishes.

1978-2000s		$1,600	$1,700

Model 655ce Jumbo 12-String
1998-present. Solid spruce top, solid maple back and sides, generally with opaque finish, on-board electronics.

1998-2003		$1,650	$1,750

Model 710
1977-present. Dreadnought-size, rosewood back and sides, spruce top.

1977-2003		$1,500	$1,700

Model 710BR
1990s. Model 710 with Brazilian rosewood.

1990s		$2,700	$2,800

Model 710ce L30 Commemorative
2004. 30th Anniversary Limited Edition, Engelmann spruce top, Indian rosewood body, on-board electronics, 30th Anniversary script logo on headstock, single-cut.

2004		$1,900	$2,100

Model 712 Grand Concert
1984-present. Grand Concert small body, solid wood, non-cut, rosewood back and sides, spruce top, cedar soundboard.

1984-2003		$1,350	$1,500

Model 712ce Grand Concert
2000-present. Cutaway, Engelmann spruce top, rosewood back and sides, on-board electronics.

2000-2003		$1,400	$1,600

Model 714 Grand Auditorium
1996-present. 15 7/8" lower bout, solid red cedar top, solid Indian rosewood back and sides.

1996-2003		$1,550	$1,750

Model 714ce Grand Auditorium
1998-present. Red cedar top, cutaway, on-board electronics.

1998-2003		$1,750	$1,950

Model 755 12-String
1990-1998. D-style, 12 strings, solid spruce top, rosewood back and sides, natural.

1990-1998		$1,600	$1,750

Taylor 655

Taylor 712

To get the most from this book, be sure to read "Using *The Guide*" in the introduction.

Taylor 912ce

Taylor NS62ce

MODEL YEAR FEATURES	EXC. COND. LOW	HIGH
Model 810 Dreadnought		
1975-present. Classic original Taylor design - early model.		
1975-2003	$1,600	$1,800
Model 810ce Dreadnought		
1998-present. Cutaway, solid sitka spruce top, Indian rosewood back and sides, on-board electronics.		
1998-2003 Brazilian rosewood option	$2,900	$3,100
1998-2003 Indian rosewood	$1,700	$2,000
Model 814 Grand Auditorium		
2005-present. Cutaway, rosewood back and sides, spruce top.		
2005	$2,150	$2,250
Model 815c Jumbo		
1993-1998. Cutaway, no electronics, solid sitka spruce top, Indian rosewood back and sides.		
1993-1998	$1,550	$1,650
Model 815ce Jumbo		
1998-present. Cutaway, solid sitka spruce top, Indian rosewood back and sides, on-board electronics.		
1998-2003	$1,600	$1,700
Model 855 Jumbo 12-String		
1993-present. Jumbo (J-200-style) 12-string, solid sitka spruce top, rosewood back and sides, natural.		
1993-2003	$1,700	$1,800
Model 910 Dreadnought		
1977-present. Maple back and sides until change to Indian rosewood in '86, spruce top, wide abalone-style rosette.		
1986-2000	$2,000	$2,500
Model 910ce Dreadnought		
1998-present. Soft cutaway, Indian rosewood back and sides, spruce top, wide abalone-style rosette.		
1998-2002	$2,200	$2,700
Model 912c Grand Concert		
1993-2002. Rosewood back and sides, abalone.		
1993-2002	$2,300	$2,500
Model 914ce		
2002-present. Soft cutaway, Indian rosewood back and sides, spruce top, on-board electronics.		
2002-2004	$2,500	$2,700
Model GSGW		
2001. Limited production of 100 guitars, grand concert size, spruce top, Zircote back and sides.		
2001	$3,500	$4,000
Model GSST		
2000. Limited production.		
2000	$4,000	$4,500
Model K10 Koa Dreadnought		
1983-present. Acoustic dreadnought, koa back and sides, spruce top, distinctive binding.		
1990s	$2,000	$2,100
Model K14c Grand Auditorium		
1998-2002. 15 3/4" lower bout, solid cedar top, solid flamed koa body, gloss finish.		
1990s	$2,200	$2,300
Model K20 Koa Dreadnought		
1983-1992. Non-cut D-style, koa top/back/sides, abalone rosette.		
1983-1992	$1,400	$1,500

MODEL YEAR FEATURES	EXC. COND. LOW	HIGH
Model K20c Koa Dreadnought		
1998-2002. Cutaway, koa body, Engelmann spruce top optional.		
1998-1999	$1,900	$2,100
Model K20ce Koa Dreadnought		
2001-present. Special order only by 2004.		
2001-2003	$2,000	$2,200
Model K55 12-String		
2001. Jumbo size 12-string, spruce top, koa back and sides.		
2001	$2,150	$2,250
Model PS12c Presentation Series		
1996-2004. Grand concert 15" lower bout, solid Englemann spruce top, solid AAA flamed koa back and sides, fancy 'Byzantine' vine inlay on fretboard.		
1996-2004	$5,000	$5,500
Model PS14BZ Special Edition		
1996. Presentation Series special edition with Englemann spruce top, Brazilian rosewood back and sides, abalone trim.		
1996	$4,500	$5,000
Model PS14c Special Edition		
2000. Presentation Series special edition with spruce top, AAA koa back and sides.		
2000	$4,800	$5,500
Model PS15 Jumbo		
1996-present. Solid Engelmann spruce top, Brazilian rosewood back and sides, scalloped X-bracing, high-end appointments.		
1996-2003	$4,800	$5,500
Model W10 Dreadnought		
1998-present. Claro walnut back and sides, optional tops include sitka spruce, Western red cedar, or claro walnut.		
1998-2003	$1,300	$1,500
Model W14ce		
2000-2003. Claro walnut back and sides, red cedar top, on-board electronics.		
2000-2003	$2,000	$2,500
Model XX-RS 20th Anniversary		
1994. Grand Auditorium 15 3/4" lower bout, spruce top, Indian rosewood back and sides.		
1994	$2,700	$2,800
Model XXV-RS 25th Anniversary		
1999-2000. D-size, spruce top, sapele back and sides.		
1999-2000	$2,100	$2,200
NS Series		
2002-present. Nylon Strung series, models include NS42ce, NS44 (ovangkol body), NS62ce (maple body) and NS74.		
2002-2004 NS42ce	$1,100	$1,200
2002-2004 NS44	$1,000	$1,100
2002-2004 NS62ce	$1,000	$1,100
2002-2004 NS74	$0	$0

Teisco

1946-1974, 1994-present. Founded in Tokyo, Japan by Hawaiian and Spanish guitarist Atswo Kaneko and electrical engineer Doryu Matsuda, the original company name was Aoi Onpa Kenkyujo;

MODEL YEAR	FEATURES	EXC. COND. LOW	HIGH

Teisco was the instrument name. Most imported into U.S. by Chicago's W.M.I. Corporation and Jack Westheimer beginning ca. '63-'64, some early ones for New York's Bugeleisen and Jacobson. Brands made by the company include Teisco, Teisco Del Rey, Kingston, World Teisco, Silvertone, Kent, Kimberly and Heit Deluxe.

In '56, the company's name was changed to Nippon Onpa Kogyo Co., Ltd., and in '64 the name changed again to Teisco Co., Ltd. In January '67, the company was purchased by Kawai. After '73, the brand was converted to Kay in U.S.; Teisco went into hiatus in Japan until being revived in the early-'90s with plexiglass reproductions of the Spectrum 5 (not available in U.S.). Some older Teisco Del Rey stock continued to be sold in U.S. through the '70s.

Electrics

1966-1969	1, 2, or 3 pickups	$100	$350
1966-1969	4 pickups or special finishes	$350	$550
1966-1969	Spectrum V	$350	$550
1968-1969	May Queen, black	$450	$600
1968-1969	May Queen, red	$550	$700

Tele-Star

1965-ca.1972. Imported from Japan by Tele-Star Musical Instrument Corporation of New York, New York. Primarily made by Kawai, many inspired by Burns designs, some in cool sparkle finishes.

Electrics

1966-1969	1, 2, or 3 pickups	$125	$250
1966-1969	4 pickups or special finishes	$250	$400
1966-1969	Amp-in-case	$150	$225
1969-1970	Double neck 6/4	$450	$650

Tennessee

1970-1993, 1996-present. Luthier Mark Taylor builds his professional and premium grade, production/custom, acoustic guitars in Old Hickory, Tennessee. He also builds mandolins, banjos and the Tut Taylor brand of resophonic guitars. Mark and his father Robert "Tut" Taylor started making the Tennessee brand of acoustic and resophonic guitars, banjos, and mandolins in '71. In '77, Tut left the company and Mark continued on as Crafters of Tennessee. In '93, Mark and Greg Rich started building instruments as Rich and Taylor. In '96, Mark resumed production under the Tennessee brand.

Texas

1959-ca. 1965. Line of aluminum neck electric solidbodies and basses made by France's Jacobacci company, which also built under its own brand. One, 2, or 3 pickups.

TheDon

Guitars made in Germany and imported into the U.S. by a guitar shop.

Thompson Guitars

1980-present. Luthier Ted Thompson builds his professional and premium grade, production/custom, flat-top, 12-string, and nylon-string guitars in Vernon, British Columbia.

Thorn Custom Guitars

2000-present. Professional and premium grade, custom/production, solid and hollowbody electrics built by luthiers Bill Thorn and his sons Bill, Jr. and Ron in Glendale, California. They started Thorn Custom Inlay in the early '90s to do custom inlay work for other builders. In '00, they added their own line of guitars.

Threet Guitars

1990-present. Premium grade, production/custom, flat-tops built by luthier Judy Threet in Calgary, Alberta.

Tilton

1850s-late 1800s. Built by William B. Tilton, of New York City. He was quite an innovator and held several guitar-related patents.

Parlor

1890s. Parlor guitar with various woods.

1890s	Diagonal grain spruce top, Brazilian	$1,800	$2,200
1890s	Pearl trim, Brazilian	$4,800	$5,200
1890s	Standard grain spruce top, Brazilian	$1,300	$1,700

Timeless Instruments

1980-present. Luthier David Freeman builds his professional, premium and presentation grade, custom, flattop, 12-string, nylon-string, and resonator guitars in Tugaske, Saskatchewan. He also builds mandolins and dulcimers.

Timm Guitars

1997-present. Professional grade, custom, flat-top, resonator and travel guitars built by luthier Jerry Timm in Auburn, Washington.

Timtone Custom Guitars

1993-present. Luthier Tim Diebert builds his premium grade, custom, solidbody, chambered-body and acoustic guitars in Grand Forks, British Columbia. He also builds basses and lap steels.

Tippin Guitar Co.

1978-present. Professional, premium and presentation grade, production/custom, flat-top guitars built by luthier Bill Tippin in Marblehead, Massachusetts.

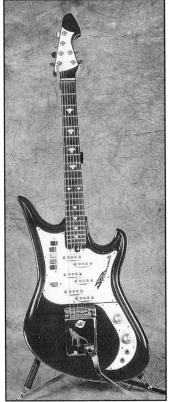

Teisco Spectrum 5

Timtone SH2

Tom Anderson Drop Top

Tony Nobles Exhibition

MODEL YEAR	FEATURES	EXC. COND. LOW	HIGH

Tobias

1977-present. Known mainly for basses, Tobias did offer guitar models in the '80s. See Bass Section for more company info.

TogaMan GuitarViol

2003-present. Premium grade, production/custom, bow-playable solidbody guitars built by luthier Jonathan Wilson in San Fernando, California.

Tokai

1947-present. Japan's Tokai Company started out making a keyboard harmonica that was widely used in Japanese schools. In the late '60s, Tokai hooked up with Tommy Moore, a successful instrument merchandiser from Fort Worth, Texas, and by '70 they were producing private label and OEM guitars. The guitars were sold in the U.S. under the brands of various importers. By the '70s, the Tokai name was being used on the instruments. Today Tokai continues to offer electrics, acoustics, and electric basses made in Japan and Korea.

ASD 403 Custom Edition

Classic offset double-cut solidbody, single-single-hum pickups, locking tremolo.

1980s		$450	$550

AST 56

Classic offset double-cut solidbody style, 3 single-coils.

1980s		$450	$550

ATE 52

Classic single-cut solidbody style, 2 single-coils.

1980s		$500	$550

Love Rock

Classic single-cut solidbody style, 2 humbuckers, figured tops at the high end.

1980s		$500	$1,000

Tom Anderson Guitarworks

1984-present. Professional and premium grade, production/custom, solidbody, semi-solidbody and acoustic guitars built by luthier Tom Anderson in Newbury Park, California.

Classic

1984-present. Double-cut solidbody, classic 3 pickup configuration, colors and appointments can vary.

1984-2000s		$1,300	$1,600

Cobra

1993-present. Single-cut solid mahogany body with figured maple top.

1993-2002		$1,600	$1,800

Drop Top

1992-present. Double-cut solidbody, single-single-hum pickups, various specs.

1992-1999		$1,500	$1,800

Hollow Classic

1996-present. Ash double-cut with tone chambers, 3 pickups.

1996-2005		$1,400	$1,800

MODEL YEAR	FEATURES	EXC. COND. LOW	HIGH

Tony Nobles

1990-present. Professional and premium grade, custom, acoustic and electric guitars built by luthier Tony Nobles in Wimberley, Texas. Tony writes a monthly repair article for Vintage Guitar magazine.

Torres (Antonio de Torres Jurado)

19th Century luthier most often associated with the initial development of the Classical Spanish guitar.

Toyota

1972-?. Imported from Japan by Hershman of New York, New York. At least 1 high-end acoustic designed by T. Kurosawa was ambitiously priced at $650.

Traphagen, Dake

1972-present. Luthier Dake Traphagen builds his premium grade, custom, nylon-string guitars in Bellingham, Washington.

Traugott Guitars

1991-present. Premium grade, production/custom, flat-top and acoustic/electric guitars built by luthier Jeff Traugott in Santa Cruz, California.

Traveler Guitar

1992-present. Intermediate grade, production, travel size electric, acoustic, classical and acoustic/electric guitars made in Redlands, California. They also make basses.

Travis Bean

1974-1979, 1999. Aluminum-necked solidbody electric guitars and basses. The company was founded by motorcycle and metal-sculpture enthusiast Travis Bean and guitar repairman Marc McElwee in Southern California; soon joined by Gary Kramer (see Kramer guitars). Kramer left Travis Bean in '75 and founded Kramer guitars with other partners. Guitar production began in mid-'76. The guitars featured carved aluminum necks with three-and-three heads with a T cutout in the center and wooden 'boards. Some necks had bare aluminum backs, some were painted black. A total of about 3,650 instruments were produced. Travis Bean guitar production was stopped in the summer of '79.

Serial numbers were stamped on headstock and were more-or-less consecutive. These can be dated using production records published by Bill Kaman in Vintage Guitar magazine. Original retail prices were $895 to $1195.

The company announced renewed production in '99 with updated versions of original designs and new models, but it evidently never got going.

MODEL YEAR	FEATURES	EXC. COND. LOW	HIGH

TB-1000 Artist
1974-1979. Aluminum neck with T-slotted headstock, double-cut archtop body, 2 humbucking pickups, 4 controls, block markers on 'board.

| 1974-1979 | | $1,500 | $3,000 |

TB-1000 Standard
1974-1979. Similar to TB-1000 Artist, but with dot inlays.

| 1974-1979 | | $1,500 | $3,000 |

TB-3000 Wedge
1976-1979. Aluminum neck with T-slotted headstock, triangle-shaped body, 2 humbucking pickups, 4 controls, block markers on 'board.

| 1976-1979 | | $1,500 | $3,000 |

TB-5000
Aluminum neck with T-slotted headstock, double-cut body, 2 single coil pickups mounted in 'guard, 2 controls, dot markers on 'board, white finish.

| 1975-1976 | | $2,000 | $4,000 |

Triggs
1992-present. Luthiers Jim Triggs and his son Ryan build their professional and premium grade, production/custom, archtop, flat-top, and solidbody guitars originally in Nashville Tennessee, and, since '98, in Kansas City, Kansas. They also build mandolins.

Acoustic/Electric Archtop
1992-present. Various archtop cutaway models.

1992-2002	Byrdland 17"	$2,500	$3,500
1992-2002	Excel 17"	$5,500	$6,500
1992-2002	Jazzmaster	$2,500	$3,500
1992-2002	New Yorker 18"	$6,500	$7,500
1992-2002	Stromberg Master 400	$7,000	$8,000

Trinity River
Acoustic and resonator guitars from Stenzler Musical Instruments of Ft. Worth, Texas. They also offer basses, mandolins, and fiddles.

True North Guitars
1994-present. Luthier Dennis Scannell builds his premium grade, custom, flat-tops in Waterbury, Vermont.

True Tone
1960s. Guitars, basses and amps retailed by Western Auto, manufactured by Chicago guitar makers like Kay. The brand was most likely gone by '68.

Double Cutaway Electric Archtop (K592)
1960s. Made by Kay and similar to their K592 double-cut thinline acoustic, 2 pickups, Bigsby tailpiece, burgundy red.

| 1960s | | $400 | $550 |

Fun Time
Early- to mid-1960s. Student 13" flat-top, painted 5-point 'guard, red sunburst finish.

| 1960s | | $50 | $75 |

Imperial Deluxe
Mid-1960s. Harmony-made (Rocket), 3 pickups, trapeze tailpiece, 6 control knobs, block markers, sunburst.

| 1960s | | $500 | $600 |

Jazz King (K573 Speed Demon)
1960s. Kay's K573 Speed Demon, 3 pickups, thinline archtop electric with F-hole, eighth note art on 'guard, sunburst.

| 1960s | | $400 | $600 |

Rock 'n Roll Electric (K100)
1960s. Kay's K100, slab body, single pickup, but with a bright red multiple lacquer finish.

| 1960s | | $150 | $225 |

Solidbody (K300 Kay)
1960s. Made by Kay and similar to their K300, double-cut, dual pickups and vibrola arm, red.

| 1960s | | $450 | $525 |

Speed Master (K6533 Value Leader Archtop)
1960s. Made by Kay and similar to their K6533 full-body electric archtop Value Leader line, eighth note art 'guard, sunburst.

| 1960s | | $175 | $250 |

Western Spanish Auditorium
Early- to mid-1960s. 15" flat-top, laminate construction, celluloid 'guard, sunburst.

| 1960s | | $150 | $200 |

Tucker
2000-present. Founded by John N. "Jack" Tucker, John Morrall, and David Killingsworth, Tucker builds professional and premium grade, production/custom, albizzia wood solidbody guitars in Hanalei, Hawaii. They also build basses.

Tut Taylor
Line of professional and premium grade, production/custom, resophonic guitars built by luthier Mark Taylor of Crafters of Tennessee in Old Hickory, Tennessee. Brand named for his father, dobro artist Tut Taylor. Taylor also builds the Tennessee line of guitars, mandolins and banjos and was part of Rich and Taylor guitars for '93-'96.

TV Jones
1993-present. Professional and premium grade, production/custom, hollow, chambered, and solid body guitars built by luthier Thomas Vincent Jones originally in California, now in Poulsbo, Washington. The instruments have either Jones or TV Jones inlaid on the headstock. He also builds pickups.

U. A. C.
1920s. Instruments built by the Oscar Schmidt Co. and possibly others. Most likely a brand made for a distributor.

1970s Travis Bean

Triggs archtop

To get the most from this book, be sure to read "Using *The Guide*" in the introduction.

Valencia JF

1970 Univox Lucy

MODEL		EXC. COND.	
YEAR	FEATURES	LOW	HIGH

Unique Guitars

2003-present. Professional and premium grade, production/custom, solidbody guitars built by luthier Joey Rico in California. He also builds basses. Joey is the son of Bernie Rico, the founder of BC Rich guitars.

Univox

1964-1978. Univox started out as an amp line and added guitars around '68. Guitars were imported from Japan by the Merson Musical Supply Company, later Unicord, Westbury, New York. Many if not all supplied by Arai and Company (Aria, Aria Pro II), some made by Matsumoku.

Univox Lucy ('69) first copy of lucite Ampeg Dan Armstrong. Generally mid-level copies of American designs.

Acoustic Flat-Top
1969-1978. Various models.

1970s		$100	$225

Bi-Centennial
1976. Offset double-cut, heavily carved body, brown stain, 3 humbucker-style pickups.

1976		$550	$900

Electric Hollowbody
Various models.

1970s		$300	$550

Electric Solidbody
Includes Flying V, Mosrite and Hofner violin-guitar copies.

1970s		$275	$600

Guitorgan FSB C-3000
1970s. Double-cut semi-hollow body, multiple controls, Guitorgan logo on headstock, footpedal.

1970s		$1,100	$1,300

USA Custom Guitars

1999-present. Professional and premium grade, custom/production, solidbody electric guitars built in Tacoma, Washington. USA also does work for other luthiers.

Vaccaro

1997-2002. Founded by Henry Vaccaro, Sr., one of the founders of Kramer Guitars. They offered intermediate and professional grade, production/custom, aluminum-necked guitars designed by Vaccaro, former Kramer designer Phil Petillo, and Henry Vaccaro, Jr., which were made in Asbury Park, New Jersey. They also built basses.

Valco

Valco, from Chicago, was a big player in the guitar and amplifier business. Their products were private branded for other companies like National, Supro, Airline, Oahu, and Gretsch.

Valencia

1985-present. Budget grade, production, classical guitars imported by Rondo Music of Union, New Jersey.

MODEL		EXC. COND.	
YEAR	FEATURES	LOW	HIGH

Valley Arts

Ca. 1977-present. Professional and premium grade, production/custom, semi-hollow and solid-body guitars built in Nashville, Tennessee. They also make basses. Valley Arts originally was a Southern California music store owned by partners Al Carness and Mike McGuire where McGuire taught and did most of the repairs. Around '77, McGuire and Valley Arts started making custom instruments on a large scale. By '83, they opened a separate manufacturing facility to build the guitars. In '92 Samick acquired half of the company with McGuire staying on for a year as a consultant. Samick offered made-in-the-U.S. production and custom models under the Valley Arts name. In '02, Valley Arts became a division of Gibson Guitar Corp., which builds the guitars in Nashville. Founders Carness and McGuire are back with the company. They reintroduced the line in January, '03.

California Pro (U.S.-made)
1983-2002. Double-cut body, six-on-a-side tuners, single/single/hum pickups, 2 knobs and switch, various colors, serial number begins with CAL.

1983-1989		$550	$650
1990-1999		$500	$650

Optek Fretlight (U.S.-made)
Double-cut body, about 126 LED lights in fretboard controlled by a scale/chord selector, black opaque.

1990		$500	$600

Standard Pro (U.S.-made)
1990-1993. Double-cut body, six-on-a-side tuners, single/single/hum pickups, 2 knobs and switch, black opaque, serial number begins with VA.

1990-1993		$500	$650

Vantage

1977-present. Budget and intermediate grade, production, acoustic and electric guitars. They also build basses. Instruments from Japan from '77-'90 and from Korea from '90-present.

Vega

1903-1980s, 1989-present. The name Vega means star and a star logo is often seen on the original Vega guitars. The original Boston-based company was purchased by C.F. Martin in '70. In '80, Martin sold the Vega trademark to Korea's Galaxy Trading Company. The Deering Banjo Company, in Spring Valley, California acquired the brand in '89 and uses it (and the star logo) on a line of banjos.

C Series Archtop
1930-1950s. Several different C-model numbers, mid-level archtops including carved solid tops with bookmatched figured maple backs, natural or sunburst.

1930s		$850	$1,100
1940s		$850	$1,100
1950s	Cutaway	$900	$1,200

MODEL YEAR	FEATURES	EXC. COND. LOW	HIGH

Duo-Tron Electric Archtop
1940s-1950s. Mid-level large body non-cut archtop, single pickup, block markers, natural or sunburst.

1940s		$1,100	$1,400
1950s		$1,100	$1,400

FT-90 Flat-Top
1960s. 15" body with narrow waist, dot markers, Vega logo, natural.

1960s		$450	$500

Parlor Guitar
Early-1900s. Small parlor-sized instrument, Brazilian rosewood back and sides, styles vary, fancy appointments associated with higher-end models, including binding, purfling and inlays.

1900s	Mid-level	$1,700	$2,000
1910s	Higher-end	$2,000	$2,500

Profundo Flat-Top
1940s-1950s. Flat-top D-style body, spruce top, mahogany or rosewood back and sides.

1940s-50s	Mahogany	$1,300	$1,600
1940s-50s	Rosewood	$2,500	$3,100

Solidbody Electric (Import)
1970s-1980s. Solidbody copies of classic designs, Vega script logo on headstock, bolt-on necks.

1970s		$225	$350

Vega, Charles
1993-present. Luthier Charles Vega builds his premium, production/custom, nylon-string guitars in Baltimore, Maryland.

Veillette
1991-present. Luthiers Joe Veillette (of Veillette-Citron fame) and Martin Keith build their professional grade, production/custom, acoustic, acoustic/electric, electric 6- and 12-string and baritone guitars in Woodstock, New York. They also build basses and mandolins.

Veillette-Citron
1975-1983. Founded by Joe Veillette and Harvey Citron who met at the New York College School of Architecture in the late '60s. Joe took a guitar building course from Michael Gurian and by the Summer of '76, he and Harvey started producing neck-thru solidbody guitars and basses. Veillette and Citron both are back building instruments.

Veleno
1967, 1970-1977, 2003-present. Premium and presentation grade, production/custom, all-aluminum electric solidbody guitars built by luthier John Veleno in St. Petersburg, Florida. First prototype in '67. Later production begins in late-'70 and lasts until '75 or '76. The guitars were chrome or gold-plated, with various anodized colors. The Traveler Guitar was the idea of B.B. King; only 10 were made. Two Ankh guitars were made for Todd Rundgren in '77. Only one bass was made. Approximately 185 instruments were made up to '77 and are sequentially numbered. In 2003, John

Veleno reintroduced his brand. See Guitar Stories Volume II, by Michael Wright, for a complete history of Veleno guitars.

Original (Aluminum Solidbody)
1973-1976. V-headstock, chrome and aluminum.

1973-1976		$7,500	$9,000

Traveler Guitar
1973-1976. Limited production of about a dozen instruments, drop-anchor-style metal body.

1973-1976		$10,000	$11,500

Ventura
1970s. Acoustic and electric guitars imported by C. Bruno Company, mainly copies of classic American models.

Hollowbody Electric Guitars
1970s. Various copy models.

1970s		$450	$525

Versoul, LTD
1989-present. Premium grade, production/custom steel-string flat-top, acoustic/electric, nylon-string, resonator, solidbody, and baritone guitars built by luthier Kari Nieminen in Helsinki, Finland. He also builds basses and sitars.

Victor Baker Guitars
1998-present. Professional and premium grade, custom, carved archtop, flat-top and solidbody electric guitars built by luthier Victor Baker in Philadelphia, Pennsylvania.

Victor Guitars
2004-present. Luthier Edward Victor Dick builds his premium grade, production/custom, steel-string acoustics in Denver, Colorado.

Victoria
1920s. Instruments built by the Oscar Schmidt Co. and possibly others. Most likely a brand made for a distributor.

Viking Guitars
1998-present. Professional and premium grade, custom, solidbody guitars made in Las Vegas, Nevada by Ed Roman.

Vincente Tatay
1894-late 1930s. Classical guitars built by luthier Vicente Tatay and his sons in Valencia, Spain.

Vinetto
2003-present. Luthier Vince Cunetto builds his professional grade, production/custom, solid, chambered and semi-hollow body guitars in St. Louis, Missouri.

Veleno Original

Versoul Buxom 6

Vox Mark VI

Vox Phantom XII

MODEL YEAR	FEATURES	EXC. COND. LOW	HIGH

Vivi-Tone

1933-ca. 1936. Founded in Kalamazoo, Michigan, by former Gibson designer Lloyd Loar, Walter Moon and Lewis Williams, Vivi-Tone built acoustic archtop guitars as well as some of the earliest electric solidbodies. They also built amps, basses and mandolins.

Guitar

1930s. Deep archtop-style body with F-holes on the backside and magnetic bridge pickup.

1930s	Rare model	$4,500	$5,000
1930s	Standard model, sunburst	$2,500	$3,000

Vox

1957-1972, 1982-present. Name introduced by Jennings Musical Instruments (JMI) of England. First Vox products were amplifiers brought to the market in '58 by Tom Jennings and Dick Denny. Guitars were introduced in '61, with an Echo Unit starting the Vox line of effects in '63. Guitars and basses bearing the Vox name were offered from '61-'69 (made in England and Italy), '82-'85 (Japan), '85-'88 (Korea), and for '98-2001 (U.S.). Vox products are currently distributed in the U.S. by Korg USA. Special thanks to Jim Rhoads of Rhoads Music in Elizabethtown, Pennsylvania, for help on production years of these models.

Apollo

1967-1968. Single sharp cutaway, 1 pickup, distortion, treble and bass booster, available in sunburst or cherry.

1967-1968		$550	$700

Bobcat

1963-1968. Double-cut semi-hollowbody style, block markers, 3 pickups, vibrato, 2 volume and 2 tone controls.

1963-1968		$700	$800

Bossman

1967-1968. Single rounded cutaway, 1 pickup, distortion, treble and bass booster, available in sunburst or cherry.

1967-1968		$500	$600

Bulldog

1966. Solidbody double-cut.

1966		$650	$850

Delta

1967-1968. Solidbody, 2 pickups, distortion, treble and bass boosters, vibrato, 1 volume and 2 tone controls, available in white only.

1967-1968		$1,050	$1,300

Folk XII

1966-1969. Dreadnought 12-string flat-top, large 3-point 'guard, block markers, natural.

1966-1969		$450	$550

Guitar-Organ

1966. Standard Phantom with oscillators from a Continental organ installed inside. Plays either organ sounds, guitar sounds, or both. Weighs over 20 pounds.

1966		$1,300	$1,700

MODEL YEAR	FEATURES	EXC. COND. LOW	HIGH

Mando Guitar

1966. Made in Italy, 12-string mandolin thing.

1966		$1,350	$1,600

Mark III

1998-2001. Teardrop reissue.

1998-2001		$675	$750

Mark VI

1965-1967. Teardrop-shaped solidbody, 3 pickups, vibrato, 1 volume and 2 tone controls.

1964-1965	England, white, Brian Jones model	$3,000	$4,000
1965-1967	Italy, sunburst	$1,000	$1,300

Mark VI Reissue

1998-2001.

1998-2001		$725	$775

Mark IX

1965-1966. Solidbody teardrop-shaped, 9 strings, 3 pickups, vibrato, 1 volume and 2 tone controls, sunburst.

1965		$850	$1,000

Mark XII

1965-1967. Teardrop-shaped solidbody, 12 strings, 3 pickups, vibrato, 1 volume and 2 tone controls, sunburst.

1965-1967		$1,000	$1,400

Phantom VI

1962-1967. Five-sided body, 6 strings, 3 pickups, vibrato, 1 volume and 2 tone controls.

1962-1964	English-made	$1,900	$2,200
1965-1967	Italian-made	$1,200	$1,500

Phantom XII

1964-1967. Five-sided body, 12 strings, 3 pickups, vibrato, 1 volume and 2 tone controls.

1964	English-made	$1,900	$2,300
1965-1967	Italian-made	$1,200	$1,600

Spitfire

1965-1967. Solidbody double-cut, 3 pickups, vibrato tailpiece.

1965-1967		$425	$500

Starstream

1967-1968. Teardrop-shaped hollowbody, 2 pickups, distortion, treble and bass boosters, wah-wah, vibrato, 1 volume and 2 tone controls, 3-way pickup selector, available in cherry or sandburst.

1967-1968		$1,000	$1,250

Starstream XII

1967-1968. 12 string Starstream.

1967-1968		$1,050	$1,300

Stroller

1961-1966. Made in England, solidbody, single bridge pickup, Hurricane-style contoured body, dot markers, red.

1961-1966		$300	$450

Student Prince

1965-1967. Mahogany body thinline archtop electric, 2 knobs, dot markers, made in Italy.

1965-1967		$375	$425

Super Ace

1963-1965. Solidbody double-cut.

1963-1965		$300	$450

MODEL YEAR	FEATURES	EXC. COND. LOW	HIGH

Super Lynx
1965-1967. Similar to Bobcat but with 2 pickups and no vibrola, double-cut, 2 pickups, adjustable truss rod, 2 bass and 2 volume controls.

1965-1967		$650	$750

Super Lynx Deluxe
1965-1967. Super Lynx with added vibrato tailpiece.

1965-1967		$650	$800

Super Meteor
1965-1967. Solidbody double-cut.

1965-1967		$300	$450

Tempest XII
1965-1967. Solidbody double-cut, 12 strings, 3 pickups.

1965-1967		$500	$600

Thunder Jet
1960s-style with single pickup and vibrato arm.

1960s		$500	$650

Tornado
1965-1967. Thinline archtop, single pickup, dot markers, sunburst.

1965-1967		$300	$400

Typhoon
1965-1967. Hollowbody single-cut, 2 pickups, 3-piece laminated neck.

1965-1967		$350	$500

Ultrasonic
1967-1968. Hollowbody double-cut, 2 pickups, distortion, treble and bass boosters, wah-wah, vibrato, 1 volume and 2 tone controls, 3-way pickup selector, available in sunburst or cherry.

1967-1968		$700	$850

Viper
1968. Double-cut, thinline archtop electric, built-in distortion.

1968		$1,050	$1,200

Walker
1994-present. Premium and presentation grade, production/custom, flat-top and archtop guitars built by luthier Kim Walker in North Stonington, Connecticut.

Wandre (Davoli)
Ca. 1956/57-1969. Solidbody and thinline hollowbody electric guitars and basses created by German-descended Italian motorcycle and guitar enthusiast, artist, and sculptor from Milan, Italy, Wandre Pioli. Brands include Wandre (pronounced Vahn-dray), Davoli, Framez, JMI, Noble, Dallas, Avalon, Avanti I and others. Until '60, they were built by Pioli himself; from '60-'63 built in Milan by Framez; '63-'65 built by Davoli; '66-'69 built in Pioli's own factory.

The guitars originally used Framez pickups, but from '63 on (or earlier) they used Davoli pickups. Mostly strange shapes characterized by neck-thru-tailpiece aluminum neck with plastic back and rosewood 'board. Often multi-color and sparkle finishes, using unusual materials like linoleum, fiberglass and laminates, metal bindings. Often the instruments will have numerous identifying names but usually somewhere there is a Wandre "blob" logo.

Distributed early on in the U.K. by Jennings Musical Industries, Ltd. (JMI) and in the U.S. by Don Noble and Company. Model B.B. dedicated to Brigitte Bardot. Among more exotic instruments were the minimalist Krundaal Bikini guitar with a built-in amplifier and attached speaker, and the "pogo stick" Swedenbass. These guitars are relatively rare and highly collectible. In '05, the brand was revived on a line of imported intermediate grade, production, solidbodies from Eastwood guitars.

Metal Solidbody

1960s		$1,500	$4,500

Warrior
1995-present. Professional, premium, and presentation grade, production/custom, acoustic and solidbody electric guitars built by luthier J.D. Lewis in Roseville, Georgia. Warrior also builds basses.

Washburn (Lyon & Healy)
1880s-ca.1949. Washburn was founded in Chicago as one of the lines for Lyon & Healy to promote high quality stringed instruments, ca. 1880s. The rights to manufacture Washburns were sold to J.R. Stewart Co. in '28, but rights to Washburn name were sold to Tonk Brothers of Chicago. In the Great Depression (about 1930), J.R. Stewart Co. was hit hard and declared bankruptcy. Tonk Brothers bought at auction all Stewart trade names, then sold them to Regal Musical Instrument Co. Regal built Washburns by the mid-'30s. The Tonk Brothers still licensed the name. These Washburn models lasted until ca. '49. In '74 the brand resurfaced.

Model 1897
High-end appointments, plentiful pearl, 18 frets, slightly larger than parlor size, natural.

1910		$2,500	$3,750

Model 1915
Brazilian rosewood back and sides.

1928		$2,000	$2,500

Style 188
Rosewood back and sides with full pearl 'board inlaid with contrasting colored pearl, pearl on edges and around soundhole.

1890s		$4,000	$4,750

Washburn
1974-present. Budget, intermediate, professional, and premium grade, production/custom, acoustic and electric guitars made in the U.S., Japan, and Korea. They also make basses, amps, banjos and mandolins.

Originally a Lyon & Healy brand, the Washburn line was revived in '74, promoted by Beckman Musical Instruments. Beckman sold the rights to the Washburn name to Fretted Instruments, Inc.

1965 Wandré Model Karak

1930s Weissenborn

Wechter Pathmaker

in '76. Guitars originally made in Japan and Korea, but production moved back to U.S. in '91. Currently Washburn is part of U.S. Music.

Washington

Washington was a brand manufactured by Kansas City, Missouri instrument wholesalers J.W. Jenkins & Sons. First introduced in 1895, the brand also offered mandolins.

Watkins/WEM

1957-present. Watkins Electric Music (WEM) was founded by Charlie Watkins. Their first commercial product was the Watkins Dominator (wedge Gibson stereo amp shape) in '57. They made the Rapier line of guitars and basses from the beginning. Watkins offered guitars and basses up to '82.

Wayne

1998-present. Professional and premium grade, production/custom, solidbody guitars built by luthiers Wayne and Michael (son) Charvel in Paradise, California. They also build lap steels.

Webber

1988-present. Professional grade, production/custom flat-top guitars built by luthier David Webber in North Vancouver, British Columbia.

Webster

1940s. Archtop and acoustic guitars, most likely built by Kay or other mass builder.

Model 16C

Acoustic archtop.

MODEL YEAR	FEATURES	EXC. COND. LOW	HIGH
1940s		$500	$600

Wechter

1984-present. Intermediate, professional and premium grade, production/custom, flat-top, 12-string, resonator and nylon-string guitars from luthier Abe Wechter in Paw Paw, Michigan. He also offers basses. The Elite line is built in Paw Paw, the others in Asia. Until '94 he built guitars on a custom basis. In '95, he set up a manufacturing facility in Paw Paw to produce his new line and in '00 he added the Asian guitars. In '04, he added resonators designed by Tim Scheerhorn. Wechter was associated with Gibson Kalamazoo from the mid-'70s to '84. He also offers the Maple Lake brand of acoustics.

Weissenborn

1910s-1937, present. Hermann Weissenborn was well-established as a violin and piano builder in Los Angeles by the early 1910s. Around '20, he added guitars, ukes and steels to his line. Most of his production was in the '20s and '30s until his death in '37. He made tenor, plectrum, parlor, and Spanish guitars, ukuleles, and mandolins, but is best remembered for his koa Hawaiian guitars that caught the popular wave of Hawaiian music. That music captivated America after being introduced to the masses at San Francisco's Panama Pacific International Exposition which was thrown in '15 to celebrate the opening of the Panama Canal and attended by more than 13 million people. He also made instruments for Kona and other brands. The Weissenborn brand has been revived on a line of reissue style guitars.

Style #1 Hawaiian

Koa, no binding, 3 wood circle soundhole inlays.

MODEL YEAR	FEATURES	EXC. COND. LOW	HIGH
1926		$2,500	$3,500

Style #2 Hawaiian

Koa, black celluloid body binding, white wood 'board binding, rope soundhole binding.

1926		$3,000	$4,000

Style #3 Hawaiian

Koa, rope binding on top, 'board, and soundhole.

1925		$3,500	$4,500

Style #4 Hawaiian

Koa, rope binding on body, 'board, headstock and soundhole.

1927		$4,000	$5,000

Tenor

1920		$1,500	$2,000

Welker Custom

Professional and premium grade, production/custom, archtop and flat-top guitars built by luthier Fred Welker in Nashville, Tennessee.

Wendler

1999-present. Intermediate and professional grade, production/custom, solidbody, electro-acoustic guitars from luthier Dave Wendler of Ozark Instrument Building in Branson, Missouri. He also builds basses. In '91, Wendler patented a pickup system that became the Taylor ES system.

Westbury-Unicord

1978-ca. 1983. Imported from Japan by Unicord of Westbury, New York. High quality original designs, generally with 2 humbuckers, some with varitone and glued-in necks.

Westone

1970s-1990, 1996-2001. Made by Matsumoku in Matsumoto, Japan and imported by St. Louis Music. Around '81, St. Louis Music purchased an interest in Matsumoku and began to make a transition from its own Electra brand to the Westone brand previously used by Matsumoku. In the beginning of '84, the brand became Electra-Westone with a phoenix bird head surrounded by circular wings and flames. By the end of '84 the Electra name was dropped, leaving only Westone and a squared-off bird with W-shaped wings logo. Electra, Electra-Westone and Westone instruments from this period are virtually identical except for the brand and logo treatment. Many of these guitars were made in very limited runs and are relatively rare. From

MODEL		EXC. COND.	
YEAR	FEATURES	LOW	HIGH

'96 to '01, England's FCN Music offered Westone branded electric and acoustic guitars. The electrics were built in England and the acoustics came from Korea.

Matsumoku-made guitars feature a serial number in which the first 1 or 2 digits represent the year of manufacture. Electra-Westone guitars should begin with either a 4 or 84.

Weymann

1864-1940s. H.A. Weymann & Sons was a musical instrument distributor located in Philadelphia that marketed various stringed instruments, but mainly known for banjos. Some guitar models made by Regal and Vega, but they also built their own instruments.

Parlor

1904-ca. 1920. Small 14 5/8" body parlor-style, fancy pearl and abalone trim, fancy fretboard markers, natural.

1910		$3,000	$3,500

Wilkanowski

Early-1930s-mid-1940s. W. Wilkanowski primarily built violins. He did make a few dozen guitars which were heavily influenced by violin design concepts and in fact look very similar to a large violin with a guitar neck.

Violin-Shaped Acoustic

1930-1945. Violin brown.

1930-1945		$15,000	$22,000

Wilkins

1984-present. Custom guitars built by luthier Pat Wilkins in Van Nuys, California. Wilkins also does finish work for individuals and a variety of other builders.

William Hall and Son

William Hall and Son was a New York City based distributor offering guitars built by other luthiers in the mid to late 1800s.

Wilson Brothers Guitars

2004-present. Production electric and acoustic guitars. They also build basses. Founded by Ventures guitarist Don Wilson.

Windsor

Ca. 1890s-ca. 1914. Brand used by Montgomery Ward for flat top guitars and mandolins made by various American manufacturers, including Lyon & Healy and, possibly, Harmony. Generally beginner-grade instruments.

Acoustic Flat-Top

1890s-1914.

1900s		$200	$325

Winston

Ca. 1963-1967. Imported from Japan by Buegeleisen and Jacobson of New York. Manufacturers unknown, but some are by Guyatone. Generally shorter scale beginner guitars.

Worland Guitars

1997-present. Professional grade, production/custom, flat-top, 12-string, and harp guitars built by luthier Jim Worland in Rockford, Illinois.

WRC Music International

1989-mid-1990s. Guitars by Wayne Richard Charvel, who was the original founder of Charvel Guitars. He now builds Wayne guitars with his son Michael.

Wright Guitar Technology

1993-present. Luthier Rossco Wright builds his unique intermediate grade, production, travel/practice steel-string and nylon-string guitars in Eugene, Oregon.

Wurlitzer

Wurlitzer marketed a line of American-made guitars in the 1920s. They also offered American- and foreign-made guitars starting in '65. The American ones were built from '65-'66 by the Holman-Woodell guitar factory in Neodesha, Kansas. In '67, Wurlitzer switched to Italian-made Welson guitars.

Model 2077 (Martin 0-K)

1920s. Made by Martin for Wurlitzer who had full-line music stores in most major cities. Size 0 with top, back and sides made from koa wood, limited production of about 28 instruments.

1922	Natural	$4,500	$5,500

Model 2090 (Martin 0-28)

1920s. Made by Martin for Wurlitzer who had full-line music stores in most major cities. Size 0 with appointments similar to a similar period Martin 0-28, limited production of about 11 instruments, Wurlitzer branded on the back of the headstock and on the inside back seam, Martin name also branded on inside seam.

1922	Natural	$6,500	$8,000

Wild One Stereo

1960s. Two pickups, various colors.

1967		$400	$800

Xaviere

Imtermediate and professional grade, prodution, solid and semi-hollow body guitars from Guitar Fetish, which also has GFS pickups.

Yamaha

1946-present. Budget, intermediate, professional, and presentation grade, production/custom, acoustic, acoustic/electric, and electric guitars. They also build basses, amps, and effects. The Japanese instrument maker was founded in 1887. Began clas-

Worland Jumbo

Wright Guitar Technology SoloEtte

Yamaha APX 9c

Yamaha RGX Standard

MODEL YEAR	FEATURES	EXC. COND. LOW	HIGH

sical guitar production around 1946. Solidbody electric production began in '66; steel string acoustics debut sometime after that. Production shifted from Japan to Taiwan (Yamaha's special-built plant) in the '80s, though some high-end guitars still made in Japan. Some Korean production began in '90s.

Serialization patterns:

Serial numbers are coded as follows: H = 1, I = 2, J = 3, etc., Z = 12

To use this pattern, you need to know the decade of production.

Serial numbers are ordered as follows: Year/ Month/Day/Factory Order

Example: NL 29159 represents a N=1987 year, L=5th month or May, 29=29th day (of May), 159=159th guitar made that day (the factory order). This guitar was the 159 guitar made on May 29, 1987.

AE-11

1966-1974. Single-cut, arched top, glued neck, 2 pickups, natural.

1966-1974		$550	$700

AE-12

1973-1977. Single-cut thinline archtop.

1973-1977		$550	$800

AE-18

1973-1977. AE-12 with upgrade inlays and gold hardware.

1973-1977		$600	$850

AE-500

1998-2000. Solidbody with rounded cutaway horn, 2 humbuckers, pearloid guard, dot markers.

1998-2000		$300	$425

AE-1200

1985-1992. Full body electric archtop, cherry sunburst.

1985-1992		$650	$850

APX-4

1992-1995. Acoustic/electric cutaway flat-top.

1992-1995		$450	$550

APX-10

1987-1994. Acoustic/electric flat-top cutaway, 2 pickups, stereo 2-way. Called APX-10T if ordered with rosewood back and sides.

1987-1994		$500	$600

DW-8 VRS

1999-2002. Dreadnought flat-top, sunburst, solid spruce top, higher-end appointments like abalone rosette and top purfling.

1999-2002		$500	$600

Eterna Acoustic

1983-1994. Folk style acoustics, there were 4 models.

1983-1994		$250	$300

FG-260

1970s. 12-string dreadnought, mahogany body.

1970s		$300	$350

FG-340

Ca. 1978-1994. Dreadnought, mahogany body, bound top.

1970s		$350	$400

FG-345

1983-1994. Bound top flat-top.

1983-1994		$350	$400

FG-410

1984-1994. Flat-top acoustic; the 410E had a pickup.

1984-1994		$350	$400

FG-412SB II 12-String

1983-1994. 12-string flat-top, sunburst.

1983-1994		$350	$425

FG-430A

1984-1994. D-style flat-top.

1984-1994		$400	$450

FG-1500

Flat-top, Brazilian rosewood.

1973		$450	$550

G-245S

1981-1985. Classical, solid spruce top, rosewood back and sides.

1981-1985		$250	$400

G-255S

1981-1985. Classical, spruce top, Indian rosewood back and sides.

1981-1985		$350	$450

Image Custom

1989-1992. Electric double-cut, flamed maple top, active circuitry, LED position markers.

1989-1992		$350	$450

L-8 Acoustic

1984-1996. Solid top dreadnought acoustic.

1984-1996		$350	$400

Pacifica (standard features)

1980s-1990s. Offset double-cut with longer horns, dot markers.

1980s		$300	$350
1990s		$300	$350

RGX Series

1988-1989. Bolt-on neck for the 600 series and neck-thru body designs for 1200 series, various models include 110 (1 hum), 211 (hum-single), 220 (2 hums), 312 (hum-single-single), 603 (3 singles), 612 (hum-single-single), 620 (2 hums), 1203S (3 singles), 1212S (hum-single-single), 1220S (2 hums).

1988-1989	Various models	$300	$400

RGZ-312

1989-1992. Offset double-cut solid body, bolt neck, 2 single-coils and 1 humbucker, dot markers.

1989-1992		$350	$400

RGZ-820R

1993-1994. Blues Saraceno Signature Model, bolt neck, 2 humbuckers, dot markers.

1993-1994		$450	$550

SA-700

1980s. Double-cut semi-hollow body, stud tailpiece, dot markers, 2 humbuckers, SA (Super Axe) Series, Super Axe script logo on headstock, SA700 logo on bell cap truss rod cover.

1980s		$850	$950

MODEL		EXC. COND.	
YEAR	FEATURES	LOW	HIGH

SA-2000
1979-1984. Double-cut semi-hollow body, stud tailpiece, block markers, 2 humbuckers, SA (Super Axe) Series, gold hardware, sunburst or burgundy finish.

| 1979-1984 | | $900 | $1,000 |

SBG-200
1983-1992. Solidbody, glued neck, unbound, dot inlays on rosewood 'board, gold hardware, white top.

| 1983-1992 | | $250 | $350 |

SBG-500
1983-1992. Electric, laminated body, set-in neck, 2 pickups, Tune-O-Matic bridge, sunburst or burgundy finish.

| 1980s | | $350 | $450 |

SBG-2000
1983-1992. Electric, double-cut beveled body, set-neck, 2 pickups.

| 1983-1992 | | $300 | $375 |

SBG-2100
1984-1992. Double-cut solidbody, set-neck.

| 1984-1992 | | $300 | $375 |

SE-250
1986-1992. Electric, offset double-cut, 2 pickups.

| 1986-1992 | | $250 | $350 |

SE-350 H
1986-1992. Solidbody, offset double-cut, 2 humbuckers.

| 1986-1992 | | $250 | $350 |

SG/SBG-3000/SG-3000 Custom/ Professional
1982-1985. Similar to SG-2000, but with solid mahogany body wings, higher output humbuckers, and abalone purfling on top.

| 1982-1985 | | $900 | $1,000 |

SG-3
1965-1966. Early double-cut solidbody with sharp horns, bolt neck, 3 hum-single pickup layout, large white guard, rotor controls, tremolo.

| 1965-1966 | | $950 | $1,150 |

SG-5/5A
1966-1971. Asymmetrical double-cut solidbody with extended lower horn, bolt neck, 2 pickups, chrome hardware.

| 1966-1971 | | $950 | $1,150 |

SG-7/7A
1966-1971. Like SG-5, but with gold hardware.

| 1966-1971 | | $950 | $1,150 |

SG-20
1972-1973. Bolt-on neck, slab body, single-cut, 1 pickup.

| 1972-1973 | | $350 | $450 |

SG-30/SG-30A
1973-1976. Slab katsura wood (30) or slab maple (30A) solidbody, bolt-on neck, 2 humbuckers, dot inlays.

| 1973-1976 | | $400 | $500 |

SG-35/SG-35A
1973-1976. Slab mahogany (35) or slab maple (35A) solidbody, bolt-on neck, 2 humbuckers, parallelogram inlays.

| 1973-1976 | | $400 | $550 |

SG-40
1972-1973. Bolt-on neck, carved body, single-cut.

| 1972-1973 | | $400 | $550 |

SG-45
1972-1976. Glued neck, single-cut, bound flat-top.

| 1972-1976 | | $500 | $650 |

SG-50
1974-1976. Slab katsura wood solidbody, glued neck, 2 humbuckers, dot inlays, large 'guard.

| 1974-1976 | | $500 | $650 |

SG-60
1972 only. Bolt-on neck, carved body, single-cut.

| 1972 | | $450 | $550 |

SG-60T
1973 only. SG-60 with large cast vibrato system.

| 1973 | | $400 | $550 |

SG-65
1972-1976. Glued neck, single-cut, bound flat-top.

| 1972-1976 | | $500 | $650 |

SG-70
1974-1976. Slab maple solidbody, glued neck, 2 humbuckers, dot inlays, large 'guard.

| 1974-1976 | | $500 | $650 |

SG-80
1972 only. Bolt-on neck, carved body, single-cut.

| 1972 | | $450 | $600 |

SG-80T
1973. SG-60 with large cast vibrato system.

| 1973 | | $450 | $600 |

SG-85
1972-1976. Glued neck, single-cut, bound flat-top.

| 1972-1976 | | $500 | $650 |

SG-90
1974-1976. Carved top mahogany solidbody, glued neck, elevated 'guard, bound top, dot inlays, chrome hardware.

| 1974-1976 | | $650 | $700 |

SG-175
1974-1976. Carved top mahogany solidbody, glued neck, elevated 'guard, abalone bound top, abalone split wing or pyramid inlays, gold hardware.

| 1974-1976 | | $750 | $850 |

SG-500/SBG-500
1976-1978, 1981-1983. Carved unbound maple top, double pointed cutaways, glued neck, 2 exposed humbuckers, 3-ply bound headstock, bound neck with clay split wing inlays, chrome hardware. Reissued as the SBG-500 (800S in Japan) in '81.

| 1976-1978 | SG-500 | $650 | $700 |
| 1981-1983 | SBG-500 | $650 | $700 |

SG-700
1976-1978. Carved unbound maple top, double pointed cutaways, glued neck, 2 humbuckers, 3-ply bound headstock, bound neck with clay split wing inlays, chrome hardware.

| 1976-1978 | | $750 | $800 |

SG-700S
1999-2001. Set neck, mahogany body, 2 humbuckers with coil tap.

| 1999-2001 | | $550 | $600 |

Yamaha SA-2000

Yamaha SG-30

To get the most from this book, be sure to read "Using *The Guide*" in the introduction.

Yamaha SG-1500

1983 Zemaitis Metal-Front

MODEL YEAR	FEATURES	EXC. COND. LOW	HIGH

SG-1000/SBG-1000
1976-1983 ('84 in Japan). Carved maple top, double pointed cutaways, glued neck, 2 humbuckers, 3-ply bound headstock, unbound body, bound neck with clay split wing inlays, gold hardware. Export model name changed to SBG-1000 in '80.

1976-1979	SG-1000	$750	$800
1980-1983	SBG-1000	$750	$800

SG-1500
1976-1979. Carved maple top, double pointed cutaways, laminated neck-thru-body neck, laminated mahogany body wings, 2 humbuckers, 5-ply bound headstock and body, bound neck with dot inlays, chrome hardware. Name used on Japan-only model in the '80s.

1976-1979		$850	$900

SG-2000/SBG-2000/SG-2000S
1976-1984 (1988 in Japan). Carved maple top, double pointed cutaways, laminated neck-thru-body neck, laminated mahogany body wings, 2 humbuckers, 5-ply bound headstock and body, bound neck with abalone split wing inlays, gold hardware. In '80, the model was changed to the SBG-2000 in the U.S., and the SG-2000S everywhere else except Japan (where it remained the SG-2000). Export model renamed SBG-2100 in '84.

1976-1984		$900	$1,000

SG-3000/SBG-3000/Custom Professional
1982-1985. SG-2000 upgrade with higher output pickups and abalone purfling on top.

1982-1985		$900	$1,000

SHB-400
1981-1985. Solidbody electric, set-in neck, 2 pickups.

1981-1985		$350	$450

SSC-500
1983-1992. Solidbody electric, 3 pickups, set-in neck.

1983-1992		$350	$450

MODEL YEAR	FEATURES	EXC. COND. LOW	HIGH

Weddington Classic
1989-1992. Electric solidbody, redesigned set-in neck/body joint for increased access to the higher frets.

1989-1992		$400	$500

Yanuziello Stringed Instruments
1980-present. Production/custom resonator and Hawaiian guitars built by luthier Joseph Yanuziello, in Toronto, Ontario.

Zeiler Guitars
1992-present. Custom flat-top, 12-string, and nylon-string guitars built by luthier Jamon Zeiler in Cincinnati, Ohio.

Zemaitis
1960-1999, 2004-present. Professional, premium, and presentation grade, custom/production, electric guitars. Tony Zemaitis (born Antanus Casimere Zemaitis) began selling his guitars in 1960. He emphasized simple light-weight construction and was known for hand engraved metal front guitars. Each hand-built guitar was a unique instrument. Ron Wood was an early customer and his use of a Zemaitis created a demand for the custom-built guitars. Approximately 6 to 10 instruments were built each year. Tony retired in '99, and passed away in '02 at the age of 67. In '04, Japan's Kanda Shokai Corporation, with the endorsement of Tony Zemaitis, Jr., started building the guitars again. KSC builds the higher priced ones and licenses the lower priced guitars to Greco.

Acoustic Models

1965	12-string, 1st year	$22,000	$26,000
1980s	12-String D-hole	$13,000	$16,000
1980s	12-string heart-hole	$24,000	$29,000
1980s	6-string D-hole	$13,000	$15,000

MODEL YEAR	FEATURES	EXC. COND. LOW	HIGH
1980s	6-string heart-hole	$19,000	$29,000
Electric Models			
1980s	Disc-front	$19,000	$24,000
1980s	Metal-front	$24,000	$29,000
1980s	Pearl-front	$29,000	$39,000
1994	"Black Pearl"	$34,000	$39,000
1995	Disc-front 40th Anniversary	$29,000	$39,000

Zen-On

1946-ca.1968. Japanese manufacturer. By '67 using the Morales brand name. Not heavily imported into the U.S., if at all (see Morales).

Acoustic Hollowbody

1946-1968. Various models.

1950s		$150	$250

Electric Solidbody

1960s. Teisco-era and styling.

1960s		$150	$250

Zeta

1982-present. Zeta has made solid, semi-hollow and resonator guitars, many with electronic and MIDI options, in Oakland, California over the years, but currently only offer basses, amps and violins.

Zim-Gar

1960s. Imported from Japan by Gar-Zim Musical Instrument Corporation of Brooklyn, New York. Manufacturers unknown. Generally shorter scale beginner guitars.

Electric Solidbody

1960s		$150	$250

Zimnicki, Gary

1980-present. Luthier Gary Zimnicki builds his professional and premium grade, custom, flat-top, 12-string, nylon-string, and archtop guitars in Allen Park, Michigan.

Zion

1980-present. Professional and premium grade, production/custom, semi-hollow and solidbody guitars built by luthier Ken Hoover, originally in Greensboro, North Carolina, currently in Raleigh.

Classic

1989-present. Double-cut solidbody, six-on-a-side headstock, opaque finish, various pickup options, dot markers.

MODEL YEAR	FEATURES	EXC. COND. LOW	HIGH
1990s	Custom quilted top	$650	$750
1995	Opaque finish	$450	$550

Graphic

1980s-1994. Double-cut basswood body, custom airbrushed body design, bolt-on neck, Green Frost Marble finish.

1990		$800	$950

Radicaster

1987-1990s. Double-cut basswood body, graphic finish, bolt-on neck, various pickup configurations, marble/bowling ball finish.

1990s		$600	$800

The Fifty

1994-present. Single-cut ash solidbody, 2 single coils, bolt-on neck.

1990s	Custom figured top	$650	$750
1990s	Natural, plain top	$500	$650

Zolla

1979-present. Professional grade, production/custom, electric guitars built by luthier Bill Zolla in San Diego, California. Zolla also builds basses, necks and bodies.

Zon

1981-present. Currently luthier Joe Zon only offers basses, but he also built guitars from '85-'91. See Bass Section for more company info.

ZZ Ryder

Solidbody electric guitars from Stenzler Musical Instruments of Ft. Worth, Texas. They also offer basses.

Zeta MIDI guitar

Zion The Fifty

Basses

Alamo Titan

Alvarez RB30SC

MODEL		EXC. COND.	
YEAR	FEATURES	LOW	HIGH

Acoustic

Ca. 1965-ca. 1987. Mainly known for solidstate amps, the Acoustic Control Corp. of Los Angeles, did offer guitars and basses from around '69 to late '74. The brand was revived a few years ago by Samick for a line of amps.

Black Widow Bass

1969-1970, 1972-1974. Around '69 Acoustic offered the AC600 Black Widow Bass (in both a fretted and fretless version) which featured an unique black equal double-cut body with German carve, an Ebonite 'board, 2 pickups, each with 1 row of adjustable polepieces, a zero fret, and a protective "spider design" pad on back. Also available was the AC650 short-scale. The '72-'74 version had the same body design, but had a rosewood 'board and only 1 pickup with 2 rows of adjustable pole pieces (the '72s had a different split-coil pickup with 4 pole pieces, 2 front and 2 back). Acoustic outsourced the production of the basses, possibly to Japan, but at least part of the final production was by Semie Moseley.

1972-1974		$550	$750

Aims

Ca. 1974-ca. 1976. Aims instruments, distributed by Randall Instruments in the mid-'70s, were copies of classic American guitar and bass models. Randall also offered a line of Aims amps during the same time.

Airline

1958-1968, 2004-present. Brand for Montgomery Ward. Built by Kay, Harmony and Valco. In '04, the brand was revived on a line of reissues from Eastwood guitars.

Electric Solidbody Bass

1958-1968	Various models	$175	$275

Pocket 3/4 Bass (Valco/National)

1962-1966. Airline brand of double-cut 'Pocket Bass,' short-scale, 2 pickups, 1 acoustic bridge and 1 neck humbucker, sunburst and other colors.

1962-1968		$650	$750

Alamo

1947-1982. Founded by Charles Eilenberg, Milton Fink, and Southern Music, San Antonio, Texas. Distributed by Bruno & Sons. See Guitar Stories Volume II, by Michael Wright, for a complete history of Alamo with detailed model listings.

Eldorado Bass (Model 2600)

1965-1966. Solidbody, 1 pickup, angular offset shape, double-cut.

1965-1966		$175	$250

Titan Bass

1963-1970. Hollowbody, 1 pickup, angular offset shape.

1963-1970		$175	$250

MODEL		EXC. COND.	
YEAR	FEATURES	LOW	HIGH

Alembic

1969-present. Professional, premium, and presentation grade, production/custom, 4-, 5-, and 6-string basses built in Santa Rosa, California. They also build guitars. Established in San Francisco as one of the first handmade bass builders. Alembic basses come with many options concerning woods (examples are maple, bubinga, walnut, vermilion, wenge, zebrawood), finishes, inlays, etc., all of which affect the values listed here. These dollar amounts should be used as a baseline guide to values for Alembic.

Anniversary Bass

1989. 20th Anniversary limited edition, walnut and vermillion with a walnut core, 5-piece body, 5-piece neck-thru, only 200 built.

1989		$1,800	$2,100

Custom Shop Built Bass

1969-present. Various one-off and/or custom built instruments. Each instrument should be evaluated individually. Prices are somewhat speculative due to the one-off custom characteristics and values can vary greatly.

1978	Dragon		
	Doubleneck	$8,000	$9,000
2000	Stanley Clarke		
	Custom	$2,800	$5,000
2004	Dragon 4-string,		
	4 made	$3,800	$4,200

Distillate Bass

1979-1991. Exotic woods, active electronics.

1979-1991	Distillate 4	$850	$1,500
1979-1991	Distillate 5	$950	$1,600

Elan Bass

1985-1996. Available in 4-, 5-, 6- and 8-string models, 3-piece thru-body laminated maple neck, solid maple body, active electronics, solid brass hardware, offered in a variety of hardwood tops and custom finishes.

1985-1996	Elan 4	$750	$1,300
1985-1996	Elan 5	$1,400	$2,400

Epic Bass

1993-present. Mahogany body with various tops, extra large pointed bass horn, maple/walnut veneer set-neck, available in 4-, 5-, and 6-string versions.

1993-1999	4-string	$950	$1,050
1993-1999	5-string	$1,200	$1,300
1993-1999	6-string	$1,200	$1,300
2000-2004	4-string	$1,300	$1,500
2000-2004	5-string	$1,600	$1,800
2000-2004	6-string	$1,600	$1,800

Essence Bass

1991-present. Mahogany body with various tops, extra large pointed bass horn, walnut/maple laminate neck-thru.

1991-1999	Essence 4	$1,400	$1,600
1991-1999	Essence 5	$1,500	$1,900
1991-1999	Essence 6	$1,500	$1,800
2000-2004	Essence 4	$1,800	$2,000
2000-2004	Essence 5	$1,900	$2,200
2000-2004	Essence 6	$1,900	$2,200

BASSES

MODEL YEAR	FEATURES	EXC. COND. LOW	HIGH

Exploiter Bass
1980s. Figured maple solidbody 4-string, neck-thru, transparent finish.
| 1984-1988 | | $1,300 | $2,000 |

Persuader Bass
1980s. Available in 4-, 5-, or 6-string.
| 1983-1991 | | $900 | $1,300 |

Series I Bass
1971-present. Mahogany body with various tops, maple/purpleheart laminate neck-thru, active electronics, available in 3 scale lengths and with 4, 5 or 6 strings.
1971-1979	Medium- or long-scale	$2,800	$3,200
1971-1979	Short-scale	$2,600	$3,000
1980-1989	Medium- or long-scale	$2,800	$3,200
1980-1989	Short-scale	$2,600	$3,000
1990-2000	All scales, highly figured top	$3,000	$3,200

Series II Bass
1971-present. Generally custom-made option, each instrument valued on a case-by-case basis, guidance pricing only.
| 1990-2000 | | $5,000 | $7,000 |

Spoiler Bass
1981-1999. Solid mahogany body, maple neck-thru, 4 or 6 strings, active electronics, various high-end wood options.
1981-1989	4-string	$1,400	$1,800
1981-1989	6-string	$1,400	$1,900
1990-1999	4-string	$1,400	$1,800

Stanley Clarke Signature Standard Bass
1990-present. Neck-thru-body, active electronics, 24-fret ebony 'board, mahogany body with maple, bubinga, walnut, vermilion, or zebrawood top, 4-, 5-, and 6-string versions.
| 1990-2000 | All scales | $1,900 | $2,200 |

Alvarez
1965-present. Imported by St. Louis Music, they offered electric basses from '90 to '02 and acoustic basses in the mid-'90s.
Electric Bass (mid-level)
| 1990s | Hollowbody | $250 | $400 |
| 1990s | Solidbody | $200 | $350 |

American Conservatory (Lyon & Healy)
Late-1800s-early-1900s. Mainly catalog sales guitars and mandolins from the Chicago maker. Mid-level Lyon & Healy offering, above their Lakeside brand, and generally under their Washburn brand.
Monster Bass G2740
Early-mid-1900s. Six-string acoustic flat-top, spruce top, birch back and sides with rosewood stain, natural. Their catalog claimed it was "Indespensable to the up-to-date mandolin and guitar club."
| 1917 | | $3,500 | $5,000 |

MODEL YEAR	FEATURES	EXC. COND. LOW	HIGH

Ampeg
1949-present. Ampeg was founded on a vision of an amplified bass peg, which evolved into the Baby Bass. Ampeg has sold basses on and off throughout its history.
AEB-1 Bass
1966-1967. F-holes thru-body, fretted, scroll headstock, pickup in body, sunburst. Reissued as the AEB-2 for '97-'99.
| 1966-1967 | | $1,700 | $1,900 |
ASB-1 Devil Bass
1966-1967. Long-horn body, fretted, triangular F-holes through the body, fireburst.
| 1966-1967 | | $2,000 | $2,800 |
AUB-1 Bass
1966-1967. Same as AEB-1, but fretless, sunburst. Reissued as the AUB-2 for '97-'99.
| 1966-1967 | | $1,700 | $1,900 |
AUSB-1 Devil Bass
1966-1967. Same as ASB-1 Devil Bass, but fretless.
| 1966-1967 | | $2,000 | $2,800 |
BB-4 Baby Bass
1962-1971. Electric upright slim-looking bass that is smaller than a cello, available in sunburst, white, red, black, and a few turquoise. Reissued as the ABB-1 Baby Bass for '97-'99.
| 1962-1971 | Solid color | $2,500 | $3,200 |
| 1962-1971 | Sunburst | $2,200 | $2,800 |
BB-5 Baby Bass
1964-1971. Five-string version.
| 1964-1971 | Sunburst | $2,500 | $3,200 |
Dan Armstrong Lucite Bass
1969-1971. Clear solid lucite body, did not have switchable pickups like the Lucite guitar.
| 1969-1971 | | $1,300 | $2,000 |
Dan Armstrong Lucite Bass Reissue
1998-2001. Lucite body, Dan Armstrong Ampeg block lettering on 'guard.
| 1998-2001 | | $725 | $825 |
GEB-101 Little Stud Bass
1973-1975. Import from Japan, offset double-cut solidbody, two-on-a-side tuners.
| 1973-1975 | | $350 | $400 |
GEB-750 Big Stud Bass
1973-1975. Import from Japan, offset double-cut solidbody, two-on-a-side tuners.
| 1973-1975 | | $350 | $400 |

Andreas
1995-present. Aluminium-necked, solidbody guitars and basses built by luthier Andreas Pichler in Dollach, Austria.

Angelica
1967-1975. Student and entry-level imports from Japan.
Electric Solidbody Bass
Japanese imports.
| 1970s | Various models | $100 | $150 |

Alembic Series I

Ampeg Dan Armstrong 1960s

Applause AE-40

1976 Aria Mach 1

MODEL YEAR	FEATURES	EXC. COND. LOW	HIGH

Apollo

Ca. 1967-1972. Entry-level instruments imported from Japan by St. Louis Music.

Electric Hollowbody Bass

Japanese imports.

1970s		$100	$200

Applause

1976-present. Intermediate grade, production, acoustic/electric basses. They also offer guitars, mandolins and ukes. Kaman Music's entry-level Ovation-styled brand. The instruments were made in the U.S. until around '82, when production was moved to Korea.nd '82, when production was moved to Korea.

AE-40 Acoustic/Electric Bass

Cutaway, flat-top acoustic/electric bass, natural.

1980s		$175	$225

Arbor

1983-present. Budget grade, production, solidbody basses imported by Musicorp (MBT). They also offer guitars.

Electric Bass

1980s	Various models	$150	$200
2000s	Various models	$75	$100

Aria/Aria Pro II

1960-present. Budget and intermediate grade, production, acoustic, acoustic/electric, solidbody, hollowbody and upright basses. They also make guitars, mandolins, and banjos. Originally branded as Aria; renamed Aria Pro II in '75; both names used over the next several year; in '01, the Pro II part of the name was dropped altogether.

Electric Bass

1980s	Various models	$225	$350

Armstrong, Rob

1971-present. Custom basses made in Coventry, England, by luthier Rob Armstrong. He also builds mandolins, flat-tops, and parlor guitars.

Artinger Custom Guitars

1997-present. Professional and premium grade, production/custom, basses built by luthier Matt Artinger in Emmaus, Pennsylvania. He also builds builds hollow, semi-hollow, and chambered solidbody guitars.

Asama

1970s-1980s. Japanese line of solidbody basses. They also offered guitars, effects, drum machines and other music products.

Audiovox

Ca. 1935-ca. 1950. Paul Tutmarc's Audiovox Manufacturing, of Seattle, Washington, was a pioneer in electric lap steels, basses, guitars and amps. Tutmarc is credited with inventing the electric bass guitar in '35, which his company started selling in the late '30s.

MODEL YEAR	FEATURES	EXC. COND. LOW	HIGH

Austin

1999-present. Budget and intermediate grade, production, basses imported by St. Louis Music. They also offer guitars, mandolins and banjos.

Avante

1997-present. Shape cutaway acoustic bass designed by Joe Veillette and Michael Tobias originally offered by Alvarez. Currently only a lower-priced baritone is offered by MusicYo.

Baldwin

1965-1970. The giant organ company got into guitars and basses in '65 when it bought Burns Guitars of England and sold those models in the U.S. under the Baldwin name.

Baby Bison Bass

1965-1970. Scroll head, 2 pickups, black, red or white finishes.

1965-1966		$600	$700
1966-1970	Model 560	$500	$600

Bison Bass

1965-1970. Scroll headstock, 3 pickups, black or white finishes.

1965-1966		$900	$1,100
1966-1970	Model 516	$800	$1,000

G.B. 66 Bass

1965-1966. Bass equivalent of G.B. 66 guitar, covered bridge tailpiece.

1965-1966		$650	$750

Jazz Split Sound Bass

1965-1970. Offset double-cut solidbody, 2 pickups, red sunburst.

1965-1966	Long-scale	$600	$700
1966-1970	Short-scale	$550	$650

Nu-Sonic Bass

1965-1966. Bass version of Nu-Sonic.

1965-1966		$500	$600

Shadows Bass/Shadows Signature

1965-1970. Named after Hank Marvin's backup band, solidbody, 3 slanted pickups, white finish.

1965-1966	Shadows	$1,200	$1,300
1966-1970	Shadows Signature	$1,000	$1,100

Vibraslim Bass

1965-1970. Thin body, scroll head, 2 pickups, sunburst.

1965-1966		$700	$800
1966-1970	Model 549	$600	$700

Barclay

1960s. Generally shorter-scale, student-level imports from Japan.

Electric Solidbody Bass

1960s	Various models	$120	$170

Bass Collection

1985-1992. Mid-level imports from Japan, distributed by Meisel Music of Springfield, New Jersey. Sam Ash Music, New York, sold the remaining inventory from '92 to '94.

MODEL YEAR	FEATURES	EXC. COND. LOW	HIGH

SB300 Series
1985-1992. Offset double-cut, bolt neck, ash or alder body, models include 300, 301 (fretless) and 302 (5-string).

1985-1992		$275	$425

SB400/SB500 Series
1985-1992. Offset double-cut, bolt neck, basswood body, active electronics, models include 401, 402 (fretless), 405 (5-string) and 501 (alder body).

1985-1992		$425	$625

SB600 Series
1985-1992. Offset double-cut, bolt neck, maple/walnut body, active electronics.

1985-1992		$650	$725

BC Rich
1966-present. Budget, intermediate, and premium grade, production/custom, import and U.S.-made basses. They also offer guitars.

Many BC Rich models came in a variety of colors. For example, in '88 they offered black, Competition Red, metallic red, GlitteRock White, Ultra Violet, and Thunder Blue. Also in '88, other custom colors, graphic features, paint-to-match headstocks, and special inlays were offered.

Bich Bass
1976-1998. Solidbody, neck-thru, 2 pickups.

1976-1983		$1,100	$1,200
1984-1993		$800	$1,200
1994-2004	New Rico-era	$800	$900

Bich Supreme 8-String Bass
Late-1970s-early-1980s.

1978-1982		$1,700	$1,900

Eagle Bass (U.S.A. assembly)
1977-1996. Curved double-cut, solidbody, natural.

1977-1979		$1,100	$1,500
1980-1989		$950	$1,400

Gunslinger Bass
1987-1999. Inverted headstock, 1 humbucker.

1987-1990		$500	$700
1991-1999		$500	$600

Ironbird Bass
1984-1998. Kinda star-shaped, neck-thru, solidbody, 2 pickups, active electronics, diamond inlays.

1980s		$650	$800

Mockingbird Bass
1976-present.

1976-1978	USA, short-horn	$1,500	$2,300
1979-1983	USA, long-horn	$1,500	$2,300
1984-1989	End 1st Rico-era	$1,500	$2,300
1994-2004	New Rico-era	$1,200	$1,600

Nighthawk Bass
1979-ca.1980. Bolt-neck.

1970s		$500	$675

NJ Bass Series
1983-present. Various models include Beast, Eagle, Innovator, Mockingbird, Virgin and Warlock.

1983-1986		$325	$450
1987-1999		$250	$400

Platinum Bass Series
1986-present. Imported versions including Eagle, Mockingbird, Beast, Warlock.

1986-1999		$275	$375

Seagull/Seagull II Bass
1972-1998.

1972-1975	Initial design	$1,000	$1,400
1976-1977	Seagull II	$900	$1,300
1980-1989		$800	$1,100
1990-1998		$700	$1,000

Son Of A Rich Bass
1977-ca.1981. Basically a bolt neck Bich, U.S. made.

1977-1981		$800	$950

ST-III Bass
Available in bolt neck and non-bolt neck (1986 price at $999 & $1299 respectively), black hardware, P-Bass/J-Bass pickup configuration, 2 tone controls, 1 volume control, jumbo frets, ebony 'board.

1987-1989	Bolt-on	$500	$600
1987-1989	Neck-thru	$600	$700

Warlock Bass (U.S.A.)
1981-present. Introduced in '81 along with the Warlock guitar, USA-made, standard bolt-on model, maple body and neck, rosewood 'board, 22/accyruzer jumbo frets, Badass II low profile bridge by '88.

1981-1989		$1,000	$1,200

Wave Bass

1980s		$1,350	$1,450

Bernie Rico Jr. Guitars
Professional and premium grade, production/custom, solidbody basses built by luther Bernie Rico, Jr. in Hesperia, California. His father founded BC Rich guitars. He also makes guitars.

Black Jack
1960s. Entry-level and mid-level imports from Japan.

Electric Solidbody Bass

1960s	Various models	$100	$175

Blade
1987-present. Intermediate and professional grade, production, solidbody basses from luthier Gary Levinson's Levinson Music Products Ltd. in Switzerland. He also builds guitars.

Bradford
1960s. House brand of W.T. Grant department store, often imported.

Electric Solidbody Bass

1960s	Various models	$100	$175

Brawley Basses
Solidbody bass guitars designed by Keith Brawley and made in Korea. The company was headquartered in Temecula, California. They also made guitars.

Artinger 5-string

1988 BC Rich Bich Bass

1979 Carvin LB-50

Conklin Groove Tools 4

MODEL YEAR	FEATURES	EXC. COND. LOW	HIGH

Brian Moore

1992-present. Brian Moore added basses in '97. Currently they offer professional grade, production, solidbody basses. They also build guitars and mandolins.

Brice

1985-present. Budget grade, production, electric and acoustic basses imported by Rondo Music of Union, New Jersey.

Bunker

1961-present. Luthier Dave Bunker builds intermediate, professional, and premium grade, production/custom, basses in Port Angeles, Washington. He also builds guitars.

Burns

1960-1970, 1974-1983, 1992-present. Intermediate and professional grade, production, basses built in England and Korea. They also build guitars.

Nu-Sonic Bass

1964-1965		$500	$600

Scorpion

2003-present. Double-cut scorpion-like solidbody.

2003-2005		$300	$350

Burns-Weill

1959. Jim Burns and Henry Weill teamed up to produce three solidbody electrics and three solidbody basses under this English brand.

Campellone

1978-present. Archtop guitar builder Mark Campellone, of Smithfield, Rhode Island, built basses in the '70s.

Canvas

2004-present. Budget and intermediate grade, production, solidbody basses made in China. They also offer guitars.

Carvin

1946-present. Intermediate and Professional grade, production/custom, acoustic and electric basses. They also build guitars and amps.

AC Series Acoustic Electric

1996-present. 4- and 5-string acoustic/electrics.

1996-2003		$400	$650

LB & V Series Solidbody Electric

Late 1970s-present. V series ran from '84 to '87.

1970s-2003		$350	$500

Solidbody Electric Basses

1960s		$400	$600

Chandler

1984-present. Premium grade, production/custom, solidbody 12-string electric basses built by luthiers Paul and Adrian Chandler in Chico, California. They also build guitars, laptops and pickups.

Charles Shifflett Acoustic Guitars

1990-present. Luthier Charles Shifflett builds his premium grade, custom, acoustic basses in High River, Alberta. He also builds flat-top, classical, flamenco, resophonic, and harp guitars, and banjos.

Charvel

1978-present. U.S.-made from '78 to '85 and a combination of imports and U.S.-made post-'85.

850 XL Bass

1988-1991. Four-string, neck-thru-body, active electronics.

1988-1991		$350	$450

CX-490 Bass

1991-1994. Double-cut, 4-string, bolt neck, red or white.

1991-1994		$200	$250

Eliminator Bass

1990-1991. Offset double-cut, active electronics, bolt neck.

1990-1991		$225	$275

Fusion V Bass

1989-1991. Five-string, offset double-cut with extreme bass horn, pearl white.

1989-1991		$600	$800

Model 1 Bass

1986-1989. Double-cut, bolt neck, 1 pickup.

1986-1989		$225	$275

Model 2 Bass

1986-1989. Double-cut, bolt neck, 2 pickups.

1986-1989		$225	$325

Model 3 Bass

1986-1989. Neck-thru-body, 2 single-coil pickups, active circuitry, master volume, bass and treble knobs.

1986-1989		$325	$425

Model 5 Bass

1986-1989. Double-cut, P/J pickups.

1986-1989		$300	$425

Star Bass

Early 1980s. Four-point solidbody, 1 pickup, brass hardware, 1-piece maple neck.

1980s		$600	$800

Surfcaster Bass

1991-1994. Semi-hollow, lipstick tube pickups.

1991-1994		$700	$900

Cipher

1960s. Student market import from Japan.

Electric Solidbody Bass

1960s. Japanese imports.

1960s		$150	$200

Citron

1995-present. Luthier Harvey Citron (of Veillette-Citron fame) builds his professional and premium grade, production/custom basses in Woodstock, New York. He also builds solidbody guitars.

MODEL YEAR	FEATURES	EXC. COND. LOW	HIGH

Clevinger
1982-present. Established by Martin Clevinger, Oakland, California. Mainly specializing in electric upright basses, but has offered bass guitars as well.
Upright Solidbody Electric Bass
1982-present. Straight vertical-shaped compact body, several options available that can increase values, black.

1982-1999		$1,700	$2,500

College Line
One of many Lyon & Healy brands, made during the era of extreme design experimentation.
Monster Bass (Style 2089)
Early-1900s. 22" lower bout, flat-top guitar/bass, natural.

1915		$4,000	$5,000

Conklin
1984-present. Intermediate, professional, and premium grade, production/custom basses from luthier Bill Conklin, of Springfield, Missouri. Conklin also offers guitars. Conklin instruments are made in the U.S. and overseas.
M.E.U. (Mobile Electric Upright) Bass
1995-present. Cello-style hollowbody, played in an upright position, 4-string or 5-string option.

1995-1999	4-string	$1,150	$1,350

Conrad
Ca.1968-1978. Student and mid-level copies imported by David Wexler, Chicago, Illinois.
Beatle Bass Copy
1970s. Hofner Beatle Bass copy.

1970s		$250	$350

Model 40096 Acoustical Slimline Bass
1970s. 2 pickups.

1970s		$200	$300

Model 40177 Violin-Shaped Bass
1970s. Scroll headstock, 2 pickups.

1970s		$225	$425

Model 40224 Bumper Bass
1970s. Ampeg Dan Armstrong lucite copy.

1970s		$225	$325

Professional Bass
1970s. Offset double-cut.

1970s		$175	$250

Professional Bison Bass
1970s. Solidbody, 2 pickups.

1970s		$175	$250

Contessa
1960s. Acoustic, semi-hollow archtop, solidbody and bass guitars made in Germany. They also made banjos.

Corey James Custom Guitars
2005-present. Professional and premium grade, production/custom solidbody basses built by luthier Corey James Moilanen in Davisburg, Michigan. He also builds guitars.

Cort
1973-present. North Brook, Illinois-based Cort offers intermediate and professional grade, production, acoustic and solidbody electric basses built in Korea. They also offer guitars.
Electric Solidbody Bass

1973-1999	Various models	$100	$325

Crafter
2000-present. Intermediate grade, production, acoustic/electric bass from Hohner. They also offer guitars.

Crafter USA
1986-present. Crafter offers intermediate grade, production, solidbody basses made in Korea. They also build guitars and amps.

Crestwood
1970s. Imported by La Playa Distributing Company of Detroit. Product line includes copies of the popular classical guitars, flat-tops, electric solidbodies and basses of the era.
Electric Bass
1970s. Includes models 2048, 2049, 2079, 2090, 2092, 2093, and 2098.

1970s		$150	$275

Crown
1960s. Violin-shaped hollowbody electrics, solidbody electric guitars and basses, possibly others. Imported from Japan.
Electric Solidbody Bass
Japanese imports.

1960s		$100	$275

Cumpiano
1974-present. Professional and premium grade, custom steel-string and nylon-string guitars, and acoustic basses built by luthier William Cumpiano in Northampton, Massachusetts.

Custom
1980s. Line of solidbody guitars and basses introduced in the early-'80s by Charles Lawing and Chris Lovell, owners of Strings & Things in Memphis.

Custom Kraft
Late-1960s. A house brand of St. Louis Music Supply, instruments built by Valco, Chicago, Illinois. They also offered guitars.
Bone Buzzer Model 12178
Late 1960s. Symmetrical double-cut thin hollow body, lightning bolt f-holes, 4-on-a-side tuners, 2 pickups, sunburst or emerald sunburst.

1968		$275	$400

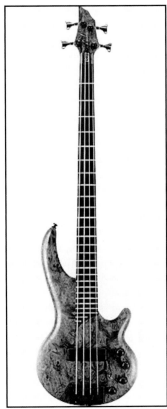

Cort Curbow 4-string

1968 Custom Kraft Bone Buzzer

BASSES

Daisy Rock Rock Candy Bass

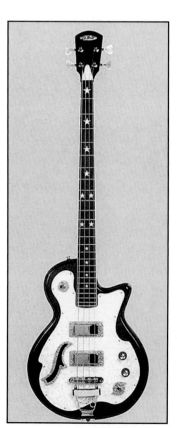

DiPinto Belvedere

D'Agostino

1976-early 1990s. Import company established by Pat D'Agostino. Solidbodies imported from EKO Italy '77-'82, Japan '82-'84, and in Korea for '84 on. Overall, about 60% of guitars were Japanese, 40% Korean.

Electric Solidbody Bass

MODEL YEAR	FEATURES	EXC. COND. LOW	HIGH
1970s	Various models	$225	$350

Daion

1978-1985. Higher quality copy imports from Japan. Original designs introduced in '80s.

Electric Basses

1978-1985	Various models	$400	$800

Daisy Rock

2001-present. Budget and intermediate grade, production, full-scale and 3/4 scale, solidbody, semi-hollow, and acoustic/electric basses. Founded by Tish Ciravolo as a Division of Schecter Guitars, initial offerings included daisy and heart-shaped electric guitars and basses.

Danelectro

1946-1969, 1997-present. Danelectro offered basses throughout most of its early history. In '96, the Evets Corporation, of San Clemente, California, introduced a line of Danelectro effects; amps, basses and guitars, many reissues of earlier instruments, soon followed. In early '03, Evets discontinued the guitar, bass and amp lines.

'58 Longhorn Bass Reissue/Longhorn Pro

1997-2003. Reissues of classic Longhorn bass.

1997-2003		$225	$275

Model 1444L Bass

Ca.1958-ca.1964. Masonite body, single-cut, 2 pickups, copper finish.

1958-1962		$650	$900
1963-1964		$550	$700

Model 3412 Shorthorn Bass

1958-ca.1966. Coke bottle headstock, 1 pickup, copper finish.

1958-1959		$650	$900
1960-1962		$600	$850
1963-1964		$550	$700
1965-1966		$500	$550

Model 3612 Shorthorn 6-String Bass

1958-ca.1966. Coke bottle headstock, 1 pickup, copper finish.

1958-1962		$1,000	$1,200
1963-1964		$800	$1,000
1965-1966		$700	$900

Model 4423 Longhorn Bass

1958-ca.1966. Coke bottle headstock, 2 pickups, copper finish.

1958-1959		$1,300	$1,700
1960-1962		$1,100	$1,700
1963-1964		$1,100	$1,500
1965-1966		$1,000	$1,500

UB-2 6-String Bass

Ca.1956-ca.1959. Single-cut, 2 pickups.

MODEL YEAR	FEATURES	EXC. COND. LOW	HIGH
1956-1959		$1,000	$1,600

Dave Maize Acoustic

1991-present. Luthier Dave Maize builds his premium grade, production/custom, acoustic basses in Cave Junction, Oregon. He also builds flat-tops.

Dean

1976-present. Intermediate and professional grade, production, solidbody, hollowbody, acoustic, and acoustic/electric, basses made overseas. They also offer guitars, banjos, mandolins, and amps.

Baby ML Bass

1982-1986. Downsized version of ML. U.S.-made.

1982-1986		$350	$400

Mach V Bass

1985-1986. U.S.-made pointed solidbody, 2 pickups, rosewood 'board.

1985-1986		$600	$800

ML Bass

1977-1986. Futuristic body style, fork headstock, U.S.-made.

1977-1983	U.S.A.-made	$1,400	$1,500
1984-1986	Korean import	$400	$450

Dean Markley

The string and pickup manufacturer offered a limited line of guitars and basses for a time in the late 1980s.

Vintage Bass

1987. Maple neck, maple or ash body, maple or rosewood 'board, solidbody, either split P-type or a P-J combination pickups.

1987		$300	$350

DeArmond

1999-2004. Electric basses based on Guild models and imported from Korea by Fender. They also offered guitars.

Decca

Mid-1960s. Solidbody basses imported from made in Japan by Teisco and imported by Decca Records, Decca headstock logo, student-level instruments. They also offered guitars and amps.

DeGennaro

2003-present. Professional and premium grade, custom/production, solidbody basses built by luthier William Degennaro in Grand Rapids, Michigan. He also builds guitars and mandolins.

DeTemple

1995-present. Premium grade, production/custom, solidbody electric basses built by luthier Michael DeTemple in Sherman Oaks, California. He also builds guitars.

MODEL		EXC. COND.	
YEAR	FEATURES	LOW	HIGH

Dillon

1975-present. Professional and premium grade, custom, acoustic basses built by luthier John Dillon in Taos, New Mexico. He also builds guitars.

Dingwall

1988-present. Luthier Sheldon Dingwall, Saskatoon, Canada, started out producing guitar bodies and necks, eventually offering complete guitars and basses. Currently Dingwall offers professional to premium grade, production/custom 4-, 5-, and 6-string basses featuring the Novax Fanned-Fret System.

DiPinto

1995-present. Intermediate and professional grade, production retro-vibe basses from luthier Chris DiPinto of Philadelphia, Pennsylvania. He also builds guitars. Until late '99, all instruments built in the U.S., since then built in Korea and the U.S.

Domino

Ca. 1967-1968. Imported from Japan by Maurice Lipsky Music of New York, mainly copies, but some original designs.

Beatle Bass
1967-1968. Beatle Bass-style.

1967-1968		$100	$300

Fireball Bass
1967-1968. Vox Phantom IV copy.

1967-1968		$100	$275

Dorado

Ca. 1972-1973. Name used briefly by Baldwin/Gretsch on line of Japanese imports.

Electric Solidbody Bass
Japanese imports.

1970s		$100	$175

Dragonfly

1994-present. Professional grade, production/custom, acoustic basses built by luthier Dan Richter in Roberts Creek, British Columbia. He also builds guitars and dulcitars.

Earthwood

1972-1985. Acoustic designs by Ernie Ball with input from George Fullerton. One of the first to offer acoustic basses.

Acoustic Bass
1972-1985. Big bodied acoustic bass alternative between Kay double bass and solidbody Fender bass.

1972-1985		$1,100	$1,400

Eastwood

1997-present. Budget and intermediate grade, production, imported solid and semi-hollowbody basses, many styled after 1960s models. They also offer guitars.

MODEL		EXC. COND.	
YEAR	FEATURES	LOW	HIGH

EKO

1959-1985, 2000-present. Built by the Oliviero Pigini Company, Italy. Original importers included LoDuca Brothers, Milwaukee, Wisconsin. Since about 2000, production, acoustic and electric EKO basses are again available and made in Italy and China. They also make guitars and amps.

Cobra II Bass
1967-ca.1969. Offset double-cut solidbody, 2 pickups.

1967-1969		$300	$400

Kadett Bass
1967-1978. Red or sunburst.

1967-1978		$300	$400

Model 1100/2 Bass
1961-1966. Jaguar-style plastic covered solidbody, 2 pickups, sparkle finish.

1961-1966		$500	$550

Model 995/2 Violin Bass
1966-ca.1969.

1966-1969		$300	$400

Rocket IV/Rokes Bass
1967-early-1970s. Rocket-shape design, solidbody, says Rokes on the headstock, the Rokes were a popular English band that endorsed EKO guitars. Marketed as the Rocket IV in the U.S. and as the Rokes in Europe. Often called the Rok. Sunburst, 1 pickup.

1967-1971		$500	$850

Electra

1971-1984. Imported from Japan by St. Louis Music.

Electric Solidbody Bass
Japanese imports, various models.

1970s		$250	$500

MPC Outlaw Bass
1970s. Has 2 separate modules that plug in for different effects, neck-thru-body.

1970s		$325	$525

Emperador

1966-1992. Student-level imports of Westheimer Musical Instruments. Early models appear to be made by either Teisco or Kawai; later models were made by Cort.

Electric Solidbody Bass
Japanese imports, various models.

1960s		$100	$225

Encore

Late 1960s-present. Budget grade, production, solidbody basses imported by John Hornby Skewes & Co. in the U.K. They also offer guitars.

Hollowbody Bass
1960s. Copy model, greenburst.

1960s		$350	$400

Engelhardt

Engelhardt specializes in student acoustic basses and cellos and is located in Elk Grove Village, Illinois.

1983 Earthwood Acoustic Bass

1967 EKO Rocket IV

1967 Epiphone Embassy

ESP Surveyor II

MODEL YEAR	FEATURES	EXC. COND. LOW	HIGH

EM-1 Maestro Bass
A popular school model upright acoustic bass, spruce top, curly maple back, rosewood trimmings, 3/4 size, sunburst.

| 1970s | | $450 | $600 |

Supreme Bass
Professional quality 3/4 size upright bass, spruce top, curly maple back, ebony trimmings.

| 1970 | | $900 | $1,200 |

Epiphone
1928-present. Epiphone didn't add basses until 1959, after Gibson acquired the brand. The Gibson Epiphones were American-made until '69, then all imports until into the '80s, when some models were again made in the U.S. Currently Epiphone offers intermediate and professional grade, production, acoustic and electric basses.

B-5 Acoustic Bass Viol
1950s. 3/4-size laminate construction.

| 1950s | | $3,000 | $4,000 |

EB-0 Bass
1998-present. SG body style, single pickup, bolt-on neck.

| 1998-2004 | | $175 | $250 |

EB-3 Bass
1999-present. SG body style, 2 pickups.

| 1999-2002 | | $275 | $375 |

EBM-4 Bass
1991-1998. Alder body, maple neck, split humbucker, white.

| 1991-1998 | | $275 | $375 |

Embassy Deluxe Bass
1963-1969. Solidbody, double-cut, 2 pickups, tune-o-matic bridge, cherry finish.

1963-1964		$1,400	$1,700
1965-1966		$1,000	$1,600
1967-1968		$900	$1,500
1969		$800	$1,400

Explorer Korina Bass
2000s. Made in Korea, Gibson Explorer body style, genuine korina body, set neck, gold hardware.

| 2000s | | $400 | $450 |

Les Paul Special Bass
1997-present. Les Paul Jr.-style slab body, single-cut, bolt-on neck, 2 humbucker pickups, sunburst.

| 1997-2004 | | $300 | $350 |

Newport Bass
1961-1970. Double-cut solidbody, 1 pickup (2 pickups optional until '63), two-on-a-side tuners until '63, four-on-a-side after that, cherry.

1961		$1,300	$1,600
1962		$1,100	$1,400
1963-1965		$900	$1,200
1966-1968		$700	$1,000
1969-1970		$600	$900

Rivoli Bass (1 pickup)
1959-1970. ES-335-style semi-hollowbody bass, two-on-a-side tuners, 1 pickup (2 in '70), reissued in '94 as the Rivoli II.

| 1959 | | $2,600 | $2,900 |
| 1960 | | $2,400 | $2,700 |

MODEL YEAR	FEATURES	EXC. COND. LOW	HIGH
1961		$2,000	$2,400
1963-1965		$1,400	$1,600
1966-1969	All finishes	$1,200	$1,500
1970	All finishes	$1,000	$1,200

Rivoli Bass (2 pickups)
1970 only. Double pickup Epiphone version of Gibson EB-2D.

| 1970 | Sunburst | $1,500 | $1,800 |

Thunderbird IV Bass
1997-present. Reverse-style mahogany body, 2 pickups, sunburst.

| 1997-2002 | | $325 | $525 |

Viola Bass
1990s-present. Beatle Bass 500/1 copy, sunburst.

| 1990-2000s | | $350 | $450 |

ESP
1975-present. Intermediate, professional, and premium grade, production/custom, electric basses. Japan's ESP (Electric Sound Products) made inroads in the U.S. market with mainly copy styles in the early '80s, mixing in original designs over the years. In the '90s, ESP opened a California-based Custom Shop.

B-1 Bass
1990s. Vague DC-style slab solidbody with bolt-on neck, ESP and B-1 on headstock.

| 1990s | | $550 | $600 |

Horizon Bass
1987-1993. Offset double-cut solidbody, 4- and 5-string versions, active electronics, 34" scale

| 1987-1993 | 4-string | $600 | $700 |

Essex (SX)
1985-present. Budget grade, production, electric basses imported by Rondo Music of Union, New Jersey. They also offer guitars.

Electric Solidbody Basses
Various models.

| 1990s | | $70 | $75 |

Evergreen Mountain
1971-present. Professional grade, custom, acoustic basses built by luthier Jerry Nolte in Cove, Oregon. He also builds guitars and mandolins.

Farnell
1989-present. Luthier Al Farnell builds his professional grade, production, solidbody basses in Ontario, California. He also offers his intermediate grade, production, C Series which is imported from China. He also builds guitars.

Fender
1946-present. Intermediate, professional, and premium grade, production/custom, electric and acoustic basses made in the U.S. and overseas. Leo Fender is the father of the electric bass. The introduction of his Precision Bass in late '51 changed forever how music was performed, recorded and heard. Leo followed with other popular models

MODEL YEAR	FEATURES	EXC. COND. LOW	HIGH

of basses that continue to make up a large part of Fender's production. Please note that all the variations of the Jazz and Precision Basses are grouped under those general headings.

Bass V
1965-1970. Five strings, double-cut, 1 pickup, dot inlay '65-'66, block inlay '66-'70.

1965-1967	Black	$2,500	$2,800
1965-1967	Blue Ice, Ocean Turquoise	$3,300	$3,800
1965-1967	Burgundy Mist	$3,600	$4,200
1965-1967	Candy Apple Red, Lake Placid Blue, Olympic White	$2,800	$3,200
1965-1967	Sunburst	$1,800	$2,100
1968-1970	Sunburst	$1,700	$2,000

Bass VI
1961-1975. Six strings, Jazzmaster-like body, 3 pickups, dot inlay until '66, block inlay '66-'75. Reintroduced as Japanese-made Collectable model '95-'98.

1961-1962	Black, blond	$4,700	$6,000
1961-1962	Burgundy Mist, Dakota Red, Fiesta Red, Sherwood Green, Shoreline Gold	$6,000	$7,800
1961-1962	Daphne Blue, Inca Silver, Sonic Blue	$5,600	$7,200
1961-1962	Foam Green, Shell Pink, Surf Green	$6,500	$8,400
1961-1962	Lake Placid Blue, Olympic White	$5,100	$6,600
1961-1962	Sunburst	$3,500	$4,500
1963	Black, blond	$4,400	$5,700
1963	Candy Apple Red, Lake Placid Blue	$4,800	$6,300
1963	Sunburst	$3,300	$4,300
1964	Lake Placid Blue	$4,700	$6,200
1964	Sunburst	$3,200	$3,800
1965	Candy Apple Red, Lake Placid Blue	$4,500	$5,000
1965	Sunburst	$3,100	$3,400
1966	Sunburst, block inlay	$2,900	$3,300
1966	Sunburst, dot inlay	$2,800	$3,200
1967	Sunburst, block inlay	$2,600	$3,100
1968	Sunburst	$2,600	$3,100
1969	Sunburst	$2,500	$2,900
1970	Sunburst	$2,400	$2,700
1971	Sunburst	$2,300	$2,600
1972	Olympic White	$3,600	$4,300
1972	Sunburst	$2,200	$2,600
1973	Sunburst	$2,100	$2,500
1974-1975	Sunburst	$1,900	$2,300

Bass VI Reissue
1995-1998. Import, sunburst.

1995-1998		$800	$900

BG-29 Bass
1995-present. Acoustic flat-top bass, single-cut, two-on-a-side tuners, Fishman on-board controls, black.

1995-2000		$325	$400

Bullet Bass (B30, B34, B40)
1982-1983. Alder body, 1 pickup, offered in short- and long-scale, red or walnut. U.S.-made, replaced by Japanese-made Squire Bullet Bass.

1982-1983		$300	$350

Squire Bullet Bass
1980s. Japanese-made, Squire-branded, replaces Bullet Bass, black.

1980s		$175	$275

Coronado I Bass
1966-1970. Thinline, double-cut, 1 pickup, dot inlay, sunburst and cherry red were the standard colors, but custom colors could be ordered.

1966-1970	Cherry red, sunburst	$750	$1,000
1966-1970	Other custom colors	$1,100	$1,400
1966-1970	White custom color	$1,000	$1,300

Coronado II Bass
1967-1972. Two pickups, block inlay, sunburst and cherry red standard colors, but custom colors could be ordered. Only Antigua finish offered from '70 on.

1967-1969	Cherry red, sunburst	$700	$1,200
1967-1969	Other custom colors	$1,100	$1,600
1967-1969	White custom color	$1,000	$1,500

HM Bass IV
1989-1991. Japanese-made, 4 strings, basswood body, no 'guard, 3 Jazz Bass pickups, 5-way switch, master volume, master TBX, sunburst.

1989-1991		$200	$300

HM Bass V
1989-1991. Five-string version of HM, sunburst.

1989-1991		$250	$350

Jazz Bass
The following are all variations of the Jazz Bass. The first four listings are for the main U.S.-made models. All others are listed alphabetically after that in the following order:

Jazz Bass
Standard Jazz Bass
American Standard Jazz Bass
American Series Jazz Bass
American Series Jazz Bass V
50th Anniversary American Standard Jazz Bass
'62 Jazz Bass
'64 Jazz Bass (Custom Shop)
'75 Jazz Bass American Vintage Series
Aerodyne Jazz Bass
American Deluxe Jazz Bass
American Deluxe Jazz V Bass
Custom Classic Jazz IV Bass
Deluxe Jazz Bass
Deluxe Jazz Bass V
Foto Flame Jazz Bass
Geddy Lee Signature Jazz Bass
Gold Jazz Bass
Highway 1 Jazz Bass
Jazz Bass Special
Jazz Plus Bass
Jazz Plus V Bass
Marcus Miller Signature Jazz Bass
Noel Redding Signature Jazz Bass

1966 Fender Bass V

1967 Fender Coronado II

BASSES

1961Fender Jazz Bass

1961 Fender Jazz Bass

Squire Jazz Bass
Standard Jazz Bass (later model)
Standard Jazz Fretless Bass (later model)
Standard Jazz V Bass (later model)
Ventures Limited Edition Jazz Bass

Jazz Bass

1960-1981. Two stack knobs '60-'62, 3 regular controls '62 on. Dot markers '60-'66, block markers from '66 on. Rosewood 'board standard, but maple available from '68 on. With the introduction of vintage reissue models in '81, Fender started calling the American-made version the Standard Jazz Bass. That became the American Standard Jazz Bass in '88 and then became the American Series Jazz Bass in 2000.

The custom colors listing are for unfaded or very slightly faded examples. Moderately faded examples will approximate values somewhat below the low end of the value range. A heavily faded example will be worth much less than the ranges shown, even if otherwise in excellent, original condition. Fade does not always mean lighter tint. A heavily faded bass will have a different tint than an unfaded one (for example, a heavily faded Lake Placid Blue can turn dark green) and will fetch values slightly higher than a standard sunburst example. Custom color Fenders can be forged and bogus finishes have been a problem. The prices in the Guide are for factory original finishes in excellent condition.

Post '71 Jazz Bass values are affected more by condition than color or neck option. The Jazz Bass was fitted with a 3-bolt neck or bullet rod in late-'74. Prices assume a 3-bolt neck starting in '75.

MODEL YEAR	FEATURES	EXC. COND. LOW	HIGH
1960	Sonic Blue	$25,000	$30,000
1960	Stack knob, sunburst	$15,000	$18,000
1960	Surf Green	$29,000	$35,000
1960	White	$23,000	$30,000
1961	Stack knob, Dakota Red, Fiesta Red	$24,000	$28,000
1961	Stack knob, Daphne Blue, Inca Silver, Sonic Blue	$22,000	$26,000
1961	Stack knob, Lake Placid Blue	$20,000	$24,000
1961	Stack knob, Sunburst	$14,000	$16,000
1962	Stack knob, black, blond	$17,000	$20,000
1962	Stack knob, Burgundy Mist, Dakota Red, Fiesta Red, Sherwood Green, Shorline Gold	$22,000	$26,000
1962	Stack knob, Daphne Blue, Inca Silver, Sonic Blue	$20,000	$24,000
1962	Stack knob, Foam Green, Shell Pink, Surf Green	$24,000	$28,000

MODEL YEAR	FEATURES	EXC. COND. LOW	HIGH
1962	Stack knob, Lake Placid Blue, Olympic White	$19,000	$22,000
1962	Stack knob, sunburst	$13,000	$15,000
1962	3 knob, black, blond	$13,000	$16,000
1962	3 knob, Burgundy Mist, Dakota Red, Fiesta Red, Sherwood Green, Shoreline Gold	$17,000	$20,000
1962	3 knob, Daphne Blue, Inca Silver, Sonic Blue	$16,000	$19,000
1962	3 knob, Foam Green, Shell Pink, Surf Green	$18,000	$22,000
1962	3 knob, Lake Placid Blue, Olympic White	$14,000	$17,000
1962	3 knob, sunburst	$10,000	$12,000
1963	Blond	$12,000	$14,000
1963	Coral Pink, match headstock	$16,000	$20,000
1963	Dakota Red, match headstock	$15,000	$19,000
1963	Lake Placid Blue	$13,000	$16,000
1963	Olympic White, match headstock	$13,000	$16,000
1963	Sonic Blue	$14,000	$17,000
1963	Sunburst	$9,000	$11,000
1964	Black, blond	$10,000	$13,000
1964	Burgundy Mist, Fiesta Red	$13,000	$17,000
1964	Candy Apple Red, match headstock	$11,000	$14,000
1964	Dakota Red, match headstock	$13,000	$17,000
1964	Lake Placid Blue, match headstock	$11,000	$14,000
1964	Olympic White	$11,000	$14,000
1964	Sherwood Green	$14,000	$17,000
1964	Sonic Blue	$12,000	$16,000
1964	Sunburst	$8,000	$10,000
1965	Black	$9,000	$10,000
1965	Blue Ice	$12,500	$13,500
1965	Burgundy Mist	$14,000	$15,000
1965	Candy Apple Red, match headstock	$11,000	$11,500
1965	Dakota Red, Fiesta Red	$12,000	$13,000
1965	Firemist Gold, match headstock	$12,500	$13,500
1965	Lake Placid Blue, match headstock	$11,000	$11,500
1965	Olympic White	$11,000	$11,500
1965	Sonic Blue, match headstock	$12,500	$13,500
1965	Sunburst	$7,000	$7,500

MODEL YEAR	FEATURES	EXC. COND. LOW	HIGH
1966	Blocks, Candy Apple Red	$7,500	$8,500
1966	Blocks, Olympic White, match headstock	$8,500	$10,000
1966	Blocks, Sonic Blue	$9,000	$10,000
1966	Blocks, sunburst	$5,000	$5,500
1966	Dots, black	$7,500	$9,000
1966	Dots, Blue Ice	$10,000	$12,000
1966	Dots, Candy Apple Red	$8,500	$10,000
1966	Dots, Foam Green	$11,500	$13,500
1966	Dots, Olympic White	$8,500	$10,000
1966	Dots, Sonic Blue	$10,000	$12,000
1966	Dots, sunburst	$5,500	$6,500
1966	Lake Placid Blue, matching headstock	$8,500	$10,000
1967	Candy Apple Red, Olympic White	$7,000	$8,000
1967	Sonic Blue	$8,000	$9,000
1967	Sunburst	$4,500	$5,000
1968	Black	$5,500	$6,000
1968	Blue Ice, Firemist Silver, Sonic Blue, Teal Green	$7,000	$8,000
1968	Candy Apple Red, Lake Placid Blue	$6,000	$7,000
1968	Sunburst	$4,000	$4,500
1969	Candy Apple Red, Lake Placid Blue, Olympic White	$5,500	$6,000
1969	Sonic Blue, Teal Green	$6,000	$7,000
1969	Sunburst	$3,500	$4,000
1970	Less common custom colors	$5,500	$6,000
1970	More common custom colors	$4,500	$5,000
1970	Sunburst	$3,000	$3,500
1971	Less common custom colors	$4,500	$5,000
1971	More common custom colors	$3,500	$4,000
1971	Sunburst	$2,500	$3,000
1972	Custom colors	$3,000	$4,000
1972	Sunburst	$2,000	$2,500
1973	Custom colors	$3,000	$4,000
1973	Sunburst	$2,000	$2,500
1974	Custom colors	$2,500	$4,000
1974	Sunburst, 4-bolt neck	$2,000	$2,500
1975	Sunburst, 3-bolt neck	$1,700	$2,000
1975	Various colors, 3-bolt neck	$1,900	$2,400
1976	Sunburst	$1,600	$2,000
1976	Various colors, 3-bolt neck	$1,800	$2,200
1977	Sunburst	$1,600	$1,900

MODEL YEAR	FEATURES	EXC. COND. LOW	HIGH
1977	Various colors, 3-bolt neck	$1,700	$2,100
1978	Sunburst	$1,600	$1,900
1978	Various colors, 3-bolt neck	$1,700	$2,000
1979	Sunburst	$1,000	$1,600
1979	Various colors, 3-bolt neck	$1,400	$1,900
1980	Sunburst	$1,000	$1,500
1980	Various colors, 3-bolt neck	$1,000	$1,500
1981	Black	$950	$1,500
1981	Black and Gold Collector's Edition	$1,100	$1,700
1981	International colors	$975	$1,600
1981	Sunburst	$875	$1,200

Standard Jazz Bass
1981-1985. Replaced Jazz Bass ('60-'81) and replaced by the American Standard Jazz Bass in '88. Name now used on import version.

1981-1982	Rare colors	$1,500	$1,900
1981-1982	Various colors	$1,200	$1,500
1982-1984	Top mounted input jack	$650	$850
1985	Japan import	$400	$700

American Standard Jazz Bass
1988-2000. Replaced Standard Jazz Bass ('81-'88) and replaced by the American Series Jazz Bass in '00. Various colors.

1988-1989		$750	$950
1990-1999		$700	$800

American Series Jazz Bass
2000-present. Replaces American Standard Jazz Bass.

2000-2004		$675	$725

American Series Jazz Bass V
2000-present. Five-string version.

2000-2004		$525	$675

50th Anniversary American Standard Jazz Bass
1996. Regular American Standard with gold hardware, 4- or 5-string, gold 50th Anniversary commemorative neck plate, rosewood 'board, sunburst.

1996		$700	$925

'62 Jazz Bass
1982-present. U.S.A.-made, reissue of '62 Jazz Bass.

1982-1985	Standard colors	$1,000	$1,200
1986-1989	Standard colors	$1,000	$1,200
1990-1999	Rare colors	$1,100	$1,300
1990-1999	Standard colors	$1,000	$1,200
2000-2003	Standard colors	$1,000	$1,100

'64 Jazz Bass (Custom Shop)
2000-present. Alder body, rosewood 'board, tortoise shell 'guard.

2000-2004	Closet Classic option	$1,700	$1,800
2000-2004	N.O.S option	$1,600	$1,700
2000-2004	Relic option	$1,900	$2,000

'75 Jazz Bass American Vintage Series
1994-present. Maple neck with black block markers.

1994-2003		$1,200	$1,250

1972 Fender Jazz Bass

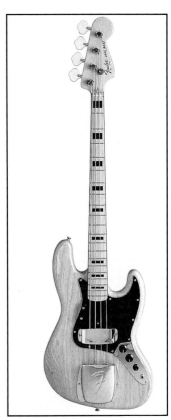

1975 Fender Jazz Bass

Fender Aerodyne Jazz Bass

Fender '62 Jazz Bass

MODEL YEAR	FEATURES	EXC. COND. LOW	HIGH
Aerodyne Jazz Bass			
2003-present. Bound basswood body, P/J pickups, Deluxe Series.			
2003-2004		$450	$475
American Deluxe Jazz Bass			
1998-present. Made in the U.S.A., active electronics, alder or ash body. Alder body colors - sunburst or transparent red, ash body colors - white, blond, transparent teal green or transparent purple.			
1998-1999		$775	$875
2000-2004		$800	$900
American Deluxe Jazz V Bass			
1998-present. Five-string model, various colors.			
1998-1999		$850	$950
Custom Classic Jazz IV Bass			
2000s		$950	$1,050
Deluxe Jazz Bass (active)			
1995-present. Made in Mexico, active electronics, various colors.			
1995-2004		$400	$500
Deluxe Jazz Bass V (active)			
1995-present. Made in Mexico, various colors.			
1995-2004		$425	$525
Foto Flame Jazz Bass			
1994-1996. Japanese import, alder and basswood body with Foto Flame figured wood image.			
1994-1996		$400	$600
Geddy Lee Signature Jazz Bass			
1998, 2004. Limited run import in '98, part of Artist Series in '04.			
1998	Black	$550	$600
2004	Artist Series	$675	$750
Gold Jazz Bass			
1981-1984. Gold finish and gold-plated hardware.			
1981-1984		$1,000	$1,300
Highway 1 Jazz Bass			
2003-present. U.S.-made, alder body, satin lacquer finish.			
2003-2004		$375	$425
Jazz Bass Special (Import)			
1984-1991. Japanese-made, Jazz/Precision hybrid, Precision-shaped basswood body, Jazz neck (fretless available), 2 P/J pickups.			
1984-1991		$400	$475
Jazz Plus Bass			
1990-1994. Alder body, 2 Lace Sensors, active electronics, rotary circuit selector, master volume, balance, bass boost, bass cut, treble boost, treble cut, various colors.			
1990-1994		$650	$700
Jazz Plus V Bass			
1990-1994. Five-string version.			
1990-1994		$700	$750
Marcus Miller Signature Jazz Bass			
1998-present. Japanese import, sunburst.			
1998-2004		$575	$625
Noel Redding Signature Jazz Bass			
1997. Limited Edition import, artist signature on 'guard, sunburst, rosewood 'board.			
1997		$575	$650

MODEL YEAR	FEATURES	EXC. COND. LOW	HIGH
Squire Jazz Bass			
1980s-present. Jazz bass import, without cover plates, various colors.			
1990s		$175	$275
2000s		$100	$125
Standard Jazz Bass (later model)			
1988-present. Imported from various countries. Not to be confused with '81-'88 American-made model with the same name.			
1988-1999		$250	$325
2000-2004		$275	$325
Standard Jazz Fretless Bass (later model)			
1994-present. Fretless version.			
1994-2004		$300	$350
Standard Jazz V Bass (later model)			
1998-present. 5-string, import model.			
1998-2004		$300	$350
Ventures Limited Edition Jazz Bass			
1996. Made in Japan, part of Ventures guitar and bass set, dark purple.			
1996		$875	$1,000
JP-90 Bass			
1990-1994. Two P/J pickups, rosewood fretboard, poplar body, black or red.			
1990-1994		$525	$575
Musicmaster Bass			
1970-1983. Shorter scale, solidbody, 1 pickup. various colors.			
1970-1983		$475	$625
Mustang Bass			
1966-1982. Shorter scale, solidbody, 1 pickup, offered in standard and competition colors, (competition colors refer to racing stripes on the body).			
1966-1969		$1,000	$1,200
1970-1979		$850	$1,100
1980-1982		$750	$1,000
Performer Bass			
1985-1986. Swinger-like body style, active electronics, various colors.			
1985-1986		$875	$1,000

Precision Bass

The following are all variations of the Precision Bass. The first four listings are for the main U.S.-made models. All others are listed alphabetically after that in the following order:

Precision Bass
Standard Precision Bass
American Standard Precision Bass
American Series Precision Bass
40th Anniversary Precision Bass (Custom Shop)
50th Anniversary American Standard Precision Bass
50th Anniversary Precision Bass
'51 Precision Bass
'55 Precision Bass (Custom Shop)
'57 Precision Bass
'57 Precision Bass (Import)
'59 Precision Bass (Custom Shop)
'62 Precision Bass

MODEL YEAR	FEATURES	EXC. COND. LOW	HIGH
'62 Precision Bass (Import)			
American Deluxe Precision Bass			
American Deluxe Precision V Bass			
Deluxe P-Bass Special			
Elite I Precision Bass			
Elite II Precision Bass			
Foto Flame Precision Bass			
Gold Elite I Precision Bass			
Gold Elite II Precision Bass			
Highway 1 Precision Bass			
Precision Bass Jr.			
Precision Bass Lyte			
Precision Bass Special			
Precision U.S. Deluxe/Plus Deluxe Bass			
Precision U.S. Plus/Plus Bass			
Squire Precision Bass Special			
Squire Precision V Bass Special			
Standard Precision Bass (later model)			
Sting Precision Bass			
Walnut Elite I Precision Bass			
Walnut Elite II Precision Bass			
Walnut Precision Bass Special			

Precision Bass

1951-1981. Slab body until '54, 1-piece maple neck standard until '59, optional after '69., rosewood 'board standard '59 on (slab until mid-'62, curved after), blond finish standard until '54, sunburst standard after that (2-tone '54-'58, 3-tone after '58). Replaced by the Standard Precision Bass in '81-'85, then the American Standard Precision in '88-'00. Renamed American Series Precision Bass in '00. Unlike the Jazz and Telecaster Basses, the Precision was never fitted with a 3-bolt neck or bullet rod.

The custom colors listings are for unfaded or very slightly faded examples. Moderately faded examples will approximate values somewhat below the low end of the value range. Fade does not always mean lighter tint. A heavily faded example will be worth much less than the ranges shown, even if otherwise in excellent, original condition. A heavily faded bass will have a different tint than an unfaded one (for example, a heavily faded Lake Placid Blue can turn dark green), and will fetch values slightly higher than a standard sunburst example. Custom color Fenders can be forged and bogus finishes have been a problem. The prices in the Guide are for factory original finishes in excellent condition.

MODEL YEAR	FEATURES	EXC. COND. LOW	HIGH
1951	Butterscotch blond, slab body	$11,500	$12,500
1952	Butterscotch blond, slab body	$10,000	$11,000
1953	Butterscotch blond, slab body	$10,000	$11,000
1954	Blond, contour body	$8,000	$9,500
1954	Butterscotch blond, slab body	$9,500	$10,500
1955	Blond, contour body	$7,200	$9,000
1956	Blond, contour body	$7,200	$9,000

MODEL YEAR	FEATURES	EXC. COND. LOW	HIGH
1956	Sunburst	$6,700	$8,000
1957	Blond, last full year	$7,300	$9,000
1957	Sunburst, anodized guard late '57	$6,700	$8,000
1957	Sunburst, white guard early '57	$6,700	$8,000
1958	Blond option	$7,300	$9,000
1958	Sunburst, anodized guard	$6,700	$8,000
1959-1960	Sunburst or blond	$6,700	$8,000
1961	Blond (see-thru)	$7,500	$9,500
1961	Dakota Red	$10,500	$12,500
1961	Daphne Blue	$10,000	$11,500
1961	Lake Placid Blue, Olympic White	$9,000	$10,500
1961	Sunburst, slab rosewood	$6,200	$7,300
1962	Curved, black	$7,000	$8,500
1962	Curved, blond	$6,000	$7,500
1962	Curved, Burgundy Mist, Dakota Red, Fiesta Red, Sherwood Green, Shoreline Gold	$9,000	$11,000
1962	Curved, Daphne Blue, Inca Silver	$8,500	$10,500
1962	Curved, Foam Green, Shell Pink, Surf Green	$10,000	$12,000
1962	Curved, Lake Placid Blue, Olympic White	$7,500	$9,500
1962	Curved, Sonic Blue	$8,500	$10,000
1962	Curved, sunburst	$5,300	$6,500
1962	Slab, black	$8,000	$9,000
1962	Slab, blond	$7,500	$8,000
1962	Slab, Burgundy Mist, Dakota Red, Fiesta Red, Sherwood Green, Shoreline Gold	$10,500	$12,000
1962	Slab, Daphne Blue, Inca Silver, Sonic Blue	$9,500	$11,000
1962	Slab, Foam Green, Shell Pink, Surf Green	$11,000	$13,000
1962	Slab, Lake Placid Blue, Olympic White	$9,000	$10,000
1962	Slab, sunburst	$6,000	$7,000
1963	Blond	$6,000	$8,000
1963	Candy Apple Red, Lake Placid Blue, Olympic White	$7,000	$9,500
1963	Dakota Red, Fiesta Red	$8,500	$11,000
1963	Sunburst	$5,000	$6,500
1964	Blond	$6,000	$7,500

1971 Fender Mustang Bass

1953 Fender Precision Bass

BASSES

1978 Fender Precision Bass (Antigua)

1983 Fender Elite II Precision

MODEL YEAR	FEATURES	EXC. COND. LOW	HIGH
1964	Burgundy Mist, Sherwood Green, Shorline Gold	$8,500	$10,500
1964	Candy Apple Red, Lake Placid Blue, Olympic White	$7,000	$8,500
1964	Fiesta Red	$8,500	$10,000
1964	Sunburst	$5,000	$6,000
1965	Black	$5,500	$7,500
1965	Blond	$5,000	$7,000
1965	Burgundy Mist	$8,000	$11,000
1965	Candy Apple Red, Lake Placid Blue, Olympic White	$6,000	$8,500
1965	Charcoal Frost	$7,500	$10,000
1965	Fiesta Red	$7,000	$9,500
1965	Sunburst	$4,000	$5,500
1965	Teal Green	$7,000	$10,000
1966	Candy Apple Red, Lake Placid Blue, Olympic White	$6,000	$7,000
1966	Firemist Gold, Blue Ice, Teal Green	$7,000	$8,000
1966	Sunburst	$4,000	$4,500
1967	Candy Apple Red	$5,500	$6,500
1967	Sunburst	$3,500	$4,500
1968	Black	$4,500	$6,500
1968	Candy Apple Red	$5,500	$7,000
1968	Sunburst	$3,500	$4,500
1969	Black, maple neck	$3,500	$3,800
1969	Black, rosewood neck	$3,400	$3,700
1969	Candy Apple Red, Lake Placid Blue, Olympic White	$3,800	$5,500
1969	Firemist Gold	$4,500	$6,500
1969	Sunburst	$2,500	$3,500
1970	Less common custom color	$4,500	$5,000
1970	More common custom color	$3,500	$4,000
1970	Sunburst, maple cap on maple	$2,600	$3,100
1970	Sunburst, rosewood	$2,500	$3,000
1971	Less common custom color	$4,000	$4,500
1971	More common custom color	$3,000	$3,500
1971	Sunburst, rosewood	$2,300	$2,600
1972	Custom colors	$2,800	$3,800
1972	Sunburst	$2,000	$2,500
1973-1974	Custom colors	$2,100	$3,600
1973-1974	Sunburst	$1,900	$2,300
1975-1976	Sunburst	$1,500	$1,800
1975-1976	Various colors	$1,700	$2,300
1977-1979	Sunburst	$1,000	$1,700
1977-1979	Various colors	$1,300	$2,000
1980-1981	Antigua	$1,300	$1,600
1980-1981	Arctic White, black	$900	$1,500

MODEL YEAR	FEATURES	EXC. COND. LOW	HIGH
1980-1981	International colors	$975	$1,600
1980-1981	Sunburst	$850	$1,400
1980-1981	Wine Red	$900	$1,300

Standard Precision Bass

1981-1985. Replaces Precision Bass, various colors. Replaced by American Standard Precision '88-'00. The Standard name is used on import Precision model for '88-present.

1981-1985		$1,000	$1,200
1985	Japan import	$400	$700

American Standard Precision Bass

1988-2000. Replaces Standard Precision Bass, replaced by American Series Precision in '00.

1988-1989	Blond, gold hardware	$850	$1,050
1988-1989	Various colors	$750	$950
1990-2000	Various colors	$700	$800

American Series Precision Bass

2000-present. Replaces American Standard Precision Bass, various colors.

2000-2002		$675	$725

40th Anniversary Precision Bass (Custom Shop)

1991. 400 made, quilted amber maple top, gold hardware.

1991		$1,400	$1,700

50th Anniversary American Standard Precision Bass

1996. Regular American Standard with gold hardware, 4- or 5-string, gold 50th Anniversary commemorative neck plate, rosewood 'board, sunburst.

1996		$700	$925

50th Anniversary Precision Bass

2001. Commemorative certificate with date and serial number, butterscotch finish, ash body, maple neck, black 'guard.

2001		$825	$900

'51 Precision Bass

2003-present. Import from Japan, does not include pickup or bridge covers as part of the package, blond or sunburst.

2003		$225	$275

'55 Precision Bass (Custom Shop)

2003-present. 1955 specs including oversized 'guard, 1-piece maple neck/fretboard, preproduction bridge and pickup covers, single-coil pickup. Offered in N.O.S., Closet Classic or highest-end Relic.

2003	Closet Classic option	$1,700	$1,800
2003	N.O.S. optioin	$1,600	$1,700
2003	Relic option	$1,900	$2,000

'57 Precision Bass

1982-present. U.S.-made reissue, various colors.

1982-1989		$950	$1,150
1990-1999		$950	$1,150

'57 Precision Bass (Import)

1984-1986. Foreign-made, black.

1984-1986		$450	$700

The *Vintage Guitar Price Guide* shows low to high values for items in all-original excellent condition, and, where applicable, with original case or cover.

MODEL YEAR	FEATURES	EXC. COND. LOW	HIGH

'59 Precision Bass (Custom Shop)
2003-present. Custom Shop built with late-'59 specs, rosewood 'board.

2003	Closet Classic option	$1,700	$1,800
2003	N.O.S. option	$1,600	$1,700
2003	Relic option	$1,900	$2,000

'62 Precision Bass
1982-present. U.S.A.-made reissue of '62 Precision, alder body.

1982-1989	Mary Kaye Blond, gold hardware	$1,050	$1,250
1982-1999	Standard colors	$950	$1,150
1990-1999	Rare colors	$1,050	$1,250
1999	Mars Music custom color	$1,050	$1,250
2000-2003	Standard colors	$850	$1,000

'62 Precision Bass (Import)
1984-1986. Foreign-made, black.

1984-1986		$450	$700

American Deluxe Precision Bass
1998-present. Made in U.S.A., active electronics, alder or ash body. Alder body colors - sunburst or transparent red. Ash body colors - white blond, transparent teal green or transparent purple.

1998-1999		$775	$875
2000-2004		$800	$900

American Deluxe Precision V Bass
1999-present. 5-string version.

1999-2000		$850	$950

Deluxe P-Bass Special
1995-present. Made in Mexico, P/J pickups, Jazz Bass neck.

1995-2003		$375	$400

Elite I Precision Bass
1983-1985. The Elite Series feature active electronics and noise-cancelling pickups, ash body, 1 pickup, various colors.

1983-1985		$800	$950

Elite II Precision Bass
1983-1985. Ash body, 2 pickups, various colors.

1983-1985		$850	$1,000

Foto Flame Precision Bass
1994-1996. Made in Japan, simulated woodgrain finish, natural or sunburst.

1994-1996		$400	$600

Gold Elite I Precision Bass
1983-1985. The Elite Series feature active electronics and noise-cancelling pickups, gold-plated hardware version of the Elite Precision I, 1 pickup.

1983-1985		$800	$950

Gold Elite II Precision Bass
1983-1985. Two pickup version.

1983-1985		$850	$1,000

Highway 1 Precision Bass
2003-present. U.S.-made, alder body, satin lacquer finish.

2003-2004		$375	$425

Precision Bass Jr.
2004-present. 3/4 size.

2004		$275	$325

Precision Bass Lyte
1992-2001. Japanese-made, smaller, lighter basswood body, 2 pickups, sunburst.

1992-2001		$525	$575

Precision Bass Special
1980-1983, 1997-1998. Active electronics, gold-plated brass hardware, 1 split-coil pickup. '90s version similar, but with chrome hardware and made in Mexico.

1997-1998	Mexico	$375	$475

Precision U.S. Deluxe/Plus Deluxe Bass
1991-1994. P-style bass with P-bass and Jazz bass pickups, concentric knobs, no 'guard models available, various colors.

1991-1994		$650	$700

Precision U.S. Plus/Plus Bass
1989-1992. P-style bass with P- and J-bass pickup, model variations, black.

1989-1992		$650	$700

Squire Precision Bass Special
1998-present. Agathis body, P/J pickups.

1998-2004		$65	$75

Squire Precision V Bass Special
2000-present. 5-string version.

2000-2004		$185	$195

Standard Precision Bass (later model)
1987-present. Traditional style, import, currently made in Mexico. Not to be confused with '81-'85 American-made model with the same name.

1987-1999		$300	$350

Sting Precision Bass
2001-present. 2-tone sunburst, 1 single-coil, Sting's signature.

2001-2004		$500	$550

Walnut Elite I Precision Bass
1983-1985. The Elite Series feature active electronics and noise-cancelling pickups. Walnut body, 1 pickup, rosewood 'board, natural.

1983-1985		$850	$1,000

Walnut Elite II Precision Bass
1983-1985. Two-pickup version.

1983-1985		$900	$1,100

Walnut Precision Bass Special
1980-1983. Precision Bass Special with a walnut body, natural.

1980-1983		$900	$1,300

Stu Hamm Urge Bass (U.S.A.)
1992-1999. Contoured Precision-style body with smaller wide treble cutaway, J and P pickups, various colors.

1992-1999		$850	$1,000

Stu Hamm Urge II Bass (U.S.A.)
1999-present. Made in the U.S.A.

1999-2004		$850	$1,000

Telecaster Bass
1968-1979. Slab solidbody, 1 pickup, fretless option '70, blond and custom colors available (Pink Paisley or Blue Floral '68-'69).

1968	Black	$2,000	$2,600
1968	Blond	$1,800	$2,300

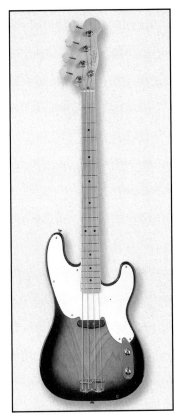

Fender '51 Precision Bass

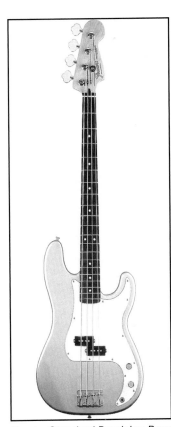

Fender Standard Precision Bass

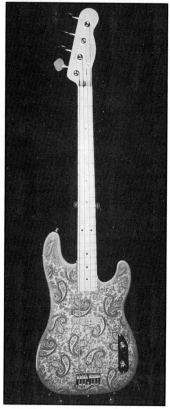

1968 Fender Telecaster Bass (Paisley)

1981 G&L L-1000

MODEL YEAR	FEATURES	EXC. COND. LOW	HIGH
1968	Blue Floral, Paisley	$6,000	$7,000
1969	4-bolt, single-coil	$1,800	$2,100
1970	4-bolt, single-coil	$1,700	$2,000
1971	4-bolt, single-coil	$1,600	$1,900
1972	4-bolt, single-coil	$1,600	$1,800
1973-1974	3-bolt, humbucker	$1,600	$1,800
1975-1976	3-bolt, humbucker	$1,300	$1,600
1977-1979	3-bolt, humbucker	$1,100	$1,500

Fernandes

1969-present. Intermediate and professional grade, production, solidbody basses. Established '69 in Tokyo. Early efforts were classical guitars, but they now offer a variety of guitars and basses.

APB-40 Bass

1990s. High-end-style copy with opaque finish, extended long bass horn, P- and J-Bass dual pickups.

1990s		$400	$450

FRB-80 Bass

FRB Series basses have active electronics, the FRB-80 has slotted neck joint construction, black.

1988		$300	$350

Copy Models

1970s. Early imports with features of classic American basses.

1970s		$300	$350

TEB-1 Bass

1993-1996.

1993-1996		$300	$400

Fina

Production acoustic basses built at the Kwo Hsiao Music Wooden Factory in Huiyang City, Guang Dong, mainland China. They also build guitars.

First Act

1995-present. Budget and professional grade, production/custom, basses built in China and their Custom Shop in Boston. They also make guitars, violins, and other instruments.

Fleishman Instruments

1974-present. Premium and presentation grade, acoustic and solidbody basses made by luthier Harry Fleishman in Sebastopol, California. He also offers electric uprights, designed by him and built in China. Fleishman also designs basses for others and is the director of Luthiers School International. He also builds guitars.

Fodera

1983-present. Luthiers Vinnie Fodera and Joseph Lauricella build their premium grade, production/custom, solidbody basses in Brooklyn, New York.

Framus

1946-1975, 1996-present. Professional and premium grade, production/custom, basses made in Germany. They also build guitars and amps. Distributed in the U.S. by Dana B. Goods.

MODEL YEAR	FEATURES	EXC. COND. LOW	HIGH

Atlantic Bass Model 5/140

1960s. Single-cut thinline with f-holes, 2 pickups, sunburst or blackrose.

1960s		$325	$525

Atlantic Bass Model 5/143

1960s. Offset double-cut thinbody with f-holes, 2 pickups, 4-on-a-side keys.

1960s		$400	$600

Atlantic Bass Model 5/144

1960s. Double-cut thinbody with f-holes, ES-335 body style, 2 pickups. Becomes Model J/144 in '70s.

1960s		$450	$650

Charavelle 4 Bass Model 5/153

1960s. Double-cut thinline with f-holes, 335-style body, 2 pickups, sunburst, cherry red or Sunset.

1960s		$500	$700

De Luxe 4 Bass Model 5/154

1960s. Double-cut thinline with sharp (acute) hornes and f-holes, 2 pickups, mute, sunburst or natural/blond. 2nd most expensive in Framus bass lineup in the mid-'60s, although not as famous as the Stone/Bill Wyman bass.

1960s		$600	$800

Electric Upright Bass

1950s. Full-scale neck, triangular body, black.

1958		$1,500	$2,000

Star Bass Series (Bill Wyman)

1959-1968. Early flyer says, "Bill Wyman of the Rolling Stones prefers the Star Bass." The model name was later changed to Framus Stone Bass. Single-cut semi-hollow body, 5/149 (1 pickup) and 5/150 (2 pickups), sunburst.

1959-1965	Model 5/150	$650	$800
1960s	Model 5/149	$600	$750

Strato De Luxe Star Bass Model 5/165

Ca. 1964-ca. 1972. Offset double-cut solidbody, 2 pickups, sunbust. There was also a gold hardware version (5/165 gl) and a 6-string (5/166).

1960s		$450	$650

Strato Star Bass Series

Ca. 1963-ca. 1972. Double-cut solidbody, 5/156/50 (1 pickup) or 5/156/52 (2 pickups), beige, cherry or sunburst.

1960s	Model 5/156/50	$300	$500
1960s	Model 5/156/52	$350	$550

T.V. Star Bass

1960s. Offset double-cut thinbody with f-holes, 2 pickups, short-scale, sunburst or cherry red. Most expensive of the '60s Framus basses, although not as popular as the Bill Wyman 5/150 model.

1960s		$550	$750

Upright Bass Viol

1946	Carved top	$3,500	$5,000

Fylde

1973-present. Luthier Roger Bucknall builds his professional and premium grade, production/custom acoustic basses in Penrith, Cumbria, United Kingdom. He also builds guitars, mandolins, mandolas, bouzoukis, and citterns.

MODEL YEAR	FEATURES	EXC. COND. LOW	HIGH

G & L

1980-present. Intermediate and professional grade, production/custom, electric basses made in the U.S. In '03, G & L introduced the Korean-made G & L Tribute Series. A Tribute logo is clearly identified on the headstock. They also build guitars.

ASAT Bass
1989-present. Single-cut, solidbody, active and passive modes, 2 humbucking pickups, various colors.

1989-1991	About 400 made	$575	$700
1992-2003		$475	$600

ASAT Commemorative Bass
1991-1992. About 150 made, 4-string ASAT commemorating Leo Fender's life.

1991-1992		$1,350	$1,600

ASAT Semi-Hollow Bass
2001-present. Semi-hollowbody style on ASAT bass.

2001-2003		$625	$800

Climax Bass
1992-1996. Single active humbucker MFD pickup.

1992-1996		$425	$550

El Toro Bass
1983-1991. Double-cut, solidbody, 2 active, smaller, humbucker pickups, sunburst.

1983-1991		$575	$900

Interceptor Bass
1984-1991. Sharp pointed double-cut, solidbody, 2 active, smaller humbucker pickups, sunburst.

1984-1991		$675	$1,000

JB-2 Bass
2001-present. Alder body, 2 Alnico V pickups.

2001-2003		$550	$700

L-1000 Bass
1980-1994. Offset double-cut, solidbody, 1 pickup, various colors.

1980-1994		$525	$700

L-1500 Bass/L-1500 Custom Bass
1997-present.

1997-2003		$475	$600

L-1505 Bass
1998-present. Five-string version, single MFD humbucker pickup.

1998-2003		$575	$650

L-2000 Bass
1980-present. Offset double-cut solidbody, 2 pickups, active electronics. Originally, the L-2000 was available with active (L-2000E) or passive (L-2000) electronics.

1980-1982		$675	$850
1983-1991	Leo signature	$675	$800
1992-2003		$575	$650

L-2000(E) Bass
1980-1982. Offset double-cut, solidbody, 2 pickups, active electronics. Originally, the L-2000 was available with active (L-2000E) or passive (L-2000) electronics.

1980-1982		$725	$850

L-2000 Custom Bass
1997. Ash top, wood-grain binding upgrade.

1997		$675	$800

L-2000 Fretless Bass
1980-1998. Fretless version.

1980-1982		$775	$900

L-2500 Bass
1997-present. Five-string, dual MFD humbucker pickups, figured tops can vary.

1997-2003		$575	$800

L-2500 Custom Bass
1997. Ash top, wood-grain binding upgrade.

1997		$675	$850

L-5000 Bass
1988-1992. Offset double-cut, solidbody, G & L Z-shaped split-humbucking pickup, 5 strings, approximately 400 made.

1988-1992		$525	$600

L-5500 Bass
1993-1997. Alder body, 5-string.

1993-1997		$575	$700

L-5500 Custom Bass
1997. Ash top, wood-grain binding upgrade.

1997		$525	$650

LB-100 Bass
1993-2000. Follow-up to earlier Legacy Bass.

1993-2000		$425	$550

Legacy Bass
1992-1993. Offset double-cut solidbody, 1split-coil pickup, renamed LB-100 in '93.

1992-1993		$550	$625

Lynx Bass
1984-1991. Offset double-cut, solidbody, 2 single-coil pickups, black.

1984-1991		$625	$750

SB 1 Bass
1982-2000. Solidbody, maple neck, body and 'board, split-humbucker pickup, 1 tone and 1 volume control.

1982-1984	1 J-style pickup	$425	$550
1985-2000	1 P-style pickup	$375	$500

SB 2 Bass
1982-present. Maple neck with tilt adjustment, 1 split-coil humbucking and 1 single-coil bridge pickups.

1982-1984	2 P-style pickups	$425	$550
1988-2003	1 P- and 1 J-style pickups	$450	$550

G.L. Stiles

1960-1994. Built by Gilbert Lee Stiles primarily in the Miami, Florida area. He also built guitars.

Electric Solidbody Bass

1970s	Various models	$350	$450

Gibson

1902-present. Professional grade, production, U.S.-made electric basses. Gibson got into the electric bass market with the introduction of their Gibson Electric Bass in '53 (that model was renamed the EB-1 in '58 and reintroduced under that name in '69). Many more bass models followed. Gibson's custom colors can greatly increase the value of older instruments. Custom colors offered from '63 to '69

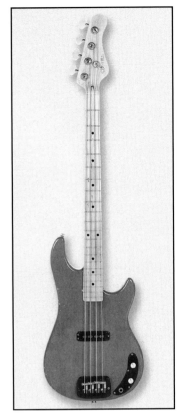

1983 G&L SB-1

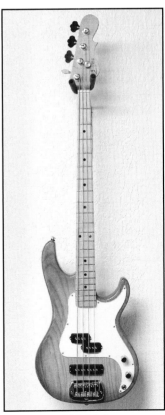

G&L SB-2

Gibson EB-0

1968 Gibson EB-3

MODEL YEAR	FEATURES	EXC. COND. LOW	HIGH

are Cardinal Red, Ember Red, Frost Blue, Golden Mist Metallic, Heather Metallic, Inverness Green, Kerry Green, Pelham Blue Metallic, Polaris White, Silver Mist Metallic.

20/20
1987-1988. Designed by Ned Steinberger, slim-wedge Steinberger style solidbody, 2 humbuckers, 20/20 logo on headstock, Luna Silver or Ferrari Red finish.

1987-1988		$1,000	$1,100

Electric Bass (EB-1)
1953-1958. Introduced as Gibson Electric Bass in '53, but was called the EB-1 by Gibson in its last year of '58, thus, the whole line is commonly called the EB-1 by collectors, reissued in '69 as the EB-1 (see EB-1 listing), brown.

1953-1958		$4,000	$5,000

EB Bass
1970 only. Renamed from Melody Maker Bass, SG body, 1 humbucker pickup.

1970		$1,000	$1,200

EB-0 Bass
1959-1979. Double-cut slab body with banjo-type tuners in '59 and '60, double-cut SG-type body with conventional tuners from '61 on, 1 pickup. Faded custom colors are of less value.

1959-1960	Cherry, slab body	$3,000	$4,000
1961	Cherry, SG body	$1,700	$2,200
1962	Cherry	$1,500	$1,800
1963-1965	Cherry	$1,300	$1,600
1966-1968	Cherry	$1,100	$1,400
1968	Black	$1,200	$1,500
1968	Burgundy Metallic	$1,500	$1,800
1968	Pelham Blue	$1,500	$2,000
1969	Cherry	$1,100	$1,300
1969	Pelham Blue	$1,500	$2,000
1970-1971	Cherry	$1,000	$1,300
1972-1974	Cherry	$900	$1,000
1975-1979	Cherry	$900	$1,000

EB-0 F Bass
1962-1965. EB-0 with added built-in fuzz, cherry.

1962		$1,500	$1,800
1963-1965		$1,300	$1,600

EB-0 L Bass
1969-1979. 34.5 inch scale version of the EB-0, various colors.

1969-1971		$1,000	$1,300
1972-1979		$900	$1,000

EB-1 Bass
1969-1972. The Gibson Electric Bass ('53-'58) is often also called the EB-1 (see Electric Bass). Violin-shaped mahogany body, 1 pickup, standard tuners.

1969-1972		$1,700	$2,000

EB-2 Bass
1958-1961, 1964-1972. ES-335-type semi-hollowbody, double-cut, 1 pickup, banjo tuners '58-'60 and conventional tuners '60 on.

1958	Sunburst, banjo tuners	$2,700	$3,000
1959	Natural, banjo tuners	$3,000	$3,500
1959	Sunburst, banjo tuners	$2,600	$2,900
1960	Sunburst, banjo tuners	$2,400	$2,700
1961	Sunburst, conventional tuners	$2,000	$2,400
1964-1965	Sunburst	$1,400	$1,600
1966-1969	Various colors	$1,200	$1,500
1967-1969	Sparkling Burgundy option	$1,500	$2,000
1970-1972	Various colors	$1,000	$1,200

EB-2 D Bass
1966-1972. Two-pickup version of EB-2, cherry, sunburst, or walnut.

1966-1969	Various colors	$1,800	$2,200
1970-1972	Sunburst	$1,500	$1,800

EB-3 Bass
1961-1979. SG-style solidbody, 2 humbuckers, solid peghead '61-'68 and '72-'79, slotted peghead '69-'71, cherry to '71, various colors after.

1961-1965		$1,800	$2,100
1965	Jack Bruce exact specs	$2,500	$3,000
1966-1968		$1,650	$2,000
1969	Slotted peghead	$1,600	$1,900
1970-1971	Slotted peghead	$1,500	$1,800
1972-1974		$1,400	$1,700
1975-1979		$1,300	$1,400

EB-3 L Bass
1969-1972. 34.5" scale version of EB-3, cherry, natural, or walnut.

1969		$1,500	$1,800
1970-1971		$1,400	$1,700
1972		$1,300	$1,600

EB-4 L Bass
1972-1975. SG-style, 1 humbucker, 34.5" scale, cherry or walnut.

1972-1975		$1,200	$1,500

EB-6 Bass
1960-1966. Introduced as semi-hollowbody 335-style 6-string with 1 humbucker, changed to SG-style with 2 pickups in '62.

1960-1961	Sunburst, 335-style	$7,000	$10,000
1962-1964	Cherry, SG-style	$8,000	$12,000
1965-1966	Cherry, SG-style	$7,000	$9,000

Explorer Bass
1984-1987. Alder body, 3-piece maple neck, ebony 'board, dot inlays, 2 humbuckers, various colors.

1984-1987		$800	$1,000

Flying V Bass
1981-1982 only. Solidbody, Flying V body.

1981-1982	Blue stain or ebony	$1,300	$1,600
1981-1982	Silverburst	$2,300	$2,700

Gibson IV Bass
1986-1988. Mahogany body and neck, double-cut, 2 pickups, black chrome hardware, various colors.

1986-1988		$450	$550

Gibson V Bass
1986-1988. Double-cut, 5 strings, 2 pickups.

1986-1988		$600	$750

The *Vintage Guitar Price Guide* shows low to high values for items in all-original excellent condition, and, where applicable, with original case or cover.

MODEL YEAR	FEATURES	EXC. COND. LOW	HIGH

Grabber Bass (G-1)
1974-1982. Double-cut solidbody, 1 pickup, bolt maple neck, maple 'board, various colors.

1974-1982		$600	$800

Grabber III Bass (G-3)
1975-1982. Double-cut solidbody, 3 pickups, bolt maple neck, maple 'board, nickel-plated hardware, various colors.

1975-1982		$700	$1,000

Les Paul Bass
1970-1971. Single-cut solidbody, 2 pickups, walnut finish, renamed Les Paul Triumph Bass '71-'79.

1970-1971		$1,400	$1,600

Les Paul Deluxe Plus LPB-2 Bass
1991-present. Same as Les Paul Special LPB-1 bass, but with flamey AAA maple top and pickup upgrade, 2 pickups, ebony 'board, active electronics, also available as 5-string.

1991-1999		$850	$900

Les Paul Signature Bass
1973-1979. Double-cut, semi-hollowbody, 1 pickup, sunburst or gold (gold only by '76).

1973-1975	Sunburst	$2,500	$2,700
1973-1979	Gold	$2,400	$2,600

Les Paul Special LPB-1 Bass
1991-1996. Two pickups, ebony 'board, active electronics, also available as 5-string.

1991-1996	Alpine White	$650	$700

Les Paul Special V Bass
1993-1996. Single-cut slab body, 5-string, 2 pickups, dot markers, black/ebony.

1993-1996		$650	$700

Les Paul Triumph Bass
1971-1979. Renamed from Les Paul Bass.

1971-1979	Various colors	$1,200	$1,400
1973-1974	White optional color	$1,300	$1,500

Melody Maker Bass
1967-1970. SG body, 1 humbucker pickup.

1967-1970		$1,000	$1,200

Q-80 Bass
1986-1988. Victory Series body shape, 2 pickups, bolt neck, black chrome hardware, renamed Q-90 in '88.

1986-1988		$600	$700

Q-90 Bass
1988-1992. Renamed from Q-80, mahogany body, 2 active humbuckers, maple neck, ebony 'board.

1988-1992		$600	$700

RD Artist Bass
1977-1982. Double-cut solid maple body, laminated neck, 2 pickups, active electronics, string-thru-body, block inlays, various colors.

1977-1982		$800	$1,000

RD Artist Custom Bass
1977-1982. Custom option with bound top, low production.

1977-1982	Sunburst, mild figure	$900	$1,200

RD Standard Bass
1977-1979. Double-cut, solid maple body, laminated neck, 2 pickups, regular electronics, string-thru-body, dot inlays, various colors.

1977-1979		$800	$1,000

Ripper Bass
1974-1982. Introduced as L-9 S Bass in '73, double-cut solidbody, glued neck, 2 pickups, string-thru-body, various colors.

1974-1982		$700	$900

SB Series Bass
1971-1978. Various models include 300 (30" scale, 1 pickup), 350 (30" scale, 2 pickups), 400 (34" scale, 1 pickup), 450 (34" scale, 2 pickups). From '75 to '78 the 450 was special order only.

1971-1973	SB-300	$500	$900
1971-1973	SB-400	$500	$900
1972-1974	SB-350	$550	$950
1972-1974	SB-450	$550	$950
1975-1978	SB-450 special order	$550	$950

Thunderbird 76 Bass
1976 only. Reverse solidbody, 2 pickups, rosewood 'board, various colors.

1976		$2,500	$2,900

Thunderbird 79 Bass
1979 only. Reverse solidbody, 2 pickups, sunburst.

1979		$1,800	$2,300

Thunderbird II Bass
1963-1969. Reverse solidbody until '65, non-reverse solidbody '65-'69, 1 pickup, custom colors available, reintroduced with reverse body for '83-'84.

1963	Sunburst, reverse	$4,500	$7,000
1964	Pelham Blue Metallic, reverse	$5,000	$8,000
1964	Sunburst, reverse	$4,500	$6,500
1965	Cardinal Red, non-reverse	$4,500	$5,000
1965	Inverness Green, non-reverse	$4,500	$5,000
1965	Sunburst, reverse	$4,000	$4,500
1966	Sunburst, non-reverse	$2,800	$3,200
1967	Sunburst, non-reverse	$2,600	$3,000
1968	Cardinal Red, non-reverse	$4,000	$4,500
1968	Sunburst, non-reverse	$2,500	$2,900
1969	Sunburst, non-reverse	$2,400	$2,800

Thunderbird IV Bass
1963-1969. Reverse solidbody until '64, non-reverse solidbody '65-'69, 2 pickups, custom colors available, reintroduced with reverse body for '86-present (see Thunderbird IV Bass Reissue).

1963	Sunburst, reverse	$5,500	$8,500
1964	Frost Blue, reverse	$7,500	$10,000
1964	Pelham Blue Metallic, reverse	$7,500	$10,000
1964	Sunburst, reverse	$5,500	$7,500

Gibson Melody Maker

1978 Gibson RD Artist

1965 Gibson Thunderbird IV

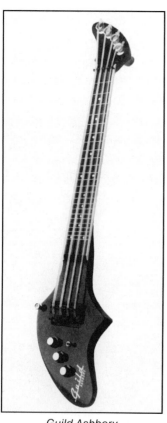

Guild Ashbory

MODEL YEAR	FEATURES	EXC. COND. LOW	HIGH
1965	Cardinal Red, non-reverse	$5,500	$6,500
1965	Inverness Green, non-reverse	$5,500	$6,500
1965	Sunburst, reverse	$5,000	$6,000
1966	Sunburst, non-reverse	$3,800	$4,300
1966	White, non-reverse	$5,000	$6,000
1967	Sunburst, non-reverse	$3,500	$4,000
1968	Sunburst, non-reverse	$3,300	$3,800
1969	Sunburst, non-reverse	$3,000	$3,500

Thunderbird IV Bass (Reissue)

1987-present. Has reverse body and 2 pickups, sunburst.

1987-1990		$1,200	$1,400
1991-2002		$1,000	$1,300
1991-2002	Rare color	$1,300	$1,500

Victory Artist Bass

1981-1985. Double-cut, solidbody, 2 humbuckers and active electronics, various colors.

1981-1985		$550	$650

Victory Custom Bass

1982-1984. Double-cut, solidbody, 2 humbuckers, passive electronics, limited production.

1982-1984		$550	$650

Victory Standard Bass

1981-1986. Double-cut, solidbody, 1 humbucker, active electronics, various colors.

1981-1986		$500	$600

Godin

1987-present. Intermediate and professional grade, production, solidbody electric and acoustic/electric basses from luthier Robert Godin. They also build guitars and mandolins.

Gold Tone

1993-present. Wayne and Robyn Rogers build their intermediate grade, production/custom acoustic basses in Titusville, Florida. They also offer lap steels, mandolins, banjos and banjitars.

Goya

1955-1996. Originally imports from Sweden, brand later used on Japanese and Korean imports.

Electric Solidbody Bass

1960s	Various models	$300	$375

Graf, Oskar

1970-present. Luthier Oskar Graf builds his premium grade, production/custom upright solidbody and acoustic basses in Clarendon, Ontario. He also builds guitars and lutes.

Granada

1970s-1980s. Japanese-made electric basses, most being copies of classic American models. They also offered guitars.

MODEL YEAR	FEATURES	EXC. COND. LOW	HIGH

Greco

1960s-present. Currently owned by Kanda Shokai, of Japan, and offering solidbody basses. They also offer guitars. Early bass models were copies of popular brands, but the by the '70s original designs appear.

Beatle Bass Copy

1970s		$350	$450

Gretsch

1883-present. Intermediate and professional grade, production, solidbody, hollow body, and acoustic/electric basses. Gretsch came late to the electric bass game, introducing their first models in the early '60s.

Bikini Doubleneck Bass

1961-1962. Solidbody electric, separate 6-string and bass-neck body units that slid into 1 of 3 body "butterflies"--1 for the 6-string only (6023), 1 for bass only (6024), 1 for doubleneck (6 and bass-6025). Components could be purchased separately. Prices here are for bass neck and 1 body.

1961-1962		$700	$900

Broadkaster Bass (7605/7606)

1975-1979. Double-cut solidbody, 1 pickup, bolt-on maple neck, natural (7605) or sunburst (7606).

1975-1979		$750	$950

Committee Bass (7629)

1977-1980. Double-cut walnut and maple soldibody, neck-thru, 1 pickup, natural.

1977-1980		$650	$750

Model 6070/6072 Bass

1968-1971. Country Gentleman thinline archtop double-cut body, fake f-holes, 1 pickup (6070) or 2 (6072), gold hardware.

1968-1971	Model 6070	$1,200	$1,500
1968-1971	Model 6072	$1,300	$1,600

G6072 Long Scale Hollow Body Bass

1998-present. Reissue of the '68 double-cut hollowbody, 2 pickups, sunburst, gold hardware.

1998-2002		$1,100	$1,275

Model 6071/6073 Bass

1968. Single-cut hollowbody, fake f-holes, 1 pickup (6071) or 2 (6073), padded back, red mahogany.

1968-1971	Model 6071	$900	$1,200
1968-1971	Model 6073	$1,000	$1,300

Model 7615 Bass

1972-1975. Offset double-cut solidbody, slotted bass horn (monkey grip), large polished rosewood 'guard covering most of the body, 2 pickups, dot markers, brown mahogany finish. Only bass offered in Gretsch catalog for this era.

1972-1975		$800	$1,000

TK 300 Bass (7626/7627)

1976-1981. Double-cut solidbody, 1 pickup, Autumn Red Stain or natural.

1976-1981		$550	$700

The *Vintage Guitar Price Guide* shows low to high values for items in all-original excellent condition, and, where applicable, with original case or cover.

MODEL		EXC. COND.	
YEAR	FEATURES	LOW	HIGH

Groove Tools

2002-2004. Korean-made, production, intermediate grade, solidbody basses that were offered by Conklin Guitars of Springfield, Missouri. They also had guitars.

GT Bass

2002-2004. Offset double-cut with large bass horn, bolt-on neck, clear hard finish, models include GT-4 (4-string), GT-5 (5-string) and GT-7 (7-string).

2002-2004	GT-4, GT-5	$400	$500
2002-2004	GT-7	$600	$800

Grosh, Don

1993-present. Professional grade, production/custom, solidbody basses built by luthier Don Grosh in Santa Clarita, California. He also builds guitars.

Guild

1952-present. Guild added electric basses in the mid-'60s and offered them until '02.

Ashbory Bass

1986-1988. 18" scale, total length 30", fretless, silicone rubber strings, active electronics, low-impedance circuitry.

1986-1988		$500	$600

B-4 E Bass

1993-1999. Acoustic/electric single-cut flat-top, mahogany sides with arched mahogany back, multi-bound, gold hardware until '95, chrome after.

1993-1999		$850	$975

B-30 E Bass

1987-1999. Single-cut flat-top acoustic/electric, mahogany sides, arched mahogany back, multi-bound, fretless optional.

1987-1999		$1,250	$1,350

B-50 Acoustic Bass

1976-1987. Acoustic flat-top, mahogany sides with arched mahogany back, spruce top, multi-bound, renamed B-30 in '87.

1976-1987		$1,250	$1,350

B-301/B-302 Bass

1976-1981. Double-cut solidbody, chrome-plated hardware. Models include B-301 (mahogany, 1 pickup), B-301 A (ash, 1 pickup), B-302 (mahogany, 2 pickups), B-302 A (ash, 2 pickups), and B-302 AF (ash, fretless).

1976-1981	B-301	$475	$600
1976-1981	B-302	$525	$650
1977-1981	B-301 A	$525	$650
1977-1981	B-302 A	$550	$675
1977-1981	B-302 AF	$525	$675

B-500 Acoustic Bass

1992-1993. Acoustic/electric flat-top, round soundhole, single-cut, solid spruce top, maple back and sides, dark stain, limited production.

1992-1993		$1,250	$1,350

Jet Star Bass

1964-1970 (limited production '68-'70). Offset double-cut solidbody, short treble horn, 1 pickup, 2-on-a-side tuners '64-'66 and 4 in-line tuners '66-'70.

1964-1966	2 on side tuners	$900	$1,100
1967-1970	4 in-line	$600	$900

MODEL		EXC. COND.	
YEAR	FEATURES	LOW	HIGH

JS I/JS II Bass

1970-1976. Double-cut solidbody, 1 pickup (JS I) or 2 (JS II), mini-switch, selector switch, renamed JS Bass 2 in '73 with carved oak leaf design available.

1970-1976	JS I	$500	$700
1970-1976	JS II	$700	$750

M-85 I/M-85 II Bass (Semi-hollow)

1967-1972. Single-cut semi-hollowbody, 1 pickup (M-85 I) or 2 (M-85 II).

1967-1972	M-85 I	$800	$1,200
1967-1972	M-85 II	$1,000	$1,400

M-85 I/M-85 II BluesBird Bass (Solidbody)

1972-1976. Single-cut solidbody archtop, Chesterfield headstock inlay, cherry mahogany, 1 humbucker pickup (I) or 2 (II).

1972-1973	M-85 I	$800	$1,200
1972-1976	M-85 II	$1,000	$1,400

MB-801 Bass

1981-1982. Double-cut solidbody, 1 pickup, dot inlays.

1981-1982		$500	$650

SB-601/SB-602/SB-602 V Pilot Bass

1983-1988. Offset double-cut solidbody, bolt-on neck, poplar body. Models include SB-601 (1 pickup), SB-602 (2 pickups or fretless) and SB-602 V (2 pickups, 5-string).

1983-1988	SB-601	$400	$600
1983-1988	SB-602	$475	$675
1983-1988	SB-602 V	$500	$700
1983-1988	SB-602, fretless	$475	$675

Starfire Bass

1965-1975. Double-cut semi-hollow thinbody, 1 pickup, mahogany neck, chrome-plated hardware, cherry or sunburst.

1965-1969	Single-coil	$1,300	$1,500
1970-1975	Humbucker	$1,200	$1,400

Starfire II Bass

1965-1978. Two-pickup version of Starfire Bass.

1965-1969	2 single-coils	$1,400	$1,600
1970-1978	2 humbuckers	$1,300	$1,500

X-701/X-702 Bass

1982-1984. Body with 4 sharp horns with extra long bass horn, 1 pickup (X-701) or 2 (X-702), various metallic finishes.

1982-1984	X-701	$725	$800
1982-1984	X-702	$825	$900

Guyatone

1933-present. Large Japanese maker which also produced instruments under the Marco Polo, Winston, Kingston, Kent, LaFayette, and Bradford brands.

Electric Solidbody Bass

1960s	Various models	$300	$425

Hagstrom

1921-1983. This Swedish guitar company first offered electric basses in '61.

Guild SB-602

1967 Guild Starfire Bass

BASSES

Hagstrom 8-string

Hamer Blitz

MODEL YEAR	FEATURES	EXC. COND. LOW	HIGH

8-String Bass
1967-1969. Double-cut solidbody, 2 pickups, various colors.

1967-1969		$1,100	$1,400

F-100 B Bass
1970s. Offset double-cut solidbody, 1 pickup, Fender style headstock.

1970s		$425	$650

Model I B Bass
1965-1966, 1971-1973. Double-cut solidbody, 2 pickups, red.

1965-1966		$425	$650

Model II B/F-400 Bass
1965-1970. Offset double-cut solidbody, 2 pickups, sunburst, called F-400 in U.S., II B elsewhere.

1965-1970		$550	$750

Swede Bass
1971-1976. Single-cut solidbody, block inlays, 2 pickups, cherry.

1971-1976		$800	$950

Swede 2000 Bass (with synth)
1977. Circuitry on this Swede bass connected to the Ampeg Patch 2000 pedal so bass would work with various synths.

1977		$800	$950

V-IN Bass/Concord Bass
1970s. Bass version of V-IN guitar, 335-style body, 2 pickups, sunburst.

1970s		$600	$700

Hallmark
1965-1967, 2004-present. Imported, intermediate grade, production, basses. Hallmark is located in Greenbelt, Maryland. They also make guitars. The brand was originally founded by Joe Hall in Arvin, California, in '65.

Hamer
1975-present. Intermediate and professional grade, production/custom, acoustic and electric basses. Founded in Arlington Heights, Illinois, by Paul Hamer and Jol Dantzig, Hamer was purchased by Kaman in '88.

8-String Bass
1990s. Special order, single-cut flat-top with soundhole, natural.

1990s		$1,400	$1,500

12-String Short-Scale Bass
1978-1996. Four sets of 3 strings - a fundamental and 2 tuned an octave higher, maple and mahogany solidbody, 30.5" scale.

1978-1996		$1,400	$1,500

Blitz Bass
1982-1990. Explorer-style solidbody, 2 pickups, bolt-on neck.

1982-1984	1st edition	$450	$850
1984-1990		$450	$700

MODEL YEAR	FEATURES	EXC. COND. LOW	HIGH

Chaparral Bass
1986-1995, 2000-present. Solidbody, 2 pickups, glued-in neck, later basses have bolt-on neck.

1986-1987	Set-neck	$400	$700
1987-1995	Bolt-on neck	$350	$550

Chaparral 5-String Bass
1987-1995. Five strings, solidbody, 2 pickups, glued-in neck, later basses have 5-on-a-side reverse peghead.

1987-1995		$350	$550

Chaparral Max Bass
1986-1995. Chaparral Bass with figured maple body, glued-in neck and boomerang inlays.

1986-1995		$500	$750

Cruise Bass
1982-1990, 1995-1999. J-style solidbody, 2 pickups, glued neck ('82-'90) or bolt-on neck ('95-'99), also available as a 5-string.

1982-1990	Set-neck	$400	$700
1995-1999	Bolt-on neck	$350	$550

Cruise Bass 5
1982-1989. Five-string version, various colors.

1982-1989		$400	$700

FBIV Bass
1985-1987. Reverse Firebird shape, 1 P-Bass Slammer and 1 J-Bass Slammer pickup, mahogany body, rosewood 'board, dots.

1985-1987		$400	$750

Standard Bass
1975-1984. Explorer-style bound body with 2 humbuckers.

1975-1979		$700	$850
1980-1984		$475	$700

Velocity 5
2002-present. Offset double-cut, long bass horn, active, 1 humbucker.

2002-2004		$175	$225

Harmony
1892-1976. Harmony once was one of the biggest instrument makers in the world, making guitars and basses under their own brand and for others.

H-22 Bass
Early-1960s-1970s. Single- or double-cut, sunburst.

1960-1970s		$275	$500

Rocket Bass
1960s-1970s. First models single-cut, later models double-cut, similar to Rocket guitar.

1960-1970s		$350	$500

Hartke
Hartke offered a line of wood and aluminum-necked basses from 2000 to 2003.

Electric Bass

2000-2003		$100	$200

Hayman
1970-1973. Solid and semi-hollow body guitars developed by Jim Burns and Bob Pearson for Ivor Arbiter of the Dallas Arbiter Company and built by Shergold in England.

MODEL YEAR	FEATURES	EXC. COND. LOW	HIGH

Heartfield

1989-1994. Distributed by Fender, imported from Japan.

DR-4 Bass

1989-1994. Double-cut solidbody, graphite reinforced neck, 2 single-coils, 4 strings, available in 5- and 6-string models.

1989-1994		$200	$350

Heit Deluxe

Ca. 1967-1970. Imported from Japan, many were made by Teisco.

Höfner

1887-present. Professional grade, production, basses. They also offer guitars and bowed instruments. Hofner basses, made famous in the U.S. by one Paul McCartney, are made in Germany.

JB-59 Upright Jazz Bass

Electric solidbody, 3/4-size, solid mahogany, pickup, preamp.

1980s		$1,100	$1,400

Model 185 Solid Bass

1962-ca. 1970. Classic offset double-cut solidbody, 2 double-coil pickups.

1960s		$400	$450

Model 500/1 Beatle Bass

1956-present. Semi-acoustic, bound body in violin shape, glued-in neck, 2 pickups, sunburst, currently listed as the 500/1 Cavern '61 Electric Bass Guitar.

1956-1959		$2,400	$3,200
1960-1961		$3,000	$3,500
1960-1961	Lefty	$3,500	$4,000
1962		$2,700	$3,300
1962	Lefty	$3,500	$4,000
1963		$2,500	$3,100
1963	Lefty	$3,500	$5,000
1964		$2,400	$3,000
1964	Lefty	$3,300	$3,800
1965		$2,300	$2,900
1965	Lefty	$3,100	$3,600
1966		$2,000	$2,500
1966	Lefty	$2,300	$2,800
1967		$1,800	$2,000
1967	Lefty	$1,900	$2,100
1968-1969	Blade pickup	$1,500	$1,700
1968-1969	Lefty, blade pickup	$1,600	$1,800
1970-1973		$1,500	$1,700
1970-1973	Lefty	$1,600	$1,800
1974-1979		$1,100	$1,500

Model 500/1 1964-1984 Bass Reissue

1984. '1964-1984' neckplate notation.

1984		$1,600	$1,700

'63 Model 500/1 Beatle Bass Reissue

1994-present. Right- or left-handed.

1990-2000s		$1,400	$1,500

Model 500/2 Bass

1965-1970. Similar to the 500/1, but with 'club' body Hofner made for England's Selmer, sunburst. Club Bass has been reissued.

1965-1970		$1,300	$1,700

Model 500/3 Senator

1962. Sunburst.

1962		$1,450	$1,700

Model 500/5 Bass

1959-1979. Single-cut body with Beatle Bass-style pickups, sunburst.

1960s		$1,700	$1,900

G5000/1 Super Beatle (G500/1) Bass

1968-present. Bound ebony 'board, gold-plated hardware, natural finish, the version with active circuit is called G500/1 Super Beatle, reissued in '94

1970s		$1,300	$1,500

President Bass

Made for England's Selmer, single-cut archtop, 2 pickups, sunburst.

1961-1962		$1,500	$1,800
1963-1965		$1,400	$1,700
1966-1967		$1,100	$1,300
1968-1969		$1,000	$1,200
1970-1972		$900	$1,100

Hohner

1857-present. Intermediate and professional grade, production, solidbody basses. Hohner has been offering basses at least since the early '70s. They also offer guitars, banjos, mandolins and ukes.

B2AFL Bass

1990-1994. Headless, 2 humbuckers, active circuitry, fretless.

1990-1994		$250	$275

B-Bass

1990-present. Solid maple neck-thru-body, rosewood 'board, 2 pickups, several options.

1990s		$250	$375

HAB-1 Acoustic/Electric Bass

1990-1993. Rounded triangular soundhole, medium-size dreadnought, single-cut.

1990-1993		$250	$375

Jack Bass

1989-1994. Headless, offset body, 2 pickups, active tone circuitry.

1989-1994		$325	$400

JJ Bass

Late 1980s-1991. Sunburst solid maple body, 2 pickups, active tone circuitry.

1980s		$250	$325

Hondo

1969-1987, 1991-present. Budget grade, production, imported acoustic and electric solidbody basses. They also offer guitars and mandolins.

Electric Solidbody Bass

1970-1990s	Various models	$125	$225

1963 Höfner 500/1

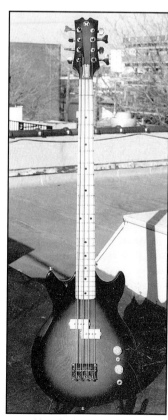

Hondo Artist 8-string

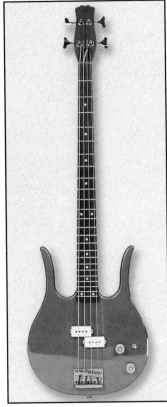

'80s Hondo H 1181

Ibanez SR-500

MODEL YEAR	FEATURES	EXC. COND. LOW	HIGH

H 1181 Longhorn Bass
Ca. 1978-1980s. Copy of Danelectro Longhorn Bass, 1 split pickup.

| 1970-1980s | | $425 | $525 |

Hopf
1906-present. From the mid-'50s to the late-'70s, Hopf offered electric basses made in their own factory and by others. Hopf currently mainly offers classical guitars and mandolins.

Hoyer
1874-present. Intermediate grade, production, electric basses. They also build guitars.

Ibanez
1932-present. Intermediate and professional grade, production, solidbody basses. They also have guitars, amps, and effects.

Axstar 50 AXB Bass
1986-1987. Headless solidbody, 1-piece maple neck, rosewood 'board, 2 humbuckers.

| 1986-1987 | | $250 | $300 |

Axstar 60 AXB Bass
1986-1987. Headless solidbody, 1-piece maple neck, ebony 'board, 2 low impedance pickups.

| 1986-1987 | | $375 | $425 |

Axstar 65 AXB Bass
1986-1987. Five-string version of the 60 AXB.

| 1986-1987 | | $325 | $425 |

Axstar 1000 AXB Bass
1986-1987. Headless alder solidbody, 1-piece maple neck-thru-body, ebony 'board, 2 low impedance pickups.

| 1986-1987 | | $350 | $400 |

BTB500 Series Bass
1999-2000. Offset double-cut ash solidbody, 2 pickups, extra long bass horn, dot markers, natural walnut.

| 1999-2000 | | $500 | $650 |

Destroyer X Series Bass
1983-1986. Futuristic-style body, P- and J-style pickups, dot markers, X Series notation on headstock, bolt neck.

| 1983-1986 | | $400 | $475 |

Model 2030 Bass
1970-1973. First copy era bass, offset double-cut, sunburst.

| 1970-1973 | | $400 | $550 |

Model 2353 Bass
1974-1976. Copy model, offset double-cut, 1 pickup, black.

| 1974-1976 | | $400 | $550 |

Model 2364B Bass
1971-1973. Dan Armstrong see-thru Lucite copy with 2 mounted humbucker pickups, clear finish.

| 1971-1973 | | $400 | $550 |

Model 2365 Bass
1974-1975. Copy model, Offset double-cut, rosewood 'board, pearloid block markers, sunburst.

| 1974-1975 | | $400 | $550 |

MODEL YEAR	FEATURES	EXC. COND. LOW	HIGH

Model 2366B/2366FLB Bass
1974-1975. Copy model, offset double-cut, 1 split-coil pickup, sunburst, FLB fretless model.

| 1974-1975 | | $400 | $550 |

Model 2385 Bass
1974-1975. Copy model, offset double-cut, 1 pickup, ash natural finish.

| 1974-1976 | | $400 | $550 |

Musician EQ Bass
1978-1979. Offset double-cut solidbody, 2 pickups, EQ, ash and mahogany body, ebony 'board, dot inlays, became the MC900.

| 1978-1979 | | $425 | $500 |

Musician MC800 Bass
1979-1980. Offset double-cut solidbody, 2 pickups, laminated neck.

| 1979-1980 | | $375 | $425 |

Musician MC900 Bass
1979-1980. MC800 with on-board 3-band EQ.

| 1979-1980 | | $425 | $500 |

Newport Bass
1974-1975. Copy model, cresting wave body, blond.

| 1974-1975 | | $550 | $650 |

PL 5050 Bass
Ca. 1985-ca. 1988. Part of the Pro Line Series.

| 1985-1988 | | $300 | $400 |

Roadstar II Bass
1982-1987. Solidbody basses, various models and colors.

| 1982-1987 | | $250 | $325 |

Rocket Roll Bass
1974-1976. Korina solidbody, V-shape, natural.

| 1974-1976 | | $1,000 | $1,100 |

SB-900 Bass
1990-1993. Ultra slim solidbody.

| 1990-1993 | | $350 | $400 |

SR-400 Bass
1993-present. Offset double-cut solidbody, long bass horn, 2 pickups.

| 1993-2003 | | $250 | $275 |

SR-405 Bass
1994-present. 5-string SR-400.

| 1994-2003 | | $250 | $275 |

SR-500 Bass
1993-1996. Offset double-cut, long bass horn, active pickups, bolt neck.

| 1993-1996 | | $300 | $400 |

SR-505 Bass
1993-1995. 5-string SR 500.

| 1993-1995 | | $350 | $450 |

Imperial
Ca.1963-ca.1970. Imported by the Imperial Accordion Company of Chicago, Illinois. Early guitars made in Italy, but by ca. '66 Japanese-made.

Electric Solidbody Bass
| 1960s | Various models | $150 | $225 |

Hollowbody Bass
1960s. Hollowbody with sharp double-cuts.

| 1960s | | $225 | $275 |

MODEL YEAR	FEATURES	EXC. COND. LOW	HIGH

Infeld

2003-present. Solidbody guitars and basses offered by string-maker Thomastik-Infeld of Vienna.

Italia

1999-present. Intermediate grade, production, solid and semi-solidbody basses designed by Trevor Wilkinson and made in Korea. They also build guitars.

J.B. Player

1980s-present. Intermediate grade, production, imported, acoustic/electric and solidbody basses. They also offer guitars, banjos and mandolins.

J.T. Hargreaves

1995-present. Luthier Jay Hargreaves builds his premium grade, production/custom, acoustic basses, in Seattle, Washington. He also builds guitars.

Jackson

1980-present. Intermediate, professional, and premium grade, production, solidbody basses. They also offer guitars. Founded by Grover Jackson, who owned Charvel.

Concert Custom Bass (U.S.-made)
1984-1995. Neck-thru Custom Shop bass.

1984-1989		$650	$725
1990-1995		$500	$625

Concert C5P 5-String (Import)
1998-2000. Bolt neck, dot inlay, chrome hardware.

1998-2000		$125	$175

Concert EX 4-String (Import)
1992-1995. Bolt neck, dot inlay, black hardware.

1992-1995		$225	$350

Concert V 5-String (Import)
1992-1995. Bound neck, shark tooth inlay.

1992-1995		$425	$550

Concert XL 4-String (Import)
1992-1995. Bound neck, shark tooth inlay.

1992-1995		$325	$450

Kelly Pro Bass
1994-1995. Pointy-cut bouts, neck-thru solidbody, shark fin marker inlays.

1994-1995		$500	$775

Piezo Bass
1986. Four piezo electric bridge pickups, neck-thru, active EQ, shark tooth inlays. Student model has rosewood 'board, no binding. Custom Model has ebony 'board and neck and headstock binding.

1986		$350	$450

Jay Turser

1997-present. Intermediate grade, production, imported semi-hollow and solidbody basses. They also offer guitars and amps.

Jerry Jones

1981-present. Intermediate grade, production, semi-hollow body electric basses from luthier Jerry Jones, and built in Nashville, Tennessee. They also build guitars and sitars.

Neptune Longhorn 4 Bass
1988-present. Based on Danelectro longhorn models, 4-string, 2 lipstick-tube pickups, 30" scale.

1988-2000		$450	$500

Neptune Longhorn 6 Bass
1988-present. 6-string version.

1988-2000		$525	$600

Johnson

Mid-1990s-present. Budget and intermediate grade, production, solidbody and acoustic basses imported by Music Link, Brisbane, California. They also offer guitars, amps, mandolins and effects.

Juzek

Violin maker John Juzek was originally located in Prague, Czeckoslovakia, but moved to West Germany due to World War II. Prague instruments considered by most to be more valuable. Many German instruments were mass produced with laminate construction and some equate these German basses with the Kay laminate basses of the same era. Juzek still makes instruments.

Kalamazoo

1933-1942, 1965-1970. Kalamazoo was a brand Gibson used on one of their budget lines. They also used the name on electric basses from '65 to '67.

Electric Bass

1960s	Bolt neck	$275	$375

Kapa

Ca. 1962-1970. Kapa was founded by Kope Veneman in Maryland.

Electric Bass

1960s	Various models	$275	$475

Kawai

1927-present. Japanese instrument manufacturer Kawai started offering guitars under other brandnames around '56. There were few imports carrying the Kawai brand until the late-'70s; best known for high quality basses. Kawai recently quit offering guitars and basses.

Electric Bass

1960s	Various models	$200	$350
1970s	Various models	$200	$350
1980s	Various models	$300	$425

Kay

Ca. 1931-present. Currently, budget grade, production, imported basses. Kay introduced upright acoustic laminate basses and 3/4 viols in '38 and electric basses in '54. *See Guitar Stories Volume II*, by Michael Wright, for a complete history of Kay with detailed model listings.

Jackson C20 Concert

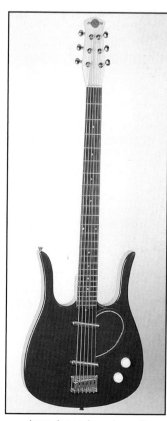

Jerry Jones Longhorn 6

'60s Kay bass

Ken Smith Black Tiger

MODEL YEAR	FEATURES	EXC. COND. LOW	HIGH

C1 Concert String Bass
1938-1967. Standard (3/4) size student bass, laminated construction, spruce top, figured maple back and sides, shaded light brown.

1938-1949		$2,000	$3,000
1950-1959		$1,800	$2,400
1960-1967		$1,800	$2,200

K-5935 Bass
1966-1968. Renumbered from 5930, plain style, double-cut solidbody.

| 1966-1968 | | $400 | $550 |

M-1 (Maestro) String Bass
1952-late-1960s. Standard (3/4) size bass, laminated construction, spruce top and curly maple back and sides. Model M-3 is the Junior (1/4) size bass, Model M-1 B has a blond finish, other models include the S-51 B Chubby Jackson Five-String Bass and the S-9 Swingmaster.

| 1952-1959 | | $1,800 | $2,400 |
| 1960-1967 | | $1,800 | $2,200 |

M-5 (Maestro) String Bass
1957-late-1960s. Five strings.

| 1957-1967 | | $2,000 | $3,000 |

Value Leader Series Bass
1960-1965. Large chrome-plated 'guard that extends from the treble cutaway to the input jack ('guard is unique to Value Leader Series), maple neck, dot markers, thinline single-cut, large Kay and K headstock logos, sunburst.

| 1960-1965 | | $350 | $450 |

Ken Smith
See listing under Smith.

Kent
1961-1969. Imported from Japan by Buegeleisen and Jacobson of New York, New York. Manufacturers unknown but many early instruments by Guyatone and Teisco.

Electric Solidbody Bass
1962-1969. Import models include 628 Newport, 634 Basin Street, 629, and 635.

| 1961-1969 | Century Red | $150 | $200 |

Semi-Hollow Electric Bass
1960s. Offset soft cutaway, single pickup, 2 control knobs.

| 1961-1969 | Sunburst | $250 | $300 |

Kingston
Ca. 1958-1967. Imported from Japan by Westheimer Importing Corp. of Chicago. Early examples by Guyatone and Teisco.

Electric Solidbody Bass

| 1960s | Various models | $125 | $175 |

MODEL YEAR	FEATURES	EXC. COND. LOW	HIGH

Klein Acoustic Guitars
1972-present. Luthiers Steve Klein and Steven Kauffman build their production/custom, premium and presentation grade acoustic basses in Sonoma, California. They also build guitars.

Klein Electric Guitars
1988-present. Lorenzo German produces his professional grade, production/custom, basses in Linden, California. He also builds guitars.

Klira
Founded in 1887 in Schoenbach, Germany, mainly making violins, but added guitars in the 1950s. The instruments of the '50s and '60s were aimed at the budget market, but workmanship improved with the '70s models.

Beatle Bass Copy
1960s. Beatle Bass 500/1 copy, sunburst.

| 1960s | | $350 | $450 |

Knutson Luthiery
1981-present. Professional grade, custom, electric upright basses built by luthier John Knutson in Forestville, California. He also builds guitars and mandolins.

Koll
1990-present. Professional and premium grade, custom/production, solidbody and chambered basses built by luthier Saul Koll, originally in Long Beach, California, and since '93, in Portland, Oregon. He also builds guitars.

Kona
2001-present. Budget grade, production, acoustic and electric basses made in Asia. They also offer guitars, amps and mandolins.

Electric Solidbody Basses

| 2001-2004 | | $70 | $80 |

Kramer
1976-1990, 1995-present. Budget grade, production, imported solidbody basses. They also offer guitars. Kramer's first guitars and basses featured aluminum necks with wooden inserts on back. Around '80 they started to switch to more economical wood necks and aluminum necks were last produced in '85. Gibson acquired the brand in '97.

250-B Special Bass
1977-1979. Offset double-cut, aluminum neck, Ebonol 'board, zero fret, 1 single-coil, natural.

| 1977-1979 | | $500 | $550 |

450-B Bass
Late-'70s-early-'80s. Aluminum neck, burled walnut body, 2 humbucking pickups, natural walnut.

| 1970s | | $500 | $550 |

BASSES

MODEL YEAR	FEATURES	EXC. COND. LOW	HIGH

650-B Artist Bass
1977-1980. Double-cut, birdseye maple/burled walnut, aluminum neck, zero fret, mother-of-pearl crowns, 2 humbuckers.

1977-1980		$550	$700

Aerostar ZX Series Bass
1986-1989. Various models include ZX-70 (offset double-cut solidbody, 1 pickup).

1986-1989	ZX-70 (Import)	$100	$200

BKL Bass
Eight strings, 2 DiMarzio pickups, 2 octaves.

1980		$525	$600

DMZ 4000 Bass
1978-1982. Bolt-on aluminum neck, slot headstock, double-cut solidbody, active EQ and dual-coil humbucking pickup, dot inlay.

1978-1981		$525	$600
1982	Bill Wyman-type	$600	$900

DMZ 4001 Bass
1979-1980. Aluminum neck, slot headstock, double-cut solidbody, 1 dual-coil humbucker pickup, dot inlay.

1979-1980		$425	$500

DMZ 5000 Bass
1979-1980. Double-cut solidbody, aluminum neck, slotted headstock, 2 pickups, crown inlays.

1979-1980		$425	$500

DMZ 6000B Bass
1979-1980. Double-cut, aluminum neck, slotted headstock, 2 pickups, crown inlays.

1979-1980		$425	$500

Duke Custom/Standard Bass
1981-1983. Headless, aluminum neck, 1 humbucker.

1981-1983		$450	$550

Duke Special Bass
1982-1985. Headless, aluminum neck, 2 pickups.

1982-1985		$425	$550

Duke Special Fretless Bass
1982-1985. Fretless version of Special.

1982-1985		$425	$550

Ferrington KFB-1/KFB-2 Acoustic Bass
1987-1990. Acoustic/electric, bridge-mounted active pickup, tone and volume control, various colors. KFB-1 has binding and diamond dot inlays; the KFB-2 no binding and dot inlays. Danny Ferrington continued to offer the KFB-1 after Kramer closed in '90.

1987-1990		$350	$475

Focus 7000 Bass
1985-1987. Offset double-cut solidbody, P and double J pickups, Japanese-made.

1985-1987		$225	$375

Focus 8000 Bass
1985-1987. Offset double-cut solidbody, Japanese-made.

1985-1987		$225	$375

Focus K-77 Bass
1984-1986. Offset double-cut solidbody, 1 pickup, Japanese-made.

1984-1986		$225	$375

Focus K-88 Bass
1984-1986. Two pickup Focus.

1984-1986		$225	$375

Forum I Bass
1988-1990. U.S.-made double-cut, neck-thru, arched top, active EMG or passive Seymour Duncan pickups.

1988-1990		$300	$375

Gene Simmons Axe Bass
1980-1981. Axe-shaped bass, slot headstock.

1980-1981		$2,250	$3,500

Pacer Bass
1982-1984. Offset double-cut solidbody, red.

1982-1984		$425	$500

Ripley Four-String Bass
1985-1987. Four-string version.

1985-1987		$375	$450

Ripley Five-String Bass
1984-1987. Offset double-cut, 5 strings, stereo, pan pots for each string, front and back pickups for each string, active circuitry.

1984-1987		$475	$550

Stagemaster Custom Bass
1981-1985, 1987-1990. First version had an aluminum neck (wood optional). Later version was neck-thru-body, bound neck, either active or passive pickups.

1987-1990		$375	$550

Striker 700 Bass
1985-1989. Offset double-cut, Korean-import, 1 pickup until '87, 2 after. Striker name was again used on a bass in '99.

1985-1987	1 pickup	$200	$325
1988-1989	2 pickups	$200	$325

XL 24 Bass
1980-1981. Odd shaped double-cut solidbody 4-string, aluminum neck, 2 pickups.

1980-1981		$350	$450

XL 8 Bass
1980-1981. Odd shaped double-cut solidbody 8-string, aluminum neck, 2 pickups, tuners mounted on both headstock and body.

1980-1981		$600	$700

KSD
2003-present. Intermediate grade, production, imported bass line designed by Ken Smith (see Smith listing) and distributed by Brooklyn Gear.

Kubicki
1973-present. Professional and premium grade, production/custom, solidbody basses built by luthier Phil Kubicki in Santa Barbara, California. Kubicki began building acoustic guitars when he was 15. In '64 at age 19, he went to work with Roger Rossmeisl at Fender Musical Instrument's research and development department for acoustic guitars. Nine years later he moved to Santa Barbara, California, and established Philip Kubicki Technology, which is best known for its line of Factor basses and also builds acoustic guitars, custom electric

'80s Kramer Duke Standard

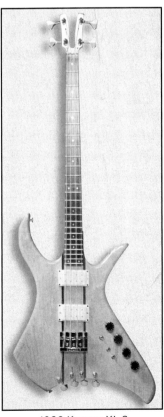

1980 Kramer XL-8

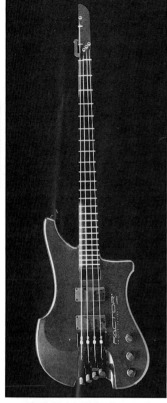

1990 Kubicki Ex Factor 4

Lakland Jerry Scheff signature

guitars, bodies and necks, and mini-guitars and does custom work, repairs and restorations.

Ex Factor 4 Bass
1985-present. Solidbody, maple body, bolt-on maple neck, 2 pickups, active electronics.

MODEL YEAR	FEATURES	EXC. COND. LOW	HIGH
1980s		$700	$1,000

Factor 4 Bass
1985-present. Solidbody, maple body, bolt-on maple neck, fretless available, 4 strings, 2 pickups, active electronics.

1980s		$900	$1,200

Factor 5-String Bass
1985-ca.1990. Solidbody, bolt-on maple neck, fretless available, 5 strings, 2 pickups, active electronics.

1980s		$900	$1,200

Kustom
1968-present. Founded by Bud Ross in Chanute, Kansas, and best known for the tuck-and-roll amps, Kustom also offered guitars and basses from '68 to '69.

Electric Hollowbody Bass

1968-1969	Various models	$750	$850

La Baye
1967. Short-lived brand out of Green Bay, Wisconsin and built by the Holman-Woodell factory in Neodesha, Kansas.

Model 2x4 II Bass
1967. Very low production, dual pickups, long-scale, small rectangle solidbody, sometimes referred to as the Bass II.

1967		$1,400	$1,700

Model 2x4 Mini-Bass
1967. Short-scale, 1 pickup, small rectangle solidbody.

1967		$1,200	$1,500

LA Guitar Factory
1997-present. Luthier Ari Lehtela builds his professional grade, production, solidbody and tone chambered basses in Charlotte, North Carolina. He also builds guitars.

Lado
1973-present. Founded by Joe Kovacic, Lado builds professional and premium grade, production/custom, solidbody basses in Lindsay, Ontario. Some model lines are branded J. K. Lado. They also build guitars.

Lafayette
Ca. 1963-1967. Sold through Lafayette Electronics catalogs. Early Japanese-made guitars from pre-copy era, generally shorter scale beginner guitars. Many made by Guyatone, some possibly by Teisco.

Lakland
1994-present. Professional and premium grade, production/custom, solid and hollowbody basses from luthier Dan Lakin in Chicago, Illinois. Lakland basses are built in the U.S. and overseas (Skyline series).

4 - 63 Classic Bass
1994-2002. Offset double-cut alder body, large bass horn, bolt neck.

MODEL YEAR	FEATURES	EXC. COND. LOW	HIGH
1994-2002		$1,600	$1,800

4 - 63 Deluxe Bass
1994-2002. Like Classic but with figured maple top on ash body.

1994-2002		$1,800	$2,000

4 - 63 Standard Bass
1994-2002. Like Classic, but with swamp ash body.

1994-2002		$1,600	$1,800

4 - 94 Classic Bass
1994-present. Offset double-cut alder body with maple top, large bass horn, bolt neck.

1994-2000		$1,600	$1,800

4 - 94 Deluxe Bass
1994-present. Like Classic but with figured maple top on ash body.

1994-2000		$1,800	$2,000

4 - 94 Standard Bass
1994-present. Like Classic, but with swamp ash body.

1994-2000		$1,600	$1,800

Joe Osborn Bass
1998-present. Fender Precision-style, 5-string, 2 P-style pickups.

1998-2003		$1,800	$2,000

Larrivee
1968-present. Founded by Jean Larrivee in Toronto and currently located in Vancouver, British Columbia, Larrivee has offered several acoustic basses over the years.

Leach
1980-present. Luthier Harvey Leach builds his premium grade, custom, acoustic basses in Cedar Ridge, California. He also builds guitars.

Linc Luthier
Professional and premium grade, custom/production, electric, acoustic and upright basses built by luther Linc Luthier in Upland, California. He also builds guitars and double-necks.

Lotus
Late-1970-present. Electric basses imported originally by Midco International, and most recently by Musicorp. They also make guitars, banjos and mandolins.

Lowrider Basses
2003-present. Professional grade, production/custom, solidbody basses made in Las Vegas, Nevada by Ed Roman.

MODEL YEAR	FEATURES	EXC. COND. LOW	HIGH

LSR Headless Instruments
1988-present. Professional grade, production/custom, solidbody headless basses made in Las Vegas, Nevada by Ed Roman. They also make guitars.

LTD
1995-present. Intermediate grade, production, Korean-made solidbody basses offered by ESP. They also offer guitars.

Lyle
Ca. 1969-1980. Japanese instruments imported by distributor L.D. Heater in Portland, Oregon.
Electric Solidbody Bass

1970s	Various models	$100	$200

Lyon by Washburn
1990s-2000s. Budget basses sold by mass merchandisers such as Target. They also offer guitars.
Electric Solidbody Bass

2000s	Various models	$75	$125

Lyric
1996-present. Luthier John Southern builds his professional and premium grade, custom, basses in Tulsa, Oklahoma. He also builds guitars.

Mako
1985-1989. Line of solidbody basses from Kaman (Ovation, Hamer). They also offered guitars and amps.
Electric Solidbody Bass

1985-1989	Student bass	$100	$125

Marco Polo
1960- ca.1964. One of the first inexpensive Japanese brands to be imported into the U.S.
Solidbody Bass

1960s	Various models	$100	$175

Marling
Ca. 1975. Budget line instruments marketed by EKO of Recanati, Italy; probably made by them, although possibly imported.
Electric Solidbody Bass
Models include the E.495 (copy of LP), E.485 (copy of Tele), and the E.465 (Manta-style).

1970s		$100	$175

Martin
1833-present. Professional grade, production, acoustic basses made in the U.S. In 1978, Martin re-entered the electric market and introduced their solidbody EB-18 and EB-28 Basses. In the '80s they offered Stinger brand electric basses. By the late '80s, they started offering acoustic basses.

B-40 Acoustic Bass
1989-1996. Jumbo-size, spruce top and Indian rosewood back and sides, mahogany neck, ebony 'board, built-in pickup and volume and tone controls. The B-40B had a pickup.

1989-1996	B-40B	$1,300	$1,700
1989-1996	Without pickup	$1,100	$1,500

B-65 Acoustic Bass
1989-1993. Jumbo-size, spruce top, maple back and sides, mahogany neck, ebony 'board with 23 frets, built-in pickup and volume and tone controls, natural.

1989-1993		$1,100	$1,700

EB-18 Bass
1979-1982. Electric solidbody, neck-thru, 1 pickup, natural.

1979-1982		$450	$650

EB-28 Bass
1980-1982. Electric solidbody.

1980-1982		$650	$850

SBL-10 Bass
Stinger brand solidbody, maple neck, 1 split and 1 bar pickup.

1980s		$150	$200

Marvel
1950s-mid-1960s. Brand used for budget instruments marketed by Peter Sorkin Company in New York, New York.
Electric Solidbody Bass

1950s	Various models	$125	$200

Messenger
1967-1968. Built by Musicraft, Inc., Messengers featured a neck-thru metal alloy neck.
Bass
1967-1968. Metal alloy neck. Messenger mainly made guitars - they offered a bass, but it is unlikely many were built.

1967-1968		$1,750	$2,750

Messenger Upright
Made by Knutson Luthiery, see that listing.

Michael Kelly
2000-present. Intermediate grade, production, acoustic/electric basses imported by Elite Music Brands of Clearwater, Florida. They also offer mandolins and guitars.

Michael Tuttle
2003-present. Luthier Michael Tuttle builds his professional and premium grade, custom, solid and hollow body basses in Saugus, California. He also builds guitars.

Microfrets
1967-1975, 2004-present. Professional grade, production, electric basses built in Myersville, Maryland. They also build guitars.

Martin B-40

Martin EB-18

Mollerup Orca 6-string

1960s Mosrite Ventures

MODEL YEAR	FEATURES	EXC. COND. LOW	HIGH

Husky Bass
1971-1974/75. Double-cut, 2 pickups, two-on-a-side tuners.

1971-1975		$550	$650

Rendezvous Bass
1970. One pickup, orange sunburst.

1970		$600	$700

Signature Bass
1969-1975. Double-cut, 2 pickups, two-on-a-side tuners.

1969-1975		$650	$750

Stage II Bass
1969-1975. Double-cut, 2 pickups, two-on-a-side tuners.

1969-1975		$650	$750

Thundermaster Bass

1969		$650	$750

Mike Lull Custom Guitars
1995-present. Professional and premium grade, production/custom, basses built by luthier Mike Lull in Bellevue, Washington. He also builds guitars.

Mitre
1983-1985. Bolt-neck solidbody basses made in Aldenville (or East Longmeadow), Massachusetts. They also built guitars.

MJ Guitar Engineering
1993-present. Luthier Mark Johnson builds his professional grade, production/custom, chambered basses in Rohnert Park, California. He also builds guitars.

Modulus
1978-present. Founded by aerospace engineer Geoff Gould, Modulus currently offers professional and premium grade, production/custom, solidbody basses built in California. They also build guitars.

Bassstar SP-24 Active Bass
1981-ca. 1990. EMG J pickups, active bass and treble circuits.

1980s		$1,000	$1,300

Flea 4 Bass
1997-present. Offset double-cut alder solidbody, also offered as 5-string.

1997-2003		$1,000	$1,200

Genesis Series Bass
1997-1998, 2003-present. Offset double-cut, 2 pickups, 4- or 5-string.

2003-2004		$800	$900

Quantum-4 Series Bass
1982-present. Offset double-cut, 2 pickups, 35" scale.

1982-2000		$1,000	$1,700

Quantum-5 Series Bass
1982-present. 5-String version.

1982-2000		$1,100	$1,750

Quantum-6 Series Bass
1982-present. 6-string version.

1982-2000		$1,200	$1,800

Mollerup Basses
1984-present. Luthier Laurence Mollerup builds his professional grade, custom/production, electric basses and electric double basses in Vancouver, British Columbia. He has also built guitars.

Moon
1979-present. Professional grade, production/custom, basses made in Japan. They also build guitars.

JB-195HS Bass
2000s. Offset double-cut, 2 pickups.

2000s		$900	$1,200

JJ Series Basses
1980s-present. Solidbody of walnut, alder, Canadian white ash, padauk, or other exotic wood, optional active circuitry, 4- and 5-string.

1987-2000		$650	$750

Moonstone
1972-present. Luthier Steve Helgeson builds his premium grade, production/custom, acoustic and electric basses in Eureka, California. He also builds guitars.

Explorer Bass
1980-1983. Figured wood body, neck-thru.

1980-1983		$1,500	$1,900

Morales
Ca.1967-1968. Made in Japan by Zen-On and not heavily imported into the U.S.

Electric Solidbody Bass

1967-1968	Various models	$125	$250

Morgan Monroe
1999-present. Intermediate grade, production, acoustic/electric basses made in Korea and distributed by SHS International of Indianapolis, Indiana. They also offer mandolins, guitars, banjos, and fiddles.

Mosrite
Semie Moseley's Mosrite offered various bass models throughout the many versions of the Mosrite company.

Brut Bass
Late-1960s. Assymetrical body with small cutaway on upper treble bout.

1960s		$950	$1,050

Celebrity Bass
1965-1969. ES-335-style semi-thick double-cut body with F-holes, 2 pickups.

1965-1966	Custom color	$900	$1,500
1965-1967	Sunburst	$700	$900
1968	Red	$700	$900
1969	Sunburst or red	$600	$800

MODEL YEAR	FEATURES	EXC. COND. LOW	HIGH

Joe Maphis Bass
1966-1969. Ventures-style body, hollow without F-holes, 2 pickups, natural.

1966-1969		$1,000	$1,400

Ventures Bass
1965-1972. Two pickups.

1965	Blue or red	$1,900	$2,400
1965	Sunburst	$1,800	$2,300
1966	Sunburst	$1,700	$2,200
1967-1968	Blue Metallic	$2,000	$3,000
1967-1968	Red Sparkle	$1,800	$2,800
1967-1968	Sunburst	$1,600	$2,000
1969	Sunburst	$1,600	$2,500
1970-1972	Sunburst	$800	$1,000

V-II Bass
1973-1974. Ventures-style, 2 humbuckers, sunburst.

1973-1974		$700	$950

MTD
1994-present. Intermediate, professional, and premium grade, production/custom, electric basses built by luthier Michael Tobias (who founded Tobias Basses in '77) in Kingston, New York. Since '00, he also imports basses built in Korea to his specifications .

Music Man
1972-present. Intermediate and professional grade, production, electric basses. They also build guitars.

Cutlass I/Cutlass II Bass
1982-1987. Ash body, graphite neck, string-thru-body.

1982-1984	CLF era Cutlass I	$1,300	$1,400
1982-1984	CLF era Cutlass II	$1,600	$1,800
1984-1987	Ernie Ball era Cutlass I	$1,000	$1,100
1984-1987	Ernie Ball era Cutlass II	$1,200	$1,400

Sabre Bass
1978-ca.1991. Double-cut solidbody bass, 3-and-1 tuning keys, 2 humbucking pickups, on-board preamp, natural.

1978-1979	CLF era	$1,000	$1,100
1980-1984	CLF era	$900	$1,000
1984-1991	Ernie Bass era	$600	$700

Stingray Bass
1976-present. Offset double-cut solidbody, 1 pickup, 3-and-1 tuners, string-thru until '80, various colors. In '05, additional pickup options available.

1976-1979	CLF era	$1,800	$2,200
1980-1984	CLF era	$1,600	$2,000
1984-1989	Ernie Ball era	$1,200	$1,800
1990-1999		$725	$825
2000-2005		$750	$850

Stingray 5-String Bass
1987-present. Active electronics, birdseye maple bolt neck, 1 humbucking pickup, 3-band EQ. In '05, additional pickup options available.

1990s		$900	$1,400

MODEL YEAR	FEATURES	EXC. COND. LOW	HIGH

Musicvox
1996-present. Intermediate grade, production, Korean-made retro-vibe guitars and basses from Matt Eichen of Cherry Hill, New Jersey.

Nady
Wireless sound company Nady Systems offered guitars and basses with built-in wireless systems for 1985-'87. The neck-thru bass was made by Fernandes in Japan and was only available for about a year.

National
Ca. 1927-present. National offered electric basses in the '60s when Valco owned the brand.

N-850 Bass
1967-1968. Semi-hollow double-cut, art deco f-holes, 2 pickups, block markers, bout control knobs, sunburst.

1967-1968		$650	$750

Val-Pro 85 Bass
1961-1962. Res-O-Glas body shaped like the U.S. map, 2 pickups, snow white, renamed National 85 in '63.

1961-1962		$925	$1,200

National Reso-Phonic
1988-present. Professional grade, production/custom, acoustic and acoustic/electric resonator basses built in San Luis Obispo, California. They also build guitars and ukes.

New York Bass Works
Luthier David Segal builds his professional and premium grade, production/custom, electric basses in New York.

Noble
Ca. 1950-ca. 1969. Distributed by Don Noble and Company of Chicago. Made by other companies.

Norma
Ca.1965-1970. Imported from Japan by Chicago's Strum and Drum.

Electric Solidbody Bass

1960s	Various models	$150	$225

Northworthy
1987-present. Professional and premium grade, production/custom, acoustic and electric basses built by luthier Alan Marshall in Ashbourne, Derbyshire, England. He also builds guitars and mandolins.

Novax
1989-present. Luthier Ralph Novak builds his fanned-fret professional grade, production/custom, solidbody basses in San Leandro, California. He also builds guitars.

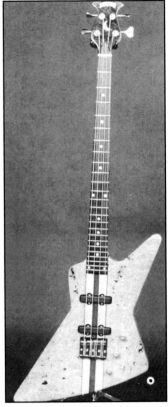

Moonstone Exploder

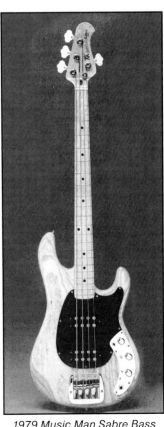

1979 Music Man Sabre Bass

MODEL YEAR	FEATURES	EXC. COND. LOW	HIGH

'77 Ovation Magnum II

Parker Fly Mojo bass

O'Hagan

1979-1983. Designed by Jerol O'Hagan in St. Louis Park, Minnesota.

Electric Solidbody Basses

1979-1983. Models include the Shark Bass, Night-Watch Bass, NightWatch Regular Bass, and the Twenty Two Bass.

1980s		$350	$500

Old Kraftsman

1930s-1960s. Brand used by the Spiegel Company. Instruments made by other American manufacturers.

Electric Solidbody Bass

1950s	Various models	$200	$350

Oncor Sound

1980-ca. 1981. This Salt Lake City-based company made both a guitar and a bass synthesizer.

Ovation

1966-present. Intermediate and professional grade, production, acoustic/electric basses. Ovation offered electric solidbody basses early on and added acoustic basses in the '90s.

Celebrity Series Bass

1990s-2000s. Deep bowl back, cutaway, acoustic/electric.

1990-2000s		$325	$400

Magnum Series Bass

1974-1980. Magnum I is odd-shaped mahogany solidbody, 2 pickups, mono/stereo, mute, sunburst, red or natural. Magnum II is with battery-powered preamp and 3-band EQ. Magnum III and IV had a new Strat-style body.

1974-1978	Magnum I	$400	$600
1974-1978	Magnum II	$450	$650
1978-1980	Magnum III	$400	$600
1978-1980	Magnum IV	$450	$650

Typhoon II/Typhoon III Bass

1968-1971. Ovation necks, but bodies and hardware were German imports. Semi-hollowbody, 2 pickups, red or sunburst. Typhoon II is 335-style and III is fretless.

1968-1971	Typhoon II	$450	$650
1968-1971	Typhoon III	$500	$700

PANaramic

1961-1963. Guitars and basses made in Italy by the Crucianelli accordion company and imported by PANaramic accordion. They also offered amps made by Magnatone.

Electric Bass

1961-1963. Double-cut solidbody, 2 pickups, dot markers, sunburst.

1961-1963		$400	$500

Parker

1992-present. Premium grade, production/custom, solidbody electric basses. They also build guitars.

Patrick Eggle Guitars

1991-present. Solidbody electric basses built in Birmingham, England. They also builds guitars.

Paul Reed Smith

1985-present. PRS added basses in '86, but by '92 had dropped the models. In 2000 PRS started again offering professional and premium grade, production, solidbody electric basses. Bird inlays can add $100 or more to the values of PRS basses listed here.

Bass-4

1986-1992. Set neck, 3 single-coil pickups, hum-cancelling coil, active circuitry, 22-fret Brazilian rosewood 'board. Reintroduced (OEB Series) in 2000s.

1986-1987		$1,300	$1,800
1988-1992		$1,200	$1,700
2000s	OEB Series	$1,300	$2,000

Bass-5

1986-1992. Five-string, set-neck, rosewood 'board, 3 single-coil pickups, active electronics. Options include custom colors, bird inlays, fretless 'board.

1986-1987		$1,300	$1,800
1988-1992		$1,200	$1,700

CE Bass 4

1986-1991. Solidbody, maple bolt neck, alder body, rosewood 'board, 4-string.

1986-1987		$1,000	$1,200
1988-1991		$900	$1,100

CE Bass 5

1986-1991. Five-string solidbody, maple bolt neck, alder body, rosewood 'board.

1986-1987		$1,200	$1,400
1988-1991		$1,100	$1,300

Curly Bass-4

1986-1992. Double-cut solidbody, curly maple top, set maple neck, Brazilian rosewood 'board (ebony on fretless), 3 single-coil and 1 hum-cancelling pickups, various grades of maple tops, moon inlays.

1986-1987		$1,700	$2,200
1988-1992		$1,600	$2,100

Curly Bass-5

1986-1992. Five-string version of Curly Bass-4.

1986-1987		$1,900	$2,400
1988-1992		$1,800	$2,300

Peavey

1965-present. Intermediate and professional grade, production/custom, electric basses. They also build guitars and amps. Hartley Peavey's first products were guitar amps and he added guitars and basses to the mix in '78.

Axcelerator Bass

1994-1998. Offset double-cut, long thin horns, 2 humbuckers, stacked control knobs, bolt neck, dot markers.

1994-1998		$275	$325

Cirrus Series Bass

1998-present. Offset double-cut, active electronics, in 4-, 5-string, and custom shop versions.

1998-2003	Cirrus 4	$700	$750

MODEL YEAR	FEATURES	EXC. COND. LOW	HIGH

Dyna-Bass
1987-1993. Double-cut solidbody, active electronics, 3-band EQ, rosewood 'board, opaque finish.

1987-1993		$200	$300

Dyna-Bass Limited
1987-1990. Neck-thru-body, ebony 'board, flamed maple neck/body construction, purple heart strips, mother-of-pearl inlays.

1987-1990		$375	$575

Forum Bass
1994-1995. Double-cut solidbody, rosewood 'board, dot inlays, 2 humbuckers.

1994-1995		$250	$300

Forum Plus Bass
1994. Forum Bass with added active electronics.

1994		$250	$325

Foundation Bass
1984-2002. Double-cut solidbody, 2 pickups, maple neck.

1984-2002		$225	$325

Foundation S Active Bass
1987-1991. Similar to Foundation S Bass with added active circuitry, provides low-impedance output, 2 pickups.

1987-1991		$250	$350

Foundation S Bass
1986-1991. Two split-coil pickups, maple body, rosewood 'board, black hardware, black painted headstock.

1986-1991		$150	$225

Fury Bass
1986-1999. Double-cut solidbody, rosewood 'board, 1 split-coil humbucker.

1986-1999		$150	$200

Fury Custom Bass
1986-1993. Fury Bass with black hardware and narrow neck.

1986-1993		$250	$300

Grind Series Bass
2001-present. Offset double-cut, neck-thru, long bass horn, 2 pickups, 4-, 5-, or 6-string.

2001-2004	Grind 4	$200	$250
2001-2004	Grind 5	$200	$270

Mildstone/Mildstone II Bass
1983-1986. Import, Fender P-Bass copy.

1983-1986		$125	$175

Millenium Series Bass
2001-present. Offset double-cut, agathis bodies, maple tops, in 4- or 5-string.

2001-2004		$125	$200

Patriot Bass
1984-1988. General J-Bass styling with larger thinner horns, 1 single-coil, maple neck.

1984-1988		$125	$175

Patriot Custom Bass
1986-1988. Patriot with rosewood neck, matching headstock.

1986-1988		$225	$275

RJ-4 Bass
1989-1991. Randy Jackson Signature model, neck-thru-body, 2 split-coil active pickups, ebony 'board, mother-of-pearl position markers.

1989-1991		$325	$450

Rudy Sarzo Signature Bass
1988-1993. Double-cut solidbody, active EQ, ebony 'board, 2 pickups.

1988-1993		$350	$475

T-20FL Bass
1980s. Fretless solidbody, 1 pickup.

1980s		$225	$300

T-40/T-40FL Bass
1978-ca.1988. Double-cut solidbody, 2 pickups. T-40FL is fretless.

1978-1988	T-40	$225	$300
1978-1988	T-40FL	$225	$300

T-45 Bass
1982-1986. T-40 with 1 humbucking pickup, and a mid-frequency rolloff knob.

1982-1986		$250	$350

TL Series Bass
1988-1998. Neck-thru-body, gold hardware, active humbuckers, EQ, flamed maple neck and body, 5-string (TL-Five) or 6 (TL-Six).

1988-1998	TL-Five	$525	$675
1989-1998	TL-Six	$725	$775

Pedulla
1975-present. Professional and premium grade, production/custom, electric basses made in Rockland, Massachusetts. Founded by Michael Pedulla, Pedulla offers various upscale options which affect valuation so each instrument should be evaluated on a case-by-case basis. Unless specifically noted, the following listings have standard to mid-level features. High-end options are specifically noted; if not, these options will have a relatively higher value than those shown here.

Buzz-4/Buzz-5 Bass
1984-present. Double-cut neck-thru solidbody, fretless, long-scale, maple neck and body wings, 2 pickups, preamp, some with other active electronics, various colors, 4-, 5-, 6-, 8-string versions.

1984-1999		$1,400	$1,500

Interceptor Bass
1980s. Double-cut, maple/walnut laminated neck-thru.

1980s		$950	$1,250

MVP Series Bass
1984-present. Fretted version of Buzz Bass, standard or flame top, 4-, 5-, 6-, 8-string versions.

1980s	MVP-4 flame top	$1,100	$1,400
1980s	MVP-4 standard top	$900	$1,200
1980s	MVP-5	$900	$1,200
1980s	MVP-6	$1,000	$1,300

Orsini Wurlitzer 4-String Bass
Mid-1970s. Body style similar to late-'50s Gibson double-cut slab body SG Special, neck-thru, 2 pickups, natural. Sold by Boston's Wurlitzer music store chain.

1970s		$900	$1,400

PRS Curly Bass 4

1983 Peavey T-45

Phantom BW

Reverend Rumblefish PJ

MODEL YEAR	FEATURES	EXC. COND. LOW	HIGH

Quilt Ltd. Bass
Neck-thru-body with curly maple centerstrip, quilted maple body wings, 2 Bartolini pickups, available in fretted or fretless 4- and 5-string models.

1987		$1,100	$1,400

Rapture 4/5 Series Bass
1995-present. Solidbody with extra long thin bass horn and extra short treble horn, 4- or 5-string, various colors.

1995-1999		$900	$1,200

Series II Bass
1987-1992. Bolt neck, rosewood 'board, mother-of-pearl dot inlays, Bartolini pickups.

1987-1992		$600	$875

Thunderbass 4/5 Series Bass
1993-present. Solidbody with extra long thin bass horn and extra short treble horn, 4- or 5-string, standard features or triple A top.

1993-1999	AAA top	$1,800	$2,000
1993-1999	Standard features	$1,400	$1,600
2000-2005	AAA top	$1,900	$2,000

Pensa (Pensa-Suhr)
1982-present. Premium grade, production/custom, solidbody basses built in the U.S. They also build guitars.

Phantom Guitar Works
1992-present. Intermediate grade, production/custom, solid and hollowbody basses assembled in Clatskanie, Oregon. They also build guitars and the MandoGuitar.

Phantom Bass
1995-present. Classic 5-sided Phantom body shape, 2 humbuckers.

1995-2000		$350	$450

Pieper
2005-present. Premium grade, production/custom, solidbody basses with interchangable necks built by luthier Robert Pieper in New Haven, Connecticut. He also builds guitars.

Premier
Ca.1938-ca.1975, 1990s-present. Budget and intermediate grade, production, import basses. They also offer guitars. Originally American-made instruments, but by the '60s imported parts were being used. Current models are imports.

Bantam Bass
1950-1970. Small body, single-cut short-scale archtop electric, torch headstock inlay, sparkle 'guard, sunburst.

1950-1970		$450	$600

Electric Solidbody Bass

1960s	Various models	$275	$350

Prestige
Professional grade, production, acoustic and electric basses from Vancouver, British Columbia. They also offer guitars.

Rarebird Guitars
1978-present. Luthier Bruce Clay builds his professional grade, production/custom, electric solidbody and hollowbody basses originally in Arvada, Colorado, but since '05 in Paonia, Colorado. He also builds guitars.

Rat Fink
2002-present. Intermediate grade, production, basses from Lace Music Products, the makers of the Lace Sensor pickup, featuring the artwork of Ed "Big Daddy" Roth. They also offer guitars and amps.

Regal
Ca. 1884-1966, 1987-present. Intermediate grade, production, acoustic wood body resonator basses from Saga. They also build guitars.

Renaissance
1978-1980. Plexiglass solidbody electric guitars and basses made in Malvern, Pennsylvania.

Plexiglas Bass
1978-1980. Plexiglas bodies and active electronics, models include the DPB bass (double-cut, 1 pickup, '78-'79), SPB (single-cut, 2 pickups, '78-'79), T-100B (Bich-style, 1 pickup, '80), S-100B (double-cut, 1 pickup, '80), and the S-200B (double-cut, 2 pickups, '80).

1978-1980		$425	$650

Renaissance Guitars
1994-present. Professional grade, custom, acoustic and solidbody basses built by luthier Rick Turner in Santa Cruz, California. He also builds guitars and ukuleles.

Reverend
1996-present. Reverend built electric basses in Warren, Michigan, from '98 to '04. They continue to build guitars.

Rumblefish
1998-2004. Offset double-cut, J-style neck and bridge pickups, 2 volumes, 1 master tone.

1998-2004		$550	$625

Rick Turner
1979-1981, 1990-present. Rick Turner has a long career as a luthier, electronics designer and innovator. He also makes the Renaissance line of guitars in his shop in Santa Cruz, California.

Rickenbacker
1931-present. Professional grade, production/custom, electric basses. They also build guitars. Rickenbacker introduced their first electric bass in '57 and has always been a strong player in the bass market.

MODEL YEAR	FEATURES	EXC. COND. LOW	HIGH

Model 2030 Hamburg Bass
1984-1997. Rounded double-cut, 2 pickups, active electronics.

1984-1989		$600	$750
1990-1997		$550	$700

Model 3000 Bass
1975-1984. Rounded double-cut, 30" scale, 1 pickup, brown sunburst.

1975-1984		$600	$850

Model 3001 Bass
1975-1984. Same as Model 3000 but with longer 33-1/2" scale, Wine Red.

1975-1984		$700	$800

Model 4000 Bass
1958-1985. Cresting wave body and headstock, 1 horseshoe pickup (changed to regular pickup in '64), neck-thru-body.

1958-1959	Autumnglo	$4,200	$5,800
1958-1959	Mapleglo	$4,700	$5,300
1960	Fireglo	$4,200	$5,300
1960	Mapleglo	$4,500	$5,300
1961	Fireglo, Mapleglo	$4,200	$5,300
1962-1964	Fireglo	$4,200	$5,300
1965-1966	Fireglo	$3,400	$4,200
1968-1969	Various colors	$2,600	$4,200
1970-1972	Various colors	$1,600	$3,000
1973-1979	Various colors	$1,100	$1,900
1980-1985	Various colors	$1,100	$1,300

Model 4000 L (Light Show) Bass
1970-1975. Model 4000 with translucent top with lights in body that lit up when played, needed external transformer.

1970-1975		$4,500	$7,500

Model 4001 Bass
1961-1965, 1968-1986. Fancy version of 4000, 1 horseshoe magnet pickup (changed to regular pickup in '64) and 1 bar magnet pickup, triangle inlays, bound neck.

1961-1965	Fireglo	$4,200	$5,800
1963-1965	Mapleglo	$4,200	$6,200
1968-1969	Mapleglo	$2,600	$4,200
1970	All colors	$2,000	$3,000
1971	All colors	$1,700	$2,600
1972	All colors	$1,600	$2,000
1973	All colors	$1,500	$1,900
1974	All colors	$1,400	$1,800
1975	All colors	$1,300	$1,700
1976-1977	All colors	$1,200	$1,700
1978	All colors	$1,100	$1,700
1979-1983	All colors	$1,100	$1,300
1984-1986	All colors	$1,100	$1,200

Model 4001 C64S Bass
2004. Recreation of Paul McCartney's 4001.

2004		$1,800	$2,200

Model 4001 CS Bass
1991-1997. Chris Squire signature model.

1991-1997	With certificate	$2,500	$3,500
1991-1997	Without certificate	$1,500	$2,500

Model 4001 FL Bass
Late-1960s-present. Fretless version of 4001 Bass, special order in '60s, various colors.

1960-1970s		$1,300	$2,700

Model 4001 Reissue Bass
1990s-2000s. Mapleglo.

1990-2000s		$950	$1,050

Model 4001 V63 Bass
1984-2000. Vintage '63 reissue of Model 4001, horseshoe-magnet pickup, Mapleglo.

1984-2000		$1,300	$1,500

Model 4001-S Bass
1964-1985. Same as Model 4000, but with 2 pickups, export model.

1980s	Special order	$1,100	$1,400

Model 4002 Bass
1967-1985. Cresting wave body and headstock, 2 humbuckers, black 'guard, checkerboard binding.

1980-1985		$2,500	$2,700

Model 4003 Bass
1979-present. Similar to Model 4001, split 'guard, deluxe features.

1979-1989		$1,300	$1,500
1990-1999		$925	$1,150
2000-2004		$925	$1,050

Model 4003 Blackstar Bass
1988-1997. Black finish version of Tuxedo Bass, black knobs, chrome and black hardware.

1988-1997		$1,000	$1,200

Model 4003 Tuxedo Bass
1980-1997. Non-deluxe feature version of Model 4003, white body with black 'guard and hardware. 100 made.

1980-1997		$800	$1,000

Model 4003-S Bass
1980-1995. Standard feature version of 4003.

1980-1989		$1,000	$1,300
1990-1995		$1,000	$1,200

Model 4003-S/5 Bass
1986-2003. 5-string Model 4003-S.

1986-2003		$1,100	$1,300

Model 4003-S/8 Bass
1986-2003. 8-string 4003-S.

1986-2003		$1,200	$1,400

Model 4004C Cheyenne/Cheyenne II
1993-present. Cresting wave, maple neck-thru-body with walnut body and head wings, gold hardware, dot inlay. Replaced by maple top 4004Cii Cheyenne II in '00.

1993-1999		$950	$1,025
2000-2004	Cheyenne II	$975	$1,050

Model 4005 Bass
1965-1984. New style double-cut hollowbody, 2 pickups, R tailpiece, cresting wave headstock.

1965-1969	Fireglo	$4,200	$5,300
1965-1969	Mapleglo	$4,400	$5,300
1966-1968	Black	$3,500	$5,300
1970-1979	Various colors	$2,000	$3,000

Rickenbacker 4001 V63

1979 Rickenbacker 4005

BASSES

Robin Freedom

1977 S.D. Curlee

MODEL YEAR	FEATURES	EXC. COND. LOW	HIGH

Model 4005 WB Bass
1966-1983. Old style Model 4005 with white-bound body.

1966	Mapleglo	$4,800	$5,800
1967-1969	Various colors	$4,800	$5,500

Model 4005-8 Bass
Late-1960s. Eight-string Model 4005.

1960s	Fireglo	$4,700	$5,500
1960s	Mapleglo	$4,800	$5,800

Model 4008 Bass
1975-1983. Eight-string, cresting wave body and headstock.

1975-1983		$1,100	$1,400

Model 4080 Doubleneck Bass
1975-1992. Bolt-on 6- and 4-string necks.

1975-1979	Jetglo or Mapleglo	$2,500	$3,400
1980-1992		$2,000	$2,900

Ritter
Production/custom, solidbody basses built by luthier Jens Ritter in Wachenheim, Germany.

RKS
2003-present. Professional and premium grade, production/custom, solidbody basses designed by Ravi Sawhney and guitarist Dave Mason and built in Thousand Oaks, California. They also build guitars.

Rob Allen
1997-present. Professional grade, production/custom, lightweight basses made by luthier Robert Allen in Santa Barbara, California.

Robin
1982-present. Founded by David Wintz and located in Houston, Texas, Robin built basses until 2000. Most basses were Japanese-made until '87; American production began in '88. They continue to build guitars and also make Metropolitan (since 1996) and Alamo (since 2000) brand guitars.

Freedom Bass
1984-1986. Offset double-cut, active treble and bass EQ controls, 1 pickup.

1984-1986		$450	$550

Freedom Bass I Passive
1986-1989. Non-active version of Freedom Bass, 1 humbucker. Passive dropped from name in '87.

1986-1989		$450	$550

Medley Bass
1984-1989. Reverse headstock, deep cutaways, 2 pickups.

1984-1989		$450	$550

Ranger Bass
1984-1997. Vintage style body with P-style and J-style pickup configuration, dot markers, medium scale from '84 to '89 and long scale from '90 to '97.

1984-1997		$575	$775

Rock Bass
2002-present. Chinese-made, intermediate and professional grade, production, bolt neck solidbody basses from the makers of Warwick basses.

Rogue
2001-present. Budget and intermediate grade, production, solidbody and acoustic/electric basses. They also offer guitars, mandolins, banjos, effects and amps.

Roland
Best known for keyboards, effects, and amps, Roland offered synthesizer-based guitars and basses from 1977 to '86.

Roman & Blake Basses
1977-2003. Professional grade, production/custom, solidbody bass guitars made in Warren, Connecticut by Ed Roman.

Roman & Lipman Guitars
1989-2000. Production/custom, solidbody basses made in Danbury, Connecticut by Ed Roman. They also made guitars.

Roman USA Basses
2000-present. Professional grade, production/custom, solidbody basses made in Las Vegas, Nevada by Ed Roman.

Rono
1967-present. Luthier Ron Oates builds his professional and premium grade, production/custom, acoustic and solidbody basses in Boulder, Colorado. He also builds guitars and mandolins.

S.D. Curlee
1975-1982. S.D. Curlee instruments were made in Illinois; S.D. Curlee International instruments were made in Japan.

Electric Solidbody Bass

1970s	Various models	$300	$500

S101
2002-present. Budget and intermediate grade, production, solidbody basses imported from China. They also offer guitars, mandolins, and banjos.

Sadowsky
1980-present. Professional and premium grade, production/custom, solidbody basses built by luthier Roger Sadowsky in Brooklyn, New York. He also builds guitars. In '96, luthier Yoshi Kikuchi started building Sadowsky Tokyo instruments in Japan; those basses are now available in the U.S.

MODEL YEAR	FEATURES	EXC. COND. LOW	HIGH

Samick

1958-2001, 2002-present. Budget, intermediate, and professional grade, production, imported acoustic and electric basses. They also offer guitars, mandolins, ukes and banjos.

Bass

1965-1999	Various models	$100	$300

Schecter

1976-present. Intermediate and professional grade, production/custom, electric basses made in the U.S. and overseas. They also offer guitars. Schecter Custom Shop basses are made in Burbank, California and their Diamond Series is made in South Korea.

Bass

1980s	Various models	$300	$450

Shergold

1968-1992. Founded by Jack Golder and Norman Houlder, Shergold originally made guitars for other brands. In '75, they started building guitars and basses under their own name. By '82, general guitar production was halted but custom orders were filled through '90. In '91, general production was again started but ended in '92 when Golder died.

Shifflett

1990-present. Luthier Charles Shifflett builds his premium grade, custom, acoustic basses in High River, Alberta. He also guitars and banjos.

Silvertone

1941- ca.1970, present. Brand used by Sears. Instruments were U.S.-made and imported.

Bass VI

One lipstick pickup.

1960s		$600	$900

Hornet

1960s. Fender-shape, 1 lipstick pickup.

1960s		$250	$400

Simmons

2002-present. Luthier David L. Simmons builds his professional grade, production/custom, 4- and 5-string basses in Hendersonville, North Carolina.

Sinister

2003-present. Intermediate and professional grade, custom/production, solidbody basses built for Sinister Guitars by luthier Jon Kammerer.

Slammer

1990-present. Budget and intermediate grade, production, basses imported by Hamer. They also offer guitars.

Smith

1978-present. Professional and premium grade, production/custom, electric basses built by luthier Ken Smith in Perkasie, Pennsylvania. Earlier models had Ken Smith on the headstock, recent models

have a large S logo. He also designs the imported KSD line of basses.

American-Made Bass

1978-2000	Various models	$1,000	$3,000

B.T. Custom VI Bass

1985-present. Six strings, double-cut, neck-thru-body.

1985-1999		$1,800	$3,500

Imported Bass

1990s	Various models	$700	$800

Specimen Products

1984-present. Luthier Ian Schneller builds his professional and premium grade, production/custom, aluminum and wood body basses in Chicago, Illinois. He also builds guitars, ukes, amps and speaker cabs.

Spector/Stuart Spector Design

1975-1990 (Spector), 1991-1998 (SSD), 1998-present (Spector SSD). Imtermediate, professional, and premium grade, production/custom, basses made in the U.S., the Czech Republic, Korea, and China. Stuart Spector's first bass was the NS and the company quickly grew to the point where Kramer acquired it in '85. After Kramer went out of business in '90, Spector started building basses with the SSD logo (Stuart Spector Design). In '98 he recovered the Spector trademark.

Bob Series Bass

1996-1999. Offset deep double-cut swamp ash or alder body, bolt neck, various colors, SSD logo on headstock, 4-string (Bob 4) or 5 (Bob 5).

1996-1999	Bob 4	$800	$1,000
1996-1999	Bob 5	$900	$1,100

NS Series Bass

1977-present. Offset double-cut solidbody, neck-thru, 1 pickup (NS-1, made into '80s) or 2 (NS-2), gold hardware.

1977-1979	NS-1	$1,100	$1,500
1977-1989	NS-2	$1,200	$1,600
1980-1985	NS-1	$1,000	$1,200
1990-2000	NS-2	$1,100	$1,300

St. Moritz

1960s. Japanese imports, generally shorter-scale, beginner basses.

Stambaugh

1995-present. Luthier Chris Stambaugh builds his professional grade, custom/production, solidbody basses in Stratham, New Hampshire. He also builds guitars.

Standel

1952-1974, 1997-present. Amp builder Bob Crooks offered instruments under his Standel brand name three different times during the '60s. See Guitar section for production details. See Amp section for more company info.

1960s Silvertone bass

Spector Spectorcore 4

Steinberger XL-2

1968 Teisco EB-200

MODEL YEAR	FEATURES	EXC. COND. LOW	HIGH
Custom Deluxe Solidbody 401 Bass			
1967-1968. Custom with higher appointments, various colors.			
1967-1968		$900	$1,200
Custom Deluxe Thinbody 402 Bass			
1967-1968. Custom with higher appointments, various colors.			
1967-1968		$1,000	$1,300
Custom Solidbody 501 Bass			
1967-1968. Solidbody, 1 pickup, various colors.			
1967-1968		$700	$900
Custom Thinbody 502 Bass			
1967-1968. Thin solidbody, 2 pickups, various colors.			
1967-1968		$800	$1,000

Steinberger

1979-present. Steinberger offers budget and intermediate grade, production, electric basses. They also offer guitars.

MODEL YEAR	FEATURES	EXC. COND. LOW	HIGH
Q-4 Bass			
1990-1991. Composite neck, Double Bass system, headless with traditional-style maple body, low-impedance pickups.			
1990-1991		$700	$900
Q-5 Bass			
1990-1991. Five-string version of Q Bass.			
1990-1991		$800	$1,000
XL-2 Bass			
1984-1993. Rectangular composite body, 4-string, headless, 2 pickups.			
1984-1989	Black	$1,200	$1,500
1990-1993	Red	$1,100	$1,300
XL-2GR Bass			
1985-1990. Headless, Roland GR synthesizer controller.			
1985-1990		$1,100	$1,300
XM-2 Bass			
1986-1992. Headless, double-cut maple body, 4-string, 2 low-impedance pickups, optional fretted, lined fretless or unlined fretless, black, red or white.			
1986-1992		$1,000	$1,200

Stevenson

1999-present. Luthier Ted Stevenson, of Lachine, Quebec, added profession grade, production/custom, basses to his product line in '05. He also builds guitars and amps.

Stewart Basses

2000-present. Luthier Fred Stewart builds his premium grade, custom/production, solidbody basses in Charlton, Maryland. He has also built guitars since '94.

Stinger

See Martin listing.

Suhr Guitars

1997-present. In '03, luthier John Suhr added professional grade, production/custom, solidbody basses, to his instrument line built in Lake Elsinore, California. He also builds guitars.

Supro

1935-1968. Supro was a budget brand for the National Dobro Company. Supro offered only two bass models in the '60s.

MODEL YEAR	FEATURES	EXC. COND. LOW	HIGH
Pocket Bass			
1960-1968. Double-cut, neck pickup and bridge mounted pickup, semi-hollow, short-scale, black.			
1960-1968		$750	$800

SX

See listing for Essex.

Tacoma

1995-present. Professional grade, production, acoustic basses produced in Tacoma, Washington. They also build acoustic guitars and mandolins.

Takamine

1962-present. Intermediate, professional and premium grade, production, acoustic and acoustic/electric basses. They also make guitars. They offered solidbody electrics for '83-'84.

Taylor

1974-present. Professional and premium grade, production, acoustic basses built in El Cajon, California.

MODEL YEAR	FEATURES	EXC. COND. LOW	HIGH
AB1 Bass			
1996-2003. Acoustic/electric, sitka spruce top, imbuia walnut back and sides, designed for 'loose' woody sound.			
1996-2003		$1,250	$1,400
AB2 Bass			
1996-2003. Acoustic/electric, all imbuia walnut body.			
1996-2003		$1,250	$1,400
AB3 Bass			
1998-2003. Acoustic/electric, sitka spruce top, maple back and sides.			
1998-2003		$1,350	$1,500

Teisco

1946-1974, 1994-present. The Japanese Teisco line started offering basses in '60.

MODEL YEAR	FEATURES	EXC. COND. LOW	HIGH
EB-100 Bass			
1968-1969. One pickup, white 'guard, blue.			
1968-1969		$125	$200
EP-200 B Bass			
1968-1969. Semi-hollowbody.			
1968-1969		$175	$250

Tele-Star

1965-ca.1972. Imported from Japan by Tele-Star Musical Instrument Corporation of New York. Primarily made by Kawai, many inspired by Burns designs, some in cool sparkle finishes.

MODEL YEAR	FEATURES	EXC. COND. LOW	HIGH
Electric Solidbody Bass			
1960s	Various models	$100	$250

MODEL		EXC. COND.	
YEAR	FEATURES	LOW	HIGH

Timtone Custom Guitars

1993-present. Luthier Tim Diebert builds his premium grade, custom, solidbody and chambered-body basses in Grand Forks, British Columbia. He also builds guitars and lap steels.

Tobias

1977-present. Founded by Mike Tobias in Orlando, Florida. Moved to San Francisco for '80-'81, then to Costa Mesa, eventually ending up in Hollywood. In '90, he sold the company to Gibson which moved it to Burbank. The first Tobias made under Gibson ownership was serial number 1094. The instruments continued to be made by the pre-Gibson crew until '92, when the company was moved to Nashville. The last LA Tobias/Gibson serial number is 2044. Mike left the company in '92 and started a new business in '94 called MTD where he continues to make electric and acoustic basses. In '99, production of Tobias basses was moved overseas. In late '03, Gibson started again offering U.S.-made Tobias instruments; they are made in Conway, Arkansas, in the former Baldwin grand piano facility. Currently Tobias offers imported and U.S.-made, intermediate and professional grade, production, acoustic and electric basses.

Basic B-4 Bass

1984-1999. 30", 32", or 34" scale, neck-thru-body in alder, koa or walnut, 5-piece laminated neck.

1984-1992		$2,000	$2,500

Classic C-4 Bass

1978-1999. One or 2 pickups, active or passive electronics, 2-octave rosewood 'board, available in short-, medium-, and long-scale models.

1978-1992		$2,300	$3,000

Classic C-5 Bass

1985-1999. 30", 32" or 34" scale, alder, koa or walnut body, bookmatched top, ebony or phenolic 'board, hardwood neck.

1985-1992		$2,300	$3,000

Classic C-6 Bass

Ca. 1986-1999. Flamed maple and padauk neck, alder body, padauk top, ebony 'board, active electronics, 32" or 34" scale.

1986-1992		$2,500	$3,200

Growler GR-5 Bass

1996-1999. 5-string, offset double-cut, bolt neck, various colors.

1996-1999		$850	$900

Killer Bee KB-5 Bass

1991-1999. Offset double-cut, swamp ash or lacewood body, various colors.

1991-1999		$1,500	$1,700

Model T Bass

1989-1991. Line of 4- and 5-string basses, 3-piece maple neck-thru-body, maple body halves, active treble and bass controls. Fretless available.

1989-1991		$1,200	$1,400

Signature S-4 Bass

1978-1999. Available in 4-, 5-, and 6-string models, chrome-plated milled brass bridge.

1978-1992		$2,200	$2,500

Standard ST-4 Bass

1992-1995. Japanese-made, 5-piece maple neck-thru, swamp ash body wings.

1992-1995		$1,100	$1,300

Toby Deluxe TD-4 Bass

1994-1996. Offset double-cut, bolt neck.

1994-1996		$550	$650

Toby Deluxe TD-5 Bass

1994-1996. 5-string version.

1994-1996		$575	$675

Toby Pro 6 Bass

1994-1996. Solidbody 6-string, Toby Pro logo on truss rod cover, neck-thru body.

1994-1996		$600	$700

Tokai

1947-present. Tokai started making guitars and basses around '70 and by the end of that decade they were being imported into the U.S. Today Tokai offers electrics, acoustics, and electric basses made in Japan and Korea.

Vintage Bass Copies

1970s-1980s. Tokai offered near copies of classic U.S. basses.

1970s		$400	$550

Tonemaster

1960s. Imported from Italy by U.S. distributor with typical '60s Italian sparkle plastic finish and push-button controls, bolt-on neck.

Electric Bass

1960s	Sparkle finish	$400	$600

Traben

2004-present. Intermediate grade, production, solidbody basses imported by Elite Music Brands of Clearwater, Florida.

Traveler Guitar

1992-present. Intermediate grade, production, travel size electric basses made in Redlands, California. They also make guitars.

Travis Bean

1974-1979, 1999. The unique Travis Bean line included a couple of bass models. Travis Bean announced some new instruments in '99, but general production was not resumed.

TB-2000 Bass

Aluminum neck with T-slotted headstock, longer horned, double-cut body, 2 pickups, 4 controls, dot markers, various colors.

1970s		$1,500	$3,000

Timtone Boomtown Bass

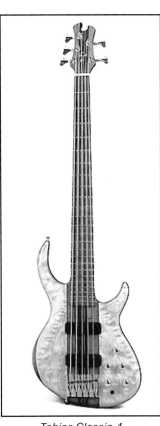

Tobias Classic 4

BASSES

1960 True Tone Bass

Univox Hi Flyer

MODEL		EXC. COND.	
YEAR	FEATURES	LOW	HIGH

Trinity River

Acoustic basses from Stenzler Musical Instruments of Ft. Worth, Texas. They also offer guitars, mandolins, and fiddles.

True Tone

1960s. Western Auto retailed this line of basses, guitars and amps which were manufactured by Chicago builders makers like Kay. The brand was most likely gone by '68.
Electric Basses

1960s		$150	$250

Tyler

Luthier James Tyler builds his professional and premium grade, custom/production, solidbody basses in Van Nuys, California. He also builds guitars.

Unique Guitars

2003-present. Professional and premium grade, production/custom, solidbody basses built by luthier Joey Rico in California. He also builds guitars.

Univox

1964-1978. Univox started out as an amp line and added guitars and basses around '69. Guitars were imported from Japan by the Merson Musical Supply Company, later Unicord, Westbury, New York. Generally mid-level copies of American designs.
Badazz Bass
1971-ca. 1975. Based on the Guild S-100.

1971-1977		$250	$400

Bicentennial
1976. Carved eagle in body, matches Bicentennial guitar (see that listing), brown stain, maple 'board.

1976		$550	$900

Hi Flyer Bass
1969-1977. Mosrite Ventures Bass copy, 2 pickups, rosewood 'board.

1969-1977		$400	$550

'Lectra (Model 1970F) Bass
1969-ca. 1973. Violin bass, walnut.

1969-1973		$300	$450

Precisely Bass
1971-ca. 1975. Copy of Fender P-Bass.

1971-1975		$250	$400

Stereo Bass
1976-1977. Rickenbacker 4001 Bass copy, model U1975B.

1976-1977		$400	$550

Vaccaro

1997-2002. They offered intermediate and professional grade, production/custom, aluminum-necked basses built in Asbury Park, New Jersey. They also built guitars.

MODEL		EXC. COND.	
YEAR	FEATURES	LOW	HIGH

Valley Arts

Ca. 1977-present. Professional and premium grade, production/custom, solidbody basses built in Nashville, Tennessee. They also make guitars.

Vantage

1977-present. Intermediate grade, production, electric basses imported from Korea (from Japan until '90). They also offer guitars.

Veillette

1991-present. Luthiers Joe Veillette and Martin Keith build their professional and premium grade, production/custom, electric basses in Woodstock, New York. They also build guitars and mandolins.

Veillette-Citron

1975-1983. Founded by Joe Veillette and Harvey Citron who met at the NY College School of Architecture in the late '60s. Joe took a guitar building course from Michael Gurian and by the Summer of '76, he and Harvey started producing neck-thru solidbody guitars and basses. Veillette and Citron both are back building instruments.

Ventura

1970s. Import classic bass copies distributed by C. Bruno (Kaman).

Versoul, LTD

1989-present. Production/custom acoustic/electric and solidbody basses built by luthier Kari Nieminen in Helsinki, Finland. He also builds guitars and sitars.

Vox

1957-1972, 1982-present. The first Vox products were amplifiers brought to market in '58 by Tom Jennings and Dick Denny. By '61 they had added instruments to the line. Guitars and basses bearing the Vox name were offered from 1961-'69 (made in England, Italy), '82-'85 (Japan), '85-'88 (Korea), and for '98-2001 (U.S.). Special thanks to Jim Rhoads of Rhoads Music in Elizabethtown, Pennsylvania, for help on production years of these models.
Apollo IV Bass
1967-1969. Single-cut hollowbody, bolt maple neck, 1 pickup, on-board fuzz, booster, sunburst.

1967-1969		$675	$775

Astro IV Bass
1967-1969. Two pickups.

1967-1969		$700	$800

Clubman Bass
1961-1966. Double-cut 2-pickup solidbody, red.

1961-1966		$350	$450

Constellation IV Bass
1967-1968. Teardrop-shaped body, 2 pickups, 1 f-hole, 1 set of controls, treble, bass and distortion boosters.

1967-1968		$650	$850

MODEL YEAR	FEATURES	EXC. COND. LOW	HIGH

Cougar Bass
1963-1967. Double-cut semi-hollow body, 2 f-holes, 2 pickups, 2 sets of controls, sunburst.

1963-1967		$650	$750

Delta IV Bass
1967-1968. Five-sided body, 2 pickups, 1 volume and 2 tone controls, distortion, treble and bass boosters.

1967-1968		$700	$900

Mark IV Bass
1963-1969. Teardrop-shaped body, 2 pickups, 1 set of controls, sunburst.

1963-1969		$950	$1,000

Panther Bass
1967-1968. Double-cut solidbody, 1 slanted pickup, rosewood 'board, sunburst.

1967-1968		$400	$550

Phantom IV Bass
1963-1969. Five-sided body, 2 pickups, 1 set of controls.

1963-1964	English made	$1,500	$1,800
1965-1969	Italian made	$1,200	$1,300

Saturn IV Bass
1967-1968. Single-cut, 2 F-holes, 1 set of controls, 1 pickup.

1967-1968		$550	$750

Sidewinder IV Bass (V272)
1967-1968. Double-cut semi-hollow body, 2 f-holes, 2 pickups, 1 set of controls, treble, bass, and distortion boosters.

1967-1968		$650	$850

Stinger Bass
1968. Teardrop-shaped, boat oar headstock.

1968		$650	$850

Wyman Bass
1966. Teardrop-shaped body, 2 pickups, 1 F-hole, 1 set of controls, sunburst.

1966		$750	$950

Wandre (Davoli)
Ca. 1956/57-1969. Italian-made guitars and basses.

Warrior
1995-present. Professional and premium grade, production/custom, solidbody basses built by luthier J.D. Lewis in Roseville, Georgia. He also builds guitars.

Warwick
1982-present. Professional and premium grade, production/custom, electric and acoustic basses made in Markneukirchen, Germany; founded by Hans Peter Wilfer, whose father started Framus guitars. They also build amps.

Corvette Standard Bass
1997-present. Offset double-cut, bubinga body, offered in 4-, 5-, and 6-string.

1997-2004		$600	$700

Jack Bruce Signature Bass
1990-1991, 2001. Based on Thumb Bass, '01 version a limited edition with 50 fretted and 50 unfretted made.

1990-1991		$1,500	$1,700

Streamer I-5 Bass
1984-present. Five-string, gold hardware, active electronics.

1984-1990s		$1,300	$1,500

Thumb/Thumb-5 Bass
1980s-present. Walnut, neck-thru, double-cut solidbody, 2 pickups.

1980-1990s		$1,100	$1,400

Washburn
1974-present. Intermediate and professional grade, production, acoustic and electric basses. Washburn instruments were mostly imports early on, U.S. production later, currently a combination of both. Washburn also offers guitars, mandolins, and amps.

Electric Bass

1980-2000s	Various models	$250	$500

Watkins
1957-present. Watkins Electric Music (WEM) was founded by Charlie Watkins. Their first commercial product was the Watkins Dominator amp in '57. They made the Rapier line of guitars and basses from the beginning. Watkins offered guitars and basses up to '82.

Rapier Bass
1957-1982. 2 pickups, red.

1960s		$375	$500

Wechter
1984-present. Professional grade, production/custom acoustic basses built by luthier Abe Wechter in Paw Paw, Michigan. He also offers U.S-made and import guitars.

Wendler
1999-present. Luthier Dave Wendler, of Ozark Instrument Building, builds his intermediate and professional grade, production/custom, solidbody, electro-acoustic basses in Branson, Missouri. He also builds guitars.

Westbury-Unicord
1978-ca. 1983. Japanese imports by Unicord.

Westone
1970s-1990. Imported from Japan by St. Louis Music.

Wilson Brothers Guitars
2004-present. Production electric basses. They also build guitars. Founded by Ventures guitarist Don Wilson.

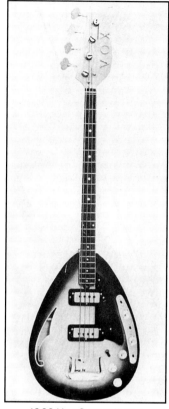

1968 Vox Constellation

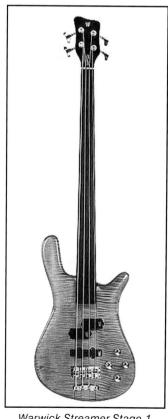

Warwick Streamer Stage 1

BASSES

Zemaitis GZB-2500

Zon Tribute

MODEL YEAR	FEATURES	EXC. COND. LOW	HIGH

Winston

Ca. 1963-1967. Imported by Buegeleisen & Jacobson of New York.

Wurlitzer

1970s. Private branded by Pedulla for the Wurlitzer music store chain. Manufacturer and retailer were both based in Massachusetts. Refer to Pedulla listing.

Yamaha

1946-present. Budget, intermediate, professional and premium grade, production, electric basses. They also build guitars. Yamaha began producing solidbody instruments in '66.

Attitude Custom Bass

1990-1994. Part of the Sheehan Series, champagne sparkle.

1990-1994		$750	$800

Electric Bass

1980-1990s	Various models	$225	$450

Zemaitis

1960-1999, 2004-present. Tony Zemaitis began selling his guitars in '60 and he retired in '99. He emphasized simple lightweight construction and his instruments are known for hand engraved metal fronts. Each hand-built custom guitar was a unique instrument. Approximately 10 custom guitars were built each year. In '04, Japan's Kanda Shokai, with the endorsement of Tony Zemaitis, Jr., started building the guitars again.

Electric Bass

1970s	Heart hole (2 made)	$25,000	$30,000
1980s	1/2 metal & spruce	$13,000	$16,000
1980s	Metal-front 4-string	$17,000	$20,000

Zen-On

1946-ca.1968. Japanese-made. By '67 using the Morales brandname. Not heavily imported into the U.S., if at all (see Morales).

Electric Solidbody Bass

1950s	Various models	$150	$200

Zeta

1982-present. Professional and premium grade, production/custom, acoustic, electric and upright basses, with MIDI options, made in Oakland, California. They also make guitars, amps and mandolins.

Crossover 4 (Model XB-304) Bass

1990s-present. Sleek offset body design, bolt-on neck, playable as strap-on or upright, natural.

1990s		$1,600	$1,800

Jazz Standard Upright Bass

1990s-present. Hourglass-shaped body, bass-viol-size version of sleek electric violin, active electronics, sunburst.

1990s		$2,300	$2,700

Zim-Gar

1960s. Japanese imports from Gar-Zim Musical Instrument Corporation of Brooklyn, New York.

Electric Solidbody Bass

1960s	Various models	$125	$200

Zolla

1979-present. Professional grade, production/custom, electric basses built by luthier Bill Zolla in San Diego, California. Zolla also builds guitars, necks and bodies.

BZ-1 Bass

1988-present. Offset double-cut solidbody, 2 pickups, offered in 4-, 5-, and 6-string versions.

1980s		$450	$600

Zon

1981-present. Luthier Joe Zon builds his professional and premium grade, production/custom, solidbody basses in Redwood City, California. Zon started the brand in Buffalo, New York and relocated to Redwood City in '87.

Legacy Elite VI Bass

1989-present. Six-string, 34" scale carbon-fiber neck, Bartolini pickups, ZP-2 active electronics.

1990s		$1,100	$1,200

Scepter Bass

1984-1993. Offset body shape, 24 frets, 1 pickup, tremolo.

1984-1993		$1,000	$1,100

ZZ Ryder

Solidbody electric basses from Stenzler Musical Instruments of Ft. Worth, Texas. They also offer guitars.

Amps

65Amps London

Acoustic 125

1977 Acoustic 135

AMPS

MODEL YEAR	FEATURES	EXC. COND. LOW	HIGH

65Amps

2004-present. Founded by Peter Stroud and Dan Boul, 65 builds tube guitar head and combo amps and speaker cabs in Valley Village, California.

Ace Tone

Late-1960-1970s. Imported from Sakata Shokai Limited of Osaka, Japan, early imported of amps and effects pedals. Later became Roland/Boss.

B-9 Amp

Late-1960s-early-1970s. Solid-state bass amp head.

1960-1970s		$100	$175

Mighty-5 Amp

Late-1960s-early-1970s. Tubes, 50-watt head.

1960-1970s		$125	$225

Acoustic

Ca.1965-ca.1987, 2001-present. The Acoustic Control Corp., of Los Angeles, California, was mostly known for solidstate amplifiers. Heads and cabinets were sold separately with their own model numbers, but were also combined (amp sets) and marketed under a different model number (for example, the 153 amp set was the 150b head with a 2x15" cabinet). The brand was revived by Samick in '01 for a line of amps.

114 Amp

Ca.1977-mid-1980s. Solidstate, 50 watts, 2x10", reverb, master volume.

1978-1984		$175	$350

115 Amp

1977-1978. Solidstate, 1x12", 50 watts, reverb, master volume.

1977-1978		$200	$375

116 Bass Amp

1978-mid-1980s. Solidstate, 75 watts, 1x15", power boost switch.

1978-1984		$225	$375

120 Amp Head

1977-mid-1980s. Solidstate head, 125 watts.

1977-1984		$175	$275

123 Amp

1977-1984. 1x12" combo.

1977-1984		$125	$225

124 Amp

1977-mid-1980s. Solidstate, 4x10", 5-band EQ, 100 watts, master volume.

1977-1984		$250	$375

125 Amp

1977-mid-1980s. Solidstate, 2x12", 5-band EQ, 100 watts, master volume.

1977-1984		$250	$375

126 Bass Amp

1977-mid-1980s. Solidstate, 100 watts, 1x15", 5-band EQ.

1977-1984		$250	$375

134 Amp

1972-1976. Solidstate, 100-125 watts, 4x10" combo.

1972-1976	125 watts	$250	$425

MODEL YEAR	FEATURES	EXC. COND. LOW	HIGH

135 Amp

1972-1976. Solidstate, 125 watts, 2x12" combo, reverb, tremolo.

1972-1976		$250	$425

136 Amp

1972-1976. Solidstate, 125 watts, 1x15" combo.

1972-1976		$250	$425

140 Bass Head

1972-1976. Solidstate, 125 watts, 2 channels.

1972-1976		$150	$250

150 Amp Head

1960s-1976. Popular selling model, generally many available in the used market. Solidstate, 110 watts until '72, 125 watts after.

1968-1976		$175	$250

150b Bass Head

1960s-1971. Bass amp version of 150 head.

1968-1971		$150	$225

153 Bass Amp Set

1960s-1971. 150b head (bass version of 150) with 2x15" 466 cabinet, 110 watts.

1968-1971		$275	$425

165 Amp

1979-mid-1980s. All tube combo, switchable to 60 or 100 watts, brown tolex.

1979-1984		$250	$375

220 Bass Head

1977-1980s. Solidstate, 5-band EQ, either 125 or 160 watts, later models 170 or 200 watts, black tolex.

1977-1984	170 or 200 watts	$175	$275

230 Amp Head

1977-1980s. Solidstate head, 125/160 watts, 5-band EQ.

1977-1984		$175	$275

260 Amp Head

1960s-1971. Solidstate, 275 watt, stereo/mono.

1968-1971		$275	$325

270 Amp Head

1970s. 400 watts.

1970s		$275	$325

320 Bass Head

1977-1980s. Solidstate, 5-band EQ, 160/300 watts, 2 switchable channels, black tolex.

1977-1984		$275	$325

360 Bass Head

1960s-1971. One of Acoustic's most popular models, 200 watts. By '72, the 360 is listed as a "preamp only."

1968-1971		$375	$525

370 Bass Head

1972-1977. Solidstate bass head, 365 watts early on, 275 later.

1972-1977	275 or 365 watts	$275	$375

402 Cabinet

1977-1980s. 2x15" bass cab, black tolex, black grille.

1977-1984		$175	$250

MODEL YEAR	FEATURES	EXC. COND. LOW	HIGH

450 Amp Head
1974-1976. 170 watts, 5-band EQ, normal and bright inputs.

1974-1976		$175	$250

455 Amp Set
1974-1976. 170 watt 450 head with 4x12" cabinet, black.

1970s	Black	$375	$525

470 Amp Head
1974-1977. 170 watt, dual channel.

1974-1977		$225	$375

G20-110 Amp
1981-mid-1980s. Solidstate, 20 watts, 1x10". The G series was a lower-priced combo line.

1981-1985		$100	$175

G20-120 Amp
1981-mid-1980s. Solidstate, 20 watts, 1x12".

1981-1985		$100	$200

G60-112 Amp
1981-mid-1980s. Solidstate, 60 watts, 1x12".

1981-1985		$125	$250

G60-212 Amp
1981-mid-1980s. Solidstate, 60 watts, 2x12".

1981-1985		$150	$275

G60T-112 Amp
1981-1987. Tube, 60 watts, 1x12".

1981-1985		$275	$375

Tube 60 Amp
1986-1987. Combo, 60 watts, 1x12", spring reverb, bright switch, master volume control, effects loop.

1986-1987		$275	$375

ADA
1977-2002. ADA (Analog/Digital Associates) was located in Berkeley, California, and introduced its Flanger and Final Phase in '77. The company later moved to Oakland and made amplifiers, high-tech signal processors, and a reissue of its original Flanger.

B-500 B Bass Power Biamp
1989-1995. 500 watts, in bi-amp mode the 2 outputs drive cabinets of 4 to 16 ohms.

1989-1995		$350	$425

Aguilar
1995-present. U.S.-made tube and solidstate amp heads, cabinets, and pre-amps from New York City, New York.

Aiken Amplification
2000-present. Tube amps, combos, and cabinets built by Randall Aiken originally in Buford, Georgia, and since '05 in Pensacola, Florida.

Aims
1970s. Aims amps were manufactured and distributed by Randall Instruments in the mid-'70s. They also offered guitars and basses.

Airline
Ca.1958-1968. Brand for Montgomery Ward, built by Kay, Harmony, and Valco.

Large Tube Amp
1960s	Various models	$225	$400

Small Tube Amp
1960s	Various models	$150	$275

Alamo
1947-1982. Founded by Charles Eilenberg, Milton Fink, and Southern Music, San Antonio, Texas, and distributed by Bruno and Sons. Alamo started producing amps in '49 and the amps were all-tube until '73; solidstate preamp and tube output from '73 to ca. '80; all solidstate for ca. '80 to '82. See Guitar Stories Volume II, by Michael Wright, for a complete history of Alamo with detailed model listings.

Birch "A" Combo Amp
1949-1962. Birch wood cabinets with A-shaped grill cutout, 2 to 5 tubes. Models include the Embassy Amp 3, Jet Amp 4, Challenger Amp 2, Amp 5, and the Montclair.

1949-1962		$150	$300

Bass Tube Amp
1960-1972. Leatherette covered, all tube, 20 to 35 watts, 15" speakers, combo or piggyback, some with Lansing speaker option. Models include the Paragon Special, Paragon Bass, Piggyback Band, Piggyback Bass, Fury Bass, and Paragon Bass (piggyback).

1960-1972		$175	$325

Small Tube Amp
1960-1972. Leatherette covered, all tube, 3 to 10 watts, 6" to 10" speakers, some with tremolo. Models include the Jet, Embassy, Challenger, Capri, Fiesta, Dart, and Special.

1960-1972		$175	$325

Mid-power Tube Amp
1960-1970. Leatherette covered, all tube, 15 to 30 watts, 12" or 15" speakers, some with tremolo and reverb, some with Lansing speaker option. Models include Montclair, Paragon, Paragon Band, Titan, and Futura.

1960-1970		$225	$500

Twin Speaker Combo (Tube/Hybrid) Amp
1973-ca.1979. Solidstate preamp section with tube output section, 20 or 70 watts, 10", 12" and 15" speaker configurations, some with reverb and tremolo. Models include the 70-watt Paragon Super Reverb Piggybacks, the 45-watt Futura 2x12, and the 20-watt Twin-Ten.

1973-1979		$225	$325

Twin Speaker Piggyback Tube Amp
1962-1972. Leatherette covered, all tube, up to 45 watts, 8", 10", 12" or 15" speaker configurations, some with tremolo and reverb, some with Lansing speaker option. Models include the Electra Twin Ten, Century Twin Ten, Futuramic Twin Eight, Galaxie Twin Twelve, Galaxie Twin Twelve Piggyback, Piggyback Super Band, Alamo Pro Reverb Piggyback, Futura, Galaxie Twin Ten, Twin-Ten, and Band Piggyback.

1962-1972		$300	$400

Aguilar DB 728

'60s Alamo Jet

1962 Alamo 2566 Century Twin Ten

AMPS

Alesis Wildfire 60

Allen Old Flame

Alessandro Redbone Special

MODEL YEAR	FEATURES	EXC. COND. LOW	HIGH

Bass Solidstate Preamp-Tube Output Amp

1973-ca.1979. Solidstate preamp section with tube output section, 35 or 40 watts, 15" speakers, combo or piggyback. Models include the Paragon Bass, Paragon Bass Piggyback, Paragon Country Western Bass, Paragon Super Bass, and the Fury Bass.

1973-1979		$125	$275

Small Solidstate Preamp-Tube Output Amp

1973-ca.1979. Solidstate preamp section with tube output section, 3 to 12 watts, 5" to 12" speaker, some with reverb. Models include the Challenger, Capri, Special, Embassy, Dart, and Jet.

1973-1979		$75	$175

Mid-power Solidstate Preamp-Tube Output Amp

1973-ca.1979. Solidstate preamp section with tube output section, 25 watts, 12" speaker, with reverb and tremolo. Models include the Montclair.

1973-1979		$125	$200

Solidstate Amp

Ca.1980-1982. All solidstate.

1980-1982		$50	$125

Alden

Small budget grade solidstate guitar and bass amps from Muse, Inc. of China.

Alesis

1992-present. Alesis has a wide range of products for the music industry, including digital modeling guitar amps. They also offer guitar effects.

Alessandro

1998-present. Tube amps built by George Alessandro in Huntingdon Valley, Pennsylvania. Founded in '94 as the Hound Dog Corporation, in '98 the company name was changed to Alessandro. The Redbone ('94) and the Bloodhound ('96) were the only models bearing the Hound Dog mark. Serial numbers are consecutive regardless of model (the earliest 20-30 did not have serial numbers). In '98 the company converted to exotic/high-end components and the name changed to Alessandro High-End Products. In '01, he added the Working Dog brand line of amps.

Allen Amplification

1998-present. Tube combo amps, heads and cabinets built by David Allen in Walton, Kentucky. He also offers the amps in kit form and produces replacement and upgrade transformers and a tube overdrive pedal.

Aloha

Late-1940s. Electric lap steel and amp Hawaiian outfits made for the Dallas-based Aloha.

MODEL YEAR	FEATURES	EXC. COND. LOW	HIGH

Ampeg

1949-present. Ampeg is primarily known for their bass amps. In the eastern United States, Ampeg was Fender's greatest challenger in the '60s and '70s bass amplifier market. St. Louis Music currently offers a line of Ampeg amps.

Amp Covering Dates:

Wood veneer	1946-1949.
Smooth brown	1949-1952.
Dot tweed	1952-1954.
Tweed	1954-1955.
Rough gray	1957-1958.
Rough tan	1957-1958.
Cream	1957-1958.
Light blue	1958.
Navy blue	1958-1962.
Blue check	1962-1967.
Black pebble	1967.
Smooth black	1967-1980.
Rough black	1967-1985.

AC-12 Amp

1970. 20 watts, 1x12", accordion amp that was a market failure and dropped after 1 year.

1970		$300	$400

AP-3550 Amp

1992-1993. Rackmount solidstate head, 350 watts or 200 watts, black metal.

1992-1993	350 watts	$225	$275

B-2 Bass Amp

1994-2000. Solidstate, 200 watts, 1x15" combo or 4x8" combo, black vinyl, black grille, large A logo.

1994-2000	1x15"	$475	$600

B-2 R Bass Head

1994-present. 200 watts, rackmount.

1994-2002		$375	$525

B-3 Amp

1995-2001. Solidstate head, 150 watts, 1x15".

1995-2001		$350	$450

B-12 N Portaflex Amp

1961-1965. 25 watts, 2x12", 2 6L6 power tubes.

1961-1965		$800	$1,000

B-12 XT Portaflex Amp

1965-1969. Tube, 50 watts, 2x12", reverb, vibrato, 2x7027A power tubes.

1965-1969		$700	$900

B-15 N (NB, NC, NF) Portaflex Amp

1960-1970. Introduced as B-15 using 2 6L6 power tubes, B-15 N in '61, B-15 NB in '62, B-15 NC with rectifier tube in '64, B-15 NF with fixed-bias 2 6L6 power tubes and 30 watts in '67, 1x15".

1960-1965		$900	$1,000
1966-1970		$800	$900

B-15 NC Portaflex Amp (2nd version)

1967-1968. A different version than the '64 to '67 version, 50 watts, 2x7027A power tubes, column 2x15" cabinet.

1967-1968		$800	$900

B-15 R Portaflex Amp (reissue)

1990s. Reissue of '65 Portaflex 1x15", blue check.

1990s		$750	$850

MODEL YEAR FEATURES	EXC. COND. LOW	HIGH

B-15 S Portaflex Amp
1971-1977. 60 watts, 2x7027A power tubes, 1x12".

| 1971-1977 | $800 | $900 |

B-18 N Portaflex Amp
1964-1969. Bass, 50 watts, 1x18".

| 1964-1965 | $850 | $1,000 |
| 1966-1969 | $800 | $950 |

B-25 Amp
1969 only. 55 watts, 2 7027A power tubes, 2x15", no reverb, guitar amp.

| 1969 | $700 | $900 |

B-25 B Bass Amp
1969-1980. Bass amp, 55 watts, 2 7027A power tubes, 2x15".

| 1969 | $700 | $900 |

B-50 R Rocket Bass Amp (reissue)
1996-2005. 50 watts, 1x12" combo, vintage-style blue check cover.

| 1996-2005 | $250 | $300 |

B-100 R Rocket Bass Amp (reissue)
1996-present. Solidstate, 100 watts, 1x15" combo bass amp, vintage-style blue check cover.

| 1996-1999 | $300 | $350 |

B-3158 B Bass Amp
1990s. Solidstate, 100 watts, 1x15", black vinyl, black grille, large A logo.

| 1990s | $500 | $575 |

BT-15 Amp
1966-1968. Ampeg introduced solidstate amps in '66, the same year as Fender. Solidstate, 50 watts, 1x15", generally used as a bass amp. The BT-15D has dual 1x15" cabinets. The BT-15C is a 2x15" column portaflex cabinet.

| 1966-1968 | $275 | $350 |

BT-18 Amp
1966-1968. Ampeg introduced solidstate amps in '66, the same year as Fender. Solidstate, 50 watts, 1x18", generally used as a bass amp. The BT-18D has dual 1x15" cabinets. The BT-18C is a 2x18" column portaflex cabinet.

| 1966-1968 | $225 | $300 |

ET-1 Echo Twin Amp
1961-1964. Tube, 30 watts, 1x12", stereo reverb.

| 1961-1964 | $575 | $700 |

ET-2 Super Echo Twin Amp
1962-1964. Tube, 2x12", 30 watts, stereo reverb.

| 1962-1964 | $625 | $750 |

G-12 Gemini I Amp
1964-1971. Tube, 1x12", 22 watts, reverb.

| 1964-1971 | $475 | $575 |

G-15 Gemini II Amp
1965-1968. Tube, 30 watts, 1x15", reverb.

| 1965-1968 | $475 | $575 |

G-110 Amp
1978-1980. Solidstate, 20 watts, 1x10", reverb, tremolo.

| 1978-1980 | $225 | $350 |

G-115 Amp
1979-1980. Solidstate, 175 watts, 1x15" JBL, reverb and tremolo, designed for steel guitar.

| 1979-1980 | $275 | $400 |

G-212 Amp
1973-1980. Solidstate, 120 watts, 2x12".

| 1973-1980 | $325 | $450 |

GS-12 Rocket 2 Amp
1965-1968. This name replaced the Reverberocket 2 (II), 15 watts, 1x12".

| 1965-1968 | $450 | $500 |

GS-12-R Reverberocket 2 Amp
1965-1969. Tube, 1x12", 18 watts, reverb. Called the Reverberocket II in '68 and '69, then Rocket II in '69.

| 1965-1969 | $450 | $500 |

GS-15-R Gemini VI Amp
1966-1967. 30 watts, 1x15", single channel, considered to be "the accordion version" of the Gemini II.

| 1966-1967 | $475 | $550 |

GT-10 Amp
1971-1980. Solidstate, 15 watts, 1x10", basic practice amp with reverb.

| 1971-1980 | $200 | $300 |

GV-22 Gemini 22 Amp
1969-1972. Tube, 30 watts, 2x12".

| 1969-1972 | $425 | $525 |

J-12 Jet Amp
1958-1964, 1967-1972. 20 watts, 1x12", 6V6GT power tubes. Second addition, also known as the Jet II, was like the J-12 D Jet but with 12AX7s.

| 1958-1963 | | $375 | $500 |
| 1967-1972 Model reappears | $325 | $425 |

J-12 A Jet Amp
1964. Jet Amp with 7591A power tubes.

| 1964 | $375 | $500 |

J-12 T Jet Amp
1965. J-12 A with revised preamp.

| 1965 | $375 | $500 |

J-12 D Jet Amp
1966. Jet Amp with new solidstate rectifier.

| 1966 | $375 | $500 |

M-12 Mercury Amp
1957-1965. 15 watts, 2 channels, Rocket 1x12".

| 1957-1959 | $550 | $700 |
| 1960-1965 | $500 | $650 |

M-15 Big M Amp
1959-1965. 20 watts, 2x6L6 power, 1x15".

| 1959 | $550 | $700 |
| 1960-1965 | $500 | $650 |

R-12 Rocket Amp
1957-1963. 12 watts, 1x12", 1 channel.

| 1957-1963 | $475 | $600 |

R-12 B Rocket Amp
1964. 12 watts, 1x12", follow-up to the R-12 Rocket.

| 1964 | $475 | $600 |

R-12 R Reverberocket Amp
1961-1963. Rocket with added on-board reverb.

| 1961-1963 | $475 | $550 |

R-12 R-B Reverberocket Amp
1964. 7591A power tubes replace R-12-R 6V6 power tubes.

| 1964 | $475 | $550 |

Ampeg B-15-N

1960s Ampeg GV-22

1959 Ampeg J-12 Jet

AMPS

AMPS

1965 Ampeg R-12-R-T Reverberocket

Ampeg SVT

Ampeg SVT 350

MODEL YEAR	FEATURES	EXC. COND. LOW	HIGH
R-12 R-T Reverberocket Amp			
1965. 7591A or 7868 power tubes, revised preamp.			
1965		$475	$550
R-12 R Reverberocket Amp (reissue)			
1996-present. 50 watts, 2xEL34 power tubes, 1x12" (R-212R is 2x12").			
1996-1999		$350	$400
R-212 R Reverberocket Combo 50 Amp (reissue)			
1996-present. 50 watts, 2x12", all tube reissue, vintage-style blue check cover, vintage-style grille.			
1996-1999		$300	$375
SB-12 Portaflex Amp			
1965-1971. 22 watts, 1x12", designed for use with Ampeg's Baby Bass, black.			
1965-1971		$550	$700
SBT Amp			
1969-1971. 120 watts, 1x15", bass version of SST Amp.			
1969-1971		$650	$800
SE-412 Cabinet			
1996-1999. 4x12" speakers.			
1996-1999		$275	$350
SJ-12 R/RT Super Jet Amp			
1996-present. 50 watts, tube, 1x12", SJ-12 RT has tremolo added.			
1996-1999		$275	$350
SS-35 Amp			
1987-1992. Solidstate, 35 watts, 1x12", black vinyl, black grille, large A logo.			
1987-1992		$125	$200
SS-70 Amp			
1987-1990. Solidstate, 70 watts, 1x12".			
1987-1990		$275	$350
SS-70 C Amp			
1987-1992. Solidstate, 70 watts, 2x10", chorus, black vinyl, black grille, large A logo.			
1987-1992		$275	$350
SVT Bass Head Amp			
1969-1985. 300 watt head only.			
1969	Stones World-Tour assoc.	$2,000	$2,200
1970-1972		$1,500	$2,000
1973-1979		$1,300	$1,500
1980-1985		$1,200	$1,300
SVT Bass Cabinets			
1969-1985. Two 8x10" cabs only.			
1969-1985		$600	$1,000
SVT Bass Amp Set			
1969-1985. 300 watt head with matching dual 8x10" cabs.			
1969	Stones World-Tour assoc.	$3,000	$3,400
1970-1972	Original matching set	$2,500	$3,200
1973-1979	Original matching set	$2,300	$2,700
1980-1985	Original matching set	$2,200	$2,500

MODEL YEAR	FEATURES	EXC. COND. LOW	HIGH
SVT-4 Pro Bass Head Amp			
1997-present. Hybrid rack-mountable, all tube preamp, MOS-FET power section yielding, 1600 watts.			
1997-2003		$750	$800
SVT-100 T Bass Combo Amp			
1990-1992. Solidstate, ultra-compact bass combo, 100 watts, 2x8".			
1990-1992		$375	$450
SVT-200 T Head Amp			
1987 only. Solidstate, 200 watts to 8 ohms or 320 watts to 4 ohms.			
1987		$400	$475
SVT-350 Head Amp			
1995-present. Solidstate head, 350 watts, graphic EQ.			
1990s		$400	$475
SVT-400 Head Amp			
1987-1997. Solidstate, 400 watts per side, rack-mountable head with advanced (in '87) technology.			
1990s		$400	$550
SVT-AV Anniversary Edition Amp			
2001		$1,050	$1,150
SVT-II Pro Bass Head Amp			
1992-present. 300 watts, rack-mountable, all tube circuit similar to original SVT, black metal.			
1992-1999		$1,000	$1,200
SVT-III Pro Bass Head Amp			
1993-present. Tube preamp section and MOS-FET power section, 350 watts, rack-mountable, black metal.			
1993-2003		$550	$700
V-2 Amp Set			
1971-1980. 60 watt head with 4x12" cab, black tolex.			
1971-1980		$650	$850
V-2 Head Amp			
1971-1980. 60 watt tube head.			
1971-1980		$375	$450
V-4 B Bass Head Amp			
1972-1980. Bass version of V-4 without reverb.			
1972-1980		$450	$600
V-4 Cabinet			
1970s. Single 4x12" cabinet only.			
1970-1980		$325	$400
V-4 Amp Stack			
1970-1980. 100 watts, wih dual 4x12" cabs.			
1970-1980	Head and cabs	$900	$1,050
1970-1980	Head only	$450	$600
V-7 SC Amp			
1981-1985. Tube, 100 watts, 1x12", master volume, channel switching, reverb.			
1981-1985		$450	$600
VH-70 Amp			
1991-1992. 70 watts, 1x12" combo with channel switching.			
1991-1992		$300	$350
VH-140 C Amp			
1992-1995. Varying Harmonics (VH) with Chorus (C), two 70-watt channel stereo, 2x12".			
1992-1995		$350	$400

MODEL YEAR	FEATURES	EXC. COND. LOW	HIGH

VH-150 Head Amp
1991-1992. 150 watts, channel-switchable, reverb.

| 1991-1992 | | $325 | $375 |

VL-502 Amp
1991-1995. 50 watts, channel-switchable, all tube.

| 1991-1995 | | $350 | $400 |

VL-1001 Head Amp
1991-1993. 100 watts, non-switchable channels, all tube.

| 1991-1993 | | $350 | $400 |

VL-1002 Head Amp
1991-1995. 100 watts, channel-switchable, all tube.

| 1991-1995 | | $400 | $450 |

VT-22 Amp
1970-1980. 100 watt combo version of V-4, 2x12".

| 1970-1980 | | $600 | $700 |

VT-40 Amp
1971-1980. 60 watt combo, 4x10".

| 1971-1980 | | $600 | $700 |

VT-60 Combo Amp
1989-1991. Tube, 6L6 power, 60 watts, 1x12".

| 1989-1991 | | $475 | $600 |

VT-60 Head Amp
1989-1991. Tube head only, 6L6 power, 60 watts.

| 1989-1991 | | $375 | $500 |

VT-120 Combo Amp
1989-1992. Tube, 6L6 power, 120 watts, 1x12", also offered as head only.

| 1989-1992 | | $525 | $650 |

VT-120 Head Amp
1989-1992. 120 watts, 6L6 tube head.

| 1989-1992 | | $425 | $550 |

Anderson Amplifiers

1993-present. Tube amps and combos built by Jack Anderson in Gig Harbor, Washington.

Aria/Aria Pro II

1960-present. The Japanese instrument builder offered a range of amps from around '79 to '89.

Ashdown Amplification

1999-present. Founded in England by Mark Gooday after he spent several years with Trace Elliot, Ashdown offers amps, combos, and cabinets.

Audiovox

Ca.1935-ca.1950. Paul Tutmarc's Audiovox Manufacturing, of Seattle, Washington, was a pioneer in electric lap steels, basses, guitars and amps.

Auralux

2000-present. Founded by Mitchell Omori and David Salzmann, Auralux builds effects and tube amps in Highland Park, Illinois.

Bacino

2002-present. Tube combo amps, heads and cabinets built by Mike Bacino in Arlington Heights, Illinois.

Bad Cat Amplifier Company

1999-present. Founded in Corona, California by James and Debbie Heidrich, Bad Cat offers class A combo amps, heads, cabinets and effects.

Baldwin

Piano maker Baldwin offered amplifiers from 1965 to '70. The amps were solidstate with organ-like pastel-colored pushbutton switches.

Exterminator Amp
1965-1970. Solidstate, 100 watts, 2x15"/2x12"/2x7", 4' vertical combo cabinet, reverb and tremolo, Supersound switch and slide controls.

| 1965-1970 | | $525 | $625 |

Model B1 Bass Amp
1965-1970. Solidstate, 45 watts, 1x15"/1x12", 2 channels.

| 1965-1970 | | $225 | $275 |

Model B2 Bass Amp
1965-1970. Solidstate, 35 watts, 1x15", 2 channels.

| 1965-1970 | | $200 | $250 |

Model C1 Custom (Professional) Amp
1965-1970. Solidstate, 45 watts, 2x12", reverb and tremolo, Supersound switch and slide controls.

| 1965-1970 | | $275 | $325 |

Model C2 Custom Amp
1965-1970. Solidstate, 40 watts, 2x12", reverb and tremolo.

| 1960s | | $225 | $275 |

Barcus-Berry

1964-present. Pickup maker Barcus-Berry offered a line of amps from '75 to '79.

Basson

2001-present. Speaker cabinets for guitar, bass and PA made by Victor Basson in Carlsbad, California.

Bedrock

1984-1997. Tube amp company founded by Brad Jeter and Ron Pinto in Nashua, New Hampshire. They produced 50 amps carrying the brand name Fred before changing the company name to Bedrock in '86. Around '88, Jay Abend joined the company, eventually becoming President. In '88, Evan Cantor joined the company as an amp designer. In '90, Jeter left Bedrock and, shortly after, Pinto and Abend moved the company to Farmington, Massachusetts. The company closed in '97.

Behringer

1989-present. Founded in Germany by Uli Behringer, offering a full line of professional audio products. In '98 they added tube, solidstate, and modeling amps. They also offer effects and guitars.

Ampeg SVT-4 Pro

Ashdown Peacemaker 60

Bad Cat Mini Cat

Blue Tone Pro 30M

Callaham EL34 Amp

Carr Mercury

Blue Tone Amplifiers

2002-present. Founded by Alex Cooper in Worcestershire, England, Blue Tone offers professional grade, production amps employing their virtual valve technology.

Bogen

1960s. Power and PA tube amps not built for guitar but used by some 1960s/1970s bands.

Bogner

1988-present. Tube combos, amp heads, and speaker cabinets from builder Reinhold Bogner of North Hollywood, California.

Brand X

2004-present. Small solidstate combo amps from Fender Musical Instruments Corporation.

Bruno (Tony)

1995-present. Tube combos, amp heads, and speaker cabinets from builder Tony Bruno of Cairo, New York.

Budda

1995-present. Amps, combos, and cabinets from San Rafael, California. They also produce effects pedals.

Burriss

2001-present. Bob Burriss builds custom and production guitar and bass tube amps, bass preamps and speaker cabinets in Lexington, Kentucky. He also builds effects.

Callaham

1989-present. Tube amp heads built by Bill Callaham in Winchester, Virginia. He also builds solidbody electric guitars.

Carl Martin

1993-present. In '05, the Denmark-based guitar effects company added tube combo amps.

Carlsbro

1959-present. Guitar, bass, and keyboard combo amps, heads and cabinets from Carlsbro Electronics Limited of Nottingham, England. They also offer PA amps and speaker cabinets.

Carr Amplifiers

1998-present. Steve Carr started producing amps in his Chapel Hill, North Carolina amp repair business in '98. The company is now located in Pittsboro, North Carolina, and makes tube combo amps, heads, and cabinets.

Hammerhead Amp
2000-present. Class A, 2 EL34 power tubes, 25 watts with 1x12", 25 watts with 2x10" or 25 watts with 2x12".

Model Year	Features	Low	High
2000-2002	1x12"	$950	$1,000

Model Year	Features	Low	High
2000-2002	2x10"	$1,000	$1,100
2003	2x12"	$1,050	$1,150

Imperial Combo Amp
2002-2004. 60 watts, with 1x15", 2x12" or 4x10".

2002-2004	1x15"	$1,450	$1,650
2002-2004	2x12"	$1,450	$1,650
2002-2004	4x10"	$1,550	$1,750

Rambler Combo Amp
1999-present. Class A, 2x6L6 power tubes, 28 watts with 1x12", 2x10", 2x12" or 1x15" speakers.

1999-2003	1x12"	$1,250	$1,450
1999-2003	1x15"	$1,350	$1,550
1999-2003	2x10"	$1,350	$1,550
1999-2003	2x12"	$1,350	$1,550

Slant 6V (Dual 6V6) Amp
1998-present. 40 watts, 2 channel, combo amp, 2x12" or 1x15", also available as a head.

1998-2002		$1,550	$1,650

Carvin

1946-present. Founded in Los Angeles by Lowell C. Kiesel who sold guitars and amps under the Kiesel name until late-'49, when the Carvin brand is introduced. They added small tube amps to their product line in '47 and today offer a variety of models. They also build guitars and basses.

Chicago Blues Box/Butler Custom Sound

2001-present. Tube combo amps built by Dan Butler of Butler Custom Sound in Elmhurst, Illinois.

Clark Amplification

1995-present. Tweed-era replica tube amplifiers from builder Mike Clark, of Cayce, South Carolina. He also makes effects.

Tyger Amp
2000-present. Classic tweed Fender 5E7 Bandmaster circuit, 3x10", 35 watts. Also available with optional 3-knob reverb and 3-position power attenuator.

2000	Non-reverb	$1,000	$1,200
2000	Reverb	$1,200	$1,400

CMI

1976-1977. Amps made by Marshall for Cleartone Musical Instruments of Birmingham, England. Mainly PA amps, but two tube heads and one combo amp were offered.

CMI Electronics

Late-1960s-1970s. CMI branded amplifiers designed to replace the Gibson Kalamazoo-made amps that ceased production in '67 when Gibson moved the electronics lab to Chicago, Illinois.

Sabre Reverb 1
Late-1960s-early-1970s. Keyboard amp, 1x15" and side-mounted horn, utilized mid- to late-'60s cabinets and grilles, look similar to mid-late '60s Gibson black tolex and Epiphone gray amp series, black or gray tolex and silver grille.

1970		$100	$150

MODEL YEAR	FEATURES	EXC. COND. LOW	HIGH

Comins

1992-present. Archtop luthier Bill Comins, of Willow Grove, Pennsylvania, introduced a Comins combo amp, built in collaboration with George Alessandro, in '03.

Cornell/Plexi

Amps based on the '67 Marshall plexi chassis built by Denis Cornell in the United Kingdom. Large Plexi logo on front.

Cosmosound

Italy's Cosmosound made small amps with Leslie rotating drums in the late '60s and '70s. They also made effects pedals.

Crafter USA

1986-present. Giant Korean guitar and bass manufacturer Crafter also builds an acoustic guitar amp.

Crate

1979-present. Solidstate and tube amplifiers distributed by St. Louis Music.

Solidstate Amp

Various student to mid-level amps, up to 150 watts.

1970s		$75	$175
1980s		$75	$175

Vintage Club 50/VC-50 Amp

1994-1999. 50-watt tube head.

1994-1999		$275	$325

Vintage Club 5212/VC-5212 Amp

1994-2001. 50 watts, 2x12" tube combo, white (earlier) or black vinyl cover, black grille.

1994-2001		$225	$300

Vintage Club 5310/VC-5310

1994-1997. 50 watts, all tube, 3x10".

1994-1997		$250	$300

Cruise Audio Systems

1999-present. Founded by Mark Altekruse, Cruise offers amps, combos, and cabinets built in Cuyahoga Falls, Ohio

Da Vinci

Late-1950s-early-1960s. Another one of several private brands (for example, Unique, Twilighter, Titano, etc.) that Magnatone made for teaching studios and accordian companies.

Model 250 Amp

1958-1962. Similar to Magnatone Model 250 with about 20 watts and 1x12".

1958-1962		$550	$650

Danelectro

1946-1969, 1997-present. Founded in Red Bank, New Jersey, by Nathan I. "Nate" or "Nat" Daniel. His first amps were made for Montgomery Ward in '47, and in '48 he began supplying Silvertone Amps for Sears. His own amps were distributed by Targ and Dinner as Danelectro and S.S. Maxwell brands. In '96,

the Evets Corporation, of San Clemente, California, reintroduced the Danelectro brand on effects, amps, basses and guitars. In early '03, Evets discontinued the guitar and amp lines, but still offers effects.

Cadet Amp

Tube, 6 watts, 1x6".

1955-1959		$200	$250
1960-1963		$150	$200
1964-1966		$125	$175
1967-1969		$100	$150

Centurion Model 275 Amp

2 6V6 power tubes for approximately 15-18 watts, 1x12", gray cover.

1959-1960		$225	$325

Corporal Model 132 Amp

Early-1960s. Low power, 2x8".

1960s		$250	$300

DM-10 Amp

Five watts, 1x6".

1960s		$125	$175

DM-25 Amp

35 watts, 1x12", reverb and tremolo.

1960s		$300	$375

DS-50 Amp

1967-1969. 50 watts, 3x10" piggyback set, reverb and tremolo, suitable for bass accordion.

1967-1969		$400	$500

DS-100 Amp

1967-1969. 100 watts, piggyback, 6x10" Jensens, reverb, tremolo, suitable for bass accordion.

1967-1969		$500	$575

Model 68 Special Amp

1950s. 20 watts, 1x12", light tweed-fabric cover, light grille, leather handle, script Danelectro plexi-plate logo.

1950s		$300	$400

Model 98 Twin 12 Amp (Series D)

1954-ca.1957. Blond tweed-style cover, brown control panel, 2x12", vibrato speed and strength, rounded front Series D.

1954-1957		$550	$750

Model 217 Twin 15 Amp

1960s. Combo amp, 100 watts, 2x15" Jensen C15P speakers, black cover, white-silver grille, 2 channels with tremolo.

1962		$450	$550

Viscount Model 142 Amp

Late-1950s. Combo amp, lower watts, 1x12", light cover, brown grille, vibrato.

1959		$325	$425

Dean

1976-present. Acoustic, electric, and bass amps made overseas. They also offer guitars, banjos, mandolins, and basses.

Dean Markley

The string and pickup manufacturer added a line of amps in 1983. Distributed by Kaman, they now offer combo guitar and bass amps and PA systems.

Chicago Blues Box Kingston

Cruise MQ4212

Danelectro Model 78 Maestro

AMPS

Demeter TGA-2.1 Inverter

Dr. Z Maz 18

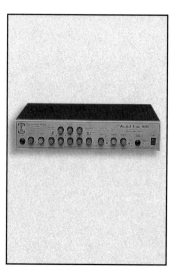

Eden WT800 Time Traveler

MODEL YEAR	FEATURES	EXC. COND. LOW	HIGH

K Series Amp

1980s. All solidstate, various models include K-15 (10 watts, 1x6"), K-20/K-20X (10 to 20 watts, 1x8", master volume, overdrive switch), K-50 (25 watts, 1x10", master volume, reverb), K-75 (35 watts, 1x12", master volume, reverb).

1986	K-15, K-20/K-20X	$65	$75
1986	K-50	$75	$100
1986	K-75	$100	$125

Decca

Mid-1960s. Small student-level amps made in Japan by Teisco and imported by Decca Records. They also offered guitars and a bass.

Demeter

1980-present. James Demeter founded the company as Innovative Audio and renamed it Demeter Amplification in '90. Located in Van Nuys, California. First products were direct boxes and by '85, amps were added. Currently they build amp heads, combos, and cabinets. They also have pro audio gear and guitar effects.

Diaz

Early-1980s-2002. Cesar Diaz restored amps for many of rock's biggest names, often working with them to develop desired tones. Along the way he produced his own line of high-end custom amps and effects. Diaz died in '02; his family announced plans to resume production of effects in '04.

Dickerson

1937-1947. Dickerson was founded by the Dickerson brothers in 1937, primarily for electric lap steels and small amps. Instruments were also private branded for Cleveland's Oahu company, and for the Gourley brand. By '47, the company changed ownership and was renamed Magna Electronics (Magnatone).

Oasis Amp

1940s-1950s. Blue pearloid cover, 1x10", low wattage, Dickerson silk-screen logo on grille with Hawaiian background.

| 1940s | Blue pearloid | $150 | $275 |

Dinosaur

2004-present. Student/budget level amps and guitar/amp packs, imported by Eleca International.

Dr. Z

1988-present. Mike Zaite started producing his Dr. Z line of amps in the basement of the Music Manor in Maple Heights, Ohio. The company is now located in its own larger facility in the same city. Dr. Z offers combo amps, heads and cabinets.

DST Engineering

2001-present. Jeff Swanson and Bob Dettorre build their amp combos, heads and cabinets in Beverly, Massachusetts. They also build reverb units.

MODEL YEAR	FEATURES	EXC. COND. LOW	HIGH

Duca Tone

The Duca Tone brand was distributed by Lo Duca Brothers, Milwaukee, Wisconsin, which also distributed EKO guitars in the U.S.

Tube Amp

12 watts, 1x12".

| 1950s | | $400 | $500 |

Dumble

1963-present. Made by Howard Alexander Dumble, an early custom-order amp maker from California. Initial efforts were a few Mosrite amps for Semie Moseley. First shop was in '68 in Santa Cruz, California.

Overdrive Special Amp and Cabinet

100 watts, 1x12", known for durability, cabinets vary.

1970s	Black	$13,000	$20,000
1980s	Black	$13,000	$20,000
1990s	Black	$13,000	$20,000

Earth Sound Research

Earth Sound was a product of ISC Audio of Huntington, New York, and offered a range of amps, cabinets and PA gear starting in the '70s.

2000 G Half-Stack Amp

1970s. 100 watts plus cab.

| 1970s | | $475 | $650 |

Amp

Various lower to mid-level KT and MV Series amplifiers.

| 1970s | | $250 | $350 |

Cabinet

| 1970s | Various models | $175 | $250 |

Eden

1976-present. Founded by David Nordschow in Minnesota as a custom builder, Eden now offers a full line of amps, combos, and cabinets for the bassist, built in Mundelein, Illinois. In '02, the brand became a division of U.S. Music Corp (Washburn, Randall). They also produce the Nemesis brand of amps.

Egnater

1980-present. Tube amps, combos, preamps and cabinets built in Michigan by Bruce Egnater.

EKO

1959-1985, 2000-present. In '67 EKO added amps to their product line, offering three piggyback and four combo amps, all with dark covering, dark grille, and the EKO logo. The amp line may have lasted into the early '70s. Since about 2000, EKO Asian-made, solidstate guitar and bass amps are again available. They also make basses and guitars.

Eleca

2004-present. Student level imported combo amps, Eleca logo on bottom center of grille.

MODEL YEAR	FEATURES	EXC. COND. LOW	HIGH

Electar

1996-present. The Gibson owned Electar brand offers tube and solidstate amps, PA gear and wireless systems. Epiphone had a line of Electar amps in the 1930s.

Electro-Harmonix

1968-1981, 1996-present. Electro-Harmonix offered a few amps to go with its line of effects. See Effects section for more company info.

Freedom Brothers Amp

Introduced in 1977. Small AC/DC amp with 2x5 1/2" speakers. E-H has reissued the similar Freedom amp.

| 1977 | | $150 | $175 |

Mike Matthews Dirt Road Special Amp

25 watts, 1x12" Celestion, built-in Small Stone phase shifter.

| 1977 | | $300 | $425 |

Elk

Late-1960s. Japanese-made by Elk Gakki Co., Ltd. Many were copies of American designs. They also offered guitars and effects.

Custom EL 150L Amp

Late-1960s. Piggyback set, all-tube with head styled after very early Marshall and cab styled after large vertical Fender cab.

| 1968 | | $350 | $425 |

Guitar Man EB 105 (Super Reverb) Amp

Late-1960s. All-tube, reverb, copy of blackface Super Reverb.

| 1968 | | $275 | $350 |

Twin Amp 60/Twin Amp 50 EB202

Late-1960s. All-tube, reverb, copy of blackface Dual Showman set (head plus horizontal cab).

| 1968 | | $350 | $425 |

Viking 100 VK 100 Amp

Late-1960s. Piggyback set, head styled after very early Marshall and cab styled after very large vertical Fender cab.

| 1968 | | $350 | $425 |

Elpico

1960s. Made in Europe, PA tube amp heads sometimes used for guitar.

PA Power Tube Amp

1960s. Tubes, 20-watt, metal case, 3 channels, treble and bass control, 2 speaker outs on front panel, Elpico logo on front, small Mexican characterization logo on front.

| 1960s | | $350 | $500 |

Emery Sound

1997-present. Founded by Curt Emery in El Cerrito, California, Emery Sound specializes in custom-made low wattage tube amps.

Epiphone

1928-present. Epiphone offered amps into the mid-'70s and reintroduced them in '91 with the EP series. Currently they offer tube and solidstate amps.

E-30 B Amp

1972-1975. Solidstate model offered similarly to Gibson G-Series (not GA-Series), 30 watts, 2x10", 4 knobs.

| 1972-1975 | | $175 | $225 |

E-60 Amp

1972-1975. Solidstate, 3 watts, 1x10", volume and tone knobs.

| 1972-1975 | | $80 | $110 |

E-70 Amp

1971-1975. Solidstate, tremolo, 1x10", 3 knobs.

| 1971-1975 | | $90 | $135 |

E-1051 Amp

1970s. Tube practice amp, 1x10".

| 1970s | | $175 | $200 |

EA-12 RVT Futura Amp

1962-1967. Low- to mid-power, 4x8", '60s gray tolex, light grille.

| 1962-1967 | | $700 | $825 |

EA-14 RVT Ensign Amp

1965-1969. Gray tolex, silver-gray grille, 50 watts, 2x12", split C logo.

| 1965-1969 | | $475 | $600 |

EA-15 RVT Zephyr Amp

1961-1965. 14 or 20 watts, 1x15", gray tolex, light grille, split C logo on panel, tremolo and reverb, script Epiphone logo lower right grille.

| 1961-1965 | | $325 | $550 |

EA-16 RVT Regent Amp

1965-1969. 25 watts, 1x12", gray vinyl, gray grille, tremolo, reverb. Called the Lancer in first year.

| 1965-1969 | | $425 | $550 |

EA-26 RVT Electra Amp

1965-1969. Gray tolex, reverb, tremolo, footswitch, 1x12".

| 1965-1969 | | $320 | $450 |

EA-32 RVT Comet Amp

1965-1967. 1x10", tremolo, reverb.

| 1965-1967 | | $325 | $450 |

EA-33 RVT Galaxie Amp

1963-1964. Gray tolex, gray grille, 1x10".

| 1963-1964 | | $424 | $500 |

EA-35 Devon Amp

1961-1963. 1x10" until '62, 1x12" with tremolo in '63.

| 1961-1963 | | $325 | $375 |

EA-50 Pacemaker Amp

1961-1969. 1x8" until '62, 1x10" after. EA-50T with tremolo added in '63. Non-tremolo version dropped around '67.

| 1961-1969 | | $200 | $275 |

EA-300 RVT Embassy Amp

1965-1969. 90 watts, 2x12", gray vinyl, gray grille, tremolo, reverb.

| 1965-1969 | | $575 | $700 |

Emery Sound Microbaby

Epiphone Electar Zephyr

1966 Epiphone EA-14 RVT Ensign

AMPS

Fender Acoustasonic SFX II

Fender Deluxe FM65R

Fender Champ 12

| MODEL | | EXC. COND. | |
YEAR	FEATURES	LOW	HIGH

EA-500T Panorama
1963-1967. 65 watts, head and large cabinet, tremolo, 1x15" and 1x10" until '64, 1x15" and 2x10" after.

1964-1967		$325	$650

EA-600 RVT Maxima Amp
1966-1969. Solidstate Epiphone version of Gibson GSS-100, gray vinyl, gray grille, two 2x10" cabs and hi-fi stereo-style amp head.

1966-1969		$525	$600

Fender

1946-present. Leo Fender's early manufacturing focus was on PA systems and he attempted to improve the inferior offerings of the day. Western Swing and Hawaiian music were popular at the time and he wanted to supply those musicians with superior products. Fender contributed many ground-breaking instruments, but Leo's primary passion was amplifiers, and of all his important contributions to musicians, none exceed those he made to the electric tube amplifier.

Tweed Fender amp circuits are highly valued because they defined the tones of rock and roll. Blackface models remained basically the same until mid-'67. Some silverface circuits remained the same as the blackface circuits, while others were changed in the name of reliability. Fender amps ruled the business until things changed in the late-'60s when powerful arena amps were introduced by the likes of Marshall.

Price Guide values are for all original, excellent condition amps. Small differences in an amp's condition can generate larger differences in selling prices. Non-original speakers will significantly reduce a pre-'68 amp's value. Reconed speakers will reduce the value, but a reconed speaker is preferable to a replacement speaker. Multi-speaker amps generally have matching speaker codes. Different speaker codes require explanation. Fender leather handles are often broken and replaced. A replacement handle drops the value of an amp. Tweed was not the best covering, being prone to stains and damage. Grille cloths should have no tears and a single tear can drop the value of an amp. Each Tweed amp should be evaluated on a case-by-case basis, and it is not unusual for a Tweed amp to have a wide range of values. Alnico speaker replacement is more significant than ceramic speaker replacement. Fender converted to ceramic about '62. Speaker replacement is of less concern in post-'70 Fender amps.

From 1953 to '67, Fender stamped a two-letter date code on the paper tube chart glued inside the cabinet. The first letter was the year (C='53, D='54, etc.) with the second the month (A=January, etc.).

The speaker code found on the frame of an original speaker will identify the manufacturer, and the week and year that the speaker was assembled. The speaker code is typically six (sometimes seven)

digits. The first three digits represent the Electronics Industries Association (E.I.A.) source code which identifies the manufacturer. For example, a speaker code 220402 indicates a Jensen speaker (220), made in '54 (4) during the second week (02) of that year. This sample speaker also has another code stamped on the frame. ST654 P15N C4964 indicates the model of the speaker, in this case it is a P15N 15" speaker. The sample speaker also had a code stamped on the speaker cone, 4965 l, which indicates the cone number. All of these codes help identify the originality of the speaker. The value ranges provided in the Guide are for amps with the original speaker and original speaker cone.

Most Fender speakers from the '50s will be Jensens (code 220). By the late-'50s other suppliers were used. The supplier codes are: Oxford (465), C.T.S. (137), Utah (328). JBL speakers were first used in the late-'50s Vibrasonic, and then in the Showman series, but JBL did not normally have a E.I.A. source code. An amp's speaker code should be reconciled with other dating info when the amp's original status is being verified.

General Production Eras:
Diagonal tweed era.
Brown tolex era.
Blackface era.
Silverface era with raised Fender logo with underlining tail.
Silverface era with raised Fender logo without underlining tail.
Silverface era with raised Fender logo with small MADE IN USA designation.

Nameplate and Logo Attribution:
Fender nameplate with city but without model name (tweed era).
Fender nameplate without city or model name (tweed era).
Fender nameplate with model name noted (tweed era).
Fender flat logo (brown era).
Fender script raised logo (blackface era).

30 Combo Amp
1979-1982. Tube amp, 30 watts, 2x10" or 1x12".

1979-1982		$475	$575

75 Combo Amp
1980-1983. Tube, 75 watts, 1x15".

1980-1983		$425	$475

85 Combo Amp
1988-1992. Solidstate, 85 watts, 1x10", black cover, silver grille.

1988-1992		$250	$300

800 Pro Bass Head Amp
2004-present. Rack-mountable, 800 watts, 5-band EQ.

2004		$500	$550

MODEL YEAR	FEATURES	EXC. COND. LOW	HIGH

Acoustasonic 30/30 DSP Amp

2000-present. Smaller portable combo Acoustasonic, brown tolex, wheat grille. Upgrade model includes DSP (Digital Signal Processor) effects.

2000-2004		$200	$225

Acoustasonic Junior/Junior DSP Amp

1998-present. Acoustic technology, 2x40 watts, 2x8" and Piezo horn, brown tolex and wheat grille.

1998-2003		$275	$350

Acoustasonic SFX/SFX II Amp

1998-present. SFX technology, 32 stereo digital present effects, 2x80 watts, 1x10" and 1x8", and Piezo horn, brown tolex and wheat grille.

1998-2002		$400	$450

AmpCan Amp

1997-present. Cylindrical can-shaped battery powered portable amp.

1997-2004		$100	$140

Bandmaster Amp

1953-1974. Wide-panel 1x15" combo '53-'54, narrow-panel 3x10" combo '55-'60, tolex '60, brownface with 1x12" piggyback speaker cabinet '61, 2x12" '62, blackface '62-'67, silverface '68-'74.

The Fender tweed 4x10" Bassman and tweed 3x10" Bandmaster amps are highly sensitive to condition. Because there are so few that are truly excellent, the price ranges listed may be misleading. Most Bassman amps are at best very good minus (VG-) because their tweed is so damaged and stained. It is also rare to find the original speakers, and if the frames are original, they have often been reconed. 4x10" Bassman and 3x10" Bandmasters that are excellent plus plus (Exc++) may have price ranges that are much higher than the values listed. It is estimated that 90% of the vintage 4x10" Bassman are really only VG or less. Because of the extreme condition factor for these tweed amps, the prices below include amps in very good (VG) condition. Therefore the condition for these listed amps is VG to Exc. Exc+ will be more than the values listed here. As per other high-end collectible, each amp should be taken on a case by case basis.

1953-1954	Tweed, 1x15"	$4,500	$5,000
1955-1958	Tweed, 3x10"	$6,500	$8,500
1959-1960	Matching trio of orig P10Rs	$1,600	$1,700
1959-1960	Tweed, 3x10"	$6,500	$9,000
1960	Brown tolex, 3x10"	$5,000	$5,500
1961	Rough white & oxblood, 1x12"	$2,000	$2,200
1961-1962	Rough white & oxblood, 2x12"	$1,900	$2,100
1963-1964	Smooth white & gold, 2x12"	$1,700	$1,900
1964-1967	Black tolex, 2x12"	$1,200	$1,400
1967-1969	Silverface, 2x12"	$900	$1,000
1970-1974	Silverface, 2x12"	$600	$800

Bandmaster Cabinet

1961-1975. 2x12" speakers.

1961-1963	Blond tolex	$750	$950
1964-1967	Blackface horizontal	$425	$550
1967-1970	Silverface vertical	$300	$350

Bandmaster Head Amp

1961-1975. Non-reverb model.

1961-1962	Rough white tolex	$900	$1,300
1963-1964	Smooth white tolex	$800	$1,100
1964-1967	Blackface, black tolex	$500	$700
1967-1969	Silverface	$400	$500
1970-1971	Silverface, black tolex	$350	$400

Bandmaster Reverb Amp

1968-1981. Cabinet for 2x12", 45 watts, silverface.

1968-1972		$900	$1,050
1973-1981		$800	$950

Bandmaster Reverb Head Amp

1968-1981. Reverb, 45 watts.

1968-1972		$500	$700
1973-1981		$400	$600

Bantam Bass Amp

1970-1972. 50 watts, large unusual 1x10" Yahama speaker.

1971-1972		$400	$550

Bassman Amp

1952-1971. Tweed TV front combo, 1x15" in '52, wide-panel '53-'54, narrow-panel and 4x10" '54-'60, tolex brownface with 1x12" in piggyback cabinet '61, 2x12" cabinet '61-'62, blackface '63-'67, silverface '67-'71, 2x15" cabinet '68-'71. Renamed the Bassman 50 in '72.

The Fender tweed 4x10" Bassman and tweed 3x10" Bandmaster amps are highly sensitive to condition. Because there are so few that are truly excellent, the price ranges listed may be misleading. Most Bassman amps are at best very good minus (VG-) because their tweed is so damaged and stained. It is also rare to find the original speakers, and if the frames are original, they have often been reconed. 4x10" Bassmans and 3x10" Bandmasters that are excellent plus plus (Exc++) may have price ranges that are much higher than the values listed. It is estimated that 90% of the vintage 4x10" Bassman are really only VG or less. Because of the extreme condition factor for these tweed amps, the prices below include amps in very good (VG) condition. Therefore the condition for these listed amps is VG to Exc. Exc+ will be more than the values listed here. As per other high-end collectibles, each amp should be taken on a case by case basis.

1952	TV front, 1x15"	$4,500	$5,000
1953-1954	Wide panel, 1x15"	$4,500	$5,000
1955-1957	Tweed, 4x10", 2 inputs	$6,500	$8,500
1957-1958	Tweed, 4x10", 4 inputs	$6,500	$8,500
1959-1960	Matching quad orig P10Qs	$1,800	$1,900
1959-1960	Tweed, 4x10", 4 inputs	$6,500	$9,000
1961	White 1x12", 6G6, tube	$2,500	$3,000
1962	White 1x12", 6G6A, s.s.	$2,300	$2,700
1963-1964	Smooth white 2x12", 6G6A/B	$2,100	$2,500

Fender Bandmaster (5E7)

1964 Fender Bandmaster head

Late-'50s Fender Bassman

AMPS

Fender Blues Junior

1960 Fender Champ

Fender Champ (5E1)

MODEL YEAR	FEATURES	EXC. COND. LOW	HIGH
1965-1966	AA165/AB165, black knobs	$1,300	$1,500
1967-1969	Silverface lg. vertical 2x15"	$900	$1,000
1970-1971	Silverface 2x15"	$600	$800

Bassman Cabinet
1961-early-1967. Blackface, 2x12" small horizontal cab, replaced in '67 with larger silverface vertical cab.

1961-1963	Blond tolex	$750	$950
1964-1967	Blackface	$425	$550
1967-1970	Silverface verticle	$300	$350

Bassman Head Amp
1961-1971. Bassman head only, no cabinet.

1961	White, 6G6, tube	$1,400	$1,600
1962	White, 6G6A, s.s.	$1,100	$1,300
1963-1964	Smooth white, 6G6A/B	$1,100	$1,300
1964	Blackface AA864, white knobs	$600	$800
1965-1967	AA165/AB165, black knobs	$550	$750
1967-1969	Silverface	$400	$500
1970-1971	Silverface, black tolex	$350	$400

Bassman '59 Reissue Amp
1990-present. Tube, 45 watts, 4x10", tweed covering.

1990s		$600	$650

Bassman Bassbreaker (Custom Shop) Amp
1998-2003. Classic Bassman 4x10" configuration. Not offered by 2004 when the '59 Bassman LTD was introduced.

1998-2003	2x12"	$775	$850
1998-2003	4x10"	$775	$850

Bassman 10 Amp
1972-1982. 4x10" combo, silverface and 50 watts for '72-'80, blackface and 70 watts after.

1972-1980	50 watts	$325	$450
1981-1982	70 watts	$350	$450

Bassman 20 Amp
1982-1985. Tubes, 20 watts, 1x15".

1982-1985		$225	$350

Bassman 25 Amp
2000-2005. Wedge shape, 1x10", 25 watts, 3-band EQ.

2000-2005		$150	$200

Bassman 50 Amp
1972-1976. 50 watts, 2x12".

1972-1976		$375	$425
1972-1976	Head only	$275	$350

Bassman 60 Amp
1972-1976, 2001-2005. 60 watts, 1x12".

1972-1976		$275	$375

Bassman 70 Amp
1977-1979. 70 watts, 2x15".

1977-1979		$400	$450

Bassman 100 Amp
1972-1979. Tube, 100 watts, 4x12".

1972-1979		$525	$575
1972-1979	Head only	$425	$450

MODEL YEAR	FEATURES	EXC. COND. LOW	HIGH

Bassman 135 Amp
1979-1983. Tube, 135 watts, 4x10".

1979-1983		$525	$575

Bassman 300 Head Amp
2002-2003, 2005-present. All tube, 300 watts, black cover, black metal grille.

2000-2003		$675	$750

Bassman 400 Combo Amp
2000-2004. Solidstate, 350 watts with 2x10" plus horn, combo, black cover, black metal grille.

2000-2004		$500	$600

Blues De Ville Amp
1993-1996. All tube Tweed Series, 60 watts, 4x10" (optional 2x12" in '94), reverb, high-gain channel, tweed cover (blond tolex optional '95 only).

1993-1996	Tweed, 4x10"	$450	$600
1994-1996	Tweed, 2x12"	$450	$600
1995	Blond tolex, 4x10"	$500	$625

Blues Deluxe Amp
1993-1996. All tube Tweed Series, 40 watts, 2 5881 output tubes, reverb, 1x12", tweed covering (blond tolex optional '95 only).

1993-1996	Tweed	$300	$400
1995	Blond	$375	$425

Blues Junior Amp
1995-present. All tube, 15 watts, 1x10", spring reverb, tweed in '95, black tolex with silver grille '96 on.

1995-2000		$300	$350

Bronco Amp
1968-1974, 1993-2001. 1x 8" speaker, all tube, 5 watts until '72, 6 watts for '72-'74, ('90s issue is 15 watts), solidstate, tweed covering (blond tolex was optional for '95 only).

1968-1974		$325	$375
1993-2001	15 watts, no reverb	$100	$175

Bullet Amp
1994-present. Solidstate, 15 watts, 1x8", with or without reverb.

1994-2000	With reverb	$100	$125
1994-2000	Without reverb	$75	$100

Capricorn Amp
1970-1972. Solidstate, 105 watts, 3x12".

1970-1972		$175	$300

Champ Amp
1953-1982. Renamed from the Champion 600. Tweed until '64, black tolex after, 3 watts in '53, 4 watts '54-'64, 5 watts '65-'71, 6 watts '72-'82, 1x6" until '57, 1x8" after.

1953-1954	Wide panel, 1x6"	$700	$900
1955-1956	Narrow panel, tweed, 1x6"	$800	$925
1956-1964	Narrow panel, tweed, 1x8"	$900	$1,100
1964	Old cab, black, 1x8", last F51	$750	$900
1964-1967	New cab, black tolex, 1x8", AA764	$450	$550
1968-1972	Silverface, 1x8"	$325	$375
1973-1982	Silverface, 1x8"	$300	$350

The **Vintage Guitar Price Guide** shows low to high values for items in all-original excellent condition, and, where applicable, with original case or cover.

MODEL YEAR	FEATURES	EXC. COND. LOW	HIGH

Champ II Amp
1982-1985. 18 watts, 1x10".

1982-1985		$325	$425

Champ 12 Amp
1986-1992. Tube, 12 watts, overdrive, reverb, 1x12".

| 1986-1992 | Black | $225 | $300 |
| 1986-1992 | Red, white, gray or snakeskin | $325 | $350 |

Champ 25 SE Amp
1992-1993. Hybrid solidstate and tube combo, 25 watts, 1x12".

| 1992-1993 | | $175 | $200 |

Champion 30/30 DSP Amp
1999-2003. Small solidstate combo, 30 watts, 1x8", reverb.

| 1999-2003 | | $75 | $125 |

Champion 110 Amp
1993-2000. Solidstate, 25 watts, 1x10", 2 channels, black tolex, silver grille.

| 1993-2000 | | $100 | $150 |

Champion 600 Amp
1949-1953. Replaced the Champion 800, 3 watts, 1x6", 2-tone tolex, TV front. Replaced by the Champ.

| 1949-1953 | | $700 | $800 |

Concert Amp
1960-1965, 1992-1995. Introduced with 40 watts and 4x10", brown tolex until '63, blackface '63-'65. In '62 white tolex was ordered by Webbs Music (CA) instead of the standard brown tolex. A wide range is noted for the rare white tolex, and each amp should be valued on a case-by-case basis. In '60, the very first brown tolex had a pink tint but only on the first year amps. Reissued in '92 with 60 watts and a 1x12".

1960	Brown (pink) tolex	$1,900	$2,400
1961-1963	Brown tolex	$1,900	$2,200
1962	White tolex (Webb Music)	$2,000	$3,500
1963-1965	Blackface	$1,400	$1,500

Concert Reverb (Pro Tube Series) Amp
2002-present. 4x10" combo, reverb, tremolo, overdrive.

| 2002-2004 | | $875 | $1,000 |

Concert 112 Amp
1982-1985. Tube, 60 watts, 1x12".

| 1982-1985 | | $525 | $625 |

Concert 210 Amp
1982-1985. Tube, 60 watts, 2x10".

| 1982-1985 | | $550 | $650 |

Concert 410 Amp
1982-1985. Tube, 60 watts, 4x10".

| 1982-1985 | | $600 | $700 |

Cyber Champ Amp
2004-present. 65 watts, 1x12", Cyber features.

| 2004 | | $250 | $325 |

Cyber Twin Combo Amp
2000-present.

| 2000-2003 | | $625 | $750 |

Deco-Tone (Custom Shop) Amp
2000s. Art-deco styling, all tube, 15 watts, 1x12", round speaker baffle opening, uses 6BQ5/ES84 power tubes.

| 2000s | | $900 | $1,000 |

Deluxe Amp
1948-1981. Name changed from Model 26 ('46-'48). 10 watts (15 by '54 and 20 by '63), 1x12", TV front with tweed '48-'53, wide-panel '53-'55, narrow-panel '55-'60, brown tolex with brownface '61-'63, black tolex with blackface '63-'66.

1948-1952	Tweed, TV front	$1,800	$2,300
1953-1954	Wide panel	$2,000	$2,500
1955-1956	Narrow panel, smaller cab	$2,500	$3,000
1956-1960	Narrow panel, slightly larger cab	$2,700	$3,100
1961-1963	Brown tolex	$1,200	$1,500
1964-1966	Black tolex	$1,000	$1,300

Deluxe Reverb Amp
1963-1981. 1x12", 20 watts, blackface '63-'67, silverface '68-'80, blackface with silver grille option introduced in mid-'80. Replaced by Deluxe Reverb II. Reissued as Deluxe Reverb '65 Reissue.

1963-1967	Blackface	$1,900	$2,200
1968-1972	Silverface	$1,000	$1,200
1973-1980	Silverface	$725	$1,075
1980-1981	Blackface	$725	$1,075

Deluxe Reverb (Solidstate) Amp
1966-1969. Part of Fender's early solidstate series.

| 1966-1969 | | $250 | $325 |

Deluxe Reverb '65 Reissue Amp
1993-present. Blackface reissue, 22 watts, 1x12".

| 1993-1999 | Black tolex | $525 | $625 |
| 1993-1999 | Blond (limited production) | $550 | $650 |

Deluxe Reverb II Amp
1982-1986. Updated Deluxe Reverb with 2 6V6 power tubes, all tube preamp section, black tolex, blackface, 20 watts, 1x12".

| 1982-1986 | | $600 | $700 |

Deluxe 85 Amp
1988-1993. Solidstate, 65 watts, 1x12", black tolex, silver grille, Red Knob Series.

| 1988-1993 | | $175 | $300 |

Deluxe 90 Amp
1999-2003. Solidstate, 90 watts, 1x12" combo, DSP added in '02.

| 1999-2002 | | $200 | $225 |
| 2002-2003 | DSP option | $250 | $300 |

Deluxe 112 Amp
1992-1995. Solidstate, 65 watts, 1x12", black tolex with silver grille.

| 1992-1995 | | $200 | $300 |

Deluxe 112 Plus Amp
1995-2000. 90 watts, 1x12", channel switching.

| 1995-2000 | | $225 | $325 |

Fender Concert (6G12)

AMPS

Fender Concert II 112

1955 Fender Deluxe

AMPS

Fender Hot Rod Deluxe

'70s Fender Musicmaster Bass

Fender Harvard

MODEL YEAR	FEATURES	EXC. COND. LOW	HIGH

Dual Professional Amp

1994-2002. Custom Shop amp, all tube, point-to-point wiring, 100 watts, 2x12" Celestion Vintage 30s, fat switch, reverb, tremolo, white tolex, oxblood grille.

1994-2002		$1,400	$1,600

Dual Showman Amp

1962-1969. Called the Double Showman for the first year. White tolex (black available from '64), 2x15", 85 watts. Reintroduced '87-'94 as solidstate, 100 watts, optional speaker cabs.

1962	Rough blond and oxblood	$2,700	$3,000
1963	Smooth blond and wheat	$2,600	$2,700
1964-1967	Black tolex, horizontal cab	$1,800	$2,200
1968	Blackface, large vertical cab	$1,000	$1,400
1968-1969	Silverface	$900	$1,100

Dual Showman Head Amp

1962-1969. Dual Showman head with output transformer for 2x15" (versus single Showman's 1x15" output ohms), blackface '62-'67, the late-'67 model logo stipulated "Dual Showman" while the '62-early-'67 head merely stated Showman (could be a single Showman or Dual Showman), '68-'69 silverface.

1962-1963	Blond	$1,400	$1,700
1964-1968	"Dual Showman" blackface	$1,050	$1,250
1968-1969	Silverface	$500	$650

Dual Showman Reverb Amp

1968-1981. Black tolex with silver grille, silverface, 100 watts, 2x15".

1968-1972		$1,000	$1,200
1973-1981		$900	$1,100

Dual Showman Reverb Head Amp

1968-1981. Amp only.

1969-1972	Includes TFL5000 series	$750	$825
1973-1981		$650	$750

Frontman Series Amp

1997-present. Student combo amps, models include 15/15B/15G/15R (15 watts, 1x8"), 25R (25 watts, 1x10", reverb).

1997-2004	15/15B/15G/15R	$50	$80
1997-2004	25R	$60	$90

H.O.T. Amp

1990-1996. Solidstate, 25 watts, 1x10", gray carpet cover (black by '92), black grille.

1990-1996		$75	$90

Harvard (Tube) Amp

1956-1961. Tweed, 10 watts, 1x10", 2 knobs volume and roll-off tone, some were issued with 1x8". Reintroduced as a solidstate model in '80.

1956-1961		$1,100	$1,400

Harvard (Solidstate) Amp

1980-1983. Reintroduced from tube model, black tolex with blackface, 20 watts, 1x10".

1980-1983		$75	$150

MODEL YEAR	FEATURES	EXC. COND. LOW	HIGH

Harvard Reverb Amp

1981-1982. Solidstate, 20 watts, 1x10", reverb, replaced by Harvard Reverb II in '83.

1981-1982		$125	$200

Harvard Reverb II Amp

1983-1985. Solidstate, black tolex with blackface, 20 watts, 1x10", reverb.

1983-1985		$125	$200

Hot Rod De Ville 212 Amp

1996-present. Updated Blues De Ville, tube, 60 watts, black tolex, 2x12".

1996-2000		$450	$550

Hot Rod De Ville 410 Amp

1996-present. Tube, 60 watts, black tolex, 4x10".

1996-2000		$450	$550

Hot Rod Deluxe Amp

1996-present. Updated Blues Deluxe, tube, 40 watts, 1x12", black tolex. Various covering optional by '98, also a wood cab in 2003.

1996-2000	Black tolex	$375	$475
1996-2000	Blond tolex option	$400	$475
1996-2000	Tweed option	$400	$475
1996-2001	Brown option	$375	$475
2003	Wood cab	$700	$775

J.A.M. Amp

1990-1996. Solidstate, 25 watts, 1x12", 4 preprogrammed sounds, gray carpet cover (black by '92).

1990-1996		$85	$100

Libra Amp

1970-1972. Solidstate, 105 watts, 4x12" JBL speakers, black tolex.

1970-1972		$275	$400

London 185 Amp

1988-1992. Solidstate, 160 watts, black tolex.

1988-1992	Head only	$175	$250

London Reverb 112 Amp

1983-1985. Solidstate, 100 watts, black tolex, 1x12".

1983-1985		$225	$350

London Reverb 210 Amp

1983-1985. Solidstate, 100 watts, black tolex, 2x10".

1983-1985		$250	$375

London Reverb Head Amp

1983-1985. Solidstate head, 100 watts.

1983-1985		$150	$275

M-80 Amp

1989-1994. Solidstate, 90 watts, 1x12". The M-80 series were also offered as head only amp.

1989-1993		$150	$275

M-80 Bass Amp

1991-1994. Solidstate, bass and keyboard amp, 160 watts, 1x15".

1991-1994		$175	$250

M-80 Chorus Amp

1990-1994. Solidstate, stereo chorus, 2 65-watt channels, 2x12", 90 watts.

1990-1994		$250	$300

M-80 Pro Amp

1992. Rackmount version of M-80, 90 watts.

1992		$125	$175

MODEL YEAR	FEATURES	EXC. COND. LOW	HIGH

Model 26 Amp
1946-1947. Tube, 10 watts, 1x10", hardwood cabinet. Sometimes called Deluxe Model 26, renamed Deluxe in '48.

1946-1947		$1,500	$2,500

Montreux Amp
1983-1985. Solidstate, 100 watts, 1x12", black tolex with silver grille.

1983-1985		$225	$350

Musicmaster Bass Amp
1970-1983. Tube, 12 watts, 1x12", black tolex.

1970-1972	Silverface	$225	$325
1973-1980	Silverface	$225	$300
1981-1983	Blackface	$225	$300

PA-100 Amp
100 watts.

1970s		$350	$450

Performer 650 Amp
1993-1995. Solidstate hybrid amp with single tube, 70 watts, 1x12".

1993-1995		$225	$275

Performer 1000 Amp
1993-1995. Solidstate hybrid amp with a single tube, 100 watts, 1x12".

1993-1995		$225	$275

Princeton Amp
1948-1979. Tube, 4.5 watts (12 watts by '61), 1x8" (1x10" by '61), tweed '48-'61, brown '61-'63, black with blackface '63-'69, silverface '69-'79.

1948-1953	TV front	$1,000	$1,200
1953-1954	Wide panel	$1,000	$1,200
1955-1956	Narrow panel, sm. Box	$1,000	$1,300
1956-1961	Narrow panel, lg. box	$1,000	$1,300
1961-1963	Brown, 6G2	$1,000	$1,100
1963-1964	Black, 6G2	$700	$850
1964-1966	Black, AA964, no grille logo	$625	$750
1966-1967	Black, AA964, raised grille logo	$600	$725
1968-1969	Silverface, alum. grille trim	$450	$550
1969-1970	Silverface, no grille trim	$425	$500
1971-1972	Silverface, AB1270	$400	$475
1973-1975	Fender logo-tail	$400	$475
1975-1978	No Fender logo-tail	$400	$475
1978-1979	With boost pull-knob	$400	$475

Princeton Reverb Amp
1964-1981. Tube, black tolex, blackface until '67, silverface after.

1964-1967	Blackface	$1,000	$1,400
1968-1972	Silverface, Fender logo-tail	$750	$900
1973-1979	Silverface, no Fender logo-tail	$650	$800
1980-1981	Blackface	$650	$800

Princeton Reverb II Amp
1982-1985. Tube amp, 20 watts, 1x12", black tolex, silver grille, distortion feature.

1982-1985		$525	$600

Princeton Chorus Amp
1988-1996. Solidstate, 2x10", 2 channels at 25 watts each, black tolex. Replaced by Princeton Stereo Chorus in '96.

1988-1996		$225	$300

Princeton 65 Amp
1999-2003. Combo 1x2", reverb, blackface, DSP added in '02.

1999-2003		$150	$200

Princeton 112/112 Plus Amp
1993-1997. Solidstate, 40 watts (112) or 60 watts (112 Plus), 1x12", black tolex.

1993-1994	40 watt	$175	$225
1995-1997	60 watt	$175	$200

Pro Amp
1947-1965. Called Professional '46-'48. 15 watts (26 by '54 and 25 by '60), 1x15", tweed TV front '48-'53, wide-panel '53-'54, narrow-panel '55-'60, brown tolex and brownface '60-'63, black and blackface '63-'65.

1947-1953	Tweed, TV front	$3,000	$4,000
1953-1954	Wide panel	$3,000	$4,000
1955	Narrow panel (old chassis)	$3,000	$4,000
1955-1959	Narrow panel (new chassis)	$3,500	$4,500
1960-1962	Brown tolex	$1,800	$2,000
1963-1965	Black tolex	$1,700	$1,900

Pro Reverb Amp
1965-1982. Tube, black tolex, 40 watts (45 watts by '72, 70 watts by '81), 2x12", blackface '65-'69 and '81-'83, silverface '69-'81.

1965-1967	Blackface	$1,700	$2,000
1968-1972	Silverface	$850	$950
1973-1980	Silverface	$800	$900
1981-1982	Blackface	$800	$900

Pro Reverb (Solidstate) Amp
1967-1969. Fender's first attempt at solidstate design, the attempt was unsuccessful and many of these models will overheat and are known to be unreliable. 50 watts, 2x12", upright vertical combo cabinet.

1967-1969		$275	$350

Pro Reverb Reissue (Pro Series) Amp
2002-present. 50 watts, 1x12", 2 modern designed channels - clean and high gain.

2002-2004		$700	$850

Pro 185 Amp
1989-1991. Solidstate, 160 watts, 2x12", black tolex.

1989-1991		$250	$325

Pro Junior Amp
1994-present. All tube, 2xEL84 tubes, 15 watts, 1x10" Alnico Blue speaker, tweed until '95, black tolex '96 on.

1994-2000		$225	$275

1957 Fender Princeton Amp

AMPS

Fender Pro (6G5A)

Fender Pro Junior

1980s Fender Showman Amp

Fender Rumble 100

1959 Fender Super Amp

MODEL YEAR	FEATURES	EXC. COND. LOW	HIGH
Prosonic Amp			
	1996-2001. Custom Shop combo, 60 watts, 2 channels, 3-way rectifier switch, 2x10" Celestion or separate cab with 4x12", tube reverb, black, red or green.		
1996-2001		$850	$900
Prosonic Head Amp			
	1996-2001. Amp head only version.		
1996-2001		$525	$650
Quad Reverb Amp			
	1971-1978. Black tolex, silverface, 4x12", tube, 100 watts.		
1971-1978		$550	$700
R.A.D. Amp			
	1990-1996. Solidstate, 20 watts, 1x8", gray carpet cover until '92, black after.		
1990-1996		$55	$65
R.A.D. Bass Amp			
	1992-1994. 25 watts, 1x10", renamed BXR 25.		
1992-1994		$55	$70
Roc-Pro 1000			
	1997-2001. Hybrid tube combo or head, 100 watts, 1x12", spring reverb, 1000 logo on front panel.		
1997-2001	Head only	$200	$230
Rumble Bass Head Amp			
	1994-1998. Custom Shop tube amp, 300 watts.		
1994-1998		$1,900	$2,200
Rumble Series Amp			
	2003-present. Solidstate bass amps, include Rumble 15 (15 watts, 1x8"), 25 (25 watts, 1x10"), 60 (60 watts, 1x12"), and 100 (100 watts, 1x15").		
2003-2004	Rumble 15	$60	$80
2003-2004	Rumble 25	$65	$85
Scorpio Amp			
	1970-1972. Solidstate, 56 watts, 2x12", black tolex.		
1970-1972		$225	$300
SFX Keyboard 200 Amp			
	1998-1999. Keyboard combo amp, digital effects, black tolex.		
1998-1999		$225	$275
SFX Satellite Amp			
	1997-2001. Hybrid tube combo or head, 100 watts, 1x12", spring reverb.		
1998-2000		$200	$250
Showman 12 Amp			
	1960-1966. Piggyback cabinet with 1x12", 85 watts, blond tolex (changed to black in '64), maroon grille '61-'63, gold grille '63-'64, silver grille '64-'67.		
1960-1962	Rough blond and oxblood	$2,800	$3,300
1963-1964	Smooth blond and gold	$2,600	$3,000
1964-1966	Black	$1,700	$2,100
Showman 15 Amp			
	1960-1968. Piggyback cabinet with 1x15", 85 watts, blond tolex (changed to black in '64), maroon grille '61-'63, gold grille '63-'64, silver grille '64-'67.		
1960-1962	Rough blond and oxblood	$2,800	$3,300
1963-1964	Smooth blond and gold	$2,600	$3,000

MODEL YEAR	FEATURES	EXC. COND. LOW	HIGH
1964-1967	Blackface	$1,700	$2,100
1967-1968	Silverface	$900	$1,000
Showman 112 Amp			
	1983-1987. Solidstate, 2 channels, 200 watts, reverb, 4 button footswitch, 5-band EQ, effects loop, 1x12".		
1983-1987		$275	$425
Showman 115 Amp			
	1983-1987. Solidstate, 1x15", 2 channels, reverb, EQ, effects loop, 200 watts, black tolex.		
1983-1987		$275	$425
Showman 210 Amp			
	1983-1987. Solidstate, 2 channels, reverb, EQ, effects loop, 2x10", 200 watts, black tolex.		
1983-1987		$275	$425
Showman 212 Amp			
	1983-1987. Solidstate, 2 channels, reverb, EQ, effects loop, 2x12", 200 watts, black tolex.		
1983-1987		$300	$475
Sidekick 10 Amp			
	1983-1985. Small solidstate Japanese or Mexican import, 10 watts, 1x8".		
1983-1985		$55	$75
Sidekick Bass 30 Amp			
	1983-1985. Combo, 30 watts, 1x12".		
1983-1985		$60	$80
Sidekick Reverb 15 Amp			
	1983-1985. Small solidstate import, reverb, 15 watts.		
1983-1985		$70	$80
Sidekick Reverb 20 Amp			
	1983-1985. Small solidstate Japanese or Mexican import, 20 watts, reverb, 1x10".		
1983-1985		$80	$90
Sidekick Reverb 30 Amp			
	1983-1985. Small solidstate Japanese or Mexican import, 30 watts, 1x12", reverb.		
1983-1985		$90	$110
Sidekick Reverb 65 Amp			
	1986-1988. Small solidstate Japanese or Mexican import, 65 watts, 1x12".		
1986-1988		$100	$120
Sidekick 100 Bass Head Amp			
	1986-1993. 100 watt bass head.		
1986-1993		$80	$100
Squire SKX 15/15R Amp			
	1990-1992. Solidstate, 15 watts, 1x8", model 15R with reverb.		
1990-1992	Non-reverb	$40	$50
1990-1992	Reverb	$55	$65
Stage 100/Stage 1000 Amp			
	1999-present. Solidstate, 1x12", combo or head only options, 100 watts, blackface. Head unit available 2004 only.		
1999-2004	Combo	$200	$275
2004	Head only	$150	$175
Stage Lead/Lead II Amp			
	1983-1985. Solidstate, 100 watts, 1x12", reverb, channel switching, black tolex. Stage Lead II has 2x12".		
1983-1985	1x12"	$175	$275
1983-1985	2x12"	$200	$300

MODEL YEAR	FEATURES	EXC. COND. LOW	HIGH

Studio Lead Amp
1983-1986. Solidstate, 50 watts, 1x12", black tolex.

1983-1986		$175	$275

Super Amp
1947-1963, 1992-1997. Introduced as Dual Professional in 1946, renamed Super '47, 2x10" speakers, 20 watts (30 watts by '60 with 45 watts in '62), tweed TV front '47-'53, wide-panel '53-'54, narrow-panel '55-'60, brown tolex '60-'64. Reintroduced '92-'97 with 4x10", 60 watts, black tolex.

1947-1952	Tweed, TV front	$3,500	$4,000
1953-1954	Tweed, wide panel	$3,500	$4,000
1955	Tweed, narrow panel, 6L6	$4,000	$5,000
1956-1957	Tweed, narrow panel, 5E4, 6V6	$3,000	$3,500
1957-1960	Tweed, narrow panel, 6L6	$4,000	$5,500
1960	Pink/brown metal knobs	$2,500	$3,000
1960	Pink/brown reverse knobs	$2,500	$3,000
1960-1962	Brown, oxblood grille, 6G4	$2,300	$2,500
1962-1963	Brown, tan/wheat grille, 6G4	$2,100	$2,400

Super Reverb Amp
1963-1982. 4x10" speakers, blackface until '67 and '80-'82, silverface '68-'80.

1963-1967	Blackface	$1,700	$2,200
1968	Silverface, AB763	$1,350	$1,450
1969-1970	Silverface	$975	$1,175
1970-1972	Silverface, AA270	$975	$1,175
1973-1980	Silverface, no MV	$850	$950
1981-1982	Blackface	$850	$950

Super Reverb '65 Reissue Amp
2001-present. 45 watts, all tube, 4x10", blackface cosmetics.

2001-2003		$775	$800

Super (4x10") Amp
1992-1997. 60 watts, 4x10", black tolex, silver grille, blackface control panel.

1992-1997		$575	$625

Super Six Reverb Amp
1970-1979. Large combo amp based on the Twin Reverb chassis, 100 watts, 6x10", black tolex.

1970-1979		$700	$800

Super 60 Amp
1989-1993. Red Knob series, 1x12", 60 watts, earlier versions with red knobs, later models with black knobs, offered in optional covers such as red, white, gray or snakeskin.

1989-1993		$225	$375

Super 112 Amp
1990-1993. Red Knob series, 1x12", 60 watts, earlier versions with red knobs, later models with black knobs, originally designed to replace the Super60 but the Super60 remained until '93.

1990-1993		$225	$375

Super 210 Amp
1990-1993. Red Knob series, 2x10", 60 watts, earlier versions with red knobs, later models with black knobs.

1990-1993		$275	$425

Super Champ Amp
1982-1986. Black tolex, 18 watts, blackface, 1x10".

1982-1986		$500	$575

Super Champ Deluxe Amp
1982-1986. Solid oak cabinet, 18 watts, upgrade 10" Electro-Voice speaker, see-thru brown grille cloth.

1982-1986		$850	$1,000

Super Twin (Non-reverb) Amp
1975-1976. 180 watts (6 6L6 power tubes), 2x12", distinctive dark grille.

1975-1976		$450	$500

Super Twin Reverb Amp
1976-1980. 180 watts (6 6L6 power tubes), 2x12", distinctive dark grille.

1976-1980		$525	$600

Taurus Amp
1970-1972. Solidstate, 42 watts, 2x10" JBL, black tolex, silver grille, JBL badge.

1970-1972		$225	$300

Tonemaster Head Amp
1993-2002. Custom Shop, hand-wired high-gain head, 100 watts, 2 channels, effects loop, blond tolex.

1993-1999		$775	$925

Tonemaster 212 Cabinet
1993-2002. Custom Shop extension cabinet for Tonemaster head, blond tolex, Oxblood grille, 2x12" Celestion Vintage 30.

1993-1999		$375	$500

Tonemaster 412 Cabinet
1993-2002. 4x12" Celestion Vintage 30 version.

1993-1999		$375	$500

Tonemaster Set Amp
1993-2002. Custom Shop, hand-wired head with Tonemaster 2x12" or 4x12" cabinet.

1993-1999	Blond and oxblood	$1,250	$1,450
1993-1999	Custom color red	$1,350	$1,550

Tremolux Amp
1955-1966. Tube, tweed, 1x12" '55-'60, white tolex with piggyback 1x10" cabinet '61-'62, 2x10" '62-'64, black tolex '64-'66.

1955-1960	Tweed, 1x12", narrow panel	$2,000	$2,400
1961	Rough white and oxblood, 1x10"	$2,000	$2,200
1961-1962	Rough white and oxblood, 2x10"	$1,900	$2,100
1962-1963	Rough white and wheat, 2x10"	$1,800	$2,000
1963-1964	Smooth white and gold, 2x10"	$1,700	$1,900
1964-1966	Black tolex, 2x10"	$1,200	$1,400

1960 Fender Super Amp

AMPS

1969 Fender Super Reverb

Fender Super Amp (6G4A)

Fender Twin Amp

Fender Twin Reverb (AB763)

1963 Fender Vibroverb Amp

MODEL YEAR	FEATURES	EXC. COND. LOW	HIGH

Twin Amp

1952-1963, 1996-present. Tube, 2x12"; 15 watts, tweed wide-panel '52-'55; narrow-panel '55-'60; 50 watts '55-'57; 80 watts '58; brown tolex '60; white tolex '61-'63. Reintroduced in '96 with black tolex, spring reverb and output control for 100 watts or 25 watts.

1952-1954	Tweed, wide panel	$5,500	$6,000
1955-1957	Tweed, 50 watts	$6,000	$8,000
1958-1959	Tweed, 80 watts	$7,000	$11,000
1960	Brown tolex, 80 watts	$7,000	$10,000
1960-1962	Rough white and oxblood	$6,000	$8,000
1963	Smooth white and gold	$5,500	$7,500

Twin Reverb (Solidstate) Amp

1966-1969. 100 watts, 2x12", black tolex.

1966-1969		$325	$500

Twin '57 Reissue Amp

2004. Custom Shop '57 tweed, low power dual rectifier model, 40 watts, 2x12", authentic tweed lacquering.

2004		$1,600	$1,800

Twin Reverb Amp

1963-1982. Black tolex, 85 watts (changed to 135 watts in '81), 2x12", blackface '63-'67 and '81-'82, silverface '68-'81, blackface optional in '80-'81 and standard in '82. Reverb reintroduced as Twin in '96.

1963-1967	Blackface	$1,975	$2,275
1968-1972	Silverface, no master vol.	$900	$1,100
1973-1975	Silverface, master vol.	$800	$975
1976-1981	Silverface, push/pull	$650	$900
1980-1982	Blackface	$650	$900

Twin Reverb '65 Reissue Amp

1992-present. Black tolex, 2x12", 85 watts.

1992-2002	High or low output	$700	$775

Twin Reverb II Amp

1983-1985. Black tolex, 2x12", 105 watts, channel switching, effects loop, blackface panel, silver grille.

1983-1985		$700	$750

Twin "The Twin"/"Evil Twin" Amp

1987-1992. 100 watts, 2x12", red knobs, most black tolex, but white, red and snakeskin covers offered.

1987-1992		$650	$725

Ultra Chorus Amp

1992-1994. Solidstate, 2x65 watts, 2x12", standard control panel with chorus.

1992-1994		$300	$325

Ultimate Chorus DSP Amp

1995-2001. Solidstate, 2x65 watts, 2x12", 32 built-in effect variations, blackface cosmetics.

1995-2001		$300	$400

Vibrasonic Amp

1959-1963. First amp to receive the new brown tolex and JBL, 1x15", 25 watts.

1959-1963		$1,950	$2,200

MODEL YEAR	FEATURES	EXC. COND. LOW	HIGH

Vibrasonic Custom Amp

1995-1997. Custom Shop designed for steel guitar and guitar, blackface, 1x15", 100 watts.

1995-1997		$650	$800

Vibro-Champ Amp

1964-1982. Black tolex, 4 watts, (5 watts '69-'71, 6 watts '72-'80), 1x8", blackface '64-'68 and '82, silverface '69-'81.

1964-1967	Blackface, AA764	$550	$625
1968-1982	Silverface	$350	$400

Vibro-King Amp

1993-present. Custom Shop combo, blond tolex, 60 watts, 3x10", vintage reverb, tremolo, single channel, all tube.

1993-1999		$1,250	$1,450

Vibro-King 212 Cabinet

1993-present. Custom Shop extension cabinet, blond tolex, 2x12" Celestion GK80.

1993-1999		$400	$500

Vibrolux Amp

1956-1964. Narrow-panel, 10 watts, tweed with 1x10" '56-'61, brown tolex and brownface with 1x12" and 30 watts '61-'62, black tolex and blackface '63-'64.

1956-1961	Tweed, 1x10"	$1,600	$1,800
1961-1962	Brown tolex, 1x12", 2x6L6	$1,800	$2,100
1963-1964	Black tolex, 1x12"	$1,950	$2,400

Vibrolux Reverb Amp

1964-1982. Black tolex, 2x10", blackface and 35 watts '64-'69, silverface and 40 watts '70-'79. Reissued in '96 with blackface and 40 watts.

1964-1967	Blackface	$2,300	$2,500
1968-1972	Silverface	$1,150	$1,400
1973-1980	Silverface	$875	$1,200
1981-1982	Blackface	$875	$1,200

Vibrolux Reverb (Solidstate) Amp

1967-1969. Fender CBS solidstate, 35 watts, 2x10", black tolex.

1967-1969		$275	$350

Vibrolux Reverb Reissue Amp

1996-present. 40 watts, 2x10", all tube, black or blond tolex.

1996-1999	Blond and tan	$700	$775
1996-2003	Black and silver	$675	$725

Vibrolux Custom Reverb Amp

2000s. Part of Professional Series, Custom Shop designed, standard factory built, 40 watts, 2x10", Vibrolux Reverb Amp on front panel, black tolex, silver grille, white knobs.

2000s		$750	$850

Vibrosonic Reverb Amp

1972-1981. Black tolex, 100 watts, 1x15", silverface.

1972-1981		$700	$750

Vibroverb Amp

1963-1964. Brown tolex with 35 watts, 2x10" and brownface '63, black tolex with 1x15" and blackface '64-'65.

1963	Brown tolex, 2x10"	$5,500	$6,750
1964	Black tolex, 1x15"	$3,400	$4,000

MODEL YEAR	FEATURES	EXC. COND. LOW	HIGH

Vibroverb '63 Reissue Amp
1990-1995. Reissue of 1963 Vibroverb, 40 watts, 2x10", reverb, vibrato, brown tolex.

1990-1995		$700	$800

Vibroverb '64 Custom Shop Amp
2003-present. Reissue of 1964 Vibroverb with 1x15" blackface specs.

2003-2004		$1,600	$1,850

Yale Reverb Amp
1983-1985. Solidstate, black tolex, 50 watts, 1x12", silverface.

1983-1985		$200	$275

Flot-A-Tone
Ca.1946-early 1960s. Flot-A-Tone was located in Milwaukee, Wisconsin, and made a variety of tube guitar and accordion amps.

Large Amp
Four speakers.

1960s		$500	$800

Small Amp
1x8" speaker.

1962		$300	$350

Framus
1946-1977, 1996-present. Tube guitar amp heads, combos and cabinets made in Markneukirchen, Germany. They also build guitars, basses, mandolins and banjos. Begun as an acoustic instrument manufacturer, Framus added electrics in the mid-'50s. In the '60s, Framus instruments were imported into the U.S. by Philadelphia Music Company. The brand was revived in '96 by Hans Peter Wilfer, the president of Warwick, with production in Warwick's factory in Germany. Distributed in the U.S. by Dana B. Goods.

Fred
1984-1986. Before settling on the name Bedrock, company founders Brad Jeter and Ron Pinto produced 50 amps carrying the brand name Fred in Nashua, New Hampshire.

Fuchs Audio Technology
2000-present. Andy Fuchs started the company, located in Bloomfield, New Jersey, in '99 to rebuild and modify tube amps. In 2000 he started production of his own brand of amps, offering combos and heads from 10 to 150 watts. They also custom build audiophile and studio tube electronics.

Fulton-Webb
Ca.1977-present. Steve Fulton and Bill Webb build their tube amp heads, combos and cabinets in Austin, Texas.

Gallien Krueger
1969-present. Gallien-Krueger has offered a variety of bass and guitar amps, combos and cabinets and is located in San Jose, California.

200G Amp
1980s. Solidstate, black tolex, black grille.

1980s		$250	$300

212GS Amp
1986-ca.1989. 140-watt mono or 70-watt stereo, 2x12", black carpet.

1986-1989		$275	$350

250ML Amp
Small practice amp, 2x4 1/2", chorus and echo.

1986-1989		$250	$350

2100CEL Digital Stereo Guitar Combo Amp
1989-1991. 200 watts (100 per channel), 2x8", EQ, compression, chorus and reverb.

1989-1991		$325	$375

Garnet
Mid 1960s-1989. In the mid '60's, "Gar" Gillies started the Garnet Amplifier Company with his two sons, Russell and Garnet, after he started making PA systems in his Canadian radio and TV repair shop. The first PA from the new company was for Chad Allen & the Expressions (later known as The Guess Who). A wide variety of tube amps were offered and all were designed by Gar, Sr. The company also produced the all-tube effects The Herzog, H-zog, and two stand-alone reverb units designed by Gar in the late '60s and early '70s. The company closed in '89, due to financial reasons caused largely by a too rapid expansion. Gar still repairs and designs custom amps.

GDS Amplification
1998-present. Tube amps, combos and speaker cabinets from builder Graydon D. Stuckey of Flint, Michigan. GDS also offers amp kits.

Genesis
Genesis was a 1980s line of student amps from Gibson.

B40 Amp
1984-late-1980s. Bass combo with 40 watts.

1984-1989		$100	$150

G Series Amps
1984-late-1980s. Small combo amps.

1984-1989	G10 (10 watts)	$50	$100
1984-1989	G25 (25 watts)	$75	$125
1984-1989	G40R (40 watts, reverb)	$125	$175

Genz Benz
1983-present. Founded by Jeff and Cathy Genzler and located in Scottsdale, Arizona, the company offers guitar, bass, and PA amps and speaker cabinets. In late 2003, Genz Benz was acquired by Kaman (Ovation, Hamer, Takamine).

El Diablo 60-C Amp
2004-present. Tubes, 60 watts, head or 1x12" combo.

2004	Combo	$750	$800
2004	Head	$600	$650

Fuchs OD Supreme

Gallien Krueger Backline 210

GDS 18W S/C

Gerhart Gilmore

Germino Lead 55

1960s Gibson Atlas

MODEL YEAR	FEATURES	EXC. COND. LOW	HIGH

George Dennis

1991-present. Founded by George Burgerstein, original products were a line of effects pedals. In '96 they added a line of tube amps. The company is located in Prague, Czech Republic.

Gerhart

2000-present. Production/custom, amps and cabinets from builder Gary Gerhart of West Hills, California. He also offers an amp in kit form.

Germino

2002-present. Tube amps, combos and cabinets built by Greg Germino in Graham, North Carolina.

Gibson

1880s (1902)-present. Gibson has offered a variety of amps since the mid-'30s to the present under the Gibson brandname and others. The price ranges listed are for excellent condition, all original amps though tubes may be replaced with affecting value. Many Gibson amps have missing or broken logos. The prices listed are for amps with fully intact logos. A broken or missing logo can diminish the value of the amp. Amps with a changed handle, power cord, and especially a broken logo should be taken on a case-by-case basis.

Atlas IV Amp
1963-1967. Piggyback head and cab, introduced with trapezoid shape, changed to rectangular cabs in '65-'66 with black cover, simple circuit with 4 knobs, no reverb or tremolo, mid-power with 2 6L6, 1x15".

1963-1965	Brown	$475	$700
1966-1967	Black	$475	$700

Atlas Medalist Amp
1964-1967. Combo version with 1x15".

1964-1967		$475	$700

B-40 Amp
1972-1975. 40 watts, 1x12".

1972-1975		$200	$275

BR-1 Amp
1945-1949. 15 watts, 1x12" field-coil speaker, brown leatherette cover, rectangular metal grille with large G.

1945-1949		$375	$475

BR-3 Amp
1946-1947. 12 watts, 1x12" Utah field-coil speaker (most BR models used Jensen speakers).

1946-1947		$325	$450

BR-4 Amp
1946-1947. 14 watts, 1x12" Utah field-coil speaker (most BR models used Jensen speakers).

1946-1947		$375	$475

BR-6 Amp
1946-1956. 10 to 12 watts, 1x10", brown leatherette, speaker opening split by cross panel with G logo, bottom mounted chassis with single on-off volume pointer knob.

1946-1947	Verticle cab	$325	$450
1948-1956	Horizontal cab	$275	$350

BR-9 Amp
1948-1953. Cream leatherette, 10 watts, 1x8". Originally sold with the BR-9 lap steel. Renamed GA-9 in '54.

1948-1953		$250	$325

Duo Metalist Amp
1967-1968. Upright vertical combo cab, tubes, faux wood grain panel, mid-power, 1x12".

1967-1968		$300	$400

EH-100 Amp
1936-1941. Electric-Hawaiian companion amp, 1x10". AC/DC version called EH-110.

1936-1941		$425	$550

EH-125 Amp
1941-1942. 1x12", rounded shoulder cab, brown cover in '41 and dark green in '42, leather handle.

1941	Brown	$550	$700
1942	Dark green	$550	$700

EH-126 Amp
1941-1942. Experimental model, 6-volt variant of EH-125, about 5 made.

1941-1942		$550	$700

EH-135 Amp
1941. Experimental model, alternating and direct current switchable, about 7 made.

1941		$600	$750

EH-150 Amp
1935-1941. Electric-Hawaiian companion amp, 1x12" ('35-'37) or 1x10" ('38-'42). AC/DC version called EH-160.

1935	13 3/4" sq. cab	$700	$900
1936-1937	14 3/4" sq. cab	$700	$900
1937-1942	15 3/8" round cab	$700	$900

EH-185 Amp
1939-1942. 1x12", tweed cover, black and orange vertical stripes, marketed as companion amp to the EH-185 Lap Steel. AC/DC version called EH-195.

1939-1942		$725	$950

EH-195 Amp
1939-1942. EH-185 variant with vibrato.

1939-1942		$900	$1,100

EH-250 Amp
1940-1942. Upgraded natural maple cabinet using EH-185 chassis, very few made, evolved into EH-275.

1940		$800	$1,000

EH-275 Amp
1940-1942. Similar to EH-185 but with maple cab and celluloid binding, about 30 made.

1940-1942		$850	$1,050

Falcon Medalist (Hybrid) Amp
1967. Transitional tube 1x12" combo amp from GA-19 tube Falcon to the solidstate Falcon, Falcon logo and Gibson logo on front panel, brown control panel, dark cover and dark grille, vertical combo cabinet.

1967		$275	$325

Falcon Medalist (Solidstate) Amp
1968-1969. Solidstate combo, 15 watts, 1x12".

1968-1969		$350	$400

MODEL		EXC. COND.	
YEAR	FEATURES	LOW	HIGH

G-10 Amp
1972-1975. Solidstate, 10 watts, 1x10", no tremolo or reverb.

1972-1975		$50	$100

G-20 Amp
1972-1975. Solidstate with tremolo, 1x10", 10 watts.

1972-1975		$100	$200

G-25 Amp
1972-1975. 25 watts, 1x10".

1972-1975		$125	$200

G-30 Amp
1972. Solidstate without tremolo or reverb, 1x12", 15 watts.

1972		$150	$225

G-35 Amp
1975. Solidstate, 30 watts, 1x12".

1975		$175	$275

G-40/G-40 R Amp
1972. Solidstate with tremolo and reverb, 40 watts, 1x12" (G-40) and 2x10" (G-40 R).

1972-1974	G-40 R	$225	$325
1972-1975	G-40	$200	$275

G-50/G-50 A/G-50 B Amp
1972, 1975. Solidstate with tremolo and reverb, models G-50 and 50 A are 1x12", 40 watts, model 50 B is a bass 1x15", 50 watts.

1972	G-50	$225	$300
1975	G-50 A	$225	$300
1975	G-50 B	$225	$300

G-55 Amp
1975. 50 watts, 1x12".

1975		$225	$300

G-60 Amp
1972. Solidstate with tremolo and reverb, 1x15", 60 watts.

1972		$250	$325

G-70 Amp
1972. Solidstate with tremolo and reverb, 2x12", 60 watts.

1972		$275	$350

G-80 Amp
1972. Solidstate with tremolo and reverb, 4x10", 60 watts.

1972		$300	$375

G-100 A/G-100 B Amp
1975. 100 watts, model 100 A is 2x12" and 100 B is 2x15".

1975	G-100 A	$300	$375
1975	G-100 B	$300	$375

G-105 Amp
1975 Solidstate, 100 watts, 2x12", reverb.

1975		$300	$375

G-115 Amp
1975. 100 watts, 4x10".

1975		$350	$425

GA-5 Les Paul Jr. Amp
1954-1957. Tan fabric cover (Mottled Brown by '47), 7" oval speaker, 4 watts. Renamed Skylark in '58.

1954		$400	$450
1955-1957		$300	$350

GA-5 Les Paul Jr. (Goldtone Series) Amp
2004. Class A, 6 watts, 1x8".

2004		$250	$350

GA-5 Skylark Amp
1957-1968. Gold cover (brown by '63 and black by '66), 1x8" (1x10" from '64 on), 4.5 watts (10 watts from '64 on), tremolo. Often sold with the Skylark Lap Steel.

1957-1962	Gold, 4.5 watts, 1x8"	$225	$300
1963	Brown, 4.5 watts, 1x8"	$225	$275
1964	Brown, 10 watts, 1x10"	$225	$275
1965-1967	Black, 10 watts, 1x10"	$225	$275
1968	Skylark, last version	$200	$225

GA-5 T Skylark Amp
1960-1967. Tremolo, 4.5 watts, gold covering and 1x8" until '63, brown '63-'64, black and 1x10" after.

1961-1962	Gold, 4.5 watts, 1x8"	$250	$325
1963	Brown, 4.5 watts, 1x8"	$250	$325
1964	Brown, 10 watts, 1x10"	$250	$325
1965-1967	Black, 10 watts, 1x10"	$275	$325

GA-6 Amp
1956-1960. Replaced the BR-6, 8 to 12 watts, 1x12", has Gibson 6 above the grille. Renamed GA-6 Lancer in '60.

1956-1960		$300	$425

GA-6 Lancer Amp
1960-1962. Renamed from GA-6, 1x12", tweed cover, 3 knobs, 14 watts.

1960-1962		$525	$650

GA-7 Amp
1955-1957. Described as "Les Paul TV Model", a basic old style GA-5 with different graphics, 4 watts, small speaker.

1955-1957		$300	$400

GA-8 Discoverer Amp
1962-1964. Renamed from GA-8 Gibsonette, gold fabric cover, 1x12", 10 watts.

1962-1964		$300	$425

GA-8 Gibsonette Amp
1952-1962. Tan fabric cover (gold by '58), 1x10", 8 watts (9 watts by '58). Name changed to GA-8 Discoverer in '62.

1952-1957	Gibsonette logo on front	$375	$450
1958-1959	Gibson logo on front	$350	$425
1960-1962	Gibson logo upper right front	$350	$425

GA-8 T Discoverer Amp
1960-1967. Gold fabric cover, 1x10", 9 watts (tan cover, 1x12" and 15 watts by '63), tremolo.

1960-1962	Tweed, 9 watts, 1x10"	$300	$475
1963-1964	Brown, 15 watts, 1x12"	$325	$375
1965-1967	Black, 15 watts, 1x12"	$300	$350

GA-9 Amp
1954-1961. Renamed from BR-9, tan fabric cover, 8 watts, 1x10". Often sold with the BR-9 Lap Steel.

1954-1956		$300	$375
1956-1957	Gibson 9 logo	$300	$375
1958-1961	Tweed, 6V6s	$400	$450

Gibson GA-5 Skylark

Gibson EH-185

'55 Gibson GA-5 Les Paul Junior

AMPS

Gibson GA-15

1965 Gibson GA-19RVT Falcon

Gibson GA-40 Les Paul Amp

MODEL YEAR	FEATURES	EXC. COND. LOW	HIGH

GA-14 Titan Amp
1959-1961. About 15 watts using 2x6V6 power tubes, 1x10", tweed cover.

1959-1961		$475	$600

GA-15 RV (Custom Shop) Amp
2002. Custom Shop built, 15 watts, 1x12", quilted maple cabinet in natural finish, companion amp to Custom Shop L-5C or Super 400 set.

2002		$1,800	$2,100

GA-15 RV Goldtone Amp
1999-2004. 15 watts, Class A, 1x12", spring reverb.

1999-2004		$325	$400

GA-15 RVT Explorer amp
1965-1967. Tube, 1x10", tremolo, reverb, black vinyl.

1965-1967		$350	$375

GA-17 RVT Scout Amp
1963-1965. Low power, 1x12", reverb and tremolo.

1963-1964	Brown	$300	$500
1965	Black	$300	$475

GA-18 Explorer Amp
1959. Tube, 14 watts, 1x10". Replaced in '60 by the GA-18 T Explorer.

1959		$475	$600

GA-18 T Explorer Amp
1959-1964. Tweed, 14 watts, 1x10", tremolo.

1959-1962		$575	$700
1963-1964		$325	$450

GA-19 RVT Falcon Amp
1961-1966. One of Gibson's best selling amps. Initially tweed covered, followed by smooth brown, textured brown, and black. Each amp has a different tone. One 12" Jensen with deep-sounding reverb and tremolo.

1961-1962	Tweed, 6V6	$625	$750
1961-1963	Smooth brown	$400	$475
1964	Textured brown	$425	$450
1965-1966	Black	$350	$450

GA-20 RVT Minuteman Amp
1965-1967. Black, 14 watts, 1x12", tube, reverb, tremolo.

1965-1967		$375	$550

GA-20 T/Ranger Amp
1956-1962. Tube, 16 watts, tremolo, 1x12". Renamed Ranger in '60.

1956-1958	2-tone	$650	$800
1959-1962	Tweed	$700	$825
1960-1962	Ranger	$500	$600

GA-20/GA-20 Crest Amp
1950-1962. Brown leatherette (2-tone by '55 and tweed by '60), tube, 12 watts early, 14 watts later, 1x12". Renamed Crest in '60.

1952-1954	Brown, 14 watts	$575	$750
1955-1958	2-tone, 14 watts	$625	$775
1959-1962	Tweed/Crest, 14 watts	$675	$800

GA-25 Amp
1947-1948. Brown, 1x12" and 1x8", 15 watts. Replaced by GA-30 in '48.

1947-1948		$425	$550

GA-25 RVT Hawk Amp
1963-1968. Reverb, tremolo, 1x15".

1963	Smooth brown	$425	$525
1964	Rough brown	$300	$525
1965-1967	Black	$300	$525
1968	Hawk, last version	$200	$300

GA-30 Amp
1948-1961. Brown until '54, 2-tone after, tweed in '60, 1x12" and 1x8", 14 watts. Renamed Invader in '60.

1948-1954	Brown	$625	$750
1955-1958	2-tone	$675	$800
1959	Tweed	$725	$850

GA-30 RV Invader Amp
1960-1961. Tweed, 1x12" and 1x8", 14-16 watts, reverb but no tremolo.

1960-1961		$950	$1,150

GA-30 RVT Invader Amp
1962-1967. Updated model with reverb and tremolo, dual speakers 1x12" and 1x8", first issue in tweed.

1962	Tweed	$850	$1,075
1963	Smooth brown	$525	$650
1964-1967	Rough brown	$525	$650

GA-35 RVT Lancer Amp
1966-1967. Black, 1x12", tremolo, reverb.

1966-1967		$400	$450

GA-40 Les Paul Amp
1952-1960. Introduced in conjunction with the Les Paul Model guitar, 1x12" Jensen speaker, 14 watts on early models and 16 watts later, recessed leather handle using spring mounting (the handle is easily broken and an unsimilar replacement handle is more common than not). Two-tone leatherette covering, '50s checkerboard grille ('52-early-'55), Les Paul script logo on front of the amp ('52-'55), plastic grille insert with LP monogram, gold Gibson logo above grille. Cosmetics changed dramatically in early/mid-'55. Renamed GA-40 T Les Paul in '60.

1952-1955	Brown 2-tone, LP grille	$850	$1,000
1955-1956	Mottled Gray 2-tone	$950	$1,300
1957-1959	2-tone	$950	$1,300
1959-1960	Tweed	$850	$1,075

GA-40 T Les Paul Amp
1960-1965. Renamed from GA-40 Les Paul, 1x12", 16 watts, tremolo. Renamed Mariner in '65-'67.

1961	Tweed	$850	$975
1962-1963	Smooth brown	$625	$700
1964-1965	Rough brown	$450	$500

GA-45 RVT Saturn Amp
1965-1967. 2x10", mid power, tremolo, reverb.

1965-1967		$475	$600

GA-50/GA-50 T Amp
1948-1955. Brown leatherette, 25 watts, 1x12" and 1x8", GA-50 T with tremolo.

1948-1955	GA-50	$1,100	$1,200
1948-1955	GA-50 T	$1,200	$1,300

GA-55 RVT Ranger Amp
1965-1967. Black cover, 4x10", tremolo, reverb.

1965-1967		$575	$700

The *Vintage Guitar Price Guide* shows low to high values for items in all-original excellent condition, and, where applicable, with original case or cover.

MODEL YEAR	FEATURES	EXC. COND. LOW	HIGH

GA-55/GA-55 V Amp
1954-1958. 2x12", 20 watts, GA-55 V with vibrato.

| 1954-1958 | GA-55 | $1,300 | $1,600 |
| 1954-1958 | GA-55 V | $1,600 | $1,800 |

GA-70 Country and Western Amp
1955-1958. 25 watts, 1x15", 2-tone, longhorn cattle western logo on front, advertised to have extra bright sound.

| 1955-1957 | 2-tone | $1,300 | $1,600 |
| 1957-1958 | Blue/blond 2-tone | $1,300 | $1,600 |

GA-75 Amp
1950-1955. Mottled Brown leatherette, 1x15", 25 watts.

| 1950-1955 | | $950 | $1,200 |

GA-75 L Recording Amp
1964-1967. 1x15" Lansing speaker, no reverb or tremolo, 2 channels, dark cover, gray grille.

| 1964-1967 | | $525 | $650 |

GA-75 Recording Amp
1964-1967. 2x10" speakers, no reverb or tremolo, 2 channels, dark cover, gray grille.

| 1964-1967 | | $525 | $650 |

GA-77 RET Amp
1964-1967. 2x10" speakers, reverb, echo, tremolo.

| 1964-1967 | | $525 | $650 |

GA-77/Vanguard Amp
1954-1960. Brown tolex, 1x15" JBL, 25 watts, 2 6L6 power tubes, near top-of-the-line for the mid-'50s. Renamed Vanguard in '60.

1954-1958	2-tone	$1,050	$1,300
1959-1960	Tweed	$1,050	$1,300
1960-1962	Vanguard, no reverb	$1,000	$1,250

GA-78 Bell Stereo Amp
1960. Gibson-branded amp made by Bell, same as GA-79 series, Bell 30 logo on front, 30 watts, 2x10" wedge cab.

| 1960 | | $1,600 | $2,400 |

GA-79 RV Amp
1960-1962. Stereo-reverb, 2x10", 30 watts.

| 1960-1961 | Tweed | $2,400 | $2,800 |
| 1962 | Gray tolex | $1,600 | $2,400 |

GA-79 RVT Multi-Stereo Amp
1961-1967. Introduced as GA-79 RVT, Multi-Stereo was added to name in '61. Stereo-reverb and tremolo, 2x10", tweed (black and brown also available), 30 watts.

1961-1962	Gray	$1,600	$2,400
1963-1964	Textured brown	$1,600	$2,400
1965-1967	Black	$1,400	$2,000

GA-80/GA-80 T/Vari-Tone Amp
1959-1961. 25 watts, 1x15", 2 channels, described as "6-in-1 amplifier with improved tremolo," 6 Vari-Tone pushbottons which give "six distinctively separate sounds," 7 tubes, tweed cover.

| 1959-1961 | | $1,200 | $1,500 |

GA-83 S Stereo-Vibe Amp
1959-1961. Interesting stereo amp with front baffle mounted 1x12" and 4x8" side-mounted speakers (2 on each side), 35 watts, Gibson logo on upper right corner of the grille, tweed cover, brown grille (late '50s Fender-style), 3 pointer knobs and 3 round knobs, 4 inputs.

| 1959-1961 | | $2,000 | $2,200 |

GA-85 Bass Reflex Amp
1957-1958. Removable head, 25 watts, 1x12", very limited production.

| 1957-1958 | | $625 | $850 |

GA-90 High Fidelity Amp
1953-1960. 25 watts, 6x8", 2 channels, advertised for guitar, bass, accordion, or hi-fi.

| 1953-1960 | | $1,050 | $1,400 |

GA-95 RVT Apollo Amp
1965-1967. 90 watts, 2x12", black vinyl, black grille, tremolo, reverb.

| 1965-1967 | | $575 | $700 |

GA-100 Bass Amp
1960-1963. Tweed, 35 watts, 1x12" cabinet, tripod was available for separate head.

| 1960-1963 | | $700 | $1,100 |

GA-200 Rhythm King Amp
1957-1962. Introduced as GA-200, renamed Rhythm King in '60, 2-channel version of GA-400. Bass amp, 60 watts, 2x12".

| 1957-1959 | 2-tone | $1,575 | $1,850 |
| 1959-1962 | Tweed | $1,575 | $1,850 |

GA-400 Super 400 Amp
1957-1962. 60 watts, 2x12", 3 channels, same size as GA-200 cab, 1 more tube than GA-200.

| 1957-1959 | 2-tone | $1,600 | $1,900 |
| 1959-1962 | Tweed | $1,600 | $1,900 |

GSS-50 Amp
1966-1967. Solidstate, 50 watts, 2x10" combo, reverb and tremolo, black vinyl cover, silver grille, no grille logo.

| 1966-1967 | | $425 | $500 |

GSS-100 Amp
1966-1967. Solidstate, 100 watts, two 24"x12" 2x10" sealed cabs, black vinyl cover, silver grille, 8 black knobs and 3 red knobs, slanted raised Gibson logo. Speakers prone to distortion.

| 1966-1967 | | $450 | $500 |

Hawk Amp
1968-1969. Solidstate, upright vertical cab, faux wood grain front panel, 15 watts, 1x10".

| 1968-1969 | | $150 | $200 |

LP-1/LP-2 Amp Set
1970. Les Paul model, piggyback amp and cab set, LP-1 head and LP-2 4x12" plus 2 horns cab, large vertical speaker cabinet, rather small compact 190 watt solidstate amp head.

| 1970 | | $300 | $425 |

Medalist 2/12 Amp
1968-1970. Vertical cabinet, 2x12", reverb and temolo.

| 1968-1970 | | $375 | $450 |

Medalist 4/10 Amp
1968-1970. Vertical cabinet, 4x10", reverb and tremolo.

| 1968-1970 | | $425 | $525 |

Mercury I Amp
1963-1965. Piggyback trapezoid-shaped head with 2x12" trapezoid cabinet, tremolo, brown.

| 1963-1965 | | $325 | $550 |

'54 Gibson GA-40
Les Paul Amp

1959 Gibson GA-55V

1962 Gibson GA-200
Rhythm King

AMPS

Gibson Thor

Ginelle El Toro Pequeno

Green amp

MODEL YEAR	FEATURES	EXC. COND. LOW	HIGH

Mercury II Amp
1963-1967. Mercury I with 1x15" and 1x10", initially trapezoid cabinets then changed to rectangular.

| 1963-1964 | Brown trapezoid cabs | $325 | $550 |
| 1965-1967 | Black rectangular cabs | $325 | $550 |

Plus-50 Amp
1966-1967. 50 watts, powered extension amplifier. Similar to GSS-100 cabinet of the same era, 2x10" cab, black vinyl cover, silver grille, slant Gibson logo.

| 1966-1967 | | $425 | $550 |

Super Thor Bass Amp
1972-1974. Solidstate, part of the new G-Series (not GA-Series), 65 watts, 2x15", black tolex, black grille, upright vertical cab with front control, single channel.

| 1972-1974 | | $275 | $375 |

Thor Bass Amp
1970-1974. Solidstate, smaller 2x10" 50 watt version of Super Thor.

| 1970-1974 | | $250 | $350 |

Titan I Amp
1963-1965. Piggyback trapezoid-shaped head and 2x12" trapezoid-shaped cabinet, tremolo.

| 1963-1965 | | $275 | $550 |

Titan III Amp
1963-1967. Piggyback trapezoid-shaped head and 1x15" + 2x10" trapezoid-shaped cabinet, tremolo.

| 1963-1964 | Brown | $325 | $650 |
| 1965-1967 | Black | $325 | $650 |

Titan V Amp
1963-1967. Piggyback trapezoid-shaped tube head and 2x15" trapezoid-shaped cabinet, tremolo.

| 1963-1964 | Brown | $325 | $650 |
| 1965-1967 | Black | $325 | $650 |

Titan Medalist Amp
1964-1967. Combo version of Titan Series with 1x15" and 1x10", tremolo only, no reverb, black.

| 1964-1967 | | $325 | $650 |

Ginelle
1996-present. Rick Emery builds his tube combo amps in West Berlin, New Jersey.

Gorilla
1980s-present. Small solidstate entry-level amps, distributed by Pignose, Las Vegas, Nevada.

Compact Practice Student Amp
1980s-present. Solidstate, 10 to 30 watts, compact design.

1980s		$30	$45
1990s		$30	$45
2000s		$35	$50

Goya
1955-1996. Goya was mainly known for acoustics, but offered a few amps in the '60s. The brand was purchased by Avnet/Guild in '66 and by Martin in the late '70s.

Green
1993-present. Amp model line made in England by Matamp (see that brand for listing), bright green covering, large Green logo on the front.

Gretsch
1883-present. In '05, Gretsch again starting offering amps after previously selling them from the 1950s to '73. Initially private branded for them by Valco (look for the Valco oval or rectangular serialized label on the back). Early-'50s amps were covered in the requisite tweed, but evolved into the Gretsch charcoal gray covering. The mid-'50s to early-'60s amps were part of the Electromatic group of amps. The mid-'50s to '62 amps often sported wrap-around and slanted grilles. In '62, the more traditional box style was introduced. In '66, the large amps went piggyback. Baldwin-Gretsch began to phase out amps effective '65, but solidstate amps continued being offered for a period of time. The '73 Gretsch product line only offered Sonax amps, made in Canada and Sho-Bud amps made in the U.S. In '05, they introduced a line tube combo amps made in U.S. by Victoria Amp Company.

Model 6150 Compact Amp
Early-1950s-1960s. Early amps in tweed, '60s amps in gray covering, no tremolo, single volume knob, no treble or bass knob, 1x8".

| 1950s | Brown tweed | $325 | $375 |
| 1960s | Gray | $275 | $350 |

Model 6151/6151 Compact Tremolo Amp
Late-1940s-late-1960s. 1x8", various covers.

1940s		$350	$400
1950s		$375	$425
1960s		$325	$375

Model 6152 Compact Tremolo Reverb Amp
Ca.1964-late-1960s. Five watts, 11x6" elliptical speaker early on, 1x12" later.

| 1964-1966 | Elliptical speaker | $525 | $575 |
| 1967-1969 | Round speaker | $500 | $550 |

Model 6154 Super-Bass Amp
Early-1960s-mid-1960s. Gray covering, 2x12", 70 watts, tube.

| 1960s | | $450 | $500 |

Model 6156 Playboy Amp
Early-1950s-1966. Tube amp, 17 watts, 1x10" until '61 when converted to 1x12", tweed, then gray, then finally black covered.

1950s	Tweed	$475	$525
1960-1962	Tweed, 1x10" or 1x12"	$475	$525
1963-1966	Black or gray, 1x12"	$475	$525

Model 6157 Super Bass (Piggyback) Amp
Mid-late-1960s. 35 watts, 2x15" cabinet, single channel.

| 1960s | | $400 | $475 |

Model 6159 Super Bass/Dual Playboy (Combo) Amp
Mid-late-1960s. 35 watts, tube, 2x12" cabinet, dual channel, black covering. Replaced by 6163 Chet Atkins Piggyback Amp.

| 1960s | | $450 | $575 |

MODEL YEAR	FEATURES	EXC. COND. LOW	HIGH

Model 6160 Chet Atkins Country Gentleman Amp

Early-late-1960s. Combo tube amp, 35 watts, 2x12" cabinet, 2 channels. Replaced by 6163 Chet Atkins Piggyback amp with tremolo but no reverb.

1960s		$475	$550

Model 6161 Dual Twin Tremolo Amp

Ca.1962-late-1960s. 19 watts (later 17 watts), 2x10" with 5" tweeter, tremolo.

1960s		$475	$600

Model 6161 Electromatic Twin Amp

Ca.1953-ca.1960. Gray Silverflake covering, two 11x6" speakers, 14 watts, tremolo, wraparound grille '55 and after.

1950s		$475	$600

Model 6162 Dual Twin Tremolo & Reverb Amp

Ca.1964-late-1960s. 17 watts, 2x10", reverb, tremolo. Vertical combo amp style introduced in '68.

1964-1967	Horizontal combo style	$600	$700
1968-1969	Vertical combo style	$400	$600

Model 6163 Chet Atkins (Piggyback) Amp

Mid-late-1960s. 70 watts, 1x12" and 1x15", black covering, tremolo, reverb.

1960s		$475	$550

Model 6164 Variety Amp

Early-mid-1960s. 35 watts, tube, 2x12".

1960s		$475	$550

Model 6165 Variety Plus Amp

Early-mid-1960s. Tube amp, 35 watts, 2x12", reverb and tremolo, separate controls for both channels.

1960s		$575	$650

Model 6166 Fury (Combo) Amp

Mid-1960s. Tube combo amp, 70 watts, 2x12", separate controls for both channels, large metal handle.

1960s		$475	$550

Model 6169 Electromatic Twin Western Finish Amp

Ca.1953-ca.1960. Western finish, 14 watts, 2-11x6" speakers, tremolo, wraparound grill '55 and after.

1950s		$1,900	$2,300

Model 6169 Fury (Piggyback) Amp

Late-1960s. Tube amp, 70 watts, 2x12", separate controls for both channels.

1960s		$500	$650

Model 6170 Pro Bass Amp

1966-late-1960s. 25 or 35 watts, depending on model, 1x15", vertical cabinet style (vs. box cabinet).

1966-1969		$350	$450

Model 7154 Nashville Amp

Introduced in 1969. Solidstate combo amp, 4' tall, 75 watts, 2x15", reverb, tremolo, magic echo.

1970s		$475	$550

Model 7155 Tornado PA System Amp

Introduced in 1969. Solidstate piggyback head and cab, 150 watts, 2 column speaker cabs, reverb, tremolo, magic echo.

1970s	2x2x15"	$475	$550
1970s	2x4x15"	$575	$650

Model 7517 Rogue Amp

1970s. Solidstate, 40 watts, 2x12", tall vertical cabinet, front control panel.

1970s		$250	$275

Rex Royal Amp

1950s. Small student compact amp, low power, 1x8", Rex Royal logo on grille, Fred Gretsch logo on back panel, single on-off volume knob.

1950s		$200	$225

Groove Tubes

1979-present. Started by Aspen Pittman in his garage in Sylmar, California, Groove Tubes is now located in San Fernando. GT manufactures and distributes a full line of tubes. In '86 they added amp production and in '91 tube microphones. Aspen is also the author of the *Tube Amp Book.*

Guild

1952-present. Guild offered amps from the '60s into the '80s. Some of the early models were built by Hagstrom.

Double Twin Amp

1953-1955. 35 watts, 2x12" plus 2 tweeters, 2-tone leatherette covered cab.

1953-1955		$475	$625

Master Amp

Ca. 1957- Ca. 1957. 2-tone tweed and leatherette combo, tremolo, Guild script logo and smaller block Master logo..

1950s		$400	$500

Maverick Amp

1960s. Dual speaker combo, verticle cab, tremolo, reverb, red/pink control panel, 2-tone black and silver grille.

1960s		$250	$350

Model One Amp

Mid-1970s-1977. 30 watts, 1x12" vertical cab combo, reverb and tremolo.

1970s		$175	$225

Model Two Amp

Mid-1970s-1977. 50 watts, 2x10" vertical cab combo, reverb and tremolo.

1977-1978		$200	$250

Model Three Amp

Mid-1970s-1977. 60 watts, 1x15" vertical cab combo, for bass, organ and guitar.

1977-1978		$225	$275

Model Four Amp

Early-1980s. Six watts.

1980s		$125	$175

Model Five Amp

Early-1980s. 10 watts, 6.25" speaker.

1980s		$135	$185

Model Six Amp

Early-1980s. Same as Model Five but with reverb.

1980s		$150	$200

Model Seven Amp

Early-1980s. Small amp for guitar, bass and keyboard, 12 watts.

1980s		$135	$185

1950s Gretsch Model 6169 Electromatic Twin

1964 Gretsch 6164 Variety

Groove Tubes Soul-O Single (head)

AMPS

Guild Thunderstar

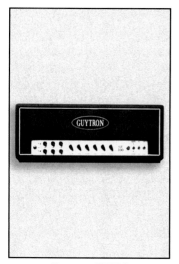

Guytron GT100

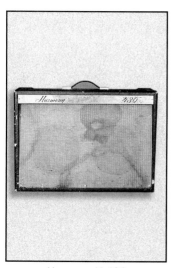

Harmony H-430

MODEL YEAR	FEATURES	EXC. COND. LOW	HIGH

Model 50-J Amp
Early-1960s. 14 watts, 1x12", tremolo, blue/gray vinyl.
| 1962-1963 | | $175 | $200 |

Model 66 Amp
1953-1955. 15 watts, 1x12", tremolo, 2-tone leatherette.
| 1953-1955 | | $200 | $275 |

Model 66-J Amp
1962-1963. 20 watts, 1x12", tremolo, blue/gray vinyl.
| 1962-1963 | | $225 | $300 |

Model 98-RT Amp
1962-1963. The only stand-alone reverb amp from Guild in the early '60s, 30 watts, 1x12", blue/gray vinyl.
| 1962-1963 | | $500 | $650 |

Model 99 Amp
1953-1955. 20 watts, 1x12", tremolo, 2-tone leatherette.
| 1953-1955 | | $300 | $350 |

Model 99-J Amp
Early-1960s. 30 watts, 1x12", tremolo, blue/gray vinyl.
| 1962-1963 | | $350 | $400 |

Model 99-U Ultra Amp
Early-1960s. Piggyback 30-watt head with optional 1x12" or 1x15" cab, cab and head lock together, tremolo, blue/gray vinyl.
| 1962-1963 | | $400 | $500 |

Model 100-J Amp
Early-1960s. 35 watts, 1x15", blue/gray vinyl.
| 1962-1963 | | $375 | $425 |

Model 200-S Stereo Combo Amp
Early-1960s. 25 watts per channel, total 50 watts stereo, 2x12", tremolo, blue/gray vinyl, wheat grille.
| 1962-1963 | | $700 | $800 |

Model RC-30 Reverb Converter Amp
Early-1960s. Similar to Gibson GA-1 converter, attaches with 2 wires clipped to originating amp's speaker, 8 watts, 1x10", blue/gray vinyl.
| 1962-1963 | | $300 | $350 |

SuperStar Amp
Ca.1972-ca.1974. 50 watts, all tubes, 1x15" Jensen speakers, vertical combo, reverb, tremolo, black vinyl cover, 2-tone black/silver grille.
| 1972-1974 | | $300 | $400 |

Thunder 1 (Model 11RVT)/T1 Amp
Introduced 1965. Combo with dual speakers and reverb, light tan cover, 2-tone tan grille.
| 1965-1968 | | $350 | $450 |

ThunderStar Bass Amp
1960s. Piggyback bass tube head or combo, 50 watts.
| 1965-1968 | | $375 | $500 |

Guyatone
1933-present. Started offering amps by at least the late '40s with their Guya lap steels. In '51 the Guyatone brand is first used on guitars and most likely amps. Guyatone also made the Marco Polo, Winston, Kingston, Kent, LaFayette and Bradford brands.

MODEL YEAR	FEATURES	EXC. COND. LOW	HIGH

Guytron
1995-present. Tube amp heads and speaker cabinets built by Guy Hedrick in Columbiaville, Michigan.

Hagstrom
1921-1983. The Swedish guitar maker built a variety of tube and solidstate amps from ca. 1961 into the '70s. They also supplied amps to Guild.

Harmony
1892-1976, late-1970s-present. Harmony was one of the biggest producers of guitars, and offered amps as well. MBT International offered Harmony amps for 2000-'02.

H Series Amp
Harmony model numbers begin with H, such as H-304, all H series models shown are tube amps unless otherwise noted as solidstate.
1940-1950s	H-200	$275	$375
1950s	H-204, 18w, 1x12"	$150	$250
1960s	H-303A, 8w, 1x8"	$100	$175
1960s	H-304, low pwr, small spkr	$150	$225
1960s	H-305A, low pwr, small spkr	$150	$250
1960s	H-306A, combo 1x12"	$175	$250
1960s	H306C, piggyback 2x12"	$450	$525
1960s	H-400, 8w, 1x8"	$100	$175
1960s	H-410A, 10w, 1x10"	$150	$225
1960s	H-415, 20w, 2x10"	$200	$275
1960s	H-420, 20w, 1x12"	$175	$250
1960s	H-430, 30w, 2x12"	$225	$300

Small Solidstate Amps
Dark covering, dark grille.
| 1970s | | $80 | $120 |

Harry Joyce
1993-2000. Hand-wired British tube amps, combos, and cabinets from builder Harry Joyce. Joyce was contracted to build Hiwatt amps in England during the '60s and '70s. He died on January 11, 2002.

Hartke
1984-present. Guitar and bass amps, combos and cabinets made in the U.S. Founded by Larry Hartke, since the mid-'80s, Hartke has been distributed by Samson Technologies. Hartke also offered basses in the past.

1-15B-XL Cab
1994-present. XL Series, 1x15" rated at 180 watts, larger cab, black cover.
| 1990s | | $225 | $275 |

4.5-XL Cab
1994-present. XL Series, 4x10" and 5" driver rated at 400 watts, larger ported cab.
| 1994-2003 | | $325 | $425 |

AMPS

MODEL YEAR	FEATURES	EXC. COND. LOW	HIGH

B 30/B 300 Bass Combo Amp
1999-present. Compact practice amp, 30 watts, 1x10", dark cover. Changed to B 300 in '05.

1999-2000		$125	$175

HA 1410 Bass Combo Amp
1994-2004. Solidstate, 140 watts, 2x10", dark cover.

1994-2004		$275	$350

HA 2000 Bass Head Amp
1992-2004. 200 watts, tube preamp, solidstate power section, tube/solidstate switchable.

1992-2004		$275	$350

HA 3500 Bass Head Amp
1992-present. Solidstate, 350 watts, 10-band graphic EQ, rack mount.

1992-1999		$350	$400
2000-2004		$375	$425

Transporter Series Cab
1990s. 1x15" cab rated 150 watts, or 4x10" rated 200-300 watts, black cover, black metal grille.

1990s	150 watts, 1x15"	$225	$275
1990s	200-300 watts, 4x10"	$250	$325

Haynes
Haynes guitar amps were built by the Amplifier Corporation of America (ACA) of Westbury, New York. ACA also made an early distortion device powered by batteries. Unicord purchased the company in around 1964, and used the factory to produce its Univox line of amps, most likely discontinuing the Haynes brand at the same time.

Jazz King II Amp
1960s. Solidstate, stereo console-style, 2x12", Haynes logo upper right side.

1960s		$200	$300

Headstrong
2003-present. Tube combo amps built by Wayne Jones in Asheville, North Carolina. They also offer a range of replacement cabinets for vintage amps.

Heritage
2004-present. Founded by Malcolm MacDonald and Lane Zastrow who was formerly involved with Holland amps. Located in the former Holland facility in Brentwood, Tennessee, they build tube combo and piggyback amps.

Hilgen
1960s. Mid-level amplifiers from Hilgen Manufacturing, Hillside, New Jersey. Dark tolex covering and swiggle-lined light color grille cloth. Examples have been found with original Jensen speakers.

Basso Grande Bass Head Amp
1960s. Brown metallic sparkle cover, 4 inputs.

1960s		$250	$300

Model T-2512 Star Amp
1960s. 25 watts, 1x12" combo, tremolo.

1960s		$250	$300

Model T-2513 Galaxie Amp
1960s. 25 watts, 1x12" piggyback cabinet, tremolo.

1960s		$250	$300

HiWatt

Bulldog SA112 Amp
1980s, 1994-present. 50 watts, combo, 1x12".

1980s		$1,000	$1,400
1990s		$700	$1,000

Bulldog SA112FL Amp
1980s-1990s. 100 watts, combo, 1x12".

1980s		$1,000	$1,400
1990s		$700	$1,000

Lead 20 (SG-20) Amp Head
1980s. Tube amp head, 30 watts, black cover, rectangular HiWatt plate logo.

1980s		$700	$1,000

Lead 50R Combo Amp
1980s. Combo tube amp, 50 watts, 1x12", reverb, dark cover, dark grille, HiWatt rectangular plate logo.

1980s		$900	$1,300

Model DR Series Amp Head
1970-1988. Tube head, 200 watts.

1970-1977		$2,000	$2,200
1978-1988		$1,900	$2,100

Model DR-103 Amp Head
1970-late-1980s, 1995-present. Tube head, 100 watts.

1970-1977		$1,800	$2,000
1978-1988		$1,700	$1,900

Model DR-504 Amp Head
1970-late-1980s, 1995-1999. Tube head amp, 50 watts.

1970-1977		$1,500	$1,700
1978-1987		$1,400	$1,600

PW-50 Tube Amp
1989-1993. Stereo tube amp, 50 watts per channel.

1989-1993		$700	$1,000

S50L Amp Head
1989-1993. Lead guitar head, 50 watts, gain, master volume, EQ.

1989-1993		$600	$900

SE 4122 4x12 Speaker Cab
1971- mid-1980s. Salt and pepper grille cloth, 4x12" Fane speakers, 300 watts.

1970s		$1,500	$1,700

Hoffman
1993-present. Tube amps, combos, reverb units, and cabinets built by Doug Hoffman from 1993 to '99, in Sarasota, Florida. Hoffman no longer builds amps, concentrating on selling tube amp building supplies, and since 2001 has been located in Pisgah Forest, North Carolina.

Hartke B120

Headstrong BL 310

HiWatt Bulldog SA112

AMPS

Holland Lil' Jimi

Holmes Pro 112

Hughes & Kettner ATS-60

MODEL YEAR	FEATURES	EXC. COND. LOW	HIGH

Hohner

1857-present. Matthias Hohner, a clockmaker in Trossingen, Germany, founded Hohner in 1857, making harmonicas. Hohner has been offering guitars and amps at least since the early '70s.

Panther Series Amps

1980s. Smaller combo amps, master volume, gain, EQ.

1980s	P-12 (12 watts)	$70	$100
1980s	P-20 (20 watts)	$75	$125
1980s	P-25R (25 watts)	$75	$125
1980s	PBK-20 bass/ keyboard (25 watts)	$75	$150

Sound Producer Series Amps

1980s. Master volume, normal and overdrive, reverb, headphone jack.

1980s	SP 35	$75	$150
1980s	SP 55	$75	$150
1980s	SP 75	$100	$175
1980s	BA 130 bass	$75	$150

Holland

1992-2004. Tube combo amps from builder Mike Holland, originally in Virginia Beach, Virginia, and since 2000 in Brentwood, Tennessee. In 2000, Holland took Lane Zastrow as a partner, forming L&M Amplifiers to build the Holland line. The company closed in '04.

Holmes

1970-late 1980s. Founded by Harrison Holmes. Holmes amplifiers were manufactured in Mississippi and their product line included guitar and bass amps, PA systems, and mixing boards. In the early '80s, Harrsion Holmes sold the company to On-Site Music which called the firm The Holmes Corp. Products manufactured by Harrison have an all-caps HOLMES logo and the serial number plate says The Holmes Company.

Performer PB-115 Bass Amp

60 watts, 1x15", black tolex.

1982		$100	$150

Pro Compact 210S Amp

60 watts, 2x10", 2 channels, active EQ, black tolex.

1982		$100	$150

Pro Compact 212S Amp

2x12" version of Pro.

1982		$125	$175

Rebel RB-112 Bass Amp

35 watts, 1x12", black tolex

1982		$75	$125

Hondo

1969-1987, 1991-present. Hondo has offered imported amps over the years. 1990s models ranged from the H20 Practice Amp to the H160SRC with 160 watts (peak) and 2x10" speakers.

Amps

1970-1990s	Various models	$25	$75

MODEL YEAR	FEATURES	EXC. COND. LOW	HIGH

Hound Dog

1994-1998. Founded by George Alessandro as the Hound Dog Corporation. Name was changed to Alessandro in 1998 (see that brand for more info).

Hughes & Kettner

1985-present. Hughes & Kettner offers a line of solidstate and tube guitar and bass amps, combos, cabinets and effects, all made in Germany.

ATS MkII 112 Combo Amp

1990-1993. MOS-FET power amp, 2-stage tube channel, transistorized clean channel, compressor, EQ, reverb. Available with 1x12", 2x12", or 4x12" cabs (GL 112, GL 212, or GL 412).

1990-1993		$275	$350

ATTAX 50 Stereo Amp

1996-2000. 40 watt 1x12" combo, black vinyl.

1996-2000		$275	$350

ATTAX 200 Stereo Amp

1994-2000. 200 watt 2x12" combo, black vinyl, tube preamp.

1994-2000		$375	$475

Duotone Amp

2000-present. 50 watt 1x12" tube combo.

2000-2004		$750	$850

Edition Tube Amp

2001-2002. 20 watt 1x12" tube combo.

2001-2002		$350	$450

Fortress Bass Preamp

1990-1994. Built-in compressor, EQ, tube preamp section.

1990-1994		$125	$175

Warp 7 Amp

2002-present. 100 watts, offered as head or 1x12" or 2x12" combo.

2002-2004	Combo	$175	$195
2002-2004	Head	$150	$160

Hurricane

1998-present. Tube guitar and harmonica combo amps built by Gary Drouin in Sarasota, Florida. Drouin started the company with harp master Rock Bottom, who died in September, 2001.

Ibanez

1932-present. Ibanez added solidstate amps to their product line in '98. They also build guitars, basses and effects.

TA Series Amp

Models include TA35 Troubadour (35 watts, 1x10").

2004	TA35	$175	$200

Idol

Late-1960s. Made in Japan. Dark tolex cover, dark grille, Hobby Series with large Idol logo on front.

Hobby Series Amps

1968	Hobby 10	$75	$90
1968	Hobby 100	$175	$250

MODEL YEAR	FEATURES	EXC. COND. LOW	HIGH
1968	Hobby 20	$100	$150
1968	Hobby 45	$150	$200
Model 007 Amp			
1968		$30	$45

Imperial

Ca.1963-ca.1970. The Imperial Accordion Company of Chicago, Illinois offered one or two imported small amps in the '60s.

Jack Daniel's

2004-present. Tube guitar amp built by Peavey for the Jack Daniel Distillery. They also offer a guitar model.

Jackson

1980-present. The Jackson-Charvel Company offered amps and cabinets in the late '80s and the '90s.

4x12" Cabinet

1990s. Red cone Jackson speakers in slant cabinet with see-thru metal grille.

1990s		$350	$475

Apogee 50 Combo Amp

1980s. Two channels, lead with boost, 2 speakers.

1980s		$800	$950

JG-2 Head Amp

Tube head, 50 watts, 2-stage preamp, midrange boost, presence, effects loop, EL34 tubes.

1980s		$325	$375

JG-3 Head Amp

Tube head, 100 watts, 2-stage preamp, midrange boost, presence, effects loop, EL34 tubes.

1980s		$350	$400

Reference 100 Head Amp

1990s. 100 watts, 3 channels, welded chromate-conversion aluminum chassis.

1994		$300	$350

Jackson-Guldan

1920s-1960s. The Jackson-Guldan Violin Company, of Columbus, Ohio, offered lap steels and small tube amps early on. They also built acoustic guitars.

Jay Turser

1997-present. Smaller, inexpensive imported solidstate guitar and bass amps. They also offer basses and guitars.

JMI (Jennings Musical Industries)

2004-present. Jennings built the Vox amps of the 1960s. They are back with tube amp heads and cabinets based on some of their classic models.

Johnson

Mid-1990s-present. Line of solidstate amps imported by Music Link, Brisbane, California. Johnson also offers guitars, basses, mandolins and effects.

Johnson Amplification

1997-present. Intermediate and professional grade, production, modeling amps and effects designed by John Johnson, of Sandy, Utah. The company is part of Harman International. In 2002, they quit building amps, but continue the effects line.

JoMama

1994-present. Tube amps and combos under the JoMama and Kelemen brands built by Joe Kelemen in Santa Fe, New Mexico.

Juke

1989-present. Tube guitar and harmonica amps built by G.R. Croteau in Troy, New Hampshire. He also built the Warbler line of amps.

Kalamazoo

1933-1942, 1965-1970. Kalamazoo was a brand Gibson used on one of their budget lines. They used the name on amps from '65 to '67.

Bass Amp

1965-1967. Enclosed back, 2x10", flip-out control panel, not a commonly found model as compared to numerous Model 1 and 2 student amps.

1965-1967		$250	$325

Lap Steel Amp

1940s. Kalamazoo logo on front lower right, low power with 1-6V6, round speaker grille opening, red/brown leatherette.

1940s		$125	$250

Model 1 Amp

1965-1967. No tremolo, 1x10", front control panel, black.

1965-1967		$125	$200

Model 2 Amp

1965-1967. Same as Model 1 with tremolo, black.

1965-1967		$150	$225

Reverb 12 Amp

1965-1967. Black vinyl cover, 1x12", reverb, tremolo.

1965-1967		$225	$325

Kay

Ca.1931-present. Kay offered amps throughout their history up to around '68 when the brand changed hands. Currently distributed in the U.S. by A.R. Musical Enterprises. See Guitar Stories Volume II, by Michael Wright, for a complete history of Kay with detailed model listings.

K506 Vibrato 12" Amp

1960s. 12 watts, 1x12", swirl grille, metal handle.

1962		$175	$250

K507 Twin Ten Special Amp

1960s. 20 watts, 2x10", swirl grille, metal handle.

1962		$225	$300

Small Tube Amps

1940s	Wood cabinet	$175	$300
1950s	Various models	$125	$175

Hurricane V-30 combo

Juke 1210

1962 Kay 703

AMPS

1963 Kay Vanguard 704

Kendrick K Spot

KJL Dirty 30

MODEL YEAR	FEATURES	EXC. COND. LOW	HIGH
1960s	Models K503, K504, K505	$100	$175

Kelemen

1994-present. Tube amps and combos under the JoMama and Kelemen brands built by Joe Kelemen in Santa Fe, New Mexico.

Kendrick

1989-present. Founded by Gerald Weber in Austin, Texas and currently located in Kempfner, Texas. Mainly known for their handmade tube amps, Kendrick also offers guitars, speakers, and effects. At the end of '03, Weber quit taking orders for most production amps, but still builds select models. They also to offer amp kits and build guitars. Gerald writes monthly columns for *Vintage Guitar* magazine and has authored books and videos on tube amps.

118 Amp
1990s. Narrow panel tweed, 5 watts, 1x8".

1990s		$500	$550

2210 Amp
1993-1995. Tweed combo, 2x10", a few were also made from '98-'03.

1993-1995		$1,100	$1,600

2410 Amp
1989-1995. Combo 4x10", a few were also made from '98-'03.

1989-1995		$1,200	$1,800

4212 Amp
1992-1995. Combo, 2x12", a few were also made from '98-'03.

1992-1995		$1,200	$1,800

Baby Huey Combo Amp
1993-1994. Special custom order, 12 made, all but 2 made from a re-manufactured Vox AC 125 chassis with special custom output transformers, a 2X12" cabinet and a Kendrick Model 1000 Reverb. Not a part of the Kendrick line.

1993-1994		$1,400	$2,000

Black Gold Stereo BG-15 Amp
1998-2003. Class A, 2x15 watt output to separate output transformer and speaker.

1998-2003		$900	$1,250

Black Gold BG-35 Amp
1997-2003. 35 watts, 1x12" or 2x10".

1997-2003		$900	$1,250

Model 4000 Special Amp Head
1990-1993. Solidstate rectifiers, 4 6L6GC output tubes, switchable to 120 or 60 watts, black tolex, only 25 made.

1990-1993		$750	$950

Sonny Boy Amp
1990s. Compact, 2 6L6 combo.

1990s		$950	$1,250

Texas Crude Gusher Amp
1995-1998. 50 watts, 2x12" or 4x10" combo.

1995-1998	2x12"	$1,200	$1,700
1995-1998	4x10"	$1,200	$1,800

The Gusher Combo Amp
1996-1998. 50 watt Texas Gusher combo, 1x15", 2x10", or 4x10", a few were also made from 2002 to '03.

1996-1998		$1,200	$1,800

Kent

Ca.1962-1969. Imported budget line of guitars and amps.

Guitar and Bass Amps
1960s. Various models.

1966	1475, 3 tubes, brown	$50	$60
1966	2198, 3 tubes, brown	$60	$70
1966	5999, 3 tubes, brown	$70	$80
1966	6104, piggyback, 12w	$110	$135
1969	6610, solidstate, small	$25	$30

Kiesel

See Carvin.

Kingston

1958-1967. Economy solidstate amps imported by Westheimer Importing, Chicago, Illinois.

Cat P-1 Amp
Mid-1960s. Solidstate, 3 watts, very small speaker, Cat Series amps have dark vinyl, dark grille. The original retail selling price in the mid-'60s was $25.99.

1960s		$30	$45

Cat P-2 Amp
Mid-1960s. Solidstate, 5 watts, very small speaker.

1960s		$35	$50

Cat P-3 Amp
Mid-1960s. Solidstate, 8 watts, 1x8".

1960s		$40	$55

Cat P-8 T Amp
Mid-1960s. Solidstate, 20 watts, 1x8", tremolo.

1960s		$40	$55

Cougar BA-21 Bass Piggyback Amp
Mid-1960s. Solidstate, 60 watts, 2x12" cab, dark vinyl, light silver grille.

1960s		$70	$150

Cougar PB-5 Bass Combo Amp
Mid-1960s. Solidstate, 15 watts, 1x8", dark vinyl cover, dark grille.

1960s		$40	$55

Lion 2000 Piggyback Amp
Mid-1960s. Solidstate, 90 watts, 2x12" cab, dark tuck-and-roll-type cover, dark grille.

1960s		$90	$175

Lion 3000 Piggyback Amp
Mid-1960s. Solidstate, 250 watts, 4x12" cab, dark tuck-and-roll-type cover, dark grille.

1960s		$120	$200

Lion AP-281 R Piggyback Amp
Mid-1960s. Solidstate, 30 watts, 2x8" cab, dark vinyl cover, light silver grille.

1960s		$55	$90

Lion AP-281 R10 Piggyback Amp
Mid-1960s. Solidstate, 30 watts, 2x10" cab, dark vinyl cover, light silver grille.

1960s		$70	$150

AMPS

MODEL		EXC. COND.	
YEAR	FEATURES	LOW	HIGH

Kitchen-Marshall

1965-1966. Private branded for Kitchen Music by Marshall, primarily PA units with block logos. Limited production.

JTM 45 MKII 45-Watt Head Amp

1965-1966. Private branded for Kitchen Music, JTM 45 Marshall with Kitchen logo plate, 45 watts.

1965-1966		$5,500	$6,500

Slant 4x12 1960 Cab

1965-1966. Slant front 4x12" 1960-style cabinet with gray bluesbreaker grille, very limited production.

1965-1966	Black on green vinyl	$4,500	$5,100

KJL

1995-present. Founded by Kenny Lannes, MSEE, a professor of Electrical Engineering at the University of New Orleans. KLJ makes tube combo amps, heads and an ABY box.

Dirty 30 Amp Head

2004-present. Tube amp head, 15/30 watts, switchable A to AB.

2004		$600	$700

Open Back Cabinet

2000s	2x10"	$325	$375

KMD (Kaman)

1986-ca.1990. Distributed by Kaman (Ovation, Hamer, etc.) in the late '80s, KMD offered a variety of amps and effects.

Koch

All-tube combo amps, heads, effects and cabinets built in The Netherlands.

Komet

Tube amp heads built with circuits designed by Ken Fischer of Trainwreck fame.

60-Watt Head Amp

2000s. 2 ECC83s, single channel and input.

2000s		$1,600	$1,800

Kona

2001-present. Budget solidstate amps made in Asia. They also offer guitars, basses and mandolins.

Krank

1996-present. Founded by Tony Dow and offering tube amp heads, combos and speaker cabinets built in Tempe, Arizona. They also build effects. The company greatly upped its distribution in '03.

Kustom

1965-present. Kustom, a division of Hanser Holdings, offers guitar and bass combo amps and PA equipment. Founded by Bud Ross in Chanute, Kansas, who offered tuck-and-roll amps as early as '58, but began using the Kustom brand name in '65. From '69 to '75 Ross gradually sold interest in the company (in the late '70s, Ross introduced the line of Ross effects stomp boxes). The brand changed hands a few times, and by the mid-'80s it was no longer in use. In '89 Kustom was in bankruptcy court and was purchased by Hanser Holdings Incorporated of Cincinnati, Ohio (Davitt & Hanser) and by '94, they had a new line of amps available.

Prices are for excellent condition amps with no tears in the tuck-and-roll cover and no grille tears. A tear in the tuck-and-roll will reduce the value, sometimes significantly.

Kustom model identification can be frustrating as they used series numbers, catalog numbers (the numbers in the catalogs and price lists), and model numbers (the number often found next to the serial number on the amp's back panel). Most of the discussion that follows is by series number (100, 200, 300, etc.) and catalog number. Unfortunately, vintage amp dealers use the serial number and model number, so the best way is to cross-check speaker and amplifier attributes. Model numbers were used primarily for repair purposes and were found in the repair manuals. In many, but not all cases, the model number is the last digit of the catalog number; for example the catalog lists a 100 series Model 1-15J-1, where the last digit 1 signifies a Model 1 amplifier chassis which is a basic amp without reverb or tremolo. A Model 1-15J-2 signifies a Model 2 amp chassis that has reverb and tremolo. In this example, Kustom uses a different model number on the back of the amp head. For the 1-15J-2, the model number on the back panel of the amp head would be K100-2, indicating a series 100 (50 watts) amp with reverb and tremolo (amp chassis Model 2).

Amp Chasis Model Numbers ('68-'72)

Model 1   Amp (basic)
Model 2   Amp with reverb
Model 3   Amp with Harmonic Clip and Boost
Model 4   Amp with reverb, tremolo, vibrato, Harmonic Clip and Selective Boost
Model 5   PA with reverb
Model 6   Amp (basic) with Selectone
Model 7   Amp with reverb, tremolo, vibrato, boost (different parts)
Model 8   Amp with reverb, tremolo, vibrato, boost (different parts)

Naugahyde Tuck-&-Roll 200 ('65-'67)

The very first Kustoms did not have the model series on the front control panel. The early logo stipulated Kustom by Ross, Inc. The name was then updated to Kustom Electronics, Inc. 1965-'67 amp heads have a high profile/tall "forehead" area (the area on top of the controls) and these have been nicknamed "Frankenstein models." The '65-'67 catalog numbers were often 4 or 5 digits, for example J695. The first digit represents the speaker type (J = Jensen, etc.), other examples are L995, L1195, L795RV, etc. Some '67 catalog numbers changed to 2 digits followed by 3 digits, like 4-D 140f, or 3-15C (3 CTS speakers), etc. Others sported 5 characters like 4-15J-1, where 4 = 4 speakers, 15 = 15" speakers, J = Jensen, and 1 = basic amp chassis with no effects. The fifth

Koch Classictone

Krank 100 Watt combo

Kustom Commander

Kustom Hustler

Kustom K-25-C

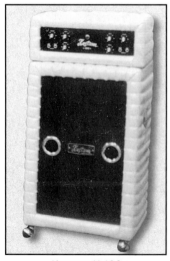

Kustom K-100

digit indicated amp chassis model number as described above.

Naugahyde Tuck-&-Roll 100/200/400 ('68-'71)

Starting in '68, the Kustom logo also included the model series. A K100, for example, would have 100 displayed below the Kustom name. The model series generally is twice the relative output wattage, for example, the 100 Series is a 50-watt amp. Keep in mind, solidstate ratings are often higher than tube-amp ratings, so use the ratings as relative measurements. Most '68-'70 Kustom catalog numbers are x-xxx-x, for example 1-15L-1. First digit represents the number of speakers, the 2nd and 3rd represent the speaker size, the fourth represents the speaker type (A = Altec Lansing, L = J.B.L., J = Jensen, C = C.T.S. Bass), the fifth digit represents the amp chassis number. The power units were interchangeable in production, so amps could have similar front-ends but different power units (more power and different effect options) and visa versa. Some '68 bass amp catalog numbers were 4 digits, for example 2-12C, meaning two 12" CTS speakers. Again, there were several different numbers used.

Kustom also introduced the 200 and 400 amp series and the logo included the series number. The catalog numbers were similar to the 100 series, but they had a higher power rating of 100 equivalent watts (200 series), or 200 equivalent watts (400 series).

Kustom U.S. Naugahyde (tuck-&-roll) covers came in 7 colors: black (the most common), Cascade (blue/green), silver (white-silver), gold (light gold), red, blue, and Charcoal (gray). The market historically shows color options fetching more. The market has not noticeably distinguished power and features options. Condition and color seem to be the most important. Gold and Cascade may be the rarest seen colors.

Naugahyde Tuck-&-Roll 150/250/300/500/600 (c.'71-c.'75)

The amp heads changed with a slightly slanted control panel and the Kustom logo moved to the right/upper-right portion of the front panel. They continued to be tuck-&-roll offered in the same variety of colors. The sales literature indicated a 150 series had 150 watts, 250 had 250 watts, etc.

Naugahyde Tuck-&-Roll SC (Self Contained) Series

Most SC combo amps were rated at 150 watts, with the 1-12SC listed at 50 watts. They were offered in 7 colors of tuck-and-roll. Again the model numbers indicate the features as follows: 4-10 SC is a 4 x 10", 2-10 SC is a 2x10", etc.

Super Sound Tuck-and-Roll Combo Series

The last tuck-and-roll combo amps with slightly smaller tucks. Amp control panel is noticeably smaller and the Kustom logo is in the right side of the control panel. Includes the following models:

Black Vinyl ('75-c.'78)

By '75 ownership changes were complete and

the colorful tuck-and-roll was dropped in favor of more traditional black vinyl. The products had a slant Kustom logo spelled-out and placed in a position on the grille similar to a Fender blackface baffle. Models included the I, II, III, and IV Lead amps. Heads with half- and full-stacks were available. Bass amps included the Kustom I, Bass I, II, III, IV, and IV SRO.

Black Vinyl "K" logo ('78-'83)

This era is easily recognized by the prominent capital K logo.

Bass V Amp

1990s. Large Kustom Bass V logo upper right side of amp, 35 watts, 1x12", black vinyl.

MODEL YEAR	FEATURES	EXC. COND. LOW	HIGH
1990s		$75	$125

Challenger Amp
1973-1975. 1x12" speaker.

1973-1975	Black	$275	$400
1973-1975	Color option	$450	$500

Hustler Amp
1973-1975. Solidstate combo amp, 4x10", tremolo, tuck-and-roll.

1973-1975	Black	$325	$400
1973-1975	Color option	$525	$600

K25/K25 C-2 SC Amp
1960s. SC (self-contained) Series, small combo tuck-and-roll, 1x12", solidstate, reverb, black control panel.

1971-1973	Black	$325	$375
1971-1973	Color option	$425	$575

K50-2 SC Amp
1971-1973. Self-contained (SC) small combo tuck-and-roll, 1x12", reverb and tremolo.

1971-1973	Black	$350	$400
1971-1973	Color option	$450	$600

K100-1 Amp Head
1968-1972. The K100-1 is the basic amp without reverb (suffix 1), 50-watt, solidstate energizer head, offered in black or several color options.

1968-1972	Black	$175	$225
1968-1972	Color option	$300	$350

K100-1 1-15C Bass Amp Set
1968-1972. K100-1 with 1-15C speaker option with matching 1x15" cab, black tuck-and-roll standard, but several sparkle colors offered, C.T.S. bass reflex speaker.

1968-1972	Black	$300	$400
1968-1972	Color option	$550	$750

K100-1 1-15L-1/1-15A-1/1-15J-1 Amp Set
1968-1972. K100-1 with matching 1x15" cab, black tuck-and-roll standard, but several colors offered, speaker options are JBL, Altec Lansing or Jensen.

1968-1972	Black	$300	$400
1968-1972	Color option	$550	$750

K100-1 1-D140F Bass Amp
1968-1972. K100-1 with matching 1x15" JBL D-140F cab, black tuck-and-roll standard, but several sparkle colors offered.

1968-1972	Black	$325	$425
1968-1972	Color option	$575	$775

K100-1 2-12C Bass Amp Set

1968-1972. K100-1 with matching 2x12" cab, black tuck-and-roll standard, but several sparkle colors offered, C.T.S. bass reflex speakers.

1968-1972	Black	$350	$450
1968-1972	Color option	$600	$800

K100-2 Reverb/Tremolo Amp Head

1968-1972. K100 50-watt solidstate energizer head with added reverb/tremolo, offered in black or several color options.

1968-1972	Black	$250	$300
1968-1972	Color option	$475	$550

K100-2 1-15L-2/1-15A-2/1-15J-2 Amp Set

1968-1972. K100-2 head and matching 1x15" cab, black tuck-and-roll standard, but several sparkle colors offered.

1968-1972	Black	$375	$475
1968-1972	Color option	$650	$800

K100-2 2-12A-2/2-12J-2 Amp Set

1968-1972. K100-2 head with matching 2x12" cab, black tuck-and-roll standard, but several sparkle colors offered.

1968-1972	Black	$425	$525
1968-1972	Color option	$675	$850

K100-5 PA Amp Head

1968-1972. 50 watts, 2 channels with 8 control knobs per channel, reverb, Kustom 100 logo located above the 4 high-impedance mic inputs.

1968-1972	Black	$250	$300
1968-1972	Color option	$400	$475

K100-6 SC Amp

1970-1972. Basic combo amp with selectone, no reverb.

1970-1972	Black	$300	$400

K100-7 SC Amp

1970-1972. Combo amp with reverb, tremolo, vibrato and boost.

1970-1972	Black	$325	$425
1970-1972	Color option	$575	$750

K100-8 SC Amp

1970-1972. Combo amp with reverb, tremolo, vibrato and boost.

1970-1972	Black	$350	$450
1970-1972	Color option	$600	$775

K100C-6 Amp

1968-1970. Kustom 100 logo middle of the front control panel, 1x15" combo, selectone option.

1968-1970	Black	$300	$400

K100C-8 Amp

1968-1970. Kustom 100 logo middle of the front control panel, 4x10" combo, reverb, tremolo, vibrato.

1968-1970	Black	$350	$450

K150-1 Amp Set

1972-1975. Piggyback, 150 watts, 2x12", no reverb, logo in upper right corner of amp head, tuck-and-roll, black or color option.

1972-1975	Color option	$400	$475

K150-2 Amp Set

1972-1975. K150 with added reverb and tremolo, piggyback, 2x12", tuck-and-roll, black or color option.

1972-1975	Color option	$575	$625

K200-1/K200B Bass Amp Head

1966-1972. Head with 100 relative watts, 2 channels, 4 controls and 2 inputs per channel, no effects. K200 heads were also offered with Reverb/Tremolo (suffix 2), Harmonic Clipper & Boost (suffix 3), and Reverb/Trem/Clipper/Boost (suffix 4). 1966 and '67 models have the "high forehead" appearance versus normal appearance by '68.

1966-1967	Black	$250	$300
1966-1967	Color option	$400	$450
1968-1972	Black	$225	$275
1968-1972	Color option	$375	$425

K200-1/K200B Bass Amp Set

1966-1972. K200 head with 2x15" cab.

1966-1967	Black	$325	$425
1966-1967	Color option	$575	$850
1968-1972	Black	$325	$425
1968-1972	Color option	$575	$850

K200-2 Reverb/Tremolo Amp Head

1966-1972. K200 head, with added reverb and tremolo (suffix 2).

1966-1967	Black	$225	$325
1966-1967	Color option	$425	$500
1968-1972	Black	$275	$300
1968-1972	Color option	$425	$500

K200-2 Reverb/Tremolo Amp and Cab Set

1966-1972. K200-2 head with 2x15" or 3x12" cab, available with JBL D-140F speakers, Altec Lansing (A) speakers, C.T.S. (C), or Jensen (J).

1966-1967	Black	$400	$500
1966-1967	Blue	$650	$850
1966-1967	Cascade	$675	$875
1966-1967	Charcoal	$650	$850
1966-1967	Gold	$675	$875
1966-1967	Red	$650	$875
1966-1967	Silver	$650	$850
1968-1972	Black	$400	$500
1968-1972	Blue	$650	$875
1968-1972	Cascade	$675	$900
1968-1972	Charcoal	$650	$875
1968-1972	Gold	$675	$900
1968-1972	Red	$650	$875
1968-1972	Silver	$650	$875

K250 Reverb/Tremolo Amp Head

1971-1975. 250 watts, tuck-and-roll cover, Kustom 250 logo on upper right section of control panel, reverb.

1971-1975	Black	$275	$325
1971-1975	Color option	$400	$500

K250 Amp and Cab Set

1971-1975. K250 head with 2x15", tuck-and-roll cover.

1971-1975	Black	$375	$500
1971-1975	Color option	$650	$875

K300 PA Amp and Speaker Set

1971-1975. Includes 302 PA, 303 PA, 304 PA, 305 PA, head and 2 cabs.

1971-1975	Color option	$700	$900

Kustom K-100-1-15

Kustom K-150-7

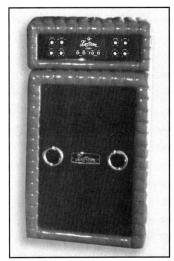

Kustom K250-2-15

Kustom K-400-2

Kustom KLA-20

Lace 20-watt

MODEL YEAR	FEATURES	EXC. COND. LOW	HIGH

K400-2 Reverb/Tremolo Amp and Cab Set
1968-1972. 200 relative watts, reverb, tremolo, with 6x12" or 8x12" cab, available with JBL D-140F speakers, Altec Lansing (A), C.T.S. (C), or Jensen (J). The K400 was offered with no effects (suffix 1), with reverb and tremolo (suffix 2), with Harmonic Clipper & Boost (suffix 3), and Reverb/Trem/Clipper/Boost (suffix 4). The 400 heads came with a separate chrome amp head stand.

1968-1972	Black	$425	$525
1968-1972	Color option	$675	$900

KBA-10 Combo Amp
Late-1980s-1990s. Compact solidstate bass amp, 10 watts, 1x8".

1990s		$50	$75

KBA-20 Combo Amp
Late-1980s-early-1990s. KBA series were compact solidstate bass amps with built-in limiter, 20 watts, 1x8".

1989-1990		$50	$75

KBA-30 Combo Amp
Late-1980s-early-1990s. 30 watts, 1x10".

1989-1990		$50	$75

KBA-40 Combo Amp
Late-1980s-early-1990s. 40 watts, 1x12".

1989-1990		$50	$90

KBA-80 Combo Amp
Late-1980s-early-1990s. 80 watts, 1x15".

1989-1990		$100	$125

KBA-160 Combo Amp
Late-1980s-early-1990s. Solidstate bass amp with built-in limiter, 160 watts, 1x15".

1989-1990		$125	$150

KGA-10 VC Amp
1999-present. 10 watts, 1x6.5" speaker, switchable overdrive.

1999-2004		$25	$50

KLA-15 Combo Amp
Late-1980s-early-1990s. Solidstate, overdrive, 15 watts, 1x8".

1989-1990		$50	$100

KLA-20 Amp
Mid-1980s-late-1980s. 1x10", MOS-FET, gain, EQ, reverb, headphone jack.

1986		$50	$100

KLA-25 Combo Amp
Late-1980s-early-1990s. Solidstate, overdrive, reverb, 25 watts, 1x10".

1989-1990		$50	$100

KLA-50 Combo Amp
Late-1980s-early-1990s. Solidstate, overdrive, reverb, 50 watts, 1x12".

1989-1990		$75	$125

KLA-75 Amp
Mid-1980s-late-1980s. 75 watts, reverb, footswitching.

1987		$100	$150

MODEL YEAR	FEATURES	EXC. COND. LOW	HIGH

KLA-100 Combo Amp
Late-1980s-early-1990s. Solidstate, reverb, 100-watt dual channel, 1x12".

1989-1990		$125	$175

KLA-185 Combo Amp
Late-1980s-early-1990s. Solidstate, reverb, 185-watt dual channel, 1x12".

1989-1990		$150	$200

KPB-200 Bass Combo Amp
1994-1997. 200 watts, 1x15".

1994-1997		$225	$275

SC 1-12 SC Amp
1971-1975. 50 watts, 1x12" Jensen speaker.

1971-1975	Black	$325	$375
1971-1975	Color option	$425	$575

SC 1-15 SC Amp
1971-1975. 150 watts, 1x15" C.T.S. speaker.

1971-1975	Black	$325	$375
1971-1975	Color option	$425	$575

SC 1-15AB SC Amp
1971-1975. 150 watts, 1x15" Altec Lansing speaker.

1971-1975	Black	$325	$375
1971-1975	Color option	$425	$575

SC 2-12A SC Amp
1971-1975. 150 watts, 2x12" Altec Lansing speakers.

1971-1975	Black	$375	$425
1971-1975	Color option	$550	$700

SC 2-12J SC Amp
1971-1975. 150 watts, 2x12" Jensen speakers.

1971-1975	Black	$375	$425
1971-1975	Color option	$550	$700

SC 4-10 SC Amp
1971-1975. 150 watts, 4x10" Jensen speakers.

1971-1975	Black	$375	$425
1971-1975	Color option	$550	$700

Lab Series
1977-1980s. Five models of Lab Series amps, ranging in price from $600 to $3,700, were introduced at the '77 NAMM show by Norlin (then owner of Gibson). Two more were added later. The '80s models were Lab Series II amps and had a Gibson logo on the upper-left front.

B120 Amp
Ca.1984. Bass combo, 120 watts, 2 channels, 1x15".

1984		$100	$150

G120 R-10 Amp
Ca.1984. Combo, 120 watts, 3-band EQ, channel switching, reverb, 4x10".

1984		$200	$250

G120 R-12 Amp
Ca.1984. Combo, 120 watts, 3-band EQ, channel switching, reverb, 2x12".

1984		$175	$225

L2 Amp Head
1977-1983. Head, 100 watts, black covering.

1977-1983		$150	$200

MODEL YEAR	FEATURES	EXC. COND. LOW	HIGH

L3 Amp
1977-ca.1983. 60 watt 1x12" combo.

1977-1983		$200	$275

L4 Amp Head
1977-1983. Solidstate, 200 watts, black cover, dark grille, large L4 logo on front panel.

1977-1983		$200	$250

L5 Amp
1977-ca.1983. Solidstate, 100 watts, 2x12".

1977-1983		$300	$450

L7 Amp
1977-1983. Solidstate, 100 watts, 4x10".

1977-1983		$300	$450

L11 Amp
1977-1983. 200 watts, 8x12", piggyback.

1977-1983		$175	$225

Lace Music Products
1979-present. Lace Music Products, which was founded by pickup innovator Don Lace Sr., added amplifiers in '96. They also offer amps under the Rat Fink and Mooneyes brands.

Lafayette
Ca.1963-1967. Japanese-made guitars and amps sold through the Lafayette Electronics catalogs.

Small Tube Amp
Japanese-made tube, gray speckle 1x12" with art deco design or black 2x12".

1960s	Black	$175	$200
1960s	Gray speckle	$150	$175

Laney
1968-present. Founded by Lyndon Laney and Bob Thomas in Birmingham, England. Laney offered tube amps exclusively into the '80s. A wide range of solidstate and tube amps are currently being offered.

100-Watt Amp Head
1968-1969. Similar to short head Plexi Marshall amp cab, large Laney with underlined "y" logo plate on upper left front corner, black vinyl cover, grayish grille.

1968-1969		$1,050	$1,300

EA-120 Amp
1990s. 120 watts, 2x10", dark vinyl cover.

1990s		$350	$400

GC-30 Amp
1990s. Compact combo amp, 30 watts, dark vinyl cover, reverb, dark see-thru grille.

1990s		$225	$275

GS-212 2x12" Cab
1980s-1990s. Rated at 150 watts, 2x12", slant front cab, black vinyl cover, metal grille.

1990s		$225	$300

GS-410 4x10" Cab
1980s-1990s. 4x10" speakers, straight-front cab, black vinyl cover, metal grille.

1990s		$225	$300

GS-412 4x12" Cab
1980s-1990s. Straight-front or slant cab, 4x12" rated at 150 watts, black vinyl cover.

1990s		$325	$425

LC-15 Amp
1990s. Compact practice amp, 15 watts.

1990s		$175	$250

MY-100 Amp Head
All tube head, 100 watts, master volume, 4-stage cascaded preamp, active boosts for treble, middle and bass.

1980s		$275	$400

MY-50 Amp Head
All tube head, 50 watts, master volume, 4-stage cascaded preamp, active boosts for treble, middle and bass.

1980s		$225	$350

Quarter Stack Amp
All tube, 2x12", self-contained, sealed back, foot-switchable reverb and overdrive, effects loop, active tone controls with push/pull switches.

1980s		$325	$400

Legend
1978-1984. From Legend Musical Instruments of East Syracuse, New York, these amps featured cool wood cabinets. They offered heads, combos with a 1x12" or 2x12" configuration, and cabinets with 1x12", 2x12" or 4x12".

A-30 Amp
Late-1970s-early-1980s. Natural wood cabinet, Mesa-Boogie compact amp appearance.

1980s		$375	$500

A-60 Amp
Late-1970s-early-1980s. Mesa-Boogie appearance, wood cabinet and grille, transtube design dual tube preamp with solidstate power section.

1980s		$375	$500

Rock & Roll 50 Combo Amp
1978-1983. Mesa-Boogie-style wood compact combo, either 1x12" or 2x12" options, tube preamp section and solidstate power supply.

1978-1979	2x12" option	$425	$500
1978-1983	1x12" option	$375	$450

Super Lead 50 Amp
Late-1970s-early-1980s. Rock & Roll 50-watt model with added bass boost and reverb, 1x12".

1978-1983		$400	$475

Super Lead 100 Amp
Late-1970s-early-1980s. Rock & Roll 100-watt model with added bass boost and reverb, 2x12".

1978-1983		$450	$525

Leslie
Most often seen with Hammond organs, the cool Leslie rotating speakers have been adopted by many guitarists. Many guitar effects have tried to duplicate their sound. And they are still making them.

Lace RF20T

Laney GG 100TI

Laney VC30-212

Little Lanilei

Louis Electric Gattone

1958 Maestro

MODEL YEAR	FEATURES	EXC. COND. LOW	HIGH

16 Rotating Speaker Cab
1960s-1970s. 1x10" or 1x12" rotating speaker (requires an amp head), black vinyl cover, silver grille, Leslie 60 logo on grille.

| 1960s | 1 cabinet | $275 | $400 |
| 1970s | 1 cabinet | $275 | $400 |

60 M Rotating Speaker Cabs
1960s-1970s. Two 1x10" rotating speaker cabs with 45-watt amp, black vinyl cover, light silver grille, Leslie logo upper left on grille.

| 1960s | 2 cabinets | $550 | $625 |

103 Amp
Two-speed.

| 1960s | | $225 | $275 |

118 Amp
1x12" Altec speaker.

| 1960s | | $250 | $300 |

125 Amp
Late-1960s. All tube amp with 2-speed rotating 1x12" speaker.

| 1960s | | $225 | $275 |

145 Amp

| 1960s | | $450 | $500 |

Line 6
1996-present. Founded by Marcus Ryle and Michel Doidic and specializing in digital signal processing in both effects and amps.

Little Lanilei
1997-present. Small handmade, intermediate grade, production/custom, amps made by Songworks Systems & Products of San Juan Capistrano, California. They also build a reverb unit and a rotary effect.

Louis Electric Amplifier Co.
1993-present. Founded by Louis Rosano in Bergenfield, New Jersey. Louis produces custom-built tweeds and various combo amps from 35 to 80 watts.

Maestro
Maestro amps are associated with Gibson and were included in the Gibson catalogs. For example, in the '62-'63 orange cover Gibson catalog, tweed Maestro amps were displayed in their own section. Tweed Maestro amps are very similar to Gibson tweed amps. Maestro amps were often associated with accordions in the early-'60s but the amps featured standard guitar inputs. Gibson also used the Maestro name on a line of effects.

The price ranges listed are for excellent condition, all original amps though tubes may be replaced without affecting value. The prices listed are for amps with fully intact logos. A broken or missing logo may diminish the value of the amp. Amps with a changed handle, power cord, and especially a broken logo, should be taken on a case-by-case basis.

Amp models in '58 include the Super Maestro

and Maestro, in '60 the Stereo Maestro Accordion GA-87, Super Maestro Accordion GA-46 T, Standard Accordion GA-45 T, Viscount Accordion GA-16 T, in '62 the Reverb-Echo GA-1 RT, Reverb-Echo GA-2 RT, 30 Stereo Accordion Amp, Stereo Accordion GA-78 RV.

GA-1 RT Reverb-Echo Amp
1961. Tweed, 1x8".

| 1961 | | $375 | $500 |

GA-2 RT Deluxe Reverb-Echo Amp
1961. Deluxe more powerful version of GA-1 RT, 1x12", tweed.

| 1961 | | $800 | $925 |

GA-15 RV/Bell 15 RV Amp
1961. 15 watts, 1x12", gray sparkle.

| 1961 | | $475 | $650 |

GA-16 T Viscount Amp
1961. 14 watts, 1x10", gray sparkle. Gibson also had a GA-16 Viscount amp from '59-'60.

| 1961 | | $375 | $550 |

GA-45 Maestro Amp
1955-1960. 16 watts, 4x8", 2-tone.

| 1955-1960 | | $700 | $800 |

GA-45 RV Standard Amp
1961. 16 watts, 4x8", reverb.

| 1961 | | $950 | $1,200 |

GA-45 T Standard Accordion Amp
1961. 16 watts, 4x8", tremolo.

| 1961 | | $750 | $875 |

GA-46 T Super Maestro Accordion and Bass Amp
1957-1961. Based on the Gibson GA-200 and advertised to be "designed especially for amplified accordions," 60 watts, 2x12", vibrato, 2-tone cover, large Maestro Super logo on top center of grille.

| 1957-1960 | | $1,475 | $1,725 |

GA-78 Maestro Series Amp
1960-1961. Wedge stereo cab, 2x10", reverb and tremolo.

1960-1961	GA-78 RV Maestro 30	$1,600	$2,400
1960-1961	GA-78 RVS	$1,600	$2,400
1960-1961	GA-78 RVT	$1,600	$2,400

GA-78 RV Amp
1960-1961. 30 watts, 2x10", wedge stereo cab, gray sparkle.

| 1960-1961 | | $1,600 | $2,400 |

Magnatone
Ca.1937-1971. Magnatone made a huge variety of amps sold under their own name and under brands like Dickerson, Oahu (see separate listings), and Bronson. They also private branded amps for several accordion companies or accordion teaching studios. Brands used for them include Da Vinci, PAC - AMP, PANaramic, Titano, Tonemaster, Twilighter, and Unique (see separate listings for those brands).

MODEL YEAR	FEATURES	EXC. COND. LOW	HIGH

Model 108 Varsity Amp
1948-1954. Gray pearloid cover, small student amp or lap steel companion amp.
1948-1954 — $250 — $350

Model 110 Melodier Amp
1953-1954. 12 watts, 1x10", brown leatherette cover, light grille.
1953-1954 — $325 — $400

Model 111 Student Amp
1955-1959. Two to 3 watts, 1x8", brown leatherette, brown grille.
1955-1959 — $225 — $275

Model 112/113 Troubadour Amp
1955-1959. 18 watts, 1x12", brown leatherette, brown grille, slant back rear control panel.
1955-1959 — $375 — $460

Model 120B Cougar Bass Amp
1967-1968. Initial Magnatone entry into the solidstate market, superseded by Brute Series in '68, 120 watts, 2x12" solidstate bass piggyback amp, naugahyde vinyl cover with polyester rosewood side panels.
1967-1968 — $175 — $275

Model 120R Sting Ray Reverb Bass Amp
1967-1968. Initial Magnatone entry into the solid-state market, superseded by Brute Series in '68, 150 watts, 4x10" solidstate combo amp, naugahyde vinyl cover with polyester rosewood side panels.
1967-1968 — $175 — $275

Model 130V Custom Amp
1969-1971. Solidstate 1x12" combo amp.
1969-1971 — $150 — $200

Model 150R Firestar Reverb Amp
1967-1968. Initial Magnatone entry into the solid-state market, superseded by Brute Series in '68, 120 watts, 2x12" solidstate combo amp, naugahyde vinyl cover with polyester rosewood side panels.
1967-1968 — $250 — $300

Model 180 Triplex Amp
Mid-to-late-1950s. Mid-level power using 2 6L6 power tubes, 1x15" and 1x8" speakers.
1950s — $400 — $500

Model 192-5-S Troubadour Amp
Early-1950s. 18 watts, 1x12" Jensen Concert speaker, brown alligator covering, lower back control panel, 3 chicken-head knobs, Magnatone script logo on front, Troubadour script logo on back control panel.
1950s — $300 — $350

Model 194 Lyric Amp
1947-mid-1950s. 1x12" speaker, old-style tweed vertical cab typical of '40s.
1940s — $300 — $350

Model 195 Melodier Amp
1951-1954. Vertical cab with 1x10" speaker, pearloid with flowing grille slats.
1951-1954 — $300 — $350

Model 196 Amp
1947-mid-1950s. Five to 10 watts, 1x12", scroll grille design, snakeskin leatherette cover.
1940s — $300 — $350

Model 199 Student Amp
1950s. About 6 to 10 watts, 1x8", snakeskin leatherette cover, metal handle, slant grille design.
1950s — $225 — $350

Model 210 Deluxe Student Amp
1958-1960. 5 watts, 1x8", vibrato, brown leatherette, V logo lower right front on grille.
1958-1960 — $250 — $300

Model 213 Troubadour Amp
1957-1958. 10 watts, 1x12", vibrato, brown leatherette cover, V logo lower right of grille.
1957-1958 — $525 — $575

Model 240 SV Magna-Chordion Amp
1967-1968. Initial Magnatone entry into the solidstate market, superseded by Brute Series in '68, 240 watts, 2x12" solidstate stereo accordion or organ amp, naugahyde vinyl cover, polyester rosewood side panels, input jacks suitable for guitar, reverb and vibrato, lateral combo cab, rear mounted controls.
1967-1968 — $275 — $300

Model 250 Professional Amp
1958-1960. 20 watts, 1x12", vibrato, brown leatherette with V logo lower right front of grille.
1958-1960 — $550 — $650

Model 260 Amp
1957-1958. 35 watts, 2x12", brown leatherette, vibrato, V logo lower right front corner of grille.
1957-1958 — $950 — $1,150

Model 262 Jupiter/Custom Pro Amp
1961-1963. 35 watts, 2x12", vibrato, brown leatherette.
1961-1963 — $675 — $750

Model 280/Custom 280 Amp
1957-1958. 50 watts, brown leatherette covering, brown-yellow tweed grille, 2x12" plus 2x5" speakers, double V logo.
1957-1958 — $1,000 — $1,300

Model 280A Amp
1958-1960. 50 watts, brown leatherette covering, brown-yellow tweed grille, 2x12" plus 2x5" speakers, V logo lower right front.
1958-1960 — $925 — $1,100

Model 410 Diana Amp
1961-1963. Five watts, 1x12", advertised as a 'studio' low power professional amp, brown leatherette cover, vibrato.
1961-1963 — $350 — $425

Model 413 Centaur Amp
1961-1963. 18 watts, 1x12", brown leatherette cover, vibrato.
1961-1963 — $525 — $575

Model 415 Clio Bass Amp
1961-1963. 25 watts, 4x8", bass or accordion amp, brown leatherette cover.
1961-1963 — $525 — $575

Model 432 Amp
Mid-1960s. Compact student model, wavey-squiggle art deco-style grille, black cover, vibrato and reverb.
1960s — $325 — $425

Magnatone Model 3802

1958 Magnatone Model 111

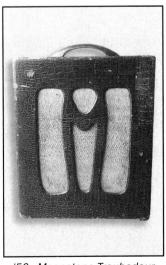
'50s Magnatone Troubadour

AMPS

Magnatone Custom 280

Magnatone 401-A

Magnatone Custom 450

MODEL YEAR	FEATURES	EXC. COND. LOW	HIGH

Model 435 Athene Bass Amp
1961-1963. 55 watts, 4x10", piggyback head and cab, brown leatherette.

1961-1963		$700	$875

Model 440 Mercury Amp
1961-1963. 18 watts, 1x12", vibrato, brown leatherette.

1961-1963		$600	$700

Model 450 Juno/Twin Hi-Fi Amp
1961-1963. 25 watts, 1x12" and 1 oval 5"x7" speakers, reverb, vibrato, brown leatherette.

1961-1963		$750	$925
1961-1963	Extension cab only	$450	$500

Model 460 Victory Amp
1961-1963. 35 watts, 2x12" and 2 oval 5"x7" speakers, early-'60s next to the top-of-the-line, reverb and vibrato, brown leatherette.

1961-1963		$800	$1,000

Model 480 Venus Amp
1961-1963. 50 watts, 2x12" and 2 oval 5"x7" speakers, early-'60s top-of-the-ine, reverb and stereo vibrato, brown leatherette.

1961-1963		$875	$1,050

Model M6 Amp
1964 (not seen in '65 catalog). 25 watts, 1x12", black molded plastic 'suitcase' amp.

1964		$375	$450

Model M7 Bass Amp
1964-1966. 38 watts, 1x15" bass amp, black molded plastic 'suitcase' amp.

1964-1966		$375	$450

Model M8 Amp
1964-1966. 27 watts, 1x12", reverb and tremolo, black molded plastic 'suitcase' amp.

1964-1966		$525	$650

Model M9 Amp
1964-1966. 38 watts, 1x15", tremolo, no reverb, black molded plastic 'suitcase' amp.

1964-1966		$575	$700

Model M10 Amp
1964-1966. 38 watts, 1x15", tremolo, transistorized reverb section, black molded plastic 'suitcase' amp.

1964-1966		$700	$800

Model M12 Bass Amp
1964-1966. 80 watts, 1x15" or 2x12", mid-'60s top-of-the-line bass amp, black molded plastic 'suitcase' amp.

1960s		$575	$700

Model M14 Amp
1964-1966. Stereo, 75 watts, 2x12" plus 2 tweeters, stereo vibrato, no reverb, black molded plastic 'suitcase' amp.

1964-1966		$700	$800

Model M15 Amp
1964-1966. Stereo 75 watts, 2x12" plus 2 tweeters, stereo vibrato, transistorized reverb, black molded plastic 'suitcase' amp.

1964-1966		$775	$875

Model M27 Bad Boy Bass Amp
1968-1971. 150 watts, 2x15" (1 passive), reverb, vibrato, solidstate, vertical profile bass amp, part of Brute Series.

1968-1971		$250	$300

Model M30 Fang Amp
1968-1971. 150 watts, 2x15" (1 passive), 1 exponential horn, solidstate, vibrato, reverb, vertical profile amp.

1968-1971		$250	$300

Model M32 Big Henry Bass Amp
1968-1971. 300 watts, 2x15" solidstate vertical profile bass amp.

1968-1971		$250	$300

Model M35 The Killer Amp
1968-1971. 300 watts, 2x15" and 2 horns, solidstate, vibrato, vertical profile amp.

1968-1971		$275	$325

Model MP-1 (Magna Power I) Amp
1966-1967. 30 watts, 1x12", dark vinyl, light grille, Magnatone-Estey logo on upper right of grille.

1966-1967		$350	$400

Model MP-3 (Magna-Power 3) Amp
1966-1967. Mid-power, 2x12", reverb, dark vinyl, light grille, Magnatone-Estey logo on upper right of grille.

1966-1967		$425	$525

Model PS150 Amp
1968-1971. Powered slave speaker cabinets, 150 watts, 2x15" linkable cabinets.

1968-1971		$175	$225

Model PS300 Amp
1968-1971. Powered slave speaker cabinets, 300 watts, 2x15" (1 passive) linkable cabinets.

1968-1971		$175	$225

Small Pearloid Amp
1947-1955. Pearloid (MOTS) covered low- and mid-power amps generally associated with pearloid lap steel sets.

1947-1955		$250	$300

Starlet Amp
1951-1952. Student model, 1x8", pearloid covering.

1951-1952		$275	$250

Starlite Model 401 Amp
Magnatone produced the mid-'60s Starlite amplifier line for the budget minded musician. Each Starlite model prominently notes the Magnatone name. The grilles show art deco wavy circles. Magnatone 1960-'63 standard amps offer models starting with 12" speakers. Starlight models offer 10" and below. Model 401 has 15 watts, 1x8" and 3 tubes.

1960s		$200	$225

Starlite Model 411 Amp
Mid-1960s. 15 watts, 1x8", 5 tubes, tremolo (not advertised as vibrato), art deco wavy grille.

1960s		$225	$250

Starlite Model 441A Bass Amp
Early-mid-1960s. Lower power with less than 25 watts, 1x15", tube amp.

1960s		$375	$400

MODEL YEAR	FEATURES	EXC. COND. LOW	HIGH

Starlite Model Custom 421 Amp
Early-mid-1960s. Tube amp, 25 watts, 1x10".
1960s $325 $400

Starlite Model Custom 431 Amp
Early-mid-1960s. Tube amp, 30 watts, 1x10", vibrato and reverb.
1960s $425 $475

Mako

1985-1989. Line of solidstate amps from Kaman (Ovation, Hamer). They also offered guitars and basses.

Marlboro Sound Works

1970-1980s. Economy amps imported by Musical Instruments Corp., Syosset, New York. Initially, Marlboro targeted the economy compact amp market, but quickly added larger amps and PAs.

GA-2 Amp
1970s. Solidstate, 3 watts, 1x8", dark vinyl cover, dark grille.
1970s $15 $20

GA-3 Amp
1970s. Solidstate, 3 watts, 1x8", tremolo, dark vinyl cover, dark grille.
1970s $20 $30

GA-20B Amp
1970s. Solidstate bass/keyboard amp, 25 watts, 1x12", dark vinyl cover, dark grille.
1970s $30 $70

GA-20R Amp
1970s. Solidstate, 25 watts, 1x12", tremolo and reverb, dark vinyl cover, dark grille.
1970s $30 $70

GA-40R Amp
1970s. Solidstate, 30 watts, 1x12", tremolo and reverb, dark vinyl cover, dark grille.
1970s $60 $100

Model 520B Amp
1970s. Solidstate, 25 watts, 1x15", bass/keyboard amp, dark vinyl cover, dark grille.
1970s $60 $100

Model 560A Amp
1970s. Solidstate, 45 watts, 2x10", dark vinyl cover, dark grille.
1970s $60 $100

Model 760A Amp
1970s. Solidstate guitar/bass/keyboard combo amp, 60 watts, 1x15", dark vinyl cover, dark grille.
1970s $60 $100

Model 1200R Head Amp
1970s. 60 watts, single channel head with reverb.
1970s $60 $100

Model 1500B Bass Head Amp
1970s. 60 watts, single channel head.
1970s $60 $100

Model 2000 Bass Amp Set
1970s. 1500B head and LS12FH 1x12" with Piezo horn cab.
1970s $60 $100

Marshall

1962-present. Drummer Jim Marshall started building bass speaker and PA cabinets in his garage in 1960. He opened a retail drum shop for his students and others and soon added guitars and amps. When Ken Bran joined the business as service manager in '62, the two decided to build their own amps. By '63 they had expanded the shop to house a small manufacturing space and by late that year they were offering the amps to other retailers. Marshall also made amps under the Park, CMI, Narb, Big M, and Kitchen-Marshall brands. Marshall continues to be involved in the company.

Mark I, II, III and IVs are generally '60s and '70s and also are generally part of a larger series (for example JTM), or have a model number that is a more specific identifier. Describing an amp only as Mark II can be misleading. The most important identifier is the Model Number, which Marshall often called the Stock Number. To help avoid confusion we have added the Model number as often as possible. In addition, when appropriate, we have included the wattage, number of channels, master or no-master info in the title. This should help the reader more quickly find a specific amp. Check the model's description for such things as two inputs or four inputs, because this will help with identification. Vintage Marshall amps do not always have the Model/Stock number on the front or back panel, so the additional identifiers should help. The JMP logo on the front is common and really does not help with specific identification. For example, a JMP Mark II Super Lead 100 Watt description is less helpful than the actual model/stock number. Unfortunately, many people are not familiar with specific model/stock numbers.

Marshall amps are sorted as follows:
AVT Series - new line for Marshall
Club and Country Series (Rose-Morris)-introduced in '78
JCM 800 Series - basically the '80s
JCM 900 Series - basically the '90s
JCM 2000 Series - basically the '00s
JTM Series
Micro Stack Group
Model Number/Stock Number (no specific series, basically the '60s, '70s) - including Artist and Valvestate models (Valvestate refers to specific Model numbers in 8000 Series)
Silver Jubilee Series

AVT 20 Combo Amp
2001-present. Solidstate, 20 watts, 12AX7 preamp tube, 1x10", Advanced Valvestate Technology (AVT) models have black covering and grille, and gold panel.
2001-2004 $175 $275

AVT 50 Combo Amp
2001-present. Solidstate, 50 watts, 1x12".
2001-2004 $325 $375

Marlboro 560A

Marshall AVT-20

Marshall AVT-50

AMPS

Marshall AVT-150

Marshall AVT-275

Marshall Club and Country 4140

MODEL YEAR FEATURES	EXC. COND. LOW	HIGH

AVT 275 Combo Amp
2001-present. Solidstate DFX stereo, 75 watts per side, 2x12".

| 2001-2004 | $675 | $750 |

AVT 412/412A Cab
2001-present. Slant half-stack 4x12" cab, 200-watt load, 25-watt Celestions.

| 2001-2004 | $275 | $400 |

AVT 412B Cab
2001-present. Straight-front half-stack 4x12" cab, 200-watt load.

| 2001-2004 | $250 | $375 |

AVT 100 Combo Amp
2001-present. Solidstate, 100 watts, tube preamp, 1x12".

| 2001-2004 | $475 | $550 |

AVT 150 Series Amp
2001-present. Solidstate, additional features over AVT 100. Combo (100 watts, 1x12"), Half-Stack (150 watts, 4x12") and Head only (150 watts).

2001-2004 Combo	$625	$675
2001-2004 Half-Stack	$850	$900
2001-2004 Head	$600	$650

Club and Country Model 4140 Amp
1978-1982. Tubes, 100 watts, 2x12" combo, Rose-Morris era, designed for the country music market, hence the name, brown vinyl cover, straw grille.

| 1978-1982 | $800 | $900 |

Club and Country Model 4145 Amp
1978-1982. Tubes, 100 watts, 4x10" combo, Rose-Morris era, designed for the country music market, hence the name, brown vinyl, straw grille.

| 1978-1982 | $800 | $900 |

Club and Country Model 4150 Bass Amp
1978-1982. Tubes, 100 watts, 4x10" bass combo, Rose-Morris era, designed for the country music market, hence the name, brown vinyl cover, straw grille.

| 1978-1982 | $700 | $800 |

DSL 201 Amp
1999-2002. 20 watts, 1x12" tube combo.

| 1999-2002 | $390 | $410 |

JCM 800 Model 1959 Amp Head
1981-1991. 100 watts.

| 1981-1991 | $850 | $1,100 |

JCM 800 Model 1987 Amp Head
1981-1991. 50 watts.

| 1981-1991 | $800 | $1,050 |

JCM 800 Model 2000 Amp Head
1981-1982. 200 watts.

| 1981-1982 | $850 | $1,100 |

JCM 800 Model 2001 Amp Head
1981-1982. Bass head amp, 300 watts.

| 1981-1982 | $850 | $1,100 |

JCM 800 Model 2203 Amp Head
1981-1990. 100 watts, master volume, reissued in '02..

| 1981-1990 | $850 | $1,100 |

JCM 800 Model 2204 Amp Head
1981-1990. 50 watts, 1 channel, 2 inputs, master volume, front panel says JCM 800 Lead Series.

| 1981-1990 | $850 | $1,100 |

JCM 800 Model 2204S Amp Head
1986-1987. Short head, 50 watts, 4x10" cab, brown grille cloth.

| 1986-1987 | $850 | $1,100 |

JCM 800 Model 2205 Amp Head
1983-1990. 50 watts, split channel (1 clean and 1 distortion), switchable, both channels with reverb, front panel reads JCM 800 Lead Series.

| 1983-1990 | $850 | $1,100 |

JCM 800 Model 2205 Limited Edition Full Stack Amp
Late-1980s. 50-watt head, 1960A slant and 1960B straight front 4x12" cabs.

| 1988 Red tolex | $1,800 | $1,900 |

JCM 800 Model 2210 Amp Head
1983-1990. 100 watts.

| 1983-1990 | $950 | $1,200 |

JCM 800 Model 4010 Combo Amp
1980-1990. 50 watts, 1x12", reverb, single channel master volume.

| 1980-1990 | $800 | $1,050 |

JCM 800 Model 4103 Combo Amp
1980-1990. Lead combo amp, 50 watts, 2x12".

| 1980-1990 | $850 | $1,100 |

JCM 800 Model 4104 Amp
1980-1990. All tube lead combo amp, 50 watts, 2x12".

| 1980-1990 Black | $850 | $1,100 |
| 1980-1990 White option | $1,000 | $1,200 |

JCM 800 Model 4210 Combo Amp
1982-1990. 50 watts, 1x12" tube combo, split-channel, single input, master volume.

| 1982-1990 | $800 | $1,050 |

JCM 800 Model 4211 Combo Amp
1983-1990. Lead combo amp, 100 watts, 2x12".

| 1983-1990 | $850 | $1,100 |

JCM 800 Model 5005 Combo Amp
1983-1990. Solidstate combo amp, 12 watts, master volume, 1x10".

| 1983-1990 | $275 | $375 |

JCM 800 Model 5010 Combo Amp
1983-1990. Solidstate combo amp, 30 watts, master volume, 1x12".

| 1983-1990 | $325 | $375 |

JCM 800 Model 5150 Combo Amp
1987-1991. Combo amp, 150 watts, specially designed 12" Celestion speaker, split channel design, separate clean and distortion channels, presence and effects-mix master controls.

| 1987-1991 | $475 | $525 |

JCM 800 Model 5212 Combo Amp
1986-1991. 2x12" split channel reverb combo.

| 1986-1991 | $500 | $550 |

JCM 800 Model 5213 Combo Amp
1986-1991. MOS-FET solidstate combo, 2x12", channel-switching, effects loop, direct output, remote footswitch.

| 1986-1991 | $375 | $425 |

MODEL YEAR	FEATURES	EXC. COND. LOW	HIGH

JCM 800 Model 5215 Combo Amp
1986-1991. MOS-FET solidstate, 1x15", Accutronics reverb, effects loop.

| 1986-1991 | | $425 | $475 |

JCM 900 2100 Mark III Amp Head
1990-1993. FX loop, 100/50-watt selectable lead head.

| 1990-1993 | | $600 | $750 |

JCM 900 2100 SL-X Amp Head
1992-1998. Hi-gain 100 watt head amp, additional 12AX7 preamp tube.

| 1992-1998 | | $600 | $750 |

JCM 900 2500 SL-X Amp Head
1990-2000. 50 watt version of SL-X.

| 1992-1998 | | $600 | $750 |

JCM 900 4100 Dual Reverb Amp Head
1990-2000. 100/50 switchable head, JCM 900 on front panel, black with black front.

| 1990-2000 | | $675 | $800 |

JCM 900 4101 Combo Amp
1990-2000. All tube, 100 watts, 1x12" combo.

| 1990-2000 | | $600 | $700 |

JCM 900 4102 Combo Amp
1990-2000. Combo amp, 100/50 watts switchable, 2x12".

| 1990-2000 | | $700 | $800 |

JCM 900 4500 Amp Head
1990-2000. All tube, 2 channels, 50/25 watts, EL34 powered, reverb, effects loop, compensated recording out, master volume, black.

| 1990-2000 | | $600 | $700 |

JCM 900 4501 Dual Reverb Combo Amp
1990-2000. 50/25 switchable, 1x12".

| 1990-2000 | | $700 | $800 |

JCM 900 4502 Combo Amp
1990-2000. 50/25 switchable, 2x12".

| 1990-2000 | | $750 | $850 |

JCM 2000 TSL 100 Amp
1998-present. Triple Super Lead, 3 channels.

| 1998-2003 | | $925 | $975 |

JCM Slash Signature Model 2555SL Amp Set
1996. Based on JCM 800 with higher gain, amp and cab set, JCM Slash Signature logo on front panel, single channel, Slash Signature 1960AV 4x12" slant cab, black.

| 1996 | | $1,700 | $1,800 |

JTM 45 Amp Head
1962-1964. Amp head, 45 watts. The original Marshall amp. Became the Model 1987 45-watt for '65-'66.

| 1962-1964 | | $9,500 | $12,000 |

JTM 45 Amp (Model 1987) Amp Head Reissue
1989-1999. Black/green tolex.

| 1988-1999 | | $625 | $750 |

JTM 45 MK IV Model 1961 4x10 Combo Amp
1965-1966. 45 watts, 4x10", tremolo, JTM 45 MK IV on panel, Bluesbreaker association.

| 1965-1966 | | $8,000 | $10,000 |

JTM 45 MK IV Model 1962 2x12 Combo Amp
1965-1966. 45 watts, 2x12", tremolo, JTM 45 MK IV on panel, Bluesbreaker association.

| 1965-1966 | | $10,000 | $12,000 |

JTM 45 Model 1987 Mark II Lead Amp Head
1965-1966. Replaced JTM 45 Amp ('62-'64), but was subsequently replaced by the Model 1987 50-watt Head during '66.

1965-1966		$5,200	$6,000
1965-1966	Rare 100-watt option	$0	$0
1965-1966	Rare trem option	$0	$0

JTM 45 Offset Limited Edition Amp Set Reissue
Introduced in 2000. Limited run of 300 units, old style cosmetics, 45-watt head and offset 2x12" cab, dark vinyl cover, light gray grille, rectangular logo plate on front of amp and cab, Limited Edition plate on rear of cab, serial number xxx of 300.

| 2000 | | $2,500 | $3,500 |

JTM 50 MK IV Model 1961 4x10 Amp
1965-1972. 50 watts, 4x10", Bluesbreaker association, tremolo, JTM 50 MK IV on front panel to '68, plain front panel without model description '68-'72.

1966-1967		$7,500	$9,000
1968		$6,500	$7,000
1969		$5,500	$6,000
1970		$4,500	$5,000
1971-1972		$3,500	$4,000

JTM 50 MK IV Model 1962 2x12 Amp
1966-1972. 50 watts, 2x12", tremolo, Bluesbreaker association, JTM 50 MK IV on front panel to '68, plain front panel without model description '68-'72.

1966-1967		$10,000	$11,500
1968	Plain panel	$9,000	$10,500
1969	Plain panel	$7,500	$8,500
1970	Plain panel	$5,500	$7,000
1971-1972	Plain panel	$4,000	$5,500

JTM 50 Model 1963 PA Amp Head
1965-1966. MK II PA head, block logo.

| 1965-1966 | | $3,000 | $3,800 |

JTM 50 Amp (Model 1962) Bluesbreaker Reissue
1989-present. 50 watts, 2x12", Model 1962 reissue Bluesbreaker.

| 1989-1999 | | $800 | $875 |

JTM 60 Mini Half-Stack Amp
1996. 60 watts, 4x10".

| 1996 | | $650 | $775 |

JTM 310 Amp
1995-1997. Tube combo, reverb, 30 watts, 2x10", effects loops, 5881 output sections, footswitchable high-gain modes.

| 1995-1997 | | $575 | $650 |

JTM 612 Combo Amp
1995-1997. Tube combo amp, 60 watts, 1x12", EQ, reverb, effects loop.

| 1995-1997 | | $575 | $650 |

Marshall JCM 2000 TSL 100

AMPS

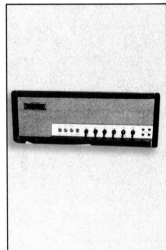

1962 Marshall JTM 45

Marshall JTM 45 Mk II Lead

Marshall Super Tremolo Mk IV

Marshal 3005 Silver Jubilee

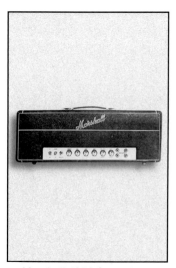

Marshall 1959 Super Lead

MODEL YEAR	FEATURES	EXC. COND. LOW	HIGH

MG 15 RCD Amp
2000-present. Solidstate, 15 watts, 1x8".

| 2000-2004 | | $95 | $100 |

MG 15MS/MSII (Micro Stack) Amp
1999-2004. 15-watt head, 1x8" slant cab and 1x8" straight cab. MSII, introduced in '02, has 10" speakers.

| 1999-2004 | | $250 | $275 |

MG100 RCD Amp Head
2000-present. Valvestate Series, made in Korea, 100 watts.

| 2000-2004 | | $250 | $300 |

Micro Stack 3005 Amp
1986-1991. Solidstate head, 12 watts, 2 1x10" stackable cabs (one slant, one straight). Standard model is black, but was also offered in white, green, red, or the silver Silver Jubilee version with Jubilee 25/50 logo.

1986-1991	Black	$325	$450
1986-1991	Green, red, white	$425	$500
1987-1989	Silver Jubilee/silver	$475	$600

Mini-Stack 3210 MOS-FET Amp Head with 2x4x10"
1984-1991. Model 3210 MOS-FET head with two 4x10" cabs, designed as affordable stack.

| 1984-1991 | | $325 | $450 |

Model 1710 Bass Cab
1990s. 1x15" speaker.

| 1990s | | $325 | $400 |

Model 1930 Popular Combo Amp
1969-1973. 10 watts, 1x12", tremolo.

| 1969-1973 | | $2,500 | $3,500 |

Model 1935A 4x12" Bass Cab
1990s. 4x12" speakers cab.

| 1990s | | $300 | $375 |

Model 1936 2x12" Cab
1981-present. 2x12" speakers, extension straight-front cab, black.

| 1981-1999 | | $250 | $325 |

Model 1958 18-Watt Lead Amp
1965-1968. 18 watts, 2x10" combo, Bluesbreaker cosmetics.

1965		$6,000	$8,000
1966		$5,500	$7,500
1967		$5,500	$6,500
1968		$5,000	$6,000

Model 1958 20-Watt Lead Amp
1968-1972. 20 watts, 2x10" combo, tremolo.

1968		$4,500	$6,000
1969		$4,000	$5,500
1970		$3,500	$4,500
1971-1972		$3,000	$4,000

Model 1959 SLP Reissue Amp Head
1992-present. SLP refers to Super Lead Plexi.

1990s	Black vinyl	$925	$1,050
1990s	Purple vinyl	$1,150	$1,400
1990s	White limited edition	$1,050	$1,300
2000s	Black vinyl	$925	$1,050

Model 1959 SLP Reissue Amp Set
1992-present. 100 watt Super Lead head and matching 4x12" slant cab.

| 1990s | Purple, full-stack, 2x4x12" | $2,500 | $3,500 |
| 1990s | Purple, half-stack, 1x4x12" | $2,000 | $2,800 |

Model 1959 Super Lead Amp
1966-1981. Two channels, 100 watts, 4 inputs, no master volume. Plexiglas control panels until mid-'69, aluminum after. See Model T1959 for tremolo version. Early custom color versions are rare and more valuable.

1966-1969	Black, plexi	$4,800	$5,500
1966-1969	Custom color, plexi	$6,500	$8,000
1969-1970	Black, aluminum	$3,300	$3,700
1969-1970	Custom color, aluminum	$4,500	$5,000
1971-1972	Black, hand-wired, small box	$1,700	$2,000
1971-1972	Custom color, hand-wired	$2,500	$3,000
1973-1975	Black, printed C.B., large box	$1,200	$1,400
1973-1975	Custom color, printed C.B.	$1,500	$1,700
1976-1979	Black	$1,200	$1,400
1976-1979	Custom color	$1,500	$1,700
1980-1981	Black	$1,000	$1,200
1980-1981	Custom color	$1,300	$1,500

Model T1959 Super Lead (Trem) Amp Head
1966-1973. Head amp, 100 watts, plexi until mid-'69, aluminum after. Tremolo version of the Model 1959 Amp.

1966-1969	Black, plexi	$4,800	$6,000
1967-1969	Custom color, plexi	$6,500	$8,000
1969-1970	Black, aluminum	$3,500	$4,200
1969-1970	Custom color, aluminum	$4,500	$5,000
1971-1973	Black, hand-wired, small box	$1,700	$2,500
1971-1973	Custom color, hand-wired	$2,500	$3,000

Model 1959 Super Lead Matching Half Stack Set
1966-1981 option. 100 watt head and matching color 4x12" cabinet. Plexiglass control panels made from '65 to mid-'69, followed by aluminum panel. Matching set requires that the head and cab are the exact matching set that came out of the factory as a set. A mismatched set that is of similar color but not built as a set is not applicable for this pricing. As is the case with all vintage amps, the speakers must be the factory original (untouched) speakers.

1966-1969	Black, plexi, weave	$8,000	$9,000
1966-1969	Custom color, plexi, weave	$12,000	$14,000
1969-1970	Black, aluminum, weave	$6,500	$7,000

MODEL YEAR	FEATURES	EXC. COND. LOW	HIGH
1969-1970	Custom color, aluminum, weave	$7,000	$8,500
1971-1972	Black, hand-wired, weave	$4,000	$5,000
1971-1972	Custom color, hand-wired, weave	$5,500	$6,500
1973-1975	Black, printed C.B., large box, checkerboard	$2,500	$3,000
1973-1975	Custom color, printed C.B., large box, checkerboard	$4,000	$5,000
1976-1979	Black	$2,300	$2,800
1976-1979	Custom color	$3,700	$4,200
1980-1981	Black	$2,000	$2,500
1980-1981	Custom color	$3,400	$3,800

Model 1959 Super Lead Matching Full Stack Set

1966-1981 option. Head with 100 watts and matching color slant and straight front 4x12" cabinets.

1966-1969	Black, plexi, weave	$12,000	$14,000
1966-1969	Custom color, plexi, weave	$18,000	$21,000

Model 1960 4x12 Slant Speaker Cabinet

1964-1979. The original Marshall 4x12" cab designed for compact size with 4x12" speakers. This first issue in '64/'65 was a 60-watt cab, from '65-'70 75 watts, from '70-'79 100 watts. After '79, models numbers contained an alpha suffix. Suffix A implies slant-angle front, suffix B implies straight-front cabinet, often the bottom cabinet of a 2-cabinet stack.

1966-1970	Black, weave	$2,500	$3,000
1966-1970	Custom color, weave	$4,500	$5,100
1971-1972	Black, weave	$2,000	$2,500
1971-1972	Custom color, weave	$2,500	$3,000
1973-1975	Black, checkerboard	$1,000	$1,250
1973-1975	Custom color, checkerboard	$2,000	$2,500
1976-1979	Black	$800	$1,000
1976-1979	Custom color	$1,800	$2,000

Model 1960 4x12 Straight Front Cabinet

1966-1970 (75 watts), 1971-1979 (100 watts).

1966-1970	Black, weave	$2,500	$3,000
1966-1970	Custom color, weave	$4,500	$5,100
1971-1972	Black, weave	$2,000	$2,500
1971-1972	Custom color, weave	$2,500	$3,000
1973-1975	Black, checkerboard	$1,000	$1,250
1973-1975	Custom color, checkerboard	$2,000	$2,500
1976-1979	Black	$800	$1,000
1976-1979	Custom color	$1,800	$2,000

Model 1960A 4x12 Slant Speaker Cabinet

1980-1983 (260 watts), 1984-1986 (280 watts, JCM 800 era), 1986-1990 (300 watts, JCM 800 era).

1980-1983	Black	$600	$800

MODEL YEAR	FEATURES	EXC. COND. LOW	HIGH
1980-1983	Custom color	$800	$1,700
1984-1986	Black	$550	$700
1984-1986	Custom color	$700	$1,700
1986-1990	Black	$500	$650
1986-1990	Custom color	$650	$1,700

Model 1960A JCM 900 4x12 Slant Speaker Cabinet

1990-2000. JCM 900 Series updated to 300 watts, stereo-mono switching.

1990-2000		$450	$575

Model 1960AV 4x12 Slant Speaker Cabinet

1990-present. JCM 900 updated, stereo/mono switching.

1990-2000	Black vinyl, black grille	$550	$700
1990s	Red vinyl, tan grille	$750	$850

Model 1960AX 4x12 Slant Speaker Cabinet

1990-present. Cab for Model 1987X and 1959X reissue heads.

1990-1999		$550	$700

Model 1960B 4x12 Straight Front Cabinet

1980-1983 (260 watts), 1984-1986 (280 watts, JCM 800 era), 1986-1990 (300 watts, JCM 800 era).

1980-1983	Black	$600	$800
1980-1983	Custom color	$800	$1,700
1984-1986	Black	$550	$700
1984-1986	Custom color	$700	$1,700
1986-1990	Black	$500	$650
1986-1990	Custom color	$650	$1,700

Model 1960B JCM 900 4x12 Straight Front Cabinet

1990-2000. JCM 900 updated cabinet, stereo/mono switching, 300 watts.

1990-2000		$450	$575

Model 1960BV 4x12 Straight Front Cabinet

1990-present. JCM 900 updated, stereo/mono switching.

1990-2000	Black vinyl, black grille	$550	$700
1990s	Red vinyl, tan grille	$750	$850

Model 1960BX 4x12 Straight Front Cabinet

1990-present. Cab for Model 1987X and 1959X reissue heads.

1990-1999		$550	$700

Model 1960TV 4x12 Slant Cabinet

1990-present. Extra tall for JTM 45, mono, 100 watts.

1990-2000		$550	$700

Model 1964 Lead/Bass 50-Watt Amp Head

1973-1976. Head with 50 watts, designed for lead or bass.

1973-1976		$1,100	$1,300

Model 1965A/1965B Cabinet

1984-1991. 140 watt 4x10" slant front (A) or straight front (B) cab.

1984-1991		$275	$350

Marshall 1959 SLP Reissue

AMPS

Marshall 1960A slant cab

1972 Marshall 1967 Major

To get the most from this book, be sure to read "Using *The Guide*" in the introduction.

Marshall 2060 Mercury

Marshall 2061x

Marshall 3203 Artist

MODEL YEAR	FEATURES	EXC. COND. LOW	HIGH

Model 1966 Cabinet
1985-1991. 150 watt 2x12" cab.

1985-1991		$275	$350

Model 1967 Major 200-Watt Amp Head
1968-1974. 200 watts, the original Marshall 200 'Pig' was not popular and revised into the 200 'Major'. The new Major 200 was similar to the other large amps and included 2 channels, 4 inputs, but a larger amp cab.

1968		$2,100	$2,400
1969		$2,000	$2,300
1970		$1,900	$2,200
1971-1974		$1,800	$2,100

Model 1967 Pig 200-Watt Amp Head
1967-early-1968 only. Head with 200 watts. The control panel was short and stubby and nicknamed the 'Pig', the 200-watt circuit was dissimilar (and unpopular) to the 50-watt and 100-watt circuits.

1967-1968		$2,000	$2,300

Model 1968 100-Watt Super PA Amp Head
1968-1975. PA head with 100 watts, 2 sets of 4 inputs (identifies PA configuration), often used for guitar.

1966-1969	Plexi	$2,700	$3,100
1969-1972	Aluminum	$1,800	$2,100

Model 1973 Amp
1965-1968. Tube combo, 18 watts, 2x12".

1965		$8,000	$10,000
1966		$7,000	$9,000
1967		$6,500	$8,500
1968		$4,500	$8,000

Model 1973 JMP Lead & Bass 20 Amp
1973 only. Front panel: JMP, back panel: Lead & Bass 20, 20 watts, 1x12" straight front checkered grille cab, head and cab black vinyl.

1973		$1,600	$1,900

Model 1974 Amp
1965-1968. Tube combo, 18 watts, 1x12".

1965		$4,500	$6,000
1966		$4,500	$5,500
1967		$4,000	$5,300
1968		$4,000	$5,000

Model 1974X Amp
2004. Reissue of 18-watt, 1x12" combo.

2004		$1,700	$1,900

Model 1987 50-Watt Amp Head
1966-1981. Head amp, 50 watts, plexiglas panel until mid-'69, aluminum panel after.

1966-1969	Black, plexi	$4,000	$5,000
1967-1969	Custom color, plexi	$6,000	$7,500
1969-1970	Black, aluminum	$3,200	$4,000
1971-1972	Hand-wired, small box	$2,000	$2,500
1973-1979	Printed C.B., large box	$1,250	$1,550
1980-1981		$1,000	$1,300

Model 1987 50-Watt Matching Set
Head and matching 4x12" cab, plexiglas control panels from '65 to mid-'69, aluminum panel after.

1966-1969	Black, plexi	$7,000	$9,000

MODEL YEAR	FEATURES	EXC. COND. LOW	HIGH
1966-1969	Custom color, plexi	$11,000	$12,500
1969	Black, aluminum	$5,700	$7,000

Model 1992 Super Bass Amp Head
1966-1981. 100 watts, plexi panel until mid-'69 when replaced by aluminum front panel, 2 channels, 4 inputs.

1966-1969	Black, plexi	$3,500	$5,000
1966-1969	Custom color, plexi	$5,000	$7,000
1969-1970	Black, aluminum	$2,500	$3,500
1971-1972	Hand-wired	$1,500	$2,200
1973-1979	Printed C.B.	$1,100	$1,400
1980-1981		$1,000	$1,300

Model 2040 Artist 50-Watt Combo Amp
1971-1978. 50 watts, 2x12" Artist/Artiste combo model with a different (less popular?) circuit.

1971-1978		$1,900	$2,100

Model 2041 Artist Head and Cab Set
1971-1978. 50 watts, 2x12" half stack Artist/Artiste cab with a different (less popular?) circuit.

1971-1978		$1,900	$2,100

Model 2046 Specialist 25-Watt Combo Amp
1972-1973. 25 watts, 1x15" speaker, limited production due to design flaw (amp overheats).

1972-1973		$700	$800

Model 2060 Mercury Combo Amp
1972-1973. Combo amp, 5 watts, 1x12", available in red or orange covering.

1972-1973	Red	$800	$900

Model 2061 20-Watt Lead/Bass Amp Head
1968-1973. Lead/bass head, 20 watts, plexi until '69, aluminum after. Reissued in '04 as the Model 2061X.

1968-1969	Black, plexi	$2,500	$3,500
1969	Black, aluminum	$1,500	$2,400

Model 2061X 20-Watt Lead/Bass Amp Head
2004. Reissue of 2061 amp head, 20 watts.

2004		$1,100	$1,250

Model 2078 Combo Amp
1973-1978. Solid-state, 100 watts, 4x12" combo, gold front panel, dark cover, gray grille.

1973-1978		$925	$1,100

Model 2103 100-Watt 1-Channel Master Combo Amp
1975-1981. One channel, 2 inputs, 100 watts, 2x12", first master volume design, combo version of 2203 head.

1975-1981		$1,350	$1,600

Model 2104 50-Watt 1-Channel Master Combo Amp
1975-1981. One channel, 2 inputs, 50 watts, 2x12", first master volume design, combo version of 2204 head.

1975-1981		$1,250	$1,500

AMPS

MODEL		EXC. COND.	
YEAR	FEATURES	LOW	HIGH

Model 2144 Master Reverb Combo Amp
1978 only. Master volume similar to 2104 but with reverb and boost, 50 watts, 2x12".

| 1978 | | $1,450 | $1,550 |

Model 2159 100-Watt 2-Channel Combo Amp
1977-1981. 100 watts, 2 channels, 4 inputs, 2x12" combo version of Model 1959 Super Lead head.

| 1977-1981 | | $1,250 | $1,400 |

Model 2203 Lead Amp Head
1975-1981. Head amp, 100 watts, 2 inputs, first master volume model design, often seen with Mark II logo.

| 1975-1981 | | $900 | $1,100 |

Model 2204 50-Watt Amp Head
1975-1981. Head amp, 50 watts with master volume.

| 1975-1981 | | $950 | $1,150 |

Model 3203 Artist Amp Head
1986-1991. Tube head version of earlier '84 Model 3210 MOS-FET, designed as affordable alternative, 30 watts, standard short cab, 2 inputs separated by 3 control knobs, Artist 3203 logo on front panel, black.

| 1986-1991 | | $350 | $450 |

Model 3210 MOS-FET Amp Head
1984-1991. MOS-FET solidstate head, refer Mini-Stack listing for 3210 with 4x10" stacked cabinets. Early-'80s front panel: Lead 100 MOS-FET.

| 1984-1991 | | $225 | $325 |

Model 3310 100-Watt Lead Amp
1988-1991. Solidstate, 100 watts, lead head with channel switching and reverb.

| 1988-1991 | | $525 | $600 |

Model 4001 Studio 15 Amp
1985-1992. 15 watts using 6V6 (only model to do this up to this time), 1x12" Celestion Vintage 30 speakers.

| 1985-1992 | | $575 | $625 |

Model 5002 Combo Amp
1984-1991. Solidstate combo amp, 20 watts, 1x10", master volume.

| 1984-1991 | | $175 | $225 |

Model 5005 Combo Amp
1984-1991. Solidstate, 12 watts, 1x10", practice amp with master volume, headphones and line-out.

| 1984-1991 | | $150 | $175 |

Model 5302 Keyboard Amp
1984-1988. Solidstate, 20 watts, 1x10", marketed for keyboard application.

| 1984-1988 | | $150 | $175 |

Model 5502 Bass Amp
1984-ca.1992. Solidstate bass combo amp, 20 watts, 1x10" Celestion.

| 1984-1992 | | $150 | $225 |

Model 6100 30th Anniversary Amp Head
1992-1995. All tube, 3 channels, 100 watts, EQ, gain, contour, full and half power modes, blue vinyl covering, front panel: 6100 LM Anniversary Series. Listed as JCM 900 6100 in '95.

| 1992-1995 | | $1,075 | $1,200 |

Model 6100 30th Anniversary Amp Set
1992-1995. Matching head with 100/50/25 watts and 4x12" cabinet (matching colors), first year was blue tolex.

| 1992 | Blue tolex | $2,500 | $3,000 |
| 1993-1995 | Purple tolex | $2,300 | $2,700 |

Model 6101 LE Combo Amp
1992-1995. 1x12", 100/50/25 switchable watts, blue/purple cover, limited edition.

| 1992-1995 | | $1,400 | $1,500 |

Model 8008 Valvestate Rackmount Amp
1991-2001. Valvestate solidstate rack mount power amp with dual 40-watt channels.

| 1991-2001 | | $200 | $275 |

Model 8010 Valvestate VS15 Combo Amp
1991-1997. Valvestate solidstate, 10 watts, 1x8", compact size, black vinyl, black grille.

| 1991-1997 | | $125 | $200 |

Model 8040 Valvestate 40V Combo Amp
1991-1997. Valvestate solidstate with tube preamp, 40 watts, 1x12", compact size, black vinyl, black grille.

| 1991-1997 | | $325 | $400 |

Model 8080 Valvestate 80V Combo Amp
1991-1997. Valvestate solidstate with tube 12AX7 preamp, 80 watts, 1x12", compact size, black vinyl, black grille.

| 1991-1997 | | $325 | $425 |

Model 8100 100-Watt Valvestate VS100H Amp Head
1991-2001. Valvestate solidstate head, 100 watts.

| 1991-2001 | | $375 | $425 |

Model 8200 200-Watt Valvestate Amp Head
1991-1998. Valvestate solidstate reverb head, 2x100-watt channels.

| 1991-1998 | | $425 | $475 |

Model 8240 Valvestate Stereo Chorus Amp
1992-1996. Valvestate, 80 watts (2x40 watts stereo), 2x12" combo, reverb, chorus.

| 1992-1996 | | $425 | $500 |

Model 8280 2x80-Watt Valvestate Combo Amp
1991-1996. Valvestate solidstate, 2x80 watts, 2x12".

| 1991-1996 | | $475 | $550 |

MS-2/R/C Amp
1990-present. One watt, battery operated, miniature black half-stack amp and cab. Red MS-2R and checkered speaker grille and gold logo MS-2C added in '93.

| 1990-2003 | | $25 | $30 |

MS-4 Amp
1998-present. Full-stack version of MS-2, black.

| 1998-2003 | | $35 | $50 |

Silver Jubilee Model 2550 50/25 (Tall) Amp Head
1987-1989. 50/25 switchable tall box head for full Jubilee stack.

| 1987-1989 | Black | $900 | $1,200 |

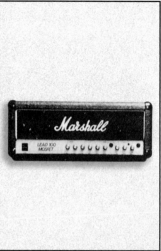
1985 Marshall 3210 head

Marshall 4101

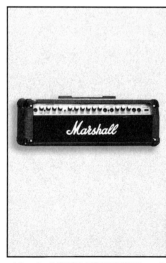
Marshall 8100 VSH100H head

AMPS

*Marshall Model 2553
50/25 Silver Jubilee*

Marshall 2558 Silver Jubilee

Matamp 1224

MODEL YEAR	FEATURES	EXC. COND. LOW	HIGH
Silver Jubilee Model 2553 (short) 2556A (mini)			
1987-1989. Short box, 100/50 watt, two 2x12".			
1987-1989		$1,900	$2,200
Silver Jubilee Model 2553 50/25 (Short) Amp Head			
1987-1989. 50/25 switchable small box head for mini-short stack.			
1987-1989		$800	$1,000
Silver Jubilee Model 2554 1x12 Combo Amp			
1987-1989. 50/25 watts, 1x12" combo using 2550 chasis.			
1987-1989		$1,200	$1,600
Silver Jubilee Model 2555 Amp with Full Stack			
1987-1989. Silver vinyl covering, chrome control panel, 100/50 watts with 2 2551A 4x12" cabinets.			
1987-1989		$2,500	$2,900
Silver Jubilee Model 2555 Amp with Half Stack			
1987-1989. 100/50 watts, one 4x12".			
1987-1989		$1,700	$2,000
Silver Jubilee Model 2556 4x12 Cab			
1987-1989. Cab with 4x12" speakers in 3 brand name options.			
1987-1989		$750	$900
Silver Jubilee Model 2556A/AV 2x12 Cab			
1987-1989. Cab with 2x12" speakers with 3 brand name options.			
1987-1989		$550	$700
Silver Jubilee Model 2558 2x12 Combo Amp			
1987-1989. 50/25 watts, 2x12" combo using 2550 chasis.			
1987-1989		$1,400	$1,800
TSL 122 Triple Super Lead Combo Amp			
1998-present. 100 watts, 3 channels, 2x12" combo.			
1998-2004		$1,050	$1,100

Martin

Martin has dabbled in amps a few times, under both the Martin and Stinger brand names.

MODEL YEAR	FEATURES	EXC. COND. LOW	HIGH
Stinger FX-1 Amp			
1988-1990. 10 watts, EQ, switchable solidstate tube-synth circuit, line out and footswitch jacks.			
1988		$100	$125
Stinger FX-1R Amp			
1988-1990. Mini-stack amp, 2x10", 15 watts, dual-stage circuitry.			
1989		$125	$175
Stinger FX-6B Amp			
1989-1990. Combo bass amp, 60 watts, 1x15".			
1989		$125	$175

Matamp

1966-present. Tube amps, combos and cabinets built In Huddersfield, England, bearing names like Red, Green, White, Black, and Blue. German-born Mat Mathias started building amps in England in

'58 and designed his first Matamp in '66. From '69 to '73, Mathias also made Orange amps. In '89, Mathias died at age 66 and his family later sold the factory to Jeff Lewis.

MODEL YEAR	FEATURES	EXC. COND. LOW	HIGH
Green GT-120 Stack			
1990s. 120 watt GT head with 4x12" straight front cab.			
1993-1999		$1,500	$2,000

Matchless

1989-1999, 2001-present. Founded by Mark Sampson and Rick Perrotta in California. Circuits based on Vox AC-30 with special attention to transformers. A new Matchless company was reorganized in 2001 by Phil Jamison, former head of production for the original company.

MODEL YEAR	FEATURES	EXC. COND. LOW	HIGH
Brave 40 112 Amp			
1997-1999. 40 watts class A, 1x12", footswitchable between high and low inputs.			
1997-1999		$1,400	$1,600
Brave 40 212 Amp			
1997-1999. 2x12" version of Brave.			
1997-1999		$1,600	$2,000
Chief Amp Head			
1995-1999. 100 watts class A, head.			
1995-1999		$2,500	$2,800
Chief 212 Amp			
1995-1999. 100 watts class A, 2x12", reverb.			
1995-1999		$2,900	$3,100
Chief 410 Amp			
1995-1999. 100 watts class A, 4x10", reverb.			
1995-1999		$2,900	$3,300
Chieftan Amp Head			
1995-1999. 40 watts class A head.			
1995-1999		$1,800	$2,200
Chieftan 112 Amp			
1995-1999. 40 watts class A, 1x12", reverb.			
1995-1999		$2,500	$2,800
Chieftan 210 Amp			
1995-1999. 40 watts class A, 2x10", reverb.			
1995-1999		$2,800	$3,100
Chieftan 212 Amp			
1995-1999. 40 watts class A, 2x12", reverb.			
1995-1999		$2,900	$3,300
Chieftan 410 Amp			
1995-1999. 40 watts class A, 4x10", reverb.			
1995-1999		$2,900	$3,300
Clipper 15 112 Amp			
1998-1999. 15 watts, single channel, 1x12".			
1998-1999		$1,000	$1,300
Clipper 15 210 Amp			
1998-1999. 15 watts, single channel, 2x10".			
1998-1999		$1,000	$1,300
Clubman 35 Amp Head			
1993-1999. 35 watts class A head.			
1993-1999		$1,800	$2,200
DC-30 Standard Cabinet			
1991-1999. 30 watts, 2x12", with or without reverb.			
1991-1999	Non-reverb	$3,100	$3,400
1991-1999	With reverb	$3,200	$3,800

MODEL YEAR	FEATURES	EXC. COND. LOW	HIGH
DC-30 Exotic Wood Cabinet Option			
1995-1999. 30 watts, 2x12", gold plating, limited production.			
1995-1999	Non-reverb	$5,300	$5,700
1995-1999	With reverb	$5,800	$6,100
EB115 Bass Cabinet			
1997-1999. 1x15" bass speaker cabinet.			
1997-1999		$450	$650
EB410 Bass Cabinet			
1997-1999. 4x10" bass speaker cabinet.			
1990s		$500	$750
ES/D Cabinet			
1993-1999. 2x12" speaker cabinet.			
1993-1999		$550	$800
ES/S Cabinet			
1991-1999. 1x12" speaker cabinet.			
1991-1999		$450	$700
ES/210 Cabinet			
1993-1999. 2x10" speaker cabinet.			
1993-1999		$500	$750
ES/410 Cabinet			
1993-1999. 4x10" speaker cabinet.			
1990s		$600	$900
ES/412 Cabinet			
1993-1999. 4x12" speaker cabinet.			
1993-1999		$650	$1,000
ES/1012 Cabinet			
1993-1999. 2x10" and 2x12" speaker cabinet.			
1993-1999		$650	$1,000
HC-30 Amp Head			
1991-1999. The first model offered by Matchless, 30 watts class A head.			
1991-1999		$2,400	$2,800
Hurricane Amp Head			
1997. 15 watts class A head.			
1997		$1,150	$1,300
Hurricane 112 Amp			
1994-1997. 15 watts class A, 1x12".			
1994-1997		$1,350	$1,500
Hurricane 210 Amp			
1996-1997. 15 watts class A, 2x10".			
1996-1997		$1,350	$1,500
JJ-30 112 John Jorgensen Amp			
1997-1999. 30 watts, DC-30 chasis with reverb and tremolo, 1x12" Celestion 30, offered in white, blue, gray sparkle tolex or black.			
1997-1999		$3,800	$4,400
Lightning 15 Amp Head			
1997. 15 watts class A head.			
1997		$1,200	$1,500
Lightning 15 112 Amp			
1994-1999. 15 watts class A, 1x12".			
1994-1999	Non-reverb	$1,500	$1,700
1997-1999	With reverb	$1,800	$2,000
Lightning 15 210 Amp			
1996-1997. 15 watts class A, 2x10".			
1996-1997	Non-reverb	$1,900	$2,100
1997	With reverb	$2,100	$2,400

MODEL YEAR	FEATURES	EXC. COND. LOW	HIGH
Lightning 15 212 Amp			
1996-1997. 15 watts class A, 2x12".			
1996-1997	Non-reverb	$2,000	$2,200
1997	With reverb	$2,300	$2,600
SC-30 Standard Cabinet Amp			
1991-1999. 30 watts class A, 1x12".			
1991-1999	Non-reverb	$2,800	$3,000
1991-1999	With reverb	$3,100	$3,400
SC-30 Exotic Wood Cabinet Amp			
1995-1999. 30 watts class A, 1x12", gold plating, limited production.			
1995-1999	Non-reverb	$5,000	$5,500
1995-1999	With reverb	$5,500	$6,000
Skyliner Reverb 15 112 Amp			
1998-1999. 15 watts, 2 channels, 1x12".			
1998-1999		$1,100	$1,400
Skyliner Reverb 15 210 Amp			
1998-1999. 15 watts, 2 channels, 2x10".			
1998-1999		$1,100	$1,400
Spitfire 15 Amp Head			
1997. 15 watts, head.			
1997		$1,100	$1,300
Spitfire 15 112 Amp			
1994-1997. 15 watts, 1x12".			
1994-1997		$1,200	$1,500
Spitfire 15 210 Amp			
1996-1997. 15 watts, 2x10".			
1996-1997		$1,400	$1,700
Starliner 40 212 Amp			
1999. 40 watts, 2x12".			
1999		$1,600	$2,000
Superchief 120 Amp Head			
1994-1999. 120 watts, class A head.			
1994-1999		$2,000	$2,500
TC-30 Standard Cabinet			
1991-1999. 30 watts, 2x10" class A, low production numbers makes value approximate with DC-30.			
1991-1999	Non-reverb	$2,800	$3,300
1991-1999	With reverb	$3,300	$3,800
TC-30 Exotic Wood Cabinet Option			
1991-1999. 30 watts, 2x10" class A, limited production.			
1991-1999	Non-reverb	$5,300	$5,800
1991-1999	With reverb	$5,800	$6,300
Thunderchief Bass Amp Head			
1994-1999. 200 watts, class A bass head.			
1994-1999		$1,100	$1,800
Thunderman 100 Bass Combo Amp			
1997-1998. 100 watts, 1x15" in portaflex-style flip-top cab.			
1997-1998		$1,400	$2,000
Tornado 15 112 Amp			
1994-1995. Compact, 15 watts, 1x12", 2-tone covering, simple controls--volume, tone, tremolo speed, tremolo depth.			
1994-1995		$900	$1,200

Matchless Chief 410

AMPS

Matchless Spitfire 112

1997 Matchless Thunderchief

Maven Peal Zeetz 0.5>50

Mesa-Boogie Lonestar Special

Mesa-Boogie Mk 1

MODEL YEAR	FEATURES	EXC. COND. LOW	HIGH

Maven Peal

1999-present. Amps, combos and cabinets built by David Zimmerman in Plainfield, Vermont (the name stands for "expert sound"). Serial number format is by amp wattage and sequential build; for example, 15-watt amp 15-001, 30-watt 30-001, and 50-watt 50-001with the 001 indicating the first amp built. S = Silver Series, no alpha = Gold Series.

Mega Amplifiers

Budget and intermediate grade, production, solidstate and tube amps from Guitar Jones, Inc. of Pomona, California.

Merlin

Rack mount bass heads built in Germany by Musician Sound Design. They also offer the MSD guitar effects.

Mesa-Boogie

1971-present. Founded by Randall Smith in San Francisco, California. Circuits styled on high-gain Fender-based chassis designs, ushering in the compact high-gain amp market. The following serial number information and specs courtesy of Mesa Engineering.

.50 Caliber/.50 Caliber+ Amp Head

Jan.1987-Dec.1988, 1992-1993. Serial numbers: SS3100 - SS11,499. Mesa Engineering calls it Caliber .50. Tube head amp, 50 watts, 5-band EQ, effects loop. Called the .50 Caliber Plus in '92 and '93.

1987-1988	Caliber	$450	$500
1992-1993	Caliber+	$450	$500

.50 Caliber+ Combo Amp

Dec.1988-Oct.1993. Serial numbers FP11,550 - FP29,080. 50 watts, 1x12" combo amp.

1988-1993		$475	$550

20/20 Amp

Jun.1995-present. Serial numbers: TT-01. 20-22 watts per channel.

1995-2001		$475	$600

50/50 (Fifty/Fifty) Amp

May 1989-2001. Serial numbers: FF001-. 100 watts total power, 50 watts per channel, front panel reads Fifty/Fifty, contains 4 6L6 power tubes.

1989-2001		$525	$625

295 Power Amp

2000s. 95 watts per channel, rack mount.

2000s		$300	$400

395 Amp

Feb.1991-Apr.1992. Serial numbers: S2572 - S3237.

1991-1992		$575	$625

Bass 400/Bass 400+ Amp Head

Aug.1989-Aug.1990. Serial numbers: B001-B1200. About 500 watts using 12 5881 power tubes. Replaced by 400+ Aug.1990-present, serial numbers: B1200- . Update change to 7-band EQ at serial number B1677.

1989-1990	Bass 400	$750	$850
1990-1999	Bass 400+	$750	$850

Blue Angel Series Amp

Jun.1994-2004. Serial numbers BA01-. Lower power combos.

Buster Bass Amp Head

Dec.1997-Jan.2001. Serial numbers: BS-1-999. 200 watts via 6 6L6 power tubes.

1997-2001		$500	$600

Buster Bass Combo Amp

1999-2001. 200 watts, 2x10", wedge cabinet, black vinyl, metal grille.

1999-2001		$550	$700

Coliseum 300 Amp

Oct.1997-2000. Serial numbers: COL-01 - COL-132. 200 watts/channel, 12 6L6 power tubes, rack mount.

1997-2000		$800	$950

D-180 Amp Head

Jul.1982-Dec.1985. Serial numbers: D001-D681. All tube head amp, 200 watts, preamp, switchable.

1982-1985		$500	$625

DC-3 Amp

Sep.1994-Jan.1999. Serial numbers: DC3-001 - DC3-4523. 35 watts, 1x12".

1994-1999		$500	$600

DC-5 Amp

Oct.1993-Jan.1999. Serial numbers: DC1024 - DC31,941. 50-watt head, 1x12" combo.

1993-1999		$625	$725

DC-10 Amp Head

May 1996-Jan.1999. Serial numbers: DCX-001 - DCX-999. Dirty/Clean (DC) 60 or 100 watts (6L6s).

1996-1999		$675	$750

Diesel Bass Cabinets

1990s-present. Designation for regular vinyl covered bass cabs after heavy-duty RoadReady cab option becomes available.

1990s	1x15" bass cab	$250	$300

F-50 Amp

2002-present. Combo, 50 watts, 1x12", AB 2 6L6 power.

2002-2004		$775	$825

Formula Preamp

Jul.1998-2002. Serial numbers: F-01. Used 5 12AX7 tubes, 3 channels.

1998-2000		$475	$550

Heartbreaker Amp

Jun.1996-2001. Serial numbers: HRT-01. 60 to 100 watts switchable, 2x12" combo, designed to switch-out 6L6s, EL34s or the lower powered 6V6s in the power section, switchable solidstate or tube rectifier.

1996-2001		$1,000	$1,100

Lonestar Series Amp

2004-present. Designed by founder Randall Smith with Doug West with focus on boutique-type amp. Class A (EL84) or AB (4 6L6) circuits, long or short head, 1x12" combo, 2x12" combo, and short head 4x10" cab, and long head 4x12" cab.

2004	1x12" combo	$1,300	$1,350
2004	2x12" combo	$1,350	$1,400
2004	4x12"	$600	$700
2004	Head, class A	$1,250	$1,300

MODEL YEAR	FEATURES	EXC. COND. LOW	HIGH
2004	Head, Class AB	$1,150	$1,200

M-180 Amp

Apr.1982-Jan.1986. Serial numbers: M001-M275.

1982-1986		$400	$650

M-2000 Amp

Jun.1995-2003. Serial numbers: B2K-01.

1995-1999		$500	$600

Mark I Combo (Model A) Amp

1971-1978. The original Boogie amp, not called the Mark I until the Mark II was issued, 60 or 100 watts, 1x12", Model A serial numbers: 1-2999, very early serial numbers 1-299 had 1x15".

1971-1972	1x15"	$950	$1,150
1971-1978	1x12"	$850	$1,050

Mark I Reissue Amp

Nov. 1989-present. Serial numbers: H001- . 100 watts, 1x12", reissue features include figured maple cab and wicker grille.

2000-2001		$650	$750

Mark II Combo Amp

1978-1980. Late-'78 1x12", serial numbers: 3000-5574. Effective Aug.'80 1x15", serial numbers: 300-559 until Mark II B replaced.

1978-1980	1x12"	$850	$1,150
1978-1980	1x15"	$850	$1,150

Mark II B Amp Head

Head only.

1981-1983		$600	$900

Mark II B Combo Amp

1980-1983. Effective Aug. '80 1x12" models, serial numbers 5575 - 110000. May '83 1x15" models, serial numbers 560 - 11000. The 300 series serial numbers K1 - K336.

1981-1983	1x12"	$850	$1,150
1981-1983	1x15"	$850	$1,150

Mark II C/Mark II C+ Amp

May 1983-Mar.1985. Serial numbers 11001 - 14999 for 60 watts, 1x15", offered with optional white tolex cover. 300 series serial numbers after C+ are in the series K337 - K422.

1983-1985		$800	$1,200
1983-1985	White tolex	$800	$1,200

Mark II C+ Head Amp

1983-1985. 60-watt head.

1983-1985		$650	$1,000

Mark III Combo Amp

Mar.1985-Feb.1999. Serial numbers: 15,000 - 28,384. 300 series serialization K500- . Graphic equalizer only Mark III since Aug.'90, 100 watts, 1x12" combo. Custom cover or exotic hardwood cab will bring more than standard vinyl cover cab.

1985-1990	Black	$800	$1,100
1985-1990	Custom color	$900	$1,200
1985-1991	Custom hardward cab	$1,000	$1,300
1990-1999	Graphic EQ, hardwood cab	$1,000	$1,300
1990-1999	Graphic EQ, standard cab	$800	$1,000

Mark III Amp Head

1985-1999. 100 watts, black vinyl.

1985-1990		$800	$950
1990-1999	Graphic EQ model	$900	$1,000

Mark III 1x12 Cab

Late-1980s-early-1990s. Typically sized 1x12" extension cab with open half back, black vinyl, black grille, not strictly for Mark III, usable for any Boogie with matching output specs, rated for 90 watts.

1988-1990s		$225	$300

Mark III 4x12 Cab

Late-1980s-early-1990s. Half stack 4x12" slant cab with open half back or straight-front cab, not strictly for Mark III, usable for any Boogie with matching output specs, often loaded with Celestion Vintage 30s, small weave grille (not see-thru crossing strips).

1988-1990s	Slant cab	$600	$650
1988-1990s	Straight-front cab	$600	$650

Mark IV Head and Half Stack Amp Set

1991-2000. Mark IV head and matching 4x12" slant half stack cab.

1991-2000		$1,600	$1,700

Mark IV/Mark IV B Combo Amp

May 1990-present. Changed to Model IV B Feb.'95, serial numbers: IV001. Clean rhythm, crunch rhythm and lead modes, 40 watts, EQ, 3-spring reverb, dual effects loops, digital footswitching.

1991-1999		$1,225	$1,375
1991-1999	Custom hardwood cab	$1,375	$1,775
2000-2003		$1,225	$1,375

Maverick Amp Head

1994-present. 35 watts, Dual Rectifier head, white/blond vinyl cover.

1994-2000		$600	$750

Maverick Combo Amp

1997-present. Dual channels, 4 EL84s, 35 watts, 1x12" or 2x12" combo amp, 5AR4 tube rectifier, cream vinyl covering. Serial number: MAV. Also available as head.

1997-2000	1x12"	$650	$850
1997-2000	2x12"	$700	$900

Maverick Half Stack Amp Set

Apr.1994-present. Serial numbers: MAV001- . 35 watts, Dual Rectifier head and half stack cab set.

1994-2000		$1,200	$1,400

M-Pulse 360 Amp

Jul.2001-2005. Serial numbers: MP3-01- . Rack mount, silver panel.

2001-2003		$650	$750

M-Pulse 600 Amp

Apr.2001-present. Serial numbers: MP6-01- . Rack mount bass with 600 watts, tube preamp.

2001-2004		$850	$950

Nomad 45 Combo Amp

Jul.1999-present. Serial numbers: NM45-01. 45 watts, 1x12, 2x12" or 4x10" combo, dark vinyl cover, dark grille.

1999-2002	1x12"	$650	$800
1999-2002	2x12"	$750	$900
1999-2003	4x10"	$775	$950

Mesa-Boogie Mk II B

Mesa-Boogie Mk I reissue

Mesa-Boogie Mk IV B reissue

AMPS

Mesa-Boogie Nomad 55

Mesa-Boogie Nomad 100

*1984 Mesa-Boogie
Son of Boogie*

MODEL YEAR	FEATURES	EXC. COND. LOW	HIGH
Nomad 55 Combo Amp			
Jul.1999-2004. Serial numbers: NM55-01. 55 watts, 1x12", 2x12" or 4x10" combo.			
1999-2001	1x12"	$800	$1,000
1999-2001	2x12"	$900	$1,100
Nomad 100 Amp Head			
Jul.1999-present. 100 watts, black cover, black grille.			
1999-2001		$825	$975
Nomad 100 Combo Amp			
Jul.1999-present. 100 watts, 1x12" or 2x12" combo, black cover, black grille.			
1999-2001	1x12"	$925	$1,125
1999-2001	2x12"	$1,025	$1,225
Powerhouse Series Bass Cabinets			
2004-present.			
2004	1x15", 400 watts	$300	$325
2004	2x10", 600 watts	$350	$375
2004	4x10", 600 watts	$375	$400
Princeton Boost Fender Conversion			
1970. Fender Princeton modified by Randall Smith, Boogie badge logo instead of the Fender blackface logo on upper left corner of the grille. About 300 amps were modified and were one of the early mods that became Mesa-Boogie.			
1970		$1,700	$2,500
Quad Preamp			
Sep.1987-1992. Serial numbers: Q001-Q2857. Optional Quad with FU2-A footswitch Aug.'90-Jan.'92, serial numbers: Q2022 - Q2857.			
1987-1992	Without footswitch	$425	$525
1990-1992	With footswitch	$500	$600
Recto Recording Preamp			
2004-present. Rack mount preamp.			
2004		$775	$825
Rect-O-Verb Combo Amp			
Dec.1998-present. Serial numbers R50-. 50 watts, 1x12", black vinyl cover, black grille.			
1998-2001		$875	$1,000
Rect-O-Verb I Amp Head			
Dec.1998-2001. Serial numbers: R50-. 50 watts, head with 2 6L6 power tubes, upgraded Apr.'01 to II Series.			
1998-2001		$825	$925
Rect-O-Verb II Amp Head			
Apr.2001-present. Upgrade, serial number R5H-750.			
2001-2003		$550	$800
Rect-O-Verb II Combo Amp			
April 2001-pressent. Upgrade R5H-750, 50 watts, AB, 2 6L6, spring reverb.			
2001-2003		$900	$925
Rect-O-Verb/Recto Cab			
1998-2001. Slant front 4x12" or 2x12" option cab, black cover, dark grille.			
1998-2001	2x12" option	$375	$475
1998-2001	4x12" slant front	$500	$575

MODEL YEAR	FEATURES	EXC. COND. LOW	HIGH
Road King Dual Rectifier Amp Head			
2002-present. Tube head, various power tube selections based upon a chasis which uses 2 EL34s and 4 6L6, 2 5U4 dual rectifier tubes or silicon diode rectifiers, 50 to 120 watts.			
2002-2004		$2,500	$2,600
RoadReady Bass Cabinets			
1990s-present. Heavy-duty flight case shell bass cabinets with metal grilles and casters.			
1990s	1x15"	$325	$425
1990s	2x12"	$425	$525
Rocket 440 Amp			
Mar.1999-Aug.2000. Serial numbers: R440-R44-1159. 45 watts, 4x10".			
1999-2000		$575	$625
Satellite/Satellite 60 Amp			
Aug.1990-1999. Serial numbers: ST001-ST841. Uses either 6L6s for 100 watts or EL34s for 60 watts, dark vinyl, dark grille.			
1990-1999		$400	$600
Solo 50 Rectifier Series I Amp Head			
Nov.1998-Apr.2001. Serial numbers: R50. 50-watt head.			
1998-2001		$850	$1,000
Solo 50 Rectifier Series II Amp Head			
Apr.2001. Upgrade, serial numbers: S50-S1709. Upgrades preamp section, head with 50 watts.			
2001		$850	$975
Son Of Boogie Amp			
May 1982-Dec.1985. Serial numbers: S100-S2390. 60 watts, 1x12", considered the first reissue of the original Mark I.			
1982-1985		$500	$700
Stereo 290 (Simul 2-Ninety) Amp			
Jun.1992-present. Serial numbers: R0001- . Dual 90-watt stereo channels, rack mount.			
1992-1999		$900	$975
Stereo 295 Amp			
Mar.1987-May 1991. Serial numbers: S001-S2673. Dual 95-watt class A/B stereo channels, rack mount. Selectable 30 watts Class A (EL34 power tubes) power.			
1987-1991		$500	$600
Strategy 400 Amp			
Mar.1987-May 1991. Serial numbers: S001-S2627. 400 to 500 watts, power amplifier with 12 6L6 power tubes.			
1987-1991		$750	$850
Strategy 500 Amp			
June 1991-April 1992. S2,552- . Rack mount, 500 watts, 4 6550 power tubes.			
1991-1992		$850	$950
Studio .22/Studio .22+ Amp			
Nov.1985-1988. Serial numbers: SS000-SS11499, black vinyl, black grille, 22 watts, 1x12". Replaced by .22+ Dec.1988-Aug.1993. Serial numbers: FP11,500 - FP28,582. 22 watts.			
1985-1988		$450	$650
1988-1993		$450	$650

The *Vintage Guitar Price Guide* shows low to high values for items in all-original excellent condition, and, where applicable, with original case or cover.

MODEL YEAR FEATURES	EXC. COND. LOW	HIGH

Studio Caliber DC-2 Amp
Apr.1994-Jan.1999. Serial numbers: DC2-01 - DC2-4247 (formerly called DC-2). 20 watts, 1x12" combo, dark vinyl, dark grille.

1994-1999	$425	$550

Studio Preamp
Aug.1988-Dec.1993. Serial numbers: SP000-SP7890. Tube preamp, EQ, reverb, effects loop.

1988-1993	$350	$450

Subway/Subway Blues Amp
Sep.1994-Aug.2000. Serial numbers: SB001-SB2515. 20 watts, 1x10".

1994-2000	$550	$600

Subway Reverb Rocket Amp
Jun.1998-Aug.2001. Serial numbers: RR1000-RR2461. 20 watts, 1x10".

1998-2001	$500	$625

Subway Rocket (no reverb) Amp
Jan.1996-Jul.1998. Serial numbers: SR001-SR2825. No reverb, 20 watts, 1x10".

1996-1998	$500	$575

Trem-O-Verb Dual Rectifier Amp Head
Jun.1993-Jan.2001. 100-watt head version.

1993-2001	$950	$1,200
1993-2001 Rack mount version	$950	$1,200

Trem-O-Verb Dual Rectifier Cab
Late-1980s-early-1990s. Half stack 4x12" slant cab with open half back, or straight-front cab, 2x12" straight-front option, not strictly for this model, useable for any Boogie with matching output specs, often loaded with Celestion Vintage 30s, small weave grille (not see-thru

1988-1990s 2x12" straight cab option	$450	$500
1988-1990s 4x12" slant cab	$550	$600
1988-1990s 4x12" straight cab	$550	$600

Trem-O-Verb Dual Rectifier Half Stack Amp
Jun.1993-Jan.2001. 100 watts, head with matching 4x12" slant cab.

2001	$1,600	$2,000

Trem-O-Verb Dual Rectifier Combo Amp
Jun.1993-Jan.2001. Serial numbers: R- to about R-21210. 100 watts, 2x12" Celestion Vintage 30.

1993-2000	$1,175	$1,375

Triaxis Preamp
Oct.1991-present. Serial numbers:T0001-. 5 12AX7 tube preamp, rack mount.

1991-2000	$975	$1,075

Triple Rectifier Amp Head
1997-present. Three-channel amp head.

1997-2003	$1,300	$1,550

V-Twin Rackmount Amp
May 1995-Jun.1998. Serial numbers: V2R-001 to V2R-2258.

1995-1998	$425	$500

Walk About M-Pulse Bass Amp Head
Sep.2001-present. Serial numbers: WK-01-. Lightweight 13 pounds, 2 12AX7s + 300 MOS-FET.

2001-2003	$500	$650

Meteoro
1986-present. Guitar, bass, harp and keyboard combo amps, heads, and cabinets built in Brazil. They also build effects.

Mission Amps
1996-present. Bruce Collins' Mission Amps, located in Arvada, Colorado, produces a line of custom-made combo amps, heads, and cabinets.

Mojave Amp Works
2002-present. Tube amp heads and speaker cabinets by Victor Mason in Apple Valley, California.

Montgomery Ward
Amps for this large retailer were sometimes branded as Montgomery Ward, but usually as Airline (see that listing).

Higher Power 1x12" Combo Amp
1950s. 1x12", about 2 6L6 power tubes, includes brown covered Maestro C Series with cloverleaf grille.

1950s	$200	$275

Lower Power 1x12" Combo Amp
1950s. 1x12" speaker, around 12 watts, includes Model 8439.

1950s	$175	$250

Mooneyes
Budget solid state amp line from Lace Music Products. They also offer amps under the Rat Fink and Lace brands. Lace has a Mooneyes guitar model line.

Morley
Late-1960s-present. The effects company offered an amp in the late '70s. See Effects section for more company info.

Bigfoot Amp
1979-ca.1981. Looks like Morley's '70s effects pedals, produced 25 watts and pedal controlled volume. Amp only, speakers were sold separately.

1979-1981	$150	$225

Mountain
Mountain builds a 9-volt amp in a wood cabinet. Originally built in California, then Nevada; currently being made in Vancouver, Canada.

Multivox
Ca.1946-ca.1984. Multivox was started as a subsidiary of Premier to manufacture amps, and later, effects.

New York 1st AVE Amp
1982. 15 watts, 1x8".

1982	$50	$80

New York 6th AVE Amp
1982. 60 watts, 1x12".

1982	$80	$110

Mesa-Boogie Son of Boogie combo

AMPS

Mission Amp

Mooneyes ME-10

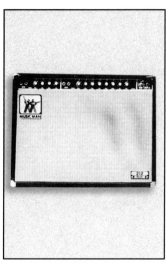

Music Man 212 Sixty Five

Music Man 115 Sixty Five

Early-'50s National/Valco

MODEL YEAR	FEATURES	EXC. COND. LOW	HIGH

Music Man

1972-present. Music Man made amps from '73 to '83. The number preceding the amp model indicates the speaker configuration. The last number in model name usually referred to the watts. RD indicated "Reverb Distortion." RP indicated "Reverb Phase." Many models were available in head-only versions and as combos with various speaker combinations.

110 RD Fifty Amp
1980-1983. 50 watts, 1x10", reverb, distortion.

1980-1983		$500	$550

112 RD Fifty Amp
1980-1983. 50 watts, 1x12", reverb, distortion.

1980-1983		$525	$575

112 RD Sixty Five Amp
1978-1983. 65 watts, 1x12", reverb, distortion.

1978-1983		$525	$575

112 RD One Hundred Amp
1978-1983. 100 watts, 1x12", reverb, distortion.

1978-1983		$525	$575

112 Sixty Five Amp
1973-1981. Combo amp, 65 watts, 1x12", reverb, tremolo.

1973-1981		$525	$575

112 RP Sixty Five Amp
1978-1983. 65 watts, 1x12", reverb, built-in phaser.

1978-1983		$500	$575

112 RP One Hundred Amp
1978-1983. Combo amp, 100 watts, 1x12", reverb, built-in phaser.

1978-1983		$525	$575

115 Sixty Five Amp
1973-1981. Combo amp, 65 watts, 1x15", reverb, tremolo.

1973-1981		$500	$575

210 HD130 Amp
1973-1981. 130 watts, 2x10", reverb, tremolo.

1973-1981		$500	$600

210 Sixty Five Amp
1973-1981. 65 watts, 2x10", reverb, tremolo.

1973-1981		$500	$600

212 HD130 Amp
1973-1981. 130 watts, 2x12", reverb, tremolo.

1973-1981		$525	$650

212 Sixty Five Amp
1973-1981. 65 watts, 2x12", reverb, tremolo.

1973-1981		$525	$650

410 Sixty Five Amp
1973-1981. 65 watts, 4x10", reverb, tremolo.

1973-1981		$550	$675

410 Seventy Five Amp
1982-1983. 75 watts, 4x10", reverb, tremolo.

1982-1983		$550	$675

HD-130 Amp
1973-1981. Head amp, 130 watts, reverb, tremolo.

1973-1981		$400	$575

RD Fifty Amp
1980-1983. Head amp, 50 watts, reverb, distortion.

1980-1983		$325	$450

Sixty Five Amp
1973-1981. Head amp, 65 watts, reverb, tremolo.

1973-1981		$325	$450

National

Ca.1927-present. National/Valco amps date back to the late-'30s. National introduced a modern group of amps about the same time they introduced their new Res-O-Glas space-age guitar models in '62. In '64, the amp line was partially redesigned and renamed. By '68, the Res-O-Glas models were gone and National introduced many large vertical and horizontal piggyback models which lasted until National's assets were assigned during bankruptcy in '69. The National name went to Chicago importer Strum N' Drum who then advertised "National is back and better than ever." Initially, Strum N' Drum had one amp, the National GA 950 P Tremolo/Reverb piggyback.

Chicago 51 Aztec/Valco Amp
Late-1940s-early-1950s. Low- to mid-power, 2x6L6, 3 oval Rola speakers, 3 baffle openings (1 for each speaker), tweed cover.

1940-1950s		$300	$500

Chicago/Valco 51 Amp
1950s. Vertical tweed cabinet, metal preamps tubes, late-1940s-early-'50s technology, 1x12".

1950s		$300	$450

Glenwood 90 (Model N6490TR) Amp
1962-1967. 35 watts, 2x12", tremolo (not listed as vibrato) and reverb.

1964-1967		$550	$650

Glenwood Vibrato (Model N6499VR) Amp
1964-1967. 70 watts, 2x12", vibrato and reverb.

1964-1967		$600	$700

Model 100 Amp
Tube amp, 40 watts, 1x12".

1940		$400	$450

Model GA 950-P Tremolo/Reverb Piggyback Amp
1970s. Strum N' Drum/National model, solidstate, 50 watts, 2-channel 2x12" and 1x7" in 32" tall vertical cabinet, black.

1970s		$175	$250

Model N6800 - N6899 Piggyback Amps
1968-1969. National introduced a new line of tube amps in '68 and most of them were piggybacks. The N6895 was sized like a Fender piggyback Tremolux, the N6875 and N6878 bass amps were sized like a '68 Fender large cab piggyback with a 26" tall vertical cab, the N6898 and N6899 were the large piggyback guitar amps. These amps feature the standard Jensen speakers or the upgrade JBL speakers, the largest model was the N6800 for PA or guitar, which sported 3x70-watt channels and 2 column speakers using a bass 2x12" + 1x3" horn cab and a voice-guitar 4x10" + 1x3" horn cab.

1968-1969	Various tube models	$200	$375

MODEL YEAR	FEATURES	EXC. COND. LOW	HIGH

Model N6816 (Model 16) Amp

1968-1969. Valco-made tube amp, 6 watts, 1x10" Jensen speaker, 17" vertical cab, tremolo, no reverb, black vinyl cover and Coppertone grille, National spelled out on front panel.

| 1968-1969 | | $125 | $175 |

Model N6820 Thunderball Bass Amp

1968-1969. Valco-made tube amp, about 35 watts, 1x15" Jensen speaker, 19" vertical cab, black vinyl cover and Coppertone grille, National spelled out on front panel.

| 1968-1969 | | $150 | $200 |

Model N6822 (Model 22) Amp

1968-1969. Valco-made, 6 watts tube (4 tubes) amp, 1x12" Jensen speaker, 19" vertical cab, tremolo and reverb, black vinyl cover and Coppertone grille, National spelled out on front panel.

| 1968-1969 | | $150 | $200 |

National Dobro Amp

1930s. Sold by the National Dobro Corp. when the company was still in Los Angeles (they later moved to Chicago). National Dobro plate on rear back panel, suitcase style case that flips open to reveal the speaker and amp, National logo on outside of suitcase. The noted price is for an all-original amp in excellent condition (this would be a rare find), there are other 1930s models included in the price range below.

| 1930s | Model B, not suitcase | $200 | $400 |
| 1930s | Suitcase style | $400 | $700 |

Sportman Amp

| 1950s | | $400 | $450 |

Student Practice Amp

1970s. Strum N' Drum era, small solidstate, single control.

| 1970s | | $25 | $35 |

Studio 10 Amp

1962-1967. Five watts, 1x3", 3 tubes, 1 channel, 1 volume control, no tone control, no reverb or tremolo.

| 1962-1963 | | $350 | $450 |
| 1964-1967 | N6410 Model | $350 | $450 |

Westwood 16 (Model N6416T) Amp

1964-1967. Five watts using 1 6V6 power, 2 12AX7 preamp, 1 5Y3GT rectifier, tremolo, 2x8", dark vinyl cover, silver grille.

| 1964-1967 | | $375 | $475 |

Westwood 22 (Model N6422TR) Amp

1964-1967. 5 watts, 2x8", reverb and tremolo, 1 channel, 6 tubes.

| 1964-1967 | | $375 | $475 |

Naylor Engineering

1994-present. Joe Naylor and Kyle Kurtz founded the company in East Pointe, Michigan, in the early '90s, selling J.F. Naylor speakers. In '94 they started producing amps. In '96, Naylor sold his interest in the business to Kurtz and left to form Reverend Guitars. In '99 David King bought the company and moved it to Los Angeles, California, then to Dallas, Texas. Currently Naylor builds tube amps, combos, speakers, and cabinets.

Nemesis

From the makers of Eden amps, Nemesis is a line of made-in-the-U.S., FET powered bass combos and extension cabinets. The brand is a division of U.S. Music Corp.

NC-200 Combo Amp

1990s. Compact style cabinet with 200 watts, solidstate, 2x10", black cover, black grille.

| 1997 | | $425 | $500 |

NC-200P Combo Amp

1990s. Compact transporter-style cabinet with 200 watts, solidstate, 4x10", black cover, black grille.

| 1997 | | $475 | $550 |

Nobel

1950-1960s. From Don Noble and Company, of Chicago, Illinois, owned by Strum N' Drum by mid-'60s.

Mid-Size Tube Amp

1950s. Low- to mid-power tube amp, Noble logo on front.

| 1950s | | $325 | $400 |

Norma

1965-1970. Economy solidstate line imported and distributed by Strum N' Drum, Wheeling (Chicago), Illinois. As noted in the National section, Strum N' Drum acquired the National brand in the '70s. Low values reflect the market's low demand for an import solidstate amp.

GA-93 Amp

1969-1970. Economy solidstate, 6 watts, 1x6", dark brown vinyl cover, dark brown grille.

| 1969-1970 | | $55 | $75 |

GA-97 T Amp

1969-1970. Economy solidstate, 13 watts, 1x8", dark brown vinyl cover, dark grille, tremolo.

| 1969-1970 | | $60 | $85 |

GA-725 B Amp

1969-1970. Economy solidstate bass amp, 38 watts, 1x10" bass speaker, dark brown vinyl cover, sparkle grille.

| 1969-1970 | | $60 | $85 |

GA-918 T Amp

1969-1970. Economy solidstate, 24 watts, 1x12", dark brown vinyl cover, dark grille, tremolo and reverb.

| 1969-1970 | | $70 | $95 |

GA-930 P (piggyback) Amp

1969-1970. Economy solidstate, 40 watts, 2x12", piggyback, dark vinyl cover, dark grille.

| 1969-1970 | | $80 | $125 |

GA-6240 Amp

1969-1970. Economy solidstate portable, 50 watts, dark vinyl cover, medium light grille.

| 1969-1970 | | $80 | $125 |

GAP-2 Amp

1969-1970. Economy solidstate, 3 watts, 1x4", dark brown vinyl cover, light brown grille.

| 1969-1970 | | $55 | $75 |

Naylor Super-Drive Sixty

National Glenwood 90

Nemesis NC-115

AMPS

MODEL YEAR	FEATURES	EXC. COND. LOW	HIGH

Oahu Holiday

Oahu

The Oahu Publishing Company and Honolulu Conservatory, based in Cleveland, Ohio, started with acoustic Hawaiian and Spanish guitars, selling large quantities in the 1930s. As electric models became popular, Oahu responded with guitar/amp sets. The brand has been revived on a line of U.S.-made tube amps.

Small Guitar/Lab Steel Amps

| 1950s | Various colors | $225 | $250 |

Oliver

Ca.1966-late-1970s. The Oliver Sound Company, Westbury, New York, was founded by former Ampeg engineer, Jess Oliver, after he left Ampeg in '65. Tube amp designs were based upon Oliver's work at Ampeg. The Oliver Powerflex Amp is the best-known design, and featured an elevator platform that would lift the amp head out of the speaker cabinet.

Model G-150R Combo Amp

2 6L6 power tubes, reverb, tremolo, black tolex with black grille, silver control panel, 40 watts, 1x15".

| 1970s | | $375 | $475 |

Model P-500 Combo Amp

All tube combo with 15" motorized amp chassis that rises out of tall lateral speaker cabinet as amp warms up.

| 1960s | | $475 | $600 |

Orbital Power Projector Amp

Late-1960s-early-1970s. Rotating speaker cabinet with horn, Leslie-like voice.

| 1970s | | $475 | $600 |

Sam Ash Oliver Amp Head

Late-1960s-early-1970s. Private branded for Sam Ash Music, about 30 watts using the extinct 7027A power tubes, Sam Ash script logo on front grille.

| 1960s | | $150 | $275 |

'70s Oliver 6200R Uniflex

Orange

1969-1981, 1995-present. Orange amps and PAs were made in England by Cliff Cooper and Matthew Mathias. The Orange-colored amps were well-built and were used by many notable guitarists. Since '95, Cliff Cooper is once again making Orange amplifiers in England, with the exception of the small Crush Practice Combo amps, which are made in Korea.

Model OR-80 Combo Amp

1970s. About 80 watts, 2x12" combo.

| 1970s | | $2,000 | $2,400 |

Model OR 80 Amp w/4x12 Bottom.

1970s. 80 watts, 4x12" straight-front cab with Orange crest on grille, orange vinyl and light orange grille.

| 1970s | | $2,400 | $3,000 |

Model OR-120 Graphic Head Amp and Half Stack

1970s. 120 watts, 4x12" straight front cab with Orange crest on grille, orange vinyl and light orange grille.

| 1970s | | $2,700 | $3,400 |

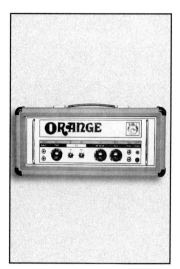

Orange Model OR-120

Model OR-120 Graphic Overdrive Amp Head

120 watts.

| 1978 | | $1,500 | $2,000 |

Model OR-200 212 Twin Amp

1970s. 120 watts, 2x12" combo, orange-vinyl, dark grille, Orange crest on grille, reverb and vibrato, master volume.

| 1970s | | $2,100 | $2,700 |

Orpheum

Late-1950s-1960s. Student to medium level amps from New York's Maurice Lipsky Music.

Small/Mid-Size Amps

Late-1950s-1960s. U.S.-made, 2 6V6 power tubes, Jensen P12R 12" speaker, light cover with gray swirl grille.

| 1959 | | $175 | $225 |

Ovation

1966-present. Kaman made few amps under the Ovation name. They offered a variety of amps under the KMD brand from '85 to around '94.

Little Dude Amp

1969-ca.1971. Solidstate combo, 100 watts, 1x15" and horn, matching slave unit also available.

| 1970s | | $175 | $250 |

The Kat (Model 6012) Amp

1970s. Solidstate, 2x12" combo.

| 1970s | | $175 | $250 |

Overbuilt Amps

1999-present. Tube amps and combos built by Richard Seccombe in West Hills, California.

PAC-AMP (Magnatone)

Late-1950s-early-1960s. Private branded by Magnatone, often for accordion studios.

Model 280-A Amp

1961-1963. About 50 watts, 2x12" + 2x5", brown leatherette, light brown grille, stereo vibrato, PAC-AMP nameplate logo.

| 1961-1963 | | $925 | $1,100 |

PANaramic (Magnatone)

1961-1963. Private branded equivalent of '61-'63 Magnatone brown leatherette series, large PANaramic logo. Many Magnatone private brands were associated with accordion companies or accordian teaching studios. PANaramic was a brand name of PANaramic accordion. They also made guitars.

Model 260/262-style Amp

1961-1963. 35 watts, 2x12", gray vinyl and light grille, vibrato, large PANaramic logo.

| 1961-1963 | | $675 | $750 |

Model 413-style Amp

1961-1963. 18 watts, 1x12", black leatherette cover, light silver grille, vibrato, large PANaramic logo.

| 1961-1963 | | $525 | $575 |

MODEL YEAR	FEATURES	EXC. COND. LOW	HIGH

Model 450-style Amp

1961-1963. 20 watts, 1x12", reverb and vibrato, reverb not generally included in an early-'60s 1x12" Magnatone amp, dark vinyl, dark cross-threaded grille, large PANaramic logo.

1961-1963		$750	$925

Paris

Master Series Amps

1960s. Compact solid-state combo, 1x12", slanted Paris logo front upper left side of grille, black tolex-style cover, silver grille (like Fender blackface), rear mounted slanted control panel.

1960s		$100	$150

Park

1965-1982, 1992-2000. Park amps were made by Marshall from '65 to '82. In the '90s, Marshall revived the name for use on small solidstate amps imported from the Far East.

G Series Amp

1990s. Student compact amps, models include G-10 (10 watts, 1x8"), G-25R (25 watts, reverb) and GB-25 (25 watts, 1x12" bass).

1990s	G-10	$40	$85
1990s	G-25R	$90	$110
1990s	GB-25	$85	$105

Model 75 Amp Head

1967-1971. Head amp, 50 watts, 2xKT88s, small-box plexi (later aluminum), black tolex.

1967-1969	Plexi	$3,900	$4,900
1969-1971	Aluminum	$3,100	$3,900

Model 1206 50-Watt Amp Head

1981-1982. 50 watts, based upon JCM 800 50-watt made at the same time period.

1981-1982		$800	$1,000

Model 1213 100-Watt Reverb Combo Amp

1970s. 100 watts, 2x12", reverb, dark vinyl, light grille, Park logo on front with elongated P.

1970s		$1,250	$1,400

Model 1228 50-Watt Lead Head Amp

1970s. 50 watts, based upon Marshall 50-watt made at the same time period.

1970s		$1,250	$1,500

Model 2046 25-Watt Combo Amp

1970s. 25 watts, 1x15", '70s era blue grille cloth, black tolex, large P Park logo upper center of grille.

1970s		$1,000	$1,300

Paul Reed Smith

1985-present. In the late '80s, PRS offered two amp models. Only 350 amp units shipped. Includes HG-70 Head and HG-212 Combo. HG stands for Harmonic Generator, effectively a non-tube, solidstate amp.

4x12" Straight-Front Cab

1989. Straight-front 4x12" black vinyl cab with silver grille, PRS logo front lower right of grille.

1989		$450	$500

HG-70 Amp Head

1989-1990. 70 watts, reverb, effects loop, noise gate. Options include 150-watt circuitry and 4x12" straight and slant cabinets, gray-black.

1989		$450	$500

HG-212 Amp

1989-1990. Combo, 70 watts, 2x12", reverb, effects loop, noise gate. Options include 150-watt circuitry and 4x12" straight and slant cabinets, gray-black.

1989		$500	$600

Peavey

1965-present. Hartley Peavey's first products were guitar amps. He added guitars to the mix in '78. Headquartered in Meridan, Mississippi, Peavey continues to offer a huge variety of guitars, amps, and PAs.

5150 212 Combo Amp

1995-2004. Combo version of 5150 head, 60 watts, 2x12", large 5150 logo on front panel, small Peavey logo on lower right of grille.

1995-2004		$500	$600

5150 EVH Head and Cab Amp Set

1995-2004. Half stack 5150 head and 4x12" cab, large 5150 logo on front of amp.

1995	Head and cab	$875	$1,000
1995	Head only	$475	$575
1996-2004	Cab only	$350	$375
1996-2004	Head and cab	$825	$925
1996-2004	Head only	$400	$500

Alphabass Amp

1988-1990. Rack mount all tube, 160 watts, EQ, includes 2x15" Black Widow or 2x12" Scorpion cabinet.

1988-1990		$300	$350

Artist Amp

120 watts, 1x12", bright and normal channels, EQ, reverb, master volume.

1970s		$225	$275

Artist 110 Amp

TransTubes, 10 watts.

1990s		$125	$150

Artist 250 Amp

1990s. 100 watts, 1x12", solidstate preamp, 4 6L6 power tubes, black vinyl cover, black grille.

1990s		$200	$250

Artist VT Amp

1990s. Combo amp, 120 watts, 1x12".

1990s		$225	$300

Audition Chorus Amp

2x10-watt channels, 2x6", channel switching, post gain and normal gain controls.

1980s		$125	$175

Audition Plus Amp

1980s. Solidstate, 20 watts, 1x10" compact practice amp, standard Peavey black tolex, black grille and slant logo.

1980s	Black Tolex	$90	$125

Overbuilt Fiscus 30 W 212 combo

Park G10

PRS HG-212

AMPS

AMPS

1977 Peavey Backstage 30

Peavey Bandit

Peavey Classic 50/212

MODEL YEAR	FEATURES	EXC. COND. LOW	HIGH

Audition 20 Amp
1980s-1990s. Compact practice amp, 20 watts, single speaker combo, black vinyl and grille.

1980-1990s		$75	$100

Audition 30 Amp
1980s-1990s. 30 watts, 1x12" combo amp, channel switching.

1980-1990s		$90	$125

Audition 110 Amp
1990s. 25 watts, 1x10" combo, 2 channels.

1990s		$90	$125

Backstage Amp
1977-mid-1980s. Master gain control, 18 watts, 1x10", 3-band EQ.

1977-1984		$60	$90

Backstage 30 Amp
30 watts, 1x8".

1980s		$90	$110

Backstage 110 Amp
Repackaged and revoiced in 1988, 65 watts, 1x10", Peavey SuperSat preamp circuitry, new power sections.

1980s		$110	$135

Backstage Chorus 208 Amp
1990s. 150 watts, 2x8", reverb, channel switching.

1990s		$150	$200

Backstage Plus Amp
1980s. 35 watts, 1x10" combo, reverb, saturation effect.

1980s		$100	$125

Bandit 75 Amp
Redesigned and renamed Bandit 112 in 1988. Channel switching, 75 watts, 1x12", 4-band EQ, reverb, post-effects loop, Superstat.

1980s		$200	$250

Bandit 112/Bandit II 112 Amp
1988-2001. 80 watts, 1x12", active EQ circuit for lead channel, active controls.

1980s	Bandit	$225	$325
1990s	Bandit II	$250	$350

Basic 40 Amp
40 watts, 1x12".

1980s		$125	$150

Basic 60 Amp
1988-1995. Solidstate combo amp, 50-60 watts, 1x12", 4-band EQ, gain controls.

1988-1995	Black	$170	$190

Basic 112 Bass Amp
2000s. 75 watts, 1x12" bass combo, 2000-era red border control panel.

2000s		$200	$225

Blazer 158 Amp
1995-present. 15 watts, 1x8", clean and distortion, now called the TransTube Blazer III.

1995-2000	Black Tolex	$65	$90

Bluesman Amp
1992. Tweed, 1x12" or 1x15".

1992		$325	$400

MODEL YEAR	FEATURES	EXC. COND. LOW	HIGH

Bravo 112 Amp
1988-1994. All tube reverb, 25 watts, 1x12", 3-band EQ, 2 independent input channels.

1988-1994		$275	$350

Classic 20 Amp
Small tube amp with 2xEL84 power tubes, 1x10", tweed cover.

1990s		$250	$300

Classic 30 Amp
1994-present. Tweed, 30 watts, 1x12", EL84 tubes.

1994-1999		$350	$400

Classic 50/212 Amp
1990-present. Combo, 50 watt, 2x12", 4 EL84s, 3 12AX7s, reverb, high-gain section.

1990-2000		$450	$500

Classic 50/410 Amp
1990-present. Combo amp, 4x10", EL84 power, reverb, footswitchable high-gain mode.

1990s		$450	$500

Classic 120 Amp
1988-ca.1990. Tube, 120 watts.

1988-1990		$350	$375

DECA/750 Amp
1989-ca.1990. Digital, 2 channels, 350 watts per channel, distortion, reverb, exciter, pitch shift, multi-EQ.

1989-1990		$275	$325

Decade Amp
1970s. Practice amp, 10 watts, 1x8", runs on 12 volt or AC.

1970s		$40	$60

Delta Blues Amp
1995-present. 30 watts, tube combo, 4 EL84 tubes, 1x15" or 2x8", tremolo, large-panel-style cab, blond tweed.

1995-2000		$325	$425

Deuce Head Amp
1975-1980s. Tube head, 120 watts.

1975-1980		$200	$250

Deuce Amp
1975-1980s. 120 watts, tube amp, 2x12" or 4x10".

1975-1980		$275	$375

Ecoustic 112 Amp
100 watts, 1x12" acoustic and mic amp, guitar input and mic input, brown vinyl, brown grille.

2000s		$200	$250

Encore 65 Amp
1990s. Compact solidstate amp, 1x12", reverb, channel switching.

1990s		$200	$225

Envoy 110 Amp
1988-2001. Solidstate, 40 watts, 1x10", patent-applied-for circuitry, TransTubes.

1988-2001		$125	$175

Heritage VTX Amp
1980s. 130 watts, 4 6L6s, solidstate preamp, 2x12" combo.

1980s		$200	$250

Jazz Classic Amp
Solidstate, 210 watts, 1x15", electronic channel switching, 6-spring reverb.

1980s		$200	$250

The *Vintage Guitar Price Guide* shows low to high values for items in all-original excellent condition, and, where applicable, with original case or cover.

MODEL YEAR FEATURES	EXC. COND. LOW	HIGH

KB-100 Amp
Keyboard amp, 1x15".
1980s — $225 — $275

LTD Amp
1975-1980s. Solidstate, 200 watts, 1x12" Altec or 1x15" JBL.
1975-1982 — $200 — $250

Mace Amp Head
Tube, 180 watts.
1980s — $275 — $300

MegaBass Amp
Rack mount preamp/power amp, 200 watts per 2 channels, solidstate, EQ, effects loop, chorus.
1980s — $250 — $300

Microbass Amp
2000s. 20 watts, 1x8" practice amp, made in China.
2000s — $75 — $100

Minx 110 Bass Amp
1988-present. Solidstate, 35 watts RMS, 1x10" heavy-duty speaker.
1988-1999 — $125 — $150

Musician Amp Head
Tube head, 200 watts.
1970s — $175 — $225

Nashville 400 Steel Guitar Amp
210 watts, 1x15" solidstate steel guitar combo amp.
1990s — $275 — $325

Nashville 1000 Steel Guitar Amp
1x15" speaker, solidstate steel guitar combo amp.
1990s — $300 — $350

Pacer Amp
1977-1980s. Master volume, 45 watts, 1x12", 3-band EQ.
1977-1985 — $135 — $150

ProBass 1000 Amp
Rack mount, effects loops, preamp, EQ, crossover, headphone output.
1980s — $175 — $200

Rage/Rage 158 Amp
1980s-1990s. Compact practice amp, 15 watts, 1x8".
1980s — $90 — $110

Reno 400 Amp
Solidstate, 200 watts, 1x15" with horn, 4-band EQ.
1980s — $200 — $250

Renown 112 Amp
1989-1994. Crunch and lead SuperSat, 160 watts, 1x12", master volume, digital reverb, EQ.
1989-1994 — $200 — $250

Renown 212 Amp
1989-1994. Crunch and lead SuperSat, 160 watts, 2x12", master volume, digital reverb, EQ.
1989-1994 — $225 — $275

Renown 400 Amp
Combo, 200 watts, 2x12", channel switching, Hammond reverb, pre- and post-gain controls.
1980s — $275 — $325

Revolution 112 Amp
2000s. 100 watts, 1x12" combo, black vinyl, black grille.
2000s — $225 — $275

Session 500 Amp
1980s. 250 watts, 1x15", standard black with metal panels appearance.
1980s — $350 — $475

Special 112 Amp
160 watts, 1x12", channel-switching, effects loops, EQ. In 1988, available in wedge-shaped enclosures slanted back 30 degrees.
1980s — $250 — $300

Special 130 Amp
1980s. 1x12", 130 watts, transtube, solidstate series.
1980s — $250 — $300

Special 212 Amp
1990s. 160 watts, 2x12", transtube, solidstate series.
1990s — $300 — $350

Studio Pro 112 Amp
Repackaged and revoiced in 1988. Solidstate, 65 watts, 1x12", Peavey SuperSat preamp circuitry, new power sections
1980s — $175 — $200

TKO-65 Bass Amp
1987-1995. Solidstate, 65 watts, 1x15".
1987-1995 — $200 — $250

TKO-75 Bass Amp
1987-1995. Solidstate, 75 watts, 1x15", EQ, compression and pre-/post-gain controls.
1987-1995 — $200 — $260

TNT-150 Bass Amp
Solidstate, 150 watts, 1x15", EQ, compression, chorus. In 1988, available in wedge-shaped enclosures slanted 30 degrees.
1980s — $275 — $325

Triple XXX Amp Head
2000s. Tube head, 120 watts.
2000s — $625 — $650

Triumph 60 Combo Amp
Tube head, effects loop, reverb, 60 watts, 1x12", multi-stage gain.
1980s — $200 — $250

Triumph 120 Amp
Tube, 120 watts, 1x12", 3 gain blocks in preamp, low-level post-effects loop, built-in reverb.
1989-1990 — $250 — $300

Ultra 112 Amp
1998-2002. 60 watts, 1x12", all tube, 2 6L6 power, black, black grille.
1998-2002 — $325 — $375

Ultra 410 Amp
1998-2002. 60 watts, 4x10".
1998-2002 — $375 — $475

Vegas 400 Amp
1980s. 210 watts, 1x15", reverb, compression feature, parametric EQ. Some musicians prefer as a steel guitar amp.
1980s — $425 — $500

Peavey Delta Blues

Peavey Musician (head)

Peavey Special 112

AMPS

Penn Signature amp

Pignose Hog

Randall RM50

MODEL YEAR FEATURES	EXC. COND. LOW	HIGH

Vintage Amp
2000s. 100 watts, 6x10",tweed combo amp.

| 2000s | $550 | $650 |

Wiggy 212 Amp
2000s. 100-watt head in mono (2x75-watt in stereo) with matching 2x12" cab, 2 EQ systems including 5-band sliders, rounded amp head cabinet.

| 2000s | $625 | $675 |

Penn
1994-present. Tube amps, combos, and cabinets built by Billy Penn, originally in Colts Neck, New Jersey, currently in Long Branch, New Jersey.

Pignose
1972-present. Made in the U.S. Pignose Industries was started by people associated with the band Chicago, including guitarist Terry Kath, with help from designers Wayne Kimball and Richard Erlund.

7-100 Practice Amp
1972-present. The original Pignose, 7"x5"x3" battery-powered portable amplifier, 1x5".

| 1972-1999 | $40 | $70 |

30/60 Amp
1978-ca.1987. Solidstate, 30 watts, 1x10", master volume.

| 1978-1987 | $120 | $170 |

60R Studio Reverb Amp
Solidstate, 30 watts.

| 1980 | $170 | $215 |

Polytone
1960s-present. Made in North Hollywood, California, Polytone offers compact combo amps, heads, and cabinets and a pickup system for acoustic bass.

Mega-Brut Amp
1990s. Mega-Brut logo on front lower right grille, black vinyl, black screen-style grille.

| 1990s | $300 | $325 |

Mini-Brut III Bass Amp
1990s. 80 watts, 1x15", footswitchable reverb and distortion.

| 1990s | $300 | $325 |

Mini-Brut IV Amp
1980s-1990s. 100 watts, 1x15", footswitchable reverb and distortion.

| 1980-1990s | $300 | $375 |

Mini-Brut V Amp
100 watts, 2x10", footswitchable reverb and distortion.

| 1980s | $375 | $400 |

RMS Pro Series Bass Amp
Rack mount, 240 watts, 2 power amps, 2 preamps, crossover for bi-amping.

| 1985 | $375 | $475 |

MODEL YEAR FEATURES	EXC. COND. LOW	HIGH

Premier
Ca.1938-ca.1975. Produced by Peter Sorkin Music Company in Manhattan. First radio-sized amplifiers introduced by '38. After World War II, established Multivox subsidiary to manufacture amplifiers ca.'46. By mid-'50s at least, the amps featured lyre grilles. Dark brown/light tan amp covering by '60. By '64 amps covered in brown woodgrain and light tan. Multivox amps were made until around '84.

B-160 Club Bass Amp
1960s. 15 to 20 watts, 1x12" Jensen speaker, '60s 2-tone brown styling, 6V6 tubes.

| 1963-1968 | $375 | $425 |

Model 50 Combo Amp
1940s-1960s. Four to 5 watts, 1x8" similar to Fender Champ circuit with more of a vertical cab.

| 1950s | $325 | $350 |

Model 76 Combo Amp
1950s. Suitcase latchable cabinet that opens out into 2 wedges, Premier 76 logo on amp control panel, 2-tone brown, lyre grille, 1x12".

| 1950s | $475 | $550 |

Model 88N Combo Amp
1950s-early-1960s. Rectangular suitcase cabinet, 2-tone tan and brown, Premier and lyre logo, 25 watts, 1x12".

| 1950s | $475 | $600 |
| 1960s | $475 | $600 |

Model 100R Amp
Combo amp, 1x12", reverb and tremolo.

| 1960s | $425 | $500 |

Twin 8 Amp
1960s. 20 watts, 2x8", tremolo, reverb.

| 1964-1966 | $525 | $600 |

Twin 12 T-12R Amp
Late-1950s. Early reverb amp with tremolo, 2x12", rectangular cabinet typical of twin 12 amps (Dano and Fender), brown cover.

| 1950s | $550 | $700 |

Quantum
1980s. Economy amps distributed by DME, Indianapolis, Indiana.

Q Terminator Economy Amps
1980s. Economy solidstate amps ranging from 12 to 25 watts and 1x6" to 1x12".

| 1980s | $35 | $75 |

Randall
1960s-present. Randall Instruments was originally out of California and is now a division of U.S. Music Corp. They have offered a range of tube and solidstate combo amps, heads and cabinets over the years.

Guitar and Bass amps
1980s-1990s. Mostly solidstate amps.

| 1980-1990s Intermediate-grade | $250 | $300 |
| 1980-1990s Student-grade | $75 | $250 |

MODEL YEAR	FEATURES	EXC. COND. LOW	HIGH

Rat Fink

2002-present. Solidstate amp line from Lace Music Products. They also sold guitars and basses under this brand and offer amps under the Mooneyes and Lace brands.

Red Bear

1994-1997. Tube amps designed by Sergei Novikov and built in St. Petersburg, Russia. Red Bear amps were distributed in the U.S. under a joint project between Gibson and Novik, Ltd. Novik stills builds amps under other brands.

MK 60 Lead Tube Amp

1994-1997. Head with 4x12" half stack, Red Bear logo on amp and cab.

1994-1997		$700	$800

Reeves Amplification

2002-present. Started by Bill Jansen, Reeves builds tube amps, combos, and cabinets based on the classic British designs of Dan Reeves.

Reverend

1996-present. Joe Naylor started building amps under the Naylor brand in '94. In '96 he left Naylor to build guitars under the Reverend brand. From '01 to '05, Reverend offered tube amps, combos, and cabinets built in Warren, Michigan, that Naylor co-designed with Dennis Kager. He also builds guitars.

Rickenbacker

1931-present. Rickenbacker made amps from the beginning of the company up to the late '80s. Rickenbacker had many different models, from the small early models that were usually sold as a guitar/amp set, to the large, very cool, Transonic.

Electro-Student Amp

Late-1940s. Typical late-'40s vertical combo cabinet, 1x12" speaker, lower power using 5 tubes, bottom mounted chassis, dark gray leatherette cover.

1948-1949		$250	$275

Model M-8 Amp

Gray, 1x8".

1950s		$300	$375
1960s		$275	$350

Professional Model 200-A Amp

1938		$275	$375

RB30 Amp

1986. Bass combo amp, 30 watts, tilted control panel, 1x12".

1986		$125	$175

RB60 Amp

1986. Bass combo amp, 60 watts, tilted control panel, 1x15".

1986		$200	$250

RB120 Amp

1986. Bass combo amp, 120 watts, tilted control panel, 1x15".

1986		$225	$300

MODEL YEAR	FEATURES	EXC. COND. LOW	HIGH

Supersonic Model B-16

4x10" speakers, gray cover.

1960s		$650	$800

TR14 Amp

1978-ca.1982. Solidstate, 1x10", reverb, distortion.

1978-1982		$175	$225

TR35B Bass Amp

1970s. Solid-state, mid-power, 1x15".

1970s		$200	$250

TR75G Amp

1978-ca.1982. 75 watts, 2x12", 2 channels.

1978-1982		$150	$200

TR75SG Amp

1978-ca.1983. 1x10" and 1x15" speakers.

1978-1982		$200	$250

TR100G Amp

1978-ca.1982. Solidstate, 100 watts with 4x12", 2 channels.

1978-1982		$250	$300

Transonic Amp

1967-1970. Trapezoid shape, 2x12", head and cabinet, Rick-O-Select.

1967-1970		$850	$1,200

Rivera

1985-present. Amp designer and builder Paul Rivera modded and designed amps for other companies before starting his own line in California. He offers heads, combos, and cabinets.

Chubster 40 Amp

2000-present. 40 watts, 1x12" combo, burgundy tolex, light grille.

2000-2003		$750	$900

Fandango 212 Combo Amp

2001-present. 55 watts, 2x12" tube amp.

2001-2002		$1,000	$1,100

Knuckle Head 55 Amp

1995-2002. 55 watts, head amp, replaced by reverb model.

1995-2002		$650	$900

Knuckle Head 100 Amp

1995-2002. 100 watt head, head amp, replaced by reverb model.

1995-2002		$700	$900

Los Lobottom/Sub 1

1999-2004. 1x12" cabinet with 300-watt powered 12" subwoofer.

1999-2004		$475	$625

M-60 Head Amp

1990s. 60 watts, head amp.

1990s		$575	$650

M-60 112 Combo Amp

1989-present. 60 watts, 1x12".

1989-1999		$650	$750

M-100 Head Amp

1990s. 100 watts, head amp.

1990s		$625	$725

M-100 212 Combo Amp

1990-present. 100 watts, 2x12" combo.

1990-1999		$725	$850

Reeves

Reverend Goblin

Rivera Knucklehead Reverb 55

Roccaforte 80 watt

1996 Roland BC-60

Savage Macht6

MODEL YEAR	FEATURES	EXC. COND. LOW	HIGH
Quiana 112 Combo Amp	*2000-present. Combo, 55 watts, 1x12".*		
2000-2002		$900	$1,000
R-30 112 Combo Amp	*1993-present. 30 watts, 1x12", compact cab, black tolex cover, gray-black grille.*		
1993-2000		$450	$650
R-100 212 Combo Amp	*1993-present. 100 watts, 2x12".*		
1993-2000		$775	$850
Suprema R-55 112/115 Combo Amp	*2000-present. Tube amp, 55 watts, 1x12" (still available) or 1x15" ('00-'01).*		
2000-2001 1x12"		$900	$1,000
2000-2001 1x15"		$950	$1,050
TBR-1 Amp	*1985-1999. First Rivera production model, rack mount, 60 watts.*		
1985-1999		$575	$875

Roccaforte Amps

1993-present. Tube amps, combos, and cabinets built by Doug Roccaforte in San Clemente, California.

Rodgers

1993-present. Custom tube amps and cabinets built by Larry Rodgers in Naples, Florida.

Rogue

2001-present. Student-level solidstate import (Korea) compact amps. They also offer guitars, mandolins, banjos, effects and basses.

MODEL YEAR	FEATURES	EXC. COND. LOW	HIGH
CG Series	*2001. Solidstate, 20-100 watts.*		
2001		$30	$150

Roland

Japan's Roland Corporation's products include amplifiers and keyboards and, under the Boss brand, effects.

MODEL YEAR	FEATURES	EXC. COND. LOW	HIGH
AC-100 Amp	*1995-present. Acoustic amp, 50 watts, 1x12" and 2x5", chorus, reverb, EQ, effects loop.*		
1995-2000		$250	$300
Bolt 60 Amp	*Early 1980s. Solidstate/tube, 1x12".*		
1980s		$225	$250
Cube 20 Amp	*1978-1982. Portable, 1x8", normal and overdrive channels, headphone jack.*		
1978-1982		$100	$200
Cube 40 Amp	*1978-1980s. Portable, 1x10", normal and overdrive channels, 40 watts.*		
1978-1983		$100	$200
Cube 60/60B Amp	*1978-1980s, 2004-present for Cube 60. 1x12", 60 watts, Cube 60 combo or Cube 60B combo bass amp.*		
1978-1983	Cube 60	$150	$225
1978-1983	Cube 60B	$150	$200

MODEL YEAR	FEATURES	EXC. COND. LOW	HIGH
Cube 100 Amp	*1978-1982. 100 watts, combo, 1x12".*		
1978-1982		$200	$300
Jazz Chorus Amp Series	*1976-present. Includes the JC-50 (1980s. 50 watts, 1x12"), JC-55 ('87-'94, 50 watts, 2x8"), JC-77 ('87-'94, 80 watts, 2x10") and the JC-120 ('76-present, 120 watts, 2x12").*		
1980s	JC-50	$300	$350
1987-1990	JC-120	$400	$500
1987-1994	JC-55	$300	$350
1987-1994	JC-77	$350	$425
Spirit 30 Amp	*1982-late 1980s. Compact, 30 watts, 1x12".*		
1980s		$125	$225
VGA3 V-Guitar Amp	*2003-present. GK digital modeling amp, 50 watts, 1x12" combo.*		
2003-2004		$300	$350
VGA5 V-Guitar Amp	*2001-2004. GK digital modeling amp, 65 watts, 1x12".*		
2001-2004		$350	$400
VGA7 V-Guitar Amp	*2000-present. 65 + 65 watts, 2x12", digital modeling with analog-style controls.*		
2000-2004		$400	$500

Sam Ash

1960s-1970s. Sam Ash Music was founded by a young Sam Ash (formerly Ashkynase - an Austro-Hungarian name) in 1924. Ash's first store was in Brooklyn, New York, and by '66 there were about four Ash stores. During this time Ash Music private branded their own amp line which was built by Jess Oliver of Oliver Amps and based upon Oliver's Ampeg designs.

MODEL YEAR	FEATURES	EXC. COND. LOW	HIGH
Sam Ash Mark II Pro Combo Amp	*1960s. 2x12" with reverb combo amp.*		
1960s		$275	$375
Sam Ash Oliver Amp Head	*Late-1960s-early-1970s. Private branded for Sam Ash Music, about 30 watts using the extinct 2x7027A power tubes, Sam Ash script logo on front grille.*		
1960s		$250	$300

Savage

Tube amps and combos built by Savage Audio in Burnsville, Minnesota.

Sceptre

1960s. Canadian-made. Sceptre script logo on upper left side of grille ('60s Fender-style and placement).

MODEL YEAR	FEATURES	EXC. COND. LOW	HIGH
Signet Amp	*1960s. Low power, 1x10", Class-A 6V6 power, Signet model name on front panel.*		
1960s		$125	$175

Selmer

1960s. The Selmer UK distributor offered mid- to high-level amps.

AMPS

MODEL YEAR FEATURES	EXC. COND. LOW	HIGH

Futurama Corvette Amp
1960s. Class A low power 1x8", volume and tone controls, plus amplitude and speed tremolo controls, large script Futurama logo on front of amp, Futurama Corvette and Selmer logo on top panel.

1960s	$425	$500

Mark 2 Treble and Bass Head Amp
1960s. About 30 watts (2xEL34s), requires power line transformer for U.S. use, large Selmer logo on grille.

1960s	$525	$700

Seymour Duncan
Pickup maker Seymour Duncan, located in Santa Barbara, California, offered a line of amps from around 1984 to '95.

84-40/84-50 Amp
1989-1995. Tube combo, 2 switchable channels, 1x12", includes the 84-40 ('89-'91, 40 watts) and the 84-50 ('91-'95, 50 watts).

1989-1991	84-40	$325	$400
1991-1995	84-50	$350	$425

Bass 300 x 2 Amp
1986-1987. Solidstate, 2 channels (300 or 600 watts), EQ, contour boost switches, effects loop.

1986-1987	$300	$425

Bass 400 Amp
1986-1987. Solidstate, 400 watts, EQ, contour boost, balanced line output, effects loop.

1986-1987	$300	$400

Convertible 100 Amp
1986-1987. Solidstate, 60 watts, effects loop, spring reverb, EQ, switchable preamp modules.

1986-1987	$375	$450

Convertible 2000 Amp
1988-1995. Solidstate, 100 watts, holds 5 interchangeable modules, 1x12", 2 switchable channels.

1988-1995	$450	$550

KTG-2075 Stereo Amp
1989-1993. Part of the King Tone Generator Series, 2 channels with 75 watts per channel.

1989-1993	$250	$300

Sho-Bud
Introduced and manufactured by the Baldwin/Gretsch factory in 1970. Distributed by Kustom/Gretsch in the '80s. Models include D-15 Model 7838, S-15 Model 7836, Twin Tube Model 7834, and Twin Trans Model 7832.

D15 Sho-Bud Double Amp
Introduced in 1970. Solidstate, 100 watts. D-15 is 2 channels, S-15 is 1 channel, both with 1x15" JBL speaker.

1970s	$325	$375

S15 Sho-Bud Single Amp
Introduced in 1972. 100 watts, 1x15" JBL, solidstate single channel combo.

1970s	$275	$325

Sho-Bass Amp
Introduced in 1972. 100 watts, 1x15", solidstate combo, black grille, black vinyl cover.

1970s	$275	$325

Twin Trans Amp
Introduced in 1972. 100 watts, solidstate combo, 2x12", reverb, black vinyl cover, dark grille, Sho-Bud script logo front upper right.

1970s	$475	$525

Twin Tube Amp
Introduced in 1972. 100 watt tube combo, 4 6L6s, 2x12", reverb, black vinyl cover, dark grille.

1970s	$725	$775

Siegmund Guitars & Amplifiers
1993-present. Chris Siegmund builds his tube amp heads, combos and cabinets in Los Angeles, California. He founded the company in Seattle, moving it to Austin, Texas for '95-'97. He also builds effects pedals and guitars.

Silvertone
1941-ca.1970, present. Brand used by Sears. All Silvertone amps were supplied by American companies up to around '66.

Model 100 Amp
Mid-late-1960s. Solidstate, piggyback amp and 2x12" cabinet with gold-label Jensen speakers.

1960s	$325	$400

Model 150 Amp
Mid-late-1960s. Solidstate, piggyback amp and 6x10" cabinet with gold-label Jensen speakers.

1960s	$450	$525

Model 1331 Amp
Ca.1954-ca.1957. Danelectro-made, luggage tweed, rounded front, a whole series made this style.

1954-1957	Tweed	$275	$350

Model 1336 (early Twin Twelve) Amp
Ca.1954-ca.1957. Danelectro-made, luggage tweed, rounded front.

1954-1957	$575	$700

Model 1340 (Student Model) Amp
Early-1950s. Tan cover, brown grille with Silvertone logo, brown sides.

1950s	$150	$200

Model 1346 (Twin Twelve) Amp
Ca.1958-ca.1961. Danelectro-made, brown control panel, 2x12", 4 6L6s, vibrato, leather handle, tan smooth leatherette cover, 2 speaker baffle openings.

1958-1961	$575	$700

Model 1391 Amp
1950s. Blond-tan tweed-cloth cover, brown grille, single small speaker, leather handle.

1950s	$175	$225

Model 1392 Amp
1950s. Student amp with tremolo, 5 control knobs, brown cover and brown grille.

1950s	$175	$225

Model 1432 Amp
Late-1950s. 1x12", low- to mid-power, 2 6L6s, late-'50s overhanging top style cabinet.

1950s	$200	$300

Savage Gläs 30

Selmer

Siegmund Midnight Blues Breaker Custom

Silvertone Model 1482

Silvertone Model 1484

Snider combo

| MODEL | | EXC. COND. | |
YEAR	FEATURES	LOW	HIGH

Model 1433 Combo Amp
Late-1950s. Tube, 30 watts, 2 6L6s, 1x15", gray cover cabinet with pronounced overhanging top, light colored grille.

1950s		$500	$575

Model 1451 Amp
Late-1950s. Three or 4 watts, 3 tubes, 1x6" or 1x8" speaker, brown sparkle cover, wheat grille, by Danelectro.

1950s	1x6"	$150	$200

Model 1457 Amp-In-Case (case only)
1960s. The amp-in-case with the electric Silvertone guitar, this is the higher powered model with tremolo and higher quality speaker.

1965	Amp only (no guitar)	$125	$150

Model 1459 Amp
1960s. Four watts, 1x6" or 1x8".

1960s		$150	$200

Model 1463 Bass 35 Amp
1960s. Solidstate, 2x12", piggyback.

1960s		$275	$325

Model 1465 Head Amp
Mid-1960s. Rectangular amp head, solidstate, 50 watts, spotted gray cover, used with Twin 12 bottom.

1960s		$175	$275

Model 1471 Amp
1x8" speaker.

1960s		$150	$200

Model 1472 Amp
1960s. 15-18 watts, 2 6V6s provide mid-level power, 1x12", front controls mounted vertically on front right side, dark cover with silver grille, large stationary handle, tremolo.

1962-1963		$250	$300

Model 1474 Amp
1960s. Mid-power, mid-level, dual speakers, tube combo amp, gray tolex, gray grille.

1960s		$425	$500

Model 1481 Amp
1960s. Low-power, student amp, 1x6", gray cover, light grille, 2 controls.

1960s		$125	$175

Model 1482 Amp
1960s. Low-power, 1x12" combo, gray tolex, silver grille, control panel mounted on right side vertically, tremolo.

1960s		$300	$400

Model 1483 Piggyback Amp
1960s. Mid-power, 1x15" piggyback tube amp, gray tolex and gray grille.

1960s		$450	$550

Model 1484 Twin Twelve Amp
1960s. Medium-power, 2x12" piggyback tube amp, classic Silvertone colors--gray cover with light grille.

1966		$500	$700

Skip Simmons
1990-present. Custom and production tube combo amps built by Skip Simmons in Dixon, California.

| MODEL | | EXC. COND. | |
YEAR	FEATURES	LOW	HIGH

SMF
Mid-1970s. Amp head and cabinets from Dallas Music Industries, Ltd., of Mahwah, New Jersey. Offered the Tour Series which featured a 150 watt head and 4x12" bottoms with metal speaker grilles and metal corners.

SMF (Sonic Machine Factory)
2002-present. Tube amps and cabinets designed by Mark Sampson (Matchless, Bad Cat, Star) and Rick Hamel (SIB effects) and built in California.

Smicz Amplification
Tube combos and extenstion cabinets built by Bob Smicz in Bristol, Connecticut.

Smith Custom Amplifiers
2002-present. All tube combo amps, heads and speaker cabinets built by Sam Smith in Montgomery, Alabama.

Smokey
1997-present. Mini amps often packaged in cigarette packs made by Bruce Zinky in Flagstaff, Arizona. He also builds Zinky amps and effects and has revived the Supro brand on a guitar and amp.

Snider
1999-present. Jeff Snider has been building various combo tube amps in San Diego, California, since '95. In '99 he started branding them with his last name.

Soldano
1987-present. Made in Seattle, Washington by amp builder Mike Soldano, the company offers a range of all-tube combo amps, heads and cabinets. They also offer a reverb unit.

Astroverb 16 Combo Amp
1997-present. Atomic with added reverb.

1997-2002		$600	$750

Atomic 16 Combo Amp
1996-2001. Combo, 20 watts, 1x12".

1996-2001		$500	$650

Decatone Amp
1998-2002. 2x12" 100-watt combo, rear mounted controls, still available as a head.

1998-2002	No footswitch	$1,650	$1,850
1998-2002	With Decatrol footswitch	$2,000	$2,150

HR 50/Hot Rod 50 Amp Head
1992-present. 50-watt single channel head.

1992-2002		$825	$950

HR 100/Hot Rod 100 Amp Head
1994-2001. 100-watt single channel head.

1994-2001		$975	$1,100

Lucky 13 Combo Amp
2000-present. 100 watts (50 also available), 2x12" combo.

2000-2002		$1,050	$1,200

MODEL YEAR	FEATURES	EXC. COND. LOW	HIGH

SLO-100 Super Lead Overdrive 100-Watt Amp
1988-present. First production model, super lead overdrive, 100 watts, snakeskin cover head amp, 4x12" cabinet.

1988-1999	Head	$1,800	$2,300
1990s	w/ cab	$2,500	$2,900

Sonax
Introduced in 1972. Budget line of solidstate amps offered by Gretsch/Baldwin, made by Yorkville Sound (Traynor) in Toronto, Canada. Introduced with dark grille and dark cover.

530-B Bass Amp
30 watts, 1x12".

1970s		$125	$200

550-B Bass Amp
50 watts, 1x15".

1970s		$150	$225

720-G Amp
Student amp, 20 watts, 2x8", reverb.

1970s		$200	$275

730-G Amp
30 watts, 2x10", reverb and tremolo.

1970s		$300	$375

750-G Amp
50 watts, 2x12", reverb and tremolo.

1970s		$375	$425

770-G Amp
75 watts, 4x10", reverb and tremolo.

1970s		$425	$475

Songworks Systems
See listing under Little Lanilei.

Sonny Jr.
1996-present. Harmonica amplifiers built by harmonica player Sonny Jr. in conjunction with Cotton Amps in Tolland, Connecticut.

Sound City
Made in England from the late-1960s to the late-'70s, the tube Sound City amps were Marshall-looking heads and separate cabinets. They were imported, for a time, into the U.S. by Gretsch.

50 PA Plus Amp
Late-1960s-late-1970s. Similar to 50 Plus but with 4 channels.

1970s		$450	$525

50 Plus/50R Amp Head
Late-1960s-late-1970s. Head amp, labeled 50 Plus or 50 R.

1960s		$450	$525
1970s		$450	$525

120/120R Amp Head
Early-late-1970s. The 120-watt head replaced the late-1960s 100-watt model.

1970s	120 no reverb	$475	$550
1970s	With reverb	$575	$650

Concord Combo Amp
80 watts, 2x12" Fane speakers, cream, basketweave grille.

1968	Cream	$525	$600

L-80 Cabinet
1970s. 4x10" cabinet.

1970s		$450	$550

X-60 Cabinet
1970s. 2x12" speaker cabinet.

1970s		$400	$500

Sound Electronics
Sound Electronics Corporation introduced a line of amplifiers in 1965 that were manufactured in Long Island. Six models were initially offered, all with tube preamps and solidstate power sections. Their catalog did not list power wattages but did list features and speaker configurations. The initial models had dark vinyl-style covers and sparkling silver grille cloth. The amps were combos with the large models having vertical cabinets, silver script Sound logo on upper left of grille. The larger models used JBL D120F and D130F speakers. Stand alone extension speakers were also available.

Various Model Amps
Mid-1960s. Includes X-101, X-101R, X-202 Bass/Organ, X-404 Bass and Organ, X-505R amps, hi-fi chassis often using 7868 power tubes.

1965		$350	$450

Sovtek
1992-2000. Sovtek amps were products of Mike Matthews of Electro-Harmonix fame and his New Sensor Corporation. The guitar and bass amps and cabinets were made in Russia.

Mig 50 Head Amp
1994-2000. Tube head, 50 watts.

1994-2000		$300	$350

Mig 60 Head Amp
1994-2000. Tube head, 60 watts, point-to-point wiring.

1994-2000		$350	$375

Mig 100 Head Amp
1992-2000. Tube head, 100 watts.

1992-2000		$375	$425

Mig 100B Head Amp
1996-2000. Bass tube head, 100 watts.

1996-2000		$350	$375

Specimen Products
1984-present. Luthier Ian Schneller added tube amps and speaker cabinets in '93. He also builds guitars, basses and ukes.

Speedster
1995-2000, 2003-present. Founded by Lynn Ellsworth, offering tube amps and combos designed by Bishop Cochran with looks inspired by dashboards of classic autos. In '03, Joe Valosay and Jevco International purchased the company and revived the brand witht the help of former owner Cory Wilds.

Soldano Lucky 13

Specimen Horn Amp

Speedster 25-Watt Deluxe

Standel Custom

Standel 100 UL15

Star Gain Star

MODEL YEAR	FEATURES	EXC. COND. LOW	HIGH

Amps were originally built by Soldono, but are now built by Speedster in Gig Harbor, Washington.

St. George

1960s. There were Japanese guitars bearing this brand, but these amps may have been built in California.

Mid-Size Tube Amp
1965. Low power, 1x10" Jensen, 2 5065 and 2 12AX7 tubes.

1960s		$200	$275

Standel

1952-1974, 1997-present. Bob Crooks started custom building amps part time in '52, going into full time standard model production in '58 in Temple City, California. In '61 Standel started distributing guitars under their own brand and others (see Guitar section for more instrument details).

By late '63 or '64, Standel had introduced solidstate amps, two years before Fender and Ampeg introduced their solidstate models. In '67 Standel moved to a new, larger facility in El Monte, California. In '73 Chicago Musical Instruments (CMI), which owned Gibson at the time, bought the company and built amps in El Monte until '74. In '97 the Standel name was revived by Danny McKinney who, with the help of original Standel founder Bob Crooks and Frank Garlock (PR man for first Standel), set about reissuing some of the early models.

A-30 B Artist 30 Bass Amp
1964-early-1970s. Artist Series, the original Standel solidstate series, 80 watts, 2x15".

1964-1969		$325	$425

A-30 G Artist 30 Guitar Amp
1964-early-1970s. Artist Series, the original Standel solidstate series, 80 watts, 2x15".

1964-1969		$400	$450

A-48 G Artist 48 Guitar Amp
1964-early-1970s. Artist Series, the original Standel solidstate series, 80 watts, 4x12".

1964-1969		$500	$600
1970s		$500	$600

A-60 B Artist 60 Bass Amp
1964-early-1970s. Artist Series, the original Standel solidstate series, 160 watts, 4x15".

1964-1969		$450	$550
1970s		$450	$550

A-60 G Artist 60 Guitar Amp
1964-early-1970s. Artist Series, the original Standel solidstate series, 160 watts, 4x15".

1964-1969		$500	$600
1970s		$500	$600

A-96 G Artist 96 Guitar Amp
1964-early-1970s. Artist Series, the original Standel solidstate series, 160 watts, 8x12".

1964-1969		$550	$800
1970s		$550	$800

C-24 Custom 24 Amp
Late-1960s-1970s. Custom Slim Line Series, solid-state, 100 watts, 2x12", dark vinyl, dark grille.

1970s		$425	$475

I-30 B Imperial 30 Bass Amp
1964-early-1970s. Imperial Series, the original Standel solidstate series, 100 watts, 2x15".

1960s		$450	$500

I-30 G Imperial 30 Guitar Amp
1964-early-1970s. Imperial Series, the original Standel solidstate series, 100 watts, 2x15".

1960s		$500	$550

Model 10L8/15L12/25L15
1953-1958. Early custom made tube amps made by Bob Crooks in his garage, padded naugahyde cabinet with varying options and colors. There are a limited number of these amps, and brand knowledge is limited, therefore there is a wide value range. Legend has it that the early Standel amps made Leo Fender re-think and introduce even more powerful amps.

1953-1958		$2,200	$3,500

S-10 Studio 10 Amp
Late-1960s-1970s. Studio Slim Line Series, solid-state, 30 watts, 1x10", dark vinyl, dark grille.

1970s		$325	$375

S-50 Studio 50 Amp
Late-1963 or early-1964-late-1960s. Not listed in '69 Standel catalog, 60 watts, gray tolex, gray grille, piggyback.

1964		$450	$550

Star

2004-present. Tube amps, combos and speaker cabinets built by Mark Sampson in the Los Angeles, California area. Sampson has also been involved with Matchless, Bad Cat, and SMF amps.

Starlite

Starlite was a budget brand made and sold by Magnatone. See Magnatone for listings.

Stella Vee

1999-present. Jason Lockwood builds his combo amps, heads, and cabinets in Lexington, Kentucky.

Stevenson

1999-present. Luthier Ted Stevenson, of Lachine, Quebec, added amps to his product line in '05. He also builds basses and guitars.

Stinger

Budget line imported by Martin.

Stramp

1970s. Stramp, of Hamburg, Germany, offered audio mixers, amps and compact powered speaker units, all in aluminum flight cases.

Solidstate amp
1970s. Solid-state amp head in metal suitcase with separate Stramp logo cabinet.

1970s		$475	$525

MODEL YEAR	FEATURES	EXC. COND. LOW	HIGH

Sunn

1965-2002. Started in Oregon by brothers Conrad and Norm Sundhold (Norm was the bass player for the Kingsman). Sunn introduced powerful amps and extra heavy duty bottoms and was soon popular with many major rock acts. Norm sold his interest to Conrad in '69. Conrad sold the company to the Hartzell Corporation of Minnesota around '72. Fender Musical Instruments acquired the brand in '85 shortly after parting ways with CBS and used the brand until '89. They resurrected the brand again in '98, but quit offering the name in '02.

200S/215B Amp & Cab Set
Late-1960s. 60 watts, 2 6550s, large verticle cab with 2x15" speakers.
1969 $700 $900

Alpha 115 Amp
1980s. MOS-FET preamp section, 1x15", clean and overdrive.
1980s $175 $250

Alpha 212 R Amp
1980s. MOS-FET preamp section, 2x12", reverb.
1980s $175 $250

Concert 215S Bass Amp Set
1970s. Solidstate head, 200 watts, Model 215S tall vertical cabinet with 2x12" Sunn label speakers, dark vinyl cover, silver sparkle grille.
1970s $450 $500

Concert Bass Head Amp
1970s. Solidstate, 200 watts.
1970s $175 $250

Concert Lead 610S Amp Set
1970s. Solidstate, 200 watts, 6x10" piggyback, reverb and built-in distortion.
1970s $475 $525

Model T Head Amp
Early-1970s.
1970s $600 $800

Model T Head Amp and Cab
1990s. Head has 100 watts, 4x12" cab, reissue model.
1990s $900 $1,000

Model T Head Amp Reissue
1990s. Reissue of '60s Model T, see thru amp grille displays tubes, dark vinyl cover.
1990s $600 $650

SB-200 Amp
1985. 200 watts, 1x15", 4-band EQ, master volume, compressor.
1985 $275 $375

Sceptre Head Amp
1968-1970s. Head amp, 60 watts, 6550 power tubes, tremolo, reverb.
1972 $300 $350

Solarus Amp
1967-1970s. Tube amp (EL34s), 40 watts (upgraded to 60 watts in '69), 2x12", reverb, tremolo.
1970s $475 $600

Sonoro Head Amp
Early-1970s. 60 watts, 2 6550s.
1970s $425 $500

SPL 7250 Amp
Dual channels, 250 watts per channel, forced air cooling, switch-selectable peak compressor with LEDs.
1989 $275 $350

Supertone

1914-1941. Supertone was a brand used by Sears for their musical instruments. In the '40s Sears started using the Silvertone name on those products. Amps were made by other companies.

Amp
1930s $150 $250

Supro

1935-1968, 2004-present. Supro was a budget brand of the National Dobro Company, made by Valco in Chicago, Illinois. Amp builder Bruce Zinky revived the Supro name for a guitar and amp model.

Bantam 1611S Amp
1961-1964. Four watts, 3 tubes, 1x 8" Jensen, petite, Spanish Ivory fabric cover, gold weave saran wrap grille.
1961-1964 $225 $250

Combo 1696T Amp
1961-1964. 24 watts, 6 tubes, 1x15" Jensen, Rhino-Hide covering in black and white, light grille, tremolo.
1961-1964 $375 $400

Comet 1610B Amp
1957-1959. Grey Rhino-Hide, 1x10".
1957-1959 $250 $375

Dual-Tone 1624T Amp
1961-1964. 17 watts, 1x12", 6 tubes, organ tone tremolo.
1961-1964 $375 $475

Dual-Tone S6424T Amp
1964-1965. 17 watts, 6 tubes, 1x12" Jensen, restyled in '64, tremolo, Trinidad Blue vinyl fabric cover, light color grille.
1964-1965   rinidad Blue vinyl cover $375 $475

Royal Reverb 1650TR Amp
1963-1964. 17 watts, 15 tubes, 2x10" Jensens, catalog says "authentic tremolo and magic-reverberation."
1963-1964 $500 $575

Super 1606S Amp
1961-1964. 4.5 watts, 3 tubes, 1x8", black and white fabric cover, light saran wrap grille.
1961-1964 $250 $325

Thunderbolt S6420(B) Bass Amp
1964-1967. 35 watts, 1x15" Jensen, introduced in the '64 catalog as a "no frills - no fancy extra circuits" amp. Sometimes referred to as the "Jimmy Page amp" based on his use of this amp in his early career.
1964-1967 $650 $950

Thunderbolt S6920 Amp
1967-1968. Redesign circuit replaced S6420B, 35 watts, 1x12".
1967-1968 $300 $325

1969 Sunn 100S

1966 Supro Thunderbolt

1964 Supro Tremo-Verb

SWR Goliath Junior III cab

Talos Basic

Teisco Checkmate 17

MODEL YEAR	FEATURES	EXC. COND. LOW	HIGH

Tremo-Verb S6422 TR Amp
1964-1965. Lower power using 4 12AX7s, 1 5Y3GT, and 1 6V6, 1x10", tremolo and reverb.

| 1964-1965 | Persian Red vinyl cover | $650 | $800 |

Trojan Tremolo 1616T/S6416T Amp
1961-1966. 5 watts, 4 tubes, 1 11"x6" oval (generally Rolla) speaker, '61-'64 black and white fabric cover and saran wrap grille, '64-'66 new larger cab with vinyl cover and light grille.

| 1961-1966 | Trinidad Blue vinyl cover | $300 | $350 |

Vibra-Verb S6498VR Amp
1964-1965. "Supro's finest amplifier," 2x35-watt channels, 1x15" and 1x10" Jensens, vibrato and reverb.

| 1964-1965 | | $550 | $625 |

SWR Sound
1984-present. Founded by Steve W. Rabe in '84, with an initial product focus on bass amplifiers. Fender Musical Instruments Corp. acquired SWR in June, 2003.

Baby Blue Studio Bass System
1990-2003. Combo, all tube preamp, 150 watts solidstate power amp, 2x8", 1x5" cone tweeter, gain, master volume, EQ, effects-blend.

| 1990-2003 | | $450 | $575 |

Basic Black Amp
1992-1999. Solidstate, 100 watts, 1x12", basic black block logo on front, black tolex, black metal grille.

| 1992-1999 | | $350 | $425 |

Goliath III Cab
1996-present. Black tolex, black metal grille, includes the Goliath III Jr. (2x10") and the Goliath III (4x10").

| 1990s | 2x10" | $400 | $475 |
| 1990s | 4x10" | $550 | $575 |

Goliath Junior Amp
1988-1991. High-end driver, 2x10", 300 watts, can function as a high-fidelity monitor or as part of a bi-amp system.

| 1988-1991 | | $400 | $450 |

Strawberry Blonde Amp
1998-present. 80 watts, 1x10" acoustic instrument amp.

| 1998-2003 | | $325 | $400 |

Studio 220 Bass Amp
1988-1995. 220 watt solidstate head, tube preamp

| 1988-1995 | | $275 | $375 |

Working Man 15 Bass Amp
1995-present. Combo amp, 1x15", 160 watts.

| 1995-2002 | | $350 | $425 |

Takt
Late-1960s. Made in Japan, tube and solidstate models.

GA Series Amps
1968. GA-9 (2 inputs and 5 controls, 3 tubes), GA-10, GA-11, GA-12, GA-14, GA-15.

| 1968 | GA-14/GA-15 | $40 | $55 |
| 1968 | GA-9 through GA-12 | $25 | $40 |

MODEL YEAR	FEATURES	EXC. COND. LOW	HIGH

Talos
2004-present. Doug Weisbrod and Bill Thalmann build their tube amp heads, combo amps, and speaker cabinets in Springfield, Virginia. They started building and testing prototypes in '01.

Tech 21
1989-present. Long known for their SansAmp tube amplifier emulator, Tech 21 added solidstate combo amps, heads and cabinets in '96.

Teisco
1946-1974, 1994-present. Japanese brand first imported into the U.S. around '63. Teisco offered both tube and solidstate amps.

Checkmate 50 Amp
Late-1950s-early-1960s. Tubes, 2 6L6s, 50 watts, 2x12" open back, reverb, tremolo, piggyback, gray tolex cover, light gray grille.

| 1960s | | $400 | $425 |

Checkmate CM-15 Amp
Late-1960s. Tubes, 15 watts.

| 1960s | | $50 | $100 |

Checkmate CM-20 Amp
Late-1960s. Tubes, 20 watts.

| 1960s | | $75 | $125 |

Checkmate CM-25 Amp
Late-1960s. Tubes, 25 watts.

| 1960s | | $100 | $150 |

Checkmate CM-60 Amp
Late-1960s. Tubes, 60 watts, piggyback amp and cab with wheels.

| 1960s | | $150 | $250 |

Checkmate CM-66 Amp
Late-1960s. Solidstate, dual speaker combo, Check Mate 66 logo on front panel.

| 1960s | | $40 | $75 |

Checkmate CM-100 Amp
Late-1960s. Tubes, 4x6L6 power, 100 watts, piggyback with Vox-style trolley stand.

| 1960s | | $275 | $400 |

King 1800 Amp
Late-1960s. Tubes, 180 watts, piggyback with 2 cabinets, large Teisco logo on cabinets, King logo on lower right side of one cabinet.

| 1960s | | $400 | $475 |

Teisco 8 Amp
Late-1960s. Five watts

| 1960s | | $25 | $45 |

Teisco 10 Amp
Late-1960s. Five watts.

| 1960s | | $25 | $45 |

Teisco 88 Amp
Late-1960s. Eight watts.

| 1960s | | $50 | $70 |

THD
1987-present. Founded by Andy Marshall and building tube amps and cabinets in Seattle, Washington.

MODEL YEAR	FEATURES	EXC. COND. LOW	HIGH

Titano (Magnatone)

1961-1963. Private branded by Magnatone, often for an accordion company or accordion studio, uses standard guitar input jacks.

Model 262 R Custom Amp

1961-1963. 35 watts, 2x12" + 2x5", reverb and vibrato make this one of the top-of-the-line models, black vinyl, light silver grille.

| 1961-1963 | | $975 | $1,275 |

Model 415 Bass Amp

1961-1963. 25 watts, 4x8", bass or accordion amp, black cover, darkish grille.

| 1961-1963 | | $525 | $575 |

Tone King

1993-present. Tube amps, combos, and cabinets built by Mark Bartel in Baltimore, Maryland. The company started in New York and moved to Baltimore in '94.

Tonemaster (Magnatone)

Late-1950s-early-1960s. Magnatone amps private branded for Imperial Accordion Company. Prominent block-style capital TONEMASTER logo on front panel, generally something nearly equal to Magnatone equivalent. This is just one of many private branded Magnatones. Covers range from brown to black leatherette and brown to light silver grilles.

Model 214 (V logo) Amp

1959-1960. Ten watts, 1x12", vibrato, brown leatherette, V logo lower right corner front, large TONEMASTER logo.

| 1959-1960 | | $525 | $575 |

Model 260 Amp

1961-1963. About 30 watts, 2x12", vibrato, brown leatherette and brown grille, large TONEMASTER logo on front.

| 1961-1963 | | $675 | $750 |

Model 380 Amp

1961-1963. 50 watts, 2x12" and 2 oval 5"x7" speakers, vibrato, no reverb.

| 1961-1963 | | $775 | $975 |

Top Hat Amplification

1994-present. Mostly Class A guitar amps built by Brian Gerhard originally in Anaheim, California, and since '05 in Fuquay-Varina, North Carolina. They also make an overdrive pedal.

Ambassador 100 TH-A100 Head Amp

Jan.1999-present. 100 watts, Class AB, 4 6L6s, reverb, dark green vinyl cover, white chicken-head knobs.

| 1999-2003 | | $1,050 | $1,250 |

Ambassador T-35C 212 Amp

1999-present. 35 watts, 2x12" combo, reverb, master volume, blond cover, tweed-style fabric grille.

| 1999-2003 | | $1,050 | $1,250 |

Club Deluxe Amp

1998-present. 20 watts, 6V6 power tubes, 1x12".

| 2000s | | $750 | $850 |

Club Royale TC-R2 Amp

Jan.1999-present. 20 watts, Class A using EL84s, 2x12".

| 1999-2003 | | $850 | $1,050 |

Emplexador 50 TH-E50 Head Amp

Jan.1997-present. 50 watts, Class AB vint/high-gain head.

| 1997-2003 | | $950 | $1,150 |

King Royale Amp

1996-present. 35 watts, Class A using 4 EL84s, 2x12".

| 1996-2003 | | $1,150 | $1,350 |

Portly Cadet TC-PC Amp

Jan.1999-present. Five watts, 6V6 power, 1x8", dark gray, light gray grille.

| 1999-2003 | | $475 | $525 |

Prince Royale TC-PR Amp

Jan.2000-2002. Five watts using EL84 power, 1x8", deep red, light grille.

| 2000-2003 | | $525 | $575 |

Super Deluxe TC-SD2 Amp

Jan.2000-present. 30 watts, Class A, 7591 power tubes, 2x12".

| 2000-2003 | | $950 | $1,150 |

Torres Engineering

Founded by Dan Torres, the company builds tube amps, combos, cabinets and amp kits in San Mateo, California. Dan wrote monthly columns for Vintage Guitar magazine for many years and authored the book Inside Tube Amps.

Trace Elliot

1978-present. Founded in a small music shop in Essex, England. Currently owned by Gibson.

TA35CR Acoustic Guitar Amp

1994-1995. Compact lateral-style cab with 2x5", 35 watts, with reverb and chorus, dark vinyl cover, dark grille.

| 1994-1995 | | $300 | $400 |

TA100R Acoustic Guitar Amp

1990-present. Compact lateral-style cab with 4x5", 100 watts, with reverb, dark vinyl cover, dark grille.

| 1990s | | $550 | $600 |

Vellocette Amp

1996-1998. 15 watt, tube, Class A, 1x10", green cover, round sound speaker hole.

| 1996-1998 | | $375 | $425 |

Trainwreck

1983-present. Founded by Ken Fischer. Limited production, custom-made amps that are generally grouped by model. Models include the Rocket, Liverpool and Express, plus variations on those themes. Each amp's value should be evaluated on a case-by-case basis. Ken wrote many amp articles for *Vintage Guitar*.

Custom Built Amp

| 1980s | High-end model | $13,000 | $15,000 |

Tone King Galaxy

Top Hat Club Royale T-20 CR

Trainwreck Express

AMPS

MODEL YEAR	FEATURES	EXC. COND. LOW	HIGH

Traynor PM-100

Tube Works 6150 DFX

Univox U130B

Traynor

1963-present. Started by Pete Traynor and Jack Long in Canada and made by Yorkville Sound.

Guitar Mate Reverb YGM3 Amp
1969-1979. 40 watts, 1x12", tube amp, black tolex, gray grille.

1969-1979		$350	$450

Mark II Bass Master Amp
1970s.

1970s		$350	$400

Mark III (YGL-3) Amp
1971-1979. All tube, 80 watts, 2x12" combo, reverb, tremolo.

1971-1979		$400	$500

YBA3 Custom Special Bass Amp Set
1967-1972. Tube head with 130 watts and 8x10" large vertical matching cab, dark vinyl cover, light grille.

1967-1972		$600	$700

True Tone

1960s. Guitars and amps retailed by Western Auto, manufactured by Chicago guitar makers like Kay.

Hi-Fi 4 (K503 Hot-Line Special) Amp
1960s. Four watts from 3 tubes, gray cabinet, gray grille, metal handle, similar to K503.

1960s		$125	$175

Vibrato 704 Amp
1960s. Solidstate, 10 watts, 1x8", white sides and gray back, gray grille.

1960s		$100	$150

Vibrato 706 Amp
1960s. Solidstate, 15 watts, 1x15", white sides and gray back, brown grille.

1960s		$125	$175

Tube Works

1987-2004. Founded by B.K. Butler in Denver, Tube Works became a division of Genz Benz Enclosures of Scottsdale, Arizona in 1997. Tube Works' first products were tube guitar effects and in '91 they added tube/solidstate amps, cabinets, and DI boxes to the product mix. In '04, Genz Benz dropped the brand.

Twilighter (Magnatone)

Late-1950s-early-1960s. Magnatone amps private branded for LoDuca Brothers. Prominent block-style capital TWILIGHTER logo on front panel, generally something nearly equal to Magnatone equivalent. This is just one of many private branded Magnatones. Covers range from brown to black leatherette, and brown to light silver grilles.

Model 213 Amp
1961-1963. About 20 watts, 1x12", vibrato, brown leatherette and brown grille.

1961-1963		$525	$575

Model 260R Amp
1961-1963. About 18 to 25 watts, 1x12", vibrato, brown leatherette cover.

1961-1963		$550	$650

MODEL YEAR	FEATURES	EXC. COND. LOW	HIGH

Model 280A Amp
Late-1950s-early-1960s. About 35 watts, 2x12", vibrato, brown leatherette cover.

1961-1963		$650	$750

Two-Rock

1999-present. Tube guitar amp heads, combos and cabinets built by Joe Mloganoski and Bill Krinard (K&M Analog Designs) originally in Cotati, California, currently in Rohnert Park. They also build speakers.

UltraSound

A division of UJC Electronics, UltraSound builds acoustically transparent amps, designed by Greg Farres for the acoustic guitarist, in Adel, Iowa.

Unique (Magnatone)

1961-1963. Private branded, typically for an accordion company or accordion studio, uses standard guitar input jacks.

Model 260R Amp
1961-1963. Based on Magnatone 260 Series amp, 35 watts, 2x12" but with reverb, black vinyl-style cover with distinctive black diamond-check pattern running through the top and sides.

1961-1963		$750	$925

Model 460 Amp
1961-1963. 35 watts, 2x12" and oval 5"x7" speakers, reverb and vibrato make it one of the top models, black vinyl, black grille.

1961-1963		$800	$975

Univox

1964-ca.1978. From '64 to early-'68, these were American-made tube amps with Jensen speakers. By '68, they were using Japanese components in American cabinets, still with Jensen speakers. Electronics were a combination of tube and transistors during this time; this type lasted until the mid-'70s. Around '71, Univox introduced a line of all solidstate amps, as well.

Bass Model U130B Amp
1976-1978. 130 watts, 1x15".

1976		$150	$225

Lead Model Tube Amp
1960s. Tube amp, 2x10".

1965-1969		$325	$400

Lead Model 65/U65RD Amp
1976-1978. Solidstate, 65 watts, reverb, 1x12", black vinyl and black grille.

1976-1978		$100	$175

Lead Model U130L Amp
1976-1978. Solidstate.

1976		$125	$200

MODEL YEAR	FEATURES	EXC. COND. LOW	HIGH

Valco

Valco, from Chicago, Illinois, was a big player in the guitar and amplifier business. Their products were private branded for other companies like National, Supro, Airline, Oahu, and Gretsch.

Vega

1903-present. The original Boston-based company was purchased by C.F. Martin in '70. In '80, the Vega trademark was sold to a Korean company.

A-49 Amp
1960s. Six watts, 1x8", tubes, tan cover.

1960s		$175	$225

Super Amp
Early 1950s. 1 6L6, 1x10", vertical combo amp typical of the era.

1950s		$300	$355

Vesta Fire

1980s. Japanese imports by Shiino Musical Instruments Corp.; later by Midco International. Mainly known for effects pedals.

Preamps

1980s	J-I, J-II	$50	$125

Power Amps

1980s	PT-I	$100	$175
1980s	PT-II	$150	$225

VHT

1989-present. Founded by Steven M. Fryette, VHT builds amps, combos, and cabinets in Burbank, California.

Pittbull Classic Combo C-100-CL
1992-1994. 4 EL34s, 2x12", 100/50/25 watt. Name changed to Pittbull 100 CL.

1992-1994		$1,400	$1,500

Pittbull Fifty-Twelve Amp
1994-1999. 50 watts, all tube preamp section, 1x12", 2x12" version still available.

1994-1999		$750	$875

Victor

Late-1960s. Made in Japan.

MA-25 Amp
Late-1960s. Student model, light cover, dark grille, solidstate, 6 controls, 2 inputs, script Victor logo.

1960s		$75	$125

Victoria

1994-present. Tube amps, combos, and reverb units built by Mark Baier in Naperville, Illinois.

Double Deluxe Amp
1994-present. 35 watts, 2x12".

1994-2004		$1,300	$1,400

Model 20112 Amp
1994-present. 20 watts, 1x12", tweed.

1994-2004		$875	$925

Model 518 Amp
1994-present. Tweed, 1x8".

1994-2004		$625	$675

Model 35210 Amp
1994-present. 35 watts, 2x10", tweed.

1994-2004		$1,300	$1,400

Model 35212-T Amp
1990s. 35 watts, 2x12", with tremolo.

1990s		$1,450	$1,550

Model 35310-T Amp
1994-present. 35 watts, 3x10".

1994-2004		$1,400	$1,500

Model 45410-T Amp
1994-present. 45 watts, 4x10" combo.

1994-2004	Tweed	$1,400	$1,500

Model 50212-T Amp
2002-2003. 50 watts, 2x12" combo.

2002-2003		$1,500	$1,600

Model 80212 Amp
1994-present. 100 watts, 2x12", tweed.

1994-2004		$1,500	$1,600

Victorilux Amp
2001-present. Victoria first offered reverb and tremolo in '01, 30 watts, 3x10", EL84s, lacquered tweed.

2001-2004		$1,600	$1,700

Vivi-Tone

1933-ca.1936. Founded in Kalamazoo, Michigan, by former Gibson designer Lloyd Loar and others, Vivi-Tone built small amps to accompany their early electric solidbody guitars. They possibly also built basses and mandolins.

Voltmaster

Trapezoid-shaped combo amps and reverb units made in Plano, Texas, in the late 1990s.

Vox

1957-1972, 1982-present. Tom Jennings and Dick Denney combined forces in '57 to produce the first Vox product, the 15-watt AC-15 amplifier. The short period between '63-'65 is considered to be the Vox heyday. Vox produced tube amps in England and also the U.S. from '64 to the early part of '66. English-made tube amps were standardized between '60 and '65. U.S.-made Vox amps in '66 were solid-state. In the mid-'60s, similar model names were sometimes used for tube and solidstate amps. In '93 Korg bought the Vox name and current products are built by Marshall.

A Vox amp stand is correctly called a "trolley" and those amps that originally came with a trolley are priced accordingly, that is the price below includes the original trolley, and an amp without the trolley will be worth less than the amount shown. Smaller amps were not originally equipped with a trolley.

AC-4 Amp
1958-1965. Made in England, early Vox tube design, 3.5 watts, 1x8", tremolo.

1958-1965		$1,500	$1,600

VHT Pitbull Super 30

Victor MA-25

Victoria Victorilux

AMPS

1963 Vox AC-2

Vox AC-50 Super Twin

Vox Pathfinder

MODEL YEAR	FEATURES	EXC. COND. LOW	HIGH

AC-10 Amp
1960-1965. Made in England, 12 watts, 1x10", tremolo, this tube version not made in U.S. ('64-'65).

1960-1965		$1,900	$2,400

AC-10 Twin Amp
1960-1965. Made in England, also made in U.S. '64-'65, 12 watts (2xEL84s), 2x10".

1960-1965		$2,100	$2,600

AC-15 Twin Amp
1958-1965. Tube, 2x12", 18 watts.

1958-1965	Black Tolex	$3,600	$4,000
1960-1965	Custom colors	$4,100	$4,500

AC-15 TBX
1996-2000. 15 watts, top boost, 1x12" Celestion (lower cost Eminence available).

1996-2000		$875	$950

AC-30 Super Twin Head Amp
1960-1965. Made in England, 30-watt head.

1960-1963	Custom color	$3,500	$3,800
1960-1965	With footswitch	$2,700	$3,000

AC-30 Twin/AC-30 Twin Top Boost Amp
1960-1965. Made in England, 30-watt head, 36 watts 2x12", Top Boost includes additional treble and bass, custom colors available in '60-'63.

1960-1963	Custom colors	$4,500	$5,400
1960-1965		$3,500	$4,400

AC-30 Reissue Models
1980s-1990s. Standard reissue and Limited edtion models with identification plate on the back of the amp. Models include the AC-30 Reissue and Reissue custom color (1980s-1990s), AC-30 25th Anniv. (1985-1986), AC-30 30th Anniv. (1991), AC-30 Collector Model (1990s, mahogany cabinet) and the AC-30HW Hand Wired (1990s).

1980s	Reissue	$1,200	$1,300
1985-1986	25th Anniv.	$1,300	$1,400
1990s	Collector Model	$2,000	$2,300
1990s	Hand wired	$2,000	$2,800
1990s	Reissue	$1,200	$1,300
1990s	Reissue custom color	$1,600	$1,700
1991	30th Anniv.	$2,000	$2,300

AC-50 Head Amp
1960-1965. Made in England, 50-watt head, U.S. production '64-'65 tube version is Westminster Bass, U.S. post-'66 is solidstate.

1960-1965		$1,500	$1,800

Berkeley II V108 (tube) Amp
1964-1966. U.S.-made tube amp, revised '66-'69 to U.S.-made solidstate model V1081, 18 watts, 2x10" piggyback.

1964-1966		$1,300	$1,400

Berkeley II V1081 (solidstate) Amp
1966-1969. U.S.-made solidstate model V1081, 35 watts, 2x10" piggyback, includes trolley stand.

1966-1969		$700	$800

Berkeley III (solidstate) Amp
1966-1969. Berkeley III logo on top panel of amp.

1966-1969		$700	$800

MODEL YEAR	FEATURES	EXC. COND. LOW	HIGH

Buckingham Amp
1966-1969. Solidstate, 70 watts, 2x12" piggyback, includes trolley stand.

1966-1969		$800	$900

Cambridge Reverb (tube) V103 Amp
1964-1966. U.S.-made tube version, 18 watts, 1x10", a Pacemaker with reverb, superceded by solidstate Model V1031 by '67.

1964-1966		$1,100	$1,200

Cambridge Reverb (solidstate) V1031 Amp
1966-1969. Solidstate, 35 watts, 1x10", model V1031 replaced tube version V103.

1966-1969		$500	$700

Cambridge 15
1999-2001. 15 watts, 1x8", tremolo.

1999-2001		$125	$175

Cambridge 30 Reverb
1999-2002. 30 watts, 1x10", tremolo and reverb.

1999-2002		$175	$275

Cambridge 30 Reverb Twin 210 Amp
1999-2002. 30 watts hybrid circuit, 2x10", reverb.

1999-2002		$275	$375

Churchill PA Head Amp and Cab Set
Late-1960s. PA head with multiple inputs and column speakers.

1960s	PA head only	$400	$500

Churchill PA V119 Head and V1091 Cab Set
Late-1960s. PA head with multiple inputs and 2 column speakers.

1960s	Head and cabs	$850	$1,000

Climax V-125/V-125 Lead Combo Amp
1970-1991. Solidstate, 125 watts, 2x12" combo, 5-band EQ, master volume.

1970-1991		$400	$700

Defiant Amp
1966-1969. Made in England, 50 watts, 2x12" + Midax horn cabinet.

1966-1969		$1,600	$1,700

Escort Amp
Late 1960s-1983. 2.5 watt battery-powered portable amp.

1968-1986		$375	$450

Essex Bass V1042 Amp
1965-1969. U.S.-made solidstate, 35 watts, 2x12".

1965-1969		$700	$850

Foundation Bass Amp
1966-1969. Solidstate, 50 watts, 1x18", made in England only.

1966-1969		$500	$650

Kensington Bass V1241 Amp
1965-1969. U.S.-made solidstate bass amp, 22 watts, 1x15", G-tuner.

1965-1969		$450	$550

Pacemaker (tube) V102 Amp
1964-1965. U.S.-made tube amp, 18 watts, 1x10", replaced by solidstate Pacemaker model V1021.

1964-1965		$750	$900

MODEL YEAR FEATURES	EXC. COND. LOW	HIGH

Pacemaker (solidstate) V1021 Amp
1966-1969. U.S.-made solidstate amp, 35 watts, 1x10", replaced Pacemaker model V102.

1967-1969	$350	$450

Pathfinder (tube) V101 Amp
1964-1965. U.S.-made tube amp, 4 watts, 1x18", '66-'69 became U.S.-made solidstate V1011.

1964-1965	$750	$850

Pathfinder (solidstate) V1011 Amp
1966-1969. U.S.-made solidstate, 25 watts peak power, 1x8".

1966-1969	$300	$400

Pathfinder 10 Amp
2002-present. Compact practice amp with 1960s cosmetics, 10 watts, 6.5" speaker.

2002-2004	$65	$90

Pathfinder 15 Amp
1998-present. 1960s cosmetics, 15 watts, 1x8".

1998-2004	$65	$90

Royal Guardsman V1131/V1132 Amp
1966-1969. U.S.-made solidstate, 50 watts piggyback, 2x12" + 1 horn, the model below the Super Beatle V1141/V1142.

1966-1969	$900	$1,200

Scorpion (solidstate) Amp
1968. Solidstate, 60 watts, 4x10" Vox Oxford speaker.

1968	$500	$700

Super Beatle V1141/V1142 Amp
1966-1967. U.S.-made 120 watt solidstate, 4x12" + 2 horns, with distortion pedal (V1141), or without (V1142).

1966-1967	$1,950	$2,150

Viscount V1151/V1152 Amp
1966-1969. U.S.-made solidstate, 70 watts, 2x12" combo.

1966-1969	$750	$800

Westminster V118 Bass Amp
1966-1969. Solidstate, 120 watts, 1x18".

1966-1969	$600	$650

V-Series
See Crate.

Wabash
1950s. Private branded amps distributed by the David Wexler company.

Model 1158 Amp
Danelectro-made, 1x15", 2x6L6 power tubes.

1955	Tweed	$150	$275

Warbler
See listing under Juke amps.

Warwick
1982-present. Combos, amp heads and cabinets from Warwick Basses of Markneukirchen, Germany.

Washburn
1974-present. Imported guitar and bass amps. Washburn also offers guitars, mandolins, and basses.

Watkins
1957-present. England's Watkins Electric Music (WEM) was founded by Charlie Watkins. Their first commercial product was the Watkins Dominator (wedge Gibson stereo amp shape) in '57, followed by the Copicat Echo in '58. They currently build accordion amps.

Clubman
1960s. Small combo amp with typical Watkins styling, blue cover, white grille.

1960s	$350	$450

Dominator V-Front Amp
Late-1950s-1960s, 2004. 18 watts, 2x10", wedge cabinet similar to Gibson GA-79 stereo amp, tortoise and light beige cab, light grille, requires 220V step-up transformer. Was again offered in '04.

1959-1962	$1,150	$1,400

White
1955-1960. The White brand, named after plant manager Forrest White, was established by Fender to provide steel and small amp sets to teaching studios that were not Fender-authorized dealers. The amps were sold with the matching steel guitar.

White (Matamp)
See Matamp listing.

Working Dog
2001-present. Lower cost tube amps and combos built by Alessandro High-End Products (Alessandro, Hound Dog) in Huntingdon Valley, Pennsylvania.

Yamaha
1946-present. Yamaha started building amps in the '60s and offered a variety of guitar and bass amps over the years. The current models are solidstate bass amps. They also build guitars, basses, effects, sound gear and other instruments.

Budokan HY-10G II Amp
1987-1992. Portable, 10 watts, distortion control, EQ.

1987-1992	$70	$100

G50-112 Amp
1983-1992. 50 watts, 1x12".

1983-1992	$250	$300

G100-112 Amp
1983-1992. 100 watts, 1x12" combo, black cover, striped grille.

1983-1992	$250	$300

G100-212 Amp
1983-1992. 100, 2x12" combo, black cover, striped grille.

1983-1992	$300	$350

JX30B Amp
1983-1992. Bass amp, 30 watts.

1983-1992	$200	$250

TA-20 Amp
1968-1972. Upright wedge shape with controls facing upwards, solidstate.

1968-1972	$150	$250

Vox Super Beatle

Watkins Dominator

Working Dog Rottweiler

AMPS

Yamaha T100 C

Zeta AP-12

Zinky 25-Watt

MODEL YEAR / FEATURES	EXC. COND. LOW	HIGH
TA-25 Amp		
1968-1972. Upright wedge shape with controls facing upwards, 40 watts, 1x12", solidstate, black or red cover.		
1968-1972	$175	$275
TA-30 Amp		
1968-1972. Upright wedge shape, solidstate.		
1968-1972	$200	$300
TA-50 Amp		
1971-1972. Solidstate combo, 80 watts, 2x12", includes built-in cart with wheels, black cover.		
1971-1972	$225	$325
TA-60 Amp		
1968-1972. Upright wedge shape, solidstate, most expensive of wedge-shape amps.		
1968-1972	$250	$300
VR4000 Amp		
1988-1992. 50-watt stereo, 2 channels, EQ, stereo chorus, reverb and dual effects loops.		
1988-1992	$275	$325
VR6000 Amp		
1988-1992. 100-watt stereo, 2 channels which can also be combined, EQ, chorus, reverb and dual effects loops.		
1988-1992	$375	$425
VX-15 Amp		
1988-1992. 15 watts.		
1988-1992	$125	$175
VX-65D Bass Amp		
1984-1992. 80 watts, 2 speakers.		
1984-1992	$150	$200
YBA-65 Bass Amp		
1972-1976. Solidstate combo, 60 watts, 1x15".		
1972-1976	$175	$225
YTA-25 Amp		
1972-1976. Solidstate combo, 25 watts, 1x12".		
1972-1976	$150	$200
YTA-300 Amp		
1972-1976. Solidstate piggyback, 200 watts, dual cabs with 2x12" and 4x12".		
1972-1976	$375	$425
YTA-400 Amp		
1972-1976. Solidstate piggyback, 200 watts, dual 4x12".		
1972-1976	$400	$450

MODEL YEAR / FEATURES	EXC. COND. LOW	HIGH
YTA-45 Amp		
1972-1976. Solidstate combo, 45 watts, 1x12".		
1972-1976	$175	$225
YTA-95 Amp		
1972-1976. Solidstate combo, 90 watts, 1x12".		
1972-1976	$200	$250
YTA-100 Amp		
1972-1976. Solidstate piggyback, 100 watts, 2x12".		
1972-1976	$250	$300
YTA-110 Amp		
1972-1976. Solidstate piggyback, 100 watts, 2x12" in extra large cab.		
1972-1976	$250	$300
YTA-200 Amp		
1972-1976. Solidstate piggyback, 200 watts, 4x12".		
1972-1976	$275	$325

Zapp

Ca.1978-early-1980s. Zapp amps were distributed by Red Tree Music, Inc., of Mamaroneck, New York.

MODEL YEAR / FEATURES	EXC. COND. LOW	HIGH
Z-10 Amp		
1978-1980s. Small student amp, 8 watts.		
1979-1982	$45	$60
Z-50 Amp		
1978-1980s. Small student amp, 10 watts, reverb, tremelo.		
1978-1982	$55	$75

Zeta

1982-present. Solid state amps with MIDI options, made in Oakland, California. They also make basses, violins and mandolins.

Zinky

1999-present. Tube head and combo amps and cabinets built by Bruce Zinky in Flagstaff, Arizona. He also builds the mini Smokey amps (since '97), effects, and has revived the Supro brand on a guitar and amp.

Effects

ADA Flanger

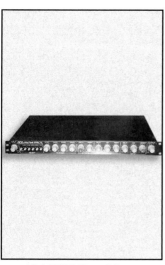

ADA TFX4 Time Effects

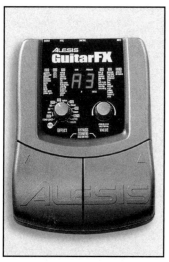

Alesis Guitar FX

MODEL YEAR	FEATURES	EXC. COND. LOW	HIGH

Ace-Tone

1968-1972. Effects from Ace Electronic Industry, which was a part of Sakata Shokai Limited of Osaka, Japan, and and also made organs, amps, etc. Their Ace-Tone effects line was available from '68-'72 and was the precedessor to Roland and Boss.

Fuzz Master FM-1
Distortion and overdrive.

1968		$125	$225

Wah Master WM-1
Filter wah.

1969		$125	$225

Acoustyx

1977-1982. Made by the Highland Corporation of Vermont.

Image Synthesizer IS-1
1977-1982.

1977-1982		$50	$60

Phase Five
1977-ca.1982. Used 6 C cell batteries!

1977-1982		$50	$60

ADA

1975-2002. ADA is an acronym for Analog/Digital Associates. The company was located in Berkeley, California, and introduced its Flanger and Final Phase in '77. The company later moved to Oakland and made amplifiers, high-tech signal processors, and a reissue of its original Flanger.

Final Phase
1977-1979. Reissued in '97.

1977-1979		$400	$450

Flanger
1977-1983, 1996-2002. Reissued in '96.

1977-1979	With control pedal	$400	$450
1977-1979	Without control pedal	$350	$400
1980-1983		$250	$300
1996-2002		$80	$100

MP-1
1987-1995. Tube preamp with chorus and effects loop, MIDI.

1987-1995	Without optional foot controller	$150	$200

MP-2
Ca.1988-1995. Tube preamp with chorus, 9-band EQ and effects loop, MIDI.

1988-1995		$225	$275

Pitchtraq
1987. Programmable pitch transposer including octave shifts.

1987		$225	$275

Stereo Tapped Delay STD-1
Introduced in 1981.

1980s		$150	$200

TFX4 Time Effects
Introduced in 1982, includes flanger, chorus, doubler, echo.

1980s		$150	$200

Aguilar

The New York, New York amp builder also offers a line of tube and solidstate pre-amps.

Akai

1984-present. In '99, Akai added guitar effects to their line of electronic samplers and sequencers for musicians.

Headrush E1
1999-present. Delay, tape echo simulations, looping recorder.

2004		$180	$190

Alamo

1947-1982. Founded by Charles Eilenberg, Milton Fink, and Southern Music, San Antonio, Texas. Distributed by Bruno & Sons. Mainly known for guitars and amps, Alamo did offer a reverb unit. See Guitar Stories Volume II, by Michael Wright, for a complete history of Alamo with detailed model listings.

Reverb Unit
1965-ca.1979. Has a Hammond reverb system, balance and intensity controls. By '73 the unit had 3 controls - mixer, contour, and intensity.

1965		$275	$350

Alesis

1992-present. Alesis has a wide range of products for the music industry, including digital processors and amps for guitars.

Effects Processors
1992-present. Various digital processors for reverb, echo, etc.

1990s		$125	$200

Allen Amplification

1998-present. David Allen's company, located in Richwood, Kentucky, mainly produces amps, but they also offer a tube overdrive pedal.

Altair Corp.

1977-1980s. Company was located in Ann Arbor, Michigan.

Power Attenuator PW-5
1977-1980. Goes between amp and speaker to dampen volume.

1977-1980		$100	$125

Amdek

Mid-1980s. Amdek offered many electronic products over the years, including drum machines and guitar effects. Most of these were sold in kit form so quality of construction can vary.

Delay Machine DMK-200
1983. Variable delay times.

1983		$100	$125

Octaver OCK-100
1983. Produces tone 1 or 2 octaves below the note played.

1983		$100	$125

MODEL YEAR	FEATURES	EXC. COND. LOW	HIGH

Ampeg

Ampeg entered the effects market in the late-1960s. Their offerings in the early-'60s were really amplifier-outboard reverb units similar to the ones offered by Gibson (GA-1). Ampeg offered a line of imported effects in '82-'83, known as the A-series (A-1 through A-9), and reintroduced effects to their product line in '05.

Analog Delay A-8
1982-1983. Made in Japan.

1982-1983		$75	$125

Chorus A-6
1982-1983. Made in Japan.

1982-1983		$50	$75

Compressor A-2
1982-1983. Made in Japan.

1982-1983		$50	$75

Distortion A-1
1982-1983. Made in Japan.

1982-1983		$50	$75

Echo Jet (EJ-12) Reverb
1963-1965. Outboard, alligator clip reverb unit with 12" speaker, 12 watts, technically a reverb unit. When used as a stand-alone amp, the reverb is off. Named EJ-12A in '65.

1963-1965		$350	$400

Echo Satellite (ES-1)
1961-1963. Outboard reverb unit with amplifier and speaker alligator clip.

1961-1963		$325	$375

Flanger A-5
1982-1983. Made in Japan.

1982-1983		$50	$75

Multi-Octaver A-7
1982-1983. Made in Japan.

1982-1983		$50	$100

Over Drive A-3
1982-1983. Made in Japan.

1982-1983		$50	$75

Parametric Equalizer A-9
1982-1983. Made in Japan.

1982-1983		$45	$70

Phaser A-4
1982-1983. Made in Japan.

1982-1983		$50	$75

Phazzer
1975-1977.

1975-1977		$50	$75

Scrambler Fuzz
1969. Distortion pedal. Reissued in '05.

1969		$75	$150

Amplifier Corporation of America

Late '60s company that made amps for Univox and also marketed effects under their own name.

Analog Man

1994-present. Founded by Mike Piera in '94 with full-time production by 2000. Located in Bethel, Connecticut, producing chorus, compressor, fuzz, and boost pedals by '03.

Aphex Systems

1975-present. Founded in Massachusetts by Marvin Caesar and Curt Knoppel, to build their Aural Exciter and other pro sound gear. Currently located in Sun Valley, California, and building a variety of gear for the pro audio broadcast, pro music and home-recording markets.

Apollo

Ca.1967-1972. Imported by St. Louis Music, includes Fuzz Treble Boost Box, Crier Wa-Wa, Deluxe Fuzz.

Crier Wa-Wa
Ca.1967-1972.

1967-1972		$100	$200

Fuzz/Deluxe Fuzz
Ca.1967-1972. Includes the Fuzz Treble Boost Box and the Deluxe Fuzz.

1967-1972		$150	$250

Arbiter

Ivor Arbiter and Arbiter Music, London, began making the circular Fuzz Face stompbox in 1966. Other products included the Fuzz Wah and Fuzz Wah Face. In '68 the company went public as Arbiter and Western, later transitioning to Dallas-Arbiter. Refer to Dallas-Arbiter for listings.

Aria

1960-present. Aria provided a line of effects, made by Maxon, in the mid-'80s.

Analog Delay AD-10
1983-1985. Dual-stage stereo.

1983-1985		$65	$75

Chorus ACH-1
1986-1987. Stereo.

1986-1987		$40	$50

Chorus CH-5
1985-1987.

1985-1987		$40	$50

Chorus CH-10
1983-1985. Dual-stage stereo.

1983-1985		$40	$50

Compressor CO-10
1983-1985.

1983-1985		$40	$50

Digital Delay ADD-100
1984-1986. Delay, flanging, chorus, doubling, hold.

1984-1986		$65	$75

Digital Delay DD-X10
1985-1987.

1985-1987		$65	$75

Distortion DT-5
1985-1987.

1985-1987		$40	$50

Distortion DT-10
1983-1985. Dual-stage.

1983-1985		$40	$50

Ampeg Chorus

Analog Man Black Cat Superfuzz

Aria CH-10 Chorus

Aria Jet Phaser RE-202

Arion Phase Shifter RE-100

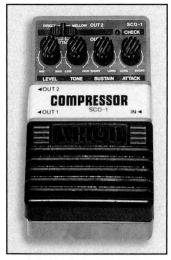

Arion Compressor SCO-1

MODEL YEAR	FEATURES	EXC. COND. LOW	HIGH
Flanger AFL-1			
1986. Stereo.			
1986		$50	$60
Flanger FL-5			
1985-1987.			
1985-1987		$50	$60
Flanger FL-10			
1983-1985. Dual-stage stereo.			
1983-1985		$50	$60
Metal Pedal MP-5			
1985-1987.			
1985-1987		$40	$50
Noise Gate NG-10			
1983-1985.			
1983-1985		$30	$40
Over Drive OD-10			
1983-1985. Dual-stage.			
1983-1985		$40	$50
Parametric Equalizer EQ-10			
1983-1985.			
1983-1985		$40	$50
Phase Shifter PS-10			
1983-1984. Dual-stage.			
1983-1984		$50	$60
Programmable Effects Pedal APE-1			
1984-1986. Compression, distortion, delay, chorus.			
1984-1986		$50	$60

Arion

1984-present. Imports distributed by Matthews and Ryan of Brooklyn, New York.

MODEL YEAR	FEATURES	EXC. COND. LOW	HIGH
Compressor SCO-1			
1985-present. Stereo, the -1 was dropped on later models.			
1985-2002		$35	$45
Distortion SDI-1			
1984-2002. Stereo, the -1 was dropped on later models.			
1984-2002		$35	$45
Hot Watt II			
1984-present. Headphone amp.			
1984-2002		$35	$45
Metal Master SMM-1			
1984-present. Stereo, the -1 was dropped on later models.			
1984-2002		$35	$45
Over Drive SOD-1			
1984-2002. Stereo, the -1 was dropped on later models.			
1984-2002		$35	$45
Parametric EQ SPE-1			
1985-late-1980s?. Stereo.			
1985-1989		$30	$40
Stereo Chorus SCH-1			
1984-present. The -1 was dropped on later models.			
1984-2002		$50	$65
Stereo Delay SAD-1			
1984-present. Analog delay.			
1984-2002		$50	$60

MODEL YEAR	FEATURES	EXC. COND. LOW	HIGH
Stereo Delay SAD-2			
Ca.1990-present.			
1990-2002		$40	$50
Stereo Flanger SFL-1			
1984-present. The -1 was dropped on later models.			
1984-2002		$35	$45
Stereo Phaser SPH-1			
1984-present. The -1 was dropped on later models.			
1984-2002		$35	$45
Tube Mania			
1987-early-1990s.			
1987-1992		$35	$45

Asama

1970s-1980s. This Japanese company offered solidbody guitars with built-in effects as well as stand-alone units. They also offered basses, drum machines and other music products.

Astrotone

Late 1960s. By Universal Amp, which also made the Sam Ash Fuzzz Boxx.

MODEL YEAR	FEATURES	EXC. COND. LOW	HIGH
Fuzz			
1966. Introduced in '66, same as Sam Ash Fuzzz Boxx.			
1966		$175	$275

ATD

Mid-1960s-early 1980s. Made by the All-Test Devices corporation of Long Beach, New York. In the mid-'60s, Richard Minz and an associate started making effects part-time, selling them through Manny's Music in New York. They formed All-Test and started making Maestro effects and transducer pickups for CMI, which owned Gibson at the time. By '75, All-Test was marketing effects under their own brand. All-Test is still around making products for other industries, but by the early to mid-'80s they were no longer making products for the guitar.

MODEL YEAR	FEATURES	EXC. COND. LOW	HIGH
PB-1 Power Booster			
1976-ca.1980.			
1979-1980		$50	$60
Volume Pedal EV-1			
1979-ca.1980.			
1979-1980		$30	$40
Wah-Wah/Volume Pedal WV-1			
1979-ca.1981.			
1979-1981		$50	$60

Audio Matrix

1979-1984. Effects built by B.K Butler in 1978 in Escondido, California. He later designed the Tube Driver and founded Tube Works in 1987. He nows operates Butler Audio, making home and auto hybrid tube stereo amps.

MODEL YEAR	FEATURES	EXC. COND. LOW	HIGH
Mini Boogee B81			
1981. Four-stage, all-tube preamp, overdrive, distortion.			
1981		$100	$135

The *Vintage Guitar Price Guide* shows low to high values for items in all-original excellent condition, and, where applicable, with original case or cover.

MODEL YEAR	FEATURES	EXC. COND. LOW	HIGH

Audioworks
1980s. Company was located in Niles, Illinois.
F.E.T. Distortion
1982.
| 1980s | | $40 | $55 |

Auralux
2000-present. Founded by Mitchell Omori and David Salzmann, Auralux builds effects and tube amps in Highland Park, Illinois.

Austone Electronics
1997-present. Founded by Jon Bessent and Randy Larkin, Austone offers a range of stomp boxes, all made in Austin, Texas.
Overdrive and Fuzz Pedals
1997-present. Various overdrive and fuzz boxes.
| 1997-2002 | | $125 | $175 |

Automagic
1998-present. Wah pedals and distortion boxes made in Germany by Musician Sound Design.
Avalanche
Brianizer
Late-1980s. Leslie effect, dual rotor, adjustable speed and rates.
| 1980s | | $75 | $90 |

Axe
1980s. Early '80s line of Japanese effects, possibly made by Maxon.

B & M
1970s. A private brand made by Sola/Colorsound for Barns and Mullens, a U.K. distributor.
Fuzz Unit
1970s. Long thin orange case, volume, sustain, tone knobs, on-off stomp switch.
| 1970s | | $275 | $325 |

Bad Cat Amplifier Company
2000-present. Founded in Corona, California by James and Debbie Heidrich, Bad Cat offers class A combo amps, heads, cabinets and effects.

Baldwin
1965-1970. The piano maker got into the guitar market when it acquired Burns of London in '65, and sold the guitars in the U.S. under the Baldwin name. They also marketed a couple of effects at the same time.

Bartolini
The pickup manufacturer offered a few effects from around 1982 to '87.
Tube-It
1982-ca.1987. Marshall tube amplification simulator with bass, treble, sustain controls.
| 1982-1987 | Red case | $80 | $90 |

Basic Systems' Side Effects
1980s. This company was located in Tulsa, Oklahoma.
Audio Delay
1986-ca.1987. Variable delay speeds.
| 1986-1987 | | $75 | $100 |
Triple Fuzz
1986-ca.1987. Selectable distortion types.
| 1986-1987 | | $50 | $60 |

BBE
1985-present. BBE, located in California, currently manufactures rack-mount effects and also owns G & L Guitars.
601 Stinger
1985-ca.1989.
| 1985-1989 | | $55 | $65 |

Behringer
1989-present. The German professional audio products company added modeling effects in '01 and guitar stomp boxes in '05. They also offer guitars and amps.

Beigel Sound Lab
1980. Music product designer Mike Beigel helped form Musitronics Corp, where he made the Mu-Tron III. In 1978 he started Beigel Sound Lab to provide product design in Warwick, New York, where in '80 he made 50 rack-mount Enveloped Controlled Filters under this brand name.

Bell Electrolabs
1970s. This English company offered a line of effects in the '70s.
Vibrato
| 1970s | | $150 | $200 |

Bennett Music Labs
Effects built in the U.S. by Bruce Bennett.

Bigsby
Bigsby has been making volume and tone pedals since the 1950s. They currently offer a volume pedal.
Foot Volume and Tone Control
| 1950s | | $125 | $175 |

Binson
Late 1950s-1982. Binson, of Milan, Italy, made several models of the Echorec, using tubes or transistors. They also made units for Guild, Sound City and EKO.
Echorec
Ca.1960-1979. Four knob models with 12 echo selections, 1 head, complex multitap effects, settings for record level, playback and regeneration. Includes B1, B2, Echomaster1, T5 (has 6 knobs), T5E, and Baby. Used a magnetic disk instead of tape. Guild later offered the "Guild Echorec by Binson" which is a different stripped-down version.
| 1960s | Tube, gold case | $500 | $700 |

Austone Soul-O-Stomp

Bad Cat 2-Tone

BBE Opto Stomp

EFFECTS

Blackbox Quicksilver

Boss Acoustic Simulator AC-2

Boss Digital Delay DD-3

MODEL YEAR	FEATURES	EXC. COND. LOW	HIGH

Bixonic

1995-present. Originally distributed by Sound-Barrier Music, Bixonic is currently distributed by Godlyke, Inc.

Expandora EXP-2000
1995-2000. Analog distortion, round silver case, internal DIP switches.

1995-2000		$175	$200

Blackbox Music Electronics

2000-present. Founded by Loren Stafford and located in Minneapolis, Minnesota, Blackbox offers a line of effects for guitar and bass.

Blackstone Appliances

1999-prresent. Distortion effects crafted by Jon Blackstone in New York, New York.

Bon, Mfg

Bon was located in Escondido, California.

Tube Driver 204
1979-ca.1981.

1979-1981		$100	$150

Boss

1976-present. Japan's Roland Corporation first launched effect pedals in '74. A year or two later the subsidiary company, Boss, debuted its own line. They were marketed concurrently at first but gradually Boss became reserved for effects and drum machines while the Roland name was used on amplifiers and keyboards. Boss still offers a wide line of pedals.

Acoustic Simulator AC-2
1997-present. Four modes that emulate various acoustic tones.

1997-1999		$55	$65

Auto Wah AW-2
1991-1999.

1991-1999		$45	$55

Bass Chorus CE-2B
1987-1995.

1987-1995		$45	$55

Bass Equalizer GE-7B
1987-1995. Seven-band, name changed to GEB-7 in '95.

1987-1995		$45	$55

Bass Flanger BF-2B
1987-1994.

1987-1994		$45	$55

Bass Limiter LM-2B
1990-1994.

1990-1994		$40	$45

Bass Overdrive ODB-3
4 1994-present.

1994-1999		$45	$55

Blues Driver BD-2
1995-present.

1995-1999		$45	$55

Chorus Ensemble CE-1
1976-1984. Vibrato and chorus.

1976-1984		$150	$250

Chorus Ensemble CE-2
1979-1982.

1979-1982		$50	$100

Chorus Ensemble CE-3
1982-1992.

1982-1992		$50	$100

Chorus Ensemble CE-5
1991-present.

1991-2004		$50	$100

Compressor Sustainer CS-1
1978-1982.

1978-1982		$75	$100

Compressor Sustainer CS-2
1981-1986.

1981-1986		$75	$100

Compressor Sustainer CS-3
1986-present.

1986-1999		$75	$100

Delay DM-2
1981-1984. Analog, hot pink case.

1981-1984		$175	$250

Delay DM-3
1984-1988.

1984-1988		$150	$200

Digital Delay DD-2
1983-1986.

1983-1986		$125	$175

Digital Delay DD-3
1986-present. Up to 800 ms of delay.

1986-1989		$125	$175
1990-2000		$100	$150

Digital Delay DD-5
1995-2005. Up to 2 seconds of delay.

1995-2005		$100	$150

Digital Delay DD-6
2003-present. Up to 5 seconds of delay

2003-2004		$60	$75

Digital Dimension C DC-2
1985-1989. Two chorus effects and tremolo.

1985-1989		$140	$150

Digital Metalizer MZ-2
1987-1992.

1987-1992		$85	$95

Digital Reverb RV-2
1987-1990.

1987-1990		$100	$150

Digital Reverb/Delay RV-3
1994-2004.

1994-2004		$100	$125

Digital Reverb RV-5
2003-present. Dual imput and dual output, four control knobs, silver case.

2003-2004		$65	$100

Digital Sampler/Delay DSD-2
1985-1986.

1985-1986		$125	$175

Digital Space-DDC-3/Digital Dimension DC-3
1988-1993. Originally called the Digital Space-D, later changed to Digital Dimension. Chorus with EQ.

1988-1993		$135	$185

MODEL YEAR FEATURES	EXC. COND. LOW	HIGH
Digital Stereo Reverb RV-70		
1994-1995. Rack mount, MIDI control, reverb/delay, 199 presets.		
1994-1995	$135	$185
Distortion DS-1		
1978-1989, 1990s-2000s.		
1978-1989	$55	$65
1990-1999	$35	$55
2000-2004	$25	$30
Dr. Rhythm DR-55		
1979-1989. Drum machine.		
1979-1989	$150	$200
Dual Over Drive SD-2		
1993-1998.		
1993-1998	$50	$60
Dynamic Wah AW-3		
2000-present. Auto wah with humanizer, for guitar or bass.		
2000-2004	$55	$65
Dynamic Filter FT-2		
1986-1988. Auto wah.		
1986-1988	$75	$100
Enhancer EH-2		
1990-1998.		
1990-1998	$40	$50
Flanger BF-1		
1977-1980.		
1977-1980	$60	$75
Flanger BF-2		
1980-present.		
1980-1989	$60	$75
1990-1999	$45	$60
Foot Wah FW-3		
1992-1996.		
1992-1996	$50	$60
Graphic Equalizer GE-6		
1978-1981. Six bands.		
1978-1981	$50	$75
Graphic Equalizer GE-7		
1981-present. Seven bands.		
1982-1989	$75	$100
1990-1999	$50	$70
Graphic Equalizer GE-10		
1976-1985. 10-band EQ for guitar or bass.		
1976-1985	$100	$125
Harmonist HR-2		
1994-1999. Pitch shifter.		
1994-1999	$75	$100
Heavy Metal HM-2		
1983-1991. Distortion.		
1983-1991	$35	$45
Hyper Fuzz FZ-2		
1993-1997.		
1993-1997	$50	$75
Hyper Metal HM-3		
1993-1998.		
1993-1998	$40	$50
Limiter LM-2		
1987-1992.		
1987-1992	$30	$40

MODEL YEAR FEATURES	EXC. COND. LOW	HIGH
Line Selector LS-2		
1991-present. Select between 2 effects loops.		
1991-2003 With adapter	$50	$75
Mega Distortion MD-2		
2003-present.		
2003-2004	$50	$60
Metal Zone MT-2		
1991-present. Distortion and 3-band EQ.		
1991-2002	$50	$75
Multi Effects ME-5		
1988-1991. Floor unit.		
1988-1991	$75	$125
Multi Effects ME-6		
1992-1997.		
1992-1997	$75	$125
Multi Effects ME-8		
1996-1997.		
1996-1997	$75	$125
Multi Effects ME-30		
1998-2002.		
1998-2002	$75	$125
Multi Effects ME-50		
2003-present. Floor unit.		
2003-2004	$175	$200
Noise Gate NF-1		
1979-1988.		
1979-1988	$45	$55
Noise Suppressor NS-2		
1987-present.		
1987-2002	$45	$55
Octaver OC-2/Octave OC-2		
1982-present. Originally called the Octaver.		
1982-2002	$60	$75
Overdrive OD-1		
1977-1985.		
1977-1979	$100	$175
1980-1985	$75	$150
Overdrive OD-3		
1997-present.		
1997-2002	$50	$75
Parametric Equalizer PQ-4		
1991-1997.		
1991-1997	$50	$75
Phaser PH-1		
1977-1981.		
1977-1981	$75	$100
Phaser PH-1R		
1982-1985. Resonance control added to PH-1.		
1982-1985	$75	$125
Pitch Sifter/Delay PS-2		
1987-1993.		
1987-1993	$100	$125
Reverb Box RX-100		
1981-mid-1980s.		
1981-1985	$75	$100
Rocker Distortion PD-1		
1980-mid-1980s. Variable pedal using magnetic field.		
1980-1985	$50	$75

Boss ME-50

Boss Noise Gate NF-1

Boss Phase Shifter PH-3

EFFECTS

Boss Tremolo TR-2

Carl Martin Hydra

Catalinabread Super Chili Picoso

MODEL YEAR	FEATURES	EXC. COND. LOW	HIGH
Rocker Volume PV-1			
1981-mid-1980s.			
1980-1985		$50	$60
Rocker Wah PW-1			
1980-mid-1980s. Magnetic field variable pedal.			
1980-1985		$60	$70
Slow Gear SG-1			
1979-1982. Violin swell effect, automatically adjusts volume.			
1979-1982		$275	$325
Spectrum SP-1			
1977-1981. Single-band parametric EQ.			
1977-1981		$275	$325
Super Chorus CH-1			
1989-present.			
1989-2002		$50	$75
Super Distortion & Feedbacker DF-2			
1984-1994. Also labeled as the Super Feedbacker & Distortion.			
1984-1994		$100	$125
Super Over Drive SD-1			
1981-present.			
1981-1989		$50	$90
1990-2002		$35	$55
Super Phaser PH-2			
1984-2001.			
1984-1989		$50	$90
1990-2001		$35	$55
Super Shifter PS-5			
1999-present. Pitch shifter/harmonizer.			
1999-2004		$100	$125
Touch Wah TW-1/T Wah TW-1			
1978-1987. Auto wah, early models were labeled as Touch Wah.			
1978-1987		$100	$125
Tremolo TR-2			
1997-present.			
1997-2002		$70	$80
Tremolo/Pan PN-2			
1990-1995.			
1990-1995		$125	$150
Turbo Distortion DS-2			
1987-present.			
1987-2002		$75	$125
Turbo Overdrive OD-2			
1985-1994. Called OD-2R after '94, due to added remote on/off jack.			
1985-1994		$75	$125
Vibrato VB-2			
1982-1986. True pitch-changing vibrato, warm analog tone, 'rise time' control allows for slow attach, 4 knobs, aqua-blue case.			
1982-1986		$375	$425
Volume FV-50H			
1987-1997. High impedance, stereo volume pedal with inputs and outputs.			
1987-1997		$50	$60
Volume FV-50L			
1987-1997. Low impedance version of FV-50.			
1987-1997		$40	$50

MODEL YEAR	FEATURES	EXC. COND. LOW	HIGH
Volume Pedal FV-100			
Late-1980s-1991. Guitar volume pedal.			
1987-1991		$40	$50

Bruno

1834-present. Music Disributor Bruno and Sons had a line of Japanese-made effects in the early '70s.

Budda

1995-present. Wahs and distortion pedals from San Rafael, California. They mainly produce amp heads, combos, and cabinets.

Burriss

Guitar effects from Bob Burriss of Lexington, Kentucky. He also builds amps.

Carl Martin

1993-present. Line of effects from Søren Jongberg and East Sound Research of Denmark. They also build amps.

Carlsbro

1959-present. English amp company Carlsbro Electronics Limited offered a line of effects from '77 to '81.

Carrotron

Late-1970s-mid-1980s. Carrotron was out of California and offered a line of effects.

Noise Fader C900B1			
1980-1982.			
1980-1982		$50	$60
Preamp C821B			
1981-ca.1982.			
1981-1982		$55	$65

Carvin

1946-present. Carvin introduced its line of Ground Effects in '02 and discontinued them in '03.

Castle Instruments

Early 1980s. Castle was located in Madison, New Jersey, and made rack-mount and floor phaser units.

Phaser III			
1980-1982. Offered mode switching for various levels of phase.			
1980-1982		$100	$175

Catalinbread

2003-present. Nicholas Harris founded Catalinbread Specialized Mechanisms of Music in Seattle, Washington, in '02 to do mods and in '03 added his own line of guitar effects.

Cat's Eye

2001-present. Dean Solorzano and Lisa Kroeker build their analog guitar effects in Oceanside, California.

EFFECTS

MODEL YEAR	FEATURES	EXC. COND. LOW	HIGH

Chandler

1984-present. Located in California, Chandler Musical Instruments offers instruments, pickups, and pickguards, as well as effects.

Digital Echo
1992-2000. Rackmount, 1 second delay, stereo.

1992-2000		$350	$450

Tube Driver
1986-1991. Uses a 12AX7 tube. Not to be confused with the Tube Works Tube Driver.

1980s	Large Box	$200	$250
1980s	Rackmount	$75	$125
1990s	Rackmount	$75	$125

Chapman

1970-present. From Emmett Chapman, maker of the Stick.

Patch of Shades
1981, 1989. Wah, with pressure sensitive pad instead of pedal. 2 production runs.

1980s		$50	$75

Chicago Iron

1998-present. Faithful reproductions of classic effects built by Kurt Steir in Chicago, Illinois.

Chunk Systems

1996-present. Guitar and bass effects pedals built by Richard Cartwright in Sydney, Australia.

Clark

1960s. Built in Clark, New Jersey, same unit as the Orpheum Fuzz and the Mannys Music Fuzz.

SS-600 Fuzz
1960s. Chrome-plated, volume and tone knobs, toggle switch.

1960s		$150	$200

Clark Amplification

1995-present. Amplifier builder Mike Clark, of Cayce, South Carolina, offers a reverb unit and started building guitar effects as well, in '98.

Colorsound

1965-present. Colorsound effects were produced by England's Sola Sound, which in '65 was founded by former Vox associate Larry Macari. The first product was a fuzzbox called the Tone Bender, designed by Gary Hurst and sold at Macari's Musical Exchange stores. The first readily available fuzz in Britain, it was an instant success. In '67, the Colorsound brand was launched. In the late-'60s, wah and fuzz-wah pedals were added, and by the end of the '70s, Colorsound offered 18 different effects, an amp, and accessories. Few early Colorsound products were imported into the U.S., so today they're scarce. Except for the Wah-Wah pedal, Colorsound's production stopped by the early '80s, but in '96 most of their early line was reissued by Dick Denny of Vox fame. Denny died in 2001. The brand is now owned by Mutronics

who offers a rack mount combination of 4 classic Colorsound effects.

Flanger

1970s		$100	$200

Fuzz Phazer
Introduced in 1973.

1970s		$150	$225

Jumbo Tonebender
1974-early 1980s. Replaced the Tonebender fuzz, with wider case and light blue lettering.

1979		$150	$250

Octivider
Introduced in 1973.

1970s		$150	$225

Overdriver
Introduced in 1972, Controls for drive, treble and bass.

1970s		$150	$225

Phazer
Introduced in 1973. Magenta/purple-pink case, slanted block Phazer logo on front.

1970s		$150	$225

Ring Modulator
Introduced in 1973. Purple case, Ring Modulator name with atom orbit slanted block logo on case.

1970s		$250	$275

Supa Tonebender Fuzz
1977-early 1980s. Sustain and volume knobs, tone control and toggle. Same white case as Jumbo Tonebender, but with new circuit.

1970s		$150	$225

Supa Wah-Swell
1970s. Supa Wah-Swell in slanted block letters on the end of the pedal, silver case.

1970s		$150	$225

Supaphase

1970s		$150	$225

Supasustain

1960s		$125	$200

Tremolo

1970s		$150	$200

Tremolo Reissue
1990s. Purple case.

1990s		$100	$125

Wah Fuzz Straight
Introduced in 1973. Aqua-blue case, Wah-Fuzz-Straight in capital block letters on end of wah pedal.

1970s		$175	$250

Wah Fuzz Swell
Introduced in 1973. Yellow case, block letter Wah Fuzz Swell logo on front, three control knobs and toggle.

1970s		$250	$350

Wah Swell
1970s. Light purple case, block letter Wah-Swell logo on front.

1970s		$225	$275

Wah Wah
1970s. Dark gray case, Wah-Wah in capital block letters on end of wah pedal.

1975		$300	$350

Chandler Tube Driver

Chunk Systems Fuzz Bass FZ002

Colorsound Sustain Module

EFFECTS

Dallas Arbiter Fuzz Face

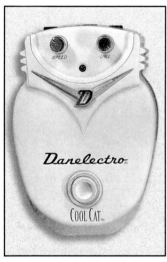

Danelectro Cool Cat

Danelectro Chicken Salad

MODEL YEAR	FEATURES	EXC. COND. LOW	HIGH
Wah Wah Reissue			
1990s. Red case, large Colorsound letter logo and small Wah Wah lettering on end of pedal.			
1990s		$75	$100
Wah Wah Supremo			
1970s. Silver/chrome metal case, Wah-Wah Supremo in block letters on end of wah pedal.			
1975		$425	$475

Companion

1970s. Private branded by Shinei of Japan, which made effects for others as well.

MODEL YEAR	FEATURES	EXC. COND. LOW	HIGH
Wah pedal			
1970s		$125	$175

Conn

Ca.1968-ca.1978. Band instrument manufacturer and distributor Conn/Continental Music Company, of Elkhart, Indiana, imported guitars and effects from Japan.

MODEL YEAR	FEATURES	EXC. COND. LOW	HIGH
Strobe ST-8 Tuner			
Late-1960s. Brown case.			
1968		$215	$225

Coron

1970s-1980s. Japanese-made effects, early ones close copies of MXR pedals.

Cosmosound

Italy's Cosmosound made small amps with Leslie drums and effects pedals in the late '60s and '70s.

Crowther Audio

1976-present. Guitar effects built by Paul Crowther, who was the original drummer of the band Split Enz, in Auckland, New Zealand. His first effect was the Hot Cake.

Crybaby

See listing under Vox for early models, and Dunlop for recent versions.

CSL

Sola Sound made a line of effects for C. Summerfield Ltd., an English music company.

Dallas Arbiter

Dallas Arbiter, Ltd. was based in London and it appeared in the late-1960s as a division of a Dallas group of companies headed by Ivor Arbiter. They also manufactured Sound City amplifiers and made Vox amps from '72 to '78. The Fuzz Face is still available from Jim Dunlop.

MODEL YEAR	FEATURES	EXC. COND. LOW	HIGH
Fuzz Face			
Introduced in 1966. The current reissue of the Dallas Arbiter Fuzz Face is distributed by Jim Dunlop USA.			
1968-1969	Red	$475	$600
1970	Red	$350	$400
1970-1976	Blue	$325	$400

MODEL YEAR	FEATURES	EXC. COND. LOW	HIGH
1977-1980	Blue	$250	$300
1981	Grey, reissue	$150	$225
1990-1999	Red, reissue	$60	$65
2000-2003	Red, reissue	$65	$70
Fuzz Wah Face			
1970s	Black	$200	$275
1990s	Reissue copy	$55	$65
Sustain			
1970s		$175	$275
Treble & Bass Face			
1960s		$200	$300
Trem Face			
Ca.1970-ca.1975. Reissued in '80s, round red case, depth and speed control knobs, Dallas-Arbiter England logo plate.			
1970-1975	Red	$250	$325
Wah Baby			
1970s. Gray speckle case, Wah Baby logo caps and small letters on end of pedal.			
1970s		$250	$350

Dan Armstrong

In 1976, Musitronics, based in Rosemont, New Jersey, introduced 6 inexpensive plug-in effects designed by Dan Armstrong. Perhaps under the influence of John D. MacDonald's Travis McGee novels, each effect name incorporated a color, like Purple Peaker. Shipping box labeled Dan Armstrong by Musitronics. They disappeared a few years later but were reissued by WD Products in '91. Since '03, Vintage Tone Project has offered the Dan Armstrong Orange Crusher. Dan Armstrong died in '04.

MODEL YEAR	FEATURES	EXC. COND. LOW	HIGH
Blue Clipper			
1976-1981. Fuzz, blue-green case.			
1976-1981		$90	$100
Green Ringer			
1976-1981. Ring Modulator/Fuzz, green case.			
1970s		$90	$100
Orange Squeezer			
1976-1981. Compressor, orange case.			
1976-1981		$90	$100
Purple Peaker			
1976-1981. Frequency Booster, light purple case.			
1976-1981		$90	$100
Red Ranger			
1976-1981. Bass/Treble Booster, light red case.			
1976-1981		$90	$100
Yellow Humper			
1976-1981. Yellow case.			
1976-1981		$90	$100

Danelectro

1946-1969, 1996-present. The Danelectro brand was revived in '96 with a line of effects pedals. They also offer the Wasabi line of effects. Prices do not include AC adapter, add $10 for the Zero-Hum adapter.

MODEL YEAR	FEATURES	EXC. COND. LOW	HIGH
Chicken Salad Vibrato			
2000-present.			
2000-2004	Orange case	$20	$25

MODEL YEAR FEATURES	EXC. COND. LOW	HIGH
Cool Cat Chorus		
1996-present.		
1996-2000	$20	$25
Corned Beef Reverb		
2000-present.		
2000-2004 Blue-black case	$20	$30
Daddy-O Overdrive		
1996-present.		
1996-2000 White case	$30	$40
Dan Echo		
1998-present.		
1998-2000	$40	$45
Fab Tone Distortion		
1996-present.		
1996-2000	$30	$40
Reverb Unit		
1965	$200	$300

Davoli

1960s-1970. Davoli was an Italian pickup and guitar builder and is often associated with Wandre guitars.

TRD

1970s. Solidstate tremolo, reverb, distortion unit.

1970s	$175	$225

Dean Markley

The string and pickup manufacturer offered a line of effects from 1976 to the early-'90s.

MODEL YEAR FEATURES	EXC. COND. LOW	HIGH
Overlord Classic Tube Overdrive		
1988-1991. Uses a 12AX7A tube, AC powered.		
1988-1991	$60	$80
Overlord III Classic Overdrive		
1990-1991. Battery-powered version of Overlord pedal. Black case with red letters.		
1990-1991	$40	$70
Voice Box 50 (watt model)		
1976-1979.		
1976-1979	$75	$125
Voice Box 100 (watt model)		
1976-1979, 1982-ca.1985.		
1976-1979	$75	$125
Voice Box 200 (watt model)		
1976-1979.		
1976-1979	$75	$125

DeArmond

In 1947, DeArmond may have introduced the first actual signal-processing effect pedal, the Tremolo Control. They made a variety of effects into the '70s, but only one caught on - their classic volume pedal. DeArmond is primarily noted for pickups.

MODEL YEAR FEATURES	EXC. COND. LOW	HIGH
Pedal Phaser Model 1900		
1974-ca.1979.		
1974-1979	$75	$125
Square Wave Distortion Generator		
1977-ca.1979.		
1977-1979	$100	$150
Thunderbolt B166		
1977-ca.1979. Five octave wah.		
1977-1979	$50	$100

MODEL YEAR FEATURES	EXC. COND. LOW	HIGH
Tone/Volume Pedal 610		
1978-ca.1979.		
1978-1979	$75	$125
Tornado Phase Shifter		
1977-ca.1979.		
1977-1979	$100	$125
Tremolo Control Model 60A/60B		
The Model 60 Tremolo Control dates from 1947 to the early-1950s. Model 60A dates from mid- to late-'50s. Model 60B, early-'60s.		
1950s 60A	$300	$375
1960s 60B	$100	$250
Twister 1930		
1980. Phase shifter.		
1980	$100	$125
Volume Pedal 1602		
1978-ca.1980s.		
1970s	$40	$60
Volume Pedal 1630		
1978-1980s. Optoelectric.		
1970s	$40	$60
Volume Pedal Model 602		
1960s.		
1960s	$40	$70
Weeper Wah Model 1802		
1970s. Weeper logo on foot pedal.		
1970s	$100	$125

DeltaLab Research

Late 1970s-early 1980s. DeltaLab, which was located in Chelmsford, Massachusetts, was an early builder of rackmount gear.

MODEL YEAR FEATURES	EXC. COND. LOW	HIGH
DL-2 Acousticomputer		
1980s. Delay.		
1980s	$75	$125
DL-4 Time Line		
1980s. Delay.		
1980s	$75	$125
DL-5		
1980s. Various digital processing effects, blue case, rackmount.		
1980s	$175	$225
DLB-1 Delay Control Pedal		
1980s. Controls other DeltaLab pedals, chrome, Morley-looking pedal.		
1980s	$50	$75
Electron I ADM/II ADM		
1980s. Blue case, rackmount effects. Models include the Electron I ADM, and the Electron II ADM.		
1980s Electron I ADM	$50	$75
1980s Electron II ADM	$75	$125

Demeter

1980-present. Located in Van Nuys, California, James Demeter and company build amp heads, combos, cabinets, pro audio gear and guitar effects.

Denio

Line of Japanese-made Boss lookalikes sold in Asia and Australia.

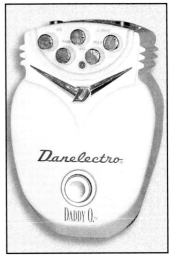

Danelectro Daddy O

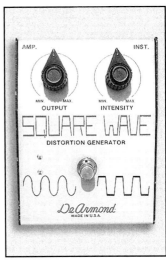

DeArmond Square Wave

DeArmond Weeper Wah

EFFECTS

Digitech PDS 2730 Hot Box

EFFECTS

Digitech Distortion PDS 1530

DOD A-B Box 270

MODEL YEAR	FEATURES	EXC. COND. LOW	HIGH

Diaz

Early 1980s-2002, 2004-present. Line of effects from the "amp doctor" Cesar Diaz. Diaz died in '02; in '04, his family announced plans to resume production.

DigiTech

The DigiTech/DOD company is in Utah and the effects are made in the U.S.A. The DigiTech name started as a line under the DOD brand in the early 1980s; later spinning off into its own brand. They also produce vocal products and studio processors and are now part of Harman International Industries.

Digital Delay PDS 1000
1985-ca.1989. One second delay.

1985-1989		$100	$150

Digital Delay and Sampler PDS 2000
1985-1991. 2 second delay.

1985-1991		$125	$175

Digital Delay PDS 2700 Double Play
1989-1991. Delay and chorus

1989-1991		$125	$175

Digital Stereo Chorus/Flanger PDS 1700
1986-1991.

1986-1991		$100	$150

Echo Plus 8 Second Delay PDS 8000
1985-1991.

1985-1991		$175	$200

Guitar Effects Processor RP 1
1992-1996. Floor unit, 150 presets.

1992-1996		$100	$150

Guitar Effects Processor RP 3
1998-2003. Floor unit.

1998-2003		$110	$150

Guitar Effects Processor RP 5
1994-1996. Floor unit, 80 presets.

1994-1996		$120	$175

Guitar Effects Processor RP 6
1996-1997. Floor unit.

1996-1997		$125	$200

Guitar Effects Processor RP 10
1994-1996. Floor unit, 200 presets.

1994-1996		$125	$175

Guitar Effects Processor RP 14D
1999. Floor unit with expression pedal, 1x12AX7 tube, 100 presets.

1999		$300	$350

Guitar Effects Processor RP 100
2000-present.

2000-2004		$100	$125

Guitar Effects Processor RP 200
2001-present. 140 presets, drum machine, Expression pedal.

2001-2004		$100	$125

Hot Box PDS 2730
1989-1991. Delay and distortion

1989-1991		$100	$125

Modulator Pedal XP 200
1996-2002. Floor unit, 61 presets.

1996-2002		$100	$125

MODEL YEAR	FEATURES	EXC. COND. LOW	HIGH

Multi Play PDS 20/20
1987-1991. Multi-function digital delay.

1987-1991		$125	$150

Pedalverb Digital Reverb Pedal PDS 3000
1987-1991.

1987-1991		$100	$125

Programmable Distortion PDS 1550
1986-1991.

1986-1991	Yellow case	$50	$75

Programmable Distortion PDS 1650
1989-1991.

1989-1991	Red case	$50	$75

Rock Box PDS 2715
1989-1991. Chorus and distortion.

1989-1991		$50	$75

Two Second Digital Delay PDS 1002
1987-1991.

1987-1991		$100	$125

Whammy Pedal WP I
1990-1993. Original Whammy Pedal, red case, reissued as WP IV in '00.

1990-1993		$375	$475

Whammy Pedal WP II
1994-1997. Can switch between 2 presets, black case.

1994-1997		$200	$275

Whammy Pedal Reissue
2000-present. Reissue version of classic WP-1 with added dive bomb and MIDI features.

2000-2004		$125	$150

DiMarzio

The pickup maker offered a couple of effects in the late-1980s to the mid-'90s.

Metal Pedal
1987-1989.

1987-1989		$50	$75

Very Metal Fuzz
Ca.1989-1995. Distortion/overdrive pedal.

1989-1995		$50	$75

DOD

DOD Electronics started in Salt Lake City, Utah in 1974. Today, they're a major effects manufacturer with dozens of pedals made in the U.S. They also market effects under the name DigiTech and are now part of Harman International Industries.

6 Band Equalizer EQ601
1977-1982.

1977-1982		$50	$70

AB Box 270
1978-1982.

1978-1982		$30	$35

American Metal FX56
1985-1991.

1985-1991		$40	$50

Analog Delay 680
1979-1982

51979-1982		$125	$150

MODEL YEAR	FEATURES	EXC. COND. LOW	HIGH
Attacker FX54			
1992-1994. Distortion and compressor.			
1992-1994		$40	$50
Bass Compressor FX82			
1987-ca.1989.			
1987-1989		$40	$50
Bass EQ FX42B			
1987-1996.			
1987-1996		$40	$50
Bass Grunge FX92			
1995-1996.			
1995-1996		$40	$50
Bass Overdrive FX91			
1998-present.			
1998-1999		$40	$50
Bass Stereo Chorus FX62			
1987-1996.			
1987-1996		$50	$60
Bass Stereo Chorus Flanger FX72			
1987-1997.			
1987-1997		$50	$60
Bi-FET Preamp FX10			
4 *1982-1996.*			
1982-1996		$30	$40
Buzz Box FX33			
1994-1996. Grunge distortion.			
1994-1996		$45	$60
Chorus 690			
41980-ca.1982. Dual speed chorus.			
19850-1982		$75	$100
Classic Fuzz FX52			
1990-1997.			
1990-1997		$35	$45
Classic Tube FX53			
1990-1997.			
1990-1997		$45	$55
Compressor 280			
1978-ca.1982.			
1978-1982		$45	$55
Compressor FX80			
1982-1985.			
1982-1985		$45	$55
Compressor Sustainer FX80B			
1986-1996.			
1986-1996		$45	$55
Death Metal FX86			
1994-present. Distortion.			
1994-1999		$35	$50
Delay FX90			
1984-ca.1987.			
1984-1987		$75	$100
Digital Delay DFX9			
1989-ca.1990.			
1989-1990		$65	$90
Digital Delay Sampler DFX94			
1995-1997.			
1995-1997		$75	$100
Distortion FX55			
1982-1986. Red case.			
1982-1986		$35	$45

MODEL YEAR	FEATURES	EXC. COND. LOW	HIGH
Edge Pedal FX87			
1988-1989.			
1988-1989		$25	$45
Envelope Filter 440			
1981-ca.1982.Reissued in '95.			
1981-1982		$65	$75
Envelope Filter FX25			
1982-1997. Replaced by FX25B.			
1982-1987		$45	$65
Envelope Filter FX25B			
1981-1987.			
1982-1987		$45	$65
Equalizer FX40			
1982-1986.			
1982-1986		$40	$55
Equalizer FX40B			
1987-present. Eight bands for bass.			
1987-1999		$40	$55
Fet Preamp 210			
4 *1981-ca.1982.*			
1981-1982		$40	$55
Flanger 670			
1981-1982.			
1981-1982		$75	$100
Gate Loop FX30			
1980s		$30	$40
Graphic Equalizer EQ-610			
1980-ca.1982. Ten bands.			
1980-1982		$50	$65
Graphic Equalizer EQ-660			
1980-ca.1982. Six bands.			
1980-1982		$40	$55
Grunge FX69			
1993-present. Distortion.			
1993-2004		$35	$50
Hard Rock Distortion FX57			
1987-1994. With built-in delay.			
1987-1994		$35	$50
Harmonic Enhancer FX85			
1986-ca.1989.			
1986-1989		$35	$50
I. T. FX100			
1997. Intergrated Tube distortion, produces harmonics.			
1997		$50	$60
Ice Box FX64			
1996-present. Chorus, high EQ.			
1996-2002		$25	$35
Juice Box FX51			
1996-1997.			
1996-1997		$30	$40
Master Switch 225			
1988-ca.1989. A/B switch and loop selector.			
1988-1989		$30	$40
Meat Box FX32			
1994-1996.			
1994-1996		$40	$50
Metal Maniac FX58			
1990-1996.			
1990-1996		$40	$50

DOD Envelope Filter FX25B

DOD Death Metal FX86

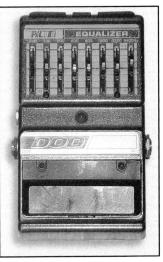

DOD Equalizer FX40B

To get the most from this book, be sure to read "Using *The Guide*" in the introduction.

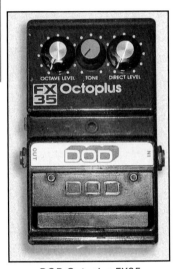

DOD Milk Box FX84

DOD Octoplus FX35

DOD Phasor 595-A

EFFECTS

MODEL YEAR	FEATURES	EXC. COND. LOW	HIGH
Metal Triple Play Guitar Effects System TR3M			
1994.			
1994		$40	$50
Metal X FX70			
1993-1996.			
1993-1996		$40	$50
Milk Box FX84			
1994-present.			
1994-1999		$40	$50
Mini-Chorus 460			
1981-ca.1982.			
1981-1982		$50	$75
Mixer 240			
1978-ca.1982.			
1978-1982		$25	$35
Momentary Footswitch			
Introduced in 1987. Temporally engages other boxes.			
1980s		$25	$35
Mystic Blues Overdrive FX102			
1998-present. Medium gain overdrive.			
1998-2004		$25	$30
Noise Gate 230			
1978-1982.			
1978-1982		$30	$40
Noise Gate FX30			
1982-ca.1987.			
1982-1987		$30	$40
Octoplus FX35			
1987-1996. Octaves.			
1987-1996		$40	$45
Overdrive Plus FX50B			
1986-1997.			
1986-1997		$35	$45
Overdrive Preamp 250			
1978-1982, 1995-present. Reissued in '95.			
1978-1982		$80	$100
1995-2002		$30	$45
Overdrive Preamp FX50			
1982-1985.			
1982-1985		$35	$45
Performer Compressor Limiter 525			
1981-1984.			
1981-1984		$55	$60
Performer Delay 585			
4 *1982-1985.*			
1982-1985		$60	$75
Performer Distortion 555			
1981-1984.			
1981-1984		$40	$50
Performer Flanger 575			
1981-1985.			
1981-1985		$40	$50
Performer Phasor 595			
1981-1984.			
1981-1984		$45	$55
Performer Stereo Chorus 565			
1981-1985.			
1981-1985	FET switching	$60	$75

MODEL YEAR	FEATURES	EXC. COND. LOW	HIGH
Performer Wah Filter 545			
1981-1984.			
1981-1984		$50	$75
Phasor 201			
1981-ca.1982. Reissued in '95.			
1981-1982		$70	$100
Phasor 401			
1978-1981.			
1978-1981		$70	$100
Phasor 490			
1980-ca.1982.			
1980-1982		$70	$100
Phasor FX20			
1982-1985.			
1982-1985		$40	$50
Psychoacoustic Processor FX87			
1988-1989.			
1988-1989		$40	$50
Punkifier FX76			
1997.			
1997		$40	$50
Resistance Mixer 240			
1978-ca.1982.			
1978-1982		$30	$35
Silencer FX27			
1988-ca.1989. Noise reducer.			
1988-1989		$35	$45
Stereo Chorus FX60			
1982-1986.			
1982-1986		$40	$50
Stereo Chorus FX65			
1986-1996. Light blue case.			
1986-1996		$40	$50
Stereo Flanger FX70			
1982-ca.1985.			
1982-1985		$40	$50
Stereo Flanger FX75			
1986-1987. Silver case with blue trim.			
1986-1987		$45	$55
Stereo Flanger FX75B			
1987-1997.			
1987-1997		$45	$55
Stereo Phasor FX20B			
1986-1999.			
1986-1999		$45	$55
Stereo Turbo Chorus FX67			
1988-1991.			
1988-1991		$40	$50
Super American Metal FX56B			
1992-1996.			
1992-1996		$35	$45
Super Stereo Chorus FX68			
1992-1996.			
1992-1996		$40	$50
Supra Distortion FX55B			
1986-present.			
1986-1999		$30	$40
Thrash Master FX59			
1990-1996.			
1990-1996		$30	$40

The *Vintage Guitar Price Guide* shows low to high values for items in all-original excellent condition, and, where applicable, with original case or cover.

MODEL YEAR	FEATURES	EXC. COND. LOW	HIGH

Votec Vocal Effects Processor and Mic preamp
1998-2001.

| 1998-2001 | | $60 | $65 |

Wah-Volume FX-17 (pedal)
1987-2000.

| 1987-2000 | | $45 | $55 |

Dredge-Tone
Located in Berkeley, California, Dredge-Tone offers effects and electronic kits.

DST Engineering
2001-present. Jeff Swanson and Bob Dettorre build reverb units in Bevly, Massachusetts. They also build amps.

Dunlop
Jim Dunlop, USA offers the Crybaby, MXR (see MXR), Rockman, High Gain, Heil Sound (see Heil), Tremolo, Jimi Hendrix, Rotovibe and Uni-Vibe brand effects.

Crybaby Bass
1985-present. Bass wah.

1985-1989		$75	$100
1990-1999		$75	$100
2000s	Black case	$30	$35

Crybaby Wah Pedal 535
1995-present. Multi-range pedal with an external boost control.

| 1995-1999 | | $70 | $90 |

Crybaby Wah-Wah GCB-95
1982-present. Dunlop began manufacturing the Crybaby in '82.

1982-1989		$55	$75
1990-1999		$45	$70
2000-2005		$40	$50

High Gain Volume + Boost Pedal
1983-1996.

| 1983-1996 | | $35 | $45 |

High Gain Volume Pedal
1983-present.

| 1983-1999 | | $40 | $50 |

Jimi Hendrix Fuzz (Round)
1987-1993.

| 1987-1993 | | $50 | $75 |

Rotovibe JH-4S Standard
1989-1998. Standard is finished in bright red enamel with chrome top.

| 1989-1998 | | $125 | $150 |

Tremolo Volume Plus TVP-1
1995-1998. Pedal.

| 1995-1998 | | $125 | $140 |

Uni-Vibe UV-1
1995-present. Rotating speaker effect.

| 1995-1999 | | $175 | $225 |
| 2000-2003 | | $175 | $200 |

Dynacord
1950-present. Dynacord is a German company that makes audio and pro sound amps, as well as other electronic equipment and is now owned by TELEX/EVI Audio (an U.S. company), which also owns the Electro-Voice brand. In the '60s they offered tape echo machines. In '94 a line of multi-effects processors were introduced under the Electro-Voice/Dynacord name, but by the following year they were just listed as Electro-Voice.

EchoCord
Introduced in 1959. Tape echo unit.

| 1960s | | $275 | $350 |

Dyno
See Dytronics.

Dytronics
Mid-1970s-early 1980s. The Japanese Dytronics company made a chorus rackmount unit for electric piano called the Dyno My Piano with flying piano keys or a lightning bolt on the front. Another version was called the Tri-Stereo Chorus and a third, called the Songbird, had a bird's head on the front.

CS-5/Dyno My Piano Tri Chorus/ Songbird
1970s. Tri-Stereo Chorus, 3 individual chorus settings which can be used all at once. Sold under all 3 brands/models.

| 1970s | | $2,500 | $3,000 |

EBow
See Heet Sound Products.

Ecco Fonic
The Ecco Fonic was distributed by Fender in 1958-'59.

Echo Unit
1958-1959. Reverb unit.

| 1958-1959 | With Brown case | $300 | $350 |

Echoplex
The Echoplex tape echo units were first sold under the Maestro brand. After Maestro dropped the Echoplex, it was marketed under the Market Electronics name from the late-'70s to the early-'80s. In the later '80s, Market Electronics was dropped from the ads and they were marketed under the Echoplex brand. Both the Market and Echoplex brands are listed here; for earlier models see Maestro. In '94, Gibson's Oberheim division introduced a rackmount unit called the Echoplex. In '01, it was relabeled as Gibson.

Echoplex EP3
1984-ca. 1988. Solidstate version.

| 1984-1988 | | $350 | $425 |

Echoplex EP4
1984-1991. Solidstate version.

| 1984-1991 | | $350 | $425 |

Dunlop Rotovibe

Dunlop Jimi Hendrix Wah

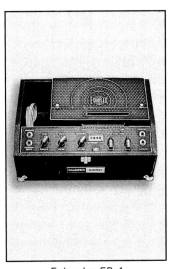

Echoplex EP-4

Effector 13 Disaster Fuzz

E-H Big Muff Pi reissue

E-H Bassballs

MODEL YEAR	FEATURES	EXC. COND. LOW	HIGH

Echoplex EP6T
1980-ca.1988. All-tube reissue of the EP2.

1980-1988		$400	$475

Effector 13
2002-present. Ever Was builds his guitar effects in Minneapolis, Minnesota. He was located in Austin, Texas until mid-'04.

EFX
1980s. Brand name of the Los Angeles-based EFX Center; they also offered a direct box and a powered pedal box/board.

Switch Box B287
1984. Dual effects loop selector.

1984		$25	$35

EKO
1959-1985, present. In the '60s and '70s EKO offered effects made by EME and JEN Elettronica, which also made Vox effects.

Electra
1971-1984. A guitar brand imported by St. Louis Music, Electra offered a line of effects in the late '70s.

Chorus 504CH
Ca.1975-ca.1980.

1975-1980		$55	$75

Compressor 502C/602C
1975-1980.

1975-1980		$45	$55

Distortion 500D
Ca.1976-ca.1980.

1976-1980		$55	$75

Flanger (stereo) 605F
Ca.1975-ca.1980.

1975-1980		$55	$75

Fuzz Wah
Ca.1975-ca.1980.

1975-1980		$75	$125

Pedal Drive 515AC
Ca.1976-ca.1980. Overdrive.

1975-1980		$40	$50

Phaser Model 501P
4 *Ca.1976-ca.1980.*

1975-1980		$50	$60

Phaser Model 875
1975-ca.1980.

1975-1980		$50	$60

Roto Phase I
1975-ca.1980. Small pocket phaser.

1975-1980		$70	$85

Roto Phase II
1975-ca.1980. Pedal phasor.

1975-1980		$80	$95

Electro-Harmonix
1968-1984, 1996-present. Founded by Mike Matthews in New York City, the company initially produced small plug-in boosters such as the LPB-1.

In '70, they unveiled the awe-inspiring Big Muff Pi fuzz and dozens of innovative pedals followed. After years of disputes, the nonunion E-H factory became the target of union organizers and a '81 union campaign, combining picketing and harrying of E-H employees, brought production to a halt. Matthews' financier then cut his funding, and in early '82, E.H. filed for bankruptcy. Later that year, Matthews was able to reopen and continue through '84. In '96, he again began producing reissues of many of his classic designs as well as new designs.

3 Phase Liner
1981.

1981		$50	$60

5X Junction Mixer
1977-1981.

1977-1981		$30	$40

10 Band Graphic Equalizer
1977-1981. Includes footswitch.

1977-1981		$60	$70

16-Second Digital Delay
Early-1980s, 2004-present. An updated version was reissued in '04.

1980s	With foot controller	$650	$800
1980s	Without foot controller	$500	$650
1990s		$325	$500
2004		$275	$375

Attack Equalizer
1975-1981. Active EQ, a.k.a. "Knock Out."

1975-1981		$150	$200

Attack/Decay
1980-1981. Tape reverse simulator.

1980-1981		$200	$225

Bad Stone Phase Shifter
1975-1981.

1970s	Three knobs	$200	$250
1970s	Two knobs, color switch	$175	$225

Bass Micro-Synthesizer
1981-1984, 1999-present. Analog synthesizer sounds, reissued in '99.

1981-1984		$225	$300
1999-2004		$150	$175

Bassballs
1978-1984, 1999-present. Bass envelope filter/distortion, reissued in '98.

1978-1984		$200	$225

Big Muff Pi
1971-1984. Sustain, floor unit, issued in 3 different looks, as described below. Reissued in '96.

1970s	Earlier black graphics, knobs in triangle pattern	$325	$375
1970s	Later red/black graphics, 1/2" letters	$150	$225
1980s	Red/black graphics, logo in 1" letters	$125	$200

MODEL YEAR	FEATURES	EXC. COND. LOW	HIGH

Big Muff Pi (reissue)
1996-present. Originally made in Russia, but currently both Russian- and U.S.-made versions are available.

| 1996-2005 | Russian-made | $40 | $45 |

Big Muff Sovtek
2000s. Big Muff Pi, Electro Harmonix, and Sovtek logos on an olive green case.

| 2000s | | $100 | $125 |

Black Finger Compressor Sustainer
1977, 2003-present. Original has 3 knobs in triangle pattern, reissued in '03.

| 1977 | | $125 | $225 |
| 2003-2004 | | $75 | $100 |

Clap Track
1980-1984. Drum effect.

| 1980-1984 | | $40 | $60 |

Clone Theory
1977-1981. Chorus effect.

| 1977-1981 | The Clone Theory logo | $150 | $175 |

Crash Pad
1980-1984. Percussion synth.

| 1980-1984 | | $40 | $60 |

Crying Tone Pedal
1976-1978. Wah-wah.

| 1976-1978 | | $175 | $225 |

Deluxe Big Muff Pi
1978-1981. Sustain, AC version of Big Muff Pi, includes a complete Soul Preacher unit.

| 1978-1981 | Red graphics | $125 | $200 |

Deluxe Electric Mistress Flanger
1977-1983, 1996-present. AC, reissued in '96.

| 1977-1979 | | $150 | $250 |
| 1980-1983 | | $125 | $175 |

Deluxe Memory Man
1977-1983, 1996-present. Echo and delay, featured 4 knobs '77-'78, from '79-'83 it has 5 knobs and added vibrato and chorus. Reissued in '96.

1977-1978	Four knobs	$225	$300
1979-1983	Five knobs	$200	$275
1996-2004		$150	$165

Deluxe Octave Multiplexer
1977-1981.

| 1977-1981 | | $200 | $250 |

Digital Delay/Chorus
1981-84. With digital chorus.

| 1981-1984 | | $250 | $300 |

Digital Rhythm Matrix DRM-15
1981-1984.

| 1981-1984 | | $225 | $250 |

Digital Rhythm Matrix DRM-16
1979-1983.

| 1979-1983 | | $225 | $250 |

Digital Rhythm Matrix DRM-32
1981-1984.

| 1981-1984 | | $225 | $250 |

Doctor Q Envelope Follower
1976-1983, 2001-present. For bass or guitar, reissued in '01.

| 1976-1983 | | $150 | $200 |
| 2001-2004 | | $30 | $35 |

Domino Theory
1981. Sound sensitive light tube.

| 1981 | | $50 | $100 |

Echo 600
1981.

| 1981 | | $175 | $225 |

Echoflanger
1977-1982. Flange, slapback, chorus, filter.

| 1977-1982 | | $200 | $250 |

Electric Mistress Flanger
1976-1984.

| 1976-1984 | | $175 | $275 |

Electronic Metronome
1978-1980.

| 1978-1980 | | $25 | $30 |

Frequency Analyzer
1977-1984, 2001-present. Ring modulator, reissued in '01.

| 1977-1984 | | $200 | $250 |

Full Double Tracking Effect
1978-1981. Doubling, slapback.

| 1978-1981 | | $100 | $150 |

Fuzz Wah
Introduced around 1974.

| 1970s | | $175 | $225 |

Golden Throat
1977-1984.

| 1977-1984 | | $300 | $400 |

Golden Throat Deluxe
1977-1979. Deluxe has a built-in monitor amp.

| 1977-1979 | | $300 | $400 |

Golden Throat II
1978-1981.

| 1978-1981 | | $150 | $225 |

Guitar Synthesizer
1981. Sold for $1,495 in May '81.

| 1981 | | $225 | $300 |

Hog's Foot Bass Booster
1977-1980.

| 1977-1978 | | $70 | $90 |

Holy Grail
2002-present. Digital reverb.

| 2002-2004 | | $80 | $90 |

Hot Foot
1977-1978. Rocker pedal turns knob of other E-H effects.

| 1977-1978 | Gold case, red graphics | $75 | $100 |

Hot Tubes
1978-1984. Overdrive, reissued in '01.

| 1978-1984 | | $125 | $200 |

Linear Power Booster LPB-1
1968-1983.

| 1976-1979 | | $55 | $80 |
| 1980-1983 | | $45 | $75 |

Linear Power Booster LPB-2
Ca.1968-1983.

| 1968-1983 | | $90 | $100 |

Little Big Muff Pi
1976-1980. Sustain, 1-knob floor unit.

| 1976-1980 | | $150 | $175 |

E-H Black Finger

E-H Little Big Muff

E-H Hot Foot

EFFECTS

E-H Octave Multiplexer

E-H Q-Tron

E-H Small Clone EH4600

MODEL YEAR FEATURES	EXC. COND. LOW	HIGH
Memory Man		
1976-1984. Analog delay, reissued in '01.		
1976-1979	$250	$300
1980-1984	$150	$250
Micro Synthesizer		
1978-1984, 1998-present. Mini keyboard phaser, reissued in '98.		
1978-1979	$225	$250
1978-1984	$225	$250
1998-2004	$150	$170
Mini Q-Tron		
2002-present. Battery-operated smaller version of Q-Tron envelope follower		
2002-2004	$40	$45
Mini-Mixer		
1978-1981. Mini mic mixer, reissued in '01.		
1978-1981	$30	$40
MiniSynthesizer		
1981-1983. Mini keyboard with phaser.		
1981-1983	$300	$400
MiniSynthesizer With Echo		
1981.		
1981	$375	$500
Mole Bass Booster		
1968-1978.		
1968-1969	$60	$80
1970-1978	$40	$60
Muff Fuzz Crying Tone		
1977-1978. Fuzz, wah.		
1977-1978	$150	$250
Octave Multiplexer Floor Unit		
1976-1980.		
1976-1980	$175	$275
Octave Multiplexer Pedal		
1976-1977, 2001-present. Reissued in '01.		
1976-1977	$150	$250
2001-2004	$40	$45
Panic Button		
1981. Siren sounds for drum.		
1981	$30	$40
Poly Chorus		
1981, 1999-present. Same as Echoflanger, reissued in '99.		
1981	$175	$200
1999-2002	$125	$150
Polyphase		
1979-1981. With envelope.		
1979-1981	$175	$225
Pulsar		
2004-present. Variable wave form tremolo.		
2004	$45	$55
Pulse Modulator		
Ca.1968 -ca.1972. Triple tremolo.		
1968-1969	$250	$325
1970-1972	$200	$250
Q-Tron		
1997-present. Envelope controlled filter.		
1997-2003	$125	$175

MODEL YEAR FEATURES	EXC. COND. LOW	HIGH
Q-Tron +		
1999-present. With added effects loop and Attack Response switch.		
1999-2003	$70	$80
Queen Triggered Wah		
1976-1978. Wah/Envelope Filter.		
1976-1978	$125	$150
Random Tone Generator RTG		
1981.		
1981	$40	$60
Rhythm 12 (rhythm machine)		
1978.		
1978	$75	$125
Rolling Thunder		
1980-1981. Percussion synth.		
1980-1981	$40	$50
Screaming Bird Treble Booster		
Ca.1968-1980. In-line unit.		
1968-1980	$75	$100
Screaming Tree Treble Booster		
1977-1981. Floor unit.		
1977-1981	$100	$150
Sequencer Drum		
1981. Drum effect.		
1981	$40	$50
Slapback Echo		
1977-1978. Stereo.		
1977-1978	$150	$200
Small Clone EH4600		
1983-1984, 1999-present. Analog chorus, depth and rate controls, purple face plate, white logo, reissued in '99.		
1983-1984	$150	$200
1999-2003	$35	$40
Small Stone Phase Shifter		
1975-1984, 1996-present. Reissued in '96 (both Russian- and U.S.-made versions reissues were made).		
1975-1979	$175	$225
1980-1984	$125	$175
Soul Preacher		
1977-1983. Compressor sustainer.		
1977-1983	$100	$150
Space Drum/Super Space Drum		
1980-1981. Percussion synthesizer.		
1980-1981	$125	$175
Switch Blade		
1977-1983. A-B Box.		
1977-1983	$45	$55
Talking Pedal		
1977-1978. Creates vowel sounds.		
1977-1978	$350	$550
The Silencer		
1976-1981. Noise elimination.		
1976-1981	$60	$80
The Wiggler		
2002-present. All-tube modulator including pitch vibrato and volume tremolo.		
2002-2004	$100	$110
The Worm		
2002-present. Wah/Phaser.		
2002-2004	$55	$65

The *Vintage Guitar Price Guide* shows low to high values for items in all-original excellent condition, and, where applicable, with original case or cover.

MODEL		EXC. COND.	
YEAR	FEATURES	LOW	HIGH

Tube Zipper
2001-present. Tube (2x12AX7EHs) envelope follower.

2001-2003		$100	$120

Vocoder
1978-1981. Modulates voice with instrument.

1978-1981	Rackmount	$425	$525

Volume Pedal
1978-1981.

1978-1981		$45	$65

Y-Triggered Filter
1976-1977.

1976-1977		$140	$160

Zipper Envelope Follower
1976-1978. The Tube Zipper was introduced in 2001.

1976-1978		$200	$300

Elk
Late-1960s. Japanese company Elk Gakki Co., Ltd. mainly made guitars and amps, but did offer effects as well.

Elka
In the late '60s or early '70s, Italian organ and synthesizer company Elka-Orla (later just Elka) offered a few effects, likely made by JEN Elettronica (Vox, others).

EMMA Electronic
Line of guitar effects built in Denmark.
ReezaFRATzitz RF-1
2004-present. Overdrive and distortion, red case.

2004		$80	$95

EMS
1969-1979. Peter Zinnovieff's English synth company (Electronic Music Studios) also offered a guitar synthesizer. The company has reopened to work on original EMS gear.

Epiphone
Epiphone pedals are labeled "G.A.S Guitar Audio System" and were offered from around 1988 to '91.
Pedals
Various models with years available.

1988-1989	Chorus EP-CH-70	$35	$45
1988-1989	Delay EP-DE-80	$45	$60
1988-1991	Compressor EP-CO-20	$35	$40
1988-1991	Distortion EP-DI-10	$35	$45
1988-1991	Flanger EP-FL-60	$40	$55
1988-1991	Overdrive EP-OD-30	$35	$45

Ernie Ball
Ernie Ball owned a music store in Tarzana, California, when he noticed the demand for a better selection of strings. The demand for his Slinky strings grew to the point where, in '67, he sold the store to concentrate on strings. He went on to produce the Earthwood brand of guitars and basses

from '72-'85. In '84, Ball purchased the Music Man company.
Volume Pedal
1977-present.

1977-2004		$35	$65

Euthymia Electronics
Line of guitar effects built by Erik Miller in Alameda, California.

Eventide
1971-present. This New Jersey electronics manufacturer has offered studio effects since the late '70s.

EXR
The EXR Corporation was located in Brighton, Michigan.
Projector
1983-ca.1984. Psychoacoustic enhancer pedal.

1983-1984		$65	$75

Projector SP III
1983-ca.1984. Psychoacoustic enhancer pedal, volume pedal/sound boost.

1983-1984		$65	$70

Farfisa
The organ company offered effects pedals in the 1960s. Their products were manufactured in Italy by the Italian accordion company and distributed by Chicago Musical Insturments.
Model VIP 345 Organ
Mid-1960s. Portable organ with Syntheslalom used in the rock and roll venue.

1960s		$500	$600

Repeater

1969		$100	$150

Sferaasound
1960s. Vibrato pedal for a Farfisa Organ but it works well with the guitar, gray case.

1960s		$275	$375

Wah/Volume

1969		$100	$150

Fender
Although Fender has flirted with effects since the 1950s (the volume/volume-tone pedal and the EccoFonic), it concentrated mainly on guitars and amps. Fender effects ranged from the sublime to the ridiculous, from the tube Reverb to the Dimension IV.
Blender Fuzz
1968-1977. Battery operated fuzz and sustain. In '05, Fender issued the Blender Custom.

1968-1969		$350	$375
1970-1977		$275	$300

Contempo Organ
1967-1968. Portable organ, all solidstate, 61 keys including a 17-key bass section, catalog shows with red cover material.

1967-1968		$525	$550

E-H Wiggler

Ernie Ball Volume Pedal

Fender Blender

EFFECTS

Fender Electronic Echo Chamber

Fender Fuzz Wah

Flip Tube Echo

MODEL YEAR	FEATURES	EXC. COND. LOW	HIGH

Dimension IV
1968-1970. Multi-effects unit using an oil-filled drum.

1968-1970		$150	$200

Echo-Reverb
1966-1970. Solidstate, echo-reverb effect produced by rotating metal disk, black tolex, silver grille.

1966-1970		$175	$300

Electronic Echo Chamber
1962-1968. Solidstate tape echo, up to 400 ms of delay, rectangle box with 2 controls '62-'67, slanted front '67-'68.

1962-1968		$275	$325

Fuzz-Wah
1968-1984. Has Fuzz and Wah switches on sides of pedal '68-'73, has 3 switches above the pedal '74-'84.

1968-1973	Switches on side	$175	$225
1974-1984	Switches above	$150	$200

Phaser
1975-1977. AC powered.

1975-1977		$125	$175

Reverb Unit
1961-1966, 1975-1978. Fender used a wide variety of tolex coverings in the early-'60s as the coverings matched those on the amps. Initially, Fender used rough blond tolex, then rough brown tolex, followed by smooth white or black tolex.

1961	Blond Tolex, Oxblood grille	$1,150	$1,450
1961	Brown Tolex	$1,000	$1,200
1962	Blond Tolex, Oxblood grille	$1,100	$1,400
1962	Brown Tolex, Wheat grille	$1,000	$1,150
1963	Brown Tolex	$800	$1,000
1963	Rough Blond Tolex	$1,000	$1,300
1963	Smooth White Tolex	$900	$1,300
1964	Black Tolex	$750	$950
1964	Brown Tolex, gold grille	$800	$1,000
1964	Smooth White Tolex	$1,000	$1,300
1965	Black Tolex	$750	$950
1966	Black Tolex	$700	$900
1966	Solidstate, flat cabinet	$150	$350
1975-1978	Tube reverb reinstated	$500	$550

Reverb Unit Reissue Models
1994-present. Reissue spring/tube Reverb Units with various era cosmetics as listed below.

1990s	'63 brown tolex	$275	$325
1990s	'63 white (limited run)	$325	$375
1990s	Blackface	$325	$350
1990s	Tweed (limited run)	$350	$400

Tone and Volume Foot Pedal
1954-1984.

1960s		$125	$175

Vibratone
1967-1972. Leslie-type speaker cabinet made specifically for the guitar, 2-speed motor.

1960s		$750	$850

MODEL YEAR	FEATURES	EXC. COND. LOW	HIGH

FlexiSound
FlexiSound products were made in Lancaster, Pennsylvania.

F. S. Clipper
1975-ca.1976. Distortion, plugged directly into guitar jack.

1975-1976		$55	$65

The Beefer
1975. Power booster, plugged directly into guitar jack.

1975		$40	$50

Flip
Line of tube effects by Guyatone and distributed in the U.S. by Godlyke Distributing.

TD-X Tube Echo
2004-present. Hybrid tube power delay pedal.

2004		$90	$100

FM Acoustics
Made in Switzerland.

E-1 Pedal
1975. Volume, distortion, filter pedal.

1975		$70	$80

Foxx
Foxx pedals are readily identifiable by their fur-like covering. They slunk onto the scene in 1971 and were extinct by '78. Made by Hollywood's Ridinger Associates, their most notable product was the Tone Machine fuzz. Foxx-made pedals also have appeared under various brands such as G and G, Guild, Yamaha and Sears Roebuck, generally without fur.

Clean Machine
1974-1978.

1974-1978		$250	$275

Down Machine
1971-1977. Bass wah.

1971-1977	Blue case	$250	$275

Foot Phaser
1975-1977.

1975-1977		$300	$650

Fuzz and Wa and Volume
1974-1978.

1974-1978		$300	$350

Guitar Synthesizer I
1975.

1975		$300	$350

O.D. Machine
1972-ca.1975.

1972-1975		$150	$200

Phase III
1975-1978.

1975-1978		$100	$150

Tone Machine
1971-1978. Fuzz with Octave.

1971-1978		$375	$400

Wa and Volume
1971-1978.

1971-1978		$200	$225

MODEL YEAR FEATURES	EXC. COND. LOW	HIGH

Wa Machine
1971-ca.1978.

| 1971-1978 | $150 | $200 |

Framptone

2000-present. Founded by Peter Frampton, Framptone offers hand-made guitar effects.

Frantone

1994-present. Effects and accessories hand built in New York City.

Fulltone

1991-present. Fulltone effects are based on some of the classic effects of the past. Fulltone was started in Los Angeles, California by Michael Fuller who says the company was born out of his love for Jimi Hendrix and fine vintage pedals.

Deja Vibe
1991-2002. UniVibe-type pedal, later models have a Vintage/Modern switch. Stereo version also available. Now offerered in Mini version.

| 1991-2004 Mono | $175 | $200 |

Deja Vibe II
1997-present. Like Deja Vibe but with built-in speed control. Stereo version also available.

| 1997-2001 Mono | $200 | $225 |

Distortion Pro
2000s. Red case, volume and distortion knobs with four voicing controls.

| 2000s | $125 | $150 |

Fat Boost
2001-present. Clean boost, silver-sparkle case, volume and drive knobs.

| 2001-2003 | $125 | $135 |

Full-Drive 2
1995-present. Blue case, four control knobs.

| 1995-2000 | $120 | $145 |

Octafuzz
1996-present. Copy of the Tycobrahe Octavia.

| 1996-1999 | $85 | $100 |

Soul Bender
1994-present. Volume, tone and dirt knobs.

| 1994-2002 | $100 | $125 |

Supa-Trem
1995-present. Black case, white Supa-Trem logo, rate and mix controls.

| 1995-2002 | $100 | $125 |

Tube Tape Echo TTE
2004-present. EchoPlex style unit with a white body and a black suitcase. Tube Tape Echo logo on top.

| 2004 | $725 | $850 |

Furman Sound

1993-present. Located in Petaluma, California, Furman makes audio and video signal processors and AC power conditioning products for music and other markets.

MODEL YEAR FEATURES	EXC. COND. LOW	HIGH

LC-2 Limiter Compressor
1990s. Rackmount unit with a black suitcase and red knobs.

| 1990s | $40 | $50 |

PQ3 Parametric EQ
1990s. Rackmount preamp and equalizer.

| 1998-1999 | $110 | $150 |

PQ6 Parametric Stereo

| 1990s | $135 | $175 |

RV1 Reverb Rackmount

| 1990s | $110 | $150 |

George Dennis

1991-present. Founded by George Burgerstein, original products were a line of effects pedals. In '96 they added a line of tube amps. The company is located in Prague, Czech Republic.

Gibson

Gibson did offer a few effects bearing their own name, but most were sold under the Maestro name (see that listing).

Echoplex Digital Pro
1994-present. Rackmount unit with digital recording, sampling and digital delay. Labeled as just Echoplex until '01 when Gibson name added.,

| 1994-2003 | $700 | $850 |

GA-3RV Reverb Unit
1964-1967. Small, compact, spring reverb unit, black tolex, gray grille.

| 1964-1967 | $325 | $400 |

GA-4RE Reverb-Echo Unit
1964-1967. Small, compact, lightweight accessory reverb-echo unit that produces complete reverberation and authentic echo, utilizes Gibson's "electronic memory" system for both reverb and echo, black tolex, gray grille.

| 1964-1967 | $450 | $550 |

Godbout

Sold a variety of effects do-it-yourself kits in the 1970s. Difficult to value because quality depends on skills of builder.

Effects Kits

| 1970s | $20 | $30 |

Goodrich Sound

Late-1970s. Goodrich was located in Grand Haven, Michigan.

Match Box 33670 Line Boost
Early-1980s. Small rectangular in and out box with control knob.

| 1980s | $45 | $55 |

Volume Pedal 6122
1979-ca.1980. Uses a potentiometer.

| 1970s | $45 | $55 |

Volume Pedal 6400ST
1979-ca.1980. Uses a potentiometer.

| 1970s | $45 | $55 |

Volume Pedal 6402
1979-ca.1980. Uses photocell.

| 1970s | $45 | $55 |

Frantone Vibutron

Fulltone Octafuzz

George Dennis Elite Wah

EFFECTS

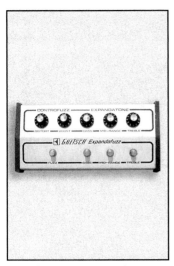

Gretsch Expandafuzz

Heil Sound Talk Box

Guyatone Silver Machine

MODEL YEAR	FEATURES	EXC. COND. LOW	HIGH

Gretsch

Gretsch has offered a limited line of effects from time to time.

Controfuzz

Mid-1970s. Distortion.

| 1970s | | $150 | $225 |

Deluxe Reverb Unit Model 6149

1963-1969. Similar to Gibson's GA-1 introduced around the same time.

| 1963-1969 | | $400 | $500 |

Expandafuzz

Mid-1970s. Distortion.

| 1970s | | $150 | $200 |

Reverb Unit Model 6144 Preamp Reverb

1963-1967. Approximately 17 watts, preamp functionality, no speaker.

| 1963-1967 | | $250 | $350 |

Tremofect

Mid-1970s. Tremolo effect, 3-band EQ, speed, effect, bass, total, and treble knobs.

| 1970s | | $225 | $300 |

Guild

Guild marketed effects made by Binson, Electro-Harmonix, Foxx, WEM and Applied in the 1960s and '70s.

Copicat

1960s-1979. Echo.

| 1970s | | $300 | $400 |

DE-20 Auto-Rhythm Unit

1971-1974. 50 watt rhythm accompaniment unit. Included 20 rhythms and a separate instrument channel with its own volume control. 1x12" plus tweeter.

| 1971-1974 | | $200 | $300 |

Echorec (by Binson)

Ca.1960-1979. This was different stripped-down version of the Binson Echorec.

| 1960s | | $375 | $475 |

Foxey Lady Fuzz

1968-1977. Distortion, sustain.

| 1968-1975 | Two knobs, made by E-H | $200 | $250 |
| 1976-1977 | 3 knobs in row, same as Big Muff | $150 | $200 |

Fuzz Wah FW-3

1975-ca.1979. Distortion, volume, wah, made by Foxx.

| 1970s | | $150 | $175 |

HH Echo Unit

1976-ca.1979.

| 1970s | | $200 | $300 |

VW-1

1975-ca.1979. Volume, wah, made by Foxx.

| 1970s | | $200 | $250 |

Guyatone

1998-present. Imported stomp boxes, tape echo units and outboard reverb units distributed by Godlyke Distributing.

MODEL YEAR	FEATURES	EXC. COND. LOW	HIGH

HAO

Line of guitar effects built in Japan by J.E.S. International, distributed in the U.S. by Godlyke.

Heathkit

1960s. Unassembled kits sold at retail.

TA-28 Distortion Booster

1960s. Fuzz assembly kit, heavy '60s super fuzz, case-by-case quality depending on the builder.

| 1960s | | $140 | $150 |

Heavy Metal Products

Mid-1970s. From Alto Loma, California, products for the heavy metal guitarist.

Raunchbox Fuzz

1975-1976.

| 1975-1976 | | $75 | $100 |

Switchbox

1975-1976. A/B box.

| 1975-1976 | | $25 | $35 |

Heet Sound Products

1974-present. The E Bow concept goes back to '67, but a hand-held model wasn't available until '74. Made in Los Angeles, California.

E Bow

1974-1979, 1985-1987, 1994-present. The Energy Bow, hand-held electro-magnetic string driver.

| 1974-1979 | | $50 | $60 |

E Bow for Pedal Steels

1979. Hand-held electro-magnetic string driver.

| 1979 | | $35 | $55 |

Heil Sound

1960-present. Founded by Bob Heil, Marissa, Illinois. Created the talk box technology as popularized by Peter Frampton. In the '60s and '70s Heil was dedicated to innovative products for the music industry. In the late-'70s, innovative creations were more in the amateur radio market, and by the '90s Heil's focus was on the home theater market. The Heil Sound Talkbox was reissued by Jim Dunlop USA in '89.

Talk Box

1976-ca.1980, 1989-present. Reissued bu Dunlop in '89.

1976-1980		$100	$125
1989-1999		$75	$85
2000-2004		$70	$80

High Gain

See listing under Dunlop.

Hohner

Hohner offered effects in the late-1970s.

Dirty Booster

1977-ca.1978. Distortion.

| 1977-1978 | | $55 | $65 |

Dirty Wah Wah'er

1977-ca.1978. Adds distortion.

| 1977-1978 | | $65 | $75 |

MODEL		EXC. COND.	
YEAR	FEATURES	LOW	HIGH

Fuzz Wah

1970s. Morley-like volume pedal with volume knob and fuzz knob, switch for soft or hard fuzz, gray box with black foot pedal.

1970s		$65	$75

Multi-Exciter

1977-ca.1978. Volume, wah, surf, tornado, siren.

1977-1978		$60	$70

Tape Echo/Echo Plus

1970s. Black alligator suitcase.

1970s		$200	$300

Tri-Booster

1977-ca.1978. Distortion, sustain.

1977-1978		$55	$65

Vari-Phaser

1977-ca.1978.

1977-1978		$55	$65

Vol-Kicker Volume Pedal

1977-ca.1978.

1977-1978		$30	$40

Wah-Wah'er

1977-ca.1978. Wah, volume.

1977-1978		$55	$65

HomeBrew Electronics

2001-present. Stomp box effects hand made by Joel and Andrea Weaver in Glendale, Arizona.

Ibanez

Ibanez effects were introduced ca. 1974, and were manufactured by Japan's Maxon Electronics. Although results were mixed at first, a more uniform and modern product line, including the now legenday Tube Screamer, built Ibanez's reputation for quality. They still produce a wide range of effects.

60s Fuzz FZ5 (Soundtank)

1991-1992, 1996-1998. Fuzz with level, tone and distortion controls, black plastic case, green label.

1990s		$30	$35

7th Heaven SH7 (Tone-Lok)

2000-2004. Lo, high, drive and level controls, gray-silver case, blue-green label.

2000-2004		$25	$35

Acoustic Effects PT-4

1993-1998. Acoustic guitar multi-effect with compressor/limiter, tone shaper, stereo chorus, digital reverb, with power supply.

1993-1998		$75	$100

Analog Delay 202 (Rack Mount)

1981-1983. Rack mount with delay, doubling, flanger, stereo chorus, dual inputs with tone and level.

1981-1983		$200	$250

Analog Delay AD9

1982-1984. 3 control analog delay, Hot Pink metal case.

1982-1984		$200	$275

Analog Delay AD-80

1980-1981. Pink case.

1980-1981		$200	$300

Analog Delay AD99

1996-1998. Reissue, 3 control knobs and on/off switch, winged-hand logo, black case.

1996-1998		$125	$150

Analog Delay AD-100 (Table Unit)

1981-1983. Stand-alone table/studio unit (not rack mount) with power cord.

1981-1983		$200	$250

Auto Filter AF9

1982-1984. Replaces AF201 model.

1982-1984		$175	$200

Auto Filter AF201

1981. Two min-max sliders, 3 mode toggle switches, orange metal case.

1981		$175	$200

Auto Wah AW5 (SoundTank)

1994-1999. Plastic case SoundTank series.

1994-1999		$35	$45

Auto Wah AW7 (Tone-Lok)

2000-present. Silver case.

2000-2004		$25	$35

Bass Compressor BP10

1986-1991.

1986-1991		$70	$80

Bi-Mode Chorus BC-9

1984. Dual channel for 2 independent speed and width settings.

1984		$75	$100

Chorus CS-505

1980-1981. Speed and depth controls, gray-blue case, stereo or mono input, battery or external power option.

1980-1981		$100	$125

Chorus Flanger CF7 (Tone-Lok)

1999-present. Speed, depth, delay, regeneration controls, mode and crazy switches.

1999-2004		$40	$45

Classic Flange FL99

1997-1999. Analog reissue, silver metal case, winged-hand artwork, 4 controls, 2 footswitch buttons.

1997-1999		$90	$110

Classic Phase PH99

1995-1999. Analog reissue, silver metal case, winged-hand artwork, speed, depth, feedback, effect level controls, intense and bypass footswitches.

1995-1999		$90	$110

Compressor CP-5 (SoundTank)

1991-1998.

1991-1998		$25	$35

Compressor Limiter CP9

1982-1984.

1982-1984		$100	$125

Compressor CP10

1986-1992.

1986-1992		$75	$80

Compressor CP-830

1975-1979.

1975-1979		$100	$125

Compressor II CP-835

1980-1981.

1980-1981		$100	$125

Hohner Tri-Dirty Booster

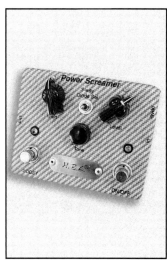

HomeBrew Power Screamer

Ibanez Classic Phase PH-99

EFFECTS

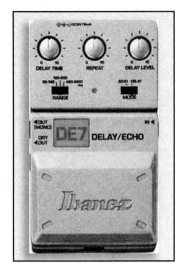

Ibanez DE7 Delay/Echo

Ibanez Flanger FL-9

Ibanez LA Metal LM7

MODEL YEAR	FEATURES	EXC. COND. LOW	HIGH
Delay Champ CD10			
1986-1989. Red case, 3 knobs.			
1986-1989		$125	$150
Delay Echo DE-7 (Tone-Lok)			
1999-present. Stereo delay/echo.			
1999-2004		$45	$55
Delay Harmonizer DM-1000			
1983-1984. Rack mount, with chorus, 9 control knobs.			
1983-1984		$175	$225
Delay III DDL20 Digital Delay			
1988-1989. Filtering, doubling, slap back, echo S, echo M, echo L, Seafoam Green coloring on pedal.			
1988-1989		$100	$125
Delay PDD1 (DPC Series)			
1988-1989. Programmable Digital Delay (PDD) with display screen.			
1988-1989		$125	$150
Digital Chorus DSC10			
1990-1992. 3 control knobs and slider selection toggle.			
1990-1992		$75	$100
Digital Delay DL5 (SoundTank)			
1991-1998.			
1991-1998		$40	$50
Digital Delay DL10			
1989-1992. Digital Delay made in Japan, blue case, 3 green control knobs, stompbox.			
1989-1992		$100	$125
Distortion DS7 (Tone-Lok)			
2000-present. Drive, tone, and level controls.			
2000-2004		$45	$50
Distortion Charger DS10			
1986-1989.			
1986-1989		$70	$90
Echo Machine EM5 (SoundTank)			
1996-1998. Simulates tape echo.			
1996-1998		$50	$60
Fat Cat Distortion FC10			
1987-1989. 3-knob pedal with distortion, tone, and level controls.			
1987-1989		$50	$75
Flanger FFL5 (Master Series)			
1984-1985. Speed, regeneration, width, D-time controls, battery or adapter option.			
1984-1985		$70	$90
Flanger FL5 (SoundTank)			
1991-1998.			
1991-1998		$30	$40
Flanger FL9			
1982-1984. Yellow case.			
1982-1984		$100	$150
Flanger FL-301			
1979-1982. Mini flanger, 3 knobs, called the FL-301 DX in late '81-'82.			
1979-1982		$100	$125
Flanger FL-305			
1976-1979. Five knobs.			
1976-1979		$100	$125

MODEL YEAR	FEATURES	EXC. COND. LOW	HIGH
Flying Pan FP-777			
1976-1979. Auto pan/phase shifter, 4 control knobs, phase on/off button, pan on/off button, silver metal case with blue trim and Flying Pan winged-hand logo.			
1976-1979		$500	$800
Fuzz FZ7 (Tone-Lok)			
2000-present. Drive, tone and level controls, gray-silver case, blue-green FZ7 label.			
2000-2004		$50	$55
Graphic Bass EQ BE10			
1986-1992. Later labeled as the BEQ10.			
1986-1992		$60	$80
Graphic EQ GE9			
1982-1984. Six EQ sliders, 1 overall volume slider, turquoise blue case.			
1982-198		$60	$80
Graphic EQ GE10			
1986-1992. Eight sliders.			
1986-1992		$60	$80
Graphic Equalizer GE-601 (808 Series)			
1980-1981. 7-slider EQ, aqua blue metal case.			
1980-1981		$75	$100
Guitar Multi-Processor PT5			
1993-1997. Floor unit, programmable with 25 presets and 25 user presets, effects include distortion, chorus, flanger, etc, green case.			
1993-1997		$100	$125
LA Metal LM7			
1988-1989. Silver case.			
1988-1989		$55	$65
LoFi LF7 (Tone-Lok)			
2000-present. Filter, 4 knobs.			
2000-2004		$25	$35
Metal Charger MS10			
1986-1992. Distortion, level, attack, punch and edge control knobs, green case.			
1986-1992		$55	$65
Metal Screamer MSL			
1985. 3 control knobs.			
1985		$55	$65
Modern Fusion MF-5 (SoundTank)			
1990-1991. Level, tone and distortion controls.			
1990-1991		$50	$55
Modulation Delay PDM1			
1988-1989. Programmable Digital Modulation pedal.			
1988-1989		$100	$125
Modulation Delay DM1000			
1983-1984. Rack mount with delay, reverb, modulation.			
1983-1984		$100	$125
Modulation Delay DM500			
1983-1984. Rack mount.			
1983-1984		$75	$100
Mostortion MT10			
1990-1992. Mos-FET circuit distortion pedal, 5 control knobs, green case.			
1990-1992		$50	$60

MODEL YEAR	FEATURES	EXC. COND. LOW	HIGH

Multi-Effect UE-300 (floor unit)
1983-1984. Floor unit, 4 footswitches for super metal, digital delay, digital stereo chorus, and master power, 3 delay modes.

1983-1984		$275	$350

Multi-effect UE-300B (floor unit)
1983-1984. Floor unit for bass.

1983-1984		$275	$350

Multi-Effect UE-400 (rackmount)
1980-1984. Rack mount with foot switch.

1980-1984		$300	$375

Multi-Effect UE-405 (rackmount)
1981-1984. Rack mount with analog delay, parametric EQ, compressor/limiter, stereo chorus and loop.

1981-1984		$300	$375

Noise Buster NB10
1988-1989. Eliminates 60-cycle hum and other outside signals, metal case.

1988-1989		$70	$75

Overdrive OD-850
1975-1979.

1975-1979		$300	$400

Overdrive II OD-855
1977-1979. Distortion, tone, and level controls, yellow/green case, large Overdrive II logo.

1977-1979		$300	$400

Pan Delay DPL10
1990-1992. Royal Blue case, 3 green control knobs.

1990-1992		$100	$125

Parametric EQ PQ9
1982-1984.

1982-1984		$85	$100

Parametric EQ PQ401
1981. 3 sliders, dial-in knob, light aqua blue case.

1981		$95	$145

Phase Tone II PT-707
1976-1979. Blue box, 1 knob, script logo for first 2 years.

1976-1979		$100	$130

Phase Tone PT-909
1979-1982. Blue box, 3 knobs, early models with flat case (logo at bottom or later in the middle) or later wedge case.

1979-1982		$140	$150

Phase Tone PT-999
1975-1979. Script logo, 1 knob, round footswitch, becomes PT-909.

1975-1979		$125	$150

Phase Tone PT-1000
1974-1975. Morley-style pedal phase, light blue case, early model of Phase Tone.

1974-1975		$200	$300

Phaser PH5 (SoundTank)
1991-1998

1991-1998		$25	$35

Phaser PH7 (Tone-Lok)
1999-present. Speed, depth, feedback and level controls.

1999-2004		$40	$45

Phaser PT9
1982-1984. Three control knobs, red case.

1982-1984		$75	$100

Powerlead PL5 (SoundTank)
1991-1998. Metal case '91, plastic case '91-'98.

1991	Metal	$30	$45
1991-1998	Plastic	$20	$25

Renometer
1976-1979. 5-band equalizer with preamp.

1976-1979		$75	$100

Rotary Chorus RC99
1996-1999. Black or silver cases available, requires power pack and does not use a battery.

1996-1999	Black case	$100	$125

Session Man SS10
1988-1989. Distortion, chorus.

1988-1989		$70	$80

Session Man II SS20
1988-1989. 4 controls + toggle, light pink-purple case.

1988-1989		$70	$80

Slam Punk SP5 (SoundTank)
1996-1999.

1996-1999		$40	$45

Smash Box SM7 (Tone-Lok)
2000-present.

2000-2004		$35	$40

Sonic Distortion SD9
1982-1984.

1982-1984		$75	$100

Standard Fuzz (No. 59)
1974-1979. Two buttons (fuzz on/off and tone change).

1974-1979		$175	$200

Stereo Box ST-800
1975-1979. One input, 2 outputs for panning, small yellow case.

1975-1979		$175	$225

Stereo Chorus CSL (Master Series)
1985-1986.

1985-1986		$70	$90

Super Chorus CS5 (SoundTank)
1991-1998.

1991-1998		$25	$35

Stereo Chorus CS9
1982-1984.

1982-1984		$75	$100

Super Metal SM-9
1984. Distortion.

1984		$75	$95

Super Stereo Chorus SC-10
1986-1992.

1986-1992		$75	$100

Super Tube Screamer ST9
1984-1985. 4 knobs, light green metal case.

1984-1985		$225	$300

Super Tube STL
1985.

1985		$75	$95

Ibanez UE-300

Ibanez Phase Tone PT-909

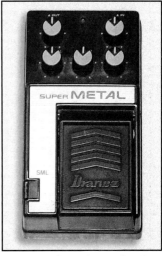

Ibanez Super Metal SM-9

EFFECTS

EFFECTS

Ibanez TS-808

Ibanez Turbo Tube Screamer TS9DX

Jacques Fuse Blower

MODEL YEAR	FEATURES	EXC. COND. LOW	HIGH
Swell Flanger SF10	*1986-1992. Speed, regeneration, width and time controls, yellow case.*		
1986-1992		$50	$55
Trashmetal TM5 (SoundTank)	*1990-1998. Tone and distortion pedal, 3 editions (1st edition, 2nd edition metal case, 2nd edition plastic case).*		
1990-1998		$20	$25
Tremolo Pedal TL5 (SoundTank)	*1995-1998.*		
1995-1998		$50	$100
Tube King TK999	*1994-1995. Has a 12AX7 tube and 3-band equalizer.*		
1994-1995	Includes power pack	$150	$200
Tube King TK999US	*1996-1998. Has a 12AX7 tube and 3-band equalizer, does not have the noise switch of original TK999. Made in the U.S.*		
1996-1998	Includes power pack	$150	$200
Tube Screamer TS5 (SoundTank)	*1991-1998.*		
1991-1998		$25	$30
Tube Screamer TS7 (Tone-Lok)	*1999-present. 3 control knobs.*		
1999-2004		$35	$40
Tube Screamer TS9	*1982-1984, 1993-present. Reissued in '93*		
1982-1984		$150	$200
1993-2004		$75	$100
Tube Screamer Classic TS10	*1986-1993.*		
1986-1993		$200	$225
Tube Screamer TS-808	*1980-1982, 2004-present. Reissued in '04.*		
1980-1981		$575	$700
Turbo Tube Screamer TS9DX	*1998-present. Tube Screamer circuit with added 3 settings for low-end.*		
1998-2004		$70	$85
Twin Cam Chorus TC10	*1986-1989. Four control knobs, light blue case.*		
1986-1989		$75	$100
Virtual Amp VA3 (floor unit)	*1995-1998. Digital effects processor.*		
1995-1998		$55	$75
VL10	*1987-1997. Stereo volume pedal.*		
1987-1997		$50	$75
Wah Fuzz Standard (Model 58)	*1974-1981. Fuzz tone change toggle, fuzz on toggle, fuzz depth control, balance control, wah volume pedal with circular friction pads on footpedal.*		
1974-1981		$225	$300
Wah WH10	*1988-1997.*		
1988-1997		$50	$75

Intersound
Made by Intersound, Inc. of Boulder, Colorado.
Reverb-Equalizer R100F
1977-1979. Reverb and 4-band EQ, fader.

1977-1979		$75	$100

J. Everman
2000-present. Analog guitar effects built by Justin J. Everman in Richardson, Texas.

Jacques
One-of-a-kind handmade stomp boxes and production models made in France. Production models are distributed in the U.S. by Godlyke Distributing.

Jan-Mar Industries
Jan-Mar was located in Hillsdale, New Jersey.
The Talker
1976. 30 watts.

1976		$75	$125

The Talker Pro
1976. 75 watts.

1976		$100	$150

Jax
1960s-1970. Japanese imports made by Shinei.
Fuzz Master

1960s		$100	$150

Vibrachorus
Variant of Univibe.

1969		$750	$1,000

Wah-Wah

1960s		$100	$150

Jersey Girl
1991-present. Line of guitar effects pedals made in Japan. They also build guitars.

Jet Sounds LTD
1977. Jet was located in Jackson, Mississippi.
Hoze Talk Box
1977. Large wood box, 30 watts.

1977		$90	$125

JHD Audio
1974-1990. Hunt Dabney founded JHD in Costa Mesa, California, to provide effects that the user installed in their amp. Dabney is still involved in electronics and builds the BiasProbe tool for tubes.
SuperCube/SuperCube II
1974-late 1980s. Plug-in sustain mod for Fender amps with reverb, second version for amps after '78.

1970s		$50	$75

Jimi Hendrix
See listing under Dunlop.

MODEL YEAR	FEATURES	EXC. COND. LOW	HIGH

John Hornby Skewes & Co.

Mid-1960s-present. Large English distributor of musical products which has also made their own brands, or self-branded products from others, over the years.

Johnson

Mid-1990s-present. Budget line of effects imported by Music Link, Brisbane, California. Johnson also offers guitars, amps, mandolins and basses.

Johnson Amplification

1997-present. Modeling amps and effects designed by John Johnson, of Sandy, Utah. The company is part of Harman International. In '02, they quit building amps, but continue the effects line.

Jordan

1960s. Jordan effects were distributed by Sho-Bud of Nashville, Tennessee.

Boss Tone Fuzz
1968-1969. Tiny effect plugged into guitar's output jack.

1968-1969		$100	$125

Compressor J-700

1960s		$75	$100

Creator Volume Sustainer

1960s		$125	$175

Gig Wa-Wa Volume

1960s		$125	$150

Phaser
Black case, yellow knobs.

1960s	Black case	$125	$150

Kay

1931-present. Kay was once one of the largest instrument producers in the world, offering just about everything for the guitarist. See Guitar Stories Volume II, by Michael Wright, for a complete history of Kay with detailed model listings.

Effects Pedals
1970s. Includes the Wah, Graphic Equalizer GE-5000, Rhythmer, and Tremolo.

1970s		$50	$75

Keeley

2001-present. Line of guitar effects designed and built by Robert Keeley in Edmond, Oklahoma. Keeley Electronics also offers a range of custom modifications for other effects.

Kendrick

1989-present. Texas' Kendrick offers guitars, amps, and effects.

ABC Amp Switcher
1990s.

1990s		$100	$140

Buffalo Pfuz
1990s.

1990s		$70	$100

Model 1000 Reverb
1991-present. Vintage style, 3 knobs: dwell, tone, and mix, brown cover, wheat grille with art deco shape.

1991-2000		$400	$450

Power Glide Attenuator
1998-present. Allows you to cut the output before it hits the amp's speakers, rack mount, metal cab.

1998-2000		$180	$200

Kent

1961-1969. This import guitar brand also offered a few effects.

Kern Engineering

Located in Kenosha, Wisconsin, Kern offers pre-amps and wah pedals.

Klon

1994-present. Originally located in Brookline, Massachusetts, and now located in Cambridge, Massachusetts, Klon was started by Bill Finnegan after working with two circuit design partners on the Centaur Professional Overdrive.

Centaur Professional Overdrive
1994-present. Gold case.

1990s		$450	$500

KMD (Kaman)

1986-ca. 1990. Distributed by Kaman (Ovation, Hamer, etc.) in the late '80s.

Effects Pedals

1986-1990	Analog Delay	$65	$90
1986-1990	Overdrive	$30	$45
1987-1990	Distortion	$30	$45
1987-1990	Flanger	$30	$50
1987-1990	Phaser	$30	$50
1987-1990	Stereo Chorus	$30	$50

Korg

Most of the Korg effects listed below are modular effects. The PME-40X Professional Modular Effects System holds four of them and allows the user to select several variations of effects. The modular effects cannot be used alone. This system was sold for a few years starting in 1983. Korg currently offers the Toneworks line of effects.

PEQ-1 Parametric EQ
1980s. Dial-in equalizer with gain knob, band-width knob, and frequency knob, black case.

1980s		$40	$50

PME-40X Professional Modular Effects System
1983-ca.1986. Board holds up to 4 of the modular effects listed below.

1983-1986		$125	$150

PME-40X Modular Effects

1983-1986	KAD-301		
	Analog Delay	$60	$70
1983-1986	KCH-301		
	Stereo Chorus	$25	$35
1983-1986	KCO-101 Compressor	$45	$55

Jan-Mar The Talker

Keeley Compressor

Kendrick Power Glide

EFFECTS

Korg Tube Works Tube Driver

Line 6 MM-4

Lock & Rock Sour Boost

MODEL YEAR	FEATURES	EXC. COND. LOW	HIGH
1983-1986	KDI-101 Distortion	$45	$55
1983-1986	KDL-301 Dynamic Echo	$90	$110
1983-1986	KFL-401 Stereo Flanger	$40	$50
1983-1986	KGE-201 Graphic EQ	$25	$35
1983-1986	KNG-101 Noise Gate	$25	$35
1983-1986	KOD-101 Over Drive	$45	$55
1983-1986	KPH-401 Phaser	$45	$55
1983-1986	OCT-1 Octaver	$70	$80

SSD 3000 Digital Delay

1980s. Rack mount, SDD-3000 logo on top of unit.

1980s		$600	$850

Krank

1996-present. Tempe, Arizona, amp builder Krank also builds effects pedals.

Laney

1968-present. Founded by Lyndon Laney and Bob Thomas in Birmingham, England, this amp builder also offered a reverb unit.

Reverberation Unit

1968-1969. Sleek reverb unit, plexi-style front panel, black vinyl cover.

1968-1969		$300	$400

Lehle

2001-present. Loop switches from Burkhard Georg Lehle of Lehle Gitarrentechnik in Voerde, Germany.

D.Loop Signal Router

2004		$150	$175

Line 6

1996-present. Effects from Marcus Ryle and Michel Doidic who were product line designers prior to forming their own design company. A sixth company telephone line was added to their product design business to handle their own product line, thus Line 6. All prices include Line 6 power pack if applicable. They also produce amps and guitars.

AM-4 Amp Modeler

Includes power pack, box and manual, yellow case.

1996-2002		$100	$125

DL-4 Delay Modeler

Includes power pack, box and manual, green case.

1996-2002		$175	$225

DM-4 Distortion Modeler

Includes power pack, box and manual, red case.

1996-2002		$100	$125

FM-4 Filter Modeler

Includes power pack, box and manual, purple case.

2000-2002		$175	$225

MM-4 Modulation Modeler

Includes power pack, box and manual, aqua blue case.

2000-2002		$150	$185

MODEL YEAR	FEATURES	EXC. COND. LOW	HIGH

POD 2.0

2000s. Amp modeler.

2000s		$150	$200

Little Lanilei

1997-present. Best known for their small hand-made amps, Songworks Systems & Products of San Juan Capistrano, California, also offers effects bearing the Little Lanilei name.

Lock & Rock

2003-present. Line of floor pedal guitar and microphone effects produced by Brannon Electronics, Inc. of Houston, Texas.

Loco Box

1982-1983. Loco Box was a brand of effects distributed by Aria Pro II for a short period starting in '82. It appears that Aria switched the effects to their own brand in '83.

Effects

1982-1983	Analog Delay AD-01	$35	$45
1982-1983	Chorus CH-01	$55	$65
1982-1983	Compressor CM-01	$35	$45
1982-1983	Distortion DS-01	$40	$55
1982-1983	Flanger FL-01	$35	$45
1982-1983	Graphic Equalizer GE-06	$25	$35
1982-1983	Overdrive OD-01	$40	$50
1982-1983	Phaser PH-01	$45	$55

Lovetone

1995-present. Hand-made analog effects from Oxfordshire, England.

Ludwig

For some reason, drum builder Ludwig offered a guitar synth in the 1970s.

Phase II Guitar Synth

1970-1971. Oversized synth, mushroom-shaped footswitches.

1970-1971	Vertical silver case	$450	$600

M.B. Electronics

Made in San Francisco, California.

Ultra-Metal UM-10

1985. Distortion.

1985		$35	$40

Maestro

Maestro was a Gibson subsidiary; the name appeared on 1950s accordian amplifiers. The first Maestro effects were the Echoplex tape echo and the FZ-1 Fuzz-Tone, introduced in the early-'60s. Maestro products were manufactured by various entities such as Market Electronics, All-Test Devices, Lowrey and Moog Electronics. In the late-'60s and early-'70s, they unleashed a plethora of pedals; some were beautiful, others had great personality. The last Maestro effects were the Silver and Black MFZ series of the late-'70s.

MODEL YEAR FEATURES	EXC. COND. LOW	HIGH
Bass Brassmaster BB-1		
1971-ca.1974. Added brass to your bass.		
1971-1974	$450	$650
Boomerang		
Ca.1969-ca.1972. Wah pedal made by All-Test Devices.		
1969-1972	$175	$200
Boomerang BG-2		
1972-ca.1976. Wah pedal made by All-Test Devices.		
1972-1976	$100	$125
Echoplex EP-1		
1962/63-mid-1960s. Original model, smaller box, tube, separate controls for echo volume and instrument volume, made by Market Electronics. Though not labeled as such, it is often referred to as the EP-1 by collectors.		
1960s Earlier small Green box	$800	$900
Echoplex EP-2		
Mid-1960s-ca.1970. Larger box than original, tube, single echo/instrument volume control, made by Market Electronics. Around '70, the EP-2 added a Sound-On-Sound feature.		
1960s Larger Green box	$800	$900
Echoplex EP-3		
Ca.1970-1977. Solidstate, made by Market Electronics, black box.		
1970-1977	$400	$550
Echoplex IV (EP-4)		
1977-1978. Solidstate, last version introduced by Maestro. See brands Market Electronics and Echoplex for later models.		
1977-1978	$375	$500
Echoplex Groupmaster		
Ca.1970-ca.1974. Two input Echoplex, solidstate.		
1970-1977	$500	$700
Echoplex Sireko ES-1		
Ca.1971-mid-1970s. A budget version of the Echoplex, solidstate, made by Market.		
1971-1975	$200	$300
Envelope Modifier ME-1		
1971-ca.1976. Tape reverse/string simulator, made by All-Test.		
1971-1976	$150	$225
Filter Sample and Hold FSH-1		
1975-ca.1976.		
1975-1976	$425	$475
Full Range Boost FRB-1		
1971-ca.1975. Frequency boost with fuzz, made by All-Test.		
1971-1975	$150	$200
Fuzz MFZ-1		
1976-1979. Made by Moog.		
1976-1979	$150	$200
Fuzz Phazzer FP-1		
1971-1974.		
1971-1974	$200	$300
Fuzz Tone FZ-1		
1962-1963. Brown, uses 2 AA batteries.		
1962-1963	$175	$225

MODEL YEAR FEATURES	EXC. COND. LOW	HIGH
Fuzz Tone FZ-1A		
1965-1967. Brown, uses 1 AA battery.		
1965-1967	$175	$225
Fuzz Tone FZ-1A (reissue)		
2000s	$65	$70
Fuzz Tone FZ-1B		
Late-1960s- early-1970s. Black, uses 9-volt battery.		
1970s	$150	$250
Fuzztain MFZT-1		
1976-1978. Fuzz, sustain, made by Moog.		
1976-1978	$200	$250
Mini-Phase Shifter MPS-2		
1976. Volume, speed, slow and fast controls.		
1976	$110	$125
Octave Box OB-1		
1971-ca.1975. Made by All-Test Devices.		
1971-1975	$225	$300
Parametric Filter MPF-1		
1976-1978. Made by Moog.		
1970s	$185	$200
Phase Shifter PS-1		
1971-1975. With or without 3-button footswitch, made by Oberheim.		
1971-1975 With footswitch	$250	$300
1971-1975 Without footswitch	$150	$250
Phase Shifter PS-1A		
1976.		
1976	$150	$250
Phase Shifter PS-1B		
1970s.		
1970s	$150	$250
Phaser MP-1		
1976-1978. Made by Moog.		
1976-1978	$100	$120
Repeat Pedal RP-1		
1970s	$200	$300
Rhythm King MRK-2		
1971-ca.1974. Early drum machine.		
1972	$200	$300
Rhythm Queen MRQ-1		
Early 1970s. Early rhythm machine.		
1970s	$125	$150
Rhythm'n Sound G-2		
Ca.1969-1970s. Multi-effect unit.		
1969-1975	$200	$300
Ring Modulator RM-1		
1971-1975.		
1971-1975 With MP-1 control pedal	$650	$700
1971-1975 Without control pedal	$550	$600
Rover Rotating Speaker		
1971-ca.1973. Rotating Leslie effect that mounted on a large tripod.		
1971-1973	$750	$900
Stage Phaser MPP-1		
1976-1978. Had slow, fast and variable settings, made by Moog.		
1976-1978	$175	$225

Maestro Fuzztain

Mestro Fuzz-Tone FZ-1A

Maestro Phase Shifter PS1-A

EFFECTS

Marshall Jackhammer JH-1

Matchless Coolbox

Moonrock

MODEL YEAR / FEATURES	EXC. COND. LOW	HIGH
Super Fuzztone FZ-1S		
1971-1975	$200	$300
Sustainer SS-2		
1971-ca.1975. Made by All-Test Devices.		
1971-1975	$100	$150
Theramin TH-1		
1971-mid-1970s. Device with 2 antennae, made horror film sound effects. A reissue Theremin is available from Theremaniacs in Milwaukee, Wisconsin.		
1971-1975	$800	$1,000
Wah-Wah/Volume WW-1		
1970s. Wah-Wah Volume logo on end of pedal, green foot pad.		
1971-1975	$150	$250

Magnatone

1937-1970s. Magnatone built very competitive amps from '57 to '66. In the early-'60s, they offered the RVB-1 Reverb Unit. The majority of Magnatone amps pre-'66 did not have on-board reverb.

Model RVB-1 Reverb Unit

1961-1966. Reverb unit that works between the guitar and amp, typical brown leatherette cover, square box-type cabinet. From '64-'66, battery operated, solidstate version of RVB-1, low flat cabinet.

1961-1963	$275	$400
1964-1966 Battery and solidstate	$200	$300

Mannys Music

Issued by the New York-based retailer.

Fuzz

1960s. Same unit as the Orpheum Fuzz and Clark Fuzz.

1960s	$225	$325

Market Electronics

Market, from Ohio, made the famous Echoplex line. See Maestro section for earlier models and Echoplex section for later versions.

Marshall

1962-present. The fuzz and wah boom of the '60s led many established manufacturers to introduce variations on the theme. Marshall was no exception, but its pedals never neared the popularity of their amps. They made another foray into stomp boxes in '89 with the Gov'nor distortion, and currently produce several distortion/overdrive units.

Blues Breaker

1992-1999. Replaced by Blues Breaker II in 2000.

1992-1999	$100	$130

Blues Breaker II Overdrive

2000-present. Overdrive pedal, 4 knobs.

2000-2004	$50	$65

Drive Master

1992-1999.

1992-1999	$70	$75

MODEL YEAR / FEATURES	EXC. COND. LOW	HIGH
Guv'nor		
1989-1991. Distortion, Gov'nor Plus introduced in 2000.		
1989-1991	$75	$100
Jackhammer		
1999-present. Distortion pedal.		
1999-2004	$55	$65
PB-100 Power Brake		
1993-1995. Speaker attenuator for tube amps.		
1993-1995	$190	$230
Shred Master		
1992-1999.		
1992-1999	$75	$100
Supa Fuzz		
Late-1960s. Made by Sola Sound (Colorsound).		
1967	$300	$400
Supa Wah		
Late-1960s. Made by Sola Sound (Colorsound).		
1969	$300	$425
Vibratrem VT-1		
1999-present. Vibrato and tremolo.		
1999-2004	$75	$85

Matchless

1989-1999, 2001-present. Matchless amplifiers offered effects in the '90s.

AB Box

1990s. Split box for C-30 series amps (DC 30, SC 30, etc.)

1990s	$175	$300

Coolbox

1997-1999. Tube preamp pedal.

1997-1999	$275	$350

Dirtbox

1997-1999. Tube-driven overdrive pedal.

1997-1999	$225	$350

Echo Box

1997-1999. Limited production because of malfunctioning design which included cassette tape. Black case, 8 white chickenhead control knobs.

1990s Original unreliable status	$300	$400
1990s Updated working order	$700	$850

Hotbox/Hotbox II

1995-1999. Higher-end tube-driven preamp pedal.

1995-1999	$375	$425

Mix Box

1997-1999. 4-input tube mixer pedal.

1997-1999	$375	$425

Reverb RV-1

1993-1999. 5 controls, tube reverb tank.

1993-1999 Various colors	$1,000	$1,300

Split Box

1990s. Tube AB box.

1997 Standard AB	$275	$325

Tremolo/Vibrato TV-1

1993-1995. Tube unit.

1993-1995	$350	$400

| MODEL | | EXC. COND. | |
| YEAR | FEATURES | LOW | HIGH |

Maxon

1970s-present. Maxon was the original manufacturer of the Ibanez line of effects. Currently offering retro '70s era stomp boxes distributed in the U.S. by Godlyke.

AD-9 Analog Delay
2001-present. Purple case.

2001-2003		$225	$275

CS-550 Stereo Chorus
2000s. Light blue case, Stereo-Chorus logo on top.

2000s		$100	$130

OD-820 Over Drive Pro
2001-present.

2001-2003		$140	$175

Mesa-Boogie

1971-present. Mesa added pre-amps in the mid '90s.

V-Twin Preamp Pedal
Dec. 1993-2004. Serial number series: V011-. 100 watts, all tube preamp, floor unit, silver case.

1993-1999		$225	$275
2000-2004	Updated bottom tone adj.	$275	$325

V-Twin Bottle Rocket
2000-2004.

2000-2004		$100	$150

Meteoro

1986-present. Guitar effects built in Brazil. They also build guitar and bass amps.

Mica

Early 1970s. These Japanese-made effects were also sold under the Bruno and Marlboro brand names.

Tone Fuzz
Silver case, black knobs.

1970s		$200	$250

Tone Surf Wah Siren
1970s. Wah pedal.

1970s		$150	$175

Wailer Fuzz

1970		$75	$100

Wau Wau Fuzz
1970s. Wau Wau Fuzz logo on end of pedal, black.

1970s		$150	$175

Moog/Moogerfooger

Robert Moog, of synth fame, introduced his line of Moogerfooger analog effects in 1998.

Misc. Effects

2004	MF-105 MuRF	$250	$275
2004	Theremin	$250	$275

Moonrock

2002-present. Fuzz/distortion unit built by Glenn Wylie and distributed by Tonefrenzy.

| MODEL | | EXC. COND. | |
| YEAR | FEATURES | LOW | HIGH |

Morley

Late-1960s-present. Founded by brothers Raymond and Marvin Lubow, Morley has produced a wide variety of pedals and effects over the years, changing with the trends. In '89, the brothers sold the company to Accutronics (later changed to Sound Enhancements, Inc.) of Cary, Illinois.

ABY Switch Box
1981-ca.1985. Box.

1981-1985		$25	$35

Auto Wah PWA
1976-ca.1985.

1976-1985		$25	$35

Bad Horsie Steve Vai Signature Wah
1997-present

1997-2004		$65	$70

Black Gold Stereo Volume BSV
1985-1991.

1985-1991		$25	$35

Black Gold Stereo Volume Pan BSP
1985-1989.

1985-1989		$30	$40

Black Gold Volume BVO
1985-1991.

1985-1991		$25	$35

Black Gold Wah BWA
1985-1991.

1985-1991		$30	$40

Black Gold Wah Volume BWV
1985-1989.

1985-1989		$30	$40

Chrystal Chorus CCB
1996-1999. Stereo output.

1996-1999		$25	$30

Deluxe Distortion DDB
1981-1991. Box, no pedal.

1981-1991		$40	$60

Deluxe Flanger FLB
1981-1991. Box, no pedal.

1981-1991		$55	$65

Deluxe Phaser DFB
1981-1991. Box, no pedal.

1981-1991		$40	$60

Distortion One DIB
1981-1991. Box, no pedal.

1981-1991		$35	$45

Echo Chorus Vibrato ECV
1982-ca.1985.

1982-1985		$150	$225

Echo/Volume EVO-1
1974-ca.1982.

1974-1982		$150	$225

Electro-Pik-a-Wah PKW
1979-ca.1982.

1979-1982		$55	$65

Emerald Echo EEB
1996-1999. 300 millisecond delay.

1996-1999	Green case	$40	$50

Jerry Donahue JD-10
1995-1997. Multi-effect, distortion, overdrive.

1995-1997		$80	$90

Maxon AD-9 Analog Delay

EFFECTS

Morley ABY

Morley Jerry Donahue JD10

Morley Swivel Tone

Mosferatu Zendrive

Multivox Basky II

MODEL YEAR	FEATURES	EXC. COND. LOW	HIGH
Power Wah PWA/PWA II			
1992-present. Wah with boost. Changed to II in '98.			
1992-2002		$40	$50
Power Wah PWO			
Ca.1969-1984.			
1969-1984		$60	$70
Power Wah/Boost PWB			
Introduced in 1973, doubles as a volume pedal.			
1970s		$70	$80
Power Wah/Fuzz PWF			
Ca.1969-ca.1984.			
1969-1984		$75	$125
Pro Compressor PCB			
1978-1984. Stomp box without pedal, compress-sustain knob and output knob.			
1978-1984		$45	$55
Pro Flanger PFL			
1978-1984.			
1978-1984		$100	$125
Pro Phaser PFA			
1975-1984.			
1975-1984		$100	$125
Rotating Sound Power Wah Model RWV			
1974-1982.			
1974-1982		$325	$375
Select-Effect Pedal SEL			
Lets you control up to 5 other pedals.			
1980s		$20	$30
Slimline Echo Volume 600			
1983-1985. 20 to 600 ms delay.			
1983-1985		$45	$55
Slimline Echo Volume SLEV			
1983-1985. 20 to 300 ms delay.			
1983-1985		$50	$60
Slimline Variable Taper Stereo Volume SLSV			
1982-1986.			
1982-1986		$70	$100
Slimline Variable Taper Volume SLVO			
1982-1986.			
1982-1986		$35	$50
Slimline Wah SLWA			
1982-1986. Battery operated electro-optical.			
1982-1986		$55	$75
Slimline Wah Volume SLWV			
1982-ca.1986. Battery operated electro-optical.			
1982-1986		$55	$75
Stereo Chorus Flanger CFL			
1980-ca. 1986. Box, no pedal.			
1980-1986		$60	$70
Stereo Chorus Vibrato SCV			
1980-1991. Box, no pedal.			
1980-1991		$80	$100
Stereo Volume CSV			
1980-ca. 1986. Box, no pedal.			
1980-1986		$30	$45
Volume Compressor VCO			
1979-1984.			
1979-1984		$30	$45

MODEL YEAR	FEATURES	EXC. COND. LOW	HIGH
Volume Phaser PFV			
1977-1984. With volume pedal.			
1977-1984		$125	$150
Volume VOL			
1975-ca.1984.			
1975-1979		$30	$45
1980-1984		$25	$40
Volume XVO			
1985-1988.			
1985-1988		$25	$40
Volume/Boost VBO			
1974-1984.			
1974-1984		$50	$60
Wah Volume CWV			
1987-1991. Box, no pedal.			
1987-1991		$65	$80
Wah Volume XWV			
1985-ca.1989.			
1985-1989		$65	$80
Wah/Volume WVO			
1977-ca.1984.			
1977-1984		$80	$100

Mosferatu

Line of guitar effects pedals built by Hermida Audio Technology.

Mosrite

Semie Moseley's Mosrite company dipped into effects in the 1960s.

Fuzzrite

1966		$175	$225

Multivox

New York-based Multivox offered a variety of effects in the 1970s and '80s.

Big Jam Effects

Multivox offered the Big Jam line of effects from 1980 to ca. '83.

MODEL YEAR	FEATURES	EXC. COND. LOW	HIGH
1980-1983	6-Band EQ	$40	$50
1980-1983	Analog Echo/Reverb	$100	$125
1980-1983	Bi-Phase 2	$50	$60
1980-1983	Chorus	$45	$55
1980-1983	Compressor	$40	$50
1980-1983	Distortion	$70	$80
1980-1983	Flanger	$50	$60
1980-1983	Jazz Flanger	$50	$60
1980-1983	Octave Box	$40	$55
1980-1983	Phaser	$40	$50
1980-1983	Spit-Wah	$40	$50
1981-1983	Noise Gate	$35	$45
1981-1983	Space Driver	$60	$70
1982-1983	Delay	$60	$70
1982-1983	Parametric EQ	$35	$45
1982-1983	Volume Pedal	$30	$35

Full Rotor MX-2

1978-ca.1982. Leslie effect.

1978-1982		$300	$350

MODEL YEAR	FEATURES	EXC. COND. LOW	HIGH
Little David LD-2			
Rotary sound effector in mini Leslie-type case.			
1970s	With pedal	$375	$450
1970s	Without pedal	$325	$375
Multi Echo MX-201			
Tape echo unit, reverb.			
1970s		$200	$250
Multi Echo MX-312			
Tape echo unit, reverb.			
1970s		$225	$300
Rhythm Ace FR6M			
27 basic rhythms.			
1970s		$60	$80

Mu-tron

1972-ca.1981. Made by Musitronics (founded by Aaron Newman), Rosemont, New Jersey, these rugged and unique-sounding effects were a high point of the '70s. The Mu-Tron III appeared in '72 and more products followed, about 10 in all. Musitronics also made the U.S. models of the Dan Armstrong effects. In '78 ARP synthesizers bought Musitronics and sold Mutron products to around '81. A reissue of the Mu-Tron III was made available in '95 by NYC Music Products and distributed by Matthews and Ryan Musical Products.

MODEL YEAR	FEATURES	EXC. COND. LOW	HIGH
Bi-Phase			
1975-ca.1981. Add $50-$75 for Opti-Pot pedal.			
1975-1981	With 2-button footswitch	$600	$750
C-100 OptiPot Control Pedal			
1975-1981	Blue case	$550	$700
C-200 Volume-Wah			
1970s		$300	$400
Flanger			
1977-ca.1981.			
1977-1981		$400	$450
III Envelope Filter			
1972-ca.1981. Envelope Filter.			
1972-1981		$400	$500
Micro V			
Ca.1975-ca.1977. Envelope Filter.			
1970s		$200	$250
Octave Divider			
1977-ca.1981.			
1977-1981		$500	$600
Phasor			
Ca.1974-ca.1976. Two knobs.			
1974-1976		$200	$300
Phasor II			
1976-ca.1981. Three knobs.			
1976-1981		$200	$300

MXR

1972-present. MXR Innovations launched its line of pedals in '72. Around '77, the Rochester, New York, company changed lettering on the effects from script to block, and added new models. MXR survived into the mid-'80s. In '87, production was picked up by Jim Dunlop. Reissues of block logo boxes can be differentiated from originals as they

MODEL YEAR	FEATURES	EXC. COND. LOW	HIGH
have an LED above the switch and the finish is slightly rough; the originals are smooth.			
6 Band Equalizer			
1975-1982.			
1975-1979		$70	$85
1980-1982		$60	$70
6 Band Equalizer M-109 (reissue)			
1987-present. Reissued by Jim Dunlop.			
1987-1999		$30	$40
10 Band Graphic Equalizer			
1975-1981.			
1975-1981	With AC power cord	$80	$100
Analog Delay			
1975-1981. Green case, power cord.			
1975-1979	Earlier 2-jack model	$300	$325
1980-1981	Later 3-jack model	$150	$200
Blue Box			
1972-ca.1978. Octave pedal, M-103.			
1970s	Earlier script logo	$225	$300
1970s	Later block logo	$175	$250
Blue Box (reissue)			
1995-present. Reissued by Jim Dunlop. Produces 1 octave above or 2 octaves below.			
1995-1999		$40	$45
Commande Overdrive			
1981-1983. The Commande series featured plastic housings and electronic switching.			
1981-1983		$40	$50
Commande Phaser			
1981-1983.			
1981-1983		$100	$110
Commande Preamp			
1981-1983.			
1981-1983		$40	$50
Commande Stereo Chorus			
1981-1983.			
1981-1983		$60	$70
Commande Stereo Flanger			
1982-1983.			
1982-1983		$70	$80
Commande Sustain			
1981-1983.			
1981-1983		$60	$70
Commande Time Delay			
1981-1983.			
1981-1983		$70	$80
Distortion +			
1972-1982.			
1970s	Earlier script logo	$185	$225
1970s	Later block logo	$85	$110
1980s	Block logo	$80	$95
Distortion + (Series 2000)			
1983-1985.			
1983-1985		$60	$70
Distortion + M-104 (reissue)			
1987-present. Reissued by Jim Dunlop.			
1980s		$55	$65
1990s		$45	$55
Distortion II			
1981-1983.			
1981-1983	With AC power cord	$140	$150

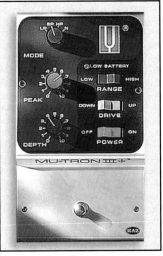

Mu-Tron III+

MXR Analog Delay

MXR Distortion +

EFFECTS

EFFECTS

MXR Phase 90

MXR Stereo Chorus

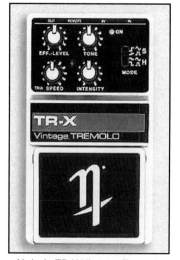

Nobels TR-X Vintage Tremolo

MODEL YEAR	FEATURES	EXC. COND. LOW	HIGH
Double Shot Distortion M-151			
2003-present. 2 channels.			
2003-2004		$65	$75
Dyna Comp			
1972-1982. Compressor.			
1970s	Earlier script logo, battery	$175	$200
1970s	Later block logo, battery	$90	$120
1980s	Block logo, battery	$65	$80
Dyna Comp (Series 2000)			
1982-1985.			
1982-1985		$65	$75
Dyna Comp M-102 (reissue)			
1987-present. Reissued by Jim Dunlop.			
1987-1999		$35	$40
Envelope Filter			
1976-1983.			
1976-1983		$125	$225
Flanger			
1976-1983, 1997-present. Analog, reissued by Dunlop in '97.			
1976-1979	AC power cord, 2 inputs	$175	$225
1980-1983	AC power cord	$100	$150
1997-2004	Dunlop reissue	$60	$70
Flanger/Doubler			
1979	Rack mount	$150	$175
Limiter			
1980-1982. AC, 4 knobs.			
1980-1982	AC power cord	$125	$200
Loop Selector			
1980-1982. A/B switch for 2 effects loops.			
1980-1982		$50	$60
Micro Amp			
1978-1983, 1995-present. Variable booster, white case, reissued in '95.			
1978-1983		$75	$100
1995-2004	M-133 reissue	$40	$45
Micro Chorus			
1980-1983. Yellow case.			
1980-1983		$125	$175
Micro Flanger			
1981-1982.			
1981-1982		$100	$150
Noise Gate Line Driver			
1974-1983.			
1970s	Script logo	$75	$125
1980s	Block logo	$75	$100
Omni			
1980s. Rack unit with floor controller, compressor, 3-band EQ, distortion, delay, chorus/flanger.			
1980s		$425	$475
Phase 45			
Ca.1976-1982.			
1970s	Script logo, battery	$125	$175
1980s	Block logo, battery	$75	$125
Phase 90			
1972-1982.			
1970s	Earlier script logo	$250	$325
1970s	Later block logo	$175	$275

MODEL YEAR	FEATURES	EXC. COND. LOW	HIGH
1980s	Block logo	$150	$200
Phase 90 M-101 (reissue)			
1987-present. Reissued by Jim Dunlop.			
1987-1989	Block logo	$60	$85
1990-1999	Block logo	$50	$75
Phase 100			
1974-1982.			
1970s	Earlier script logo	$250	$325
1970s	Later block logo, battery	$175	$275
Phaser (Series 2000)			
1982-1985. Series 2000 introduced cost cutting die-cast cases.			
1982-1985		$60	$85
Pitch Transposer			
1980s		$400	$475
Power Converter			
1980s		$45	$60
Smart Gate M-135			
2002-present. Noise-gate, single control, battery powered.			
2002-2004		$60	$70
Stereo Chorus			
1978-1985. With AC power cord.			
1978-1979		$175	$275
1980-1985		$150	$200
Stereo Chorus (Series 2000)			
1983-1985. Series 2000 introduced cost cutting die-cast cases.			
1983-1985		$55	$75
Stereo Flanger (Series 2000)			
1983-1985. Series 2000 introduced cost cutting die-cast cases, black with blue lettering.			
1983-1985		$60	$80
Super Comp M-132			
2002-present. Dunlop MXR, 3 knobs, battery powered.			
2002-2004		$40	$55

Nobels

1997-present. Offered by Musicorp. German-designed effects.

ODR-1

1997-present. Overdrive.

1997-2002		$30	$40

TR-X Tremolo

1997-present. Tremolo effect using modern technology, purple case.

1997-1999		$30	$40

Nomad

Fuzz Wah

1960s. Import from Japan, similar looking to Morley pedal with depth and volume controls and fuzz switch, silver metal case and black foot pedal.

1960s		$75	$125

MODEL YEAR FEATURES	EXC. COND. LOW	HIGH

Olson

Olson Electronics was in Akron, Ohio.

Reverberation Amplifier RA-844

1967. Solidstate, battery-operated, reverb unit, depth and volume controls, made in Japan.

1967	$100	$150

Ovation

1970s. Well known for original design flat tops, Ovation ventured into the solidstate amp and effects market in the early '70s.

K-6001 Guitar Preamp

1970s. Preamp with reverb, boost, tremolo, fuzz, and a tuner, looks something like a Maestro effect from the '70s, reliability may be an issue.

1970s	$100	$125

PAIA

1967-present. Founded by John Paia Simonton in Edmond, Oklahoma, specializing in synthesizer and effects kits. PAIA did make a few complete products but they are better known for the various electronic kit projects they sold. Values on kit projects are difficult as it depends on the skills of the person who built it.

Roctave Divider 5760

Kit to build analog octave divider.

1970s	$70	$85

Park

1965-1982, 1992-2000. Sola/Colorsound made a couple of effects for Marshall and their sister brand, Park. In the '90s, Marshall revived the name for use on small solidstate amps.

Pax

1970s. Imported Maestro copies.

Fuzz Tone Copy

1970s	$125	$150

Octave Box Copy

1970s. Dual push-buttons (normal and octave), 2 knobs (octave volume and sensitivity), green and black case.

1970s	$125	$150

Pearl

Pearl, located in Nashville, Tennessee, and better known for drums, offered a line of guitar effects in the 1980s.

Analog Delay AD-08

1983-1985. Four knobs.

1983-1985	$100	$150

Analog Delay AD-33

1982-1984. Six knobs.

1982-1984	$175	$225

Chorus CH-02

1981-1984. Four knobs.

1981-1984	$75	$100

Chorus Ensemble CE-22

1982-1984. Stereo chorus with toggling between chorus and vibrato, 6 knobs.

1982-1984	$125	$175

Compressor CO-04

1981-1984.

1981-1984	$50	$75

Distortion DS-06

1982-1986.

1982-1986	$40	$60

Flanger FG-01

1981-1986. Clock pulse generator, ultra-low frequency oscillator.

1981-1986	$75	$100

Graphic EQ GE-09

1983-1985.

1983-1985	$40	$55

Octaver OC-07

1982-1986.

1982-1986	$75	$100

Overdrive OD-05

1981-1986.

1981-1986	$75	$100

Parametric EQ PE-10

1983-1984.

1983-1984	$45	$60

Phaser PH-03

1981-1984. Four knobs.

1981-1984	$75	$100

Phaser PH-44

1982-1984. Six knobs.

1982-1984	$150	$175

Stereo Chorus CH-22

1982-1984.

1982-1984 Blue case	$75	$125

Thriller TH-20

1984-1986. Exciter.

1984-1986 Black case, four knobs	$175	$225

Peavey

1965-present. Peavey made stomp boxes from '87 to around '90. They offered rack mount gear after that.

Accelerator Overdrive AOD-2

1980s	$30	$35

Biampable Bass Chorus BAC-2

1980s	$30	$35

Companded Chorus CMC-1

1980s	$25	$30

Compressor/Sustainer CSR-2

1980s	$35	$40

Digital Delay DDL-3

1980s	$30	$35

Digital Stereo Reverb SRP-16

1980s	$50	$55

Dual Clock Stereo Chorus DSC-4

1980s	$30	$35

Hotfoot Distortion HFD-2

1980s	$25	$30

PedalDoctor FX

1996-present. Tim Creek builds his production and custom guitar effects in Nashville, Tennessee.

Olson Reverberation Amplifier RA-844

Pearl CO-04 Compressor

Peavey Companded Chorus CMC-1

EFFECTS

Pedalworx Texas Two Step

EFFECTS

ProCo Juggernaut

Red Witch Deluxe Moon Phaser

MODEL YEAR	FEATURES	EXC. COND. LOW	HIGH

Pedalworx

2001-present. Bob McBroom and George Blekas build their guitar effects in Manorville, New York and Huntsville, Alabama. They also do modifications to wahs.

Pharaoh Amplifiers

1998-present. Builder Matt Farrow builds his effects in Raleigh, North Carolina.

Premier

Ca.1938-ca.1975, 1990-present. Premier offered a reverb unit in the '60s. See Guitar section for more company info.

Reverb Unit
1961-late-1960s. Tube, footswitch, 2-tone brown.

1960s		$250	$300

Prescription Electronics

1994-present. Located in Portland, Oregon, Prescription offers a variety of hand-made effects.

Dual-Tone
1998-present. Overdrive and distortion.

1998-2002		$165	$175

Throb
1996-present. Tremolo.

1996-2000		$165	$175

Yardbox
1994-present. Patterned after the original Sola Sound Tonebender.

1994-1999		$90	$125

ProCo

1974-present. Located in Kalamazoo, Michigan and founded by Charlie Wicks, ProCo produces effects, cables and audio products.

Rat
1979-1987. Fuzztone, large box until '84. The second version was 1/3 smaller than original box. The small box version became the Rat 2. The current Vintage Rat is a reissue of the original large box.

1979-1984	Large box	$200	$250
1984-1987	Compact box	$100	$150

Rat 2
1987-present.

1987-1999		$75	$100
2000-2004		$40	$50

Turbo Rat
1989-present. Fuzztone with higher output gain, slope-front case.

1989-2000		$40	$50

Vintage Rat
1992-present. Reissue of early-'80s Rat.

1992-2002		$40	$50

Pro-Sound

The effects listed here date from 1987, and were, most likely, around for a short time.

MODEL YEAR	FEATURES	EXC. COND. LOW	HIGH

Chorus CR-1

1980s		$25	$40

Delay DL-1
Analog.

1980s		$35	$55

Distortion DS-1

1980s		$20	$35

Octaver OT-1

1980s		$25	$40

Power and Master Switch PMS-1

1980s		$15	$25

Super Overdrive SD-1

1980s		$20	$35

Radial Engineering

1994-present. Radial makes a variety of products in Port Coquitlam, British Columbia, including direct boxes, snakes, cables, splitters, and, since '99, the Tonebone line of guitar effects.

Rapco

The Jackson, Missouri based cable company offers a line of switch, connection and D.I. Boxes.

The Connection AB-100
1988-present. A/B box

1988-1999		$25	$35

Real McCoy Custom

1993-present. Wahs and effects by Geoffrey Teese. His first wah was advertised as "the Real McCoy, by Teese." He now offers his custom wah pedals under the Real McCoy Custom brand. He also used the Teese brand on a line of stomp boxes, starting in '96. The Teese stomp boxes are no longer being made.

Red Witch

2003-present. Analog guitar effects, designed by Ben Fulton, and made in Paekakariki, New Zealand.

Reverend

1996-present. Reverend offered its Drivetrain effects from '00 to '04. They also build guitars.

RGW Electronics

2003-present. Guitar effects built by Robbie Wallace in Lubbock, Texas.

Rockman

See listings under Scholz Research and Dunlop.

Rocktek

1986-present. Imports formerly distributed by Matthews and Ryan of Brooklyn, New York; currently handled by D'Andrea USA.

Effects
1986-present.

1986-2003	Delay	$30	$40
1986-2003	Distortion	$15	$25

MODEL YEAR	FEATURES	EXC. COND. LOW	HIGH
1986-2003	Overdrive	$15	$20
1986-2003	Super Delay	$30	$40
1986-2004	6 Band EQ	$15	$25
1986-2004	Bass EQ	$15	$25
1986-2004	Chorus	$15	$25
1986-2004	Compressor	$15	$25
1986-2004	Flanger	$15	$20
1986-2004	Metal Worker	$15	$20
1986-2004	Phaser	$15	$20
1990-2003	Vibrator Tremolo	$15	$20

Rocktron

1980s-present. Rocktron is a division of GHS Strings and offers a line of amps, controllers, stomp boxes, and preamps.

Austin Gold Overdrive
1997-present. Light overdrive enhancement without changing guitar-amp tone.

1997-2004		$25	$35

Banshee Talk Box
1997-present. Includes power supply.

1997-2004		$65	$80

Hush Rack Mount
1980s-present.

2000-2004		$50	$100

Hush Pedal
1996-present. Pedal version of rackmount Hush.

1996-2004		$25	$35

Rampage Distortion
1996-present. Sustain, high-gain and distortion.

1996-2004		$25	$35

Surf Tremolo
1997-2000.

1997-2000		$60	$80

Tsunami Chorus
1996-present. Battery or optional AC adapter.

1996-2004	Battery power	$40	$50
1996-2004	With power supply	$50	$60

Vertigo Vibe
2003-present. Rotating Leslie speaker effect.

2003-2004	Battery power	$50	$60
2003-2004	With power supply	$60	$70

XDC
1980s. Rack mount stereo preamp, distortion.

1980s		$100	$150

Roger Mayer Electronics

1964-present. Roger Mayer started making guitar effects in England in '64 for guitarists like Jimmy Page and Jeff Beck. He moved to the U.S. in '69 to start a company making studio gear and effects. Until about 1980, the effects were built one at a time in small numbers and not available to the general public. In the '80s he started producing larger quantities of pedals, introducing his rocket-shaped enclosure. He returned to England in '89.

Axis Fuzz
Early 1980s-present.

1987-1999		$125	$150

Classic Fuzz
1987-present. The Fuzz Face.

1987-1999		$175	$200

Metal Fuzz
Early 1980s-1994.

1987-1994		$125	$150

Mongoose Fuzz
Early 1980s-present.

1987-1999		$175	$200

Octavia
Early 1980s-present. Famous rocket-shaped box.

1981-1999		$150	$200

VooDoo-1
Ca.1990-present.

1990s		$175	$300

Rogue

2001-present. Budget imported guitar effects. They also offer guitars, basses, mandolins, banjos, ukes and amps.

Roland

Japan's Roland Corporation first launched effect pedals in 1974; a year or two later the subsidiary company, Boss, debuted its own line. They were marketed concurrently at first, but gradually Boss became reserved for effects and drum machines while the Roland name was used on amplifiers and keyboards.

Analog Synth SPV
1970s. Multi-effect synth, rack mount.

1970s		$700	$900

Bee Baa AF-100
1975-ca.1980. Fuzz and treble boost.

1975-1980		$300	$350

Bee Gee AF-60
1975-ca.1980. Sustain, distortion.

1975-1980		$75	$125

Double Beat AD-50
1975-ca.1980. Fuzz wah.

1975-1980		$175	$200

Expression Pedal EV-5

1970s		$50	$75

Expression Pedal EV-5 Reissue
2000s. Black pedal, blue foot pad.

2000s		$25	$30

Guitar Synth Pedal GR-33 and Pickup GK-2A
2000-present. Requires optional GK-2A pickup, blue case.

2000-2003		$475	$550

Human Rhythm Composer R-8
1980s. Drum machine, key pad entry.

1980s		$250	$350

Human Rhythm Composer R-8 MK II
2000s. Black case.

2000s		$300	$400

Jet Phaser AP-7
1975-ca.1978. Phase and distortion.

1975-1978		$225	$250

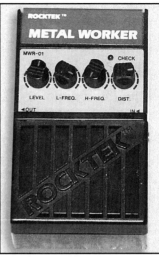

Rocktek Metalworker

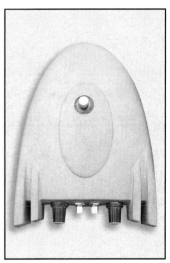

Roger Mayer Octavia

Roland Jet Phaser AP-7

EFFECTS

Ross Distortion

Scholz Acoustic Guit Pedal

SIB Mr. Fazeadelic

MODEL YEAR	FEATURES	EXC. COND. LOW	HIGH
Phase Five AP-5	*1975-ca.1978.*		
1975-1978		$200	$225
Phase II AP-2	*1975-ca.1980. Brown case.*		
1975-1980		$100	$150
Space Echo Unit	*1974-ca.1980. Tape echo and reverb, various models.*		
1970s	RE-101	$400	$550
1970s	RE-150	$400	$550
1970s	RE-301	$400	$550
1970s	RE-501	$450	$600
Vocoder SVC-350	*Late-1970s-1980s. Vocal synthesis (vocoder) for voice or guitar, rack mount version of VP-330.*		
1980		$550	$700
Vocoder VP-330 Plus	*Late-1970s-1980s. Analog vocal synthesis (vocoder) for voice or guitar, includes 2 1/2 octaves keyboard.*		
1978-1982		$700	$900
Wah Beat AW-10	*1975-ca.1980.*		
1975-1980		$100	$125

Ross

Founded by Bud Ross, who also established Kustom, in Chanute, Kansas, in the 1970s. Ross produced primarily amplifiers. In about '78, they introduced a line of U.S.-made effects. Later production switched to the Orient.

MODEL YEAR	FEATURES	EXC. COND. LOW	HIGH
10 Band Graphic Equalizer			
1970s		$80	$100
Compressor	*1970s. Gray case.*		
1970s		$250	$300
Distortion	*1978-ca.1980. Brown.*		
1979-1980		$75	$125
Flanger	*1977-ca.1980. Red.*		
1977-1980		$100	$150
Phase Distortion R1	*1979. Purple.*		
1979		$100	$125
Phaser	*1978-ca.1980. Orange.*		
1978-1980		$80	$100
Stereo Delay	*1978-ca.1980.*		
1978-1980		$125	$175

Rotovibe

See listing under Dunlop.

Sam Ash

1960s-1970s. Sam Ash Music was founded by a young Sam Ash (nee Askynase) in '24. Ash's first store was in Brooklyn, and was relocated to a better part of town in '44. By '66, there were about four Ash stores. During this time, Ash Music private branded their own amps and effects.

MODEL YEAR	FEATURES	EXC. COND. LOW	HIGH
Fuzzz Boxx	*1966-1967. Red, made by Universal Amplifier Company, same as Astrotone Fuzz.*		
1967		$200	$225
Volume Wah	*Italian-made.*		
1970s		$175	$200

Schaller

1970s. German-made guitar effects.

Scholz Research

1982-present. Started by Tom Scholz of the band Boston. In '95, Jim Dunlop picked up the Rockman line (see Dunlop).

MODEL YEAR	FEATURES	EXC. COND. LOW	HIGH
Power Soak			
1980s		$100	$160
Rockman			
1980s		$70	$130
Rockman X100	*Professional studio processor.*		
1980s		$100	$150
Soloist	*Personal guitar processor.*		
1980s		$50	$80

Seamoon

1973-1977, 1997-2002. Seamoon made effects until '77, when Dave Tarnowski bought up the remaining inventory and started Analog Digital Associates (ADA). He reissued the brand in '97.

MODEL YEAR	FEATURES	EXC. COND. LOW	HIGH
Fresh Fuzz	*1975-1977. Recently reissued by ADA.*		
1975-1977		$150	$200
Funk Machine	*1974-1977. Envelope filter. Recently reissued by ADA.*		
1974-1977		$175	$225
Studio Phase	*1975-1977. Phase shifter.*		
1975-1977		$75	$125

Sekova

Mid-1960s-mid-1970s. Entry level instruments imported by the U.S. Musical Merchandise Corporation of New York.

Shinei

Japanese imports. Shinei also made effects for Univox and probably others.

MODEL YEAR	FEATURES	EXC. COND. LOW	HIGH
Fuzz Wah			
1970s		$125	$175
Resly (repeat time) Machine	*Black case, 3 speeds.*		
1970s		$400	$500

Sho-Bud

1956-1980. This pedal steel company offered volume pedals as well.

MODEL YEAR	FEATURES	EXC. COND. LOW	HIGH
Volume Pedal			
1965		$90	$95

EFFECTS

SIB

Effects pedals from Rick Hamel, who helped design SMF amps.

Siegmund Guitars & Amplifiers

1993-present. Los Angeles, California amp and guitar builder Chris Siegmund added effects to his product line in '99.

Snarling Dogs

1997-present. Started by Charlie Stringer of Stringer Industries, Warren, New Jersey in '97. Stringer died in May '99. The brand is now carried by D'Andrea USA.

Sobbat

1995-present. Line of effects from Kinko Music Company of Kyoto, Japan.

Sola/Colorsound

1965-present. Sola was founded by London's Macari's Musical Exchange in '65. Sola made effects for Vox, Marshall, Park, and B & M and later under their own Colorsound brand. Refer to Colorsound for listings and more company info.

Soldano

1987-present. Seattle, Washington amp builder Soldano also builds a reverb unit.

Songbird

See Dytronics.

South Hawk

Hawk I Fuzz

MODEL YEAR	FEATURES	EXC. COND. LOW	HIGH
1975		$100	$125

LTD

| 1975 | Silver case, slider | $100 | $125 |

Speedster

1995-2000, 2003-present. Speedster added American-made guitar effects pedals to their product line in '04.

Stinger

Stinger effects were distributed by the Martin Guitar Company from 1989 to '90.

Effects

MODEL YEAR	FEATURES	EXC. COND. LOW	HIGH
1989-1990	CH-70 Stereo Chorus	$25	$55
1989-1990	CO-20 Compressor	$35	$55
1989-1990	DD-90 Digital Delay	$45	$65
1989-1990	DE-80 Analog Delay	$50	$70
1989-1990	DI-10 Distortion	$40	$65
1989-1990	FL-60 Flanger	$40	$65
1989-1990	OD-30 Overdrive	$40	$65
1989-1990	TS-5 Tube Stack	$45	$65

Studio Electronics

1989-present. Synth and midi developer Greg St. Regis' Studio Electronics added guitar pedal effects to their line in '03.

Subdecay Studios

2003-present. Brian Marshall builds his guitar effects in Woodinville, Washington.

Supro

1935-1968. Supro offered a few reverb units in the '60s.

500 R Standard Reverb Unit

1962-1963. Outboard reverb unit.

MODEL YEAR	FEATURES	EXC. COND. LOW	HIGH
1962-1963		$300	$350

Sweet Sound

1994-present. Line of effects from Bob Sweet, originally made in Trenton, Michigan, currently in Coral Springs, Florida.

Systech (Systems & Technology in Music, Inc)

1975-late-1970s. Systech was located in Kalamazoo, Michigan.

Effects

MODEL YEAR	FEATURES	EXC. COND. LOW	HIGH
1975-1979	Envelope and Repeater	$75	$125
1975-1979	Envelope Follower	$75	$125
1975-1979	Flanger	$75	$125
1975-1979	Harmonic Energizer	$150	$225
1975-1979	Overdrive Model 1300	$75	$125
1975-1979	Phase Shifter Model 1200	$75	$125

T.C. Electronics

1976-present. Brothers Kim and John Rishøj founded TC Electronic in Risskov, Denmark, and made guitar effects pedals for several years before moving into rack-mounted gear. Currently they offer a wide range of pro audio gear.

Booster + Distortion

MODEL YEAR	FEATURES	EXC. COND. LOW	HIGH
1980s		$325	$400

Dual Parametric Equalizer

| 1980s | | $275 | $350 |

Stereo Chorus/Flanger

Introduced in 1982, and reissued in '91.

| 1980s | | $175 | $225 |

Sustain + Equalizer

| 1980s | | $225 | $300 |

T.C. Jauernig Electronics

2004-present. Tim Jauernig, of Rothschild, Wisconsin, built effects for several years before launching his T.C. Jauernig brand in '04.

Tech 21

1989-present. Tech 21 offers a variety of products out of New York City.

Sansamp

1989-present. Offers a variety of tube amp tones.

MODEL YEAR	FEATURES	EXC. COND. LOW	HIGH
1989	1st year	$125	$175
1990-1999		$100	$125

XXL Pedal

1995-2000. Distortion, fuzz.

| 1995-2000 | | $50 | $75 |

*Snarling Dogs
Bawl Buster Bass Wah*

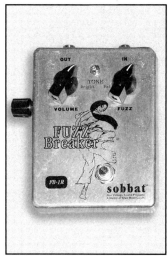

Sobbat FB-1R Fuzz Breaker

T.C. Jauernig Luxury Drive

EFFECTS

Tycobrahe Parapedal

EFFECTS

Univox Univibe

T-Rex BetaVibe

MODEL YEAR	FEATURES	EXC. COND. LOW	HIGH

Teese

Geoffrey Teese's first wah was advertised as "the Real McCoy, by Teese." He now offers his custom wah pedals under the Real McCoy Custom brand. The Teese brand was used on his line of stomp boxes, starting in '96. The Teese stomp boxes are no longer being made.

Thomas Organ

The Thomas Organ Company was heavily involved with Vox from 1964 to '72, importing their instruments into the U.S. and designing and assembling products, including the wah-wah pedal. Both Thomas Organ and JMI, Vox's European distributor, wanted to offer the new effect. The problem was solved by labeling the Thomas Organ wah the Crybaby. The Crybaby is now offered by Dunlop. Refer to Vox listing for Crybaby Stereo Fuzz Wah, Crybaby Wah, and Wah Wah.

Tonebone

See Radial Engineering listing.

Top Gear

1960s-1970s. Top Gear was a London music store. Their effects were made by other manufacturers.

Rotator
Leslie effect.

1970s		$100	$175

Top Hat Amplification

1994-present. The Anaheim, California, amp builder also offers effects.

Tremolo

See listing under Dunlop.

T-Rex

2003-present. Made in Denmark and imported by European Musical Imports.

Tube Works

1987-2004. Founded by B.K. Butler (see Audio Matrix) in Denver, Colorado, Tube Works became a division of Genz Benz Enclosures of Scottsdale, Arizona in 1997 which dropped the brand in 2004. They also offered tube/solidstate amps, cabinets, and DI boxes.

Blue Tube
1989-2004. Overdrive bass driver with 12AX7A tube.

1989-2004		$100	$150

Real Tube
Ca.1987-2004. Overdrive with 12AX7A tube.

1987-1999		$100	$150

Tube Driver
1987-2004. With tube.

1987-2004	With tube	$100	$150

Tycobrahe

The Tycobrahe story was over almost before it began. Doing business in 1976-1977, they produced only three pedals and a direct box, one the fabled Octavia. The company, located in Hermosa Beach, California, made high-quality, original devices, but they didn't catch on. Now, they are very collectible.

Octavia
1976-1977. Octave doubler.

1976-1977		$750	$950

Parapedal
1976-1977. Wah.

1976-1977		$750	$950

Pedalflanger
1976-1977. Blue pedal-controlled flanger.

1976-1977		$750	$950

Uni-Vibe

See listings under Univox and Dunlop.

Univox

Univox was a brand owned by Merson (later Unicord), of Westbury, New York. It marketed guitars and amps, and added effects in the late-'60s. Most Univox effects were made by Shinei, of Japan. They vanished in about '81.

EC-80 A Echo
Early-1970s-ca.1977. Tape echo, sometimes shown as The Brat Echo Chamber.

1970s		$95	$135

EC-100 Echo
Tape, sound-on-sound.

1970s		$105	$145

Echo-Tech EM-200
Disc recording echo unit.

1970s		$130	$170

Micro 41 FCM41 4 channel mixer

1970s		$35	$50

Micro Fazer
1970s. Phase shifter.

1970s		$75	$100

Noise-Clamp EX110

1970s		$45	$55

Phaser PHZ1
AC powered.

1970s		$50	$75

Pro Verb
1970s. Reverb (spring) unit, black tolex, slider controls for 2 inputs, 1 output plus remote output.

1970s		$80	$100

Square Wave SQ150
Introduced in 1976, distortion, orange case.

1970s		$75	$125

Super-Fuzz
1968-1970s. Early transistor effect, made by Shinei.

1971	Gray box, normal bypass switch	$225	$300
1973	Unicord, various colors, blue bypass pedal	$225	$300

Uni-Comp
Compression limiter.

1970s		$50	$100

MODEL YEAR	FEATURES	EXC. COND. LOW	HIGH
Uni-Drive			
1970s		$150	$200
Uni-Fuzz			
1960s. Fuzz tone in blue case, 2 black knobs and slider switch.			
1960s		$275	$375
Uni-Tron 5			
A.k.a. Funky Filter, envelope filter.			
1975		$125	$200
Uni-Vibe			
Introduced around 1969, with rotating speaker simulation, with pedal.			
1960s		$900	$1,050
1970s		$800	$950
Uni-Wah Wah/Volume			
1970s		$100	$125

Vesta Fire

Ca.1981-ca.1988. Brand of Japan's Shiino Musical Instrument Corp.

Effects

1981-1988	Digital Chorus/ Flanger FLCH	$35	$50
1981-1988	Distortion DST	$35	$50
1981-1988	Flanger	$35	$50
1981-1988	Noise Gate	$25	$40
1981-1988	Stereo Chorus SCH	$35	$50

Vintage Tone Project

2003-present. Line of guitar effects made by Robert Rush and company in Lafayette, Colorado. They also build reissues of Dan Armstong's '70s effects.

VooDoo Lab

1994-present. Line of effects made by Digital Music Corp. in California.

Analog Chorus
1997-present.

1997-2004		$100	$120

Bosstone
1994-1999. Based on '60s Jordan Electronics Fuzz.

1994-1999		$70	$75

Microvibe
1996-present. UniVibe swirl effect.

1996-2004		$55	$65

Overdrive
1994-2002. Based on '70s overdrive.

1994-2002		$55	$65

Super Fuzz
1999-present.

1999-2004		$75	$90

Tremolo
1995-present.

1995-2004		$55	$75

Vox

1957-present. Vox offered a variety of guitars, amps, organs and effects. Ca. '66, they released the Tone Bender, one of the classic fuzzboxes of all time. A year or so later, they delivered their greatest contribution to the effects world, the first wah-wah pedal. The American arm of Vox (then under Thomas Organ) succumbed in '72. In the U.K., the company was on-again/off-again.

Clyde McCoy Wah-Wah Pedal
Introduced in 1967, reissued in 2001-present. Clyde's picture on bottom cover.

1967	Clyde's picture	$700	$900
1968	No picture	$550	$750
2001-2004	Model V-848	$85	$100

Crybaby Wah
Introduced in 1968. The Thomas Organ Company was heavily involved with Vox from '64 to '72, importing their instruments into the U.S. and designing and assembling products. One product developed in conjunction with Vox was the wah-wah pedal. Both Thomas Organ and JMI, Vox's European distributor, wanted to offer the new effect. The problem was solved by labeling the Thomas Organ wah the Crybaby. The original wahs were built by Jen in Italy, but Thomas later made them in their Chicago, Illinois and Sepulveda, California plants. Thomas Organ retained the marketing rights to Vox until '79, but was not very active with the brand after '72. The Crybaby brand is now offered by Dunlop.

1960s	Jen-made	$200	$250
1970	Sepulveda-made	$125	$175

Double Sound
Jen-made, Double Sound model name on bottom of pedal, double sound derived from fuzz and wah ability.

1970s		$200	$250

Flanger

1970s		$200	$250

King Wah
Chrome top, Italian-made.

1970s		$100	$200

Stereo Fuzz Wah

1970s		$150	$200

Tone Bender V-828
1966-1970s. Fuzz box, reissued as the V-829 in '94.

1966	Gray	$300	$400
1969	Black	$250	$350

V-807 Echo-Reverb Unit
Solidstate, disc echo.

1967		$275	$375

V-837 Echo Deluxe Tape Echo
Solidstate, multiple heads.

1967		$350	$450

V-846 Wah
1969-1970s. Chrome top, Italian-made.

1969	Transitional Clyde McCoy	$500	$650
1970s		$300	$400

V-847 Wah
1992-present. Reissue of the original V-846 Wah.

1992-2000		$65	$80

Valvetronix Tonelab
2003-present. Multi-effect modeling processor, 12AX7 tube preamp.

2003-2004		$400	$425

Vesta Fire Distortion DST

Vox Clyde McCoy Wah

Vox King Wah

EFFECTS

Wasabi AS-1

Xotic AC Booster

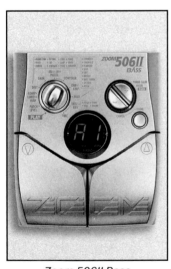

Zoom 506II Bass

MODEL YEAR	FEATURES	EXC. COND. LOW	HIGH

Volume Pedal
Late 1960s. Reissued as the V850.

1960s		$50	$100

Wasabi
2003-present. Line of guitar effect pedals from Danelectro.

Washburn
Washburn offered a line of effects from around 1983 to ca. '89.

Effects

1980s	Analog Delay AX:9	$30	$35
1980s	Flanger FX:4	$35	$40
1980s	Phaser PX:8	$40	$45
1980s	Stack in a Box SX:3	$30	$35

Watkins/WEM
1957-present. Watkins Electric Music (WEM) was founded by Charlie Watkins. Their first commercial product was the Watkins Dominator (wedge Gibson stereo amp shape) in '57, followed by the Copicat Echo in '58.

Copicat Tape Echo
1958-1970s, 1985-present. The Copicat has been reissued in various forms by Watkins.

1960s	Solidstate	$300	$400
1960s	Tube	$700	$1,000

Way Huge Electronics
1995-1998. Way Huge offered a variety of stomp boxes, made in Sherman Oaks, California.

WD Music
Since 1978, WD Music has offered a wide line of aftermarket products for guitar players. In '91, they introduced a line of effects that were copies of the original Dan Armstrong color series (refer to Dan Armstrong listing).

Blue Clipper
1991-present. Fuzz.

1991-2002		$30	$45

Orange Squeezer
1991-present. Signal compressor.

1991-2002	Light Orange case	$40	$50

Purple Peaker
1991-present. Mini EQ.

1991-2002		$40	$50

Westbury
1978-ca.1983. Brand imported by Unicord.

Tube Overdrive
1978-1983. 12AX7.

1978-1983		$150	$200

Whirlwind
1980s. Whirlwind called Rochester, New York, home.

Commander
Boost and effects loop selector.

1980s		$75	$100

MODEL YEAR	FEATURES	EXC. COND. LOW	HIGH

Wurlitzer
1960s. Wurlitzer offered the Fuzzer Buzzer in the 1960s, which was the same as the Clark Fuzz.

Xotic Effects
2001-present. Hand-wired effects made in Los Angeles, California, and distributed by Prosound Communications.

Yamaha
1946-present. Yamaha has offered effects since at least the early '80s. They also build guitars, basses, amps, and other musical instruments.

Analog Delay E1005
1980s. Free-standing, double-space rack mount-sized, short to long range delays, gray case.

1980s		$160	$180

Yubro
Yubro, of Bellaire, Texas, offered a line of nine effects in the mid- to late-'80s.

Analog Delay AD-800
300 ms.

1980s		$75	$125

Stereo Chorus CH-600

1980s		$50	$75

Zinky
1999-present. Guitar effects built by Bruce Zinky in Flagstaff, Arizona. He also builds amps and has revived the Supro brand on a guitar and amp.

Zoom
Effects line from Samson Technologies Corp. of Syosset, New York.

503 Amp Simulator
1998-2000.

1998-2000		$25	$40

504 Acoustic Pedal
1997-2000. Compact multi-effects pedal, 24 effects, tuner, replaced by II version.

1997-2000		$25	$40

505 Guitar Pedal
1996-2000. Compact multi-effects pedal, 24 effects, tuner, replaced by II version.

1996-2000		$30	$40

506 Bass Pedal
1997-2000. Compact multi-effects bass pedal, 24 effects, tuner, black box, orange panel. Replaced by II version.

1997-2000		$35	$45

507 Reverb
1997-2000.

1997-2000		$25	$40

1010 Player
1996-1999. Compact multi-effects pedal board, 16 distortions, 25 effects.

1996-1999		$40	$75

The *Vintage Guitar Price Guide* shows low to high values for items in all-original excellent condition, and, where applicable, with original case or cover.

Steels and
Lap Steels

1960 Alamo Embassy

Aria lap steel

STEELS & LAPS

MODEL YEAR	FEATURES	EXC. COND. LOW	HIGH

Airline
Ca. 1958-1968. Name used by Montgomery Ward for instruments built by Kay, Harmony and Valco.

Lap Steel

1960s	Rec-O-Glas/plastic	$500	$600
1960s	Wood	$175	$250

Rocket 6-String Steel
Black and white, 3 legs, Valco-made.

1964		$325	$375

Student 6 Steel

1958	Black	$125	$150

Alamo
1947-1982. The first musical instruments built by Alamo, of San Antonio, Texas, were lap steel and amp combos with early models sold with small birch amps. See *Guitar Stories Volume II*, by Michael Wright, for a complete history of Alamo with detailed model listings.

Hawaiian Lap Steels
1947-ca. 1967. Models include the '50s Challenger and Futuramic Dual Eight, the '50s and early-'60s Embassy (pear-shape) and Jet (triangular), the early-'60s Futuramic Eight and Futuramic Six, and the late-'60s Embassy (triangular Jet).

1950s		$125	$200

Alkire
1939-1950s. Founded by musician and teacher Eddie Alkire, the instruments may have been built by another company.

E-Harp 10-String Steel
1939-1950s. Similar to Epiphone lap steel with Epi-style logo, offered in lap steel or console.

1940s		$600	$875
1950s		$600	$875

Alvarez
Ca. 1966-present. Imported by St. Louis Music from mid-'60s.

Model 5010 Koa D Steel-String

1960s		$275	$325

Aria
1960-present. Aria offered Japanese-made steels and lap steels in the '60s.

Asher
1982-present. Intermediate, professional and premium grade, production/custom, solidbody, semi-hollow body and acoustic lap steels built by luthier Bill Asher in Venice, California. He also builds guitars.

Ben Harper Model
1998-2001. Limited edition of 70, electric lap steel version of Weissenborn guitars, mahogany body, 8 tone chambers, koa top and fretboard, natural oil or lacquer finish.

2005		$1,700	$2,200

MODEL YEAR	FEATURES	EXC. COND. LOW	HIGH

Audiovox
Ca. 1935-ca. 1950. Paul Tutmarc's Audiovox Manufacturing, of Seattle, Washington, was a pioneer in electric lap steels, basses, guitars and amps.

Lap Steel

1940s		$825	$950

Lap Steel and Amp Set

1940s		$1,250	$1,300

Bigsby
1947-1965. All handmade by Paul Arthur Bigsby, in Downey, California. Bigsby was a pioneer in developing pedal steels and they were generally special order or custom-made and not mass produced. The original instruments were made until '65 and should be valued on a case-by-case basis. Models include the Single Neck pedal steel, Double 8 pedal steel, 8/10 Doubleneck pedal steel, Triple 8 pedal steel (all ca. '47-'65), and the '57-'58 Magnatone G-70 lap steel. A solidbody guitar and a pedal steel based upon the original Paul Bigsby designs were introduced January, 2002.

Triple 8-String Neck Steel
1947-1965. Bigsby steel were generally special order or custom-made and not mass produced. Instruments should be valued on a case-by-case basis.

1947-1959	Natural	$2,700	$5,000

Blue Star
1984-present. Intermediate grade, production/custom, lap steels built by luthier Bruce Herron in Fennville, Michigan. He also builds guitars, mandolins, dulcimers, and ukes.

Bronson
George Bronson was a steel guitar instructor in the Detroit area from the 1930s to the early '50s and sold instruments under his own brand. Most instruments and amps were made by Rickenbacker, Dickerson or Valco.

Melody King Model 52 Lap Steel
Brown bakelite body with 5 gold cavity covers on the top, made by Rickenbacker.

1950s		$575	$725

Carvin
1946-present. Founded by Lowell C. Kiesel who produced lapsteels under the Kiesel brand for 1947-'50. In late '49, he renamed the instrument line Carvin after sons Carson and Galvin. Until '77, they offered lap, console, and pedal steels with up to 4 necks.

Double 6 Steel With Legs

1960s		$600	$700

Double 8 Steel With Legs

1960s	Sunburst	$650	$750

Electric Hawaiian Lap Steel

1950s		$225	$300

MODEL YEAR	FEATURES	EXC. COND. LOW	HIGH

Single 8 With Legs

Large block position markers, 1 pickup, 2 knobs, blond finish.

1960s		$450	$550

Chandler

1984-present. Intermediate grade, production/custom, solidbody Weissenborn-shaped electric lapsteels built by luthiers Paul and Adrian Chandler in Chico, California. They also build guitars, basses and pickups.

Cromwell

1935-1939. Budget model brand built by Gibson and distributed by various mail-order businesses.

Lap Steel

Charlie Christian bar pickup.

1939	Sunburst	$275	$375

Danelectro

1946-1969, 1997-present. Known mainly for guitars and amps, Danelectro did offer a few lap steels in the mid-'50s.

Lap Steels

1950s		$250	$350

Denley

1960s. Pedal steels built by Nigel Dennis and Gordon Huntley in England. They also made steels for Jim Burns' Ormston brand in the '60s.

Dickerson

1937-1948. Founded by the Dickerson brothers in '37, primarily for electric lap steels and small amps. Besides their own brand, Dickerson made instruments for Cleveland's Oahu Company, Varsity, Southern California Music, Bronson, Roland Ball, and Gourley. The lap steels were often sold with matching amps, both covered in pearloid mother-of-toilet-seat (MOTS). By '48, the company changed ownership and was renamed Magna Electronics (Magnatone).

Lap Steel with matching amp

1950s. Gray pearloid with matching amp.

1950s		$450	$550

Dobro

1929-1942, ca.1954-present. Dobro offered lap steels from '33 to '42. Gibson now owns the brand and recently offered a lap steel.

Hawaiian Lap Steel

1933-1942		$350	$450

Lap Steel Guitar and Amp Set

1930s-1940s. Typical pearloid covered student 6-string lap steel and small matching amp (with 3 tubes and 1 control knob).

1933-1942	White pearloid	$450	$550

Dwight

1950s. Private branded instruments made by National-Supro.

Lap Steel

1950s. Pearloid, 6 strings.

1950s	Gray pearloid	$350	$425

Emmons

1970s-present. Owned by Lashley, Inc. of Burlington, North Carolina.

Lashley LeGrande III Steel

2001-present. Double-neck, 8 pedals, 4 knee levers, 25th Anniversary.

2001		$2,000	$3,000

S-10 Pedal Steel

Single 10-string neck pedal steel.

1970s		$800	$1,300

English Electronics

1960s. Norman English had a teaching studio in Lansing, Michigan, where he gave guitar and steel lessons. He had his own private-branded instruments made by Valco in Chicago.

Tonemaster Lap Steel

Cream pearloid, 6 strings, 3 legs, Valco-made.

1960s		$250	$300

Epiphone

1928-present. The then Epiphone Banjo Company was established in '28. Best known for its guitars, the company offered steels from '35 to '58 when Gibson purchased the brand.

Century Lap Steel

1939-1957. Rocket-shaped maple body, 1 pickup, metal 'board, 6, 7 or 8 strings, black finish.

1939-1957		$325	$425

Electar Hawaiian Lap Steel

1935-1937. Wood teardrop-shaped body, bakelite top, black, horseshoe pickup, 6 string.

1935-1937		$425	$475

Electar Model M Hawaiian Lap Steel

1936-1939. Metal top, stair-step body, art deco, black ('36-'37) or gray ('38-'39), 6, 7 or 8 strings.

1936-1939		$350	$450

Zephyr Hawaiian Lap Steel

1939-1957. Maple stair-step body, metal 'board, 6, 7 or 8 strings.

1939-1949	Black, with white top	$550	$700
1950-1957	Sunburst	$550	$700

Kent Hawaiian Lap Steel

1949-1953. Guitar-shaped maple body, 6 strings, lower-end of Epiphone Hawaiian line.

1949-1953		$300	$375

Solo Console Steel

1939-1954. Maple with white mahogany laminated body, black binding, black metal 'board, 6, 7 or 8 strings.

1939-1954		$450	$550

Triple-Neck Console Steel

1954-1957. Three neck version of Solo, sunburst or natural finish.

1954-1957		$700	$900

Chandler Lectraslide

1941 Epiphone Electar Zephyr

STEELS & LAPS

1948 Fender Princeton

STEELS & LAPS

Fender Champion

MODEL YEAR	FEATURES	EXC. COND. LOW	HIGH

Fender

1946-present. Fender offered lap and pedal steels from '46 to '80.

400 Pedal Steel

1958-1976. One 8-string neck with 4 to 10 pedals.

1960s	Blond	$600	$1,000

800 Pedal Steel

1964-1976. One 10-string neck, 6 to 10 pedals.

1964-1976	Sunburst	$700	$1,100

1000 Pedal Steel

1957-1976. Two 8-string necks and 8 or 10 pedals.

1957-1976	Natural, 8 pedals	$900	$1,300
1957-1976	Sunburst, 10 pedals	$900	$1,300
1957-1976	Sunburst, 8 pedals	$900	$1,300

2000 Pedal Steel

1964-1976. Two 10-string necks, 10 or 11 pedals, sunburst.

1964-1976	10 pedals	$1,200	$1,600

Artist Dual 10 Pedal Steel

1976-1981. Two 10-string necks, 8 pedals, 4 knee levers, black or mahogany.

1976-1981		$600	$1,000

Champion Lap Steel

1949-1955. Covered in what collectors call mother-of-toilet-seat (MOTS) finish, also known as pearloid. Replaced by Champ Lap Steel.

1949-1955	Tan	$700	$775
1949-1955	White or yellow pearloid	$700	$775

Champ Lap Steel

1955-1980. Replaced Champion Lap Steel.

1955-1959	Tan	$700	$775
1960-1969	Tan	$650	$725
1970-1980	Tan	$500	$650

Deluxe Steel

1949-1950. Strings-thru-pickup, Roman numeral markers, became the Deluxe 6 or Deluxe 8 Lap Steel in '50.

1946	Wax	$850	$1,050
1947-1950	Blond or Walnut	$850	$1,050

Deluxe 6/Stringmaster Single Steel

1950-1981. Renamed from the Deluxe, 6 strings, 3 legs.

1950-1959	Blond or Walnut	$800	$1,000
1960-1969	Blond or Walnut	$750	$1,000
1970-1981	Black or White	$750	$900

Deluxe 8/Stringmaster Single Steel

1950-1981. Renamed from the Deluxe, 8 strings, 3 legs.

1950-1969	Blond or Walnut	$800	$1,050
1970-1981	Black or White	$750	$950

Dual 6 Professional Steel

1950-1981. Two 6-string necks, 3 legs optional, blond or walnut.

1952-1981	Blond	$800	$1,100
1952-1981	Walnut	$900	$1,000

Dual 8 Professional Steel

1946-1957. Two 8-string necks, 3 legs optional, blond or walnut.

1946-1957	Blond	$1,000	$1,300
1946-1957	Walnut	$900	$1,100

MODEL YEAR	FEATURES	EXC. COND. LOW	HIGH

K & F Steel

1945-1946. Made by Doc Kauffman and Leo Fender, strings-thru-pickup.

1945-1946	Black	$1,350	$1,500

Organ Button Steel

1946-1947.

1946-1947	Wax	$900	$1,000

Princeton Steel

1946-1948. Strings-thru-pickup, Roman numeral markers.

1946-1948	Wax	$650	$750

Stringmaster Steel (two-neck)

1953-1981. The Stringmaster came in 3 versions, having 2, 3 or 4 8-string necks (6-string necks optional).

1953-1959	Blond (light finish)	$1,500	$1,900
1953-1959	Walnut (dark finish)	$1,200	$1,500
1960-1969	Blond (light finish)	$1,400	$1,700
1960-1969	Walnut (dark finish)	$1,000	$1,400
1970-1981	Blond or Walnut	$1,000	$1,300

Stringmaster Steel (three-neck)

1953-1981.

1953-1959	Blond (light finish)	$2,200	$2,500
1953-1959	Walnut (dark finish)	$1,700	$2,200
1960-1969	Blond (light finish)	$1,900	$2,400
1960-1969	Walnut (dark finish)	$1,400	$1,800
1970-1981	Blond (light finish)	$1,500	$1,700
1970-1981	Walnut (dark finish)	$1,100	$1,400

Stringmaster Steel (four-neck)

1953-1968.

1953-1959	Blond (light finish)	$2,400	$2,800
1953-1959	Walnut (dark finish)	$1,900	$2,500
1960-1968	Blond (light finish)	$2,100	$2,700
1960-1968	Walnut (dark finish)	$1,600	$2,100

Studio Deluxe Lap Steel

1956-1981. One pickup, 3 legs.

1956-1981	Blond	$725	$775

Framus

1946-1977, 1996-present. Imported into the U.S. by Philadelphia Music Company in the '60s. Brand revived in '96, and distributed in the U.S. by Dana B. Goods.

Deluxe Table Steel 0/7

1970s	White	$300	$350

Student Hawaiian Model 0/4

1970s	Red	$175	$225

G.L. Stiles

1960-1994. Gilbert Lee Stiles made a variety of instruments, mainly in the Miami, Florida area. See Guitar section for more company info.

Doubleneck Pedal Steel

1970s		$475	$600

Gibson

1902-present. Gibson offered steels from '35-'68.

MODEL YEAR	FEATURES	EXC. COND. LOW	HIGH
BR-4 Lap Steel			
1947. Guitar-shaped of solid mahogany, round neck, 1 pickup, varied binding.			
1947	Sunburst	$425	$525
BR-6 Lap Steel			
1947-1960. Guitar-shaped solid mahogany body, square neck (round by '48).			
1947-1960		$425	$525
BR-9 Lap Steel			
1947-1959. Solidbody, 1 pickup, tan.			
1947-1949	Non-adj. Poles	$350	$450
1950-1959	Adj. Poles	$450	$550
1950-1959	Matching Steel and Amp	$700	$800
Century 6 Lap Steel			
1948-1968. Solid maple body, 6 strings, 1 pickup, silver 'board.			
1948-1968		$550	$650
Century 10 Lap Steel			
1948-1955. Solid maple body, 10 strings, 1 pickup, silver 'board.			
1948-1955	Black	$550	$650
Console Grand Steel			
1938-1942, 1948-1967. Hollowbody, 2 necks, triple-bound body, standard 7- and 8-string combination until '42, double 8-string necks standard for '48 and after.			
1938-1942	Sunburst	$1,000	$1,300
1948-1967	Sunburst	$1,000	$1,300
Consolette Table Steel			
1952-1957. Rectangular korina body, 2 8-string necks, 4 legs, replaced by maple-body Console after '56.			
1952-1957		$1,000	$1,200
Console Steel (C-530)			
1956-1966. Replaced Consolette during '56-'57, double 8-string necks, 4 legs optional.			
1956-1966	With legs	$900	$1,100
EH-100 Lap Steel			
1936-1949. Hollow guitar-shaped body, bound top, 6 or 7 strings.			
1936-1939		$650	$850
1940-1949		$550	$750
EH-125 Lap Steel			
1939-1942. Hollow guitar-shaped mahogany body, single-bound body, metal 'board.			
1939-1942	Sunburst	$750	$950
EH-150 Lap Steel			
1936-1943. Hollow guitar-shaped body, 6 to 10 strings available, bound body.			
1936	1st offering metal body	$2,500	$3,000
1937-1939	Sunburst	$950	$1,150
1940-1943	Sunburst	$850	$1,000
EH-150 Lap Steel Matching Set (guitar and amp)			
1936-1942. Both electric Hawaiian steel guitar and amp named EH-150, with matching tweed guitar case.			
1936-1939	Guitar with Christian pickup	$2,000	$2,200
1940-1942		$1,600	$1,800

MODEL YEAR	FEATURES	EXC. COND. LOW	HIGH
EH-150 Doubleneck Electric Hawaiian Steel			
1937-1939. Doubleneck EH-150 with 7- and 8-string necks.			
1937-1939		$2,700	$3,000
EH-185 Lap Steel			
1939-1942. Hollow guitar-shaped curly maple body, triple-bound body, 6, 7, 8 or 10 strings.			
1939-1942	Sunburst, lap steel and amp	$1,900	$2,300
1939-1942	Sunburst, lap steel only	$1,300	$1,800
EH-500 Skylark Lap Steel			
1956-1968. Solid korina body, 8-string available by '58.			
1956-1968	Natural	$850	$950
EH-620 Steel			
1955-1967. Eight strings, 6 pedals.			
1955-1967	Natural	$750	$900
EH-630 Electraharp Steel			
1941-1967. Eight strings, 8 pedals (4 in '49-'67). Called just EH-630 from '56-'67.			
1941-1967	Sunburst	$900	$1,000
EH-820 Steel			
1960-1966. Two necks, 8 pedals, Vari-Tone selector.			
1960s	Cherry	$1,000	$1,300
Royaltone Lap Steel			
1950-1952, 1956-1957. Symmetrical wavy body, volume and tone knobs on treble side of pickup, Gibson silk-screen logo, brown pickup bridge cover, updated guitar-shaped body style for '56-'57.			
1950-1952	Symmetrical body	$800	$900
1956-1957	Guitar-shaped body	$500	$800
Ultratone Lap Steel			
1946-1959. Solid maple body, plastic 'board, 6 strings.			
1940s	White	$800	$1,000
1950s	Dark Blue or Seal Brown	$850	$1,050

Gold Tone

1993-present. Wayne and Robyn Rogers build their intermediate grade, production/custom lap steels in Titusville, Florida. They also offer basses, mandolins, banjos and banjitars.

Gourley

See Dickerson listing.

Gretsch

1883-present. Gretsch offered a variety of steels from 1940-'63. Gretsch actually only made 1 model; the rest were built by Valco. Currently they offer 2 lap steel models.

Electromatic Console (6158) Twin Neck Steel

1949-1955. Two 6-string necks with six-on-a-side tuners, Electromatic script logo on end cover plates, 3 knobs, metal control panels and knobs, pearloid covered.

1949-1955		$700	$900

Gibson Royaltone

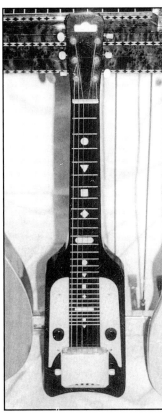

1950s Gretsch Electromatic

STEELS & LAPS

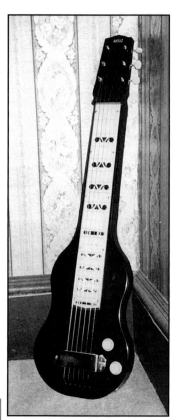

Kiesel lap steel

Harmony Roy Smeck

MODEL YEAR	FEATURES	EXC. COND. LOW	HIGH

Electromatic Standard (6156) Lap Steel
1950-1955.

| 1950-1955 | Brown Pearloid | $500 | $600 |

Electromatic Student (6152) Lap Steel
1949-1955. Square bottom, pearloid cover.

| 1949-1955 | Brown Pearloid | $375 | $450 |

Jet Mainliner (6147) Steel
1955-1963. Single-neck version of Jet Twin.

| 1955-1963 | | $500 | $600 |

Jet Twin Console (6148) Steel
1955-1963. Valco-made, 2 6-string necks, six-on-a-side tuners, Jet Black.

| 1955-1963 | | $700 | $900 |

Guyatone

1933-present. Large Japanese maker. Brands also include Marco Polo, Winston, Kingston, Kent, LaFayette and Bradford. They offered lap steels under various brands from the '30s to the '60s.

Lap Steels

| 1960s | | $250 | $300 |

Table Steels
Three legs, 2 pickups.

| 1960s | | $325 | $375 |

Harmony

1982-1976. Founded by Wilhelm Schultz and purchased by Sears in 1916. The company evolved into the largest producer of stringed instruments in the U.S. in the '30s. They offered electric lap steels by '36.

Lap Steels

1936-1959	Various models	$250	$450
1960s	Painted body	$250	$450
1960s	Pearloid body	$300	$450

Jackson-Guldan

1920s-1960s. The Jackson-Guldan Violin Company, of Columbus, Ohio, offered lap steels and small tube amps early on. They also built acoustic guitars.

K & F (Kaufman & Fender)

See listing under Fender.

Kalamazoo

1933-1942, 1946-1947, 1965-1970. Budget brand produced by Gibson in Kalamazoo, Michigan. They offered lap steels in the '30s and '40s.

Lap Steels
1938-1942, 1946-1947.

| 1938-1942 | Sunburst | $200 | $375 |
| 1946-1947 | Sunburst or plain brown | $200 | $375 |

Kay

Ca. 1931-present. Huge Chicago manufacturer Kay offered steels from '36 to '60 under their own brand and others. See Guitar Stories Volume II, by Michael Wright, for a complete history of Kay with detailed model listings.

MODEL YEAR	FEATURES	EXC. COND. LOW	HIGH

K-24 Deluxe Steel

| 1950s | Honey Sunburst | $275 | $400 |
| 1960s | | $275 | $400 |

Lap Steel
1940s. Kay crest logo.

| 1940s | Blond | $275 | $400 |

Lap Steel with matching amp

| 1940s | Dark mahogany | $400 | $550 |
| 1950s | Green | $400 | $550 |

Kiesel

1946-1949. Founded by Lowell Kiesel as L.C. Kiesel Co., Los Angeles, California, but renamed Carvin in '49. Kiesel logo on the headstock.

Bakelite Lap Steel
1946. Small guitar-shaped bakelite body, 1 pickup, 2 knobs, diamond markers.

| 1946 | | $275 | $400 |

Lapdancer

2001-present. Intermediate and professional grade, custom/production, lap steels built by luthier Loni Specter in West Hills, California.

Maestro

A budget brand made by Gibson.

Lap Steel
Pearloid, 1 pickup, 6 strings.

| 1940s | | $275 | $350 |
| 1950s | | $250 | $300 |

Magnatone

Ca. 1937-1971. Magnatone offered lap steels from '37 to '58. Besides their own brand, they also produced models under the Dickerson, Oahu, Gourley, and Natural Music Guild brands.

Lyric Doubleneck Lap Steel
Ca.1951-1958. Model G-1745-D-W, 8 strings per neck, hardwood body.

| 1951-1958 | | $350 | $550 |

Maestro Tripleneck Steel
Ca.1951-1958. Model G-2495-W-W, maple and walnut, 8 strings per neck, legs.

| 1951-1958 | | $550 | $700 |

Pearloid (MOTS) Lap Steels
1950s. These were often sold with a matching amp; price here is for lap steel only.

| 1950s | | $200 | $375 |

Lap Steel and Amp MOTS Set
Late-1940s-mid-1950s. Matching pearloid acetate covered lap steel and small amp.

| 1948-1955 | | $550 | $675 |

Marvel

1950-mid 1960s. Budget brand marketed by the Peter Sorkin Company of New York.

Electric Hawaiian Lap Steel

| 1950s | | $150 | $250 |

May Bell

See listing under Slingerland.

STEELS & LAPS

MODEL YEAR	FEATURES	EXC. COND. LOW	HIGH

McKinney
Lap Steel

1950s	White Pearloid	$300	$350

Melobar

1970-present. Designed by Walt Smith, of Smith Family Music, Melobar instruments feature a guitar body with a tilted neck, allowing the guitarist to play lap steel standing up. The instrument was developed and first made in Ed and Rudy Dopyera's Dobro factory. Most were available in 6-, 8-, or 10-string versions. Ted Smith took over operations from his father. Ted retired in late 2002.

6-String Electric Steel

1990s. Solidbody cutaway body shape, portable Melobar-style.

1990s		$625	$700

10-String Electric Steel

1970s. Double-cut guitar-shaped body, portable Melobar-style. Similar model currently offered as the Skreemr.

1970s		$750	$900

Skreemr Electric Steel

Early 1990s-present. The classic Melobar in a V (Skreemr SK2000) or double-cut (Skreemr) version, available in 6-, 8- and 10-string versions.

1990s	6-string version	$550	$650

V-10 Power-Slide Guitar

1982-early 1990s. Solidbody, V-shaped body, tilted neck, 10 strings (6- or 8-string models were available). Similar model now called the Skreemr SK2000.

1980s		$750	$900

X-10 Power-Slide Guitar

1981-early 1990s. Solidbody, futuristic body shape, tilted neck, 10 strings (6- or 8-string models were available). Called the Power-Slide One in early literature.

1980s		$750	$900

National

Ca. 1927-present. Founded in Los Angeles as the National String Instrument Corporation in '27, the brand has gone through many ownership changes over the years. National offered lap steels from '35 to '68.

Chicagaon Lap Steel

1948-1961. Gray pearloid, metal hand rest.

1948-1961		$350	$450

Console (Dual 8) Steel

1939-1942. Two 8-string necks, parallelogram markers, black top with white sides.

1939-1942		$975	$1,050

Dynamic Lap Steel

1941-1968. New Yorker-style body, 6 strings, 3 detachable screw-in legs added by '56.

1941-1965	Lap steel	$400	$500
1956-1968	With legs	$450	$550

Electric Hawaiian Lap Steel

1935-1937. Cast aluminum round body, 1 pickup, square neck, 6 or 7 strings.

1935-1937	6 strings	$700	$800
1935-1937	7 strings	$750	$850

Grand Console Steel

1947-1968. Two 8-string necks, Totem Pole 'board markers.

1947-1959		$525	$675
1960-1968		$500	$600

New Yorker Lap Steel

1939-1967. Introduced as Electric Hawaiian model in '35, square end body with stair-step sides, 7 or 8 strings, black and white finish.

1939-1949		$600	$675
1950-1959		$500	$575
1960-1967		$400	$475

Princess Lap Steel

1942-1947. Strings-thru-pickup, parallelogram markers, white pearloid.

1942-1947		$350	$450

Rocket One Ten Lap Steel

1955-1958. Rocket-shaped, black and white finish.

1955-1958		$350	$450

Trailblazer Steel

1948-1950. Square end, numbered markers, black.

1948-1950		$350	$450

Triplex Chord Changer Lap Steel

1949-1958. Maple and walnut body, 2 knobs, natural.

1949-1958		$350	$450

Nioma

Regal and others (maybe Dickerson?) made instruments for this brand, most likely for a guitar studio or distributor.

Lap Steel

1930s	Pearloid	$225	$300

Oahu

1926-1985. The Oahu Publishing Company and Honolulu Conservatory, based in Cleveland, published a very popular guitar study course. They sold instruments to go with the lessons, starting with acoustic Hawaiian and Spanish guitars, selling large quantities in the '30s. As electric models became popular, Oahu responded with guitar-amp sets. Lap steel and matching amp sets were generally the same color; for example, yellow guitar and yellow amp, or white pearloid guitar and white amp. These sets were originally sold to students who would take private or group lessons. The instruments were made by Oahu, Valco, Harmony, Dickerson, and Rickenbacker and were offered into the '50s and '60s.

Dianna Lap Steel

1950s. Oahu and Diana logos on headstock, Oahu logo on fretboard, fancy bridge, pleasant unusual sunburst finish.

1950s		$500	$600

Hawaiian Lap Steel

1930s	Sunburst	$275	$375
1940s	Pearloid, Supro-made	$300	$400
1950s	Pearloid or painted	$275	$400

Melobar Skreemr

1940 Oahu Tonemaster

STEELS & LAPS

Rickenbacker seven-string

Rickenbacker Model B-6

MODEL YEAR	FEATURES	EXC. COND. LOW	HIGH

Lap Steel/Amp Set
See also Lap Steel Oahu Amp listing in the Guide's amp section.

1930s	Pearloid, small rectangular amp	$475	$600
1930s	Sunburst, mahogany	$425	$550
1950s	White Valco Amp, 1x10"	$450	$500
1950s	Yellow Valco amp	$450	$500

Lolana
1950-1951, Late-1950s. Gold hardware, 2 6-string necks. Early model is lap steel, later version a console.

1950-1951	Lap	$500	$600
1950s	Console	$700	$800

Ormston
1966-1968. Pedal steels built in England by Denley and marketed by James Ormston Burns between his stints with Burns London, which was bought by America's Baldwin Company in '65, and the Dallas Arbiter Hayman brand.

Premier
Ca.1938-ca.1975, 1990s-present. Premier made a variety of instruments, including lap steels, under several brands.

Recording King
Ca. 1930-1943. Brand used by Montgomery Ward for instruments made by Gibson, Regal, Kay, and Gretsch.

Electric Hawaiian Lap Steel
1930s		$375	$450

Roy Smeck Model AB104 Steel
1938-1941. Pear-shaped body, 1 pickup.

1940s		$375	$450

Regal
Ca. 1884-1954. Regal offered their own brand and made instruments for distributors and mass-merchandisers. The company sold out to Harmony in '54.

Electric Hawaiian Lap Steel
1940s		$175	$275

Octophone Steel
1930s		$350	$500

Reso-phonic Steel
1930s. Dobro-style resonator and spider assembly, round neck, adjustable nut.

1930s		$850	$1,100

Rickenbacker
1931-present. Rickenbacker produced steels from '32 to '70.

Acadamy Lap Steel
1946-1947. Bakelite student model, horseshoe pickup, replaced by the Ace.

1946-1947		$350	$400

MODEL YEAR	FEATURES	EXC. COND. LOW	HIGH

Ace Lap Steel
1948-1953. Bakelite body, 1 pickup.

1948-1953		$350	$400

DC-16 Steel
1950-1952. Metal, double 8-string necks.

1950-1952		$700	$800

Electro Doubleneck Steel
1940-1953. Two bakelite 8-string necks.

1940-1953		$1,100	$1,400

Electro Tripleneck Steel
1940-1953. Three bakelite 8-string necks.

1940-1953		$1,200	$1,500

Model 59 Lap Steel
1937-1943. Sheet steel body, 1 pickup.

1937-1943		$650	$750

Model 100 Lap Steel
1956-1970. Wood body, 6 strings, block markers, light or silver gray finish.

1956-1970		$450	$500

Model A-22 "Frying Pan" Steel
1932-1950, 1954-1958. Frying Pan Electro Hawaiian Guitar, cast aluminum body, 1 pickup, slotted peghead.

1932-1936		$1,500	$1,600

Model B Steel
1935-1955. Bakelite body and neck, 1 pickup, string-thru-body, decorative metal plates, 6 strings.

1935-1955	Black	$900	$1,000

Model BD Steel
1949-1970. Bakelite body, 6 strings, deluxe version of Model B, black.

1949-1960		$650	$700

Model CW-6 Steel
1957-1961. Wood body, grille cloth on front, 6 strings, 3 legs, renamed JB (Jerry Byrd) model in '61.

1957-1961	Walnut	$650	$750

Model DW Steel
1955-1961. Wood body, double 6- or 8-string necks, optional 3 legs.

1955-1961	8-string necks	$700	$1,000

Model G Lap Steel
Ca.1948-1957. Chrome-plated ornate version of Silver Hawaiian, gold hardware and trim, 6 or 8 strings.

1948-1957		$600	$700

Model S/NS (New Style) Steel
1946-early-1950s. Sheet steel body, 1 pickup, also available as a doubleneck.

1946-1949	Gray Sparkle	$600	$700
1946-1949	Gray, metal body	$600	$700
1946-1949	Grayburst	$600	$700

Model SD Steel
1949-1953. Deluxe NS, sheet steel body, 6, 7 or 8 strings, Copper Crinkle finish.

1949-1953		$550	$600

Silver Hawaiian Lap Steel
1937-1943. Chrome-plated sheet steel body, 1 horseshoe pickup, 6 strings.

1937-1943		$900	$1,000

STEELS & LAPS

MODEL YEAR	FEATURES	EXC. COND. LOW	HIGH

Roland Ball
See Dickerson listing.

Sherwood
c.1950s. Private brand made by Chicago manufacturerers such as Kay.
Deluxe Lap Steel
1950s. Symmetrical body, bar pickup, volume and tone controls, wood body, sunburst, relatively ornate headstock with script Sherwood logo, vertical Deluxe logo, and lightning bolt art.

1950s		$400	$450

Sho-Bud
1956-1980. Founded by Shot Jackson in Nashville. Distributed by Gretsch. They also had guitar models. Baldwin bought the company in '79 and closed the factory in '80.
Maverick Pedal Steel
Ca. 1970-1980. Beginner model, burl elm cover, 3 pedals.

1970-1980		$500	$700

Pro I
1970-1980. Three pedals, natural.

1970-1975	Round front pre-1976	$650	$800
1976-1980	Square front later model	$800	$1,000

Pro II
1973-1980. Birdseye maple, double 10-string necks, natural.

1970-1975	Round front pre-1976	$750	$950
1976-1980	Square front later model	$950	$1,100

Pro III
1975-1980. Metal necks.

1970-1975	Round front pre-1976	$850	$1,000
1976-1980	Square front later model	$1,000	$1,200

Super Pro
1977-1980. Doubleneck 10 strings, 8 floor pedals, 6 knee levers, Jet Black.

1977-1980		$1,400	$1,500

Silvertone
1940-1970. Brand name for instruments sold by Sears.
Six-String Lap Steels

1950s	Standard finish	$175	$275
1950s	White pearloid	$200	$325
1960s		$150	$250

Slingerland
1916-present. Offered by Slingerland Banjos and Drums. They also sold the May Bell brand. Instruments were made by others and sold by Slingerland in the '30s and '40s.

May Bell Lap Steel
1930s. Guitar-shaped lap steel with May Bell logo. This brand also had '30s Hawaiian and Spanish guitars.

1930s	Black	$225	$425

Supertone
1914-1941. Brand name for Sears which was replaced by Silvertone. Instruments made by Harmony and others.
Electric Hawaiian Lap Steel

1930s	Various models	$250	$450

Supro
1935-1968. Budget brand of the National Dobro Company.
Clipper Lap Steel
1941-1943. One pickup, bound rosewood 'board, dot inlay, brown pearloid.

1941-1943		$275	$325

Comet Lap Steel
1947-1966. One pickup, attached cord, painted-on 'board, pearloid.

1947-1949	Gray pearloid	$225	$300
1950-1959	White pearloid	$250	$325
1960-1966	White pearloid	$200	$275

Comet Steel (with legs)
1950s-1960s. Three-leg 6-string steel version of the lap steel, 2 knobs, Supro logo on cover plate, 1 pickup.

1960s	Black and White	$600	$700

Console 8 Steel
1958-1960. Eight strings, 3 legs, black and white.

1958-1960		$600	$700

Irene
1940s. Complete ivory pearloid cover including headstock, fretboard and body, Roman numeral markers, 1 pickup, 2 control knobs, hard-wired output cord.

1940s		$300	$400

Jet Airliner Steel
1962-1964. One pickup, totem pole markings, 6 or 8 strings, pearloid, National-made.

1962-1964	Red	$225	$300

Professional Steel
Light brown pearloid.

1950s		$250	$325

Special Steel
1955-1962. Pearloid lap steel, student model, large script "Special" logo near pickup on early models, red until '57, white after.

1955-1957	Red pearloid	$225	$300
1957-1962	White pearloid	$225	$300

Spectator Steel
1952-1954. Wood body, 1 pickup, painted-on 'board, natural.

1952-1954		$175	$275

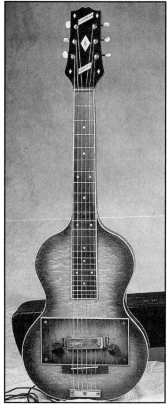

Slingerland Songster

1930s Supro Hawaiian Electric

STEELS & LAPS

Timtone Lapdog

Wayne lap steel

STEELS & LAPS

MODEL YEAR	FEATURES	EXC. COND. LOW	HIGH

Student De Luxe Lap Steel
1952-1955. One pickup, pearloid, large script "Student De Luxe" logo located near pickup, replaced by Special in '55.

1952-1955	Black and white, or red, pearloid	$300	$375
1952-1955	Natural wood or white paint	$275	$300

Supreme Lap Steel
1947-1960. One pickup, painted-on 'board, brown pearloid until ca.'55, then red until ca.'58, Tulip Yellow after that.

1947-1960		$300	$375

Supro 60 lap steel and amp-in-case
Late 1930s-early '40s. Supro 60 logo near the single volume knob, long horizontal guitar case which houses a small tube amp and speaker, the case cover folds out to allow for ventilation for the tubes, the amp was made by National Dobro of Chicago.

1939-1941	White pearloid, black amp case	$750	$850

Twin lap steel
1948-1955. Two 6-string necks, pearloid covering, renamed Console Steel in '55.

1948-1955		$500	$600

Teisco
1946-1974. The Japanese guitar-maker offered many steel models from '55 to around '67. Models offered '55-'61: EG-7L, -K, -R, -NT, -Z, -A, -S, -P, -8L, -NW, and -M. During '61-'67: EG-TW, -O, -U, -L, -6N, -8N, -DB, -DB2, -DT, H-39, H-905, TRH-1, Harp-8 and H-850.

Hawaiian Lap Steels
1955-1967		$150	$250

Timtone Custom Guitars
1993-present. Luthier Tim Diebert builds his professional grade, custom, lap steel guitars in Grand Forks, British Columbia. He also builds guitars and basses.

True Tone
1960s. Brand name sold by Western Auto (hey, everybody was in the guitar biz back then). Probably made by Kay or Harmony.

Lap Steel
1960s. Guitar-shaped, single-cut, 1 pickup.

1960s		$225	$300

Varsity
See Dickerson listing.

Vega
1903-present. The original Boston-based company was purchased by C.F. Martin in '70. In '80, the Vega trademark was sold to a Korean company. The company was one of the first to enter the electric market by offering products in '36 and offered lap steels into the early '60s.

DG-DB Steel
Two necks, 8 strings.

1950s		$600	$700

Odell Lap Steel
White pearloid.

1950s		$300	$400

Other Lap Steels
1930s		$350	$450
1940s	Art deco-style	$350	$450

Wabash
Brand name of Larry Wexler and Company of Chicago.

Lap Steel (Hawaiian Scene tailpiece)
Natural, 12 frets.

1950s		$225	$325

Wayne
1998-present. Luthiers Wayne and Michael Charvel, of Paradise, California, added intermediate grade, production, lap steel guitars to their line in '04. They also build guitars.

White
1955-1960. The White brand, named after plant manager Forrest White, was established by Fender to provide steel and small amp sets to teaching studios that were not Fender-authorized dealers. A standard guitar was planned, but never produced.

6 String Steel
1955-1956. White finish, block markers, 2 knobs, 3 legs. The 6 String Steel was usually sold with the matching white amp Model 80. Possibly only 1 batch of these was made by Fender in October/November '55.

1955-1956		$700	$825

Mandolins

1920 American Conservatory Style A

Andersen Stringed Instruments mando

MODEL YEAR	FEATURES	EXC. COND. LOW	HIGH

Airline

Ca. 1958-1968. Brand for Montgomery Ward. Instruments were built by Kay, Harmony and Valco.

Electric Mandolin (Kay K390)

Early-1960s. In '62 the K390 was advertised as the Kay Professional Electric Mandolin. Venetian shape with sunburst spruce top, curly maple back and sides, tube-style pickup, white 'guard, rope-style celluloid binding.

1962		$350	$550

Mandolin (lower end)

1960s. Acoustic, plainer features.

1960s		$250	$350

Allen

1982-present. Premium grade, production resonators, steel-string flat-tops, and mandolins built by Luthier Randy Allen, Colfax, California.

Alvarez

C.1966-present. An import brand for St. Louis Music, Alvarez currently offers intermediate grade, production, mandolins.

Model A Mandolins

Classic F-style mandolin features, round soundhole or F-holes. Models include the A700 and A910.

1970s		$350	$600

American Conservatory (Lyon & Healy)

Late-1800s-early-1900s. Mainly catalog sales of guitars and mandolins from the Chicago maker. Marketed as a less expensive alternative to the Lyon & Healy Washburn product line.

Arched Back Mandolins

1910s. Flat back with a mild arch, standard appointments, nothing fancy.

1910s		$325	$375

Bowl Back Mandolin Style G2603

Early-1900s. Bowl back-style, 28 rosewood ribs (generally more ribs and use of rosewood ribs versus mahogany indicates higher quality), color corded soundhole and edge inlay, inlaid tortoise shell celluloid guard plate underneath strings and below the soundhole, bent top, butterfly headstock inlay.

1917		$325	$400

Bowl Back Mandolin Style G2604

Early-1900s. Bowl back-style, 42 rosewood ribs (generally more ribs incidated higher quality), extra fancy color corded soundhole and edge inlay around, extra fancy inlaid tortoise shell celluloid guard plate underneath strings and below the soundhole, bent top, butterfly headstock inlay.

1917		$475	$525

Andersen Stringed Instruments

1978-present. Luthier Steve Andersen builds his premium grade, production/custom mandolins in Seattle, Washington. He also builds guitars.

Apitius

1976-present. Luthier Oliver Apitius builds his premium and presentation grade, production/custom, mandolins in Shelburne, Ontario.

Applause

1994-present. Applause currently offers intermediate grade, production, mandolins. Kaman Music's entry-level Ovation-styled import brand added mandolins in '94.

MAE148 Mandolin

1994-present. Acoustic/electric import.

1990s	Black	$250	$275

Aria/Aria Pro II

1960-present. Intermediate grade, production, acoustic and electric mandolins from Aria/Aria Pro II, which added Japanese and Korean mandolins to their line in '76.

AM200/BS Style A Mandolin

1994-present. Beginner-grade import, pear-shaped body, sunburst.

1990s		$175	$300

AM300/BS Style F Mandolin

1990s. F-style, sunburst.

1990s		$325	$425

AM600 Style F Mandolin

1990s		$375	$475

PM750 Style F Mandolin

Mid-1970s. F-style Loar copy, sunburst.

1976		$400	$525

Armstrong, Rob

1971-present. Custom mandolins made in Coventry, England, by luthier Rob Armstrong. He also builds basses, flat-tops, and parlor guitars.

Atkin Guitars

1993-present. Luthier Alister Atkin builds his production/custom mandolins in Canterbury, England. He also builds flat-top guitars.

Austin

1999-present. Budget and intermediate grade, production, mandolins imported by St. Louis Music. They also offer guitars, basses and banjos.

Bacon & Day

Established in 1921 by David Day and Paul Bacon, primarily known for fine quality tenor and plectrum banjos in the '20s and '30s.

Mandolin Banjo "Orchestra"

1920s. Mandolin neck and banjo body with open back, headstock with Bacon logo.

1920s		$350	$450

Senorita Banjo Mandolin

1930s		$400	$550

Silverbell #1 Banjo Mandolin

1920s. Fancy appointments, closed-back resonator.

1920s		$1,000	$1,100

MODEL		EXC. COND.	
YEAR	FEATURES	LOW	HIGH

Bauer (George)

1894-1911. Luthier George Bauer built guitars and mandolins in Philadephhia, Pennsylvania. He also built instruments with Samuel S. Stewart (S.S. Stewart).

Acme Professional (bowl back)
1890s. 29 ribs Brazilian, fancy styling.

1890s		$300	$400

Beltone

1920s-1930s. Acoustic and resonator mandolins and banjo-mandolins made by others for New York City distributor Perlberg & Halpin. Martin did make a small number of instruments for Beltone, but most were student-grade models most likely made by one of the big Chicago builders.

Bertoncini Stringed Instruments

1995-present. Luthier Dave Bertoncini mainly builds flat-top guitars in Olympia, Washington, but has also built mandolins.

Bigsby

Ca. 1947-present. Guitar builder Paul Arthur Bigsby also built 6 electric mandolins.

Bishline Guitars

1985-present. Luthier Robert Bishline builds custom-made mandolins in Tulsa, Oklahoma. He also builds flat-tops, resonators and banjos.

Blue Star

1984-present. Luthier Bruce Herron builds his intermediate grade, production/custom, electric solidbody mandolins in Fennville, Michigan. He also builds guitars, lap steels, dulcimers, and ukes.

Bohmann

1878-ca.1926. Established by Czechoslavakian-born Joseph Bohmann in Chicago, Illinois.

Fancy Bowl Mandolin
Spruce top, marquetry trimmed, inlay, pearl.

1890		$400	$550

Brandt

Early 1900s. John Brandt started making mandolin-family instruments in Chicago, Illinois around 1898.

Mandola
1900s. Spruce top, rosewood body, scroll headstock, pearl and abalone fretboard binding.

1900		$1,100	$1,300

Presentation Mandolin
Spruce top, tortoise shell-bound.

1900s		$700	$900

Breedlove

1990-present. Founded by Larry Breedlove and Steve Henderson. Professional and premium grade, production/custom, mandolins made in Tumalo, Oregon. They also produce guitars.

Alpine Master Class
2000s. O-style body, spruce/maple.

2000s		$1,900	$2,100

K-5 Mandolin
Asymmetric carved top, maple body.

1990s		$1,600	$1,800

Olympic Mandolin
Solid spruce top, teardrop-shaped, oval soundhole, highly flamed maple back, sunburst.

1990s		$1,200	$1,350

Quartz OF/OO Mandolin
2000s. Basic A-style body with f-holes.

2000s		$800	$900

Brian Moore

1992-present. Moore offers premium grade, production/custom, semi-hollow electric mandolins. They also build guitars and basses.

Bruno and Sons

1834-present. Established in 1834 by Charles Bruno, primarily as a distributor, Bruno and Sons marketed a variety of brands, including their own; currently part of Kaman. In the '60s or '70s, a Japanese-made solidbody electric mandolin was sold under the Bruno name.

Banjo Mandolin
Open back, 10" model.

1920s		$300	$375

Bowl Back Mandolin
1890s-1920s. Brazilian rosewood, spruce, rosewood ribs.

1920s		$300	$400

Calace

1825-present. Nicola Calace started The Calace Liuteria lute-making workshop in 1825 on the island of Procida, which is near Naples. The business is now in Naples and still in the family.

Lyre/Harp-Style Mandolin
Late-1800s-early-1900s. Lyre/harp-style, 8 strings, round soundhole, slightly bent top. Condition is important for these older instruments and the price noted is for a fully functional, original or pro-restored example.

1900		$900	$1,500

Carvin

1946-present. Carvin offered solidbody electric mandolins from around '56 to the late '60s, when they switched to a traditional pear-shaped electric/acoustic.

MB Mandolins
1956-1968. Solidbody, 1 pickup, single-cut Les Paul shape until '64, double-cut Jazzmaster/Strat shape after. Models include the #1-MB and the #2-MB, with different pickups.

1950s		$650	$800

Breedlove Olympic

Carvin 1-MB

MANDOLINS

Collings MT2

D'Angelico

MODEL		EXC. COND.	
YEAR	FEATURES	LOW	HIGH

Clifford

Clifford mandolins were manufactured by Kansas City, Missouri instrument wholesalers J.W. Jenkins & Sons. First introduced in 1895, the brand also offered guitars.

Collings

1986-present. Professional and premium grade, production/custom, mandolins built in Austin, Texas. Collings added mandolins to their line in '99. They also build guitars.

MF

1999-present. F-style, carved top and back.

1999-2004		$3,000	$3,500

MT

1999-presnt. A-style, 2 f-holes, carved top and back, matte finish, tortoise-bound top.

1999-2004		$1,500	$1,800

MT2

1999-present. MT with high gloss finish, ivoroid body, neck and headstock binding.

1999-2004		$2,200	$3,000

Conrad

Ca. 1968-1977. Imported from Japan by David Wexler and Company, Chicago, Illinois. Mid- to better-quality copy guitars, mandolins and banjos.

Crafter

2000-present. Line of intermediate grade, production, acoustic and acoustic/electric mandolins from Hohner. They also offer guitars and a bass.

Crestwood

1970s. Copy models imported by La Playa Distributing Company of Detroit.

Mandolin

Includes models 3039 (electric A-style), 3041 (bowl back-style, flower 'guard), 3043 (bowl back-style, plain 'guard), 71820 (A-style), and 71821 (F-style).

1970s		$100	$275

Cromwell

1935-1939. Private branded instruments made by Gibson at their Parsons Street factory in Kalamazoo, Michigan. Distributed by a variety of mail order companies such as Continental, Grossman, and Richter & Phillips.

GM-4 Mandolin

1935-1939. Style A, f-holes, solid wood arched top, mahogany back and sides, block capital letter Cromwell headstock logo, dot markers, elevated 'guard, sunburst.

1935-1939		$700	$800

D'Angelico

1932-1964. Handcrafted by John D'Angelico. Models include Excel, Teardrop, and Scroll. Appointments can vary from standard to higher-end so each mandolin should be evaluated on a case-by-case basis.

MODEL		EXC. COND.	
YEAR	FEATURES	LOW	HIGH

Mandolin

1932-1949. Various models and appointments.

1932-1949	High-end appointments	$22,000	$25,000
1932-1949	Plain styling, lower range	$2,200	$3,000
1932-1949	Plain, non-elevated pickguard	$8,000	$10,000

D'Aquisto

1965-1995. James D'Aquisto apprenticed under D'Angelico. He started his own production in '65.

Mandolin

1970s. Various models and appointments.

1970s	Only 3 made	$26,000	$30,000

Dean

1976-present. Intermediate grade, production, acoustic and acoustic/electric mandolins made overseas. They also offer guitars, banjos, basses, and amps.

Dearstone

1993-present. Luthier Ray Dearstone builds his professional and premium grade, custom, mandolin-family instruments in Blountville, Tennessee. He also builds guitars and violins.

DeCava Guitars

1983-present. Premium grade, production/custom, mandolins built by luthier Jim DeCava in Stratford, Connecticut. He also builds guitars, ukes, and banjos.

DeGennaro

2003-present. Professional and premium grade, custom/production, acoustic and electric mandolins built by luthier William Degennaro in Grand Rapids, Michigan. He also builds guitars and basses.

DeLucia, Vincenzo

1910s-1920s. Luthier Vincenzo DeLucia built mandolins in Philadelphia, Pennsylvania.

Mandolin

Early-1900s. High quality material, rosewood body, fine ornamentation.

1910s		$900	$1,100

Dennis Hill Guitars

1991-present. Premium grade, production/custom, mandolins built by luthier Dennis Hill in Panama City, Florida. He has also built dulcimers, guitars, and violins.

Ditson

Mandolins made for the Oliver Ditson Company of Boston, an instrument dealer and music publisher. Turn of the century and early-1900s models were bowl back-style with the Ditson label. The '20s Ditson Style A flat back mandolins were made by

MANDOLINS

MODEL YEAR	FEATURES	EXC. COND. LOW	HIGH

Martin. Models were also made by Lyon & Healy of Boston, often with a Ditson Empire label.

Style A Mandolin
1920s. Style A flat back made by Martin, mahogany sides and back, plain ornamentation.

1920s		$800	$950

Victory Bowl Back Mandolin
1890s. Brazilian rib bowl back-style with fancy inlays.

1890s		$500	$800

Dobro
1929-1942, 1954-present. Dobro offered mandolins throughout their early era and from the '60s to the mid-'90s.

Mandolin (wood body)
Resonator on wood body.

1930s		$1,000	$1,300
1940s		$1,000	$1,300
1960s		$850	$1,100

Dudenbostel
1989-present. Luthier Lynn Dudenbostel builds his limited production, premium and presentation grade, custom, mandolins in Knoxville, Tennessee. Started with guitars and added mandolins in '96, started full-time building in '95.

F-5 (Loar) Style
1996-2005. About 30 made.

1996-2005		$24,000	$26,000

Eastman
1992-present. Intermediate and professional grade, production, mandolins built in China. Eastman added mandolins in '04. They also build guitars, violins, and cellos.

EKO
1961-1985, 2000-present. The Italian-made EKOs were imported by LoDuca Brothers of Milwaukee. The brand was revived around 2000, but does not currently include mandolins.

Baritone Mandolin
1960s. Baritone mandolin with ornate inlays.

1960s		$325	$400

Octave Mandolin
1960s. Octave mandolin with ornate inlays.

1960s		$325	$400

Epiphone
1928-present. Intermediate grade, production, acoustic mandolins. Epiphone has offered several mandolin-family models over the years. Those from the '30s to the '60s were U.S.-made, the later models imported.

Adelphi Mandolin
1932-1948. A-style body, maple back and sides, f-holes, single-bound top and back.

1945-1946		$500	$700

MM50
1998-present. Import f-style with The Epiphone logo.

1998-2004		$400	$500

Strand Mandolin
1932-1958. Walnut back and sides, F-holes, multibound, sunburst.

1944		$600	$700

Venetian Electric Mandolin
1961-1970. Gibson-made, pear-shaped body, 4 pole P-90 'dog-ear' mounted pickup, volume and tone knobs, dot markers, sunburst finish.

1961-1964		$1,200	$1,700
1965-1970		$1,000	$1,500

Zephyr Mandolin
1939-1958. A-style, electric, F-holes, maple body, 1 pickup, slotted block inlay.

1950s		$550	$700

Esquire
1930s. Student level instruments with painted Esquire logo and painted wood grain.

Mandolins
1930s. Laminate A-style wood body, sunburst.

1930s		$175	$225

Euphonon
1934-1944. Euphonon was a brand of the Larson Brothers of Chicago. The brand was introduced so Larson could compete in the guitar market with the new larger body 14-fret guitar models. Production also included mandolins, and most models were A-style, with teardrop body and flat backs.

Mandolin
1934-1944. Various models and appointments, each mandolin should be evaluated on a case-by-case basis.

1934-1944		$4,000	$10,000

Everett Guitars
1977-present. Luthier Kent Everett, of Atlanta, Georgia, mainly builds guitars, but has also built mandolins.

Evergreen Mountain
1971-present. Professional grade, custom, mandolins built by luthier Jerry Nolte in Cove, Oregon. He also builds guitars and basses.

Fairbanks (A.J.)
1875-ca.1920s. Primarily known for banjos, Fairbanks also offered mandolins.

Mandolin
1890-1910. Typical late-1890s bent top-style mandolin, with decorated top and rope-style binding.

1900s	Natural		$250	$350

Fender
1946-present. Intermediate grade, production, acoustic and acoustic/electric mandolins. Fender also offered an electric mandolin for 20 years.

Epiphone MM-50

Evergreen Mountain

MANDOLINS

Flatiron A-5

Flatiron Festival

MODEL YEAR	FEATURES	EXC. COND. LOW	HIGH

Mandolin
1956-1976. Electric solidbody, often referred to as the Mandocaster by collectors.

1956-1957	Blond	$2,500	$3,000
1958-1959	Sunburst	$2,200	$2,600
1960-1961	Sunburst	$2,000	$2,500
1962-1963	Sunburst	$2,000	$2,300
1964-1965	Sunburst	$1,800	$2,100
1966-1970	Sunburst	$1,600	$1,900
1971-1976	Sunburst	$1,500	$1,700

Fine Resophonic
1988-present. Professional grade, production/custom, wood and metal-bodied resophonic mandolins built by luthiers Mike Lewis and Pierre Avocat in Vitry Sur Seine, France. They also build guitars and ukes.

Flatiron
1977-2003. Gibson purchased Flatiron in 1987. Production was in Bozeman, Montana until the end of '96, when Gibson closed the Flatiron mandolin workshop and moved mandolin assembly to Nashville, Tennessee. General production tapered off after the move and Flatirons were available on a special order basis for a time.

Festival Series
F-holes, maple body and neck, carved spruce top, ebony board.

1977-1987	Style A	$1,000	$1,550
1977-1987	Style F	$2,000	$2,500
1988-1995	Style A	$900	$1,400
1988-1995	Style F	$1,700	$2,200

Model 1 Mandolin
Oval shape, spruce top, maple body, rosewood board.

1977-1987	Pre-Gibson	$400	$550
1988-1995	Gibson Montana	$350	$500

Model 2 Mandolin
Oval body, curly maple (MC) or birdseye maple (MB) back and sides, spruce top, ebony 'board.

1977-1987	Pre-Gibson	$400	$550
1977-1995	Flamed koa back and sides	$550	$725
1988-1995	Gibson Montana	$350	$500

Model 2MW Mandola

1977-1987	Pre-Gibson	$550	$650
1988-1995	Gibson Montana	$500	$600

Model 3 Octave Mandolin
Oval shape, birdseye maple (MB) or curly maple (MC) body, spruce top, ebony 'board, longer scale.

1977-1987	Natural, bird's-eye back and side	$700	$900
1988-1995	Gibson Montana	$625	$800

Performer Series
Spruce top, maple body, nickel hardware.

1977-1987	Style A	$800	$900
1977-1987	Style F	$1,600	$1,800
1988-1995	Cadet	$475	$550
1988-1995	Style A	$725	$800
1988-1995	Style F	$1,450	$1,600

MODEL YEAR	FEATURES	EXC. COND. LOW	HIGH

Signature Series
Introduced in the 1996 catalog, flamed maple body and neck, carved spruce top, rosewood or ebony board.

1996-2003	A-5	$1,400	$1,700
1996-2003	A-5 Artist	$1,400	$1,700
1996-2003	A-5 Junior	$1,100	$1,200
1996-2003	F-5 Artist (Modified Fern)	$3,000	$3,700

Fletcher Brock Stringed Instruments
1992-present. Custom mandolin-family instruments made by luthier Fletcher Brock originally in Ketchum, Idaho, and currently in Seattle, Washington. He also builds guitars.

Framus
1946-1977, 1996-present. Founded in Erlangen, Germany by Fred Wilfer. In the '60s, Framus instruments were imported into the U.S. by Philadelphia Music Company. They offered acoustic and electric mandolins. The brand was revived in '96.

12-string mandolin

1960s		$325	$350

Freshwater
1992-present. Luthier Dave Freshwater and family build mandolin family instruments in Beauly, Inverness, Scotland. They also build bouzoukis, dulcimers and harps.

Mandolin/Mandolin Family
2000s. Lateral Freshwater logo on headstock.

2000s		$450	$550

Fylde
1973-present. Luthier Roger Bucknall builds his intermediate and professional, production/custom mandolins and mandolas in Penrith, Cumbria, United Kingdom. He also builds guitars and basses, bouzoukis, and citterns.

G.L. Stiles
1960-1994. Built by Gilbert Lee Stiles in Florida. He also built acoustics, solidbodies, basses, steels, and banjos.

Mandolin

1960s		$400	$550

Galiano/A. Galiano
New Yorkers Antonio Cerrito and Raphael Ciani offered instruments built by them and others under the Galiano brand during the early 1900s.

Mandolin
Bowl back, some fancy appointments.

1920s		$300	$400

Giannini
1900-present. Acoustic mandolins built in Salto, SP, Brazil near Sao Paolo. They also build guitars, violas, and cavaquinhos.

MODEL		EXC. COND.	
YEAR	FEATURES	LOW	HIGH

Gibson

1880s-present. Orville Gibson created the violin-based mandolin body-style that replaced the bowl back-type. Currently Gibson offers professional, premium and presentation grade, production/custom, mandolins.

Special Designations:

Snakehead headstock: 1922-1927 with production possible for a few months plus or minus.

Lloyd Loar era: Mid-1922-late 1924 with production possible for a few months plus or minus.

A Mandolin

1902-1933. Oval soundhole, snakehead headstock '22-'27, Loar era mid-'22-late-'24.

1902-1909	Orange Top	$1,000	$1,300
1910-1918	Orange Top	$1,200	$1,500
1918-1921	Brown	$1,400	$1,700
1922-1924	Loar era	$2,500	$2,800
1925-1933		$2,200	$2,500

A Junior Mandolin

1920-1927. The Junior was the entry level mandolin for Gibson, but like most entry level Gibsons (re: Les Paul Junior), they were an excellent product. Oval soundhole, dot markers, plain tuner buttons. Becomes A-0 in '27.

| 1920-1927 | Sheraton Brown | $1,200 | $1,400 |

A-0 Mandolin

1927-1933. Replaces A Jr., oval soundhole, dot inlay, brown finish.

| 1927-1933 | | $1,400 | $1,550 |

A-00 Mandolin

1933-1943. Oval soundhole, dot inlay, carved bound top.

| 1933-1943 | Sunburst | $1,500 | $1,850 |

A-1 Mandolin

1902-1918, 1922-1927, 1933-1943. Snakehead headstock '23-'27.

1902-1918	Orange	$1,200	$1,700
1922-1924	Loar era	$2,500	$3,500
1925-1927	Black	$2,500	$3,000
1927	Not snaked	$2,400	$2,800
1927	Snaked	$2,500	$3,000
1932	Re-introduced, oval	$2,400	$2,800
1933-1943	Sunburst, F-holes	$2,000	$2,400

A-2/A-2Z Mandolin

1902-1908, 1918-1922. A-2Z '22-'27. Renamed A-2 '27-'28. Snakehead headstock '23-'27. Lloyd Loar era mid-'22-late-'24.

1902-1908	Orange	$1,900	$2,100
1918-1921	Brown	$2,000	$2,200
1918-1922	White (optional)	$2,300	$2,700
1922-1924	Loar Era	$3,800	$4,300
1925-1928		$2,800	$3,000

A-3 Mandolin

1902-1922. Oval soundhole, single-bound body, dot inlay.

| 1902-1905 | Various colors | $2,100 | $2,300 |
| 1906-1922 | Various colors | $2,300 | $2,800 |

A-4 Mandolin

1902-1935. Oval soundhole, single-bound body, dot inlay, snakehead '23-'27.

1902-1917	Various colors	$2,000	$2,400
1918-1921	Dark mahogany	$2,400	$2,700
1922-1924	Loar era	$4,700	$5,300
1925-1935	Various colors	$3,000	$3,500

A-5 Mandolin

1957-1979. Oval soundhole, maple back and sides, dot inlay, scroll headstock, sunburst.

1957-1964		$2,500	$2,900
1965-1969		$2,400	$2,800
1970-1979		$2,200	$2,600

A-5 G Mandolin

1988-1996. Less ornate version of the A-5 L, abalone fleur-de-lis headstock inlay.

| 1988-1996 | | $1,400 | $1,500 |

A-5 L Mandolin

1988-present. A-5-style body, raised 'board, flower-pot headstock inlay, curly maple and spruce.

| 1988-1999 | Sunburst | $2,200 | $2,400 |

A-9 Mandolin

2002-present. Spruce top, maple back and sides, black bound top, satin brown finish.

| 2002-2004 | | $925 | $950 |

A-12 Mandolin

1970-1979. F-holes, long neck, dot inlay, fleur-de-lis inlay, sunburst.

| 1970-1979 | | $1,600 | $1,900 |

A-40 Mandolin

1948-1970. F-holes, bound top, dot inlay, natural or sunburst.

1948-1949		$1,100	$1,350
1950-1964		$1,000	$1,250
1965-1970		$900	$1,050

A-50 Mandolin

1933-1971. A-style oval bound body, F-holes, sunburst.

1933-1941	Larger 11.25" body	$1,300	$1,500
1942-1965	Smaller 10" body	$1,100	$1,400
1966-1971		$950	$1,200

A-C Century Mandolin

1935-1937. Flat back, bound body, oval soundhole.

| 1935-1937 | Sunburst | $2,900 | $3,200 |

Army and Navy Special Style DY/Army-Navy Mandolin

1918-1922. Lower-end, flat top and back, round soundhole, no logo, round label with model name. Reintroduced as Army-Navy (AN Custom) '88-'96.

| 1918-1922 | Brown stain | $900 | $1,000 |

C-1 Mandolin

1932. Flat top, mahogany back and sides, oval soundhole, painted on 'guard, a '32 version of the Army and Navy Special. This model was private branded for Kel Kroydon in the early-'30s.

| 1932 | Natural | $950 | $1,100 |

Gibson A Junior

Gibson A-5

MANDOLINS

Gibson F-4

1927 Gibson F-5

MANDOLINS

MODEL YEAR	FEATURES	EXC. COND. LOW	HIGH
EM-100/EM-125 Mandolin			
1938-1943. Initially called EM-100, renamed EM-125 in '41-'43. Style A (pear-shape) archtop body, 1 blade pickup, 2 knobs on either side of bridge, dot markers, tortoise 'guard, sunburst.			
1938-1940	EM-100	$1,800	$2,000
1941-1943	EM-125	$1,700	$1,900
EM-150 Mandolin			
1936-1971. Electric, A-00 body, 1 Charlie Christian pickup early on, 1 P-90 later, bound body, sunburst.			
1936-1940	Charlie Christian pickup	$2,000	$2,400
1941-1949	Rectangular pickup	$1,600	$2,000
1949-1965	P-90 pickup	$1,600	$2,000
1966-1971	P-90 pickup	$1,400	$1,600
EM-200/Florentine Mandolin			
1954-1971. Electric solidbody, 1 pickup, gold-plated hardware, 2 control knobs, dot markers, sunburst. Called the EM-200 in '60 and '61.			
1954-1960	Florentine	$2,300	$2,500
1960-1961	Renamed EM-200	$2,100	$2,400
1962-1971	Renamed Florentine	$2,000	$2,300
F-2 Mandolin			
1902-1934. Oval soundhole, pearl inlay, star and crescent inlay on peghead.			
1902-1909	3-point	$3,300	$4,000
1910-1917	2-point	$3,300	$4,000
1918-1921	2-point	$4,000	$5,000
1922-1924	Loar era	$5,500	$7,000
1925-1934		$3,500	$4,500
F-3 Mandolin			
1902-1908. Three-point body, oval soundhole, scroll peghead, pearl inlayed 'guard, limited production model, black top with red back and sides.			
1902-1908		$3,700	$4,900
F-4 Mandolin			
1902-1943. Oval soundhole, rope pattern binding, various colors.			
1902-1909	3-point	$4,000	$5,000
1910-1917	2-point	$4,500	$5,000
1918-1921	2-point	$5,500	$6,000
1922-1924	Loar era	$7,000	$9,000
1925-1943		$4,500	$5,500
F-5 Mandolin			
1922-1943; 1949-1980. F-holes, triple-bound body and 'guard. The '20s Lloyd Loar era F-5s are extremely valuable. Reintroduced in '49 with single-bound body, redesigned in '70.			
1922-1924	Loar era	$125,000	$135,000
1925-1928	Fern, Master-built	$70,000	$77,000
1928-1929	Fern, not Master-built	$60,000	$67,000
1930-1931	Fern peghead inlay	$50,000	$57,000
1932-1935	Fern peghead inlay	$40,000	$52,000
1936-1940	Fern (limited production)	$37,000	$48,000
1940-1943	Fleur-de-lis peghead inlay	$30,000	$39,000

MODEL YEAR	FEATURES	EXC. COND. LOW	HIGH
1949	Flower pot, mahogany neck	$9,000	$15,000
1950-1953	Flower pot, maple neck	$8,000	$8,500
1954	Flower pot peghead inlay	$7,500	$8,000
1955-1956	Flower pot peghead inlay	$7,000	$7,500
1957-1959	Flower pot peghead inlay	$6,500	$7,000
1960-1965		$4,500	$5,500
1966-1969	Sunburst	$4,000	$5,000
1971-1980	Sunburst	$3,200	$4,000
F-5 Bella Voce Mandolin			
1989. Custom Shop master-built model, high-end materials and construction, engraved tailpiece with "Bella Voce F-5", sunburst.			
1989		$8,500	$8,800
F-5 L Mandolin			
1978-present. Reissue of Loar F-5, gold hardware, fern headstock inlay (flowerpot inlay with silver hardware also offered for '88-'91), sunburst.			
1978-1984	Kalamazoo-made	$4,200	$4,900
1984-1999		$4,000	$4,900
F-5 Master Model			
2003-present. F-holes, triple-bound body and guard, red spruce top, maple back and sides, flowerpot inlay.			
2003-2004		$10,000	$11,000
F-5 V Mandolin			
1990s. Based on Lloyd Loar's original F-5s of 1922-24, varnish Cremona Brown sunburst finish.			
1990s		$6,500	$6,800
F-5 Wayne Benson Signature			
2003. Limited edition of 50, solid spruce top, figured maple back, sides and neck, gold hardware, vintage red satin.			
2003		$5,200	$5,500
Bill Monroe Model F Mandolin			
1992-1995. Limited run of 200.			
1992-1995	Sunburst	$7,000	$10,000
Sam Bush F-5 Mandolin			
2000-present. Artist Series model, carved spruce top, gold hardware, built at Opry Mill plant in Nashville.			
2000-2002		$4,500	$5,500
F-7 Mandolin			
1934-1940. F-holes, single-bound body, neck and 'guard, fleur-de-lis peghead inlay, sunburst.			
1934-1937		$8,500	$9,500
F-9 Mandolin			
2002-present. F-5 style, carved spruce top, no inlays, black bound body.			
2002-2004		$1,825	$1,975
F-10 Mandolin			
1934-1936. Slight upgrade of the '34 F-7 with extended 'board and upgraded inlay, black finish.			
1934-1936		$8,500	$9,500

MODEL YEAR	FEATURES	EXC. COND. LOW	HIGH

F-12 Mandolin
1934-1937, 1948-1980. F-holes, bound body and neck, scroll inlay, raised 'board until '37, 'board flush with top '48-on, sunburst.

1934-1937		$8,000	$9,000
1948-1959		$3,700	$4,000
1960-1969		$3,200	$3,700
1970-1980		$2,400	$3,300

H-1 Mandola
1902-1936. Has same features as A-1 mandolin, but without snakehead headstock.

1902-1908	Orange	$2,000	$2,200
1918-1921	Brown	$2,100	$2,300
1922-1924	Loar era	$3,800	$4,300
1925-1928		$2,800	$3,000

H-1 E Mandola
Late-1930s. Limited number built, electric with built-in adjustable bar pickup, sunburst.

1938		$3,800	$4,000

H-2 Mandola
1902-1922. Has same features as A-4 mandolin.

1902-1917	Various colors	$2,500	$3,000
1918-1921	Dark Mahogany	$2,800	$3,500

H-4 Mandola
1910-1940. Same features as F-4 mandolin.

1910-1921		$4,500	$5,500
1922-1924	Loar era	$7,000	$9,000
1925-1940		$5,500	$8,800

H-5 Mandola
1923-1929 (available by special order 1929-1936), 1990-1991. Same features as the high-end F-5 Mandolin. This is a very specialized market and instruments should be evaluated on a case-by-case basis.

1923-1924	Loar ear	$55,000	$65,000
1925-1928	Fern, Master-built	$40,000	$45,000
1928-1929	Fern, not Master-built	$35,000	$40,000
1990-1991	Limited production	$5,000	$5,600

K-1 Mandocello
1902-1943. Same features as H-1 mandola, off & on production, special order available.

1902-1908	Orange	$3,000	$3,500
1918-1921	Brown	$3,500	$4,000
1922-1924	Loar era	$6,000	$8,000
1925-1943		$3,300	$3,600

K-2 Mandocello
1902-1922. Same features as A-4 mandolin.

1902-1917	Black or Red mahogany	$3,500	$4,000
1918-1922		$4,000	$4,500

K-4 Mandocello
1912-1929 (offered as special order post-1929). Same features as F-4 mandolin, sunburst.

1912-1921		$6,000	$7,000
1922-1924	Loar era	$10,000	$14,000
1925-1929		$6,500	$7,500

M-6 (octave guitar)
2002-present. A-style mandolin body, short-scale 6-string guitar neck.

2002-2004		$1,300	$1,400

MB-1 Mandolin Banjo
1922-1923, 1925-1937.

1922-1923		$1,000	$1,200
1925-1937		$1,000	$1,200

MB-2 Mandolin Banjo
1920-1923, 1926-1937.

1920-1923		$1,100	$1,300

MB-3 Mandolin Banjo
1923-1939.

1923-1939		$1,500	$1,600

MB-4 Mandolin Banjo
1923-1932. Fleur-de-lis inlay.

1923-1932		$1,600	$1,700

MB-Junior Mandolin Banjo
Open back, budget level.

1924-1925		$700	$800

Style J Mando Bass
1912-1930 (special order post-1930). A-style body, 4 strings, round soundhole, bound top, dot inlay.

1912-1930		$3,000	$4,000

Style TL-1 Tenor Lute Mandolin

1924-1926		$1,500	$2,500

Gilchrist
1978-present. Premium and presentation grade, custom, mandolins made by luthier Steve Gilchrist of Warrnambool, Australia. Custom ordered but were also initially distributed through Gruhn Guitars, Nashville, Tennessee and then exclusively by Carmel Music Company. Designs are based upon Gibson mandolins built between 1910 and '25.

Model 5 Mandolin
1978-present. Based on the Gibson '22-'24 Loar-era F-5 mandolin, Gilchrist slant logo, spruce top, flamed maple back, sides, and neck, ebony 'board, multiple binding, sunburst.

1978-1995	Sunburst	$18,000	$22,000
1996-2003	Sunburst	$20,000	$24,000

Givens
1962-1992. Luthier R. L. (Bob) Givens handcrafted about 800 mandolins and another 700 in a production shop.

A Mandolin
1962-1975. Early production A-style.

1962-1975		$1,500	$2,500

A-3 Mandolin
Mid-1970s-mid-1980s. Distinguished by use of decal (the only model with Givens decal).

1975-1988		$1,300	$2,300

A-4 Mandolin
1988-1993. No 'board binding, simple block-like multiple-line RL Givens inlay, nicer maple.

1988-1993		$1,000	$2,000

A-5 Mandolin
1988-1993. Bound 'board, pearl headstock inlay.

1988-1993		$1,200	$2,200

A-6 (Torch) Mandolin
1988-1992. Torch inlay (the only model with this), gold hardware, snowflake markers.

1988-1992		$2,300	$3,300

Gibson K-2 mandocello

Givens A-4

MANDOLINS

Godin A-8

Gold Tone GM-110

MODEL YEAR	FEATURES	EXC. COND. LOW	HIGH

A-6 Custom Mandolin
1991-1992. Elaborate customized A-6 model.

1991-1992		$3,000	$4,000

F-5 (Fern) Mandolin
1973-1985. Givens' own version with fern ornamentation.

1973-1985		$3,300	$4,300

F-5 (Loar) Mandolin
1962-1972. Givens' own version based upon the Loar model F-5.

1962-1972		$3,300	$4,300

F-5 (Torch) Mandolin
1988-1992. Givens F-5 with torch inlay (the only F model with this).

1988-1992		$5,500	$7,500

F-5 (Wheat Straw) Mandolin
1986-1988. Givens F-5-style with wheat straw ornamentation.

1986-1988		$4,800	$6,000

Godin
1987-present. Intermediate grade, production, acoustic/electric mandolins from luthier Robert Godin. They also build basses and guitars.

A-8 Mandolin
2000-present. Single-cut chambered body, acoustic/electric.

2000-2003		$550	$600

Gold Tone
1993-present. Wayne and Robyn Rogers build their intermediate grade, production/custom mandolins in Titusville, Florida. They also offer lap steels, basses, banjos and banjitars.

Goya
1955-present. Korean-made mandolins. They also build guitars and banjos. Originally made in Sweden, by the late '70s from Japan, then from Korea.

Mandolin

1960s	Japan/Korea	$140	$160
1960s	Sweden Built	$200	$300
1970s	Sweden Built	$175	$275

Gretsch
1883-present. Gretsch started offering mandolins by the early 1900s. Currently Gretsch does not offer mandolins.

New Yorker Mandolin
Late 1940s-late 1950s. Teardrop shape, F-holes, arched top and back, spruce top, maple back, sides, and neck, rosewood 'board.

1950s		$450	$575

GTR
1974-1978. GTR (for George Gruhn, Tut Taylor, Randy Wood) was the original name for Gruhn Guitars in Nashville, Tennessee (it was changed in '76). GTR imported mandolins and banjos from Japan. An A-style (similar to a current Gibson A-5 L) and an F-style (similar to mid- to late-'20s F-5 with fern pattern) were offered. The instruments were made at the Moridaira factory in Matsumoto, Japan by factory foreman Sadamasa Tokaida. Quality was relatively high but quantities were limited.

A-Style Mandolin
1974-1978. A5-L copy with GTR logo on headstock.

1974-1978		$1,400	$1,600

F-Style Mandolin
1974-1978. F-5 Fern copy with slant GTR logo on headstock, handmade in Japan.

1974-1978	Sunburst	$2,400	$2,600

Harmony
1982-1976. Founded by Wilhelm Schultz in 1892, and purchased by Sears in 1916. The company evolved into one of the largest producers of stringed instruments in the U.S. in the '30s.

Baroque H35/H835 Electric Mandolin
Late 1960s-early 1970s. Electric version of Baroque H425 with single pickup and two controls.

1969-1970	H35	$350	$425
1971-1976	H835	$325	$400

Baroque H425/H8025 Mandolin
F-style arched body, extreme bass bout pointy horn, close grained spruce top, sunburst.

1969-1970	H425	$300	$350
1971-1976	H8025	$250	$325

Lute H331/H031 Mandolin
1960s-1970s. A-style, flat top and back, student level.

1960s	H331	$100	$150
1970s	H8031	$90	$140

Monterey H410/H417/H8017 Mandolin
A-style arched body with f-holes, sunburst.

1950s	H410	$145	$200
1960s	H410	$135	$185
1960s	H417	$160	$210
1970s	H410	$125	$175
1970s	H8017	$150	$200

Heiden Stringed Instruments
1974-present. Luthier Michael Heiden builds his premium grade, production/custom mandolins in Chilliwack, British Columbia. He also builds guitars.

Heritage
1985-present. Started by former Gibson employees in Gibson's Kalamazoo, Michigan plant, Heritage offered mandolins for a number of years.

H-5 Mandolin
1986-1990s. F-style scroll body, f-holes.

1980s		$3,000	$4,000

Höfner
1887-present. Hofner has offered a wide variety of instruments, including mandolins, over the years. They currently do not offer a mandolin

MODEL YEAR	FEATURES	EXC. COND. LOW	HIGH

Model 545/E545 Mandolin

1960s. Pear-shaped A-style with catseye F-holes, block-style markers, engraved headstock, Genuine Hofner Original and Made in Germany on back of headstock, transparent brown.

1968-1969	545 (acoustic)	$325	$425
1968-1969	E545 (acoustic-electric)	$425	$475

Hohner

1857-present. Intermediate grade, production, acoustic and acoustic/electric mandolins. They also offer guitars, basses, and ukes.

Hondo

1969-1987, 1991-present. Budget grade, production, imported mandolins. They also offer basses and guitars. Hondo also offered mandolins from around '74 to '87.

Mandolin

1974-1987. Hondo offered F-style, A-style, and bowl back mandolin models.

1970s	Acoustic	$100	$150
1970s	Acoustic-electric	$150	$200

Hopf

1906-present. Professional grade, production/custom, mandolins made in Germany. They also make basses, guitars and flutes.

Howe-Orme

1893-early-1900s. Edward Howe patented a guitar-shaped mandolin on November 14, 1893.

Mandola

1893-early-1900s. Guitar body-style with narrow waist, not the common mandolin F- or S-style body, pressed (not carved) spruce top, mahogany back and sides, flat-top guitar-type trapeze bridge, decalomania near bridge.

1890s	Natural	$1,400	$1,700

Ibanez

1932-present. Ibanez offered mandolins from '65 to '83. In '04 they again added mandolins to the product line.

Model 513 Mandolin

1974-1979. A-5 copy with double cutaways, oval sound hole, dot markers.

1974-1979	Sunburst	$325	$425

Model 514 Mandolin

1974-1979. Arched back, spruce, rosewood, dot inlays.

1974-1979	Sunburst	$325	$400

Model 524 Artist Mandolin

1974-1978. F-5 Loar copy, solid wood carved top and solid wood carved top and solid wood back.

1974-1978	Sunburst	$750	$950

Model 526 (electric) Mandolin

1974-1978. A-style body, single pickup, two control knobs, sunburst.

1974-1978		$400	$450

Model 529 Artist Mandolin

1982-1983. F-5 Loar era copy, solid wood carved top and solid wood spruce top and solid maple sides and back.

1982-1983	Sunburst	$800	$1,000

Imperial

1890-1922. Imperial mandolins were made by the William A. Cole Company of Boston, Massachusetts.

Bowl Back Mandolin

1890s		$275	$375

J.B. Player

1980s-present. Budget grade, production, imported mandolins. They also offer basses, banjos and guitars.

J.R. Zeidler Guitars

1977-present. Luthier John Zeidler builds his premium grade, custom, mandolins in Wallingford, Pennsylvania. He also builds guitars.

John Le Voi Guitars

1970-present. Production/custom, mandolin family instruments built by luthier John Le Voi in Lincolnshire, United Kingdom. He also builds guitars.

Johnson

Mid-1990s-present. Budget and intermediate grade, production, mandolins imported by Music Link, Brisbane, California. Johnson also offers guitars, amps, basses and effects.

MA Series A-Style Mandolin

Mid-1990s-present. Import, A-style copy, plain Johnson logo on headstock. Several levels offered; the range shown is for all value levels.

1990s		$90	$175

MF Series F-Style Mandolin

Mid-1990s-present. Import, F-style copy, plain Johnson logo on headstock. Several levels offered; the range shown is for all value levels.

1990s	Sunburst	$150	$300

K & S

1992-1998. Mandolins and mandolas distributed by George Katechis and Marc Silber and handmade in Paracho, Mexico. They also offered guitars and ukes.

Kalamazoo

1933-1942, 1946-1947, 1965-1970. Budget brand produced by Gibson in Kalamazoo, Michigan. They offered mandolins until '42.

Kalamazoo/Oriole A-Style Mandolin

1930s. Kalamazoo and Oriole on the headstock, KM/A-style.

1930s		$800	$950

Hohner HMA

Kalamazoo A-style

MANDOLINS

1950s Kay K73

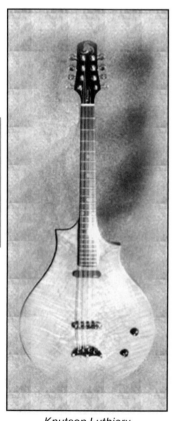

*Knutson Luthiery
Electric Octave*

MODEL YEAR	FEATURES	EXC. COND. LOW	HIGH
KM-11 Mandolin			
1935-1941. Gibson-made, A-style, flat top and back, round soundhole, dot inlay.			
1930s	Sunburst	$700	$850
KM-21 Mandolin			
1936-1940. Gibson-made, A-style, F-holes, arched bound spruce top and mahogany back.			
1930s	Sunburst	$800	$950
KMB Mandolin/Banjo			
1930s. Banjo-mandolin with resonator.			
1930s		$425	$475

Kay

1931-present. Located in Chicago, Illinois, the Kay company made an incredible amount of instruments under a variety of brands, including the Kay name. From the beginning, Kay offered several types of electric and acoustic mandolins. In '69, the factory closed, marking the end of American-made Kays. The brand survives today on imported instruments. See Guitar Stories Volume II, by Michael Wright, for a complete history of Kay with detailed model listings.

MODEL YEAR	FEATURES	EXC. COND. LOW	HIGH
K68/K465 Concert Mandolin			
1952-1968. Pear-shape, close-grain spruce top, genuine mahogany back and sides. Renamed the K465 in '66. Kay also offered a Venetian-style mandolin called the K68 in '37-'42.			
1952-1968	Natural	$200	$250
K73 Mandolin			
1939-1952. Solid spruce top, maple back and sides, A-style body, F-holes, cherry sunburst.			
1939-1952		$200	$250
K390/K395 Professional Electric Mandolin			
1960-1968. Modified Venetian-style archtop, 1 pickup, F-hole, spruce top, curly maple back and sides, sunburst finish. Renamed K395 in '66.			
1960-1968		$350	$550
K494/K495 Electric Mandolin			
1960-1968. A-style archtop, single metal-covered (no poles) pickup, volume and tone control knobs, the K494 was originally about 60% of the price of the K390 model (see above) in '65. Renamed K495 in '66.			
1960-1968	Sunburst	$350	$450

Kay Kraft

1931-1937. First brand name of the newly formed Kay Company. Brand replaced by Kay in '37.

MODEL YEAR	FEATURES	EXC. COND. LOW	HIGH
Mandolin			
1931-1937. Kay Kraft offered Venetian- and teardrop-shaped mandolins.			
1931-1937		$275	$350

Kel Kroyden (by Gibson)

1930-1937. Private branded budget level made by Gibson.

MODEL YEAR	FEATURES	EXC. COND. LOW	HIGH
KK-20 (Style C-1) Mandolin			
1930-1933. Flat top, near oval-shaped body, oval soundhole, natural finish, dark finish mahogany back and sides.			
1930-1933		$600	$800

Kent

1961-1969. Japanese-made instruments. Kent offered teardrop, A style, and bowlback acoustic mandolins up to '68.

MODEL YEAR	FEATURES	EXC. COND. LOW	HIGH
Acoustic Mandolin			
1961-1968. Kent offered teardrop, A-style, and bowlback acoustic mandolins up to '68.			
1961-1968		$100	$150
Electric Mandolin			
1964-1969. Available from '64-'66 as a solidbody electric (in left- and right-hand models) and from '67-'69 an electric hollowbody Venetian-style with F-holes (they called it violin-shaped).			
1964-1969		$150	$200

Kentucky (Saga M.I.)

1977-present. Brand name of Saga Musical Instruments currently offering budget, intermediate, and professional grade, production, A- and F-style mandolins.

MODEL YEAR	FEATURES	EXC. COND. LOW	HIGH
KM Series			
2000s	KM-140 A-style	$100	$125
2000s	KM-150 A-style	$125	$150
2000s	KM-630 F-style	$300	$450
2000s	KM-700 F-style	$375	$425
2000s	KM-800 F-style	$400	$450

Kingston

Ca. 1958-1967. Japanese imports. See Guitar section for more company info.

MODEL YEAR	FEATURES	EXC. COND. LOW	HIGH
Acoustic Mandolin			
1960s		$125	$175
EM1 Electric Mandolin			
1964-1967. Double-cut solidbody electric, 15.75" scale, 1 pickup.			
1960s		$125	$200

Knutsen

1890s-1920s. Luthier Chris J. Knutsen of Tacoma/Seattle, Washington.

MODEL YEAR	FEATURES	EXC. COND. LOW	HIGH
Harp Mandolin			
1910s. Harp mandolin with tunable upper bass bout with 4 drone strings, and standard mandolin neck. The mandolin version of a harp guitar.			
1910s		$4,200	$5,200

Knutson Luthiery

1981-present. Professional and premium grade, custom, acoustic and electric mandolins built by luthier John Knutson in Forestville, California. He also builds guitars and basses.

Kona

2001-present. Budget grade, production, acoustic mandolins made in Asia. They also offer guitars, basses and amps.

MANDOLINS

MODEL YEAR	FEATURES	EXC. COND. LOW	HIGH

La Scala

Ca. 1920s-1930s. A brand of the Oscar Schmidt Company of New Jersey, used on guitars, banjos, and mandolins. These were often the fanciest of the Schmidt instruments.

Lakeside (Lyon & Healy)

Late-1800s-early-1900s. Mainly catalog sales of guitars and mandolins from the Chicago maker. Marketed as a less expensive alternative to the Lyon & Healy Washburn product line.

Style G2016 12-String Mandolin

Early-1900s. 12-string, 18 mahogany ribs with white inlay between, celluloid guard plate, advertised as "an inexpensive instrument, possessing a good tone, correct scale, and durable construction."

1917		$275	$400

Lakewood

1986-present. Luthier Martin Seeliger builds his professional grade, production/custom, mandolins in Giessen, Germany. He also builds guitars.

Larson Brothers (Chicago)

1900-1944. Made by luthiers Carl and August Larson and marketed under a variety of names including Stetson, Maurer, and Prairie State.

Bowl Back Mandolin

1900s. Neopolitan-style (bowl back) with 36 Brazilian rosewood ribs, spruce top, engraved rosewood 'guard, fancy abalone trim and headstock inlay.

1900		$450	$600

Flat Back Mandolin

1910s. Brazilian rosewood back and sides, standard appointments, dot markers, rope binding.

1910s		$700	$800

Harp-Mandolin Style 35

1920s. Harp-style body with extended upper bass bout horn without drone strings.

1920		$4,200	$6,200

Levin

1900-1973. Acoustic mandolins built in Sweden. Levin was best known for their classical guitars, which they also built for other brands, most notably Goya. They also built ukes.

Lotus

Late-1970-present. Acoustic mandolins imported by Midco International. They also offered banjos and guitars.

Lyon & Healy

1964-ca. 1945. Lyon & Healy was a large musical instrument builder and marketer, and produced under many different brands.

Style A Mandocello

Scroll peghead, symmetrical 2-point body, natural.

1910s		$4,000	$8,000
1920s		$4,000	$8,000

Style A Professional Mandolin

Violin scroll peghead, natural.

1918		$3,000	$4,000

Style B Mandolin

Maple back and sides, 2-point body, natural.

1920		$1,600	$2,000

Style C Mandolin

1920s. Like Style A teardrop Gibson body style, oval soundhole, carved spruce top, carved maple back, natural.

1920s		$1,600	$2,000

Lyra

1920s-1930s. Private brand made by Regal, Lyra name plate on headstock.

Style A (scroll) Mandolin

1920s-1930s. Scroll on upper bass bout.

1925-1935		$400	$450

Maccaferri

1923-1990. Mario Maccaferri made a variety of instruments over his career. He produced award-winning models in Italy and France until he fled to the U.S. due to WW II. He applied the new plastic to a highly successful line of instruments after the war. A mandolin was about the only stringed instument they didn't offer in plastic. His Europe-era instruments are very rare.

Mandolins/Mandolas made by Maccaferri: 1928-ca. '31: No. 1 Mandolone, No. 2 Mandoloncello, No. 3 Mandola Baritono, No. 4 Mandola Tenore, No. 5 Mandola Soprano, No. 6 Mandolino, No. 7 Quartino.

Martin

1833-present. Martin got into the mandolin market in 1896 starting with the typical bowl back designs. By 1914, Gibson's hot selling, innovative, violin-based mandolin pushed Martin into a flat back, bent top hybrid design. By '29, Martin offered a carved top and carved back mandolin. Most models were discontinued in '41, partially because of World War II. Currently Martin offers only a Backpacker mandolin.

Style 0 Mandolin

1905-1925. Bowl back-style, 18 rosewood ribs, solid peghead.

1905-1925		$800	$900

Style 00 Mandolin

1908-1925. Bowl back-style, 9 rosewood ribs (14 ribs by '24), solid peghead.

1908-1925		$600	$800

Style 000 Mandolin

1914 only. Bowl back, solid peghead, dot inlay, 9 mahogany ribs.

1914		$500	$700

Style 1 Mandolin

1898-1924. Bowl back, German silver tuners, 18 ribs.

1898-1924		$850	$950

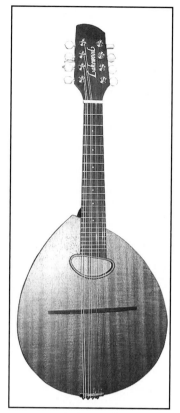

Lakewood

1925 Martin Style E

MANDOLINS

Martin 2-15

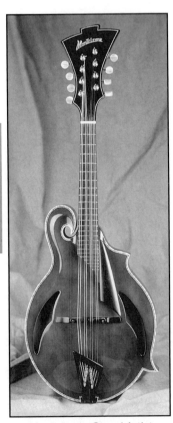

Monteleone Grand Artist

MODEL YEAR	FEATURES	EXC. COND. LOW	HIGH

Style 2 Mandolin
1898-1924. Bowl back, 26 rosewood ribs, higher appointments than Style 1.

1898-1924		$900	$1,000

Style 2-15 Mandolin
1936-1964. Carved spruce top, maple back and sides, F-hole, single-bound back, solid headstock.

1936-1964		$1,100	$1,400

Style 2-20 Mandolin
1936-1941. Carved spruce triple-bound top and bound maple back and sides, F-hole, dot inlay.

1936-1942		$1,900	$2,100

Style 2-30 Mandolin
1937-1941. Carved spruce top and maple back and sides, multi-bound, F-holes, diamond and square inlays.

1937-1941		$2,900	$3,400

Style 5 Mandolin
1898-1920. Bowl back, vine inlay, abalone top trim.

1898-1899		$2,000	$2,400
1900-1909		$1,900	$2,400
1910-1920		$1,900	$2,400

Style 6 Mandolin
1898-1921. Bowl back, top bound with ivory and abalone, vine or snowflake inlay.

1919	Snowflake inlay	$2,400	$2,700

Style A Mandolin
1914-1995. Flat back, oval soundhole, dot inlay, solid headstock.

1914-1919		$900	$1,200
1920-1939		$950	$1,200
1940-1949		$850	$1,100
1950-1969		$750	$1,000
1970-1995		$650	$900

Style AK Mandolin
1920-1937. Koa wood version of Style A, flat back.

1920-1937		$1,100	$1,500

Style B Mandolin
1914-1946, 1981-1987. Flat back with bent top, spruce top and rosewood back and sides, herringbone back stripe, multi-bound.

1910s		$1,100	$1,500
1920s		$1,100	$1,500

Style BB Mandola
1917-1921, 1932-1939. Brazilian rosewood, herringbone trim, features like Style B mandolin. This is the only Mandola offered.

1917-1921		$1,500	$2,000

Style E Mandolin
1915-1937. Flat back, rosewood back and sides, bent spruce top, Style 45 snowflake fretboard inlay and other high-end appointments. Highest model cataloged.

1915-1919		$4,500	$5,000
1920-1929		$4,000	$4,500
1930-1937		$4,000	$4,500

Maurer

Maurer Mandolins from the 1930s include Style 30 Flat Model, Style 40, Octave Mandola Style 45, Mandocello Style 50, and Mandola Tenor.

MODEL YEAR	FEATURES	EXC. COND. LOW	HIGH

Mandolin
Brazilian rosewood, birdseye maple, bowl back.

1930		$900	$1,200

May Flower

1890s-1910s. H. J. Flower's Chicago-based May Flower Music Company offered bowl back mandolins that he may or may not have built. There were also May Flower harp guitars built by others.

Bowl Back Mandolin
1901-1920s. Mid-level bowl back-style with 19 rosewood ribs and mid-level appointments.

1900s		$750	$1,100

Menzenhauer & Schmidt

1894-1904. Founded by Frederick Menzenhauer and Oscar Schmidt International. Menzenhauer created the guitar-zither in the U.S. He had several patents including one issued in September 1899 for a mandolin-guitar-zither. Control of operations quickly went to Oscar Schmidt.

12-String Mandolin
1890s. Bowl back mandolin with 3 strings per course that were tuned in octaves, designed during an experimental era for mandolin-related instrumetns, 13 rosewood ribs, spruce top, inlays.

1890s		$200	$275

Michael Kelly

2000-present. Intermediate and professional grade, production, imported, acoustic and acoustic/electric mandolins. They also offer guitars and basses.

Michael Lewis Instruments

1992-present. Luthier Michael Lewis builds his premium grade, custom, mandolins in Grass Valley, California. He also builds guitars.

Mid-Missouri

1995-present. Intermediate grade, production, acoustic and electric mandloins and mandolas built by luthier Michael Dulak in Columbia, Missouri.

M Series Mandolin
1995-1999. Teardrop A-style body, solid spruce top, solid maple, mahogany or rosewood back and sides.

1995-1999	M-1	$400	$450
1995-1999	M-2	$450	$500
1995-1999	M-3	$500	$550
1995-1999	M-4	$550	$600

Mirabella

1997-present. Professional and premium grade, mandolins built by luthier Cristian Mirabella in Babylon, New York. He also builds guitars and ukes.

Monteleone

1971-present. Primarily a guitar maker, luthier John Monteleone also builds presentation grade, custom, mandolins in West Islip, New York.

MODEL YEAR	FEATURES	EXC. COND. LOW	HIGH
Grand Artist Mandola			
1990-1995		$23,000	$25,000
Grand Artist Mandolin			
1990s. Style F body, spruce top, curly maple back and sides, dot markers.			
1990-1995	Sunburst	$23,000	$25,000
1996-2003		$24,000	$26,000
Radio Flyer Mandolin			
1990s. Style F body with variations on the F-style theme.			
1990s		$28,000	$32,000
Style B Mandolin			
1980s. Long A body style with long F-holes, flamed curly maple back and sides, elongated fretboard over body.			
1988	Sunburst	$14,000	$16,000

Moon

1979-present. Intermediate and professional grade, production/custom, acoustics and acoustic/electric mandolins and mandolas built by luthier Jimmy Moon in Glasgow, Scotland. They also build guitars.

Morales

Ca.1967-1968. Japanese-made, not heavily imported into the U.S.

MODEL YEAR	FEATURES	EXC. COND. LOW	HIGH
Electric Mandolin			
1967-1968.			
1967		$225	$300

Morgan Monroe

1999-present. Intermediate and professional grade, production, acoustic mandolins made in Korea and distributed by SHS International of Indianapolis, Indiana. They also offer guitars, basses, banjos, and fiddles.

Mozzani

Late-1800s-early-1900s. Founder Luigi Mozzani was an Italian (Bologna) master luthier and renowned composer and musician. There are original Mozzani-built mandolins and also factory-built instruments made later at various workshops.

MODEL YEAR	FEATURES	EXC. COND. LOW	HIGH
Mandolin			
Factory-built bowl back model.			
1920s		$275	$400
Original Bowl Back Mandolin			
Late-1800s-early-1900s. Handcrafted by Luigi Mozzani, about 24 ribs, soundhole ornamentation, snowflake-like markers.			
1904		$1,200	$1,500

National

Ca.1927-present. The National brand has gone through many ownership changes and offered resonator mandolins from around 1927 to '41. Currently, National does not offer a mandolin.

MODEL YEAR	FEATURES	EXC. COND. LOW	HIGH
Style 0 Mandolin			
1931-early-1940s. Metal body with Hawaiian scenes, single-cone resonator.			
1930s	Hawaiian scene	$3,000	$4,000

MODEL YEAR	FEATURES	EXC. COND. LOW	HIGH
Style 1 Mandolin			
1928-1936. Plain metal body, tri-cone resonator.			
1928-1936	Single cone	$2,000	$2,500
1928-1936	Tricone version	$3,500	$4,000
Style 2 Mandolin			
1928-1936. Metal body with rose engraving, tri-cone resonator.			
1928-1936	Single cone	$4,000	$5,000
1928-1936	Tricone version	$6,000	$7,000
Style 3 Mandolin			
1930s	Single cone	$5,000	$6,500
1930s	Tricone version	$6,000	$7,500
Style 97 Mandolin			
1936-1940. Metal body, tri-cone resonator.			
1936-1940		$4,000	$8,000
Triolian Mandolin			
1928-1940. Metal body with palm trees, single-cone resonator.			
1928-1940	Single cone	$1,500	$2,200

Northworthy

1987-present. Professional and premium grade, production/custom, mandolin-family instruments built by luthier Alan Marshall in Ashbourne, Derbyshire, England. He also builds guitars.

Nugget

1970s-present. Luthier Mike Kemnitzer builds his premium grade mandolins in Central Lake, Michigan.

Nyberg Instruments

1993-present. Professional grade, custom, mandolins and mandolas built by luthier Lawrence Nyberg in Hornby Island, British Columbia. He also builds guitars, bouzoukis and citterns.

O'Dell, Doug

See listing under Old Town.

Old Hickory

2005-present. Budget grade, production, imported F- and A-style acoustic mandolins from Musician's Wholesale America, Nashville, Tennessee. They alos offer banjos.

MODEL YEAR	FEATURES	EXC. COND. LOW	HIGH
Style A Mandolin			
2005	M-1 lowest level	$40	$60
2005	AC-1 mid-level	$75	$100
2005	FC-100 highest level	$125	$200

Old Kraftsman

1930s-1960s. Brand name used by the Siegel Company on instruments made by Kay and others (even Gibson). Quality was mixed, but some better-grade instruments were offered.

MODEL YEAR	FEATURES	EXC. COND. LOW	HIGH
Mandolin			
1950s		$200	$350

Old Town

1974-present. Luthier Doug O'Dell builds his professional and premium grade, production/custom acoustic and electric mandolins in Ohio.

Moon Master Series

National Style 2

MANDOLINS

Ovation

Regal Fancy Scroll

MODEL		EXC. COND.	
YEAR	FEATURES	LOW	HIGH

EM-10 Electric Mandolin
1980s-present. Double-cut, flamed maple top, 1 pickup, 2 control knobs.

1980s		$1,850	$1,950

Old Wave
1990-present. Luthier Bill Bussmann builds his professional and premium grade, production/custom, mandolins and mandolas in Caballo, New Mexico. He has also built guitars and basses.

Orpheum
1897-1942, 1944-early 1970s, 2001-present. Currently intermediate grade, production, mandolins. They also offer guitars. An old brand often associated with banjos, 1930s branded guitars sold by Bruno and Sons. 1950s branded guitars and mandolins sold by Maurice Lipsky Music, New York, New York.

Electric Mandolin Model 730 E
1950s. Private branded for Maurice Lipsky. Cataloged as a student model designed for ensemble playing. A-style body, single neck bar pickup, 2 side-mounted knobs, spruce top, maple back and sides, dot markers, sunburst.

1950s		$500	$600

Model No. 2 Mandolin-Banjo
1920s. Mandolin neck on small banjo body, fancy headstock and fretboard inlay, carved heel.

1920s		$500	$600

Oscar Schmidt
1879-ca. 1939, 1979-present. Currently offering budget and intermediate grade, production, mandolins. They also offer guitars, banjos, and autoharps. The original Schmidt company offered innovative mandolin designs during the 1900-'30 mandolin boom.

Mandolin Harp Style B
1890s. More zither-autoharp than mandolin, flat autoharp body with soundhole.

1890s		$100	$125

Sovereign Mandolin
1920s. Bowl back, bent top, rope-style binding, mahogany ribs, dot inlay, plain headstock.

1920s	Natural	$175	$300

Ovation
1966-present. Known for innovative fiberglass-backed bowl back acoustic and acoustic/electric guitars, Ovation added mandolins in '94 and currently offers intermediate and professional grade, production, mandolins.

Celebrity Mandolin
1994-present. Single-cut, small Ovation body, Ovation headstock.

1990s	Red Sunburst	$400	$500

P. W. Crump Company
1975-present. Luthier Phil Crump builds his custom mandolin-family instruments in Arcata, California. He also builds guitars.

Penco
Ca. 1974-1978. Japanese-made copies of classic American mandolins. They also made guitars, basses and banjos.

Phantom Guitar Works
1992-present. Intermediate grade, production, solidbody MandoGuitars assembled in Clatskanie, Oregon. They also build guitars and basses.

Phoenix
1990-present. Premium grade, production/custom, mandolins built by luthier Rolfe Gerhardt (formerly builder of Unicorn Mandolins in the '70s) in South Thomaston, Maine. Gerhard's Phoenix company specializes in a 2-point Style A (double-cut) body style.

Bluegrass (double-point) Mandolin
1990-present. Double-point shallow body voiced for bluegrass music, adirondack spruce top, figured maple body.

1990s	Sunburst	$1,500	$1,900

Premier
Ca.1938-ca.1975, 1990s-present. Brand produced by Peter Sorkin Music Company in New York City. Around '57 the company acquired Strad-O-Lin and many of their mandolins were offered under that brand. By '75, the Premier brand went into hiatus. The Premier brand currently appears on Asian-made solidbody guitars and basses.

Ramsey
1990s. Built by luthier John Ramsey of Colorado Springs, Colorado.

Randy Wood Guitars
1968-present. Premium and presentation grade, custom/production, mandolins, mandolas, and mandocellos built by luthier Randy Woods in Bloomingdale, Georgia. He also builds guitars and banjos.

Ratliff
1982-present. Professional and premium grade, production/custom, mandolin family instruments built in Church Hill, Tennessee.

R-5 Mandolin
1990s-present. F-5 style, carved spruce top, figured maple back and sides.

1995-2004		$2,000	$2,200

Recording King
1929-1943. Montgomery Ward house brand. Suppliers include Gibson, Kay, Regal, and Gretsch.

Mandolin (Gibson-made)
1929-1940. A-style body.

1930s	Sunburst	$450	$600

MODEL YEAR	FEATURES	EXC. COND. LOW	HIGH

Regal

Ca.1884-1954. Large Chicago-based manufacturer which made their own brand name and others for distributors and mass merchandisers. Absorbed by the Harmony Company in 1955.

Mandolin

1920s	Flat-top A-style	$375	$500
1930s	Sunburst, standard model	$375	$500
1930s	Ultra Grand Deluxe model	$700	$1,000

Octophone Mandolin

1920s. Octave mandolin, long body with double points, round soundhole.

1920s		$700	$1,000

Resonator Mandolin

1950s		$375	$500

Rigel

1990-present. Professional and premium grade, production/custom mandolins and mandolas built by luthier Pete Langdell in Hyde Park, Vermont.

A-Plus Series

1990s-present. A-style body, carved spruce top, maple back and sides, dot markers.

1990s	A-Plus (f-holes)	$1,400	$1,500
1990s	A-Plus (oval soundhole)	$1,000	$1,100

Classic S

2000s	Double cutaway, f-holes	$1,900	$2,100

Model G-110 Mandolin

1990-present. Maple neck, back and sides, red spruce top, f-holes.

1990s	Sunburst	$2,300	$2,600

Roberts

1980s. Built by luthier Jay Roberts of California.

Tiny Moore Jazz 5 Mandolin

1980s. Based on Bigsby design of the early-1950s as used by Tiny Moore, five-string electric.

1985	Sunburst	$1,600	$1,800

Rogue

2001-present. Budget grade, production, imported mandolins. They also offer guitars, basses, ukes, banjos, effects and amps.

Rono

1967-present. Luthier Ron Oates builds his professional grade, production/custom, electric mandolins in Boulder, Colorado. He also builds basses and guitars.

S. S. Stewart

Late-1800s-early-1900s. S.S. Stewart of Philadelphia was primarily known for banjos. Legend has it that Stewart was one of the first to demonstrate the mass production assembly of stringed instruments.

Mandolin Banjo

Early-1900s. Mandolin neck and a very small open back banjo body, star inlay in headstock.

1900s		$325	$450

Samick

1958-2001, 2002-present. Budget and intermediate grade, production, imported acoustic and acoustic/electric mandolins. They also offer guitars, basses, ukes and banjos.

Sammo

1920s. Labels in these instruments state they were made by the Osborne Mfg. Co. with an address of Masonic Temple, Chicago, Illinois. High quality and often with a high degree of ornamentation. They also made ukes and guitars.

Sawchyn

1972-present. Intermediate and professional grade, production/custom, mandolins built by luthier Peter Sawchyn in Regina, Saskatchewan. He also builds flat-top and flamenco guitars.

Sekova

Mid-1960s-mid-1970s. Entry level, imported by the U.S. Musical Merchandise.

Electric Mandolin

1960s-1970s. Kay-Kraft-style hollowbody with F-holes, 1 pickup and Sekova logo on the headstock.

1965-1970s		$175	$300

Silvertone

1941-ca.1970. Brand name used by Sears on their musical instruments.

Mandolin

Arched top and back.

1940s	Sunburst	$175	$300
1950s	Sunburst	$175	$300

Smart Musical Instruments

1986-present. Premium and presentation grade, custom, mandolin family instruments built by luthier A. Lawrence Smart in McCall, Idaho. He also builds guitars.

Sovereign

Ca. 1899-ca. 1938. Sovereign was originally a brand of the Oscar Schmidt company of New Jersey. In the late '30s, Harmony purchased several trade names from the Schmidt Company, including Sovereign. Sovereign then ceased as a brand, but Harmony continued using it on a model line of Harmony guitars.

Mandolins

1920s. Old-style bent top.

1920s		$250	$400

Stahl

William C. Stahl instruments were "made" (per their literature they were not manufactured) in Milwaukee, Wisconsin, in the early-1900s. Models

Rigel A-Plus Oval Deluxe

Sawchyn Custom A-Style

MANDOLINS

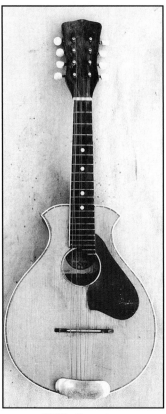

1920s Supertone

Tacoma M-3

MODEL YEAR	FEATURES	EXC. COND. LOW	HIGH

included Style 4 (22 ribs) to Style 12 Presentation Artist Special. The more expensive models were generally 44-rib construction.

Arched Back Presentation

1910s. Brazilian rosewood back and sides, very fancy abalone appointments.

| 1910s | | $2,000 | $4,000 |

Bowl Back Mandolin (deluxe professional model)

Rosewood, 40 ribs.

| 1910s | | $800 | $1,200 |

Bowl Back Mandolin (mid-level)

Pearl floral design on 'guard, 32 ribs.

| 1910s | | $350 | $550 |

Stathopoulo

1903-1916. Original design instruments, some patented, by Epiphone company founder A. Stathopoulo.

A-Style Mandolin

1903-1916. A-style with higher-end appointments, bent-style spruce top, figured maple back and sides.

| 1912 | | $800 | $1,200 |

Stefan Sobell Musical Instruments

1982-present. Luthier Stefan Sobell builds his premium grade, production/custom, mandolins in Hetham, Northumberland, England. He also builds guitars, citterns and bouzoukis.

10-String Mandolin

| 1988 | | $2,500 | $2,700 |

Stella

Ca. 1899-1974, present. Stella was a brand of the Oscar Schmidt Company which was an early contributor to innovative mandolin designs and participated in the 1900-'30 mandolin boom. Pre-World War II Stella instruments were low-mid to mid-level instruments. In '39, Harmony purchased the Stella name and '50s and '60s Stella instruments were student grade, low-end instruments. The Stella brand has been reintroduced by MBT International.

Banjo-Mandolin

1920s. One of several innovative designs that attempted to create a new market, 8-string mandolin neck with a banjo body, Stella logo normally impressed on the banjo rim or the side of the neck.

| 1920s | | $150 | $275 |

Bowl Back Mandolin

1920s. Typical bowl back, bent top-style mandolin with models decalomania, about 10 (wide) maple ribs, dot markers.

| 1920s | | $100 | $225 |

Pear-Shape Mandolin

1940s-1960s. Harmony-made lower-end mandolins, pear-shaped (Style A) flat back, oval soundhole.

1940s	Natural	$175	$250
1950s		$175	$250
1960s	Sunburst	$175	$250

Sterling

Early-1900s. Distributed by wholesalers The Davitt & Hanser Music Co.

Stiver

Professional and premium grade, custom/production, mandolins built by luthier Lou Stiver in Pennsylvania.

Strad-O-Lin

Ca.1920s-ca.1960s. The Strad-O-Lin company was operated by the Hominic brothers in New York, primarily making mandolins for wholesalers. In the late '50s, Multivox/Premier bought the company and used the name on mandolins and guitars.

Baldwin Electric Mandolin

1950s. A-Style, single pickup, tone and volume knobs, spruce top, maple back and sides, Baldwin logo on headstock.

| 1950s | Natural | $325 | $425 |

Junior A Mandolin

1950s. A-Style, Stradolin Jr. logo on headstock, dot markers.

| 1950s | Sunburst | $275 | $375 |

Stromberg-Voisinet

1921-ca.1932. Marketed Stromberg (not to be confused with Charles Stromberg of Boston) and Kay Kraft brands, plus instruments of other distributors and retailers. Became the Kay Musical Instrument Company. By the mid-'20s, the company was making many better Montgomery Ward guitars, banjos and mandolins, often with lots of pearloid. The last Stromberg acoustic instruments were seen in '32.

Mandolin

1921-1932. Vague two point A-style.

| 1921-1932 | | $250 | $300 |

Superior

1987-present. Intermediate grade, production/custom mandolin-family instruments made in Mexico for George Katechis Montalvo of Berkeley Musical Instrument Exchange. They also offer guitars.

Supertone

1914-1941. Brand used by Sears before they switched to Silvertone. Instruments made by other companies.

Mandolin

Spruce top, mahogany back and sides, some with decalomania vine pattern on top.

| 1920s | | $225 | $350 |
| 1930s | Decalomania vine pattern | $225 | $350 |

Supro

1935-1968, 2004-present. Budget line from the National Dobro Company. Amp builder Bruce Zinky revived the Supro name for a guitar and amp model.

MODEL YEAR	FEATURES	EXC. COND. LOW	HIGH

T30 Electric Mandolin
1950s		$375	$525

T. H. Davis
1976-present. Premium grade, custom, mandolins built by luthier Ted Davis in Loudon, Tennessee. He also builds guitars.

Tacoma
1995-present. Intermediate, professional and premium grade, production, mandolins made in Tacoma, Washington. They also build guitars and basses.

M-1/M-1E Mandolin
1999-present. Solid spruce top, mahogany back and sides, typical Tacoma body-style with upper bass bout soundhole.

1999-2004	M-1 acoustic	$300	$375
1999-2004	M-1E acoustic/ electric	$350	$425

M-3E Mandolin
1999-2004. Acoustic/electric, upper bass bout sound hole. Acoustic M-3 still available.

1999-2004		$575	$600

Tennessee
1970-1993, 1996-present. Luthier Mark Taylor builds his professional and premium grade, production/custom, mandolins in Old Hickory, Tennessee. He also builds guitars, mandolins, banjos and the Tut Taylor brand of resophonic guitars.

Timeless Instruments
1980-present. Luthier David Freeman builds his intermediate grade, mandolins in Tugaske, Saskatchewan. He also builds guitars and dulcimers.

Triggs
1992-present. Luthiers Jim Triggs and his son Ryan build their professional and premium grade, production/custom, mandolins in Kansas City, Kansas. They also build guitars. They were located in Nashville, Tennessee until '98.

Trinity River
Mandolins from Stenzler Musical Instruments of Ft. Worth, Texas. They also offer guitars, basses, and fiddles.

Unicorn
1970s-late 1980s. Luthier Rolfe Gerhardt (currently luthier for Phoenix Mandolins) founded Unicorn in the mid-'70s. Gerhardt built 149 mandolins before selling Unicorn to Save Sjnko in '80. Sinko closed Unicorn in the late-'80s.

F-5 Style Mandolin
1976-1980	Sunburst	$1,000	$2,000

MODEL YEAR	FEATURES	EXC. COND. LOW	HIGH

Vega
1903-present. The original Boston-based company was purchased by C.F. Martin in '70. In '80, the Vega trademark was sold to a Korean company. Vega means star and a star logo is often seen on the original Vega instruments.

Lansing Special Bowl Mandolin
Spruce top, abalone, vine inlay.

1890s		$500	$650

Little Wonder Mandolin Banjo
Maple neck, resonator.

1920s		$450	$600

Mando Bass Mandolin
1910s-1920s. Large upright bass-sized instrument with bass tuners, body-style similar to dual-point A-style, scroll headstock.

1920s		$2,500	$3,700

Mandolin Cittern
1910s. 10-string (five double strings tuned in 5ths), vague A-style with oval soundhole and cylinder back, natural.

1910s		$1,800	$2,200

Style 202 Lute Mandolin
Early-1900s. Basic A-style with small horns, natural spruce top, mahogany sides and cylinder back, dot markers.

1910s		$700	$850

Style A Mandolin
1910s		$500	$625

Style F Mandolin
1910s. Scroll upper bass bout, oval soundhole, Vega and torch inlay in headstock.

1910s		$900	$1,000

Style K Mandolin Banjo
1910s		$350	$550
1920s		$350	$550
1930s		$350	$550

Style L Banjo Mandolin
1910s. Open back banjo body and mandolin 8-string neck.

1910s		$800	$900

Super Deluxe Mandolin
1939	Sunburst	$650	$750

Tubaphone Style X Mandolin Banjo
1923		$650	$750

Veillette
1991-present. Luthiers Joe Veillette and Martin Keith build their professional grade, production/custom, mandolins in Woodstock, New York. They also builds basses and guitars.

Vinaccia
Italian-made by Pasquale Vinaccia, luthier.

Bowl Back Mandolin
High-end appointments and 'guard, 30 rosewood ribs.

1900-1920s		$2,500	$3,000

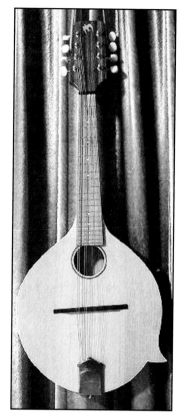
Timeless Instruments

Triggs mando

MANDOLINS

Weber Style Yellowstone

Wurlitzer Mandolin Banjo

MANDOLINS

MODEL YEAR	FEATURES	EXC. COND. LOW	HIGH

Vivi-Tone

1933-ca. 1936. Lloyd Loar's pioneering guitar company also built early electric mandolins and mandocellos in Kalamazoo, Michigan.

Electric Mandocello

1933-1935. Traditonal guitar-arch body, Vivi-Tone silkscreen logo on headstock.

1933-1935		$5,500	$6,000

Electric Mandola

1933-1935. Traditonal European teardrop/pear-shaped top, Vivi-Tone silkscreen logo on headstock.

1933-1935		$4,500	$5,000

Electric Mandolin

1933-1935. Vivi-Tone silkscreen logo on headstock.

1933-1935		$4,000	$4,500

Ward

Depression era private brand made by Gibson's Kalamazoo factory.

Style A Mandolin

1930s. Style A body with round soundhole and flat top and back, dot markers, mahogany back and sides, silkscreened Ward logo.

1935	Sunburst	$325	$400

Washburn (Lyon & Healy)

1880s-ca.1949. Washburn was founded in Chicago as one of the lines for Lyon & Healy to promote high quality stringed instruments, ca. 1880s. The rights to Washburn were sold to Regal which built Washburns by the mid-'30s until until ca. '49. In '74 the brand resurfaced.

Bowl Back Mandolin

Lyon and Healy sold a wide variety of bowl back mandolins, Brazilian ribs with fancy inlays and bindings.

1890s	Fancy inlays and bindings	$600	$900
1890s	Plain appointments	$300	$400
1900s	Fancy inlays and bindings	$600	$900
1900s	Plain appointments	$300	$400
1910s	Standard appointments	$300	$400

Style A Mandolin

Brazilian rosewood.

1920s		$900	$1,000

Style E Mandolin

1915-1923. Brazilian rosewood.

1915-1923		$1,000	$1,200

Washburn (Post 1974)

1974-present. Currently, Washburn offers imported intermediate and professional grade, production, mandolins.

Mandolin/Mandolin family

1974-present.

1974-2005		$300	$600

MODEL YEAR	FEATURES	EXC. COND. LOW	HIGH

Washington

Washington mandolins were manufactured by Kansas City, Missouri instrument wholesalers J.W. Jenkins & Sons. First introduced in 1895, the brand also offered guitars.

Weber

1996-present. Intermediate, professional, and premium grade, production/custom, mandolins, mandolas, and mandocellos. In '96, Gibson moved the manufacturing of Flatiron mandolins from Bozeman, Montana, to Nashville, Tennessee. Many former Flatiron employees, including Bruce Weber, formed Sound To Earth, Ltd., to build Weber instruments in Belgrade, Montana.

Aspen #1

1990s. Celtic teardrop A-style body, solid spruce top, maple sides and back, natural finish, Weber and Celtic knot headstock logo.

1990s		$775	$825

Beartooth

2000s	A-style, f-holes	$1,700	$1,800

Style F Yellowstone Mandolin

1996-present. Style F mandolin built with solid spruce top and flamed maple back and sides.

1998	Sunburst	$1,900	$2,200

Weymann

1864-1940s. H.A. Weymann & Sons was a musical instrument distributor located in Philadelphia. They also built their own instruments.

Keystone State Banjo Mandolin

Maple rim and back, ebony fretboard.

1910s		$300	$400

Model 20 Mando-Lute

1920s. Lute-style body, spruce top, flamed maple sides and back, rope binding, deluxe rosette.

1920s	Natural	$600	$750

Model 40 Mandolin Banjo

1910s-1920s. Mandolin neck on a open banjo body with a larger sized 10" head.

1920s	10" or 11" rim	$450	$600

Wurlitzer

The old Wurlitzer company would have been considered a mega-store by today's standards. They sold a wide variety of instruments, gave music lessons, and operated manufacturing facilities.

Mandolin

Koa.

1920		$500	$700

Mandolin Banjo

1900s. Mandolin neck on open back banjo body, plain-style.

1900s		$200	$275

Zeta

1982-present. Professional grade, production, acoustic/electric mandolins made in Oakland, California. They also make basses, amps and violins.

Ukuleles

Ukulele Identification: The Numbers Game

It's been said that you just can't play a sad song on a ukulele. More suited to the likes of happy hula music and Tin Pan Alley tunes than any song in a minor key, the uke has been cheering up strummers and listeners alike for over a century. Find yourself the owner of an unmarked vintage uke, however, and you're likely to be singing a very sad song, indeed.

Fear not. Even though a great many ukuleles were never marked and seem to defy every attempt at identification, there actually is a hidden system. And although a uke's features may not offer any easy answers, you can at least find out what model it is.

First, a little history. The uke craze caught on fast, and from the time of its invention in the late 1800s it was clear the ukulele was going to be a hot item, one for which small-scale production wouldn't meet demand. And like all manufactured goods, it was crucial to create a line of models, composed of a few styles with unique and identifiable features. This was still early, mind you, and ukuleles of different sizes hadn't yet come into being. A uke was just a uke, at roughly 22" inches long and 6" wide, it was what we think of today as a soprano, except it was just a ukulele-sized uke.

As the most prolific of Hawaiian ukulele makers (like Kumalae, Manuel Nunes, and Kamaka) began churning out product, it became apparent that a standardized numbering system would be just the ticket to simplify the ornamentation levels and justify a pricing scheme. As quick as you could say "King Kamehameha," ukes were designed in styles 1, 2, and 3. And while all ukuleles produced in Hawaii during these years featured koa-wood bodies and necks, the degree of ornamentation varied with the style number in a careful and predictable way.

Style 1, the plainest and least expensive model, featured only a decorated soundhole. This usually took the form of either a colored wood rosette (called "rope") around the soundhole, or a rosette of concentric bands of lighter wood. This inlaid motif was a quick, inexpensive procedure, but was also functional, creating a barrier against cracking and damage to the delicate soundhole edge.

Style 2 added rope binding that matched the soundhole rosette to the top edge of the body, and sometimes (albeit rarely) on the back, as well.

Style 3, the fanciest, continued the rope on the surface (center, edges, or both) of the fingerboard, and often onto the peghead.

While variations that resulted in additional binding were common, styles 1, 2, and 3 continued as standard ukulele archetypes even as mainland manufacturers jumped on the bandwagon decades later. Indeed, C.F. Martin's first ukulele models were – you guessed it – 1, 2, and 3, the three degrees of ornamentation carried over from the earlier Hawaiian makers. And while Martin didn't offer koa wood until a few years later, and pushed the envelope a bit by putting dark rosewood body binding onto their Style 1, their inspiration for a trio of introductory models was unmistakable. When additional models were added to tap into an exploding uke market, Martin used an O to denote a plain model, and the regal number 5 (skipping 4 entirely) to describe its pearl-trimmed presentation model.

One after the other, American manufacturers – regardless of their existing instrument numbering systems – issued ukulele lines based upon a simple triad of models. Gibson offered its Uke 1, Uke 2, and Uke 3 for more than 50 years; National issued its nickel-silver-bodied resonator ukes in styles 1, 2, and 3, each with a different level of engraving. Weissenborn made Hawaiian guitars in four distinct styles, ukes in the familiar three. Seemingly, the only ukuleles that sidestepped the numbers were the stenciled fare from companies like Harmony and Regal. After all, how can you number a painted girl in a canoe?

So remember: 1 – fancy soundhole; 2 – fancy soundhole and body; 3 – fancy sound hole, body, and fingerboard.

And while you may never be sure whether that ukulele you've been scratching your head about is a Kumalae, a Kamaka, or a Kent, at least you now can rest assured you know what style it is.

R.J.Klimpert
Thatukeguy@earthlink.net

Kumalae Style 1

Kumalae Style 2

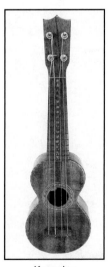
Kumalae Style 3

Kamaka Pineapple Uke Style-3

Martin 2K

Gibson UKE-2

The *Vintage Guitar Price Guide* shows low to high values for items in all-original excellent condition, and, where applicable, with original case or cover.

MODEL		EXC. COND.	
YEAR	FEATURES	LOW	HIGH

Aero Uke

1920s. Never branded, but almost certainly produced by Chicago's Stromberg-Voisenet Company, the precursor of Kay, the Aero Uke is an instrument quite unlike any other. With its spruce-capped body resembling an old-timey airplane wing and a neck and headstock that approximate a plane's fuselage, this clever '20s offering cashed in on the Lindbergh craze (like the Harmony Johnny Marvin model with its airplane-shaped bridge), and must have been a big hit at parties.

Aero Uke
Airplane body.

1927	Black deco on wing	$1,600	$2,000
1927	Gold deco on wing	$1,800	$2,200

Aloha

1935-1960s. The Aloha brand turns up on numerous vastly different ukes. In fact, the variety of features exhibited by Aloha ukuleles leads the modern observer to believe that the ukes that bear this headstock decal were made by as many as a dozen different manufacturers, each with access to the same logo. Many were undoubtedly Island-made, with all koa bodies and some with fancy rope binding; others bear unmistakable mainland traits. Some of these have a more traditional look and are stamped Akai inside the soundhole, while still others, strongly resembling mainland C.F. Martins in design, typically sport a decal of the Sam F. Chang curio shop on the reverse of the headstock.

Akai Soprano Ukulele
Koa construction.

1930s		$350	$500

Soprano Ukulele
Koa body, plain.

1950s		$350	$500

Applause

1976-present. Kaman Music's entry-level Ovation-styled import brand Applause currently offers budget and intermediate grade, production, soprano and tenor ukuleles.

Bear Creek Guitars

1995-present. Intermediate and professional grade ukuleles built by luthier Bill Hardin in Kula, Hawaii. He also builds guitars.

Beltona

1990-present. Production metal body resonator ukuleles made in New Zealand by Steve Evans and Bill Johnson. Beltona was originally located in England. They also build guitars.

Blue Star

1984-present. Intermediate grade, production/custom, acoustic and electric ukuleles built by luthier Bruce Herron in Fennville, Michigan. He also builds guitars, mandolins, dulcimers and lap steels.

Bruno

1834-present. This New York distributor certainly subcontracted all of its ukulele production to other manufacturers, and as a result you'd be hard pressed to find two identical Bruno ukes.

Soprano Ukulele

1920s	Koa, rope soundhole	$300	$400
1930s	Koa, rope bound body	$350	$400

DeCava Guitars

1983-present. Professional grade, production/custom, ukuleles built by luthier Jim DeCava in Stratford, Connecticut. He also builds guitars, banjos, and mandolins.

Del Vecchio Dinamico

With a design patterned after the pioneering work of Dobro and National, this Brazilian company produced a full line of resonator instruments, all constructed of native Brazilian rosewood, from the 1950s onward.

Resonator Ukulele
Brazilian rosewood.

1950s		$700	$850
1980s		$700	$850

Ditson

1916-1930. Don't be fooled. While some of the ukes that were commissioned by this East Coast music publisher and chain store were actually manufactured by C.F. Martin, Martin was by no means the sole supplier. The Martin-made instruments often bear a Martin brand as well as a Ditson one, or, barring that, at least demonstrate an overall similarity to the rest of the ukes in the regular Martin line, both on the inside and out.

Soprano Ukulele

1922	as Martin Style 1 K	$1,500	$2,000
1922	as Martin Style 1 M	$900	$1,000
1922	as Martin Style 2 K	$1,500	$2,300
1922	as Martin Style 2 M	$1,200	$1,300
1922	as Martin Style 3 K	$2,400	$3,200
1922	as Martin Style 3 M	$2,500	$2,800
1922	as Martin Style 5 K	$6,000	$8,000
1922	as Martin Style O	$800	$900

Dobro

1929-1942, ca. 1954-present. The ukulele version of the popular amplifying resonator instruments first produced in California, the Dobro uke was offered in 2 sizes (soprano and tenor), 2 styles (F-holes and screen holes), and 2 colors (brown and black). Models with Dobro headstock decals are often outwardly indistinguishable from others bearing either a Regal badge or no logo at all, but a peek inside often reveals the presence of a sound well in the belly of the former, making them the more desirable of the two.

Aloha "Islands" Uke

Dobro resonator

ca. 1916 Earnest Kaai

UKULELES

Favilla

Flamingo

Gibson Uke 1

MODEL YEAR	FEATURES	EXC. COND. LOW	HIGH

Resonator Ukulele
Wood body.

1930s	F-holes, Regal-made	$500	$900
1930s	Screen holes	$600	$900

Earnest Kaai

Hawaiian Earnest Kaai was many things (teacher, songbook publisher, importer/exporter) during the early part of the 20th century, but ukulele manufacturer was certainly one job that he couldn't add to his resume. Still, scads of ukes proudly bear his name, in a variety of different styles and variations. Even more puzzling is the fact that while some appear to actually have been island-made, an equal number bear the telltale signs of mainland manufacture.

Soprano Ukulele
Koa body.

1920	Rope bound top/back	$500	$700
1925	Abalone trim top, paper label	$800	$1,000
1925	Unbound, decal logo	$300	$500
1930	Rope bound soundhole only	$400	$600

Favilla

1890-1973. The small New York City family-owned factory that produced primarily guitars also managed to offer some surprisingly high quality ukes, the best of which rival Martin and Gibson for craftsmanship and tone. As a result, Favilla ukuleles are a real value for the money.

Baritone Ukulele
Plain mahogany body.

1950s		$400	$500

Soprano Ukulele

1950s	Mahogany body, triple bound	$500	$600
1950s	Plain mahogany body	$400	$500
1950s	Teardrop-shaped, birch body	$400	$500
1950s	Teardrop-shaped, stained blue	$400	$500

Fender

Fender offered Regal-made ukuleles in the 1960s, including the R-275 Baritone Ukulele.

Fin-der

1950s. The pitch of this short-lived plastic ukulele was apparently the ease of learning, since the included instructional brochure helped you to "find" your chords with the added help of rainbow of color-coded nylon strings.

Diamond Head Ukulele
Styrene plastic, in original box.

1950s		$150	$200

Fine Resophonic

1988-present. Intermediate and professional grade, production/custom, wood and metal-bodied resophonic ukuleles built by luthiers Mike Lewis

MODEL YEAR	FEATURES	EXC. COND. LOW	HIGH

and Pierre Avocat in Vitry Sur Seine, France. They also build guitars and mandolins.

Flamingo

1950s. If swanky designs and hot-foil stamped into the surface of these '50s swirly injection molded polystyrene ukes didn't grab you, certainly the built-in functional pitch pipe across the top of the headstock would. And I ask you, who can resist a ukulele with built-in tuner?

Soprano Ukulele

1955	Brown top, white 'board	$125	$150
1955	White top, brown 'board	$125	$150

Gibson

1880s (1902)-present. A relative late-comer to the uke market, Gibson didn't get a line off the ground until 1927, fully 9 years after Martin had already been in production. Even then they only produced 3 soprano styles and 1 tenor version. Worse still, they never made any ukes in koa, sticking to the easier-to-obtain mahogany.

Nonetheless, Gibson ukuleles exhibit more unintentional variety than any other major maker, with enough construction, inlay, binding, and cosmetic variations to keep collectors buzzing for many a year to come. In general, the earliest examples feature a Gibson logo in script, later shortened to just Gibson. Post-war examples adopted the more square-ish logo of the rest of the Gibson line, and, at some point in the late '50s, began sporting ink-stamped serial numbers on the back of the headstock like their guitar and mandolin brethren.

ETU 1 Ukulele
Electric tenor, unbound body, square black pickup, 88 made.

1949		$3,000	$4,500

ETU 3 Ukulele
Electric tenor, triple bound body, square pickup, rare.

1953		$5,000	$6,500

TU-1 Ukulele
Tenor, called the TU until 1 added in 1949, mahogany body, sunburst finish.

1930s		$750	$1,000

Uke-1 Ukulele
Soprano, plain mahogany body.

1927		$600	$750
1951	Red SG guitar-like finish	$600	$750

Uke-2 Ukulele
Soprano, mahogany body.

1934	Triple bound	$700	$900

Uke-3 Ukulele
Soprano, dark finish, diamonds and squares inlay.

1933		$1,200	$1,500

UKULELES

MODEL YEAR	FEATURES	EXC. COND. LOW	HIGH

Graziano

1969-present. Luthier Tony Graziano has been building ukuleles almost exclusively since '95 in his Santa Cruz shop. Like many, he sees the uke as the instrument of the new millennium, and his entirely handmade, custom orders can be had in a variety of shapes, sizes, and woods.

Gretsch

1883-present. The first (and most desirable) ukuleles by this New York manufacturer were actually stamped with the name Gretsch American or with interior brass nameplates. Subsequent pieces, largely inexpensive laminate-bodied catalog offerings, are distinguished by small round Gretsch headstock decals, and a lack of any kerfed linings inside the bodies.

Plain Soprano Ukulele

Natural mahogany body, no binding.

1950s		$150	$200

Round Ukulele

Round body, blue to green sunburst.

1940		$150	$200

Soprano Ukulele

1940s	Koa wood body, fancy 'board inlay	$650	$750
1940s	Mahogany body, fancy 'board inlay	$600	$750
1940s	Unbound body, engraved rose in peghead	$800	$900
1950s	Darker finish, bordered in dark binding	$250	$450

Guild

1952-present. By rights this fine East Coast shop should have produced a full line of ukes to complement its impressive flat and carved-top guitar offerings. Alas, a lone baritone model was all that they could manage. And it's a darned shame, too.

B-11 Baritone Ukulele

1963-1976. Mahogany body, rosewood 'board.

1960s		$400	$550

Harmony

1892-1976, late 1970s-present. This manufacturer surely produced more ukuleles than all other makers put together. Their extensive line ran the gamut from artist endorsed models and ukes in unusual shapes and materials, to inexpensive but flashy creations adorned with eye-catching decals and silk screening. The earliest examples have a small paper label on the back of the headstock, and a branded logo inside the body. This was replaced by a succession of logo decals applied to the front of the headstock, first gold and black, later green, white, and black. By the '60s Harmony had become so synonymous with ukulele production that they were known around their Chicago locale as simply "the ukulele factory," as in, "Ma couldn't come

to the bar-b-que on-a-counta she got a job at the ukulele factory."

Baritone Ukulele

Bound mahogany body.

1960s		$250	$350

Concert Ukulele

Mahogany body, bound, concert-sized.

1935		$250	$300

Harold Teen Ukulele

Carl Ed cartoon decals on front.

1930	Red or Gray-blue	$200	$400
1930	Yellow	$300	$450

Johnny Marvin Tenor Ukulele

Sports an airplane bridge.

1930s	Flamed koa	$550	$800
1930s	Sunburst mahogany	$400	$550

Roy Smeck Concert Ukulele

Concert-sized, sunburst spruce top.

1935		$400	$500

Roy Smeck Ukulele

Mahogany body.

1955	Plastic 'board	$150	$200
1955	Wood 'board	$350	$450

Roy Smeck Vita Ukulele

Pear-shaped body, seal-shaped F-holes.

1926		$550	$750

Tiple Ukulele

Multicolored binding, 10 steel strings.

1935		$600	$850

Ukulele

1930	Koa body, unbound	$250	$500
1935	Plain mahogany body, unbound	$300	$400

Hilo Bay Ukuleles

2003-present. Intermediate grade, production, tenor ukuleles made in Cebu City, Philippines for Hilo Guitars and Ukuleles of Hilo, Hawaii.

Johnson

Mid-1990s-present. Budget ukuleles imported by Music Link of Brisbane, California. They also offer guitars, amps, mandolins and effects. Most notable of the Johnson ukes are the National metal-bodied uke copies, which come surprisingly close to the look and feel of the originals, at an unfathomably low price.

K & S

1992-1998. Ukes distributed by George Katechis and Marc Silber and handmade in Paracho, Mexico. They also offered guitars. In '98, Silber started marketing the ukes under the Marc Silber Guitar Company brand and Katechis continued to offer instruments under the Casa Montalvo brand.

Kamaka

Part of the second wave of ukulele builders on the Hawaiian islands (after Nunes, Dias, and Santos) Kamaka distinguished itself first with ukes of extremely high quality, subsequently with the most

Gibson Uke 3 Rare version

1920s Harmony Roy Smeck Vita

UKULELES

Johnson UK-998

Kamaka Pineapple Uke Style-3

Kumalae Fancy Uke

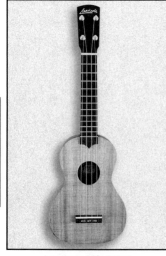

Larrivee US-01KA

enduring non-guitar-derived designs, the Pineapple Uke, patented in 1928. Kamaka is the only maker which has been in continuous production for nearly a hundred years, offering Hawaiian-made products from native woods in virtually every size and ornamentation.

Baritone Uke
Koa body, extended 'board.

Model Year	Features	Exc. Cond. Low	High
1990		$600	$900

Concert Uke
Koa body, extended rosewood 'board.

Model Year	Features	Exc. Cond. Low	High
1975		$250	$500

Lili'u Uke
Concert-sized koa body.

Model Year	Features	Exc. Cond. Low	High
1965	8 strings	$500	$700
1985	6 strings	$500	$700

Pineapple Uke

Model Year	Features	Exc. Cond. Low	High
1925	Pineapple art painted onto top or back	$1,300	$1,500
1930	Monkeypod wood, plain, unbound	$600	$950
1930	Rope bound top only, koawood body	$800	$1,000
1935	Rope bound soundhole only	$700	$900
1960	Koa body, unbound, 2 Ks logo	$500	$600
1970	Koa body, extended rosewood 'board	$350	$650

Tenor Uke
Koa body, extended rosewood 'board.

Model Year	Features	Exc. Cond. Low	High
1955		$300	$750

Kent

1961-1969. Large, student quality ukes of laminated construction were offered by this Japanese concern throughout the '60s.

Baritone Ukulele
Mahogany body, bound top, bound back.

Model Year	Features	Exc. Cond. Low	High
1960s		$150	$250

Knutsen

1890s-1920s. While Christopher Knutsen was the inventor of flat-topped harp instruments featuring an integral sound chamber on the bass side of the body, he almost certainly left the manufacturing to others. Striking in both concept and design, Knutsen products nonetheless suffer from compromised construction techniques.

Harp Taro Patch
Koa body, large horn chamber, 8 strings, unbound.

Model Year	Features	Exc. Cond. Low	High
1915		$3,000	$4,000

Harp Uke
Koa body, large horn chamber.

Model Year	Features	Exc. Cond. Low	High
1915	Bound	$2,000	$3,500
1915	Unbound	$1,500	$2,500

Kumalae

Along with Kamaka, Kumalae was also of the second wave of Hawaiian uke makers. Jonah Kumalae's company quickly snagged the prestigious Gold Award at the Pan Pacific Exhibition in 1915, and the headstock decals and paper labels aren't about to let you forget it, either. Many assume that these all date from exactly that year, when in fact Kumalaes were offered right up through the late 1930s.

Soprano Ukuele

Model Year	Features	Exc. Cond. Low	High
1930	Unbound body	$500	$700

Soprano Ukulele
Figured koa body.

Model Year	Features	Exc. Cond. Low	High
1919	Bound top, back, 'board	$700	$1,000
1920	Rope bound top/back	$500	$700
1927	As 1919 but with fiddle-shaped peghead	$800	$1,500
1933	Rope bound soundhole only	$500	$700

Tenor Ukulele
Koa body, unbound top and back.

Model Year	Features	Exc. Cond. Low	High
1930		$700	$900

Lanikai

2000-present. Line of budget and intermediate grade, production, koa or nato wood, acoustic and acoustic/electric, ukuleles distributed by Hohner.

Larrivee

1968-present. This mainstream guitar manufacturer has an on-again off-again relationship with the ukulele, having occasionally produced some superb examples in various sizes, woods and degrees of ornamentation. They introduced 3 ukulele models in '00. They also build guitars.

Le Domino

This line of striking ukuleles turned the popularity of domino playing into a clever visual motif, displaying not only tumbling dominos on their soundboards and around their soundholes, but 'board markers represented in decal domino denominations (3, 5, 7, 10, 12, etc.). The ukuleles were, in fact, produced by at least 2 different companies - Stewart and Regal - but you can scarcely tell them apart.

Concert Ukulele
Concert size, black-finish, white bound, dominos.

Model Year	Features	Exc. Cond. Low	High
1932		$1,000	$1,200

Soprano Ukulele
Domino decals.

Model Year	Features	Exc. Cond. Low	High
1930	Black finish, white bound	$500	$650
1940	Natural finish, unbound	$150	$250

Leonardo Nunes

Leonardo was the son of Manuel, the self professed inventor of the Ukulele. Whether actually the originator or not, Dad was certainly on the

UKULELES

MODEL YEAR	FEATURES	EXC. COND. LOW	HIGH

ship that brought the inventor to the islands in 1879. Leonardo, instead of joining up and making it Manuel & Son, set out on his own to produce ukes that are virtually indistinguishable from pop's. All constructed entirely of koa, some exhibit considerable figure and rope binding finery, making them as highly desirable to collectors as Manuel's.

Radio Tenor Ukulele
Koa body, bound top, back and neck.

1935		$1,500	$2,000

Soprano Ukulele
Figured koa body.

1919	Bound top/ back/'board	$750	$1,100
1920	Rope bound top/back	$750	$1,000
1927	Bound body/ 'board/head	$1,200	$1,600
1930	Unbound body	$500	$750
1933	Rope bound soundhole only	$600	$800

Taro Patch Fiddle
Koa body, unbound top and back.

1930		$1,500	$2,000

Tenor Ukulele
Koa body, unbound top and back.

1930		$800	$1,100

Levin
1900-1973. Ukuleles built in Sweden. Levin was best known for their classical guitars, which they also built for other brands, most notably Goya. They also built mandolins.

Loprinzi
1972-present. Intermediate and professional grade, production/custom, ukuleles built in Clearwater, Florida. They also build guitars.

Lyon & Healy
1880s-ca.1949. During different periods several different makers constructed ukes bearing this stamp – often with an additional Washburn tag as well. After initial production by Lyon & Healy, instrument manufacture then apparently bounced between Regal, Stewart, and Tonk Brothers all within a span of only a few short years. Adding to the confusion, ukes surface from time to time bearing no maker's mark that can be reasonably attributed to Lyon & Healy. Suffice it to say that the best of these ukes, those displaying the highest degrees of quality and ornamentation, rival Gibson and Martin for collectability and tone and beauty.

Bell-shaped Ukulele
Mahogany body.

ca. 1927		$1,200	$1,500

Camp Ukulele
Round nissa wood body, black binding.

1935		$150	$250

Concert Ukulele
Mahogany body, bound top and back.

1930		$1,500	$1,750

Shrine Ukulele
Triangular body, green binding.

1930	Mahogany	$1,000	$1,200
1933	Koa	$1,200	$1,500

Soprano Ukulele
Mahogany body.

1930	Unbound	$500	$700
1932	Bound top/back	$500	$700

Soprano Ukulele (Koa body)

1927	Bound top, pearl rosette	$1,750	$2,000
1934	Bound top/back	$750	$850
1935	Pearl bound top/back	$5,000	$7,000

Tenor Ukulele
Mahogany body, bound top and back.

1933		$1,500	$2,200

Maccaferri
1923-1990. Between the time he designed the Selmer guitar that became instantly synonymous with Django's gypsy jazz and his invention of the plastic clothespin, guitar design genius and manufacturing impresario Mario Maccaferri created a line of stringed instruments revolutionary for their complete plastic construction. The ukuleles were by far the greatest success, and most bore the tiny Maccaferri coat of arms on their tiny headstock.

Baritone Ukulele
Polystyrene cutaway body.

1959		$100	$200

Islander Ukulele
Polytyrene plastic body, crest in peghead.

1953		$100	$200

Playtune Ukulele
Polystyrene body.

1956		$100	$200

TV Pal Deluxe Ukulele
Extended 'board.

1960		$100	$200

TV Pal Ukulele
Polystyrene plastic body.

1955		$100	$200

Magic Fluke Company
1999-present. Budget grade, production, ukuleles made in New Hartford, Connecticut. With a clever design, exceptional quality, dozens of catchy finishes, and surprisingly affordable prices, it's little wonder that these little wonders have caught on. Riding – if not almost single-handedly driving – the coming third wave of uke popularity (the '20s and '50s were the first and second), Dale and Phyllis Webb of the Magic Fluke, along with Phyllis' brother, author Jumpin' Jim Beloff, are downright ukulele evangelists. The Fluke is the first new uke that you're not afraid to let the kid's monkey pick up, and with their addition of the slightly smaller

Leonardo Nunes

1920s Lyon & Healey Leland

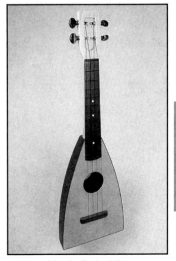

Magic Fluke Uke

UKULELES

Marc Silber Frisco

Martin Style O

Martin Style 1-K

Flea, they're so far the only producer of a good quality instrument to learn on.

Manuel Nunes

The self-professed father of the ukulele was at least one of the first makers to produce them in any quantity. Beginning after 1879, when he and the first boat load of Portuguese settlers landed in Hawaii, until at least the 1930s, Manuel and his son Leonardo (see Leonardo Nunes section) produced some of the most beautiful and superbly crafted ukes offered by any Island maker.

Soprano Ukulele
Koa body.

MODEL YEAR	FEATURES	EXC. COND. LOW	HIGH
1919	Figured koa body, bound top, back, 'board	$1,000	$1,500
1920	Rope bound top/back	$800	$1,200
1927	Bound body, 'board/head	$1,000	$1,500
1930	Unbound body	$700	$900
1933	Rope bound soundhole only	$700	$900

Taro Patch Fiddle
Koa body.

1930	Rope bound top/back	$2,000	$2,500
1930	Unbound top/back	$1,500	$2,000

Tenor Ukulele
Koa body, unbound top and back.

1930		$900	$1,200

Marc Silber Guitar Company

1998-present. Mexican-made ukes from designer Marc Silber of Berkley, California. He also offers guitars. His Frisco Uke takes its inspiration from the inimitable Roy Smeck Vita Uke (see Harmony), but without the whimsy of the original.

Martin

1833-present. The C.F. Martin Company knew they wanted in on the uke craze, and toyed with some prototypes as early as 1907 or so, but didn't get around to actually getting serious until '16. The first of these were characterized by rather more primitive craftsmanship (by stringent Martin standards), bar frets, and an impressed logo in the back of the headstock. By '20, koa became available as a pricey option, and by the early '30s, regular frets and the familiar Martin headstock decal had prevailed. Martin single-handedly created the archetype of the mainland uke and the standard by which all competitors are measured.

Martin has recently re-entered the ukulele market with its budget Mexican-made model S-0, and Backpacker Uke.

Style 0 Ukulele
Unbound mahogany body.

1920	Wood pegs	$500	$700
1953	Patent pegs	$500	$700

Style 1 Taro Patch
Mahogany body, 8 strings, rosewood bound.

MODEL YEAR	FEATURES	EXC. COND. LOW	HIGH
1933		$1,250	$1,750

Style 1 Ukulele
Mahogany body.

1940	Rosewood bound top only	$600	$800
1950	Tortoise bound top only	$600	$800
1960	Tortoise bound top only	$500	$800
1967	Tortoise bound top only	$500	$800

Style 1-C Concert Ukulele
Concert-sized mahogany body, bound top.

1950		$1,100	$1,500

Style 1-C K Concert Ukulele
Concert-sized koa body, bound top.

1950		$2,000	$2,500

Style 1-K Taro Patch
Style 1 with koa wood body.

1940		$1,500	$2,500

Style 1-K Ukulele
Koa body, rosewood bound top.

1922	Wood pegs	$1,500	$1,700
1939	Patent pegs	$1,500	$2,000

Style 1-T Tenor Ukulele
Tenor-sized mahogany body, bound top only.

1940		$1,300	$1,500

Style 2 Taro Patch
Mahogany body, 8 strings, ivoroid bound.

1931		$1,500	$2,000

Style 2 Ukulele
Mahogany body, ivoroid bound top and back.

1922		$900	$1,100
1935		$900	$1,100
1961		$800	$1,200

Style 2-K Taro Patch
Style 2 with koa wood body.

1937		$1,700	$2,500

Style 2-K Ukulele
Figured koa body, bound top and back.

1923		$2,000	$2,500
1939	Patent pegs	$2,000	$2,500

Style 3 Taro Patch
Mahogany body, 8 strings, multiple bound.

1941		$2,000	$3,500

Style 3 Ukulele
Mahogany body.

1925	Kite inlay in headstock	$1,500	$2,500
1940	B/W lines in ebony 'board	$1,500	$2,500
1950	Extended 'board, dots	$1,500	$2,500

Style 3-C K Concert Ukulele
Same specs as 3K, but in concert size.

1930		$7,000	$10,000

Style 3-K Taro Patch
Style 3 with koa wood body.

1929		$3,000	$4,500

UKULELES

MODEL YEAR	FEATURES	EXC. COND. LOW	HIGH

Style 3-K Ukulele
Figured koa body.

1924	Bow-tie 'board inlay	$3,500	$4,500
1932	B/W lines, diamonds, squares	$3,500	$4,500
1940	B/W lines and dot inlay	$3,500	$4,500

Style 5-K Ukulele
Highly figured koa body, all pearl trimmed.

1926		$7,000	$10,000

Style 5-M Ukulele
1941. Same as 5K, but mahogany body.

1941		$12,000	$15,000

Style 51 Baritone Ukulele
Mahogany body, bound top and back.

1966		$1,000	$1,500

Style T-15 Tiple Ukulele
Mahogany body, 10 metal strings, unbound.

1971		$500	$750

Style T-17 Tiple Ukulele
Mahogany body, unbound top and back.

1950		$750	$1,000

Style T-28 Tiple Ukulele
Rosewood body, bound top and back.

1969		$1,200	$1,500

Michael Dunn Guitars
1968-present. Luthier Michael Dunn builds a Knutsen-style harp uke in New Westminster, British Columbia. He also builds guitars.

Mirabella
1997-present. Professional grade, custom ukuleles built by luthier Cristian Mirabella in Babylon, New York. He also builds mandolins and guitars.

National
Ca. 1927-present. To capitalize on the success of their amplifying guitars, the Dopyera brothers introduced metal-bodied ukuleles and mandolins as well. Large, heavy, and ungainly by today's standards, these early offerings nonetheless have their charms. Their subsequent switch to a smaller body shape produced an elegant and sweet-sounding resonator uke that soon became much sought after.

Style 1 Ukulele
Nickel body.

1928	Tenor, 6" resonator	$2,500	$4,000
1933	Soprano	$2,500	$4,000

Style 2 Ukulele
Nickel body, engraved roses.

1928	Tenor	$4,000	$5,000
1931	Soprano	$4,000	$5,000

Style 3 Ukulele
Nickel body, lilies-of-the-valley.

1929	Tenor	$4,000	$6,000
1933	Soprano	$5,000	$8,000

Style O Ukulele
Metal body, soprano size, sandblasted scenes.

1931		$2,000	$3,000

Triolian Ukulele

1928	Tenor, sunburst painted body	$1,400	$2,000
1930	Soprano, sunburst painted body	$1,600	$2,200
1934	Soprano, wood-grained metal body	$1,200	$1,600

National Reso-Phonic
1988-present. Successors to the National name, with the designs and patented amplifying resonator assemblies of the original National models, they offer professional grade, production, single cone ukuleles from their shop in San Luis Obispo, California. They also build guitars and basses.

Oscar Schmidt
1879-ca. 1939, 1979-present. The same New Jersey outfit responsible for Leadbelly's 12-string guitar offered ukes as well during the same period. Many of these were odd amalgams of materials, often combining koa, mahogany, and spruce in the same instrument. Since 1979, when the name was acquired by the U.S. Music Corp. (Washburn, Randall, etc.) they have offered a line of budget grade, production, Asian-made ukes. They also offer guitars, mandolins, and banjos.

Soprano Ukulele
Spruce top, bound mahogany body.

1930		$250	$400

Pegasus Guitars and Ukuleles
1977-present. Professional grade, custom, ukulele family instruments built by luthier Bob Gleason in Kurtistown, Hawaii, who also builds steel-string guitars.

Polk-a-lay-lee
1960s. These inexplicably shaped oddities were produced by Petersen Products of Chicago ca. the mid-'60s, and anecdotal Midwestern lore has it that their intent was to be offered as giveaways for the Polk Brothers, a local appliance chain. This may be how they ended up, although the gargantuan original packaging makes no reference to any such promotion. The box does call out what the optional colors were. Many have noted the striking resemblance to the similarly named wares of the Swaggerty company (see Swaggerty) of California, who also offered brightly colored plywood-bodied ukes in comically oversized incarnations, but who was copying whom has yet to be determined.

Ukulele
Long boat oar body, uke scale, brown, natural, red, or black.

1965		$300	$400

Michael Dunn Harp Uke

Pegasus Artist Series tenor 6-string

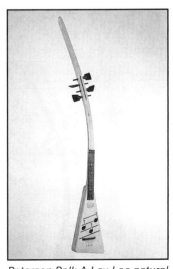

Petersen Polk-A-Lay-Lee natural uke

UKULELES

Regal

Regal Jungle Uke

Sammo

Regal

Ca. 1884-1966, 1987-present. Like the other large 1930s Chicago makers, Harmony and Lyon & Healy, the good ukes are very very good, and the cheap ukes are very very cheap. Unlike its pals, however, Regal seems to have produced more ukuleles in imaginative themes, striking color schemes, and in more degrees of fancy trim, making them the quintessential wall-hangers. And lucky for you, there's a vintage Regal uke to suit every décor.

Carson Robison Ukulele

Top sports painted signature, cowboy scene.

MODEL YEAR	FEATURES	EXC. COND. LOW	HIGH
1935		$600	$1,000

Jungle Ukulele

Birch body, covered in leopard skin fabric.

1950		$500	$900

Resonator Ukulele

Black body, F-holes, see Dobro uke.

1934		$1,000	$1,500

Soprano Ukulele (birch)

Birch body.

1931	Brown sunburst	$175	$300
1931	Nautical themes, various colors	$175	$250
1945	Painted body, victory themes	$450	$800

Soprano Ukulele (koa)

Koa body, multicolored rope bound top.

1930		$250	$300

Soprano Ukulele (mahogany)

Mahogany body.

1930	Multiple bound top	$450	$700
1935	Spruce top, inlays	$350	$700
1940	Extended 'board	$250	$300

Tiple Ukulele

1930	Birch body stained dark, black binding	$300	$450
1935	Spruce top, mahogany body, fancy binding	$400	$550

Wendall Hall Red Head Ukulele

Koa body, celebrity decal on headstock.

1935		$500	$700

Renaissance Guitars

1994-present. In '05 luthier Rick Turner added a line of acoustic and acoustic/electric ukuleles built in Santa Cruz, California. He also builds guitars and basses.

Rogue

2001-present. Budget grade, production, imported ukuleles. They also offer guitars, basses, mandolins, banjos, effects and amps.

S. S. Stewart

Not much is known about the ukuleles of this Philadelphia firm, except that they were most certainly sub-contracted from another maker or makers.

Soprano Ukulele

Mahogany body, bound top and back.

MODEL YEAR	FEATURES	EXC. COND. LOW	HIGH
1927		$200	$400

Samick

1958-2001, 2002-present. Budget grade, production, imported ukuleles. They also offer guitars, basses, mandolins and banjos.

Sammo

Flashy internal paper labels trumpet that these ukes (mandolins and guitars, too) were products of the Osborne Mfg. Co. Masonic Temple, Chicago-Illinois and what the heck any of that means is still open to modern speculation. Your guess is as good as mine. Still, the high quality and often opulent degree of ornamentation that the instruments exhibit, coupled with even the vaguest implication that they were made by guys wearing fezzes and/or men who ride around in tiny cars at parades is all the reason we need to buy every one we see.

Soprano Ukulele

1925	Figured maple body, 5-ply top, back binding	$300	$500
1925	Unbound koa body, fancy headstock shape	$300	$500

Silvertone

1941-ca. 1970, present. Silvertone was the house brand of Sears & Roebuck and most (if not all) of its ukes were manufactured for them by Harmony.

Soprano Ukulele

Mahogany body, Harmony-made.

1950	Sunburst	$150	$250
1950	Unbound	$150	$250
1955	Bound	$150	$250
1960	Green	$150	$250

Slingerland

Banjo ukuleles bearing this brand (see Slingerland Banjo uke section below) were certainly made by the popular drum company (banjos being little more than drums with necks, after all). Slingerland standard ukuleles, on the other hand, bear an uncanny resemblance to the work of the Oscar Schmidt company.

Soprano Ukulele

Koa body, rope bound top and soundhole.

1920		$250	$400

Specimen Products

1984-present. Luthier Ian Schneller builds his professional grade, production/custom, ukuleles in Chicago, Illinois. He also builds guitars, basses, amps and speaker cabs. Schneller has built some of the most offbeat, endearing - and high quality - custom ukuleles available.

MODEL YEAR	FEATURES	EXC. COND. LOW	HIGH

Sterling

The miniscule reference buried deep within the headstock decal to a T.B. Co. can only mean that the Sterling ukulele somehow fits into the mind-numbing Tonk Bros./Lyon & Healy/Regal/S.S. Stewart manufacturing puzzle. Nonetheless, the brand must have been reserved for the cream of the crop, since the Sterling ukes that surface tend to be of the drop-dead-gorgeous variety.

Soprano Ukulele
Flamed koa, multiple fancy binding all over.

1935		$1,500	$2,000

Stetson

Popular misconception – to say nothing of wishful thinking and greed – has it that all instruments labeled with the Stetson brand were the work of the Larson Brothers of Chicago. While a few Stetson guitars and a very few mandolins may be genuine Larson product, the ukuleles surely were made elsewhere.

Soprano Ukulele
Mahogany body, single bound top and back.

1930		$200	$300

Supertone

1914-1940s. For whatever reason, Supertone was the name attached to Sears' musical instruments before the line became Silvertone (see above). These, too, were all Harmony-made.

Soprano Ukulele (koa)
Koa body, Harmony-made.

1935	Rope bound	$250	$500
1943	Unbound	$150	$400

Soprano Ukulele (mahogany)
Mahogany body, Harmony-made.

1930	Unbound	$150	$350
1940	Bound	$150	$350

Swaggerty

Not enough is known of this West Coast company, except that their product line of unusually shaped 4 stringed novelty instruments oddly mirrors those made by Petersen Products in Chicago at the same time (see Polk-a-lay-lee). The two companies even seem to have shared plastic parts, such as 'boards and tuners. Go figure.

Surf-a-lay-lee Ukulele
Plywood body, long horn, green, yellow, or orange

1965		$250	$400

Tabu

The Tabu brand on either the back of a ukulele's headstock or inside its soundhole was never an indication of its original maker. Rather, it was intended to assure the purchaser that the uke was, indeed of bona fide Hawaiian origin. So rampant was the practice of mainland makers claiming Island manufacture of their wares that in the late 'teens Hawaii launched a campaign to set the record straight, and – lucky for you – a nifty little brand

was the result. The Tabu mark actually was used to mark the ukes of several different makers.

Soprano Ukulele
Figured koa body.

1915	Rope bound	$700	$900
1915	Unbound	$500	$800

Vega

Famous for their banjos, the Vega name was applied to a sole baritone uke, tied with the endorsement of 1950s TV crooner Arthur Godfrey.

Arthur Godfrey Baritone Ukulele
Mahogany body, unbound.

1955	Mahogany	$400	$500

Washburn

See Lyon & Healy.

Weissenborn

1910s-1937. The mainland maker famous for their hollow-necked Hawaiian guitars was responsible for several uke offerings over the course of its 20-or-so-year run. Like their 6-stringed big brothers, they were the closest thing to Island design and detail to come from the mainland.

Soprano Ukulele

1920	Rope bound	$1,300	$1,500
1920	Unbound	$1,200	$1,400

Weymann

Renowned for fine tenor banjos, Weyman affixed their name to a full line of soprano ukes of varying degrees of decoration, quite certainly none of which were made under the same roof as the banjos. Most were C.F. Martin knock-offs.

Soprano Ukulele

1925	Mahogany, unbound	$500	$700
1930	Koa, fancy pearl vine 'board inlay	$1,300	$1,500

Banjo Ukuleles
Bacon

This legendary Connecticut banjo maker just couldn't resist the temptation to extend their line with uke versions of their popular banjos. As with Gibson, Ludwig, Slingerland, and Weyman, the banjo ukuleles tended to mimic the already proven construction techniques and decorative motifs of their regular banjo counterparts. In materials, finish, and hardware, most banjo ukes share many more similarities with full sized banjos than differences. The banjo ukes were simply included as smaller, plainer, variations of banjos, much as concert, tenor, and baritone options fleshed out standard ukulele lines.

Banjo Ukulele
Walnut rim, fancy 'board inlays.

1927		$1,000	$1,200

Silver Bell Banjo Ukulele
Engraved pearloid 'board and headstock.

1927		$1,750	$2,000

Supertone Cheerleader

Weissenborn

Weissenborn

UKULELES

Gibson BU 3

Ludwig Banjo Uke

MODEL YEAR	FEATURES	EXC. COND. LOW	HIGH

Dixie

With chrome plated all-metal design, there's only one word for these banjo ukes, "shiny." Their bodies, necks, and frets are die cast together in zinc (think Hot Wheels cars and screen door handles), the Dixie must have made the perfect indestructible instrument for Junior's birthday back in the 1960s. Similar to one made by Werko.

Banjo Ukulele

One-piece, all-metal construction.

1960		$75	$125

Gibson

BU-1 Banjo Uke

Small 6" head, flat panel resonator.

1928		$300	$550

BU-2 Banjo Uke

8" head, dot inlay.

1930		$500	$750

BU-3 Banjo Uke

8" head, diamond and square inlay.

1935		$1,000	$1,250

BU-4 Banjo Uke

8" head, resonator and flange.

1932		$1,000	$1,600

BU-5 Banjo Uke

8" head, resonator and flange, gold parts.

1937		$1,500	$2,000

Le Domino

Banjo Ukulele

Resonator, decorated as Le Domino uke.

1933		$350	$500

Ludwig

The Ludwig was then, and is today, the Cadillac of banjo ukes. British banjo uke icon George Formby's preference for Ludwig continues assuring their desirability, while the fact that they were available in only a couple of models, for a few short years, and in relatively small production numbers only adds to the mystique.

Banjo Uke

1928	Flange w/ crown holes, nickel or gold plated parts	$2,500	$3,500
1930	Ivoroid headstock overlay w/ art deco detail	$2,000	$2,500

Wendell Hall Professional Banjo Uke

Walnut resonator, flange with oval holes.

1927		$1,500	$2,000

MODEL YEAR	FEATURES	EXC. COND. LOW	HIGH

Lyon & Healy

Banjo Uke

Walnut neck and resonator, fancy pearl inlay.

1935		$2,000	$2,500

Paramount

1920s-1942, Late 1940s. The William L. Lange Company began selling Paramount banjos, guitar banjos and mandolin banjos in the early 1920s. Gretsch picked up the Paramount name and used it on guitars for a time in the late '40s.

Banner Blue Banjo Uke

Brass hearts 'board inlay, walnut neck.

1933		$750	$1,250

Regal

Banjo Ukulele

Mahogany rim, resonator, fancy rope bound.

1933		$300	$500

Richter

Allegedly, this Chicago company bought the already-made guitars, ukes, and mandolins of other manufacturers, painted and decorated them to their liking and resold them. True or not, they certainly were cranked out in a bevy of swanky colors.

Banjo Uke

Chrome plated body, 2 f-holes in back.

1930		$250	$350
1930	Entire body/neck painted	$250	$350

Slingerland

May Bell Banjo Uke

Walnut resonator with multicolored rope.

1935		$350	$450

Werko

These Chicago-made banjo ukuleles had construction similar to the Dixie brand, and except for the addition of a swank layer of blue sparkle drum binding on the rim, you would be hard pressed to tell them apart.

Banjo Uke

Chrome-plated metal body and neck.

1960		$75	$150

Weymann

Banjo Uke

Maple rim, open back, ebony 'board.

1926		$1,000	$1,200

Banjos

1932 Gibson Mastertone Granada. Photo courtesy George Gruhn.

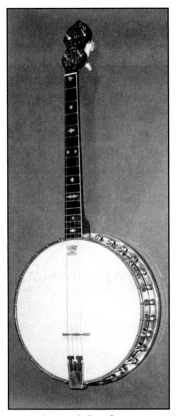

Bacon & Day Super

Deering Maple Brothers

MODEL YEAR	FEATURES	EXC. COND. LOW	HIGH

Bacon & Day

1921-1967. David Day left Vega to join up with Fred Bacon in '21. Gretsch purchased Bacon & Day in '40, and ran the Bacon line until '67.

Blue Bell

1922-1939	Tenor	$1,350	$1,600

Blue Ribbon 17

1933-1939	Tenor	$450	$550

Ne Plus Ultra

1920s	Tenor	$7,500	$9,000
1930s	Tenor	$7,500	$9,000
1950s	Tenor	$2,500	$3,000
1960s	Tenor	$2,500	$3,000

Senorita

1930	Plectrum, pearloid, resonator	$1,000	$1,200
1950s	4-string	$450	$700

Silver Bell #1

1922-1939	Tenor	$1,500	$1,750

Silver Bell Montana #1

1933-1939	Tenor	$2,000	$2,400

Sultana #1

1933-1939	Tenor	$2,250	$2,600

Super

1920	Tenor	$1,000	$1,200
1927	5-string, fancy appt., flamed resonator	$3,400	$3,600

Benary and Sons

1890-1899. Manufactured by the James H. Buckbee Co. for music instrument wholesaler Robert Benary.

Celebrated Benary

1890-1899. 5-string, open back, plain appointments.

1890-1899		$500	$600

Boucher

1830s-1850s. William Boucher's operation in Baltimore is considered to be one of the very first banjo-shops. Boucher and the Civil War era banjos are rare. The price range listed is informational guidance pricing only. The wide range reflectrs conservative opinions. 150 year old banjos should be evaluated per their own merits.

Boucher banjos

1840s		$3,000	$15,000

Buckbee

1863-1897. James H. Buckbee Co. of New York was the city's largest builder. The company did considerable private branding for companies such as Benery, Dobson, and Farland.

Buckbee 5-string

1890-1897. 5-string, open back, plain appointments.

1890-1897		$400	$500

MODEL YEAR	FEATURES	EXC. COND. LOW	HIGH

Cole

1890-1919. W.A. Cole, after leaving Fairbanks-Cole, started his own line in 1890. He died in 1909 but the company continued until 1919.

Eclipse

1890-1919	Flower inlays, dots	$1,650	$2,200
1890-1919	Man-in-the-moon inlays	$2,250	$3,000

Deering

1975-present. Greg and Janet Deering build their banjos in Spring Valley, California. In 1978 they introduced their Basic and Intermediate banjos. They also offer banjos under the Vega and Goodtime brands.

Ditson

1916-1930. The Oliver Ditson Company of Boston offered a variety of musical instruments.

Tenor Banjo

1920. 4-string, resonator with typical appointments.

1920		$600	$700

Dobson

1880s. Brothers Henry, George, and Edgar Dobson were banjo teachers and performers in the 1880s. They designed banjos that were built for them by manufactures such as Buckbee of New York.

Epiphone

1873-present. Epiphone started offering banjos in the early 1920s, if not sooner, offering them up to WW II. After Gibson bought the company in '57, they reintroduced banjos to the line, which they still offer.

EB-44 Campus

1960s. Long neck, folk-era 5-string banjo.

1960s		$700	$800

Electar (electric) Tenor Bnajo

1930s. Maple body, 1 pickup, 3 knobs.

1930s		$1,300	$1,400

Recording B

1930s	Tenor	$2,450	$2,750

Recording Concert C Special

1930s. Tenor, maple body, fancy appointments, resonator.

1932		$3,400	$3,500

TB-100

1960s	Tenor	$800	$900

Fairbanks/Vega Fairbanks/ A.C. Fairbanks

1875-1919. From 1875 to 1880, A. C. Fairbanks built his own designs in Boston. In 1880, W. A. Cole joined the company, starting Fairbanks & Cole, but left in 1890 to start his own line. The company went by Fairbanks Co. until it was purchased by Vega in 1904. The banjos were then branded Vega Fairbanks until 1919.

MODEL YEAR	FEATURES	EXC. COND. LOW	HIGH

Acme (F & C)
1880-1890. 5-string, open back, fancy markers.

1880-1890		$900	$1,000

Senator No. 1/Fairbanks 3
1900s	5-string	$1,300	$1,500

Vega Lady's Banjo
1913		$800	$900

Whyte Laydie #2
1901-1904	5-string	$2,900	$3,700

Whyte Laydie #7
1901-1904	5-string	$8,000	$9,000
1909	5-string	$8,000	$9,000

Farland
Ca. 1890-1920s. Buckbee and others made instruments for New York banjo teacher and performer A. A. Farland.

Concert Grand
1900-1920	5-string	$1,400	$1,550

Fender
1946-present. Fender added banjos to their product mix in the late 1960s, and continue to offer them.

Allegro (Tenor or 5-string)
Late 1960s-1970s.

1960s		$750	$900

Leo Deluxe
1970s

1970s		$1,500	$1,600

Framus
1946-1977, 1996-present. The new Framus company, located in Markneukirchen, Germany, continues to offer banjos.

5-string Model
1960s		$150	$275

Gibson
1880s (1902)-present. Gibson started making banjos in 1918, and continues to manufacture them. Vega and Gibson were the only major manufacturing companies that offered banjos in their product catalog in the '50s.
    RB prefix = regular banjo (5-string)
    TB prefix = tenor banjo (4-string, tenor tuning)
    PB prefix = plectrum banjo (4-string, plectrum tuning)

All American
1930-1937. Tenor banjo, fancy appointments, historic art, gold hardware.

1930-1937		$10,000	$13,000

Bella Voce
1927-1931. Tenor banjo, fancy appointments, flower-pattern art, gold hardware.

1927-1931		$9,000	$15,000

Earl Scruggs
1984-present. 5-string, high-end appointments.

1980s		$2,800	$3,000
1990s		$2,800	$3,000
2000s		$2,800	$2,900

ETB Electric Tenor Banjo
1937-1941	Christian pickup	$2,000	$2,500

Florentine Plectrum
1925-1930	2 piece flange	$11,000	$15,000

Florentine Tenor
1927-1937. High-end appointments, gold hardware.

1927-1937		$8,500	$9,500

Granada Earl Scruggs
With high-end replacement tone ring.

1988-1999		$3,300	$3,650

Granada RB
1925-1939. 5-string banjo with either a 2 piece flange (1925-1930), or a 1 piece flange (1933-1939).

1925-1930		$23,000	$28,000
1933-1939	Flat head tone ring	$125,000	$180,000

Granada TB
1925-1939. Tenor banjo with either a 2 piece flange (1925-1930), or a 1 piece flange (1933-1939).

1925-1930		$18,000	$25,000
1933-1939	Flat head tone ring	$87,000	$125,000

PB-4
1925-1940. Plectrum banjo with either a 2 piece flange (1925-1932), or a 1 piece flange (1933-1940).

1925-1927	Ball bearing tone ring	$2,250	$3,500
1928-1932	Archtop	$3,350	$4,000
1933-1940	Archtop	$7,800	$12,000
1933-1940	Flat head tone ring	$65,000	$87,000

RB Jr.
1924-1925. 5-string, budget line, open back.

1924-1925		$1,100	$1,300

RB-00
1933-1939		$1,900	$2,100

RB-1
1930-1932	1 piece flange	$2,900	$3,100
1933-1939	Diamond flange	$2,500	$2,750
1933-1939	w/ high-end replacement tone ring	$4,000	$4,400

RB-2
1933-1939		$8,000	$8,700

RB-3
1960s	RB-3 Reno	$2,500	$3,500

RB-4
1922-1937. 5-string banjo with either a 2 piece flange (1925-1931), or a 1 piece flange (1933-1937). Trap or non-trap door on earlier models (1922-1924).

1922-1924	Trap or non-trap door	$2,300	$3,500
1925-1931	Archtop, resonator	$16,000	$22,000
1933-1937	Archtop	$30,000	$40,000
1933-1937	Flat head tone ring	$80,000	$120,000

Fender FB59

Gibson PB-4

BANJOS

Gretsch tenor

Kay KBJ24

MODEL YEAR	FEATURES	EXC. COND. LOW	HIGH
RB-6			

1927-1937. 5-string banjo with fancy appointments.

MODEL YEAR	FEATURES	EXC. COND. LOW	HIGH
1927-1933	Archtop	$15,000	$25,000
1933-1937	Flat head tone ring	$125,000	$180,000
RB-11			
1933-1939		$5,200	$5,700
RB-175			

1962-1973. 2000s. Open back, long neck typical of banjos of the 1960s. Models include the RB-175, RB-175 Long Neck, RB-175 Folk.

1962	RB-175	$1,000	$1,100
1962-1964	Long Neck	$1,000	$1,200
1965-1969	Folk	$1,000	$1,200
1970-1973	RB-175	$900	$1,000
RB-250			
1964-1968	Flat head tone ring	$2,000	$2,100
1970s	Mastertone	$1,500	$2,000
1980s	Mastertone	$1,500	$2,000
RB-800			
1971-1979		$2,600	$2,900
1980s		$2,600	$2,900
TB			
1919		$1,000	$1,200
TB-00			
1939		$2,500	$2,750
TB-1			

1922-1939. Tenor banjo with a 1 piece flange.

1922-1924	Trap door	$700	$850
1933-1939	Simple hoop tone ring	$2,850	$3,200
TB-1 Conversion			

1922-1939. TB-1 with a 5-string conversion and a flat head tone ring.

1933-1939		$3,400	$3,750
TB-2			
1922-1928	Wavy flange	$575	$700
1933-1939	Pearloid board	$3,300	$4,000
TB-3			

1927-1939. Tenor banjo with either a 2 piece flange (1927-1931), or a 1 piece flange (1933-1939).

1925-1926	Ball-bearing tone ring	$2,000	$3,000
1927-1931	40 or no hole ring	$3,000	$3,800
1933-1939	40 or no hole ring	$7,000	$10,000
1933-1939	Flat head tone ring	$21,000	$30,000
1933-1939	Wreath, archtop	$15,000	$17,000
TB-4			
1922-1924	Trap door	$1,300	$1,500
TB-5			
1922-1924	Trap door	$1,500	$1,800
TB-11			
1933-1939		$3,000	$3,400
TB-11 Conversion			

1933-1939. TB-11 with a 5-string conversion and a flat head tone ring.

1933-1939		$3,750	$4,000
TB-100			
1963-1967		$850	$1,250

Gretsch

1883-present. Gretsch offered banjos in the '20s and again in the '50s and '60s.

Broadcaster Banjo

1932-1939. Tenor or 5-string banjo with pearloid head and board.

1932-1939	5-string	$800	$1,400
1932-1939	Tenor	$500	$900

Orchestella

1925-1929. Tenor or 5-string banjo with gold engravings.

1925-1929	5-string	$2,750	$3,250
1925-1929	Tenor	$800	$1,100

Tenor short-scale

1925-1929	Plain styling	$150	$300

GTR

1974-1978. GTR (for George Gruhn, Tut Taylor, Randy Wood) was the original name for Gruhn Guitars in Nashville, and they imported mandolins and banjos from Japan.

GTR 5-string banjo copy

1970s		$1,000	$1,100

Kalamazoo

1933-1942, 1965-1970. Budget brand built by Gibson. Made flat-tops, solidbodies, mandolins, lap steels, banjos and amps.

Kalamazoo banjos

1935-1940	Plectrum	$400	$500
1935-1941	5-string	$500	$600

Kay

Ca. 1931 (1890)-present. Kay was a huge manufacturer and built instruments under their name and for a large number of other retailers, jobbers, and brand names.

Student Tenor Banjo

1950s		$300	$350

Kel Kroyden (by Gibson)

1930-1937. Private branded budget level instruments made by Gibson.

Kel Kroyden banjo

1933-1937	Conversion	$3,650	$3,900
1933-1937	Tenor	$2,000	$2,500

Keystone State

1920s. Brand of banjos built by Weymann.

Style 2

1920s. Tenor, resonator, fancy appointments.

1920s		$1,100	$1,200

Lange

1920s-1942, Late 1940s. The William L. Lange Company began selling Paramount banjos, guitar banjos and mandolin banjos in the early 1920s. Gretsch picked up the Paramount name and used it on acoustics and electrics for a time in the late '40s. See Paramount for more listings.

Tourraine Deluxe

1920s	Tenor	$350	$500

The **Vintage Guitar Price Guide** shows low to high values for items in all-original excellent condition, and, where applicable, with original case or cover.

MODEL		EXC. COND.	
YEAR	FEATURES	LOW	HIGH

Leedy

1989- Founded in Indianapolis by U. G. Leedy, the company started making banjos in 1924. Leedy was bought out by C. G. Conn in '30.

Solotone

1924-1930	Tenor	$700	$900

Ludwig

The Ludwig Drum Company was founded in 1909. They saw a good business opportunity and entered the banjo market in '21. When demand for banjos tanked in '30, Ludwig dropped the line and concentrated on its core business.

Bellevue

1920s. Tenor, closed-back banjo with fancy appointments.

1920s		$800	$900

Big Chief

1930. Carved and engraved plectrum banjo.

1930		$7,500	$9,500

Capital

1920s. Tenor banjo, resonator and nice appointments.

1920s		$800	$1,200

Commodore

1930s. Tenor or plectrum, with gold hardware and fancy appointments.

1930s	Tenor	$1,400	$1,800
1932	Plectrum	$2,000	$2,400

Deluxe

1930s. Engraved tenor, with gold hardware.

1930s		$2,750	$3,250

Dixie

1930s	Tenor	$400	$450

Kenmore Plectrum Banjo

1920s	Open back	$700	$800

Kenmore Tenor Banjo

1920s	Resonator	$500	$600

Kingston

1924-1930	Tenor	$750	$900

Standard Art Tenor Banjo

1924-1930. Tenor banjo with fancy appointments.

1924-1930		$3,850	$4,500

The Ace

1920s. Tenor banjo, resonator and nickel appointments.

1920s		$1,200	$1,400

ODE/Muse

1961-1980. Founded by Charles Ogsbury in Boulder, Colorado, purchased by Baldwin in '66 and moved to Nashville, Gretsch took over in '76. Muse was a retail store brand of banjos produced by ODE from '61 to '66. In '71, Ogsbury started the OME Banjo Company in Colorado.

Model C

1976-1980. 5-string banjo, resonator and fancy markers.

1976-1980		$1,300	$2,000

Model D

1970s-1980. 5-string banjo, resonator and gold engravings.

1970s		$1,900	$2,800

Orpheum

1897-1922. Lange and Rettberg purchased the J.H. Buckbee banjo factory in 1897 and started making banjos under the Orpheum label. William Lange took control in 1922 and changed the name to Paramount.

Model #2

1920-1922	5-string	$2,800	$3,000
1920-1922	Tenor	$1,000	$1,500

Paramount

1921-1935. William Lange and his Paramount company are generally accredited with commercializing the first modern flange and resonator in 1921.

Aristocrat

1921-1935	Plectrum	$1,450	$2,150
1921-1935	Tenor	$1,250	$1,850

Aristocrat Special

1921-1935. Plectrum banjo with fancy appointments.

1921-1935		$2,900	$3,000

Junior

1921-1935	Plectrum	$850	$1,100
1921-1935	Tenor, resonator	$750	$950

Leader

1921-1935	Plectrum	$1,000	$1,200
1921-1935	Tenor	$850	$1,050

Style 1

1921-1935	Plectrum	$450	$625
1921-1935	Tenor	$400	$550

Style 2

1921-1935. Tenor banjo, resonator and plain appointments.

1921-1935		$500	$600

Style A

1921-1935. Models include the Style A Tenor, Plectrum, and the 5-string (with resonator and fancy appointments).

1921-1935	5-string	$2,300	$2,500
1921-1935	Plectrum	$1,035	$1,150
1921-1935	Tenor	$900	$1,000

Style B

1921-1935. Models include the Style B Tenor, and the Plectrum (with resonator and fancy appointments).

1921-1935	Plectrum	$1,000	$1,150
1921-1935	Tenor	$900	$1,000

Style C

1921-1935. Models include the Style C Tenor, Plectrum, and the 5-string (with resonator and fancy appointments).

1921-1935	5-string	$3,000	$3,750
1921-1935	Plectrum	$1,700	$2,250
1921-1935	Tenor	$1,100	$1,450

Style D

1921-1935	Plectrum	$2,200	$2,800
1921-1935	Tenor	$1,950	$2,450

Orpheum tenor

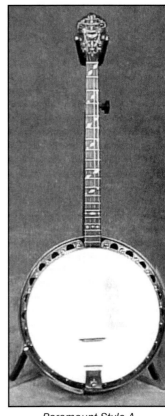

Paramount Style A

BANJOS

Slingerland tenor

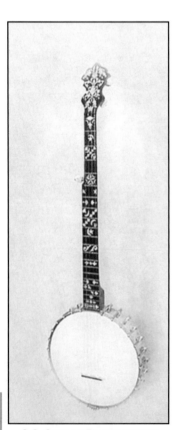

S.S. Stewart Thoroughbred

MODEL YEAR	FEATURES	EXC. COND. LOW	HIGH
Style E			
1921-1935	Plectrum	$2,300	$2,875
1921-1935	Tenor	$2,000	$2,500
Style F			
1921-1935	Plectrum	$3,700	$4,150
1921-1935	Tenor	$3,250	$3,600
Super/Super Paramount			
1921-1935	Plectrum	$4,150	$4,800
1921-1935	Tenor	$3,600	$4,200
Trooper			
1921-1935	Plectrum	$700	$775
1921-1935	Tenor	$600	$675

Silvertone

1941-ca. 1970, present. Brand of Sears instruments which replaced their Supertone brand in '41. Currently, Samick offers a line of amps under the Silvertone name.

Silvertone 5-string banjo copy

1960s		$300	$400

Slingerland

1930s-mid-1940s. The parent company was Slingerland Banjo and Drums, Chicago, Illinois. The company offered other stringed instruments into the '40s. Slingerland Drums is now owned by Gibson.

Student/economy tenor banjo

1930s. Models include the Tenor, Student, and Maybell series banjos.

1930s		$300	$600

S.S. Stewart

1878-1904. S.S. Stewart of Philadelphia is considered to be one of the most important and prolific banjo manufacturers of the late 19th century. It's estimated that approximately 25,000 banjos were made by this company.

MODEL YEAR	FEATURES	EXC. COND. LOW	HIGH
American Princess (5-string)			
1890s	10" rim	$900	$1,200
Banjeaurine			
1890. 5-string banjo, 10" head with and open back.			
1890		$1,200	$1,300
Universal Favorite			
1892	11" head	$900	$1,200

Studio King

1930s. Banjos made by Gibson, most likely for a mail-order house or a jobber.

Studio King banjo

1933-1937	Original 5-string	$2,250	$2,500
1933-1937	Tenor	$1,000	$1,300

Superb

1920s. Private brand made by Epiphone.

Tenor Banjo

Mayfair Tenor, resonator.

1920s		$400	$500

Supertone

1914-1941. Brand used by Sears, Roebuck and Company for instruments made by various American manufacturers, including its own Harmony subsidiary Harmony. In '40, Sears began making a transition to the Silvertone brand.

Prairie Wonder

1925. 5-string, open back banjo.

1925		$300	$600

Tilton

1850s-late 1800s. Built by William B. Tilton, of New York City. He was quite an innovator and held several instrument-related patents. He also built guitars.

MODEL YEAR	FEATURES	EXC. COND. LOW	HIGH

Vega

1903-1980s, 1989-present. Vega of Boston got into the banjo business in 1904 when it purchased Fairbanks. Vega and Gibson were the only major manufacturing companies that offered banjos in their product catalog in the 1950s. The Deering Banjo Company acquired the brand in '89 and uses it on a line of banjos.

Artist Professional #9
1923-1929	Tenor	$2,500	$2,800

Folk Wonder
1960s	5-string	$850	$1,000

Little Wonder
1920s	Plectrum	$600	$650
1920s	Tenor	$500	$600

Pete Seeger
1958-1966. 5-string, long neck banjo.
1958-1964	Folk era	$2,800	$3,300
1965-1966		$1,500	$2,300

Professional
1960. 5-string banjo with a Tubaphone tone ring.
1960		$1,300	$1,400

Regent
1920s. 5-string banjo with an open back and dot markers.
1920s		$1,800	$2,000

Style 9
1920s. Tenor banjo with fancy appointments.
1920s		$1,400	$1,500

Style M
1920s. Tenor banjo, models include the Style M and the Style M Tubaphone.
1920s	Style M	$1,850	$1,950
1920s	Tubaphone	$900	$1,500

Style X
1926	Tenor	$2,000	$2,800

Tubaphone #3
1923-1929	Plectrum	$1,150	$1,350
1929-1928	5-string	$3,000	$3,500

V-45
1970. Plectrum banjo, flat head tone ring, fancy appointments.
1970		$2,900	$3,000

Vegaphone Professional
1960s	5-string	$900	$1,000

Whyte Laydie #3
1923-1928	5-string	$3,300	$3,750

Whyte Laydie Style R
1930s. Tenor banjo with closed back.
1930s		$1,200	$1,300

Washburn (Lyon & Healy)

1880s-ca.1949. Washburn was the brand name of Lyon & Healy of Chicago. They made banjos from 1880-1929.

Irene 5-string
1920s		$750	$800

Weymann

1864-1940s. They Weymann company was founded in 1864 and got seriously into the banjo manufacturing business in 1917. They manufactured banjos until around 1930.

Orchestra
1920s	Style A Plectrum	$800	$1,000
1924-1928	#1 Tenor	$800	$1,000
1924-1928	#2 Tenor	$1,000	$1,200

Style #6
1924-1928	Black walnut	$4,000	$5,000

Yosco

1900-1930s. Lawrence L. Yosco was a New York City luthier building guitars, round back mandolins and banjos under his own brand and for others.

Style 3 Tenor
1920s		$1,300	$1,400

Vega tenor

Washburn 5183 tenor

BANJOS

Bibliography

'50s Cool: Kay Guitars, by Jay Scott, 1992, Seventh String Press, Inc.

50 Years of Fender, by Tony Bacon, 2000, Miller Freeman Books.

Acoustic Guitars and Other Fretted Instruments, A Photographic History, by George Gruhn and Walter Carter, 1993, GPI Books.

Acoustic Guitar magazine, various issues, String Letter Publishing.

Acquired of the Angels, by Paul William Schmidt, 1998, Scarecrow Press.

American Basses, by Jim Roberts, 2003, Backbeat Books.

American Guitars, An Illustrated History, by Tom Wheeler, 1992, Harper Collins.

American's Instrument, The Banjo in the Nineteenth Century, by Philip F. Gura and James F. Bollman, 1999, University of North Carolina Press.

Ampeg - The Story Behind The Sound, by Gregg Hopkins and Bill Moore, 1999, Hal Leonard Publishing.

Amps! The Other Half of Rock 'n' Roll, by Ritchie Fliegler, 1993, Hal Leonard publishing.

Analog Man's Guide to Vintage Effects, by Tom Hughes, 2004, Musicians Only Publishing.

The Bass Book, A Complete Illustrated History of Bass Guitars, by Tony Bacon and Barry Moorhouse, 1995, Miller Freeman Books.

The Boss Book, 2001, Hal Leonard Publishing.

The Burns Book, by Paul Day, 1990, PP Publishing and The Bold Strummer.

Classic Guitars U.S.A., by Willie G. Moseley, 1992, Centerstream.

The Classical Guitar Book, by Tony Bacon, et al., 2002, Balafon Books.

The Complete History of Rickenbacker Guitars, by Richard R. Smith, 1987, Centerstream.

Cowboy Guitars, by Steve Evans and Ron Middlebrook, 2002, Centerstream.

Custom Guitars, A Complete Guide to Contempory Handcrafted Guitars, 2000, String Letter Publishing.

The Custom Guitar Shop and Wayne Richard Charvel, by Frank W/m Green, 1999, Working Musician Publications.

A Desktop Reference of Hip Vintage Guitar Amps, by Gerald Weber, 1994, Kendrick Books.

Electric Guitars and Basses, A Photographic History, by George Gruhn and Walter Carter, 1994, GPI Books.

Elektro-Gitarren Made in Germany, by Norbert Schnepel and Helmuth Lemme (German, with English translation), 1987, Musik-Verlag Schnepel-Lemme oHG.

Epiphone: The Complete History, by Walter Carter, 1995, Hal Leonard publishing.

Epiphone: The House of Stathopoulo, by Jim Fisch & L.B. Fred, 1996, Amsco Publications.

The Fender Amp Book, by John Morrish, 1995, Balafon Books and GPI Books.

Fender Amps: The First Fifty Years, by John Teagle and John Sprung, 1995, Hal Leonard Publishing.

The Fender Bass, by Klaus Blasquiz, 1990, Mediapresse.

The Fender Bass, An Illustrated History, by J.W. Black and Albert Molinaro, 2001, Hal Leonard Publishing.

The Fender Book, by Tony Bacon and Paul Day, 1992, Balafon and GPI Books.

Fender: The Sound Heard 'Round the World, by Richard R. Smith, 1995, Garfish Publishing.

The Fender Stratocaster, by Andre Duchossoir, 1988, Mediapresse.

The Fender Telecaster, by Andre Duchossoir, 1991, Hal Leonard Publishing.

G&L: Leo's Legacy, by Paul Bechtoldt, 1994, Woof Associates.

Gibson Electrics, The Classic Years, by A. R. Duchossoir, 1994, Hal Leonard Publishing.

Gibson's Fabulous Flat-Top Guitars, by Eldon Whitford, David Vinopal, and Dan Erlewine, 1994, GPI Books.

Gibson Guitars: 100 Years of An American Icon, by Walter Carter, 1994, W. Quay Hays.

The Gibson Les Paul Book, A Complete History of Les Paul Guitars, by Tony Bacon and Paul Day, 1993 Balafon Books and GPI Books.

The Gibson Super 400, Art of the Fine Guitar, by Thomas A. Van Hoose, 1991, GPI Books.

Gibson Shipping Totals 1948-1979, 1992, J.T.G.

The Gretsch Book, by Tony Bacon & Paul Day, 1996, Balafon Books and GPI Books.

Gruhn's Guide to Vintage Guitars, 2nd Edition, by George Gruhn and Walter Carter, 1999, Miller Freeman Books.

The Guild Guitar Book: The Company and the Instruments 1952-1977, by Hans Moust, 1995, GuitArchives Publications.

Guitar Identification: Fender-Gibson-Gretsch-Martin, by Andre Duchossoir, 1983, Hal Leonard Publishing Corporation.

Guitar People, by Willie G. Moseley, 1997, Vintage Guitar Books.

Guitar Player magazine, various issues, Miller Freeman.

Guitar Stories, Vol. I, by Michael Wright, 1994, Vintage Guitar Books.

Guitar Stories, Vol. II, by Michael Wright, 2000, Vintage Guitar Books.

Guitar World magazine, various issues, Harris Publications.

The Guitars of the Fred Gretsch Company, by Jay Scott, 1992, Centerstream.

Guitars From Neptune, A Definitive Journey Into Danelectro-Mania, by Paul Bechtoldt, 1995, Backporch Publications.

Guitar Graphics, Vol. 1 (Japanese), 1994, Rittor Music Mooks.

The Guru's Guitar Guide, by Tony Bacon and Paul Day, 1990, Track Record and The Bold Strummer.

The History and Artistry of National Resonator Instruments, by Bob Brozman, 1993, Centerstream.

The History of Marshall, by Michael Doyle, 1993, Hal Leonard Publishing.

The History of the Ovation Guitar, by Walter Carter, 1996, Hal Leonard publishing.

Ibanez, the Untold Story, by Paul Specht, Michael Wright, and Jim Donahue, 2005, Hoshino (U.S.A.) Inc.

The Martin Book, by Walter Carter, 1995, Balafon Books and GPI Books.

Martin Guitars, A History, by Mike Longworth, 1988, 4 Maples Press.

Martin Guitars: An Illustrated Celebration of America's Premier Guitarmaker, by Jim Washburn & Richard Johnston, 1997, Rodale Press, Inc.

Musicial Merchandise Review magazine, various issues, Symphony Publishing.

The Music Trades magazine, various issues, Music Trades Corporation.

The Official Vintage Guitar Magazine Price Guide, all editions.

The PRS Guitar Book, by Dave Burrluck, 1999, Outline Press, London.

The Rickenbacker Book, by Tony Bacon & Paul Day, 1994, Balafon Books and GFI Books.

Stellas & Stratocasters, by Willie G. Moseley, 1994, Vintage Guitar Books.

Stompbox, by Art Thompson, 1997, Miller Freeman Books.

The Tube Amp Book, 4th Edition, by Aspen Pittman, 1993, Groove Tubes.

The Ultimate Guitar Book, by Tony Bacon and Paul Day, 1991, Alfred A. Knopf.

Vintage Guitar magazine, various issues, Vintage Guitar, Inc.

VG Classics magazine, various issues, Vintage Guitar, Inc.

The Vox Story, A Complete History of the Legend, by David Peterson and Dick Denney, 1993, The Bold Strummer, Ltd.

Washburn: Over One Hundred Years of Fine Stringed Instruments, by John Teagle, 1996, Amsco Publications.

Various manufacturer catalogs, literature, and web sites.

Dealer Directory
A GEOGRAPHICAL GUIDE

AUSTRALIA
Ric's Vintage Guitars
Contact: Richard Zand-Vliet
Studio 3-13 James St.
Fremantle 6160
West Australia
Phone: international +61 8 9433265
Phone: local 08-94332625
ric@ricsvintageguitars.com
www.ricsvintageguitars.com

CANADA
Capsule Music
Contact: Mark or Peter Kesper
921 Queen St. W.
Toronto, Ontario M6J 1G5
Phone: 416-203-0202
contact@capsulemusic.com
www.capsulemusic.com

Folkway Music
Contact: Mark Stutman
163 Suffolk Street West
Guelph, Ontario N1H2N7
Phone: 519-763-5524
info@folkwaymusic.com
www.folkwaymusic.com

The Twelfth Fret Inc.
Contact: Grant MacNeill and David
 Wren
2132 Danforth Avenue
Toronto, Ont., Canada M4C 1J9
Phone: 416-423-2132
Fax: 416-423-0012
sales@12fret.com
www.12fret.com

ENGLAND
Ampaholics
Contact: Paul GT
P.O. Box 542
Surrey, GU1 12F, England
Phone: +44-1483-825102
Fax: +44-1483-825102
www.ampaholics.org.uk

Watford Valves & Speakers
Contact: Derek Rocco
Bricket Wood, Street Albans.
Herts. England AL2 3TS
Phone: 44-1923-893270
Fax: 44-1923-679207
sales@watfordvalves.com
www.watfordvalves.com

ITALY
Real Vintage
Contact: Nino Fazio
via Manzoni, 13

98057 Milazzo ME, Italy
Phone: +39-090-40646
realvintage@realvintage.it
www.realvintage.it

UNITED STATES
Alabama
Elite Music Sales
Contact: Brian Hinton
1737 Eastern Blvd.
Montgomery, AL 36117
Phone: 334-215-0215
Fax: 334-215-0216
sales@elitemusicsales.com
www.elitemusicsales.com

Arizona
Antique Electronic Supply
Contact: Brian Campanella
6221 South Maple Avenue
Tempe, AZ 85283
Phone: 480-820-5411
Fax: 800-706-6789
info@tubesandmore.com
www.tubesandmore.com

CE Distribution
Contact: Noreen Cravener
6221 South Maple Avenue
Tempe, AZ 85283
Phone: 480-755-4712
Fax: 480-820-4643
info@cedist.com
www.cedist.com

Willies Music
Contact: Willie
P.O. Box 1090
Dewey, AZ 86327
Phone: 928-632-0528
Fax: 928-632-9052
Cell: 928-713-3956
willieduck@yahoo.com

Arkansas
Blue Moon Music, Inc.
Contact: Les Haynie
3107 North College Ave.
Fayetteville, AR 72703-2609
Phone: 479-521-8163
blumnmus@aol.com

California
A Brown Soun
23 Joseph Ct.
San Rafael, CA 94903
Phone: 415-479-2124
Fax: 415-479-2132
abs@abrown.com
www.abrown.com

AA-Ibanez/Gibson Guitar Collector
All 1970s - '80s Japanese Relics
 - Archtops/Semi-hollows/Solids
Phone: 310-672-2432
bluesfingers@earthlink.net

Aantone's Music
Contact: Antone
36601 Newark Boulevard #11
Newark, CA 94560
Phone: 510-795-9170
Fax: 510-795-9170
aantones@pacbell.net
www.aantones.com

Bad Cat Amps
Contact: James Heidrich
PMB #406, 2621 Green River Road
Corona, CA 92882
Phone: 909-808-8651
Fax: 909-279-6383
badcatamps@earthlink.net
www.badcatamps.com

Bill Lawrence Pickups
Contact: Bill or Becky Lawrence
1785 Pomona Road, Unit D
Corona, CA 92880
Phone: 909-737-5853
Fax: 909-737-7834
becky@billlawrence.com
billlawrence.com

Buffalo Bros. Guitars
Contact: Gary Bibb
2270-C Camino Vida Roble
Carlsbad, CA 92009
Phone: 760-431-9542
Fax: 760-431-9532
BuffaloBros@aol.com
www.buffalobrosguitars.com

California Vintage Guitar and Amps
5244 Van Nuys Blvd.
Sherman Oaks, CA 91401
Phone: 818-789-8884
www.californiavintageguitarandamp.
 com

Chandler Musical Instruments
Contact: Paul
Phone: 530-899-1503
www.chandlerguitars.com
www.pickguards.us

Demeter Amplification
Contact: James Demeter

15730 Stagg Street
Van Nuys, CA 91406
Phone: 818-994-7658
Fax: 818-994-0647
info@demeteramps.com
www.demeteramps.com

Emery Sound
Contact: Curtis Emery
Phone: 510-236-1176
www.emerysound.com

Eric Schoenberg Guitars
Contact: Eric
106 Main Street
Tiburon, CA 94920
Phone: 415-789-0846
eric@om28. com
www.om28.com

Folk Music Center & Museum
220 Yale Ave.
Claremont, CA 91711
Phone: 909-624-2928
folkmusiccenter@verizon.net
www.folkmusiccenter.com

Freedom Guitar, Inc.
Contact: Dewey L. Bowen
6334 El Cajon Boulevard
San Diego, CA 92115
Phone: 800-831-5569
Fax: 619-265-1414
info@freedomguitar.com
www.freedomguitar.com

Fretted Americana
23901 Calabasas Rd., Ste 2024
Calabasas, CA 91302
Phone: 818-222-4113
Fax: 818-222-6173
vgm@frettedamericana.com
www.frettedamericana.com

Guitar Center (CA)
7425 Sunset Boulevard
Hollywood, CA 90046
Phone: 323-874-2302
 323-874-1060
Fax: 323-969-9783
www.vintageguitars.net

Guitar Heaven (CA)
Contact: Frank Benna
1934 Oak Park Blvd.
Pleasant Hill, CA 94523-4601
Phone: 925-687-5750
guitarheaven@juno.com
www.guitarheaven.com

Guitar Slam
info@guitarslam.com
www.guitarslam.com

Mercury Magnetics
Contact: Paul Patronette
Chatsworth, CA
Phone: 818-998-7791
Fax: 818-998-7835
sales@mercurymagnetics.com
www.mercurymagnetics.com

Neal's Music
Contact: Neal and Cathy Shelton
16458 Bolsa Chica Road PMB133
Huntington Beach, CA 92647
Phone: 714-901-5393
Fax: 714-901-5383
nealmuzic@aol.com
www.nealsmusic.com

Norman's Rare Guitars
Contact: Norman Harris
18969 Ventura Blvd.
Tarzana, CA 91356-3229
Phone: 818-344-8300
Fax: 818-344-1260
normsgtrs@aol.com
www.normansrareguitars.com

Players Vintage Instruments
P.O. Box 445
Inverness, CA 94937-0445
Phone: 415-669-1107
Fax: 415-669-1102
info@vintageinstruments.com
www.vintageinstruments.com

Soest Guitar Shop
Contact: Steve Soest
760 North Main Street Suite D
Orange, CA 92668
Phone: 714-538-0272
Fax: 714-532-4763
soestguitar@earthlink.net
www.soestguitar.com

Virtual Vintage Guitars
Contact: Jason C. Allen
Phone: 949-635-9797
sales@virtualvintageguitars.com
www.virtualvintageguitars.com

Virtuoso Polish and Cleaner
The Virtuoso Group, Inc.
P.O. Box 9775
Canoga Park, CA 91309-0775
Phone: 818-992-4733
virtuosopolish@sbcglobal.net
www.virtuosopolish.com

Wings Guitar Products, Inc.
Contact: Art Wiggs
5622 Comanche Court
San Jose, CA 95123
Phone: 408-225-2162
Fax: 408-225-5147

Connecticut
Analog Man Guitar Effects
Contact: Mike Piera
36 Tamarack Avenue #343
Danbury, CT 06811
Phone: 203-778-6658
AnalogMike@aol.com
www.analogman.com

Guitar Hanger
Contact: Rick Tedesco
61 Candlewood Lake Road
Brookfield, CT 06804
Phone: 203-740-8889
Fax: 203-740-2730
sales@guitarhanger.com
www.guitarhanger.com

Delaware
ACME Guitar Works
Phone: 302-836-5301
www.acmeguitarworks.com

Florida
Andy's Guitars
Contact: Andy
1208 North Monroe Street
Tallahassee, FL 32303
Phone: 850-224-9944
Fax: 850-224-5381
info@andysguitars.com
www.andysguitars.com

Crescent City Music
Contact: Allen Glenn
111 North Summit Street
Crescent City, FL 32112
Phone/Fax: 386-698-2873
Phone: 386-698-2874
ccmusic@crescentcitymusic.biz
www.crescentcitymusic.biz

Dixie Guitar Traders
Contact: Glen Helfer
5068 North Dixie Highway
Ft. Lauderdale, FL 33334
Phone: 954-772-6900
dixieguitartrade@bellsouth.net

Kummer's Vintage Instruments
Contact: Timm Kummer
Phone: 954-752-6063
prewar99@aol.com
www.kummersvintage.com

Legends Music, Inc.
Contact: Kent Sonenberg
4340 West Hillsborough Avenue
Tampa, FL 33614
Phone: 813-348-0688
Fax: 813-348-0689
ksonenbl@tampabay.rr.com
www.legendsguitars.com

Music Magic
Contact: Robert Graupera
6850 SW 81 Terrace
Miami, FL 33143

Phone: 305-975-6656
UsedGuitar@aol.com
www.magicguitars.com

Georgia
Atlanta Vintage Guitars
Contact: Frank Moates
561 Windy Hill Road
Smyrna, GA 30080
Phone: 770-433-1891
Fax: 770-433-1858
atlantavintage@bellsouth.net
www.atlantavintageguitars.com

Dreamcatcher Guitars
Contact: Eddie Mathis
26 Webb Street Suite. 1
Roswell, GA 30075
Phone: 877-241-2359
Fax: 770-587-9962
em@gtrs4u.com
www.dreamcatcherguitars.com

Midtown Music
Contact: David Tiller
3326 N. Druid Hills Rd.
Decatur, GA 30033
Phone: 404-325-0515
Fax: 404-252-2243
midtownmusic@mindspring.com
www.midtownmusic.com

Hawaii
Coconut Grove Music
Contact: Fred Oshiro
418 Kuulei Road
Kailua, HI 96734
Phone: 808-262-9977
Fax: 808-263-7052
cgmusic@lava.net
www.coconutgrovemusic.com

Illinois
Butler Custom Sound/Chicago Blues Box
770 N. Church Rd., #1
Elmhurst, IL 60126
Phone: 630-832-1983
www.chicagobluesbox.com

Chicago Music Exchange
Contact: Scott Silver
3316 N. Lincoln Ave.
Chicago, IL 60657
Phone: 773-477-0830
Fax: 773-477-0427
sales@chicagomusicexchange.com
www.chicagomusicexchange.com

Guitar Works Ltd
Contact: Steve or Terry
709 Main Street
Evanston, IL 60202
Phone: 847-475-0855
Fax: 847-475-0715
guitarworksltd@aol.com
www.guitarworksltd.com

Make 'n Music
Contact: Teddy
1455 W. Hubbard St.
Chicago, IL 60622
Phone: 312-455-1970
info@makenmusic.com
www.makenmusic.com

Music Gallery
Contact: Frank
2558 Greenbay Road
Highland Park, IL 60035
Phone: 847-432-6350 / 847-432-8883
MusicGlry@aol.com
www.musicgalleryinc.com

RWK Guitars
P.O. Box 1068
Highland Park, IL 60035
Phone: 847-432-4308
Bob@RWKGuitars.com
www.RWKGuitars.com

Indiana
Hoosierdad's Music
Contact: James Peltz
4609 Grape Rd. Ste. A5
Mishawaka, IN 46545-8257
Phone: 574-277-5038
Fax: 574-247-9486
www.hoosierdad.com

WeberVST
Speakers, Amp Kits, components, tools and attenuators
Contact: T.A. Weber
329 E Firmin Street
Kokomo, IN 46902
Phone: 765-452-1249
www.webervst.com
www.weberspeakers.com

Kansas
E.M. Shorts Guitars
Contact: Jon Ray
2525 East Douglas Avenue
Wichita, KS 67211
Phone: 800-835-3006
Fax: 316-684-6858
wbic@wichitaband.com
www.wichitaband.com

Overland Express Guitars
Contact: David Schaefer
10739 West 109th Street
Overland Park, KS 66210
Phone: 913-469-4034
Fax: 913-469-9672
dave@overlandexpress.com
www.overlandexpress.com

Kentucky
Guitar Emporium
1610 Bardstown Road
Louisville, KY 40205
Phone 502-459-4153
Fax: 502-454-3661
guitar-emporium@mindspring.com

www.guitar-emporium.com

Louisianna
International Vintage Guitars
Contact: Steve Staples
1011 Magazine Street
New Orleans, LA 70130
Phone: 504-524-4557
Fax: 504-524-4665
guitars@webcorral.com
www.webcorral.com

Maryland
Garrett Park Guitars, Inc.
Contact: Rick Hogue
150 East Jennifer Road 150-0
Annapolis, MD 21401
Phone: 401-573-0500
Fax: 401-573-0502
gpguitars@toad.net
www.gpguitars.com

Guitar Exchange
Contact: Bruce Sandler
740 Frederick Road
Baltimore, MD 21228
Phone: 410-747-0122
Fax: 410-747-0525

Jim's Guitars Inc.
Contact: Jim Singleton
706 Frederick Rd.
Baltimore, MD 21228-4501
Phone: 866-787-2865
Fax: 410-744-0010
info@jimsguitars.com
www.jimsguitars.com

Nationwide Guitars
Contact: Bruce Rickard
P.O. Box 2334
Columbia, MD 21045
Phone: 410-997-7440
Fax: 410-997-7440
nationwideguitars@comcast.net
www.nationwideguitars.com

Southworth Guitars
Contact: Gil Southworth
7845 Old Georgetown Road
Bethesda, MD 20814
Phone: 301-718-1667
Fax: 301-718-0391
southworthguitar@aol.com
www.southworthguitars.com

Massachusetts
Bay State Vintage Guitars
Contact: Craig D. Jones
295 Huntington Avenue, Room 304
Boston, MA 02115
Phone: 617-267-6077

Cold Springs Electrical Works
Contact: Norm Moren
332 Rock Rimmon Road
Belchertown, MA 01007
Phone: 413-323-8869

norm@coldspringselectricalworks.
  com
www.coldspringselectricalworks.com

Lucchesi Vintage Instruments
Contact: Frank Lucchesi
108 Cottage St.
Easthampton, MA 01027
Phone: 413-527-6627
info@lucchesivintageinstruments.
  com
www.lucchesivintageinstruments.
  com

Michigan
Elderly Instruments
Contact: Stan Werbin
1100 North Washington
P.O. Box 14210 -VGF
Lansing, MI 48901
Phone: 517-372-7890
Fax: 517-372-5155
elderly@elderly.com
www.elderly.com

Huber & Breese Music
33540 Groesbeck Highway
Fraser, MI 48026
Phone: 586-294-3950
Fax: 586-294-7616
handbmusic@sbcglobal.net
www.huberbreese.com

Rockin' Daddy's
Contact: Randy Volin
P.O. Box 210368
Auburn Hills, MI 48321
Fax: 248-420-8499
randy@randyvolin.com
www.rockindaddys.com

Minnesota
Schaefer Guitars
Contact: Ed Schaefer
4221 West 4th Street
Duluth, MN 55807
Phone: 218-624-7231
sguitars@airmail.net
www.schaeferguitars.com

Solidbodyguitar.com
Contact: Bruce Barnes
2566 Highway 10
Mounds View, MN 55112
Phone: 763-783-0080
Fax: 763-783-0090
solidbodyguitar@quest.net
www.solidbodyguitar.com

Willie's American Guitars
254 Cleveland Avenue South
St. Paul, MN 55105
Phone: 651-699-1913
Fax: 651-690-1766
info@williesguitars.com
www.williesguitars.com

Missouri

Eddie's Guitars
Contact: Ed Putney
7362 Manchester Rd.
St. Louis, MO 63143-3108
Phone: 314-781-7500
Fax: 314-781-7510
eddiesguitars@sbcglobal.net
www.eddiesguitars.com

Fly By Night Music
Contact: Dave Crocker
103 South Washington
Neosho, MO 64850-1816
Phone: 417-451-5110
Show number: 800-356-3347
crocker@joplin.com
www.texasguitarshows.com

Grubville Guitars
Contact: Glen Meyers
P.O. Box 14
Grubville, MO 63041
Phone: 636-274-4738
Fax: 636-285-9833
glencogg@aol.com
grubvilleguitars.com

Hazard Ware Inc./ Killer Vintage
Contact: Dave
P.O. Box 190561
St. Louis, MO 63119
Phone: 314-647-7795
        800-646-7795
Fax: 314-781-3240
www.killervintage.com

Nevada
AJ's Music In Las Vegas
Contact: Peter Trauth
2031 W. Sunset Rd.
Henderson, NV 89014-2120
Phone: 702-436-9300
Fax: 702-436-9302
pete@ajsmusic.com
www.ajsmusic.com

Cowtown Guitars
2797 South Maryland Parkway, Ste.
  14
Las Vegas, NV 89109
Phone: 888-682-3002
Fax: 702-866-2520
www.cowtownguitars.com

New Hampshire
Retro Music
Contact: Jeff Firestone
38 Washington Street
Keene, NH 03431
Phone/Fax: 603-357-9732
retromusic@verizon.com
www.retroguitar.com

New Jersey
Dr. Bob's Guitar & Stringed Instrument Repair
Contact: Robert "Dr. Bob" Pinaire
Princeton, NJ Area

Phone: 609-921-1407 or 888-921-2461
Fax: 609-434-1643
swtsongman@aol.com
www.DrBobsMusic.com

Fuchs Audio Technology
Contact: Annette Fuchs
73 Collins Avenue
Bloomfield, NJ 07003-4504
Phone: 973-893-0225
sales@fuchsaudiotechnology.com
fuchsaudiotechnology.com

Golden Age Fretted Instruments
Contact: John Paul Reynolds
309 South Avenue W.
Westfield, NJ 07090
Phone: 908-301-0001
Fax: 908-301-1199
info@goldenageguitars.com
www.goldenageguitars.com

Hi Test Guitars
341 Westwind Court
Norwood, NJ 07648
Phone/Fax: 201-750-2445
By appointment Mon.-Sat. 11-6 EDT

Hoboken Vintage Guitars
Contact: Jim Pasch
164 1st Street
Hoboken, NJ 07030-3544
Phone: 201-222-8977
Fax: 201-222-9127
hoboken@extend.net
www.hobokenvintage.com

Lark Street Music
479 Cedar Lane
Teaneck, NJ 07666
Phone: 201-287-1959
Larkstreet@aol.com
www.larkstreet.com

New Jersey Guitar & Bass Center
Contact: Jay Jacus
995 Amboy Avenue
Edison, NJ 08837
Phone: 732-225-4444
Fax: 732-225-4404
NJGtrBass@aol.com
www.members.aol.com/NJGtrBass

Pick of the Ricks
Contact: Chris Clayton
17 Clementon Rd. at Twin Roads
  Plaza
Berlin, NJ 08009
Phone: 856-767-5820
Fax 856-627-4053
sales@pickofthericks.com
www.pickofthericks.com

Russo Music Center
Contact: Joe Carroll
1989 Arena Dr.
Hamilton, NJ 08610-2428
Phone: 800-847-8776

joe.c@russomusic.com
www.russomusic.com

New York
Bernunzio Vintage Guitars
Contact: John Bernunzio
875 East Avenue
Rochester, NY 14607
Phone: 585-473-6140
Fax: 585-442-1142
info@bernunzio.com
www.bernunzio.com

Diamond Strings
Contact: Bruce Diamond
20 Shaftsbury Rd.
Rochester, NY 14610
Phone: 585-424-3369
dstrings@rochester.rr.com
diamondstrings.com

Imperial Guitar and Soundworks
Contact: Bill Imperial
99 Route 17K
Newburgh, NY 12550
Phone: 845-567-0111
igs55@aol.com
www.imperialguitar.com

Keyboard Instrument Rentals
Vintage Effects, Guitars and Amps
1697 Broadway Ste 504
New York, NY 10019
Phone: 212-245-0820
Fax: 212-245-8858
keyboardrentals@aol.com

KORG USA
www.korg.com

Laurence Wexer Ltd.
Contact: Larry
251 East 32nd Street #11F
New York, NY 10016
Phone: 212-532-2994
info@wexerguitars.com

Ludlow Guitars
Contact: Robert
164 Ludlow Street
New York, NY 10002
Phone: 212-353-1775
Fax: 212-353-1749
www.ludlowguitars.com

Mandolin Brothers, Ltd.
629 Forest Avenue
Staten Island, NY 10310
Phone: 718-981-3226/8585
Fax: 718-816-4416
mandolin@mandoweb.com
www.mandoweb.com

Michael's Music
Contact: Michael Barnett
29 West Sunrise Highway
Freeport, NY 11520
Phone: 516-379-4111

Fax: 516-379-3058
michaelsmusic@optonline.net
www.michaelsmusic.com

Mirabella Guitars & Restorations
Contact: Cris Mirabella
P.O. Box 482
Babylon, NY 11702
Phone: 631-842-3819
Fax: 631-842-3827
mirguitars@aol.com
www.mirabellaguitars.com

Rudy's Music
Contact: Rudy
169 West 48th Street
New York, NY 10036
Phone: 212-391-1699
info@rudysmusic.com
www.rudysmusic.com

Rumble Seat Music
Contact: Eliot Michael
121 West State St.
Ithica, NY 14850
Phone: 607-277-9236
Fax: 607-277-4593
rumble@rumbleseatmusic.com
www.rumbleseatmusic.com

Straight Shooter Guitars
Contact: John DeSilva
Syosset, NY
Phone: 516-993-9893
straightshooter@optonline.net
www.straightshooterguitars.com

We Buy Guitars
David Davidson
705A Bedford Ave.
Bellmore, NY 11710
Phone: 516-221-0563
Fax: 516-221-0856
webuyguitarsl@aol.com
www.webuyguitars.com

We Buy Guitars
Richie Friedman
705A Bedford Ave.
Bellmore, NY 11710
Phone: 516-221-0563
Fax: 516-221-0856
webuyguitars@aol.com
www.webuyguitars.com

We Buy Guitars
Tom Dubas
705A Bedford Ave.
Bellmore, NY 11710
Phone: 516-221-0563
Fax: 516-221-0856
webuyguitars2@aol.com
www.webuyguitars.com

North Carolina
Bee-3 Vintage

Contact: Gary Burnette
25 Arbor Lane
Ashville, NC 28805
Phone: 828-298-2197
bee3vintage@hotmail.com
www.bee3vintage.com

Carr Amplifiers
Contact: Steve
433 West Salisbury St.
Pittsboro, NC 27312
Phone: 919-545-0747
Fax: 919-545-0739
info@carramps.com
www.carramps.com

Legato Guitars
Contact: Bill Fender
1121C Military Cutoff Rd. #342
Wilmington, NC 28405
By Appointment Only
bf@legatoguitars.com
www.legatoguitars.com

Maverick Music
Contact: Phil Winfield
8425 Old Statesville Rd., Ste 19
Charlotte, NC 28269-1828
Phone: 704-599-3700
Fax: 704-599-3712
sales@maverick-music.com
www.maverick-music.com

Top Hat Amplification
Contact Brian Gerhard
5316 Millstone Creek Dr.,
Fuquay-Varina, NC 27526
Phone 919-762-9688
tophatamps@aol.com
www.tophatamps.com

Ohio
DHR Music
PO Box 43209
Cincinnati, OH 45243
Phone: 513-272-8004
Fax: 513-530-0229
dhrmusic@hotmail.com
www.dhrmusic.com

Fretware Guitars
Contact: Dave Hussung
400 South Main
Franklin, OH 45005
Phone: 937-743-1151
Fax: 937-743-9987
guitar@erinet.com
www.fretware.cc

Gary's Classic Guitars
Contact: Gary Dick
Cincinnati, OH
Phone: 513-891-0555
Fax: 513-891-9444
garysclssc@aol.com
www.garysguitars.com

Mike's Music

Contact: Mike Reeder
2615 Vine Street
Cincinnati, OH 45219
Phone: 513-281-4900
Fax: 513-281-4968
www.mikesmusicohio.com

String King Products
Contact: John Mosconi
P.O. Box 9083
Akron, OH 44305
Phone: 330-798-1055

Oklahoma
Strings West
Contact: Larry Briggs
P.O. Box 999
20 E. Main Street
Sperry, OK 74073
Phone: 800-525-7273
Fax: 918-288-2888
larryb@stringswest.com
www.stringswest.com

Oregon
McKenzie River Music
455 West 11th
Eugene, OR 97401
Phone: 541-343-9482
Fax: 541-465-9060
www.McKenzieRiverMusic.com

Pennsylvania
Guitar-Villa – Retro Music
Contact: John Slog
216A Nazareth Pike
Bethlehem, PA 18020
Phone: 610-746-9200
Fax: 610-746-9135
gvilla@guitar-villa.com
www.guitar-villa.com

Guitar-Villa – Retro Music
Contact: John Slog
30 S. Westend Boulevard.
Quakertown, PA 18951
Phone: 215-536-5800
gvilla@guitar-villa.com
www.guitar-villa.com

JH Guitars
Contact: Jim Heflybower
Pennsylvania
Phone: 610-363-9204
Fax: 610-363-8689
JHGuitars@webtv.net
www. jhguitars.com

Vintage Instruments & Frederick W. Oster Fine Violins
Contact: Fred W. Oster
1529 Pine Street
Philadelphia, PA 19102
Phone: 215-545-1100
www.vintage-instruments.com

Rhode Island
PM Blues Guitar Heaven

Contact: Paul Moskwa 401-722-5837
  Shawn Reilly 401-724-1144
bluespm@aol.com
www.pmblues.com

VintageMarshall.com
Contact: Paul Moskwa 401-722-5837
  Shawn Reilly 401-724-1144
Avintagemarshall@aol.com
www.vintagemarshall.com

Tennessee
Gruhn Guitars
Contact: George Gruhn
400 Broadway
Nashville, TN 37203
Phone: 615-256-2033
Fax: 615-255-2021
gruhn@gruhn.com
www.gruhn.com

Music Room Guitars
Contact: Brad Gibson
5103 Kingston Pike
Knoxville, TN 37919
Phone: 865-584-0041
Toll Free: 877-584-0099
mrgknox@aol.com

PedalDoctor FX
Contact: Tim Creek
412 Newbary Ct.
Franklin, TN 37069
Phone: 615-260-5651
doc@pedaldoctor.com
www.pedaldoctor.com

Showcase Custom Cases
Contact: Ken Burbage
2153-A Utopia Ave.
Nashville, TN 37211-2051
Toll Free: 866-306-9119
         615-256-9119
Fax: 615-254-0167
showcaseken@juno.com
www.showcasecases.com

Texas
Allparts
13027 Brittmoore Park Drive
Houston, TX 77041
Phone: 713-466-6414
allpartgtr@aol.com
www.allparts.com

Anderson Guitar Gallery
Contact: Steve Anderson
6811 Oak St.
Frisco, TX 75034
Phone: 214-387-4050
info@andersonguitargallery.com
www.andersonguitargallery.com

Charley's Guitar Shop
Contact: Clay and Sheila Powers
2720 Royal Ln. Ste.100
Dallas, TX 75229-4727
Phone: 972-243-4187

Fax: 972-243-5193
shop@charleysguitar.com
www.charleysguitar.com

Dallas Guitar Show
Contact: Mark Pollock
Booth Info: dallas@guitarshow.com
Contact: Jimmy Wallace
Band Music Info: james.
  wallace17@gte.net
www.guitarshow.com

Durham Electronics
Contact: Alan Durham
Austin, TX USA
Phone: 512-581-0663
alan@durhamelectronics.com
www.durhamelectronics.com

Eugene's Guitars Plus
Contact: Eugene Robertson
2010 South Buckner Boulevard
Dallas, TX 75217-1823
Phone: 214-391-8677
pluspawnguitars@yahoo.com
www.texasguitarshows.com

Hill Country Guitars
Contact: Kevin Drew Davis
111 Old Kyle Rd. #200
Wimberley, TX 78676-9701
Phone: 512-847-8677
Fax: 512-847-8699
info@hillcountryguitars.com
www.hillcountryguitars.com

Jimmy Wallace Guitars
Contact: Jimmy Wallace
3622 Shoreside Dr.
Garland, TX 75043
Phone: 972-740-9925
orders@jimmywallaceguitars.com
www.jimmywallaceguitars.com

Kendrick Amplifiers
Route. 2 P.O. Box 871
Kempner, TX 76539
Phone: 512-932-3130
Fax: 512-932-3135
kendrick@kendrick-amplifiers.com
www.kendrick-amplifiers.com

Southpaw Guitars
Contact: Jimmy
5813 Bellaire Boulevard
Houston, TX 77081
Phone: 713-667-5791
Fax: 713-667-4091
southpawguitars@sbcglobal.net
www.southpawguitars.com

Texas Amigos Guitar Shows
Arlington Guitar Show (The 4
  Amigos)
Contact: John or Ruth Brinkmann
Phone: 800-329-2324
Fax: 817-473-1089
web: www.texasguitarshows.com

Chicago/Austin Guitar Show
Contact: Dave Crocker
Phone: 800-356-3347
Fax: 817-473-1089
crocker@joplin.com
www.texasguitarshows.com

California World Guitar Shows
Contact: Larry Briggs
Phone: 800-525-7273
Fax: 918-288-2888
larryb@stringswest.com
www.texasguitarshows.com

Transpecos Guitars
Contact: Mark Pollock
311 E. Holland Ave.
Alpine, TX 79830
Phone: 432-837-0101
mtp@transpecosguitars.com
www.transpecosguitars.com

Van Hoose Vintage Instruments
Contact: Thomas Van Hoose
2722 Raintree Drive
Carrollton, TX 75006
Phone: (days) 972-250-2919 or (eves)
  972-418-4863
Fax: 972-250-3644
tv0109@flash.net
www.vanhoosevintage.com

Waco Vintage Instruments
Contact: John Brinkman
1275 North Main Street, Ste #4
Mansfield, TX 76063
Phone: 817-473-9144
Guitar Show Phone: 888-473-6059

Utah
Intermountain Guitar and Banjo
Contact: Leonard or Kennard
712 East 100 South
Salt Lake City, UT 84102
Phone: 801-322-4682
Fax: 801-355-4023
guitarandbanjo@earthlink.com
www.guitarandbanjo.net

Virginia
Authentic Guitars
Contact: Michael Hansen
12715-Q Warwick Blvd.
Newport News, VA 23606
Phone: 757-595-4663
www.AuthenticGuitars.com

Authentic Guitars - 2nd Store
Contact: Michael Hansen
5251-42 John Tyler Highway
Williamsburg, VA 23185
Phone: 757-259-9711
www.AuthenticGuitars.com

**Callaham Vintage Guitars &
Amps**
Contact: Bill Callaham

114 Tudor Drive
Winchester, VA 22603
Phone: 540-955-0294 - Shop
callaham@callahamguitars.com
www.callahamguitars.com

Vintage Sound
Contact: Bill Holter
P.O. Box 11711
Alexandria, VA 22312
Phone: 703-914-2126
Fax: 703-914-1044
bhvsound@vintagesound.com
www.vintagesound.com

Washington
Emerald City Guitars
Contact: Jay Boone
83 South Washington in Pioneer
  Square
Seattle, WA 98104
Phone: 206-382-0231
jayboone@emeraldcityguitars.com

Gregg Rogers Guitars
Contact: Gregg or Marcia Rogers
32069 Lyman Hamilton Hwy
Sedro Woolley, WA 98284
Phone: 360-826-4860
Fax: 360-826-4860
grguitars@msn.com
www.GRGuitars.com

Guitarville
Contact: Tommy Steinley
19258 15th Avenue North East
Seattle, WA 98155-2315
Phone: 206-363-8188
Fax: 206-363-0478
gv@guitarville.com
www.guitarville.com

Jet City Guitars LLC
Contact: Allen Kaatz
2212 Queen Anne Ave. N., Box 134
Seattle, WA 98109
Phone: 206-361-1365
ark@jetcityguitars.com
www.jetcityguitars.com

Wisconsin
Bizarre Guitars
Contact: Brian Goff
2501 Waunona Way
Madison, WI 53713
Phone: 608-235-3561
bdgoff@sbcglobal.net
www.bizarreguitars.com

Dave's Guitar Shop
Contact: Dave Rogers
1227 South 3rd Street
La Crosse, WI 54601
Phone: 608-785-7704
Fax: 608-785-7703
davesgtr@aol.com
www.davesguitar.com

Index

Bold Page numbers indicate first listing

Bold Page numbers indicate first listing

Bold Page numbers indicate first listing

Bold Page numbers indicate first listing

Bold Page numbers indicate first listing

FOR 20 YEARS, *VINTAGE GUITAR* MAGAZINE HAS BEEN THE #1 SOURCE

for information and values on used and vintage gear. With its expanded 2006 edition of ***The Official Vintage Guitar Price Guide***, *VG* offers 1,000 photos and even more background and prices on over 1,300 brands of **Electric Guitars, Acoustic Guitars, Amplifiers, Basses, Effects, Lap Steels, Steels, Ukuleles, Mandolins, and Now Banjos!**

"*The VG Price Guide* really is the Bible of current values of vintage guitars. We recommend it to all of our Guitar Center stores as *the* reference." **– Dave Belzer, Hollywood Guitar Center**

"As a musician, collector, and lover of fine vintage guitars, *The VG Price Guide* is an indispensable tool. Just as *Vintage Guitar* magazine is an educational textbook, *The Guide* makes the perfect companion. I recommend it to anyone who's serious about guitars. I've certainly referred to it often in the quest for the perfect guitar."
– Greg Martin, The Kentucky HeadHunters

"Gil and Alan have done an impeccable job of gathering and analyzing the vast amount of information that make *The Guide* an invaluable tool. Next guitar show, bring extra money – and don't forget *The Guide!*" **– Nate Westgor, Willie's American Guitars**

"Money for nothing and my chicks for free, *The VG Price Guide* is the only one for me!"
– Jim Singleton, Jim's Guitars

VINTAGE GUITAR BOOKS

EXCLUSIVELY DISTRIBUTED BY

Hal•Leonard®

U.S. $24.95

ISBN 1-884883-17-6

0 73999 31329 1

HL00331329

9 781884 883170

52495